AF696995

A Guide to Reviewing
Economics
Free Enterprise in Action

Economics: Free Enterprise in Action develops economic understanding through a well organized, comprehensive presentation of fundamental economic principles and concepts.

The list below is a brief guide to key features of ***Economics: Free Enterprise in Action.*** Page references provide examples of these features.

A clear consistent organization promotes understanding:

- ▶ UNIT OPENERS (pages 166–167) include colorful photographs illustrating unit themes and list chapter titles.
- ▶ CHAPTER OPENERS (pages 168–169) feature high-interest photographs, content-related quotes, and chapter outlines of section titles and major headings.
- ▶ NUMBERED SECTIONS (page 175) divide chapter topics into manageable learning segments.

The skills program continually develops four strands:

- ▶ READING SKILLS, through READING ABOUT ECONOMICS (pages 40–41) and USING PRIMARY SOURCES (pages 379, 381).
- ▶ WRITING SKILLS, through WRITING ABOUT ECONOMICS (pages 110–111) and numerous writing activities (pages 118, 138).
- ▶ THINKING SKILLS, through THINKING ABOUT ECONOMICS (pages 78–79) and higher-level thinking questions in SECTION, CHAPTER, and UNIT REVIEWS (pages 147, 162, 164).
- ▶ GRAPHIC INTERPRETATION SKILLS, through INTERPRETING THE VISUAL RECORD (pages 52–53) and abundant maps, charts, and diagrams (pages 83–85).

Motivating special features enrich and extend the narrative:

- ▶ An ILLUSTRATED OVERVIEW OF ECONOMICS (pages 1–17) introduces basic economic concepts through exciting photographs and diagrams.
- ▶ CASE STUDY (page 184), in every chapter, demonstrates economic concepts in action.
- ▶ DECISION MAKERS IN THE ECONOMY (page 181), in every chapter, profiles successful business people and government officials.
- ▶ ISSUES IN ECONOMICS (pages 182–183), in every unit, explores current economic topics.
- ▶ HIGHLIGHTS IN ECONOMICS (page 173), in every unit, discusses historical turning points that have influenced the United States economy.

Extensive study aids help students learn:

- ▶ CHAPTER STUDY GUIDES (page 170) alert students to important concepts and vocabulary before chapter study begins.
- ▶ KEY VOCABULARY is highlighted in boldfaced type and defined in context (page 179), reinforced in reviews (page 186), and included in the GLOSSARY (pages 555, 556).
- ▶ SECTION REVIEWS (page 333) help assess comprehension of content.
- ▶ CHAPTER SUMMARIES (page 459) present brief reviews of chapter topics to reinforce main ideas.
- ▶ CHAPTER REVIEWS (pages 138–139) and UNIT REVIEWS (pages 164–165) reinforce and extend learning.

A complete Reference Library contains an ATLAS OF ECONOMICS (page 466), a WORLD ECONOMIC DATA FILE (page 481), a CHRONOLOGY OF ECONOMIC EVENTS (page 499), an EVERYDAY ECONOMICS HANDBOOK (page 507), a CAREERS IN THE MARKETPLACE (page 539), a GLOSSARY (page 545), and an INDEX (page 560).

The fully annotated Teacher's Edition provides background information (page 49), additional learning activities (page 47), and teaching strategies (page 54).

HBJ Harcourt Brace Jovanovich, Inc.
School Department

N

PROMOTE ECONOMIC LITERACY!

ECONOMICS: FREE ENTERPRISE IN ACTION

Economics: Free Enterprise in Action develops understanding of the components and benefits of the free enterprise system in the United States This highly readable, well-organized textbook explores the roles of markets and government in the American economic system, compares economic systems of the world, and presents high-interest consumer economics topics.

- **Comprehensive content** helps ensure economic literacy—from concepts such as scarcity and choice to issues such as trade tariffs. *See pages P2 and P3.*
- **Thorough development of economic skills**—through four strands—provides the tools for continued expansion of economic knowledge. *See page P4.*
- **Emphasis on critical thinking** develops effective decision-making and problem-solving skills—including organizing, interpreting, analyzing, and classifying ideas; seeing relationships; and using economic imagination. *See page P5.*
- **Motivating features** present a variety of real-world applications that enliven the textbook and heighten student interest. *See pages P6 and P7.*
- **Consistent reviews** promote understanding of economic vocabulary and concepts, reinforce critical-thinking skills, provide practice in consumer skills, and suggest individual and group projects. *See pages P8 and P9.*
- **Valuable teaching support** facilitates lesson preparation with detailed lesson plans and teaching strategies, as well as numerous resources for review, enrichment, and evaluation. *See page P10.*

Completely correlated with the Joint Council for Economic Education's Master Curriculum and Framework

COMPREHENSIVE CONTENT LOGICALLY ORGANIZED!

An Illustrated Overview of Economics (not shown) introduces basic economic concepts through the use of photographs and diagrams. Topics include "The Nature of Economics," "Features of Free Enterprise," and "Comparative Economic Systems."

A **High-interest photographs**—depicting the focus of each chapter—promote student interest.

B **Chapter Openers** feature engaging, content-related quotes that offer opportunities for class discussion.

C **Chapter Outlines** guide reading through a brief overview of chapter content.

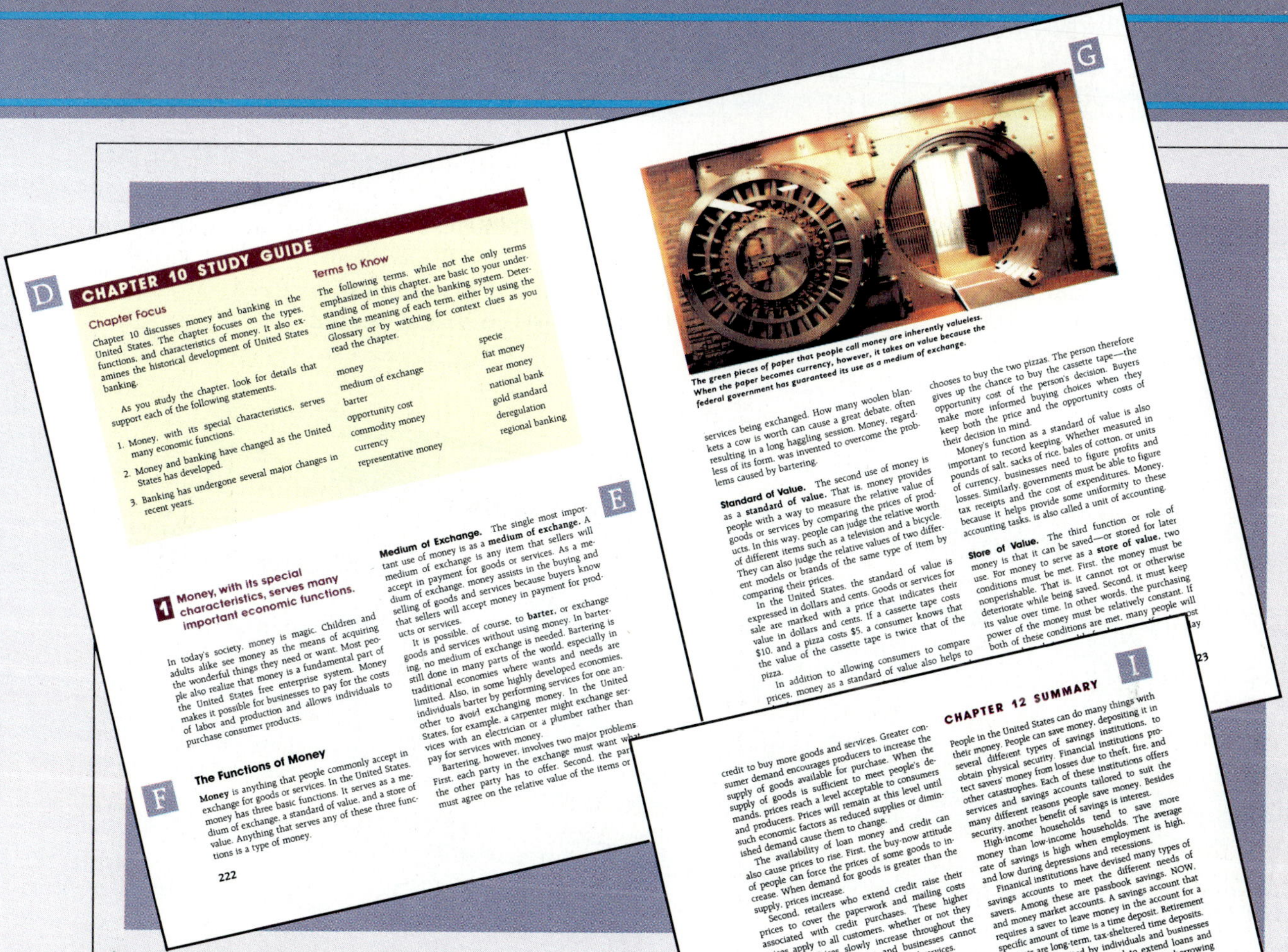

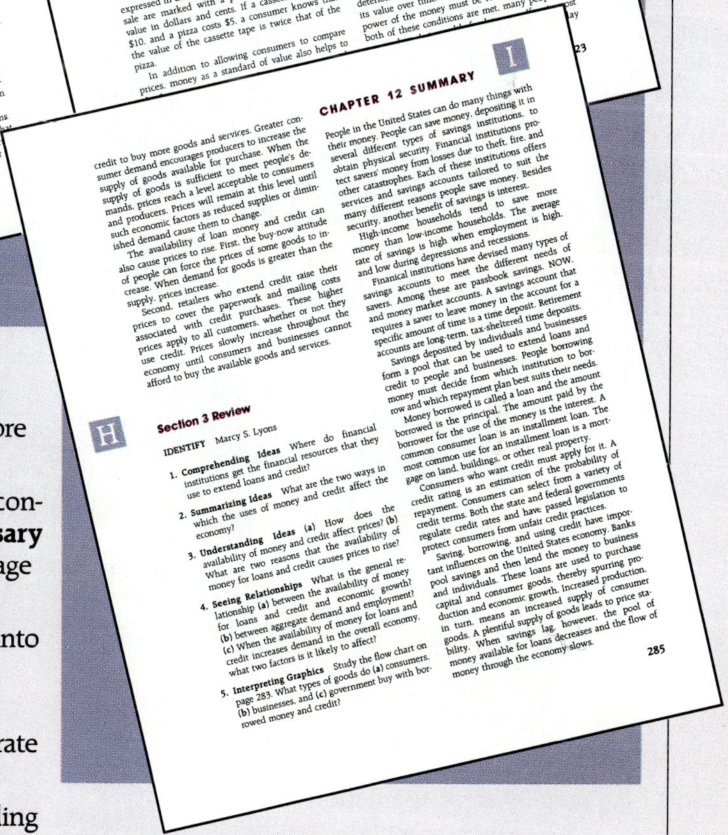

D **Chapter Study Guides** alert students to important concepts and vocabulary before chapter study begins.

E **Important economic terms**—defined in context—appear in boldfaced type. The **Glossary** (not shown) contains an entry with a page reference for each boldfaced term.

F **Concise sections** divide chapter topics into manageable learning segments.

G **Vivid photographs, charts, and graphs** enhance comprehension and help illustrate complex topics.

H **Section Reviews** help assess understanding and integrate critical-thinking skills with section content.

I **Chapter Summaries** provide succinct reviews of chapter topics to reinforce understanding.

Sample pages are reduced. Actual sizes are 8″ x 10″ *(Pupil's Edition)*.

ECONOMIC SKILLS
THOROUGHLY DEVELOPED!

In every chapter, a strong skills program includes a practical, high-interest feature that develops and reinforces skills in four strands:

Reading About Economics
Writing About Economics
Thinking About Economics
Interpreting the Visual Record

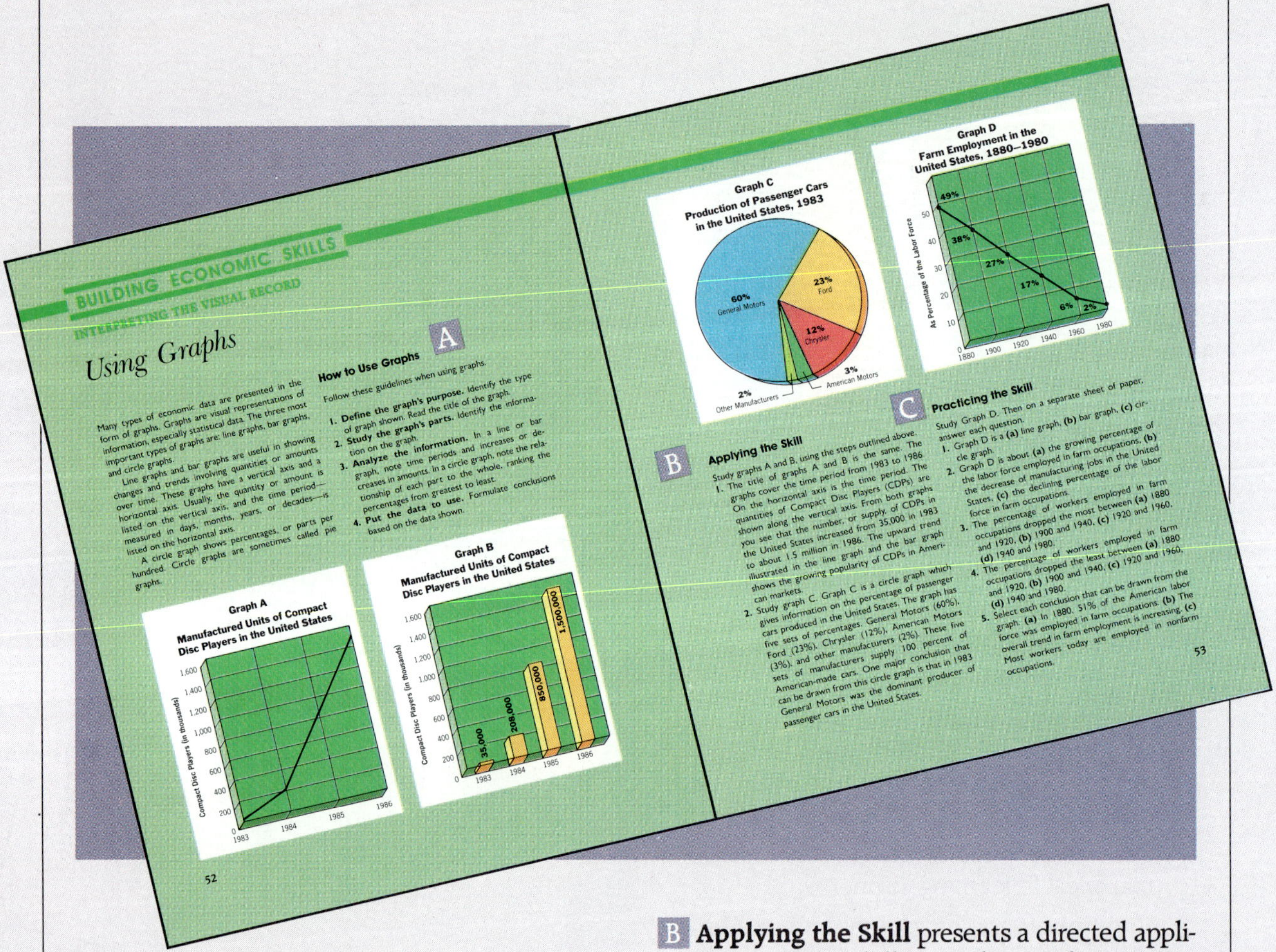

BUILDING ECONOMIC SKILLS

INTERPRETING THE VISUAL RECORD

Using Graphs

Many types of economic data are presented in the form of graphs. Graphs are visual representations of information, especially statistical data. The three most important types of graphs are: line graphs, bar graphs, and circle graphs.

Line graphs and bar graphs are useful in showing changes and trends involving quantities or amounts over time. These graphs have a vertical axis and a horizontal axis. Usually, the quantity or amount is listed on the vertical axis, and the time period—measured in days, months, years, or decades—is listed on the horizontal axis.

A circle graph shows percentages, or parts per hundred. Circle graphs are sometimes called pie graphs.

A **How to Use Graphs**

Follow these guidelines when using graphs.

1. **Define the graph's purpose.** Identify the type of graph shown. Read the title of the graph.
2. **Study the graph's parts.** Identify the information on the graph.
3. **Analyze the information.** In a line or bar graph, note time periods and increases or decreases in amounts. In a circle graph, note the relationship of each part to the whole, ranking the percentages from greatest to least.
4. **Put the data to use.** Formulate conclusions based on the data shown.

52

B **Applying the Skill**

Study graphs A and B, using the steps outlined above.

1. The title of graphs A and B is the same. The graphs cover the time period from 1983 to 1986. On the horizontal axis is the time period. The quantities of Compact Disc Players (CDPs) are shown along the vertical axis. From both graphs you see that the number, or supply, of CDPs in the United States increased from 35,000 in 1983 to about 1.5 million in 1986. The upward trend illustrated in the line graph and the bar graph shows the growing popularity of CDPs in American markets.
2. Study graph C. Graph C is a circle graph which gives information on the percentage of passenger cars produced in the United States. The graph has five sets of percentages. General Motors (60%), Ford (23%), Chrysler (12%), American Motors (3%), and other manufacturers (2%). These five sets of manufacturers supply 100 percent of American-made cars. One major conclusion that can be drawn from this circle graph is that in 1983 General Motors was the dominant producer of passenger cars in the United States.

C **Practicing the Skill**

Study Graph D. Then on a separate sheet of paper, answer each question.

1. Graph D is a **(a)** line graph, **(b)** bar graph, **(c)** circle graph.
2. Graph D is about **(a)** the growing percentage of the labor force employed in farm occupations, **(b)** the decrease of manufacturing jobs in the United States, **(c)** the declining percentage of the labor force in farm occupations.
3. The percentage of workers employed in farm occupations dropped the most between **(a)** 1880 and 1920, **(b)** 1900 and 1940, **(c)** 1920 and 1960, **(d)** 1940 and 1980.
4. The percentage of workers employed in farm occupations dropped the least between **(a)** 1880 and 1920, **(b)** 1900 and 1940, **(c)** 1920 and 1960, **(d)** 1940 and 1980.
5. Select each conclusion that can be drawn from the graph. **(a)** In 1880, 51% of the American labor force was employed in farm occupations. **(b)** The overall trend in farm employment is increasing. **(c)** Most workers today are employed in nonfarm occupations.

53

A **Step-by-step instructions** clearly explain each skill.

B **Applying the Skill** presents a directed application of the skill—complete with answers.

C **Practicing the Skill** provides an opportunity for immediate independent practice.

Sample pages are reduced. Actual sizes are 8" x 10" *(Pupil's Edition)*.

CRITICAL THINKING CONSISTENTLY EMPHASIZED!

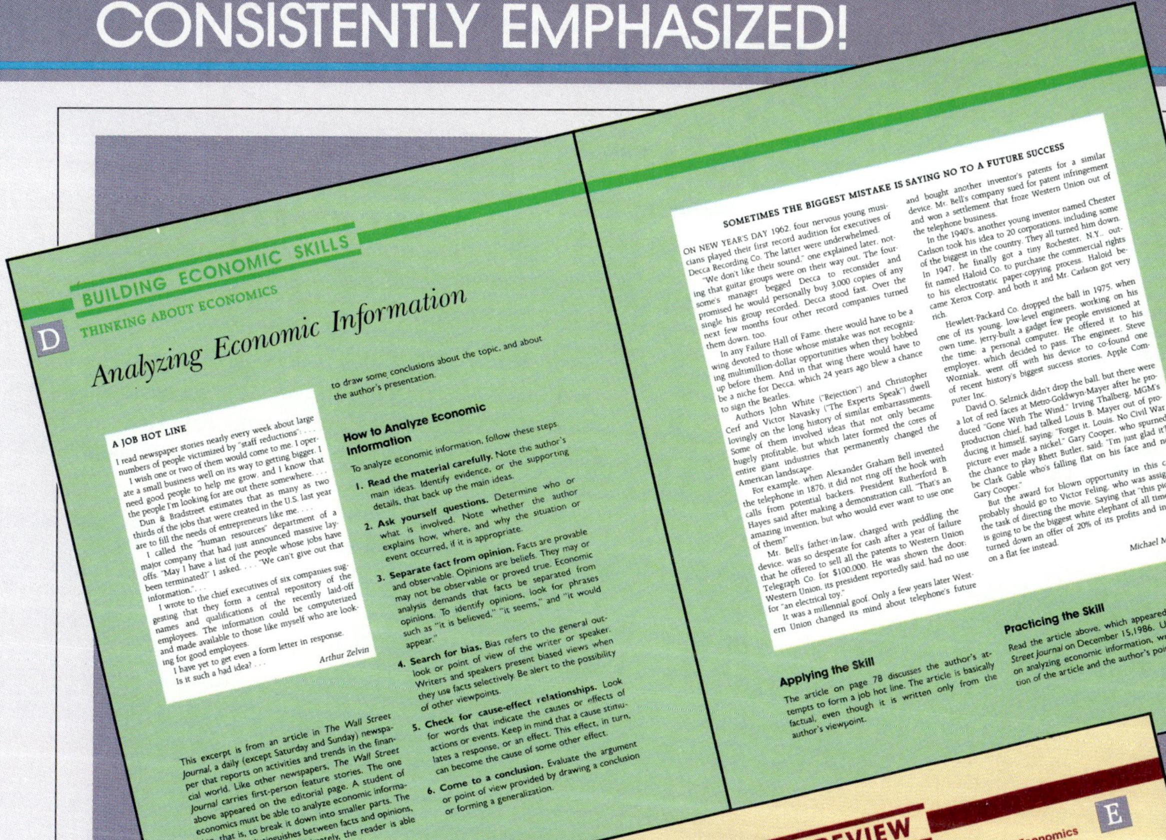

BUILDING ECONOMIC SKILLS

THINKING ABOUT ECONOMICS

D

Analyzing Economic Information

How to Analyze Economic Information

To analyze economic information, follow these steps.

1. **Read the material carefully.** Note the author's main ideas. Identify evidence, or the supporting details, that back up the main ideas.
2. **Ask yourself questions.** Determine who or what is involved. Note whether the author explains how, where, and why the situation or event occurred, if it is appropriate.
3. **Separate fact from opinion.** Facts are provable and observable. Opinions are beliefs. They may or may not be observable or proved true. Economic analysis demands that facts be separated from opinions. To identify opinions, look for phrases such as "it is believed," "it seems," and "it would appear."
4. **Search for bias.** Bias refers to the general outlook or point of view of the writer or speaker. Writers and speakers present biased views when they use facts selectively. Be alert to the possibility of other viewpoints.
5. **Check for cause-effect relationships.** Look for words that indicate the causes or effects of actions or events. Keep in mind that a cause stimulates a response, or an effect. This effect, in turn, can become the cause of some other effect.
6. **Come to a conclusion.** Evaluate the argument or point of view provided by drawing a conclusion or forming a generalization.

A JOB HOT LINE

SOMETIMES THE BIGGEST MISTAKE IS SAYING NO TO A FUTURE SUCCESS

Applying the Skill

Practicing the Skill

78 79

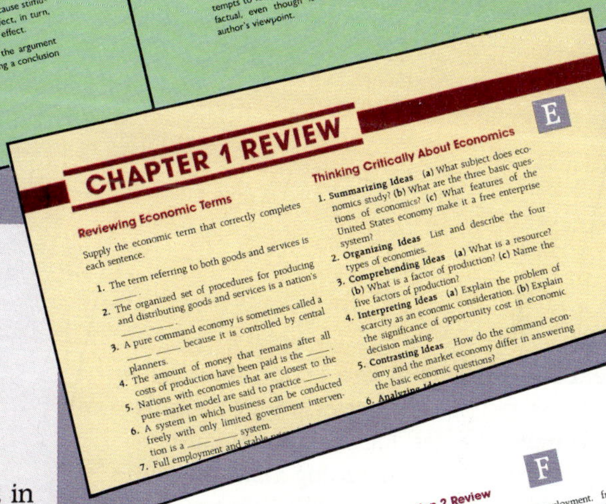

E

CHAPTER 1 REVIEW

Reviewing Economic Terms

Thinking Critically About Economics

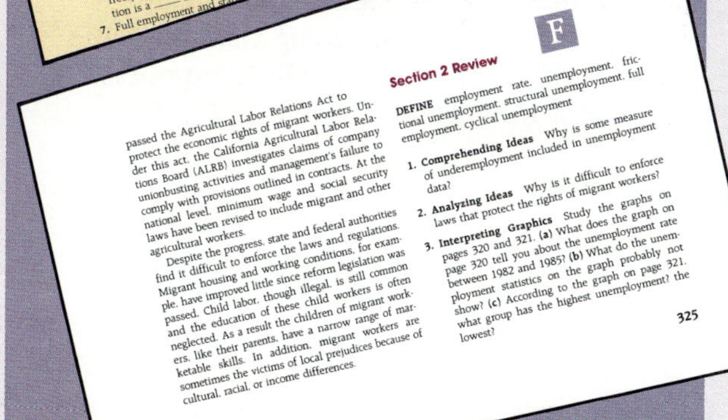

F

Section 2 Review

325

D **Thinking About Economics** applies specific critical-thinking skills to economics.

E **Thinking Critically About Economics,** in each Chapter Review, reinforces a variety of critical-thinking skills—clearly identified in boldface headings.

F **Section Reviews** consistently develop critical-thinking skills such as interpreting, comparing, and analyzing ideas.

MOTIVATING FEATURES
ENGAGINGLY REALISTIC!

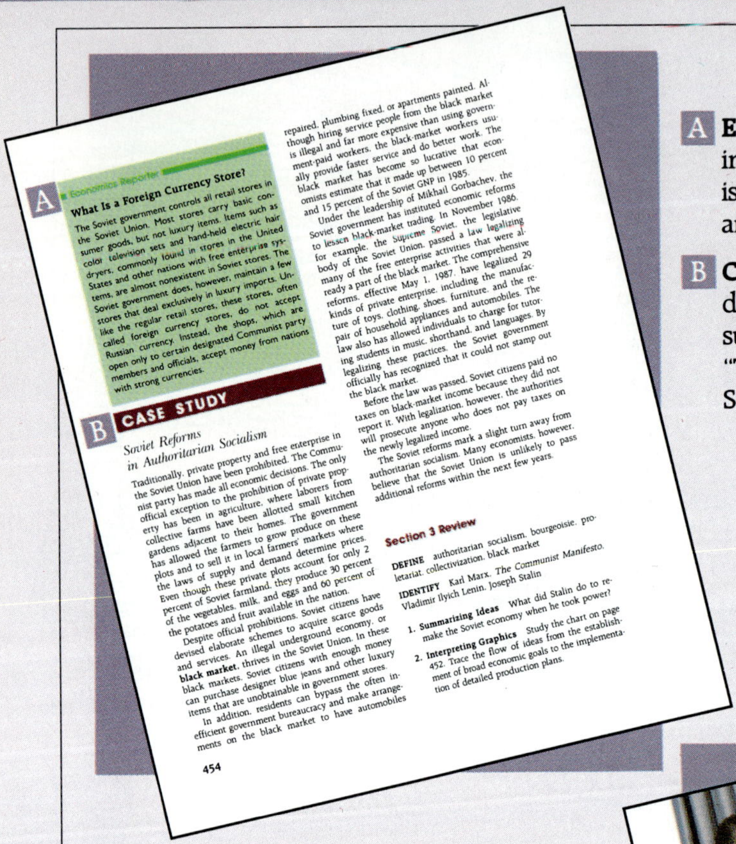

A ■ Economics Reporter

What Is a Foreign Currency Store?

The Soviet government controls all retail stores in the Soviet Union. Most stores carry basic consumer goods, but not luxury items. Items such as color television sets and hand-held electric hair dryers, commonly found in stores in the United States and other nations with free enterprise systems, are almost nonexistent in Soviet stores. The Soviet government does, however, maintain a few stores that deal exclusively in luxury imports. Unlike the regular retail stores, these stores, often called foreign currency stores, do not accept Russian currency. Instead, the shops, which are open only to certain designated Communist party members and officials, accept money from nations with strong currencies.

B **CASE STUDY**

Soviet Reforms in Authoritarian Socialism

Traditionally, private property and free enterprise in the Soviet Union have been prohibited. The Communist party has made all economic decisions. The only official exception to the prohibition of private property has been in agriculture, where laborers from collective farms have been allotted small kitchen gardens adjacent to their homes. The government has allowed the farmers to grow produce on these plots and to sell it in local farmers' markets where the laws of supply and demand determine prices. Even though these private plots account for only 2 percent of Soviet farmland, they produce 30 percent of the vegetables, milk, and eggs and 60 percent of the potatoes and fruit available in the nation.

Despite official prohibitions, Soviet citizens have devised elaborate schemes to acquire scarce goods and services. An illegal underground economy, or **black market**, thrives in the Soviet Union. In these black markets, Soviet citizens with enough money can purchase designer blue jeans and other luxury items that are unobtainable in government stores.

In addition, residents can bypass the often inefficient government bureaucracy and make arrangements on the black market to have automobiles repaired, plumbing fixed, or apartments painted. Although hiring service people from the black market is illegal and far more expensive than using government-paid workers, the black-market workers usually provide faster service and do better work. The black market has become so lucrative that economists estimate that it made up between 10 percent and 15 percent of the Soviet GNP in 1985.

Under the leadership of Mikhail Gorbachev, the Soviet government has instituted economic reforms to lessen black-market trading. In November 1986, for example, the Supreme Soviet, the legislative body of the Soviet Union, passed a law legalizing many of the free enterprise activities that were already a part of the black market. The comprehensive reforms, effective May 1, 1987, have legalized 29 kinds of private enterprise, including the manufacture of toys, clothing, shoes, furniture, and the repair of household appliances and automobiles. The law also has allowed individuals to charge for tutoring students in music, shorthand, and languages. By legalizing these practices, the Soviet government officially has recognized that it could not stamp out the black market.

Before the law was passed, Soviet citizens paid no taxes on black-market income because they did not report it. With legalization, however, the authorities will prosecute anyone who does not pay taxes on the newly legalized income.

The Soviet reforms mark a slight turn away from authoritarian socialism. Many economists, however, believe that the Soviet Union is unlikely to pass additional reforms within the next few years.

Section 3 Review

DEFINE authoritarian socialism, bourgeoisie, proletariat, collectivization, black market

IDENTIFY Karl Marx, *The Communist Manifesto*, Vladimir Ilyich Lenin, Joseph Stalin

1. **Summarizing Ideas** What did Stalin do to remake the Soviet economy when he took power?
2. **Interpreting Graphics** Study the chart on page 452. Trace the flow of ideas from the establishment of broad economic goals to the implementation of detailed production plans.

454

A **Economics Reporter** presents brief insights into economic concepts, institutions, and issues, including oil leases, *Consumer Reports*, and greenmail.

B **Case Study**—integrated into each chapter—demonstrates economic concepts in action, such as "Comparable Worth and Fair Pay," "The Compact Disc Revolution," and "The Social Security System Today."

C DECISION MAKERS IN THE ECONOMY

Reverend Leon Sullivan

Reverend Leon Sullivan, a black Baptist minister in Philadelphia, is a vehement opponent of the South African system of apartheid. As a means of combating racial discrimination in businesses in South Africa, he introduced the Sullivan Principles in 1977.

The Sullivan Principles consist of six requirements for businesses. They must desegregate all parts of the workplace. They must provide equal employment practices for all employees. They must offer equal pay for equal work to all employees. They must develop programs to train nonwhites for supervisory, administrative, clerical, and technical jobs. They must work to increase the number of nonwhites in managerial and supervisory positions. They must also work to improve the quality of their employees' lives outside the workplace.

All United States companies operating in South Africa were asked to adopt the principles voluntarily. By October 1985, 175 United States companies had agreed to follow Sullivan's guidelines, and he had begun to urge companies in Great Britain, France, and Germany to comply as well.

Sullivan also began to question whether stronger measures than the original principles are needed to eliminate apartheid. Although Sullivan would still prefer to bring about change through the original principles, he now believes that more stringent economic measures may be necessary.

Sullivan's most recent call is for all foreign corporations to leave South Africa unless apartheid is abolished by May 1987.

this privilege, however, during the Korean War. In the mid-1980s, some American businesspeople were lobbying Congress to restore most-favored-nation status to the Soviet Union. By the beginning of 1987, that status had not yet been restored.

The Trade Expansion Act of 1962. The Trade Expansion Act of 1962 renewed and expanded the Reciprocal Trade Agreements Act of 1934. The 1962 act encouraged further tariff reductions and provided for worker retraining programs and other benefits to workers and firms hurt by foreign competition. These benefits are called **trade adjustment assistance.** The Trade Expansion Act of 1962 gave Presidents Kennedy and Johnson enough authority to push for important free-trade reforms during the 1960s.

The Trade Reform Act of 1974. The Trade Reform Act of 1974 further increased the President's authority to cut tariffs and expand benefits to displaced workers. Under the provisions of this act, the President was empowered to eliminate any tariff of 5 percent or less, and to cut by 60 percent any tariffs greater than 5 percent. The act also increased financial and other benefits to displaced workers, firms, and geographical areas that were especially hard hit by foreign competition. Congress regularly voted for additional trade adjustment funding during the 1980s.

World Regional Trade Organizations

Many nations have formed regional trade organizations and reduced or eliminated trade barriers

405

C **Decision Makers in the Economy** profiles business people and government officials who have affected local, national, and world economics—including Lilia Clemente, investment analyst, and Phil Gramm, U.S. Senator from Texas.

Sample pages are reduced. Actual sizes are 8" x 10" *(Pupil's Edition).*

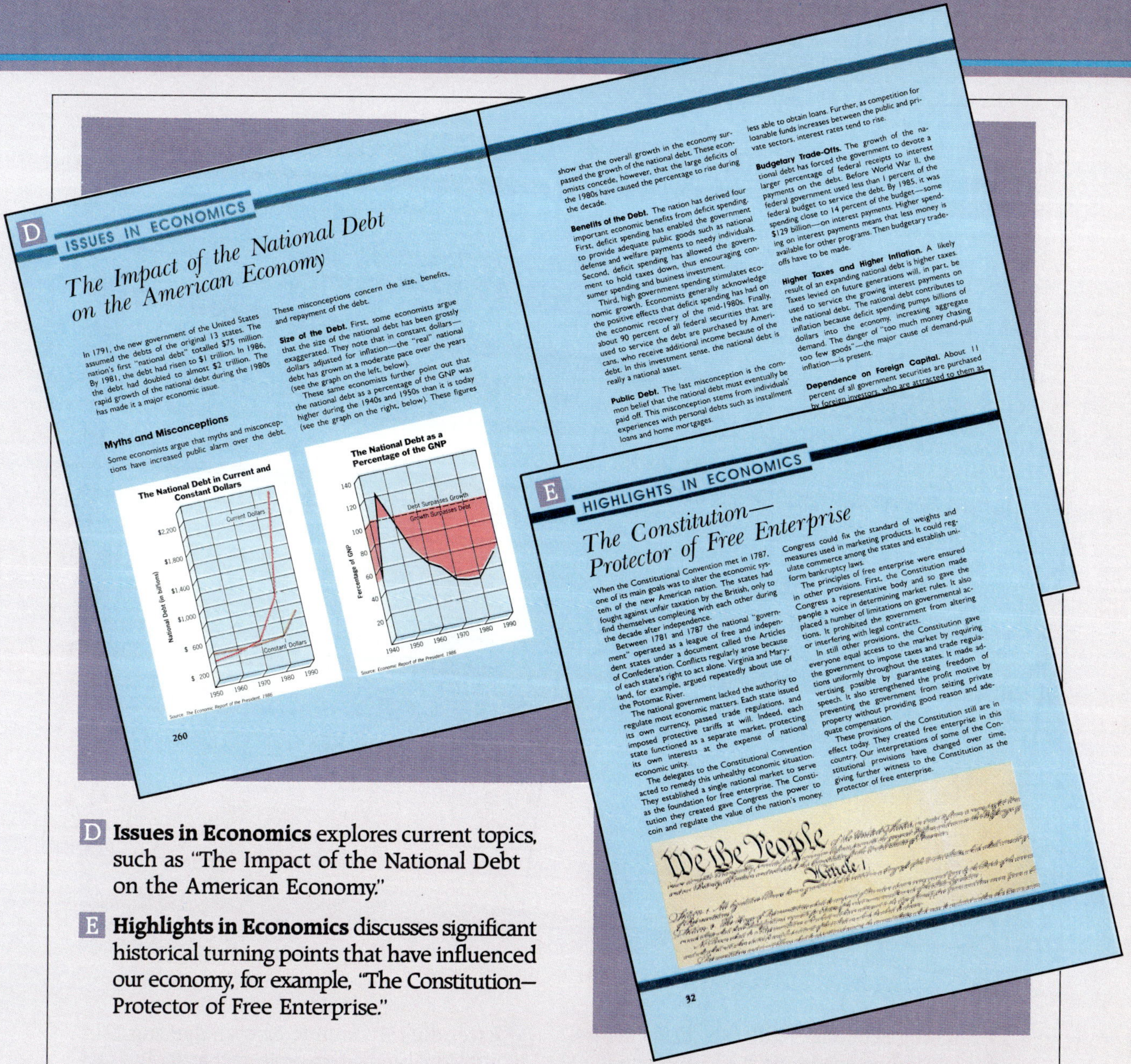

D **Issues in Economics** explores current topics, such as "The Impact of the National Debt on the American Economy."

E **Highlights in Economics** discusses significant historical turning points that have influenced our economy, for example, "The Constitution–Protector of Free Enterprise."

Valuable Reference Library in Each Student Book

- Atlas of Economics
- World Economic Data
- Chronology of Economic Events
- Everyday Economics Handbook
- Careers in the Marketplace
- Glossary
- Index

COMPLETE REVIEWS CAREFULLY SEQUENCED!

A **Reviewing Economic Terms** reinforces key vocabulary introduced in the chapter.

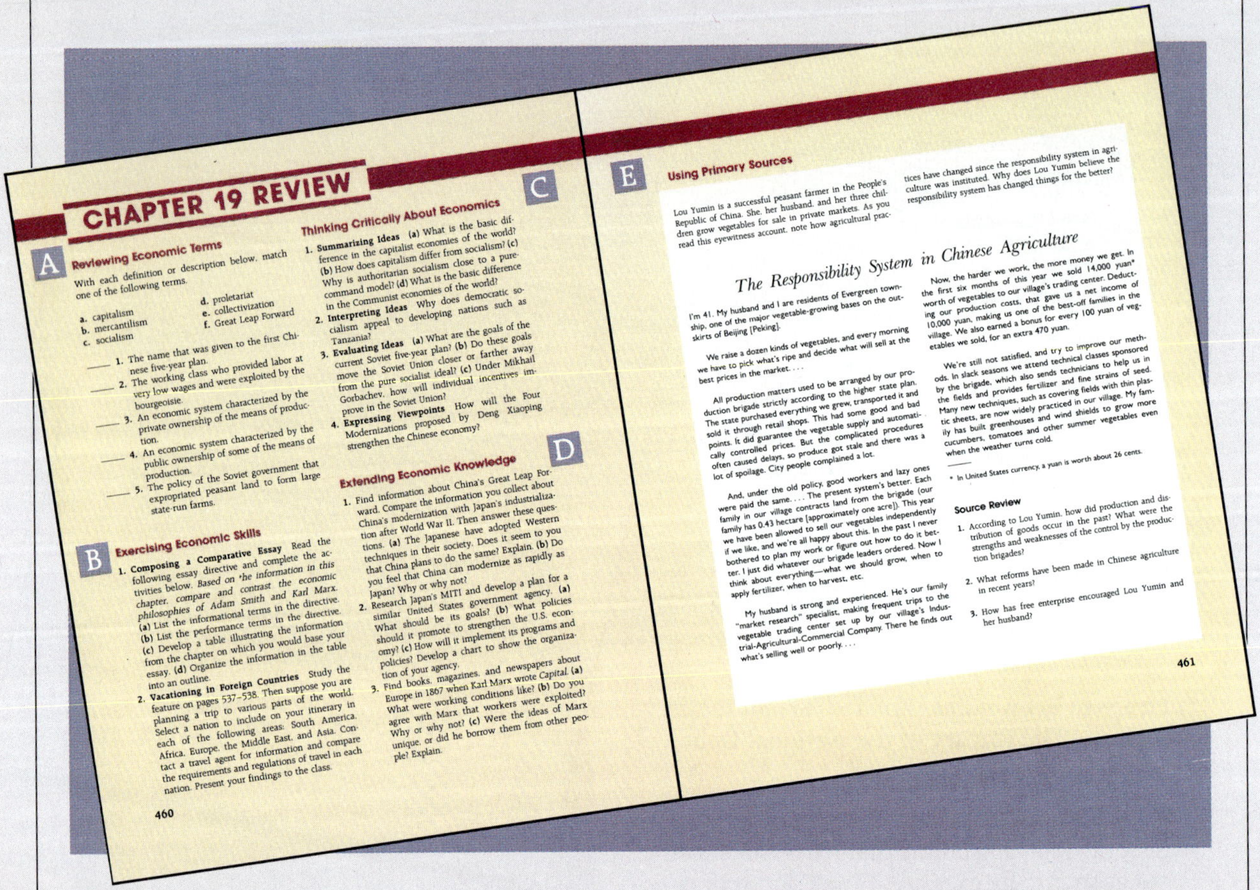

CHAPTER 19 REVIEW

A

Reviewing Economic Terms

With each definition or description below, match one of the following terms.

a. capitalism
b. mercantilism
c. socialism
d. proletariat
e. collectivization
f. Great Leap Forward

____ 1. The name that was given to the first Chinese five-year plan.
____ 2. The working class who provided labor at very low wages and were exploited by the bourgeoisie.
____ 3. An economic system characterized by the private ownership of the means of production.
____ 4. An economic system characterized by the public ownership of some of the means of production.
____ 5. The policy of the Soviet government that expropriated peasant land to form large state-run farms.

B

Exercising Economic Skills

1. **Composing a Comparative Essay** Read the following essay directive and complete the activities below. *Based on the information in this chapter, compare and contrast the economic philosophies of Adam Smith and Karl Marx.* **(a)** List the informational terms in the directive. **(b)** List the performance terms in the directive. **(c)** Develop a table illustrating the information from the chapter on which you would base your essay. **(d)** Organize the information in the table into an outline.
2. **Vacationing in Foreign Countries** Study the feature on pages 537–538. Then suppose you are planning a trip to various parts of the world. Select a nation to include on your itinerary in each of the following areas: South America, Africa, Europe, the Middle East, and Asia. Contact a travel agent for information and compare the requirements and regulations of travel in each nation. Present your findings to the class.

460

C

Thinking Critically About Economics

1. **Summarizing Ideas** **(a)** What is the basic difference in the capitalist economies of the world? **(b)** How does capitalism differ from socialism? **(c)** Why is authoritarian socialism close to a pure-command model? **(d)** What is the basic difference in the Communist economies of the world?
2. **Interpreting Ideas** Why does democratic socialism appeal to developing nations such as Tanzania?
3. **Evaluating Ideas** **(a)** What are the goals of the current Soviet five-year plan? **(b)** Do these goals move the Soviet Union closer or farther away from the pure socialist ideal? **(c)** Under Mikhail Gorbachev, how will individual incentives improve in the Soviet Union?
4. **Expressing Viewpoints** How will the Four Modernizations proposed by Deng Xiaoping strengthen the Chinese economy?

D

Extending Economic Knowledge

1. Find information about China's Great Leap Forward. Compare the information you collect about China's modernization with Japan's industrialization after World War II. Then answer these questions. **(a)** The Japanese have adopted Western techniques in their society. Does it seem to you that China plans to do the same? Explain. **(b)** Do you feel that China can modernize as rapidly as Japan? Why or why not?
2. Research Japan's MITI and develop a plan for a similar United States government agency. **(a)** What should be its goals? **(b)** What policies should it promote to strengthen the U.S. economy? **(c)** How will it implement its programs and policies? Develop a chart to show the organization of your agency.
3. Find books, magazines, and newspapers about Europe in 1867 when Karl Marx wrote *Capital*. **(a)** What were working conditions like? **(b)** Do you agree with Marx that workers were exploited? Why or why not? **(c)** Were the ideas of Marx unique, or did he borrow them from other people? Explain.

E

Using Primary Sources

Lou Yumin is a successful peasant farmer in the People's Republic of China. She, her husband, and her three children grow vegetables for sale in private markets. As you read this eyewitness account, note how agricultural practices have changed since the responsibility system in agriculture was instituted. Why does Lou Yumin believe the responsibility system has changed things for the better?

The Responsibility System in Chinese Agriculture

I'm 41. My husband and I are residents of Evergreen township, one of the major vegetable-growing bases on the outskirts of Beijing [Peking].

We raise a dozen kinds of vegetables, and every morning we have to pick what's ripe and decide what will sell at the best prices in the market. . . .

All production matters used to be arranged by our production brigade strictly according to the higher state plan. The state purchased everything we grew, transported it and sold it through retail shops. This had some good and bad points. It did guarantee the vegetable supply and automatically controlled prices. But the complicated procedures often caused delays, so produce got stale and there was a lot of spoilage. City people complained a lot.

And, under the old policy, good workers and lazy ones were paid the same. . . . The present system's better. Each family in our village contracts land from the brigade (our family has 0.43 hectare [approximately one acre]). This year we have been allowed to sell our vegetables independently if we like, and we're all happy about this. In the past I never bothered to plan my work or figure out how to do it better. I just did whatever our brigade leaders ordered. Now I think about everything—what we should grow, when to apply fertilizer, when to harvest, etc.

My husband is strong and experienced. He's our family "market research" specialist, making frequent trips to the vegetable trading center set up by our village's Industrial-Agricultural-Commercial Company. There he finds out what's selling well or poorly. . . .

Now, the harder we work, the more money we get. In the first six months of this year we sold 14,000 yuan* worth of vegetables to our village's trading center. Deducting our production costs, that gave us a net income of 10,000 yuan, making us one of the best-off families in the village. We also earned a bonus for every 100 yuan of vegetables we sold, for an extra 470 yuan.

We're still not satisfied, and try to improve our methods. In slack seasons we attend technical classes sponsored by the brigade, which also sends technicians to help us in the fields and provides fertilizer and fine strains of seed. Many new techniques, such as covering fields with thin plastic sheets, are now widely practiced in our village. My family has built greenhouses and wind shields to grow more cucumbers, tomatoes and other summer vegetables even when the weather turns cold.

* In United States currency, a yuan is worth about 26 cents.

Source Review

1. According to Lou Yumin, how did production and distribution of goods occur in the past? What were the strengths and weaknesses of the control by the production brigades?
2. What reforms have been made in Chinese agriculture in recent years?
3. How has free enterprise encouraged Lou Yumin and her husband?

461

B **Exercising Economic Skills** provides activities for expanding economic study and consumer skills.

C **Thinking Critically About Economics** provides additional opportunities for applying higher-level thinking skills.

D **Extending Economic Knowledge** suggests individual and group projects that apply a variety of skills, including use of primary sources.

E **Using Primary Sources**—a primary source reading with introduction and questions—provides an opportunity to see how classical and contemporary economic thinkers view past and present issues.

Sample pages are reduced. Actual sizes are 8″ x 10″ *(Pupil's Edition)*.

F **Reviewing Economic Ideas** presents questions that focus on important unit concepts and information.

G **Connecting Economic Ideas** contains higher-level thinking questions that ask students to synthesize ideas from the unit.

H **Investigating Economic Issues** provides opportunities for skills applications related to **Issues in Economics.**

I **Applying Economics** suggests additional individual and group projects that extend skills development.

J **Using Primary Sources** offers an excerpt from a speech, document, law, essay, or eyewitness account that reinforces and extends unit content.

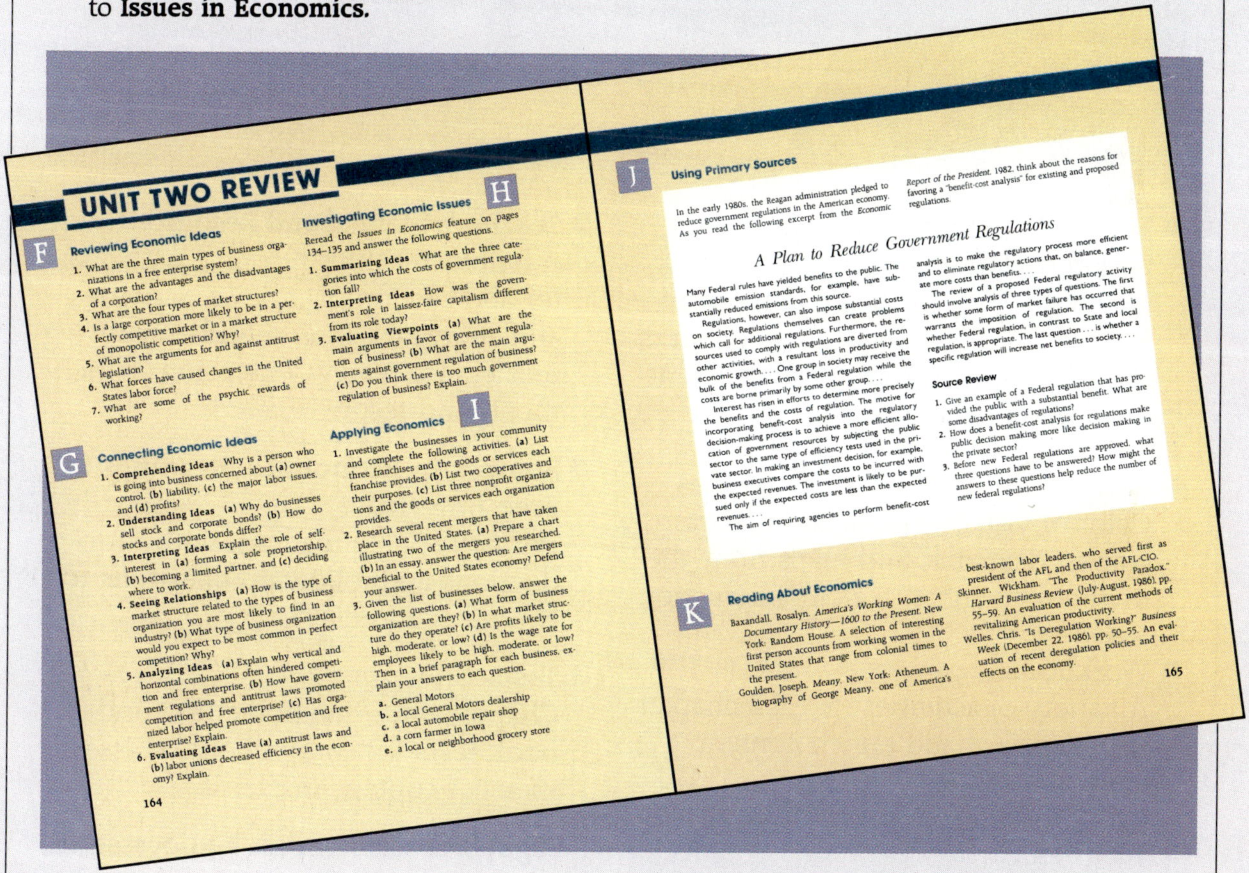

UNIT TWO REVIEW

F

Reviewing Economic Ideas

1. What are the three main types of business organizations in a free enterprise system?
2. What are the advantages and the disadvantages of a corporation?
3. What are the four types of market structures?
4. Is a large corporation more likely to be in a perfectly competitive market or in a market structure of monopolistic competition? Why?
5. What are the arguments for and against antitrust legislation?
6. What forces have caused changes in the United States labor force?
7. What are some of the psychic rewards of working?

G

Connecting Economic Ideas

1. **Comprehending Ideas** Why is a person who is going into business concerned about (a) owner control, (b) liability, (c) the major labor issues, and (d) profits?
2. **Understanding Ideas** (a) Why do businesses sell stock and corporate bonds? (b) How do stocks and corporate bonds differ?
3. **Interpreting Ideas** Explain the role of self-interest in (a) forming a sole proprietorship, (b) becoming a limited partner, and (c) deciding where to work.
4. **Seeing Relationships** (a) How is the type of market structure related to the types of business organization you are most likely to find in an industry? (b) What type of business organization would you expect to be most common in perfect competition? Why?
5. **Analyzing Ideas** (a) Explain why vertical and horizontal combinations often hindered competition and free enterprise. (b) How have government regulations and antitrust laws promoted competition and free enterprise? (c) Has organized labor helped promote competition and free enterprise? Explain.
6. **Evaluating Ideas** Have (a) antitrust laws and (b) labor unions decreased efficiency in the economy? Explain.

H

Investigating Economic Issues

Reread the *Issues in Economics* feature on pages 134–135 and answer the following questions.

1. **Summarizing Ideas** What are the three categories into which the costs of government regulation fall?
2. **Interpreting Ideas** How was the government's role in laissez-faire capitalism different from its role today?
3. **Evaluating Viewpoints** (a) What are the main arguments in favor of government regulation of business? (b) What are the main arguments against government regulation of business? (c) Do you think there is too much government regulation of business? Explain.

I

Applying Economics

1. Investigate the businesses in your community and complete the following activities. (a) List three franchises and the goods or services each franchise provides. (b) List two cooperatives and their purposes. (c) List three nonprofit organizations and the goods or services each organization provides.
2. Research several recent mergers that have taken place in the United States. (a) Prepare a chart illustrating two of the mergers you researched. (b) In an essay, answer the question: Are mergers beneficial to the United States economy? Defend your answer.
3. Given the list of businesses below, answer the following questions. (a) What form of business organization are they? (b) In what market structure do they operate? (c) Are profits likely to be high, moderate, or low? (d) Is the wage rate for employees likely to be high, moderate, or low? Then in a brief paragraph for each business, explain your answers to each question.

a. General Motors
b. a local General Motors dealership
c. a local automobile repair shop
d. a corn farmer in Iowa
e. a local or neighborhood grocery store

164

J

Using Primary Sources

In the early 1980s, the Reagan administration pledged to reduce government regulations in the American economy. As you read the following excerpt from the *Economic Report of the President*, 1982, think about the reasons for favoring a "benefit-cost analysis" for existing and proposed regulations.

A Plan to Reduce Government Regulations

Many Federal rules have yielded benefits to the public. The automobile emission standards, for example, have substantially reduced emissions from this source.

Regulations, however, can also impose substantial costs on society. Regulations themselves can create problems which call for additional regulations. Furthermore, the resources used to comply with regulations are diverted from other activities, with a resultant loss in productivity and economic growth. . . . One group in society may receive the bulk of the benefits from a Federal regulation while the costs are borne primarily by some other group. . . .

Interest has risen in efforts to determine more precisely the benefits and the costs of regulation. The motive for incorporating benefit-cost analysis into the regulatory decision-making process is to achieve a more efficient allocation of government resources by subjecting the public sector to the same type of efficiency tests used in the private sector. In making an investment decision, for example, business executives compare the costs to be incurred with the expected revenues. The investment is likely to be pursued only if the expected costs are less than the expected revenues. . . .

The aim of requiring agencies to perform benefit-cost analysis is to make the regulatory process more efficient and to eliminate regulatory actions that, on balance, generate more costs than benefits. . . .

The review of a proposed Federal regulatory activity should involve analysis of three types of questions. The first is whether some form of market failure has occurred that warrants the imposition of regulation. The second is whether Federal regulation, in contrast to State and local regulation, is appropriate. The last question . . . is whether a specific regulation will increase net benefits to society. . . .

Source Review

1. Give an example of a Federal regulation that has provided the public with a substantial benefit. What are some disadvantages of regulations?
2. How does a benefit-cost analysis for regulations make public decision making more like decision making in the private sector?
3. Before new Federal regulations are approved, what three questions have to be answered? How might the answers to these questions help reduce the number of new federal regulations?

K

Reading About Economics

Baxandall, Rosalyn. *America's Working Women: A Documentary History—1600 to the Present*. New York: Random House. A selection of interesting first person accounts from working women in the United States that range from colonial times to the present.

Goulden, Joseph. *Meany*. New York: Atheneum. A biography of George Meany, one of America's best-known labor leaders, who served first as president of the AFL and then of the AFL-CIO.

Skinner, Wickham. "The Productivity Paradox." *Harvard Business Review* (July-August, 1986), pp. 55–59. An evaluation of the current methods of revitalizing American productivity.

Welles, Chris. "Is Deregulation Working?" *Business Week* (December 22, 1986), pp. 50–55. An evaluation of recent deregulation policies and their effects on the economy.

165

K **Reading About Economics** extends unit content with an annotated bibliography of suggested student readings.

TEACHING SUPPORT

CONVENIENTLY PRACTICAL!

- **Teacher's Resource Package**
A rich package featuring Unit Transparencies, the *Teacher's Manual and Resource Guide*, a binder, and dividers with color-coded tabs for convenient organization and storage

- **Chapter and Atlas Transparencies**
Colorful visuals that include charts, graphs, diagrams, and maps from the textbook to enhance group instruction

- **Workbook**
A variety of activities for each chapter that reinforce and enrich content

- ***Economics: Free Enterprise in Action* Test Bank**
A microcomputer software program that enables teachers to test the content they want by selecting from a comprehensive bank of test items or by writing their own

- **Teacher's Manual and Resource Guide**
A helpful teaching resource with chapter and section overviews, activities, and strategies—plus abundant copying masters for review, extension, enrichment, and testing

- **Sources in Economics: Readings in Free Enterprise**
Primary source readings with introductions and follow-up questions to extend economic study

- **Tests**
Chapter, unit, mid-book, and end-of-book tests for comprehensive assessment of content mastery

- **Light-Side Economics: Audiocassettes to Accompany *Economics: Free Enterprise in Action****
Recordings that clarify basic economic concepts through amusing situations and examples

**Audio reports in this package were originally broadcast on National Public Radio's daily news and information programs "All Things Considered" and "Morning Edition." For National Public Radio's Catalog offering 700 educational broadcasts along with the NPR station list, write to Pamela Gouge, NPR Cassette Publishing, 2025 M Street NW, Washington, DC, 20036.*

Teacher's Edition

ECONOMICS

Free Enterprise in Action

David E. O'Connor

HBJ Harcourt Brace Jovanovich

Orlando San Diego Chicago Dallas

An annotated Teacher's Edition is not automatically included with each shipment of a classroom set of textbooks. However, an annotated Teacher's Edition will be forwarded when requested by a teacher, an administrator, or a representative of Harcourt Brace Jovanovich, Inc.

The annotated Teacher's Edition of *ECONOMICS: Free Enterprise in Action* is complemented by the Teacher's Manual and Resource Guide. When used with the pupil's textbook, the Teacher's Edition and the Teacher's Manual and Resource Guide provide a complete economics program.

Copyright © 1988 by Harcourt Brace Jovanovich, Inc.

All rights reserved. No part of this publication may be reproduced or transmitted in any form or by any means, electronic or mechanical, including photocopy, recording, or any information storage and retrieval system, without permission in writing from the publisher.

Requests for permission to make copies of any part of the work should be mailed to: Permissions, Harcourt Brace Jovanovich, Publishers, Orlando, Florida 32887

Printed in the United States of America

ISBN 0-15-374201-1

ANSWER KEY CONTENTS

INTRODUCTION

OBJECTIVES OF THE TEXTBOOK

ECONOMICS: Free Enterprise in Action provides teachers and students with a comprehensive study of the basic concepts, principles, and practices of economics. The textbook is designed to meet three major goals. First, the textbook helps students develop an understanding of the principles that underlie the United States free enterprise system. Second, the textbook helps students understand the operations of the United States economy. Third, the textbook helps students develop an appreciation for the benefits of living in a nation that enjoys a free enterprise system.

Clear, Logical Framework

ECONOMICS: Free Enterprise in Action achieves its first and second goals through its clearly logical organization and highly readable text. Believing strongly in the need to bring economics to life, the author has written a narrative that makes complex economic concepts easily understandable to students and teachers alike. Headings and subheadings in every chapter provide a workable outline and overview. Paragraphs center on one clearly explained idea and present a logical flow of ideas from topic to topic.

Contemporary Applicability

To provide students with an understanding of the applicability of economics to their everyday lives, the textbook personalizes the study of economics. Each chapter begins with a quotation from a prominent economist or successful entrepreneur that sets the tone of the chapter. Each CHAPTER and UNIT REVIEW includes a primary source reading that enriches the students' understanding of the concepts and principles presented in each chapter or unit.

ECONOMICS: Free Enterprise in Action further personalizes the study of economics through its emphasis on people and the ways that economics influences the lives of ordinary Americans. Further applications of economic concepts and principles are made in the various features that are a part of each unit and chapter. For more information on these features, see pages A 2–A 4.

Benefits Of The Free Enterprise System

The third goal of the textbook is met in several ways. First, the textbook stresses the benefits of the American free enterprise system—a theme that is carried throughout the textbook and is further reinforced through the study of the last unit, which stresses comparative economics.

In this unit, students learn about the international dimension of economics. This unit gives students opportunities to compare the benefits of the free enterprise system learned in the first five units with the other economic systems in use worldwide.

Second, the textbook includes an *Everyday Economics Handbook* (see text pages 507–538), which introduces students to specific skills that will help them become wise consumers. Each consumer skill is correlated with the content of a chapter, and is reinforced with a suggested application on the CHAPTER REVIEW page. The consumer orientation is continued in *Careers in the Marketplace* (see text pages 539–544), a selection of careers that students can pursue.

SKILLS PROGRAM

The skills program advances all the major goals of *ECONOMICS: Free Enterprise in Action.* The skills program starts with built-in study aids that facilitate student reading and learning. Each chapter begins with a clear outline of topics (e.g., text pages 121, 243, and 385). Each chapter provides a STUDY GUIDE that provides students with a reading focus and a selected list of vocabulary terms. Each vocabulary term is highlighted in boldface type, is clearly defined in context, and is further defined in the *Glossary.*

A major component of the skills program is a skills presentation in each chapter. For examples of the skills program, see text pages 78–79, 110–111, and 366–367.

ORGANIZATION OF THE TEXTBOOK

Special care has been taken to make the overall organization of *ECONOMICS: Free Enterprise in Action* easy to use for students and teachers alike. In the chapter-by-chapter development, the textbook includes a number of teaching devices that help in organizing teaching strategies.

ILLUSTRATED OVERVIEW OF ECONOMICS

A 17-page ILLUSTRATED OVERVIEW OF ECONOMICS begins the textbook. This introduction to the textbook uses colorful and informative photographs and captions to familiarize the students with the most basic concepts of economics. As a prologue, the ILLUSTRATED OVERVIEW OF ECONOMICS serves the time-honored purpose of providing students with a basic framework on which to build a sound economic structure.

UNITS

ECONOMICS: Free Enterprise in Action is divided into six units, each of which begins with a special two-page unit opener that includes a dramatic full-page picture and a list of chapter titles (see text pages 18–19). The unit opener gives students a quick preview of the major topics that will be studied in the unit. Study aids at the end of each unit review main ideas, reinforce economic study skills, provide opportunities for enrichment, and give students practice in using primary sources. (For more on unit study aids, see pages A 3–A 4.)

CHAPTERS

The author has organized *ECONOMICS: Free Enterprise in Action* into 19 chapters, each of which provides a thorough discussion of a particular topic in the study of economics. Each chapter begins with a special two-page chapter opener that includes a dramatic full-page picture, a quotation from a notable economist or business leader, and a list of section titles and major section headings (see text pages 20–21). The quotation sets the tone for the chapter and helps stimulate student interest in the topic about to be studied.

SECTIONS

Each chapter of *ECONOMICS: Free Enterprise in Action* is divided into numbered sections. The titles of these sections, which are complete sentences, give students a summary statement of the section's major idea. Each of the 67 sections is suitable for a daily lesson in most economics classes. The organization into only 67 sections ensures that teachers will have adequate time for enrichment activities and tests.

THE REFERENCE LIBRARY

ECONOMICS: Free Enterprise in Action includes a valuable Reference Library (text pages 465–594). THE REFERENCE LIBRARY begins with a 15-page *Atlas of Economics* that includes 16 economic-data maps. The atlas also includes 7 charts and graphs, including "The Winners of the Nobel Memorial Prize in Economics." THE REFERENCE LIBRARY continues with the *World Economic Data File*, an 18-page section that provides relevant economic data on each of the world's independent nations.

A *Chronology of Major Economic Events* is a five-page section that provides a capsulized glimpse of major economic events and that allows students to integrate economic events with history.

The *Everyday Economics Handbook* is a 31-page feature that presents 19 how-to essays on being wise consumers, each one correlated to the chapter indicated by the essay's number.

Careers in the Marketplace provides a selection of 24 different careers, each of which has been keyed to an applicable section of the textbook through an annotation in the TEACHER'S EDITION.

THE REFERENCE LIBRARY concludes with a 12-page *Glossary* and a 32-page *Index*. For the convenience of students and teachers, side tabs make each of the components of THE REFERENCE LIBRARY visible and easy to locate.

FEATURES OF THE TEXTBOOK

Woven into the textbook are a number of skill and comprehension programs that accomplish essential economic goals in both the cognitive and affective learning areas. These valuable programs combine with the main text to provide students with the necessary instruction to become informed and effective contributors to the free enterprise system.

THE SKILLS PROGRAM

Believing that successful skills instruction depends upon a systematic presentation, *ECONOMICS: Free Enterprise in Action* has integrated with content a comprehensive skills instruction. Each of the 19 chapters includes a self-contained skills lesson, entitled BUILDING ECONOMIC SKILLS, easily recognizable on green-tinted pages. Each of these lessons promotes the mastery of a specific skill from one of four skill strands.

All skill lessons are closely tied to the content of the chapters in which they appear. Students are led through the various skills on a step-by-step basis, focusing on one learning operation at a time. After directed application of the skill, students are given an opportunity to practice the skill independently.

The skills are reinforced in the CHAPTER REVIEWS under the heading *Exercising Economic Skills.* Questions in each SECTION REVIEW and CHAPTER REVIEW provide further reinforcement.

THE ENRICHMENT PROGRAM

ECONOMICS: Free Enterprise in Action contains six types of enrichment features, each designed to enliven the study of economics and help students apply economics to everyday life.

Decision Makers In The Economy

Selected individuals of economic significance are succinctly profiled in DECISION MAKERS IN THE ECONOMY, a series of one-half page illustrated features (for example, see text page 24). These biographical vignettes include successful entrepreneurs and others who in one way or another have had an effect on the American economy.

Economics Reporter

Recognizing the need to show the connection between what is being read in the textbook with what is being said about economics in newspapers and newsmagazines and on television, the textbook includes a wide variety of short features entitled ECONOMICS REPORTER (see text page 47). Each chapter includes at least one ECONOMICS REPORTER. These features are set off with a green-tinted box and are presented in the textbook where specific correlation with the narrative content can most effectively be made.

Case Study

The chapter narrative includes a CASE STUDY that profiles enterprising Americans, key economic trends, or successful institutions that are models of economics in action (see text page 86). Clearly labeled CASE STUDY, the feature is positioned near the discussion of the principle or theory to which it makes application.

Highlights In Economics

Each of the six units of *ECONOMICS: Free Enterprise in Action* includes a HIGHLIGHTS IN ECONOMICS feature (see text page 124). These features, which are presented against a blue-tinted background, discuss significant turning points or moments in the history of economics. Their placement in the textbook is such that the impact of the event or events on economics can be most clearly understood by the students.

Issues In Economics

Each unit includes a two-page feature entitled ISSUES IN ECONOMICS (see text page 82). These features explore contemporary economic issues as they relate to the United States, and include such topics as "The Underground Economy—What It Means to a Nation" (see text page 350) and "The Impact of Multinational Corporations on the Developing World" (see text page 428).

Using Primary Sources

The second page of each CHAPTER REVIEW and UNIT REVIEW is called Using Primary Sources and contains a reading that further applies, extends, and enriches the students' study of economics. The feature begins with a brief introduction that details the background of the source. A Source Review provides a means of evaluating student comprehension of material.

THE STUDY AID PROGRAM

ECONOMICS: Free Enterprise in Action provides students and teachers with a comprehensive study aid program. Study aids are located at the beginning of each chapter as well as at the end of each section, chapter, and unit.

Chapter Study Guides

Each chapter begins with a one-half page CHAPTER STUDY GUIDE (see text page 22). The first part of the STUDY GUIDE, entitled Chapter Focus, includes a short introductory paragraph and a list of section titles. By using the Chapter Focus, teachers and students can quickly preview the key concepts of economics that are discussed in the chapter.

The second part of the CHAPTER STUDY GUIDE, entitled Terms to Know, is part of the textbook's comprehensive vocabulary program. It provides a selected list of important terms that are discussed and defined in the chapter.

Section Reviews

A SECTION REVIEW concludes each section of a chapter (see text page 26) and may have as many as three parts. The first part, DEFINE, asks the students to review boldfaced terms that were discussed in the section. The second part, IDENTIFY, asks students to identify people, legislation, and agencies described in the section. The third part consists of numbered questions to reinforce knowledge of key facts and main ideas. Each question is labeled with the critical thinking skill the students need to apply in order to answer the question.

The Answer Key in the TEACHER'S EDITION provides suggested, or model, answers to the questions in each SECTION REVIEW.

Chapter Reviews

Each chapter concludes with a two-page CHAPTER REVIEW designed to help students review and develop information in the text.

Reviewing Economic Terms. This first part of the CHAPTER REVIEW measures students' understanding of the economic terms introduced in the chapter.

Exercising Economic Skills. This two-part section reinforces the skill presentations for each chapter. The component includes one exercise for the skill lesson from the chapter and one exercise relating to the relevant section of the *Everyday Economics Handbook* in THE REFERENCE LIBRARY.

Thinking Critically About Economics. This section consists of questions that require the students to recall and interpret factual information presented in the chapter. Each question has a label that clearly indicates the skill students need to apply in answering the question.

Extending Economic Knowledge. This section provides three enrichment suggestions geared toward students with specific abilities. The first activity is basic and well within the reach of all students; the second is for students of average ability; and the third is for students who enjoy challenging activities.

Using Primary Sources. The second page of each CHAPTER REVIEW presents a primary source reading that is preceded by a brief introduction and followed by questions that help students analyze what they have read.

The Answer Key of the TEACHER'S EDITION provides suggested, or model, answers to the questions and exercises in the CHAPTER REVIEWS.

Unit Reviews

The two-page UNIT REVIEWS provide students with an opportunity to synthesize the material within a unit, enabling them to arrive at unit understanding. The UNIT REVIEWS in *ECONOMICS: Free Enterprise in Action* have six main parts (see text pages 92–93).

Reviewing Economic Ideas. This first part asks students to recall factual information from the various chapters of the unit. The questions often assist students in integrating factual information from the various chapters of the unit.

Connecting Economic Ideas. This part includes critical thinking questions that help students to bring the ideas from the various chapters together in a needed synthesis.

Investigating Economic Issues. This part consists of critical thinking questions based on the unit feature, ISSUES IN ECONOMICS, and helps students relate the economic concepts studied in the unit to current national and world developments.

Applying Economics. This part gives students the chance to go beyond the text by completing special projects and assignments.

Using Primary Sources. This part of the UNIT REVIEW asks students to interpret primary source materials.

Further Reading. The last part of each UNIT REVIEW provides students with an annotated bibliography of high-interest books relating to the material in the unit.

The Answer Key of the TEACHER'S EDITION also provides suggested, or model answers for relevant portions of each UNIT REVIEW.

ADDITIONAL LEARNING AIDS

ECONOMICS: Free Enterprise in Action also includes a variety of other learning aids to help both students and teachers.

Vocabulary Aids

Great care has been taken to make the textbook content clear and interesting to students. An important part of this task has involved the treatment of key economics terms. Such terms are set in boldface type and defined in context. Reinforcement of vocabulary development takes place in SECTION REVIEWS and CHAPTER REVIEWS. For the teacher's convenience, the Answer Key provides model answers.

Glossary. The Glossary in THE REFERENCE LIBRARY contains definitions for all terms that are boldfaced in the textbook. The Glossary also includes references indicating on which pages of the textbook the boldfaced terms appear.

Preteaching Vocabulary. Teachers are alerted to important vocabulary terms in each chapter of the textbook. This feature, found in the TEACHER'S MANUAL AND RESOURCE GUIDE, lists important terms and gives the page on which each term is boldfaced (see page TM 2 for an example).

Graphics And Other Illustrations

Graphs and charts are invaluable tools to economists as they work to explain concepts and theories. With this in mind, the textbook includes 114 colorful graphs and charts in the textbook. The narrative fully explains each graphic so that students may refer to the graph or chart as they read the text. In addition, the many full-color photographs throughout the textbook provide real-life examples of the concepts being studied.

THE TEACHER'S EDITION

This annotated TEACHER'S EDITION includes an Answer Key insert that provides suggested answers to all review questions. Annotations on the pupil pages provide additional teaching and learning strategies, and supply relevant cross-references.

THE TEACHER'S MANUAL AND RESOURCE GUIDE

The Teacher's Manual and Resource Guide (TMRG) is designed to help the busy teacher effectively use the textbook. The TMRG contains the Teacher's Manual and 12 different sets of copying masters that provide the teacher with additional resources for review, enrichment, and evaluation. The Teacher's Manual provides overviews of each unit, chapter, and section. It suggests unit goals and chapter objectives. It gives assistance in the preteaching of each chapter's vocabulary. It provides introductory and teaching strategies that are geared to student ability levels. It also suggests key study questions and provides answers to the study questions as key understandings.

AN INTRODUCTION TO ECONOMICS

CHAPTER

1 Economics and Economic Systems (text pages 20–43)

Section 1 Review (text page 26)

DEFINE

economics: Study of the choices people make to satisfy wants and needs.

consumer: Person who buys goods and services.

producer: Person who makes the goods and provides the services for consumers.

factor of production: Resource used to produce goods or services.

entrepreneurship: Risk taking and organizational abilities involved in starting a new business or introducing a new product to consumers.

trade-off: Sacrifice made when a resource used to produce one item cannot be used to produce another.

opportunity cost: Value of what a person gives up to get something else.

production possibilities curve: Graph that shows all the possible combinations of two goods or services that can be produced within a given time.

IDENTIFY

Henry F. Henderson: Entrepreneur and founder of Henderson Industries, the first black-owned company to manufacture equipment for the People's Republic of China.

1. **(a)** A capital good is a manufactured resource used to produce a finished product. A consumer good is the finished product that the consumer buys. **(b)** A lawn mower becomes a capital good when it is used in a business.
2. **(a)** People and nations alike must make economic choices because neither has enough resources to satisfy all wants and needs. **(b)** Factors of production are natural, human, and capital resources used to produce goods and services.
3. First, scientists and inventors use technology to produce new products. Second, entrepreneurs are needed to produce and market the new products created by the scientists and inventors. Third, entrepreneurs continually seek technological improvements to increase the efficiency of their businesses.
4. A trade-off is the sacrifice people give up of one good or service in order to obtain another, while the value of what people give up is called the opportunity cost.
5. Scarcity contributes to the need to make economic decisions because people's needs and wants are greater than the resources available to satisfy them. People must therefore make economic decisions about how to use best their available resources to satisfy the greatest number of needs and wants.
6. It is impossible to move from point **B** to point **F** on the curve on page 25 because point **F** lies outside the curve, indicating that current technology and other resources make production at that level an impossibility.

Section 2 Review (text page 31)

DEFINE

economic system: Organized set of procedures a nation uses in producing and distributing goods and services.

market: Place where goods and services are exchanged freely.

profit: Amount of money that remains after costs of production have been paid.

IDENTIFY

Adam Smith: Scottish economist (1723–1790) who wrote *An Inquiry into the Nature and Causes of the Wealth of Nations* (1776) in which he explained how self-interest helps the pure market economy grow, and government regulation hinders individual self-interest in regulating the market.

1. **(a)** The four types of economic systems are traditional, command, market, and mixed. **(b)** The Dinka of the southern Sudan, the Berbers of North Africa, and the aborigines of Australia have traditional economies. The Old Kingdom of ancient Egypt, the Chou Dynasty of China, and feudal Europe had command economies. A pure market economy exists only in theory. A mixed economy practices either capitalism (the United States and Japan), authoritarian socialism (the Soviet Union and People's Republic of China), or democratic socialism (Great Britain and Sweden).
2. In a capitalist system, individuals largely answer the basic economic questions, while under Communism the roles of individuals are limited because government planners determine the basic economic answers.
3. **(a)** A pure market economy seldom exists because it would be impracticable and unprofitable for individuals to produce all goods and services. A pure command economy no longer exists because no single person, such as the pharaoh in ancient Egypt, owns all the natural, human, and capital resources or can single-handedly determine the answers to all economic questions. **(b)** In a free economy, the "invisible hand of self-interest" regulates economic growth through the cumulative self-interest of individuals who unknowingly do what is best for the economy.

Section 3 Review

(text page 39)

DEFINE

free enterprise system: Economic system in which business is conducted freely with limited government interference.

private property: Goods that are owned by individuals or businesses rather than by the government.

contract: Legally binding agreement, either oral or written, between people to buy and sell goods and services.

competition: Economic rivalry that exists among businesses selling similar products.

standard of living: Economic measurement of well-being, usually by the average amount of goods an individiaul can consume over a given period of time.

circular flow model: Chart that shows how the exchanges are made in resource market, product market, and money payments.

IDENTIFY

public sector: Segment of the economy that includes the economic activities that are under the direct control of local, state, and federal governments.

private sector: Segment of the economy that includes the economic activities of households and private businesses.

1. **(a)** Answers will vary. Students might point out that the free enterprise system is important in the United States because people are free to exchange goods and services, work at a job of their own choosing, use their resources as they wish, and own and operate businesses. **(b)** Competition in a free enterprise system prevents one producer from controlling the market, promotes business efficiency, and encourages the improvement of existing products and the creation of new ones.
2. **(a)** The features of the United States economy are that Americans as individuals have the right to own private property and enter into contracts, make choices through the price system, engage in free enterprise and competition, make decisions based on self-interest and the profit motive, and do these things with limited government interference. **(b)** The goals of the United States economy are economic freedom, or freedom of choice in the marketplace; economic efficiency, or making the best use of scarce resources; economic equity,

or ensuring that all members of society share in the costs and benefits equally; economic security, or the private and public protection of people from poverty, unemployment, business failures, and medical emergencies; economic stability, or the ensuring of full employment and stable prices; and economic growth, or increasing the amount of goods and services each worker can produce.

3. Answers will vary. For example, some students may feel that economic freedom is the most important goal because it allows people to make economic choices. Some students may feel that economic efficiency is the most important goal because it allows the nation to produce the most products from its resources, helping preserve some of the resources for future citizens. Some students may feel that economic equity is the most important goal because it helps provide opportunities for all Americans to participate in and benefit from the economy. Some students may feel that economic security is the most important goal because it protects people from poverty and emergency situations. Some students may feel that economic stability is the most important goal because it relieves the tensions and other negative social costs caused by unemployment and wildly fluctuating prices. Some students may feel that economic growth is the most important goal because it allows the United States to become stronger and raises the nation's standard of living.

4. **(a)** The chart shows how the three major participants—households, government, and business—interact in the United States economy. **(b)** The arrows represent the direction of payments for goods and services in the United States economy.

Building Economic Skills *(text pages 40–41)*

See the annotations on text page 41.

Chapter 1 Review *(text pages 42–43)*

REVIEWING ECONOMIC TERMS

1. product
2. economic system
3. planned economy
4. profit
5. capitalism
6. free enterprise
7. economic stability
8. Adam Smith
9. circular flow model
10. standard of living

EXERCISING ECONOMIC SKILLS

1. Student lists should include the following features: DECISION MAKERS IN THE ECONOMY—Michael R. Hollis, page 24; CASE STUDY—The Mbuti of Central Africa, page 29; HIGHLIGHTS IN ECONOMICS—The Constitution: Protector of Free Enterprise, page 32; ECONOMICS REPORTER—What Are the Private Sector and the Public Sector?, page 34.

2. Answers will vary.

THINKING CRITICALLY ABOUT ECONOMICS

1. **(a)** Economics studies the choices people make in an effort to satisfy their wants and needs, and examines how people use scarce resources to produce and consume goods and services. **(b)** The three basic questions of economics are (1) What goods and services should be produced? (2) How should these goods and services be produced? and (3) For whom should these good and services be produced? **(c)** The United States is a free enterprise economy because individuals have the rights to own private property and enter into contracts, to make personal choices and to communicate those choices through the price system, to engage in free enterprise and competition, to make decisions based on self-interest and the profit motive, and to do all these things with a minimum of government regulation and intervention.

2. A *traditional economy* is based on the family or the tribe, and it conducts its business in a time-honored fashion with almost no change from the way things were done by the group's ancestors. In a *pure market economy*, individuals determine the answers to the three basic questions of what

goods are to be produced, how they are to be produced, and who will receive them. In a *pure command economy*, the government determines everything. Most economies in the world today are *mixed economies* classified according to the degree of government control: capitalism with the least government control, authoritarian socialism with the most, and democratic socialism with considerable government control but the retention of basic human rights.

3. **(a)** A resource is anything that people use to make or obtain what they need or want. **(b)** Resources that can be used to produce goods and services are called factors of production. **(c)** The five factors of production are natural resources, human resources, capital resources, technology, and entrepreneurship.

4. **(a)** Scarcity forces individuals, businesses, and governments to make choices among alternative wants and needs. Scarcity also explains why it is not always possible to achieve *all* of the nation's economic goals. **(b)** Opportunity cost is significant in economic decision making because policymakers, in choosing among the alternatives, must determine which costs are acceptable.

5. In a command economy, the government has complete control over the three basic economic questions of what goods and services are to be produced, who will produce them, and who will receive them. In a market economy, individuals make those decisions.

6. **(a)** The goals of the United States economy are *economic freedom*, or freedom of choice in the marketplace concerning how to dispose of income, where to work, how to invest or save, and what business decisions to make; *economic efficiency*, or making the best use of scarce resources; *economic equity*, sometimes called economic justice, which means policymakers must ensure that all members of society share in the costs and benefits of the free enterprise system in a relatively equal way; *economic security*, referring to private and public efforts to protect people from poverty, unemployment, business and bank failures, and disastrous medical costs; *economic stability*, or achieving full employment and stable prices; *economic growth*, or increasing the amount of goods and services each worker in society can produce. **(b)** Answers will vary. For example, students may point out that businesspeople will use the most advanced technology available because of its economic efficiency. Such technology may conflict with economic stability because it causes people to lose their jobs.

USING PRIMARY SOURCES

1. Friedman interprets "free market capitalism" as equality of opportunity.

2. The myth is that free market capitalism increases the inequalities between the rich and the poor. Friedman dispels the myth by making two main points. First, wherever the free market system operates, ordinary people have attained the highest levels of living. Second, the gap between rich and poor was wider in feudal societies and is wider in today's centrally planned societies than it is in today's free market economies.

3. He defines equality as an outcome—the opportunity everyone has to make choices. He claims that the use of force to achieve equality will destroy freedom.

4. Friedman believes capitalism provides equality of opportunity and greater freedom. A free society releases the energy and abilities of the people, making it the fairest and most efficient economic system.

CHAPTER

2 Demand in the Marketplace

(text pages 44–57)

Section 1 Review

(text page 48)

DEFINE

demand: Amount of a good or service a consumer is willing and able to buy at various prices during given time periods.

purchasing power: Amount of money that individuals have available to spend on goods and services.

utility: Amount of satisfaction that an individual receives from consuming a product.

1. **(a)** First, the consumer must be *willing* and *able* to buy at various prices. Second, demand must be for a *given period of time.* **(b)** The law of demand states that an increase in price causes a decrease in the quantity demanded, while a decrease in price causes an increase in the quantity demanded. **(c)** The substitution effect refers to the tendency of consumers to substitute a lower-priced product for a relatively more expensive product.
2. The demand curve plots information from the demand schedule.

Section 2 Review (text page 50)

DEFINE

elasticity of demand: Degree to which changes in a good's price affect the quantity demanded by consumers.

1. **(a)** Elastic demand is illustrated when a small increase in a good's price causes a major increase in the quantity demanded and when a small decrease in a good's price causes a major increase in the quantity demanded. **(b)** The second description fits the elastic demand for Company BCT's tapes because a small decrease in the tape's price causes a notable increase in demand.
2. **(a)** Answers will vary. **(b)** Answers will vary.
3. The basic difference in elastic demand and inelastic demand is the impact that a change in price has on demand for the product. *Elastic demand* for a product means that the demand for the product changes significantly when there is a change in the product's price. *Inelastic demand* for a product means that the demand for that product does not change significantly regardless of the change in price.
4. **(a)** People Express increased demand for its service by offering lower prices than its competition. **(b)** The substitution effect worked at first in People Express's favor in that travelers switched to People Express because of the low fares. Later, travelers switched away from People Express because competing airlines offered matching or lower fares than People Express, more on-time flights, and more complete service.
5. On the graph on page 49, the slope of the line showing elastic demand is much steeper than that shown on the graph on page 50, illustrating elastic demand.

Building Economic Skills (text pages 52–53)

See the annotations on text page 53.

Section 3 Review (text page 55)

DEFINE

substitute good: Item that can be used to replace the purchase of other items when prices rise.

complementary good: Item that is commonly used with another item, such as a paint brush with paint.

IDENTIFY

Wilma P. Mankiller: First woman leader of a major Indian nation, the Cherokees, whose goals for the Cherokees are solving unemployment, lack of education, and inadequate health care.

1. The determinants of demand are consumer *tastes and preferences*, a nonprice factor that can shift over time; *market size*, or the number of potential buyers for a product; *people's income*, with an increase in income, people have more money to spend on goods and services; *prices of related complementary or substitute goods*, an increase or decrease in which will affect the demand for a particular good; and *consumer expectations* about future disposable income.
2. A change in market size might result from production decisions such as the decision to launch a major advertising campaign, or from government policies such as opening trade with the People's Republic of China.

3. Answers will vary. For example, a student graph illustrating an increase in income will show a shift to the right on the demand curve.

Chapter 2 Review

(text pages 56–57)

REVIEWING ECONOMIC TERMS

1. e; 2. b; 3. a; 4. c.

EXERCISING ECONOMIC SKILLS

1. Student graphs should resemble the following graph.

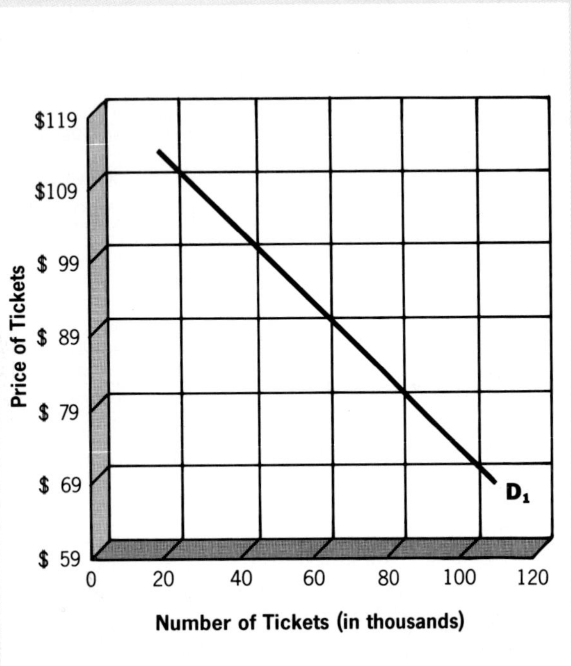

2. Answers will vary.

THINKING CRITICALLY ABOUT ECONOMICS

1. **(a)** The major factors affecting demand are price, consumer tastes and preferences, the size of the market, people's income, the prices of related goods, and consumer expectations. **(b)** Price affects some products differently from others because of elasticity of demand. **(c)** Answers will vary. For example, students may note that a larger market means increased demand, while a smaller market means decreased demand.

2. Diminishing marginal utility is the phenomenon that after a certain point, as more units of a product are consumed, the satisfaction from consuming additional units declines. Examples will vary.

3. Answers will vary. Students should be able to explain why the nonprice factor they selected is the most important influence on the demand for the product they selected.

USING PRIMARY SOURCES

1. Marshall defines economics as "a study of men as they live and move and think in the ordinary business of life."

2. Marshall says that economics is more exact than other social sciences because the motives for economic behavior can be measured more precisely than the motives for social behavior. Money is important because it serves as the precise measure for economic laws.

3. Marshall says that the study of economics is less exact than the physical sciences because human behavior cannot be measured exactly like the law of gravitation.

4. Marshall defines *economic law* as a statement of economic tendency "in which the strength of the motives chiefly concerned can be measured by a money price." *Economic law* is a statement of economic tendencies affecting human conduct whereas *social law* is a statement of social tendencies expected of members of a social group under certain conditions. The terms are similar in that both refer to human conduct, and because there is "no hard and sharp line of division" between those social laws which may or may not also be regarded as economic laws. The definitions are important to the study of economics because they establish a criteria for measuring economic behavior.

CHAPTER

3 Supply in the Marketplace

(text pages 58–73)

Section 1 Review

(text page 62)

DEFINE

supply: Quantity of goods and services that producers offer; directly related to the prices producers charge.

law of supply: Principle which states that producers supply more products when they can charge higher prices and fewer products when they must charge lower prices.

supply schedule: Table that lists each quantity of a product that producers are willing to supply at various market prices.

supply curve: Graph that plots the information found in a supply schedule to illustrate what quantity of a product producers are willing to supply at various market prices.

revenue: Money a business takes in from the sale of the goods it produces.

cost of production: Wages and salaries, rents, interest, and payments to other entrepreneurs and resource suppliers.

1. **(a)** Profit is the major determinant of a producer's supply schedule because the quantity offered at each price is based on the amount of profit that producers make at each price. **(b)** Profits direct the use of resources because entrepreneurs will use resources to produce goods as long as the profit is attractive to them. **(c)** When companies in a business make a profit, other entrepreneurs are encouraged to open competing businesses. When companies fail to make an attractive profit, entrepreneurs are discouraged from entering the business.
2. **(a)** Price is directly related to supply because producers supply more products when they can charge higher prices and fewer products when they must charge lower prices. **(b)** Revenue and profit are directly related because a producer makes a profit when the money taken in from the sale of goods is greater than the cost of their production.
3. Both curves plot information from a schedule, but a demand curve slopes downward and a supply curve slopes upward.
4. As a producer, you would be willing and able to produce more of a product at a high price rather than a low price when demand for the product remains high because your profits would be increased.

Section 2 Review

(text page 64)

DEFINE

elasticity of supply: Degree to which a good's supply is affected by changes in price.

1. Elastic supply exists when producers significantly change production in response to relatively small increases or decreases in the product's price. Inelastic supply exists when, regardless of price, producers are unable or unwilling to increase or decrease the supply of a product.
2. **(a)** The graphs on page 63 illustrate the difference between elastic and inelastic demand by showing that there is a small slope for elastic supply, but a very steep slope for inelastic supply, even with price increases in both posters and computer design systems. **(b)** If the price of posters rose to $4.50, the supply would increase even more rapidly than on the present graph. **(c)** There would be little change in the supply because the number of designs is limited, regardless of price.

Building Economic Skills

(text page 66)

Student overviews should resemble the overview shown on page A 12.

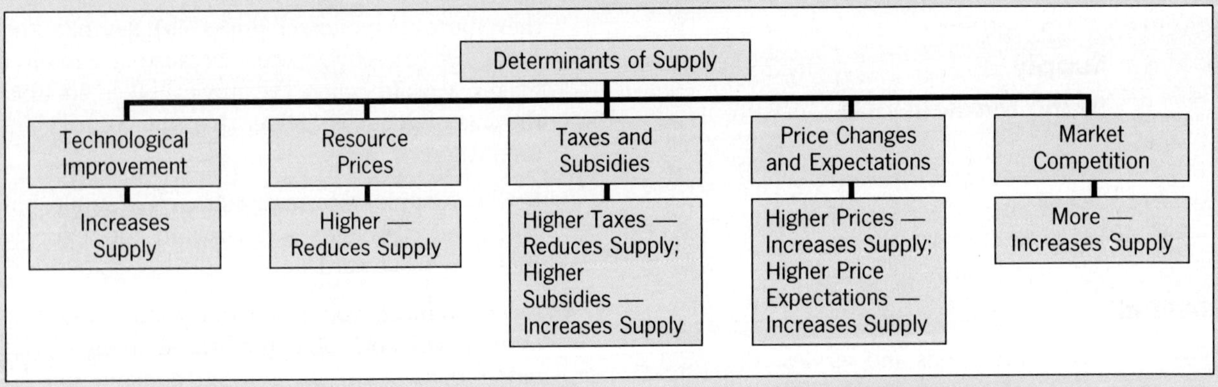

Section 3 Review

(text page 68)

DEFINE

technology: Use of science to create new products or more efficient ways to produce products.

venture capital: Money invested in high-risk but promising new businesses; also known as risk capital.

competition: Economic rivalry among businesses selling similar products.

IDENTIFY

Romesh Wadhwani: Entrepreneur born in Bombay, India, who in the early 1980s founded American Robot, a company that offered second-phase robotics involving the total automation and computerization of a factory, including administration as well as assembly-line production.

Robert A. Swanson: Co-founder in 1976 and chief executive officer of Genentech, Inc., a pioneer in recombinant DNA and gene-splicing for the pharmaceutical industry, a major new industry for the twenty-first century.

1. **(a)** The nonprice determinants of supply are the following: *technological improvement*, the new scientific knowledge used to change the methods of production; *resource prices*, the prices paid for materials or wages; *taxes*, levies imposed on the product that add to production costs and reduce the supply, and *subsidies*, money grants that reduce production costs and increase the supply; *price changes*, changes in the prices of other products that shift a supply curve; *price expectations*, attitudes about future prices that affect current supply; and *market competition*, the incentives for producers to enter or to exit a field. **(b)** Technological improvement increases supply by either lowering production costs or improving the goods themselves, or both. **(c)** Market competition affects supply through the entry of more producers into a field where demand is great or profit expectations are high, and the exit of producers from the field when consumer demand is low and profit expectations are low.
2. **(a)** A *change in quantity supplied* means a change in the amount of a product for sale because of a change in price, while a *change in supply* means that the entire supply schedule has changed. **(b)** A tax is added to production costs and reduces the supply because sellers must raise prices to make a profit comparable to the pretax profit. As a grant of money, a subsidy reduces production costs and increases the supply because more goods can be purchased without an increase in costs.
3. **(a)** The subject of the graph is the effects of decreasing competition on supply. **(b)** Decreased competition causes a shift to the left because there is a smaller supply of products.

Section 4 Review

(text page 71)

DEFINE

overhead: Fixed costs for producers.

total cost: Sum of the fixed and variable costs of production.

marginal cost: Variable expense incurred by producing one more unit of output.

1. **(a)** The costs of production affect supply because they determine how much it costs producers to produce a product and are a major factor in setting the price of the product. In addition, costs and price interact to determine the profit margin, which directly influences the amount of a product producers are willing to supply. When production costs increase, producers usually raise the price of the product to cover the increased costs and to protect their profit margin. If consumers are unwilling to pay the higher price, producers will not produce as much of the product and the supply will decrease. When production costs decrease, producers will usually supply more of the product at the market price because their profit margin is larger. **(b)** The law of diminishing marginal returns states that as more of one resource is added to a fixed supply of other resources, the output per unit of input may increase for a time, but eventually the rate of increase of productivity will diminish.

2. **(a)** A fixed cost—interest payments, rent, taxes, salaries—remains the same whether the producer makes nothing, very little, or large quantities. A variable cost—usually associated with labor and raw materials—changes with changes in output. **(b)** A total cost is the sum of fixed and variable costs of production, while average total costs are the sum of the average fixed costs and the average variable costs.

3. At zero output, a firm's total costs are equal to its fixed costs, but as production increases, so do the total costs as the variable costs are added to the fixed costs.

4. **(a)** The addition of more labor hurt Dynamic Tees' production. **(b)** Additional workers hurt production because Dynamic Tee's reached the point of diminishing returns, where the addition of another worker contributed less to the production of shirts than the previous worker did. **(c)** The optimal number of employees is 5 (point **E**).

Chapter 3 Review

(text pages 72–73)

REVIEWING ECONOMIC TERMS

1. d; **2.** b; **3.** a; **4.** f; **5.** e.

EXERCISING ECONOMIC SKILLS

1. Student overviews should resemble the following overview.

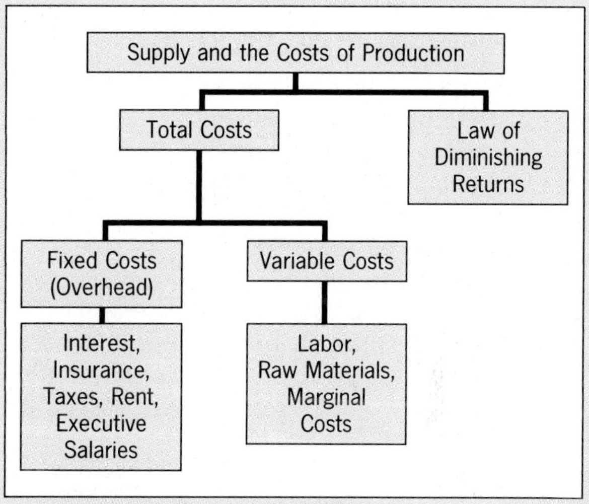

2. Answers will vary.

THINKING CRITICALLY ABOUT ECONOMICS

1. **(a)** Profit is the amount of money that producers make after all the costs of production have been paid. Making a profit, is in the producers' self-interest. To make a profit, producers must provide the goods and services that consumers want at prices consumers are willing and able to pay. **(b)** A good's elasticity of supply is determined by changes in price. **(c)** The determinants of supply are the following: *technological improvement*, the new scientific knowledge used to change the methods of production; *resource prices*, the price paid for materials and wages; *taxes*, levies imposed on a product that are additional production costs, and *subsidies*, money grants that reduce production costs; *price changes*, changes in the prices of other products that shift a supply curve; *price expectations*, attitudes about future prices that affect current supply; and *market competition*, the incentive for producers to enter or exit the field. **(d)** Producers

must consider fixed costs, variable costs, total costs and average total costs, and marginal costs in making production decisions.

2. Elastic supply exists when producers significantly change production in response to relatively small increases or decreases in the product's price. Inelastic supply exists when producers are unable or unwilling to increase or decrease the supply of a product, regardless of price. Perfectly inelastic supply exists when, regardless of price, producers cannot increase the quantity supplied.

3. *Technological improvement* can lower production costs and increase supply by improving the methods of production. An *increase in resource prices* for materials and the wages paid to workers raises the cost of production and reduces supply. *Higher taxes* on the product add to production costs and reduce supply, while *higher subsidies* reduce production costs and increase supply. *Increases in the prices of other products* may lead to increased supply. *Expectations of future price increases* may also increase current supply. *Increased market competition* increases the supply of a good.

4. Variable costs are important to a producer's production decision making because an employer may have to hire or lay off workers because of demand, or the cost of raw materials used in a good may be too expensive to increase production.

USING PRIMARY SOURCES

1. Alvin Toffler states that in an unchanging society permanence was the ideal and people built things to last, but in a society with rapidly advancing technology, it is easier and less expensive to replace a good than it is to repair it.

2. The economics of transience exists because (1) advancing technology lowers the costs of manufacture much more rapidly than the costs of repair, (2) advancing technology does not allow improvement upon a product, so producers build for the short term rather than the long term, and (3) uncertainty about the future but certainty of the inevitability of change causes producers to hesitate to commit large resources to rigidly fixed objects intended to serve unchanging purposes.

3. Product obsolescence occurs when a product is no longer useful, the fear of which impels producers to make innovations while consumers prefer rented, disposable, or temporary products. Obsolescence occurs when a product deteriorates to the point at which it cannot perform its original functions, when a new product is made that performs the functions more effectively, and when the needs of the consumer change.

CHAPTER

4 The Price System in the Marketplace

(text pages 74–75)

Building Economic Skills

(text pages 78–79)

See the annotation on text page 79.

Section 1 Review

(text page 81)

DEFINE

price system: Economic system based on the principles that everything bought or sold in a market has a price and that price is a good measure of what products should be produced, how they should be produced, and for whom they should be produced.

IDENTIFY

Walter B. Wriston: Former chief executive officer of Citicorp, the largest banking organization in the United States. Opposed to trade protectionism, Wriston believes that the world economy is a single global market, not a collection of separate national markets, created through technological advances that allow information and money to travel great distances in seconds.

1. **(a)** The price system is based on two principles: that everything bought and sold has a price, and that price is a good measure of what products should be produced, how they should be produced, and for whom they should be produced.

(**b**) Prices communicate by telling consumers how much it costs to produce a product, and consumers respond by purchasing or not purchasing a product.

2. (**a**) Producers' self-interest is to make the maximum profit. (**b**) Consumers' self-interest is to buy a product at the lowest possible price.

3. (**a**) The level of prices provide incentives for resource owners to sell their resources to producers, for producers to produce goods and services, and for consumers to purchase goods and services. (**b**) The information function is important in the resource market because without price information managers of businesses would not know in advance how much to pay for natural, human, and capital resources.

Section 2 Review

(text page 87)

DEFINE

market equilibrium: Condition in which supply and demand for a product are equal, making the prices charged for a product relatively stable.

surplus: Condition in which the quantity of a good produced exceeds the quantity demanded at the price offered.

shortage: Condition in which the quantity of a good demanded exceeds the quantity supplied at the price offered.

1. The market equilibrium is the best balance between consumer self-interest and producer self-interest because supply and demand are equal and prices are relatively stable.

2. Changing consumer tastes affect price by raising prices with increased demand and lowering prices with reduced demand.

3. At point **A**, the demand for motor scooters at a price of $1,500 is 100,000. At point **B**, the company would produce 500,000 scooters to sell at $1,500. At point **C**, the company would produce only 100,000 scooters to sell at $500. At point **D**, consumer demand for scooters at $500 is 500,000. The equilibrium point, $\mathbf{E_1}$, shows that supply and demand are equal when 300,000 scooters are produced to sell at $1,000 each. The shaded area below $\mathbf{E_1}$ indicates a condition in which a shortage would exist. The shaded area above $\mathbf{E_1}$ indicates a condition in which a surplus would exist.

Section 3 Review

(text page 89)

DEFINE

externalities: Negative side effects, or social costs, of a producer's or consumer's actions on people not connected with the production or consumption of the good.

price ceiling: Government regulation that prohibits prices from rising above a certain maximum level.

price floor: Government regulation that prohibits prices from falling below a certain minimum level.

1. (**a**) The price system pulls together the decisions of consumers and producers to bring about market equilibrium. (**b**) The price system contributes to economic freedom because it allows individuals and businesses to interact and cooperate freely.

2. (**a**) Price controls affect demand and result in shortages because consumers demand more products than the producer is willing to supply at the legal price. (**b**) Price floors result in surpluses because a guaranteed minimum price encourages producers to maintain a high level of production. The oversupply provides more products than the consumer is willing to buy at the fixed low price. (**c**) The government has set price floors to stabilize agricultural products. (**d**) Price controls ensure a supply of agricultural products and enable farmers to cover their production costs.

3. (**a**) Efficiency is important to an economic system to moderate the use of scarce resources. (**b**) Answers will vary. Some students may feel that the producer should pay the costs because the process of production is the cause of the

problem. Other students may feel that the costs should remain as social costs because if the producers pay the costs, prices will increase too much.

4. **(a)** *Proponents* of the price system argue that the price system forces producers to make the goods and services that the public wants in the most efficient manner. The price system also allows for personal freedom and economic cooperation between individuals and businesses. *Opponents* of the price system argue that the system works against the free enterprise system because only a few large producers are able to achieve maximum efficiency. When these large producers control the marketplace, competition declines, the price system weakens, and the consumer suffers. Opponents also point out that the price system does not take into account externalities, nor does it set prices for all the goods and services in the economy, such as local government water and sewer rates and public utility rates. **(b)** Answers will vary. For example, students may support the price system because it allows freedom in the marketplace through the economic activities of individuals and businesspeople cooperating freely through the price system. The alternative is a directed, controlled economy, the opposite of the free enterprise system.

Chapter 4 Review

(text pages 90–91)

REVIEWING ECONOMIC TERMS

1. price system
2. market equilibrium
3. surplus
4. externalities
5. price ceiling

EXERCISING ECONOMIC SKILLS

1. **(a)** The excerpt describes OPEC's activities. **(b)** *Who:* The Organization of Petroleum Exporting Countries; *What:* A cartel formed to regulate the production and sale of oil; *Where:* The Middle East, North Africa, and South America; *When:* Since 1960; *Why:* To control world oil prices; *How:* By limiting the supply of oil and setting "official" prices. **(c)** Answers will vary. Many students, however, may feel the excerpt presents only facts. **(d)** Answers will vary. Many students, however, will feel the author has no bias. **(e)** OPEC's control of oil's supply and price has caused the price of oil to rise significantly since 1960. The United States alliance with Israel caused OPEC to use oil as a political weapon against the United States.

2. Answers will vary.

THINKING CRITICALLY ABOUT ECONOMICS

1. **(a)** Self-interest motivates producers to produce more goods and services when higher prices can be charged and fewer goods and services when lower prices can be charged, while self-interest motivates consumers to demand more goods and services at lower prices. **(b)** The equilibrium point is the point on a graph at which the supply and demand curves meet. It means that the supply and demand for a product are equal, and that the price charged for a product is stable. **(c)** The price system contributes to market equilibrium by determining that point at which the needs of both producers and consumers are best satisfied.

2. **(a)** Prices communicate by having producers tell consumers how much it costs to produce a product, and consumers say how much they are willing to pay for a product. **(b)** The price system coordinates market activities in the private sector by providing information, offering incentives, and establishing limits on buying.

3. **(a)** The functions of the price system are to provide information to resource owners, producers, and consumers; to provide incentives for resource owners, producers, and consumers about buying decisions; and to place limits on the availability of products and resources to those who can afford to buy them. **(b)** Answers will vary. For example, students may consider the information function as most important because in a free enterprise system businesspeople need to know how much they must pay for natural, human, and capital resources that make up the factors of production.

4. **(a)** Personal freedom is important in the United States economy because it allows for a competitive price system that forces producers to make the goods and services that the public wants in the most efficient manner, using the best techniques at the lowest cost. **(b)** Personal freedom influences the price system because individuals and businesses cooperate freely through the price system. The alternative is a directed, involuntary economy.

5. **(a)** Price ceilings and price floors are designed to protect consumers and producers by stabilizing prices and enabling some producers, particularly farmers, to cover their production costs. Price controls, however, often result in surpluses or shortages in production and prevent the market from reaching equilibrium. **(b)** Price ceilings and price floors are adopted because the price system cannot reach equilibrium on its own, but once the price controls are instituted, they fail because the price system is unable to eliminate the resulting surpluses or shortages.

USING PRIMARY SOURCES

1. Adam Smith wrote that a commodity's natural price was affected by the rent on the land, the wages of labor, and the costs of raising, preparing, and bringing a good to market.

2. Natural price is the precise selling price of a commodity at the real costs to the seller who brought it to market.

3. Effectual demand regulates the market price of a good through the quantity actually brought to market and the demand of those willing to pay the natural price.

4. A commodity's market price would be higher than its natural price when its quantity is less than the effectual demand. The price would be lower when the quantity is more than the effectual demand.

5. A commodity's natural price and its market price are the same when the supply meets the demand. It is in the best interests of producers and consumers to match supply and effectual demand, because producers will sell their goods, consumers will satisfy their wants or needs, and both will be satisfied with the price.

Unit One Review

(text pages 92–93)

REVIEWING ECONOMIC IDEAS

1. **(a)** A good is a physical object that can be purchased, and a service is an action or activity done for others for a fee. **(b)** A need is a good or service necessary for survival, while a want is a good or service that people consume beyond what is needed for survival.

2. **(a)** A traditional economy looks to the past for the answers to the three basic economic questions of what to produce, how to produce it, and for whom should it be produced. **(b)** The government answers these questions in a command economy. **(c)** Individuals answer the basic economic questions in a market economy.

3. The three main types of mixed economies are *capitalism*, in which individuals own and control the factors of production, and the government intervenes on a limited basis; *authoritarian socialism*, or Communism, in which the government owns or controls almost all the means of production and undertakes centralized economic planning; and *democratic socialism*, in which the government owns some of the factors of production and determines economic planning through elected officials, but is a system in which basic human rights are protected.

4. **(a)** The main features of the United States economy are that individuals have the right to own private property and enter into contracts, make personal choices and communicate those choices through the price system, engage in free enterprise and competition, make decisions based on self-interest and the profit motive, and face only limited government intervention and regulation. **(b)** The goals of the United States economy are *economic freedom*, or freedom of choice in the marketplace; *economic efficiency*, or making the best use of scarce resources; *economic equity*, or ensuring that all members of society share equally in the costs and benefits of the free enterprise system; *economic security*, or the private and public protection of people from poverty, unemployment, business failures, and emergencies; *economic stability*, or the ensuring of full employment and stable prices; and *economic*

growth, or increasing the amount of goods and services each worker can produce.

5. **(a)** The determinants of demand are *consumer tastes and preferences,* a nonprice factor that can shift over time; *market size,* or the number of potential buyers for a product; *income,* the amount of money people have to spend on goods and services; *prices of related complementary or substitute goods,* an increase or decrease in which will affect the demand for a particular good; and *consumer expectations about disposable income*—fears of a decrease or hopes of an increase in income will affect demand for a particular good. **(b)** The determinants of supply are *technological improvement,* the new scientific knowledge used to change the methods of production; *resource prices,* the prices paid for materials or wages; *taxes,* levies imposed on the product that add to production costs and reduce supply, and *subsidies,* money grants that reduce production costs and increase supply; *price changes,* changes in the price of other goods that affect current supply; *price expectations,* attitudes about price changes that affect current supply; and *market competition,* the incentives for producers to enter or exit the marketplace. **(c)** The functions of price are to provide information to resource owners, producers, and consumers; provide incentives to act in self-interest in a market system; and to place limitations on consumer buying.

6. **(a)** The law of demand states that an increase in price causes a decrease in the quantity demanded, while a decrease in price causes an increase in the quantity demanded. **(b)** The law of supply states that producers supply more products when they can charge higher prices and few products when they must charge lower prices. **(c)** The law of diminishing marginal utility states that as more units of a product are consumed, the utility received from consuming each additional unit declines. **(d)** The law of diminishing returns states that as more of one resource—such as labor—is added to a fixed supply of other resources—such as natural resources and capital—the output per unit of input may increase for a time, but eventually the rate of increase of productivity will diminish.

CONNECTING ECONOMIC IDEAS

1. **(a)** An entrepreneur in a capitalist economy undertakes the financial risks in providing the capital to start a new business or to introduce a new product. If successful, the new business or new product contributes to economic growth by providing gainful employment to workers to produce the good to satisfy consumer demand. **(b)** Entrepreneurship does not play a major role in Communist economies because central planners make economic decisions of what goods to produce, leaving no room for the individual entrepreneur.

2. Scarcity is a basic fact of economic life because human needs and wants are usually greater than the resources available to satisfy them. Efficiency is an important economic goal because it makes the best use of scarce resources. It is measured by how many goods and services a nation's workers can produce.

3. Without the profit motive in the free enterprise system, there would be no incentive for investment and thus no means of achieving economic growth.

4. **(a)** Answers will vary. Students might point out that the self-interest of individuals seeking profit in the marketplace could only work where a large measure of economic freedom exists. **(b)** Demand and supply interact to bring about market equilibrium. **(c)** Both laws predict that as more units are produced and consumed, there are diminishing returns for producers and consumers.

5. **(a)** They both reduce demand. **(b)** Opportunity costs affect supply because when economic choices are made, the supply of the chosen products decreases while the supply of those products not chosen does not decrease. The substitution effect affects supply because as prices rise, people substitute lower-priced products for the relatively more expensive product, thereby decreasing the supply of the substitute products.

6. Answers will vary. For example, students may feel the laws favor entrepreneurs because entrepreneurs have many ways to influence demand and supply. Other students may feel that the

laws do not favor entrepreneurs because entrepreneurs seem to have little control over demand in the price system. Examples will vary.

INVESTIGATING ECONOMIC ISSUES

1. **(a)** OPEC is the Organization of Petroleum Exporting Countries. **(b)** A cartel is a group that is formally bound together to regulate the production and sale of a good or service.

2. **(a)** Oil shortages created by OPEC's production ceilings caused gasoline prices in the United States to rise during the 1970s. **(b)** People's incomes, lowered because of a severe recession, combined with serious efforts at energy conservation to reduce demand for oil products in the United States in the late 1970s and early 1980s. **(c)** Gasoline prices fell during the 1980s because there were oil surpluses.

3. **(a)** A cartel affects supply by agreeing to production limits. **(b)** It affects price by setting the price, rather than letting the market determine price.

4. **(a)** Positive effects on the world economy as a result of the OPEC cartel's actions during the 1970s were that oil-consuming nations were forced to adopt energy conservation measures. Oil-producing nations improved their economies through the increased revenues. **(b)** Negative effects of OPEC actions were high inflation throughout the world, shortages in oil products, reduced business activity, and a cutback in services and public projects in the developing nations. **(c)** Answers will vary. Students might point out that OPEC's actions forced the world to take energy conservation seriously, to build fuel-efficient automobiles and trucks, raise thermostats in the hot summer and lower them in the winter, and to seek alternatives for oil-based products. On the negative side, students might indicate that the high inflation hurt most world economies and that it was not eradicated everywhere by a disruption of the OPEC cartel in the 1980s. Overall, a lesson in economics was learned about the dangers of monopolies in upsetting the balance in the world economy.

USING PRIMARY SOURCES

1. OPEC's ability to dictate world oil prices is limited by low worldwide demand caused by the stockpiling of cheap oil by oil companies and consumers.

2. OPEC is also limited in its ability to dictate oil prices because of disagreement within the cartel about production limitations; some members wish to continue pumping oil and Iraq is exempt from the quotas.

3. Non-OPEC oil-producing nations have not limited production despite low demand, and some oil-producing nations refuse to go along with OPEC unless the OPEC nations hold to their own agreement.

TEACHER'S NOTES

BUSINESS IN THE FREE ENTERPRISE SYSTEM

CHAPTER

5 Business Organizations

(text pages 96–119)

Section 1 Review

(text page 108)

DEFINE

liability: Debt or amount of money owed by a business.

stockholder: Individual who invests in a corporation by buying shares of stock.

stock: Certificate of ownership in the corporation.

preferred stock: Share of ownership in a corporation that offers a fixed dividend paid from profits before dividends on common stock.

corporate bond: Certificate, offering a fixed interest rate, issued by a corporation in exchange for money borrowed from investors.

articles of incorporation: Application for a corporate charter with a state in which a corporation will have its headquarters.

IDENTIFY

Small Business Administration: Independent government agency that aids, counsels, assists, and protects the interests of small business owners.

chief executive officer: Highest ranking executive in a corporation.

Portia Issacson: Founder, president, and chief executive officer of Future Computing Inc., a consulting firm that analyzes market trends in the personal computer industry.

Lee Iacocca: President of the Chrysler Corporation who saved Chrysler from financial disaster and is best known for his straightforward approach to business.

1. **(a)** The three forms of business organization are sole proprietorship, partnership, and corporation. **(b)** In a sole proprietorship, the owner has complete business control. In a general partnership, control is shared among the partners. In a limited partnership, the partners rarely have any control over business decisions. In a corporation, the board of directors sets the overall policies and goals with the corporate officers making the day-to-day decisions.

2. **(a)** **Sole Proprietorship** *Advantages* A sole proprietorship is easy to form; the proprietor makes all the decisions, which generally saves time and allows for quick responsiveness to trends; and the sole proprietor gets all of the profits. *Disadvantages* The proprietor must make all the business decisions and has unlimited liability if the business suffers losses. **General Partnership** *Advantages* A partnership is easy to form and partners bring additional capital or expertise to the business venture. General partnerships can specialize, assigning specific business duties to different partners. General partners also share decision making, and decisions made after discussion are often more informed than those without the benefit of additional opinions. *Disadvantages* Each general partner has unlimited liability. Shared decision making can lead to arguments and conflicts among the partners. The life of the partnership is dependent on the willingness and ability of the general partners to stay in business together. Profits are shared among the partners. **Limited Partnership** *Advantages* The chief advantage of a limited partnership is that each partner is liable only to the limit of his investment in the partnership. *Disadvantage* The chief disadvantage in a limited partnership is that limited partners rarely take an active role in business decisions. **(b)** Answers will vary. For example, stu-

dents may feel that the general partnership is the best type of business organization because partners can specialize and decision making is shared. Some students may feel that a sole proprietorship is the best type of organization because the proprietor makes all the decisions and receives all the profits. Some students may feel that limited partnerships are the best type of organization because liability is limited and limited partners do not have to take an active role in business decisions.

3. **(a)** According to the graph on page 105, the top two categories are natural resources (4) and automotive (2). **(b)** Answers will vary. For example, students may point out that petroleum products provide a majority of the fuel used in the United States. Automobiles, ships, and trains run on oil or oil products. Oil is also used to generate much of the nation's electricity.

Building Economic Skills *(text pages 110–111)*

1. The informational terms are technical efficiency, production process, and businesses.
2. **(a)** The subject is the technical efficiency of the production process. **(b)** The main idea is the factors that influence technical efficiency of businesses.
3. The performance terms are state and identify.
4. Student overviews should resemble the following overview.

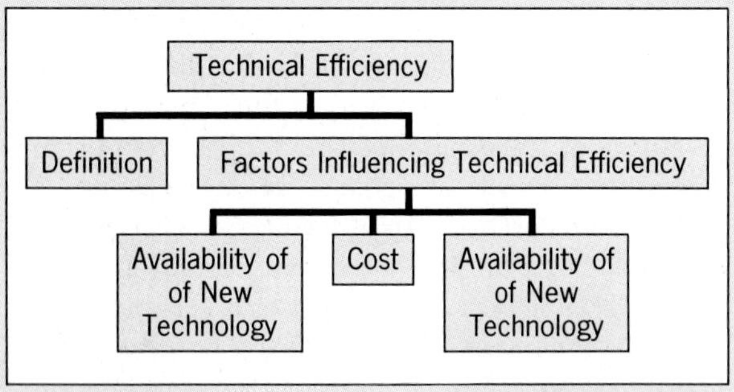

5. Essays will vary.

Section 2 Review *(text page 114)*

DEFINE

merger: Business arrangement in which one company absorbs another.

horizontal combination: Merger between two or more companies that produce the same good or service or dominate one phase of a service or of a good's production.

vertical combination: Merger between two or more companies that are involved in different phases of a service or of a good's production.

conglomerate combination: Merger between two or more companies producing or marketing different products.

subsidiary: Company that retains its corporate identity after its acquisition by another company.

1. **(a)** A *horizontal combination* is a merger between two or more companies that produce the same good or service or dominate one phase of a service or of a good's production. A *vertical combination* is a merger between two or more companies that are involved in different phases of a service or the production of the same good. A *conglomerate combination* is a merger between two or more companies producing or marketing different products. **(b)** Answers will vary. For example, students may use the Standard Oil Company of the late 1800s as an example of a horizontal combination, the United States Steel Corporation of the late 1800s as an example of a vertical combination, and the International Telephone and Telegraph Corporation (ITT) before its forced divestment by the government in the 1980s as an example of a conglomerate combination.
2. **(a)** Answers will vary. For example, students may note that as a result of a merger a corporation can borrow more money for further expansion, can diversify its product line by acquiring a different business with an established market, and can save money because buying an existing

business is often less expensive than starting a new one. **(b)** Corporate methods and philosophies of merged companies often conflict and the conglomerate's resources may be drained by one or more unprofitable subsidiaries. **(c)** Answers will vary. For example students may feel the acquired subsidiary benefits because it becomes part of a larger corporate entity, with increased capital and marketing.

3. Horizontal combinations have often resulted in a monopoly because as the combination absorbed more and more of the companies producing a good or service, the competition was reduced and eventually the combination took control of the production of that good or service.

4. The recent trend has been toward corporate combinations because government efforts to spur economic growth have resulted in more lenient regulation of mergers. Corporations, realizing mergers can help generate more cash for further expansion and provide tax benefits, have sought companies to acquire.

5. Students who agree may feel that corporate combinations do contribute to the economic growth of the nation because the conglomerates are better able to compete on the international market. Students who disagree may feel that unlimited corporate combinations will lead to a few huge companies controlling most areas of production and sales, a situation that could stifle economic growth by eliminating small businesses.

6. According to the chart, a horizontal combination can eventually control most or all of the producers of a service or good. They can then set prices and establish quality as they see fit because there is no competition. A vertical combination can control most of the costs of production by acquiring sources of raw materials and methods of transporting goods. It can then reduce its price until it drives competitors out of business, eliminating competition and leaving the market open to its product at its price. A conglomerate combination seems less likely to create a monopoly or control an industry because it is a combination of a variety of unrelated businesses. Therefore it is less likely to be able to arbitrarily set high prices that hurt consumers.

Section 3 Review

(text page 117)

DEFINE

franchise: Contract in which a company known as a franchiser agrees to let another person or group known as a franchisee establish an enterprise, using its name to sell goods or services.

cooperative: Business that is owned by the people who use its services.

credit union: Cooperative in which members pool their savings and borrow money at low rates of interest.

1. **(a)** The five basic types of cooperatives are purchasing cooperatives, marketing cooperatives, housing cooperatives, credit unions, and service cooperatives. **(b)** A condominium is a housing cooperative.

2. **(a)** The guiding force of a majority of for-profit businesses is the profit motive. A nonprofit organization, however, provides goods and services without seeking profits for distribution to individual members. It seeks only to make enough money to perform its functions, and unlike profit-oriented companies, a nonprofit organization is not taxed by state or federal governments. **(b)** Answers will vary. For example, students may note that people often form nonprofit organizations for charitable, religious, educational, and cultural purposes.

3. **(a)** Answers will vary. For example, students may point out that people in a particular area may need a specific good or service that they cannot obtain from any existing company. Individually, they do not have the capital to provide the good or service, but collectively, they do. So they start a cooperative to provide the needed good or service and share the expenses and work. **(b)** Answers will vary. Some students will note that service cooperatives are often found in rural areas. Others may note, however, that housing cooperatives and credit unions are found in urban areas.

4. **(a)** *Benefits* The franchisee can take advantage of national advertising and promotional operations,

as well as the experience and training in setting up a franchise provided by the parent company. Many parent companies also provide some form of financial assistance to a franchisee. *Costs* A fee is required from the franchisee to the franchiser for the use of the parent company's name along with a percentage of the profit. Also, franchisees often must follow strict corporate guidelines in operating the business. **(b)** The franchiser reduces the costs of production by receiving a franchise fee from the franchisee. Also, the franchiser gains a new outlet for its products. **(c)** Answers will vary. For example, a franchiser may suffer a considerable amount of unfavorable publicity from a franchisee who does not uphold the company's standards. Also, when a franchisee goes bankrupt, the franchiser will be liable for some of the debts.

5. Answers will vary. For example, students may feel that a high percentage of the businesses in their community are franchises. Others may cite the familiar look franchises give the city streets in different cities and towns.

Chapter 5 Review

(text pages 118–119)

REVIEWING ECONOMIC TERMS

1. b; **2.** f; **3.** a; **4.** d; **5.** e; **6.** c.

EXERCISING ECONOMIC SKILLS

1. **(a)** The informational terms contained in the essay directive are advantage, disadvantage, and three types of business organizations. **(b)** The subject is the advantages and disadvantages of the three types of business organizations. **(c)** The performance terms stated in the directive are compare, determine, and defend.

2. Answers will vary.

THINKING CRITICALLY ABOUT ECONOMICS

1. **(a)** The most common forms of business organization in the American free enterprise system are sole proprietorships, partnerships, and corporations. **(b)** Answers will vary. For example, students may point out that size often enables the corporation to reduce production costs. **(c)** A franchise is a business started by a franchisee who, for a fee and a share of the profits, is allowed by the franchiser to use its name and products. A cooperative is a business formed by a group of people for the use of the members. A nonprofit organization is a business that puts all profits back into the organization.

2. Answers will vary. For example, students may note that the money raised and reinvested by a nonprofit organization is not taxed.

3. Answers will vary. For example, students may point out that many owners cannot put a price on the hard work and effort that went into starting the business. Many owners also fear that the corporation will change the name and cheapen the product, or otherwise undo the work that the sole proprietor put into creating the company.

4. **(a)** The business organization that represents the largest percentage of businesses is sole proprietorships. **(b)** The business organization that has the largest percentage of total sales is the corporation. **(c)** The graphs on page 102 illustrate that sole proprietorships may be the most numerous type of business, but the total business sales of sole proprietorships are small compared with those of corporations.

USING PRIMARY SOURCES

1. Answers will vary. For example, the entrepreneurial revolution is a profound change in attitudes about small to mid-level businesses brought about by rapid technological change and a greater educational level of the population. It has come into being because society recognizes the value, importance, and productivity of the entrepreneurial business unit.

2. Answers will vary. For example, small and mid-sized companies can adapt to change, bring new products to market, generate jobs, and create new wealth.

3. The six reasons that Bernard A. Goldhirsh states for the "entrepreneurial explosion" in the United States are as follows. (1) We have become a very wealthy, middle-class country. (2) Sixty percent of the households in the under-50 age bracket now have two wage earners. (3) The economy has shifted into the service sector or knowledge business. (4) A larger portion of our population has attained higher education. (5) A profound change in attitudes about small to mid-level businesses has been brought about by rapid technological change. (6) Young entrepreneurs are redefining the relationship between risk and personal fulfillment. It has come into being because change can only be handled by the entrepreneurial sector.

CHAPTER

6 Competition and Market Structure *(text pages 120–139)*

Section 1 Review *(text page 126)*

DEFINE

market structure: Term used to describe competition in the marketplace.

perfect competition: Type of industry that is the most competitive because it has many buyers and sellers, none of whom control prices.

pure monopoly: Condition in which a single firm controls the total production or sale of a good or service.

natural monoply: Condition in which a single firm most efficiently produces or sells a good or service.

government monopoly: Condition in which government at any level owns and operates a monopoly.

geographic monopoly: Condition in which a firm is the only producer or seller of a good or service in a specific location.

IDENTIFY

ENIAC: Machine that ushered in the modern era of computers.

1. **(a)** The four conditions present in perfect competition are that a particular product must have many sellers and buyers, the product being offered by one firm must be comparable to products offered by competing firms, buyers must have easy access to information on the products and prices available, and entrance to and exit from the industry must be relatively easy and inexpensive. **(b)** The three conditions that exist in a monopoly are that one firm is the sole producer or seller of a product, no substitute good is available, and there are prohibitive barriers to entry into the industry.
2. Answers will vary. For example, students may note that a large number of competitors means businesses must be more creative in attracting customers.
3. **(a)** In perfect competition, demand and supply have more influence on a product's price than they do in a monopoly. **(b)** In a monopoly, producers have control of the price without regard to supply or demand.
4. **(a)** and **(b)** See the following continuum.

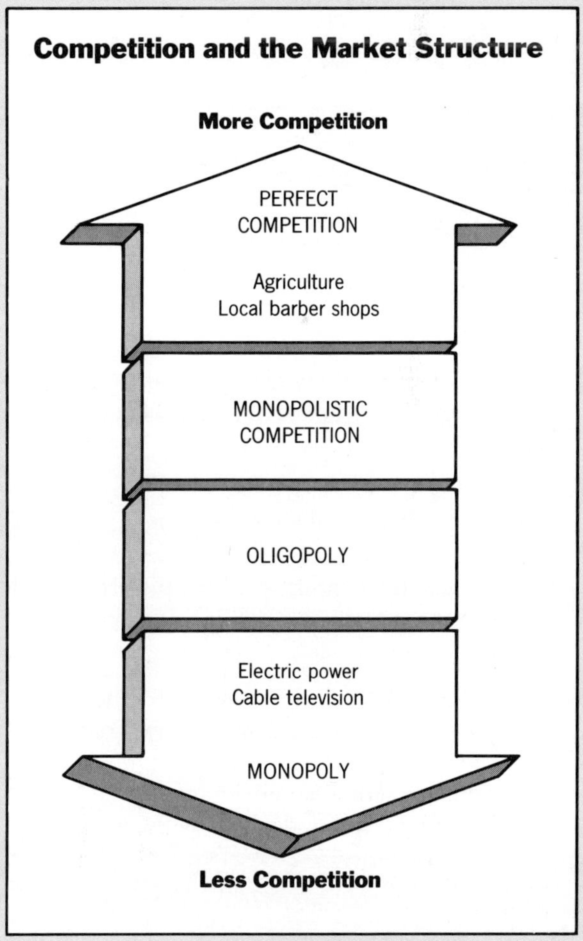

Section 2 Review (text page 129)

DEFINE

monopolistic competition: Condition that occurs when a good or service has numerous buyers and sellers, similar but differentiated products are offered for sale, buyers are well informed about differentiated products, and firms can easily enter or leave an industry.

product differentiation: Market structure that results when sellers emphasize the differences among competing products in order to increase sales.

competitive advertising: Information that tries to persuade consumers that a product is better than substitute goods.

IDENTIFY

Fortune 500 Company: Company on the list of the largest corporations in the United States, published annually by *Fortune* magazine.

Ted Turner: Successful Atlanta-based entrepreneur who recognized the potential of cable television and used Channel 17 (WTBS) as a basis to launch a national cable network. Turner also started the innovative Cable News Network (CNN), which provides news 24 hours a day.

1. In nonprice competition firms within an industry compete in areas other than price, using nonprice methods.
2. **(a)** The fast-food industry has a few large companies and numerous smaller competitors. None of the companies controls the market or prices. **(b)** The fast-food industry needs advertising to establish an identity in its highly competitive market.
3. Some of the techniques used by businesses to succeed in a market characterized by monopolistic competition are to create brand name loyalty, to develop good reputations for quality, and to be friendly and prompt in dealings with customers.

Building Economic Skills (text pages 130–131)

1. **(a)** The central characters are Teddy Roosevelt, trusts, and Uncle Sam. **(b)** The artist has used recognizable symbols for Roosevelt and Uncle Sam and has labeled the trusts.
2. Uncle Sam represents the United States.
3. **(a)** It exaggerates his facial features and portrays him as a cowhand. **(b)** His toughness is being exaggerated.
4. **(a)** Roosevelt is busting a bucking bronco labeled "trusts." **(b)** Roosevelt seems to be winning.
5. **(a)** Answers will vary. For example, students may assume that it takes place in the early 1900s because Roosevelt became President in 1901 and then became active in trustbusting. Roosevelt is dressed as a cowhand because of earlier days spent on cattle ranches in the West. **(b)** Reforms of government and business were taking place.
6. **(a)** Answers will vary. For example, students may feel that Roosevelt is rescuing the United States by breaking the trusts. **(b)** Answers will vary. For example, students may feel that the cartoonist favored Roosevelt's trustbusting because he is successfully riding the bronco.

Section 3 Review (text page 133)

DEFINE

oligopoly: Type of imperfect competition in which only a few large companies control an industry.

differentiated oligopoly: Type of imperfect competition in which a few producers dominate the production of similar products.

pure oligopoly: Type of imperfect competition in which a few producers dominate the production of an identical product.

collusion: Condition in which leaders of competing firms set production levels or prices for products, presenting a clear danger to free competition.

1. **(a)** In an oligopoly, the four characteristics are that the largest three or four firms in the industry must produce 70 percent or more of the industry's total output, differentiated products are for sale, information about a product must be readily available, and substantial barriers to entry into the industry must exist. **(b)** In an oligopoly, price is determined by brand name loyalty, nonprice competition, and price leadership.

2. **(a)** The differences between price leadership and collusion are that in *price leadership* one firm, normally the largest, offers its new product at a certain price, hoping that competing firms will set similar prices, while in *collusion* the leaders of competing firms together set production levels or prices for products. Price leadership is legal and collusion is not. **(b)** The basic difference between a pure oligopoly and a differentiated oligopoly is that in a *pure oligopoly*, a few producers dominate the production of an *identical* product whereas in a *differentiated oligopoly*, a few producers dominate the production of a *similar* product.

3. The major advantage is a concentrated market in which brand name loyalty and advertising can capture a large percentage of the customers.

4. It is easier to make a profit in a oligopolistic market structure because some control over prices is possible, while in perfect competition there is little control over prices.

Section 4 Review

(text page 137)

DEFINE

trust: Huge monopoly created through a merger and cutthroat competition in the United States after the Civil War.

laissez-faire: Form of capitalism in which individuals make all the economic decisions and the government does not interfere.

economies of scale: Benefit received by large firms that are able to take advantage of mass production techniques to lower unit production costs.

1. **(a)** Government has permitted certain monopolies to exist to promote business efficiency and for the general welfare of the people. **(b)** Answers will vary. For example, students may identify the nuclear power industry, which is a government monopoly, and Western Union, which has a monopoly on the transmission of money from one part of the country to another.

2. The basic purpose of United States antitrust legislation has been to ensure that free competition exists in the marketplace.

Chapter 6 Review

(text pages 138–139)

REVIEWING ECONOMIC TERMS

1. market structure
2. monopoly
3. natural monopoly
4. nonprice competition
5. oligopoly
6. price leadership
7. technological monopoly
8. product differentiation
9. antitrust legislation

EXERCISING ECONOMIC SKILLS

1. **(a)** President Reagan is hanging from the leash. **(b)** Uncle Sam represents the American people. **(c)** The cartoonist represents the deficit with a large, mean-looking dog. **(d)** Answers will vary. Most students may note, however, that the cartoonist probably views the deficit as harmful, comparing it as he does to a large monstrous animal that is dangerous and difficult to control. **(e)** Answers will vary. Some students may note, however, that the deficit, despite Reagan's campaign promises to reduce it, has actually grown larger since Reagan took office.

2. **(a)** Answers will vary. Students may mention the quality of service, special services, and discounts as the most important things to consider. **(b)** Answers will vary. **(c)** Answers will vary. **(d)** Answers will vary.

THINKING CRITICALLY ABOUT ECONOMICS

1. **(a)** Competition is the economic rivalry that oc-

curs among businesses when producers in a given industry attempt to gain a larger share of the market. **(b)** The four conditions that exist in monopolistic competition are that a particular good or service has many sellers and buyers available, the good or service being offered by one competing firm is similar or identical to those offered by other firms, buyers have easy access to information on the products and prices available, and entrance to and exit from the industry is relatively inexpensive and easy. **(c)** An oligopoly is a type of market in which only a few producers dominate the production of an identical product. **(d)** The federal government has passed antitrust legislation to protect competition in the United States economy.

2. Easy access to information is vital in perfect competition because consumers must have information upon which to base purchasing decisions and producers must have information upon which to base production decisions.

3. Yes, it is possible for prices determined in a monopoly to be lower than those determined in perfect competition because a monopoly can almost completely control production costs.

4. **(a)** Answers will vary. For example, students may feel that antitrust legislation has allowed individuals to enter sole proprietorships, thereby protecting economic freedom. **(b)** Answers will vary. For example, students may feel that the government should regulate business more than it currently does to guard against arbitrary and unfair prices.

USING PRIMARY SOURCES

1. The Sherman Antitrust Act tries to protect competitive markets in the United States by declaring illegal all monopolies, trusts, contracts, or conspiracies that restrain trade or commerce in the United States or with foreign nations. The legislation applies to every person, contract, combination in the form of a trust, or conspiracy. It applies to all individuals, corporations, and associations.

2. According to Section 4, the court system is to institute proceedings when necessary to prevent and restrain violations of the act.

3. The penalities listed in Section 1 of the Sherman Antitrust are that any individual or company deemed guilty of a misdemeanor, on conviction, shall be punished by a fine not exceeding $5000, or by imprisonment for one year, or by both punishments. The penalities in Section 7 are that a person who is injured as a result of a restraint of trade may sue and recover threefold the damages sustained and the costs of the suit.

CHAPTER

7 The Labor Force in the United States

(text pages 140–165)

Section 1 Review

(text page 147)

DEFINE

labor force: All people who are at least 16 years old and who are working or looking for work.

industrialization: Process by which a nation's economy is transformed from an agricultural one to one based on the mechanization of all major forms of production.

labor-intensive: Economy that produces goods through human and animal power.

capital-intensive: Economy that produces goods through machine power rather than through animal or human power.

derived demand: Need for workers that results from a shift in consumers' tastes and preferences and a subsequent demand for new goods and services.

IDENTIFY

affirmative action: Policy that aims to eliminate racial and sexual bias in employment practices, especially in firms doing business with the federal government. It can force the establishment of quotas for hiring and promoting women and minorities.

1. The labor force has fewer unskilled and semiskilled workers, fewer agricultural workers,

more women and minority workers, and more highly educated workers.

2. **(a)** As a result of industrialization, the United States economy changed from labor-intensive to capital-intensive. The rise of the factory system brought more and more unskilled and semi-skilled workers into the force. **(b) and (c)** Until recently, most workers in the United States labor force were white males. Legislation has promoted more equitable opportunities for women and minorities, increasing their numbers in the labor force. **(d)** Answers will vary. For example, some students may feel that industrialization has had the greatest impact on the labor force because many new types of jobs are continually being created. Some may feel that the women's rights movement has had the greatest impact because it has increased job opportunities for women. Others may feel that antidscrimination laws have had the greatest impact because they have opened opportunities to all Americans and have encouraged fairer hiring and promotion practices.

3. **(a)** The categories of occupation in the graph on page 145 in which there are higher percentages of females than males are service and technical, sales, and administrative. **(b)** Answers will vary. For example, when women began entering the labor force in numbers, only certain jobs were open to them. Women are still concentrated in these categories.

Section 2 Review *(text page 151)*

DEFINE

wage rate: Hourly, weekly, monthly, or yearly pay that a worker receives.

minimum wage: Lowest compensation that employers can legally pay a worker for a job.

labor union: Organization of workers that negotiates with employers for better wages, improved working conditions, and job security.

IDENTIFY

right-to-work law: Law that established the open shop, which employs both union and nonunion members.

comparable worth: Issue which maintains that salaries should be paid according to the skill levels involved and not by whether the job is held by a man or a woman.

1. **(a)** The major forces that determine wages are the interaction of the demand and supply of labor, governmental regulation, and the negotiations of organized labor. **(b)** The minimum-wage legislation has helped determine wage rates.

2. Wages are like prices because they are determined by supply and demand, competition, and the fluctuations of the business cycle.

3. Supply and demand interact to determine wages because if an occupation has a large supply of workers and a relatively low demand for them, the wage rate tends to be low. When the supply of workers in an occupation is limited and the demand for them is high, the wage rate tends to be high.

4. **(a)** Answers will vary. **(b)** The region of the nation in which the most states have a right-to-work law is the South. **(c)** The region of the nation in which no states have right-to-work laws is the Northeast.

Building Economic Skills *(text page 155)*

Student time lines should resemble the time line on page A 30.

Section 3 Review *(text page 161)*

DEFINE

collective bargaining: Process in which union representatives speak for all their members in an effort to negotiate a contract with management.

IDENTIFY

Samuel Gompers: Head of the Cigarmakers Union who in 1886 organized a loose association of local craft unions into the American Federation of Labor (AFL).

AFL-CIO: Union formed when the American Federation of Labor (AFL), and the Congress of Industrial Organizations (CIO) merged in 1955.

Lynn Williams: Current president of the United Steelworkers of America, considered by many to be the prototype of the modern union president.

1. The shift from a manufacturing-oriented to a service-oriented economy, antiunion campaigns by businesses and government, and negative perceptions of unions by the public have led to a decline of unions.
2. Labor's principal weapons are the *strike*, or work stoppage; the *boycott*, in which an attempt is made to get the consumer to support a strike by not buying the product of the company labor is striking against; the *secondary boycott* (though illegal), in which the union attempts to get the consumer not to buy products from businesses that carry goods from the company that the union is striking; and the *picket*, in which union members march to call attention to their grievances in hopes of gaining support from other workers and the public. **(b)** Management uses the *lockout*, in which workers are prevented from returning to the factory to work, and therefore are not paid; *strikebreaking*, in which new workers are given the jobs of the striking workers; and *union-busting*, decertification of the union and the defusing of any potential strikes.

Chapter 7 Review

(text pages 162–163)

REVIEWING ECONOMIC TERMS

1. labor force
2. labor-intensive
3. derived demand
4. wage rate
5. minimum wage
6. labor union
7. strike

EXERCISING ECONOMIC SKILLS

1. Answers will vary. For example, see the time line on page A 31.
2. Answers will vary.

THINKING CRITICALLY ABOUT ECONOMICS

1. **(a)** More women, minorities, and highly educated workers have entered the labor force in the last 25 years. **(b)** The three forces that determine wage rates are the supply and demand of labor—the number of workers available and needed by a particular business; governmental regulation—laws regulating how much an employer must pay an employee; and the negotiations of organized labor—contracts that include specific wage demands. **(c)** Labor unions were established because of management's lack of concern about working conditions, hours, wages, and benefits. Individually, workers had no real power in their

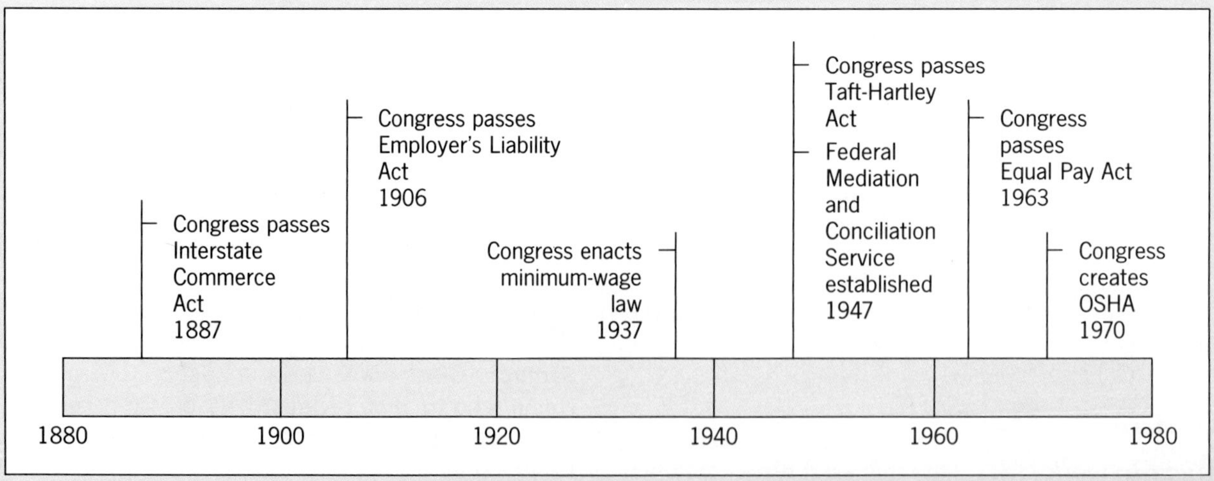

dealings with management. When an entire factory joined together, however, management was forced to listen to workers' demands.

2. The five major labor issues are *wages and fringe benefits*—what workers get for their labor; *working conditions*—clean, neat, and safe work areas; *job security*—freedom from fear of loosing a job without just cause; *union security*—the right to organize and join a union; and *grievance procedures*—steps that workers or management may take when work-related disputes arise.

3. Self-interest affects contract negotiations in a number of ways. Union negotiators desire to get all the benefits they feel workers deserve. The workers also want wages to keep pace with inflation and want to achieve a higher standard of living. Management wants to keep down the cost of production, of which wages and salaries are a major item.

4. Answers will vary. For example, students may note that the increased participation by women in the labor force has led to the two-paycheck family, which means more money for consumer goods.

5. **(a)** Labor unions negotiate for the highest possible wages, often boosting pay. Government regulations set a minimum wage, keeping starting wages at a certain level. The demand for and supply of labor have varying influences on wages. When demand is high and supply is low, wages are high. When demand is low, or supply large, pay is relatively low. **(b)** Answers will vary. For example, some students may feel union negotiations have the greatest impact because in unionized businesses today wages are often much higher than in nonunion businesses. Some may feel that the government's minimum-wage law has the greatest impact today because its sets the starting point for all wages. Others may feel that supply and demand has the greatest impact because employers must be willing to pay wages that are high enough to attract workers into job categories in which the demand is high.

6. **(a)** The five-year period in which the minimum wage increased the least is 1950–1955. **(b)** The five-year period in which the minimum wage increased the most is 1975–1980. **(c)** Answers will vary. For example, students may claim that wages increased little between 1950 and 1955 because the cost of living increased only moderately, and that the cost of living increased significantly between 1975 and 1980 and wages increased significantly to keep pace.

USING PRIMARY SOURCES

1. Samuel Gompers calls unions "organizations of necessity" because he felt unions were needed to

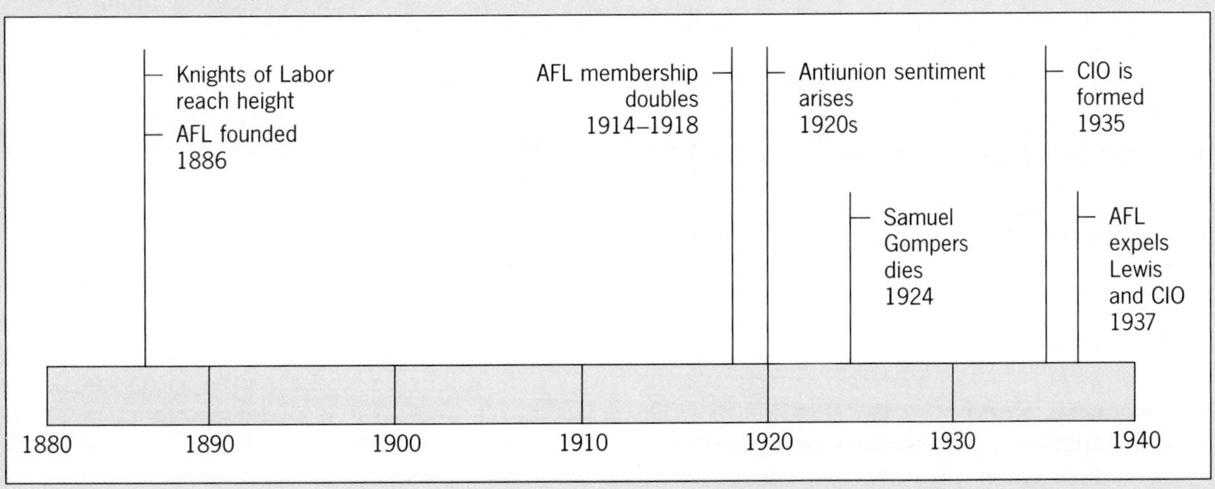

protect and defend workers from encroachment, injustice, and wrong. The group that Gompers felt needed unions the most was the working class. Gompers said that unions were needed because there had been no progress in improving the plight of workers without them.

2. Gompers blamed many of the workers for their own misery because they accepted through their own ignorance the terrible working conditions. Gompers also felt that state and federal governments shared the blame.

3. Gompers felt unions could achieve economic and social reform by recognizing that there was a need for reform, and then electing pro-unionists at all levels of government and the courts. Gompers expected that it would take a considerable amount of time to realize the goals he had set. He knew that it would not happen "over night."

4. Among Gompers' goals were the election of working people to all levels of government and the courts, the freedom of children from the same level of drudgery as their parents, and the protection of workers' rights to a higher and better life, and to share in the products of their labor.

5. Answers will vary. Students may feel if Gompers were alive today, he would think that workers have, for the most part, a better life and are enjoying the fruits of their labors.

Unit Two Review

(text pages 164–165)

REVIEWING ECONOMIC IDEAS

1. The three types of business organizations in a free enterprise system are sole proprietorships, partnerships, and corporations.

2. *Advantages* The advantages of a corporation are that its stockholders have limited liability, the management is separated from the ownership, and capital is easier to raise. *Disadvantages* The disadvantages of a corporation are slow decision making, taxation of corporate profits, and the lack of a sense of pride, accomplishment, and personal satisfaction for corporate stockholders in their roles as corporate owners because they are far removed from the actual running of the business.

3. The four types of market structures are perfect competition, monopolistic competition, oligopoly, and monopoly.

4. A large corporation is more likely to be in a market structure of monopolistic competition. Most corporations are large and dominate one phase of production or sales of a product.

5. The arguments for antitrust legislation are that such legislation protects consumers because monopolies and other unfair business practices are outlawed, and competition in the marketplace is preserved. Critics of antitrust legislation argue that government interference is not good for business. They claim that government regulations cost businesses money and limit their ability to compete in the marketplace. These regulation-induced costs cause lower business productivity and higher prices. Critics also believe that many regulations on business are unnecessary because businesses acting in their own self-interest will take voluntary action to prevent some of the abuses that antitrust legislation is intended to stop. Most of all, some critics charge, antitrust legislation takes away from business some freedom to control business operations.

6. Immigration, industrialization, increasing numbers of women in the workforce, antidiscrimination laws, and higher educational attainment by workers have caused changes in the nation's labor force.

7. Working brings pride and satisfaction in a job well-done and the status and respect that accompanies the job.

CONNECTING ECONOMIC IDEAS

1. **(a)** A person entering business is concerned about owner control because leadership and decision making are central to the success or failure of a business. **(b)** A businessperson also is concerned with liability in case the company has financial problems. **(c)** An entrepreneur must be

concerned about labor issues because the business must get and keep workers. **(d)** An entrepreneur is concerned about profit because it is the reason that most people begin a business and it is the focus of business operations.

2. **(a)** Both stocks and corporate bonds are sold by companies to raise operating capital. **(b)** A individual stock is a certificate of ownership in the company, entitling the holder to a voice in the company's operation. A corporate bond is a certificate issued by the company for an amount of money borrowed from the holder of the bond. It is a debt owed by the company to the corporate bond holder.

3. **(a)** In a sole proprietorship, self-interest is the key. A person starts a business and makes the decisions in his or her best interests. **(b)** A limited partner's self-interest is focused on security because a limited partner is willing to sacrifice a share of the company's profits and control in return for limited liability. **(c)** Deciding where to work involves a high degree of self-interest. In most instances when a worker has the opportunity to choose where to work, he or she will always opt for the job that offers more money, more prestige, better working conditions, and a greater chance for advancement.

4. **(a)** The type of market structure is directly related to the type of business organization most likely to be found operating in an industry because the market structure determines the level of competition and the efficiency with which businesses in that industry must operate. **(b)** Many sole proprietorships would be found because there are many sellers competing in a perfectly competitive market structure.

5. **(a)** Answers will vary. For example, students may note that vertical and horizontal combinations often restrained free competition by setting artifically low price levels to drive out any competition and then raising the prices once the total control of a good or service was assured. **(b)** Government regulations protect the consumer from unfair prices and restraint of trade posed by business consolidation or monopoly. **(c)** Answers will vary. For example, students may feel that organized labor has always promoted the idea of free enterprise because such a system means more jobs for the workers as new companies are created under free enterprise.

6. **(a)** Answers will vary. For example, some students may feel that antitrust laws have stifled business efficiency because they hinder a corporation's ability to expand in order to better compete in domestic and world markets. Others may feel that antitrust laws have not decreased efficiency because they have promoted competition in the marketplace, which usually results in the most efficient use of resources. **(b)** Answers will vary. For example, some students may feel that organized labor has blocked business efficiency by opposing modernization because it feared a loss of jobs from such technological unemployment. Others may feel that labor unions have not blocked efficiency because collective bargaining has resulted in improved working conditions which allow workers to be more prodcutive.

INVESTIGATING ECONOMIC ISSUES

1. The three categories into which the costs of government regulation fall are financial costs, lower productivity, and less consumer choice in the marketplace.

2. In laissez-faire capitalism, the government had no official role, while today government regulates many facets of business.

3. **(a)** Supporters of government business regulation point out that regulation promotes competition and health and safety in the workplace, and protects consumers as well as savers and investors. **(b)** Critics charge that government regulations increase financial costs to businesses, lower business productivity, and limit consumer choice. **(c)** Answers will vary. For example, some students may feel that governmental regulation is too restrictive and does not allow business to be competitive with businesses in nations with fewer governmental regulations. Others may feel that there is not too much governmental regulation because of the physical and psychological benefits such regulation provides for workers.

USING PRIMARY SOURCES

1. One federal regulation that has provided the pub-

lic with a substantial benefit is automobile emission standards. One disadvantage of regulations is that they are often costly for companies to implement.

2. Benefit-cost analysis is based on efficiency, making public decision making similar to private decision making.

3. The three questions that have to be answered are whether some form of market failure has occurred that warrants the imposition of regulation; whether federal regulations, in contrast to state and local regulations, are appropriate; and whether a specific regulation will increase net benefits to society. Answers will vary. For example, students may feel that such a questioning process helps reduce the number of new federal regulations because it requires the government to see if its current regulations cover the subject.

UNIT THREE

(text pages 166–217)

GOVERNMENT AND THE ECONOMY

CHAPTER

8 The Role of Government in the Economy

(text pages 168–191)

Section 1 Review

(text page 174)

IDENTIFY

New Deal: Legislation formulated during Franklin Roosevelt's first and second administrations to solve the problems of the Great Depression.

1. The programs and policies of the New Deal increased the government's economic power and involvement in the nation's economy.
2. **(a)** State and local government has experienced the greatest increases since 1935. **(b)** The number of federal employees exceeded the number of state and local employees in 1945. **(c)** The number decreased.

Building Economic Skills

(text pages 176–177)

1. The headline of the news article is "The Budget is Congress' Problem Again."
2. **(a)** The article was written on July 21, 1986. **(b)** The author is Howard Gleckman.
3. **(a)** *Who:* The Supreme Court, the President, the Congress, and nonelected administration officials; **(b)** *What:* Congress' reassumption of the responsibility for controlling federal spending following the Supreme Court's action; **(c)** *Where:* Washington; **(d)** *When:* December 1985 to July 1986.
4. **(a)** *How:* Congress has to control the deficit through a joint resolution. **(b)** *Why:* Politicians do not want to increase taxes or make necessary spending cuts, and the President continues to send unrealistic budgets to Congress.
5. Answers will vary. For example, some students may feel that the article objectively presents the facts of the Supreme Court's action. Other students, however, may feel that the author is not objective because he expresses a strong point of view that Congress will do nothing to cut the deficit.

Section 2 Review

(text page 186)

DEFINE

public good: Good or service that the government provides for everyone.

privatization: Sale of government property or the relinquishment of certain government services to private businesses.

business cycle: Sequential rise and fall of the economy.

IDENTIFY

Occupational Safety and Health Administration: Branch of the Labor Department that enforces safety and health regulations in the workplace.

Office of Consumer Affairs: Federal agency responsible for consumer protection.

Barbara Mikulski: Democratic Senator from Maryland elected in 1986, former social worker and congresswoman, who takes an active interest in consumer affairs and the rights of the disadvantaged.

Social Security: Program that provides income security for the elderly, the disabled, and their dependents.

1. **(a)** The four major functions of government are to regulate economic activity, provide public

goods, promote economic well-being, and stabilize the economy. **(b)** Stabilizing the economy is assumed largely by the federal government.

2. **(a)** A transfer payment is money that the government collects in taxes from one group of citizens and redistributes to another group of citizens. **(b)** A subsidy is a government transfer payment or other assistance to business. **(c)** Transfer payments redistribute money and goods to the needy, while subsidies help businesses that provide certain basic goods and services to continue operations.

3. The five categories of citizens who receive Social Security benefits are retired workers, widows and widowers, children, wives and husbands, and disabled workers.

Section 3 Review

(text page 189)

DEFINE

interest group: Organization of citizens having common interests and goals.

lobbyist: Person hired by an interest group to express the group's point of view to policymakers.

IDENTIFY

Political Action Committee: Special interest group set up by trade and professional associations, corporations, and labor unions to collect and distribute campaign contributions to candidates likely to support their cause.

1. **(a)** Individuals have an opportunity to make their opinions known through voting. **(b)** Interest groups help influence government economic actions by influencing elected representatives.

2. **(a)** The six economic goals that serve as criteria for evaluating government policies are economic freedom, economic efficiency, economic equity, economic security, economic stability, and economic growth. **(b)** Economic equity and economic security to promote the economic well-being of many disadvantaged Americans seemed more important economic goals in the 1960s. **(c)** Economic efficiency, economic stability, and economic growth seemed more important goals to bring the nation from the recession of the early 1980s. **(d)** Answers will vary. Students may consider economic freedom an important goal in 1776 because a major cause of the Revolutionary War was the colonists' protests against British economic policies.

Chapter 8 Review

(text pages 190–191)

REVIEWING ECONOMIC TERMS

1. f; **2.** b; **3.** a; **4.** e; **5.** g; **6.** c; **7.** d.

EXERCISING ECONOMIC SKILLS

1. **(a)** The author believes that the responsibility for controlling federal spending lies with elected officials—the President and Congress. **(b)** The Gramm-Rudman Act gave the responsibility for controlling federal spending to the Comptroller General. **(c)** The author believes that the Gramm-Rudman Act erodes representative democracy by giving major decision-making responsibility to nonelected officials. **(d)** The author is not optimistic about Congress cutting the budget deficit because politicians do not always enact the necessary measures or tax increases.

2. Answers will vary.

THINKING CRITICALLY ABOUT ECONOMICS

1. **(a)** The roles of government in the economy are to promote competition, to provide public goods, to promote economic well-being, and to stabilize the economy. **(b)** To promote *competition*, the government makes and enforces antitrust regulations, prevents the abuse of laborers and monitors and sets standards for working conditions, and protects consumers. To provide *public goods*, the government operates and maintains goods and services needed by everyone when they are not supplied by private production. To promote *economic well-being*, the government transfers money between groups through transfer pay-

ments and subsidies. To *stabilize the economy*, the government uses fiscal policy, monetary policy, and wage and price controls to smooth out the fluctuations in the business cycle.

2. **(a)** The growth of government has been caused by population growth, an increase in the size and number of traditionally disadvantaged groups, changing attitudes about the role of government, a rising standard of living, and national emergencies. **(b)** The number of federal employees has generally risen, while the number of state and local government employees has risen dramatically. In dollars, government spending has soared, while as a percentage of the GNP, it has risen more modestly. **(c)** Citizens can influence government economic policies by voting for elected officials with similar philosophies or by belonging to an interest group.

3. **(a)** *Fiscal policy* is developed by Congress and the President, and it allows the government to use its taxing and spending powers to stabilize the economy. *Monetary policy* is formulated by the Federal Reserve Board, and it seeks to stabilize the economy by modifying the nation's money supply in response to economic pressures. The federal government uses *wage and price controls* to set limits on wages and prices during times of emergency such as war. The government uses fiscal policy, monetary policy, and wage and price controls to steer a middle course between recession and inflation. To effectively stabilize the economy, these policies must be coordinated. **(b)** Answers will vary. Students who feel fiscal policy is the most effective method may think that government spending and taxing policies have a more immediate and predictable effect on the economy than the other methods. Students who feel that monetary policy is the most effective method may cite the size of the money supply and interest rates as the key determinants of aggregate demand and therefore the key point of attack in stabilizing the economy. Students who feel price controls are the most effective method may think that price controls can be applied selectively rather than tampering with the entire economy.

4. **(a)** *Advantages* The arguments in favor of privatization are that private firms can operate certain industries more efficiently than the government, government should not be a competitor with private business, and selling government enterprises is a means to reduce the federal deficit. *Disadvantages* The arguments against privatization are that certain public goods and services should continue under government control because they are essential to the well-being of users, and the government has tremendous resources at its disposal to meet special business needs and circumstances. **(b)** The Grace Commission said the federal government could save $11.2 billion over three years through privatization. **(c)** Answers will vary. For example, students may feel that privatization improves economic efficiency because businesses can provide certain goods and services more efficiently than government can provide them.

5. Students who agree may feel that more privatization provides more opportunities for entrepreneurs to start businesses. Students who disagree may note that the government provides public goods that are available to everyone, while private production of these goods may exclude certain users.

USING PRIMARY SOURCES

1. Countervailing power refers to the power blocs such as big government and labor unions that are needed to balance the power of big business.

2. Galbraith says that a large and disadvantaged group such as labor most needs the government's countervailing power. American workers have benefited from the countervailing power of the government through federal protection of union organizing under the Wagner Act and through minimum-wage legislation. The government helps groups in the private sector through direct and indirect assistance.

3. The government's role in the economy has expanded through its support of groups such as labor unions and farmers. Galbraith favors big government because it has contributed to the self-confidence and well-being of disadvantaged groups. Reformers have avoided groups seeking countervailing power because the notion of government support is not yet accepted "in the accredited structure of American economic and political science."

CHAPTER

9 Financing in the Public Sector

(text pages 192–217)

Section 1 Review

(text page 196)

DEFINE

tax: Mandatory payment that individuals and firms make to the government to cover the costs of public goods and services.

tax rate: Percentage of a person's income that is taken by the government.

sales tax: Levy on the sale of some goods or services.

ability-to-pay principle: Criterion of tax fairness which holds that people with higher incomes and wealth should pay higher taxes, while people with lower incomes or wealth should pay lower taxes.

benefits-received principle: Criterion of tax fairness which holds that people who benefit directly from certain public goods and services should pay for them.

1. **(a)** Taxes in the United States are used to finance government operations and functions and have an influence on economic behavior. **(b)** Government can discourage the consumption of a product by adding a tax; it can encourage the production and consumption of a product, provide incentives to spend more or save more, and encourage certain activities such as relocations of businesses by eliminating or by reducing a tax.
2. The three types of taxes in the United States are the *progressive tax* such as the individual income tax that takes a higher percentage of income from a high-income person than from a low-income person, the *proportional tax* such as some state income taxes that takes the same percentage of income from an individual regardless of income level, and the *regressive tax* such as the sales tax that takes a higher percentage of income from a low-income person than from a high-income individual.
3. A sales tax is a regressive tax because people with low incomes generally spend a higher percentage and save a lower percentage of their income than do people with high income. If low-income persons pay a sales tax on all that they buy, then they pay a proportionally higher tax rate than those with higher incomes.
4. Answers will vary. Some students may feel that the the ability-to-pay principle is the fairer of these two because the people with greater wealth can better afford to pay taxes. Other students may feel that the benefits-received principle is the fairer because it requires users to pay for goods and services.

Section 2 Review

(text page 203)

DEFINE

excise tax: Levy on the production or sale of a particular good or service.

estate tax: Levy on the assets of a person who has died.

gift tax: Levy on the transfer of any gift of value, such as money or personal property.

customs duty: Levy on an imported good brought into the United States from another country.

grant-in-aid: Transfer payment from the federal government to state or local governments.

property tax: Levy that individuals and firms pay on their assets.

tax break: Deduction that a person is allowed to subtract from gross income.

1. **(a)** The three major types of federal taxes are the individual income tax, corporate income tax, and the Social Security tax. **(b)** The individual income tax is levied on an individual's wages or salary, interest, dividends, and tips. **(c)** The corporate income tax is levied on a business corporation's profits.
2. The Social Security tax is proportional because it takes a set percentage of an employee's salary. It

is regressive because a higher percentage is taken from a low salary than a high salary.

3. **(a)** Tax receipts from individual income taxes increased by $244.1 billion from 1970 to 1985. **(b)** Individual income taxes as a percentage of federal tax receipts decreased 1.1 percent from 1970 to 1985. **(c)** Answers will vary. For example, students may note that the other sources of government revenue have increased at least as much as individual income.

Section 3 Review (text page 205)

DEFINE

federal budget: Federal government's plan for the use of government revenues.

1. **(a)** Between the mid-1800s and the early 1900s, the need for a federal budget increased because of the increased spending in the Civil War and World War I, the need to check political and financial corruption, and the general spirit of reform during the Progressive Era. **(b)** The wartime spending increase was so great that it required a more formal process for planning future revenues and expenditures. Bribery and corruption on the part of some government officials in the awarding of contracts required a budget to make government revenue collection and spending more systematic. Progressive reformers believed that centralized decision making would permit federal resources to be used in a more efficient and fairer manner. **(c)** The *President* submits a detailed budget proposal to Congress. *Congress* reviews the proposed budget and makes a final allocation of funds. Congress and the President make trade-offs when devising the federal budget because scarcities of revenues restrict the number of programs that the government can fund.

2. **(a)** The percentage of the federal budget allocated to social programs dropped from a high of 54 percent in 1980 and 1981 to a low of 49 percent in 1986 and 1987. **(b)** The defense budget rose from a low of 22 percent during the Carter administration in 1980 to a high of 28 percent in 1987.

Building Economic Skills (text pages 206–207)

1. **(a)** The main idea of the passage is that unfair and oppressive taxes in the United States work to the disadvantage of American firms in competition with foreign firms. **(b)** Taxes must be reduced to restore American competitiveness.

2. A single-cause fallacy is that taxes alone are responsible for the losses on foreign and domestic markets by United States firms.

3. An irrelevant-evidence fallacy is that although the United States GNP is more than $4 trillion, American firms are taxed unfairly. This argument says nothing about why heavy taxation caused American firms to lose out to foreign competition. There is no evidence that a $4 trillion GNP, high taxes on United States firms, and the success of foreign competitors are related.

4. A majority-view fallacy is that "everybody knows" that high tax rates in the United States put American firms at a disadvantage. Other nations also may have high tax rates, but may be successful in meeting foreign competiton.

Section 4 Review (text page 213)

DEFINE

budget deficit: Financial situation that occurs when government expenditures are greater than government revenues.

budget surplus: Financial situation that occurs when government revenues are greater than government expenditures.

national debt: Total amount of money that the federal government owes to its creditors.

debt ceiling: Legislation that limits how much the federal government can borrow.

IDENTIFY

Phil Gramm: Senator from Texas, who co-initiated the Gramm-Rudman-Hollings Balanced Budget and Emergency Deficit Reduction Control Act of 1986, who favors a reduction in the size of the federal government, and who switched from the Democratic to the Republican Party in 1983.

1. **(a)** Deficit spending is an intentional government policy of appropriating more money for its programs than it is able to cover with its revenues. **(b)** The federal government can balance the budget by increasing revenues or decreasing expenditures. **(c)** In the mid-1980s, the federal government tried to reduce government expenditures by stepping up its campaign against waste and fraud, eliminating or reducing the cost of some programs, and establishing maximum payments for certain medical services provided for by Medicare.

2. Answers will vary. Increases in the federal budget deficit are reflected in the rapidly rising national debt.

Chapter 9 Review

(text pages 214–215)

REVIEWING ECONOMIC TERMS

1. taxes
2. tax rate
3. proportional tax
4. national debt
5. deficit spending
6. Social Security Taxes
7. customs duty
8. regressive tax

EXERCISING ECONOMIC SKILLS

1. **(a)** This statement is an example of a single-cause fallacy because there were other factors that contributed to the collapse of several Texas banks. **(b)** This statement is an example of a irrelevant-evidence fallacy because there is no evidence that increased salaries have caused deceased performance. **(c)** This statement is an example of a majority-view fallacy because it states "everyone knows."

2. Answers will vary.

THINKING CRITICALLY ABOUT ECONOMICS

1. **(a)** Governments collect taxes to finance their operations, provide public goods, and redistribute money. **(b)** Governments raise revenues through the levying of taxes and the sales of government bonds and securities. **(c)** The federal budget includes expenditure plans, revenue estimates, and deficit projections. **(d)** A budget deficit occurs when the government borrows money to pay some of its bills. A national debt is the total amount of money that a nation owes its creditors.

2. **(a)** The ability-to-pay principle of taxation states that people with greater income or wealth should pay a higher tax and that people with a lower income or wealth should pay a lesser tax. The benefits-received principle states that people who benefit directly from certain public goods and services should pay for them. **(b)** Proponents of the benefits-received principle argue that it is fair because it resembles the marketplace in that people are free to choose which government goods to use and to pay for, and that the principle increases government efficiency by encouraging government to produce reasonably priced public goods that are in high demand.

3. **(a)** Students should note that an increase in the corporate income tax is usually passed on to consumers as increased prices. Corporations pass on this increase in production cost so they can maintain their profit margin. **(b)** Students should note that an increase in the individual income tax reduces aggregate demand. Eventually businesses must reduce supply and cut back on production. Aggregate demand is reduced because the government is taking money that previously could have been spent on consumer goods.

USING PRIMARY SOURCES

1. Adam Smith's four maxims of a fair tax system are that people ought to contribute to the support of the government in proportion to their abilities; a person's tax should be certain and not arbitrary; a tax ought to be levied at the time or in the manner most convenient for payment; and a tax ought not be a burden to the taxpayer or a great benefit to the tax collector.

2. The four economic and social problems of overly burdensome taxation are salaries that eat up the greater share of the tax, a tax so heavy that it discourages industry, a tax so ruinous that it encourages evasion, and tax collecting so frequently imposed that it causes people to feel oppressed.

3. Answers will vary. Students might point out that a budget is designed to allocate revenues for government salaries in the most efficient manner, a progressive income tax is designed to be fair to taxpayers and not so heavy as to encourage evasion—for which severe penalties exist—and the time for tax collecting is known by the citizens (April 15).

Unit Three Review

(text pages 216–217)

REVIEWING ECONOMIC IDEAS

1. Government has increased in the twentieth century because of population growth, an increase in the size and number of disadvantaged groups, changing attitudes about government, increased citizen expectations of government, and recent national emergencies.

2. Government regulates the economy by promoting competition and protecting consumers.

3. The government stabilizes the economy to avoid periods of inflation and recession through its fiscal policy, which uses taxing and spending powers, and its monetary policy, which modifies the nation's money supply.

4. Evaluations are based on how well government actions fulfill the nation's economic goals.

5. Governments levy taxes to raise revenues and in so doing influence the economic behaviors of individuals and businesses.

6. The ability-to-pay principle is based on a progressive tax, which taxes wealthy people more than less wealthy people, and the benefits-received principle is a proportional tax, which taxes users at equal rates.

7. The tax burden on United States citizens is relatively low.

8. **(a)** A progressive tax is a type of tax that takes a higher percentage of income from a high-income person than from a low-income person. **(b)** A proportional tax is a type of tax that takes the same percentage of income from individuals at all income levels. **(c)** A regressive tax is a type of tax that takes a larger percentage of income from low-income groups than from high-income groups.

CONNECTING ECONOMIC IDEAS

1. **(a)** Government spending has increased dramatically in recent years. Because government revenues have not increased as rapidly as government spending, the national debt has increased. **(b)** Answers will vary. Students may feel that changing public attitudes toward government have allowed government involvement in more areas, thus increasing the national debt.

2. **(a)** Economic equity and economic security are promoted by the Social Security system. **(b)** A regressive tax places a proportionally larger burden on those with lower incomes, reducing their economic equity. **(c)** Economic freedom is reduced when the government increases taxes because taxpayers have less money after taxes with which to make economic choices.

3. **(a)** Some people feel a sales tax is an unfair type of tax because it is regressive. **(b)** Answers will vary. Some students may feel that the corporate income tax is fairest because it is a cost of operating in the United States economy. Other may think that estate or gift taxes are fairest because the government is not taking away something that has been earned with those taxes.

4. **(a)** Students may feel that the public desire for a stable economy makes increasing government involvement in the economy inevitable. **(b)** Answers will vary.

5. Students who agree may point out that more government agencies are available to deal with the economic problems of the disadvantaged and other special interest groups. Students who disagree may point out that increased government makes it more difficult for the government to be responsive to the needs of special interest groups.

INVESTIGATING ECONOMIC ISSUES

1. Target groups include the chronically unemployed and workers who have been displaced by plant closings, relocation, and automation.

2. **(a)** Labor unions support retraining programs because they reduce technological unemployment. **(b)** The telephone and automobile industries have instituted successful retraining programs. **(c)** Both programs have met with good success, training hundreds of workers for new jobs.

3. **(a)** The Jobs Corps is a federal worker retraining program. **(b)** The program is aimed at the hard-core unemployed.

4. The goal of workfare programs is immediate, short-term employment, while worker training and retraining programs teach marketable employment skills for the longer term.

5. Students who agree may feel these programs should be paid for by private businesses, which benefit directly from such programs. Students who disagree may think that programs that are run by private businesses will not do much for the chronically unemployed.

USING PRIMARY SOURCES

1. The goals of the Job Corps are to provide occupational training for economically disadvantaged young men and women.

2. Four eligibility requirements for participation in the Job Corps are to be between the ages of 14 and 22, to be economically disadvantaged and require additional education and training for secure and meaningful employment, to live in an environment characterized by cultural deprivation or a disruptive homelife, and to have the capacity and aspiration to complete the Job Corps program.

3. The Job Corps provides education, vocational training, work experience, physical rehabilitation and development, and counseling. The Job Corps also helps people choose realistic career goals.

FINANCIAL INSTITUTIONS

CHAPTER

10 Money and the Banking System

(text pages 220–241)

Section 1 Review

(text page 226)

DEFINE

money: Any item that people commonly accept in exchange for goods or services.

barter: Exchange of goods and services without using money.

opportunity cost: Value of what a person gives up to get something else.

currency: Coins and paper money.

specie: Gold or silver coins.

demand deposit: Funds payable on demand to the holder of a check; also known as a checking account.

1. Money was invented out of the need to have a portable medium of exchange, to have a way of judging the relative value of goods and services, and to provide a store of value.
2. Commodity money differs from fiat money in the value of the item that serves as money. Commodity money has an intrinsic value. Fiat money, on the other hand, has value because a government says it has value.
3. **(a)** The three basic functions money serves are as a medium of exchange, a standard of value, and a store of value. **(b)** The five characteristics of money are durability, portability, divisibility, stability in value, and acceptability. **(c)** The three categories of money are commodity money, representative money, and fiat money.
4. **(a)** The new dollar has a polyester security thread that is visible only when the bill is held up to light. Old dollars do not have a security thread. **(b)** It was developed to combat counterfeiting.
5. **(a)** United States coins and paper money are fiat money because they receive their value from government decree rather than from the value of their composition. **(b)** Time deposits are considered to be near money because although they cannot be used to directly buy goods or pay debts, they can be easily converted into cash.

Section 2 Review

(text page 231)

DEFINE

national bank: Financial institution chartered by the federal government.

gold standard: Monetary system in which paper money is fully backed by and convertible into gold.

commercial bank: Financial institution that lends money; accepts savings and checking deposits; and transfers money among businesses, other banks, and financial institutions, and individuals.

IDENTIFY

Alexander Hamilton: First Secretary of the Treasury, who believed that a strong, centralized banking system was necessary if the United States expected to develop its industries and commerce. He proposed that a national bank have the power to handle government funds, charter and monitor other banks throughout the country, and issue currency.

American Eagle: First gold coin minted by the United States government as legal tender since the early 1930s.

1. The system created a national currency and a dual banking system that brought uniformity and government control of money and banking.

2. Both Thomas Jefferson and James Madison were states' right advocates. They feared that the concentration of economic power at the national level would weaken the economic and political freedom of the individual states.

3. **(a)** The main types of financial institutions are commercial banks, savings and loan associations, mutual savings banks, and credit unions. **(b)** Insured commercial banks generally have the most assets.

Building Economic Skills *(text pages 232–233)*

1. **(a)** The chart's title is "A Three-Sector Circular Flow of Goods and Services." **(b)** The three sectors are households, government, and business firms.

2. There are twelve arrows on the chart.

3. **(a)** Taxes and resources flow from households to government. **(b)** Services and money payments flow from government to households. **(c)** Money payments and services flow from government to businesses. **(d)** Products and taxes flow from businesses to government.

4. They are called taxes.

5. The correct answer is ***c***.

6. The chart on page 232 is a two-sector chart and the one on page 37 is a three-sector chart.

Section 3 Review *(text page 239)*

DEFINE

deregulation: Process by which the government lifts some of its restrictions on an industry.

automatic teller machine (ATM): Automated device that handles many routine banking tasks.

debit card: Plastic card that can be inserted in a point-of-sale terminal allowing a buyer to transfer funds from the buyer's account to the seller's account to pay for purchases.

float time: Period between purchase and payment when a credit card is used.

IDENTIFY

Peter T. Buchanan: Became president of First Boston Corporation in 1978 when it was almost out of business. Under Buchanan's direction, First Boston prospered and earned $94.7 million in profits in 1985. First Boston has also exhibited strong leadership in acquisitions and mergers.

1. The federal government deregulated the banking system to develop more competition in the industry.

2. **(a)** There are a number of advantages to regional banking. Smaller banks are now allowed to merge with out-of-state banks. Out-of-state banks may build branch offices in other states where the state government is agreeable to such an expansion. Regional banking has allowed larger banks to offer a wider variety of services to customers. **(b)** The major aspects of automatic banking are automatic teller machines, automatic clearing house services, point-of-sale terminals, and electronic home banking.

3. Yes. Had all S & Ls been insured under the FSLIC, a panic would have been less likely because the resources of the federal government are considerably greater than those of the private insurers. The troubled S & Ls could have given the first panicked customers their money, and other nervous customers would have been reassured about the safety of their deposits.

Chapter 10 Review *(text pages 240–241)*

REVIEWING ECONOMIC TERMS

1. barter
2. gold standard
3. fiat money
4. savings and loan associations
5. money
6. panic run
7. commodity money
8. deregulation
9. medium of exchange

EXERCISING ECONOMIC SKILLS

1. Answers will vary.
2. Answers will vary. Students should develop a chart similar to the chart shown on page 270 of the textbook.

THINKING CRITICALLY ABOUT ECONOMICS

1. **(a)** Money is important in record keeping because it helps provide a uniform way for government to figure tax receipts and expenditures and for businesses to figure profits and losses. **(b)** The United States developed a central banking system to ensure banking uniformity and public credibility. **(c)** Some bankers feel that branches of out-of-state banks and larger state banks may be unresponsive to local needs and may have a competitive edge over smaller local banks.
2. **(a)** Jackson vetoed the Second Bank of the United States because he was a strong supporter of states' rights and he did not trust a single institution controlling the nation's money. **(b)** States began to require that banks hold a specie reserve of a certain percentage of their notes in an effort to restore the public's faith in state banks.
3. In 1791 Congress established a central bank. President Jackson's veto of legislation in 1832 that would have extended the Bank's charter led to the fall of the national bank and the rise of state and local banks. The panic of 1837 caused people to lose confidence in state banks. The financial stress of the Civil War convinced Congress it must create a national banking system. This system, begun in 1863, established a national currency and a dual banking system of national and state banks. In 1913 Congress established the Federal Reserve System to further guide and supervise banking.
4. The principal advantage in not requiring a currency to be backed by a reserve of specie is that government can put more money into circulation.
5. Students who agree may feel that a "holiday" was necessary in order to reorganize banking and to reestablish public confidence in banks. Students who disagree may feel that FDR's action was an unnecessary intrusion of government into banking and into the economy.

USING PRIMARY SOURCES

1. The four reasons that Congress offers to justify deregulating interest rates paid by depository institutions are that the regulation of interest rates discourages persons from saving money, creates inequities for depositors, impedes the ability of depository institutions to compete for funds, and does not achieve the purpose of providing an even flow of funds for home mortgage lending.
2. The purpose of the Depository Institutions Deregulation Act of 1980 is to provide for the orderly phaseout and the ultimate elimination of the limitations on the maximum rates of interest and dividends. Taking the ceiling off the interest rates allows banks to compete for the savings dollar by offering higher interest rates.
3. It promotes competition by allowing banks to compete for customers' business by offering different rates of interest.
4. The function of the Deregulation Committee is to provide for the orderly phaseout and the ultimate elimination of the limitations on the maximum rates of interest and dividends that may be paid on deposits and accounts and to work toward providing all depositors with a market rate of return on their savings as rapidly as economic conditions warrant. The Deregulation Committee is composed of the Secretary of the Treasury, the Chairman of the Board of Governors of the Federal Reserve System, the Chairman of the Board of Directors of the Federal Deposit Insurance Corporation, the Chairman of the Federal Home Loan Bank Board, the Chairman of the National Credit Union Administration Board, and the Comptroller of the Currency.

CHAPTER

11 The Nation's Federal Reserve System

(text pages 242–265)

Section 1 Review

(text page 249)

DEFINE

central bank: Depository for a nation's funds and a place where banks bank.

pyramided reserves: System designed to avoid economic panics by requiring local banks to deposit some of their reserves with larger city banks. Larger city banks deposit some of their own reserves in the largest banks, which in turn, use some of these deposits to extend loans while holding the rest in reserve.

IDENTIFY

National Monetary Commission: Group chaired by Senator Nelson Aldrich from 1908 to 1911, which identified banking problems and made recommendations that led to the passage of the Federal Reserve Act.

1. The three periods in the development of central banking in the United States are from the 1780s to 1860s, which was a time of debate and experimentation; from the 1860s to 1913, during which a national banking system was created; and the current period, from 1913 to the present, in which banking reforms under the guidance of the Federal Reserve System have taken place.
2. The two major decision-making bodies in the Federal Reserve System are the Board of Governors and the Federal Open Market Committee.
3. The Federal Reserve System is different from any other central bank in the world because it is organized on both the national and state levels.
4. Goals and policies flow from the Board of Governors to the Federal Open Market Committee and to the Federal Advisory Council, to the Federal Reserve and Federal Branch banks, and to the 5,800 member banks and other depository institutions.

Section 2 Review

(text page 252)

DEFINE

check clearing: Method of crediting and debiting checking accounts.

1. **(a)** The services the Federal Reserve provides to the federal government are that it serves as the depository for federal revenues, it holds a checking account for the Treasury on which the Treasury writes checks to cover all government payments, it serves as a federal bookkeeper, and it serves as a financial adviser to the government. **(b)** The main services the Fed provides to banks are clearing checks and making loans to banks.
2. The buying and selling of government securities allows the Fed to regulate the money supply and to provide the government with the cash it needs to finance public goods and services.
3. The Federal Reserve regulates banks by examining the financial activities of member banks, by regulating bank mergers, and by chartering bank holding companies.
4. The Bureau of Printing and Engraving sends the new currency, most of it in Federal Reserve Notes, to the 12 Federal Reserve Banks. The Federal Reserve Banks exchange the new currency for the worn-out notes that are sent to it by banks.
5. The basic role of the Federal Reserve in clearing Mr. Walker's check is to communicate between the local banks in Dallas and Atlanta, and to oversee the adjustments in each bank's cash reserves.

Building Economic Skills

(text pages 256–257)

1. The subject is the growth of the money supply from 1975 to 1985.
2. The annual supply of money in the M1, the M2, the M3, and the L are given.
3. The information is given for the years 1975 through 1985.

4. It is recorded in billions of dollars.

5. The 1985 figures are as of May 1985, the (NA) in column L stands for data not available, and the source is *Statistical Abstract of the United States, 1986.*

6. The correct answer is ***a.***

7. In the years 1979 and 1980, the supply of money in M2 remained constant.

Section 3 Review

(text page 258)

DEFINE

money supply: Amount of money in circulation.

monetary policy: Program of the Federal Reserve Board designed to control the nation's money supply and credit.

aggregate demand: Total spending in the economy.

reserve requirement: Percentage of money deposited in checking and savings accounts that must be held by banks either in their own vaults or at the district Federal Reserve Bank.

discount rate: Interest rate that the Federal Reserve charges member banks for the use of its money.

prime rate: Interest that a bank charges on loans to its best business customers.

open market operation: Buying and selling of government securities by the Federal Reserve.

margin requirement: Percentage of cash required of an investor to buy stocks, options, warrants, and convertible bonds.

1. **(a)** The general purpose of monetary policy is to regulate aggregate demand or the total spending in the economy. **(b)** The three key components of the Federal Reserve's monetary policy are the reserve requirement, the discount rate, and open market operations.

2. M2 is a broader measure of the money supply than M1 because M2 includes money market accounts, money-market mutual fund shares, and other savings deposits as well as the money counted in M1.

3. When the Federal Reserve sells securities, the amount of money in circulation decreases because the Fed receives money as payments for the securities.

4. **(a)** The goal of an *easy-money policy* is to expand the money supply, increase aggregate demand, and promote economic growth, while the goal of a *tight-money policy* is to reduce the money supply and aggregate demand. **(b)** In an *easy-money policy,* interest rates are lowered to increase borrowing, while in a *tight-money policy,* interest rates are raised to restrict borrowing and the use of credit.

5. **(a)** The prime rate was highest in 1981. **(b)** In 1986, the prime rate was 10 percent. **(c)** Since 1981, both the prime rate and the discount rate have shown an overall decrease.

Section 4 Review

(text page 263)

IDENTIFY

Paul Volcker: Appointed Chairman of the Federal Reserve Board of Governors in 1979 and later reappointed in 1983 by President Reagan. During Reagan's first term, Volcker built a reputation for his firm and decisive battle against inflation.

1. The five limitations are difficulties in forecasting business activity, time lags in the formulation and implementation of monetary policies, judgments in setting priorities and weighing tradeoffs, lack of coordination among government agencies, and a lack of consensus among government leaders about the goals of monetary policy.

2. **(a)** Economic forecasts are predictions of future levels of business activity that are used by the government to develop and check economic policies. Forecasts are important because they provide assumptions on which policies are made, and incorrect forecasts can lead to inappropriate policy decisions. **(b)** The term *time lag* refers to the delays that occur between government imple-

mentation of policy and the policy's impact on the economy. **(c)** Trade-offs in monetary policy occur because a policy used to remedy one problem may make another problem worse.

3. Monetary policy is ineffective in battling stagflation because it is designed to fight *either* inflation *or* unemployment and recession, and stagflation is characterized by *both.*

4. Answers will vary. Some students may feel that difficulties in forecasting business activity are the most serious limitation because they make it very difficult to formulate successful policies. Some students may feel that time lags are the most serious limitation because they make it difficult to affect change immediately. Some students may feel that judgments in setting priorities and weighing trade-offs is the most serious limitation because judgments are often based on data that is difficult to collect and interpret, especially data related to the prediction of business activity. Some students may feel that a lack of coordination among government programs and policies is the most serious limitation because programs and policies often work against each other. Some students may feel that disagreement over policy goals is the most serious limitation because as long as such uncertainties exist, it is impossible for the Fed to develop policies that solve complex economic problems.

Chapter 11 Review

(text pages 264–265)

REVIEWING ECONOMIC TERMS

1. d; **2.** b; **3.** g; **4.** f; **5.** c; **6.** a; **7.** e.

EXERCISING ECONOMIC SKILLS

1. **(a)** The largest number of S & Ls is found in the category in which assets are between $100 million and $499 million. **(b)** The largest number of mutual savings banks is found in the category in which assets are between $100 million and $499 million. **(c)** The largest number of credit unions is found in the category in which assets are less than $1 million. **(d)** Answers will vary. For example, some students may conclude that because mutual savings banks are both the fewest in number and have the least total assets, they must serve a very specific group of clients rather than the general public.

2. **(a)** Answers will vary. All the applications will ask for the same demographic information and credit history. **(b)** Answers will vary. The applications may ask for different amounts of detail in certain information categories, especially in work and credit history. **(c)** Answers will vary. Most students will note, however, that the most important information usually is work and credit history.

THINKING CRITICALLY ABOUT ECONOMICS

1. **(a)** A central bank holds the government's funds, provides banking uniformity, and helps establish public credibility. **(b)** The Fed's seven services are clearing checks, extending loans to banks and the government, transferring funds nationwide, supervising and regulating member banks, serving as the government's fiscal agent, distributing paper money, and regulating the money supply. **(c)** The Fed's major functions are regulating the money supply and formulating monetary policy. **(d)** The five limitations that the Federal Reserve considers when establishing a monetary policy are difficulties in forecasting business activity, time lags in the formulation and implemention of monetary policies, judgments in setting priorities and in the weighing of trade-offs, lack of coordination among government agencies in the formulation of economic policies, and lack of consensus among government leaders about the goals of monetary policy.

2. **(a)** There are 12 Federal Reserve District banks. **(b)** There are 25 Federal Reserve Branch banks.

3. The Federal Reserve is concerned with stability and growth and was intentionally created to be an independent body so it would not be subject to political pressure. The President and Congress who determine fiscal policy goals must be responsive to the electorate and be open to political compromise. Federal Reserve monetary policy often involves choosing unpopular political actions that reduce the availability of credit and economic activity.

4. **(a)** The "lender of last resort" is a financial institution that is strong enough to make funds available in a time of economic emergency or to remedy the effects of natural disasters, or to counter seasonal fluctuations. Without such a lender, the economic fabric of the nation would be severely damaged because of lack of capital at critical times. **(b)** The Federal Reserve grants loans for fairly predictable seasonal events that deplete cash reserves in banks; for floods, hurricanes, tornadoes, and earthquakes and other natural disasters which necessitate large cash withdrawals and a high demand for new loans from area banks; and for other financial emergencies.

USING PRIMARY SOURCES

1. The Federal Reserve Board is now called the Federal Reserve Board of Governors. Members of the board were chosen by the President of the United States with the advice and consent of the Senate. The seven members are still chosen by the President with the advice and consent of the Senate.

2. The act states that "the President shall have due regard to a fair representative of different commercial, industrial, and geographical divisions of the country." Ideally, members representing commercial, industrial, and geographical divisions of the country should be appointed to the board.

3. The Federal Reserve Board of Governors is empowered to examine the finances and operations of its member banks, it can control the issue and retirement of Federal Reserve Notes, it can suspend or remove any official or director of any member bank, it can write off any doubtful or worthless assets from the books of member banks, and it can suspend the operations of any member bank for violation of any provision of the act.

4. The Federal Advisory Council acts as a link between the Federal Reserve Board of Governors and its member banks and helps the board supervise the Federal Reserve System by recommendations and information supplied to the board by member banks. The members of the Federal Advisory Council are chosen by each Federal Reserve Bank's board of directors and there is one member for every Federal Reserve District—a total of 12. Since the Federal Advisory Council members represent the districts, they can keep the Federal Reserve Board of Governors supplied with the information they need to know to formulate the correct monetary policies for the nation as well as acting as a forum for the policies of the Federal Reserve to its member banks.

CHAPTER

12 Saving, Borrowing, and Using Credit

(text pages 266–287)

Section 1 Review

(text page 273)

DEFINE

spending: Consumption of disposable income.

saving: Nonconsumption of disposable income.

savings rate: Percentage of disposable income deposited into savings accounts.

liquidity: Condition that indicates the ease with which accounts or property can be converted into cash with little or no loss in interest payments or capital.

1. **(a)** The savings options available to savers are regular savings accounts, money market accounts, NOW and Super-NOW accounts, certificates of deposit, government bonds and other treasury investments, and retirement accounts. **(b)** The benefits that depositors receive from their savings are security and interest. **(c)** For most savings accounts, the trade-off for a higher interest rate is reduced liquidity.

2. One disadvantage of time deposits is that there is a financial penalty if money is withdrawn prior to the maturity date.

3. **(a)** A retirement account is a long-term, tax-sheltered time deposit. **(b)** People open retirement accounts to plan for financial security after the age of 59.

4. **(a)** Portugal has the highest savings rate.

(b) Answers may vary. For example, students may suggest that the people in Portugal have fewer consumer goods available on which to spend their money than the people in the other selected nations shown on the chart.

Building Economic Skills *(text pages 274–275)*

See the annotation on text page 274.

Section 2 Review *(text page 282)*

DEFINE

credit: Purchase of goods and services without the actual transfer of money on the promise to pay later.

principal: Amount borrowed in a loan.

finance charge: Total cost of credit expressed in dollars and cents.

bankruptcy: Legal declaration of an inability to pay debts.

usury: Charging of interest at a rate higher than the law allows.

IDENTIFY

"smart" card: Credit card with a microchip that details the user's credit history. The card has been developed to guard against credit abusers and is programmed to stop any further granting of credit after an established credit limit has been reached.

1. **(a)** The 4-Cs that help creditors to determine a credit rating are character, capacity to pay, capital, and credit history. **(b)** A creditor evaluates information about a consumer and assigns that person a credit rating. Often the information used by the creditor comes from a credit bureau, a business that specializes in collecting financial information about consumers.

2. In a *regular charge account*, payment for the purchase amount is made at the end of a 30-day period; in a *revolving charge account*, the customer's additional purchases, up to a stated credit limit, are added to the previous month's balance, and the customer must make a minimum monthly payment with interest charged on the unpaid balance; in a *installment charge account*, the purchaser pays for the items purchased in a number of equal payments with interest spread over a period of time. The monthly payments on an installment credit account include an interest charge.

3. **(a)** The two measures of the cost of credit are the finance charge and the annual percentage rate (APR). **(b)** The APR is the better gauge because it can be used to compare credit costs.

4. **(a)** Bankruptcies field under *Chapter 7* allow debtors to write off most of their debts. Bankruptcies filed under *Chapter 11* allow debtors to delay payments while undergoing financial reorganization. Bankruptcies filed under *Chapter 13* allow debtors to repay a percentage of their debts to every creditor. **(b)** Bankruptcy is the last resort for credit abuse because it has serious consequences. Bankruptcy information stays on an individual's credit history for 10 years, making it nearly impossible during that 10-year period to get any credit.

5. **(a)** Between 1978 and 1981, the number of bankruptcies increased significantly. **(b)** Answers will vary. Students might infer that 1978 to 1981 was a period of recession.

Section 3 Review *(text page 285)*

IDENTIFY

Marcy S. Lyons: Assistant vice president at the San Francisco office of the First National Bank of Chicago. She seeks out potential clients among companies that do business overseas and helps them create an account with First National.

1. The financial resources come from money put into savings in financial institutions.

2. The uses of money and credit affect the economy

by stimulating economic growth and by promoting economic stability.

3. **(a)** Usually when money is available, consumers spend more and prices rise. The higher spending encourages producers to increase the supply. When the supply is sufficient to meet demand, prices reach a level acceptable to consumers and producers. **(b)** The two reasons that the use of loan money and credit can cause prices to rise are that the buy-now attitude of people can force the prices of some goods to increase, and that retailers who extend credit raise their prices to all customers to cover the additional costs, such as paperwork and mailing costs, associated with credit purchases.

4. **(a)** A greater availability of money for loans and credit spurs economic growth. **(b)** The relationship between aggregate demand and employment is that when the aggregate demand is high, employment is usually high. **(c)** When credit increases demand in the overall economy, it is likely to effect both production and employment.

5. **(a)** Consumers buy consumer goods. **(b)** Businesses buy capital goods. **(c)** The government buys public goods.

Chapter 12 Review

(text pages 286–287)

REVIEWING ECONOMIC TERMS

1. h; **2.** a; **3.** d; **4.** e; **5.** g; **6.** b; **7.** f; **8.** c.

EXERCISING ECONOMIC SKILLS

1. Answers will vary.

2. Answers will vary.

THINKING CRITICALLY ABOUT ECONOMICS

1. **(a)** People save money to make a down payment on a major purchase, to set aside money to meet large expected bills, to have a reserve to meet unexpected expenses, and to save for major expenses in the future. **(b)** People borrow money to enjoy a purchase while paying off the debt and to extend the payments for expensive items by paying them over a period of time.

2. **(a)** The two economic goals affected by the availability of money and credit are economic growth and economic stability. **(b)** The goals of economic stability and economic growth conflict because fast growth is inherently more unstable than moderate growth. The greater the expansion of credit, for example, the greater the chance for corresponding periods of decline.

3. **(a)** The greater the liquidity is, the smaller the interest paid on the account. **(b)** Financial institutions charge a heavy penalty for withdrawing money from the account before it matures because the institution uses the money and if people withdrew their savings before the maturity of the account, the bank would experience cash-flow problems.

4. Answers will vary. Students who agree may feel that the government should encourage people to increase their savings because an increase in savings will make more funds available for investment. Students who disagree may feel that if the economy is overstimulated, inflation will occur.

5. **(a)** In dollar value, the outstanding nonmortgage consumer credit has risen rapidly. **(b)** As a percentage of the consumer debt, the outstanding nonmortgage consumer credit rate has fluctuated between 19 and 23 percent. **(c)** In dollar value, the outstanding nonmortgage consumer credit should continue to rise sharply, while as a percentage of the consumer debt it should rise modestly.

USING PRIMARY SOURCES

1. The 1974 Equal Credit Opportunity Act protects women and single people.

2. Borrowers of different races, colors, religions, and national origins are guaranteed equal access to credit under the amendments of 1976. It is unlawful for creditors to deny credit on the basis of race, color, religion, national origin, sex, marital status, or age; because all or part of the applicant's income derives from any public assistance program; or because the applicant has in good faith exercised any right under the Consumer Credit Protection Act.

3. A creditor may ask about a borrower's marital status to ascertain the creditor's rights and remedies applicable to the particular extension of credit. They may ask about age, or receipt of public assistance to ascertain the amount and probable continuance of income levels, credit history, or other pertinent elements of credit worthiness. The creditor must determine if the person who desires to borrow money is a good credit risk, and such questions help the creditor determine ability to repay the loan.

CHAPTER

13 Investment and Investors

(text pages 288–309)

Section 1 Review

(text page 293)

DEFINE

investment: Condition in which people exchange their money for something of value and expect to earn a profit from this purchase in the future.

capital accumulation: Expansion of capital goods in the economy.

venture capital: Money invested in a high-risk but promising business; also known as risk capital.

spending and saving plan: Personal or household budget that is the starting point for all personal financial planning.

fixed expenses: Costs that remain constant from month to month.

flexible expenses: Costs that vary from month to month.

diversification: Variety of investments combining several investment goals—security, high yield, and growth.

1. **(a)** Two types of investments are financial investments and real investments. **(b)** The difference between a financial investment and a real investment is that in a financial investment property is bought and sold in a transfer from one person or group to another; whereas in a real investment investors use money to create a new capital good.

2. **(a)** A savings account is the most risk-free way to save money because most deposits are protected by federal and state insurance plans. **(b)** Many investors are willing to make financial and real investments because they offer higher returns on their money than savings deposits.

3. Real investment by private firms and by the government promotes economic growth by increasing the number of capital goods used in the economy and by encouraging research and development and the application of new technology to production.

4. **(a)** The economic infrastructure consists of roads, bridges, harbors, airports, other transportation facilities, and public schools and universities. **(b)** Improvements created from real investment help business and spur economic growth because the elements of the economic infrastructure support business activities.

5. Both are long-range economic plans. A *retirement plan*, a type of long-term savings plan, helps a person accumulate wealth for use after retirement. An *estate plan* provides for the orderly transfer of any remaining wealth after a person's death.

Section 2 Review

(text page 297)

DEFINE

dividend: Return stockholders receive on investments in corporate stocks.

common stock: Share of ownership in a corporation that offers a variable dividend determined by the corporation's board of directors.

stock split: Increase in the number of shares of a company that occurs when the company's directors and shareholders declare that each old share can be converted into a specified number of new shares.

stockbroker: Person who links buyers and sellers of stocks and bonds; also known as a broker.

market analyst: Individual who researches individual firms and evaluates their strengths and weaknesses.

mutual fund: Pool of money from investors to purchase a variety of securities.

investment bank: Financial institution frequently used by corporations when they issue new stock, buy out controlling interests in another company, or trade large blocks of other stocks.

syndicate: Group of investment banks that spreads the work and risk of marketing a new stock issue or reselling a large stock purchase in a process called syndication.

1. Changes in technology have improved the speed and accuracy of stock transactions.
2. Dividends for preferred stock are always paid and are paid from profits before the company pays dividends on common stock.
3. **(a)** The advantages of investing in a mutual fund are that the fund allows an individual to invest smaller amounts with less risk; the pooled funds have a greater potential for gain; and mutual funds hold a variety of stocks, reducing the possibility of a loss due to the poor performance of one stock. **(b)** Investors who hold only a few shares of stock have little power in shaping policies of public corporations because the largest corporations have thousands of shareholders, some of whom control large blocks of stocks. Because votes are cast according to the number of shares an investor has, a small investor is easily outvoted by a larger investor.
4. **(a)** The number of stockholders decreased. **(b)** Answers will vary. For example, students might suggest that a recession during those years meant less money was available to be invested in the stock market.

Building Economic Skills *(text pages 298–299)*

See annotation on text page 299.

Section 3 Review *(text page 303)*

DEFINE

bull market: Condition in the stock market noted for investor optimism that prices will rise and marked by a steady rise in the Dow Jones Industrial Average.

bear market: Condition in the stock market noted for investor anticipation that prices will fall and marked by a steady decline in the Dow Jones Industrial Average.

prospectus: Fact sheet containing data on a company's finances used by investors to evaluate securities offered for sale.

IDENTIFY

Dow Jones Industrial Average: Index of stock prices of selected companies.

greenmail: Wall Street's name for a hostile merger attempt.

Ivan Boesky: Well-known risk arbitrageur who made huge profits in trading shares in companies' stocks because he had information obtained in his role as an insider trader. The Securities and Exchange Commission investigated Boesky's activities and forced him to pay a $100 million fine—$50 million in settlement for illegal profits and a $50 million penalty.

1. **(a)** The major determinant of stock prices is demand for the stock. **(b)** Corporate financial strength, investor expectations, and external factors over which neither the firm or the stock market has control influences demand for the stock.
2. The Clayton Antitrust Act puts limits on the types of stocks corporations can buy. The SEC evaluates securities trading, licenses all stock exchanges to ensure that they conform to certain rules and regulations, and regulates stockbrokers and brokerage houses.
3. The actions by the Securities and Exchange Commission against insider trading have protected small investors because an investor using inside

information not available to the general public may unfairly affect the demand and price of an investment.

4. (a) A greenmailer threatens a hostile takeover by buying enough of a company's stock, usually with the idea of reselling the stock to the company at a higher price. (b) Answers will vary. Students who agree may feel that greenmailers take unfair advantage of a company's financial situation. Students who disagree may feel that greenmail is a legitimate part of free enterprise.

Section 4 Review

(text page 305)

DEFINE

futures market: Trading in which contracts are made to sell securities or commodities such as agricultural products, industrial goods, and gold and silver at a future date.

IDENTIFY

programmed trading: Buying and selling stocks and futures under the direction of a computer program.

1. The chief advantages are that *real estate* appreciates or grows more valuable over time; *government bonds* pay fixed and often higher interest rates than are paid on savings accounts and are backed by the federal government; *corporate bonds* also pay fixed and often higher interest rates and the interest on the bonds must be paid in good times and in bad; *futures markets* pay potential higher returns because prices are eventually determined by the open market.

2. The return on corporate bonds is normally less than that of government bonds. The government bonds may pay a lower rate of interest because they have the advantage of tax-exemption. The real interest rate on corporate bonds, however, is greater after taxes are paid on corporate-bond income.

3. The futures market is considered more of a risk than the purchase of common stock because the price of the commodity, or future, on the open market may rise far above that which is listed on the contract. The business or investor must then honor the contract and deliver the commodity to the investor at the lower price. There also is risk involved in investing in common stock. The risk in stock is more long-term than the risk in futures because usually the demise of a company and the faltering of its stock happens over a number of years. In addition, stock prices are less prone to the affects of natural occurrences such as the weather than are futures.

Chapter 13 Review

(text pages 306–307)

REVIEWING ECONOMIC TERMS

1. real investment
2. mutual fund
3. bull market
4. prospectus
5. capital gain
6. risk capital
7. bear market
8. syndication
9. economic infrastructure

EXERCISING ECONOMIC SKILLS

1. Answers will vary.

2. Answers will vary. The prospectus will usually contain a company's financial information, such as gross income, net income, and profits. It may also include a brief history of the company, a review of the corporate structure, and information on the company's officers.

THINKING CRITICALLY ABOUT ECONOMICS

1. (a) A real investment uses money to create a new good, while financial investment produces no new good. (b) Most investments involve risk because of the possibility that the investor will lose money. (c) The Securities and Exchange Commission was created to regulate the sale of securities because abuses in the system helped to bring on the stock market crash in 1929.

2. Stock for some companies is sold on the over-the-counter market rather than at a stock exchange because the company does not meet the standards for stock transactions set by the nation's stock exchanges.

3. Investment banks are interested in forming syndicates to trade in stock because such an operation spreads the work and risk of buying and reselling a large stock purchase, and the banks can collect a commission on the transactions.

4. Stockholders are owners of the corporation, and each share represents a percentage of the ownership.

5. A growth stock is a share of ownership in a company whose growth rate is faster than other companies or the economy as a whole. The growth stock pays no dividends, but becomes more valuable with time as the company grows. Investors buy growth stocks as a long-term investment. An income stock has high current earnings and pays consistent dividends. An income stock, however, is more susceptible to economic downturns than is a growth stock.

6. Investors' expectations about the future may cause the price of a stock to rise when investors increase their demand for a stock because they expect it to increase in value. They cause a price to fall when they sell the stock because they believe a stock's value will decrease.

7. An investor or market analyst would want to look at *The Wall Street Journal* or *Forbes* because these publications contain expert advice on individual firms or on the stock market itself.

USING PRIMARY SOURCES

1. Carnegie viewed the rich as the trustees of society's wealth. He called them trustees because the excess wealth should be placed in a trust which would be administered by them. Carnegie felt that these trustees should live modest lives, shunning displays or extravagance.

2. Carnegie believed that a trustee's ability to accumulate money was important to society because the wealth could be used to improve the condition of the people. Answers will vary. For example, students may recall that the captains of industry used the surplus wealth to build industry by funding various vertical and horizontal combinations.

3. Carnegie believed that causes worthy of support are ones that benefit the community, improve public taste, and improve the general condition of the people. Answers will vary. For example, students may feel that Carnegie's philanthropy was an investment in America's society and culture because in bettering the lives of all citizens, it created a better society, better markets for industry, and a more promising future.

4. Carnegie feels that "indiscriminate charity" is an obstacle to the improvement of society because it might be used to help the lazy, the drunken, and the unworthy. Carnegie felt that the best rule for charity was giving to those who would help themselves.

Unit Four Review

(text pages 308–309)

REVIEWING ECONOMIC IDEAS

1. Money serves as a medium of exchange, a store of value, and a standard of value. It provides the market with the economic fuel it needs to function effectively.

2. **(a)** The United States went off the gold standard in 1934, but continued to hold gold reserves as partial backing of currency until 1968. **(b)** The government went off the gold standard so that it could put more money in circulation in an effort to soften the Great Depression.

3. The purpose of desposit insurance is that it insures deposits up to the limit ($100,000), guaranteeing that depositors will be able to withdraw their funds in the event of a bank failure. It also has the ability to stop panic withdrawals.

4. The monetary tools of the Federal Reserve are the discount rate, reserve requirement, and open market operations.

5. The forms of money that are included in M1 are all currency in circulation, the value of all traveler's checks, and all checking accounts.

6. The government adopts an easy-money policy when it wants to encourage economic growth.

7. **(a)** People in the United States save an average of 6 percent of their disposable income. **(b)** Americans save less than the people in most other

countries shown on the chart. Only people in Finland are shown as saving less than people in the United States.

8. Real investment creates capital goods.

9. **(a)** Stock represents ownership in a corporation. **(b)** The advantage of buying preferred stock over common stock is that preferred stock pays a guaranteed dividend, and it pays its dividend from profits before the dividends for common stock are paid. **(c)** A corporate bond is a certificate, offering a fixed interest rate, issued in exchange for money borrowed from investors.

CONNECTING ECONOMIC IDEAS

1. The trade-offs are the greater security and liquidity of regular savings accounts versus the higher risk and potential for greater return on investment when investing in the stock market.

2. Improvements in the infrastructure are an investment in economic growth because an improved infrastructure helps businesses carry out their operations. Such improvements are an investment in economic equity because the components of the economic infrastructure are public goods.

3. **(a)** Money and credit are necessary for increased investment and economic growth. An easy-money policy provides money to fund economic expansion, while a tight-money policy restricts economic expansion. **(b)** The size of the money supply is directly related to the growth of the economy. The size of the money supply determines the amount of money available for government spending, private consumption, and corporate and other business investments.

4. Savings deposits, time deposits, and stocks are similar because each investment pays a return on the money invested. They are different because they have different risk factors, liquidity, and other specific points.

5. **(a)** Unions are made up of many hundreds of workers. Taken singly, workers do not have economic power. By pooling their resources in a credit union, workers generate considerable revenue which the credit union can then use to lend money to its members at lower-than-bank rates. **(b)** The principal reason that 12 separate Federal Reserve Banks were created rather than one large one was to spread the power of the Fed among its banks and not concentrate it in one location.

6. As interest rates increase, economic activities decrease because consumers cannot afford to borrow money or use credit to make purchases. As aggregate demand decreases in response to high interest rates, production and eventually supply decrease.

INVESTIGATING ECONOMIC ISSUES

1. Misconceptions concerning the national debt are in the areas of size, benefits, and repayment of the debt. Some economists feel that the debt is exaggerated. Others feel that the debt has a number of benefits derived from deficit spending, and 90 percent of the bonds used to service the debt are purchased by Americans. Also, many people feel that the debt must be repaid because of their experience with installment finance. Some economists feel that this is an unnecessary fear.

2. **(a)** Economists have determined that the national debt has five potential consequences: tighter credit markets, additional budgetary trade-offs, higher taxes, higher inflation, and an increasing dependence on foreign capital to finance the debt. **(b)** Deficit spending has allowed the government to provide adequate public goods such as national defense and welfare payments to needy individuals. It has allowed the government to hold down taxes, thus encouraging consumer spending and business investment. It has stimulated economic growth, especially during the economic recovery of the mid-1980s. It serves as a national investment because about 90 percent of all federal securities that are used to service the debt are purchased by Americans.

3. Answers will vary. Students who agree may feel that the national debt has a negative impact because the government uses a larger percentage of the national budget to pay the interest on the debt, which means less money is available for important social and defense programs. They may also feel that the increasing size of the national debt will cause higher taxes for future generations. Students who disagree may feel that the national debt is beneficial because it pumps billions of dollars into the economy, fueling eco-

nomic growth and recovery from economic downturns.

4. **(a)** The trend has shown a strong upward surge of the national debt to a high of $2.2 trillion in 1986. **(b)** The trend in the national debt as a percentage of the GNP has been down during the 1950s and through the early 1980s where it has again begun an upward surge. **(c)** Throughout the 1950s and 1960s, even though the size of the debt was becoming larger, the debt as a percentage of the GNP fell because the economy was in a period of growth. In the 1980s, with the debt in dollars still growing, the percentage has also grown because the economy is slowing down and is not generating as much overall revenue.

USING PRIMARY SOURCES

1. The government should limit or eliminate transfer payments and entitlements.
2. A welfare state is a nation in which the productive people have only residual claim to what is left of their income and wealth after all levels of government are finished redistributing it to the politically deserving. He says a welfare state exists in the United States because our poverty programs are so generous that most welfare recipients do not try to work themselves out of poverty any more.
3. A welfare state is harmful to *private investment* because government spending crowds out private investment. It is harmful to *private property rights* because the government takes so much of a person's income and wealth to redistribute that many people are discouraged from innovative attempts to accumulate wealth. A welfare state is harmful to *personal incentives and self-reliance* because it provides such generous and free welfare to a large segment of the population. A welfare state "institutionalizes poverty" by making it easier for people to receive welfare than it is for them to find productive work.

TEACHER'S NOTES

SETTING AND MEETING ECONOMIC GOALS

CHAPTER 14

Inflation, Recession, and Unemployment (text pages 312–335)

Section 1 Review (text page 318)

DEFINE

inflation: Increase in the average price level of all goods and services.

deflation: Decline in the average price level of all goods and services.

disinflation: Reduction of inflation.

Consumer Price Index: Government measure that charts changes in prices paid by consumers for goods and services.

Produce Price Index: Government measure that charts the changes in the average prices of goods sold by producers in all stages of processing.

demand-pull inflation: Increase in the price level of all goods and services that occurs when aggregate demand increases at a faster rate than aggregate supply.

wage-price spiral: Condition in which workers, particularly those represented by unions, bargain for pay increases that are greater than the inflation rate, leading to higher inflation.

1. Inflation decreases aggregate demand, leading to an increase in supply until producers cut back production levels of goods and services.
2. A creditor would be more unhappy than a debtor with inflation because the dollars received in repayment of a loan have less buying power than the dollars originally loaned.
3. Consumer Price Index rose steadily from 1970 to 1985.

Section 2 Review (text page 325)

DEFINE

employment rate: Percentage of employed labor force 16 years of age or older.

unemployment: Situation that occurs when a number of people do not have jobs but actively seek employment.

frictional unemployment: Situation that occurs when workers are temporarily between jobs.

structural employment: Situation that occurs when changes in the economy eliminate jobs or generate jobs for which unemployed workers are not qualified.

full employment: Lowest level of unemployment that is possible in an economy, generally occurring when about 95 percent of the labor force has jobs.

cyclical unemployment: Situation that occurs when people are out of work because of economic downturns.

1. The unemployment figures measure only those who are looking for jobs. Many people are working less than full time and not earning an adequate income, which is also a significant measurement of the underutilization of labor resources in a nation.
2. It is difficult to enforce laws protecting the rights of migrant workers because the migrant workers move from one political jurisdiction to another. Also, because migrant workers often have little education, they are unaware of their rights, and because migrant workers depend on temporary, low-paying jobs, they seldom complain about illegal practices.
3. **(a)** The unemployment rate decreased between 1982 and 1985. **(b)** The statistics probably do not show hidden unemployment, or people who have given up looking for work, and underem-

ployment, or people who are working at jobs beneath their skill level. **(c)** Males 16–19 years old have the highest rate of unemployment (19.5 percent). Men 20 years old or older and white workers have the lowest, each at 6.2 percent.

Building Economic Skills *(text pages 326–327)*

Answers will vary. The following answers are sample responses for each of the economic decisions listed on text page 327.

THE IMMIGRATION REFORM AND CONTROL ACT

1. **(a)** The decision was to offer amnesty and legalization to aliens who entered the United States illegally before January 1, 1982, and could prove they had lived continuously in the country since before 1982. **(b)** The influx of illegal aliens was increasing and the Census Bureau estimated that there were between 3.5 and 6 million illegal aliens in the United States by 1986. Employment of undocumented aliens stirred fierce controversy because many Americans felt that the employment of illegal aliens cost Americans jobs and lowered the pay rate for certain jobs. Students may provide additional relevant historical conditions.

2. The government could have increased its efforts to stop the illegal entry of aliens into the nation, or it could have continued its present policies, ignoring the increasing controversy. Some students may provide other alternatives.

3. **(a)** The *costs* include increased federal expenditures for a 50 percent increase in the Border Patrol, for the prosecution of aliens with forged documents, and for additional welfare recipients; possible increased hiring discrimintation against Hispanics, Asians, and other minorities by employers fearing the law; and frustration over the difficulty of enforcing the law. The *benefits* include increased tax revenues from aliens who register and are added to tax roles; increased pay rates for certain jobs; and a reduction of the resentment felt for immigrants, especially those emigrating from Latin America and Asia. Students may provide additional costs and benefits. **(b)** Answers will vary. Some students may note that policymakers recognized the growing problem of illegal immigration into the United States and decided that the enactment of the law was the best way to solve the problem.

4. Answers will vary. Students who feel its is a "good" decision may feel that the employment and economic problems caused by illegal aliens are a serious problem and that this law will help solve it. Students who feel it is a "bad" decision may feel that the law will cause increased discrimination or higher taxes.

WORKFARE LEGISLATION

1. **(a)** The decision was made by some states to require welfare recipients deemed employable to work for their benefits. **(b)** In the 1980s, concerns over the size of the national debt and deficit spending spurred welfare reform. Certain welfare programs seemed wasteful and sometimes unjust, and many reformers agreed that a new system that established incentives to encourage those who can work to do so would be an improvement over the old system. Students may provide additional relevant historical conditions.

2. Decision makers could have allowed the system to continue to operate unchanged, or they could have abolished the programs that distributed money to the unemployed. Students may provide additional alternatives.

3. **(a)** The *costs* include increased expenditures for the staff necessary to run the programs, and the frustration of being unable to motivate some people to take and keep jobs. The *benefits* include helping individuals and families to become self-reliant and reducing welfare expenditures as people become self-supporting. Students may provide additional costs and benefits. **(b)** Answers will vary. Students may feel that policymakers selected this alternative because it is fair and does help people become self-sufficient.

4. Answers will vary. Students who think it is a "good" decision may feel that it is only fair that welfare recipients who can work for their benefits do so. Students who think it is a "bad" decision may feel that it fails to solve the social and

economic problems that cause the unemployment of certain individuals and groups.

FAIR LABOR STANDARDS ACT

1. **(a)** Congress decided to establish a law to protect workers against unfair employment practices by setting a maximum work week and a minimum wage, and by restricting child labor. **(b)** In the early 1900s, working conditions were unsafe and unsanitary, wages were low, and child labor was widespread. Early attempts at labor reform legislation were declared unconstitutional. The Great Depression crystallized the relationship between employer and employee and the New Deal opened the door for increased government regulation of the workplace. Students may provide additional relevant historical conditions.

2. The government could have avoided involvement, allowing labor unions to try to solve the problem without government help; or it could have asked for voluntary agreements from employers to improve working conditions. Students may provide additional alternatives.

3. **(a)** The *costs* include increased expenditures for personnel to enforce compliance with the law, higher prices throughout the economy caused by the increase in workers' pay, and the failures of businesses that could not afford to comply with the law. The *benefits* include the improved quality of life for the nation, the improved health of many workers, a higher standard of living for most workers, and increased aggregate demand created by additional pay. Students may provide additional costs and benefits. **(b)** Answers will vary. Students may feel that policymakers selected this alternative because labor unions and legislative attempts at improving working conditions had not been successful and because employers were not likely to voluntarily raise pay and improve conditions.

4. Answers will vary. Students who think it is a "good" decision may feel that higher pay and improved working conditions have an important positive effect on society and the economy. Students who think it is a "bad" decision may feel that the problem should have been solved without government intervention, avoiding additional government expenditures and involvement.

EXECUTIVE ORDER NO. 11246

1. **(a)** The federal government decided to issue an order requiring businesses that receive federal money to follow a policy of preferential treatment to women and minorities to ensure nondiscrimination in hiring and promoting women and minority workers. Goals were established to increase the employment of women and minorities. **(b)** In the 1950s and 1960s, the Civil Rights Movement made the American public conscious of discrimination throughout society. As a result of the movement, Congress passed the Civil Rights Act of 1964. The act outlawed discrimination by employers and labor unions. The government decided to take antidiscrimination a step further by supporting affirmative action. Students may provide additional relevant historical conditions.

2. The government could have stopped its antidiscrimination push with the Civil Rights Act of 1964; or to ensure fair hiring and promoting practices, the government could have taken over all the personnel duties of private businesses. Students may provide additional alternatives.

3. **(a)** The *costs* include increased expenditures to enforce the order, frustration caused by dealing with an attitude such as prejudice, and the controversy surrounding providing preferential treatment in a society based on personal initiative and equality. The *benefits* include fairer hiring and promoting practices for all workers and the discovery of many talented people who may have previously been overlooked because of their sex or minority status. Students may provide additional costs and benefits. **(b)** Answers will vary. Students may feel that policymakers selected this alternative because it extended the spirit of antidiscrimination contained in the Civil Rights Act of 1964 and seemed the only way to ensure fairness in hiring and promotion.

4. Answers will vary. Students who think it was a "good" decision may feel that the government needed to establish preferential treatment for minorities and women because society had not provided equal opportunities for them. Students who think it was a "bad" decision may feel that preferential treatment for minorities and women was unfair to men.

Section 3 Review

(text page 329)

DEFINE

stagflation: Condition that results when high unemployment and high inflation rates simultaneously plague the economy.

production disincentive: Cause of slowdown in industrial output that contributes to stagflation.

1. The traditional pattern has been that when there is high unemployment, the low aggregate demand resulted in a low inflation rate. Conversely, when employment was high, the increased demand put pressure on prices to rise. In the late 1970s and early 1980s, the rates of inflation and unemployment were both relatively high.
2. **(a)** An expectation of inflation will cause current consumption to increase. **(b)** The increase in consumption when prices are lower will put pressure on prices to increase.
3. Even though unemployment remained high at 7 percent, stagflation has not occurred because unemployment dropped to about 4 percent.

Section 4 Review

(text page 333)

DEFINE

business cycle: Sequential rise and fall of the economy.

Gross National Product: Dollar value of all new, final products produced in a nation each year; increases and decreases measure business cycles.

1. **(a)** Business activities and cycles are measured by changes in the Gross National Product. **(b)** The phases of the business cycle are expansion, or a period of growth, which increases to a peak that indicates a generally prosperous economy; followed by a period of decline called a contraction. The lowest point is the trough, which indicates that aggregate demand, production, and employment are at their lowest point.
2. The three types of indicators are *leading indicators*, such as the size of the money supply; *coincident indicators*, such as the sales volume of business; and *lagging indicators*, such as the unemployment rate.
3. The number of new business permits issued and orders for capital goods are examples of a leading economic indicator.
4. If people expect a contraction (or recession) in the business cycle, they may save more income to prepare for it. Decreased demand contributes to the contraction. If people expect an expansion in the business cycle, they may spend more. Increased spending contributes to the expansion.
5. When unemployment is high, and production and aggregate demand are at their lowest point, a nation is in the trough of the contraction phase of the business cycle.

Chapter 14 Review

(text pages 334–335)

REVIEWING ECONOMIC TERMS

1. aggregate demand
2. structural unemployment
3. inflation
4. disincentive
5. recession
6. trough
7. frictional unemployment
8. stagflation

EXERCISING ECONOMIC SKILLS

1. Answers will vary.
2. Answers will vary.

THINKING CRITICALLY ABOUT ECONOMICS

1. **(a)** Price fluctuations threaten the stability of the economy because inflation, deflation, and disinflation alter consumers' purchasing power and affect economic growth. **(b)** High unemployment destabilizes the economy because it adversely affects income and spending, business production and capital investment, and the economy's short-term and long-term performance. **(c)** Stagflation occurs because of high government spending, inflationary expectations, a growing labor force, and production disincentives. **(d)** The business cycle helps economists to better predict price and employment fluctuations.

2. **(a)** Current dollars are a basic measure of the present value of money, while constant dollars have been adjusted for inflation. **(b)** Constant dollars are a more significant measure because they show real growth, not just price changes.

3. Leading indicators illustrate in what direction the economy is heading. For example, if the average work week increases, it means that more labor resources are being put to work. When more resources are put into production, expansion usually results.

4. A investor would favor government policies aimed at reducing inflation over policies aimed at reducing unemployment because reducing inflation would protect an investment's real gain.

USING PRIMARY SOURCES

1. Discrimination reduces employment opportunities for minorities.

2. Discrimination costs the victims lost employment opportunities; it costs the discriminator opportunities to make money.

3. Public utilities have zero costs of discrimination because extra costs of discrimination are passed on to the consumer and costs of reducing discrimination also go to the consumer because the government regulates the prices charged by utilities. The costs of discrimination are less severe in highly competitive industries because these industries have a disproportionate overrepresentation of minorities.

CHAPTER

15 Measures and Causes of Economic Growth

(text pages 336–357)

Section 1 Review

(text page 341)

DEFINE

net exports: Value of the goods and services that a country sells to other countries less the value of goods and services that the country buys from other countries.

consumer good: Good that a consumer buys.

capital good: Building, structure, machinery, or tool that is used in the production process.

government good: Item that national, state, and local governments purchase.

implicit GNP price deflator: Measure of price changes in economic output that estimates the average price level of all consumer, capital, and government goods and services produced in a given year.

real per capita GNP: Real GNP divided by the total population.

per capita money GNP: Measure used to compare economic growth and the standard of living when reliable data on inflation is unavailable.

IDENTIFY

Simon Kuznets: Economist known as the father of the Gross National Product (GNP) because of his development of procedures for measuring national economic performance; awarded Nobel Prize for Economics in 1971.

1. Consumption, investment, government spending, and net exports make up the GNP.

2. Used automobiles were counted as a part of the GNP when they were purchased by their first users. If the used automobiles were counted each time they changed owners, it would be additional counting of actual production.

3. When the money GNP is greater than the real GNP, the standard of living has decreased due to the effects of inflation.

Building Economic Skills *(text pages 342–343)*

1. **(a)** The thesis is that the Tax Reform Act of 1986 is a piece of historic legislation because it simplifies the tax codes. **(b)** The author notes that hundreds of additions and exceptions to the tax code are wiped out by the Tax Reform Act.

2. **(a)** There are few facts presented. **(b)** The author feels that the Tax Reform Act is an outstanding improvement, fixing "a problem that has been festering for decades."

3. The author is George J. Church.

4. Answers will vary. Some students may feel the author does make a logical defense because he cites the the new direction the Tax Reform Act will give to taxation. Other students may feel his defense is not logical because he presents few solid facts. Yes, the author uses the majority-view fallacy when he states, "And everybody knows the political process does not work that way."

5. The author's point of view, while positive on the Tax Reform Act, is negative about Congressional and Presidential efforts to streamline the tax code.

Section 2 Review

(text page 345)

DEFINE

depreciation: Value of capital that is used up each year to keep a nation's capital stock intact.

Net National Product: Gross National Product less depreciation.

national income: Total amount of money that everyone in the economy earns.

indirect business tax: Government levy on a firm's output rather than on the firm itself.

personal income: Total amount of income that individuals receive before paying taxes.

disposable income: Personal income less income taxes.

1. Net National Product is a more accurate measurement of an increase in productivity than the GNP because only the net gain in capital goods indicates increased productivity. In Net National Product, the amount invested to replace worn-out equipment has been subtracted because there was no increase in total capital goods.

2. Transfer payments are included as personal income and not national income because they are money transferred from one person to another and, therefore, were counted as a part of national income when originally earned.

3. The key word in national income is *earn.* Three fourths of the national income is earned by people, who are the suppliers of factors of production and earn their living from contributing to the production process.

Section 3 Review

(text page 352)

DEFINE

capacity utilization rate: Information calculated by the government to show how much of the nation's total capital goods are being used to produce goods.

IDENTIFY

enterprise zone: Zone established by state government to promote economic growth in a distressed geographical area.

Philip B. Crosby: Founder of Philip Crosby Associates and developer of a theory of quality, which stresses that no defects are acceptable.

1. **(a)** Machinery and buildings are the capital resources, **(b)** workers are human resources, and **(c)** ore is a natural resource.

2. **(a)** Public education is an investment in labor, or human, resources. **(b)** Investment in public education increases the quality of labor resources.

3. The dips in capacity utilization rates for 1974–1975 and 1980–1982 mean that industries are not operating at full capacity, and that the economy is undergoing a recession.

Section 4 Review

(text page 355)

DEFINE

urbanization: Movement of people from rural areas to cities.

IDENTIFY

acid rain: Form of pollution caused when sulfur and other pollutants released into the atmosphere by factory smokestacks combine with water vapor and fall to the ground, polluting the air, soil, and water.

1. Economic growth leads to increased consumption of goods and services and an improved standard of living. A higher standard of living leads to decreased crime and other social problems. Economic growth also leads to increased government revenues, which can be used to provide more services and security.
2. Pollution is often considered a social cost of production because the costs of cleanup often cannot be assigned to a producer. The costs, therefore, must be assigned to society, making them social costs. Further, the opportunity cost of using government revenues to clean up pollution is the reduction of other programs so it is a social cost because it may adversely affect the quality of life.
3. Given limited resources within the economy, each dollar spent on capital or on research and development reduces the amount available in the short run for consumption.

Chapter 15 Review

(text pages 356–357)

REVIEWING ECONOMIC TERMS

1. Gross National Product (GNP)
2. economic growth
3. capacity utilization rate
4. real per capita GNP
5. disposable income
6. capital goods

EXERCISING ECONOMIC SKILLS

1. Answers will vary.
2. Answers will vary. Many students, however, may recommend that the retired couple invest in a stock market mutual fund, thereby pooling their small amount of money with money from other investors; the young college graduate invest in a bond market mutual fund; and the millionaire invest in a money market mutual fund.

THINKING CRITICALLY ABOUT ECONOMICS

1. **(a)** Comparisons of economic growth and standards of living are difficult to measure among nations because growth is measured in different ways and statistical data are collected with varying degrees of accuracy. **(b)** Disposable income (DI) is an important indicator of a nation's economic health and of an individual's standard of living because DI most accurately reflects how much income people have to satisfy their needs and wants. **(c)** A scarcity of natural resources inhibits economic growth because a nation must depend on other countries to supply natural resources, and must trade money or other resources to acquire the natural resources or finished products they need.
2. **(a)** Real per capita GNP is generally considered the most significant measurement of economic well-being. **(b)** It may be a false indicator if the goods and services produced are not evenly distributed, or if a very large portion represents government spending or investment that does not result in consumption.
3. Answers will vary. Students may focus on the deterioration of the quality of life, the nonmaterial aspects of living, as the main social cost of economic growth. Students may discuss problems such as pollution, the stress of a rapid pace of life, and the strain on local governments to provide police and fire protection and adequate schools.
4. The phrase "the cost of capital accumulation is reduced consumption," means that the money given to capital accumulation cannot be used for consumption in the short run. Consumption is the opportunity cost of the capital accumulation.
5. Students who disagree may note that spending on the problem of acid rain will reduce the resources available for consumption. Because the costs probably cannot be assigned to specific polluters, the costs may have to be paid in taxes. If private firms are made to pay the costs, higher prices will result. Students who agree may cite

the health of individuals or the needed improvement to the environment as their primary concern.

USING PRIMARY SOURCES

1. Lee Iacocca defines industrial policy as the use of government to help restructure and revitalize older American industries so they can meet the challenge of foreign competition.
2. There is resistance to an industrial policy in the United States because some people think having such a policy is an attack on capitalism and that it too closely resembles the Soviet Union with its five-year plans. An industrial policy will make government more active in economic planning.
3. Iacocca's six basic elements of a United States industrial policy are (1) to achieve energy independence, (2) limit Japan's market share in certain critical industries, (3) cut costs in federal entitlement programs, (4) make special education grants for high technology, (5) get new incentives to increase research and development in private industry and accelerate modernization, and (6) rebuild highways, bridges, railroads, and waterways for commerce.
4. Answers will vary. Students might indicate that Iacocca's six-point program will help achieve long-term economic efficiency, economic stability, and economic growth, but economic equity and economic freedom may suffer in the short term.

CHAPTER

16 The Nation's Fiscal Policy

(text pages 358–381)

Section 1 Review

(text page 365)

DEFINE

fiscal policy: Program of the government designed to stabilize the business cycle and reduce unemployment through the use of federal taxing and spending powers.

investment tax credit: Incentive that permits businesses to deduct from corporate income tax a percentage of money spent on new capital.

automatic stabilizers: Built-in features of federal tax and spending programs that activate nondiscretionary fiscal policy.

multiplier effect: Term that explains how small changes in income ripple through the economy and eventually cause a much larger change in spending.

marginal propensity to consume: Fraction of additional income that people spend.

marginal propensity to save: Fraction of additional income that people save.

IDENTIFY

Council of Economic Advisers: Group of professional economists who develop and recommend to the President national economic policies.

1. An investment tax credit is an example of a discretionary fiscal policy.
2. Keynes reasoned that increasing aggregate demand would stimulate the economy, causing an expansion of the business cycle.
3. If the marginal propensity to consume is 80 percent and 10 million new dollars are injected into the economy, the resulting total spending increase is \$40 million ($1 \div 1 - 0.80 = 1 \div 0.25 = 4$; \$10 million $\times$ 4 = \$40 million).
4. If taxes are cut and federal spending increases, aggregate demand would increase.

Building Economic Skills

(text pages 366–367)

1. **(a)** The subject of the table is sources of personal income from 1945 to 1985. **(b)** The source of the table is the *Economic Report of the President, 1986.*

2. **(a)** Gross personal income in 1945 was $172.4 billion. **(b)** PI was $3,443.3 billion in 1985.

3. **(a)** PI increased the most between 1975 and 1985. **(b)** Other income as a percentage of gross personal income has increased from 31 percent in 1945 to 43 percent in 1985.

4. **(a)** PI increased by $3,270.9 billion. **(b)** Wages and salaries increased by $1,843.2 billion. **(c)** Other income increased by $1,427.7 billion.

5. **(a)** Answers will vary. Students may recognize, however, that gross personal income has increased enormously. **(b)** Answers will vary. Students may note, however, that income from other sources has increased more dramatically than income from wages and salaries.

Section 2 Review

(text page 371)

IDENTIFY

Office of Management and Budget: Department that assists the President in preparing the budget, supervises administration of the budget, reviews the structure and operation of the executive branch and recommends reforms for greater efficiency and effectiveness, and coordinates proposed legislation coming from various executive departments and agencies.

Ray Rodriguez: Director of Institute for Business and Industrial Training in Colorado Springs, which trains or retrains workers for jobs and encourages the startup of small businesses that can work by contract.

1. Timing problems, forecasting problems, political constraints, and unpredictable economic behavior limit the effectiveness of fiscal policy in regulating aggregate demand.

2. A restrictive policy, whether increased taxes or less spending, will slow economic growth because reduced spending slows economic activity.

3. The marginal propensity to consume must be accurately predicted to forecast the effect of a tax cut.

4. **(a)** President Kennedy's spending reduced unemployment and raised inflation slightly. **(b)** President Johnson's tax cut and Great Society programs further reduced unemployment and increased inflation substantially.

Section 3 Review

(text page 377)

DEFINE

supply-side economics: Fiscal policy that provides incentives for producers to increase aggregate supply.

Say's Law: Economic principle formulated by Jean-Baptiste Say which declares that supply creates its own demand.

IDENTIFY

Arthur B. Laffer: Economist and leading proponent of supply-side economics, whose Laffer Curve illustrates that higher taxes slow productivity by decreasing profits, thus removing the incentive to invest and produce.

1. Tax cuts for individuals and businesses, reduced federal spending on social programs, and regulatory reform made up President Reagan's supply-side policy.

2. Supply-siders contend that regulations are a disincentive to producers because regulations inhibit investment and production.

3. The Laffer Curve shows the relationship between tax rates and revenues.

Chapter 16 Review

(text pages 378–379)

REVIEWING ECONOMIC TERMS

1. c; **2.** e; **3.** f; **4.** a; **5.** d; **6.** b.

EXERCISING ECONOMIC SKILLS

1. Answers will vary.
2. Answers will vary.

THINKING CRITICALLY ABOUT ECONOMICS

1. Laffer's theory states that lower tax rates will provide an incentive to increase investment and production. Increased production will generate greater tax revenues.
2. Keynes said that government spending will increase employment which in turn will increase aggregate demand, stimulating the business cycle.
3. The progressive income tax acts as an automatic stabilizer in a period of high wage inflation because, as incomes increase and demand increases, the tax rate increases. The higher tax rate somewhat reduces the increase in demand, reducing the inflationary effect.
4. Regulations may increase the cost of production or limit the ability to use resources. These reduce the potential of profit and, thus, are a production disincentive.
5. Laffer argues that a reduction in tax rates may be an incentive to invest, produce, or earn more income. The larger tax base will increase revenues. Laffer contends that there will be an optimum tax rate at which revenues are maximized.

USING PRIMARY SOURCES

1. Keynes said that the government can affect consumption by an extension of central controls to ensure full employment. The present system has broken down over the determination of the volume of employment, not the direction.
2. Keynes said full employment will be ensured by government controls that curb the excesses of capitalistic individualism.
3. The advantages of individualism are decentralization and self-interest. Individualism is the best safeguard of personal liberty through its allowance of the exercise of choice. Individualism also is the best safeguard of the variety of life, a condition that is lost in totalitarian states.

Unit Five Review

(text pages 380–381)

REVIEWING ECONOMIC IDEAS

1. It is considered full employment when about 95 percent of the labor force has jobs. At a given time, 5 percent of the people will be voluntarily unemployed and looking for a new job.
2. The four phases of the business cycle are expansion, peak, contraction, and trough.
3. **(a)** GNP measures the total value of all final goods and services produced in a nation in one year. **(b)** The four components of the GNP are consumption, government spending, investment, and net exports.
4. Transfer payments are not considered a part of the GNP because they simply transfer income from one person to another and do not result in an increase in production.
5. Water and air are included as natural resources.
6. The multiplier is 10 ($1 \div 1 - 0.90 = 1 \div 0.1 = 10$).
7. A supply-side proponent would favor less government regulation.
8. The Laffer Curve is a diagram developed by Arthur B. Laffer that illustrates how tax cuts affect tax revenues and economic growth.

CONNECTING ECONOMIC IDEAS

1. To stimulate investment, the government could use a tax deduction to encourage businesses to invest in new capital.
2. **(a)** Policies that are aimed at inflation tend to slow economic growth. The trade-off is generally higher unemployment. **(b)** Answers will vary. For example, students may feel that the fight against inflation is a longer-range goal while unemployment is a short-term problem.
3. Fiscal policies are slow to be implemented and their effects are slow to be felt, so often the business cycle changes before the policies can be implemented or take effect.
4. Fewer restrictions on business and increasing competition in some industries will encourage more competitors to enter those fields. If the re-

strictions increase costs, their elimination will enhance profit potential.

5. Students can argue the logic of Say's Law. Supply creates its own demand. As goods are supplied, people are hired to produce those goods. The income derived increases demand, or the increased supply keeps prices down. When prices are relatively low, consumers will purchase more.

6. The goals of Keynesian demand-management proponents and supply-sider economists concerning economic growth are very similar. The difference between the two economic philosophies is the point in the circular flow at which the injection of money takes place. Demand stimulates supply, and supply can stimulate demand.

INVESTIGATING ECONOMIC ISSUES

1. **(a)** The two segments of the underground economy are unreported legal business activity and unreported illegal business activity. **(b)** Unreported legal business activity includes wage earners who fail to report all or part of their income in order to avoid taxes. Unreported illegal business activity includes people engaged in illegal businesses to avoid paying taxes and to avoid criminal prosecution. **(c)** The underground economy costs the United States government about $100 billion in lost revenues. **(d)** The GNP does not include income from underground economic activities. If it did the GNP would be far larger.

2. **(a)** The United States government catches most tax evaders through tax audits. **(b)** The IRS believes tax audits are successful because it gains $10.40 in new tax revenue for every dollar spent on the audit. **(c)** Tax amnesty allows tax evaders to pay delinquent tax bills without financial or criminal penalties. **(d)** A tax amnesty might be more successful than harsh penalties because people who are afraid of being caught would be more likely to come forward to settle their tax bills with an amnesty than if they were to be punished.

USING PRIMARY SOURCES

1. Underground economies exist because production units are unregulated and untaxed, and productivity runs high.

2. The costs of underground economies are that they pay no taxes, thus making it more difficult for governments to have funds for necessary goods and services.

3. The benefits of underground economies are that they provide goods more efficiently than those produced in regular channels, and employ people at higher wages than the prevailing wage. The benefits are necessary in nations with no market economy, such as the Soviet Union, because the underground economy delivers products otherwise unavailable and contributes as much as 20 percent to the GNP.

TEACHER'S NOTES

UNIT SIX

(text pages 382–463)

INTERNATIONAL ECONOMICS

CHAPTER

17 International Trade

(text pages 384–409)

Section 1 Review

(text page 391)

DEFINE

international trade: Voluntary exchange of goods and services between the people in different nations.

absolute advantage: Ability of one nation to produce a product at a lower cost than a second nation, given the same resources.

comparative advantage: Ability of one nation to produce an item at a lower opportunity cost relative to other products than a second nation.

trade surplus: Condition in which the value of a nation's imports is greater than the value of its imports.

1. When countries specialize, they choose to limit their production to those things that they produce most efficiently. At the same time, they decide not to produce those things at which they are less efficient, but may need. Specializing countries become economically interdependent on trade with other nations to supply the products they need but do not produce.
2. The nation has an unfavorable balance of trade when more money and goods are flowing to other nations than are flowing into the country.
3. **(a)** A surplus occurred in the years 1973 and 1975. **(b)** The United States trade deficit exceeded $140 million in 1985.

Building Economic Skills

(text pages 392–393)

Answers will vary.

Section 2 Review

(text page 397)

DEFINE

devaluation: Reduction of the value of a nation's currency in relation to currencies of other nations.

floating exchange rate: System in which supply and demand determine the value of a currency.

1. Until 1973, the foreign exchange rate fixed the value of the dollar at $35 per ounce of gold. Today the rate floats according to the demand and supply of the currency.
2. A strong dollar affects trade by increasing the price of a foreign product imported into the United States, but it also decreases the demand for United States goods in foreign nations.
3. **(a)** The daily trading volume is greatest on the London money market. **(b)** Most are in Europe. **(c)** Answers will vary. Students may note that international banking services began in Europe, and Europe remains the hub of currency exchange. They may also note that Europe is a crossroads of international trade, necessitating a large number of trading centers.

Section 3 Review

(text page 402)

DEFINE

trade barrier: Specific government action that protects domestic industries and jobs from foreign competition.

revenue tariff: Tax on imports designed to raise money for the government.

protective tariff: Tax on imports designed to protect domestic industries from foreign competition.

free trade: Policy advocating the lifting of government regulations on international trade.

1. The three types of trade barriers are an import quota, a tariff, and a voluntary trade agreement.

2. A protective tariff increases the price of imported goods by adding the amount of the tariff to the price of the imported goods making them more expensive in the United States market.

3. **(a)** The year that the United States had the lowest average tariff was 1982. The year that the United States had the highest average tariff was 1930. **(b)** In the 1920s, the economic climate of the United States was good, profits were up, and the United States was enjoying unprecedented prosperity. In 1929, United States industries were devastated by the Great Depression, and tariff barriers went up to protect industries during the period of economic recovery.

Section 4 Review

(text page 407)

DEFINE

most-favored-nation status: United States policy that automatically extends any trade benefits granted one nation to other nations with the same status.

trade adjustment assistance: Government program that provides for worker retraining and other benefits to workers and firms hurt by foreign competition.

IDENTIFY

Reverend Leon Sullivan: Baptist Minister from Philadelphia and a strong opponent of apartheid, who developed the six Sullivan Principles to guide United States and foreign businesses operating in South Africa.

1. The Reciprocal Trade Agreements Act gave the President the power to reduce tariffs and the Congress the power to grant most-favored-nation status.

2. The purpose of a regional trade organization is to break trade barriers and encourage cooperation between the member nations, which usually have close geographic, political, and economic ties.

3. **(a)** Two important changes in international trade in the 1980s are the building of plants by foreign firms in the countries in which they do business and joint ownership agreements among multinational firms. **(b)** The building of plants by foreign firms in the countries in which they do business allows the firms to avoid some shipping fees, protective tariffs, and quotas. The host nation benefits through increased employment and an injection of money into the economy. Joint ownership agreements allow multinationals to share the investment risk and also open markets that were previously closed to some firms.

Chapter 17 Review

(text pages 412–413)

REVIEWING ECONOMIC TERMS

1. e; **2.** a; **3.** b; **4.** d; **5.** i; **6.** g; **7.** h; **8.** f.

EXERCISING ECONOMIC SKILLS

1. **(a)** Student charts should resemble the chart on page A 73. **(b)** Answers will vary.

2. Answers will vary.

THINKING CRITICALLY ABOUT ECONOMICS

1. **(a)** Nations engage in international trade to acquire products they cannot or choose not to produce. **(b)** Nations restrict free trade because they want to protect domestic industries and jobs from foreign competition and for political reasons. **(c)** The Trade Expansion Act of 1962, the Trade Reform Act of 1974, and the GATT rounds are recent examples of international cooperation.

2. **(a)** Excessive paperwork is time-consuming and often frustrating, so many companies will avoid it by not exporting their goods or services to nations requiring it. **(b)** Licensing fees also raise the price of a product, which may reduce the product's competitiveness in foreign nations.

3. The more a nation specializes, the more economically interdependent it becomes. As a nation specializes, it limits the products it produces to those for which it has the best comparable advantages.

It chooses not to produce products for which the comparable advantage is not so great. The more it limits the number of different products it produces, the more economically interdependent it is on other nations to supply the products it needs but chooses not to produce.

4. A nation can consider devaluating its currency by selling it on the open market. The increased supply of currency will lower its relative value and make goods from that country cheaper in other countries. The nation may also consider subsidies to companies whose foreign trade is affected. The subsidies would allow the companies to reduce the price of their products overseas.

5. A nation with an absolute advantage in almost all products can still gain from trade because its comparative advantage in some products will be greater than its comparative advantage in others, and it will be more efficient to produce only those products for which it has the greatest comparative advantage and to trade for the products it chooses not to produce.

6. Supporters of a United States industrial policy feel it is necessary for national security. These advocates claim that certain industries are vital to the production of key defense products and that if the United States is dependent on other nations for these products, its national defense is in jeopardy.

USING PRIMARY SOURCES

1. Fair trade means markets are open to all nations and competition takes place under internationally agreed upon trading rules. The United States supports fair trade because it will enable greater sales, which will increase profitability and result in a higher standard of living. Fair trade is beneficial because trade barriers will be removed and a more open world economy will exist.

2. The guiding principle is that opening foreign markets to enable greater United States sales is preferable to closing United States markets to foreigners.

Two Commentaries on the Federal Budget

	Lee	Gleckman
Main Thesis	President Reagan hopes to reduce the federal budget through privatization, or selling off the federal government's properties.	Congress, not nonelected officials, has to act to reduce federal budget deficits. The Gramm-Rudman Act had eroded democracy by shifting authority to the Comptroller-General.
Supporting Evidence	Budget Director James C. Miller has put power authorities, airports, petroleum reserves, and loans on the block.	The Supreme Court declared a key provision of Gramm-Rudman Act of 1985 unconstitutional, and put federal spending back in the hands of the elected officials.
Conclusions	Privatization is a *political* move, not an economic measure, because only about 1% ($8.5 billion) of the government's revenues would derive from privatization. Privatization is not the way to cut the budget; its main goal is to reduce the government's role in the economy.	Budget is a *political* move. Even though Congress has control of the budget, and this is where it ought to be, the budget is not likely to get reduced because of politics.
Assumptions	President Reagan believes the government should get out of business and stop competing with the private sector.	Politicians are not willing to make the necessary tax increases or cuts in Social Security and food stamps and other programs for the poor;, so reducing the budget becomes an impossible task.

3. The President wants future GATT rounds to deal with the trade in services and the protection of intellectual property. These areas are important to the United States economy because the United States is a world leader in each and increased world trade in these areas would increase United States trade profitability.

4. Because the United States is a world leader in research creativity and innovation, it is necessary to develop international agreements that protect such intellectual properties.

5. The administration feels that all markets should be open to all nations.

CHAPTER

18 Economic Growth in the Developing World *(text pages 410–437)*

Section 1 Review *(text page 415)*

DEFINE

population growth rate: Annual increase in a nation's population, expressed as a percentage.

subsistence agriculture: Farming in which families grow just enough to meet basic needs and crop surpluses for trade are seldom produced.

1. **(a)** The definition includes the size and sophistication of a nation's industrial, service, and agricultural sectors. **(b)** According to economists, there are 30 developed nations in the world. **(c)** Economists say that there are 130 developing nations in the world.

2. Colonialism gave people in many Third World nations a glimpse of the modern world that resulted in rising expectations. When the colonies began to achieve independence, however, they found that their economies were ill-equipped to compete successfully in world markets. The economic activities of colonial powers had provided few jobs for members of colonial populations or generated little capital beyond the amount that made its way back to the colonial powers. The people of the newly independent nations had little education, little business or political experience, and little else with which to work except nationalistic pride and in some cases resentment against the colonialism that had oppressed them.

3. In developing nations, rapid population growth usually drains the nation's resources. The nation cannot increase the production of goods and services or raise the people's standard of living.

4. The nations should be classified as follows. *Low-income developing nations:* China, Ethiopia, Ghana, Haiti, India, Kenya, Pakistan, Tanzania, and Zaire; *middle-income developing nations:* Bolivia, Chile, Egypt, El Salvador, Hungary, Israel, Mexico, Nicaragua, Nigeria, Peru, Philippines, Thailand, Turkey, and Yugoslavia; *developed nations:* France, Italy, Saudi Arabia, Singapore, the United Kingdom, and the United States.

Section 2 Review *(text page 420)*

DEFINE

one-crop economy: System of production in which a nation concentrates on a single item.

capital formation: Accumulation of the financial resources and capital goods necessary for sound economic development.

default: Action by which a nation fails to pay its foreign debts, wiping them off the books.

nationalization: Process by which a government assumes ownership and control of a business or property after compensating the former owner.

expropriation: Process by which a government seizes ownership and control of a business or property without compensating the former owner.

1. **(a)** To achieve economic growth, a nation must increase its per capita output of goods and services, improve the quantity and quality of the factors of production, and effectively use its resources. **(b)** Obstacles are the scarcity and underutilization of resources and the lack of natural, human, capital resources and entrepreneurs.

2. When a country depends on one crop, it runs the

risk that the price of that crop will fall and reduce its only source of revenue.

3. The key to economic development is the improvement of the quality or quantity of the factors of production. Education improves the quality of a nation's human resources, setting the stage for economic development.

4. Students should note that the overall debt of the developing nations rose steadily between 1977 and 1986.

Building Economic Skills *(text pages 424–425)*

1. **(a)** The title of the map is World Labor in Agriculture. **(b)** The map shows the percentage of the world's people in agriculture.

2. **(a)** The categories are 1–25 percent; 26–50 percent; 51–75 percent; 76–100 percent; and data not available. **(b)** Red represents the lowest percentage. **(c)** Yellow represents the highest percentage. **(d)** 13 (Guyana, Suriname, French Guiana, Iceland, The Gambia, Guinea-Bissau, Namibia, Botswana, Gabon, Equatorial Guinea, Oman, United Arab Emirates, and Kampuchea [Cambodia]).

3. **(a)** Nations shown on the map in which less than 26 percent of the labor force are engaged in agriculture are: Algeria, Argentina, Australia, Austria, Belgium, Bulgaria, Canada, Chile, Cuba, Czechoslovakia, Denmark, East Germany, France, Finland, Hungary, Ireland, Israel, Italy, Japan, Jordan, Kuwait, Libya, Netherlands, New Zealand, Norway, Singapore, Soviet Union, Spain, Sweden, Switzerland, Trinidad and Tobago, United Kingdom, United States, Uruguay, Venezuela, and West Germany. **(b)** Answers will vary. Students may note, however, that many of the nations located in North America and Europe devote less than 26 percent of their labor force to agriculture.

4. **(a)** Most are in Africa. **(b)** Answers will vary. Students may note, however, that many of the African nations south of the Sahara still devote more than 75 percent of their labor force to agriculture.

5. Answers will vary. Students may note that these nations are likely to be characterized by subsistence farming.

Section 3 Review *(text page 426)*

DEFINE

development plan: Outline of how a nation's resources should be use to meet its economic goals.

land reform: Redistribution of arable land from a few major landowners to a larger number of the peasants who work the land.

1. **(a)** The chief characteristic is that decisions are made by the government through central planning. **(b)** The chief characteristic is decentralized decision making. **(c)** The main *advantage* is that it allows the government to direct the use of resources toward specific economic goals. The *disadvantages* are the inefficiency with which a bureaucracy formulates and implements goals and plans, the resistence to change of a bureaucratic system regardless of trends in the economy, and the occasional corruption of the bureaucracy. **(d)** The main *advantage* is free enterprise. The *disadvantage* is that there are few direct controls on the use of resources. This is a disadvantage because the government generally has only indirect controls at its disposal, making it difficult to eliminate inefficiency or to direct growth.

2. **(a)** In a capitalist economy, individual incentives encourage risk taking and enterprise. The opportunity to make a profit using privately owned resources stimulates economic activity. **(b)** Incentives have little effect in a socialist economy because the government has predetermined the answers to the basic economic questions.

3. Expanded agricultural production is particularly important to developing nations because more and better food improves the quality of the human resources and allows the use of capital and human resources for growth rather than for food production and acquisition.

Section 4 Review *(text page 435)*

DEFINE

foreign aid: Money, products, and services that governments extend to other nations.

economic assistance: Financial and technical aid, loans, and cash grants that governments extend to other nations and that contribute directly to economic development.

IDENTIFY

Barber Conable: As President of the World Bank, Conable helps to set and implement the policies through which the Bank lends $15 billion a year. During his tenure, the Bank has stiffened its loan conditions to tie economic reforms to the granting of loans.

1. Funds are available from domestic savings, multinational corporations, banks, nonprofit organizations, foreign governments and international development organizations.
2. The biggest roadblock is the political and economic instability of some developing nations.
3. Students who agree may feel that aid to developing nations helps to improve the political and economic stability of developing countries. A politically and economically stable world is important to the success of American business both at home and abroad. Students who disagree may feel that the benefits of such aid are difficult to measure, that it often helps only a few people in a given nation, and that nations that are not allied with the United States do not deserve United States aid.

Chapter 18 Review

(text pages 436–437)

REVIEWING ECONOMIC TERMS

1. International Monetary Fund
2. socialist
3. expropriation
4. green revolution
5. foreign aid
6. development plan
7. Agency for International Development

EXERCISING ECONOMIC SKILLS

1. Answers will vary.
2. **(a)** Answers will vary. Students may note that they can usually obtain a passport at the post office or federal courthouse, as well as at other specially designated places. **(b)** Answers will vary. Students who were born in the United States must have their birth certificate. Students who were born as United States citizens in other countries must have a government citizenship certificate. Students who are naturalized citizens must have their naturalization certificates. **(c)** Answers will vary.

THINKING CRITICALLY ABOUT ECONOMICS

1. **(a)** The common characteristics of developing nations are low per capita GNP, lack of resources, rapid population growth and traditional agricultural economies. **(b)** Scarcity and underutilization of resources and adverse environmental factors often hinder progress. **(c)** Developing nations rely on domestic savings, foreign businesses and nonprofit organizations, foreign governments, and international development organizations for funds.
2. People with rising expectations anticipate a steady and rapid economic growth. In developing nations, however, steady and rapid economic growth is rare because the nations must develop so many phases of the economy before growth takes off. When the reality of slow, hesitant growth conflicts with rising expectations, people are often disillusioned with the new ways and revert to their traditional ways of life.
3. Answers will vary. For example, students may say that economic development directed by central planners might force the people to abandon their traditional ways of life as the government determines what and how much they are to produce.
4. Students who agree may feel that decentralized decision making more successfully involves the entire society in economic development. Students who disagree may note that centralized decision making has clearer economic goals and more direct control of resources.
5. **(a)** The chart compares the gross sales income for certain large MNCs and the GNPs of selected nations. **(b)** Answers will vary. Students may note, however, that the chart does show that some multinational corporations have greater economic power than some sovereign nations.

USING PRIMARY SOURCES

1. Ward defines technology as applied science. Technology results in an increase in productivity.
2. According to Ward, the expenses that would be incurred in building a large power station include the costs of leveling the site; constructing roads; assembling materials, machines, and generators; and developing skills in workers.
3. Technology costs money, and money for capital investment comes from savings. Also, in the long run, technology can help producers produce more with less resources, creating further potential for saving.
4. Capital can be used to create private enterprises, and they, in turn, can produce profits, which can be used for further capital investment. A general tax can also be levied to raise money for capital investment.

CHAPTER

19 Comparative Economic Systems

(text pages 438–463)

Section 1 Review

(text page 442)

DEFINE

mercantilism: Economic doctrine calling for government regulation of the economy in order to accumulate greater wealth for a nation.

IDENTIFY

Adam Smith: Scottish philosopher who wrote *An Inquiry into the Nature and Causes of the Wealth of Nations* and developed the laissez-faire school of economics, which called for a free economic system with no government inference or control.

1. **(a)** The rise of new nations in Europe created a need for national currencies and banking systems, two key institutions of capitalism. **(b)** Capitalism is characterized by the private ownership of the means of production and individual economic decision making.
2. **(a)** Under mercantilism a nation's wealth was measured in terms of gold, silver, and an excess of exports over imports. **(b)** Government leaders granted trading monopolies, raised tariff barriers, and established colonies to supply industries with raw materials.
3. Adam Smith's criticism was that mercantilism interfered with economic growth because government interference took away private incentive and competition.
4. The Japanese economy is more closely regulated by the government than that of the United States. The government planning agency MITI helps to coordinate the industrial policy, while the United States had no counterpart to MITI. The United States leaves coordination up to individual initiative.

Section 2 Review

(text page 445)

DEFINE

socialism: Broad term used to describe many types of noncapitalist economic systems in which the government owns all or part of the means of production.

democratic socialism: Economic system in which the government owns some of the factors of production, but individuals maintain basic human rights and have control over economic planning through the election of government officials.

IDENTIFY

Julius K. Nyerere: President of Tanzania from 1961 to 1985. During Nyerere's long presidency, Tanzania adopted democratic socialism based on nationalization, villagization, and ujamaa.

1. The harsh working conditions and the poor quality of life for workers in the capitalist nations was the chief concern of the reformers.
2. Tanzania enjoys political stability, a relatively low infant mortality, a 79 percent literacy rate, and a variety of social programs.

3. The trade-off for the broader range of government services is high taxes and the resulting reduction in consumption.

Building Economic Skills *(text pages 446–447)*

1. Informational terms contained in the essay directive are central planning, Soviet Union, and The People's Republic of China.
2. The performance terms in the directive are compare and contrast.
3. Charts should resemble the chart below.
4. Outlines should resemble the following.
   I. Introduction
   II. Similarities in the decision-making process in the Soviet Union and in the People's Republic of China
      A. Who makes the planning decisions?
      B. How do the economic goals compare?
      C. How do the results compare?
   III. Differences in the decision-making process in the Soviet Union and the People's Republic of China
      A. How is the central planning organized?
      B. How do the economic goals contrast?
      C. How do the results contrast?
5. Essays will vary.

Section 3 Review *(text page 454)*

DEFINE

authoritarian socialism: Economic system in which the government owns or controls almost all of the means of production; also known as Communism.

bourgeoisie: According to Marx, merchant class who took control of the means of production during the early Industrial Revolution and exploited the working class, or proletariat.

proletariat: According to Karl Marx, the working class who provided labor at very low wages.

Central Planning Under Authoritarian Socialism

	Soviet Union	People's Republic of China
Structure and Leadership	Communist Party under Mikhail Gorbachev directs five-year plan, 1986–1990.	Communist Party under Deng Xiaoping directs economic policy of the Four Modernizations in agriculture, industry, science and technology, and defense.
Goals	To modernize capital stock, improve productivity among Soviet workers, improve the quality of Soviet products, reduce corruption among bureaucratic planners and managers, and stamp out abuses of the black market economy.	To transform China into a modern industrialized nation and to end the failures of overcentralized planning by introducing market incentives.
Methods	Give more authority to plant managers; allow the legalization of private enterprise in some fields.	State planners set production goals and some quotas, but plant managers have power to hire and fire workers and determine what goods to produce beyond quotas. Peasants can sell some crops on open market for profit. Free-trade zones allow foreign investment.
Results	Soviet Union's agriculture still remains a weak part of the economy and imports of food are required. Black market thrives. Gorbachev's reforms represent only a slight turning away from the authoritarian socialist model.	China has achieved greater output and a greater variety of consumer goods. By providing an incentive borrowed from capitalism, Deng Xiaoping's reforms seemingly indicate a lessening of state control on the economy.

collectivization: Policy of the Soviet government that completely expropriated peasant land to form large state-run farms.

black market: Illegal underground economy.

IDENTIFY

Karl Marx: The author of *The Communist Manifesto* and *Capital,* who viewed economics as a struggle between capitalism and the proletariat, with the workers eventually winning and setting up a classless society.

The Communist Manifesto: Pamphlet written in 1848 by Karl Marx and Friedrich Engels, which outlines the program of revolutionary change advocated by the Communist League, an international workers' organization.

Vladimir Ilyich Lenin: Leader of the Bolsheviks during the 1917 Russian Revolution. He started War Communism and later the New Economic Policy, which restored some private incentives, but left large industries in the hands of the government.

Joseph Stalin: Lenin's successor, who abolished the NEP, instituted strict central planning, eliminated private property, and established the five-year plan that set long-term economic goals and allocated scarce resources.

1. Stalin dismantled Lenin's reforms, stopped private enterprise, and adopted a rigid system of central planning.
2. The Council of Ministers establishes broad economic goals and sends them to the Gosplan, which outlines how the Council's goals are to be met. The Gosplan sends its outline to the Ministries, which refine the draft and return it to the Gosplan. The Gosplan sends the final draft to the Council of Ministers, who sends it to The Supreme Soviet for final approval. The Supreme Soviet sends the detailed production plans to hundreds of thousands of enterprises.

Section 4 Review

(text page 459)

DEFINE

iron rice bowl: System in China under which workers receive the same low wages regardless of their productivity.

contract responsibility system: Agricultural reform in China after 1978, permitting peasants to lease state-owned land and sell a certain portion of their crops on the open market.

free-trade zone: Area in China where foreign corporations are offered tax incentives to invest and build in return for providing capital, technology, and management to strengthen China's economy.

IDENTIFY

Deng Xiaoping: Head of government of the Peoples' Republic of China. Chairman Deng is dedicated to modernizing China, and has instituted economic reforms that combine aspects of free enterprise with a Communist government philosophy.

1. The second economy improves productivity in Hungary by allowing workers with individual incentive to hold second jobs.
2. The current economic goals are based on market incentives to improve productivity and the standard of living of citizens. The four modernizations in China all contain individual incentives.
3. The greatest conflict is between the older, more traditional elements of the Communist Party and the younger reformers. The new system is potentially more unstable. Problems of inflation and unemployment are new to most people in China.

Chapter 19 Review

(text pages 460–461)

REVIEWING ECONOMIC TERMS

1. f; **2.** d; **3.** a; **4.** c; **5.** e.

EXERCISING ECONOMIC SKILLS

1. **(a)** The informational terms are based on the information in the chapter, economic philosophies, Adam Smith, and Karl Marx. **(b)** The directional terms are compare and contrast. **(c)** and **(d)** Student charts and outlines should resemble the chart and outline on page A 80.

I. Introduction
II. Comparing the economic philosophies of Adam Smith and Karl Marx
   A. What did they write and what schools did they found?
   B. How did each view the role of the individual in the economy?
   C. How did each view the role of government in the economy?
   D. How did each view profit?
III. Conclusions

2. Answers will vary.

THINKING CRITICALLY ABOUT ECONOMICS

1. **(a)** The basic difference is the amount of government involvement in the economy. **(b)** In capitalism, individuals own and control the means of production, while in socialism the government owns and controls most of the means. **(c)** Authoritarian socialism is close to a pure-command model because the government makes all the economic decisions. **(d)** The basic difference is the amount of individual incentive permitted in the economy.

2. Democratic socialism appeals because it offers a greater degree of economic equality to the people. It is a combination of private enterprise and central planning that aids the progress of economic development.

3. **(a)** The goals of the current five-year plan call for building of more capital stock, improved productivity, more competitiveness on the world market for Soviet products, and a streamlined bureaucracy. **(b)** The Soviet Union is moving further away from the socialist system because more power is being given to lower-level production managers, and incentive is being introduced into the industrial areas of the Soviet Union. **(c)** Incentives will help productivity because the workers will share in the increase. Reward will be more directly related to effort.

4. The Four Modernizations in China will make the economy stronger by increasing efficiency and output. Individual incentives will motivate workers to produce. An increase of exports will give the People's Republic of China the capital necessary for growth.

USING PRIMARY SOURCES

1. Production was determined by the Production Brigade and the state bought the goods, transported them, and sold them through retail shops. The system did guarantee a steady vegetable supply and stable prices but the production system was complicated and delays developed, produce got stale, and often spoilage occurred.

2. Land is contracted from the production brigade by farmers, who can sell their vegetables to any-

Economic Theories of Smith and Marx

	Adam Smith	Karl Marx
Economic System	Author of *Wealth of Nations;* advocate of laissez-faire capitalism.	Author of *The Communist Manifesto* and *Capital;* advocate of authoritarian socialism, or Communism.
Role of Individual	Individual's self-interest works in the best interest of the marketplace and the prosperity of the economy.	The state more important than the individual. Looks at history as a series of class struggles that determine political and social change.
Role of Government	Government should not intervene in economic affairs.	In theory, government no longer needed after the ideal Communist society was created; in practice, strong role in planning under Communism.
Profit	Profit motive makes for a free and efficient economic system.	Profit is gained by one class through exploitation of another.

one at a price that the farmers set. The farm family determines how and what they will plant and how much produce they will market.

3. She is now encouraged to improve the family's standard of living. She and her husband attend technical classes to get information on what to plant and on when and how to fertilize. They have built a greenhouse and wind shields to grow more produce during colder times.

Unit Six Review

(text pages 462–463)

REVIEWING ECONOMIC IDEAS

1. The Trans-Gabon Railway was funded entirely through domestic savings.
2. A nation can determine its areas of competitive advantage by calculating the economic benefits received from producing various goods and services.
3. The power of the President of the United States to cut tariffs and expand benefits to workers is strengthened by the Act.
4. It raises the prices of exported goods, making them less competitive in foreign markets.
5. The GATT rounds have worked continuously to equalize trade barriers around the world.
6. Three regional trade organizations are the European Communities, or Common Market; the Latin American Free Trade Association; and the Council for Mutual Economic Assistance. The Common Market has eliminated many trade barriers in Western Europe. The Latin American Free Trade Association has been instrumental in lowering trade barriers between some of South America's largest industrial nations, and the Council for Mutual Economic Assistance has reduced trade barriers in Eastern Europe.
7. The four social factors that work against a nation's economic planning and development are tradition, attitudes towards work, rigid class structure, and rising expectation.

CONNECTING ECONOMIC IDEAS

1. If the price of a commodity on which a country depends for income falls significantly, that country's currency will also fall in value.
2. **(a)** The socialist model appeals to developing countries because it offers a more equal distribution of wealth to citizens. The socialist model also offers a faster transition from undeveloped to developed status. **(b)** Many developing nations have only a partially literate populace, and although they are trying to upgrade their educational level, a majority must use the socialist system because it allows those people in the nation with the capabilities and education to make the decisions that control the economy in a centralized way.
3. With increased exports China will be able to accumulate the currency to purchase needed imports, and will be able to accumulate the capital for investment within the country. Increased tax revenues will be another benefit to the Chinese economy.
4. **(a)** A country which is dependent on exports for the accumulation of capital may want to limit the outflow of that capital. One way to do this is to limit imports. **(b)** Most developing countries need exports to survive and will not be able to acquire needed goods and services or working capital if developed nations put up trade barriers.
5. **(a)** Foreign aid helps nations to build their infrastructures and meet basic needs so that capital can be accumulated for growth. Aid also helps stabilize the political and economic situations, making trade safer. **(b)** Since a stable currency and economic climate is necessary for continued free trade, the United States gains in two ways from foreign aid. First, that aid allows a country to build up their own industries and to increase the living standard of the people. Second, the development of a higher standard of living will provide more profitable markets for United States products in that country.
6. **(a)** The Smoot-Hawley tariff raised the prices of imports tremendously, thereby reducing United States trade. Many nations reciprocated, closing foreign markets around the world. Lack of foreign markets for goods decreased the demand for goods worldwide, and resulted in decreased production that fueled the Great Depression. **(b)** An

argument against the Smoot-Hawley tariff would include these points. Anytime a prohibitive protective tariff is passed, production efficiency will decrease, the demand for goods will decrease, markets decrease, and government revenues from trade decrease. These results trigger a business slowdown and a loss of government goods and services.

INVESTIGATING ECONOMIC ISSUES

1. **(a)** A multinational is a firm located in an industrialized country that produces or sells goods in other countries. **(b)** The four reasons that multinational firms invest in foreign countries are to reduce production costs, to reduce corporate taxes, to avoid trade barriers, and to expand more readily the market for their goods. **(c)** The three topics that economists cover when they attempt to determine how powerful a multinational is in a country are employment opportunities for people in the developing country, the potential for economic growth, and influence in changing the quality of life for people in the developing nations.
2. The ways in which developing countries have sought to control multinational companies in their countries is by requiring the multinational to form joint partnerships. They also use multinationals to help stimulate local business, and they have enacted strict tax codes, and laws requiring multinationals to export a certain percentage of their output to protect local manufacturers. They can, of course, threaten to nationalize or expropriate the firm. Some nations require multinationals to train local people for skilled jobs, and they integrate them into the company.
3. Critics say that although multinationals provide some jobs, they take even more jobs away because many local competitors are forced out of business and multinationals build capital-intensive plants in a labor-intensive economy. Also, multinationals usually create many low-skill jobs. They rarely train local residents for upper-level jobs, giving them instead to people that they bring into the country.
4. Supporters of multinationals say that they provide additional factors of production to the local economy because they can borrow money on the international market to finance building projects for the lowest possible price. They help to create global markets for products. In some areas, multinationals have distributed goods from local competing companies.

USING PRIMARY SOURCES

1. Multinationals use their integrating ability to develop large production facilities with access to markets in the developed world.
2. People and their competitive instincts propel development, and education integrates industry and competition into economic development. Developed nations have already done this, and developing nations must learn from them. To find out how it was done by the developed nation, young people from the developing nation must come to the developed country to study and learn, and take the knowledge with them to their home country. Multinationals can help by assigning younger, able people from its affiliate in the developing country for three to five years to managerial and professional work in one of the developed countries. These people will learn how to manage the type of individuals it takes to create an integrated industrial system.
3. According to Drucker, economic self-sufficiency is not possible, even for the best endowed country. Multinationals possess the capacity to cross international boundaries so they can help integrate the production capacities of developing countries into the world economy.

ECONOMICS
Free Enterprise in Action

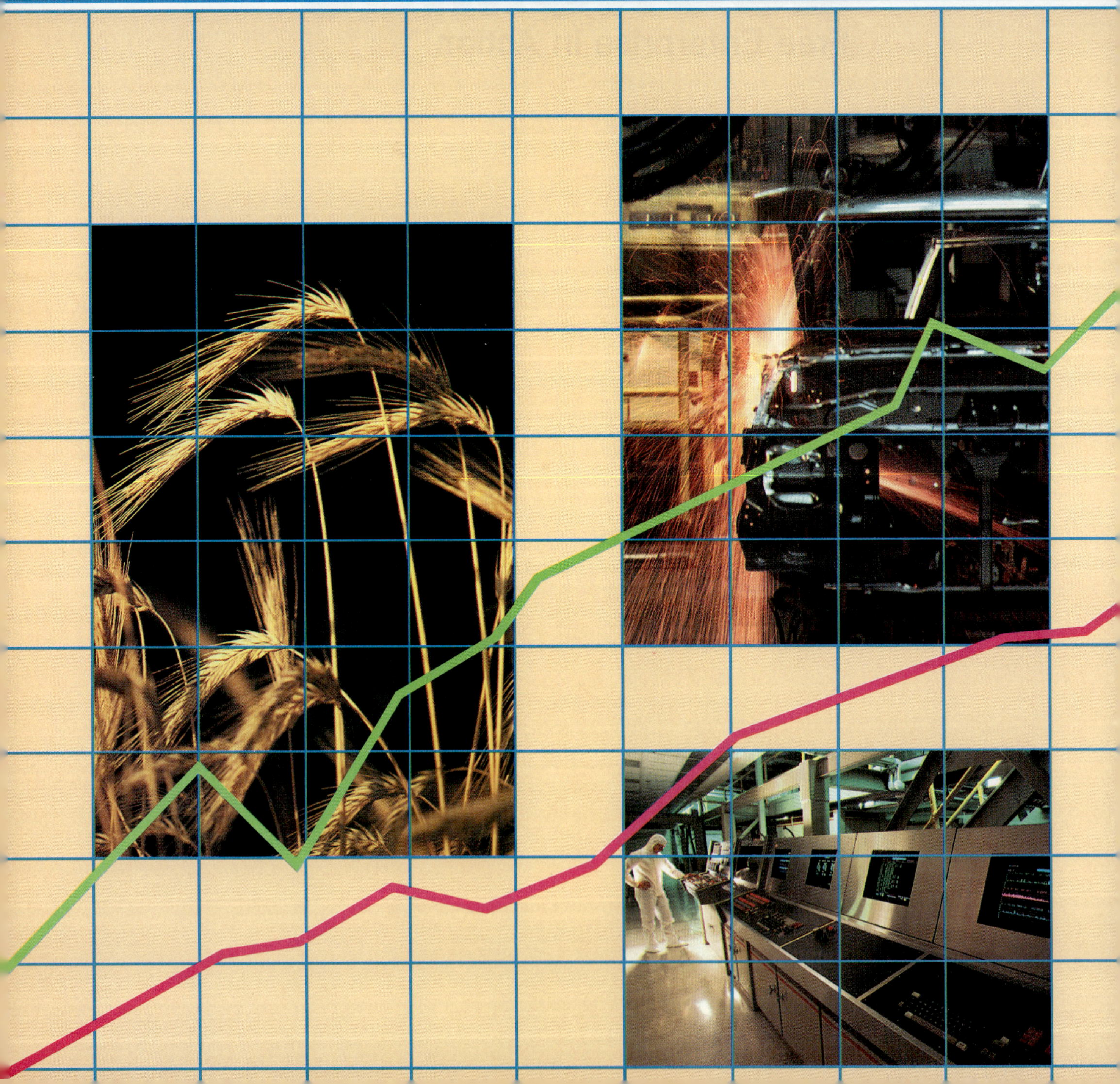

ECONOMICS

Free Enterprise in Action

David E. O'Connor

HBJ Harcourt Brace Jovanovich
Orlando San Diego Chicago Dallas

THE AUTHOR

David E. O'Connor is an experienced secondary social science teacher with a special interest in economics. He has been associated with the Connecticut Joint Council on Economic Education (JCEE) and its Developmental Economics Education Program (DEEP) in the Edwin O. Smith School since 1978 and has been a member of the JCEE regional advisory board since 1980.

CONTENT SPECIALISTS

Douglas Haskell
Greater Cincinnati Center for Economic Education
University of Cincinnati
Cincinnati, Ohio

John Pisciotta
Center for Private Enterprise
Baylor University
Waco, Texas

Gary Stone
Center for Economic Education
Winthrop College
Rock Hill, South Carolina

Gary F. Young
Center for Economic Education
University of Tennessee at Martin
Martin, Tennessee

Robert Pennington
Center for Economic Education
University of Central Florida
Orlando, Florida

Dick J. Puglisi
Center for Economic Education
University of South Florida
Tampa, Florida

Jo Ann Sweeney
Center for the Advancement of Economic Education
University of Texas
Austin, Texas

CURRICULUM SPECIALISTS

Susan S. Averill
Evans High School
Orlando, Florida

Phyllis Darling
Clark County Schools
Las Vegas, Nevada

Randall Felton
Leon County Schools
Tallahassee, Florida

Barbara Moore
Center for Economic Education
University of Central Florida
Orlando, Florida

James Betres
Center for Economic Education
Rhode Island College
Providence, Rhode Island

Ouida Dickey
Center for Economic Education
Berry College
Mount Berry, Georgia

Jennifer Giles
Trinity High School
Euless, Texas

Warren Tracy
Duval County Schools
Jacksonville, Florida

FIELD TEST TEACHERS

Kenneth Barnes
Elyria High School
Elyria, Ohio

John Edwards
Edgewater High School
Orlando, Florida

Warren Linton
Lake Gibson High School
Lakeland, Florida

Kathy Nadler
Thomas Jefferson High School
Los Angeles, California

Gary Cagiano
Fort Meade High School
Fort Meade, Florida

Jerry Gruss
Lakewood High School
Lakewood, Ohio

Rene Marfull
James Lick High School
San Jose, California

Donald R. White
Belmont High School
Belmont, Massachusetts

Curtis Calamari
Admiral King High School
Lorain, Ohio

OTHER CONTRIBUTORS

Walter Buenger
Texas A & M University

Robert Calvert
Texas A & M University

Henry C. Dethloff
Texas A & M University

Howard Yeargan
Southwest Texas State University

Copyright © 1988 by Harcourt Brace Jovanovich, Inc.

All rights reserved. No part of this publication may be reproduced or transmitted in any form or by any means, electronic or mechanical, including photocopy, recording, or any information storage and retrieval system, without permission in writing from the publisher.

Requests for permission to make copies of any part of the work should be mailed to:
Permissions, Harcourt Brace Jovanovich, Publishers, Orlando, Florida 32887

ACKNOWLEDGMENTS:
For permission to reprint copyrighted material, grateful acknowledgment is made to the following sources:

Bantam Books, Inc.: From *IACOCCA: An Autobiography* by Lee Iacocca, with William Novak. Copyright © 1984 by Lee Iacocca. All rights reserved. *Basic Books, Inc., Publishers:* From "The Economics of Discrimination" in *Markets and Minorities* by Thomas Sowell. Copyright © 1981 by The International Center for Economic Policy Studies. *Cambridge University Press and Harcourt*
(Acknowledgments continue on page 592.)

Printed in the United States of America

ISBN 0-15-374200-3

Contents

GUARANTEED
LOWEST PRICES!
"NOBODY BEATS OUR PRICES!"
5%
WE GUARANTEE OUR STORE PRICES TO BE LOWER OR AS LOW AS ANY OF OUR COMPETITOR'S ADVERTISED PRICES—OR
WE'LL SELL IT TO YOU AND KNOCK AN ADDITIONAL 5% OFF THEIR PRICE!

UNIT TWO BUSINESS IN THE FREE ENTERPRISE SYSTEM

ERA
Bold
cheer
Bright
Solo
Oxydol
Fab
BORAX
COLD POWER
Dash

DISTRICT COUNCIL 9 OF PAINTERS LOCAL UNION 51
NOTICE TO PUBLIC
STOP ILLEGAL ALIENS FROM TAKING AMERICANS' JOBS!

UNIT FOUR FINANCIAL INSTITUTIONS

BROADWAY
WALL ST

UNIT FIVE SETTING AND MEETING ECONOMIC GOALS 310

14 Inflation, Recession, and Unemployment 312

16 The Nation's Fiscal Policy 358

UNIT SIX INTERNATIONAL ECONOMICS

19 Comparative Economic Systems 438

THE REFERENCE LIBRARY 465

BUILDING ECONOMIC SKILLS

PRIMARY SOURCES

CASE STUDIES

ECONOMICS REPORTER

DECISION MAKERS IN THE ECONOMY

HIGHLIGHTS IN ECONOMICS

ISSUES IN ECONOMICS

CHARTS, GRAPHS, TABLES, AND MAPS

*Graphics appearing in skills

ILLUSTRATED OVERVIEW OF ECONOMICS

Even before you begin a formal study of economics, you may already know a few things about the subject. You may know, for example, that economics is about money. It is also about jobs and businesses and banks. But that is only part of what you will be studying in economics. The Illustrated Overview of Economics gives you an introduction to the major concepts and issues that are a part of the free enterprise system of the United States.

- **The Nature of Economics**
- **The Factors of Production**
- **Basic Economic Activities**
- **Features of Free Enterprise**
- **Goals of Free Enterprise**
- **Business Organizations**
- **The Circular Flow in the Economy**
- **The Global Nature of Economics**
- **Comparative Economic Systems**

THE NATURE OF ECONOMICS

Needs, wants, scarcity, choices—the interaction of these ideas forms the basis of economics. Economics is the study of the choices people make in an effort to satisfy their needs and wants. It is a study that can lead to more effective and responsible decision making by individuals, as well as society as a whole.

Goods and services (left) are the key to satisfying people's needs and wants. A good is a physical object that can be purchased. A service is an action or activity done for others for a fee. Both goods and services are known as products. The people who buy products are known as consumers. The goods they buy are called consumer goods.

Wants (above) go beyond what people need for survival. Jewelry, stereos, and swimming pools are examples of wants.

Needs (below) are those goods and services that are necessary for survival. Food, clothing, and shelter are examples of needs.

People's needs and wants are often greater than the resources available to satisfy them. Scarcity, the lack of available resources, forces people to choose how best to use the resources available to them (right) in order to satisfy the greatest number of needs and wants.

THE FACTORS OF PRODUCTION

Resources used to produce the goods and services that satisfy people's needs and wants are called factors of production. Economists usually identify natural resources, human resources, and capital resources as the main factors of production.

Natural resources (above) are items provided by nature. When a natural resource is used to produce goods and services, it is considered to be a factor of production.

Technicians, farmers, teachers, surgeons, clerks, and workers of all kinds provide human resources (below). Any human effort, either physical or intellectual, that is exerted in the production process is a human resource.

Capital resources are money and capital goods. Money is used to purchase items necessary to the production process. Capital goods are the buildings, structures, machinery, and tools that are used to produce goods and services.

BASIC ECONOMIC ACTIVITIES

By definition, any activity related to meeting people's needs and wants can be considered an economic activity. The various basic economic activities can be grouped into three categories—those which take materials from the earth, those which manufacture products, and those which provide services to consumers.

The most basic economic activities are those in which materials are taken from the earth. These activities include farming, mining, drilling, and fishing.

Activities in which products are manufactured form the second category of economic activities. These manufacturing activities (left) largely depend on materials taken from the earth. Businesses that carry out manufacturing activities include steel mills, automobile assembly plants, electronics manufacturers, and textile mills.

Activities in which services are provided (left and above) form the third category of economic activities. Restaurants, dry cleaners, law firms, landscaping companies, and automobile repair shops are examples of businesses that carry out service-related activities.

FEATURES OF FREE ENTERPRISE

Freedom is the principle on which the United States was founded. More than 200 years later, freedom serves as the nation's political foundation. Freedom is also the cornerstone of the American economic system. The American economic system often is called the free enterprise system because of the freedoms of the marketplace.

Owning private property (left) is one of the most basic freedoms of the American free enterprise system. Goods that are owned by individuals or businesses, rather than by the government, are private property. In the United States, individuals and businesses are free to buy as much private property as they can afford and sell as much as they wish.

Individuals and businesses in the United States are free to enter into contracts (right). Contracts, whether they are oral or written, are legally binding agreements to buy and sell goods.

Individuals in the United States are free to make personal choices and to communicate those choices through the price system. As shoppers, consumers cast "dollar votes" for the products they buy. The dollar votes of consumers help producers determine what products to produce and what prices to ask for those products.

Individuals in the United States are free to engage in free enterprise and competition. That is, individuals are free to work and to choose where they will work. They also are free to open their own businesses (right), to choose the type and quantity of goods and services to produce, and to choose the manner in which to produce them.

According to the Scottish economist Adam Smith, self-interest is the force that directs the actions of individuals and businesses in the market system (left). Individuals in the United States are free to look after their own self-interests and to make profits. Profit is the money that remains after all of the costs of production have been paid.

The American economic system is largely free from government interference. The government does, however, play a role in regulating the economy. For example, the government sets laws and rules that businesses must follow, such as health and safety standards. The government raises money through taxation. The government also works to keep the economy stable (right).

GOALS OF FREE ENTERPRISE

Individuals must make economic choices in an effort to satisfy their needs and wants. Nations, too, must make economic choices. To help make such choices, nations set overall economic goals. In the American economy, policymakers keep six major goals in mind.

A major goal of the American economic system is to maintain economic freedom. Consumers must be free to choose what to buy. Workers (right) must be free to choose their occupations. Businesspeople must be free to open new businesses.

Another goal of the American free enterprise system is economic efficiency, to make the best use of scarce resources. The nation's businesses are constantly looking for better ways to produce more goods and services in less time and at less cost (left). Economic efficiency is measured by how many goods and services a nation's workers produce.

A sense of justice for all is a part of America's heritage. In economic terms, this sense of justice is known as the goal of economic equity. Questions of fairness are often difficult to decide. Yet policymakers in the United States attempt to ensure that all individuals share in the costs and benefits of the free enterprise system in a relatively equal way (right).

Another goal of the American free enterprise system is the goal of economic security. Individuals as well as the American government work toward this goal. One way individuals can help protect themselves against the unexpected is by buying different kinds of insurance (left).

To operate smoothly, the American free enterprise system must be stable. Achieving the goal of economic stability involves achieving full employment and maintaining stable prices. A certain amount of unemployment always exists (right). Nevertheless, policymakers work to provide jobs for as many people as possible and keep constant the overall level of prices.

Another goal of the American free enterprise system is economic growth (left). The aim of economic growth is to increase the amount of goods and services that each worker in the economy can produce.

BUSINESS ORGANIZATIONS

Businesses are the means by which products are made available to satisfy people's needs and wants. Today, there are millions of businesses in the United States. Each is organized in a special way. The most common forms of business organization are sole proprietorships, partnerships, and corporations. Businesses also can be organized as franchises, cooperatives, or nonprofit organizations.

A sole proprietorship (left) is a business that is owned and controlled by one person. Sole proprietorships are the oldest, simplest, and most common form of business organization found in the United States.

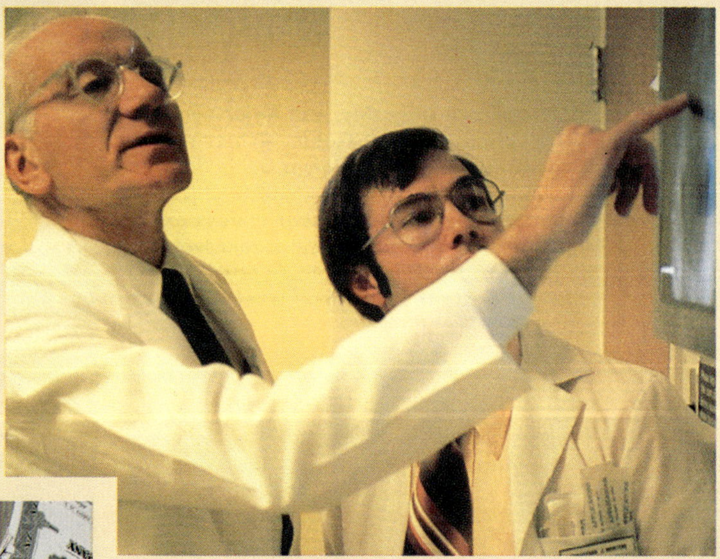

A partnership (right) is a business that is owned and controlled by two or more people. This type of business organization is the least common found in the United States.

A corporation is a business organization that is treated by law as if it were a person. Corporations, for example, can buy and sell property, enter into contracts, and sue or be sued in court. Yet corporations are owned by individuals known as stockholders, who buy shares of stock (left). Stocks are the certificates of ownership in a corporation.

Many hotel and motel chains (left) and restaurants are operated under franchise agreements. A franchise is a contract in which a company agrees to let another person or group start a business using its name to sell goods or services. The parent company is called the franchiser. The person or group who opens the franchise is called the franchisee.

A nonprofit organization (below) provides goods and services without seeking profits for distribution to individual members. Such organizations often promote charitable works, religious activities, and educational and cultural programs.

A cooperative, or co-op (above), is a business that is owned by the people who use its services. Types of cooperatives include purchasing cooperatives, marketing cooperatives, housing cooperatives, credit unions, and service cooperatives.

THE CIRCULAR FLOW IN THE ECONOMY

In the American free enterprise system, resources, products, and money are exchanged, or flow, among households, businesses, and the government. This interaction can be illustrated by a diagram, or model. The model has two parts. The upper part represents the product market. The lower part represents the resource market.

In the product market, goods and services, or products (left, below), are exchanged for money payments. Businesses produce and sell these products to households and the government. Households and the government, in turn, make money payments to the businesses in exchange for the products.

In the resource market, resources (left and below) are exchanged for money payments. Households sell their resources to businesses and the government. In return, businesses and the government make money payments to the households. The money payments that households receive are known as income.

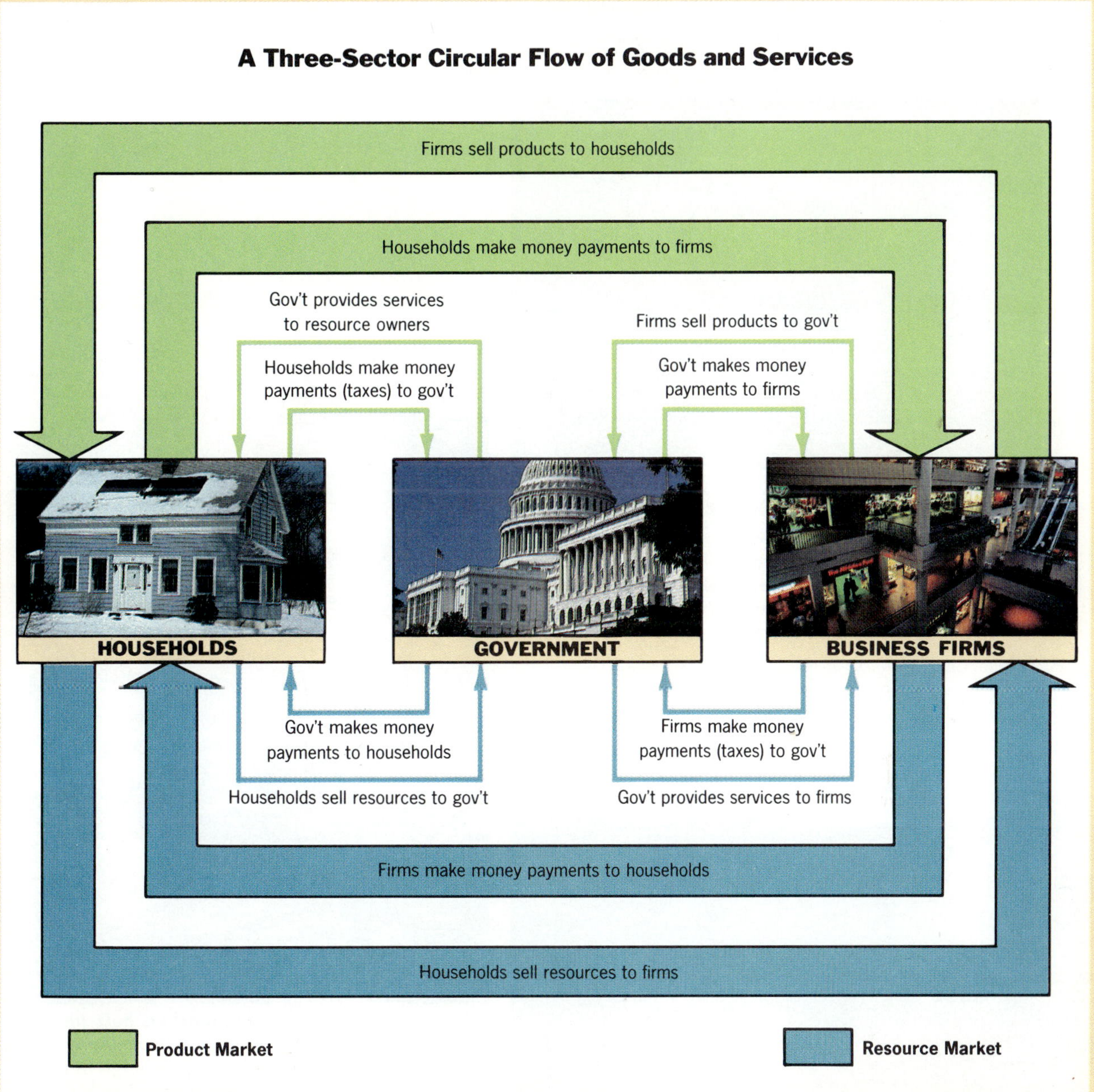

The circular flow model (above) is used by economists to illustrate the two types of flows that are at work in the American economic system. The first is the resource-product flow between households, business firms, and governments. The second is the money flow that takes place as resources and products are exchanged between households, business firms, and governments.

THE GLOBAL NATURE OF ECONOMICS

No nation's economic system is completely independent. The economy of one nation can affect, and be affected by, the economies of nations thousands of miles away. Interdependence links the economic systems of all of the nations of the world.

New techniques in communication have made nearly split-second verbal and written exchanges possible. These developments and many more have made today's world seem to be a smaller place (above).

With the use of advanced telecommunications equipment (above), currency does not need to be physically transported from one place to another. Instead, the paper accounts of firms and banks are automatically changed as withdrawals and receipts of money are recorded.

Foreign exchange markets help individuals, businesses, and governments exchange foreign currencies. Foreign exchange markets are networks of major commercial and investment banks that link the economies of the world.

International trade is the voluntary exchange of goods and services among people in different nations (right). Nations everywhere seek a favorable balance of trade. The balance of trade is the difference between the value of a nation's imports and its exports.

The world's natural resources, human resources, and capital resources—the factors of production—are distributed unevenly (left). The availability of resources largely determines the kinds of products that a nation will import and export.

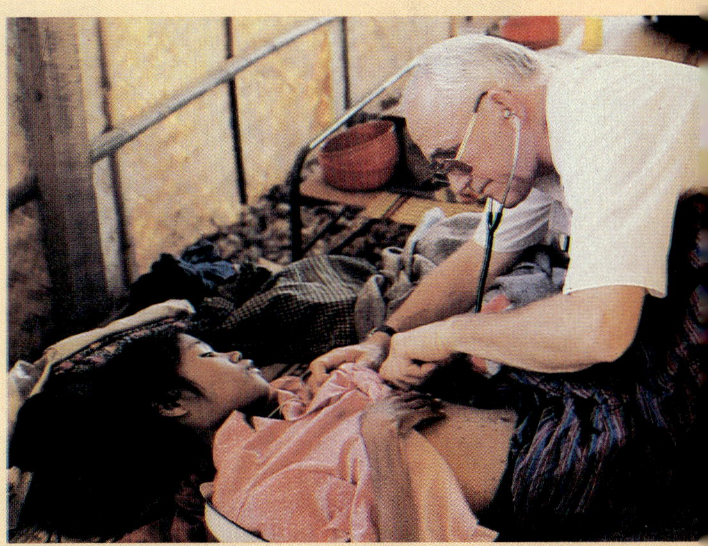

Many of the poorer, less industrialized nations, often called developing nations, receive economic assistance (right) from a variety of sources. Among these are foreign businesses and nonprofit organizations, foreign governments, and international development organizations.

COMPARATIVE ECONOMIC SYSTEMS

Most of the nations of the world today have mixed economies. Depending on the degree of government control over the economy, the type of mixed economy found in a nation can be based on democratic socialism, authoritarian socialism, or capitalism.

Under democratic socialism, the people retain basic human rights. The people also retain some degree of control over economic planning through the election of government officials. The government, however, owns all or part of certain basic industries. Sweden (right) and Great Britain (below) are examples of nations with economic systems based on democratic socialism.

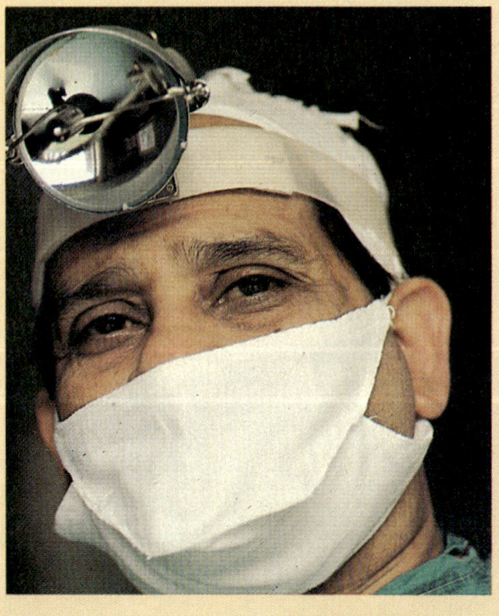

Under authoritarian socialism, or Communism, the government owns and controls nearly all of the means of production. A major feature of authoritarian socialism is central planning, in which government leaders set rigid short-term and long-term production goals. The Soviet Union (left and above) and the People's Republic of China are examples of countries with economic systems based on authoritarian socialism.

Capitalism is a system based on freedom—the basic freedoms of the marketplace. Individuals taking part in the free exchange of goods (top and center) and services (below) guide the economies of capitalistic nations. In the American free enterprise system, the government intervenes in the economy only on a limited basis. In capitalistic nations such as Japan and South Korea, however, the government plays a larger role in economic decision making.

UNIT ONE

AN INTRODUCTION TO ECONOMICS

CHAPTER 1

See Chapter Overview, p. TM 2.
See Chapter Objectives, p. TM 2.
See Introducing the Chapter, p. TM 2.
See Extending Economic Knowledge on text p. 42.

Economics and Economic Systems

Our society is what we make it. We can shape our institutions. Physical and human characteristics limit the alternatives available to us. But none prevents us, if we will, from building a society that relies primarily on voluntary cooperation to organize both economic and other activity.

Milton and Rose Friedman

1 Economics examines how people use scarce resources to produce and consume goods and services.

- The Factors of Production
- Trade-offs and Opportunity Costs
- Production Possibilities

2 The answers to the basic economic questions are determined by a nation's economic system.

- Answering Basic Questions
- Answers in Traditional Economies
- Answers in Command Economies
- Answers in Market Economies
- Answers in Mixed Economies

3 The features and goals of the United States economy are based on a system of free enterprise.

- The Features of the United States Economy
- The Goals of the United States Economy
- Economic Goals in Conflict
- The Circular Flow Model of the Economy

CHAPTER 1 STUDY GUIDE

Chapter Focus

Chapter 1 examines scarcity and the need for choosing how best to use scarce resources. The chapter then describes the four major types of economic systems—traditional, command, market, and mixed. It explains how each system answers the basic economic questions of what, how, and for whom to produce goods and services. The chapter also discusses the features and goals of the United States economy. Finally it presents the circular flow model, which describes how resources, products, and money payments are exchanged in the economy.

As you study the chapter, look for the details that support each of the following statements.

1. Economics examines how people use scarce resources to produce and consume goods and services.
2. The answers to the questions of what, how, and for whom to produce are determined by a nation's economic system.
3. The features and goals of the United States economy are based on a system of free enterprise.

See Preteaching Vocabulary, p. TM 2.

Terms to Know

The following terms, while not the only terms emphasized in this chapter, are basic to your understanding of economics and economic systems. Determine the meaning of each term, either by using the Glossary or by watching for context clues as you read the chapter.

economics
consumer good
factor of production
capital good
technology
entrepreneurship
trade-off
production possibilities curve
traditional economy
command economy
market economy
mixed economy
free enterprise system
circular flow model

See Key Study Questions and Key Understandings, p. TM 3.

1 Economics examines how people use scarce resources to produce and consume goods and services.

See Suggested Teaching Strategies, p. TM 3.

The study of the choices people make in an effort to satisfy their wants and needs is called **economics.** Wants and needs refer to people's desires to consume certain goods and services. In economic terms, a **good** is a physical object that can be purchased. A record, a house, and a car are examples of a good. A **service** is an action or activity done for others for a fee. Lawyers, plumbers, teachers, and taxicab drivers perform services. The term *product* often is used to refer to both goods and services.

The people who wish to buy goods and services are called **consumers** and the goods that they buy are called **consumer goods.** The people who make the goods and provide the services that satisfy consumers' wants and needs are called **producers.**

Economists generally classify as **needs** those ◆ goods or services that are necessary for survival. Food, clothing, and shelter are considered needs. **Wants** are those goods or services that people consume beyond what is needed for survival.

The need for making choices arises from the problem of scarcity. Scarcity exists because people's wants and needs are greater than the resources available to satisfy them. Thus people must choose how best to use their available resources to satisfy the greatest number of wants and needs.

The Factors of Production

A resource is anything that people use to make or obtain what they want or need. Resources that can be used to produce goods and services are called

 ◆ Discussion topic: The role of money in satisfying wants and needs.

◆ **factors of production.** Economists usually divide these factors of production into three categories: (1) natural resources, (2) human resources, and (3) capital resources. Today, many economists have added technology and entrepreneurship to this list.

Natural Resources. Items provided by nature that can be used to produce goods and to provide services are called **natural resources.** Natural resources are found in or on the earth or in the earth's atmosphere. Examples of natural resources on the earth are fertile land, vegetation, animals, and bodies of water. Minerals and petroleum are examples of natural resources that are found in the earth. Atmospheric resources include the sun, wind, and rain. A natural resource is considered a factor of production only when it is used to produce goods and to provide services.

Human Resources. Anyone who works is considered a **human resource.** Any human effort that is exerted in the production process is classified as a human resource. The effort can be either physical or intellectual. Assembly-line workers, ministers, professional sports figures, physicians, store clerks, and sanitation engineers are all human resources.

Capital Resources. The money and capital goods that are used to produce consumer products are called **capital resources. Capital goods** include the buildings, structures, machinery, and tools that are used in the production process. Department stores, factories, industrial machinery, dams, ports, wrenches, hammers, and surgical scalpels are all examples of capital goods.

Economists make an important distinction between capital goods and consumer goods. Capital goods are the manufactured resources that are used in producing finished products. Consumer goods are the finished products—the goods and services that consumers buy. Some products can be either capital goods or consumer goods, depending on how they are used. A bicycle purchased for personal use is a consumer good. The same is not true when the bicycle is purchased by a New York messenger service. Because the messenger service will use the bicycle to make deliveries—to provide a service—the bicycle is considered a capital good.

Technology. The use of science to create new products or more efficient ways to produce products is called **technology.** Technology makes the other factors of production—natural, human, and capital

As individuals have become more aware of the scarcity of resources, they have increased their efforts to recycle items such as aluminum and paper.

◆ Class activity: Have the students list the factors of production that were required in the production of objects in the room.

DECISION MAKERS IN THE ECONOMY

Henry F. Henderson, Jr.

Henry F. "Hank" Henderson, Jr., is an entrepreneur. Henderson, who graduated from college with a degree in electronics, started his own electrical contracting business in 1954 when he was 26 years old. Today, Henderson Industries has annual sales of $24 million. Among the electrical equipment produced by the company are control panels for drawbridges and manufacturing plants.

Like many entrepreneurs, Henderson began his business on a very limited budget. With a $5,000 bank loan, Henderson set up shop in the basement of his New Jersey home. His wife, Ethel, acted as receptionist whenever the corporate telephone rang in the kitchen.

As business increased, Henderson moved his company from the basement of his home to his garage. By 1969, his business had outgrown his house. Henderson mortgaged his home to help finance the construction of a 17,000 square-foot factory. He later expanded the factory to 30,000 square feet.

In the early years, Hank Henderson made all of his business contacts by telephone. Today, his clients are scattered around the world. A 1983 contract with the Ta Chung Hua Rubber Plant made Henderson Industries the first black-owned company to manufacture equipment for the People's Republic of China.

Hard work, careful planning, and the willingness to explore new markets have paid off for Hank Henderson. Through his efforts, Henderson Industries has grown from a small, home-based enterprise to a major manufacturer of electrical equipment.

resources—more productive. Technological advances in the computer industry, for example, have increased efficiency in the workplace. In some highly automated plants, computers even direct production by issuing electronic instructions to robots on the assembly line.

Entrepreneurship. The risk-taking and organizational abilities involved in starting a new business or in introducing a new product to consumers are called **entrepreneurship.** The term *entrepreneurship* is derived from a French word meaning "to undertake." The goal of entrepreneurship is to create a new mix of the other factors of production and thereby create something of value. The **entrepreneur** is a person who attempts to start a new business or introduce a new product. The entrepreneur risks failing in return for the financial gain that is possible if the business venture is a success.

Trade-offs and Opportunity Costs

Choosing among alternative uses for available resources forces people to make sacrifices. If a resource is used to produce one thing, that same resource cannot be used to produce something else. One item is sacrificed for another. In economic terms, this sacrifice is called a **trade-off.** The cost of this sacrifice—the value of what is given up to obtain that item—is called the **opportunity cost.**

Trade-offs and opportunity costs are realities that ◆ people face every day. Consider the following example. Molly Mason has two events she would like to attend in the same week—a concert and a professional football game. Tickets for the concert and the football game cost the same amount. Unfortunately, Mason has only enough money to purchase one ticket. She must make a trade-off because she cannot afford to buy two tickets. She must give up one

◆ Have the students read "Preparing a Personal Budget" on pages 508–509 of the *Everyday Economics Handbook* and answer the questions that follow.

of the choices. If she spends money on a ticket to the concert, the alternative choice—the ticket to the football game—is the opportunity cost of buying the concert ticket.

The above example is a simple, two-item choice. Most choices, however, involve many more trade-offs. When resources are used to build a factory, the trade-off is not between the factory and one other use of the resources. The natural, human, and capital resources, and the necessary technology and entrepreneurship that go into building the factory could be used in varying combinations to produce a wide range of goods and services. It is important to ◆ consider trade-offs when making economic choices.

Production Possibilities

Trade-offs and opportunity costs can be illustrated using a production possibilities curve. A **production possibilities curve** shows all of the possible combinations of two goods or services that can be produced within a stated time period, given two important assumptions. First, it is assumed that the amount of available resources, including technology, will not change during the period being studied. Second, it is assumed that all of the natural, human, and capital resources and available technology are being used in the most efficient manner possible.

The above assumptions are important because they determine which production combinations will fall on the curve and which will not. All of the combinations on the curve meet these assumptions. Combinations that lie inside (below) the curve, on the other hand, represent the inefficient use of existing resources. Combinations that lie outside (above) the curve represent production impossibilities, given existing technology. Each production combination is measured in terms of opportunity costs. More of one good can be produced only at the expense of producing less of the other good.

A production possibilities curve is a model, which is a simplified version of reality. Because a model represents rather than mirrors reality, the real world does not necessarily operate as it does in the model. The model, however, makes it possible to determine what would happen in the real world if certain assumptions were met. A model is only as good as the assumptions on which it is based. If the assumptions mirror closely what happens in the real world, the model will be a helpful tool. The production possibilities curve is an example of a helpful model.

The Production Possibilities Curve

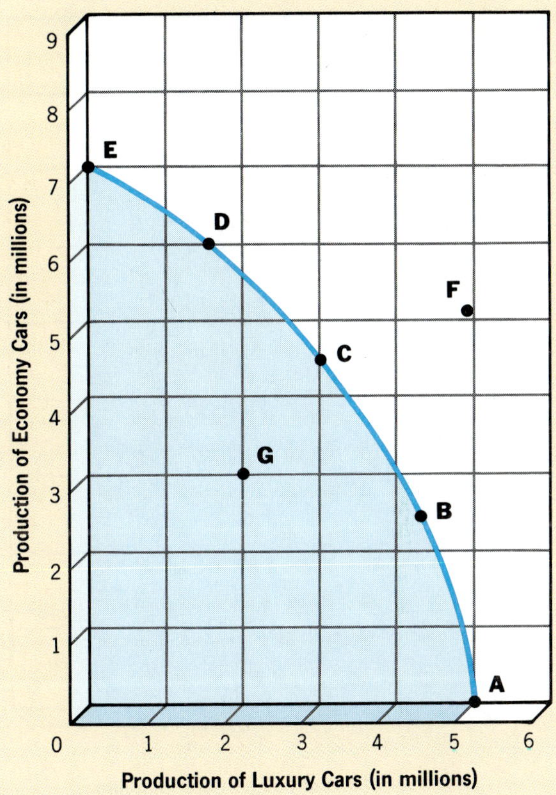

Current Production Possibilities. The graph on this page shows the possible production options that would be available to the United States automotive industry if it were to concentrate its current resources on the production of economy and luxury cars. Like all production possibilities curves, this curve is based on the assumptions of a fixed amount of resources and the efficient use of those resources.

The curve that connects points **A** through **E** shows the production combinations that meet the stated assumptions. At point **A**, all resources are devoted to the production of luxury cars. Point **E** represents the other extreme—all resources are devoted to the production of economy cars. In each case, the opportunity cost of producing one class of cars is the entire production capacity of the other class of cars.

◆ Discussion topic: The role that time plays in opportunity costs.

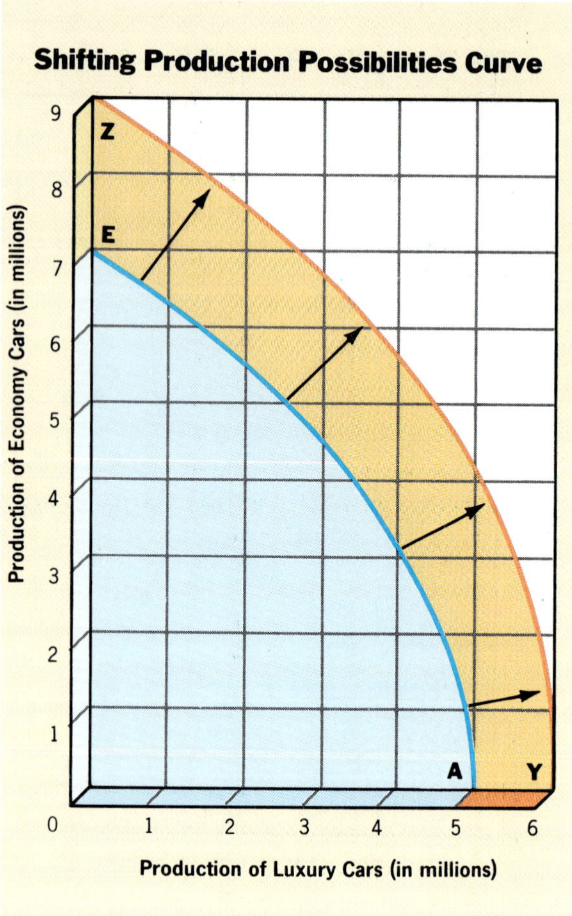

Given the varied tastes of consumers, it is unlikely that the automotive industry would choose to limit its production to either luxury or economy cars. Instead, it would most likely produce some combination of the two classes of cars. These combinations are represented by points **B, C,** and **D** on the curve. In terms of opportunity costs, the cost of producing a certain number of one class of cars would be the number of cars of the other class that could not be produced.

Two additional points, **F** and **G,** are included in the graph. Point **F,** which lies outside the curve, is a production impossibility given the current levels of technology and other resources. No matter how the automotive industry mixes the existing factors of production, it cannot produce at this high a level. Point **G,** which lies inside the curve, represents the inefficient use of resources. If the existing factors of production are used more efficiently, the industry should be able to produce at a level represented by one of the points on the production possibilities curve.

Future Production Possibilities. In the real world, technology and the other factors of production do not remain constant. When advancements in technology and resources occur, the entire production possibilities curve changes. A new curve is formed to the right of the old curve. Economists say that the curve has "shifted" to the right.

The production possibilities curve on this page shows a shift to the right. The new curve, which connects points **Y** and **Z,** represents the expanded production that results from advances in technology or resources. Once the new curve is established, the old assumptions of fixed resources and efficiency go into effect. If the assumptions change—if new technology or resources become available—the curve once again shifts to the right.

See Suggested Assignments, p. TM 3.

Section 1 Review See Answers, p. A 5.

DEFINE economics, consumer, producer, factor of production, entrepreneurship, trade-off, opportunity cost, production possibilities curve

IDENTIFY Henry F. Henderson, Jr.

1. **Comprehending Ideas** How does scarcity contribute to the need to make economic decisions?
2. **Comparing Ideas** **(a)** What are the major differences between a capital good and a consumer good? **(b)** When does a lawn mower become a capital good?
3. **Summarizing Ideas** **(a)** Why do people and nations have to make economic choices? **(b)** What are the factors of production upon which people and nations base their economic decisions?
4. **Seeing Relationships** What is the relationship between entrepreneurship and technology?
5. **Analyzing Ideas** What is the difference between a trade-off and an opportunity cost?
6. **Interpreting Graphics** Study the graph on page 25. Why is it impossible to move from point **B** to point **F** on the graph on page 25?

See Key Study Questions and Key Understandings, p. TM 4.

2 The answers to the basic economic questions are determined by a nation's economic system.

See Suggested Teaching Strategies, p. TM 4.

Nations, like people, are affected by scarcity. Nations, like people, do not have enough resources to satisfy all of their wants and needs. Thus nations—in reality their national leaders—must make choices concerning how best to use available resources.

Answering Basic Questions

Nations make these choices by answering the three basic questions of economics. (1) What goods and services should be produced? (2) How should these goods and services be produced? (3) For whom should these goods and services be produced?

Production Choices. The question of what goods and services to produce involves several factors. A nation must decide what percentage of its resources will be devoted to producing capital goods and what percentage will be devoted to producing consumer goods. Once the percentage is determined, the nation must decide what types of capital and consumer goods will be produced.

Resource Choices. The question of how goods and services should be produced involves determining how best to employ the nation's natural, human, and capital resources. Production can be simple—based primarily on human labor—or complex—based primarily on the use of machines.

Distribution Choices. The question of for whom these goods and services should be produced can be answered in several ways. A nation can choose to have everyone receive an equal share of what is produced. It is truer to reality, however, that some people will receive more goods and services than other people. If the distribution is unequal, the nation must determine who will receive what goods and services and in what amounts.

The type of economic system a nation has determines how it answers these three basic questions. An **economic system** is the organized set of procedures that a nation follows in producing and distributing goods and services. Economists have identified four types of economic systems. A nation has either a traditional, a command, a market, or a mixed economy.

Examples of traditional and mixed economies can be found in various parts of the world today. Pure command and pure market economies, however, are models. No nation actually has a pure command or a pure market economy. In the pure-command model, the government controls the use of all resources and dictates the answers to the basic economic questions. In the pure-market model, on the other hand, individuals and privately owned firms control the use of resources and answer the basic economic questions.

The majority of nations in the world are mixed economies. The economies of these nations combine elements of both the pure-command and the pure-market models. Mixed economies that are closer to the pure-command model are often classified as command economies. Mixed economies that are closer to the pure-market model are often classified as market economies.

Answers in Traditional Economies

A **traditional economy** looks to the past for the answers to the three basic economic questions. Present economic activities are based on tradition—the customs, habits, laws, and religious beliefs that were developed by the group's ancestors.

In a traditional economy, the same products are produced in the same ways in which they have been produced for generations. Economic activities tend to be centered around the family and the tribal or other social unit. Jobs and the skills needed to carry them out are passed from parent to child. Men and women often perform different duties. The goods and services that are produced are usually distributed equally among the group's members. Change occurs slowly because economic activities are based on how things have been done in the past. When change does occur, people in traditional societies often resist it.

Traditional economic systems still exist in parts of Latin America, Asia, Africa, and the Middle East. For example, the Dinka of central Africa still herd their cattle and grow their crops on the plains of

Text continues on page 29.

◆ Have the students use Rostow's economic stages to look for examples of nations which are in transition.

In some areas of the world, such as Malaysia (top left), Indonesia (top right), and Egypt (middle), and in some traditional Indian villages in the United States (bottom), daily life has changed little for centuries.

southern Sudan as they have done for centuries. Examples of other traditional economies include the Bushmen of the Kalahari Desert, the nomadic Berbers of northern Africa, and the aborigines of Australia. The Mbuti of central Africa are another example of people organized into a traditional economic system.

CASE STUDY

The Mbuti of Central Africa

The Mbuti are inhabitants of the Ituri Forest in the central African nation of Zaire. The Mbuti live, work, and travel in small groups, or bands, of 30 people or less. Band members view themselves as a family. The 35,000 Mbuti live in harmony with the forest, adapting to their natural environment rather than trying to dominate it.

The Mbuti are food gatherers and hunters. The Ituri Forest supplies an abundance of natural resources. The Mbuti gather roots, mushrooms, fruits, berries, and nuts and hunt for wild game. The Mbuti do not cultivate the land or keep herds of animals. Because the Mbuti are hunters and gatherers, they must follow the food. Consequently, the bands are nomadic and rarely stay in one place for more than a month.

Almost every person in the Mbuti band is a human resource. Tradition dictates which jobs will be done by men and which will be done by women. Tradition also dictates what duties children will perform. The main duty of all band members is the provision of food. The men hunt and the women and children gather and prepare the food.

The capital resources used by the Mbuti have changed little over the years. The men use such items as nets, spears, bows, and arrows, which are sometimes dipped in poison. These items are classified as capital resources because they are used to produce food. In recent years, the Mbuti have obtained metal machetes and knives from neighboring tribes. The Mbuti must trade for these items because they do not possess the necessary capital or technology to produce metal implements.

Answers in Command Economies

A pure **command economy** relies on officials in the government to answer the three basic economic questions. The officials—called central planners—have the authority to determine what products will be produced. They determine the methods that will be used to produce the products. They also determine who will receive the products once they are produced. Individual members of a nation with a pure command economy have little or no say in economic decisions. The government maintains complete control over the factors of production. Command economies are often called planned economies because they are controlled by central planners.

While pure command economies no longer exist, they were once quite common. For example, in the Old Kingdom period of Egyptian history (2700–2200 B.C.), the monarch controlled the economy of Egypt. The monarch owned the land, controlled all trade, collected taxes, and supervised the building of the kingdom's dams, canals, and granaries.

In China during the Chou Dynasty (1122–249 B.C.), emperors were able to control resources by distributing land to subordinates called vassals. The vassals pledged their military and political loyalty to the emperor in return for the emperor's grant of land.

A similar system existed in western Europe during the Middle Ages. Monarchs granted land—called fiefs—to vassals in exchange for loyalty. These vassals were often called lords. They lived in manor houses, which sometimes took the form of castles. **Manorialism** was the name given to this type of command economy. The head of the manor, or lord, had absolute control over the use of human, natural, and capital resources on the manor.

Answers in Market Economies

A pure **market economy** relies on individuals to answer the three basic economic questions. Individuals, rather than the government, own and control the factors of production. The government has no say in what, how, and for whom goods are produced. People are free to buy, sell, and produce whatever they wish and work wherever they want. The only control is that which is provided by the market itself. ◆

The **market**—sometimes called the **marketplace**—is defined as any situation where goods or

◆ **Have the students read "Economists" on page 541 of *Careers in the Marketplace.***

Adam Smith (1723–1790) was the first economist to claim that manufacturing, rather than farming, was the economy's most important source of wealth.

services are exchanged freely. Adam Smith (1723–1790), the Scottish economist, was one of the first people to attempt to explain how the market operates in a pure market economy. He published his explanation in his book, *An Inquiry into the Nature and Causes of the Wealth of Nations,* published in 1776.

According to Smith, in the absence of governmental interference, the market is controlled by the invisible hand of self-interest. According to Smith, in a market exchange, each person attempts to gain as much as possible from the transaction. Smith argued that the promotion of self-interest benefits all of society by helping the economy to grow. He attributed the growth to an invisible hand that leads individuals to unknowingly do what is best for all of society when they protect their own self-interests. Smith believed that government intervention weakened the ability of the invisible hand of self-interest to regulate the market.

The types of products available and the cost of these products are two important features of a market economy regulated by self-interest. If consumers are to promote their own self-interest, they must purchase the goods and services they desire at the lowest prices possible. Producers, on the other hand, promote their own self-interest by receiving the ◆ most profit from the sale of their products. **Profit** is the amount of money that remains after all of the costs of production have been paid. In order to maximize profits, producers must sell the right products at the right prices. By buying a certain good and not another, consumers send signals to producers about what to produce and in what quantities.

Answers in Mixed Economies

A **mixed economy** combines elements of the pure-market and the pure-command economic models. Virtually all of the nations in the world today have mixed economies. The mixed economies of these nations represent a wide range of economic practices that need to be classified. Thus economists classify nations with mixed economies according to the degree of government control.

Capitalism. Nations with economies that are closest to the pure-market model are said to practice **capitalism.** In an economic system based on capitalism, individuals own and control the factors of production. The government provides some regulations, but its intervention is limited.

The economies in the United States, Hong Kong, Singapore, Japan, South Korea, and the Republic of China (Taiwan) are classified as capitalistic. All of these nations rely on private ownership and control of the vast majority of businesses.

Although private ownership and control is the guiding force in capitalist economies, the government does have a limited influence on economic activities. Through taxation and spending policies, the government redistributes wealth and provides such services as education, social welfare programs, and national defense. Government regulations, such as health and safety standards in the workplace, also affect these economies to varying degrees. In Japan and South Korea, the government also takes an active role in economic planning.

Authoritarian Socialism. Nations that are closest to the pure-command model are said to practice **authoritarian socialism,** also referred to as **Communism.** In economies based on authoritarian socialism, the government owns or controls almost all of the means of production.

The Soviet Union, the People's Republic of China, Cuba, and Albania are examples of economies based on authoritarian socialism. In these countries, the government owns and controls most of the factors of production. Government planners, to a large extent, answer the basic economic questions by devising five-year plans for the use of the nation's

◆ **Report topic: How the marketplace would be different if profit were regulated by the government.**

resources. The governmental long-range planning limits the decision-making role of individuals. Recent trends in the Soviet Union and the People's Republic of China, however, indicate a slight shift away from rigid central planning toward individual decision making. This trend will be examined further in Chapter 19.

Democratic Socialism. In between capitalism and authoritarian socialism is **democratic socialism.** In democratic socialism, the government owns some of the factors of production. Under democratic socialism, however, individuals maintain basic human rights and control over economic planning through the election of government officials.

The economies of Great Britain, France, West Germany, Sweden, and many other western European nations are based on democratic socialism. While most factors of production are owned and controlled by private individuals, the government owns some industries. In most instances, government ownership and control is confined to such important industries as energy production and manufacturing of industrial goods.

Many developing nations in Africa, the Middle East, Latin America, and Asia also have economies based on democratic socialism. **Developing nations** is the term given to the poorer, less industrialized countries of the world. Tanzania, Angola, and Mozambique are examples of developing nations that practice democratic socialism.

See Suggested Assignments, p. TM 4.

Section 2 Review See Answers, p. A 5.

DEFINE economic system, market, profit

IDENTIFY Adam Smith

1. **Organizing Ideas** **(a)** List the four general categories of economies. **(b)** Produce an example of each category.
2. **Contrasting Ideas** How do capitalism and Communism differ in determining who answers the basic economic questions?
3. **Analyzing Ideas** **(a)** Why does a pure market economy or a pure command economy seldom exist? **(b)** How does the "invisible hand of self-interest" operate in a free economy?

See Key Study Questions and Key Understandings, p. TM 5.

3 The features and goals of the United States economy are based on a system of free enterprise.

See Suggested Teaching Strategies, p. TM 5.

The economy of the United States, as already stated, leans heavily toward the market model. In the ◆ United States individuals are free to exchange their goods and services, seek jobs of their own choosing, use their resources as they wish, and own and operate businesses. Because of these freedoms, the economy of the United States is sometimes referred to as a free enterprise system. Enterprise is simply another word for business. Thus a **free enterprise system** is a system in which business can be conducted freely with only limited government intervention.

The Features of the United States Economy

The free enterprise system of the United States is based on five features. (1) In the United States, individuals have the right to own private property and enter into contracts. (2) Individuals have the right to make personal choices and to communicate those choices through the price system. (3) Individuals have the right to engage in free enterprise and competition. (4) Individuals have the right to make decisions based on self-interest and the profit motive. (5) The United States has a limited amount of government regulation and intervention. It is the final feature, limited government intervention and regulation, that separates the United States economy from the pure-market model.

Private Property and Contracts. Goods that are owned by individuals and by businesses, rather than by the government, are considered **private property.** A person's house, car, and furniture are examples of private property. A business's private property might include a factory, office building, machinery and other equipment, and the land on which the factory and office buildings are located. Individuals and business owners can use their property or dispose of it as they wish. They can buy as much private property as they can afford. They also

Text continues on page 33.

◆ Discussion topic: Discuss some specific examples of how our economy is mixed (government regulation in food and drugs; government regulation of minimum and maximum wages).

The Constitution— Protector of Free Enterprise

When the Constitutional Convention met in 1787, one of its main goals was to alter the economic system of the new American nation. The states had fought against unfair taxation by the British, only to find themselves competing with each other during the decade after independence.

Between 1781 and 1787 the national "government" operated as a league of free and independent states under a document called the Articles of Confederation. Conflicts regularly arose because of each state's right to act alone. Virginia and Maryland, for example, argued repeatedly about use of the Potomac River.

The national government lacked the authority to regulate most economic matters. Each state issued its own currency, passed trade regulations, and imposed protective tariffs at will. Indeed, each state functioned as a separate market, protecting its own interests at the expense of national economic unity.

The delegates to the Constitutional Convention acted to remedy this unhealthy economic situation. They established a single national market to serve as the foundation for free enterprise. The Constitution they created gave Congress the power to coin and regulate the value of the nation's money. Congress could fix the standard of weights and measures used in marketing products. It could regulate commerce among the states and establish uniform bankruptcy laws.

The principles of free enterprise were ensured in other provisions. First, the Constitution made Congress a representative body and so gave the people a voice in determining market rules. It also placed a number of limitations on governmental actions. It prohibited the government from altering or interfering with legal contracts.

In still other provisions, the Constitution gave everyone equal access to the market by requiring the government to impose taxes and trade regulations uniformly throughout the states. It made advertising possible by guaranteeing freedom of speech. It also strengthened the profit motive by preventing the government from seizing private property without providing good reason and adequate compensation.

These provisions of the Constitution still are in effect today. They created free enterprise in this country. Our interpretations of some of the Constitutional provisions have changed over time, giving further witness to the Constitution as the protector of free enterprise.

We the People of the United States, in Order to form a more perfect Uni
insure domestic Tranquility, provide for the common defence, promote the general Welfare, and secure the Blessings of
and our Posterity, do ordain and establish this Constitution for the United States of America.

Article. I.

Section. 1. All legislative Powers herein granted shall be vested in a Congress of the United States, which shall consist of
of Representatives.

Section. 2. The House of Representatives shall be composed of Members chosen every second Year by the People of the severa
in each State shall have Qualifications requisite for Electors of the most numerous Branch of the State Legislature.

No Person shall be a Representative who shall not have attained to the Age of twenty five Years, and been seven Years a Ci
and who shall not, when elected, be an Inhabitant of that State in which he shall be chosen.

Representatives and direct Taxes shall be apportioned among the several States which may be included within this Union, accor can sell as much as they wish, providing a buyer is willing and able to purchase the property.

Individuals also have the right to enter into agreements with one another to buy and sell goods and services. These agreements are called **contracts.** A contract can be either oral or written, but regardless of its form, it is legally binding. In other words, all of the people who have entered into the contract must actually do what they have said they will do. If any person fails to fulfill the terms of the contract, the courts may be asked to step in to ensure that the agreement is carried out or that a satisfactory compromise is reached.

Choice and the Price System. Property owners, laborers, and consumers in the United States enjoy freedom of choice. Property owners are free to use or dispose of their private property as they choose. Laborers are free to pursue job opportunities. Consumers are free to buy those goods and services that best meet their wants and needs.

That all people are consumers is a basic economic fact. Many people do not realize, however, that consumers have a key role to play in the decisions that businesses make. Consumer demand, more than any other single factor, gives producers signals about what to produce and in what quantities. In economic terms, **demand** is the amount of a good or service a consumer is willing and able to buy at various prices during a given time period.

Demand in the marketplace directly affects the price system. The price system is a type of communication system that tells producers the kinds and quantities of products that consumers want and need. By looking at how consumers cast their dollar votes, producers can determine what they should produce in order to obtain the highest profit.

Higher sales and higher prices are signals to producers to increase production of a good or service. Higher sales and higher prices also are signals to other firms to enter the market in search of profit. Conversely, slower sales and lower prices are signals to producers to decrease production and possibly exit from the market in search of other markets that are more profitable.

Free Enterprise and Competition. Freedom of enterprise guarantees businesspeople the right to choose the type and quantity of goods and services to produce and the manner in which to produce them. This right, however, carries with it the responsibility of accepting the consequences of business decisions. In other words, businesspeople have the freedom to succeed as well as the freedom to fail in the marketplace.

Items such as diamonds, which have a high demand but a limited supply, tend to be expensive to buy.

Success or failure in the marketplace often results from a firm's ability to compete with other businesses producing similar products. **Competition** is the name given to the economic rivalry that exists among businesses selling the same or similar products. Competition is important because it prevents one producer from controlling the market, promotes business efficiency, and encourages producers to improve existing products and develop new ones.

Self-Interest and Profit. As Adam Smith indicated, self-interest is the force that directs the actions of individuals and firms in a market system. Consumers prefer to buy goods at lower prices rather than at higher prices. Laborers prefer to work at higher-paying jobs rather than at lower-paying jobs. Businesses prefer to sell goods at higher prices rather than at lower prices.

It is in a businessperson's self-interest to make a profit. As mentioned earlier, profit is the money that remains after all of the costs of production have been paid. If a business is unable to make a profit, the business will fail. The desire to make a profit is the reason people invest time, money, and energy in business endeavors. Economists label this reason the profit motive.

Economics Reporter

What Are the Private Sector and the Public Sector?

The private sector includes the economic activities of households and private businesses. By households, economists mean all persons who live in the same residence whether one person, a family, or unrelated individuals sharing a residence. Private businesses are all businesses owned by individuals or groups of individuals. Businesses owned or controlled by the government are not included in the private sector. The public sector includes economic activities that are under the direct control of local, state, and federal governments. Raising money through taxes, spending the money that has been raised, and regulating certain aspects of the economy are examples of public-sector actions.

Limited Government Interference. Although businesses in the United States operate with a fair amount of freedom, the government plays a key role in regulating the economy. For example, the government regulates the economy by establishing laws and rules that individuals and businesses must follow. The government raises money through taxation and spends the tax dollars on goods and services for members of society.

Public education and national defense are two services paid for through state and federal taxes, respectively. The government also uses the money raised through taxes to redistribute wealth by providing assistance to needy individuals and to struggling businesses. Finally, the government attempts to keep the economy stable by holding down prices and unemployment and by encouraging economic growth.

The Goals of the United States Economy

Economic goals are the general objectives that an economic system strives to achieve. All nations establish economic goals. By setting goals, a nation's policymakers can better choose how to use scarce resources. Economic goals make it easier to determine the trade-offs involved in each choice.

The economy of the United States has six major goals. These goals are (1) economic freedom; (2) economic efficiency; (3) economic equity, or justice; (4) economic security; (5) economic stability; and (6) economic growth.

Economic Freedom. The goal of **economic freedom** refers to efforts to maintain freedom of choice in the marketplace. In a free enterprise system, consumers must be free to decide how to spend their scarce income on goods and services. Workers must be free to choose an occupation, change jobs, or join a union. Savers and investors must be free to decide when, where, and how to save or invest their money. Businesspeople must be free to change from one business to another and to expand or fold existing ones.

Economic Efficiency. The goal of **economic efficiency** refers to efforts to make the best use of scarce resources. Economic efficiency can be measured by how many goods and services a nation's workers can produce. The more products an individual worker can produce, the more efficient the economy.

Economic Equity. The goal of **economic equity,** sometimes called economic justice, is difficult to define because it deals with questions of fairness and of right and wrong. Policymakers are often confronted with problems demanding a fair or just decision. By studying the costs and benefits of a proposed course of action, policymakers can better judge what is fair or right. Policymakers in the United States attempt to ensure that members of society share in the costs and benefits of the free enterprise system in a relatively equal way.

Economic Security. The basic goal of **economic security** refers to a nation's efforts to protect its members from poverty, business and bank failures, medical emergencies, and other emergency situations that would have a negative effect on its members' economic well-being. Economic security can result from individual actions or from government actions. For example, individuals can guard against the unexpected by purchasing different types of insurance or by saving a portion of their money. Governments at the local, state, and national levels promote economic security through such actions as providing unemployment compensation, insuring bank deposits, and giving economic assistance to slumping businesses.

Economic Stability. The basic goal of **economic stability** involves two concerns—achieving full employment and achieving stable prices. **Full employment** is the lowest level of unemployment that is possible in the economy. Full employment does not mean that everyone who wants to work has a job. A certain amount of unemployment always exists. Economists disagree on the maximum percentage of the labor force that can be unemployed during periods of full employment. Some economists say that full employment exists when no more than 4 percent of the labor force is unemployed. Other economists set the figure as high as 7 percent.

Price stability is achieved when the overall price level of the goods and services available in the economy is relatively constant. It is important to note that price stability refers to the prices of all products taken together, not to changes in the price of an individual product.

Economic Growth. The goal of **economic growth** refers to efforts to increase the amount of goods and services each worker in the economy can produce. The distinction between simply increasing the economy's production and increasing the production from each worker is important. If total production increases more slowly than the population increases, each worker actually produces less. Lower production from each worker means that fewer goods and services are available to consume. A decrease in the number of available goods and services results in a decline in the standard of living in a nation. **Standard of living** refers to the economic well-being of people. Economists measure the standard of living by how much, on average, every person in a nation is able to consume in a given period of time—usually one year.

Clubs such as 4-H and Junior Achievement help to ensure economic growth by providing training for the next generation of businesspeople.

Economic Goals in Conflict

While most people in the United States would agree that the six goals of the economy are desirable, obstacles often prevent their achievement. Many factors also bring the various economic goals into conflict.

Setting Priorities. Scarcity forces individuals, businesses, and governments to make choices among alternative wants and needs. Scarcity is one reason why it is not always possible to achieve *all* of the nation's economic goals. Consequently, policymakers must first determine which goals are most important given a nation's needs at the time. For example, during the prosperity of the 1920s, the goals of economic freedom, efficiency, and growth tended to dominate. By the 1930s, however, the poverty created by the Great Depression made economic security and equity the most important goals.

Conflicting Group Interests. Even at a single point in history, conflicts among goals arise because different groups in the nation have different needs. The elderly and poverty-stricken, for example, are more concerned with economic security and equity than with the other economic goals. Businesspeople, on the other hand, want to emphasize economic growth and efficiency.

In addition to deciding which goals to stress, a nation's policymakers must decide how to achieve those goals. Policymakers often have conflicting ideas about the best means to achieve the selected goals. These differences are not always easy to resolve.

Solving Goal Conflicts. Even when conflicts between different groups of policymakers are resolved, actual policies may cause conflicts between various goals. In the mid-1980s, for example, Congress considered reducing the minimum wage for teenagers to decrease youth unemployment. Supporters of the reduced minimum wage for teenagers argued that this plan would promote economic stability—especially full employment—by increasing the size of the labor force. Opponents countered that reducing the minimum wage for teenagers would affect the goal of economic equity. Teenagers would be forced to work for lower wages than those paid to adult workers. Other opponents claimed that economic security for adult workers would be decreased because employers would hire the lower-paid teenagers in place of adult workers.

If a nation is to maintain economic equity, it must balance the needs of the entire society with the needs of special groups, such as the elderly.

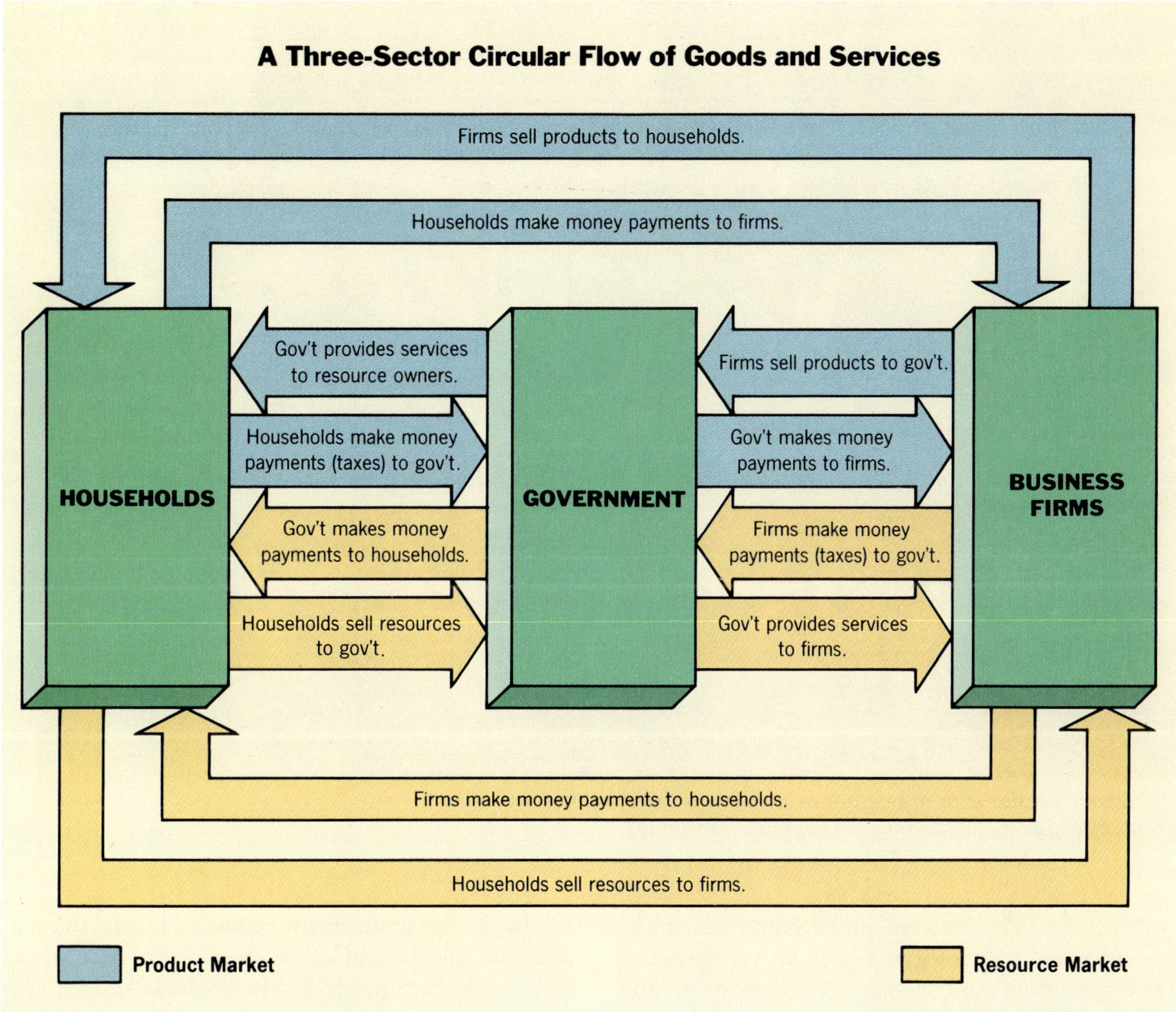

The Circular Flow Model of the Economy

The **circular flow model** shows how resources, products, and money payments are exchanged in the United States economy. The model, shown in the diagram above, is a simplified view of how the economy functions and how the three major participants—households, the government, and business firms—interact.

The Markets. The circular flow model is divided in half. The top half is the **product market.** The product market represents all of the exchanges of goods and services in the economy. Business firms produce products for sale to households and the government. Households and the government, in turn, make money payments to the business firms in exchange for the products.

The bottom half of the model is the resource market. The **resource market** represents the exchange of resources between households—the individuals who own the factors of production—and business firms and the government—the users of the resources.

The money payments that households receive from business firms and the government in exchange for the households' resources are called **income.** Households receive income in the form of rents (in exchange for natural resources), wages (in

The flower vendor is as important as a huge corporation in helping to circulate products and money through the economy.

exchange for labor), interest (in exchange for capital resources and technology), and profit (in exchange for entrepreneurship). Rents, wages, interest, and profits provide the motive for people to work, save, invest, and produce.

The Flows. In the product market, products are exchanged for money payments. In the resource market, resources are exchanged for money payments. Thus, there are two types of exchanges taking place. These exchanges involve two different types of flows—the flow of resources and products and the flow of money payments. The flows are represented by the arrows in the diagram on page 37.

The resource and product flow shows how resources are converted into finished products and then distributed throughout the economy. Households supply the resources to business firms and the government in the resource market. Business firms then produce products, which are sold to households and the government in the product market. Likewise, the government produces goods and services for the benefit of business firms and households. The government produces goods and services by using the resources it purchases from households in the resource market.

The second flow is the money flow. In the resource market, business firms and the government make money payments to households in exchange for the households' resources. Once households receive their money payments, they continue the money flow by purchasing products in the product market. By doing this, households return money to the business firms. Business firms then use the money payments to purchase additional resources from households. The money flow also is continued by the money payments that business firms and households make to the government. These money payments take the form of taxes paid to the government. The government uses the money payments to provide goods and services to business firms and households.

See Suggested Assignments, p. TM 5

Section 3 Review See Answers, p. A 6.

DEFINE free enterprise system, private property, contract, competition, standard of living, circular flow model

IDENTIFY public sector, private sector

1. **Summarizing Ideas** **(a)** Discuss the importance of free enterprise in the United States. **(b)** What is the role of competition in a free enterprise system?
2. **Organizing Ideas** **(a)** Outline the features of the United States economy. **(b)** Describe the goals of the United States economy.
3. **Evaluating Ideas** Which economic goal do you feel is the most important? Why?
4. **Interpreting Graphics** Study the chart on page 37. **(a)** What does the chart show? **(b)** What do the arrows on the chart represent?

CHAPTER 1 SUMMARY

Scarcity is the basic fact of economic life. Human wants and needs are always greater than the resources available to satisfy them. Thus choices must be made concerning how best to use the limited resources available. Economics is the study of the choices people make in an effort to satisfy their wants and needs.

A resource is anything that can be used to satisfy a want or need. Resources that can be used to produce goods and services are called factors of production. Economists generally recognize five categories of resources: natural resources, human resources, capital resources, technology, and entrepreneurship.

If a resource is used to produce one item, that same resource cannot be used to produce another item. One item must be sacrificed for the other item. Economists call this sacrifice a trade-off and the sacrificed item an opportunity cost. Production possibilities curves can be used to analyze the trade-offs and opportunity costs involved in producing specific combinations of goods and services.

All nations must answer the three basic questions of economics: (1) What goods and services should be produced? (2) How should these goods and services be produced? (3) For whom should these goods and services be produced? How a nation answers these questions is determined by its economic system.

An economic system is the organized set of procedures that a nation follows in producing and distributing goods and services. Economists have identified four types of economic systems: traditional, command, market, and mixed. In the pure command economy, the government controls economic decision making. In the pure market economy, individuals control economic decision making.

The pure command economy and the pure market economy are models that represent the two extremes of government control. No nation actually has a pure command or a pure market economy. Traditional economies and mixed economies, on the other hand, are actual systems.

The majority of nations in the world have mixed economies. Mixed economies have elements of both the pure-command and the pure-market models. Because mixed economies vary greatly in their characteristics, economists classify them according to their degree of government control. Nations closest to the pure-market model are said to practice capitalism. Nations closest to the pure-command model are said to practice authoritarian socialism. Nations with systems between these two extremes are said to practice democratic socialism.

The economic system of the United States leans heavily toward the pure-market model. Because the economic system of the United States is based on freedom of choice, it is often referred to as a free enterprise system.

In the free enterprise system of the United States, individuals have the right to own private property and enter into contracts; make personal choices and communicate those choices through the price system; engage in free enterprise and competition; and make decisions based on self-interest and the profit motive. Only a limited amount of government intervention exists in the economy. These five features of the free enterprise system assist the economy in reaching six goals. These goals are economic freedom, economic efficiency, economic equity, economic security, economic stability, and economic growth.

Economists use the circular flow model to show how resources, products, and money payments are exchanged in the free enterprise system of the United States.

READING ABOUT ECONOMICS

Using Textbook Features

Within any textbook is a vast amount of information that you have to make your own. To help you understand this information, the textbook has been divided into many parts, each of which has its own function. Some parts help you preview the information you are about to study. Other parts help you study that information. Still other parts help you review what you have just studied. Learning to use the textbook and its parts wisely is an important first move in your study of economics.

The study of economics involves the use of more than one set of tools. The economics textbook itself is just one of these sets. In succeeding chapters you will read about other sets of tools that help you study.

How to Use the Textbook

To get the most from the textbook, use these guidelines.

1. **Use the Table of Contents.** Familiarize yourself with the textbook's Table of Contents, which begins on page v. The Table of Contents gives you an overview of the topics covered and of the textbook's organization.
2. **Study each unit's opening pages.** Begin the study of each unit by taking time to study the unit's opening pages. For example, review the opening pages of Unit One (pages 18-19). Read the unit label and the unit title, and the titles of the chapters in the unit. Consider the relation of the illustration to the unit theme.
3. **Begin at the beginning.** Turn to pages 20-21 for the opening of Chapter 1. Ask yourself questions about what you see on these pages: chapter title, chapter quote, section titles, and a full-page illustration. Note the connection between this page and the chapter's theme.

   Now turn to page 22. Examine the feature labeled "Chapter 1 Study Guide." Read the Chapter Focus which directs you in your study of the chapter. Study the list of terms under the label "Terms to Know." Knowing the meaning of these terms will give you a good understanding of the chapter's material.
4. **Preview the chapter.** Skim the chapter, noting the first section title (page 22) and the other section titles. Under each section title, note the subheadings that give you clues about the details supporting the section's main idea. Note the charts, photographs, and other visuals within each section. Take time to read the captions. Glance at the first Section Review (page 26). Previewing gives you the framework around which the chapter is constructed.
5. **Read the chapter carefully.** Use the textbook's clues to help you get the most out of your reading of a chapter. First, use the headings and subheadings as clues to main ideas and supporting details.

   Second, pay attention to words printed in bold black type. These important **boldfaced terms** are highlighted to call attention to their meaning, which can be determined from the sentences around them. Third, on each page review the illustrations and the captions that accompany them before moving on to the next page. Relate the information in the illustrations to the content of your reading. Finally, use the Review at the end of each section to check your reading.
6. **Study the special features.** Each chapter and unit has several special features that add to your knowledge of economics. When you read the features depends on your learning style. *When* you read them is not as important as being sure you *do* read them.

7. **Summarize the chapter.** Each chapter ends with a Chapter Summary (page 39). The Chapter Summary helps you to recap the main ideas of the chapter.
8. **Review the chapter.** The textbook provides a Chapter Review (pages 42-43) and a Unit Review (pages 92–93) to help you check and pinpoint the information that is important.
9. **Use the Reference Section.** The Reference Section is your library of information. It begins on page 465. Familiarize yourself with it now, so you may utilize it later.

Applying the Skill

Complete the following activities.

1. Turn to the Table of Contents. Use it to find the answer to these questions. (a) How many units and chapters does the text have? (b) What is the title of the primary source found on the page labeled "Chapter 7 Review"?

   If you answered that the textbook has 6 units and 19 chapters, and that the title of the primary source on the page labeled "Chapter 7 Review" is "A Philosophy of Unionism in the United States," then you have used the Table of Contents correctly.
2. Turn to the Glossary (page 545) and answer these questions. (a) What is the first entry under "M"? (b) What is the definition of the term **product market?** If you discovered that the first entry under "M" is **M1** and that **product market** is defined as *total exchanges of goods and services in an economy,* you have made good use of the Glossary.

Practicing the Skill

The titles, headings, and subheadings of Chapter 1 can be used to formulate a working outline. Study the sample outline on this page. Compare the outline items with the headings and subheadings of Chapter 1. On a sheet of paper, copy the outline, filling in the missing parts.

Economics and Economic Systems

I. **Economics examines how people use scarce resources to produce and consume goods and services.**
   A. **The Factors of Production**
      1. Natural Resources
      2. Human Resources
      3. Capital Resources
      4. Technology
      5. Entrepreneurship
   B. **Trade-offs and Opportunity Costs**
   C. Production Possibilities
      1. Current Production Possibilities
      2. Future Production Possibilities

II. **The answers to the basic economic questions are determined by a nation's economic system.**
   A. **Answering Basic Questions**
      1. Production Choices
      2. Resource Choices
      3. Distribution Choices
   B. Answers in Traditional Economies
   C. **Answers in Command Economies**
   D. **Answers in Market Economies**
   E. Answers in Mixed Economies
      1. Capitalism
      2. Authoritarian Socialism
      3. Democratic Socialism

III. **The features and goals of the United States economy are based on a system of free enterprise.**
   A. The Features of the United States Economy
      1. Private Property and Contracts
      2. Choice and the Price System
      3. Free Enterprise and Competition
      4. Self-Interest and Profit
      5. Limited Government Interference
   B. The Goals of the United States Economy
      1. Economic Freedom
      2. Economic Efficiency
      3. Economic Equity
      4. Economic Security
      5. Economic Stability
      6. Economic Growth
   C. **Economic Goals in Conflict**
      1. Setting Priorities
      2. Conflicting Group Interests
      3. Solving Goal Conflicts
   D. The Circular Flow Model of the Economy
      1. The Markets
      2. The Flows

CHAPTER 1 REVIEW

For Answers to Chapter 1 Review, see p. A 7.

Reviewing Economic Terms

Supply the economic term that correctly completes each sentence.

1. The term referring to both goods and services is ______.
2. The organized set of procedures for producing and distributing goods and services is a nation's ______ ______.
3. A pure command economy is sometimes called a ______ ______ because it is controlled by central planners.
4. The amount of money that remains after all costs of production have been paid is the ______.
5. Nations with economies that are closest to the pure-market model are said to practice ______.
6. A system in which business can be conducted freely with only limited government intervention is a ______ ______ system.
7. Full employment and stable prices is the goal of ______ ______.
8. One of the first people to attempt to explain how the market operates in a pure market economy was the Scottish economist ______ ______.
9. How resources, products, and money are exchanged in the United States economy is illustrated by the ______ ______ ______.
10. The overall economic well-being of people is often called their ______ ______ ______.

Exercising Economic Skills

1. **Using Textbook Features** Turn to the Table of Contents. Use it to list the titles and page locations of the special features in Chapter 1.
2. **Preparing a Personal Budget** Study the feature on pages 508–509. Then **(a)** list the expenses you anticipate you will have for one week. Be sure to include all your expenses, no matter how small. **(b)** Record all your expenses for one week. **(c)** Divide your weekly expenses into fixed and flexible expenses and label them according to the major expense categories discussed on pages 508–509. **(d)** In a paragraph, explain how you think you could reduce your weekly expenses.

Thinking Critically About Economics

1. **Summarizing Ideas** **(a)** What subject does economics study? **(b)** What are the three basic questions of economics? **(c)** What features of the United States economy make it a free enterprise system?
2. **Organizing Ideas** List and describe the four types of economies.
3. **Comprehending Ideas** **(a)** What is a resource? **(b)** What is a factor of production? **(c)** Name the five factors of production?
4. **Interpreting Ideas** **(a)** Explain the problem of scarcity as an economic consideration. **(b)** Explain the significance of opportunity cost in economic decision making.
5. **Contrasting Ideas** How do the command economy and the market economy differ in answering the basic economic questions?
6. **Analyzing Ideas** **(a)** List and describe the economic goals of the United States economy. **(b)** What conflict exists between economic efficiency and economic stability?

Extending Economic Knowledge

1. **(a)** List three products for which you think demand will increase in the next five years. **(b)** What changes in the factors of production do you think will be necessary to meet the increased demand for each product? **(c)** List three resources that you think will be scarcer in five years than they are today. **(d)** What products do you think this increased scarcity will affect?
2. **(a)** From newspapers or magazines, collect one article that deals with economic choice on an international level, one that deals with economic choice on a national level, and one that deals with economic choice on a state or local level. **(b)** To accompany each article, write a statement that explains the opportunity cost involved in the economic choice.
3. Draw a production possibilities curve that illustrates what effect technological advancement would have on the production of luxury automobiles in the United States.

Using Primary Sources

Milton Friedman (1912–) is the author of many books on economics and one of the most influential economists in the United States. In *Free to Choose: A Personal Statement* (1980), co-authored with his wife Rose, Friedman argues that capitalism is the fairest and most productive type of economic system. As you read the following excerpt from the book, consider why Friedman believes that the economic freedoms under capitalism promote economic equity, efficiency, and growth.

Capitalism, Freedom, and Equality

Everywhere in the world there are gross inequalities of income and wealth. They offend most of us. Few can fail to be moved by the contrast between the luxury enjoyed by some and the grinding poverty suffered by others.

In the past century a myth has grown up that free market capitalism—equality of opportunity as we have interpreted that term—increases such inequalities, that it is a system under which the rich exploit the poor.

Nothing could be further from the truth. Wherever the free market has been permitted to operate, wherever anything approaching equality of opportunity has existed, the ordinary man has been able to attain levels of living never dreamed of before. Nowhere is the gap between rich and poor wider, nowhere are the rich richer and the poor poorer, than in those societies that do not permit the free market to operate. That is true of feudal societies like medieval Europe, India before independence, and much of modern South America, where inherited status determines position. It is equally true of centrally planned societies, like Russia [the Soviet Union] or China [the People's Republic] or India since independence, where access to government determines position. It is true even where central planning was introduced, as in all three of these countries, in the name of equality.

Russia [the Soviet Union] is a country of two nations: a small privileged upper class of bureaucrats, Communist party officials, technicians; and a great mass of people living little better than their great-grandparents did. . . .

China [the People's Republic], too, is a nation with wide differences in income—between the politically powerful and the rest; between city and countryside; between some workers in the cities and other workers. . . . We must conclude that China is far from a society of complete equality. . . .

A society that puts equality—in the sense of equality of outcome—ahead of freedom will end up with neither equality nor freedom. The use of force to achieve equality will destroy freedom. . . .

On the other hand, a society that puts freedom first will, as a happy by-product, end up with both greater freedom and greater equality. Though a by-product of freedom, greater equality is not an accident. A free society releases the energies and abilities of people to pursue their own objectives. It prevents some people from arbitrarily suppressing others. It does not prevent some people from achieving positions of privilege, but . . . those positions of privilege . . . are subject to continued attack by other able, ambitious people. Freedom . . . preserves the opportunity for today's disadvantaged to become tomorrow's privileged. . . .

Source Review

For Answers to Source Review, see p. A 8.

1. How does Friedman interpret the term "free market capitalism"?
2. Friedman states that a myth concerning capitalism has evolved over the past century. What is this myth? What arguments does Friedman make to dispel this myth?
3. Friedman contrasts the terms equality and equal opportunity. How does Friedman define equality? What does he say about the use of force to achieve equality?
4. Why does Friedman believe that capitalism is the fairest and most efficient type of economic system?

EATON'S
GOURMET PASSAGE

CHAPTER 2

See Chapter Overview, p. TM 6.
See Chapter Objectives, p. TM 6.
See Introducing the Chapter, p. TM 6.
See Extending Economic Knowledge on text p. 56.

Demand in the Marketplace

We might as well reasonably dispute whether it is the upper or the lower blade of a pair of scissors that cuts a piece of paper, as whether value is governed by [demand] or [supply].

Alfred Marshall

1 The forces affecting demand play a major role in the free enterprise system.

- The Law of Demand
- A Demand Schedule
- A Demand Curve

2 Price does not affect the demand for all products to the same degree.

- Elastic Demand
- Inelastic Demand

3 In addition to price, five nonprice factors affect demand.

- Consumer Tastes and Preferences
- Market Size
- Income
- Prices of Related Goods
- Consumer Expectations

CHAPTER 2 STUDY GUIDE

Chapter Focus

Chapter 2 analyzes the factors that determine demand in the free enterprise system. The chapter discusses the law of demand and the degree to which price affects demand for all products. The chapter concludes with a discussion of the five nonprice factors that determine demand.

As you study the chapter, look for the details that support each of the following statements.

1. The forces affecting demand play a major role in the free enterprise system.
2. Price does not affect the demand for all products to the same degree.
3. In addition to price, five nonprice factors affect demand.

See Preteaching Vocabulary, p. TM 6.

Terms to Know

The following terms, while not the only terms emphasized in this chapter, are basic to your understanding of demand. Determine the meaning of each term, either by using the Glossary or by watching for context clues as you read the chapter.

demand
purchasing power
income effect
substitution effect
utility
diminishing marginal utility
demand schedule
demand curve
elastic demand
inelastic demand
substitute good
complementary good

See Key Study Questions and Key Understandings, p. TM 7.

1 The forces affecting demand play a major role in the free enterprise system.

See Suggested Teaching Strategies, p. TM 7.

In economic terms, demand is more than simply wanting something. Rather, **demand** is the amount of a good or service a consumer is willing and able to buy at various prices during a given time period.

◆ This definition of demand contains two important conditions. First, the consumer must be *willing* and *able* to buy the good or service. In other words, the person must want the product and be able to pay for it. Second, demand for the product must be examined for a *specific time period*—a day, a week, a month, a year, or some other definite period. The time period under study must be specific because various factors that change over time can affect the demand for a product.

To understand the significance of the two conditions, consider the following example. Mike Morris is shopping for a new car. He is looking for a car that meets certain requirements—good gas mileage, a reputation for few repairs, a good safety record, and an attractive design. Mike would love to have a Mercedes Benz. He thinks it meets all of his requirements. But the price of the Mercedes Benz is more than he is willing and able to pay. Regretfully, Mike has to look for another kind of car to buy. Mike Morris, at this particular time, does not add to the demand for Mercedes Benz automobiles. This does not mean, however, that Mike might not find himself both willing and able to buy a Mercedes Benz at some time in the future.

The Law of Demand

In a free enterprise system, an inverse, or opposite, relationship between price and demand exists. The **law of demand** states that an increase in price causes a decrease in the quantity demanded, while a decrease in price causes an increase in the quantity demanded. For example, if the price of compact disc players rises from $300 to $400, consumers will be willing and able to buy fewer compact disc players. In other words, the price increase will lead to a decrease in the quantity demanded. If the price for the

◆ Have the students read "Shopping Wisely" on pages 510–511 of the *Everyday Economics Handbook* and answer the questions that follow.

players falls to $200, however, the quantity demanded will increase.

Three economic concepts can be used to explain the law of demand. These concepts are (1) the income effect, (2) the substitution effect, and (3) diminishing marginal utility.

Income Effect. The amount of money that individuals have available to spend on goods and services is referred to as their **purchasing power.** As the purchasing power of individuals increases, their demand for goods and services also increases. An individual's purchasing power is affected by the prices charged for goods and services. When the price of a product is lowered, an individual can buy more of the product with the same amount of income. When the price of a product is increased, an individual can buy less of the product with the same amount of income. The increase or decrease in purchasing power brought on by changes in prices is called the **income effect.**

Substitution Effect. The substitution effect also influences the demand for a good or service. The **substitution effect** refers to the tendency of consumers to substitute a lower-priced product, such as a generic product, for a relatively more expensive product. As the price of a product increases, the demand for lower-priced alternative products also increases. For example, when the price of steak increases, the demand for chicken—a lower-priced substitute—increases.

Diminishing Marginal Utility. The amount of satisfaction an individual receives from consuming a product affects demand for that product. In economic terms, the amount of satisfaction that an individual receives from consuming a product is called **utility.** While it might seem that utility would increase as more and more of a product is consumed, this does not happen. In reality, as more units of a product are consumed, the utility received from consuming each additional unit declines. Economists label this phenomenon the law of **diminishing marginal utility.** As utility declines, demand for the product also declines. At some point, an individual will consume more of a product only if the price is lowered.

Consider the following example of diminishing marginal utility. Betty Baxter is in a Wednesday night bowling league. Her team is tied for first place. The final night of the league is the next Wednesday night. Baxter decides to spend Saturday afternoon practicing for Wednesday night's series in hopes of sharpening her game for the league championship.

Economics Reporter

What Are Generic Products?

Generic products are nonbrand name products. The characteristics of these products are the same as brand name products. Popular in Europe, generic products were first introduced to United States markets in 1977. They sell for up to 40 percent less than brand names. Generic products had their highest United States sales in 1982, at the height of the last recession when consumer purchasing power was very low. Generic products still occupy store shelves. Retailers and manufacturers feel that if the economy slows down or inflation increases, expansion of the generic market is always possible.

Higher prices cause many shoppers to substitute less expensive packaged meats for fresh-cut meats.

The Demand for Car Stereos

Demand Schedule

Price per Car Stereo	Car Stereos Demanded
$210	0
$190	1,000
$170	2,000
$150	3,000
$130	4,000
$110	5,000
$ 90	6,000

Demand Curve

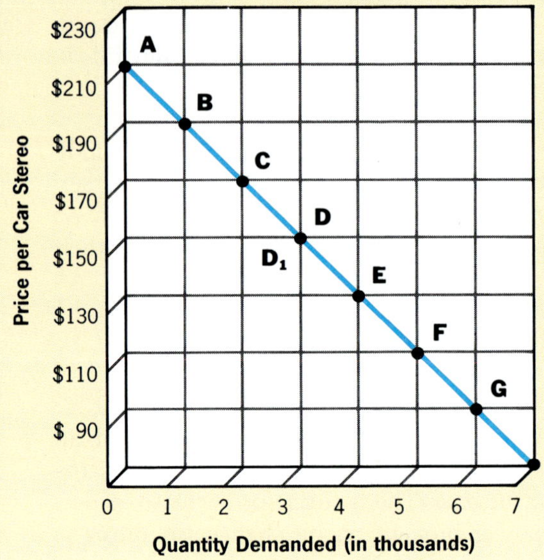

The bowling alley charges $1.00 for each game on Saturday afternoon. Baxter gladly pays the $1.00 for her first game. The utility that she receives from the game is worth the $1.00 price. So are the next four games. The fifth game she bowls, however, provides her with slightly less satisfaction than the first four. Through the next three games, she receives less satisfaction from each game she bowls. At this point, Baxter will bowl an additional game only if the price is lowered.

A Demand Schedule

Economists often construct a **demand schedule** to show the inverse relationship between the price of a good or service and the quantity consumers demand. This schedule lists the quantity of goods that consumers are willing and able to buy at a series of possible prices for the good.

Consider the example of car stereos as shown in the demand schedule on this page. The schedule shows that as prices increase from $90 to $210, the quantity demanded decreases. The quantity demanded will be 6,000 stereos when the price is $90. None, however, will be purchased when the price is $210 a stereo.

A Demand Curve

Economists also construct demand curves to illustrate patterns of demand. A **demand curve** plots the information from the demand schedule to illustrate the inverse relationship between price and the quantity demanded. The demand curve $\mathbf{D_1}$ shows all of the possible combinations of prices and quantities demanded at points **A** through **G.** The curve slopes downward, reflecting the greater quantity that consumers will buy at lower prices.

See Suggested Assignments, p. TM 7.

Section 1 Review See Answers, p. A 8.

DEFINE demand, purchasing power, utility

1. **Summarizing Ideas** **(a)** What are the two conditions contained in the definition of demand? **(b)** What is the law of demand? **(c)** What is the substitution effect?
2. **Interpreting Graphics** Study the graphics on page 48. What is the relationship between the demand schedule and the demand curve?

See Key Study Questions and Key Understandings, p. TM 8.

2 Price does not affect the demand for all products to the same degree.

See Suggested Teaching Strategies, p. TM 8.

Changes in a good's price often affect demand. The degree to which changes in a good's price affect the quantity demanded by consumers is called the **elasticity of demand.** The demand for a good or service can be elastic or inelastic.

Elastic Demand

Elastic demand exists when a small *increase* in a good's price causes a major *decrease* in the quantity demanded. Elastic demand also exists when a small *decrease* in a good's price causes a major *increase* in the quantity demanded. In general, items that are not necessities or for which there are many substitutes have elastic demand.

For most people, blank cassette tapes are not necessities. These are products for which demand is elastic. Several companies compete to sell blank tapes in the United States, contributing to this elastic demand. For example, Company BCT tries to increase its share of the market by decreasing the price of its tapes from $2.50 to $1.50. Other companies producing tapes, on the other hand, keep the price of their blank tapes at $2.50. The demand for Company BCT's tapes is most likely to increase dramatically as shown on the graph on this page. The demand curve D_1 is almost horizontal, showing that even a small decrease in the price of Company BCT's tapes causes a large increase in the quantity demanded. At point **A**, for example, the quantity demanded is only 100,000 tapes. By dropping the price just $1.00—from $2.50 to $1.50—the quantity demanded increases to 600,000.

The demand for blank cassette tapes is elastic. The demand for the tapes is elastic because many companies offer similar products. If Company BCT is the only company selling blank cassette tapes in the United States, the company can increase its price without suffering a decline in sales. Competition, however, means that price increases will decrease the quantity demanded so drastically that all companies will try to keep prices low in order to compete in the marketplace.

Elastic Demand for Blank Cassette Tapes

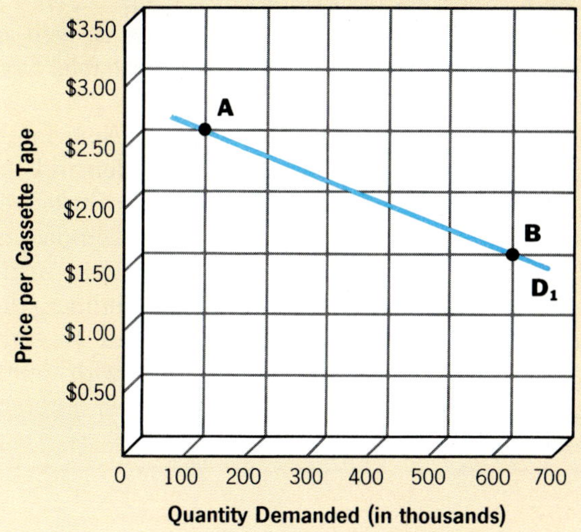

CASE STUDY

Elastic Demand and People Express

In 1981 a new airline, People Express, began offering low-cost flights from Newark, New Jersey, to several cities across the United States. The flights did not offer the complimentary meals or baggage handling that most competing airlines offered. The lower fares, however, attracted so many passengers that the airline rapidly expanded. By 1985, People Express had added routes throughout the United States and Europe.

By 1986, however, People Express was in financial trouble. Buoyed by optimistic plans for the future, the airline had added several routes that attracted too few passengers to be profitable. People Express also bought several other airlines that proved unprofitable. In addition, full-service airlines, those that offered complimentary meals and baggage handling, cut their fares to compete with People Express fares. Finally, People Express acquired a reputation for late flights and poor service. The inconveniences suffered by customers led many of them to fly with other airlines.

People Express is an example of elastic demand in action in the free enterprise system. By offering

◆ Deregulation of the airline industry also paved the way for other airlines, such as Presidential Airways and Florida Express, to offer low-cost service.

slightly lower prices, the airline significantly increased demand for its flights. Even though airline travel for most People Express passengers was not a necessity and substitutes—other airlines as well as other modes of transportation—were available, travelers took advantage of the low fares.

Other airlines responded by lowering their fares. As increased competition lessened the demand for People Express flights, the airline became a takeover target. In December of 1986, Texas Air Corporation acquired People Express. The acquisition made Texas Air, which also owns four other airlines, the largest airline carrier in the United States. In early 1987, Texas Air merged People Express with Continental Airlines and dropped the People Express name.

Inelastic Demand

◆ **Inelastic demand** exists when a change in a good's price has little impact on the quantity demanded. A good that is viewed as a necessity and has few substitutes often has an inelastic demand.

Inelastic Demand for Home Heating Oil

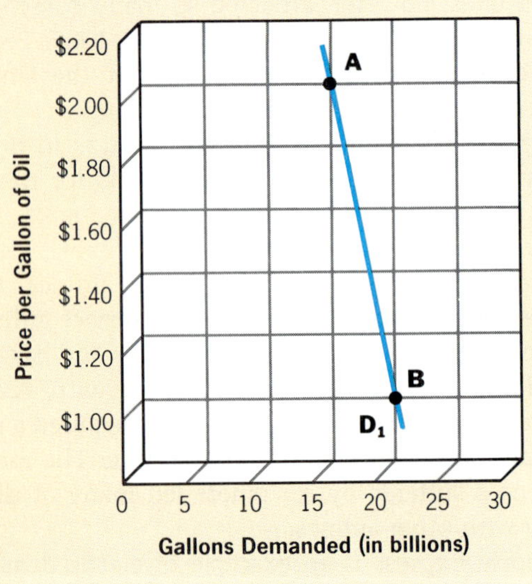

Home heating oil is an example of a good with an inelastic demand. Many homes in the United States are heated with oil. During the cold winter months, especially in climates that have severely low winter temperatures, home heating oil is essential for survival. Wood, coal, and natural gas are substitutes for heating oil. But changing to a substitute means spending a substantial amount of money to install a new heating system.

The graph on this page illustrates the inelastic demand curve for home heating oil. The demand curve $\mathbf{D_1}$ is almost vertical, showing that even after a large decrease in the price of a gallon of heating oil there is a relatively small change in the quantity demanded. At point **A**, for example, the price per gallon is \$2.00. At this price the quantity demanded throughout the United States is 15 billion gallons. If the price for each gallon decreases to \$1.00, the quantity demanded increases to 20 billion gallons, representing only a 25 percent increase ($20b - 15b = 5b$; $5b \div 20b = 0.25$, or 25%) in the quantity demanded, compared to a 100 percent decrease (\$2.00 − \$1.00 = \$1.00; \$1.00 ÷ 2.00 = 0.50 or 50%) in the product's price.

See Suggested Assignments, p. TM 8.

Section 2 Review See Answers, p. A 9.

DEFINE elasticity of demand

1. **Summarizing Ideas** **(a)** Describe the two cause-effect relationships that illustrate elastic demand. **(b)** Which of the two descriptions fits the elastic demand for Company BCT's tapes? Why?
2. **Understanding Ideas** **(a)** List five items that have an elastic demand. **(b)** List five items that have an inelastic demand.
3. **Comparing Ideas** Explain the difference between elastic demand and inelastic demand.
4. **Analyzing Ideas** **(a)** What factor was most responsible for increasing the demand for People Express tickets? **(b)** Explain how the substitution effect affected People Express.
5. **Interpreting Graphics** Study the graphs on pages 49 and 50. How do the two graphs illustrate the difference between elastic demand and inelastic demand?

 ◆ Discussion topic: Whether insulin is an example of inelastic demand.

DECISION MAKERS IN THE ECONOMY

Wilma P. Mankiller

Wilma P. Mankiller became the first female leader of a major American Indian nation when she was installed as Principal Chief of the Cherokee Nation on December 14, 1985. Mankiller had been elected Deputy Principal Chief in 1983 as the running mate of Ross O. Swimmer. After Swimmer left to head the United States Bureau of Indian Affairs, Mankiller automatically was named to serve out the remainder of his term.

Mankiller has said that running the 67,000-member Cherokee tribe is "like running a tiny, tiny country." The Cherokees are the second-largest nation in the United States after the Navajos. As the Cherokee chief, Mankiller must oversee 45,000 acres of land in northeastern Oklahoma. She also directs the Cherokees' many businesses, which include a motel and restaurant, a cattle and poultry ranch, a greenhouse, and an electronics manufacturing firm. In addition, she administers federal and state-funded assistance that totals approximately $20 million a year.

Mankiller's specific goals as leader include tackling three continuing problems among the Cherokees. They are unemployment, lack of education, and inadequate health care. She also wants to reduce the Cherokees' dependence on federal funds. Mankiller hopes to find new sources of income and new businesses to operate. Her goal is particularly important because of recent and projected cuts in the federal budget. Mankiller already has convinced many people that she can achieve her stated objectives.

See Key Study Questions and Key Understandings, p. TM 9.

3 In addition to price, five nonprice factors affect demand.

See Suggested Teaching Strategies, p. TM 9.

When economists develop a simple demand curve like the one on page 48, they are looking at the effect of price on the quantity demanded at a specific point in time. Changes in the quantity demanded indicate movement along the demand curve.

As the demand curve shows, a decrease in the price of blank cassette tapes has resulted in an increase in the quantity demanded—from point **A** to point **B.** In this example, nonprice factors that might affect demand are held constant. These nonprice factors, which are known collectively as the **determinants of demand,** include (1) consumer ◆ tastes and preferences, (2) the size of the market, (3) people's income, (4) the prices of related goods, and (5) consumer expectations.

Over time, however, the nonprice factors fluctuate. Changes in demand resulting from these fluctuations create an entirely new demand curve. In economic terms, the old demand curve has shifted. When the nonprice factors increase demand, the entire curve shifts to the right. When the nonprice factors decrease demand, the entire curve shifts to the left.

Consumer Tastes and Preferences

One of the most important of the nonprice factors that can change over time and shift the demand curve to the right or left is consumer tastes and preferences. The popularity of different rock groups, for example, has changed over the years. When a group's popularity increases, the demand for the group's appearances in concerts and on television

Text continues on page 54.

◆ Have the students read "Market Researchers" on page 543 of *Careers in the Marketplace.*

BUILDING ECONOMIC SKILLS

INTERPRETING THE VISUAL RECORD

Using Graphs

Many types of economic data are presented in the form of graphs. Graphs are visual representations of information, especially statistical data. The three most important types of graphs are: line graphs, bar graphs, and circle graphs.

Line graphs and bar graphs are useful in showing changes and trends involving quantities or amounts over time. These graphs have a vertical axis and a horizontal axis. Usually, the quantity or amount is listed on the vertical axis, and the time period—measured in days, months, years, or decades—is listed on the horizontal axis.

A circle graph shows percentages, or parts per hundred. Circle graphs are sometimes called pie graphs.

How to Use Graphs

Follow these guidelines when using graphs.

1. **Define the graph's purpose.** Identify the type of graph shown. Read the title of the graph.
2. **Study the graph's parts.** Identify the information on the graph.
3. **Analyze the information.** In a line or bar graph, note time periods and increases or decreases in amounts. In a circle graph, note the relationship of each part to the whole, ranking the percentages from greatest to least.
4. **Put the data to use.** Formulate conclusions based on the data shown.

Graph A

Manufactured Units of Compact Disc Players in the United States

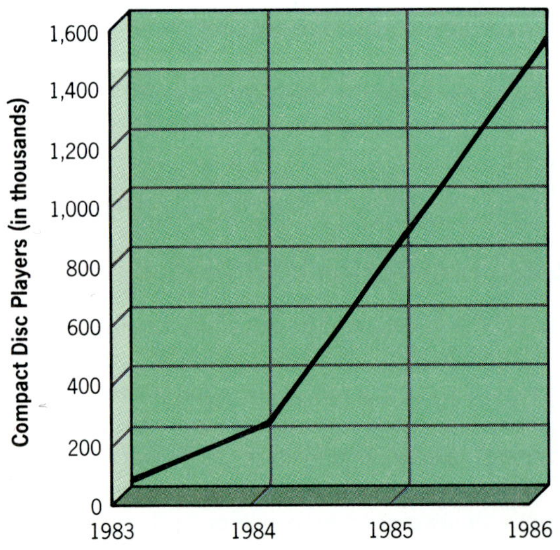

Graph B

Manufactured Units of Compact Disc Players in the United States

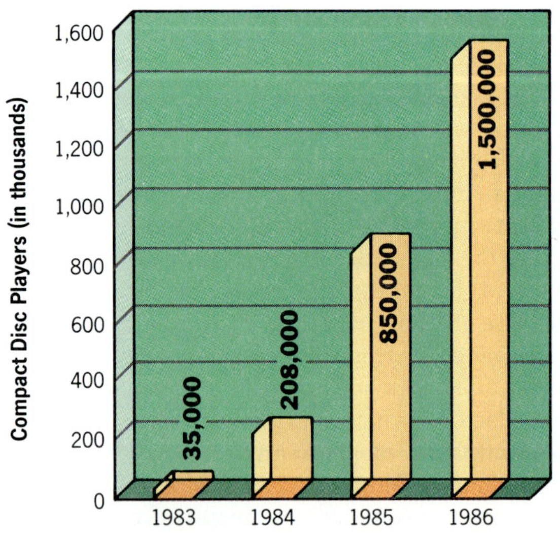

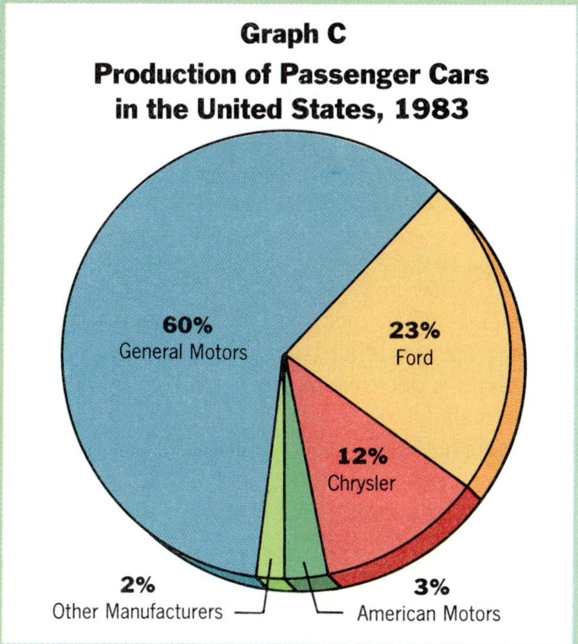

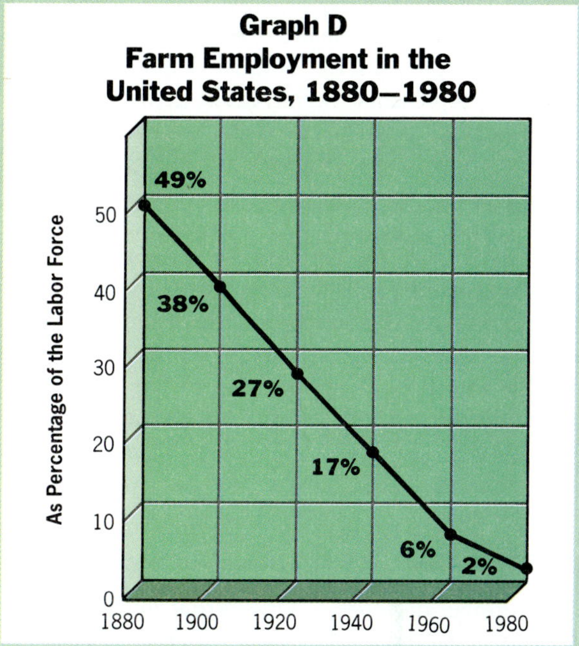

Applying the Skill

Study graphs A and B, using the steps outlined above.

1. The title of graphs A and B is the same. The graphs cover the time period from 1983 to 1986. On the horizontal axis is the time period. The quantities of Compact Disc Players (CDPs) are shown along the vertical axis. From both graphs you see that the number, or supply, of CDPs in the United States increased from 35,000 in 1983 to about 1.5 million in 1986. The upward trend illustrated in the line graph and the bar graph shows the growing popularity of CDPs in American markets.
2. Study graph C. Graph C is a circle graph which gives information on the percentage of passenger cars produced in the United States. The graph has five sets of percentages. General Motors (60%), Ford (23%), Chrysler (12%), American Motors (3%), and other manufacturers (2%). These five sets of manufacturers supply 100 percent of American-made cars. One major conclusion that can be drawn from this circle graph is that in 1983 General Motors was the dominant producer of passenger cars in the United States.

Practicing the Skill

Study graph D. Then on a separate sheet of paper, answer each question.

1. Graph D is a **(a)** line graph, **(b)** bar graph, **(c)** circle graph.
2. Graph D is about **(a)** the growing percentage of the labor force employed in farm occupations, **(b)** the decrease of manufacturing jobs in the United States, **(c)** the declining percentage of the labor force in farm occupations.
3. The percentage of workers employed in farm occupations dropped the most between **(a)** 1880 and 1920, **(b)** 1900 and 1940, **(c)** 1920 and 1960, **(d)** 1940 and 1980.
4. The percentage of workers employed in farm occupations dropped the least between **(a)** 1880 and 1920, **(b)** 1900 and 1940, **(c)** 1920 and 1960, **(d)** 1940 and 1980.
5. Select each conclusion that can be drawn from the graph. **(a)** In 1880, 51% of the American labor force was employed in farm occupations. **(b)** The overall trend in farm employment is increasing. **(c)** Most workers today are employed in nonfarm occupations.

Practicing the Skill Answers: 1. (a), 2. (c), 3. (a), 4. (d), 5. (c)

increases. Likewise, the demand for the group's recorded music increases.

The left-hand graph on this page illustrates the favorable shift in demand for Group X's cassette tapes. **D_1** represents the original demand for these tapes. **D_2** represents the increased demand. The **D_2** curve, by shifting to the right, shows that consumers are willing to buy more of this group's tapes at each price.

A group's popularity may decrease the following year, decreasing the demand for the group's tapes. The right-hand graph on this page shows the shift to the left as this important determinant of demand—tastes and preferences—moves in an unfavorable direction. **D_3**, by shifting to the left, shows that consumers want fewer of this group's tapes at ◆ each price.

Market Size

The number of potential buyers that might demand a particular product determines market size. If the market size is large, producers can anticipate high demand. If the market size is small, producers can anticipate low demand.

The size of a market sometimes results from economic decisions. For example, a company producing pineapple-grapefruit juice might try to increase the number of buyers by launching a national advertising campaign—a private sector economic decision.

The government might also initiate policies that increase the market for American products. The opening of trade with the People's Republic of China in the early 1980s, for example, created a sizable market for American goods.

Income

In general, when people's income increases, the demand for goods and services increases. On the other hand, a decrease in the general level of income decreases demand.

Although the demand for most goods increases as income rises, a few exceptions exist. Suppose, for example, that a family eats beef once each week for dinner. As the household's income increases, the family switches from less expensive ground beef to higher-priced steak. Thus, the higher income leads to an increase in the demand for steak. The higher income, on the other hand, also causes the demand for ground beef to decrease. In this instance, the substitution effect is working in reverse. The higher-priced steak is being substituted for the lower-priced hamburger.

The Effects of Changing Tastes and Preferences on Demand

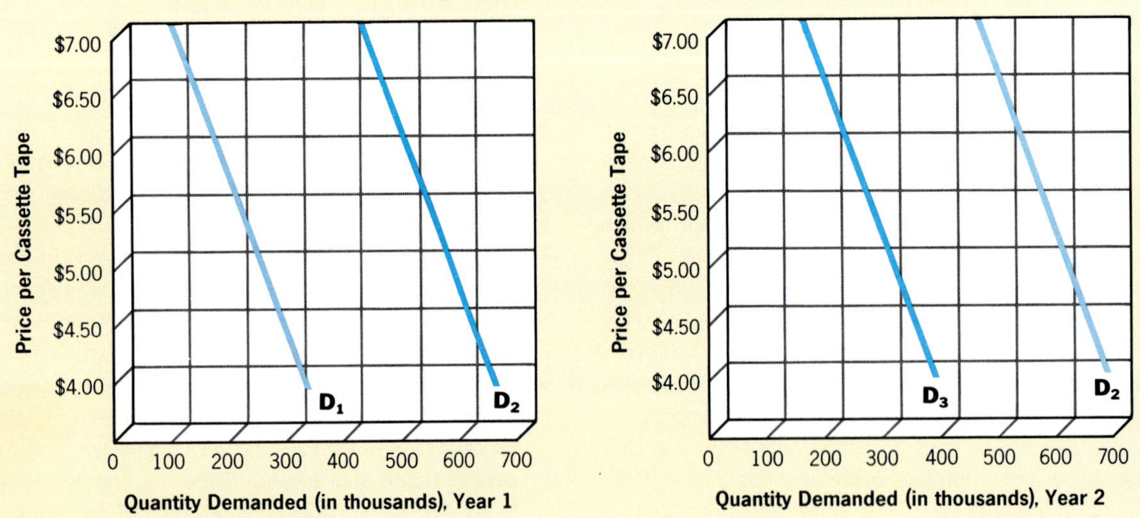

 ◆ Report topic: Why consumer tastes change as people get older.

Prices of Related Goods

The demand for one good is often connected to the demand for other goods related to it. **Related goods** are often classified as either substitute goods or complementary goods.

Substitute goods are goods that can be used to replace purchases of other goods when prices rise. Price changes for one good often affect demand for the possible substitutes of that good. For example, price changes for butter can affect the demand for margarine. When the price of butter increases, people consume less butter, using margarine in place of butter. The demand for margarine, as a substitute good, then increases. When the price of butter decreases, on the other hand, the overall demand for margarine often decreases.

Complementary goods are goods that are commonly used with other goods. Paint applicators and paint, for example, are complementary goods. An increase in the price of one of the complementary goods causes demand for both goods to decline. A decrease in the price of one of the complementary goods causes the demand for both goods to increase.

Rob's Paint Store, for example, regularly sells paint for $20 a gallon. To increase sales, Rob reduces the price for a gallon of paint to $15. He anticipates that the lower sale price will increase demand for the paint. At the same time, he expects the demand for paint applicators to increase, reasoning that people will need to apply the newly purchased paint. Conversely, when the paint returns to its regular price of $20 a gallon, the demand for both paint and paint applicators will drop.

Consumer Expectations

People's expectations of their future incomes also affect demand. If, for example, a person anticipates a substantial raise in wages, he or she might decide to increase the demand for goods now. When consumers are optimistic about their future incomes, the general level of demand for all products in the economy increases.

If, on the other hand, a person anticipates a lower income because of a strike or a plant closing, he or she will probably put off major purchases. When consumers are pessimistic about their future incomes, the general level of demand for all products in the economy decreases.

Section 3 Review See Answers, p. A 9.

DEFINE substitute good, complementary good

IDENTIFY Wilma P. Mankiller

1. **Organizing Ideas** List and describe the determinants of demand.
2. **Interpreting Ideas** What are some of the factors that bring about a change in market size?
3. **Interpreting Graphics** Study the graphs on page 54. Draw a graph showing the effect of a change in one of the other determinants of demand.

CHAPTER 2 SUMMARY

Demand is the amount of a good or service a consumer is willing and able to buy at various prices during a given time period. In a free enterprise system, price is one of the most important factors affecting demand. The law of demand states that an increase in price decreases the amount demanded, while a decrease in price increases the amount demanded. Economists use demand schedules and demand curves to chart how much changes in prices alter the quantity demanded.

The demand for goods can be either elastic or inelastic. When a small increase in a good's price causes a major decrease in the quantity demanded or when a small decrease in a good's price causes a major increase in the quantity demanded, demand is elastic. In contrast, inelastic demand occurs when a change in a good's price has little impact on the quantity demanded.

When economists study demand at a specific point in time, they hold the nonprice determinants of demand constant and look at the effect of price on quantity demanded. Changes in quantity demanded result in movement along the demand curve.

Economists also look at changes in demand over time. When economists study changes in demand over time, they are interested in the nonprice determinants of demand. The nonprice determinants of demand are consumer tastes and preferences, market size, people's income, the prices of related goods, and consumer expectations. Changes in any one of these factors produce an entirely new demand curve.

See Suggested Assignments, p. TM 9.

CHAPTER 2 REVIEW

For Answers to Chapter 2 Review, see p. A 10.

Reviewing Economic Terms

With each definition or description below, match correctly one of the following terms.

a. elasticity of demand
b. utility
c. substitute good
d. demand
e. elastic demand

_____ **1.** The amount of a product a consumer is willing and able to buy at various prices during a given time.
_____ **2.** The amount of satisfaction that an individual receives from consuming a product.
_____ **3.** The degree to which a change in a product's price affects the quantity demanded by consumers.
_____ **4.** Item that can be purchased in place of another product when price increases.

Exercising Economic Skills

1. **Using Graphs** Given the imaginary demand schedule below, develop an elastic demand graph that illustrates the experiences of People Express in the mid-1980s.

Demand Schedule

Flights from Newark, NJ to Chicago	
Price	Tickets Purchased
$69	100,000
$79	80,000
$89	60,000
$99	40,000
$109	20,000

2. **Shopping Wisely** Study the feature on pages 510–511. Then select three products to price at a grocery store or drug store. Compare the prices of the generic brands of the products to the name brands. Also compare the unit prices of the products. Prepare a chart to present your findings to the class.

Thinking Critically About Economics

1. **Summarizing Ideas** **(a)** What are the major factors affecting demand? **(b)** Why is a price's effect on some items different from its effect on others? **(c)** Select one determinant of demand and describe how a change in it affects demand.
2. **Interpreting Ideas** Describe the law of diminishing marginal utility, using your favorite product as an example.
3. **Evaluating Ideas** Which determinant of demand is most important? Why?

Extending Economic Knowledge

1. Interview a merchant in your town to discover what effect a recent price change has had in demand for a product. Ask: Was the price change an increase or decrease? What were the reasons for the change in price? Did product sales level off or have they continued to increase or decrease? Present your findings to the class.
2. Using the demand schedule below, complete the following activities. **(a)** Construct a demand curve. **(b)** Use the information on the graph to explain the law of demand for medium-sized pizzas.

Demand Schedule for Medium-Sized Pizzas

Price	Amount Purchased
$5.00	50,000
$6.00	40,000
$7.00	30,000
$8.00	20,000
$9.00	10,000

3. Write a paragraph identifying a product for which demand is highly elastic and a product for which demand is highly inelastic. Write a second paragraph answering the question: Why is demand for some products more elastic than demand for other products?

Using Primary Sources

Alfred Marshall (1842–1924) was a noted English economist and mathematician. In his classic *Principles of Economics*, which was published in 1890, Marshall examined the nature of economics and economic laws. As you read the following excerpts, consider why Marshall believes economics is more "exact" than the other social sciences. Why does he consider economics to be less exact than the physical sciences?

Economics and Economic Laws

Economics is a study of men as they live and move and think in the ordinary business of life. But it concerns itself chiefly with those motives which affect, most powerfully and most steadily, man's conduct in the business part of his life. . . . The steadiest motive to ordinary business work is the desire for the pay which is the material reward of work. The pay may be on its way to be spent selfishly or unselfishly, for noble or base ends; and here the variety of human nature comes into play. But the motive is supplied by a definite amount of money: and it is this definite and exact money measurement of the steadiest motives in business life, which has enabled economics far to outrun every other branch of the study of man. Just as the chemist's fine balance has made chemistry more exact than most other physical sciences; so this economist's balance, rough and imperfect as it is, has made economics more exact than any other branch of social science. But of course economics cannot be compared with the exact physical sciences: for it deals with the ever changing and subtle forces of human nature. . . .

The laws of economics are to be compared with the laws of the tides, rather than with the simple and exact law of gravitation. For the actions of men are so various and uncertain, that the best statement of tendencies, which we can make in a science of human conduct, must needs be inexact and faulty. This might be urged as a reason against making any statements at all on the subject; but that would be almost to abandon life. Life is human conduct, and the thoughts and emotions that grow up around it. . . .

The term "law" means then nothing more than a general proposition or statement of tendencies, more or less certain, more or less definite. . . .

Thus a law of social science, or a *Social Law,* is a statement of social tendencies; that is, a statement that a certain course of action may be expected under certain conditions from the members of a social group.

Economic laws, or statements of economic tendencies, are those social laws which relate to branches of conduct in which the strength of the motives chiefly concerned can be measured by a money price.

There is thus no hard and sharp line of division between those social laws which are, and those which are not, to be regarded also as economic laws. For there is a continuous gradation from social laws concerned almost exclusively with motives that can be measured by price, to social laws in which such motives have little place; and which are therefore generally as much less precise and exact than economic laws. . . .

Source Review

For Answers to Source Review, see p. A 10.

1. How does Marshall define *economics*?
2. Why does Marshall state that economics is more "exact" than the other social sciences? Why is the use of money so important to his explanation?
3. Why does Marshall say that the study of economics is less exact than the study of the physical sciences?
4. How does Marshall define the term *economic law*? What is the difference between the terms *economic law* and *social law*? How are the definitions of these terms similar? Why are these definitions important to the study of economics?

CHAPTER 3

See Chapter Overview, p. TM 10.
See Chapter Objectives, p. TM 10.
See Introducing the Chapter, p. TM 10.
See Extending Economic Knowledge on text p. 72.

Supply in the Marketplace

Without development there is no profit, without profit no development. For the capitalist system, it must be added further that without profit, there would be no accumulation of wealth.

Joseph A. Schumpeter

1 The forces affecting supply play major roles in the free enterprise system.

- The Law of Supply
- The Supply Curve
- The Profit Motive

2 Price does not affect the supply of all products to the same degree.

- Elastic Supply
- Inelastic Supply

3 In addition to price, six nonprice factors affect supply.

- Technological Improvement
- Resource Prices
- Taxes and Subsidies
- Price Changes and Expectations
- Market Competition

4 The cost of production affects the supply of goods and services.

- The Costs of Production
- The Law of Diminishing Returns

CHAPTER 3 STUDY GUIDE

Chapter Focus

Chapter 3 analyzes the factors that determine supply in the free enterprise system. The chapter examines the law of supply and the degree to which price affects the supply of products. The chapter also discusses the six nonprice factors that determine supply.

As you study the chapter, look for details that support each of the following statements.

1. The forces affecting supply play major roles in the free enterprise system.
2. Price does not affect the supply of all products to the same degree.
3. In addition to price, six nonprice factors affect supply.
4. The cost of production affects the supply of goods and services.

See Preteaching Vocabulary, p. TM 10.

Terms to Know

The following terms, while not the only terms emphasized in this chapter, are basic to your understanding of supply in the free enterprise system. Determine the meaning of each term, either by using the Glossary or by watching for context clues as you read the chapter.

profit	determinant of supply
supply	technology
law of supply	subsidy
supply schedule	competition
supply curve	venture capital
revenue	law of diminishing returns
cost of production	
elastic supply	
inelastic supply	

See Key Study Questions and Key Understandings, p. TM 11.

1 The forces affecting supply play major roles in the free enterprise system.

See Suggested Teaching Strategies, p. TM 11.

◆ The major incentive for producers is profit. **Profit** is the amount of money that producers make after all of the costs of production have been paid. In order to make a profit, producers must be able to provide the goods and services that consumers want at prices consumers are willing and able to pay.

The Law of Supply

The quantity of goods and services that producers offer at each price is called **supply.** Supply is directly related to the prices that producers can charge for their products. Producers supply more products when they can sell them at higher prices and fewer products when they must sell them at lower prices. This tendency to vary production based on price is called the **law of supply.**

The law of supply can be illustrated using a supply schedule. A **supply schedule** is a table that lists each quantity of a product that producers are willing to supply at various market prices. As can be seen in the supply schedule on page 61, the quantity of products supplied increases as the price charged for the product increases. The quantity that is offered at each price is based on the amount of profit that producers make at each price.

Consider the following example. Audio Blast Manufacturing specializes in making car stereos. The owners of Audio Blast Manufacturing have determined that the cost of producing a single car stereo is $90. To help plan how many car stereos to produce, the owners developed a supply schedule similar to the one on page 61.

The supply schedule lists the range of prices for car stereos—from $90 to $210. Audio Blast Manufacturing will not produce any stereos for $90 because they would not make a profit at this price. Audio Blast Manufacturing, however, would like to produce the stereos at a price of $210 because this would bring in the highest profit—$120 a stereo.

◆ Profit is characteristic of the free enterprise system. The opportunity for individuals to make a profit is limited in other economic systems.

The Supply Curve

The information that is contained in a supply schedule also can be presented in graph form. A graph that plots the information found in a supply schedule is called a **supply curve.** The supply curve shows the direct relationship between price and the quantity of the product that is supplied.

The supply curve on this page plots the supply schedule for Audio Blast Manufacturing. On the vertical axis are the various prices that Audio Blast Manufacturing can charge for a car stereo. On the horizontal axis are the various quantities of car stereos the company is able to supply. The number of car stereos that Audio Blast Manufacturing is willing to supply at each price is indicated by the curve $\mathbf{S_1}$.

A supply curve slopes upward. A demand curve slopes downward. The difference in the direction of the two types of curves is due to the different relationship supply and demand each has with price. In the case of supply, as price increases, the quantity supplied also increases. Thus the supply curve slopes upward. In the case of demand, as price increases, the quantity demanded decreases. Thus the demand curve slopes downward.

The Profit Motive

Profit is the key consideration when producers determine a supply schedule. A business makes a profit when its **revenues**—the money it takes in from the sale of goods—are greater than its **cost of production**—the wages and salaries, rents, interest, and payments to other entrepreneurs and resource suppliers.

The owners of Audio Blast Manufacturing have already used a supply schedule to determine that the cost of producing each stereo is $90. The manufacturer then calculates the profit at each price by subtracting the cost for producing a stereo from the price asked for a stereo. At the $90 price, for example, Audio Blast Manufacturing makes no profit ($90 – $90 = $0.00). At the $150 price, however, Audio Blast Manufacturing earns a $60 profit on each stereo sold ($150 – $90 = $60).

Profit is the incentive for all producers, not just Audio Blast Manufacturing, to produce. Profits not only affect the individual business but also help direct the use of resources in the entire market. For example, when car stereo manufacturers are able to charge $210 for each stereo and sell thousands of stereos a year, they know that demand is high and

The Supply of Car Stereos

Supply Schedule

Price per Car Stereo	Car Stereos Supplied
$210	6,000
$190	5,000
$170	4,000
$150	3,000
$130	2,000
$110	1,000
$ 90	0

Supply Curve

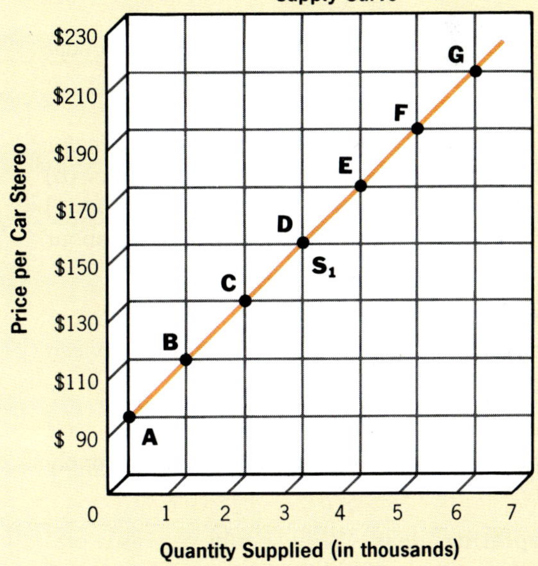

People enter businesses to make a profit. If the demand for T-shirts falls off, the owner of this shop might decide to sell another product.

that production should be continued or increased. On a broader scale, the car stereo manufacturers' successes signal other entrepreneurs about opening competing businesses. If, on the other hand, the manufacturers can charge only $90 a stereo, this may signal lower demand. The manufacturers may decrease or stop the production of car stereos, and other businesspeople may be discouraged from starting competing businesses.

See Suggested Assignments, p. TM 11.

Section 1 Review

See Answers, p. A 11.

DEFINE supply, law of supply, supply schedule, supply curve, revenue, cost of production

1. **Summarizing Ideas** **(a)** Why is profit the major determinant of a producer's supply schedule? **(b)** How does profit direct the use of resources? **(c)** How does profit signal other entrepreneurs about opening competing businesses?
2. **Seeing Relationships** Describe the relationships **(a)** between price and supply, **(b)** between revenue and profit.
3. **Comparing Ideas** What are the similarities and differences between a demand curve and a supply curve?
4. **Interpreting Ideas** Why should you, as a producer, be willing and able to produce more of your product at a high price rather than at a low price?

See Key Study Questions and Key Understandings, p. TM 12.

2 Price does not affect the supply of all products to the same degree.

See Suggested Teaching Strategies, p. TM 12.

Changes in a good's price affect the quantity supplied by the producer. The degree to which a good's supply is affected by changes in price is called the **elasticity of supply.** The supply of a good or service can be elastic or inelastic. ◆

Elastic Supply

An **elastic supply** exists when producers significantly change production in response to relatively small increases or decreases in the product's price. Supplies are easily expanded when market conditions are favorable and easily reduced when market conditions are unfavorable.

In elastic supply situations, producers must be prepared to change production rates to meet changing consumer demand. For example, in the mid-1980s dozens of companies produced coins, posters, and other items to commemorate the 1986 passing of Halley's comet. Expecting revenues to top a half billion dollars in 1986, these businesspeople catered to a short-lived but profitable fad. Supplies of T-shirts, musical records, and posters of popular television and music personalities also are elastic because they can be made quickly without large amounts of capital and skilled labor.

◆ Remind the students that demand can also be elastic or inelastic.

The graph to the right illustrates an elastic supply curve for posters of television and music personalities. The curve S_1 is almost horizontal, showing that a small change in the price of posters causes a large change in the quantity of posters supplied. At point **A**, for example, producers supply 100,000 posters at $1.50 each. At point **B**, however, producers supply 700,000 posters because the price has increased to $2.50 each. The relatively small rise in price causes producers to drastically increase the production of posters.

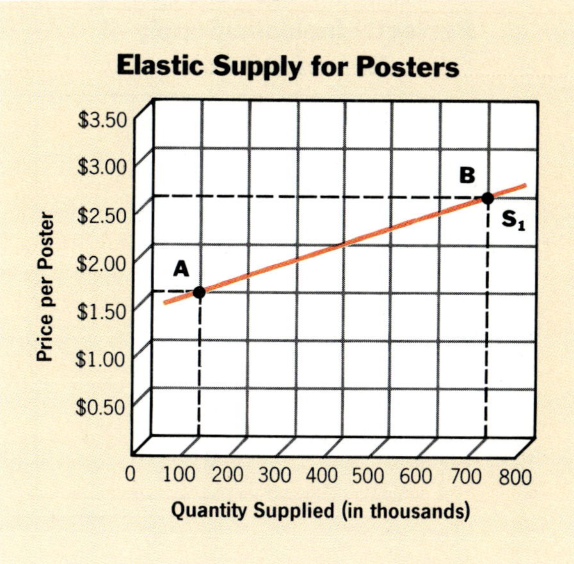

Inelastic Supply

An **inelastic supply** exists when, regardless of price, producers are unable or unwilling to increase or decrease the supply of a product. The supply is inflexible and cannot be easily expanded or reduced in response to price changes or other market conditions.

Goods and services that have an inelastic supply typically involve great expense, time, and resources to produce. The supply may be limited by the scarcity of natural resources such as gold and other precious metals or by the scarcity of human resources such as highly trained workers.

Regardless of the high prices paid for the design of computer systems, for example, the small number of skilled engineers and the length of time needed to develop a system limits the number of computer systems that can be designed. The graph to the right shows an inelastic supply curve for computer system designs. The curve S_1 is almost vertical because no matter how much the price for computer system designs rises, the number of computer systems that can be developed is limited. At point **A**, 2,000 computer systems are designed at $5,000 per system. At point **B**, only 4,000 computer systems are designed despite a price increase to $50,000 per system. While the number of computer systems designed increases by a relatively small amount (2,000), the price per design climbs from $5,000 to $50,000.

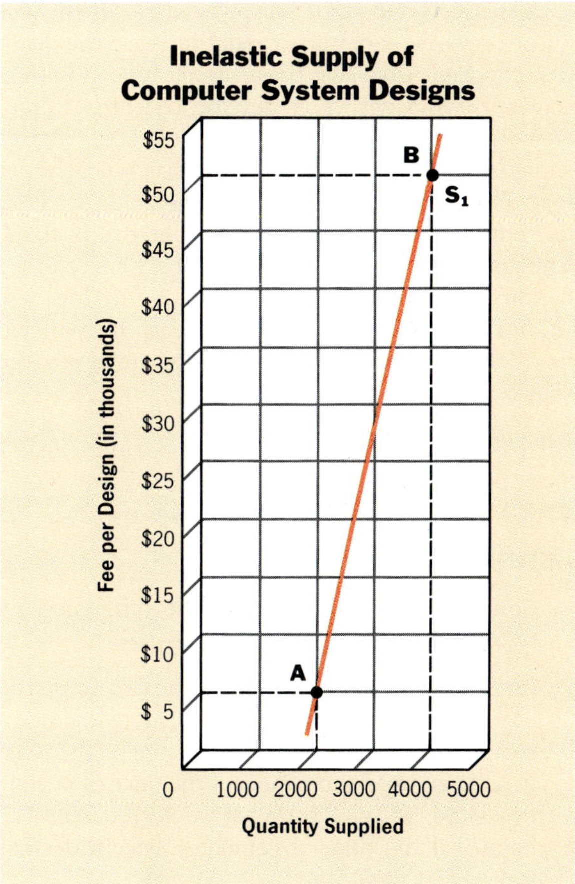

The supply of a product may also be limited by the need for large capital resources. People wishing to enter new businesses, for example, often have a difficult time gathering the necessary real capital—equipment, buildings, machinery, or cash—to begin production.

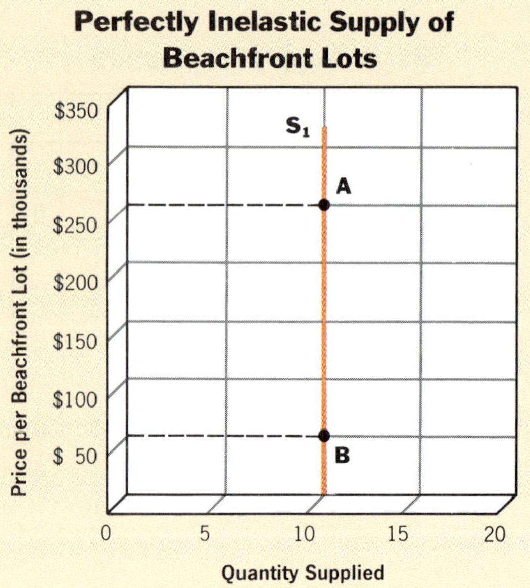

A perfectly inelastic supply exists when producers, regardless of price, cannot increase the quantity supplied. Consider the example of a building contractor who wishes to develop beachfront property. The building contractor divides 4,000 feet of shoreline property into 10 equal-sized beachfront lots. The market will determine the price for each lot, but the supply of shoreline properties is fixed. The graph above shows that the supply curve $\mathbf{S_1}$ for beachfront lots is vertical. At point **A**, the lots will sell for $250,000 each. At point **B**, each lot will sell for $50,000. Regardless of the price, however, the supply is perfectly inelastic.

See Suggested Assignments, p. TM 12.

Section 2 Review See Answers, p. A 11.

DEFINE elasticity of supply

1. **Contrasting Ideas** What is the difference between elastic and inelastic supply?
2. **Interpreting Graphics** Study the two graphs on page 63. **(a)** How do the graphs illustrate the difference between elastic and inelastic supply? **(b)** What would you expect to happen if the price of posters rose to $4.50? Why? **(c)** What would you expect to happen if the price of computer system designs rose to $100,000? Why?

See Key Study Questions and Key Understandings, p. TM 13.

3 In addition to price, six nonprice factors affect supply.

See Suggested Teaching Strategies, p. TM 13.

Like demand, supply is affected by factors other than price. In studying supply, it is just as important to make a distinction between a change in the quantity supplied and a change in supply. A change in the *quantity supplied* means a change in the amount of a product for sale because of a change in price. Such a change is represented by the movement from one point to another point on a supply curve.

A *change in supply*, however, means that the entire supply schedule has changed. This change in supply is represented by the creation of a new supply curve. In economic terms, the curve is said to shift. An increase in supply shifts the curve to the right along the horizontal axis. A decrease in supply shifts the curve to the left.

The cause of a change in supply is a change in one or more of the six nonprice **determinants of supply.** These nonprice determinants of supply are (1) technological improvement, (2) resource prices, (3) taxes and subsidies, (4) the prices of other goods, (5) price expectations, and (6) market competition. Change in one of these nonprice factors causes a change in the total supply of a good or a service.

Technological Improvement

Technology is the science of production. Technological improvement uses new knowledge to change methods of production. It also uses new knowledge to change the goods themselves. Technological improvement often lowers production costs and thereby increases supply. With lower production costs, businesses find it profitable to offer a larger amount of a product at each price. ◆

Improvements in laser technology, for example, have led to advances in communications, medicine, and manufacturing. By the mid-1980s, laser technology was revolutionizing the music industry. Compact disc players (CDPs) and compact discs (CDs) soared in popularity in the United States and abroad. Producers of CDPs and CDs had used new technology to increase their supplies of these products. The graph on page 65 shows how the supply curve would shift to the right—from $\mathbf{S_1}$ to $\mathbf{S_2}$—as a result of the increase in supply brought about by changes in technology.

 ◆ Report topic: The effect of technology on health care.

CASE STUDY

Robotics and Technological Change

American Robot is one of the leading manufacturers of robots in the United States. Founded by Romesh Wadhwani in the early 1980s, American Robot employed only 25 workers in 1982. By the mid-1980s, the young company's work force had grown to 250, and its sales had increased from $3 million to $20 million.

Wadhwani, an immigrant born in Bombay, India, assessed the potential market for robotics in the United States. Competition was strong. Many robotic companies, most of them Japanese firms, existed. But relatively few industrial contracts were available.

Wadhwani also recognized that American Robot would have to overcome two obstacles to succeed in this highly competitive market. First, the company had to secure enough capital to finance an aggressive marketing campaign. Second, the company needed to finance the research and development of a product that was distinguishable from and superior to existing robots on the market.

Wadhwani secured financial backing from corporate giants such as Ford and BMW (Bavarian Motor Works). Large companies often take a risk in promising new businesses. The money invested in these firms is called **venture capital.** In return for their money, investors expect a high return on the investment and hope to benefit directly from the technological breakthroughs made by the new company.

The major attraction offered by American Robot was its product—a "second-phase" robotic system. Second-phase robotics involves the total automation of a factory, with computers directing both the administrative and production tasks. American Robot's computer-integrated manufacturing system, or CIM, differs from "first-phase" robotics that did solely assembly-line jobs.

American Robot's CIM system, dubbed Merlin, has captured the imagination of major businesses worldwide. By the mid-1980s, Merlins were the only American robots being marketed in Japan. Major European automotive producers, such as Volkswagen and BMW, were using Merlin to monitor different aspects of auto production. By the mid-1980s, Merlins were being used by 40 of the world's top 100 corporations.

Resource Prices

A resource is anything that is used in the production of a product. The prices paid for materials and the wages paid to workers are the two primary resource costs.

Lower resource prices result in an increase in the amount of a product a producer can supply at the cost of production. Resource prices can be lowered in only a few ways. Less expensive or more efficient methods for processing natural resources and more efficient use of labor are common ways to lower resource prices. Improved mining processes, for example, have reduced the costs of many minerals used in the production of finished products and the use of robotics in some industries has reduced labor costs.

Taxes and Subsidies

Taxes imposed on the producers of a product also affect supply. Taxes add to production costs and therefore reduce supply. The tax shifts the supply curve upward by the amount of the tax. For example, if the government imposes a $2 excise tax on a pair of earrings, sellers who were willing to offer 500,000 pairs of earrings at $20 a pair must now offer them at $22 a pair to make the same profit.

Text continues on page 67.

The Effects of Technological Change on Supply

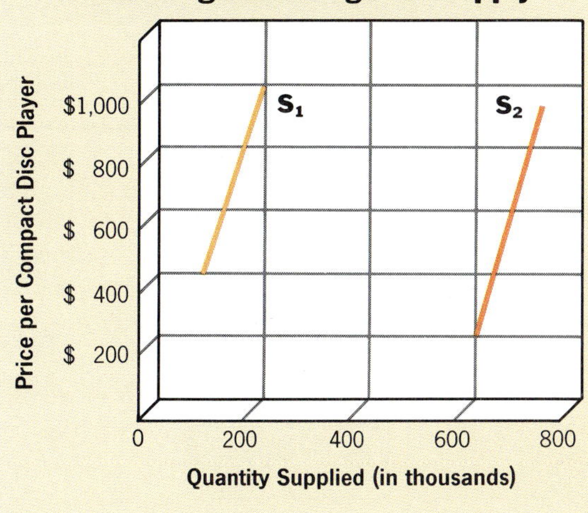

BUILDING ECONOMIC SKILLS

WRITING ABOUT ECONOMICS

Developing a Structured Overview

A student of economics is required to read and to remember a great deal of information. One way to help you remember what you have read is to develop a structured overview, which is a kind of outline.

How to Develop a Structured Overview

To develop a structured overview, follow these steps.

1. **Identify the major ideas.** Read the information, observing headings for each major idea or main topic.

2. **Identify categories and supporting details.** Find the major categories under which the material is organized. Look for key words that point to supporting details.

3. **Structure the headings and categories.** Form an overview by structuring the headings and categories as shown below.

Applying the Skill

Skim Section 1 of this chapter on the forces affecting supply. The main theme of the section is the relationship between supply and price, so that becomes the title of the structured overview below. Note that the section covers three main topics: (1) supply, (2) the way businesses determine the quantity of supply, and (3) the profit motive. In a structured overview of Section 1, then, these three headings would indicate the main topics.

Read through the section again. Note that after a definition of supply, two topics are discussed: the law of supply and the supply schedule. Law of supply and supply schedule are entered as subtopics of supply on the structured overview. Supporting material defining the law of supply and the supply schedule belongs under each of these categories. Check the structured overview for Section 1 below.

Practicing the Skill See Answers, p. A 11.

Read Section 3 of this chapter. Then develop a structured overview on a separate sheet of paper.

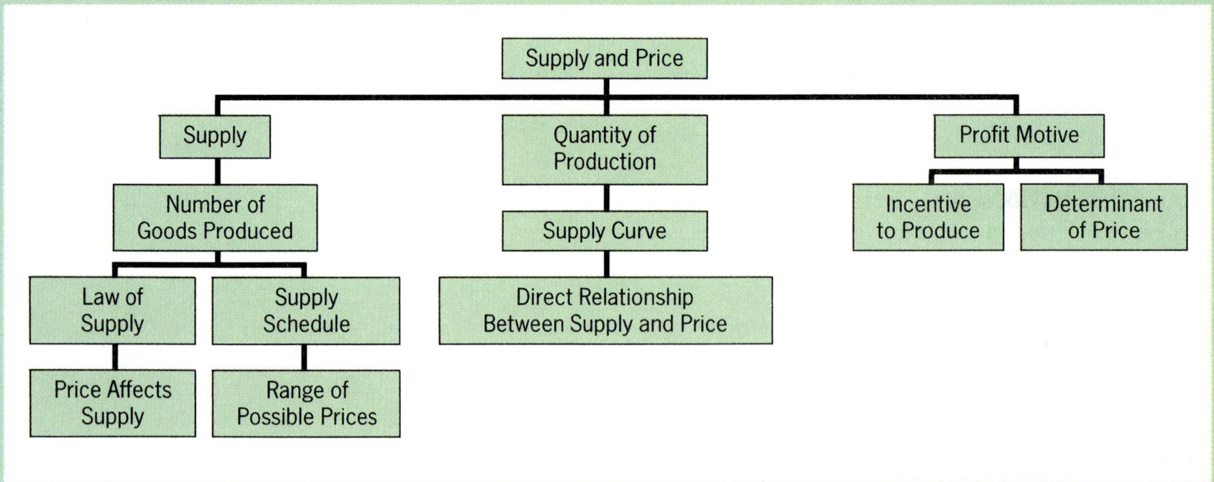

DECISION MAKERS IN THE ECONOMY

Robert A. Swanson

Robert A. Swanson is co-founder and chief executive officer of Genentech, Inc. As CEO, he was the first person to recognize that new technology in the biological sciences could be used to fill immediate needs in the market for medicines.

He and biochemist Herbert W. Boyer realized that the large numbers of natural proteins found in recombinant DNA and recovered by gene-splicing could form the basis of a profitable pharmaceutical business.

The history of Genentech, Inc., founded by Swanson and Boyer in 1976, has proved their gamble correct. In 1982, Genentech, Inc., produced synthetic insulin, which became the first recombinant-DNA drug on the market. It quickly showed a profit because it was less expensive to produce than other forms of insulin. In 1985, the company received approval for Protropin, a hormone used to treat pituitary dwarfism. In only 10 weeks, $5 million worth of sales were recorded. Testing for Activate, a drug designed to treat the 1.5 million people who develop heart-threatening blood clots each year, is in its final test stages. Meanwhile, research continues on other drugs.

According to the Congressional Office of Technology Assessment, products of recombinant-DNA technology by the year 2000 may account for an annual $15 billion in sales. Swanson's foresight has helped to create a major new industry. It also illustrates the effects of technology on supply.

Subsidies, grants of money or benefits to private businesses, reduce production costs and increase supply. For example, the tax-supported educational system provides the skilled labor needed by industry at no cost to industry. If businesses had to pay for the training of their technical, scientific, and administrative personnel, production costs would skyrocket and supply would decrease.

Price Changes and Expectations

Changes in the prices of other products can also shift a product's supply curve. This is especially true of agricultural products where, for example, a decline in the price of wheat may cause farmers to produce more corn at each price. Conversely, a rise in the price of wheat may influence farmers to produce and sell less corn. Thus, the price of wheat has a dramatic impact on corn's supply curve.

Many producers base current production goals on future price expectations. It is difficult, however, to generalize about the effects of future price expectations on current supplies because various producers view the effects differently. Manufacturers, for example, may expand production in response to expected price increases, causing increased supplies of their product. Farmers, on the other hand, may withhold part of their current supply in anticipation of a future rise in prices for their product, decreasing supplies of their product. In either case, however, expectation concerning the future price of a product affects the current supply of that product.

Market Competition

Competition also has a bearing on supply. The economic rivalry among producers or sellers of similar goods for customers or markets is called

■ Economics Reporter

What Is Direct Marketing?

Through direct marketing, the producer approaches the consumer on a one-to-one basis, either by the use of printed matter or through ◆ sales representatives. In direct marketing, retailers and wholesalers are excluded. The consumer deals only with the manufacturer. Consumer products such as Tupperware and Avon are direct marketed as are specialized industrial goods.

competition. The larger the number of producers or sellers competing in a market, the greater is the supply. As more producers enter a field of production, the supply increases and the supply curve shifts to the right. When producers leave a field of production, the supply usually decreases. The supply curve then shifts to the left.

Consumer demand and anticipated profits attract producers into a field or cause them to exit from a field. The incentive for producers to enter a field is greater when consumer demand and profits are higher. The incentive for producers to enter a field is less and the desire for them to exit from a field is greater when consumer demand and profits are lower.

One business that has attracted new producers in recent years is the limited-service motel such as Econo Lodge. These motels offer rates that are 20 to 60 percent lower than full-service hotel and motel chains such as Holiday Inn and Hilton. Limited-service motels, however, offer fewer services for guests than full-service hotel and motel chains. Today, the limited-service motels are the fastest-growing and most profitable segment of the $36-billion lodging industry. From 1980 to 1987, the supply of limited-service motel rooms increased by more than 75 percent, causing the supply curve for limited-service motels to shift to the right.

Producers have also exited from certain industries in recent years. American companies, for example, were once the world leaders in the production of motorcycles. Foreign competition, especially from Japan, has caused many firms in the United States to leave this once-profitable market. The graph on this page illustrates the decline in the supply of American-made motorcycles. On the graph, $\mathbf{S_1}$ represents the original supply and $\mathbf{S_2}$ represents the new and smaller supply.

See Suggested Assignments, p. TM 13.

The Effects of Decreasing Competition on Supply

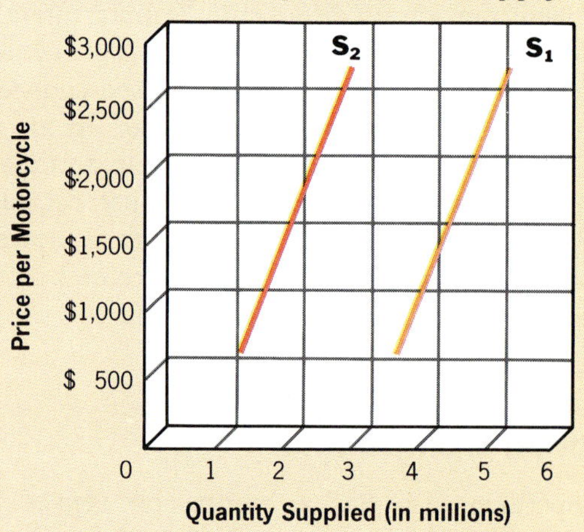

Section 3 Review See Answers, p. A 12.

DEFINE technology, venture capital, competition

IDENTIFY Romesh Wadhwani, Robert A. Swanson

1. **Summarizing Ideas** **(a)** Name and describe the nonprice determinants of supply. **(b)** How does technological improvement affect supply? **(c)** Explain the effect of market competition on supply.
2. **Contrasting Ideas** **(a)** What is the difference between a *change in quantity supplied* and a *change in supply?* **(b)** Why does a tax affect supply differently than a subsidy?
3. **Interpreting Graphics** Study the graph on page 68. **(a)** What is the subject of the graph? **(b)** Why does decreased competition cause the supply curve to shift to the left?

◆ Many clothing manufacturers also use direct marketing when they send catalogs to consumers and accept telephone and mail orders.

See Key Study Questions and Key Understandings, p. TM 14.

4 The cost of production affects the supply of goods and services.

See Suggested Teachings Strategies, p. TM 14.

Production decisions are influenced by productivity and the costs of production. Manufacturers must analyze production costs before making their supply decisions. To more easily analyze their costs and make their supply decisions, most manufacturers divide their costs into several different categories.

The storing and transporting of agricultural goods is one of the production costs faced by farmers.

The Costs of Production

Changes in the costs of production can affect the supply of goods. Producers must pay the cost of production, which may change over time. Production costs are generally divided into fixed costs, variable costs, and total costs. Producers also calculate the average total costs and marginal costs of production. Analyzing these costs of production helps producers determine production goals and profit margins.

Fixed Costs. The costs that producers incur whether they produce nothing, very little, or large quantities are their **fixed costs.** Total fixed costs are called **overhead.** Fixed costs include interest payments on loans and bonds, insurance premiums, local and state property taxes, rent payments, and executive salaries. Fixed costs also include the wear and tear on and aging of capital goods. Machine parts, for example, eventually break. As the machine gets older, it is less valuable. The significance of fixed costs is that they do not change as output changes.

Variable Costs. A second category of costs—costs that change with changes in output—are **variable costs.** Unlike fixed costs, which are usually associated with such capital goods as machinery, salaries, and rent, variable costs are usually associated with labor and raw materials.

Variable costs reflect the costs of items that businesses can control or alter in the short run. Wages, for example, are a variable cost because more employees may be hired as production increases and some employees may be laid off as production decreases.

Total Costs and Average Total Costs. The sum of the fixed and variable costs of production is the **total costs.** At zero output, a firm's total costs are equal to its fixed costs. Then as production increases, so do the total costs as the increasing variable costs are added to the fixed costs.

Producers are equally concerned with their per unit production costs. The average total costs of production are the sum of the average fixed costs and the average variable costs. Each of these average costs is calculated by dividing the cost by the total units produced.

Marginal Costs. One final measure of costs is **marginal costs**—the extra costs incurred by producing one more unit of output. Marginal costs are an increase in variable costs because fixed costs do not change.

Marginal costs identify the costs over which a business has the most direct control. More specifically, they indicate the costs of producing the last unit of output and the cost that can be saved by reducing output by one unit. Many businesses make marginal production decisions—decisions to produce a few more or a few less units of output. Marginal costs allow the business to determine the profitability of increasing or decreasing production by a few units.

The Law of Diminishing Returns

To help determine the best combination of resources in the production process, businesses must consider the **law of diminishing returns.** The law of diminishing returns states that as more of one resource—such as labor—is added to a fixed supply of other resources—such as natural resources and capital—the output per unit of input may increase for a time. Eventually, however, the rate of increase of productivity will diminish.

The law of diminishing returns tries to isolate the impact that varying a single type of resource has on the overall production of a good. Often, businesses use labor as the variable. By changing the number of laborers, a business can experience increasing returns, diminishing returns, or negative returns.

The graph below illustrates the law of diminishing returns, using Dynamic Tees, a T-shirt manufacturer, as an example. As a businessperson, the owner of Dynamic Tees makes a graph to note changes in the number of T-shirts produced in the shop. On the graph, the vertical axis represents the total output of T-shirts produced by Dynamic Tees' employees each day. The horizontal axis represents the number of workers employed by Dynamic Tees. Capital and natural resources are fixed, or constant, in this example. The variable resource is labor.

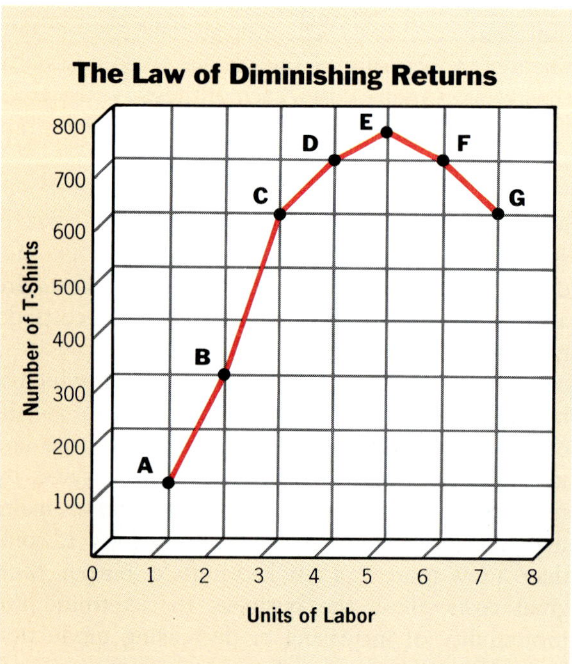

After opening the shop, the owner of Dynamic Tees discovers that a large demand has developed for one of the novelty T-shirts produced in the shop. The 100 T-shirts that Dynamic Tees' one worker can produce, which is shown at point **A,** are insufficient to meet demand. The owner then hires an additional worker. The two workers can now specialize. One worker can prepare and attach a design stencil to each T-shirt. The other worker can then apply the paint. Time is saved because the worker applying the paint does not have to stop to attach a stencil to each T-shirt. As a result, Dynamic Tees' production of T-shirts jumps to 300, shown at point **B,** an increase of 200 T-shirts (300 – 100 = 200).

The 200-unit increase in production is an example of increasing returns. Increasing returns occur when the additional labor resource—or any variable resource—adds more to the total production than the previous one. The second worker adds 200 units to the total production, compared to just 100 units contributed by the first worker.

By hiring a third worker, shown at point **C,** the owner of Dynamic Tees again experiences increasing returns. The third worker is able to remove the stencils and fold the T-shirts once the paint dries. The third worker adds 300 (600 – 300 = 300) units to the overall production of T-shirts, compared to just 200 units added by the second worker.

A point of diminishing returns is reached at point **D.** Diminishing returns occur when the addition of another unit of a resource contributes less to the overall production of a good than the addition of the previous unit did. Although total production of T-shirts increases at point **D,** it increases at a lower, or diminishing rate—an increase of only 100 units (700 – 600 = 100) compared to the previous laborer's contribution of 300 units. Again at point **E,** the business experiences diminishing returns, as the addition of a fifth worker adds only 50 T-shirts (750 – 700 = 50) to the total production.

A point of negative returns is reached at points **F** and **G.** Negative returns occur when an additional resource hurts production to the point that the firm's total output drops. At point **F,** for example, the addition of a sixth worker causes the total production to fall by 50 units. The addition of a seventh laborer results in a drop of another 100 T-shirts.

Have the students read "Reading the Want Ads" on page 512 of the *Everyday Economics Handbook* and answer the questions that follow.

High production costs, low market prices, and an oversupply of agricultural goods have prevented many farmers from making a profit.

A business experiences negative returns when the factors of production are grossly imbalanced. In the case of Dynamic Tees, too many workers might cause overcrowding in the shop, production bottlenecks, and poor supervision of workers by the owner. In addition, the overcrowding might cause low worker morale, which would further erode productivity.

See Suggested Assignments, p. TM 14.

Section 4 Review See Answers, p. A 12.

DEFINE overhead, total cost, marginal cost

1. **Summarizing Ideas** **(a)** Why do the costs of production affect the supply of a product? **(b)** State the law of diminishing marginal returns.
2. **Contrasting Ideas** What is the difference **(a)** between fixed cost and variable cost? **(b)** between total cost and average total cost?
3. **Seeing Relationships** What is the relationship between total costs and variable costs?
4. **Interpreting Graphics** Study the graph on page 70. **(a)** What additional resource hurt Dynamic Tees' production? **(b)** Why? **(c)** What is the optimal number of employees for Dynamic Tees?

CHAPTER 3 SUMMARY

Many economic factors affect the supply of a product. The major influence, however, is price because the quantity of a product offered for sale varies with its price. This relationship is graphically illustrated by supply schedules and supply curves. Profit is the key consideration when producers determine a supply schedule.

Change in a product's price affects the product's supply. When a change in price results in a significant change in the supply, the supply is elastic. When a change in price causes little change in supply, the supply is inelastic. In cases where price change results in no supply change, the supply is perfectly inelastic. The elasticity of the supply indicates businesses' ability and willingness to respond to market pressures.

Six nonprice factors also influence supply. When changes in one or more of these factors cause increased supplies, the supply curve shifts to the right. Changes that result in decreased supplies cause a shift of the supply curve to the left.

Production decisions are affected by the costs of production and productivity. In figuring the costs of production, business owners are concerned with fixed costs, variable costs, total costs, average total costs, and marginal costs. When deciding how best to increase production, business owners must consider the law of diminishing returns.

CHAPTER 3 REVIEW

For Answers to Chapter 3 Review, see p. A 13.

Reviewing Economic Terms

With each definition or description below, match correctly one of the following terms.

a. determinant of supply
b. variable cost
c. law of supply
d. profit
e. supply
f. fixed cost

_____ **1.** The amount of money producers make after all the costs of production are paid.
_____ **2.** A cost that changes with changes in output.
_____ **3.** A nonprice factor that may cause a change in supply.
_____ **4.** A cost that producers incur whether they produce nothing, very little, or large quantities.
_____ **5.** The quantity of a product that producers offer for sale at each price.

Exercising Economic Skills

1. **Developing a Structured Overview** Reread Section 4 of this chapter. Then develop a structured overview of the section.
2. **Reading the Want Ads** Study the feature on page 512. Then study the classified section of your local newspaper to find and list at least three advertised jobs in which you are interested. **(a)** For each job on your list, describe the qualifications needed for the job, **(b)** show how you are qualified for the job, and **(c)** explain how you plan to apply for the job.

Thinking Critically About Economics

1. **Summarizing Ideas** **(a)** What is profit, why is it important, and how is it gained by producers? **(b)** What determines a good's elasticity of supply? **(c)** Name and describe the determinants of supply. **(d)** What are the major types of production costs that producers must consider in making production decisions?
2. **Contrasting Ideas** What are the differences between elastic supply, inelastic supply, and perfectly inelastic supply?
3. **Organizing Ideas** Explain the effect that an increase in each determinant of supply may have on a product's supply.
4. **Analyzing Ideas** Why are variable costs important to a producer's production decisions? Explain.

Extending Economic Knowledge

1. Suppose you owned a sporting goods store and your supplier charged you $24.00 for top-of-the-line tennis shoes. **(a)** How much would you charge your customers for the tennis shoes? **(b)** What price would you charge if your cost from the supplier increased to $24.20? Why?
2. Using the supply schedule below during a given week, complete the following activities. **(a)** Construct a supply curve for medium-sized pizzas. **(b)** Use the information on the graph to explain the law of supply for medium-sized pizzas. **(c)** Indicate on the supply curve the shift that occurs if technological improvement enabled producers to produce twice as many medium-sized pizzas.

Supply Schedule for Medium-Sized Pizzas

Price	Quantity Supplied
$5.00	0
$6.00	5,000
$7.00	10,000
$8.00	15,000
$9.00	20,000

3. Productivity and production costs are the key influences of production decisions. Select a business that interests you. **(a)** Research the business to discover its method of operation and the resources it uses in production. **(b)** Make a list of all the costs that the business might incur in its operations. Include all costs, no matter how small. **(c)** Divide the costs on your list into two categories—fixed costs and variable costs—and total the estimated costs for each category. **(d)** Write a paragraph in which you identify where you would cut costs to increase profits.

Using Primary Sources

Alvin Toffler (1928–) is a leading American futurist. His best-selling book, *Future Shock* (1970), commented on the rapid social and technological changes taking place in the United States. One important change Toffler observed concerned "the economics of impermanence." As you read the following excerpts, consider the causes of impermanence. Why do human wants and needs change? What impact does the economics of impermanence have on the marketing of goods?

The Economics of Impermanence

In the past, permanence was the ideal. . . . Man built to last. He had to. As long as the society around him was relatively unchanging each object had clearly defined functions, and economic logic dictated the policy of permanence. . . .

As the general rate of change in society accelerates, however, the economics of permanence are—and must be—replaced by the economics of transience [impermanence].

First, advancing technology tends to lower the costs of manufacture much more rapidly than the costs of repair work. [Manufacturing] is automated, [repair work] remains largely a handcraft operation. This means that it often becomes cheaper to replace than to repair. It is economically sensible to build cheap, unrepairable, throwaway objects, even though they may not last as long as repairable objects.

Second, advancing technology makes it possible to improve the object as time goes by. The second-generation computer is better than the first, and the third is better than the second. . . . It often makes hard economic sense to build for the short term rather than the long. . . .

Third, as change accelerates and reaches into more and more remote corners of the society, uncertainty about future needs increases. Recognizing the inevitability of change, but unsure as to the demands it will impose on us, we hesitate to commit large resources for rigidly fixed objects intended to serve unchanging purposes. . . .

It is important here to turn for a moment to the notion of obsolescence [condition of no longer being useful]. For the fear of product obsolescence drives businessmen to innovation at the same time that it impels the consumer toward rented, disposable or temporary products. The very idea of obsolescence is disturbing to people bred on the ideal of permanence, and it is particularly upsetting when thought to be planned. Planned obsolescence has been the target of . . . much recent social criticism. . . .

Some businessmen conspire to shorten the useful life of their products in order to guarantee replacement sales. . . . Similarly, . . . many of the annual model changes with which American (and other) consumers are increasingly familiar are not technologically substantive [advancements in technological progress]. . . .

Clearly, obsolescence occurs . . . under three conditions. It occurs when a product literally deteriorates to the point at which it can no longer fulfill its functions. . . .

Obsolescence also occurs when some new product arrives on the scene to perform these [same] functions more effectively than the old product. . . .

But obsolescence also occurs when the needs of the consumer change, when the functions to be performed by the product are themselves altered. . . . A car, for example, is more than a conveyance [a means of transport]. It is an expression of the personality of the user, a symbol of status, [and] a source of that pleasure associated with speed.

Source Review

For Answers to Source Review, see p. A 14.

1. How does Toffler contrast the present economics of impermanence, or transience, with the past policy of permanence?
2. According to Toffler, what three factors contribute to the economics of transience?
3. How does Toffler define "product obsolescence"? Under what condition does obsolescence occur?

GUARANTEED
LOWEST PRICES!
"NOBODY BEATS OUR PRICES!"
DO IT YOURSELF
5%
WE GUARANTEE OUR STORE PRICES TO BE LOWER OR AS LOW AS ANY OF OUR COMPETITOR'S ADVERTISED PRICES-OR
WE'LL SELL IT TO YOU AND KNOCK AN ADDITIONAL 5% OFF THEIR PRICE!
NO SALES TO DEALERS
A COPY OF COMPETITOR'S ADVERTISEMENT MUST BE PRESENTED TO VERIFY PRICE.
ITEM MUST COME FROM OUR PRESENT STOCK AND BE IDENTICAL ITEM AND BRAND... CLOSEOUTS, CLEARANCES,
AD MISTAKES OR ERRORS CANNOT BE HONORED. COMPETITOR MUST BE WITHIN A 10 MILE RADIUS OF OUR

CHAPTER 4

See Chapter Overview, p. TM 16.
See Chapter Objectives, p. TM 16.
See Introducing the Chapter, p. TM 16.
See Extending Economic Knowledge on text p. 90.

The Price System in the Marketplace

Certainly no business can stand to pay out more than it makes. When you pump water out of a well at a faster rate than the water flows, the well goes dry.

Henry Ford

1 In a free enterprise economy, supply and demand are coordinated through the price system.

- The Need for Compromise
- The Information Function
- The Incentive Function
- The Limitation Function

2 In a free enterprise economy, the price system produces market equilibrium.

- Equilibrium Price and Quantity
- Changes in Supply and Demand

3 The price system in a free enterprise economy has defenders and critics.

- A Defense of the Price System
- Opposition to the Price System

CHAPTER 4 STUDY GUIDE

Chapter Focus

Chapter 4 examines the role of the price system in free enterprise. Economic graphs are used to illustrate how the price system regulates the forces of supply and demand. The chapter also examines the strengths and weaknesses of the price system.

As you study the chapter, look for the details that support each of the following statements.

1. In a free enterprise economy, supply and demand are coordinated through the price system.
2. In a free enterprise economy, the price system produces market equilibrium.
3. The price system in a free enterprise economy has defenders and critics.

See Preteaching Vocabulary, p. TM 16.

Terms to Know

The following terms, while not the only terms emphasized in this chapter, are basic to your understanding of the price system. Determine the meaning of each term, either by using the Glossary or by watching for context clues as you read the chapter.

price system
market equilibrium
equilibrium point
surplus
shortage
externalities
price ceiling
price floor

See Key Study Questions and Key Understandings, p. TM 17.

1 In a free enterprise economy, supply and demand are coordinated through the price system.

See Suggested Teaching Strategies, p. TM 17.

Self-interest plays a major role in guiding the actions of producers and consumers in a free enterprise economy. ◆ Self-interest motivates producers to produce more goods and services when higher prices can be charged and fewer goods and services when lower prices can be charged. Self-interest motivates consumers to demand more goods and services at lower prices than at higher prices. Unfortunately, the self-interest of producers and consumers are in conflict.

The Need for Compromise

For the market to function efficiently, producers and consumers must compromise. Producers have to be able to sell products at prices that are high enough to cover the costs of production and still earn a profit. Consumers, on the other hand, need to be offered products that can be purchased at affordable prices.

In order to reach a compromise, producers and consumers must be able to communicate so that they can coordinate production decisions. In a free enterprise economy, these functions of communication and coordination are carried out through the **price system.** The price system is based on two principles. The first principle is that everything bought and sold in a market has a price. The second principle is that price is a good measure of what products should be produced, how they should be produced, and for whom they should be produced.

It sounds strange to say that prices communicate, but that is what they do. Prices are the way in which producers tell consumers how much it costs to produce a product. In essence, a producer is saying, "If you want this product in this quantity, you will have to pay this price." Consumers respond by purchasing or not purchasing the product. By purchasing the product, a consumer is saying, "Yes, I want this product and I am willing to pay this price." By not purchasing the product, the

◆ Have the students read "Applying for a Job" on pages 512–514 of the *Everyday Economics Handbook* and answer the questions that follow.

◆ *Consumer Reports* **carries no advertisements so that it will not become dependent on advertising revenues and thus biased toward particular companies.**

consumer is saying, "No, I do not want this product at this price."

If consumers do not purchase the product at the asked-for price, the producer must determine whether it is possible to charge a lower price and still make a profit. The producer's decision is communicated through a change in price. In a free enterprise economy, the price system eventually leads to a compromise between the needs of producers and the needs of consumers. The price system thus coordinates market activities in the private sector by providing information, offering incentives, and establishing limits on buying.

Economics Reporter

What Is *Consumer Reports?*

Consumer Reports is a magazine that helps educate consumers by providing technical guidance. The publication started as *Consumers Union Reports* in 1936 with a circulation of more than 4,000 copies. The magazine carries no advertisements and previews a wide range of consumer needs and products. *Consumer Reports* tests products scientifically and has professional consultants examine a variety of services. The product or service is rated as best buy, acceptable, or not acceptable. The best buy is considered the best value for the money, not necessarily the best product. Today *Consumer Reports* has a circulation of 3.5 million across the United States, with advocacy offices in Washington, D.C.; San Francisco; and Austin, Texas. ◆

The Information Function

Prices provide information to resource owners, producers, and consumers. Buying and selling would be impossible in many instances in the free enterprise economy of the United States without access to price information. In the resource market, for example, managers of businesses must know in advance how much they must pay for the natural, human, and capital resources that make up the factors of production. Conversely, the owners of resources need information about the wages they can expect to pay, the amount of interest they have to pay on business loans, and the interest they may receive on money in the bank. In the product market, consumers need to know the prices of finished goods and services in order to make informed buying decisions.

Text continues on page 80.

How shoppers spend their money guides producers in deciding what goods to produce and how much to charge for them.

BUILDING ECONOMIC SKILLS

THINKING ABOUT ECONOMICS

Analyzing Economic Information

A JOB HOT LINE

I read newspaper stories nearly every week about large numbers of people victimized by "staff reductions": . . .

I wish one or two of them would come to me. I operate a small business well on its way to getting bigger. I need good people to help me grow, and I know that the people I'm looking for are out there somewhere. . . .

Dun & Bradstreet estimates that as many as two thirds of the jobs that were created in the U.S. last year are to fill the needs of entrepreneurs like me. . . .

I called the "human resources" department of a major company that had just announced massive layoffs. "May I have a list of the people whose jobs have been terminated?" I asked. . . . "We can't give out that information,". . .

I wrote to the chief executives of six companies suggesting that they form a central repository of the names and qualifications of the recently laid-off employees. The information could be computerized and made available to those like myself who are looking for good employees.

I have yet to get even a form letter in response.

Is it such a bad idea? . . .

Arthur Zelvin

This excerpt is from an article in *The Wall Street Journal,* a daily (except Saturday and Sunday) newspaper that reports on activities and trends in the financial world. Like other newspapers, *The Wall Street Journal* carries first-person feature stories. The one above appeared on the editorial page. A student of economics must be able to analyze economic information, that is, to break it down into smaller parts. The analysis then distinguishes between facts and opinions, and causes and effects. Ultimately, the reader is able to draw some conclusions about the topic, and about the author's presentation.

How to Analyze Economic Information

To analyze economic information, follow these steps.

1. **Read the material carefully.** Note the author's main ideas. Identify evidence, or the supporting details, that back up the main ideas.
2. **Ask yourself questions.** Determine who or what is involved. Note whether the author explains how, where, and why the situation or event occurred, if it is appropriate.
3. **Separate fact from opinion.** Facts are provable and observable. Opinions are beliefs. They may or may not be observable or proved true. Economic analysis demands that facts be separated from opinions. To identify opinions, look for phrases such as "it is believed," "it seems," and "it would appear."
4. **Search for bias.** Bias refers to the general outlook or point of view of the writer or speaker. Writers and speakers present biased views when they use facts selectively. Be alert to the possibility of other viewpoints.
5. **Check for cause-effect relationships.** Look for words that indicate the causes or effects of actions or events. Keep in mind that a cause stimulates a response, or an effect. This effect, in turn, can become the cause of some other effect.
6. **Come to a conclusion.** Evaluate the argument or point of view provided by drawing a conclusion or forming a generalization.

SOMETIMES THE BIGGEST MISTAKE IS SAYING NO TO A FUTURE SUCCESS

ON NEW YEAR'S DAY 1962, four nervous young musicians played their first record audition for executives of Decca Recording Co. The latter were underwhelmed.

"We don't like their sound," one explained later, noting that guitar groups were on their way out. The foursome's manager begged Decca to reconsider and promised he would personally buy 3,000 copies of any single his group recorded. Decca stood fast. Over the next few months four other record companies turned them down, too.

In any Failure Hall of Fame, there would have to be a wing devoted to those whose mistake was not recognizing multimillion-dollar opportunities when they bobbed up before them. And in that wing there would have to be a niche for Decca, which 24 years ago blew a chance to sign the Beatles.

Authors John White ("Rejection") and Christopher Cerf and Victor Navasky ("The Experts Speak") dwell lovingly on the long history of similar embarrassments. Some of them involved ideas that not only became hugely profitable, but which later formed the cores of entire giant industries that permanently changed the American landscape.

For example, when Alexander Graham Bell invented the telephone in 1876, it did not ring off the hook with calls from potential backers. President Rutherford B. Hayes said after making a demonstration call, "That's an amazing invention, but who would ever want to use one of them?"

Mr. Bell's father-in-law, charged with peddling the device, was so desperate for cash after a year of failure that he offered to sell all the patents to Western Union Telegraph Co. for $100,000. He was shown the door: Western Union, its president reportedly said, had no use for "an electrical toy."

It was a millennial goof. Only a few years later Western Union changed its mind about telephone's future and bought another inventor's patents for a similar device. Mr. Bell's company sued for patent infringement and won a settlement that froze Western Union out of the telephone business.

In the 1940's, another young inventor named Chester Carlson took his idea to 20 corporations, including some of the biggest in the country. They all turned him down. In 1947, he finally got a tiny Rochester, N.Y., outfit named Haloid Co. to purchase the commercial rights to his electrostatic paper-copying process. Haloid became Xerox Corp. and both it and Mr. Carlson got very rich.

Hewlett-Packard Co. dropped the ball in 1975, when one of its young, low-level engineers, working on his own time, jerry-built a gadget few people envisioned at the time: a personal computer. He offered it to his employer, which decided to pass. The engineer, Steve Wozniak, went off with his device to co-found one of recent history's biggest success stories, Apple Computer Inc.

David O. Selznick didn't drop the ball, but there were a lot of red faces at Metro-Goldwyn-Mayer after he produced "Gone With The Wind." Irving Thalberg, MGM's production chief, had talked Louis B. Mayer out of producing it himself, saying: "Forget it, Louis. No Civil War picture ever made a nickel." Gary Cooper, who spurned the chance to play Rhett Butler, said: "I'm just glad it'll be Clark Gable who's falling flat on his face and not Gary Cooper."

But the award for blown opportunity in this case probably should go to Victor Fleming, who was assigned the task of directing the movie. Saying that "this picture is going to be the biggest white elephant of all time," he turned down an offer of 20% of its profits and insisted on a flat fee instead.

Michael M. Miller

Applying the Skill

The article on page 78 discusses the author's attempts to form a job hot line. The article is basically factual, even though it is written only from the author's viewpoint.

Practicing the Skill

Read the article above, which appeared in the *Wall Street Journal* on December 15,1986. Using the steps on analyzing economic information, write an evaluation of the article and the author's point of view.

Practicing the Skill Answers: The article written by Michael Miller describes factual events from the author's point of view. This biased account of incidences where people and companies passed up great opportunities for money or success fails to give the viewpoints of the "losers." It is possible that they were able to turn the apparent mistake into an opportunity.

DECISION MAKERS IN THE ECONOMY

Walter B. Wriston

Before his retirement, Walter B. Wriston was the chief executive officer (CEO) of Citicorp, the largest banking organization in the United States. Recently, Wriston has written a book, *Risk and Other Four-Letter Words,* in which he discusses the economic theories that guided his decisions as Citicorp's CEO.

Wriston believes that technological breakthroughs have changed the nature of the world economy. With advances in telecommunications, information and money travel around the world in seconds. As a result, the world now thinks as one market, not as a collection of separate national markets.

According to Wriston, a world that thinks as one market should be treated as one market. In his view, governments should not pass protectionist measures designed to benefit their own industries at the expense of industries in other countries. Wriston argues that trade encourages trade, but restrictions on imports disrupt economic activity both at home and abroad.

In Wriston's words, the global market is "the greatest data processor in existence." When left to itself, the global market adjusts as necessary to all the various conditions that affect supply and demand. When governments interfere within nations, between nations, and among nations, they send out confusing signals and hinder the market's natural responsiveness. To Wriston, free trade is necessary to the development of a rational and healthy world economy.

The Incentive Function

Prices provide an incentive for resource owners to sell their resources, producers to furnish products, and consumers to make purchases. Each group tends to act in its own self-interest in a free enterprise market system. To a producer, profit guides all business decisions. High prices for the output are an incentive to the producers to produce more product. The consumer generally wants low prices. Low prices are an incentive for the consumer to buy more product. On the other hand, lower prices for the producer's output may be a deterrent to production. Workers, savers, investors, and other consumers also consider the incentives offered by the price system before making personal decisions about jobs, savings options, and investment opportunities.

The Limitation Function

Prices also place limits on consumer buying. Goods, services, and resources are for sale in a free enterprise system. Buyers, however, must have enough money to purchase the products before exchanges can take place. People tend to buy more product at the more affordable lower prices than at the less affordable higher prices. Price, therefore, serves to ◆ limit the availability of products and resources to those who can afford to pay.

In a free enterprise system, there is a continuous give and take among producers, resource owners, and consumers. The supply and demand for goods and services change regularly. These changes can be seen everywhere—at the grocery store, the sandwich shop, and the department store.

◆ **Report topic: How the availability of credit affects consumer buying.**

Lower prices are an incentive to buy for most consumers. Low prices and the opportunity to negotiate price attract customers to flea markets (top). One way that grocery stores (bottom) attract customers is through sales.

The shift in popularity from pinball machines to video games provides a good example of how the price system communicates necessary changes in the market and helps to coordinate those changes. In the 1960s and early 1970s, pinball machines provided entertainment for many people.

During the 1970s and 1980s, however, video games became popular, causing the demand for pinball machines to decline. The change in demand was reflected in lower profits for the producers of pinball machines and for the arcade operators and other pinball machine owners, who made them available to the public. Producers cut back on the production of pinball machines and increased the production of video-game machines. Arcade operators and other owners were forced to replace pinball machines with video-game machines because of the changing tastes and preferences of their customers.

See Suggested Assignments, p. TM 17.

Section 1 Review

See Answers, p. A 14.

DEFINE price system

IDENTIFY Walter B. Wriston

1. **Interpreting Ideas** **(a)** Upon what two principles is the price system based? **(b)** How do prices communicate?

2. **Seeing Relationships** **(a)** What role does self-interest play in guiding the actions of producers? **(b)** What role does self-interest play in guiding the actions of consumers?

3. **Analyzing Ideas** **(a)** What is the incentive function? **(b)** Why is the information function important in the resource market?

The OPEC Cartel—Supply and Demand at Work

In 1960, five oil-producing nations—Saudi Arabia, Kuwait, Iraq, Iran, and Venezuela—founded the Organization of Petroleum Exporting Countries, or OPEC. Shortly thereafter Indonesia, Algeria, Nigeria, Gabon, Libya, Qatar, Ecuador, and the United Arab Emirates joined OPEC.

OPEC is a cartel, a group that is formally bound together to regulate the production and sale of a good or service. The OPEC cartel imposes "production ceilings" on its members. It also sets the price for the oil that its member nations sell.

The governments of the 13 OPEC nations were able to control the supply and the selling price of oil in their countries by nationalizing, or taking over, private firms (see the graph on page 83).

Limiting Supply to Create an Oil Shortage

During the 1960s, the OPEC cartel was weak, disorganized, and ineffective in its efforts to limit the supply of oil. Throughout the 1960s, the average price of oil remained under $2* per 42-gallon (152-liter) barrel. In the 1970s, OPEC slowly increased the price of its oil. In 1973, after an Arab nation's defeat in a war with Israel, the Arab members of OPEC influenced the cartel to impose an oil embargo on the United States, Israel's chief ally. The cartel thus made oil a political weapon.

The oil embargo unified and strengthened the cartel. Even after the cartel lifted the oil embargo in 1974, the cartel continued to limit the world's supply of oil and to increase its control over the world oil market. The "official" price of OPEC oil jumped from $11.51 a barrel in 1975 to $34.00 a barrel in 1981.

OPEC's control also affected the spot market, the term used to indicate unofficial transactions between major oil producers and consumers. The price paid for oil on the spot market reflects the true market value of oil. Unofficial prices on the spot market hovered as high as $40 a barrel during most of this period. By imposing production ceilings, OPEC kept the oil supply below the world's demand for oil. The result was an oil shortage.

Reducing Demand to Create an Oil Glut

During the 1980s, a drastic change in the international oil market took place. Faced with a shortage, the world markets found ways to reduce demand. The reduction, coupled with other factors, created an oil glut, or an oversupply of oil.

One factor that altered the oil supply in world markets was the increased production of oil by non-OPEC nations, the major independent producers. These non-OPEC nations included Mexico, Canada, the United Kingdom, and the United States. By the mid-1980s, the United States and the United Kingdom each were producing more oil than Saudi Arabia. In 1981, Saudi Arabia had produced more than 10 million barrels of oil a day. By 1985, in its intent to hold down the world's supply and maintain OPEC price levels, Saudi Arabia was producing less than 2 million barrels a day.

Another force that helped create the oil glut was widespread "cheating" by OPEC members in an effort to increase their revenues. The cheating took place in several ways. Some OPEC members offered buyers under-the-table "discounts." Other OPEC members quietly exceeded their production quotas. Iran and Iraq, for example, needed money to finance the war against each other that began in 1981 and continues today.

---

*All dollar figures are equal to U.S. dollars.

The decline in demand stemmed from two major forces. First, a worldwide recession began in 1980 that decreased the need for oil in the major oil-consuming nations. Second, conscious efforts to conserve energy also took place.

People everywhere lowered thermostats on furnaces in winter and raised them on air-conditioning units in the summer. People began to demand more fuel-efficient automobiles and trucks. At the same time, the United States lowered the speed limits on interstate highways and urged states to do likewise on state road systems.

In 1979, world oil production stood at 63 million barrels of oil a day. OPEC's share of the world's total oil output dropped from a high of 56 percent in 1973 to 32 percent in 1985.

OPEC and the World Economy

The steady rise in OPEC oil prices during the 1970s had both positive and negative effects on the world economy. On the positive side, oil-consuming nations were forced to use their energy resources more efficiently. In the oil-producing nations, the economies improved, enabling these nations to provide additional services to their people.

On the negative side, higher prices for oil brought about inflation—a general increase in price levels—in many nations. The high prices paid for oil also resulted in shortages of gasoline, home heating oil, and other petroleum-based products. High fuel costs hurt business activity in the industrialized nations of the world. The developing world, which relies on inexpensive oil for producing cheap fertilizer, was also hit hard.

The drop in oil prices in the 1980s also affected the world economy. On the positive side, prices for necessities such as gasoline and home heating oil were lowered. Businesses, encouraged by the low energy costs, began to expand and modernize. On the negative side, oil-producing nations had to cut back on their public-service projects.

The oil situation of the 1970s and 1980s is a real-life lesson in economics. It reminded people of the dangers of monopolies. It also reminded people that, whenever the economy is out of balance, the forces of supply and demand will continue to work until a balance is restored. ◆

OPEC's Share of the World Oil Market

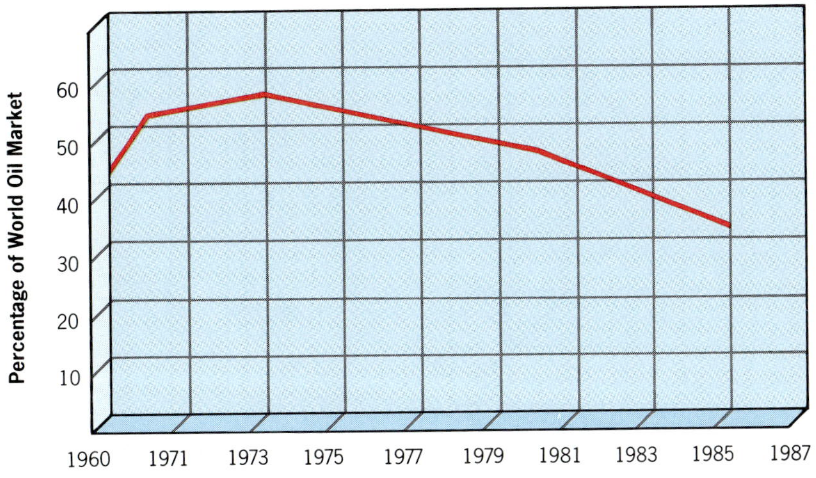

◆ Discussion topic: How the forces of supply and demand are similar to the system of checks and balances in American government.

See Key Study Questions and Key Understandings, p. TM 18.

2 In a free enterprise economy, the price system produces market equilibrium.

See Suggested Teaching Strategies, p. TM 18.

The needs of producers and consumers are best met at a point called the market equilibrium. **Market equilibrium** occurs when the supply and demand for a product are equal, and the prices charged for the product are relatively stable. The market equilibrium is established by combining the supply and demand curves for a product on the same graph. The point at which these two curves intersect is called the **equilibrium point.**

Equilibrium Price and Quantity

The forces of supply and demand in the marketplace determine the equilibrium price and quantity of a product. Combining a supply curve and a demand curve for a product on the same graph makes it possible to see how the interests of producers and consumers can be balanced.

The supply curve $\mathbf{S_1}$ and the demand curve $\mathbf{D_1}$ for motor scooters are shown below on the left. The vertical axis lists the possible prices for a motor scooter. The horizontal axis lists the quantity supplied and the quantity demanded. The two curves intersect at the equilibrium point $\mathbf{E_1}$. The equilibrium point is the equilibrium price of $1,000 and the equilibrium quantity of 300,000 motor scooters.

The market equilibrium is the best balance between the self-interests of suppliers and consumers. When a producer supplies a product at a quantity that is higher than the equilibrium point, a surplus occurs. In a **surplus,** the quantity produced exceeds the quantity demanded at the price offered. When a producer supplies a product at a quantity that is lower than the equilibrium point, then a shortage occurs. In a **shortage,** the quantity demanded exceeds the quantity supplied at the price offered (see the graph below to the right).

A Surplus Example. Consider the following example. Run-Rite Motors decides to produce 500,000 scooters and to sell them for $1,500 each (point **B** in the graph below). But at the $1,500 price, Run-Rite Motors sells only 100,000 motor scooters. The firm has produced a surplus of 400,000 motor scooters (500,000 − 100,000 = 400,000). Faced with the surplus, Run-Rite Motors decides to lower its price

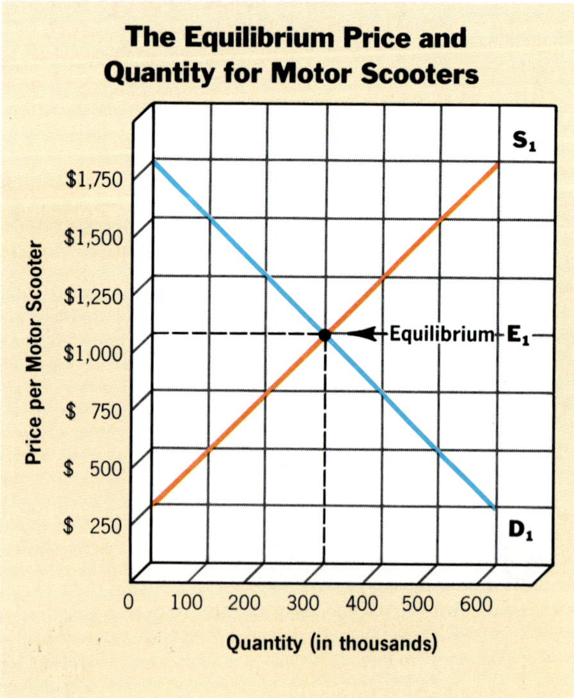

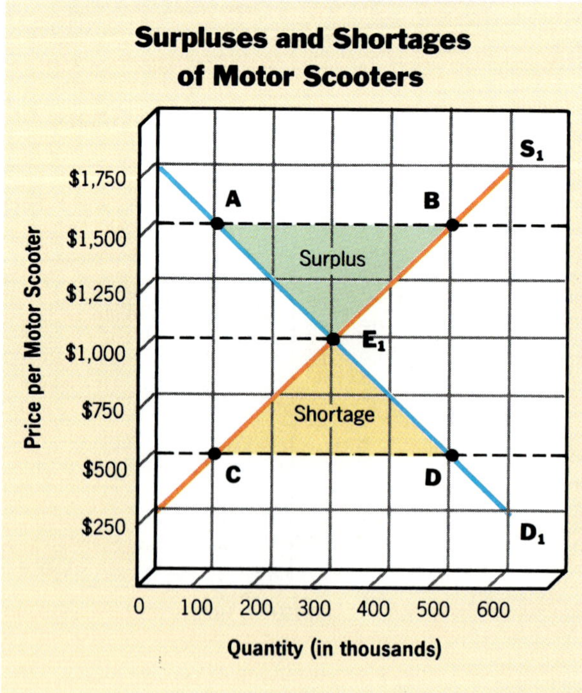

in order to increase consumer demand. Run-Rite Motors continues to offer the scooters at the lower price until the surplus is eliminated—in other words, until the equilibrium point is reached.

A Shortage Example. Suppose, on the other hand, that Run-Rite Motors decides to produce 100,000 motor scooters and to sell them for $500 each (point **C** in the graph on page 84). At the $500 price, Run-Rite Motors is faced with an incredible demand for 500,000 motor scooters. Presented with a shortage of 400,000 scooters (500,000 – 100,000 = 400,000), Run-Rite decides to raise the selling price to decrease consumer demand. Run-Rite continues to offer the scooters at the higher price until the shortage is eliminated—in other words, until the equilibrium point is reached.

While Run-Rite Motors is an individual firm, the same process of price determination is taking place in every other motor-scooter manufacturing firm.

Changing Equilibrium with a Favorable Shift in Supply

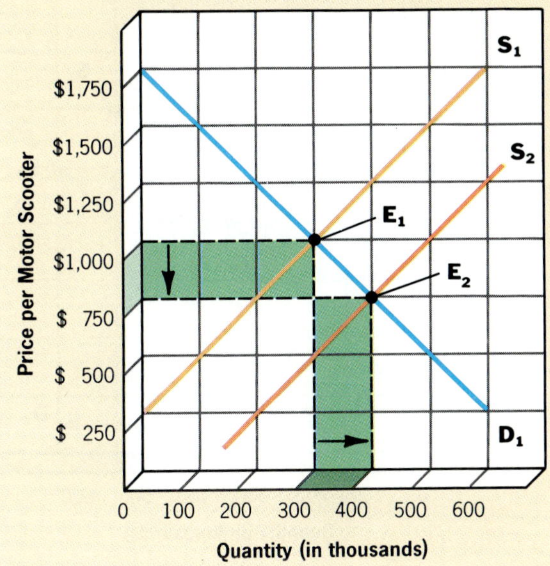

Changes in Supply and Demand

Changes in any of the five nonprice determinants of demand cause the entire demand curve to shift either to the left or to the right. For a review of these nonprice determinants of demand, see Chapter 2. Changes in any of the six nonprice determinants of supply cause the entire supply curve to shift either to the left or to the right. For a review of these six nonprice determinants of supply, see Chapter 3.

The Effect of Automation. In the real world, changes in supply and demand often affect market ◆ equilibrium. Again, take the example of Run-Rite Motors. Suppose that one or more of the determinants of supply changes in the manufacturer's favor. Run-Rite's profit picture has enabled it to automate its factories. Automation increases production and lowers production costs. The technological change causes the entire supply curve to shift to the right, as shown in the graph on this page.

If demand remains constant and the supply increases, Run-Rite Motors will be able to produce more scooters at a lower price. In this case, the new equilibrium $\mathbf{E_2}$ is at the intersection of the demand curve $\mathbf{D_1}$ and the new supply curve $\mathbf{S_2}$. At this point, the new equilibrium price has fallen to $750, while the new equilibrium quantity has increased to 400,000 motor scooters. The "old" supply curve $\mathbf{S_1}$ no longer reflects Run-Rite Motors' supply schedule. The manufacturer is now willing to produce more motor scooters at each price.

Electronic scanners read price codes, enabling stores to speed up the check-out process. The increased productivity helps stores lower production costs.

◆ Note that automation also affects people. Some jobs cease to exist when companies increase automation. Automation may also create new jobs that require technical training to equip workers with new skills.

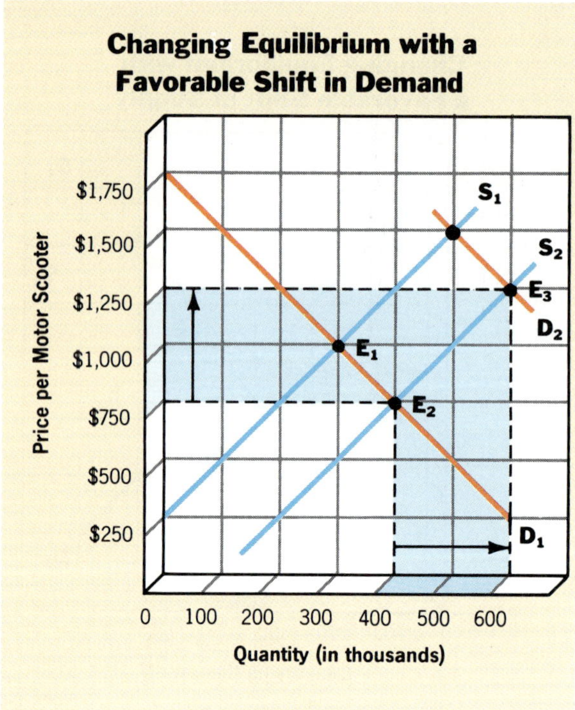

The Effect of Changing Tastes. Suppose now that consumer tastes, one of the determinants of demand, also change. Run-Rite Motors has developed advertising aimed at the youth market. The advertising shows football players and rock stars riding Run-Rite's motor scooters. The young people respond with an increased demand for Run-Rite's and other manufacturers' motor scooters. The total size of the market—and total demand—increases substantially. This favorable change in demand is shown in the graph above.

In the graph, the original curve $\mathbf{D_1}$ has shifted to the right. The new curve is labeled $\mathbf{D_2}$. The $\mathbf{D_2}$ curve represents the new, larger market for motor scooters. The point at which the new demand curve intersects with the $\mathbf{S_2}$ supply curve is the new market equilibrium. The new equilibrium point is labeled $\mathbf{E_3}$ on the graph. The equilibrium price has increased from $750 to $1,250 a motor scooter. The equilibrium quantity has increased from 400,000 to 600,000 motor scooters. The "old" demand curve $\mathbf{D_1}$ no longer reflects the demand schedule. At each and every price along the $\mathbf{D_2}$ curve, consumers are now willing and able to buy more motor scooters than they were earlier.

CASE STUDY

The Compact Disc Revolution

Levels of supply and demand are constantly changing in a free enterprise system. Some products decrease in popularity. Others increase in popularity. Changes for a good in either its supply or its demand cause the price and quantity of the good to increase or decrease.

The arrival of the compact disc (CD) and the compact disc player (CDP) has caused a significant change in the recording industry. CDs and CDPs were originally developed by Sony of Japan and Philips of the Netherlands. In a joint business venture in 1978, the two companies produced the world's first laser-based music system. After its introduction into the United States in 1983, this technological marvel became the fastest-selling machine in the history of home electronics.

Before the 1980s, the supply of CDPs and CDs had been initially limited by the relatively small number of firms producing them and the high costs of production. By the mid-1980s, however, the recording industry had overcome many production obstacles. By 1985, for example, about 50 firms in the world were producing CDPs, while 13 companies—including one in the United States—were producing CDs.

By decreasing the costs of production, producers have been able to drastically reduce prices for CDs and CDPs. CDPs cost over $1,000 in 1983. In 1985, they cost less than $200. CDs cost about $20 in 1983. Two years later, they cost $12 to $14. Lower production costs also have resulted in an increase in the quantity of CDs and CDPs available for sale. The supply of CDPs increased from 35,000 in 1983 to about 600,000 in 1985. The supply of CDs increased from 770,000 in 1983 to about 15 million in 1985.

The demand for CDPs and CDs has continued to increase. The profits to producers have increased, too. The determinants of demand most favoring CDPs and CDs have included favorable shifts in consumer tastes and preferences, the increase in the size of the market, and the prices of related goods.

Consumer tastes and preferences have been affected by the purity of sound produced by the CDs and CDPs. The variety of models of CDPs—home versions, automobile systems, the boom box version, the portable model, and even a jukebox model—

also has added to consumer demand. In addition, prices for CDs and CDPs have compared favorably with the prices of such substitute goods as turntables, cassette players, and LP albums and cassettes. First-time buyers are now more likely to consider buying the lower-priced compact disc systems than the higher-priced conventional systems. As a result, the size of the market has expanded worldwide.

Producers of audio equipment also hope that the growing popularity of the CDPs will cause an increase in demand for their complementary goods, such as amplifiers and speakers.

See Suggested Assignments, p. TM 18.

Section 2 Review See Answers, p. A 15.

DEFINE market equilibrium, surplus, shortage

1. **Interpreting Ideas** Why is market equilibrium the best balance between consumer self-interest and producer self-interest?
2. **Analyzing Ideas** What effect do changing consumer tastes have on price?
3. **Interpreting Graphics** Review the graph on page 84 showing surpluses and shortages of motor scooters. Describe in at least one full sentence what is shown at points **A, B, C, D,** and $\mathbf{E_1}$ on the graph.

See Key Study Questions and Key Understandings, p. TM 19.

3 The price system in a free enterprise economy has defenders and critics.

See Suggested Teaching Strategies, p. TM 19.

In a free enterprise economy, the competitive price system pulls together the decisions of consumers and producers, so that market equilibrium results. Ideally, producers will produce goods consumers want at prices satisfying to both. However, the price system does not always work as expected, and outside forces can cause a disruption of the market equilibrium.

A Defense of the Price System

Proponents of the competitive price system argue that the price system forces producers to make the goods and services that the public wants in the most efficient manner. Efficiency means that producers must use the best techniques at the lowest cost in producing the goods that people want.

Supporters of the price system also argue that it allows for personal freedom. The economic activities of individuals and businesses cooperate freely through the price system. The alternative is a directed, involuntary economy—the opposite of the free enterprise system.

Opposition to the Price System

The price system is not without its critics. Some economists believe that the price system works against the free enterprise system because only a very few large producers are able to achieve maximum efficiency. Because of their size and level of efficiency, these few producers are able to control the marketplace. When competition declines because of fewer producers, the price system weakens and the consumers suffer.

The price system helps to keep prices low by encouraging competition among suppliers.

Opponents of the price system argue that agriculture is one area in which the price system inadequately regulates the market.

Negative Social Costs. Opponents also argue that the price system does not take into account all of the costs of production. The production of goods sometimes results in negative side effects, or social costs, that affect people not connected with the production or consumption of the goods. These negative social costs are called **externalities.**

Environmental pollution is a good example of an ◆ externality. The air pollution emitted by some factory smokestacks is an externality that can affect a wide geographical area. Water pollution caused by chemical wastes discharged from a manufacturing plant is another example of an externality. The monetary costs of dealing with the health and environmental problems brought on by pollution are not reflected in the price of the products produced by the offending manufacturers. Thus the effectiveness of the price system as a mechanism for controlling market actions is weakened.

Government Regulation of Prices. Critics also point out that the price system does not set prices for all goods and services in the economy. Some prices are set by the government. For example, local governments set the rates for water and sewer services. State governments regulate companies that provide certain essential goods or services. State regulation of public utilities, for example, requires that state agencies or legislatures approve rate increases before the increases are passed along to consumers.

Price Stabilization. Finally, critics insist that the price system is ineffective. The inability of the price system to stabilize prices sometimes results in government intervention. When government leaders feel that prices are rising or falling too quickly, they sometimes institute price ceilings or price floors.

A **price ceiling** is a government regulation that prohibits prices from rising above a certain maximum level. Price ceilings make it illegal to charge prices above the established level. A **price floor** is a government regulation that prohibits prices from falling below a certain minimum level. It is illegal for producers to drop their prices below the established level. Price floors are much more common than price ceilings. The government often sets price floors for agricultural products in an effort to help farmers cover their production costs.

Most economists do not favor the use of price ceilings and price floors because of the effect that

◆ **Discussion topic: The government requires automobile manufacturers to install antipollution devices on new automobiles even though the devices lower gas mileage. Examine the social benefits versus the economic costs of this regulation.**

price controls have on demand in the marketplace. Price ceilings tend to result in shortages. The inability of producers to raise prices above a certain level means that demand in the marketplace cannot be regulated by manipulating price. Consumers then demand more products than producers are willing to supply at the legal price.

On the other hand, price floors tend to result in surpluses. A guaranteed minimum price encourages producers to maintain a high level of production. The high level of production results in more products than consumers are willing to buy at the mandated price. Once again, the inability of producers to raise and lower prices according to the operations of supply and demand prevents the market from reaching equilibrium.

Price ceilings and price floors present an interesting paradox. Price controls are adopted because the price system is unable to reach equilibrium on its own. Once the price controls are instituted, however, they fail because the price system is unable to eliminate the resulting surpluses and shortages.

See Suggested Assignments, p. TM 19.

Section 3 Review See Answers, p. A 15.

DEFINE externalities, price ceiling, price floor

1. **Summarizing Ideas** **(a)** How does the price system work to bring about market equilibrium? **(b)** How does it contribute to economic freedom?
2. **Organizing Ideas** **(a)** What is often the result of price controls? Why? **(b)** What is often the result of price floors? Why? **(c)** Which type of price control has the United States government established to stabilize agricultural products? **(d)** Why are price controls for agricultural products necessary?
3. **Analyzing Ideas** **(a)** Why is efficiency important to an economic system? **(b)** Since the price system does not take into account externalities, who should pay for externalities such as pollution? Why?
4. **Evaluating Ideas** **(a)** Describe the arguments for and against the price system. **(b)** Which argument do you find most convincing? Why?

CHAPTER 4 SUMMARY

Self-interest plays a major role in guiding the actions of producers and consumers. Self-interest brings the actions of producers and consumers into conflict, however. In a free enterprise economy, a compromise between the conflicting self-interests of producers and consumers is achieved through the operations of the price system. The price system is the communication process that enables producers and consumers to coordinate production decisions to achieve a balance in the marketplace between supply and demand. First, the price system coordinates market activities by providing information on the price levels that consumers consider acceptable. Second, the price system coordinates market activities by providing incentives for producers and consumers to engage in market exchanges. Third, it coordinates market activities by placing limits on consumer buying.

The market equilibrium is the point at which the needs of producers and consumers are best met. The market equilibrium is established by combining the supply and demand curves for a product on the same graph. The point at which the two curves intersect is the equilibrium point.

When producers supply a product at a quantity higher than the equilibrium point, a surplus occurs. When producers supply a product at a quantity that is below the equilibrium point, a shortage occurs. The market is brought back into equilibrium by altering the price of the product, thereby affecting demand.

The price system as a mechanism for achieving market equilibrium enjoys widespread support in the United States. The price system, however, is not without its critics. Among the criticisms of the price system are that it limits competition, fails to take into account externalities, fails to set prices for all goods and services, and cannot always achieve price stability.

When price stability cannot be achieved, the government sometimes institutes price ceilings and price floors. A price ceiling establishes the highest price that can be charged for a product. A price floor establishes the lowest price that can be charged for a product. While price ceilings and price floors stabilize prices, they often lead to shortages in the case of price ceilings and to surpluses in the case of price floors.

CHAPTER 4 REVIEW

For Answers to Chapter 4 Review, see p. A 16.

Reviewing Economic Terms

Supply the economic term that correctly completes each sentence.

1. Consumers and producers communicate through the _____ _____.
2. When the supply and the demand for a product are equal and the product's price is relatively stable, _____ _____ occurs.
3. In a _____, the quantity produced exceeds the quantity demanded at the price offered.
4. Negative social costs are called _____.
5. A government regulation that prohibits prices from rising above a set level is a _____ _____.

Exercising Economic Skills

1. **Analyzing Economic Information** Read *A Change in Direction for OPEC* on page 93. **(a)** State the main idea. **(b)** Answer the who, what, where, when, why, and how questions. **(c)** List the opinions, if any, stated by the author. **(d)** Describe the author's bias, if any. **(e)** Identify two cause-effect relationships.
2. **Applying for a Job** Study the feature on pages 512–515. Then **(a)** make a list of your special interests, **(b)** identify possible jobs or careers in which you could pursue one or more of your special interests, and **(c)** secure more information about one of these careers.

Thinking Critically About Economics

1. **Summarizing Ideas** **(a)** How does producer and consumer self-interest conflict? **(b)** What does the equilibrium point represent? **(c)** What is the relationship between the price system and market equilibrium?
2. **Organizing Ideas** **(a)** How do prices communicate? **(b)** How does the price system coordinate market activities?
3. **Interpreting Ideas** **(a)** What are the functions of the price system? **(b)** Which function do you consider the most important? Why?
4. **Analyzing Ideas** **(a)** Discuss the importance of personal freedom in the United States economy. **(b)** What influence does personal freedom have on the price system?
5. **Evaluating Ideas** **(a)** Describe the positive and negative aspects of price ceilings and price floors. **(b)** Evaluate the use of price ceilings and price floors to correct the price system.

Extending Economic Knowledge

1. Write a paragraph in which you **(a)** describe the effect you think high salaries for professional athletes will have on the supply of athletes, **(b)** explain why high salaries will have that effect on the supply of athletes, and **(c)** predict the effect on the supply of athletes if salaries are significantly reduced.
2. Using the demand and supply schedules below, complete the following activities. **(a)** Plot the demand curve and the supply curve on the same graph. **(b)** Mark the market equilibrium point with an $\mathbf{E_1}$. **(c)** Use the information on the graph to state the equilibrium price and the equilibrium quantity for medium-sized pizzas. **(d)** Construct a new graph that illustrates the shift that occurs in demand and equilibrium price if consumer preference for medium-sized pizzas increases.

Medium-Sized Pizzas

Demand Schedule		Supply Schedule	
Price	Quantity	Price	Quantity
$5.00	50,000	$5.00	0
$6.00	40,000	$6.00	5,000
$7.00	30,000	$7.00	10,000
$8.00	20,000	$8.00	15,000
$9.00	10,000	$9.00	20,000

3. Research the price supports established by the United States government on peanuts or another farm product. Then write an essay evaluating the effects of the price support on that product in the marketplace.

Using Primary Sources

Adam Smith (1732–1790) was a philosopher and economist from Scotland. His greatest work, *An Inquiry into the Nature and Causes of the Wealth of Nations*, was published in 1776. In this book, Smith supported economic freedom in the marketplace. As you read the following excerpts, think about how a commodity's "natural price" is determined. Why is a commodity's natural price often different from its "market price"?

The Natural and Market Price of Commodities

There is in every society or neighbourhood an ordinary or average rate both of wages and profit in every different employment of labour and stock. This rate is naturally regulated, . . . partly by the general circumstances of the society . . . and partly by the particular nature of each employment.

There is likewise in every society or neighbourhood an ordinary or average rate of rent, which is regulated too, . . . partly by the general circumstances of the society or neighbourhood in which the land is situated, and partly by the natural or improved fertility of the land.

These ordinary or average rates may be called the natural rates of wages, profit, and rent. . . .

When the price of any commodity is neither more nor less than what is sufficient to pay the rent of the land, the wages of the labour, and the profits of the stock employed in raising, preparing, and bringing it to market, according to their natural rates, the commodity is then sold for what may be called its natural price.

The commodity is then sold precisely for what it is worth, or for what it really costs the person who brings it to market. . . .

The actual price at which any commodity is commonly sold is called its market price. . . .

The market price of every particular commodity is regulated by the proportion between the quantity which is actually brought to market, and the demand of those who are willing to pay the natural price of the commodity. . . . Such people may be called the effectual demanders, and their demand the effectual demand. . . . A very poor man may be said in some sense to have a demand for a coach and six [horses]; he might like to have it; but his demand is not an effectual demand, as the commodity can never be brought to market in order to satisfy it.

When the quantity of any commodity which is brought to market falls short of the effectual demand, . . . [a] competition will immediately begin among them [potential buyers], and the market price will rise more or less above the natural price. . . .

When the quantity brought to market exceeds the effectual demand, . . . [some] part must be sold to those who are willing to pay less. . . . The market price will sink more or less below the natural price. . . .

When the quantity brought to market is just sufficient to supply the effectual demand and no more, the market price naturally comes to be either exactly, or as nearly as can be judged of, the same with the natural price. . . .

The quantity of every commodity brought to market naturally suits itself to the effectual demand. It is the interest of all those who employ their land, labour, or stock, in bringing any commodity to market, that the quantity never should exceed the effectual demand; and it is the interest of all other people that it never should fall short of that demand.

Source Review

For Answers to Source Review, see p. A 17.

1. According to Adam Smith, what are three costs of production that affect a commodity's "natural price"?
2. In a sentence, define "natural price."
3. How does Smith distinguish between "effectual demand" and "demand"?
4. When would a commodity's market price be higher than its natural price? When would a commodity's market price be lower than its natural price?
5. When is a commodity's natural price and market price the same? Why is it in the best interests of both producers and consumers to match the supply of a commodity with its effectual demand?

UNIT ONE REVIEW

For Answers to Unit One Review, see p. A 17.

Reviewing Economic Ideas

1. What is the difference **(a)** between a good and a service? **(b)** between a need and a want?
2. Where are the answers to the basic economic questions found in **(a)** a traditional economy, **(b)** a command economy, and **(c)** a market economy?
3. Describe the three main types of mixed economies.
4. **(a)** What are the main features of the United States economy? **(b)** Name and describe the goals of the United States economy.
5. Identify **(a)** the determinants of demand, **(b)** the determinants of supply, and **(c)** the functions of price.
6. Restate and explain **(a)** the law of demand, **(b)** the law of supply, **(c)** the law of diminishing marginal utility, and **(d)** the law of diminishing marginal returns.

Connecting Economic Ideas

1. **Summarizing Ideas** **(a)** What is the role of entrepreneurship in a capitalist economy? **(b)** Does entrepreneurship play a major role in Communist economies? Why or why not?
2. **Organizing Ideas** Explain the influences of scarcity and the resulting need for efficiency as an economic goal.
3. **Interpreting Ideas** Explain how the profit motive affects a nation's economic growth.
4. **Seeing Relationships** **(a)** How are economic freedom, self-interest, and the profit motive related to economic decision making? **(b)** What two factors interact to produce market equilibrium? **(c)** How are the laws of diminishing marginal utility and diminishing returns related?
5. **Analyzing Ideas** What effect do opportunity costs and the substitution effect have on **(a)** demand and **(b)** supply ?
6. **Evaluating Ideas** Based on what you have read in this unit, do you think the laws of demand and supply favor entrepreneurs? Why or why not? Support your argument with real examples.

Investigating Economic Issues

Reread the *Issues in Economics* feature on pages 82–83 and answer the following questions.

1. **Organizing Ideas** **(a)** What does the term OPEC stand for? **(b)** What is a cartel?
2. **Seeing Relationships** What effect did OPEC's production ceilings during the 1970s have on the oil supply and on gasoline prices? **(b)** In the late 1970s, what two factors contributed to decreasing demand for gasoline in the United States? **(c)** Why did gasoline prices fall in the early 1980s?
3. **Analyzing Ideas** How does a cartel affect **(a)** supply and **(b)** price?
4. **Evaluating Ideas** **(a)** What were the positive effects on the world economy of the actions of the OPEC cartel during the 1970s? **(b)** What were the negative effects on the world economy of the actions of the OPEC cartel during the 1970s? **(c)** Overall, have the actions of the OPEC cartel had a positive or negative effect on the world economy? Explain.

Applying Economics

1. Suppose you and a group of classmates were shipwrecked. **(a)** What is the first thing you would do in organizing an economic system for the group? **(b)** Which type of economy would you recommend to answer the basic economic questions in this situation? Why?
2. Collect six articles from newspapers or magazines that illustrate the major points of this unit. For each article, write a paragraph that describes the main idea of the article and what the article illustrates about economics.
3. **(a)** Research a product of interest to you to find its price and the approximate quantity produced last year. **(b)** With the statistics you have researched as a guide, develop imaginary demand and supply schedules. **(c)** Using the imaginary demand and supply schedules, plot a demand curve and supply curve on the same graph. **(d)** Mark the equilibrium point on the graph with an $\mathbf{E_1}$ and indicate the areas where surpluses and shortages would occur.

Using Primary Sources

In August of 1986, the OPEC oil ministers announced that the cartel was abandoning its eight-month-old policy of unlimited production. In its place, OPEC established "voluntary" quotas. As you read the following excerpts from *The Economist*, a leading British newsmagazine, note the difficulties OPEC will face in abiding by these voluntary production targets.

A Change in Direction for OPEC

The plan is likely to run into problems on the side of both demand and supply. Demand is likely to be low even by October [1986], because the buildup in OPEC production in the past few months . . . has enabled oil companies and consumers to stockpile lots of cheap oil. Even a cold northern winter in 1986–87 will not take much pressure off the producers as it normally does.

On the side of supply, individual OPEC members will still have every incentive to pump out more oil than the world needs. Quite how fragile the new agreement is became plainer as successive oil ministers started to talk about it. Both Saudi Arabia and Kuwait, which will have to make the biggest production cuts to meet their . . . quotas, say they intend to turn on the taps again at the first sign of any other member country welshing on the deal. Those who have fought long-running battles within OPEC for higher quotas, such as the United Arab Emirates, say they have only postponed, not given up, their campaigns. Iraq, which is conveniently exempt from the new agreement, will continue to produce flat out to sustain its stuttering effort in the Gulf war. . . .

Despite the [price] crash, oil demand in the rich countries has not picked up much. And little non-OPEC production has closed down. . . . Britain has refused to have anything to do with any global production-rationing deal. Some other oil producers are more sympathetic. After the [OPEC] announcement from Geneva, Mexico and Malaysia both said . . . that they would cut their output too. They will continue this policy only if OPEC convinces them that its members can keep their own new act together.

Source Review

For Answers to Source Review, see p. A 19.

1. What "demand" factors limit OPEC's ability to dictate oil prices on world markets?
2. What "supply" factors limit the cartel's ability to dictate oil prices?
3. How have non-OPEC oil producers responded to OPEC's call for production quotas?

Reading About Economics

Canterbury, E. Ray. *The Making of Economics*, 3rd Ed. Belmont, California: Wadsworth Publishing. A survey of economists, their theories, and different economic systems, with emphasis on Adam Smith and the free market system.

Friedman, Milton and Rose. *Free to Choose: A Personal Statement.* San Diego: Harcourt Brace Jovanovich. An attack on the intervention in the United States economy by government agencies, with proposals for an economic Bill of Rights as amendments to the United States Constitution.

Heilbroner, Robert L. *The Worldly Philosophers: The Lives, Times, and Ideas of the Great Economic Thinkers*, 5th ed. rev. New York: Simon and Schuster. A survey of the great economists from Adam Smith's time to the present.

Heilbroner, Robert L. and Lester C. Thurow. *Five Economic Challenges.* Englewood Cliffs, N.J.: Prentice-Hall. General discussion of inflation, recession, government's influence on the economy, the dollar's fluctuating exchange rate, and the economics of the energy crisis.

Puth, Robert C. *American Economic History.* New York: The Dryden Press. A history of the development of the American economy.

See Unit Materials, p. TM 20.
See Multimedia Guide, p. TM 21.
See Applying Economics on text p. 164.

UNIT TWO

BUSINESS IN THE FREE ENTERPRISE SYSTEM

CHAPTER 5

See Chapter Overview, p. TM 22.
See Chapter Objectives, p. TM 22.
See Introducing the Chapter, p. TM 22.
See Extending Economic Knowledge on text p. 118.

Business Organizations

I learned to keep going, even in bad times. . . . I learned that there are no free lunches. And I learned about the values of hard work. In the end, you've got to be productive. That's what made this country great—and that's what's going to make us great again.

Lee Iacocca

1 In a free enterprise system, businesses can be organized in a number of ways.

- Sole Proprietorships
- Partnerships
- Corporations

2 Corporations can expand by combining one business with other businesses.

- Types of Corporate Combinations
- Trends in Corporate Combinations
- The Impact of Corporate Combinations

3 Businesses also can be organized as franchises, cooperatives, and nonprofit organizations.

- Franchises
- Cooperatives
- Nonprofit Organizations

CHAPTER 5 STUDY GUIDE

Chapter Focus

Chapter 5 presents an overview of how businesses can be organized in a free enterprise system. It examines the three most common types of business organizations, which are sole proprietorships, partnerships, and corporations. The chapter also discusses corporate mergers and other forms of business organization.

As you study the chapter, look for the details that support each of the following statements.

1. In a free enterprise system, businesses can be organized in a number of ways.
2. Corporations can expand by combining one business with other businesses.
3. Businesses also can be organized as franchises, cooperatives, and nonprofit organizations.

See Preteaching Vocabulary, p. TM 22.

Terms to Know

The following terms, while not the only terms emphasized in this chapter, are basic to your understanding of types of business organizations. Determine the meaning of each term, either by using the Glossary or by watching for context clues as you read the chapter.

sole proprietorship	horizontal combination
liability	vertical combination
partnership	conglomerate combination
corporation	subsidiary
stockholder	franchise
stock	cooperative
merger	nonprofit organization

See Key Study Questions and Key Understandings, p. TM 23.

1 In a free enterprise system, businesses can be organized in a number of ways.

See Suggested Teaching Strategies, p. TM 23.

Most people at some time in their lives dream of starting their own business. For many people, owning a business represents the opportunity to be their own boss and to reap well-deserved rewards. Organizing, building, and operating a business, however, is considerably more work than just dreaming a great idea, inventing a better mousetrap, or opening up a lemonade stand in the front yard.

In the American free enterprise system, people who wish to own a private business have the opportunity to select the type of organization that best suits their business needs. The most common forms are sole proprietorships, partnerships, and corporations.

Sole Proprietorships

A business owned and controlled by one person is a **sole proprietorship.** Sole proprietorships are the oldest, simplest, and most common of all types of businesses.

Because the financial resources available to one person often are limited, sole proprietorships tend to be enterprises that require small amounts of capital to start and operate. Many doctors, dentists, lawyers, bakers, and beauticians organize as sole proprietors to provide professional services. Other services offered by sole proprietors include plumbing, carpentry, dry cleaning, and lawn care. Many construction companies, small "mom-and-pop" grocery stores, florists, other small retail stores, farms, real estate firms, and insurance firms also are organized as sole proprietorships.

Advantages of Proprietorships. There are many advantages to organizing a business as a sole proprietorship. Chief among the advantages is that sole proprietorships are an easy type of business to form. In addition to requiring small amounts of capital, forming a sole proprietorship involves few legal considerations. No complicated legal documents have to be filed with the state or federal government in order to start a sole proprietorship.

The major legal and governmental restrictions involve zoning laws and licensing. Sole proprietorships, like all businesses, must observe zoning laws. Zoning laws stipulate the areas of a city or county in which various types of businesses can operate. In addition, sole proprietorships usually must obtain various business licenses from the city and county before they can open for business. Some professionals—such as doctors, lawyers, and beauticians—also must be licensed by the state.

A second advantage of sole proprietorships is profit. Sole proprietors receive the entire profit from their business activities. Keeping all of the profit is appealing to many individuals because profit is the chief motivating factor for starting a business. The chances of making a fortune from a small investment are slim, but fortunes sometimes have been made by business people who started out as sole proprietors. The possibility of wealth that feeds the entrepreneurial spirit is at the basis of the free enterprise system.

A third advantage of sole proprietorships is control. Sole proprietors, who have ownership and control of their businesses, can make business decisions quickly. They can respond quickly to correct problems or to take advantage of opportunities. Sole proprietors can hire or fire workers without the paperwork usually demanded by larger firms. Similarly, sole proprietors can increase or decrease the number of items being produced or sold without the group decision making often utilized in larger firms. They also can respond more quickly than owners of larger firms to changes and trends in the marketplace.

Finally, sole proprietorships offer owners a high degree of personal satisfaction. Much satisfaction stems from the control they have over their own businesses. When proprietors succeed, they do so on their own merits because they are their own bosses. Success brings with it financial and psychological rewards in the form of profits, prestige, and a sense of accomplishment.

Disadvantages of Proprietorships. Sole proprietorships also have disadvantages. One of the major disadvantages is the unlimited liability that proprietors face. **Liability** is the debt, or amount of money, owed by the business. From a legal standpoint, sole proprietors personally are responsible for all business debts. Sometimes business losses are so

For many sole proprietors, the rewards of owning their own businesses outweigh the risks involved.

great that sole proprietors cannot pay their suppliers or repay their loans. To cover their debts, sole proprietors then have to forfeit their personal property as well as their businesses. Most failures of sole proprietorships, as with other business organizations, are covered by state and federal bankruptcy laws (see Chapter 12).

A second disadvantage is the burden of sole responsibility for all aspects of running the business. Proprietors typically must perform the roles of market analyst, chief salesperson, accountant, and recordkeeper. With responsibilities so varied, proprietors need to be competent and efficient in many fields to be successful. In addition, the frustration created by such varied demands may result in loss of personal satisfaction and sense of accomplishment that is so important to sole proprietors.

A third disadvantage is the limited potential for ◆ business growth that is attached to most sole proprietorships. Proprietors usually start their businesses by borrowing small sums of money and putting up collateral to guarantee repayment of the loans. **Collateral** is anything of value that a borrower has that can be used to guarantee that a loan will be repaid. A sole proprietor's collateral is usually limited. It may include such things as the business itself, the inventory of unsold merchandise, and even the proprietor's house and other personal possessions. Creditors, however, are hesitant to offer

◆ Report topic: Why sole proprietorships have the highest failure rate and make the least profit.

loans that exceed the value of collateral. Like other businesses, sole proprietorships need capital to grow and modernize. But unless the collateral of a sole proprietorship increases, the sole proprietor lacks access to increasing amounts of credit.

A final disadvantage of sole proprietorships is lack of longevity. Sole proprietorships often have a shorter life span than other types of business organizations. The success of the business depends on the health, commitment, and competence of one person. The risk of failure is greater when the entire business rests on one person. This fact alone accounts for the many business failures found among sole proprietorships.

Partnerships

A **partnership** is a business that is owned and controlled by two or more people. Partnerships are the least common type of business organization in the United States (see the graph on page 102).

As in the case of sole proprietorships, partnerships are concentrated in businesses that require relatively small amounts of money to start and operate. Small retail stores, farms, and construction companies often are organized as partnerships. People in service occupations, such as doctors, lawyers, accountants, and photographers, also form partnerships. Many of these partnerships may have started as sole proprietorships.

A partnership begins when two or more people agree to operate a business together. In order to avoid later conflicts, the partners usually formulate a written agreement called a partnership contract. A **partnership contract** outlines the distribution of profits and losses. It details the specific responsibilities of each partner and includes provision for adding or dropping partners and dissolving the partnership.

Partnerships take different forms. In a **general partnership,** partners enjoy equal decision-making authority and have unlimited liability. In a **limited partnership,** the partners join as an investment,

Partnerships allow doctors to share the expenses of maintaining offices and the responsibilities of providing care for their patients.

rarely take an active role in business decisions, and their liability is limited to the amount of money invested in the business. The personal property of limited partners, such as houses or cars, cannot be touched by creditors should the business fail.

Some of the disadvantages of sole proprietorships can be overcome by forming a partnership. Trade-offs, however, are involved. While a partnership solves some problems, it may create others.

Advantages of Partnerships. Partnerships share one advantage with proprietorships in that both are relatively easy to form and require a small amount of money to start and operate. Partnerships also are subject to the same zoning and licensing restrictions as proprietorships.

A second major advantage of partnerships is specialization. Specific business duties can be assigned to different partners depending on the provisions of the partnership contract. Unlike the owner of a sole proprietorship, partners are better able to specialize in those areas of the business in which their skills and talents can be best used. For example, Tracy Michaels, Patti Palmer, and Laura Lewis are partners in a local retail store. Palmer is an excellent accountant and money manager. Michaels is a skilled salesperson. Lewis, the third partner, is skilled in merchandising and keeps the shelves well stocked with a wide variety of goods.

A third advantage of partnerships is shared decision making. When partners take the time to consult with each other on business matters, mistakes are likely to be minimized. Decisions made after discussion and debate often are more informed decisions than those made without the benefit of additional opinions.

A fourth advantage of partnerships is the sharing of business losses. The sharing of losses may enable a partnership to survive the same type of situation that brings a sole proprietor to failure. Furthermore, partnerships usually are in a better position than sole proprietorships to obtain needed capital to finance business expansion and modernization. Creditors are more likely to extend larger loans to partnerships than to sole proprietorships because the risk is shared among the partners, but is the full responsibility of the sole proprietor.

Finally, as owners of businesses, partners often feel the same pride, sense of accomplishment, and personal satisfaction that sole proprietors feel.

Economics Reporter

What Is the Small Business Administration?

The Small Business Administration (SBA) is an independent government agency created by Congress to aid, counsel, assist, and protect the interests of small business owners. Its aim is to ensure that small businesses receive a fair share of government purchases, contracts, and subcontracts. Among the services offered by the SBA are financial assistance, managerial and technical assistance, and aid in investigating policy decisions that affect small businesses. The SBA also helps women and minorities overcome prejudice encountered in starting a small business. It gives special assistance to the handicapped and to nonprofit organizations that employ them.

Disadvantages of Partnerships. Partnerships, while easing some of the problems associated with sole proprietorships, still have disadvantages. One of the major disadvantages is the unlimited liability attached to general partnerships. Each general partner has an active role in the business, and each is personally responsible for all debts incurred by the business. General partners may lose more than their original investments.

A second disadvantage of partnerships is that disagreements or other conflicts may arise among partners. Partners may have different personalities and different styles of management. One person may have poor communication skills and fail to relay important information either to the other partner or partners or to the employees. Partners with opposing views may fail to reach a necessary compromise. Partnership conflicts lower employee morale, delay important business decisions, and lessen the efficiency of the total operation. Disagreements also can lessen the personal satisfaction of the partners and even lead to a breakup of the partnership.

A final disadvantage is that the life of the partnership is dependent on the willingness and ability of the partners to continue in the business together. Sickness, death, conflict among partners, and other problems can end the partnership.

Business Organizations

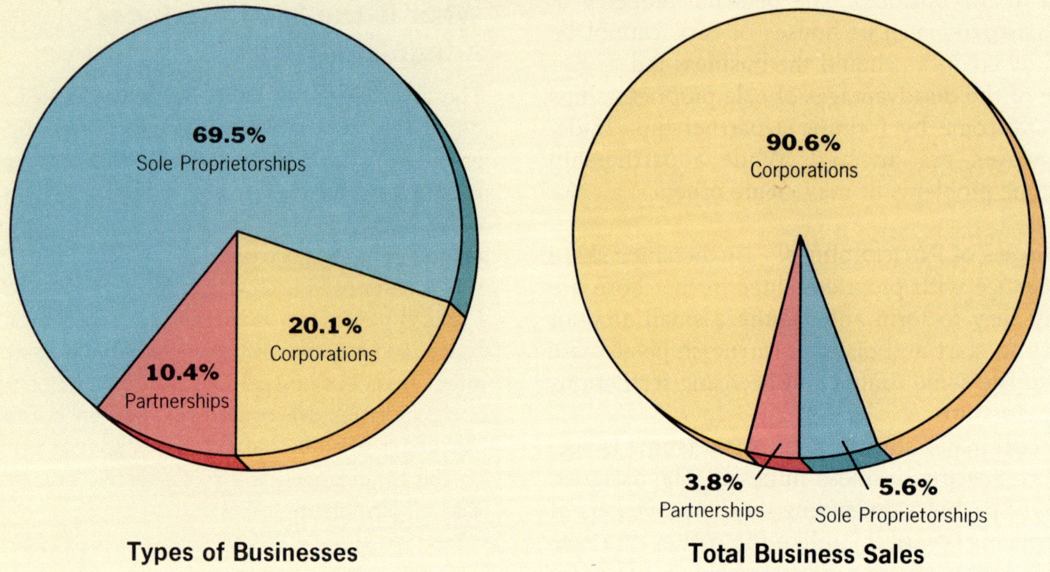

Source: *Statistical Abstract of the United States, 1986*

Corporations

◆ A **corporation** is a business organization that is treated by law as if it were an individual person. A corporation can do everything that a sole proprietorship or a partnership can do. It can, for example, buy property and resources, hire workers, make contracts, pay taxes, sue others and be sued, and produce and sell products. A corporation, however, is owned by stockholders. **Stockholders** are individuals who invest in a corporation by buying shares of stock. **Stocks** are the certificates of ownership in the corporation. Stockholders invest in a corporation in order to make a profit.

About 20 percent of the businesses in the United States are organized as corporations. The 20 percent, however, produce approximately 91 percent of total sales in the nation. Corporations are considered to be the most influential type of business organization because they account for the vast majority of sales in the economy. The graphs on this page show the percentage of businesses organized as sole proprietorships, partnerships, and corporations and the percentage of total sales that each type of organization produces annually.

Types of Corporations. A corporation may be either publicly owned or closed. A publicly owned corporation allows its shares to be purchased by anyone who chooses to invest in the business. Most corporations today are publicly owned. A closed corporation is owned by a limited number of stockholders. People outside of this limited group may not buy shares in the corporation.

Many businesses begin as closed corporations. At some point, however, they sell stock to the public and become publicly owned. For example, the Ford Motor Company was a closed corporation until the mid-1950s. The Ford family, and later the Ford Foundation, a philanthropic organization established by the Ford family in 1936, controlled the company's stock.

From 1946 through 1954, the company financed a major modernization and expansion of its facilities with funds that came totally from within the corporation. The expansion rescued Ford from losses totalling $10 million a month and brought it to a respectable place among industries in the United States.

Then in January 1956, Ford Motor Company issued 10,200,000 shares of stock, thereby becoming a

◆ ***Inc.* after the name of a business stands for *Incorporated* and means that the business is a corporation.**

publicly owned corporation. The sale represented the largest stock offering to that date, beating the record set by General Motors in 1955 when it issued 4,380,683 shares of stock.

Corporate Stocks and Bonds. The selling of stock is the method used by businesses to raise operating capital. Corporations issue either common stock or preferred stock. Ownership of **common stock** gives stockholders a voice in how the corporation is run and a share in whatever dividends it produces. A **dividend** is the amount of money paid to the investor in return for his or her investment. The dividends on common stock are determined by the **board of directors.** These are the individuals who set the policies and goals of the corporation. The board of directors may decide to pay very small dividends or no dividends at all. **Preferred stock** carries guaranteed dividends to its owners. Preferred stock owners, however, usually have no voice in how the company is run.

In addition to issuing common and preferred stocks, corporations may issue corporate bonds to raise money for expansion and modernization. A **corporate bond** is a certificate issued by a corporation in exchange for money borrowed from investors. When a corporation issues bonds, it promises to repay the principal plus interest to the investor. The **principal** is the original amount of money that was borrowed. **Interest** is the predetermined amount the borrower must pay for the use of those funds. A bond indicates that the corporation is in debt to the holder of the bond. A stock, on the other hand, is a certificate of ownership.

Corporate Formation. Forming a corporation is a more complex process than starting a sole proprietorship or partnership. Individuals wishing to incorporate a business generally need the assistance of a lawyer because the process involves much paperwork and many legal restrictions.

Obtaining a corporate charter is the first step in the incorporation process. A **corporate charter** is a license granted by the state that gives a business the right to operate as a corporation. The license is obtained by filing an application with the state in which the corporation will have its headquarters. The application is referred to as the **articles of incorporation.** Information contained in the articles of incorporation includes six items.

Economics Reporter

What Is a Chief Executive Officer?

The chief executive officer (CEO) is the highest ranking executive in a corporation. CEOs generally are appointed by the board of directors, the governing body of the corporation. Many CEOs also hold the title of company president. The position of chief executive officer is very powerful. For example, CEOs often have the authority to appoint the other corporate officers. Corporations tend to reflect the values and desires of their chief executive officers because of the amount of authority vested in the position.

1. It states the name and purpose of the proposed corporation.
2. It includes the address of the corporate headquarters.
3. It indicates the number of shares of stock the corporation will have the authority to issue.
4. It states the amount of money to be raised by issuing stock.
5. It contains the name and address of the major corporate officer.
6. It specifies the length of time the corporation will exist—either indefinitely or for a definite period of time.

Once the corporate charter is obtained, the corporation must raise funds and elect a full board of directors.

State laws require that an individual run a series of legal notices in the newspaper announcing the intent to do business under a fictitious name. This is the type of notice required by Florida.

NOTICE UNDER FICTITIOUS NAME STATUTE

TO WHOM IT MAY CONCERN

Notice is hereby given that the undersigned pursuant to the "Fictitious Name Statute," Chapter 865.09, Florida Statutes, will register with the County Comptroller, in and for Orange County, Florida, upon receipt of proof of the publication of this notice, the fictitious name, to-wit:

CAMPUS MOTORS

under which I expect to engage in business at 555 West Allen Highway, Orlando, Florida, 32819.

That the party interested in said business enterprise is as follows:

Martha R. Thomas

Dated at Orlando, Orange County, Florida, December 16, 1986

LS-000(4) Dec. 21, 28, 1986
Jan. 4, 11, 1987

◆ As of 1985, General Motors had 2,001,000 stockholders.

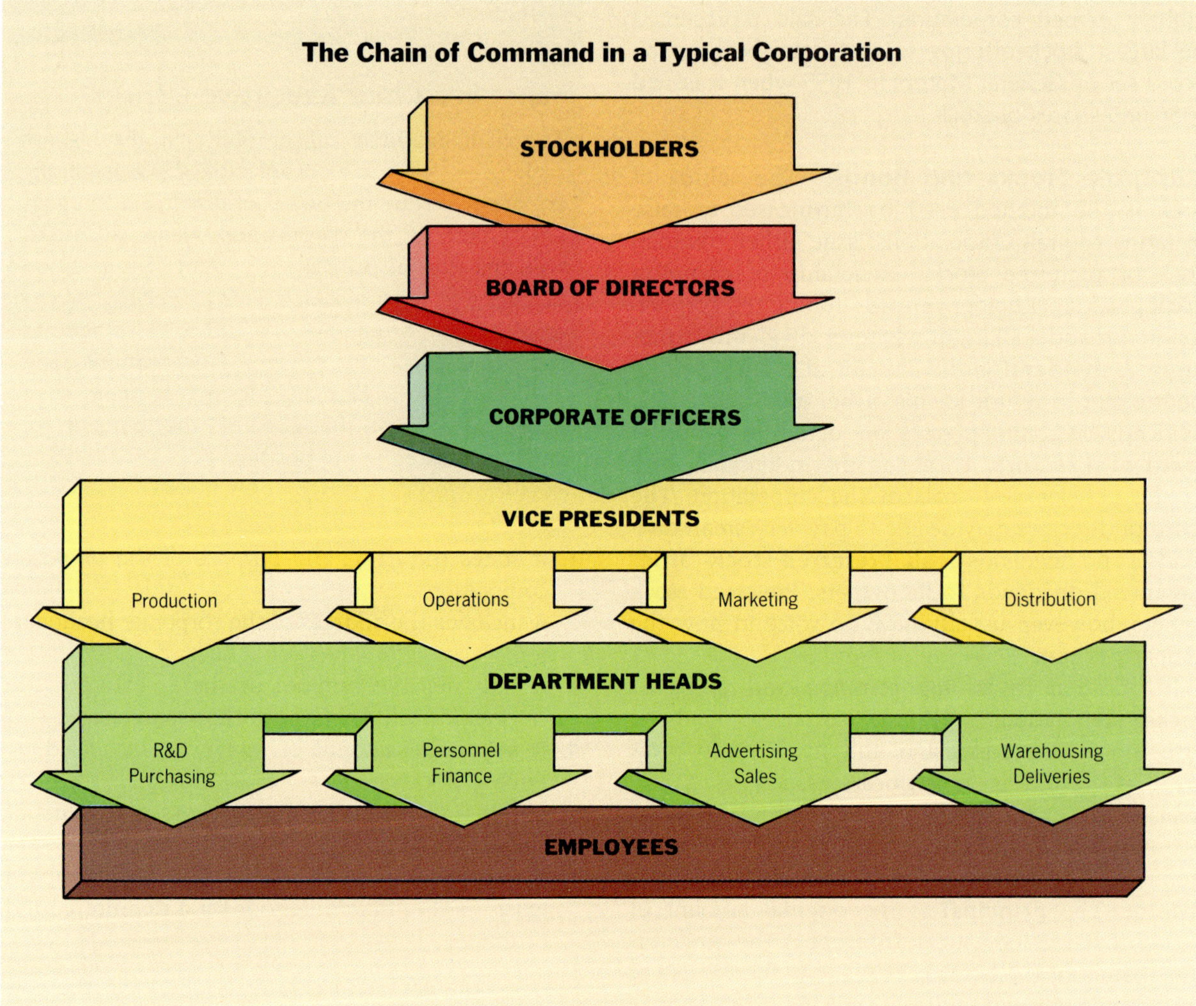

◆ **Corporate Decision Making.** The board of directors, which is elected by the stockholders, is the most important decision-making body in the corporation. The board sets corporate policies and goals. For example, the board decides what products will be produced and in what quantity. The board also establishes how much of the corporation's profits will go to stockholders and how much will be kept for expansion and modernization. In addition, the board selects the corporation's top officers. These officers include the chief executive officer (CEO), the president, one or more vice presidents, the secretary, and the treasurer.

In most corporations, the officers make the day-to-day decisions. The board of directors entrusts the officers with these decisions because the officers are professional managers. The top officers in a corporation advise the board and suggest policies and production plans. Once these policies and plans have been approved, the officers see that the orders are carried out by the corporation's various department heads. The diagram above shows the structure of a typical corporation. Specific corporation structures vary somewhat from the diagram because corporations differ in size and in the goods and services they produce.

◆ **Have the students read "Systems Analysts" on page 544 of *Careers in the Marketplace.***

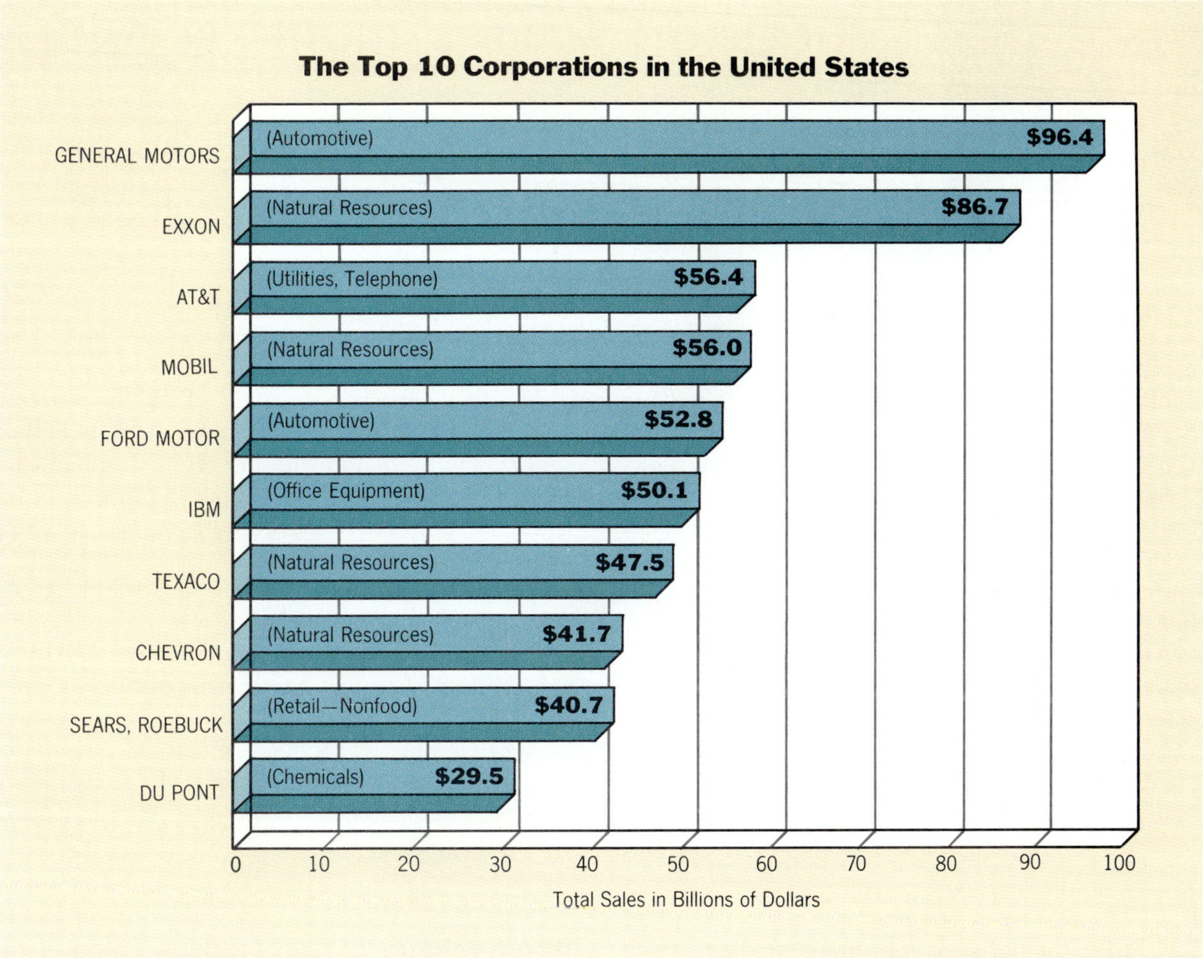

Top Corporations. Corporations dominate most of the heavy industries in the United States, such as steel production, mining, and automobile manufacturing. Three examples of industrial companies organized as corporations are General Motors, Exxon, and United States Steel, which changed its name to ◆ USX in 1986.

Many major wholesalers and retailers also are corporations. For example, Sears, Roebuck and Company, the largest retail chain in the United States, is organized as a corporation. By the mid-1980s, Sears, Roebuck and Company had about 800 retail stores operating nationwide. Other corporations provide such services as selling real estate or insurance. The graph on this page shows the top 10 United States corporations in terms of total sales in 1986.

Advantages of Corporations. It is necessary to look at the advantages of corporations from two viewpoints: that of the stockholders and that of the business itself.

For stockholders, the major advantage is limited liability. If the corporation fails, the loss to stockholders is limited to the amount invested. A stockholder's personal property and assets may not be seized to pay corporate debts. A second advantage for stockholders is profit. The corporate form of organization allows investors to earn dividends without actually doing any work for the corporation.

From the viewpoint of the corporation, one of the major advantages is the separation of ownership from the management. By separating management from ownership, the corporation can assign specialists to complex tasks. Professional managers, those

◆ **Point out to the students that the free enterprise system is the only economic system that allows private ownership of large corporations.**

DECISION MAKERS IN THE ECONOMY

Portia Isaacson

Portia Isaacson is a classic example of a successful entrepreneur. As founder, president, and chief executive officer of Future Computing, Inc., Isaacson has made a name for herself as an authority on market trends in the personal computer industry.

Isaacson did not start out at the top of the business world. She grew up on a small, struggling dairy farm in Oklahoma. By the time she was 21, Isaacson was receiving welfare payments to help support her three children.

How did Isaacson go on to establish a successful market research and consulting firm? She got the training she needed, eventually earning two masters' degrees and a doctorate in computer science. Isaacson then set out to become well known in her field by writing papers and speaking at conferences. When she founded Future Computing in 1980, Isaacson already had many contacts she could draw on for business.

In 1981, Isaacson learned of IBM's plans to market a new personal computer. In a published report, she predicted that the IBM PC would have a dramatic effect on the computer market. When Isaacson's prediction proved correct, her company began to be taken seriously.

By 1984, Isaacson's clients included IBM, Apple, AT&T, Eastman Kodak, Sears, and Xerox. In the same year, she sold Future Computing to McGraw-Hill for $8 million plus a percentage of future profits. Isaacson felt the sale was necessary because Future Computing needed access to corporate management experience. As part of the corporate merger, Portia Isaacson continues to run Future Computing.

who make the decisions concerning production and marketing of the corporation's products, possess the skills to make sound decisions. The corporation can also hire additional specialists, such as lawyers and accountants to advise the professional management team.

A second major advantage of corporations from the business viewpoint is the ease with which capi- ◆ tal can be raised. Corporations issue stock and sell bonds to raise capital to finance growth, research and development, and modernization.

The final major advantage of corporations from the business viewpoint is their longevity. A corporation often continues in existence after the death of its founder and original management. This long life span is possible because the pool of owners and management constantly changes. Shares of stock are bought and sold. Corporate directors, officers, and employees are hired and fired. The death of a stockholder, the transfer of stock, and changes in corporate personnel do not end the corporation.

Disadvantages of Corporations. Most of the disadvantages of corporations are viewed from the corporate side rather than from the stockholder side. Stockholders, however, are faced with at least one disadvantage. Stockholders earn a profit without actually working for the company. Individual stockholders may feel no great sense of pride, accomplishment, and personal satisfaction in their roles as corporate owners because they are far removed from the actual running of the business.

For corporations, one of the major disadvantages is the slowness of the decision-making process. In a corporation, especially a large one, decision making usually involves extensive study of the issues by specialists and discussion and debate among managers. Proposals pass through a chain of command before final decisions are made. The process can be further slowed if disagreements occur between top-level managers and the board of directors over such matters as policies and production targets. In addition, governmental regulations and restrictions that

◆ **Have the students read "Stockbrokers" on page 543 of *Careers in the Marketplace*.**

apply only to corporations and that must be followed often delay the carrying out of decisions.

For some people, the way corporate profits are taxed is another disadvantage. These people claim that corporate profits undergo double taxation—once as dividends and again as corporate profits. When a corporation distributes profits to its stockholders, the government views these dividends as income to the stockholder. The stockholder, therefore, must pay an income tax on this money. The income of a corporation is also taxed because a corporation is treated under the law as a person. Critics of this process claim that it is unfair to tax the same profits twice.

Lee Iacocca maintains that government intervention in the economy is necessary at times.

CASE STUDY

◆ *Lee Iacocca*

Lee Iacocca is one of the most recognized business leaders in the United States. Born to Italian immigrant parents, Lido Anthony—Lee—Iacocca learned early the value of hard work and of seizing business opportunities.

Iacocca began his career in the automotive industry in 1946 as a salesperson at Ford Motor Company. Over the years, he climbed the corporate ladder. In 1970, Ford's board of directors named Iacocca president of the company. He held this position until 1978 when the competing Chrysler Corporation named him as its president. In 1979, Chrysler's board of directors named Iacocca chief executive officer (CEO).

One of the most important reasons for Iacocca's business success has been his sales skills. As a salesperson, Iacocca has "sold" himself as well as cars. He was successful in marketing Ford automobiles in the 1960s and 1970s. For example, under his direction in 1964, the Ford Mustang broke the single-year sales record. Twenty years later Iacocca was a part of another record-breaking performance when the Chrysler Corporation earned $2.4 billion in profits in a single year.

Lee Iacocca's success at Chrysler is, in part, a result of his decisions concerning the product line. It also is due, however, to his ability to communicate with consumers in the United States. Between 1980 and 1985, Chrysler's television advertisements, which featured Iacocca, reached 97 percent of all households in the United States. Reflecting his straightforward approach to business, Iacocca's message was direct: "If you can find a better car, buy it."

Iacocca also has been successful at "selling" himself to Chrysler's employees—from top management to assembly-line workers—and to the thousands of dealers that sell Chrysler products. His past business successes, hard work, and image as a plain-spoken "can do" executive have inspired worker confidence. He has also impressed top management with his decision-making skills, which Iacocca calls management by consensus. The managers tell Iacocca what they think, then he decides on a course of action.

Iacocca's views on how to improve United States industry and its position in world markets have gained national attention in recent years. While Iacocca is a firm believer in the merits of capitalism, he has become a supporter of government intervention in the economy. First, he feels that the federal government should devise an "industrial policy," as many other nations have done, to encourage certain industries and discourage less profitable or less efficient ones. Second, Iacocca favors governmental aid to ailing industries. For example, he lobbied in Washington, D.C., to obtain $1.5 billion in federally guaranteed loans to help save the Chrysler Corporation from bankruptcy in the early 1980s. Third, to protect manufacturing jobs in the United States, Iacocca supports such restrictions on trade as import tariffs and import quotas.

◆ **Lee Iacocca's book, *Iacocca: An Autobiography,* was on the bestseller list in 1984.**

To many, Iacocca has become a type of industrial folk hero who has achieved success through his own efforts, talents, and ambition. To these people, he represents the fulfillment of the American dream. His civic-mindedness also has contributed to this image. For example, Iacocca has served as the chairperson of the Statue of Liberty–Ellis Island Commission, which was responsible for the multimillion-dollar restoration of the Statue of Liberty and Ellis Island. These two projects commemorate the contributions of immigrants—including Iacocca's parents—to the United States. He also has established the Lee Iacocca Foundation, which provides financial assistance to hospitals and other worthwhile causes.

Lee Iacocca has a vision of capitalism that differs from the visions of Milton Friedman and Adam Smith. The major differences are in the realm of government intervention in the economy. His contrasting views reflect the legitimate differences of opinion permitted in the American political and economic systems.

See Suggested Assignments, p. TM 23.

Section 1 Review See Answers, p. A 21.

DEFINE liability, stockholder, stock, preferred stock, corporate bond, articles of incorporation

IDENTIFY Small Business Administration, chief executive officer, Portia Isaacson, Lee Iacocca

1. **Understanding Ideas** **(a)** What are the three major types of business organizations? **(b)** Explain the role control plays in each type of organization.
2. **Evaluating Ideas** **(a)** What are the advantages and disadvantages of sole proprietorships and partnerships? **(b)** Based on your comparisons of the advantages and disadvantages, which type of business organization do you think is the best type of business organization? Why?
3. **Interpreting Graphics** Study the graph on page 105. **(a)** Into what two categories do most top ten corporations fall? **(b)** What economic factors might explain the fact that four of the top ten businesses in the United States are oil companies?

See Key Study Questions and Key Understandings, p. TM 24.

2 Corporations can expand by combining one business with other businesses.

See Suggested Teaching Strategies, p. TM 24.

Some of the advantages enjoyed by corporations stem from the size. Large corporations are better able to carry out such tasks as raising capital for business expansion and hiring professional managers and other specialists. Throughout the history of the United States, corporations have increased in size in two major ways. They have either expanded from within by building new facilities, or they have legally combined, or merged with another business.

Types of Corporate Combinations

The most common way of joining businesses is through mergers. A **merger** occurs when one company absorbs another. In a merger, the absorbed company often is forced to abandon its identity.

In the 1980s, the number of mergers increased ◆ dramatically. Between 1980 and 1985, more than 60 of the top 500 corporations in the United States merged with other companies. Multibillion-dollar corporate mergers in the mid-1980s included Nestlé's acquisition of Carnation, Capital Cities Communications' acquisition of the American Broadcasting Corporation (ABC), and General Motors' acquisition of Hughes Aircraft Company. In 1985 alone, more than 3,000 mergers or acquisitions occurred.

Three types of business mergers take place—horizontal combinations, vertical combinations, and conglomerate combinations. The diagram on page 109 illustrates examples of these types of business combinations.

Horizontal Combinations. A merger between two or more companies that produce the same good or service or dominate one phase of the production of a good is a **horizontal combination.** The Standard Oil Company provides a classic example of a horizontal combination. In the 1870s, John D. Rockefeller and his associates formed the Standard Oil Company of Ohio.

Over the next 12 years, Rockefeller's group purchased refineries throughout the United States. By 1882, Standard Oil controlled almost all of the

◆ A merger is not a trust unless a court rules that the merger violated the Sherman Antitrust Act by leading to restraint of trade.

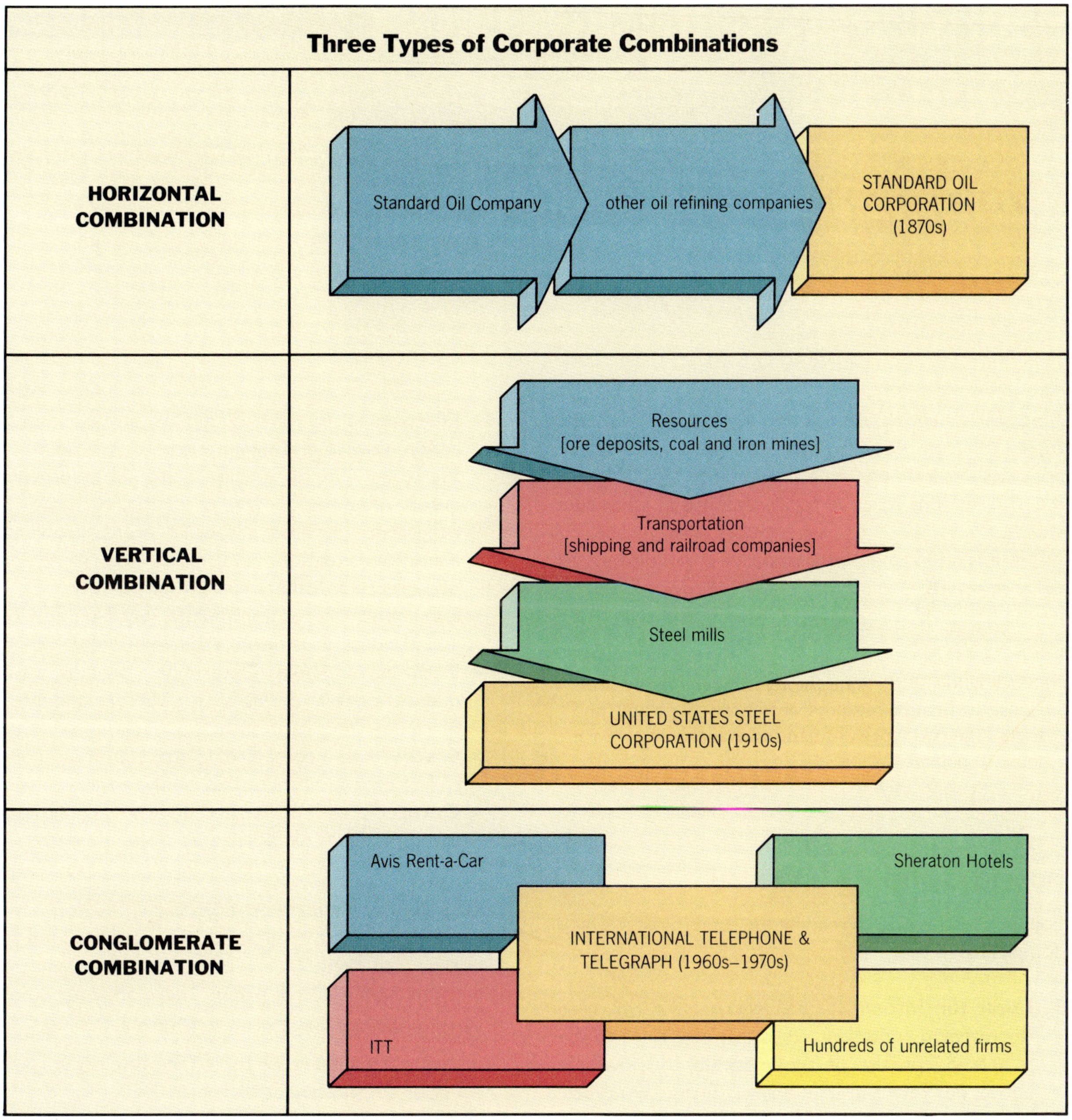

country's oil industry. The Standard Oil Trust was formed in 1882 to unify the management of the various companies under Standard Oil's control. In the same year, Standard Oil of New Jersey was chartered as one of the companies within the trust.

The supreme court of Ohio forced Standard Oil to dissolve the trust in 1892. All of the companies in the trust had to once again operate as independent companies. In 1899, Standard Oil of New Jersey was reorganized in an attempt to retain control of the companies that had once been a part of the trust. Standard Oil of New Jersey exchanged shares of its stock for shares of stock in various companies. The exchange resulted in Standard Oil of New Jersey having stock in about 20 companies.

Text continues on page 112.

WRITING ABOUT ECONOMICS

Composing an Essay

An essay is a short composition written on a specific topic. You compose an essay when you write a report, answer a thought question on a test, or follow a set of directions that call for a response in your own words.

Here is an example of a directive that demands an essay response.

> ESSAY DIRECTIVE: State the reasons why many firms choose to finance business operations (5 points), and discuss the two types of financing available to corporations (10 points).

How to Compose an Essay

Follow these steps in reading an essay directive and composing an essay.

1. **Look for informational terms.** As you read the directive, note key terms that give clues to the expected content of the essay. In the example above, key terms include finance, firms, two types, and corporations.

2. **Determine the essay's scope.** Determine the subject of the essay. Note whether the directive asks you to address one main idea or several main ideas.

3. **Note the performance terms.** Performance terms are the words in the essay directive that indicate what you are supposed to do. These are some of the most common performance terms:
   - **Discuss:** Tell in some detail; assess the reasons, action, results, and significance.
   - **Identify:** Cite a specific name of a person, group, organization, law, or nation; or name an occurrence such as a specific event, problem, issue, or situation; and relate the name or occurrence to other relevant information.
   - **Describe:** Create a complete word picture of an individual, institution, action, or event.
   - **Explain, or Show:** Determine a process, a sequence, or relationship such as before and after or cause-effect relationship.
   - **State:** Make a complete, formal statement consisting of several sentences on the topic.
   - **Compare or Contrast:** Indicate similarities and differences or differences alone.

4. **Develop a structured overview.** As you have already learned, a structured overview is a kind of outline (see page 66). It is most effective when it is written on a sheet of paper. There are four steps to developing a structured overview.

   a. State the subject, or topic. The title often gives clues to the subject or topic.

   b. Identify the main ideas. Section titles often give clues to main ideas.

   c. Identify subheadings, or supporting details, of the main ideas

   d. Diagram the information so it is easily followed.

5. **Write the essay.** Follow the directive in the first column.

Applying the Skill

See Step 1 for the informational terms of the essay directive on page 110. The subject is the financing of businesss operations. You should have provided information on two main points: the reasons why businesses finance business operations, and the types of financing used by corporations.

The first main point includes all types of businesses—sole proprietorships, partnerships, corporations, and other forms of business organizations. The second main point narrows the scope of the essay to the corporation. Pages 102–108 of this chapter provided the necessary background information.

Note the value assigned to each part of the essay. The part worth the most points should have the most detail. The sample essay below devotes one paragraph to the reasons for business financing, and one paragraph to the types of financing used by a corporation. The introduction states the subject of the essay. The conclusion restates the major points of the essay and reinforces the points made in the introduction.

Practicing the Skill See Answers, p. A 22.

Read the following essay directive. Then on a separate sheet of paper, complete the activities and answer the questions below.

ESSAY DIRECTIVE: Several factors affect technical efficiency in the production process. State what technical efficiency means (5 points). Identify three important factors that influence technical efficiency of businesses (15 points).

1. List the informational terms in the directive.
2. **(a)** What is the subject of the essay directive? **(b)** List the directive's main ideas.
3. List the performance terms in the essay directive.
4. Draw a structured overview of your response to the essay directive.
5. Write an essay response to the directive.

SAMPLE ESSAY

INTRODUCTION	It is common for firms in the United States to finance business operations. Financing involves obtaining outside capital. All types of businesses are able to finance their operations through debt financing. Equity financing, however, is reserved for only corporations.
REASONS FOR FINANCING	There are two important reasons why businesses finance production. First, businesses raise needed capital for day-to-day operations when a temporary shortage of cash occurs. Secondly, businesses use financing for new building projects. These projects include expenditures for plant modernization and plant expansion.
TYPES OF FINANCING	Corporations use debt financing and equity financing. Debt financing involves borrowing money. In short-term debt financing, a corporation borrows money for short periods of time—usually less than one year. In long-term debt financing, the repayment schedule for loans is greater than one year. Corporations also issue bonds to investors as a method of long-term debt financing. Many bonds mature from 20 to 30 years after they are issued. Equity financing is a second way that corporations raise needed capital. Equity financing involves the issuing of preferred stock and common stock. By issuing stock, the corporation sells part ownership in the firm to investors.
CONCLUSION	In short, financing allows firms to supplement their business revenues with outside sources of capital. While all types of business organizations raise capital through debt financing, only corporations are permitted to raise money through equity financing.

Some people fear that the increased merger activity of the 1980s may result in too much power being placed in the hands of too few people.

◆ In 1911, the U.S. Supreme Court ruled that Standard Oil of New Jersey had too much control over the refining of oil. The ruling once again forced Standard Oil of New Jersey to sell off parts of its business operations. Even after the sell off, however, Standard Oil of New Jersey remained the largest individual corporation in the United States.

In 1972, Standard Oil of New Jersey changed its name to the Exxon Corporation. Today, Exxon is the second largest industrial corporation in the United States and the largest petroleum company in the world.

Vertical Combinations. A merger between two or more companies that are involved in different phases of the production of the same good or service is a **vertical combination.** The founding of the United States Steel Corporation in 1901 combined companies involved in different phases of the production and distribution of steel. The combined companies owned ore deposits, iron mines, coal mines, shipping companies, railroads, and steel mills. United States Steel's founder, J. Pierpont Morgan, built the world's first billion-dollar corporation through the merging of these varied companies.

Today, the company produces nearly 25 percent of the steel manufactured in the United States and 6 percent of the steel produced in the free world. In addition to steel and its other original business interests, the company now produces oil and gas products. It manufactures oil-field drilling and pumping equipment and basic materials for the plastics industry, and agricultural and industrial chemicals. It also develops, leases, and finances real estate. In 1986, United States Steel changed its name to USX to reflect the diversity of the corporation's interests.

Conglomerate Combinations. A merger between two or more companies producing or marketing different products is a **conglomerate combination.** While horizontal and vertical combinations have been common since the mid-1800s, conglomerate combinations did not become common until the 1960s and 1970s.

The classic example of a conglomerate is the International Telephone and Telegraph Corporation (ITT). Until the 1950s, ITT manufactured only telecommunications equipment. During the 1960s and 1970s, however, ITT acquired hundreds of **subsidiaries**—acquired companies that have not

◆ Until the late 1800s, the federal government did little to regulate the trusts.

been forced to abandon their corporate identities. The subsidiaries, which did business in many fields, included such companies as Avis Rent-a-Car, Howard Sams Publishers, Continental Baking, and Sheraton Hotels.

Today, ITT owns companies in more than 80 countries and is involved in such varied enterprises as the production of frozen foods and plumbing supplies and the operation of computer services, consumer finance companies, and hotels. Although ITT is second only to American Telephone and Telegraph in the production of telecommunications equipment, these products account for only about 25 percent of ITT's annual sales.

In a move designed to retain competent and knowledgeable decision makers, subsidiaries often are allowed to keep their own top management. For example, when General Motors (GM) acquired ◆ Hughes Aircraft Company in the mid-1980s, GM basically permitted Hughes to conduct its own affairs. Similarly, when International Business Machines (IBM) purchased Rolm Corporation, IBM allowed Rolm to decide for itself how to produce and market its telecommunications equipment.

Trends in Corporate Combinations

The trend toward conglomerate combinations began in the 1960s and carried into the 1970s. Conglomerate mergers helped to build corporate empires for ITT, Gulf & Western, and many other major producers. During the 1980s, however, a trend toward vertical and horizontal combinations redeveloped. Companies in the 1980s tended to merge with other companies that produced the same or related goods or services. For example, when the Chevron Corporation merged with Gulf in 1984, two oil giants were combined. The Chevron–Gulf merger remains the largest corporate combination in United States history. Combinations within the airline and communication industries are also common.

While the current trend is toward horizontal and vertical combinations, conglomerate combinations still occur. For example, the 1986 conglomerate merger between General Electric (GE) and Radio Corporation of America (RCA) represents the largest non-oil merger in United States history. It cost GE over $6.2 billion to acquire a controlling interest in RCA.

The Impact of Corporate Combinations

Some economists see corporate mergers as having a positive impact on the United States economy. Others are concerned about the dangers of corporate combinations.

Advantages of Combinations. One of the major business advantages of corporate mergers is efficiency. By centralizing decision making within an industry, corporate combinations, especially horizontal and vertical combinations, can increase efficiency. Costs also can be cut by eliminating unnecessary or overlapping jobs and departments.

A second business advantage of mergers is that buying an existing business is often far less expensive than building new plants, hiring new employees, or acquiring additional capital in order to expand. In most mergers, the acquiring corporation obtains additional capital resources and experienced management and employees.

A third business advantage of mergers is that the increased size of merged corporations often makes it possible to borrow more capital. This additional capital can be used for such improvements as enlarging the sales force or modernizing production facilities. In general, larger corporations also are able to compete more effectively in the marketplace.

Corporate mergers also may provide an advantage for stockholders in acquired companies. Mergers and rumors of pending mergers often increase the stock value of acquired companies. Companies that are the target of acquisition attempts by more than one corporation may experience even larger increases in the value of their stock. By bidding against one another, the competing companies drive up the value of the stock of the company they are attempting to buy. When stock values increase, stockholders receive a greater return on their investment.

Disadvantages of Combinations. Corporate combinations may result in disadvantages for the merged corporation, stockholders, and consumers. Corporate mergers sometimes have negative consequences for the merged corporations, both from the standpoint of corporate performance and from the standpoint of worker satisfaction.

In some instances, especially in conglomerates, the managers of merged corporations may not have

◆ **Corporate combinations can also involve companies in different countries. In 1980, for example, American Motors combined with the French automaker, Renault.**

Several airline mergers in the 1980s have been unsuccessfully opposed by the employees and unions of the acquired airlines.

the necessary skills to supervise the production of newly acquired goods and services. Lack of supervisory skills can result in decreased efficiency and profits.

Mergers also may result in added unemployment because of changes in business operations. Employees may be reshuffled and some people may be laid off. The employees who stay on the job sometimes suffer from low morale due to altered job descriptions or other negative changes that occur in ◆ the workplace.

While mergers usually are beneficial for stockholders in the acquired company, almost half of all major mergers in the United States result in a decrease in the value of the purchasing corporation's stock. Consequently, the purchasing company's stockholders experience at least a temporary drop in the value of their investment.

For consumers, one of the major disadvantages of corporate mergers is that they often lead to decreased competition in the marketplace. This lack of competition may result in higher prices for consumers. It also may limit the choices available to consumers by reducing the number of competing goods and services.

Section 2 Review

See Answers, p. A 22.

DEFINE merger, horizontal combination, vertical combination, conglomerate combination, subsidiary

1. **Summarizing Ideas** **(a)** Describe the types of business combinations. **(b)** Give an example of each of the three types of mergers.
2. **Comprehending Ideas** **(a)** What are the advantages of corporate mergers? **(b)** What are the disadvantages of corporate mergers? **(c)** Who benefits most from a corporate merger? Why?
3. **Interpreting Ideas** Why have horizontal combinations often resulted in a monopoly?
4. **Analyzing Ideas** Explain why the recent trend has been toward corporate combinations.
5. **Evaluating Ideas** Defend or refute this statement: Corporate combinations contribute to the nation's economic growth.
6. **Interpreting Graphics** Study the chart on page 109. Why do conglomerate combinations seem better for consumers than horizontal or vertical combinations?

See Suggested Assignments, p. TM 24.

◆ Displaced workers often lose all insurance and retirement benefits and because of age or extensive experience have difficulty finding other jobs.

See Key Study Questions and Key Understandings, p. TM 25.

3 Businesses also can be organized as franchises, cooperatives, and nonprofit organizations.

See Suggested Teaching Strategies, p. TM 25.

Sole proprietorships, partnerships, and corporations are not the only ways in which businesses are organized. Three additional forms of business organizations are franchises, cooperatives, and nonprofit organizations.

Franchises

A **franchise** is a contract in which a company agrees to let another person or group establish an enterprise using its name to sell goods or services. The parent company is called the **franchiser.** The person or group who wants to open the franchise is called the **franchisee.**

Many persons today operate businesses under franchise agreements. Among these businesses are hotel and motel chains such as Holiday Inn, restaurants such as Burger King, copying and printing centers such as Sir Speedy, and computer stores such as ComputerLand. The ComputerLand franchise, for example, was founded in 1976. By 1986, ComputerLand had contracts with over 800 franchisees in 24 countries. In this 10-year period, ComputerLand became the world's largest chain of computer stores. ◆

Operating a franchise has both costs and benefits. The costs to the franchisee include a fee required by the franchisee in exchange for the use of the parent company's name and a stated percentage of the profits made by the franchisee. Franchise restrictions may be considered as costs. For example, the franchisee is required to uphold quality standards. The franchisee must also follow the guidelines on the type of service that the franchisee must offer.

The benefits to the franchisee include financial assistance, training for employees and management personnel, and national advertising, in addition to the use of the parent company's well-known name.

The growing popularity of franchises gives city streets around the United States a similar appearance.

◆ Have the students read "Interpreting Warranties" on page 515 of the *Everyday Economics Handbook* and answer the questions that follow.

Purchasing cooperatives enable consumers to buy products, such as food, at reduced prices.

A marketing cooperative helps artisans and artists reduce the costs of selling their works.

Cooperatives

A second type of business organization is a cooperative. A **cooperative**, or co-op, is a business that is owned by the people who use its services. The five basic types of cooperatives are purchasing cooperatives, marketing cooperatives, housing cooperatives, credit unions, and service cooperatives.

A **purchasing cooperative** is a retail store that is owned and operated by its customers. Because purchasing cooperatives buy in large quantities, they are able to purchase goods from farmers, private manufacturers, and wholesalers at reduced prices. Purchasing cooperatives pass these savings on to their members. Some cooperatives also sell goods to nonmembers at regular prices. The two main types of purchasing cooperatives are consumer cooperatives, which sell food, household supplies, and other goods, and farm purchasing cooperatives, which sell farm supplies.

A **marketing cooperative** is a group of farmers who join together in an effort to get higher prices for their goods. Marketing cooperatives collect, process, sell, and ship their members' goods. Many cooperatives have their own processing plants and warehouses. Sunkist citrus, Land O' Lakes dairy products, and Sun-Maid raisins are examples of well-known cooperative brands.

A **housing cooperative** is a corporation formed ◆ by members to buy the buildings in which they live. Although individual members own shares in the corporation, they usually do not own the property. The corporation owns the property and members have the right to occupy a house or apartment in the cooperative. Members of housing cooperatives share costs of maintaining the buildings in which they live.

A **credit union** is a cooperative in which members pool their savings. When members need to borrow money, they can do so from the credit union at lower rates of interest than from other types of financial institutions. Members of credit unions generally share some common bond, such as membership in the same labor union or church or employment in the same company. Credit unions are the most common form of cooperative in the United States.

◆ Housing cooperatives are often referred to as co-ops.

A **service cooperative** provides services to its members. For example, some service cooperatives generate and sell electrical power or provide telephone service in rural areas. Other cooperatives of this type provide their members with such services as health care or legal assistance.

Nonprofit Organizations

Nonprofit organizations represent a third type of specialized business organization. A **nonprofit organization** provides goods or services without seeking profits for distribution to individual members. Any profits that may be earned are put back into the organization.

Nonprofit organizations, which are often involved in charitable works, religious activities, and educational and cultural programs, are not taxed by the government. Examples of nonprofit organizations include the Boy Scouts of America, the Girl Scouts, and the Young Men's Christian Association. Revenues for most nonprofit organizations come from the sale of their products, fees for their services, or charitable contributions.

See Suggested Assignments, p. TM 25.

Section 3 Review See Answers, p. A 23.

DEFINE franchise, cooperative, credit union

1. **Organizing Ideas** **(a)** What are the five basic types of cooperatives? **(b)** A condominium is what type of cooperative?
2. **Comparing Ideas** **(a)** Compare for-profit businesses with nonprofit organizations. **(b)** Why would people form a nonprofit organization?
3. **Analyzing Ideas** **(a)** Why would a group of people form a cooperative? **(b)** Are cooperatives more common in urban or rural areas? Why?
4. **Evaluating Ideas** **(a)** Describe the benefits and costs of franchises for the franchisee. **(b)** What benefits does the franchiser gain from a franchise contract? **(c)** What possible costs might a franchise contract have for a franchiser?
5. **Interpreting Graphics** Study the picture on page 115. State a generalization about franchises that can be formed from the picture.

CHAPTER 5 SUMMARY

In a market economy, businesses can be organized as sole proprietorships, partnerships, and corporations. Sole proprietorships are the oldest and least complicated form of business organization. A sole proprietorship relies on the work and organizational abilities of one person. Obtaining resources can be the most difficult part of running a sole proprietorship. Business debt also can present a problem because a sole proprietor has unlimited liability for business debt.

Partnerships, which spread the risk and work load among partners, are of two kinds. In a general partnership, partners assist in running the business and accept complete liability for the business. In a limited partnership, the limited partners invest in the business, but rarely assist in day-to-day operations. The liability of limited partners is restricted to the amount of their investment.

The corporation is a complex form of business organization. It is managed by professionals and supervised by a board of directors. Under the law, the corporation is treated as if it were an individual. Like individuals, corporations can enter into contracts, merge with other firms, and expand their operations through the sale of stocks and corporate bonds.

Corporations are able to expand their operations by combining, or merging, with other firms. Horizontal combinations occur between two or more companies that produce the same goods or services. Vertical combinations are mergers between two or more companies that are involved in different phases of the production of the same good or service. A conglomerate combination occurs between two or more companies producing or marketing different products.

Franchises, cooperatives, and nonprofit organizations are three additional types of business organizations. In a franchise, one business agrees to let another business use its name to sell goods or services. A cooperative is a voluntary association of people in some kind of business activity. Kinds of cooperatives include purchasing, marketing, housing, and service cooperatives, as well as credit unions. Nonprofit organizations provide goods or services but do not seek profits for individual members. These organizations are not taxed by the government.

CHAPTER 5 REVIEW

For Answers to Chapter 5 Review, see p. A 24.

Reviewing Economic Terms

With each definition or description below, match one of the following terms.

a. partnership
b. sole proprietorship
c. conglomerate combination
d. stock
e. dividends
f. collateral
g. corporate bond

_____ **1.** A business that is owned and controlled by one person.

_____ **2.** Anything of value that a borrower can use to guarantee a loan.

_____ **3.** A business that is owned and controlled by two or more people.

_____ **4.** A certificate of corporate ownership.

_____ **5.** The amount of money paid to investors in return for their investments.

_____ **6.** A merger between two or more companies producing or marketing different products.

Exercising Economic Skills

1. **Composing an Essay** Read the following essay directive and answer the questions below. *Compare the advantages and disadvantages of the three types of business organizations (15 points). Determine which of the three you think is the most advantageous form of business organization and defend your selection (10 points).* **(a)** What are the informational terms stated in the essay directive? **(b)** What is the subject of the directive? **(c)** What are the performance terms stated in the directive? **(d)** Develop a structured overview of your response.
2. **Interpreting Warranties** Study the feature on page 515. Then select a specific type of product and compare the warranties offered by at least two different manufacturers. **(a)** Visit a local store or stores to study the terms of different warranties. **(b)** Write a paragraph in which you describe the differences, if any, that you found among the warranties from different manufacturers. **(c)** Write a second paragraph in which you evaluate the warranties according to the coverage they provide.

Thinking Critically About Economics

1. **Summarizing Ideas** **(a)** What are the most common forms of business organization in the American free enterprise system? **(b)** Why is size often an advantage for corporations? **(c)** Briefly describe a franchise, a cooperative, and a nonprofit organization.
2. **Understanding Ideas** What are the benefits of forming a nonprofit organization?
3. **Analyzing Ideas** Why do owners of sole proprietorships often refuse to sell their businesses to corporations that seek to buy them?
4. **Interpreting Graphics** Study the graphs on page 102. **(a)** Which type of business organization represents the largest percentage of businesses? **(b)** Which type of business organization has the largest percentage of total sales? **(c)** In general, what do these graphs illustrate about business organizations and total sales?

Extending Economic Knowledge

1. Select at least three local sole proprietorships and interview the owners. Find out **(a)** how each person got started in business, **(b)** how business is presently going, **(c)** what specific problems the business faces, and **(d)** what the future prospects of the business are. Present your findings either as a written or oral report.
2. Contact your local government to collect information about starting a business. Study the local, state, and federal regulations for starting each type of business organization. In an essay, compare the regulations that apply to starting each type of business organization.
3. **(a)** Choose a product or service and form an imaginary business to produce that product or service. **(b)** Determine which type of business organization would best produce your product or service. **(c)** Establish a chain of command within your organization. **(d)** Describe your general business operations. **(e)** Figure your production costs, product price, anticipated sales and revenues, and profits. **(f)** Submit a folder containing a complete profile of your imaginary company.

Using Primary Sources

In a speech delivered to the Pittsburgh Advertising Club in 1985, Bernard A. Goldhirsh comments on the entrepreneurial environment in the United States. As you read the following excerpts from this speech, think about the reasons why a favorable entrepreneurial climate exists in the United States today. How does capitalism encourage entrepreneurship?

The Entrepreneurial Explosion

The fact is, a profound transformation is taking place throughout the business landscape. It is an entrepreneurial revolution. It has come into being because society has come to recognize the value, importance, and productivity of the entrepreneurial business unit. The awesome capabilities of the small to mid-sized companies to adapt to change, to bring new products to market, to generate jobs, and to create new wealth has been recognized by government, academia, capital sources, students, and top management in our largest corporations. . . . Small firms are producing up to 80 percent of all the new jobs created. . . .

There are a number of reasons for this entrepreneurial explosion.

First, we have become a very wealthy, middle-class country. Professional and managerial incomes are higher than ever before.

Second, 60 percent of the households in the under-50 age bracket now have two wage earners. The rise of the working woman makes it possible for one partner to go out and take a risk without the fear of not being able to feed one's family or pay the rent.

Third, the shift of the economy into the service sector or knowledge business is fueling the entrepreneurial fire. Here the key is the relatively low capital requirements to enter some of the small but emerging growth businesses.

Fourth, . . . we are the first nation to provide higher education to so large a proportion of our population. And I hope that this is one area that is not going to be cut back because it undergirds everything else. . . .

Fifth, many economists argue convincingly that in times of rapid technological change it is only the entrepreneurial sector that can bring new products to market in the time frames required to be competitive. . . .

A sixth reason for accelerating entrepreneurism is that college graduates are redefining the relationship between risk and personal fulfillment. In the sixties, joining the Peace Corps was perceived as a far better option than starting a business. In many circles the idea of working to turn a profit was scorned, as if to say that those who were generating profits were not also generating products, jobs, and playing a key role in the creating of a better economy.

Now we have college graduates who aren't necessarily reaching for the hand of the first established company to come along offering them security. They are thinking in terms of risks. . . .

To summarize, we are entering an era where mature industries are being restructured and new industries, the rising stars, are being born. . . . We take it as an article of faith that the powerful forces generating the technological and entrepreneurial revolutions are now beginning to transform this nation and we intend to be a part of this experience.

Source Review

For Answers to Source Review, see p. A 24.

1. What is the entrepreneurial revolution? How has it come into being?
2. What capabilities do the small to mid-sized companies have that the larger corporations do not have?
3. What six reasons does Bernard A. Goldhirsh offer for the "entrepreneurial explosion" in the United States?

DETERGENT PLUS FABRIC SOFTENER
Bold 3
1. CLEANS
2. SOFTENS
3. CONTROLS STATIC
NEW! CLEANS EVEN BETTER IN WARM AND COLD WATER!
ALL TEMPERATURE cheer
IMPROVED FOR COOLER WATER WASHING
Tide
AMERICA'S FAVORITE
Tide's In... Dirt's Out
229
229
229
ALL TEMPERATURE CONCENTRATED DETERGENT
Bright
for a brighter wash every time
359
229
229
229
Oxydol
FOR SPARKLING WHITES
Full Power Detergent + Color Safe Bleach
239
359
359
COLD POWER
CLEANS...BRIGHTENS ...SAVES ENERGY IN COLD WATER
concentrated detergent
Dash
3 powerful dirt dissolvers for a remarkably clean wash
Super value!
Purex
all temperature heavy duty detergent
239
382
215
359
239

CHAPTER 6

See Chapter Overview, p. TM 26.
See Chapter Objectives, p. TM 26.
See Introducing the Chapter, p. TM 26.
See Extending Economic Knowledge on text p. 138.

Competition and Market Structure

There are no barriers to someone with a good idea going out in the organization and making things happen. People feel a tremendous mobility to move across and up. It is like America.

Ken Olsen

1 Perfect competition has many sellers of the same product, while pure monopoly has only one.

- Perfect Competition Market Conditions
- Perfect Competition and Price
- Perfect Competition in Action
- Pure Monopoly Market Conditions
- Pure Monopoly and Price
- Pure Monopoly in Action

2 Under monopolistic competition, product differentiation is vital.

- Monopolistic Competition and Market Conditions
- Monopolistic Competition and Price
- Monopolistic Competition in Action

3 Under oligopoly, a few firms dominate the market.

- Market Structure in Oligopoly
- Oligopoly and Price
- Oligopoly in Action

4 The government has a varied record of regulating competition.

- Early Trust and Antitrust Legislation
- Progressive Era Legislation
- Current Antitrust Policy

CHAPTER 6 STUDY GUIDE

Chapter Focus

Chapter 6 considers the four types of market structure that exist in the economy of the United States: perfect competition, pure monopoly, monopolistic competition, and oligopoly. The chapter also examines the past and present role of government in preserving and encouraging competition.

As you study the chapter, look for the details that support each of the following statements.

1. Perfect competition has many sellers of the same product, while pure monopoly has only one.
2. Under monopolistic competition, product differentiation is vital.
3. Under oligopoly, a few firms dominate the market.
4. The government has a varied record of regulating competition.

See Preteaching Vocabulary, p. TM 26.

Terms to Know

The following terms, while not the only terms emphasized in this chapter, are basic to your understanding of competition and market structure. Determine the meaning of each term, either by using the Glossary or by watching for context clues as you read the chapter.

market structure	product differentiation
perfect competition	nonprice competition
pure monopoly	oligopoly
natural monopoly	pure oligopoly
technological monopoly	differentiated oligopoly
government monopoly	collusion
geographic monopoly	trust
monopolistic competition	economies of scale

See Key Study Questions and Key Understandings, p. TM 27.

1 Perfect competition has many sellers of the same product, while pure monopoly has only one.

See Suggested Teaching Strategies, p. TM 27.

Competition is the economic rivalry that occurs among businesses when producers in a given industry attempt to gain a larger share of the market. Economists use the term **market structure** to describe how competitive specific industries are.

Perfect competition and pure monopoly are the opposite extremes of the market structure continuum (see the diagram on page 123). **Perfect competition** exists when there are many buyers and sellers, none of whom control prices. In contrast, **pure monopoly** exists when a single firm controls the total production or sale of a good or service.

Perfect Competition Market Conditions

The most competitive type of industry is that with perfect competition. Four conditions must be present in the market structure for perfect competition to exist.

First, a particular good or service must have many sellers and buyers available. In addition, each seller must account for just a small share of the overall sales in the market. The goal of these sellers is to attract enough buyers to their businesses to earn a profit.

Second, the good or service being offered by one competing firm must be similar or identical to those offered by other firms. In such a situation, buyers may choose freely from the selection.

Third, buyers must have easy access to information on the products and prices available. This information allows buyers to make intelligent choices about which goods to purchase based on price and quality.

Fourth, entrance to and exit from the industry must be relatively easy and inexpensive. In a purely competitive market structure, firms can easily enter a profitable industry or leave an unprofitable one. Low start-up costs, the need for little technical know-how, and the lack of control existing companies have in the industry determine the ease a new firm has in gaining entry.

Perfect Competition and Price

In perfectly competitive industries, no one firm controls the price of a good. Suppose, for example, that thousands of firms are producing identical note pads that sell for $2. If one firm raises the price of its note pads to $2.10, buyers will simply buy from another firm. Conversely, no firm would need to cut its prices because it sells enough note pads to make a profit at $2. Lowering prices would merely mean lower profits. Economists state that prices in perfect competition are set by the marketplace rather than by individual firms.

Perfect Competition in Action

No industries are purely competitive in the United States today. Some industries, however, lean toward perfect competition.

Agriculture, with its hundreds of products and thousands of independent farmers, comes close to being a model of perfect competition. Thousands of farmers compete to sell their products to millions of buyers. No single agricultural producer is large enough to affect the price of an agricultural product such as corn or peaches. The products are uniform, and buyers are aware of product information, especially price information, which prevents one producer from demanding a higher price than another producer of an identical product. Although the high price of farmland prevents many people from entering farming, farmers who already own land can easily decide other crops are more profitable and grow them—restricted of course by climate and soil.

Pure Monopoly Market Conditions

The conditions necessary for the existence of pure monopoly are very different from those necessary for the existence of perfect competition. In general, pure monopolies exist when three specific conditions are present.

First, one firm is the sole producer or seller of a good or service. This condition distinguishes a monopoly from the three other market structures—perfect competition, monopolistic competition, and oligopoly as shown in the chart on this page. Even though monopolies do not have to compete with other firms for a share of the market, monopolies often advertise their product or service to promote the company's image.

Second, no close substitute goods are available. ◆ Electric power companies are examples of monopolies because each company is the exclusive supplier of electricity in a specific geographic area. While consumers may choose to substitute kerosene lamps and wood stoves for electricity, these substitutes are not close substitutes.

Third, prohibitive barriers to entry in the industry must exist. Most often high investment costs and the need for technological expertise prevent firms from trying to enter monopolistic markets. In addition, a number of legal restrictions make entry into government-supported monopolies nearly impossible. For example, governments give telephone companies exclusive rights to provide service in a specific area. Other telephone companies are barred from entering the market.

Competition and the Market Structure

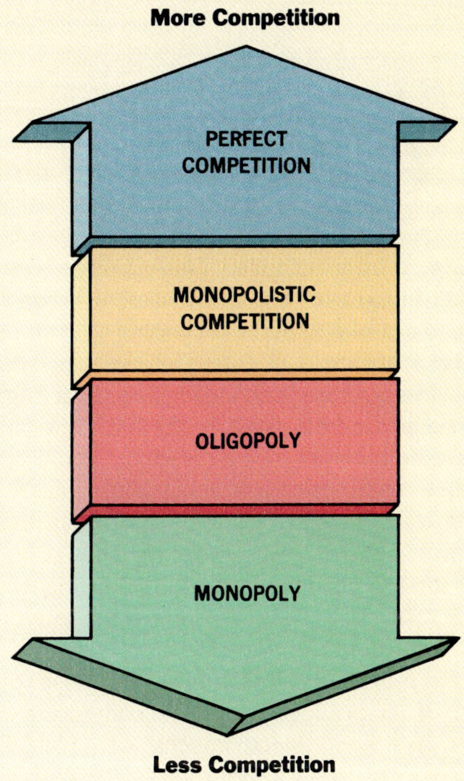

◆ Have the students read "Choosing a Long-Distance Telephone Service" on pages 516–517 of the *Everyday Economics Handbook* and answer the questions that follow.

HIGHLIGHTS IN ECONOMICS

Beginnings in Computer Technology

◆ In 1946, a machine called ENIAC (Electronic Numerical Integrator and Computer) ushered in the modern era of computer technology.

John Mauchly, a scientist at the University of Pennsylvania's Moore School of Electrical Engineering, had presented plans for ENIAC several years earlier. He believed such a computer could speedily produce ballistics-trajectory tables, which were desperately needed during World War II. When the United States government signed a contract in 1943 for the development of ENIAC, Mauchly and fellow scientist J. Presper Eckert went to work.

The machine the two scientists produced could operate more quickly than even the most sophisticated of its predecessors. The computers of the 1930s had been electromechanical. ENIAC was electronic. It used vacuum tubes, rather than slow-moving electromagnetic switches, to store and process information. As a result, it could perform 5,000 additions or subtractions per second, a rate that was 1,000 times faster than before.

Since ENIAC's unveiling in 1946, further advances in computer technology have made this landmark machine look, in the words of *Time* magazine, like a "big dimwit." Compared with today's computers having similar functions, ENIAC was enormous. It consisted of some 18,000 vacuum tubes, 70,000 resistors, 10,000 capacitors, and 6,000 switches. It weighed 30 tons and filled a room the size of a two-car garage.

ENIAC had other problems in addition to its size. Tubes burned out at the rate of two a day. Each time a tube failed, the machine stopped working, and a technician had to search through a maze of parts for the one that needed to be replaced. Technicians also had to rewire ENIAC whenever the machine needed to change operations, a process that usually took several days.

The transistor, the silicon chip, and other subsequent inventions have enabled scientists to produce computers that are many times smaller, faster, and easier to operate than ENIAC. These new computers also can perform a great variety of functions. Yet ENIAC was a marvel for its time and represented a major breakthrough in computer technology.

Pure Monopoly and Price

As the only producer or seller of a good, a monopoly has a great deal of control over prices. Nevertheless, the law of demand works even in monopolistic markets. If the price of a good is set too high, buyers will buy less or stop buying the good entirely. Excessively high prices also attract competing firms to the industry. The high prices make the high initial investment costs and the risks of starting a new business worthwhile to an entrepreneur. In addition, local, state, and national governments sometimes monitor and dictate the quantity, quality, and price of the product of a legal monopoly.

In many foreign countries, airlines are monopolies. For example, only Aviaco, an airline owned by the Spanish government, provides service between Spanish cities. In theory, Aviaco has the freedom to charge any price for airline tickets. In reality, however, Aviaco must consider the law of demand when setting fares. If the price is too high, travelers will use alternate forms of transportation, such as

◆ Report topic: How the computer revolution is changing life in the United States.

One response to strong foreign competition has been the bumper-sticker campaign urging Americans to buy products manufactured in the United States of America (USA).

automobiles, trains, or buses. In addition, the Spanish government sets limits on what fares Aviaco charges.

Pure Monopoly in Action

The United States government has determined that four types of monopolies in the United States are beneficial to the entire economy and are thus legal enterprises. These monopolies include natural monopolies, technological monopolies, government monopolies, and geographic monopolies.

Natural Monopoly. In some industries, competition is inconvenient, impractical, and unworkable. In these industries, a single firm most efficiently produces or sells a good or service. Economists call such an industry a **natural monopoly.**

Public utilities are the leading examples of natural monopolies. The government gives utility companies the exclusive right to provide service in a specific geographic region. In return, the government closely regulates the natural monopoly to ensure that it provides quality service at reasonable prices. In the communications industry, the American Telephone & Telegraph Company (AT&T) long had a natural monopoly on telephone service. The court-ordered breakup of the AT&T network ended this natural monopoly in 1984.

Technological Monopoly. A **technological monopoly** occurs when a firm develops new technology that changes the way goods are produced or creates an entirely new product. General Dynamics, for example, is the only defense contractor in the United States with the technology to build Trident submarines. In effect this corporation has a technological monopoly on the production of Trident submarines.

◆ Firms and individuals apply for patents to protect their technological discoveries. A patent grants a firm or individual the exclusive right to produce, use, or dispose of an invention or discovery for 17 years. Thus, the firm has a 17-year monopoly over the invention.

Patent laws encourage firms to invest in the research and development of new products and production techniques. In 1985, the Patent and Trademark office issued 77,251 patents on inventions and production processes. The new and protected technology helps firms to gain an advantage over competitors. For this reason, individual firms and the government vigorously protect patents.

In a 10-year-long patent infringement case, the Polaroid Corporation accused the Eastman Kodak Company of infringing on seven Polaroid instant photography patents. In 1986, the Supreme Court upheld a lower court ruling that had convicted Kodak of stealing trade secrets from Polaroid. The court ordered Kodak to give up its instant photography product line.

◆ In the late 1800s, some government officials wanted to close the Patent Office because they believed that everything that could be invented had already been patented.

The Norris Dam on the Clinch River is part of the Tennessee Valley Authority.

Written works and works of art are protected in much the same way as scientific works. By granting a copyright, the United States Copyright Office gives authors, composers, and artists exclusive rights to publish, duplicate, perform, display, or sell their creative works. The huge income from the works of recording artists, for example, makes protection of the works extremely important to those artists. This legal protection encourages creative and artistic efforts, just as patent laws encourage industrial research and development.

Government Monopoly. The third type of legal monopoly is the **government monopoly,** a monopoly owned and operated by any level of government. Towns and cities own and operate water and sewer services as government monopolies. The states control the building and maintenance of roads, bridges, and canals as government monopolies. The federal government dominates mail delivery through the Postal Service, a government monopoly. Although the government allows private companies to provide overnight mail service at premium prices, the Postal Service is the only firm that can offer low-cost regular mail. ◆ The Tennessee Valley Authority (TVA), the major producer of electricity in the southeastern United States, is also a federal government monopoly.

Government monopolies exist in response to a public need the private sector of the economy has not met. Most government monopolies tend to provide goods or services that enhance the general welfare rather than seek profits. For this reason, the public generally supports government monopolies.

Geographic Monopoly. A geographic monopoly is the fourth type of legal monopoly. A **geographic monopoly** occurs when a firm is the only producer or seller of a good or service in a specific location. A general store in a remote community, for example, has a geographic monopoly on the sale of many common household items and food if no competitor exists in the area. Geographic monopolies form when business or the potential for profit is insufficient to attract a competitor to the area.

Geographic monopolies have declined because Americans are more mobile today than in the past. Consumers have access to public or private transportation and can travel longer distances to shop. Increasingly, consumers are shopping by direct mail and phone, which gives them rapid contacts with stores on a national level.

See Suggested Assignments, p. TM 27.

Section 1 Review See Answers, p. A 25.

DEFINE market structure, perfect competition, pure monopoly, natural monopoly, government monopoly, geographic monopoly

IDENTIFY ENIAC

1. **Summarizing Ideas** **(a)** What conditions are present in perfect competition? **(b)** What conditions are present in a monopoly?
2. **Comprehending Ideas** How does the number of competitors affect the market structure?
3. **Comparing Ideas** Compare how price is determined in **(a)** perfect competition and **(b)** a monopoly.
4. **Interpreting Graphics** Study the chart on page 123. **(a)** Draw a market structure continuum similar to the one on page 123. **(b)** In the sections of the arrow labeled "Perfect Competition" and "Monopoly," write the names of two types of businesses or industries that fit the description of that part of the continuum.

 ◆ Many people believe that the government should sell the TVA.

See Key Study Questions and Key Understandings, p. TM 28.

2 Under monopolistic competition, product differentiation is vital.

See Suggested Teaching Strategies, p. TM 28.

When competition is not perfect, it is called imperfect competition. One type of imperfect competition is monopolistic competition.

Monopolistic Competition and Market Conditions

Monopolistic competition exists when four conditions are present in the market structure. First, numerous buyers and sellers of the good or service must exist. As with perfect competition, monopolistic competition requires that firms act independently. Many firms share the existing market, but no single firm is large enough to change the overall supply or price of the good.

Second, firms must offer similar but differentiated products for sale. In **product differentiation,** sellers emphasize the differences among competing products in order to increase sales. These differences can be real, but often they are insignificant. Firms achieve product differentiation by advertising brand names or small differences in the design and color of the product. Producers of designer jeans, for example, emphasize the style and the names of the designers in their expensive advertising campaigns. Designer jeans that cost $75 and bargain jeans that cost $15 have few differences other than price. Yet many consumers buy the more expensive brands because of the designer's name and because they believe that the expensive jeans are more stylish.

Third, buyers must be well informed about differentiated products. To educate buyers, monopolistic competitors rely on informative advertising and competitive advertising. **Informative advertising** is intended to provide consumers with information on the price, quality, and special features of specific products. Ads for refrigerators that emphasize the convenience, price, and dependability of a particular product are examples of informative advertising.

Competitive advertising tries to persuade consumers that the product being advertised is better than substitute goods. Ads for refrigerators or Cadillacs are examples of competitive advertising. In general, firms use competitive advertising more than informative advertising under conditions of monopolistic competition. In many cases, however, the same advertisement is both competitive and informative.

The fourth condition is that firms be able to enter or exit an industry with relative ease. Few legal, financial, or other restrictions exist. Firms that cannot afford to develop product differentiation, and bear heavy advertising costs, however, will be unable to enter the industry.

Economics Reporter

What Is a Fortune 500 Company?

The editors of *Fortune*, a leading business magazine, publish an annual list of the largest industrial corporations in the United States. The list is referred to as the Fortune 500. All Fortune 500 companies operate in the areas of manufacturing or mining. The primary criterion for ranking on this list is the volume of yearly sales. The ranking lists a corporation's total assets, net income, stockholder's return on investment, number of employees, assets per employee, and sales per employee. The Fortune 500 list also indicates the corporations that are profitable stock investments and leaders in the domestic market.

Monopolistic Competition and Price

Monopolistic competitors have some control over the price of a good or service. This limited control stems from the producer's ability to achieve product differentiation and create buyer loyalty to the brand name and the product through advertising.

Monopolistic competitors often use **nonprice competition** to control prices. An example of nonprice competition is advertising the brand name or special features of a product.

A firm that succeeds in developing brand name loyalty can marginally increase the price of the product without losing its customers. In this sense, the market structure is monopolistic. Monopolistic competitors realize, however, that they are subject to the law of demand. If a producer increases the price of a good too much, buyers will switch to a competitor's product. In this respect, the market structure is competitive.

DECISION MAKERS IN THE ECONOMY

Ted Turner ◆

Ted Turner, one of the nation's best-known entrepreneurs, has helped to change the nature of the television industry. Quick to recognize the potential of cable television, he has used it to gain entry into a market once dominated by the three major networks: ABC, NBC, and CBS.

Turner got his start in 1963 when he successfully rebuilt his family's failing billboard advertising business. In 1970, he bought Channel 17 (now WTBS) in Atlanta. Under Turner's management, the station captured a 16-percent share of the local audience.

Even as Channel 17 was becoming a huge success in Atlanta, Turner was well aware that cable television might someday enable him to reach viewers throughout North America. Then in 1975, the Federal Communications Commission (FCC) relaxed its rules concerning access to cable systems. In the same year, RCA launched its first commercial communications satellite. By the end of 1976, Channel 17 had become one of the satellite's full-time users.

At the end of 1978, Channel 17 counted 50,000 homes a month as part of its audience. WTBS's rapid growth in market share led to an equally rapid increase in the station's worth.

Turner has continued to expand his television operations. In 1980, he launched Cable News Network (CNN), a cable television station providing the news 24 hours a day. In late 1981, he launched CNN2, which presents the news in a more concise format. Although Turner would still like to own a major network, he has already proved that new networks can enter the industry and compete successfully.

Monopolistic Competition in Action

Numerous examples of monopolistic competition exist in the United States economy. Producers of facial tissues, gasoline, and home heating oil, for example, compete in monopolistic competitive markets. In each case, producers attempt to create brand name loyalty for similar and even identical products.

Monopolistic competition also exists in some service industries. Competing airlines, for example, may offer customers a variety of services different from those of their competitors: wider and more comfortable seats, meals on flights, and reading material or movies for entertainment. They build reputations and gain customer loyalty by being prompt and friendly. Although the airlines prefer nonprice competition, harmful price wars often occur.

CASE STUDY

Monopolistic Competition and Food Franchising

One area of the United States economy where monopolistic competition is evident is food franchising. In food franchising, individuals pay an initial fee to a corporation for the privilege of using the corporation's name and selling the corporation's products.

The fast-food hamburger industry is an excellent example of franchising as monopolistic competition. Although three giant corporations—McDonald's, Wendy's, and Burger King—dominate the industry, thousands of small competitors exist throughout the nation. In addition, no single firm can affect supply

◆ Ted Turner was the captain of *Courageous*, the yacht that won the America's Cup in 1977.

McDonald's and Popeyes are two companies that have been successful in using franchising as a method to expand their businesses.

or price. If McDonald's raises its prices too much, consumers will buy hamburgers from competitors.

To obtain a franchise from McDonald's, Burger King, or Wendy's, an investor must pay the corporation an initial fee that ranges from about $500,000 to more than $1 million. In return, the investor receives training from the corporation as well as a restaurant and all of the capital needed to begin operating. While the individual investor owns the business, the parent corporation sets prices, monitors quality, and sells the investor all the equipment and food necessary to operate the business.

It is often easy to enter the fast-food hamburger industry. Individuals, for example, can set up their own independent hamburger stands without much investment. In addition, while purchasing a franchise from one of the big three corporate leaders is certainly not inexpensive, the purchase is within the reach of many investors. To enter the national market as a competitor to McDonald's, Burger King, or Wendy's, however, would require an initial investment of billions of dollars. Such huge investments are beyond the reach of almost all investors.

As in most cases of monopolistic competition, the fast-food hamburger industry spends millions of dollars on advertising. In the mid-1980s, the advertising campaigns of McDonald's, Wendy's, and Burger King, which cost more than $500 million, became so fierce that the news media labeled them the "Burger Wars." Each corporation's campaigns stressed small differences in their products in order to build consumer loyalty. In addition, the firms used catchy phrases and songs, and comparisons of how their hamburgers were superior to those of the competition to win a larger share of the market.

Franchising exists in many areas of the United States economy. Many restaurants, grocery stores, convenience stores, and fast-food outlets are franchise operations that allow individual investors with limited capital to set up a business.

See Suggested Assignments, p. TM 28.

Section 2 Review See Answers, p. A 26.

DEFINE monopolistic competition, product differentiation, competitive advertising

IDENTIFY Fortune 500 Company, Ted Turner

1. **Summarizing Ideas** What is the purpose of nonprice competition?
2. **Comprehending Ideas** **(a)** Why is the fast-food industry an example of monopolistic competition? **(b)** Why is advertising important in the fast-food industry?
3. **Interpreting Ideas** What techniques do businesses use to succeed in a market characterized by monopolistic competition?

BUILDING ECONOMIC SKILLS

INTERPRETING THE VISUAL RECORD

Analyzing Editorial Cartoons

An editorial cartoon is a drawing that presents a point of view on an economic, political, or social issue or topic. Editorial cartoons have been used throughout United States history to influence public opinion. Some cartoons present a positive point of view. Most editorial cartoons, however, are critical of a policy, event, person, or group. Editorial cartoons typically are found in the editorial sections of newspapers and newsmagazines.

The two most important techniques that cartoonists use to express their message are caricature and symbolism. A caricature is a drawing that exaggerates or distorts physical features.

Symbolism is the use of one thing to represent another idea, feeling, or object. Common symbols for the United States, for example, include the bald eagle and Uncle Sam. Cartoonists often include titles, captions, or other labels to get across their messages.

How to Analyze an Editorial Cartoon

To analyze an editorial cartoon, follow these steps.

1. **Identify the caricatures.** Identify the people or objects being characterized. Note whether the cartoon figures contain any exaggerations or distortions. Determine whether the cartoonist's point of view is positive or negative.
2. **Identify the symbols used.** Determine the meaning of each symbol. State how the symbols are connected to the message being communicated by the editorial cartoonist. Decide how the symbols clarify the message.
3. **Read all labels.** Editorial cartoonists often use labels to identify people, objects, events, or ideas. Determine how the labels help express the cartoonist's point of view.
4. **Read the caption.** Many cartoons carry a caption in addition to their labels. If the cartoon has a caption, state the relationship of the caption to the editorial cartoon. Determine whether the viewpoint being expressed is that of the cartoonist, the cartoon figure, or other persons or institutions shown in the cartoon.

BRONCO BUSTING IN THE WEST
"Amuses us and don't hurt the hoss"

Applying the Skill

Study the editorial cartoon on page 130. Note that it appeared in the magazine *Puck* in 1889, shortly before the debate on the Sherman Antitrust Act began in Congress. The caricatures of the trusts, or monopolies, show huge, distorted bodies. These huge bodies are meant to symbolize the trusts' power over the senators. The moneybags that form the bodies of the trusts are marked with dollar signs ($). The top hats worn by the trusts are a traditional symbol for capitalists. The labels in the cartoon identify specific trusts. Some of these trusts are the paper bag trust, the coal trust, the sugar trust, the iron trust, and the steel beam trust. Notice that the monopolists' entrance to the Senate chamber is open, while the peoples' entrance is closed. The sign at the rear of the chamber says, "This is a Senate of the monopolists, by the monopolists, and for the monopolists." The cartoon's caption—"Bosses of the Senate"—reinforces the cartoon's point of view that monopolies control this branch of Congress.

Practicing the Skill See Answers, p. A 26.

Study the editorial cartoon above. Then, on a separate sheet of paper, answer each question.

1. **(a)** Who are the central figures in the editorial cartoon? **(b)** How do you know?
2. What symbol is being used to represent the United States?
3. **(a)** Why is the cartoonist's depiction of Teddy Roosevelt a caricature? **(b)** What feature of Roosevelt's personality is being exaggerated?
4. **(a)** What action is taking place in the cartoon? **(b)** Who seems to be winning the struggle?
5. **(a)** When is the struggle taking place? **(b)** What types of reforms were underway during the Progressive Era?
6. **(a)** How would you explain the message of the cartoon? **(b)** What is the cartoonist's viewpoint?

See Key Study Questions and Key Understandings, p. TM 29.

3 Under oligopoly, a few firms dominate the market.

See Suggested Teaching Strategies, p. TM 29.

Monopolistic competition is one type of imperfect competition. **Oligopoly,** in which a few large firms control an industry, is the second type. A **pure oligopoly** exists when a few producers dominate the production of an identical product, such as oil, lumber, aluminum, or steel. A **differentiated oligopoly** exists when a few producers dominate the production of similar products, such as automobiles, breakfast cereals, or television sets.

Market Structure in Oligopoly

Oligopolies exist when four conditions are present in the market structure. First, few producers or sellers of a good or service exist. Having few producers or sellers distinguishes an oligopolistic market structure from those of perfect competition and monopolistic competition. An industry is classified as an oligopoly when the largest three or four firms in the industry produce 70 percent or more of the industry's total output (see the chart on page 133).

The cost of capital equipment makes it difficult for new firms to enter the automotive industry.

Second, firms offer similar or identical yet differentiated goods or services for sale. Oligopolies consider it important for buyers to perceive differences between competing products. The differences may be real or imaginary and, as with monopolistic competition, advertising influences buyers' perceptions.

Third, as in perfect and monopolistic competition, information about a product must be readily available. The three or four dominant firms in the industry often use advertising to remind buyers of brand name products already on the market. They use informative advertising to introduce a new product to potential buyers.

Fourth, substantial barriers to entry into the industry must exist. The three major barriers are money, technical knowledge, and loyalty to existing brand name products. Because many firms in an oligopoly are large firms, potential competitors must raise billions of dollars to build and equip a plant, hire workers, and buy natural resources. Technical knowledge, especially in high-technology industries such as computers that require extensive research and development, is expensive and time consuming. New firms also face competition from established firms with brand name products, whose buyers remain loyal to them.

Oligopoly and Price

Like monopolistic competitors, oligopolies can control price to some degree by creating brand name loyalty and engaging in nonprice competition. Oligopolies can also control the price of a good through price leadership. **Price leadership** often originates with the largest firm in an industry, which offers its new product at a certain price, hoping that the competing firms will set similar prices for their products.

If the competing firms in the oligopoly do follow the leader, a single firm then has succeeded in setting the price of the good. If the competition does not follow the leader's price, the leading firm may be forced to change its price so that it is in line with the prices of the competition. Price leadership is an accepted method of determining a price for a product in oligopolistic markets.

Price leadership is legal. Collusion is not. **Collusion** occurs when leaders of competing firms set production levels or prices for products. Collusion presents a clear danger to free competition.

Comparing Market Structures

	PERFECT COMPETITION	MONOPOLISTIC COMPETITION	OLIGOPOLY	PURE MONOPOLY
NUMBER OF FIRMS IN INDUSTRY	Very Many	Many	Few (Three or Four)	One
MARKET CONCENTRATION	Low	Low	High	Absolute
TYPE OF PRODUCT	Similar or Identical	Similar or Identical	Similar or Differentiated	Unique (No Substitutes)
AVAILABILITY OF INFORMATION	Much (Product Advertising)	Much (Product Advertising)	Much (Product Advertising)	Less (Product and Institutional Advertising)
ENTRY INTO INDUSTRY	Very Easy	Fairly Easy	Difficult	Prohibitive
CONTROL OVER PRICES	None	Little	Some	Much
INDUSTRY EXAMPLES	Agriculture	Personal Computers Airlines	Automobiles Breakfast Cereals	Electric Power Cable Television

Oligopoly in Action

Oligopolies exist in many industries in the United States. Oligopolies often form as a result of the failure of less efficient businesses in a particular industry, such as occurred in the automobile industry between 1920 and the 1960s. In the 1920s, more than 300 companies in the United States manufactured automobiles. Competition, however, caused the less efficient companies to fail so that after Studebaker failed in 1966 only four automobile manufacturers remained: General Motors, Ford, Chrysler, ◆ and American Motors.

Oligopolies in the United States economy are not guaranteed a fixed share of the industry's market. Firms must keep up with consumer demands for new and better products because substitute goods are readily available. The Chrysler Corporation's near collapse by the early 1980s is a good reminder that a brand name alone cannot hold consumer loyalty.

Section 3 Review See Answers, p. A 26.

DEFINE oligopoly, differentiated oligopoly, pure oligopoly, collusion

1. **Comprehending Ideas** **(a)** What conditions exist in an oligopolistic market structure? **(b)** How is price determined in an oligopoly?
2. **Contrasting Ideas** **(a)** What are the differences between price leadership and collusion? **(b)** What is the basic difference bet· een a pure oligopoly and a differentiated oligopoly?
3. **Interpreting Ideas** What is the major advantage for business of an oligopoly?
4. **Interpreting Graphics** Study the chart on this page. According to the information on the chart, is it easier to make a profit in a perfectly competitive or oligopolistic market structure? Why?

See Suggested Assignments, p. TM 29.

◆ American Motors is by far the smallest American automobile manufacturer.

ISSUES IN ECONOMICS

The Costs and Benefits of Government Regulation

During the first century of United States history, the government supported laissez-faire capitalism. Businesses were allowed to function with few governmentally imposed restrictions or regulations. Since the 1880s, however, support for laissez-faire capitalism has given way to increased government involvement in business.

The effect of government regulations on the economy is the subject of heated national debate. Many persons believe that government regulations serve the public interest by performing such functions as protecting competition and promoting health and safety. Other people believe that government's involvement in business hurts the economy. The validity of both viewpoints can be analyzed by examining the costs and benefits of government regulations.

Economic Costs of Government Regulations

Businesses, consumers, and taxpayers incur costs as a result of government regulations. Generally, these costs fall into three categories: (1) financial costs, (2) lower productivity, and (3) less consumer choice in the marketplace.

Financial Costs. Businesses must bear the financial burden of higher production costs when they conform to pollution control, occupational safety, and other government standards. Regulations imposed by the Nuclear Regulatory Commission (NRC), for example, have contributed to the skyrocketing cost of constructing nuclear power plants. Some economists estimate that businesses spend more than $100 billion annually to comply with state and federal regulations.

Consumers and taxpayers also bear financial costs. Consumers pay more for many goods and services because businesses increase their prices in order to pass on higher production costs to consumers. Similarly, taxpayers incur financial costs of more than $6 billion a year. These tax payments fund support for the approximately 50 independent regulatory commissions and agencies that enforce government regulations.

Lower Business Productivity. Businesses must devote resources to comply with the guidelines of government regulations. These resources could otherwise go toward investment in new capital or toward research and development that would tend to increase productivity.

Critics of government regulation of business, such as Milton Friedman, point to statistical evidence showing that regulations have lowered productivity. Productivity has dropped as the number of government regulations has increased. Between 1949 and 1969, the average output per worker in the United States increased by more than 3 percent per year. As regulatory control expanded during the 1970s, however, the increase in productivity was only 1.5 percent. Productivity continues to show declines through the 1980s.

Limited Consumer Choice. Regulations can prohibit the manufacture of medicines, toys, and other products that do not meet specified standards. The prohibitions sometimes run counter to the desires of consumers. If the products were available, consumers would purchase them. In these instances, government regulations, rather than consumer choices, affect producers' decisions about what to produce and consumers' decisions about what products to buy.

Criticism and Deregulation. Critics believe that many of these regulations are unnecessary. They believe that businesses, acting in their own self-interest, will take voluntary precautions to provide a safe workplace and quality products. They also note that such private organizations as the Better Business Bureau, Consumers' Research, and the Consumers' Union could handle many problems related to quality and safety in the workplace.

The public's support for deregulating the economy was evident in the Presidential elections of 1980 and 1984. President Ronald Reagan's economic platform called for the elimination of regulations that were wasteful or counter-productive. As a result, the government budget cutting during the 1980s has included cuts in regulatory agencies such as the Consumer Product Safety Commission (CPSC) and the Federal Trade Commission (FTC). In 1986, the Reagan administration even proposed the elimination of the Interstate Commerce Commission (ICC).

Economic and Social Benefits

An analysis of the economic and social benefits of government regulations must focus on how these rules serve the public interest. In a sense, regulatory commissions and agencies are "watchdogs" for the government. The measure of their effectiveness is how well they protect businesses, consumers, workers, savers, and investors.

Preserving Competition. The ICC, the FTC, and other regulatory agencies were created to stop monopolies from controlling industries by investigating violations of antitrust laws. Thus, government regulations protect the right of countless smaller businesses to compete with larger ones.

Protecting Consumers. As early as 1906, the Congress established the Food and Drug Administration (FDA) to guarantee the safe consumption of food and medicine. Later the FTC and the FCC protected consumer choice by working to ensure that consumers were informed about products and unfair and deceptive practices. More recently, the Consumer Product Safety Commission was established as an umbrella organization to guarantee product safety and provide information to buyers.

Protecting Workers. The Occupational Safety and Health Administration (OSHA) was created in 1970 to ensure that working conditions were safe. OSHA regulations cover many aspects of the workplace, including safe levels of noise and heat.

The process toward equal opportunities in the labor market, especially for women and for blacks, Hispanics, and other minority groups, gained momentum with the creation of the Equal Employment Opportunity Commission (EEOC) in 1964.

Protecting Savers and Investors. Federal insurances, such as the Federal Deposit Insurance Corporation (FDIC), insure savers' deposits and impose regulations on insured bank and nonbank financial institutions. In addition, the Securities and Exchange Commission (SEC) establishes rules for the issue, sale, and purchase of stock and thus protects investors in the United States stock market.

Cost-Benefit Analysis

In 1981, the Office of Management and Budget (OMB) ordered regulatory commissions and agencies to submit cost-benefit analyses for proposed regulations whenever compliance would cost an industry more than $100 million. The OMB is a federal bureau that reviews budget requests submitted by various government agencies and makes budget recommendations to the President. To secure approval of new regulations, the regulators must prove that the benefits to the public are greater than the costs of compliance. In a sense, this policy regulates the regulators.

Examining regulations in terms of their costs and benefits, however, is a difficult task because the dollar value of certain elements under study must be determined. For example, how does one compare the cost of OSHA's workplace regulations to the life of a human being?

See Key Study Questions and Key Understandings, p. TM 30.

4 The government has a varied record of regulating competition.

See Suggested Teaching Strategies, p. TM 30.

Over the past century, the federal government has acted to protect competition in the United States economy. At the same time, local, state, and national governments have permitted certain legal monopolies to exist to promote business efficiency and the general welfare of the people.

Early Trust and Antitrust Legislation

After the Civil War ended in 1865, captains of industry used mergers and cutthroat competition to create huge monopolies called **trusts** in oil, meat ◆ packing, sugar, coal, tobacco, and steel. At first the federal government did nothing to interfere with these trusts. By the 1880s, however, the government, aware of the trend toward industrial consolidations, passed laws to protect competition in the United States economy. The chart on this page describes the major features of these laws.

The passage of the Interstate Commerce Act in 1887 and the Sherman Antitrust Act in 1890 began a new era in the relationship between business and government. Called **antitrust legislation,** these acts were designed to monitor and regulate big business, prevent monopolies from forming, and break up existing monopolies.

The Sherman Antitrust Act of 1890 continues to be the cornerstone of antitrust legislation in the United States. Most of the antitrust legislation that followed further defined the principles embodied in the Sherman Antitrust Act. These principles are most clearly stated in Sections 1 and 2 of the Sherman Antitrust Act as described on the chart.

The Sherman Antitrust Act's failure to define key terms such as "trust" and "restraint of trade" made the act sometimes ineffective. The act also ran contrary to the laissez-faire attitude that had dominated government-business relations since the beginning of the republic. The economic theory of **laissez-faire** states that economic systems prosper only when the government does not interfere with or regulate business in any way. For these reasons, most of the antitrust cases brought against firms in the 1890s were unsuccessful.

Progressive Era Legislation

The success of the Sherman Antitrust Act during the reform-minded Progressive Era (1901–1920)

United States Antitrust Legislation

YEAR	LEGISLATION	PURPOSE
1887	Interstate Commerce Act	Created the Interstate Commerce Commission (ICC) to oversee railroad rates; today the ICC regulates railroads, motor vehicles, and other freight carriers.
1890	Sherman Antitrust Act	Prohibited any agreements, contracts, or conspiracies that would restrain interstate trade or cause monopolies to form.
1914	Clayton Antitrust Act	Clarified and strengthened the Sherman Antitrust Act by prohibiting price discrimination, local price cutting, interlocking directorates, mergers that reduce competition, and exclusive sales contracts.
1914	Federal Trade Commission Act	Created the Federal Trade Commission (FTC) to investigate charges of unfair methods of competition and commerce.
1936	Robinson–Patman Act	Protected small retail businesses by prohibiting wholesalers from charging small retailers higher prices than they charged large retailers and by prohibiting large retailers from setting artificially low prices (also called the Antiprice Discrimination Act).
1950	Celler–Kefauver Act	Strengthened the Clayton Antitrust Act by preventing mergers and the purchase of competitors' assets when such acquisition would substantially reduce competition (also called the Celler Antimerger Act).

◆ Journalists called muckrakers exposed corrupt practices in business. Ida Tarbell wrote a series on the Standard Oil Company in *McClure's* magazine, and Upton Sinclair's *The Jungle* exposed unsanitary conditions in the meat-packing industry.

reflected the popular demand that government correct certain political and economic problems. Other Progressive Era antitrust legislation paved the way for vigorous antitrust actions. The Clayton Antitrust Act and the Federal Trade Commission Act, both passed in 1914, spelled out specific types of illegal business practices. The Robinson-Patman Act of 1936 and the Celler-Kefauver Act of 1950 were extensions of Progressive Era legislation.

During the 1960s and 1970s, antitrust legislation was strictly interpreted and enforced by the Antitrust Division of the Department of Justice. For example, the federal government's antitrust case against American Telephone and Telegraph (AT&T) broke up the world's largest corporation by 1984. AT&T was forced to divest itself of 22 local telephone companies, worth about $80 billion. In 1985, about 1,000 voluntary corporate divestitures worth about $30 billion occurred. The AT&T divestiture, on the other hand, was a mandatory divestiture. It is a landmark antitrust case because it dissolved the world's largest natural monopoly.

◆ Current Antitrust Policy

Despite its antitrust case against AT&T, the federal government generally softened its policies toward corporate mergers during the 1980s. Nevertheless, by the mid-1980s a national debate over antitrust policy had developed. At the center of the controversy was Section 7 of the Clayton Act. Section 7 made it illegal for firms to buy the assets—real capital, property, resources—of a competitor if "the effect of such acquisition may be substantially to lessen competition, or tend to create a monopoly."

Critics of the Clayton Act argued that Section 7 prevented horizontal mergers that could make United States industries more efficient and enable companies to benefit from the economies of scale. **Economies of scale** exist when firms are large enough to take advantage of mass production techniques that result in lower per unit production costs. Lower per unit production costs mean that a firm is more profitable.

Supporters of the Clayton Act countered that the looser interpretation of the Clayton Act during the 1980s was already giving United States firms the chance to consolidate and benefit from the economies of scale.

See Suggested Assignments, p. TM 30.

◆ Discussion topic: The current administration's stand on prosecuting trusts.

Section 4 Review See Answers, p. A 27.

DEFINE trust, laissez-faire, economies of scale

1. **Analyzing Ideas** **(a)** Why has the government permitted certain legal monopolies to exist? **(b)** Give two examples of legal monopolies that currently exist in the United States.
2. **Interpreting Graphics** Study the chart on page 136. According to the chart, what has been the basic purpose of United States antitrust legislation?

CHAPTER 6 SUMMARY

The most competitive type of market structure is perfect competition. Perfectly competitive market structures include many buyers and sellers, similar products for sale, and easy entry to and exit from the industry. Perfect competition is rare in the United States, but agriculture approximates it.

Pure monopoly, which exists when a single firm controls the total production or sale of a good or service, is the opposite of perfect competition. For pure monopolies to exist, no close substitute goods can be available and prohibitive barriers to entry in the industry must be present. The four types of monopolies that are legal in the United States include natural monopolies, technological monopolies, government monopolies, and geographic monopolies.

Monopolistic competition is a third type of market structure. Monopolistic competition is possible when numerous buyers and sellers of a good or service exist, firms offer similar but differentiated products for sale, buyers are well informed about differentiated products, and firms are able to enter or exit an industry easily.

The final type of market structure is the oligopoly, in which a few large firms control an industry. Oligopolies are possible when few producers or sellers exist, firms offer similar or identical yet differentiated goods or services, information about products is readily available, and substantial barriers to entry into the industry exist.

Since the 1880s, the United States has regulated competition in the United States economy. The Interstate Commerce Act and the Sherman Antitrust Act were the first attempts at this regulation. Today the Sherman Antitrust Act is still the cornerstone of antitrust regulation in the United States.

CHAPTER 6 REVIEW

For Answers to Chapter 6 Review, see p. A 27.

Reviewing Economic Terms

Supply the economic term that correctly completes each sentence.

1. Economists use the term _____ _____ to describe the competition among specific industries.
2. When a single firm controls the total production or sale of a product, a _____ exists.
3. A single firm that most efficiently produces or sells a product is called a _____ _____.
4. Monopolistic competitors often use several types of _____ _____ to control prices.
5. A type of monopolistic competition in which a few large firms control an industry is _____.
6. When the largest firm offers a new product at a certain price and competitors set similar prices, price has been determined by _____ _____.
7. When a firm develops new technology that changes the way goods are produced or creates an entirely new product, _____ _____ occurs.
8. Emphasizing the differences among competing items is _____ _____.
9. Laws designed to prevent monopolies are called _____ _____.

Exercising Economic Skills

1. **Analyzing Editorial Cartoons** Study the cartoon on page 372. **(a)** Who is dangling from deficit's leash? **(b)** In this cartoon, who do you think Uncle Sam represents? **(c)** What does the cartoonist use to represent the deficit? **(d)** Why do you think the cartoonist represents the deficit this way? **(e)** What is the cartoonist's message?
2. **Choosing a Long-Distance Telephone Service** Study the feature on pages 516–517. Then check the latest telephone bill sent to your house. **(a)** What do you think are the main considerations in selecting a long-distance telephone company? **(b)** What is the name of your long-distance telephone company? **(c)** What special services of the long-distance company does your family use? **(d)** What influenced your family's choice of a long-distance telephone company?

Thinking Critically About Economics

1. **Summarizing Ideas** **(a)** In business, what is competition? **(b)** What conditions exist in monopolistic competition? **(c)** What is an oligopoly? **(d)** Why has the federal government passed antitrust legislation?
2. **Seeing Relationships** What is the role of easy access to information in perfect competition?
3. **Analyzing Ideas** Is it possible for the prices determined in a monopoly to be lower than those determined in perfect competition? Explain.
4. **Evaluating Ideas** **(a)** How has antitrust legislation benefited society? **(b)** Should the government regulate business more or less? Explain.

Extending Economic Knowledge

1. Ask at least three businesspeople in your community the following questions.
   - **a.** How much competition does your business have?
   - **b.** How important to your business is advertising?
   - **c.** Describe your advertising approach, including how often and where you advertise.
   - **d.** How do you determine prices?
2. Describe the type of market structure in which each of the following businesses operates in your community.
   - **a.** a hair salon
   - **b.** a stockbroker
   - **c.** the local Buick dealership
   - **d.** a wheat farmer
   - **e.** a local restaurant
   - **f.** a chain of local restaurants
   - **g.** a fast-food franchise
3. **(a)** Select five of the businesses listed in Question 2 of Extending Economic Knowledge and classify each business in its proper market structure. **(b)** Then in a paragraph for each business, explain how changing the market to include first the state and then the nation affects the classification of each of the five businesses. **(c)** In a second paragraph for each business, explain how the size of the market area influences production, pricing, and advertising decisions.

Congressional passage of the Sherman Antitrust Act of 1890 marked the beginning of a new era of government regulation in the public interest. As you read the following excerpts of the Sherman Antitrust Act, note how this legislation was intended to protect competition in the American economy. What penalties for monopolistic practices are listed under the provisions of the act?

The Sherman Antitrust Act of 1890

SEC. 1. Every contract, combination in the form of trust or otherwise, or conspiracy, in restraint of trade or commerce among the several States, or with foreign nations, is hereby declared to be illegal. Every person who shall make any such contract or engage in any such combination or conspiracy, shall be deemed guilty of a misdemeanor, and, on conviction thereof, shall be punished by fine not exceeding five thousand dollars, or by imprisonment not exceeding one year, or by both said punishments, in the discretion of the court.

SEC. 2. Every person who shall monopolize, or attempt to monopolize, or combine or conspire with any other person or persons, to monopolize any part of the trade or commerce among the several States, or with foreign nations, shall be deemed guilty of a misdemeanor, and, on conviction thereof, shall be punished by fine not exceeding five thousand dollars, or by imprisonment not exceeding one year, or by both said punishments, in the discretion of the court.

SEC. 3. Every contract, combination in form of trust or otherwise, or conspiracy, in restraint of trade or commerce in any Territory of the United States or of the District of Columbia, or . . . with foreign nations, . . . is hereby declared illegal. . . .

SEC. 4. The several circuit courts* of the United States are hereby invested with jurisdiction to prevent and restrain violations of this act; and it shall be the duty of the several district attorneys of the United States, in their respective districts, under the direction of the Attorney General, to institute proceedings in equity to prevent and restrain such violations. . . . When the parties complained of shall have been duly notified of such petition the court shall proceed, as soon as may be, to the hearing and determination of the case; and . . . the court may at any time make such temporary restraining order or prohibition as shall be deemed just in the premises. . . .

SEC. 7. Any person who shall be injured in his business or property by any other person or corporation by reason of anything forbidden or declared to be unlawful by this act, may sue . . . without respect to the amount in controversy, and shall recover threefold the damages by him sustained, and the costs of suit, including a reasonable attorney's fee.

SEC. 8. That the word "person," or "persons," wherever used in this act shall be deemed to include corporations and associations existing under or authorized by the laws of either the United States, the laws of any of the Territories, the laws of any State, or the laws of any foreign country.

* In 1911 circuit courts were abolished. Enforcement of the Sherman Act was reassigned to district courts.

Source Review

For Answers to Source Review, see p. A 28.

1. Sections 1, 2, and 3 of the Sherman Antitrust Act state the aim of this legislation. How does the act try to protect competitive markets in the United States? To whom does this legislation apply?
2. According to Section 4, what is the role of the court system in administering the Sherman Antitrust Act?
3. The Sherman Antitrust Act lists several types of penalties for firms that violate the act. What penalties are listed in Section 1? What penalties are listed in Section 7?

DISTRICT
COUNCIL 9
OF
PAINTERS
LOCAL UNION
51
NOTICE TO PUBLIC
STOP
ILLEGAL ALIENS
FROM TAKING
AMERICANS' JOBS!

CHAPTER 7

See Chapter Overview, p. TM 31.
See Chapter Objectives, p. TM 31.
See Introducing the Chapter, p. TM 31.
See Extending Economic Knowledge on text p. 162.

The Labor Force in the United States

If we can distribute high wages, then that money is going to be spent. It will serve to make storekeepers and distributors and manufacturers and workers in other lines more prosperous. Their prosperity will show up in our sales.

Henry Ford

1 The labor force is constantly undergoing changes.

- Technological Shift
- Women in the Labor Force
- Higher Educational Attainment
- Antidiscrimination Laws
- Conditions Affecting Labor Supply

2 Several forces influence the determination of wages in the United States economy.

- Supply and Demand
- Government Regulations
- Organized Labor

3 Labor unions have helped improve conditions for workers in the United States.

- The Growth of Labor Unions
- Government Responses to Unions
- Major Labor Issues
- Contract Negotiations
- Strikes and Management Responses
- The Future of Labor Unions

CHAPTER 7 STUDY GUIDE

Chapter Focus

Chapter 7 discusses the composition of the labor force in the United States. It goes on to discuss decision making in the labor force and the determination of wages in various occupations. The chapter also describes the role of unions in the United States labor movement, their origins and development; the collective bargaining process; and union responses in the 1980s to declining union membership.

As you study the chapter, look for the details that support each of the following statements.

1. The labor force is constantly undergoing changes.
2. Several forces influence the determination of wages in the United States economy.
3. Labor unions have helped improve conditions for workers in the United States.

See Preteaching Vocabulary, p. TM 31.

Terms to Know

The following terms, while not the only terms emphasized in this chapter, are basic to your understanding of the labor force in the United States. Determine the meaning of each term, either by using the Glossary or by watching for context clues as you read the chapter.

labor force
industrialization
labor-intensive
capital-intensive
derived demand
wage rate
minimum wage
labor union
collective bargaining
mediation
arbitration
strike

See Key Study Questions and Key Understandings, p. TM 32.

1 The labor force is constantly undergoing changes.

See Suggested Teaching Strategies, p. TM 32.

The **labor force** includes all people who are at least 16 years old and who are working or looking for work. In the United States, more than 116 million people—almost two thirds of all people 16 years of age or older—are members of the labor force.

More than 98 percent of all people who are employed or looking for work are members of the civilian labor force. Less than 2 percent are members of the armed forces or are employed by the military.

The United States labor force has changed in several ways. The first major change occurred with the technological shift of the economic base caused by **industrialization**,* which resulted in the appearance of many new occupations. The second was a sharp increase in the number of women working outside the home.

The third major change was reflected in the higher levels of education attained by today's workers. Finally, the composition and distribution of the labor force has been significantly altered by the application of antidiscrimination laws.

Technological Shift

The Industrial Revolution, which began in England during the 1700s, gradually changed the world's economy. Industrialization shifted the economy of the United States from an agricultural to a manufacturing base. The reliance on technology and capital ◆ that accompanied industrialization resulted in a vast increase in the number and kinds of goods and services available.

Industrialization deeply affected the kinds and numbers of occupations among the labor force in the United States (see the graph on page 143). In the late 1700s, more than 90 percent of the labor

---

* Industrialization is the process by which a nation's economy is transformed from an agricultural one to one based on the mechanization of all major forms of production.

◆ The Industrial Revolution in the United States began in the 1790s when Samuel Slater built a textile factory in Rhode Island.

Service industries are the fastest-growing segment of the United States labor force. The capital-intensive nature of many service industries is evident in this photograph of Census Bureau workers inputting data.

force was engaged in mainly agricultural occupations. The economy was **labor-intensive,** producing goods through animal and human power. Industrialization in the 1800s transformed the United States economy from one that was labor-intensive to one that was capital-intensive. In a **capital-intensive** economy, goods are produced with machine power rather than with animal or human power. Productivity increases. As machine power replaced human and animal power in agriculture, the demand for agricultural workers decreased. As more factories were built, the demand for manufacturing workers ◆ increased.

In 1850, the percentage of people working in agriculture had dropped to 63.7 percent. In 1900, it had dropped to 37.5 percent. Today, less than 3 percent of the labor force work in agriculture. More than 85 percent work in service and manufacturing occupations. For more information about the shift from a farm to a nonfarm economy, see the graph on page 144.

The United States Labor Force

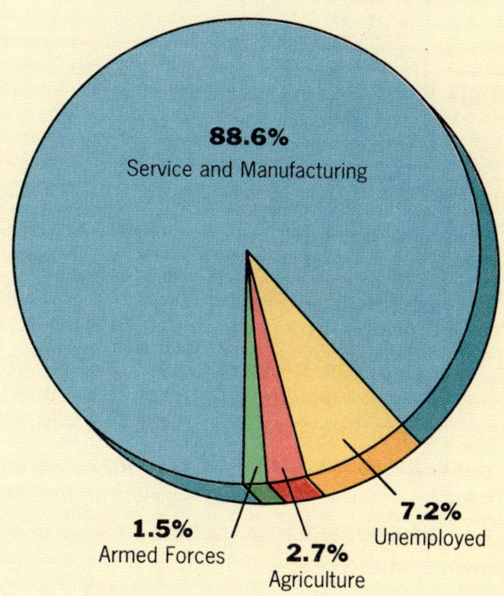

Source: *Statistical Abstract of the United States, 1986*

◆ **Have the students read "Tool-and-Die Makers" on page 544 of *Careers in the Marketplace.***

Occupational Changes in the United States Labor Force

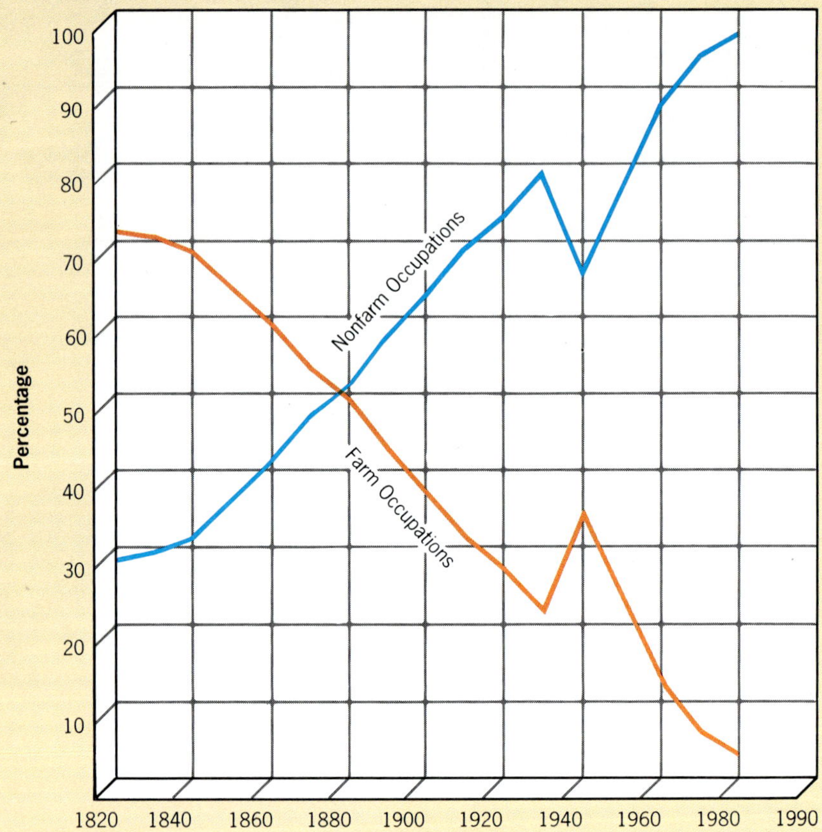

Sources: *Historical Statistics of the United States, Colonial Times to 1970, Part 1*
Statistical Abstract of the United States, 1986

Women in the Labor Force

In 1900, women working outside the home made up only 19 percent of the civilian labor force. Today, women make up about 44 percent of the civilian labor force.

A number of reasons account for the increase of women in the labor force. During World War I and World War II, women worked outside their homes in defense plants, replacing men who had joined the military. The millions of women who joined the labor force in those times of national emergency helped establish a pattern for work outside of the home and contributed to a change in society's attitude toward women.

Other trends in United States society also have contributed to an increase of women working outside the home as members of the labor force. Many women today have educations that are comparable to those of men. Women with such extensive education are thus able to compete with men for jobs previously closed to women. Newer attitudes toward family size have led to lower birthrates in the United States. Affordable day-care centers have also increased in number. Women in the United States ◆ today thus have the freedom to choose motherhood as well as a career outside the home. In addition, rising costs have almost made two incomes in a family a necessity. Finally, legislation protecting equal access to jobs also has increased employment opportunities for women.

In recent years, women have begun to enter such traditionally male-dominated fields as engineering, science, construction, and medicine. The percentage

◆ **Discussion topic: The effect of the increased entry of women into the labor force on present-day male workers.**

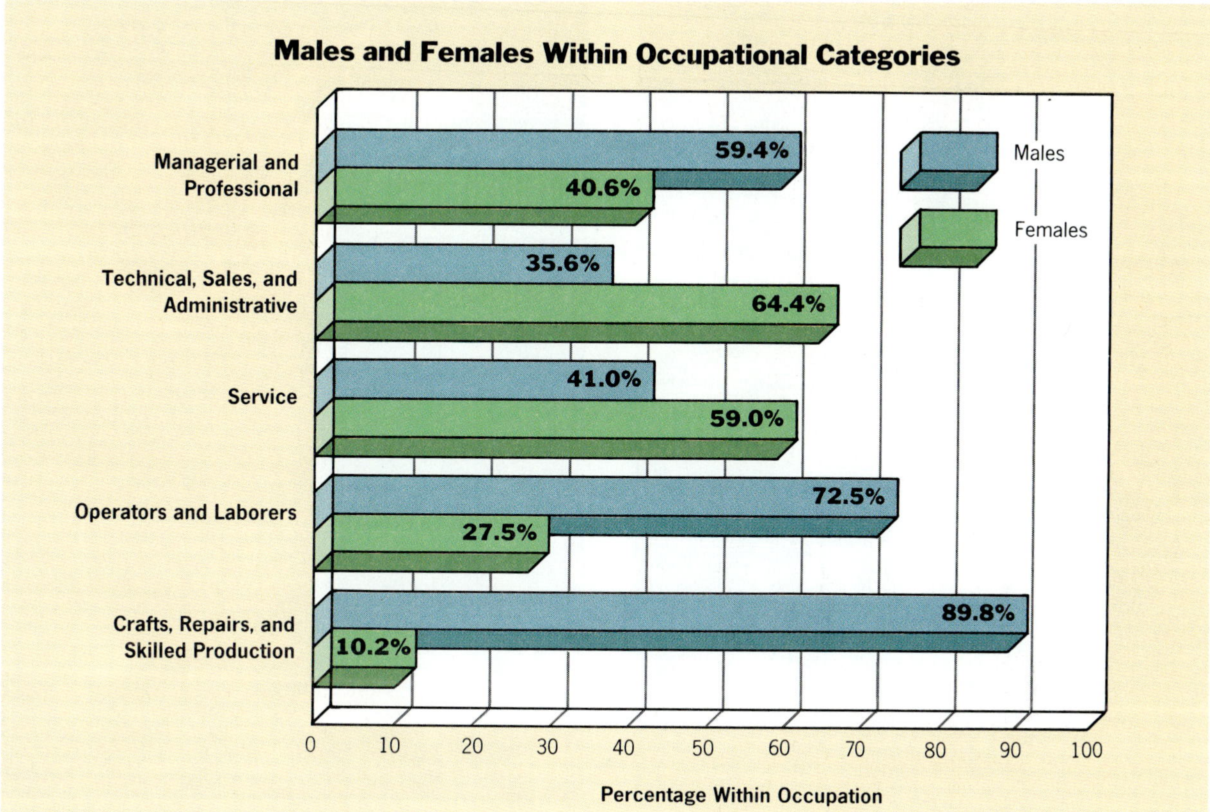

Source: *Statistical Abstract of the United States, 1986*

of women in these occupations, however, remains low. Most women in the labor force are found in lower-paying occupations. As a result, the median wage paid to women continues to lag behind that of men. The graph on this page shows the percentage of males and females within occupational categories and the continuing gap in the median wage of male and female workers.

Higher Educational Attainment

Today about 80 percent of the civilian labor force has earned a high school diploma. In addition, more than 20 percent of the labor force has completed at least four years of college.

A direct relationship exists between education levels and job stability. Most workers 35 years of age and younger have completed more years of schooling than the majority of workers 45 and older. The average worker under age 35 stays at one job for about 2.5 years. In contrast, workers 45 and older, of whom only about one in two has a high school diploma, average 12 years at one job.

A direct relationship between level of education and income also exists. In general, workers with 16 years or more of education have better jobs and higher salaries than workers with less education. For example, according to a report from the Bureau of the Census in 1986, college graduates earned a median salary of $31,449, compared to median salaries of $22,418 for high school graduates and $14,849 for high school dropouts. ◆

Antidiscrimination Laws

During the 1960s, Congress passed a series of laws aimed at protecting workers from discrimination in hiring, promotion, and firing. The Equal Pay Act of 1963 mandates that female workers who do the same jobs as male workers receive the same rates of pay as male workers.

◆ **In 1983, the average annual pay for all workers was highest in Alaska ($28,739) and lowest in South Dakota ($12,099).**

The Civil Rights Act of 1964 has helped many groups, such as women and the handicapped, enter fields that were formerly closed to them.

The Civil Rights Act of 1964 protects workers from employer discrimination based on race, sex, religion, or national origin. The act specifically prevents unions from discriminating against blacks by segregating, expelling, or excluding them. In addition, the Civil Rights Act established the Equal Employment Opportunity Commission (EEOC). The chief task of the EEOC is to monitor and enforce the act's provisions.

The Age Discrimination Act of 1967 protects workers between the ages of 40 and 65 against age discrimination. Congress passed a law in 1986 that prohibits a company from forcibly retiring an employee in some cases. This bill was sponsored by Congressman Claude Pepper of Florida.

In 1965, President Lyndon Johnson established affirmative action policies through Executive Order No. 11246. The policies were aimed at eliminating racial and sexual bias in employment practices, particularly in firms doing business with the federal government.* By 1968, the Department of Labor had established what amounted to quotas for hiring and promoting women and minorities.

Affirmative action policies have stirred up controversy between employees and employers. Supporters of affirmative action argue that the policies are the only sure way to prevent discrimination in employment practices. Opponents of affirmative action argue that affirmative action is itself a form of discrimination because it gives preferential treatment to one group of citizens over another. ◆

* Affirmative action applies only to those businesses receiving government money. State and local governments may require such businesses to prepare an affirmative action plan, and many do.

◆ **Report topic: The effectiveness of affirmative action in eliminating discrimination.**

Conditions Affecting Labor Supply

Several conditions affect the supply of labor. They are immigration, consumer tastes and preferences, and technological change.

◆ **Immigration.** External influences are outside forces that can change the supply of workers in an occupation. Throughout the nation's history, immigration has been an important source of labor force expansion. During the 1800s and early 1900s, for example, successive waves of immigrants increased the labor force primarily with unskilled laborers. In recent years, immigrants from Asia, Latin America, and other regions have expanded the various levels of the labor force.

Consumer Tastes and Preferences. The demand for labor is determined by the needs of producers. Consumers, however, have a strong influence in determining producers' needs.

When consumers' tastes and preferences shifted from the horse and buggy to the automobile in the early 1900s, the demand for skilled carriage workers declined. Demand for industrial workers in the automobile plants, on the other hand, increased. This example illustrates **derived demand**—the need for workers that results from a shift in consumers' tastes and preferences and a subsequent demand for new goods and services. When consumer demand for a particular product increases, the producer of the product hires more workers to supply the higher level of output needed to satisfy the increased demand.

Conversely, when demand for a product decreases, the producer needs fewer workers to supply the required output. The General Tire plant in Waco, Texas, illustrates the effect that a shift in consumer preferences has on the derived demand for workers. The Waco, Texas, plant produced bias-ply tires. In the early 1980s, consumer preferences shifted from bias-ply tires to radial tires. At the time, foreign tire manufacturers captured 25 percent of the United States tire market. The result of the derived demand was that the plant's management had to lay off 2,000 workers and eventually had to close the plant.

Technological Change. Technological change has affected producers' demand for workers in virtually all sectors of the economy. In agriculture, for example, mechanization has led to a decrease in the number of farm workers. Automation in the industrial and service sectors of the economy also has reduced the need for certain types of production and clerical jobs.

See Suggested Assignments, p. TM 32.

Economics Reporter

What Is Affirmative Action?

The policy of affirmative action has been established to overcome past injustices to women and minorities. Affirmative action provides preferential treatment to women and minorities to ensure nondiscrimination for them in hiring and promotions. The goal of affirmative action is to increase the number of women and minority employees in the United States. The opponents of affirmative action argue that the policy leads to reverse discrimination. Proponents argue that only through affirmative action can past injustices be corrected.

Section 1 Review

See Answers, p. A 28.

DEFINE labor force, industrialization, labor-intensive, capital-intensive, derived demand

IDENTIFY affirmative action

1. **Summarizing Ideas** Describe the major changes that the United States labor force has undergone since 1900.
2. **Interpreting Ideas** Explain how each of the following affected the labor force: **(a)** industrialization, **(b)** the women's rights movement, and **(c)** antidiscrimination laws. **(d)** Which of the three factors do you feel has had the greatest impact on the United States labor force? Why?
3. **Interpreting Graphics** Study the graph on page 145. **(a)** In which categories of occupation are there higher percentages of females than males? **(b)** State a generalization that explains why there are more females than males employed in those specific categories.

◆ In 1984, 544,000 immigrants were admitted to the United States.

See Key Study Questions and Key Understandings, p. TM 33.

2 Several forces influence the determination of wages in the United States economy.

See Suggested Teaching Strategies, p. TM 33.

A **wage rate** is the hourly, weekly, monthly, or yearly pay that a worker receives. Wage rates are determined by three major forces. They are the interaction of supply and demand, the process of governmental regulation, and the negotiations of organized labor.

Supply and Demand

Supply and demand interact to determine wages just as they determine prices. When an occupation has a large supply of workers and a relatively low demand for them, the wage rate tends to be low. High wage rates, on the other hand, occur when the supply of workers in an occupation is limited and the demand for them is high.

The number of people willing and able to enter an occupation is determined by the number of skills ◆ needed in the occupation, the conditions under which people must work, and the kinds of nonmonetary rewards that people seek. Still other influences help determine which occupations will have a high or low salary. These are chiefly immigration, consumer tastes and preferences, and technological change.

Skill Level. Jobs that demand a high level of education and training, previous job experiences, or the presence of natural abilities have a limited supply of workers. Relatively few people, for example, attain the skills or abilities required for professional sports and precision craftwork. Hence, the limited number of workers in these fields contributes to high wages. Occupations that call for workers with no specialized skills or training or that call for training in the use of simple equipment have larger supplies of workers. These large supplies of workers contribute to lower wages for these occupations.

Working Conditions. In most workplaces, health and safety concerns, noise levels, and cleanliness are carefully regulated and implemented. But in some high-risk occupations, the workplace itself or the duties the workers must perform are especially dangerous. Two obvious examples are nuclear power plant operations and crime fighting. In these occupations, salaries sometimes are higher than for occupations with low risks to life and limb.

Many travel agencies now use a computerized registration and scheduling system, thereby changing the skills needed to be a travel agent.

◆ Report topic: The type of career a student expects to choose and the salary level that can be expected.

Psychic Rewards. Many people have nonmonetary, internal reasons for working. These reasons are called psychic, or intrinsic, rewards. Psychic rewards include a worker's pride and satisfaction in his or her work and the status, prestige, or respect that accompanies a job.

People who are highly motivated toward a particular psychic reward are often willing to accept lower salaries than another type of job calling for a comparable level of skill and training. For example, teaching and social work offer high psychic rewards and are relatively low paying. In such professions, the psychic rewards ensure a high supply of workers.

Location. The physical location of a job also affects supply. Jobs in distant or remote locations, such as on offshore oil rigs, often require employers to pay high wages to ensure an adequate supply of workers. Engineers, building contractors, and other specialists who are recruited to work in developing nations also receive high salaries. Workers performing the same jobs in more desirable locations generally receive lower wages.

Minimum Hourly Wage Rates, 1950–1985

Year	Minimum Hourly Wage Rates
1950	$0.75
1955	$0.75
1960	$1.00
1965	$1.25
1970	$1.60
1975	$2.10
1980	$3.10
1985	$3.35

Source: *Statistical Abstract of the United States, 1986.*

Government Regulations

In the United States economy, government plays a direct role in the determination of a minimum wage through the passage of legislation. A **minimum wage** is the lowest wage that employers can legally pay a worker for a job.

In 1938, the Fair Labor Standards Act established the first minimum wage of $0.25 an hour. The act applied the minimum wage only to businesses engaged in interstate commerce—trade across state boundaries—and excluded farm workers, maids, and other domestics. Later, the courts extended the Fair Labor Standards Act to cover additional categories of occupations. For example, the Supreme Court ruled in *Garcia* v. *San Antonio Metropolitan Transit Authority* (1985) that the federal minimum wage and overtime provisions should be applied to 7 million employees of state and local governments. Today, more than 80 percent of all employees are covered by the minimum-wage law, which presently sets the minimum wage at $3.35 an hour. For changes in the minimum hourly wage rates from 1950 through 1985, see the chart on this page.

The minimum wage, however, has both supporters and opponents. Supporters argue that it ensures a basic salary for all covered workers. Opponents argue that the minimum wage has increased the costs of production for producers, making it too expensive for some employers to hire additional workers. In recent years, the most hotly debated minimum-wage issue has been its application to teenagers.

Many people favor setting a lower minimum ◆ wage for teenagers. They say that a lower wage would encourage business to hire teenagers, who have high unemployment rates. They further argue that the decrease in teenage unemployment would make youth employment programs unnecessary, thus saving the government money.

Those opposed to lowering the minimum wage contend that a lower wage would be discriminatory and would encourage employers to hire teenagers rather than older workers. They also argue that lower wages for teenagers would hurt the economy. They say that lower wages would mean that teenagers would have less income and would buy less. The lower consumption by teenagers would contribute to lower business activity in many sectors of the economy, especially those that cater to teenage tastes.

◆ **Discussion topic: Whether the government should set a lower minimum wage for teenagers.**

Economics Reporter

What Is a Right-to-Work Law?

Right-to-work laws are established by states to forbid union shops, which are workplaces for union members only. Under union-shop rules, all workers in a particular workplace must join a union within a specified period of time to keep their jobs. The Taft-Hartley Act gave the states the power to pass right-to-work laws. Right-to-work laws establish the open shop, which employs both union and non-union members. Twenty-one states have passed right-to-work laws. The map on this page shows these 21 states.

Organized Labor

By organizing into labor unions, workers themselves have helped determine wage rates. A **labor union** is an organization of workers that negotiates with employers for better wages, improved working conditions, and job security. The two major types of labor unions are craft unions and industrial unions.

A craft union is composed only of skilled workers such as plumbers, electricians, and carpenters in a trade or industry. The International Union of Bricklayers and Allied Craftsmen is an example of a craft union. An industrial union includes all workers whether they are unskilled, semiskilled, or skilled. The United Auto Workers is an example of an industrial union.

Labor unions help determine wages in two important ways. First, union negotiators speak for all workers in the union. Operating from a position of unity gives the union its strength. This strength enables the union to exert pressure on management during contract negotiations.

Second, craft unions often restrict entry into skilled occupations. Some craft unions require that all new workers qualify for membership by completing apprenticeships. Craft unions defend apprenticeship programs as a way to ensure quality workmanship and as a means of protecting job

States with Right-to-Work Laws

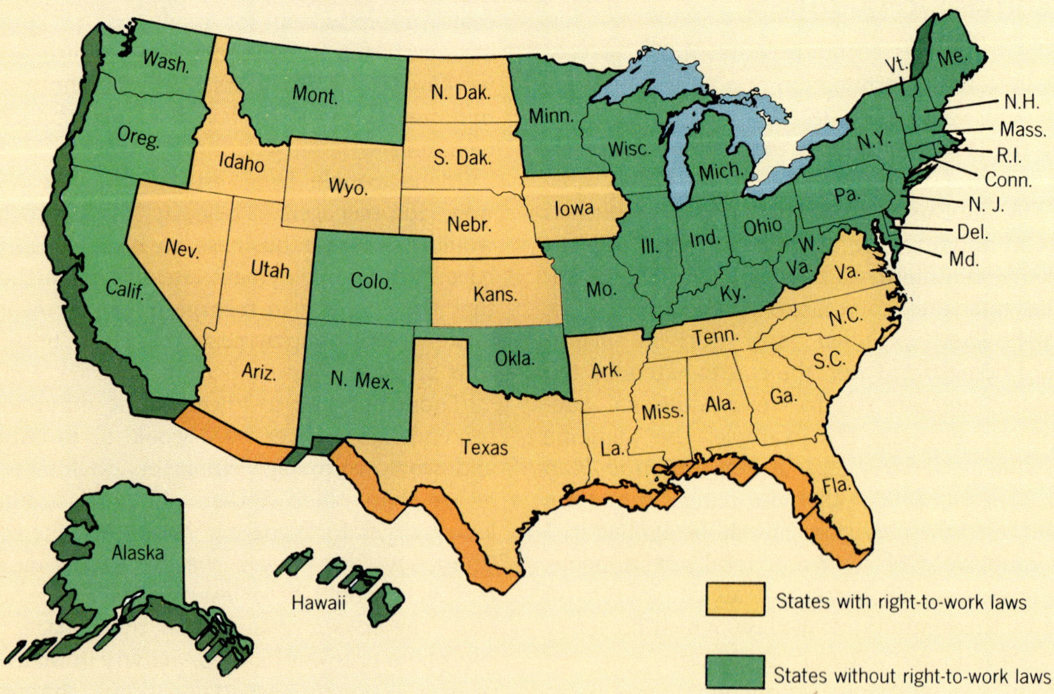

Have the students read "Understanding Your Rights as an Employee" on pages 517–519 of the *Everyday Economics Handbook* and answer the questions that follow.

security. Critics of apprenticeship programs, however, accuse unions of discriminating against minorities by rejecting them for apprenticeship programs.

CASE STUDY

Comparable Worth and Fair Pay

During the 1980s, a new movement began to promote wage fairness through the idea of comparable worth. As an issue, comparable worth centers on the wage and salary differences between occupations traditionally dominated by women and those traditionally dominated by men. Supporters of comparable worth maintain that salaries should be paid according to the skill levels involved and not by whether the job is held by a man or a woman.

Supporters of comparable worth argue that female workers have been discriminated against in the past by employers who have offered women lower wage rates than those offered to men in the same occupations. The supporters note that earnings for women have traditionally been about 60 percent those of men. Supporters of comparable worth include such women's groups as the National Organization for Women (NOW) and such unions as the American Federation of State, County and Municipal Employees (AFSCME).

Opponents of comparable worth deny that sex discrimination has influenced wage rates. Instead, they point to the interaction of supply and demand as the main determinants of fair wage rates for occupations. As a strong opponent of comparable worth, the National Association of Manufacturers contends that classifying jobs on the basis of skills, working conditions, and responsibilities would upset the interaction of supply and demand in the labor market.

The federal courts, state legislatures, and unions ◆ have had to settle the issue of fair pay for women. In 1983, a federal district court ruled in favor of comparable worth in a suit brought against the state of Washington. The court awarded almost $1 billion in back pay and damages to female government employees because the state had been paying them much less than it paid male employees in comparable positions. In 1985, however, a federal court of appeals overturned the 1983 decision. Some states, such as Connecticut, Iowa, Minnesota, New York, and Wisconsin, have enacted legislation to ensure pay equity between the sexes.

Differences in wage rates between men and women are often the subject of heated debate.

See Suggested Assignments, p. TM 33.

Section 2 Review See Answers, p. A 29.

DEFINE wage rate, minimum wage, labor union

IDENTIFY right-to-work law, comparable worth

1. **Understanding Ideas** **(a)** What are the major forces that determine wages? **(b)** What governmental regulation has helped determine wage rates?
2. **Comparing Ideas** How are wages like prices?
3. **Analyzing Ideas** Explain how the supply of and demand for labor interact to determine wages.
4. **Interpreting Graphics** Study the map on page 150. **(a)** Does your state have a right-to-work law? **(b)** In what region of the nation do most of the states have right-to-work laws? **(c)** What states have no right-to-work laws?

◆ The Civil Rights Act of 1964 bars discrimination against women and minorities. Many companies now specify that they are "Equal Opportunity Employers" and their want ads do not specify male or female.

See Key Study Questions and Key Understandings, p. TM 34.

3 Labor unions have helped improve conditions for workers in the United States.

See Suggested Teaching Strategies, p. TM 34.

The United States labor movement began very early in the history of the nation. In 1786, for example, Philadelphia printers staged the nation's first planned strike or work stoppage. In 1792, Philadelphia shoemakers founded the nation's first craft union. It was not until the 1900s, however, that labor unions became more powerful.

The Growth of Labor Unions

Industrialization wrought sweeping changes within the United States economy, chief of which was the transformation into a manufacturing-based nation. During this transformation, wealth became a chief element dividing laborers and owners of factories, mills, mines, and other businesses. In addition, as the wealth of business leaders grew, so did their power over common laborers and other employees.

In the early years of industrialization, individual laborers had no power to bargain with management. Management set the pay and the hours worked. Many laborers worked 12- to 14-hour days in unsafe, noisy, and unsanitary workplaces. Workers received few, if any, benefits and had no job security whatever. In 1860, the average work week for a factory laborer was 66 hours. Workers responded by forming a number of labor unions.

The Knights of Labor. The most successful of the early unions was the Knights of Labor, which attempted to form one union for all workers. Under a loosely structured organization, the Knights brought skilled and unskilled workers from a wide variety of crafts and industries together. At the height of its power in 1886, the Knights had nearly 700,000 members.

The Knights of Labor supported the eight-hour workday, an end to child labor, and a system of worker cooperatives to replace capitalism. The Knights of Labor hoped to achieve social and political reform through radical political action.

Terrence Powderly (center) led the Knights of Labor to the height of their power in the 1880s.

After helping to found the AFL–CIO in 1955, George Meany led the union for the next 24 years.

More than one quarter of all union members in the United States are employed in some type of manufacturing.

The loose structure of the Knights of Labor and its support of radical political change, however, eventually led to its downfall. The Knights attracted more unskilled workers than skilled workers. As the Knights made major attempts to improve the working conditions of unskilled workers, skilled members refused to support the union's actions. Once the Knights lost the support of skilled workers, the union began to lose power. By 1900, it was no longer a major force in the labor movement. The union was dissolved in 1917.

The American Federation of Labor. The modern period of the United States labor movement began in 1886 with the reorganization of a loose association of local craft unions into the American Federation of Labor (AFL). Samuel Gompers, the first president of the AFL, felt that a successful union should be more interested in higher wages and better working conditions than in political change.

Gompers rejected radical change, believing that unions should try to make the existing economic system responsive to the needs of organized workers. Gompers made the AFL a successful union by negotiating with management for higher wages, shorter hours, better working conditions, and more benefits. With this strategy, Gompers attained recognition for the union.

The AFL was a federation of self-governing craft unions. Workers first had to organize on the local level and then apply for membership in the AFL. The AFL accepted only unions composed of skilled workers. It excluded women and blacks from membership. ◆

The AFL expanded steadily. By the time World War I began in 1914, the AFL had 2 million members. By the end of the war, its membership had doubled.

The 1920s, however, were difficult for labor unions. Internal struggles plagued the AFL. Opponents challenged Gompers' leadership. At his death in 1924, the presidency of the union changed hands, but the internal struggles did not disappear. A strong antiunion sentiment arose after World War I. Businesses, enlisting the aid of the government and the courts, attacked organized labor. Many business owners set up open shops, where workers were prohibited from joining unions.

◆ **Have the students read "Electricians" on page 541 of *Careers in the Marketplace*.**

Many state and local government workers are represented by the American Federation of State, County, and Municipal Employees (AFSCME).

The massive unemployment during the Great Depression further decreased the AFL's membership. The continuing internal disputes, particularly over union membership, resulted eventually in the formation of a separate union.

The Congress of Industrial Organizations. The origins of the Congress of Industrial Organizations (CIO) date back to 1935 when John L. Lewis—the president of the United Mine Workers of America (UMWA)—organized the Committee for Industrial Organizations. Through this committee, Lewis defied the AFL's leadership by organizing unskilled and semiskilled industrial workers in one union.

By 1937, Lewis, and all of the industrial unions that he had helped organize, were expelled from ◆ the AFL. A year later, Lewis became the president of the newly named Congress of Industrial Organizations. Under his leadership, millions of industrial workers, including women, blacks, and other minorities, were organized. Large industrial unions that joined the CIO included the United Steel Workers, the United Automobile Workers (UAW), and Lewis' own UMWA, which later withdrew.

The AFL–CIO. By the mid-1950s, union leaders in the AFL and CIO recognized that laborers, regardless of skill or occupation, had similar economic concerns. In 1955, the American Federation of Labor and the Congress of Industrial Organizations merged to form the AFL–CIO. Today, this gigantic union includes 94 different unions. Its membership is about 13 million.

Other Unions. Another 4.5 million workers belong to the International Brotherhood of Teamsters, the United Mine Workers of America, the United Steel Workers, and the International Brotherhood of Electrical Workers. These four unions, as well as 120 other small unions, are independent and not affiliated with the AFL–CIO.

Government Responses to Unions

The government's responses to unionism have changed throughout United States history. During

Text continues on page 156.

◆ **Discussion topic: Why the AFL was more successful than the Knights of Labor.**

BUILDING ECONOMIC SKILLS

INTERPRETING THE VISUAL RECORD

Understanding Time Lines

Time lines are used to show the sequence of events over time. By organizing information chronologically, it is easier to see relationships between events. In the study of economics, time lines are especially useful when determining cause-effect relationships.

How to Understand a Time Line

When reading a time line, follow these steps.

1. **Determine its framework.** Identify the years covered and the intervals into which the time line is divided.
2. **Supply missing information.** Note each event listed on the time line. Determine other important events, people, or places that are associated with the event.
3. **Note the sequence of events.** Ask yourself how each event on the time line relates to each previous event and each subsequent event. Note especially cause-effect relationships.
4. **Name the time line.** Assign a title to the time line. Base the title on the type of events listed.
5. **Use the time line as a summary.** Use the events listed to write a summary of the period.

Applying the Skill

Study the time line below, following the steps that help you understand a time line. The time line covers the period from 1930 to 1960. The time line is divided into three 10-year intervals. The events listed on the time line trace major developments in the American labor movement. It focuses on the division of the American Federation of Labor (AFL) into two unions—the AFL and the Congress of Industrial Organizations (CIO)—in the late 1930s, and the merger of these unions into the AFL–CIO in 1955. One possible title for the time line is "The Founding of the AFL–CIO." You can use the Chronology on textbook pages 499–506 to help you fill in some of the missing events. For example, not shown are the first sit-down strike in the late 1930s and some of the major legislation that influenced the history of unionism in the United States.

Practicing the Skill See Answers, p. A 29.

Use the Chronology on textbook pages 499–506 or the chart on page 156 of the text to develop a time line of major labor legislation in the United States.

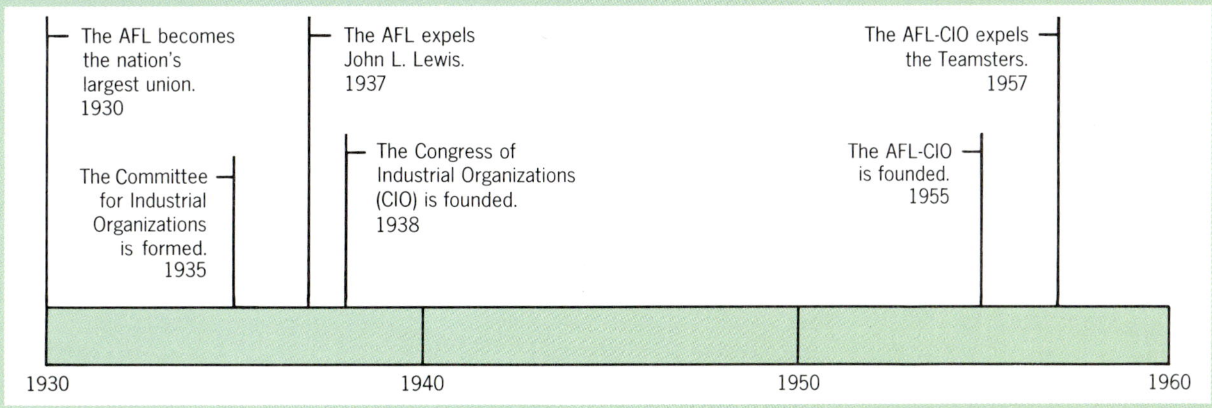

the 1800s, government at all levels generally favored business interests over those of labor unions. In the famous Baltimore and Ohio Railroad strike of 1877, for example, government troops were ordered to crush the strike and restore railway service. The violent confrontations between federal troops and strikers resulted in 26 deaths and millions of dollars in property damage. During the 1900s, legislation tended to be prounion. Since 1940, on the other hand, legislation has tended to place limits on the power of unions. For a description of the major labor legislation of the twentieth century, see the chart on this page.

Major Labor Issues

The labor movement in the United States has traditionally been concerned with practical "bread-and-butter" issues, rather than with economic theories. ◆ In negotiations between labor and management today, five major issues are usually discussed. They are wages and fringe benefits, working conditions and hours, job security, union security, and grievance procedures.

Wages and Fringe Benefits. A labor contract sets wage rates for employees. These wage rates are usually based on the type of job and the number of

Legislation Affecting Organized Labor

YEAR	LEGISLATION	PURPOSE
1914	Clayton Antitrust Act	The act exempted unions from antitrust suits and gave labor the right to strike, picket, and boycott a firm's products in an effort to settle contract disputes. The act also made it more difficult for businesses to obtain injunctions. The act was not always effective because courts often sided with business.
1932	Norris–LaGuardia Act	The act guaranteed the right to join unions and engage in normal union activities, outlawed yellow-dog contracts, and further restricted the issuing of court injunctions during labor disputes.
1935	Wagner Act	Also called the National Labor Relations Act, the act guaranteed workers the right to form unions and bargain collectively. It required management to bargain in good faith and refrain from unfair labor practices. It also established the National Labor Relations Board.
1938	Fair Labor Standards Act	Also called the Wages and Hours Law, the act established a minimum wage and set a maximum workweek of 44 hours (which was later reduced to 40 hours). The act also guaranteed time-and-a-half pay for overtime and restricted child labor.
1947	Taft–Hartley Act	Also called the Labor–Management Relations Act, the act reversed some of the union gains by outlawing closed shops. It allowed states to enact right-to-work laws, prohibiting union shops. It required unions to give 60-days notice before striking and allowed federal injunctions to block strikes for up to 80 days. It also outlawed union campaign contributions to national political candidates and prohibited federal government employees from striking.
1959	Landrum–Griffin Act	Also called the Labor Reform Act, the act was passed in an effort to prevent corrupt union practices. It required union officials to be elected democratically. It required that union funds be recorded with the Department of Labor. It also set up strict guidelines to be followed in establishing unions and conducting union activities.

◆ **Have the students read "Labor Relations Specialists" on page 542 of *Careers in the Marketplace.***

years a worker has been on the job. The contract also outlines the wage policy for overtime beyond the maximum 40-hour limit. In addition, some contracts include a cost-of-living adjustment, or COLA. COLAs automatically adjust a worker's wages to match an increase in the inflation rate, thus protecting a worker's purchasing power.

Fringe benefits include nonwage payments to workers. The most common fringe benefits included in labor contracts are paid sick days, holidays, and vacations; health and life insurance; and retirement programs. Many companies also include profit sharing and employee stock ownership plans (ESOPs) as benefits. Under profit sharing, a firm distributes a portion of its profits to workers. An ESOP allows employees to become part owners in the firm. Profit sharing and ESOPs provide an incentive for workers to become more productive.

Economics Reporter

What Is Profit Sharing?

Profit sharing is a plan in which a corporation distributes a predetermined share of its profits to qualified employees. The amount distributed rarely exceeds 10 percent of the firm's net profits and generally requires the shareholders' approval. Employees may collect their share of the profit at regular intervals, usually after 10 years of service, or reinvest it in the company. Profit-sharing plans often help to lower employee turnover in a company and provide incentives for employees to increase productivity and reduce waste.

Working Conditions. Desirable working conditions include a clean and safe workplace, clearly defined and challenging work responsibilities, and reasonable working hours. Some companies, such as General Motors at its Saturn automobile plant, are experimenting with self-directing teams of workers to improve working conditions. These self-directing teams are responsible for producing a larger section of an automobile, thus instilling pride and satisfaction in the work effort. Further, job rotation among team members allows workers to learn and use new skills.

Job Security. The legal system provides some job security for workers. Laws, for example, prevent an employer from firing an employee because of race, sex, religion, age, or union activity. Most contracts also seek to protect job security through the seniority system. Seniority is based on the number of years a worker has been employed by the firm. Labor contracts usually protect seniority because they generally stipulate that workers with the least seniority are the first to lose their jobs during layoffs.

At times the seniority system has come into conflict with the government's affirmative action program (see page 147). Under affirmative action, firms doing business with the federal government must employ a certain percentage of minority and female employees. Yet, minority and female employees usually have less seniority than other groups of workers. Under the rules of seniority, they should be the first to be laid off. Their layoffs, however, mean that the firm's percentage of minority and female workers falls below the federal requirement. To keep in compliance, firms often violate seniority rules.

Union Security. In its broadest sense, union security involves the right of workers to organize and join a union. This right is enforced by the National Labor Relations Board (NLRB). To form a union, workers must follow two steps. First, at least 30 percent of a firm's employees must sign a petition informing the NLRB that they want an election to determine whether or not the employees favor unionization. Second, the NLRB conducts the election, using a secret ballot. If the majority of the workers favor unionization, the NLRB recognizes the union as the exclusive bargaining unit for the employees.

Grievance Procedures. Grievance procedures are the sets of steps that labor or management may take when work-related disputes arise. Such disputes often result when labor or management feels that the other side has violated provisions outlined in the contract. These grievances, or formal complaints, are usually resolved internally by committees made up of representatives of the union and the management.

If this procedure does not resolve the problem, a neutral arbiter is brought in under the auspices of the National Labor Relations Board. Both sides must

◆ **Point out to students that under many profit-sharing plans, workers who leave the company with less than 10 years service can collect only a percentage of their account.**

During the 1980s, strikes and threats of strikes have sometimes been ineffective weapons against management attempts to reduce worker benefits.

agree to abide by the decision of the arbiter and provide that person with all relevant information. This arbitration is considered to be a part of the collective bargaining process.

Contract Negotiations

The process in which union representatives speak for all their members in an effort to negotiate a new contract with management is known as **collective bargaining.** In most cases collective bargaining results in a contract settlement.

The most important factor that contributes to contract settlements is self-interest. It is in a laborer's self-interest to be employed and to earn an income. It is in an employer's self-interest to ensure that production continues. A firm cannot earn a profit unless it produces goods or services to sell in the marketplace.

When labor and management are deadlocked, they may resort to **mediation.** In mediation, negotiators call in a respected and neutral third party, or mediator, to listen to the arguments of both sides and suggest ways in which agreement may be reached.

Both private citizens and government agencies offer mediation services. In 1985, for example, Richard Nixon mediated a labor conflict between baseball umpires and the owners of major league teams. The Federal Mediation and Conciliation Service (FMCS), which the Taft-Hartley Act of 1947 established, mediates thousands of disputes every year at no charge to either side in the dispute.

At times, neither collective bargaining nor mediation results in a contract settlement. A third way to reach a contract agreement is through **arbitration.** Like mediation, arbitration calls for the assistance of an arbitrator to arrive at a contract. Like a mediator, an arbitrator is a neutral third party. Unlike a mediator, however, an arbitrator offers specific terms in the settlement of a contract. Two types of arbitration exist. They are advisory arbitration and binding arbitration.

In advisory arbitration, one or both sides may reject the arbitrator's settlement. In binding arbitration, negotiators on both sides must accept the arbitrator's decisions. Binding arbitration is sometimes used in negotiations between public-sector employees, who are not allowed to strike, and the government. Binding arbitration is also used in professional sports to settle differences between the salaries asked for by athletes and those offered by the club owners.

Strikes and Management Responses

When union representatives and management are unable to reach an agreement through collective bargaining, mediation, or arbitration, unions can resort to a **strike.** Unions can halt production by calling a strike until their contract demands are met. Traditionally, the majority of strikes are called over wage disputes. Strikes have also been called to settle disputes over how the plant is run and to improve

DECISION MAKERS IN THE ECONOMY

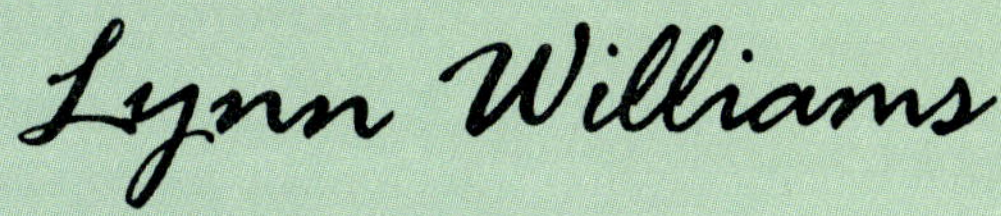

Lynn Williams, president of the United Steelworkers of America, represents a new style of leadership in American labor unions. Williams believes fervently in the value of unions. At the same time, however, he takes a businesslike approach to the task of union negotiations. He is always willing to compromise when industry conditions make compromise necessary.

Williams knows that unionism has its critics. Some critics say that unions have outlived their purpose. Others say that unions, with their demands for high wages and import restrictions, reduce the ability of American industry to compete with foreign industry. Williams argues that unions are necessary to the American free enterprise system. He claims that unions force industry owners to think of workers as human beings. According to Williams, the government should issue import restrictions to ensure that American companies can continue to pay well and therefore to support the country's high standard of living.

Worker involvement in managerial decisions is a focal point for Williams as he tries to bring in new union members. He would like to see labor and management work with, instead of against, each other in finding solutions to industry problems. Williams believes that workers' involvement in managerial decisions could help to revive the troubled steel industry and give a new sense of purpose to unions in this country.

benefits and working conditions. Three tactics are commonly used in carrying out strikes. They are picketing, boycotting, and coordinated campaigning.

Picketing. The tactic of picketing serves three major purposes. It informs the public that a strike is in progress. It arouses public support. It also discourages nonstrikers from entering the premises. ◆

Boycotting. An organized effort to stop buying a firm's products until the strike is resolved is called a **primary boycott.** On a local level, strikers organizing a primary boycott rely on word of mouth or the local media to publicize the boycott. Localized primary boycotting is effective only when the majority of the firm's income is derived from local sales.

Primary boycotts also can be carried out on a national level. During the late 1960s, for example, Cesar Chavez, director of the United Farm Workers' Organizing Committee (UFWOC), organized a primary boycott against California grape producers. The boycott on behalf of the striking migrant workers received extensive coverage in the national media. In 1970, the grape producers finally agreed to the UFWOC's demands.

A **secondary boycott** is a refusal to buy products or services of any firm that does business with a company whose employees are on strike. Secondary boycotts are often used against retail stores that sell products manufactured by the struck employer.

Coordinated Campaigning. During the 1970s and 1980s, some union organizers began using a coordinated campaign to win favorable contract settlements. By the mid-1980s, the AFL–CIO described coordinated campaigns as effective means to put pressure on companies. A coordinated campaign involves the use of picketing as well as primary and secondary boycotts.

The Amalgamated Clothing and Textile Workers Union (ACTWU) was the first union to successfully launch a coordinated campaign when it struck the

◆ Point out that picketing, which often receives wide media coverage, may influence the public's perception of labor unions.

J. P. Stevens Company in 1980. In 1985 and 1986, the United Food and Commercial Workers (UFCW) union used a coordinated campaign against the George A. Hormel Company. In this coordinated campaign, the UFCW picketed and boycotted corporations and banks that did business with the Hormel company. Union members also distributed leaflets to local residents and to other unions to gain support for UFCW demands.

Management Responses. To fight strikes, management can use lockouts and injunctions. Lockouts occur when an employer closes a plant's doors until a suitable contract agreement is reached. Employers also can ask the government to issue an injunction to prevent workers from striking. Although restrictions have been placed on the issuing of court injunctions, the Taft-Hartley Act permits the issuing of an injunction when a strike threatens the health or safety of people. In 1978, for example, President Carter agreed to an injunction against the United Mine Workers of America (UMWA). The UMWA continued to strike, but the injunction prompted serious collective bargaining that resulted in a contract settlement between the UMWA and management.

Union Membership in the United States

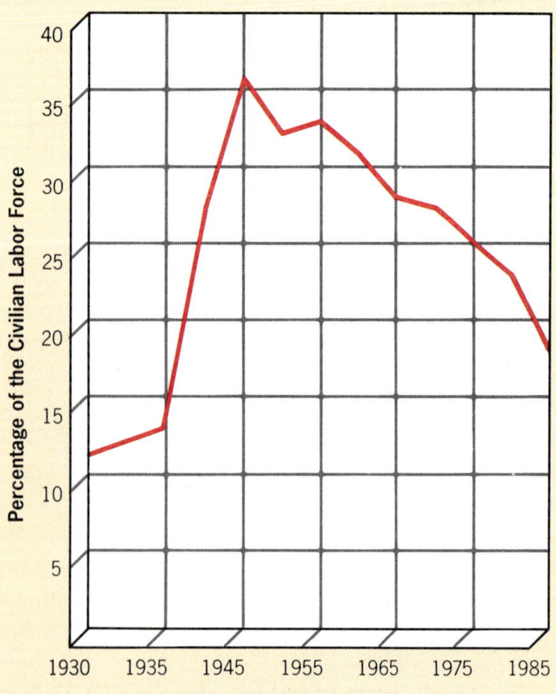

Source: United States Bureau of Labor Statistics, 1986

The Future of Labor Unions

The 1980s has been a time of crisis for the labor movement in the United States. Recent economic, social, and political changes have resulted in a dramatic drop in union membership as shown in the graph on this page.

Economic Shift. One factor contributing to the decline in union membership since 1950 has been a shift from a manufacturing-oriented to a service-oriented economy. Blue-collar workers in the manufacturing sector traditionally have provided a solid backbone for labor unions. White-collar and service workers—the fastest-growing employee groups—have had low rates of union participation.

Efforts to Weaken Unionism. Some firms have hired specialists called union busters to discourage workers from joining unions. Other firms have hired union busters to conduct decertification campaigns in which workers are encouraged to end union affiliations. Still other companies have relocated from large manufacturing cities of the North and Midwest where unionism is strong to Sun Belt cities where unionism is relatively weak. Finally, to show their workers that unions are unnecessary, some nonunion companies have kept their wages and benefits as good as or better than those negotiated through collective bargaining at union plants.

Government Actions. In 1981, for example, the Professional Air Traffic Controllers Organization (PATCO)—a union of federal workers responsible for directing the movement of aircraft during takeoffs and landings—went on strike. Citing the no-strike clause of the Taft-Hartley Act, President Reagan demanded that PATCO order the air traffic controllers to return to work. ◆

When PATCO refused, President Reagan declared the strikers to be in violation of the law and fired all 12,000 strikers. This mass firing reinforced the decline in unionism in the public sector that had begun during the late 1970s. Further contributing to the decline has been the National Labor Relations Board (NLRB). The NLRB, which hears cases involv-

◆ **Have the students read "Air Traffic Controllers" on page 540 of *Careers in the Marketplace.***

ing labor-management disputes, has become more sympathetic to business during the 1980s.

Negative Public Perception. A final contributing factor to slumping union memberships is the negative perception of unionism that some people have. This negative perception includes a belief that corruption is present in all labor unions.

Union Responses. Unions have responded to the crisis in the United States labor movement by attempting to adapt to the times. As union membership has declined and business and government have taken a stronger stand against organized labor, unions have adopted a more cooperative spirit in their dealings with management. For example, during the 1980s, labor and management agreed to wage and benefit reductions in the steel, automotive, and meatpacking industries to help save companies from bankruptcy.

In addition, labor and management have united on other national issues. For example, both labor and management have supported government protectionist policies to reduce foreign competition in the United States markets. They also have opposed skyrocketing insurance costs for businesses.

To attract new groups of workers to unions, organized labor has adopted new issues to include in their collective bargaining efforts. Many of the new contract issues for the 1980s concerned psychic rewards such as the quality of life in the workplace, more worker involvement in decision making on the job, the development of personal skills, and programs that provide an opportunity for climbing the career ladder. Other issues such as company day-care facilities and comparable worth clauses cater to parents, women, and other specific groups.

Unions have further attempted to increase membership by providing their union organizers with better training. Unions conduct workshops to develop recruitment skills. Unions are also hiring more professional union organizers to explain the benefits of union membership to nonunion workers.

Finally, unions have begun to experiment with incentives to encourage union membership. In 1986, for example, the AFL–CIO test marketed credit cards with discount interest rates to increase union membership. Unions also have considered other incentives, such as life and health plans, retirement accounts, and group legal services to encourage memberships.

See Suggested Assignments, p. TM 34.

Section 3 Review See Answers, p. A 29.

DEFINE collective bargaining

IDENTIFY Samuel Gompers, AFL–CIO, Lynn Williams

1. **Summarizing Ideas** What factors have contributed to the decline of labor unions?
2. **Understanding Ideas (a)** List and describe the techniques used by labor to influence management when collective bargaining fails. **(b)** What techniques does management use to respond to labor in such situations?

CHAPTER 7 SUMMARY

The United States labor force, which has 116 million members, includes all people who are at least 16 years old and who are working or looking for work. The labor force has undergone numerous changes throughout the nation's history. Among these changes are a shift from agricultural to service and manufacturing occupations, a sharp increase in the number of women in the labor force, and a higher level of education among workers.

Forces that determine the wage rates in the labor force include the interaction of supply and demand, government regulations, and the actions of organized labor. Skill level, working conditions, psychic rewards, job location, and external forces determine the supply of workers in a particular occupation, while consumer tastes and preferences and technological change affect demand.

In the 1900s, labor unions became increasingly powerful. Today, the AFL–CIO, with its 13 million members, is the largest and most powerful labor organization in the United States.

Labor unions engage in collective bargaining, mediation, and arbitration to improve working conditions and wages for their members. If an agreement is not reached, unions can resort to such tactics as strikes, picketing, and boycotts. Management can counter these tactics with lockouts and injunctions. While unions remain a powerful force in the United States labor market in the 1980s, the shift to white-collar occupations and a negative perception have led to declines in union membership.

CHAPTER 7 REVIEW

For Answers to Chapter 7 Review, see p. A 30.

Reviewing Economic Terms

Supply the economic term that correctly completes each sentence.

1. All people who are at least 16 years old and are working or are seeking work are included in the _____ _____.
2. Goods are produced by machine power rather than animal and human power in a _____ _____ economy.
3. The need for workers that results from a shift in consumers' tastes and preferences is _____ _____.
4. The hourly, weekly, monthly, or yearly pay workers receive is their _____ _____.
5. The lowest wage an employer can legally pay an employee is the _____ _____.
6. An organization of workers that negotiates with employers for better wages and working conditions is a _____ _____.
7. Workers often stop work, or _____, in an attempt to influence contract negotiations.

Exercising Economic Skills

1. **Understanding Time Lines** Reread pages 152–154 and 156. Then develop a time line tracing the development of labor unions in the United States from 1880 to 1940.
2. **Understanding Your Rights as an Employee** Study the feature on pages 517–519. Then study either the National Labor Relations Act, the Fair Labor Standards Act, or the Civil Rights Act of 1964 and compose an essay in which you discuss how the act will affect you as a member of the United States labor force.

Thinking Critically About Economics

1. **Summarizing Ideas** **(a)** Describe the changes the United States labor force has undergone in the last 25 years. **(b)** List and briefly explain the three forces that determine wage rates. **(c)** Why were labor unions established?
2. **Comprehending Ideas** Describe the five major labor issues and explain why each issue is important to workers.
3. **Seeing Relationships** How does self-interest affect contract negotiations?
4. **Analyzing Ideas** How has the increased participation of women in the labor force affected the overall economy?
5. **Comparing Ideas** **(a)** Discuss the effects of labor unions, government regulations, and supply and demand on wages. **(b)** Which seems to have the greatest impact today? Explain.
6. **Interpreting Graphics** Study the chart on page 149. **(a)** In what five-year period did the minimum wage increase the least? **(b)** In what five-year period did it increase the most? **(c)** State two generalizations, one that explains each of the facts you stated in the first two parts of this question.

Extending Economic Knowledge

1. Interview a person who worked during the Great Depression, a person who worked in the early 1950s at a job similar to that of the first person you interviewed, and two people who are working at similar jobs today. Ask each person **(a)** what wage rate they received and **(b)** why they think wages for similar jobs are so much higher today. Write a paragraph in which you discuss your findings.
2. Research the Lowell Female Labor Reform Association, an organization of female textile workers. Prepare an oral or written report on **(a)** the conditions that led to the formation of the association and **(b)** the actions taken by the association.
3. Contact a union representative in your community to obtain a collective bargaining agreement. Study the agreement. **(a)** In a paragraph, summarize the most important aspects of the agreement. **(b)** In a second paragraph, evaluate the agreement, first from an employee's point of view and then from management's point of view. **(c)** In a final paragraph, discuss whether you think the contract favors labor or management.

Using Primary Sources

Samuel Gompers (1850–1924) was the leading spokesman for the American labor movement during the late 1800s and early 1900s. He helped found the American Federation of Labor (AFL) in 1886, and served, except for one year, as that organization's president until his death in 1924. In a speech in 1898 to the AFL convention Gompers defended trade unions. As you read the following excerpts, note how Gompers viewed the role of unions in United States society. How could union goals be achieved?

A Philosophy of Unionism in the United States

The trade unions are ... not the creation of any man's brain. They are organizations of necessity. They were born of the necessity of the workers to protect and defend themselves from encroachment, injustice and wrong. They are the organizations of the working class, for the working class, by the working class; grappling with economic and social problems as they arise, dealing with them in a practical manner to the end that a solution commensurate with the interests of all may be attained. ...

... No intelligent workman who has passed years of his life in the study of the labor problem, expects to wake up any fine morning to find the hopes of these years realized over night. ...

Much of our misery as enforced wage-workers ... is the result of the ignorance of so many in our own class who accept conditions by their own volition. The more intelligent ... seek to benefit themselves and their fellow men through trade unions and trade union action. ...

We want legislation in the interest of labor; ... executed by labor men; we want trade unionists in Congress and more trade unionists in the State legislatures, in our municipal councils and in our executive offices; we want trade unionists on the magisterial benches [the judiciary], and those convinced of the justice of our cause ... in the highest offices of our land. ...

Today modern society is beginning to realize that the trade unions are the only hope of our civilization, ...

The toilers of our country look to you [trade unionists] to devise the ways and means by which a more thorough organization of the wage-earners may be accomplished. ... Let us see to it that they [our children] are not ... brought to a premature death by early drudgery ... [in the] factory and the workshop. To protect the workers in their inalienable rights to a higher and better life; to protect them, not only as equals before the law, but also in their rights to the product of their labor; ... to this the workers are entitled beyond ... doubt. With nothing less ought they, or will they, be satisfied. ... No higher or nobler mission ever fell to the lot of a people than that committed to the working class—a class of which we have the honor to be members.

Source Review

For Answers to Source Review, see p. A 31.

1. Why does Samuel Gompers call unions the "organizations of necessity"? What group of people needs the unions the most? Why?
2. According to Gompers, who is the most to blame for the misery of wage earners? Who else shares in the blame?
3. In Gompers' view, how can unions achieve economic and social reform? How long will labor's struggles last?
4. Gompers names a number of goals to be realized through trade unions. List these goals.
5. If Gompers were alive today, which goals would he feel have been achieved? Which would he feel have not been fully achieved? What new goals might he add to the list?

UNIT TWO REVIEW

For Answers to Unit Two Review, see p. A 32.

Reviewing Economic Ideas

1. What are the three main types of business organizations in a free enterprise system?
2. What are the advantages and the disadvantages of a corporation?
3. What are the four types of market structures?
4. Is a large corporation more likely to be in a perfectly competitive market or in a market structure of monopolistic competition? Why?
5. What are the arguments for and against antitrust legislation?
6. What forces have caused changes in the United States labor force?
7. What are some of the psychic rewards of working?

Connecting Economic Ideas

1. **Comprehending Ideas** Why is a person who is going into business concerned about **(a)** owner control, **(b)** liability, **(c)** the major labor issues, and **(d)** profits?
2. **Understanding Ideas** **(a)** Why do businesses sell stock and corporate bonds? **(b)** How do stocks and corporate bonds differ?
3. **Interpreting Ideas** Explain the role of self-interest in **(a)** forming a sole proprietorship, **(b)** becoming a limited partner, and **(c)** deciding where to work.
4. **Seeing Relationships** **(a)** How is the type of market structure related to the types of business organization you are most likely to find in an industry? **(b)** What type of business organization would you expect to be most common in perfect competition? Why?
5. **Analyzing Ideas** **(a)** Explain why vertical and horizontal combinations often hindered competition and free enterprise. **(b)** How have government regulations and antitrust laws promoted competition and free enterprise? **(c)** Has organized labor helped promote competition and free enterprise? Explain.
6. **Evaluating Ideas** Have **(a)** antitrust laws and **(b)** labor unions decreased efficiency in the economy? Explain.

Investigating Economic Issues

Reread the *Issues in Economics* feature on pages 134–135 and answer the following questions.

1. **Summarizing Ideas** What are the three categories into which the costs of government regulation fall?
2. **Interpreting Ideas** How was the government's role in laissez-faire capitalism different from its role today?
3. **Evaluating Viewpoints** **(a)** What are the main arguments in favor of government regulation of business? **(b)** What are the main arguments against government regulation of business? **(c)** Do you think there is too much government regulation of business? Explain.

Applying Economics

1. Investigate the businesses in your community and complete the following activities. **(a)** List three franchises and the goods or services each franchise provides. **(b)** List two cooperatives and their purposes. **(c)** List three nonprofit organizations and the goods or services each organization provides.
2. Research several recent mergers that have taken place in the United States. **(a)** Prepare a chart illustrating two of the mergers you researched. **(b)** In an essay, answer the question: Are mergers beneficial to the United States economy? Defend your answer.
3. Given the list of businesses below, answer the following questions. **(a)** What form of business organization are they? **(b)** In what market structure do they operate? **(c)** Are profits likely to be high, moderate, or low? **(d)** Is the wage rate for employees likely to be high, moderate, or low? Then in a brief paragraph for each business, explain your answers to each question.

   a. General Motors
   b. a local General Motors dealership
   c. a local automobile repair shop
   d. a corn farmer in Iowa
   e. a local or neighborhood grocery store

Using Primary Sources

In the early 1980s, the Reagan administration pledged to reduce government regulations in the American economy. As you read the following excerpt from the *Economic Report of the President*, 1982, think about the reasons for favoring a "benefit-cost analysis" for existing and proposed regulations.

A Plan to Reduce Government Regulations

Many Federal rules have yielded benefits to the public. The automobile emission standards, for example, have substantially reduced emissions from this source.

Regulations, however, can also impose substantial costs on society. Regulations themselves can create problems which call for additional regulations. Furthermore, the resources used to comply with regulations are diverted from other activities, with a resultant loss in productivity and economic growth. . . . One group in society may receive the bulk of the benefits from a Federal regulation while the costs are borne primarily by some other group. . . .

Interest has risen in efforts to determine more precisely the benefits and the costs of regulation. The motive for incorporating benefit-cost analysis into the regulatory decision-making process is to achieve a more efficient allocation of government resources by subjecting the public sector to the same type of efficiency tests used in the private sector. In making an investment decision, for example, business executives compare the costs to be incurred with the expected revenues. The investment is likely to be pursued only if the expected costs are less than the expected revenues. . . .

The aim of requiring agencies to perform benefit-cost analysis is to make the regulatory process more efficient and to eliminate regulatory actions that, on balance, generate more costs than benefits. . . .

The review of a proposed Federal regulatory activity should involve analysis of three types of questions. The first is whether some form of market failure has occurred that warrants the imposition of regulation. The second is whether Federal regulation, in contrast to State and local regulation, is appropriate. The last question . . . is whether a specific regulation will increase net benefits to society. . . .

Source Review

For Answers to Source Review, see p. A 33.

1. Give an example of a Federal regulation that has provided the public with a substantial benefit. What are some disadvantages of regulations?
2. How does a benefit-cost analysis for regulations make public decision making more like decision making in the private sector?
3. Before new Federal regulations are approved, what three questions have to be answered? How might the answers to these questions help reduce the number of new federal regulations?

Reading About Economics

Baxandall, Rosalyn. *America's Working Women: A Documentary History—1600 to the Present.* New York: Random House. A selection of interesting first person accounts from working women in the United States that range from colonial times to the present.

Goulden, Joseph. *Meany.* New York: Atheneum. A biography of George Meany, one of America's best-known labor leaders, who served first as president of the AFL and then of the AFL-CIO.

Skinner, Wickham. "The Productivity Paradox." *Harvard Business Review* (July-August, 1986), pp. 55–59. An evaluation of the current methods of revitalizing American productivity.

Welles, Chris. "Is Deregulation Working?" *Business Week* (December 22, 1986), pp. 50–55. An evaluation of recent deregulation policies and their effects on the economy.

See Unit Materials, p. TM 37.
See Multimedia Guide, p. TM 37.
See Applying Economics on text p. 216.

UNIT THREE

GOVERNMENT AND THE ECONOMY

CHAPTER 8

See Chapter Overview, p. TM 38.
See Chapter Objectives, p. TM 38.
See Introducing the Chapter, p. TM 38.
See Extending Economic Knowledge on text p. 190.

The Role of Government in the Economy

By failing to exploit the opportunity to expand public production we are missing opportunities for enjoyment which otherwise we might have had. . . . It is scarcely sensible that we should satisfy our wants in private goods with reckless abundance, while in the case of public goods . . . we practice extreme self-denial.

John Kenneth Galbraith

1 Government at all levels has increased in size during the twentieth century.

- Spurs to Government Growth
- Growth in Government Spending

2 Governments play several roles in the United States economy.

- Regulating Economic Activity
- Providing Public Goods
- Promoting Economic Well-Being
- Stabilizing the Economy

3 Citizens evaluate and influence the performance of government economic policies.

- Evaluating Government Performance
- Influencing Economic Policy

CHAPTER 8 STUDY GUIDE

Chapter Focus

Chapter 8 examines the functions of government in the nation's economy and discusses the growth of government at all levels during the twentieth century. The chapter discusses each role and its performance in influencing public policy.

As you study the chapter, look for the details that support each of the following statements.

1. Government at all levels has increased in size during the twentieth century.
2. Governments play several roles in the United States economy.
3. Citizens evaluate and influence the performance of government economic policies.

See Preteaching Vocabulary, p. TM 38.

Terms to Know

The following terms, while not the only terms emphasized in this chapter, are basic to your understanding of government's role in the United States economy. Determine the meaning of each term, either by using the Glossary or by watching for context clues as you read the chapter.

- public goods
- privatization
- transfer payment
- subsidies
- business cycle
- fiscal policy
- monetary policy
- wage and price control
- market failure
- interest group
- lobbyist

See Key Study Questions and Key Understandings, p. TM 39.

1 Government at all levels has increased in size during the twentieth century.

See Suggested Teaching Strategies, p. TM 39.

In recent years, several factors have caused governments at every level to grow in size and take on many additional responsibilities. Today, government is the nation's largest employer and largest business, and citizens must deal each day with an increasing number of government agencies and employees.

Spurs to Government Growth

Five key factors have spurred government expansion. They are population growth, an increase in the size of traditionally disadvantaged groups, changing attitudes about the role of government, a rising standard of living, and national emergencies.

◆ **Population Expansion.** Meeting the needs of an expanding population means increasing the number of government employees. In 1930, for example, federal, state, and local governments employed 3.2 million workers. By 1985 governments employed more than 16 million workers (see the graph on page 171).

The population of the United States has more than tripled since 1900, when it was 76 million. By 1986, the population of the United States was more than 240 million, making the United States the fourth most populous nation in the world. Other more populous nations are the People's Republic of China (1.1 billion), India (750 million), and the Union of Soviet Socialist Republics (280 million). Population expansion requires additional public goods and services, the goods and services that only government can provide.

Disadvantaged Groups. Traditionally disadvantaged groups, such as minorities and the poor, have grown at a much faster rate than the total population of the United States. Thus, minorities and the poor represent an increasingly larger proportion of the total population. By 1984, more than 46 million people, nearly 20 percent of the population, were classified as nonwhite—Hispanic, black,

◆ Discussion topic: The effects of population shifts as unemployed workers relocate to areas of the country where more jobs are available.

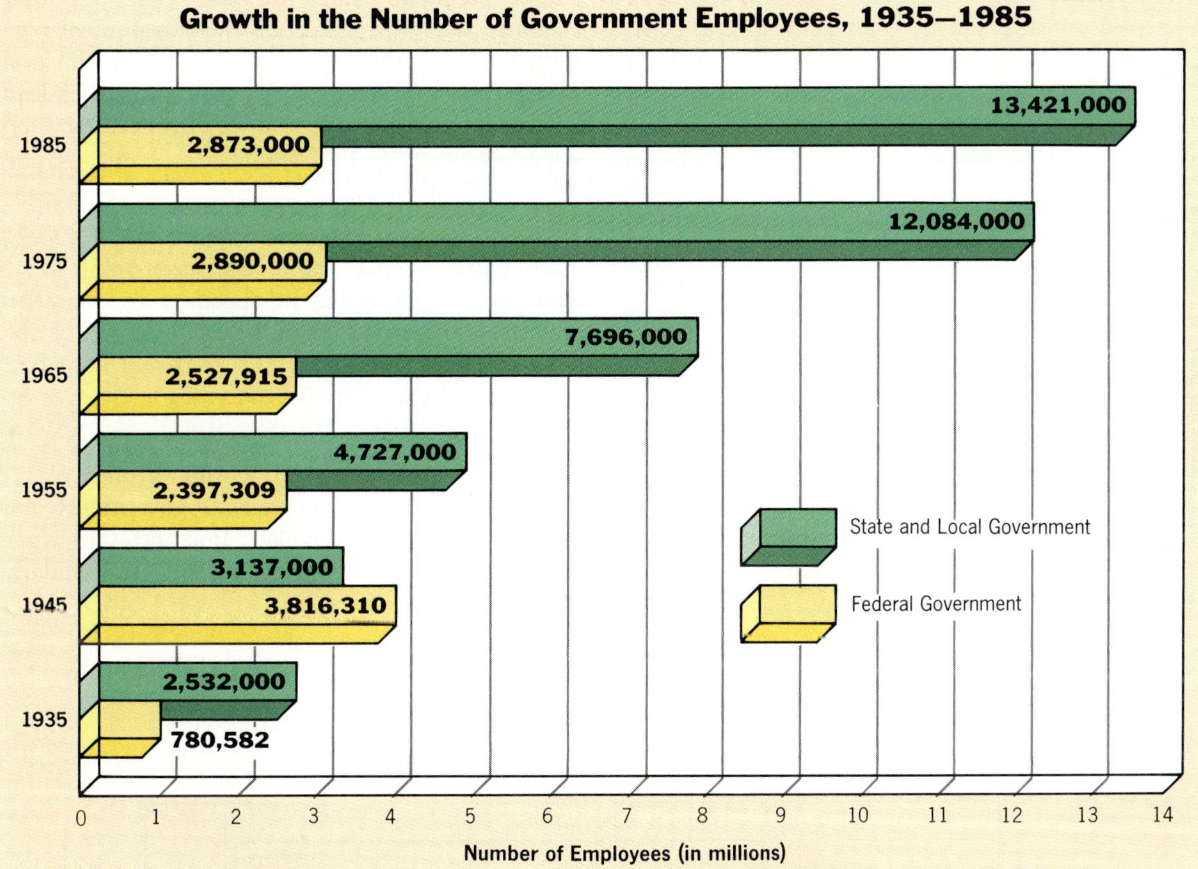

Sources: *Statistical History of the United States, Colonial Times to 1970*
Statistical Abstract of the United States, 1986
Economic Report of the President, 1986

Government growth has followed from the need to provide more public services, such as rapid transit, to an expanding urban population.

Asians, Native Americans. About 38 million people, 14 percent of the population, were classified as poor. Government assistance programs, established to meet the basic needs of disadvantaged people, have had to expand to keep up with the growth of the disadvantaged population.

Changing Attitudes. Before the Great Depression of the 1930s, most Americans supported the laissez-faire doctrine that rejected government intervention in the economy. The severity of the Great Depression, however, caused many people to change their minds about government intervention in the economy. Many supported an expanded role for government as a way to end the depression and to reform the economic system.

Government's success in ending the depression has convinced many people that government has a role in the nation's economy. Many New Deal reform programs remain an integral part of government today. Acceptance of the government's enlarged role in the economy cuts across all social classes and includes both business and labor leaders. Today, government is involved in almost every aspect of the economy.

Citizen Expectations. As the standard of living rises, citizens expect more and better public goods and services. Government spending in education, medical and health care, and welfare as well as special projects such as the space program have been encouraged by a booming economy. ◆

National Emergencies. During World War I, the number of civilian federal government employees more than doubled, from 402,000 workers in 1914 to 855,000 workers in 1918. Similarly,

Growth in Government Spending, 1945–1985

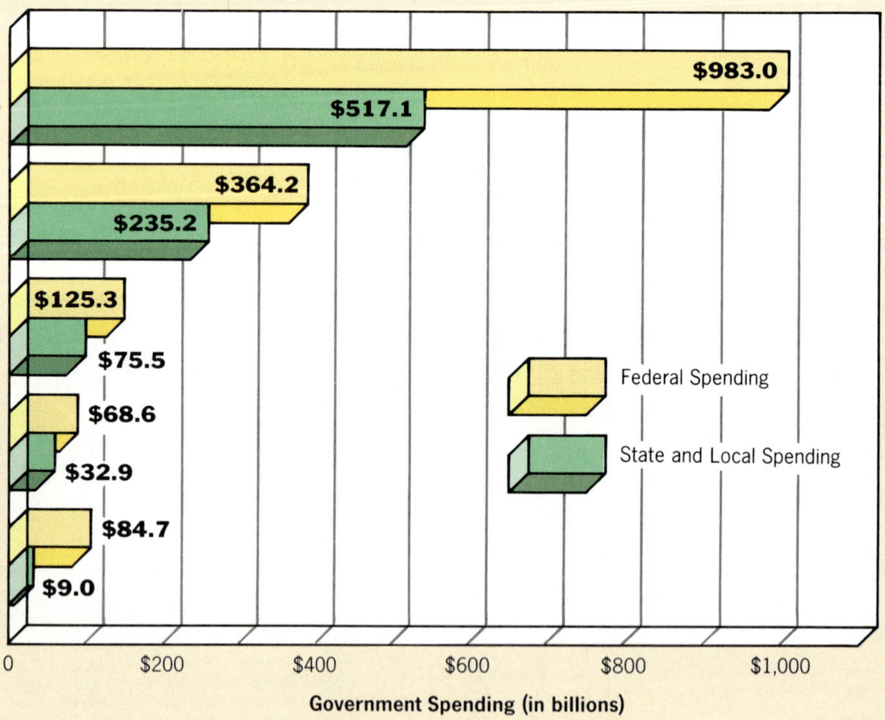

Source: *Economic Report of the President, 1986*

◆ Inform students that government assistance includes the food-stamp program in which people with incomes below a certain level buy coupons at a discounted rate. The coupons can be used as cash to purchase food.

HIGHLIGHTS IN ECONOMICS

The New Deal—Changing the Nation's Economic Course

Franklin D. Roosevelt promised the American people a "New Deal" at his inauguration for the Presidency in 1932. Economists, historians, and others now use the phrase to refer to the years 1933 through 1938 to characterize the legislation enacted in that period.

Most of this legislation was designed to solve the problems of the Great Depression and so is economic in its import. In general, the New Deal legislation gave the federal government much more economic power that it had ever had before.

The first and largest spurt of New Deal legislation passed Congress in 1933. This new legislation stemmed from a belief that a quick economic recovery needed government involvement. With the Agricultural Adjustment Act (1933) and the National Industrial Recovery Act (1933), the government began to regulate competition in agriculture and industry. Banking reform measures gave the government supervisory power over the troubled banking system and created the Federal Deposit Insurance Corporation (FDIC). Other laws required federal regulation of the securities market and created agencies such as the Tennessee Valley Authority, which involved the government in planning how to use natural and human resources.

In 1935, the second spurt of New Deal legislation took place. Recovery was slow, prompting Congress to take a different approach. This spurt of legislation focused less on market conditions and more on the needs of individual people and groups. The most important law passed was the Social Security Act (1935). This act created a system through which the government would provide the nation's citizens with some measure of financial security.

In 1938, the last year of the New Deal, no specific piece of legislation was as significant as the government's espousal of Keynesian economic theory. The government used the theory to justify the deficit spending that was necessary to finance the new social welfare programs and other kinds of government expansion enacted through New Deal legislation.

The programs and policies of the New Deal have had a lasting impact on government's role in the economy. The federal subsidies for agriculture, the FDIC, and other programs begun by the New Deal still serve as major elements in the nation's economic structure. The federal government continues to play a large and powerful role in regulating economic activity because of these elements.

◆ the number of federal employees increased during World War II from about 1 million in 1940 to almost 4 million employees in 1945, the final year of World War II. While the number of federal employees dropped after each war, the number never fell to prewar levels and the government continued many programs begun during each emergency.

Growth in Government Spending

Government spending began to grow rapidly in the 1940s in response to wartime needs and the increased involvement of government in everyday economic affairs (see the graph on page 172). Spending by all governments in the United States in 1950 was

◆ Have the students read "Mail Carriers" on page 543 of *Careers in the Marketplace.*

How a Federal Dollar Is Spent

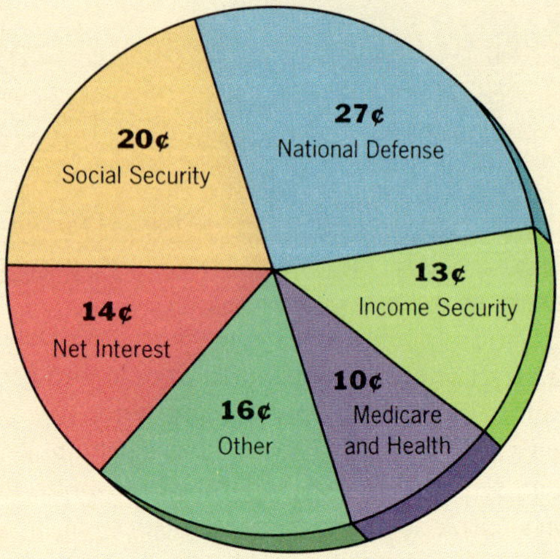

How a State Dollar Is Spent

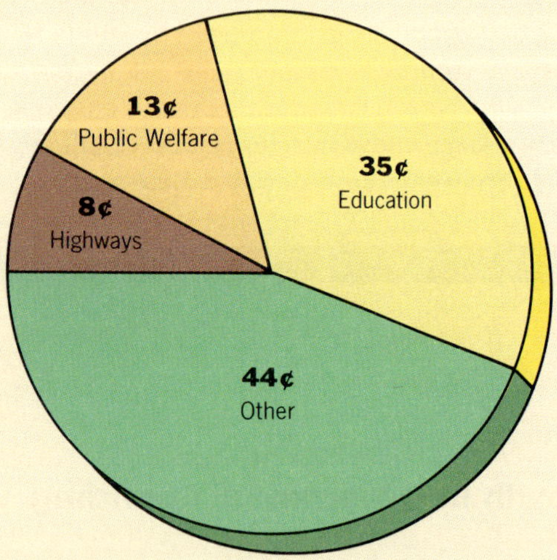

about $70 million. By 1985, total government expenditures had risen to almost $1.5 trillion, or almost $6,250 for every man, woman, and child in the United States. The federal government alone spent close to $1 trillion. For a breakdown of federal spending, see the top graph on this page.

Though total spending by the federal government has grown dramatically since 1970, federal spending as a percentage of the Gross National Product (GNP) has risen at a more modest pace. From 1970 to 1985, for example, federal spending increased from $208 billion to $983 billion, an increase of $775 billion or 372 percent. During the same period, federal spending as a percentage of the GNP fluctuated between 19.4 percent and 24.7 percent annually.

State and local governments also spend large sums of money—a total of more than $500 billion in 1985. Spending by state governments, for example, rose from about $11 billion in 1950 to more than $233 billion in 1985. During the same time period, spending by local governments increased from $17 billion to more than $332 billion.

The largest expenditures in state and local budgets are generally for education, public welfare, and road construction and maintenance. These categories ◆ account for about 56 percent of all state and local spending. The remaining 44 percent of state and local spending pays for public libraries, hospitals and health care, police and fire protection, public buildings, sanitation services, and government administration. For a breakdown of state spending, see the bottom graph on this page.

See Suggested Assignments, p. TM 39.

Section 1 Review See Answers, p. A 35.

IDENTIFY New Deal

1. **Analyzing Ideas** How did the New Deal change the nation's economic course?

2. **Interpreting Graphics** Study the graph on page 171. **(a)** Which level of government has experienced the greatest increases since 1935? **(b)** What is the only year shown on the graph in which the number of federal employees exceeded the number of state and local government employees? **(c)** What happened to the number of federal employees between 1975 and 1985?

◆ Inform students that the federal government often helps state and local governments by helping fund such projects as roads and public parks.

See Key Study Questions and Key Understandings, p. TM 40.

2 Governments play several roles in the United States economy.

See Suggested Teaching Strategies, p. TM 40.

The role of governments in the economic system of the United States has changed dramatically during the nation's history. From the late 1700s through the late 1800s, popular acceptance of the economic doctrine of laissez-faire limited government's role in the economy. People considered government intervention in the economy a threat to individualism and a challenge to capitalism. Governments, therefore, imposed few regulations and provided relatively few public goods or services.

As government grew during the 1900s, however, it assumed additional functions that began to affect the economy. Governments began to regulate businesses and offer consumers protection, to provide public goods, to promote economic well-being for certain individuals and groups, and to stabilize the economy. Today federal, state, and local governments share the first three roles, while economic stabilization is primarily the function of the federal government.

Economics Reporter

What Is the Occupational Safety and Health Administration?

The Occupational Safety and Health Administration (OSHA) is the branch of the Labor Department that enforces safety and health regulations in the workplace. OSHA conducts inspections and cites businesses for any violations. OSHA regulations cover approximately 65 million workers and more than 5 million companies involved in interstate commerce.

Since its formation in 1969, OSHA has had both opponents and supporters. Businesses claim that compliance with the inflexible regulations leads to higher production costs. Supporters of OSHA point out that in 1969, 15,000 employees in the private sector died because of accidents in the workplace. These supporters believe that the regulations helped decrease the number of work-related deaths to only 3,750 in 1985.

Regulating Economic Activity

In their regulatory roles, governments establish the rules and procedures that guide the conduct of economic activity. Government regulations affect all individuals and businesses participating in the United States economy.

Promoting Competition. Government regulation of business enterprises usually seeks to promote competition in the marketplace, to prevent the abuse of laborers, and to minimize the negative side effects of production.

The government promotes competition by making and enforcing antitrust legislation that prevents the formation of monopolies and breaks up existing ones. The Sherman Antitrust Act of 1890 was the first major piece of antitrust legislation in the United States. Later legislation has clarified and strengthened the Sherman Antitrust Act.

The government prevents the abuse of laborers by making and enforcing regulations that protect workers from discrimination in hiring or promotions because of age, sex, race, religion, or national origin.

The government also monitors and sets standards for working conditions. Federal agencies such as the Office of Economic Opportunity (OEO) and the Occupational Safety and Health Administration (OSHA) monitor business practices and punish violators. In 1986, for example, OSHA levied a $1.4 million fine on Union Carbide Corporation for willful violations of safety rules at its plant in Institute, West Virginia, where a chemical discharge the previous year had injured 130 local residents.

Government regulations also are aimed at minimizing the negative side effects that sometimes accompany economic activities. Examples of such side effects include pollution, traffic congestion, and soil erosion. The Environmental Protection Agency, Nuclear Regulatory Commission, and other government agencies establish and enforce regulations that try to limit the negative side effects of business operations.

In 1986, for example, the Department of Agriculture instituted a policy aimed at protecting the nation's fertile soil by cutting financial aid to farmers who allowed soil erosion on their farms to continue.

Protecting Consumers. Most government regulations protect individual consumers in the economy.

Text continues on page 178.

READING ABOUT ECONOMICS

Interpreting News Articles

Newspaper and newsmagazine articles on economic information report on current economic events, issues, problems, and policies—usually in an objective style—in contrast to editorials, which express an opinion, or a point of view about an issue or topic.

The standard news article follows a basic format. A headline first presents the main idea of the article. Next, a dateline states where and when the article was written. A byline follows if the author of the article is to be credited. The first, or "lead," paragraph or paragraphs states key information, including who is involved, what the situation is, and when and where the situation occurred. The remainder of the article usually explains the hows and whys of the report.

You have already studied how to analyze economic information (Chapter 4, pages 78–79) and how to analyze editorial cartoons (Chapter 6, pages 130-131). You may wish to review these skills.

How to Interpret a News Article

To interpret a news article, follow these steps.

1. **Read the headline.** Note the article's main idea.
2. **Check for a dateline and byline.** If available, note when and where the article was written, and by whom.
3. **Read the lead paragraph.** Note the answers to the who, what, where, and when questions.
4. **Read the rest of the article.** Determine the answers to the how and why questions.
5. **Identify bias.** Identify whether any words and phrases are indicative of a judgment or express an emotion. Note whether the author uses them to express a point of view.

REAGAN'S BUDGET: SELLING OFF THE GOVERNMENT

BY LEE SMITH

AFTER SEVERAL YEARS of a brilliant run in Britain, privatization is moving onto center stage in the U.S. When President Reagan sent his otherwise unsurprising budget message to Congress on February 5 [1986], he put the spotlight on what for the U.S. is a new idea: selling off some of the government's property and turning over some of its services to private enterprise. Noting that over the years the government has become ever more deeply involved in commerce, Reagan said, "In most cases it would be better for the government to get out of the business and stop competing with the private sector . . . I propose that we begin that process."

Reagan's budget director, James C. Miller III, has put power authorities, airports, petroleum reserves, and loans on the block. But he is not about to hold a garage sale. In fiscal 1987, which begins this October 1, the Administration wants to realize about $8.5 billion through privatization, only about 1% of the $850.4 billion in revenues it expects.

The debut of privatization got mixed reviews at best. The purists complain that the Administration should sell off more assets. That way it would not have to cut back on popular benefits in order to reduce the deficit. Political theorists point out that much of what passes for privatization in the budget is actually something else—a transfer of property from the federal government to state and local authorities, which they call devolution, not privatization.

A close look at the privatization proposals shows that some are one-shot deficit reductions that will cost the government revenue in the future. Others will make little difference to the deficit, and quite a few won't happen. The Administration's plan to sell off the government is a political, not an economic measure. Privatization will help the President come closer to one of his primary goals: a reduction of the role of the U.S. government in the economy. . . .

6. Analyze the article. Think about the type of data provided in the article. Decide whether the article identifies the sources from whom any information was received. Determine the reliability of the data. If the data seems reliable, use it to draw conclusions or form generalizations.

Applying the Skill

Read the news article on page 176. The headline indicates that the main idea is President Reagan's plan to sell off some government assets. The article was written for *Fortune* magazine, on March 3, 1986, by Lee Smith. The lead paragraph provides these answers.

- **Who:** President Reagan, Budget Director James C. Miller III, and Congress.
- **What:** President Reagan's budget message to Congress which supports privatization.
- **Where:** The Capitol, Washington, D.C.
- **When:** February 5, 1986.

The remainder of the article answers these questions.

- **How:** Privatization occurs by selling government assets, such as power authorities, airports, and petroleum reserves, to companies in the private sector.
- **Why:** The major reason is political, to reduce the role of government in the economy; privatization can also help reduce budget deficits and take government out of the business of competing with private firms.

The story appears objective. Both sides of the issue are briefly stated. The author does not express a point of view. The use of the word "brilliant" in the lead paragraph tends to slant the story in favor of privatization in Britain.

Practicing the Skill See Answers, p. A 35.

Read the news article on this page, which appeared in the July 21, 1986, issue of *Business Week*. On a separate sheet of paper, answer these questions.

1. What is the headline of the news article?
2. **(a)** When was it written? **(b)** by whom?
3. How does the lead paragraph answer the questions **(a)** who? **(b)** what? **(c)** where? **(d)** when?
4. How does the rest of the article answer the questions **(a)** how and **(b)** why?
5. Is the article objective? Explain.

THE BUDGET IS CONGRESS' PROBLEM AGAIN

BY HOWARD GLECKMAN

By declaring a key provision of the Gramm-Rudman Act unconstitutional, the Supreme Court has put the business of controlling federal spending back where it belongs—in the hands of elected officials. The lawmakers who passed the act last December [1985] may yet find a maneuver that will let them meet this year's deficit target on paper without actually making the difficult cuts. But the longer Congress and the Administration wait, the harder it will be for them to get the budget under control.

There's more at stake than mere numbers. The federal budget helps define the government's role in national life. Gramm-Rudman eroded representative democracy by shifting those decisions from Congress and the President to unelected officials.

Both the Administration and Capitol Hill were responsible for this unhealthy situation. In approving the law [Gramm-Rudman], Congress created a process called "sequesteration," under which across-the-board cuts would be ordered by the Comptroller General without any votes being taken. President Reagan, after six years of failing to control the budget deficit, signed Gramm-Rudman into law. But then he made it all but impossible for Congress to comply by refusing to compromise on his own fiscal 1987 budget.

The untouchables. Thanks to the court decision, the deficit problem is back in Congress' lap. If the lawmakers want to cut the budget deficit, they will have to vote to do so in a joint resolution, not pass the buck to a civil servant. "We will see if the President and the Congress have the guts to make the tough decisions," says Representative Leon E. Panetta (D-Calif.), a former member of the House Budget Committee. There is much talk on the Hill that lawmakers will find the courage to do what they have been unable to do for five years. Regrettably, it's hard to see why.

As a result, there's little chance the fiscal 1987 Gramm-Rudman deficit target of $144 billion will be met. Politicians probably won't enact the necessary cuts or tax increases. Social security is off limits. Programs for the poor, such as food stamps and aid to children, are relatively untouchable. President Reagan has ruled out any significant tax increases and is fighting to maintain his defense buildup. So Congress is left to try to find the money needed to balance the budget

(Text of article continues on page 589.)

In addition to those regulations that protect workers, federal and state laws protect consumers, savers, borrowers, and investors.

Federal regulations set up agencies that establish guidelines to help guarantee the rights of consumers. For example, the Food and Drug Administration and Consumer Product Safety Commission protect people from unsafe foods, medicines and other drugs, toys, ◆ and other products.

The Federal Trade Commission and Federal Communications Commission ensure that advertising and sales practices are ethical, truthful, and fair. The Office of Consumer Affairs coordinates the actions of federal agencies and commissions on behalf of consumers. Individuals can also register their concerns and complaints directly with most federal agencies.

The federal government insures savings deposits (see Chapter 12), and monitors the business practices of insured banks to guarantee their compliance with banking laws (see Chapter 10). Federal credit laws also protect borrowers. The Securities and Exchange Commission (SEC) protects investors against fraud in the securities trade (see Chapter 13). It sets procedures for the registration and sale of stocks and the licensing of securities dealers. The SEC is empowered to punish any violators.

Many state governments and local governments have developed regulations that further protect consumers and borrowers. These regulations require the compliance of all businesses that operate within the state or local boundaries. Most state and local regulatory agencies, like their federal counterparts, accept consumer complaints.

The United States Department of Agriculture (USDA) was created by an act of Congress on May 15, 1862. The duties of the USDA include the inspection and grading of the United States food supply.

◆ **Inform students that the FDA requires thorough testing of new medications before approving them for distribution. The FDA initiated these requirements, which often take years to complete, to protect consumers from any harmful side effects of proposed medication.**

Providing Public Goods

Governments receive most of their revenues from taxes and use most of these tax dollars to provide public goods. **Public goods** are goods and services provided for everyone by the government. An individual's use of a public good does not reduce another person's enjoyment of the same good. Furthermore, government cannot prevent any individual from benefiting from a public good, although everyone does not have to use the good. Governments provide public goods for the well-being of citizens and because private production cannot meet public demand. National defense, public education, and federal highways are examples of public goods.

Shared Responsibility. Except for national defense, which is provided solely by the federal government, responsibility for public goods is often shared by federal, state, and local governments. For example, the courts, the nation's legal system, the correction departments, and the law enforcement agencies are all found at all three government levels. One level of government often has the primary responsibility for a public good, but it receives assistance from the other government levels. Local government, for example, directs public education but receives state and federal funding to help pay the costs.

Privatization. In recent years, privatization, a new concept regarding government production, administration, and ownership of public goods, has gained national attention. **Privatization** refers to either the sale of government property or the relinquishment of certain government services to private businesses. Garbage collection has long been privatized in many cities, and governments are contracting for more private services. Some smaller airports no longer have Federal Aviation Administration staffs in their control towers. Some for-profit hospital chains now operate formerly public hospitals.

Supporters justify privatization in three ways. First, they argue that private firms can operate certain industries more efficiently than the government. A case in point is the United States Postal Service. It faces considerable competition because users have turned to more efficient private carriers such as Federal Express and Airborne Freight for quick mail delivery.

Economics Reporter

What Is the Office of Consumer Affairs?

The federal agency responsible for consumer protection is the United States Office of Consumer Affairs. President Richard M. Nixon created the office in 1971, making it part of the Executive Office of the President. In 1973, he moved it to the Department of Health and Human Resources. The main purposes of the Office of Consumer Affairs are to give advice and provide information to consumers, and to direct people to the government agency that can help resolve their complaints.

Second, they argue that the government should not be a competitor with private business. The Federal Housing Administration (FHA), for example, provides loans in direct competition with private financial institutions. In addition, government resources and regulations permit the FHA to offer loans at a lower interest rate than those charged by private financial institutions.

Third, they point to the need to reduce the federal deficit, which the sale of some public properties and services would help. The Grace Commission reported that the federal government could save $11.2 billion over three years through the privatization of certain federal properties. Some of these include Dulles and National Airports in Washington, D.C., all military commissary stores and government vehicles, and most of the operations of the Coast Guard. In addition, supporters of privatization point to Great Britain's success in raising over $11 billion since 1979 through the sale of certain government goods and services.

Opponents of privatization counter that most public goods and services should continue under government control because they are essential to the well-being of users. Opponents also point to the tremendous resources at government disposal to meet special business needs and circumstances. The largest federal public employees' union, the American Federation of State, County, and Municipal Employees (AFSCME), also opposes privatization because it fears that employee layoffs, inefficiencies, and corruption will result from the private management of essential services.

Report topic: The privatization of the Postal Service.

The federal government ensures that handicapped commuters have access to public transportation.

In addition to delivering mail, the Postal Service is responsible for the enforcement of postal laws.

Promoting Economic Well-Being

The third major economic role of government is promoting economic well-being. To fulfill this function, governments redistribute tax revenues to individuals or businesses that need specific assistance. Groups such as the poor, the elderly, and the ill receive tax moneys. Such government payments are called **transfer payments.** In transfer payments, the government transfers money from one group of citizens to another group of citizens. Individuals receive transfer payments through entitlement programs such as public assistance and social insurance.

Public Assistance and Social Insurance. The government transfers income to individuals through entitlement programs which, by federal law, are the right of the recipients. Some entitlement programs provide incomes for households, while others finance medical care, higher education, housing, and job training or retraining programs.

Some entitlement programs are wholly financed and administered by the federal government. The federal government, for example, provides monthly Social Security payments to elderly and disabled people and their dependents. It distributes $12 billion worth of food stamps annually to 20 million low-income Americans. Other entitlement programs are sponsored jointly by federal, state, and local governments. These include the Aid to Families with Dependent Children (AFDC), reduced prices for transportation, food deliveries to individual homes, and other aids to the sick, disabled, elderly, and the poor.

Federal and state governments also administer unemployment insurance programs. In most states, workers who are temporarily unemployed through no fault of their own are entitled to receive a percentage of their regular wages for a period of time, usually 26 weeks, while they seek a new job. The payments, called unemployment compensation, are paid by both federal and state funds.

During the fiscal year that ended in June 1986, 68 percent of the dislocated workers who had completed the job training program administered by the Labor Department found new jobs.

DECISION MAKERS IN THE ECONOMY

Barbara Mikulski

Barbara Mikulski (Democrat from Maryland), is a former social worker and member of Baltimore's City Council. She was first elected to the United States House of Representatives in 1976, serving four consecutive terms until her election to the Senate in 1986.

Mikulski is a well-known consumer "activist," who works to promote the rights and welfare of women, children, minorities, the elderly, and consumers. She has tried to obtain funds for the prevention of domestic violence and for the care of battered spouses and children. She has urged the establishment of both national health insurance and a child health insurance program. She has also initiated efforts to regulate hospital costs.

Economic equity and economic security are always at or near the top of Mikulski's list of economic priorities. She believes that all Americans should have access to adequate jobs, education, and health care, and that the government must help to provide these necessities. In her opinion, the country needs a strong federal government with the financial resources to guarantee a relatively high standard of living for everyone.

In 1986 Mikulski ran for the United States Senate. She won the Senate race over Linda Chavez, the Republican candidate. As a Senator representing the entire state of Maryland, Mikulski is sure to remain an influential advocate of the needs of disadvantaged people.

Subsidies. Government transfer payments and other assistance to businesses are called business entitlements, or **subsidies.** These grants are intended for business rather than personal expenses. Governments at all levels subsidize business activity in the agricultural and nonagricultural sectors of the economy.

Each year governments grant subsidies totalling billions of dollars to private businesses and public agencies to ensure continued service or production of certain goods. The government, for example, assumes some of the financial costs of subways, bus lines, commuter trains, and other means of mass transportation. In this way, the government ensures that the service will be available and affordable for users.

Farmers receive government subsidies in the forms of price supports, crop control, and easy credit. Easy credit means money is available and affordable to borrowers. Price supports guarantee farmers a set price for grains, cotton, tobacco, dairy, and other eligible products. Fruit, meats, and vegetables are usually not eligible for price supports.

Crop-control guidelines stabilize or reduce the production of certain crops by paying farmers not to produce them. The goal of crop control is to bring the supply of agricultural products into balance with the demand for these products and, thereby, assure farmers a higher price for those products.

During the past 20 years, the government also has subsidized farmers by extending to them easy credit to pay for new land and equipment, to refinance past debts, or to meet current financial emergencies. In the 1980s, however, easy credit has had unhappy results for many farmers. Crop surpluses and low crop prices have made it impossible for many farmers to repay their debts. Some farmers who could not meet loan payments were forced to sell their farms.

Text continues on page 184.

ISSUES IN ECONOMICS

Worker Training and Retraining Programs

Worker training programs and worker retraining programs teach laborers marketable job skills to prepare them for long-term and gainful employment. Broad popular support exists for worker training and retraining programs. Agreement is mixed, however, on who should benefit from such programs and how they should be administered.

Groups Benefiting From Training and Retraining Programs

Private and public worker retraining programs assist different "target groups." Some programs target the "hard-core," or chronically unemployed—those with little education, few skills, and irregular work histories. Other worker training and retraining programs target workers who have been displaced because of plant closings, relocations, or automation. Changes in the job market or the economy have cost 11.5 million American workers their jobs between 1979 and 1984.

Training and retraining programs for hard-core unemployed seek to reduce the number of people relying on public assistance. Aid to Families with Dependent Children (AFDC) alone costs taxpayers about $14 billion annually.

Unions and Private-Sector Retraining Programs

Labor unions have made retraining programs a high priority in many recent contract negotiations. ◆ Organized labor is a particularly strong supporter of worker retraining. Through the cooperation of management and laborers, many successful retraining programs have been developed.

The "Aim To Learn and Succeed," or Atlas program is one successful retraining program. The Atlas program is a $36 million benefit that resulted from negotiations between the 650,000-member Communications Workers of America (CWA) and American Telephone and Telegraph (AT&T).

Since 1983, Atlas has retrained thousands of workers in the fast-changing telecommunications industry. Classroom instruction acquaints trainees with new technology in the field and upgrades their skills. In effect, Atlas anticipates technological changes that will affect the workplace, and prepares workers to fit into new systems.

Other union-negotiated contracts include similar retraining programs. A recent agreement between the United Automobile Workers (UAW) and GM and Ford included moneys for worker retraining. Retraining in the auto industry was especially important for two reasons. First, new skills were required to keep pace with technological changes in the workplace. Second, foreign competition in the auto market was hurting workers' job security. Thus, learning marketable skills was seen as a way to prepare for possible lay-offs.

Cost is the major obstacle to worker retraining programs in the private sector. For corporations and other businesses, the money spent on worker retraining programs, like other items in a union contract, becomes a cost of production. Higher production costs often result in lower corporate profits or in higher consumer prices. Many individuals and firms, therefore, look to government to increase its worker-retraining efforts.

The Role of Government Worker-Retraining Programs

Government at all levels—local, state, and national—has devised programs to train and retrain workers. These programs are aimed at the hard-core unemployed and displaced workers.

◆ Have the students read "Understanding Contract Obligations" on pages 519–520 of the *Everyday Economics Handbook* and answer the questions that follow.

Retraining The Hard-Core Unemployed. The federal government has experimented with a number of worker training and retraining programs since the 1960s. For example, under the provisions of the Economic Opportunity Act of 1964, the Job Corps and the Neighborhood Youth Corps Work Training Program were established. The Neighborhood Youth Corps proved ineffective, but the Job Corps expanded during the 1970s and 1980s.

The Youth Employment and Demonstration Projects Act (1977) increased the government's commitment to the Job Corps. Until 1986, the Job Corps was a $600 million annual program. It operated 107 residential job-training centers, and trained 40,000 workers annually for employment in the private sector. In 1986, however, budget cuts slowed the Job Corps's progress. Many critics of the budget cuts think that the government should continue to fully fund the Job Corps program.

A number of individual states have developed retraining programs for the chronically unemployed. California has training programs to teach job skills to AFDC recipients. Child care and assistance in the job search are also part of the program. In Massachusetts, a worker training program has placed 23,000 former welfare recipients in jobs between 1983 and 1985. Further, 86 percent stayed off the welfare rolls, saving the state government millions of dollars in public assistance payments.

Retraining Displaced Workers. In 1982 Congress established the Job Training Partnership Act, the most important federal retraining program for displaced workers. Displaced workers are those who have lost their jobs because of technological change, plant closings or relocations, and other factors beyond their control.

Under the provisions of the Job Training Partnership Act, state and local governments receive grants of money from the federal government. These grants, which total $225 million annually, are used by local governments to subsidize worker retraining programs conducted by private firms.

The Trade Adjustment and Assistance Act of 1974 funds a retraining program for workers who have lost their jobs because of foreign competition. By 1985, the federal government was supplying $26 million annually for this program. In 1986, Congress expanded the program and its budget.

State programs also have been developed to retrain displaced workers. More than a dozen states sponsor retraining programs that offer retraining while maintaining unemployment benefits.

California administers its program through the Employment Training Panel (ETP). The ETP targets experienced workers that have been laid off, or those who may soon be displaced. Then, in cooperation with private firms, the ETP places workers in specialized training programs conducted by private firms. These firms pay for the initial training costs. The firms are reimbursed for the training costs by the ETP after they have hired the trainee for full-time employment. The California model for worker retraining received national attention during the mid-1980s.

Workfare Programs. Worker training and retraining programs teach marketable skills to workers who are unemployed, or who will soon become unemployed. These programs look to the long-term benefits of a skilled work force—higher worker productivity and independence, and relief for taxpayers who would otherwise have to support public assistance programs.

Workfare, or "make-work," programs, on the other hand, simply place people in jobs as a way to increase their personal incomes. The goal is immediate, or short-term, employment. The "public works" programs that were initiated during the Great Depression were workfare programs. In the 1980s, over 20 states instituted workfare programs. Workfare demands that able-bodied welfare recipients accept make-work jobs in exchange for their benefits.

The issue of worker training and retraining is likely to attract greater amounts of attention in the 1980s and beyond than ever before. Differing views about funding and administration are likely to increase as the pace of technological change and worker displacement increases.

CASE STUDY

The Social Security System

Before the Great Depression, no comprehensive federal program provided income security for the elderly, the disabled, and their dependents. Before the 1930s, people viewed income security as an individual responsibility rather than a function of the government. But after the Great Depression wiped out the lifetime savings of millions of Americans, people began to look to the federal government for income security. The government responded with the Social Security Act of 1935, which created the Social Security system.

Social Security provides a regular income and medical care to eligible retired or disabled workers and their families. To be eligible for full Social Security benefits, a worker must be 65 years old and have worked for a specified period of time during which Social Security taxes were paid. Reduced benefits are available to retired workers at age 62.

Most Social Security beneficiaries are retired workers (see the graph below). Social Security payments to beneficiaries vary in size, according to individual household circumstances. To help beneficiaries cope with inflation, the Social Security system makes a yearly cost-of-living adjustment, which ◆ increases payments as prices rise.

The Social Security system has grown rapidly since its beginning in the 1930s. In 1985, the government paid Social Security benefits to 37 million people at an annual cost of $189 billion. The Social Security payout accounts for 20 percent of all federal expenditures. The 1985 Social Security payout was double the amount spent on Social Security in 1978.

To fund Social Security, the government collects Social Security taxes from workers who are currently employed. It then redistributes the money as retirement, disability, and death benefits. The system is intergenerational, meaning that current Social Security contributions pay benefits to an older generation. About 95 percent of all wage earners contribute to Social Security.

Amendments to the Social Security Act made during the mid-1960s created two companion programs, Medicare and Medicaid. These two programs expand medical coverage for the elderly, the disabled, and the poor. Medicare provides hospital and medical insurance to people who are 65 years of age and older. In 1985, the federal government spent $66 billion on Medicare.

Medicaid, a program sponsored jointly by federal and state governments, provides hospitalization and health care to the blind, the disabled, and the poor. In 1985, federal, state, and local governments expended more than $34 billion on the Medicaid program.

The Distribution of Social Security Benefits

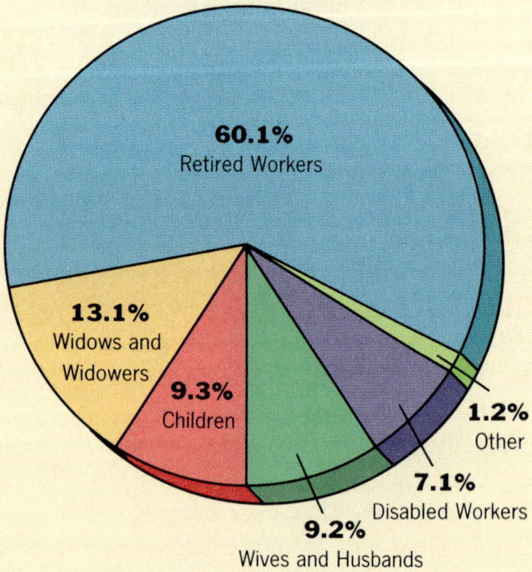

Source: *Statistical Abstract of the United States, 1986*

Stabilizing the Economy

Government's expanded role in the economy allows it to promote the general welfare of the American people, a goal established for government by the Constitution. In large part, the government has sought to achieve this goal by stabilizing the economy, the fourth economic function of government and a role assumed largely by the federal government.

Government Economic Policies. Throughout United States history, periods of economic prosper-

 ◆ Discussion topic: How inflation affects persons on fixed incomes.

ity have been followed by periods of recession and even depression. This sequential rising and falling of the economy is called the **business cycle.**

Before the 1930s, the government did not attempt to stabilize this business cycle. But during the Great Depression and especially during and after World War II, the government began to play a major role in managing the economy. It has attempted to steer the economy on a middle course between inflation and recession. To achieve this goal, the government today relies on its fiscal policy, its monetary policy, and wage and price controls.

Through the **fiscal policy** developed by Congress and the President, the government uses its taxing and spending powers to stabilize the economy. To fight recession, for example, the government reduces taxes and increases spending. To combat inflation, on the other hand, the government increases taxes and reduces spending.

Monetary policy, formulated by the Federal ◆ Reserve Board, seeks to stabilize the economy by modifying the nation's money supply in response to certain economic pressures. To effectively stabilize the economy, the fiscal policy and the monetary policy must be coordinated.

On occasion, the federal government also uses wage and price controls to stabilize the economy. Considered a drastic economic measure and usually imposed only during wartime, **wage and price controls** set limits on increases in certain wages and prices. Wage and price controls were used during World War II and the Korean War and only once in peacetime in 1971 when President Nixon imposed a 90-day freeze on wages and prices.

Rather than set actual controls, most Presidents have preferred to establish wage and control guidelines. These guidelines suggest to business and industry voluntary limits on wage and price increases.

Before 1971, an International Monetary Fund agreement enabled foreign countries to request gold in exchange for the currency they received from their trading partners. In 1971, President Richard Nixon abandoned this agreement, fearing that the country's growing trade deficit would result in the depletion of its gold reserves.

◆ Discussion topic: How fiscal policy differs from monetary policy.

Garbage strikes are an unpleasant reminder of our dependence on public goods and services.

Market Failure Responses. The government also attempts to ensure economic stability by eliminating any **market failures** that may disrupt the market economy. The five major types of market failures are inadequate business competition, the negative side effects of business, the inability or unwillingness of private enterprise to produce public goods, inadequate knowledge of market conditions, and immobility of the factors of production.

Inadequate business competition occurs when one or a few businesses dominate a field and control the price and supply of a good. The government responds to inadequate competition with regulations that prohibit and dissolve monopolies and open the field to new competitors.

A second type of market failure is caused by aspects of a business operation that negatively affect persons not connected with the business. These negative side effects might include such health and safety hazards as air and water pollution. When these hazards are present, the government responds to them by imposing specific standards that are designed to minimize the negative side effects. ◆

A third type of market failure is the inability or unwillingness of private enterprise to produce public goods. This type of market failure occurs when private enterprise lacks the skill, the resources, or the legal right to produce a needed good or service. In such cases, the government produces and distributes the good to the citizens. The redistribution of income through transfer payments is a government response to this type of market failure.

The fourth type of market failure occurs when consumers have inadequate knowledge of market conditions. When consumers, borrowers, investors, or workers lack reliable information upon which to make informed marketplace decisions, market problems occur. The government responds to this fourth type of market failure by ensuring that information is available to the public. Two agencies that act as consumer watchdogs are the Consumer Protection Agency and the Securities and Exchange Commission.

The fifth type of market failure is immobility of the factors of production. This failure occurs when workers' skills become obsolete because of technological or other changes. It also occurs when entrepreneurs lack capital and are unable to improve their financial situations. The government responds to these problems by providing education and job training for workers and by providing subsidies and tax incentives to businesspeople needing capital.

See Suggested Assignments, p. TM 40.

Section 2 Review

See Answers, p. A 35.

DEFINE public good, privatization, business cycle

IDENTIFY Occupational Safety and Health Administration, Office of Consumer Affairs, Barbara Mikulski, Social Security

1. **Summarizing Ideas** **(a)** What are the four major functions of government? **(b)** Which function is assumed largely by the federal government?
2. **Comprehending Ideas** **(a)** What is a transfer payment? **(b)** What is a subsidy? **(c)** How does each type of payment promote economic wellbeing?
3. **Interpreting Graphics** Study the graph on page 184. Excluding the category of "other," list the five categories of citizens that receive Social Security benefits.

◆ **Have the students read "Consumer Safety Inspectors" on page 540 of *Careers in the Marketplace.***

See Key Study Questions and Key Understandings, p. TM 41.

3 Citizens evaluate and influence the performance of government economic policies.

See Suggested Teaching Strategies, p. TM 41.

The government's growth at all levels has enabled it to provide more and better public goods and services, better income security and medical security, and more economic stability. At the same time, however, government involvement in the economy has been controversial because it has meant higher financial costs to businesses and individuals and more regulations on economic activity. Such controversy has led individuals and businesses to evaluate and attempt to influence government economic policies.

The redevelopment of downtown areas is one way the federal government promotes economic growth.

Evaluating Government Performance

◆ In a democratic society, citizens evaluate the performance of government policies. Such evaluations are based on how well government actions help the nation achieve its economic goals, given the constraints placed on the government. The six economic goals that serve as criteria for evaluating government policies are economic freedom, economic efficiency, economic equity, economic security, economic stability, and economic growth. (For a complete review of these economic goals, see Chapter 1.)

Economic freedom refers to the marketplace freedoms enjoyed by businesses, consumers, workers, savers, borrowers, and investors, and is the basis for the free enterprise system. Economic efficiency, making the best use of resources, considers the costs and benefits of economic decisions and determines which solution is best for the economy. Economic equity means an economic policy is fair to individuals and groups in the nation. Economic security provides for the general well-being of citizens through programs such as income and savings security and medical insurance. Economic stability is generally reflected by full employment and stable prices. Economic growth means that, on average, the real value of all goods and services produced in the economy each year for each person has risen.

Any policy used to manage the economy is likely to be controversial. In fact, the most controversial issue of all is whether government should manage the economy at all. Once the decision to manage the economy is made, then controversy usually arises over the best way to manage it. For example, in fighting inflation should taxes be raised, spending decreased, or both? Should the money supply be tightened by raising interest rates? Should wage and price controls be imposed? Each choice has pros and cons—gains for one group in the economy and losses for another group.

Policymakers, therefore, must assign each economic goal a relative importance, which changes as national conditions and attitudes change. During the mid-1960s, for example, economic equity and security were high priorities in President Lyndon B. Johnson's Great Society program. Higher taxes were needed to finance these programs, which were designed to promote the economic well-being of many disadvantaged Americans.

During the serious recession of the early 1980s, on the other hand, economic efficiency, stability, and growth became high priorities. The Reagan administration instituted income-tax cuts to stimulate the sluggish economy. The tax cuts resulted in substantial cuts in social programs.

Tuning the machinery of the economy is a complicated task that is made more complicated by scarcities of money, resources, and time. Because of these constraints, it is sometimes impossible to implement programs that are desirable to all groups. Evaluators must consider such constraints when determining the success of government policies in achieving the nation's economic goals.

◆ You may wish to remind students that the United States is one of the few nations in the world where citizens are allowed to openly criticize government policies.

Some interest groups use protests as a method to bring their needs to the attention of the federal government and the public.

Influencing Economic Policy

In the United States, individuals, working alone or in groups, can affect the policies and direction of government. By becoming informed and by voting, Americans can influence the passage of economic policies.

The Role of Individuals. Elections are a barometer of public opinion because people vote for candidates who most closely reflect their own beliefs and values. Citizens who are at least 18 years old have the right to vote in local, state, and federal elections. Through voting, they have an opportunity to make their opinions heard.

Individuals can influence economic policies by electing to public office representatives with an economic philosophy similar to their own. For example, the landslide victories of President Ronald Reagan over his Democratic opponents in the 1980 and 1984 elections indicated broad support for his economic plans. Elected representatives are especially sensitive to public opinion because they must satisfy constituents if they hope to be reelected. ◆

The Role of Interest Groups. Interest groups affect government economic actions by influencing elected representatives. An **interest group** is an organization of citizens having common interests and goals. Some interest groups have a broad-based

◆ Point out to students that individuals may also influence economic decision making by writing to their elected representatives.

Economics Reporter

What Is a Political Action Committee?

One result of the government reforms enacted by Congress after the Watergate affair in 1974 was the creation of Political Action Committees (PACs). PACs are special interest groups set up by trade and professional associations, corporations, and labor unions to collect and distribute campaign contributions to candidates likely to support their causes. PACs have grown in number and in size over the years and have become a dominant force in national political campaigns.

appeal because they discuss issues affecting large segments of the population. Common Cause, for example, is concerned with the rights of all citizens and attracts members from all segments of society. Similarly, Ralph Nader's Public Citizen, Inc., works on behalf of all consumers.

Other interest groups have a more concentrated appeal. The American Association of Retired Persons (AARP) works on behalf of the elderly and is a vocal supporter of Medicare and Medicaid legislation and ◆ age-discrimination laws. In the United States, interest groups represent diverse ethnic and minority groups, labor unions, farmers, and businesspeople. Some interest groups, such as those that represent labor unions and the elderly, have millions of members and have considerable influence because of the money and votes under their control. Such influence makes interest groups powerful political and economic forces in a democratic society.

Most interest groups place their concerns in the hands of a lobbyist. A **lobbyist** is a person who is hired by an interest group to express the group's point of view to policymakers. Lobbying groups affect government policies at all levels of government, and large-sized interest groups such as the real estate industry and the medical profession employ many lobbyists.

Lobbyists exert pressure on elected officials mainly through the allocation of political campaign contributions. Candidates can expect the support of the interest group only so long as they support the group's position on key issues. Often interest groups are able to exert their influence in situations where individuals acting singly would have little effect.

See Suggested Assignments, p. TM 41.

◆ Class activity: Have the students research the current impact of "Farm Aid" versus government subsidies (private solutions versus government solutions).

Section 3 Review

See Answers, p. A 36.

DEFINE interest group, lobbyist

IDENTIFY Political Action Committee

1. **Summarizing Ideas** How can **(a)** individuals and **(b)** interest groups help determine economic policies?
2. **Analyzing Ideas** **(a)** List the six economic goals that serve as the criteria for evaluating government policies. **(b)** Which economic goals seemed most important during the mid-1960s? Explain. **(c)** Which economic goals seemed most important during the mid-1980s? Explain. **(d)** Which economic goals were probably most important in 1776? Explain.

CHAPTER 8 SUMMARY

In the twentieth century, government on all levels has grown in size and complexity due to a variety of factors. Government's rapid growth makes it the nation's largest employer and largest business.

Government involvement in the United States economy has gone from the laissez-faire policy of the early years to the considerable regulation of today. By regulating business and protecting individuals, providing public goods, promoting economic well-being, and stabilizing the economy, government helps promote the general welfare of all Americans. Despite fears by some Americans that government tampering with the free enterprise system would be harmful, most government policies and programs have met with success.

In the free enterprise environment of a representative democracy such as the United States, individuals and groups can influence government economic policies. They do this by exercising their right to vote. Individuals can ensure the election of representatives who will enact acceptable economic policies. Interest groups, through campaign contributions, block voting of their members, and the help of lobbyists can influence both the election and policymaking of public officials. Because of these opportunities to influence the policymakers, economic programs and policies generally reflect the opinions of a majority of the nation's voters.

CHAPTER 8 REVIEW

For Answers to Chapter 8 Review, see p. A 36.

Reviewing Economic Terms

With each definition or description below, match one of the following terms.

a. monetary policy	**e.** public good
b. business cycle	**f.** privatization
c. interest group	**g.** fiscal policy
d. transfer payment	**h.** market failure

_____ **1.** Sale of government property or the relinquishment of government services to private businesses.

_____ **2.** Sequential rise and fall of the economy.

_____ **3.** Program formulated by the Federal Reserve's Board of Governors to control the nation's money supply and credit.

_____ **4.** Good or service provided for everyone by the government.

_____ **5.** Program formulated by Congress and the President to stabilize the business cycle and reduce unemployment by the use of federal taxing and spending powers.

_____ **6.** Organization of citizens with common interests and goals.

_____ **7.** Tax money collected by government and redistributed to groups such as the poor, the elderly, and the ill.

Exercising Economic Skills

1. **Interpreting News Articles** Reread the excerpt from the news article on page 177 and answer the following questions. **(a)** Who does the author feel should have the responsibility for controlling federal spending? **(b)** Who was given this responsibility under the Gramm-Rudman Act? **(c)** Why, according to the author, does the Gramm-Rudman Act erode representative democracy? **(d)** Is the author optimistic that Congress will hit the deficit target? Why or why not?
2. **Understanding Contract Obligations** Study the feature on pages 519–520. Then draw up a sample contract for work you would consider doing for a fee, such as babysitting, washing cars, or cutting grass. Be sure that your contract meets all the basic contract criteria.

Thinking Critically About Economics

1. **Comprehending Ideas** **(a)** What are the government's roles in the United States economy? **(b)** What actions does the government take in each of its economic roles?
2. **Summarizing Ideas** **(a)** What factors have caused the growth of government? **(b)** Describe the growth in government size and in government spending. **(c)** In what ways can citizens influence government economic policies?
3. **Comparing Ideas** **(a)** Compare the government's use of fiscal policy, monetary policy, and price controls to stabilize the economy. **(b)** Which one achieves stabilization most effectively?
4. **Analyzing Ideas** **(a)** What are the advantages and disadvantages of privatization? **(b)** How much did the Grace Commission say the federal government could save through privatization? **(c)** How does privatization affect economic efficiency?
5. **Evaluating Viewpoints** Defend or refute this statement: Increased privatization promotes economic freedom.

Extending Economic Knowledge

1. Select a state or local public service such as the school district, police or fire department, library system, road maintenance department, park service, or postal service. Answer the following questions about the public service you have selected. **(a)** What are the benefits to the public? **(b)** What are the annual financial costs? **(c)** Are there any other costs? If so, what are they? **(d)** In your opinion, is the public service worth the costs? Explain.
2. Interview three local businesspeople about the effects of government regulation on their businesses. Find out from each person the effect that government regulations have on his or her business operations.
3. Transfer payments are a controversial economic activity of the government. Research the topic and prepare a position paper in which you support or oppose transfer payments.

Using Primary Sources

John Kenneth Galbraith (1908–) is a controversial American economist. In *American Capitalism: The Concept of Countervailing Power* (1956), Galbraith supported an expanded role for government in the economy. He argued that power blocs, such as "big government" and labor unions, were needed to balance the power of big business. He coined the term "countervailing power" to describe these power blocs. As you read the following excerpts, consider how the government serves as a countervailing power in the American economy. How has this role expanded the size of government since the 1930s?

Big Government and Countervailing Power

There are strong incentives in the modern economy for developing countervailing power. . . . [The] group that seeks countervailing power is, initially, a numerous and disadvantaged group which seeks organization because it faces, in its market, a much smaller and much more advantaged group. . . .

Labor sought and received it in the protection and assistance which the Wagner Act provided to union organization. Farmers sought and received it in the form of federal price supports to their markets. . . . Unorganized workers have sought and received it in the form of minimum wage legislation. . . .

The groups that sought the assistance of government in building countervailing power sought that power in order to use it against market authority [monopolists and big business] to which they had previously been subordinate. . . .

As noted, farmers, workers and numerous other groups have sought and received government assistance, either in the form of direct support to their market power or in support to organization which in turn made market power possible. In short, the government has subsidized with its own power the countervailing power of workers, farmers, and others. . . . This assistance, clearly, explains some part of the self-confidence and well-being which these groups display today.

Yet few courses of policy have ever been undertaken more grudgingly and with a greater sense of guilt. . . .

The principal reason for this sense of guilt, no doubt, is that the notion of a government subsidy of its power to groups seeking to develop countervailing power has never enjoyed a place in the accredited structure of American economic and political science. Accordingly the unfinished tasks of developing such power have never had a place on the reformer's calendar. The reformer, in fact, has almost invariably been overtaken by the action. When the groups in question have developed enough influence to obtain government assistance on their own behalf they have simply gone ahead and got it without blessing or benefit of doctrine. As the role of countervailing power comes to be understood, we can expect that much of the anxiety that is evoked by government support to the process will disappear.

Source Review

For Answers to Source Review, see p. A 37.

1. What is the concept of countervailing power?
2. According to John Kenneth Galbraith, which groups in society are most in need of the government's countervailing power? How have American workers benefitted from the countervailing power of the government? How does the government help groups in the private sector develop their own countervailing power?
3. According to Galbraith, how has countervailing power increased the size and role of government in the economy? Why does he favor "big government"? Why have reformers avoided groups seeking to develop countervailing power?

CHAPTER 9

See Chapter Overview, p. TM 42.
See Chapter Objectives, p. TM 42.
See Introducing the Chapter, p. TM 42.
See Extending Economic Knowledge on text p. 214.

Financing in the Public Sector

Finance is the art of passing currency from hand to hand until it finally disappears.

Robert W. Sarnoff

1 The government levies taxes on the people to raise revenue.

- The Role of Taxes
- Types of Taxes
- Fairness in Taxation

2 All levels of government raise revenues through taxation.

- Federal Taxes
- State and Local Taxes
- The Tax Burden in the United States

3 Formulating a federal budget requires trade-offs.

- The Creation of a Federal Budget
- Trade-offs

4 Federal budget deficits serve to increase the national debt.

- Federal Budget Deficits
- The National Debt
- Balancing the Federal Budget

CHAPTER 9 STUDY GUIDE

Chapter Focus

Chapter 9 considers how federal, state, and local governments raise revenues through taxation. The three types of taxation in the United States economy are progressive taxes, proportional taxes, and regressive taxes. The chapter discusses the importance of the federal budget, the problem of the federal deficit, and government financing of needed programs.

As you study the chapter, look for the details that support each of the following statements.

1. The government levies taxes on the people to raise revenue.
2. All levels of government raise revenues through taxation.
3. Formulating a federal budget requires trade-offs.
4. Federal budget deficits serve to increase the national debt.

See Preteaching Vocabulary, p. TM 42.

Terms to Know

The following terms, while not the only terms emphasized in this chapter, are basic to your understanding of financing in the public sector. Determine the meaning of each term, either by using the Glossary or by watching for context clues as you read the chapter.

progressive tax
proportional tax
regressive tax
ability-to-pay principle
benefits-received principle
individual income tax
corporate income tax
excise tax
estate tax
property tax
budget deficit
budget surplus
deficit spending
national debt

See Key Study Questions and Key Understandings, p. TM 43.

1 The government levies taxes on the people to raise revenue.

See Suggested Teaching Strategies, p. TM 43.

Governments throughout history have levied taxes on people. **Taxes** are mandatory payments that individuals and firms make to the government to cover the costs of public goods and services.

The Role of Taxes

In the United States, taxes have two important roles. ◆ The government collects tax revenues to finance its operations and functions. Taxes pay for the following functions of government: regulation, providing public goods, and redistribution.

The government also levies taxes to influence the economic behavior of individuals and firms. Many taxes influence consumer behavior. The federal and state governments, for example, place excise taxes on some commodities such as tobacco, alcohol, and gasoline. The purposes of excise taxes are to raise revenue for the government, discourage the use of goods such as tobacco and alcohol, and ration goods during wars and other national emergencies. Excise taxes also raise the prices of some goods. The increased prices serve to restrict consumption of these goods because of the law of demand.

On a larger scale, the federal government affects the buying behavior of all consumers through its taxation policies. For example, by increasing the federal income tax, the government reduces the disposable income consumers have available. Less disposable income, in turn, means lower demand for goods and services.

The economic behavior of firms is also influenced by taxes. For example, state and local governments encourage firms to relocate in their areas by offering low property taxes and other tax breaks as incentives. Some Sun Belt states have successfully used tax incentives to attract industries from other parts of the country. Other tax incentives encourage plants to relocate in depressed sections of cities, to increase the purchase of new capital, or to step up the research and development of new products.

◆ Before the passage of the Seventeenth Amendment in 1913, which provided for the direct election of United States senators, members of the House of Representatives were the only elected Congressional officials. This is why the Constitution specifies that all revenue bills must originate in the House.

The Regressive Effect of State Sales Taxes

	Annual Income	Amount of Taxable Goods Purchased	Sales Tax in State A	Total Sales Tax Paid to State A	Total Sales Tax Payment as a Percentage of Total Income
Wage Earner 1 (low-income)	$10,000	$5,000	5%	$250 (.05 × $5,000 = $250)	2.5% ($250 ÷ $10,000 = .025, or 2.5%)
Wage Earner 2 (high-income)	$50,000	$15,000	5%	$750 (.05 × $15,000 = $750)	1.5% ($750 ÷ $50,000 = .015, or 1.5%)

Types of Taxes

The three types of taxes in the United States economy are progressive taxes, proportional taxes, and regressive taxes. Each tax affects the taxpayer in a different way.

Progressive Taxes. A **progressive tax** is a type of tax that takes a larger percentage of income from a high-income person than from a low-income person. The most important progressive tax in the United States is the federal income tax.

Under current income-tax laws, there are different tax rates and different tax brackets for people with different levels of income. The **tax rate** is the percentage of a person's income that is taken by the government.

A tax bracket is expressed as a percentage of taxable income. Under the 1986 tax reform, the lowest tax bracket for 1987 carries an 11 percent rate, with a taxable income of $3,000 or less. The highest tax bracket carries a 38.5 percent rate with a taxable income that ranges from $45,000 to $90,000. The four main categories of taxpayers are single persons; married, filing separately; heads of households; and married, filing joint returns.

Proportional Taxes. Some states have proportional income taxes, also called "flat-rate income taxes." A **proportional tax** takes the same percentage of income from individuals at all income levels.

To illustrate how this type of tax affects taxpayers, consider the following example. Suppose a state has a 5 percent proportional income tax. A person earning $100,000 per year pays $5,000 in taxes (.05 × $100,000 = $5,000). A second person earning $10,000 per year, on the other hand, pays $500 ◆ (.05 × $10,000 = $500).

Regressive Taxes. A **regressive tax** is a type of tax that takes a larger percentage of income from low-income groups than from high-income groups. State sales taxes are one kind of regressive tax. A **sales tax** is a tax levied on the sale of some goods or services. Forty-five states and the District of Columbia have sales taxes that range from 3 percent to 7.5 percent. In addition, many cities such as Chicago, Dallas, Los Angeles, New Orleans, and New York City have city sales taxes.

To show the impact of a sales tax on high-income and low-income households, consider the example in the table on this page, which assumes the following circumstances.

1. Wage Earner 1 has an annual income of $10,000, and buys $5,000 worth of taxable goods each year.
2. Wage Earner 2 has an annual income of $50,000, and buys $15,000 worth of taxable goods each year.
3. Both wage earners live in State A, which has a 5 percent sales tax.

Under these circumstances, Wage Earner 1 pays $250 in sales taxes, which is $500 less than Wage Earner 2, who pays $750 in sales taxes ($750 − $250 = $500). Yet the $250 paid by Wage Earner 1 represents 2.5 percent of his or her total income, compared with just 1.5 percent for Wage Earner 2.

◆ **Report topic: Lower-income families and the fairness of proportional taxes.**

The basic reason for the disparity in amounts is that high-income households save and invest more of their money than low-income households. The money that is saved or invested is not subject to sales taxes. Wage Earner 2 needed $15,000, which is less than one third of the earner's total income, to meet his or her needs. Wage Earner 1, on the other hand, needed $5,000, which is one half of his or her income, to buy goods subject to sales taxes.

Fairness in Taxation

What is a "fair" tax? To a large extent, the concept of tax fairness depends on individual economic values. Two principles of taxation have traditionally been used to judge fairness in taxation: the ability-to-pay principle and the benefits-received principle.

Ability-to-Pay Principle. One criterion of tax fairness is the **ability-to-pay principle.** Under the ability-to-pay principle of taxation, people with more income or wealth should pay more in taxes. Those with lesser income or wealth should pay lesser amounts in taxes.

Economists distinguish between "ability-to-pay based on income" and "ability-to-pay based on wealth." Ability-to-pay based on income means that people who have more income—from wages or salaries, interest or dividend payments, rents, or other payments—should pay more in taxes. Ability-to-pay based on wealth, on the other hand, means that people who have more personal assets—houses or other real estate, stocks or bonds, savings accounts, and consumer durables—should pay more in taxes.

The federal income tax derives from the ability-to-pay based on income principle of taxation because the federal income tax is a progressive tax. Federal inheritance taxes and estate taxes, on the other hand, tax wealth that has been acquired during a person's lifetime. These taxes are based on the ability-to-pay based on wealth principle.

Supporters of the ability-to-pay criterion argue that it is fair because the heaviest tax burden falls on those people who can most afford to pay. Critics of the ability-to-pay principle counter that high taxes reduce people's economic incentives.

Benefits-Received Principle. The benefits-received principle is the other criterion of tax fairness. The **benefits-received principle** states that people who benefit directly from certain public goods and services should pay for them.

The excise tax on gasoline is the classic example of a tax based on the benefits-received principle. The government uses revenues from the excise tax on gasoline to build and maintain highways, bridges, and mass transit systems. Only people who drive on the highways, and who obviously must buy gasoline to do so, pay the tax.

The benefits-received criterion for tax fairness, like the ability-to-pay criterion, has its supporters and critics. Supporters argue that the benefits-received principle is fair because it resembles the transactions that take place in the marketplace. In other words, people are able to choose which government goods to use and to pay for. In addition, supporters note that the benefits-received principle increases government efficiency by encouraging the government to produce reasonably priced public goods that are in high demand.

Critics of the benefits-received criterion point to its limitations. First, critics note that it is impossible to determine an exact per-capita cost for many public goods such as national defense or local fire protection. Second, the people who receive the most benefits from public goods and services are least able to pay for them.

Most people consider the tax system of the United States to be fair, because some taxes are based on the ability-to-pay principle and others are based on the benefits-received principle. ◆

See Suggested Assignments, p. TM 43.

Section 1 Review See Answers, p. A 38.

DEFINE tax, tax rate, sales tax, ability-to-pay principle, benefits-received principle

1. **Comprehending Ideas** **(a)** What roles do taxes have in the United States? **(b)** How do taxes influence economic behavior?
2. **Summarizing Ideas** Describe the three types of taxes in the United States and give an example of each type.
3. **Interpreting Ideas** Explain why a sales tax is actually a regressive tax.
4. **Evaluating Ideas** Which of the principles of taxation is the fairer to United States taxpayers?

◆ Have the students read "Tax Auditors" on page 544 of *Careers in the Marketplace.*

See Key Study Questions and Key Understandings, p. TM 44.

2 All levels of government raise revenues through taxation.

See Suggested Teaching Strategies, p. TM 44.

As the role of government has expanded during the ◆ twentieth century, so has the cost of government. The bulk of these costs are paid for with tax revenues. The remainder are financed through borrowing like the sale of government bonds and other securities to the public. The graph below shows how tax receipts have risen from 1945 to 1985.

Both federal and state dollars go into the provision of such public services as waste-water treatment and pollution control.

Federal Taxes

Federal taxes raise revenues to support the federal government in its roles of regulation, providing public goods, and redistribution. The three major types

Total Tax Receipts, 1945–1985

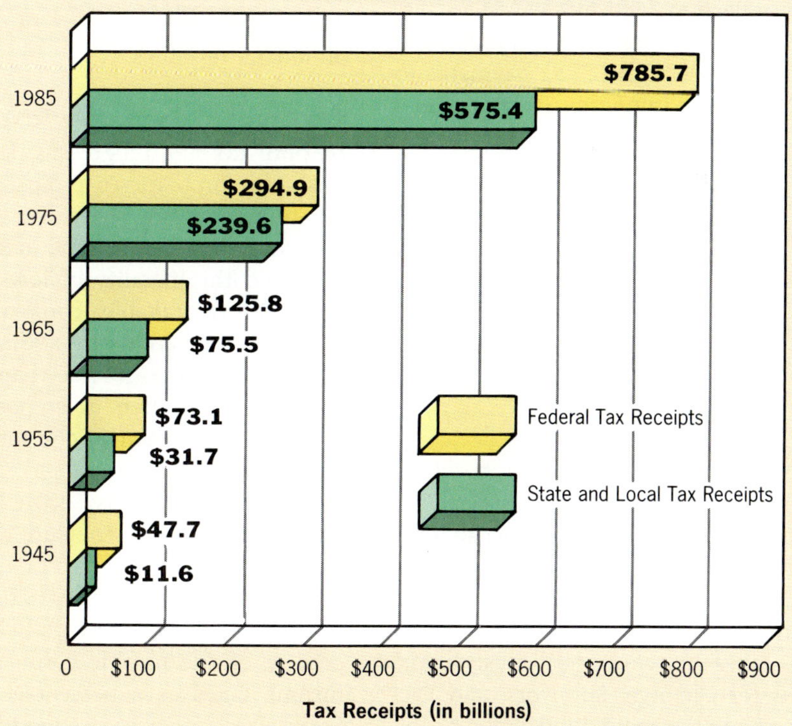

Source: *Economic Report of the President, 1986*

◆ Discussion topic: The connection between government expansion and twentieth-century wars. (During wars government expenditures exceed tax revenues. The government borrows to finance the war. As a result, the national debt increases dramatically. During this century, the nation has fought World War I, World War II, in Korea, and in Vietnam.)

of federal taxes are individual income taxes, corporate income taxes, and Social Security taxes.

The bar graphs and pie charts on page 199 compare the sources of federal government revenues in 1970 and 1985. Revenues from the three taxes represented 90 percent of all federal tax receipts in 1985. The remaining 10 percent of federal receipts came from other taxes, including excise taxes, estate and gift taxes, and customs duties.

Individual Income Taxes. The **individual income tax** is a tax on an individual's income, including wages or salaries, interest, dividends, and tips. Beginning in 1984, a portion of Social Security payments was also included in taxable income. The individual income tax is a progressive tax based on the ability-to-pay principle of taxation. Tax rates for 1987 range from a low of 11 percent to a high of 38.5 percent. Close to half of all federal revenues come from the individual income tax.

Wage earners pay individual income taxes through a payroll withholding system. Employers deduct tax money from employees' paychecks and forward it to the Internal Revenue Service (IRS). The IRS is the branch of the Treasury Department responsible for tax collection. The pay-as-you-go system of tax collection also applies to self-employed workers who pay regular estimated tax payments to the IRS. **Estimated tax payments** are approximations of what is owed to the government. All individual income tax returns for each calendar year must be filed with the IRS by April 15 of the following year. **Tax returns** list a person's income and any payments or refunds that are due.

The pay-as-you-go system of collection eases the payment of taxes for wage earners. It also provides a regular flow of revenues to the Treasury, thus reducing the government's need to borrow money.

Social Security Taxes. The letters FICA, which are seen on payroll check stubs, stand for the Federal Insurance Contribution Act. It is this act that set out the procedures for paying **Social Security taxes.** Like federal income taxes, FICA taxes are withheld by employers and sent to the government, which places the FICA taxes in two special trust funds. One trust fund is for Old Age, Survivors, and Disability Insurance. The other trust fund is for hospitalization insurance under Medicare. Each trust fund provides assistance to people eligible for Social Security benefits.

FICA taxes are both proportional and regressive. The FICA tax is proportional because it takes a set percentage of an employee's wages. In 1986, the first $42,000 in wages were taxed at a uniform 7.15 percent, a sum matched by the employer. The FICA tax is 12.3 percent for self-employed people. Up to this point, FICA taxes are proportional because the same percentage applies to everyone's income.

FICA taxes become regressive beyond $42,000 because that amount is the maximum amount of wages subject to FICA taxes. The maximum FICA payment, therefore, is $3,003 (.0715 × $42,000 = $3,003). This maximum FICA tax applies to a worker who earns $42,000 as well as to a worker who earns $200,000 per year. FICA taxes are regressive because a larger percentage is taken out of a lower salary, while a smaller percentage is taken out of a higher salary. For the $42,000 income, the percentage is 7.15. For the higher income, the percentage is just 1.5.

FICA taxes are the second largest and the fastest-growing source of revenue for the federal government. By 1985, FICA taxes represented 36 percent of the government's receipts, a 50-percent jump from 1970, when they accounted for about 23 percent of all federal revenues.

Corporate Income Taxes. The **corporate income tax** is a progressive federal tax levied on a business corporation's profits. Historically, the corporate income tax was never as steeply progressive as the individual income tax. In 1984, Congress corrected the inequity of low-tax rates on the first $100,000 of taxable corporate income of large, wealthy corporations by adding a 5 percent tax on corporate income greater than $1 million but less than $1.405 million. A corporation with a taxable income greater than $1.405 million pays a tax of 46 percent.

Many corporations, however, pay taxes at reduced rates because they are eligible for tax breaks, such as those designed to promote plant modernization and expansion. Corporations may also deduct for charitable contributions, which are limited to 10 percent of the taxable corporate income. Corporate income taxes as a percentage of Internal Revenue Service receipts have declined from about 17 percent in 1970 to 8.5 percent in 1985.

Comparison of Tax Receipts of the Federal Government, 1970 and 1985

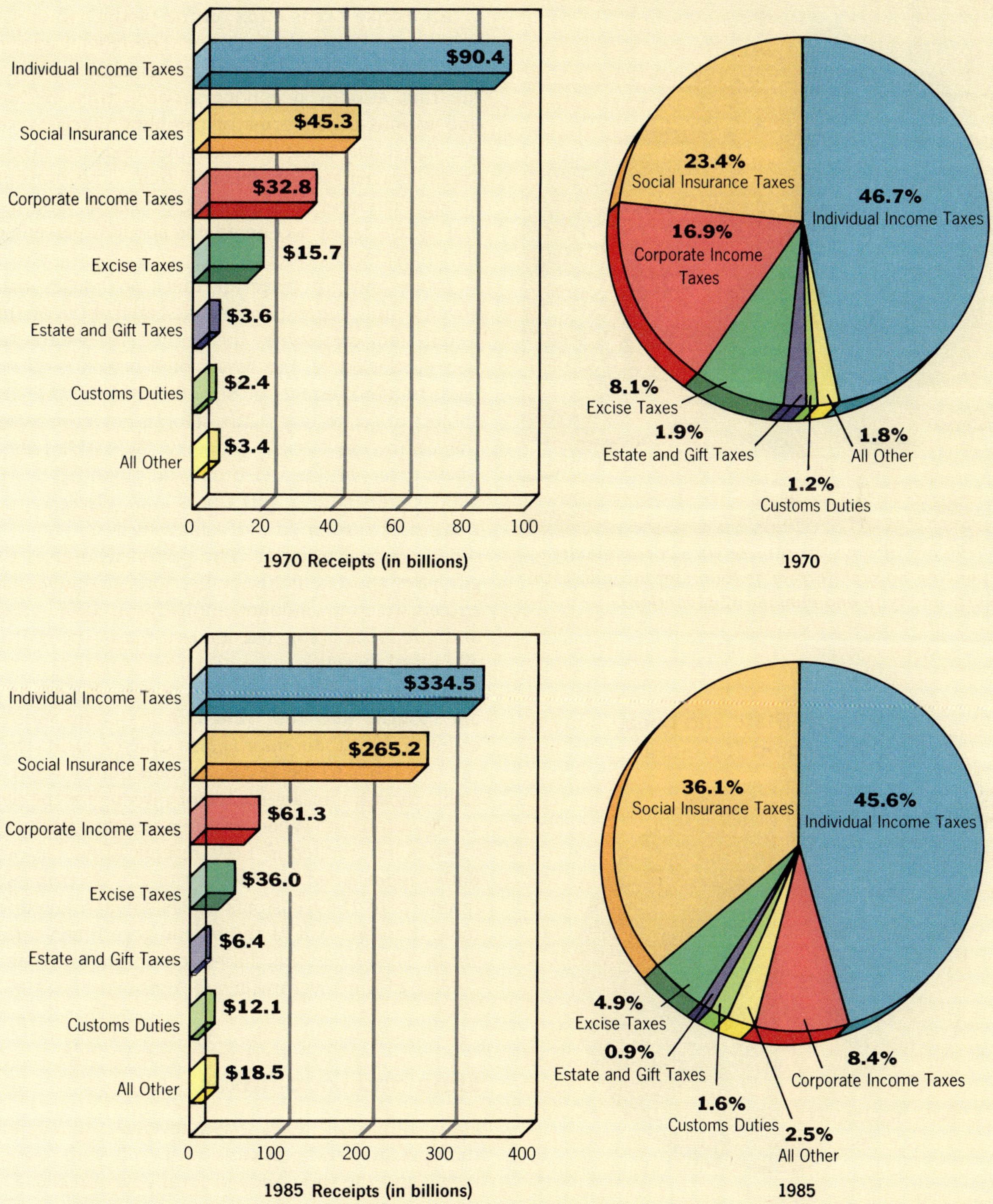

Sources: *Economic Report of the President, 1986*
The Statistical History of the United States

Individuals' income-tax returns vary in complexity depending on such factors as source of income, total assets, and type and number of deductions.

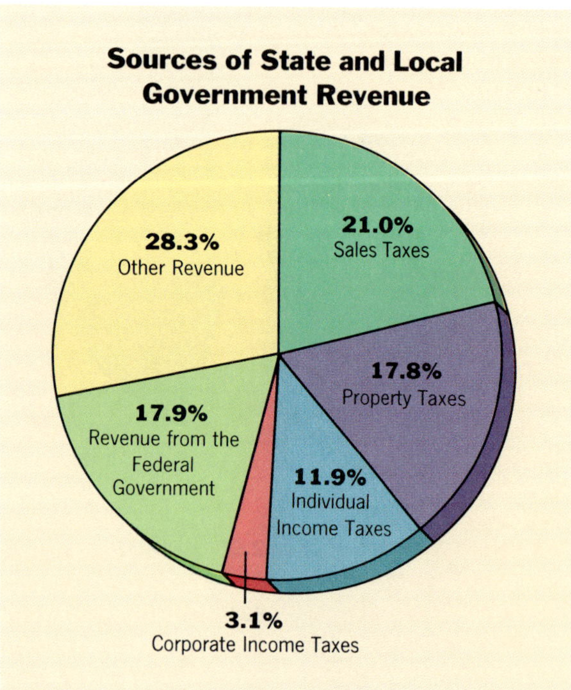

Other Taxes and Revenues. Excise taxes, estate and gift taxes, and customs duties represent another 10 percent of all federal revenues.

An **excise tax** is a tax on the production or sale of a particular good or service. The federal government places excise taxes on gasoline, tobacco, firearms, alcohol, telephone services, tires, betting, and various other forms of gambling. Excise taxes are regressive taxes because they tend to take a larger percentage of income from lower-income groups than from higher-income groups. In 1985, federal excise taxes accounted for about 5 percent of the government's revenues.

Estate and gift taxes are taxes on houses, cars, jewelry, and other personal assets that are transferred from one owner to another. An **estate tax** is a tax levied on the assets of a person who has died. In 1986, estates of $500,000 or less were not subject to estate taxes. Tax reform, however, raised the ceiling on taxable property. By 1987, federal estate taxes will be levied only on properties worth $600,000 or more. A **gift tax** is a tax placed on the transfer of certain gifts of value, such as money or other personal property. The person who gives the gift pays the tax if his or her gifts to individuals exceed a certain amount annually. In 1985, estate and gift taxes accounted for less than 1 percent of all federal revenues.

A **customs duty** is a tax on imported goods that are brought into the United States from another country. A customs duty is also called a tariff. From the late 1700s to the 1890s, customs duties were the single most important source of revenue for the federal government. When President George Washington was inaugurated in 1789, revenues from customs duties represented 99.5 percent of the government's revenues. In 1889, customs duties still accounted for more than one half of the federal government's revenues. Today, customs duties account for less than 2 percent of the government's receipts. ◆

State and Local Taxes

State and local taxes raise revenues to support the operation and programs of the 50 state governments and the thousands of local governments. The three most important state and local taxes are sales taxes, property taxes, and individual income taxes. The graph to the left shows that the revenues

◆ **Have the students read "Customs Inspectors" on page 541 of *Careers in the Marketplace.***

In addition to the national office, the IRS operates 10 regional offices, such as this one in Chicago, and 60 district offices.

generated from these three taxes comprise about one half of all receipts by state and local governments. Another significant source of state and local revenue—close to $100 million—is money provided by the federal government through grants-in-aid. A federal **grant-in-aid** is a transfer payment from the federal government to state or local governments.

Sales Taxes. A sales tax is a regressive tax levied on certain goods and services by state or local governments. It is a regressive tax because it takes a larger portion of income from low-income groups than from high-income groups. Some states that have sales taxes do not tax food, medicine, children's clothing, or other necessities. These exemptions soften the economic burden of sales taxes on low- and moderate-income groups. Sales taxes may be deducted from federal income taxes, but excise taxes may not. Alaska, Delaware, Montana, New Hampshire, and Oregon do not have sales taxes.

Property Taxes. Individuals and firms pay a tax called a **property tax** on their assets. Most property taxes are levied on houses, factory buildings, condominiums, the land on which they are built, and undeveloped real estate holdings. Some states tax personal property such as household furnishings, boats, and jewelry. Each of the 50 states has a different definition of "property" and each determines which types of property it will tax.

Local governments rely on property taxes to finance education, police and fire protection, and sanitation. More than 80 percent of local government revenue comes from property taxes.

The property tax is a controversial tax, despite its use by state and local governments to meet local needs. Property taxes are controversial because they do not take into account a person's income. For example, consider a retired couple. The couple lives on a fixed income. But they own a three-bedroom home on a large lot. The retired couple would very

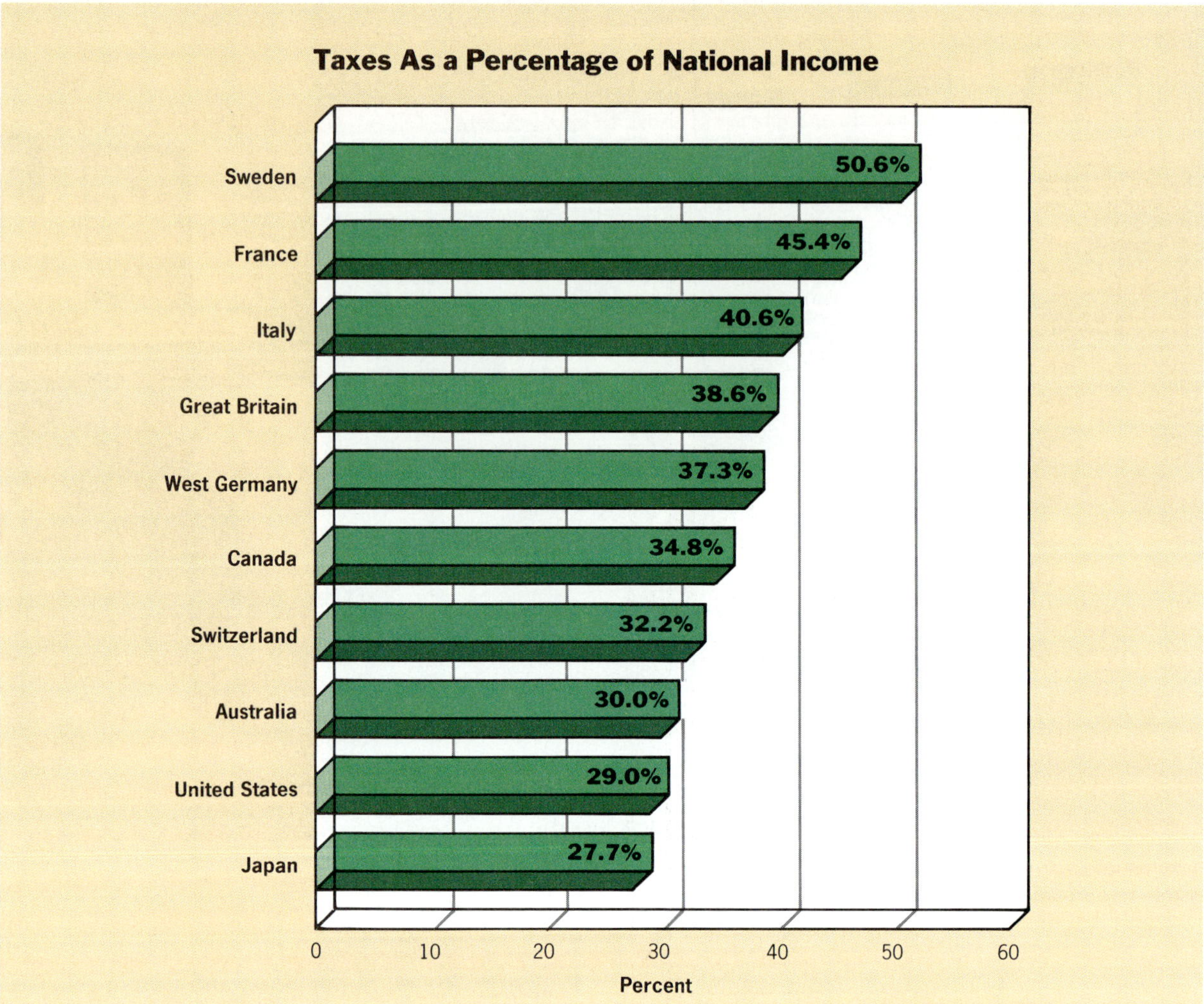

Source: Organization for Economic Cooperation and Development (OECD)

likely pay more in property taxes than a high-income couple living in a condominium apartment. Property owners incur a "penalty" because they own real or personal property.

Another limitation of property taxes is that tax assessors find it difficult to judge the true value of many properties. The taxes levied on two similar properties may vary a great deal depending on who conducted the assessment.

Critics of a reliance on local property taxes to provide public goods and services also point to the resulting inequalities. Local governments that are able to collect enough property taxes can provide quality education, recreation facilities, police and fire protection, and other services. Towns and cities that are unable to raise enough money through property taxes, however, sometimes provide inadequate public goods and services.

Individual Income Taxes. In addition to the federal government, some states and a few cities tax ◆ individual income taxes. States use either the "graduated income tax" or the "flat-rate income tax" to calculate a person's income tax. Like the federal income tax, the graduated income tax is a progressive tax. The higher the person's income, the higher the tax rate is. The flat-rate income tax, on the other hand, is a proportional tax.

◆ **All states except Florida, Nevada, South Dakota, Texas, Washington, and Wyoming have income taxes. Connecticut taxes only dividend and interest income. Florida has an intangible property tax that taxes income from stocks and bonds.**

The Tax Burden in the United States

Federal, state, and local governments take in taxes about 29 cents of every dollar earned in the United States. Compared to the taxes levied by other highly industrialized capitalist nations on their taxpayers, the tax burden on Americans is relatively low. The graph on page 202 compares the tax burdens of taxpayers in the 10 leading industrialized nations. Americans pay less in personal income taxes, Social Security taxes, corporation taxes, and sales and excise taxes than citizens in most other countries. Americans pay more in property taxes, however, than citizens elsewhere.

Personal and business tax breaks built into the tax system help explain the relatively low tax payments in the United States. **Tax breaks** are deductions that people are allowed to subtract from their gross income. Tax breaks are sometimes called tax loopholes.

Personal tax breaks include tax deductions for state and local taxes, mortgage interest payments, sales taxes, charitable contributions, and Social Security benefits. Business tax breaks include deductions for depreciation, the purchase of new capital, and research and development costs. Tax breaks cost the federal government about $400 billion in lost revenue in 1986. ◆

See Suggested Assignments, p. TM 44.

Section 2 Review See Answers, p. A 38.

DEFINE excise tax, estate tax, gift tax, customs duty, grant-in-aid, property tax, tax break

1. **Summarizing Ideas** **(a)** What are the three major types of federal taxes? **(b)** On what is individual income tax levied? **(c)** On what is corporate income tax levied?
2. **Analyzing Ideas** Explain why the Social Security tax is proportional and regressive.
3. **Interpreting Graphics** Study the graphs on page 199. **(a)** In dollars, what was the change in tax receipts from individual income taxes between 1970 and 1985? **(b)** In percentage of federal tax receipts, what was the change in receipts from individual income taxes during the same period? **(c)** State a conclusion that you can draw from these two statistics.

See Key Study Questions and Key Understandings, p. TM 45.

3 Formulating a federal budget requires trade-offs.

See Suggested Teaching Strategies, p. TM 45.

A **federal budget** is the federal government's plan for the use of government revenues. The budget plans expenditures, estimates government revenues, and projects deficits. In the process of determining the best uses of its resources, federal decision makers consider the trade-offs of their decisions. State and local governments formulate budgets in a similar manner. The current budgetary process has evolved over the past 200 years.

The Creation of a Federal Budget

Until 1921, the United States had no formal process for planning future revenues and expenditures. The various federal departments simply made requests for funds as moneys were needed. Government revenues, derived mainly from customs duties, usually were sufficient to meet the monetary needs of the government departments. From the mid-1800s to the early 1900s, increased wartime spending, political

The federal budget must include money for new projects such as this dam in Bonneville, Oregon.

◆ Under the Tax Reform Law of 1986, fewer tax deductions are allowed.

and financial corruption, and the spirit of Progressive reform worked to change the haphazard allocation of federal funds.

Federal spending for all programs was just $63 million in 1860, the year before the outbreak of the Civil War. By 1865, the final year of the war, federal spending had jumped to $1 billion—16 times the 1860 level. World War I caused a further expansion of federal spending. The increased spending required a more formal process for planning future revenues and expenditures.

The need to check political and financial corruption was a second factor favoring the creation of a federal budget. The bribery of public officials by those seeking government contracts or other favors occurred frequently. People believed that a federal budget would make the collection and spending of government revenues more systematic. They also believed it would cut down on financial and political corruption.

Third, the federal budget became a part of the general spirit of reform during the Progressive Era (1900–1920). Progressives like President Theodore Roosevelt believed that centralized decision making would permit federal resources to be used in a more efficient and fair manner.

In response to these forces, Congress passed the Budget and Accounting Bill in 1921. Under this legislation, the President was empowered to formulate and present an annual federal budget for Congressional action. The Office of Management and Budget (OMB), a part of the executive branch, was charged with devising the President's budget proposal.

Further budgetary reforms passed in 1974 established an orderly, but complex, process that the executive and legislative branches of the federal government must follow when devising a budget. The Congressional Budget Office (CBO), created in 1974, and the Budget Committees in the House of Representatives and the Senate review the budget proposals. These Congressional groups analyze spending priorities and how revenues will be raised, and make reports to the House and Senate.

Trade-offs

Congress and the President are forced to make trade-offs when devising a federal budget because scarcities of resources, especially money, restrict the number of programs that the government can afford to fund.

In committee hearings such as this one, the House and Senate receive information about which trade-offs to choose in balancing the federal budget.

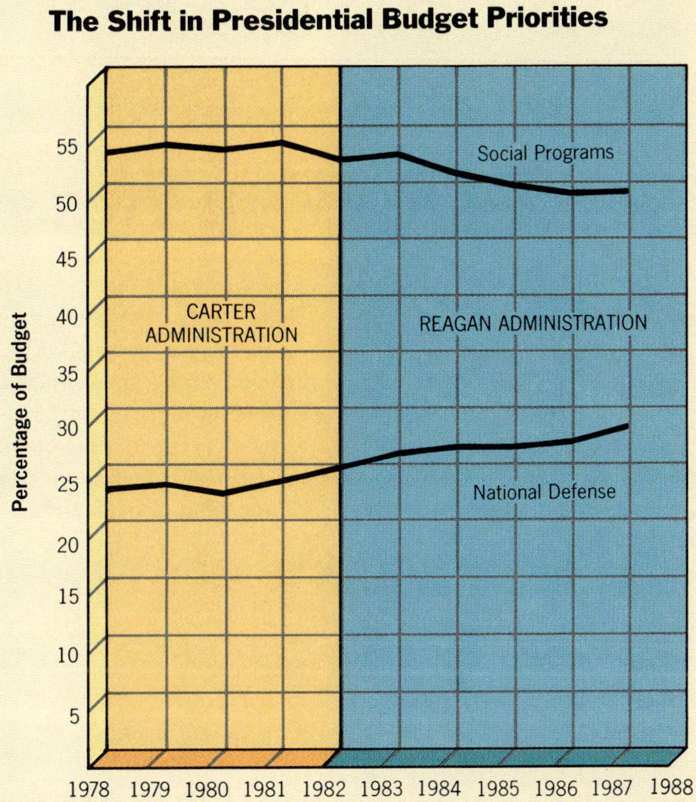

Source: *Economic Report of the President, 1986*

The decisions that Congress and the President make have a cost. While some programs gain funding, others receive cuts in funding or are dropped completely from the budget. The programs that are cut or dropped represent the opportunity costs of the public decision-making process. As alternative uses of the nation's money, these cut or dropped programs are traded-off to finance the programs that are kept and fully funded.

Major debates on the federal budget tend to concentrate on spending for defense programs over spending for social programs, sometimes referred to as the debate over "guns or butter." The graph on this page illustrates the increase in the percentage of the federal budget devoted to defense and the decline in the percentage devoted to social programs from 1978 to 1987.

Section 3 Review

See Answers, p. A 39.

DEFINE federal budget

1. **Summarizing Ideas** **(a)** What factors between the mid-1800s and early 1900s created a need for a federal budget? **(b)** How did each factor lead to the creation of the federal budget? **(c)** How do the President and Congress interact to create a budget?
2. **Interpreting Graphics** Study the graph on this page. **(a)** How did the percentage of the federal budget allocated to social programs change from its high point to its low point? **(b)** What was the change in the percentage allocated for defense from its low point to its high point?

See Suggested Assignments, p. TM 45.

Determining Fallacies in Reasoning

Students of economics are often called upon to analyze and evaluate economic statements and viewpoints. To do this, it is necessary to recognize fallacies in reasoning. A fallacy in reasoning is either an unsound and unsupported argument, or an erroneous conclusion. Refer to the following list of fallacies, which are categorized under the headings cause-effect fallacies and fallacies of proof.

CAUSE–EFFECT FALLACIES

Some errors in reasoning occur in determining cause-effect relationships. The three most common cause-effect fallacies are as follows.

- Single-Cause Fallacy—identifying only one cause for a major event. For example, the statement "interest payment on the national debt caused record-breaking federal budget deficits during the 1980s" contains a single-cause fallacy. Several factors, such as increased federal spending for national defense and for social programs, contributed to the $200 billion deficit.

  The single-cause fallacy should not be confused with accurate statements about the main causes of economic actions, behaviors, events, or conditions. An economist who writes about a "major cause" or "the main cause" of an event is ranking causes by importance. The economist, however, is not attributing the event to one cause and excluding other possible explanations or causes.

- Correlation-as-Cause Fallacy—identifying an event that occurs at the same time as another event as the cause of the event. The following statements illustrate the correlation-as-cause fallacy. "Federal budgetary deficits occurred during the Presidential administrations of Franklin D. Roosevelt, Harry Truman, and Jimmy Carter. All three of these Presidents were Democrats. Therefore, Democrats cause budget deficits." The occurrence of budget deficits during the administrations of these three Democratic Presidents does not mean Democrats cause deficits. In fact, budgetary deficits occurred during the Republican administrations of Eisenhower, Nixon, Ford, and Reagan.

- Previous-Event-as-Cause Fallacy—identifying an event that occurred before another event as the cause of the second event when, in fact, the two events were not directly related. The reasoning is that if Event A happened before Event B, it must have caused Event B. An example of this fallacy in reasoning is the statement: "The election of President Wilson in 1912 enabled Congress to pass the 16th Amendment in 1913." In fact, the approval of the 16th Amendment to the Constitution, which established a national income tax, was the result of many factors during the Progressive Era that led to widespread support for the tax.

FALLACIES OF PROOF

When a conclusion is erroneously drawn from evidence, a fallacy of proof occurs. In the study of economics, fallacies of proof often result when facts are misused or misinterpreted. The three most common fallacies of proof are as follows.

- Insufficient-Evidence Fallacy—using insufficient data in an effort to prove a major thesis. For example, suppose an economist is trying to prove that the overall tax burden in the United States is lighter than the tax burden in most other highly industrialized nations. To prove this thesis, the economist must collect and compare tax data about many industrialized nations. If the economist collects tax data only about Japan and Australia and considers the thesis proved, the economist has committed an insufficient-proof fallacy.

- Irrelevant-Evidence Fallacy—using unrelated information to prove a major thesis. Continuing the example of the economist above, suppose the economist collected data about many low-income, agriculture-based nations as well as a few industrialized nations to prove the thesis. Any conclusions based on the evidence are erroneous because tax data about low-income nations are irrelevant to the thesis.

- Majority-View Fallacy—arguing that because "everyone" says something is so, it must be true. For example, the statement "Everyone knows that American citizens pay a greater percentage of their incomes to the government than taxpayers in other industrialized nations" is a majority-view fallacy. Although this may be a widely held view, it is not supported by the facts.

How to Recognize Fallacies

To recognize fallacies in economic reasoning, follow these guidelines.

1. **Read the statement carefully.** Identify the main idea and the conclusion.
2. **Identify fallacies in reasoning.** Ask how each conclusion was reached.
3. **Evaluate the statement or argument.** Determine the validity of the statement based on the reasoning and the evidence presented.

Applying the Skill

Read the passage at the top of the next column. Then identify the fallacies in the statement.

The main idea of the passage is that spending on national defense is solely responsible for the increase in the national debt during the 1980s. It concludes that a balanced budget is possible only if the government makes large cuts in the defense budget.

There are two fallacies in reasoning in the passage. The first fallacy is a single-cause fallacy—that the sole reason for the increases in the budget is defense spending. Actually, several factors contributed to the soaring national debt. The second fallacy is the insufficient-evidence fallacy. That is, the author failed to provide data or evidence that linked defense spending with the growth of the national debt. The author also failed to provide specific information on other sources contributing to the debt increases. Nor did the author provide an evaluation of other possible solutions to the soaring national debt.

> Between 1981 and 1986, the national debt in the United States doubled from $1 trillion to $2 trillion. This marked increase in the national debt is the result of excessive federal spending for national defense. During this period, in fact, the government spent over $1 trillion on national defense. Clearly, to achieve a balanced budget, the federal government must drastically reduce defense appropriations.

Practicing the Skill See Answers, p. A 39.

Read the following passage. Then on a separate sheet of paper, answer the questions below. You may wish to review Chapter 9 before searching for errors in reasoning.

> Everybody knows that the high tax rates in the United States put American firms at a disadvantage when competing with firms operating in other nations. The reason why American firms are losing their hold on foreign and domestic markets is the oppressive tax burden. The Gross National Product of the United States is over $4 trillion—the highest in the world. Yet American firms are taxed at an unfairly high rate. To restore the competitiveness of American firms in international markets, taxes must be reduced.

1. **(a)** What is the main idea of the passage? **(b)** What conclusion does the author draw?
2. Identify a single-cause fallacy in the passage and explain why it is a single-cause fallacy.
3. Identify an irrelevant-evidence fallacy and explain why it is an irrelevant-evidence fallacy.
4. Identify a majority-view fallacy and explain why it is a majority-view fallacy.

See Key Study Questions and Key Understandings, p. TM 46.

4 Federal budget deficits serve to increase the national debt.

See Suggested Teaching Strategies, p. TM 46.

In most years since the 1930s, increases in federal spending were not matched by increases in government revenues. By the mid-1980s, annual deficits increased to over $200 billion and the total national debt passed the $2 trillion mark.

Federal Budget Deficits

The federal budget indicates how the government plans to raise and use government revenues. The budget shows how the government will borrow money to pay the debts that occur when the government's expenditures exceed its revenues.

A federal **budget deficit** occurs when the government borrows money to pay some of its bills. The government borrows money by selling its IOUs—savings bonds and other securities—to investors. A **budget surplus**, on the other hand, occurs when government revenues are greater than government expenditures. The last government surplus occurred in 1969.

Economists use the term **deficit spending** to refer to the intentional government policy of appropriating more money for its programs than it is able to cover with its revenues. Deficit spending causes budget deficits. The graph below shows that deficit spending has increased dramatically since 1974, the last year of a balanced budget. Deficit spending averaged $5.7 billion a year in the 1960s, $36.5 billion a year in the 1970s, and $123.2 billion a year in the 1980s.

Federal Budget Surpluses and Deficits, 1960–1986

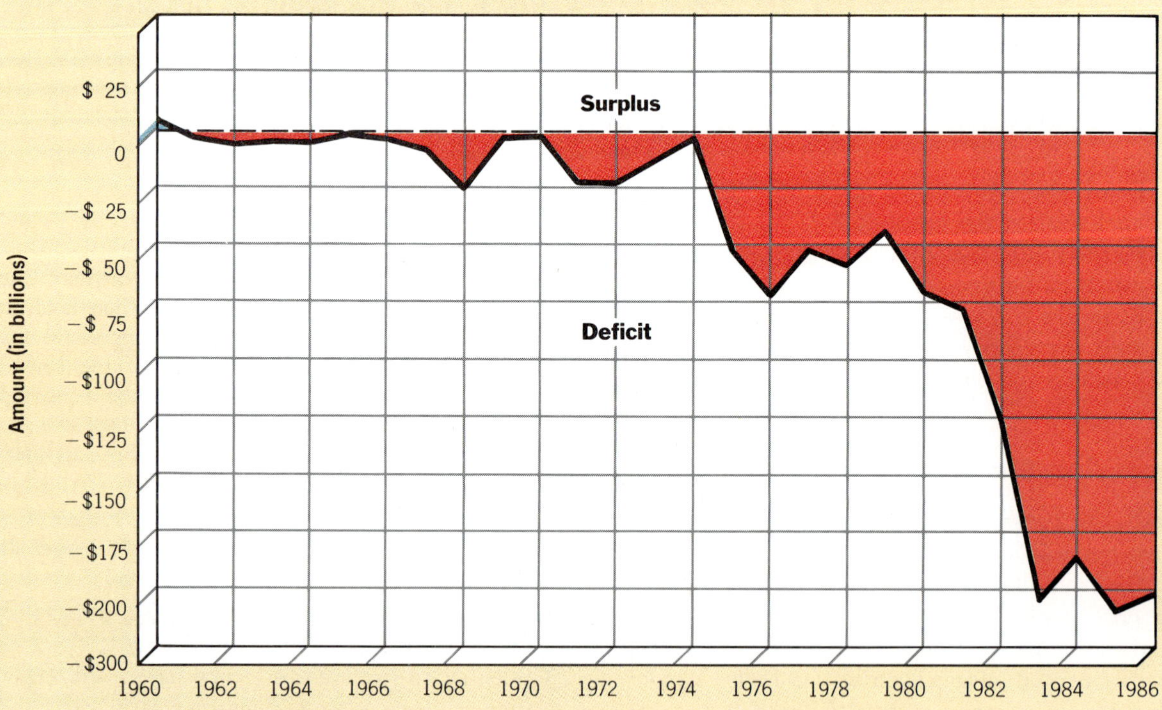

Source: *Economic Report of the President, 1986*

National emergencies, the need for additional public goods and services, economic stabilization policies, and the changing role of government in the United States economy are the main causes for budget deficits. National emergencies during the Civil War, World War I, World War II, the Korean War, and the Vietnam War resulted in deficit spending. The federal government has also employed deficit spending in an effort to win the costly arms race between the United States and the Soviet Union that has arisen since World War II.

In providing public goods, the federal government may use deficit spending for roads and bridges, airports, or dams. Most people in the United States tend to support the purchase of public goods even when deficit spending is necessary because they view these purchases as investments in the nation's future.

A third reason the federal government uses deficit spending is to stabilize the economy by fighting inflation and recession. The federal government first used deficit spending to stimulate the economy, or "prime the pump," during the Great Depression. The federal government has since used deficit spending to fight recessions. During recessions, the federal government decreases taxes and increases its spending programs, putting money back into the economy. With money more available, individuals and firms are thus able to buy more goods and services. Higher production and employment usually result, bringing the recession to an end. Deficit spending as a stabilization policy, however, is not without cost. Lower taxes and higher government spending create budget deficits.

The federal government's emphasis on promoting the economic well-being of its citizens is the fourth reason for budget deficits. During the 1980s, about one half of all federal expenditures went for social programs that serve as a "safety net" for the nation's poor, the elderly, and the handicapped. Before the Great Depression and the recovery, relief, and reform efforts of the New Deal and subesequent administrations' efforts, there were few safety-net social programs.

The National Debt

◆ The **national debt** is the total amount of money that the federal government owes to its creditors.

Economics Reporter

How Much Is a Trillion Dollars?

The budget proposed by President Reagan for the 1987 fiscal year was about a trillion dollars. A trillion dollars in numbers is $1,000,000,000,000. A third of the United States Gross National Product is one trillion dollars. One trillion dollars in one-dollar bills laid end to end would form 3,803 full circles around the earth. If a trillion dollars were divided equally among every person in the United States when the population was 237 million, each person would receive almost $5,000.

The graph on this page shows the creditors of the federal government. Each time the government uses deficit spending to finance its programs, it accumulates more debt. The annual budget deficit contributes to the growth of the national debt.

Creditors of the Federal Government

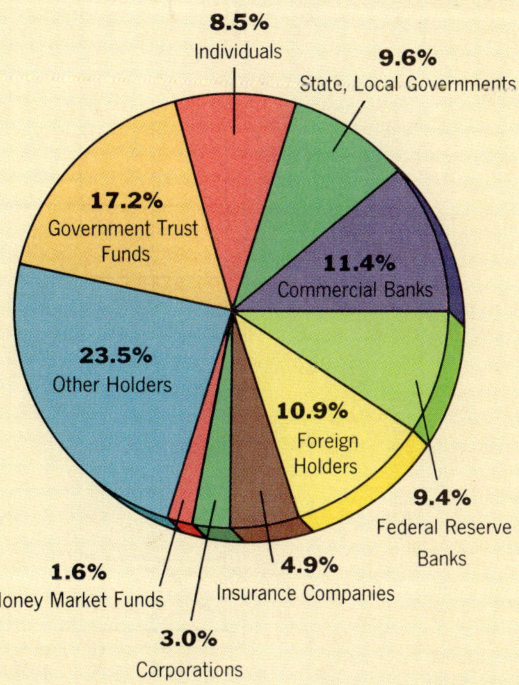

Sources: *U.S. News and World Report*
Office of Management and Budget, Department of the Treasury

◆ **Have the students read "Understanding Tax Reform" on pages 520–521 of the *Everyday Economics Handbook* and answer the questions that follow.**

Growth of the National Debt. Under the provisions of the Constitution of the United States, the federal government assumed all outstanding debts of the original 13 states. The national debt in 1789 totalled $75 million. During George Washington's administration, the government first decided to sell government securities to finance its deficit spending, a money-raising method that has since continued.

Since Washington's Presidency, the national debt has fluctuated. Federal budget deficits have increased the size of the national debt, while budget surpluses have reduced it.

The national debt surpassed the $1 billion mark for the first time during the Civil War. In 1917, the year the United States entered World War I, the national debt was about $3 billion. By 1919, the debt had climbed to more than $25 billion. The graph on this page shows the growth in the national debt from 1940, the year before the United States entered World War II, to 1986. Since World War II, the national debt has increased steadily. In 1981, it topped the $1 trillion mark. Within five years, the national debt doubled again.

Debt Ceilings. Public concern about the size of the national debt has led Congress to approve debt ceilings. A **debt ceiling** legislates limits on the size of the national debt. The debt ceiling of $11 billion approved during World War I was soon abandoned because of the government's need for credit. In 1918 the national debt increased to $12.5 billion, and by 1919 this debt had doubled.

The National Debt, 1940–1986

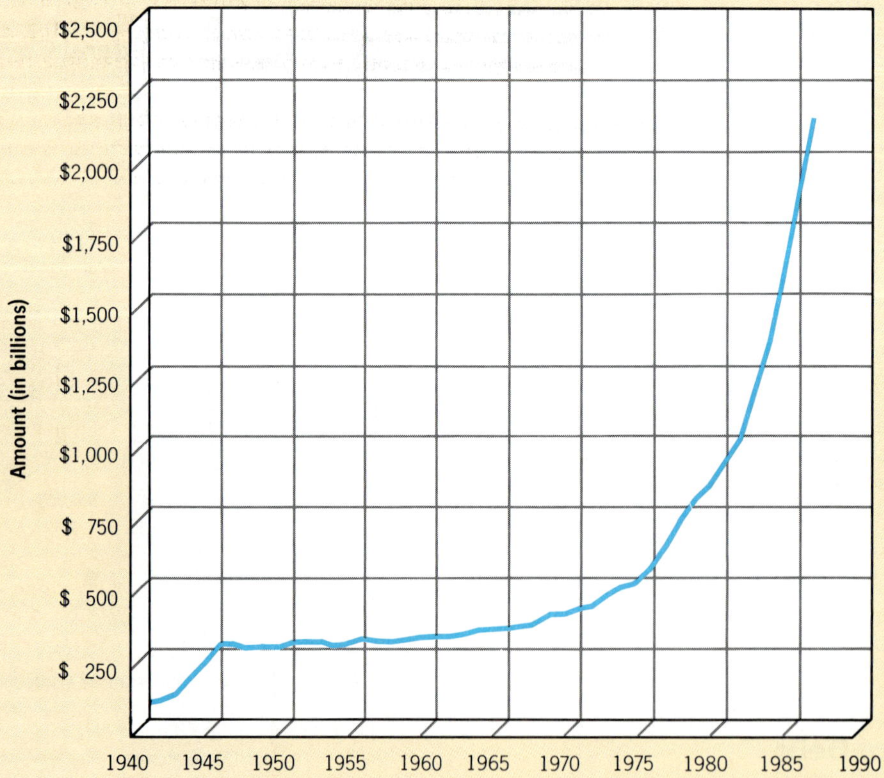

Source: *Economic Report of the President, 1986*

The President and his Cabinet are often at odds with the House and Senate over the best means of balancing the federal budget.

In 1947, a "permanent" debt ceiling of $275 billion was instituted. But the inability to escape deficit spending has forced the government to regularly raise the debt ceiling. In 1986, Congress raised the debt ceiling to $2 trillion. The ceiling is expected to be raised to $3 trillion by 1988.

Economic Impact of the National Debt. Economists disagree about how the national debt and the annual federal budget deficit affect the economy. Some economists argue that the benefits achieved from annual deficit spending and the subsequent rise in the national debt exceed the costs. They note how government spending programs improve the quality of life for the people.

Other economists counter that the short-term and long-term economic costs of the debt are severe. They argue that the annual deficits and the national debt should be reduced. For further information on this controversy, see pages 260–261.

Balancing the Federal Budget

The high federal deficits and the consequent rapid ◆ rise of the national debt have caused policymakers to look for ways to balance the federal budget. The two ways to balance the budget are to increase revenues or to decrease expenditures.

Increases in Government Revenues. The most important tool that the federal government has used to increase revenues is taxation. In recent years, however, the government's ability to raise taxes has been limited. The Economic Recovery Act of 1981, for example, reduced income taxes during the early 1980s. President Reagan also pledged not to raise taxes during his second term of office.

The government has other methods of raising revenues. The Tax Equity and Fiscal Responsibility Act of 1982 has raised additional revenues by strictly enforcing existing tax laws. The Deficit Reduction Act of 1984 has raised government revenues by establishing stricter tax recordkeeping procedures and closing some tax loopholes. These acts have targeted people who evade taxes. The IRS estimates that the federal government has lost $100 billion a year from tax cheating.

During the 1980s, the government has raised additional money by withholding money from federal employees' wages and from income tax returns of people who had not paid government loans. The Department of Education, for example, expected to collect $15 billion in student loans that had gone into default by tapping the income tax returns of more than 1 million former students.

◆ Discussion topic: Whether economic stability demands a balanced budget.

DECISION MAKERS IN THE ECONOMY

Phil Gramm

Phil Gramm is a first-term United States Senator from Texas. He entered Congress in 1979 as a Democrat serving in the House of Representatives. He soon realized that his political beliefs were more Republican than Democratic. In 1983, he changed parties. In 1984, he won his Senate seat as a Republican. It was his initial idea that eventually became the Gramm-Rudman-Hollings Balanced Budget and Emergency Deficit Reduction Control Act of 1985.

Gramm believes strongly in the free enterprise system. His main goal as a legislator has been to reduce the size of the federal government. He also wants to return some of its power, especially that relating to personal finances, to the average citizen. A smaller federal government, he argues, will lead to a stronger economy.

The Gramm-Rudman-Hollings Act was designed with these beliefs in mind. By requiring the government to operate on a balanced budget, it could provide a permanent check on government growth.

Phil Gramm's budget-balancing law will certainly have a major effect on the economy if it can be successfully enforced. Gramm himself fervently believes that it will eventually lead to increased prosperity for all Americans.

Decreases in Government Expenditures. Another way the government can balance the federal budget is by decreasing spending. Federal spending had increased to $946 billion by 1985. Government expenditures had become so large that many policymakers agreed that federal spending had to be brought under control.

In response to this need, the government stepped up its campaign against waste and fraud. Several defense contractors, for example, were fined and obliged to pay the government back for fraudulent billings. Similarly, IRS computer checks on households receiving public assistance through AFDC, food stamps, and Medicaid weeded out people who were not eligible for benefits under these social programs.

The government also eliminated or reduced the cost of some programs. In the mid-1980s, for example, the Department of Defense halted work on the multibillion dollar DIVAD antiaircraft weapon, and the government abandoned the Synfuel Corporation (SFC). The SFC was established in 1980 to assist private firms in the production of gasoline and oil from coal, tar sands, and shale. Most of the $19 billion originally budgeted for the SFC was never spent. The government also established maximum payments for certain medical services provided for Medicare recipients.

Legislating a Balanced Budget. Despite government actions to increase revenues and decrease expenditures, the remedies did not succeed in bringing federal deficits under control during the 1980s. This failure gave rise to proposals to legislate a balanced budget.

One proposal called for a constitutional amendment to balance the budget, permitting federal borrowing during peacetime only if 60 percent of Congress approved. The balanced budget amendment gained the support of President Reagan. The amendment, however, failed to win the necessary two-thirds vote in Congress.

Another proposal, the Gramm-Rudman-Hollings Balanced Budget and Emergency Deficit Reduction Control Act of 1985, initiated a five-year phase-in program to balance the budget.

◆ **Discussion topic: Programs that should be cut or eliminated to lower government spending.**

CASE STUDY

Gramm-Rudman-Hollings Balanced Budget Act of 1985

The President signed the Gramm-Rudman-Hollings Balanced Budget Act into law in December 1985. The law instructs the President to submit federal budget proposals to Congress. These proposals must meet preset deficit-reduction targets requiring annual cuts in the deficit of $36 billion each fiscal year from 1987 to 1991. The goal of the deficit-reduction law is to achieve a balanced budget by 1991.

Gramm-Rudman-Hollings also includes a provision for "automatic" budget cuts should the President and Congress not be able to meet the stated deficit-reduction targets. The size of the automatic cuts depends on how much the budget proposal exceeds the deficit-reduction target.

To illustrate the impact of the automatic debt-reduction process, suppose the proposed budget for fiscal 1990 included a $200 billion deficit. Assume also that this figure is $56 billion over the target deficit of $144 billion ($200 − $144 = $56). Thus, $56 billion would have to be cut from the budget.

The OMB, CBO, and the General Accounting Office (GAO) are responsible for estimating budget deficits. The GAO has the final decision about projected deficits if disagreements arise among the groups. The GAO also determines exactly how much money will be trimmed from various federal agencies and departments.

The automatic cuts apply to defense and nondefense areas of the budget. About one half of the total reduction comes from the defense budget. The other half comes from all other eligible areas. A number of programs are exempt from mandatory cuts including transfer payments to individuals and interest on the national debt.

In February 1986, a federal court ruled that part of the Gramm-Rudman-Hollings law is unconstitutional because it gives too much power to the Comptroller General. The Comptroller General is responsible for determining how much money is to be cut from each department and agency. In effect, the judges have rejected the idea that Congress can hand over its legislative powers to unelected bureaucrats. The decision has been appealed to the United States Supreme Court, which has not yet ruled on the lower court's decision.

See Suggested Assignments, p. TM 46.

Section 4 Review See Answers, p. A 39.

DEFINE budget deficit, budget surplus, national debt, debt ceiling

IDENTIFY Phil Gramm

1. **Summarizing Ideas** **(a)** What is deficit spending? **(b)** What are two ways the federal government can balance the budget? **(c)** What actions did the federal government take in the mid-1980s to decrease government expenditures?
2. **Interpreting Graphics** Compare the graphs on pages 208 and 210. State a generalization that explains the trends in both the national debt and federal surpluses and deficits illustrated by these two graphs.

CHAPTER 9 SUMMARY

Federal, state, and local governments in the United States must finance their operations through various kinds of taxes. The federal government raises 90 percent of its revenues through individual income taxes, corporate income taxes, and Social Security taxes. Excise taxes, estate taxes, gift taxes, and customs duties comprise the remaining 10 percent of federal taxes. State and local governments raise revenues through individual income taxes, sales taxes, and property taxes.

People judge how fair all taxes are by the ability-to-pay principle and the benefits-received principle. Taxes in the United States are a mix of the two.

All governments in the twentieth century formulate budgets to help them plan sources of revenues and the amounts and direction of expenditures. The federal government has full-time executive and legislative offices which work only on the budget.

Federal spending in particular has grown by leaps and bounds. Deficit spending since the end of World War II has caused great increases in the annual budget deficits. By the mid-1980s, the national debt of the United States passed the $2 trillion mark. Since 1947, Congress has legislated higher and higher debt ceilings. Some concerned citizens and legislators believe that an amendment requiring the federal government to have balanced budgets should be added to the United States Constitution.

CHAPTER 9 REVIEW

For Answers to Chapter 9 Review, see p. A 40.

Reviewing Economic Terms

Supply the economic term that correctly completes each sentence.

1. The mandatory payments that individuals and firms make to the government to cover the costs of public goods are ____.
2. The percentage of a person's income that is taken by the government is the ____ ____.
3. A tax that takes the same percentage from individuals at all income levels is a ____ ____.
4. The total amount of money that the federal government owes its creditors is the ____ ____.
5. The intentional government policy of appropriating more money for its programs than it is able to cover with its revenues is ____ ____.
6. Taxes that are withheld by employers and placed by government in two special trust funds are ____ ____ ____.
7. A tax on a good brought into the United States from another country is a ____ ____.
8. A tax that takes a larger percentage of income from low-income groups than from high-income groups is a ____ ____.

Exercising Economic Skills

1. **Determining Fallacies in Reasoning** Refer to the skill lesson on pages 206–207 and classify each of the following fallacies.
   a. The decline in the oil industry in Texas caused the collapse of several Texas banks.
   b. The high salaries paid to baseball players has resulted in a decline in performance because they do not work as hard as in the past.
   c. Everyone knows that the national debt was responsible for the most recent recession.
2. **Understanding Tax Reform** Study the feature on pages 520–521. Then review newspapers and magazines to find an article on tax reform. **(a)** What is the main idea of the article? **(b)** What is the author's opinion or point of view? How do you know? **(c)** Identify any fallacies contained in the article and classify them according to the categories on pages 206–207.

Thinking Critically About Economics

1. **Summarizing Ideas** **(a)** Why do governments collect taxes? **(b)** In what ways do governments raise revenues? **(c)** What is included in the federal budget? **(d)** What is a budget deficit and a national debt?
2. **Interpreting Ideas** **(a)** Explain the two principles of taxation. **(b)** What are the arguments for the benefits-received principle of taxation?
3. **Seeing Relationships** **(a)** What effect does an increase in the corporate income tax have on consumers? Why? **(b)** What effect does an increase in the individual income tax have on corporations? Why?

Extending Economic Knowledge

1. In a paragraph, explain your decision in the following situation. Suppose you are a city commissioner and the city has just sold a city-operated hospital for $10 million. Given the following alternatives and costs, how would you vote to spend the money?
   a. replace the 100-year-old hall — $5 million
   b. build a new city park — $2 million
   c. build a library branch — $3 million
   d. replace the old and overcrowded high school — $7 million
   e. purchase needed new equipment for all city departments — $6 million
   f. put money into savings at 10 percent annual interest — none
2. Contact a local government agency such as the school system, police or fire department, or library system. Find out **(a)** from what sources the department's operating budget comes, **(b)** how much this fiscal year's budget was, and **(c)** for what the department spends its money. Prepare a chart to illustrate your findings.
3. The increasing size of the national debt is a controversial subject. Research both sides of the issue and prepare a position paper stating your view on this question: Should the federal government be required by law to take steps to reduce the national debt?

Using Primary Sources

Adam Smith (1732–1790) was a prominent economist from Scotland. In *An Inquiry Into the Nature and Causes of the Wealth of Nations* (1776), Smith established four maxims, or norms, on which a fair tax system is based. As you read the excerpts below, identify the four maxims of taxation. Are these maxims being applied in any way in the tax system of the United States today?

The Four Maxims of Taxation

Before I enter upon the examination of particular taxes, it is necessary to premise [state] the four following maxims with regard to taxes in general.

I. The subjects of every state ought to contribute towards the support of the government, as nearly as possible, in proportion to their respective abilities; that is, in proportion to the revenue which they respectively enjoy under the protection of the state. . . .

II. The tax which each individual is bound to pay ought to be certain, and not arbitrary. The time of payment, the manner of payment, the quantity to be paid, ought all to be clear and plain to the contributor, and to every other person. Where it is otherwise, every person subject to the tax is put more or less in the power of the tax-gatherer, who can either aggravate the tax upon any obnoxious contributor, or extort, by the terror of such aggravation, some present or perquisite [privilege] to himself. . . .

III. Every tax ought to be levied at the time, or in the manner, in which it is most likely to be convenient to pay it. A tax upon the rent of land or of houses, payable at the same term at which such rents are usually paid, is levied at the time when it is most likely to be convenient for the contributor to pay; or, when he is most likely to have the wherewithal to pay. Taxes upon such consumable goods as articles of luxury, are all finally paid by the consumer, and generally in a manner that is very convenient for him. He pays them little by little, as he has occasion to buy the goods. . . .

IV. Every tax ought to be so contrived as both to take out and to keep out of the pockets of the people as little as possible. . . . A tax may either take out or keep out of the pockets of the people a great deal more than it brings into the public treasury, in the four following ways. First, . . . salaries may eat up the greater part of the produce of the tax . . . and . . . impose another additional tax upon the people. Secondly, it [taxation] may obstruct the industry of the people, and discourage them from applying to [investing in] certain branches of business which might give maintenance and employment to the great multitudes. . . . Thirdly, . . . it may frequently ruin them [tax evaders], and thereby put and end to the benefit the community might have received from the employment of their capitals. . . . Fourthly, by subjecting the people to the frequent visits . . . of the tax-gatherers it may expose them to much unnecessary trouble, vexation, and oppression. . . . It is in some one or other of these four different ways that taxes are frequently so much more burdensome to the people than they are beneficial to the sovereign.

Source Review

For Answers to Source Review, see p. A 40.

1. According to Smith, what are the four maxims of a fair tax system? State each maxim in a sentence.
2. Smith believes that taxes should take as little money as possible out of the pockets of taxpayers. What four economic and social problems are likely to result from overly burdensome taxation?
3. In what ways are Smith's four maxims of taxation included in the tax system of the United States?

UNIT THREE REVIEW

For Answers to Unit Three Review, see p. A 41.

Reviewing Economic Ideas

1. Why has the size of government increased during the twentieth century?
2. How does government regulate the economy?
3. How does the government stabilize the economy through its fiscal and monetary policies?
4. On what criteria do citizens in a democratic society evaluate the performance of government economic policies?
5. Why do governments levy taxes?
6. How do the two principles of taxation differ?
7. How does the tax burden of United States citizens compare with the tax burdens of citizens in other nations?
8. What is **(a)** a progressive tax, **(b)** a proportional tax, and **(c)** a regressive tax?

Connecting Economic Ideas

1. **Seeing Relationships** **(a)** How are the growth in the size of government and the increasing national debt related? **(b)** Which of the factors that have led to a growth in the size of government do you feel has contributed the most to the national debt? Why?
2. **Interpreting Ideas** **(a)** What economic goals are promoted by the Social Security System? **(b)** Explain the possible conflict between economic equity and regressive taxes. **(c)** How is economic freedom affected when the government increases taxes?
3. **Comprehending Ideas** **(a)** Why do some people feel that a sales tax is an unfair type of taxation? **(b)** Which tax do you think is the fairest? Why?
4. **Analyzing Viewpoints** **(a)** Why do many people think that increasing government involvement in the economy is inevitable? **(b)** Explain why you agree or disagree with the previous statement.
5. **Evaluating Viewpoints** Defend or refute this statement: The increased size of government increases economic equity by providing greater opportunities for special interest groups and their activities.

Investigating Economic Issues

1. **Summarizing Ideas** What are the target groups at which worker retraining programs are aimed?
2. **Interpreting Ideas** **(a)** Why do labor unions support retraining programs? **(b)** What two industries have instituted major worker retraining programs? **(c)** With what success have the programs met?
3. **Comprehending Ideas** **(a)** What is the Job Corps? **(b)** What is the Job Corps' target group?
4. **Contrasting Ideas** How are workfare programs different from worker training and worker retraining programs?
5. **Evaluating Viewpoints** Defend or refute this statement: Worker training and retraining programs should be the responsibility of private business.

Applying Economics

1. Suppose you are a United States Senator. **(a)** Using percentages, indicate how you would allocate budget spending among the following government programs and **(b)** defend your allocations.
   - **a.** Education
   - **b.** Agriculture
   - **c.** National Defense
   - **d.** Social Welfare
   - **e.** Transportation
   - **f.** Health and Safety
   - **g.** Other
2. Research worker training and retraining programs. Write an essay in which you **(a)** describe the programs available through government funding and private business and **(b)** compare the successes of publicly funded and privately funded worker training and retraining programs.
3. Research the economic programs and policies established by the federal government that continue today. Select three of the programs and policies and in a paragraph for each selection, answer these questions. **(a)** Why was the program or policy started? **(b)** How have the goals, purposes, and effects of the program or policy changed since the New Deal? **(c)** What would be the effects on the economy if the program or policy were discontinued?

Using Primary Sources

The Job Corps was founded in 1964 to provide occupational training for unemployed youth. In 1982, the Job Corps was absorbed into the larger Job Training Partnership Act. As you read the excerpts below, consider how the Job Corps helps the youth to gain marketable skills. Who is eligible to participate in the program?

The Job Corps

Sec. 421. This part of the Job Training Partnership Act maintains a Job Corps for economically disadvantaged young men and women. The purpose of this part is to assist young individuals who need and can benefit from an unusually intensive program, operated in a group setting, to become more responsible, employable, and productive citizens.

Sec. 423. To become an enrollee in the Job Corps, a young man or woman must be an eligible youth who—

(1) has attained age 14 but not attained age 22 at the time of enrollment.

(2) is economically disadvantaged . . . and who requires additional education, training, or intensive counseling and related assistance in order to secure and hold meaningful employment, participate successfully in regular school work, qualify for other suitable training programs, or satisfy Armed Forces requirements. . . .

(3) is currently living in an environment so characterized by cultural deprivation, a disruptive homelife, or other disorienting conditions. . . .

(4) is determined . . . to have the present capacities and aspirations needed to complete and secure the full benefit of the Job Corps. . . .

Sec. 428. Each Job Corps center shall provide enrollees with an intensive, well-organized, and fully supervised program of education, vocational training, work experience, planned vocational and recreational activities, physical rehabilitation and development, and counseling. To the fullest extent feasible, the required program shall include activities to assist enrollees in choosing realistic career goals, coping with problems they may encounter in home communities, or in adjusting to new communities, and planning and managing their daily affairs in a manner that will best contribute to long-term upward mobility. Center programs shall include required participation in center maintenance work to assist enrollees in increasing their sense of contribution, responsiblity, and discipline.

Source Review

For Answers to Source Review, see p. A 42.

1. What are the goals of the Job Corps?
2. List four eligibility requirements for participation in the Job Corps.
3. What specific types of programs does the Job Corps provide to enrollees? In terms of employment skills and attitudes, how do these programs help prepare enrollees for employment in the economy?

Reading About Economics

Hughes, Jonathan R. T. *The Governmental Habit.* New York: Basic Books. A historical look at the growth of government involvement and an examination of the growing public acceptance of big government and its role in the economy.

Samuel, Peter. "Battling the Budget Bulge—Gracefully." *Reason* (May 1984), pp. 34, 36–39. A recap of Grace Commission suggestions on cutting the federal budget and spending.

Silk, Leonard. *Economics in Plain English: All You Need to Know About Economics—in Language Anyone Can Understand.* New York: Simon and Schuster. A readable review of the economic concepts presented by Adam Smith, Thomas Malthus, and Karl Marx. It also discusses other basic economic concepts and understandings in easy-to-read language and presents an evaluation of recent international and domestic financial trends in trade, banking, and governmental fiscal and monetary policies.

10

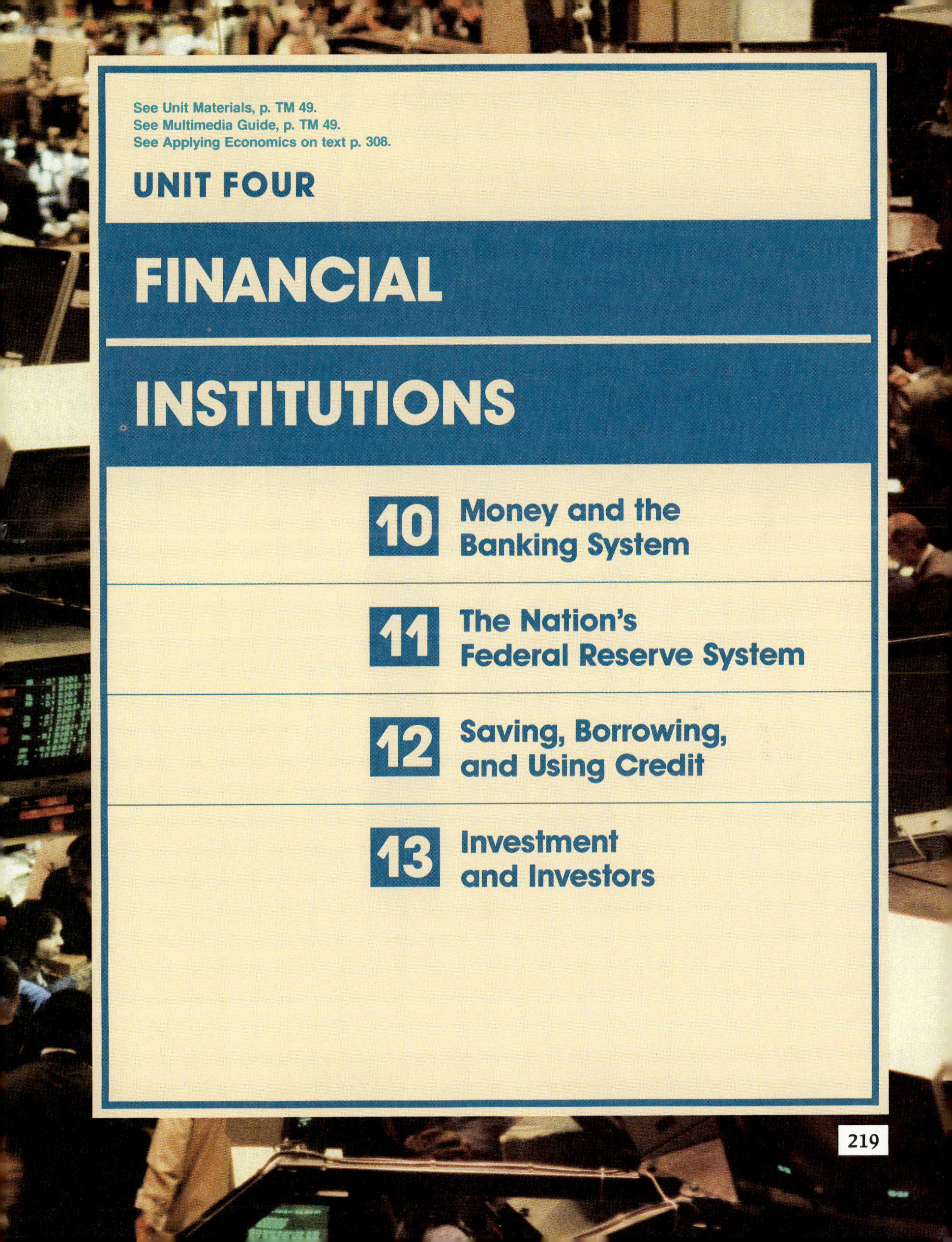

See Unit Materials, p. TM 49.
See Multimedia Guide, p. TM 49.
See Applying Economics on text p. 308.

UNIT FOUR

FINANCIAL INSTITUTIONS

BANK OF STOCKTON
DONALD D. BOSCOE
&
MARVIN MARKS
ATTORNEYS AT LAW
TIME TO
MAIN
SAN JOAQUIN
ONE WAY
BANK OF STOCKTON
ESTABLISHED 1867
COMMERCIAL · SAVINGS · TRUST

CHAPTER 10

See Chapter Overview, p. TM 50.
See Chapter Objectives, p. TM 50.
See Introducing the Chapter, p. TM 50.
See Extending Economic Knowledge on text p. 240.

Money and the Banking System

A power has risen up in the government greater than the people themselves, consisting of many and various and powerful interests . . . and held together by the cohesive power of the vast surplus in the banks.

John C. Calhoun

1 Money, with its special characteristics, serves many important economic functions.

- The Functions of Money
- Characteristics of Money
- Sources of Money's Value
- Types of Money

2 Money and banking have changed as the United States has developed.

- Money and Banking to 1860
- A National Banking System, 1860 to 1913
- Banking Reform and Regulation, 1913 to the Present
- Types of Financial Institutions

3 Banking has undergone several major changes in recent years.

- Banking Deregulation
- Automatic Banking
- Financial Troubles in Banking

CHAPTER 10 STUDY GUIDE

Chapter Focus

Chapter 10 discusses money and banking in the United States. The chapter focuses on the types, functions, and characteristics of money. It also examines the historical development of United States banking.

As you study the chapter, look for details that support each of the following statements.

1. Money, with its special characteristics, serves many economic functions.
2. Money and banking have changed as the United States has developed.
3. Banking has undergone several major changes in recent years.

See Preteaching Vocabulary, p. TM 50.

Terms to Know

The following terms, while not the only terms emphasized in this chapter, are basic to your understanding of money and the banking system. Determine the meaning of each term, either by using the Glossary or by watching for context clues as you read the chapter.

money	specie
medium of exchange	fiat money
barter	near money
opportunity cost	national bank
commodity money	gold standard
currency	deregulation
representative money	regional banking

See Key Study Questions and Key Understandings, p. TM 51.

1 Money, with its special characteristics, serves many important economic functions.

See Suggested Teaching Strategies, p. TM 51.

In today's society, money is magic. Children and adults alike see money as the means of acquiring the wonderful things they need or want. Most people also realize that money is a fundamental part of the United States free enterprise system. Money makes it possible for businesses to pay for the costs of labor and production and allows individuals to purchase consumer products.

The Functions of Money

Money is anything that people commonly accept in exchange for goods or services. In the United States, money has three basic functions. It serves as a medium of exchange, a standard of value, and a store of value. Anything that serves any of these three functions is a type of money.

Medium of Exchange. The single most important use of money is as a **medium of exchange.** A medium of exchange is any item that sellers will accept in payment for goods or services. As a medium of exchange, money assists in the buying and selling of goods and services because buyers know that sellers will accept money in payment for products or services.

It is possible, of course, to **barter,** or exchange goods and services without using money. In bartering, no medium of exchange is needed. Bartering is still done in many parts of the world, especially in traditional economies where wants and needs are limited. Also, in some highly developed economies, ◆ individuals barter by performing services for one another to avoid exchanging money. In the United States, for example, a carpenter might exchange services with an electrician or a plumber rather than pay for services with money.

Bartering, however, involves two major problems. First, each party in the exchange must want what the other party has to offer. Second, the parties must agree on the relative value of the items or the

 ◆ Exchanging services is part of the underground economy.

The green pieces of paper that people call money are inherently valueless. When the paper becomes currency, however, it takes on value because the federal government has guaranteed its use as a medium of exchange.

services being exchanged. How many woolen blankets a cow is worth can cause a great debate, often resulting in a long haggling session. Money, regardless of its form, was invented to overcome the problems caused by bartering.

Standard of Value. The second use of money is as a **standard of value.** That is, money provides people with a way to measure the relative value of goods or services by comparing the prices of products. In this way, people can judge the relative worth of different items such as a television and a bicycle. They can also judge the relative values of two different models or brands of the same type of item by comparing their prices.

In the United States, the standard of value is expressed in dollars and cents. Goods or services for sale are marked with a price that indicates their value in dollars and cents. If a cassette tape costs $10, and a pizza costs $5, a consumer knows that the value of the cassette tape is twice that of the pizza.

In addition to allowing consumers to compare prices, money as a standard of value also helps to clarify **opportunity costs.** Suppose a person with $10 to spend has narrowed the choices to a cassette tape or two pizzas. Next, suppose the person chooses to buy the two pizzas. The person therefore gives up the chance to buy the cassette tape—the opportunity cost of the person's decision. Buyers make more informed buying choices when they keep both the price and the opportunity costs of their decision in mind.

Money's function as a standard of value is also important to record keeping. Whether measured in pounds of salt, sacks of rice, bales of cotton, or units of currency, businesses need to figure profits and losses. Similarly, governments must be able to figure tax receipts and the cost of expenditures. Money, because it helps provide some uniformity to these accounting tasks, is also called a unit of accounting.

Store of Value. The third function or role of money is that it can be saved—or stored for later use. For money to serve as a **store of value,** two conditions must be met. First, the money must be nonperishable. That is, it cannot rot or otherwise deteriorate while being saved. Second, it must keep its value over time. In other words, the purchasing power of the money must be relatively constant. If both of these conditions are met, many people will accumulate their wealth for later use. If not, most people will be hesitant about saving money today that will be worth little or nothing tomorrow.

This Middle Eastern woman's money chains are a way of telling others of her family's wealth and standing in the community.

Characteristics of Money

To be used as money, an item must have certain characteristics. The five major characteristics of money are durability, portability, divisibility, stability in value, and acceptability.

Durability. Durability refers to money's ability to be used over and over again. Eggs would be a poor choice for money because they are fragile and perishable. Metals such as gold and silver, however, are ideal because they withstand wear and tear well. In fact, many coins minted in ancient times are still in existence.

Portability. Money's ability to be carried from one place to another and transferred from one person to another is its portability. As a medium of exchange, money must be convenient for people to use. Items that are difficult to carry make poor money. Large stones, such as those used on the island of Yap in the South Pacific, are not as portable as the paper money and coins used in much of the world.

Divisibility. Divisibility refers to money's ability to be divided into smaller units. In the United States, the dollar is divisible into any amount between 1 and 100. Combining the various coins in the United States economy permits buyers and sellers to make transactions of any size. Divisibility also enhances money's use as a standard of value because exact price comparisons between products can be made.

Stability in Value and Acceptability. For money to be useful as a store of value, it must be stable ◆ in value. Stability in value encourages saving and maintains money's purchasing power. Most people who save money are confident that it will have approximately the same value when they want to buy something with it as it had when they put it into savings.

Acceptability means that people are willing to accept money in exchange for their goods or services. People accept money because they know they, in turn, can spend it for other products. Visitors to the United States from a Pacific island where shells are used as money, for example, would have trouble buying goods with their shells. Shopkeepers would not accept the shells because they cannot be used to buy more merchandise. Of course, Western visitors to the Pacific island might find their paper money worthless there.

Sources of Money's Value

Money must have and retain value. All money falls into three categories according to what gives the money its value. The three categories of money are commodity money, representative money, and fiat money.

Commodity Money. An item that has a value of its own and that is also used as money is called **commodity money.** Throughout history, societies have used many commodities as money. The ancient Romans sometimes used salt as money. Precious metals such as gold and silver, and gems such as rubies, emeralds, and diamonds, have often been used as money. All of these things have been used as money because people decided that the commodities had value and could be used in trade for goods or services.

Often, commodity money is the most convenient type of money available. For example, tobacco was

◆ **Inform students that under the Articles of Confederation (1781–1787) each state had the right to coin and regulate the value of money. Because of problems created by this system, the United States Constitution reserves to the federal government the right to coin and regulate the value of money.**

used as money in Virginia in the early 1600s, partially because it was the colony's major crop. In 1618, the governor of the Virginia colony established an official price—or standard of value—for tobacco. By the 1630s, the Massachusetts Bay Colony also had established an official price for commodities such as corn, furs, cattle, wool, and wampum.

The majority of nations in the world today use **currency**—coins and paper bills—for money. The Lydians, an ancient people in Asia Minor, minted the world's first coins about 700 B.C. The Chinese developed the first paper currency, perhaps as early as A.D. 1000 or A.D. 1100.

Representative Money. Money that has value because it can be exchanged for something valuable is **representative money.** The first use of representative money in colonial America occurred in the late 1600s. In 1690, the Massachusetts Bay Colony issued "bills of credit" to help finance its war with the Indians. Printed on these bills of credit was the amount of money colonists had loaned to the Massachusetts government. These bills could be redeemed with the colony's treasurer at a later date as payment for taxes. Other colonies soon followed the Massachusetts example and issued bills of credit that could be redeemed for **specie**—gold or silver coins.

During the American Revolution (1776–1783), the Continental Congress issued representative money, called Continentals, to finance the war for independence from Great Britain. The Continentals, however, could not be redeemed for gold or silver because the government had little specie. The Continentals lost much of their value, and colonists often refused to accept them.

Today in the United States, checks are representative money. Checks can be exchanged for currency as long as the check writer has sufficient funds on account.

Fiat Money. Value is attached to **fiat money** because a government decree, or fiat, says that it has value. Coins and United States paper money, called Federal Reserve notes, are examples of fiat money. Each Federal Reserve note carries the inscription, "This note is legal tender for all debts, public and private." In addition, the materials used to produce United States coins are worth much less than the face value of the coins. For example, the copper and nickel used in making a quarter are worth about 2 cents, far less than the 25-cent value of the coin. The money has value, however, because the government says that citizens must accept paper money and coins for all transactions.

Economics Reporter

What Is the New Dollar?

A new process for printing dollars is being created to fight counterfeiters who are using sophisticated color copiers to produce bogus paper money. The Secret Service, the agency in charge of combating counterfeiting, believes that approximately $8 million in bogus currency is in circulation. One agency projects that by 1990, 90,000 people will have access to sophisticated color photocopiers capable of producing counterfeit money. To prepare against this potential for massive counterfeiting, the new dollar bill will have a polyester security thread that is visible only when the bill is held up to light. Other changes proposed by Congress and Treasury officials include using multicolor arrangements and holographs that are three dimensional and uncopyable.

Types of Money

Money comes in all shapes and sizes. The items used as money are a reflection of the society in which they are used. United States money includes coins, paper money, checks, and near money.

Coins and Paper Money. Coins and paper money make up the United States currency. Coins, which make up about 6 percent of the money supply, are made by the Bureau of the Mint, a part of the Department of the Treasury. Federal Reserve notes account for about 25 percent of the total United States money supply and are printed by the Bureau of Engraving and Printing in Washington, D.C. Although the government held some gold and silver as partial backing for paper money until 1968, present-day Federal Reserve notes are not backed by specie. It is money only because the United States government has made it so by law.

Checks. Checks, or checkbook money, make up the largest segment of the United States money supply. Checks represent more than 70 percent of the money supply, and nearly 90 percent of the transactions are completed by writing checks. Because checks are payable to the holder of the check on demand, checking accounts are often called **demand deposits.**

Checks are representative money because they stand for the amount of money in a person's account. They are generally accepted because the bank must pay the amount of the check when it is presented for payment. Checks, therefore, are considered money because they are a medium of exchange, a standard of value, and a store of value.

Near Money. Other financial assets are very similar to money. These assets, such as savings accounts and time deposits, are called **near money** and are not usually considered part of the nation's money supply. Though they are easily accessible, these accounts cannot be used directly to buy goods or pay debts. Depositors, for example, cannot pay bills directly from their savings accounts. Since funds in these accounts can be easily converted into cash, however, they are considered near money.

See Suggested Assignments, p. TM 51.

Section 1 Review

See Answers, p. A 43.

DEFINE money, barter, opportunity cost, currency, specie, demand deposit

1. **Comprehending Ideas** Why was money invented?
2. **Contrasting Ideas** How does commodity money differ from fiat money?
3. **Summarizing Ideas** **(a)** What are the three basic functions of money? **(b)** What are the five characteristics of money? **(c)** What are the three categories of money?
4. **Understanding Ideas** **(a)** How is the "new" United States dollar different from other dollars? **(b)** Why was it developed?
5. **Interpreting Ideas** **(a)** Why are United States coins and paper money classified as fiat money? **(b)** Why are time deposits considered near money?

See Key Study Questions and Key Understandings, p. TM 52.

2 Money and banking have changed as the United States has developed.

See Suggested Teaching Strategies, p. TM 52.

The histories of American money and banking are interwoven with the history of the United States. The American monetary and banking systems have gone through three periods of development. During each of these periods, stability and progress in the nation's money and banking systems has increased.

Money and Banking to 1860

The first period, from the 1780s to 1860, was a time of experimentation and debate in American banking. During this period, money and banking were part of a larger battle between Federalists and advocates of states' rights. ◆ States' rights advocates believed in the supremacy of state governments over the national government. Federalists, on the other hand, believed that the authority of the national government should be supreme. This political issue affected money and the banking system in the early republic.

Money and Banking in the Young Nation. The failure of the Continentals that were printed during the American Revolution caused national leaders during the 1780s and 1790s to seek a more stable form of money and a stronger banking system. Though the nation's leaders agreed on these goals, they disagreed about how to reach them.

Federalists, such as Alexander Hamilton, believed that a strong, centralized banking system was necessary if the United States expected to develop its industries and commerce. As Secretary of the Treasury, Hamilton proposed that a national bank have the power to handle the government's funds, charter and monitor other banks throughout the country, and issue currency.

Advocates of states' rights, such as Thomas Jefferson and James Madison, opposed the national bank because they feared that the concentration of economic power at the national level would weaken the economic and political power of individual states. Jefferson and Madison supported a decentralized banking system in which the states, rather than the federal government, would charter and regulate the banks within their borders.

◆ Remind students that the advocates of states' rights were also called Anti-Federalists.

A National Bank. Hamilton's views prevailed. In 1791, Congress established the First Bank of the United States as a private business. Its 20-year charter, or legal permission to operate, outlined the ◆ bank's responsibilities, which included the issuing of representative money in the form of bank notes. These bank notes were backed by gold and silver specie. The First Bank also had supervisory powers over other banks nationwide.

A year later, Congress established a national coinage system, and the federal government began to mint gold and silver coins. It also established the dollar as the official unit of currency.

The First Bank of the United States brought some order to monetary and banking systems in the United States. It was particularly successful in regulating banks chartered by states. The First Bank of the United States, for example, required state banks to hold gold and silver for exchange. When Congress failed to renew the First Bank's 20-year charter in 1811, the number of state banks increased almost threefold, from 90 in 1811 to 250 in 1816. Without federal regulation, these state banks often issued far more currency than they could back with gold and silver. The effect was that many banks were unable to redeem paper money, causing a loss of confidence in the bank and the money.

The chaos in the nation's banking system between 1811 and 1816 caused Congress to once again establish a national bank in 1816. The Second Bank of the United States slowly restored confidence in the banking system, and in the representative money that state banks issued.

The Second Bank, however, was not without its critics, and it operated in a climate of distrust. Opponents argued that the concentration of wealth in the federal banking system gave the federal government too much power. Other critics argued that the bank restricted economic growth by failing to provide enough credit and currency for the needs of the nation. Still others claimed the bank issued too much credit and currency.

Among the duties of the United States Mint are the manufacturing of coins and the processing and storage of gold and silver bullion.

◆ **Remind students that the United States Constitution does not specify that Congress may authorize a national bank. Congress was able to do so, however, because of the "elastic clause," which gives Congress the power to make laws that are "necessary and proper" for executing other powers. The elastic clause is found in Article I, Section 8, of the United States Constitution.**

The Fall of the National Bank. The general distrust for the Second Bank became an issue in the Presidential election of 1828. This widespread distrust helped elect Andrew Jackson, a vocal critic of the bank, to the Presidency. In 1832, four years before the official end of the Second Bank's charter, President Jackson vetoed legislation that would have extended the bank's charter for another 20 years. Jackson's withdrawal of government funds in 1833 further blocked the Second Bank's effectiveness for the remaining three years of its life.

The fall of the Second Bank again caused a rise in the number of state banks. Between 1830 and 1837, the number of state banks doubled. These state banks, each issuing their own currencies, extended more and easier credit. They also kept smaller and smaller reserves of gold and silver to back the growing supply of paper money. By 1837, people found it increasingly difficult to exchange their paper money for gold or silver. Public confidence in the notes issued by state banks diminished, and many state banks failed when they were unable to redeem their bank notes in specie.

The banking crisis of 1837, however, did not revive public support for another national bank. Instead, individual states coped with the banking crisis by imposing stricter guidelines on state banks. Most states, for example, adopted the Second Bank's policy requiring state banks to hold a specie reserve equal to a certain percentage, usually 25 percent, of the notes they issued.

A National Banking System, 1860 to 1913

Between 1860 and 1913, a national banking system was created in the United States. The system brought more uniformity and stability to money and banking. During this period of time, the federal government created the dual banking system comprised of state and national banks.

The Need to Improve Banking. The fall of the Second Bank in 1836, and the lack of uniformity among the nation's state banks, created a patchwork banking system by the mid-1800s. By 1860, about 1,500 of the nation's 1,600 state banks were issuing paper money of questionable value. The currency problems, along with problems in raising money for the Civil War, convinced national leaders that the United States needed a better banking system. For these reasons, Congress took steps to establish a national banking system.

The first Congressional action was to issue currency to pay Northern war expenses. By the end of the Civil War in 1865, $450 million in currency was in circulation. Called greenbacks or United States notes, this fiat money was backed only by the federal government's promise to repay the note's face value at some future date.

A National System of Banking. The next step Congress took was to pass the National Banking Acts of 1863 and 1864. These acts gave the federal government the power to charter national banks, issue a national currency through the national banks, and require banks to hold gold and silver reserves. The government's power to charter national banks created a dual banking system composed of national banks and state banks. **National banks** were chartered by the federal government. Individual states chartered and regulated the state banks.

A further decision by the federal government was to issue a national currency through the national banks. This decision led to the eventual elimination of the 1,600 different state-bank currencies in use in the 34 states. Most of these state-bank currencies were good for local purchases only and relied on the strength and reputation of a single bank for their value. A national currency provided a nationally acceptable medium of exchange and stabilized the entire economic system.

After the Civil War, Congress took still further actions to support the national currency as a stable medium of exchange. First, Congress tied the paper money to gold with the passage of the Coinage Act of 1873. The Gold Standard Act of 1900 committed the government to the **gold standard**—a monetary system in which paper money is fully backed by and convertible into gold.

A national system of banking increased public confidence in paper currency and in the banking system. It did not, however, provide for an efficient way to regulate the amount of money circulating in the economy. Further, the system lacked any central organization.

During the Civil War, the Confederate government printed more than $1 billion in Confederate bank notes. After the war, the bank notes became worthless because no government guaranteed their value.

Banking Reform and Regulation, 1913 to the Present

The third period, from 1913 to the present, has been a period of reform and regulation. The banking system has experienced many successes as well as failures.

The Federal Reserve System. In 1913, Congress passed the Federal Reserve Act, establishing the Federal Reserve System, or Fed. The Fed became the nation's central bank. All national banks were required to join the Fed. State banks were free to join, or to operate as nonmember banks. Today about 4,750 national banks and about 1,050 state banks are Fed members.

The Fed administers this banking system through 12 Federal Reserve banks, each representing a section of the United States. A Board of Governors, appointed by the President and confirmed by the Senate, sets Fed policy. The Fed is controlled, but not owned, by the government. The more than 5,800 member banks, however, are the Fed's owners.

In its early years, the Fed experienced both success and failure. The chief success was the Fed's ability to provide the government and other banks with enough credit to finance the United States effort during World War I. Its chief failure was its inability to control credit during the 1920s. In fact, the overextension of credit and the resulting borrower defaults were major causes of the Great Depression of the 1930s.

New Deal Banking Reforms. During the Great Depression, financial panic swept the nation. Many savers withdrew their deposits from banks, causing many banks to fail. Between 1930 and 1933, more than 5,100 banks failed, some 4,000 in 1933 alone.

Franklin D. Roosevelt's election to the Presidency in 1932 brought immediate and lasting changes to the monetary and banking systems. Promising a "New Deal" to the nation's people, Roosevelt sought to restore public confidence in the economy.

With his first move, Roosevelt closed the nation's banks on March 5, 1933. The order for the "bank holiday" allowed banks to reopen only after federal auditors judged them to be financially sound. Most banks were reopened within a few weeks. Certification by the auditors helped restore confidence in the reopened banks and soon people and businesses began to use them.

Economics Reporter

What Is a Gold American Eagle?

Gold coins have not been legal tender in the United States since the early 1930s. The Gold Bullion Act that President Reagan signed in 1985, however, once again allows the United States government to mint gold coins. The American Eagle gold coin comes in denominations of $5, $10, $25, and $50. Each coin contains a different amount of gold, with the $50 coin containing a full ounce of gold. The actual price at which the gold coins sell, however, is higher than the face value of the coin. Most people who buy the gold coins do so as an investment, hoping that the coins will rise in value. In 1986, the $50 Gold American Eagle was selling for about $450.

The Banking Act of 1933, also known as the Glass-Steagall Banking Act, prohibited the Fed's member banks from selling stocks and bonds. The act also established a temporary Federal Deposit Insurance Corporation (FDIC), which insured each savings account up to $2,500. The Banking Act of 1935 made the FDIC permanent and expanded its insurance to $20,000 for each account. Today, depositors' money is insured up to $100,000 for each account.

The Gold Reserve Act removed the United States from the gold standard. The act prohibited the use of gold coins and the redemption of Federal Reserve notes at banks. By 1971, this act was expanded to prevent foreign nations from redeeming United States dollars for United States gold. The Gold Reserve Act also made it illegal for United States citizens to hold gold, a policy that was reversed in 1975. Further, Federal Reserve notes were no longer to be backed by gold.

Types of Financial Institutions

Savers can deposit their money in several different types of financial institutions, which offer different services and different interest rates. As with any financial investment, a saver who wants to maximize returns needs to comparison shop for a financial institution. The most common type of financial institutions are commercial banks, savings and loan associations, mutual savings banks, and credit unions. The chart on page 231 shows the types of financial institutions in the United States and the percentage of total assets deposited in each type of institution.

Commercial Banks. More than 15,000 commercial banks exist in the United States. Commercial banks with "national" in their titles are chartered by the federal government. All other commercial banks are chartered by the states in which they operate.

In the 1800s, commercial banks were institutions for business and commerce. In the early 1900s, commercial banks began to offer services for individuals for checking, savings deposits, and loans. Today, commercial banks control the largest amount of money in savings and checking accounts and generally offer customers the widest range of services of all financial institutions.

The main functions of **commercial banks** are to lend money; accept savings and checking deposits; ◆ and transfer money among businesses, other banks and financial institutions, and individuals. Commercial banks make about 20 percent of all loans to homeowners and almost 50 percent of all other time-payment loans.

Savings and Loan Associations. Like commercial banks, **savings and loan associations** lend money and accept deposits. Savings and loan associations were begun as "home-building societies" in the mid-1800s. Members deposited money into a large general fund and took turns borrowing it until each member was able to build a house. Today the nation has more than 4,600 savings and loan associations. Individuals and families are still their chief customers.

Recent federal regulations and laws have allowed savings and loan associations to expand. They may now offer many of the same services available at commercial banks, such as credit cards and insured deposits. Nearly 90 percent of the loans made by savings and loan associations, however, are still used to buy homes and account for about 50 percent of the nation's mortgage loans. Interest rates on both savings accounts and loans vary widely among savings and loan associations.

Mutual Savings Banks. About 460 savings banks exist in the United States. Most are located in

◆ Have the students read "Keeping a Checking Account" on pages 522–523 of the *Everyday Economics Handbook* and answer the questions that follow.

Selected Financial Institutions in the United States, 1984

Assets (in millions)	Insured Commercial Banks	S & Ls	Mutual Savings Banks[1]	Credit Unions[2]
Less than $1.0	11	70	—	7,346
$1–$4.9	320	130	—	4,688
$5–$9.9	1,150	135	1	1,284
$10–$24.9	4,064	422	7	1,051
$25–$49.9	3,761	600	3	403
$50–$99.9	2,741	671	57	266
$100–$499.0	1,956	1,034	136	139
$500 or more	478	329	63	7
Totals	14,481	3,391	267	15,144

[1]Excludes federally chartered mutual savings banks.
[2]Excludes nonfederally insured state-chartered credit unions and federally insured corporate credit unions.

Source: *Statistical Abstract of the United States, 1986*

New England and the Middle Atlantic States. **Mutual savings banks** were first set up in the early 1800s to serve savers who wished to make small deposits that were not welcomed by large commercial banks. Often a mutual savings bank has "farmer's" or "seaman's" in its title to indicate the group it originally served.

Like a savings and loan association, most business for a mutual savings bank comes from savings deposits and home loans. About 75 percent of the loans made by mutual savings banks are to buy homes. These loans make up about 10 percent of the nation's mortgages. Mutual savings banks also make installment loans, but these loans account for only 1 percent of the nation's installment loans. Interest rates for loans at mutual savings banks are often slightly lower than those at commercial banks.

Credit Unions. Employees of large businesses and members of large labor unions often set up **credit unions.** Today in the United States approximately 21,000 credit unions exist. Credit unions are owned and operated by their members. When credit union members deposit money, they purchase shares that pay interest. Credit unions use this savings-deposit pool to supply low-cost loans to credit union members. Credit unions usually offer higher interest rates on savings and lower interest rates on loans than other financial institutions. Personal, automobile, and home improvement loans account for the majority of the loan activity in credit unions, although some large credit unions also offer mortgage loans.

See Suggested Assignments, p. TM 52.

Section 2 Review

See Answers, p. A 43.

DEFINE national bank, gold standard, commercial bank

IDENTIFY Alexander Hamilton, American Eagle

1. **Comprehending Ideas** Explain how the national banking system improved banking.
2. **Interpreting Viewpoints** What were the concerns of Thomas Jefferson and James Madison over a central bank?
3. **Interpreting Graphics** Study the chart on this page. **(a)** What are the four main types of financial institutions in the United States? **(b)** Which type of financial institution generally has the most assets?

BUILDING ECONOMIC SKILLS

INTERPRETING THE VISUAL RECORD

Understanding Flow Charts

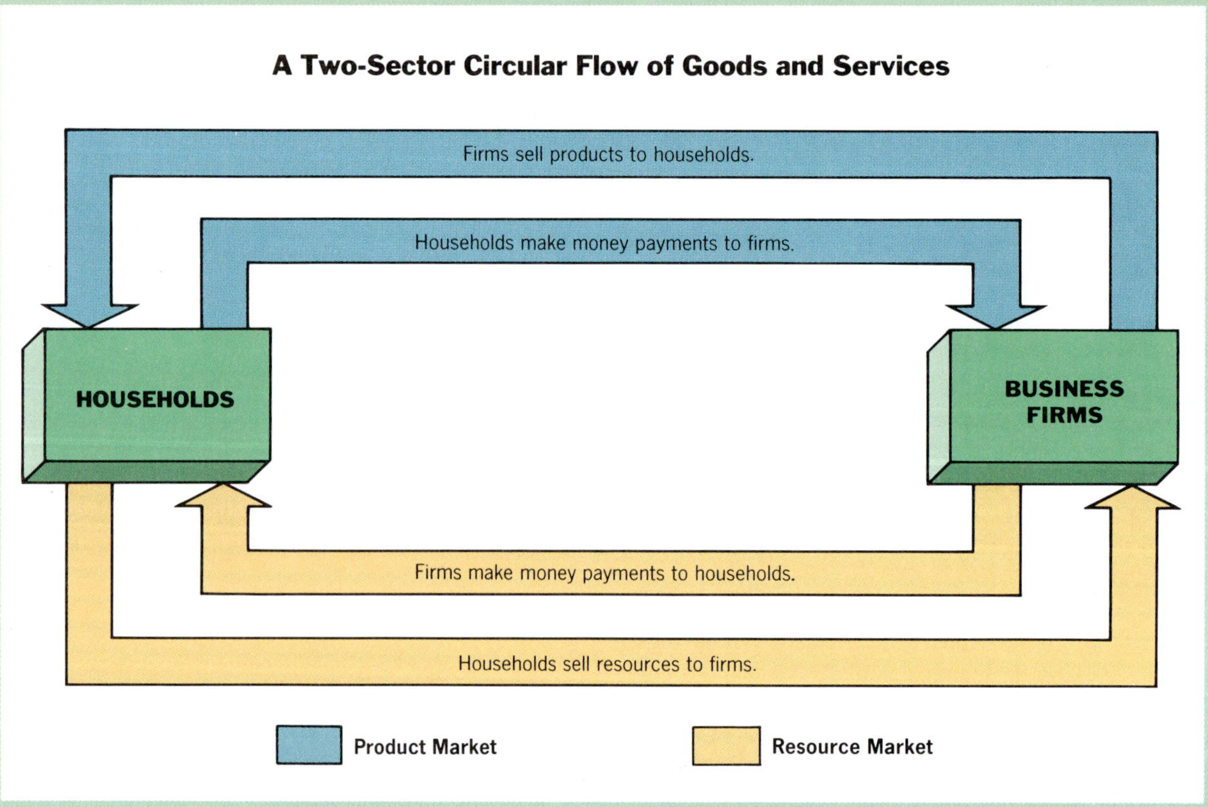

Economists often use flow charts, such as the one above, to show a sequence of events, the steps in a process, or the organization or structure of things. Interpreting information in flow charts enables the student of economics to discover important economic relationshps.

How to Understand Flow Charts

Follow these guidelines when reading a flow chart.

1. **Define the chart's purpose.** Note the chart's title and subtitles. Note all other labels. Study the information presented on the flow chart.

2. **Study the parts, or sections, of the chart.** Identify the information given in each of the chart's segments. Define key economic terms contained on the chart.

3. **Analyze the information.** Note directional lines or arrows. When tracing steps in a process, organize the data in chronological order. Look for cause-effect relationships among the data on the chart. Note intervals of time between steps in a process or in a sequence of events. When studying the organization of something, note relationships among component parts.

4. **Put the data to use.** Draw conclusions or formulate generalizations from the data.

Applying the Skill

Study the flow chart on page 232, which illustrates the two-sector circular flow of goods and services between households and business firms. The title of the chart indicates the chart's purpose, which is to show the flow of goods and services in two sectors of the economy.

Two arrows are shown at the top of the chart. The first arrow shows the flow of goods and money from business firms to households in the product market. The second arrow shows the flow of goods and services from households to business firms, again in the product market. The key indicates that these two arrows show the flow of goods and services in the product market. Two arrows are also shown on the bottom part of the chart. The outside arrow shows the flow of resources and money payments in a resource market. The inside arrow shows the flow of money payments made by firms to households.

One conclusion that can be drawn from the data on the chart is that money circulates continuously through the economy. Households make money payments to firms, and firms make money payments to households.

Practicing the Skill See Answers, p. A 44.

Study the flow chart on text page 37. Then on a separate sheet of paper, answer the following questions.

1. **(a)** What is the title of the chart? **(b)** What are the three sectors referred to in the title?

2. How many arrows are there on the chart?

3. **(a)** What items flow from households to government? **(b)** from government to households? **(c)** from government to business firms? **(d)** from business firms to government?

4. According to the chart, what are money payments by households and business firms to the government called?

5. A conclusion that can be drawn from the chart is **(a)** Firms pay more money to households than households pay to firms, **(b)** Firms pay higher taxes than households, **(c)** Government provides services to both businesses and households, **(d)** The resource market is more important than the product market to the economy.

6. How does the chart on page 232 differ from the chart on page 37?

See Key Study Questions and Key Understandings, p. TM 53.

3 Banking has undergone several major changes in recent years.

See Suggested Teaching Strategies, p. TM 53.

Several key changes have occurred in banking in the 1980s. Four major trends in banking, banking deregulation, expansion of banking services, automation, and bank failures, are responsible for the major ◆ changes in banking.

Banking Deregulation

Deregulation occurs when the government lifts some of its restrictions on an industry. Banking deregulation has resulted in more competition and greater uniformity in banking, and the rise of interstate, or regional, banking in the United States.

Deregulation has enabled S & Ls and other nonbank financial institutions to offer many of the same services as commercial banks.

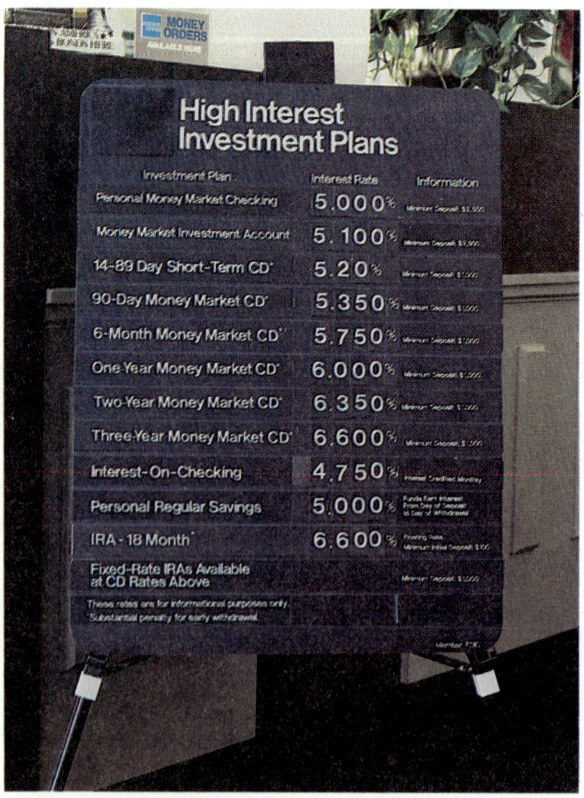

Changes in the Laws. Banking deregulation began in 1980, when Congress passed the Depository Institutions Deregulation and Monetary Control Act. This act eliminated many of the traditional differences between financial institutions. In effect, the act's provisions affecting interest rates, checking accounts, and required reserves made banking more competitive and uniform.

The first major provision deregulated interest rates. Deregulation allows financial institutions to more freely compete for people's deposits, which are the major source of their loanable funds, by offering varied interest rates.

The second major provision removed restrictions on financial institutions' ability to offer checking accounts or checking-type accounts. This provision officially ended the monopoly on checking accounts held by commercial banks. Other financial institutions may now offer similar types of checking accounts.

The third important segment of the law required that all financial institutions hold substantial reserves. This provision strengthened the banking system by ensuring that all banks had sufficient reserves to meet unexpected customer demands for their money.

While deregulation gave banks and other financial institutions more freedom to compete against one another, the government was also increasing its surveillance of federally chartered banks. The goals of this surveillance were to minimize risky loans by monitoring loaning practices, and to enforce existing regulations. During the mid-1980s, the government sent examiners to many of the nation's federally chartered banks. In 1985, bank examiners fined the Bank of Boston and the San Francisco-based Crocker Bank for not reporting a number of cash transactions to the government. The Bank of Boston was fined $500,000 and the Crocker Bank $2.25 million. In 1986, the Bank of America, the nation's second largest bank, was fined $4.8 million for similar violations.

Regional and National Banking. A major change in banking as a result of deregulation has been the growth of **regional banking.** Since the 1920s, banks and their branches had been limited by law to their home states. In 1985, however, the Supreme Court ruled that the states, rather than the

◆ Have the students read "Tellers" on page 544 of *Careers in the Marketplace.*

federal government, should regulate regional banking. The ruling allowed banks to merge with other banks or build branch offices in other states, where state legislatures were agreeable to the expansion. Many banking experts view this trend toward regional banking as beneficial, primarily because larger banks can offer a wider variety of services to customers.

Many bankers foresee problems in regional banking. Smaller banks fear that larger banks from distant regions will be unresponsive to customers' needs. In addition, smaller banks fear that the mere size of the larger banks gives the larger banks a competitive edge. For example, the four largest banks in New York City have combined assets of $326 billion compared to the combined assets of $311 billion of all banks in the 10-state Southeastern region. Small banks also fear hostile mergers, in which banks that wish to remain independent are absorbed by larger banks.

Larger banks—especially those in New York, Texas, and California—support full interstate banking, or nationwide banking. Nationwide banking would allow any bank to build or merge with banks in any state. Supporters of nationwide banking claim that present regulations discriminate against the larger banks. These supporters argue that the move to national banking would create more competitive markets. Further, they note that "bigness" in the banking industry would allow it to benefit from the economies of scale.

Many banking experts believe that nationwide banking will replace regional banking by the early 1990s. In 1985 alone, Alaska, Arizona, Maine, New York, South Dakota, and Washington had already opened their doors to any bank.

Automatic Banking

A second major trend of the 1980s is banking automation. Banking automation relies on the use of computers to handle many types of banking transactions. In 1978, the Electronic Funds Transfer Act paved the way for computer systems to handle many banking functions. Electronic Funds Transfer (EFT) increases banks' efficiency by allowing them to immediately record banking transactions by computer rather than on paper. It also saves banks money by decreasing the number of workers needed for banking operations.

Statewide and nationwide automatic teller systems have given individuals increased access to their money.

Automatic Teller Machines. Since the late 1970s, financial institutions have been using ◆ **automatic teller machines** (ATMs). Many routine banking tasks that had been handled by bank tellers are now handled by ATMs. Bank customers, for example, make deposits or withdrawals from savings or checking accounts at ATMs. They also make payments on bank loans or transfer money from one account to another automatically. Plastic ATM cards, along with a **personal identification number** (PIN) that is keyed into the ATM, allow customers to use ATMs 24 hours per day. By 1986, more than 135 million ATM cards were in circulation. In addition, the 60,000 ATMs accounted for about 9 percent of all banking transactions in the United States.

◆ Discussion topic: Whether the United States still needs nationwide banking.

Few banking experts believe that the large-scale banking failures that occurred during the Great Depression are possible today.

Automatic Clearing House Services. Another service based on EFT technology is **automatic clearing house services** (ACH), a system that transfers money from a customer's account to that of creditors. In other words, ACH pays people's bills for them. Usually, ACH pays regular monthly bills, such as home mortgage payments or rents, insurances, and utility bills.

Point-of-Sale Terminals. Introduced in the early 1980s, point-of-sale terminals, or POS terminals, are located in stores or other businesses. POS transactions involve the direct transfer of money from buyers' bank accounts to sellers' bank accounts. Buyers pay for goods at the checkout counter by inserting a plastic card, called a **debit card,** into the terminal. If buyers have enough money in their accounts to cover the purchases, money is automatically transferred from the buyers' accounts to the sellers' accounts. By 1986, POS terminals were in use at many gas stations and convenience food stores in the United States.

Some banking experts believe that the use of debit cards will soon replace the use of checks in the American economy. They note that debit cards help merchants by ending the risk of bad checks and the inconvenience and expense of processing credit-card transactions. Consumers also benefit because they do not need to carry cash or checks. They can also regularly check the amount of money remaining in their accounts by inserting their cards into POS terminals.

The use of debit cards, however, has some drawbacks. For example, debit cards can only be used in stores with POS terminals. In addition, consumers are accustomed to the **float time** offered by credit cards. When consumers can make a credit-card purchase at the beginning of a billing period, they do not have to pay the bill until the end of the billing period. The time between the purchase and the payment is the float time. Finally, the technology is new and fairly expensive for businesses and banks. As a result, the fees for using debit cards are high, discouraging their use. ◆

Today, less than 3 percent of the adult population in the United States uses debit cards, compared to about 88 percent who use checks. Some debit card systems, however, are successful. Florida's Honor system, for example, has issued over 4 million debit cards. The Honor system is owned and operated by nine large Florida banks, and handles about 90,000 debit card transactions per month. The Mobil Oil Corporation also has installed thousands of POS terminals at its gas stations, hoping their convenience will attract customers from competing stations.

◆ **Have the students read "Banking Officers" on page 540 of *Careers in the Marketplace.***

Electronic Home Banking. The fourth aspect of automated banking is electronic home banking and the use of personal computers (PCs). **Electronic home banking** links PCs in homes with the bank's computers. Bank records can be accessed and many transactions done by home computer. Home banking provides convenience to customers and helps banks by making the recording of transactions less costly and time-consuming.

By 1986, about 50 banks had established home computer links with about 60,000 customers. One of the nation's largest banks, New York's Chemical Bank, has home-computer ties with more than 21,000 customers through its Pronto system.

Bank Closures, 1980–1986

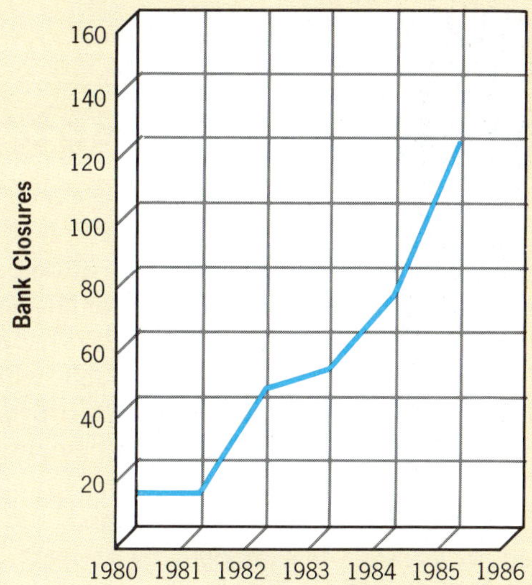

Sources: *Statistical Abstract of the United States, 1986*
Federal Deposit Insurance Corporation

Financial Troubles in Banking

The third major trend of the 1980s is the growing number of **bank failures** and near failures in the banking system. A bank fails when it no longer has enough assets on deposit to cover its accounts. Federal regulators close the bank when this happens. The trend in bank failures is shown in the graph on this page. Banks are considered near failures when government regulators suspend their banking operations and take over their management. These financial troubles have shaken the public's confidence in banking.

A Rough Time for Banking. More banks have failed in the 1980s than in any decade since the depression. Between 1980 and 1985, the number of FDIC-insured banks that failed rose from 10 to more than 100. Added to this total are the numerous near failures and banks in serious difficulty.

Not included in this total, for example, is the 1984 near collapse of the nation's seventh-largest commercial bank, Continental Illinois National Bank and Trust Company of Chicago. Its $1.1 billion in losses represented the second-largest banking loss in the history of United States banking. The FDIC bailout of Continental cost $4.5 billion. In 1985, however, the bank earned $151 million. In 1986, it announced plans to acquire three suburban Chicago banks.

Despite Continental's recovery, financial woes have continued. BankAmerica, the nation's second-largest bank to New York's Citicorp, posted three consecutive quarterly losses, including a $640 million dollar loss in the second quarter of 1986. In November 1986, First Interstate Bancorp made a merger offer intended to infuse money into asset-poor BankAmerica. In July 1986, the First National Bank and Trust of Oklahoma City collapsed. Its losses of $1.6 billion surpassed even Continental Illinois' losses. The FDIC was forced in 1986 to adopt a policy that promises to rescue all banks, regardless of size, in the event of bank collapse. ◆

Other Banking Crises. Other financial concerns troubled the United States banking community in the 1980s. The Farm Credit System (FCS), a network of 37 banks that offers loans to farmers nationwide through so-called "farm banks," suffered from a wave of loan defaults in the 1980s. Many farmers were unable to make payments on property and equipment that had been purchased with FCS credit. As the nation's sixth-largest financial institution with about $71 billion in outstanding loans, the FCS was on the verge of bankruptcy by 1986. The FCS continued to lobby in Washington, D.C., for federal assistance to help cover its multibillion dollar losses.

◆ Report topic: How the "upstreaming" of loans tied Continental Illinois to Penn Square and led to Continental's fall.

DECISION MAKERS IN THE ECONOMY

Peter T. Buchanan

First Boston Corporation, one of the nation's largest investment banks, was almost out of business in 1978, the year it earned only $1 million. That same year Peter T. Buchanan became president of First Boston, and in 1982 he became chief executive officer as well. Under Buchanan's management, the bank made a dramatic turnaround. By September 1985, it had earned $94.7 million and was expected to increase that amount to at least $120 million by the end of the year.

As the highest-ranked official of First Boston, Buchanan is responsible for the coordination of many different departments, the most profitable of which is mergers and acquisitions. The department worked on almost every major oil merger of the early 1980s. It also played a role in Philip Morris's buyout of General Foods.

Other departments within First Boston earn much less than mergers and acquisitions; yet they, too, are essential to First Boston's total success. To compete with other major investment banks, First Boston must offer a full range of investment services. Buchanan must decide when to take profits from one department to support the activities of another.

Managing a full-service bank the size of First Boston is no easy matter. Nevertheless, Peter Buchanan has successfully balanced the needs of First Bank's various divisions with the institution's overall goals.

CASE STUDY

Savings and Loan Associations in Crisis

The most visible crisis in United States banking during the 1980s involved savings and loan associations (S&Ls). Coupled with the rising number of commercial- and savings-bank failures, and the near bankruptcy of the Farm Credit System, the S&L crisis further eroded public confidence in United States financial institutions.

A number of factors contributed to the S&L crisis. First, many loans granted in the early 1980s to S&L customers, both individuals and businesses, were classified as nonperforming. That is, borrowers were not making payments on the loans. This situation caused some S&Ls to close and some to be absorbed by larger financial institutions. Other S&Ls continued to operate without earning a profit. By 1985, industry experts estimated that about 17 percent of the nation's 3,500 S&Ls were either not profitable or insolvent. A financial institution is declared insolvent when its assets are not enough to pay off its debts if the institution closed its doors.

Another factor contributing to the S&L crisis was that some S&Ls were privately insured. About 30 states approved private deposit insurance during the mid-1980s, allowing state-chartered S&Ls to choose private insurance instead of insurance provided by the Federal Savings and Loan Insurance Corporation (FSLIC). By 1986, nearly 18 percent of the nation's S&Ls had chosen private insurance. Private insurance plans, however, lacked the financial resources to handle S&L failures in some states.

The problems experienced by S&Ls were most serious in Ohio and Maryland. In 1985, a rash of panic runs on privately insured S&Ls in Ohio forced the governor to temporarily close 69 institutions. A

panic run occurs when many depositors withdraw their deposits at the same time.

The panic originated with the closing of Cincinnati's Home State Savings, which had made a series of bad investments. Ohio's "thrift holiday" (S&Ls are called thrifts because they offer lower interest rates on loans.) was likened to F.D.R.'s "bank holiday" of 1933. S&Ls in Ohio were not allowed to reopen until federal auditors judged them to be sound.

In Maryland in the mid-1980s, 102 S&Ls also were privately insured. Like the Ohio thrifts, the private insurance provided by the Maryland Savings-Share Insurance Corporation was insufficient to cover the losses if a major run on the 102 non-FSLIC institutions occurred. Still shaken by the Ohio crisis a few months earlier, and by banking improprieties at one S&L—Baltimore's Old Court Savings & Loan—panicky depositors ran to withdraw their savings. To halt the panic run, Maryland's governor was forced for a time to limit individual withdrawals to $1,000.

By the mid-1980s, the federal and state governments were taking steps to correct the problems of banking improprieties and sagging public confidence. The most important reform was to encourage privately insured thrifts, through legislation and public pressure, to join the FSLIC. Some states, such as Maryland, enacted legislation to require S&Ls to join the federal agency.

Membership in FSLIC is beneficial to S&Ls and their customers for three reasons. First, the FSLIC guarantees depositors' money up to $100,000 for each account. This guarantee reduces the risk of saving in S&Ls and thereby reduces the likelihood of panic runs on S&Ls. Second, FSLIC-membership requires additional federal supervision and regulation of S&Ls. Federal supervision makes banking improprieties and risky loans less possible. Third, the FSLIC assumes responsibility for finding a buyer for troubled S&Ls if failure is imminent. This service saves many S&Ls from collapse.

See Suggested Assignments, p. TM 53.

Section 3 Review See Answers, p. A 44.

DEFINE deregulation, automatic teller machine (ATM), debit card, float time

IDENTIFY Peter T. Buchanan

1. **Summarizing Ideas** Why did the government deregulate the banking system?
2. **Comprehending Ideas (a)** What are the advantages of regional banking? **(b)** What are the major aspects of automatic banking?
3. **Evaluating Ideas** Would mandatory deposit insurance have prevented panic runs on S & Ls in Ohio in 1985? Explain your reasoning.

CHAPTER 10 SUMMARY

Money is a key to the economic process. For centuries, people traded and bartered, but money made more sophisticated transactions possible. The basic functions of money are as a medium of exchange, a standard of value, and a store of value. To best accomplish these functions, money should be durable, portable, divisible, have stability of value, and have acceptability. Different societies use different items as money. Some societies rely on commodity money. Some societies use representative money, and some societies use fiat money. Coins and paper money, which is fiat money, and checks and near money, which are representative money, serve as money in the United States.

Like money, banking has evolved to meet the needs of the people in the changing United States society. Problems with the First and Second Banks of the United States led to a period of open banking. During this period, state and wildcat banks boomed. Financial panics and the Civil War, however, convinced Congress to reestablish a national banking system. Further troubles and panics led to the development of the Federal Reserve and the beginning of the modern banking system. Today, Americans can choose from a wide variety of financial institutions, including commercial banks, savings and loan associations, and credit unions.

Banking has changed rapidly in recent years. Federal banking deregulation has led to competition and reorganizations in the banking industry. These changes have led to an expansion of banking services. Technological advances have led to banking automation. These changes and economic fluctuations have resulted in financial troubles throughout the banking system. Even more banking changes loom on the horizon as banking deals with these changes and the changes in United States society.

CHAPTER 10 REVIEW

For Answers to Chapter 10 Review, see p. A 44.

Reviewing Economic Terms

Supply the economic term that correctly completes each sentence.

1. The direct exchange of goods and services without a medium of exchange is called ____.
2. The legal requirement that the currency of the United States be backed by specie reserves is called the ____ ____.
3. Money that has value because of a government decree is called ____ money.
4. Financial institutions that are created primarily to make mortgage loans are called ____ ____ ____ ____.
5. Anything that people commonly accept in exchange for goods and services is ____.
6. When many depositors withdraw their deposits at the same time a ____ ____ occurs.
7. In colonial Virginia, tobacco—an example of ____ ____ money—was traded for other goods and services.
8. The lifting of some of the government's restrictions on banking is a process called ____.
9. Because buyers and sellers agree to accept money in payment for goods or services, money's single most important use is as a ____ ____ ____.

Exercising Economic Skills

1. **Understanding Flow Charts** Study the flow chart on page 232. Then find a flow chart in a newspaper or magazine (*USA Today* and the *New York Times* often use flow charts to illustrate information). Using a paragraph for each flow shown, explain the various flows involved in the chart.
2. **Keeping a Checking Account** Study the feature on pages 522–523. Then secure information from a local bank about the types of checking accounts it offers. Develop a chart that lists the following for each account: **(a)** name, **(b)** specific requirements, and **(c)** special features. **(d)** In a paragraph, specify which account you would recommend to a recent high school graduate with $1,000 to put into a savings account and explain why you recommended that particular account.

Thinking Critically About Economics

1. **Summarizing Ideas** **(a)** Why is money's function as a standard of value so important in record keeping? **(b)** Why did the United States develop a central banking system? **(c)** Why do some bankers oppose the idea of regional banking?
2. **Understanding Ideas** **(a)** Why did President Andrew Jackson veto the Second Bank of the United States? **(b)** Why did some states begin to require that banks hold a specie reserve of a certain percentage of their notes?
3. **Organizing Ideas** Trace the development of the United States banking system.
4. **Interpreting Ideas** What is the advantage of not requiring a currency to be backed by a reserve of specie?
5. **Evaluating Ideas** Defend or refute this statement: President Roosevelt was right to declare a "bank holiday."

Extending Economic Knowledge

1. Research the various forms of money that have been used throughout history. **(a)** Prepare a chart or poster with at least five examples of items formerly used as money. **(b)** For each item shown on the chart as money, summarize the conditions or problems that would limit the use of the item as money today.
2. Contact an official at a local financial institution to find out how the Depository Institutions Deregulation and Monetary Control Act of 1980 has affected its business. Ask: **(a)** What changes in business operations have taken place since the act's passage? **(b)** How has competition changed? **(c)** What new approaches to banking has the bank taken since the act went into effect? **(d)** Has the act had a positive or negative effect on business? on banking in general?
3. Study newspaper or magazine accounts of the near collapse of the Continental Illinois Bank of Chicago in 1984. **(a)** Propose a regulation that would have prevented the bank's potential collapse. **(b)** Would this regulation be supported by most financial institutions? Why or why not?

Using Primary Sources

The Depository Institutions Deregulation Act is a major section in the larger Depository Institutions Deregulation and Monetary Control Act of 1980. The Depository Institutions Degregulation Act set in motion a process to deregulate the banking industry that was completed in 1986. As you read the following excerpts from the act, consider how this legislation seeks to make the banking industry more competitive. Why did Congress believe that a more competitive banking industry would benefit the economy?

The Depository Institutions Deregulation Act of 1980

Sec. 201. This title may be cited as the "Depository Institutions Deregulation Act of 1980."

Sec. 202. (a) The Congress hereby find that—

(1) limitations on the interest rates which are payable on deposits and accounts discourage persons from saving money, create inequities for depositors, impede the ability of depository institutions to compete for funds, and have not achieved their purpose of providing an even flow of funds for home mortgage lending; and

(2) all depositors, and particularly those with modest savings, are entitled to receive a market rate of return on their savings as soon as it is economically feasible for depository institutions to pay such a rate.

(b) It is the purpose of this title [Title II] to provide for the orderly phase-out and the ultimate elimination of the limitations on the maximum rates of interest and dividends which may be paid on deposits and accounts by depository institutions by extending the authority to impose such limitations for 6 years, subject to specific standards designed to ensure a phase-out of such limitations to market rates of interest. . . .

Sec. 203. (b) The Deregulation Committee shall consist of the Secretary of the Treasury, the Chairman of the Board of Governors of the Federal Reserve System, the Chairman of the Board of Directors of the Federal Deposit Insurance Corporation, the Chairman of the Federal Home Loan Bank Board, and the Chairman of the National Credit Union Administration Board, who shall be voting members, and the Comptroller of the Currency who shall be a nonvoting member of the Deregulation Committee. The Deregulation Committee shall hold public meetings at least quarterly. . . . The Deregulation Committee may not take any action unless such action is approved by a majority vote of the voting members of the Deregulation Committee. . . .

Sec. 204. (a) The Deregulation Committee shall . . . provide for the orderly phase-out and the ultimate elimination of the limitations on the maximum rates of interest and dividends which may be paid on deposits and accounts as rapidly as economic conditions warrant. The phase-out of such limitations may be achieved by the Deregulation Committee by the gradual increase in such limitations applicable to all existing categories of accounts, the complete elimination of the limitations applicable to particular categories of accounts, the creation of new categories of accounts not subject to limitations or which limitations set at current market rates, any combination of the above method, or any other method.

(b) The Deregulation Committee shall work toward providing all depositors with a market rate of return on their savings with due regard for the safety and soundness of depository institutions. . . .

Source Review

For Answers to Source Review, see p. A 45.

1. What four reasons does Congress offer to justify deregulating interest rates paid by depository institutions to depositors?
2. What is the purpose of the Depository Institutions Deregulation Act of 1980? How does the elimination of interest ceilings help depositors receive a "market rate of return on their savings"?
3. How does deregulation in the banking industry promote competition among financial institutions?
4. What is the function of the Deregulation Committee? Who comprises the committee?

CHAPTER 11

See Chapter Overview, p. TM 54.
See Chapter Objectives, p. TM 54.
See Introducing the Chapter, p. TM 54.
See Extending Economic Knowledge on text p. 264.

The Nation's Federal Reserve System

[United States monetary policy in 1985] was the classic illustration of the power of very big money, through its proxy the Federal Reserve, which really runs the U.S. economy, sacrificing U.S. jobs and farms on the altar of Wall Street financial solvency.

Warren T. Brookes

1 The Federal Reserve System is the central bank of the United States.
- The History of Central Banking
- The Organization of the Federal Reserve System
- Features of the System

2 The Federal Reserve System and its services strengthen the United States economy.
- The Fed's Banking Services
- The Fed's Services to the Federal Government

3 The Federal Reserve's monetary policy promotes economic growth and stability.
- The Money Supply
- Monetary Policy
- Components of Monetary Policy

4 Monetary policy in the United States economy has limitations.
- Economic Forecasting and Time Lags
- National Priorities and Trade-offs
- Lack of Coordinated Economic Policies
- Disagreements Over Policy Goals

CHAPTER 11 STUDY GUIDE

Chapter Focus

Chapter 11 examines the history, organization, and functions of the Federal Reserve System. The chapter discusses how the Federal Reserve regulates monetary policy and what effects and limitations this has on the economy.

As you study the chapter, look for the details that support each of the following statements.

1. The Federal Reserve System is the central bank of the United States.
2. The Federal Reserve System and its services strengthen the United States economy.
3. The Federal Reserve's monetary policy promotes economic growth and stability.
4. Monetary policy in the United States economy has its limitations.

See Preteaching Vocabulary, p. TM 54.

Terms to Know

The following terms, while not the only terms emphasized in this chapter, are basic to your understanding of the Federal Reserve System. Determine the meaning of each term, either by using the Glossary or by watching for context clues as you read the chapter.

central bank
member bank
check clearing
money supply
M1
M2
monetary policy
easy-money policy
tight-money policy
reserve requirement
discount rate
prime rate
open market operation
moral suasion
margin requirement

See Key Study Questions and Key Understandings, p. TM 55.

1 The Federal Reserve System is the central bank of the United States.

See Suggested Teaching Strategies, p. TM 55.

Central banking in the United States has gone through three distinct periods of development. The first period, from the 1780s to the 1860s, was a time of debate and experimentation. The second period, from the 1860s to 1913, witnessed the creation of a national banking system. The third and current period in the development of banking is characterized by banking reforms and regulation guided by the ◆ Federal Reserve System.

The History of Central Banking

The history of central banking in the United States has been stormy. It began with the founding of the First Bank of the United States during the administration of President George Washington (1789–1797) and continued to evolve into today's Federal Reserve System.

The Idea of Central Banking. During the early years of the nation, the central bank issue was part of a larger battle between the Federalists and Antifederalists, or states' rights advocates. A **central bank,** a depository for federal funds and place where banks bank, seemed to the Antifederalists to concentrate all financial power in the national government's hands.

Congressional support for the Federalist view, however, led to the establishment of the First Bank of the United States as a private business in 1791. The bank's 20-year charter authorized it to issue currency and to serve as the official depository for the federal government's funds. As a private corporation, the Bank of the United States also accepted deposits from other banks and carried on normal commercial activities without government intervention. The 20-year charter of the Second Bank of the United States (1816–1836) gave it similar powers.

The First and Second banks of the United States strengthened the nation's monetary and banking

◆ In many nations, such as France, the government owns both the central bank and the commercial banks.

HIGHLIGHTS IN ECONOMICS

The Founding of the Federal Reserve System

The Federal Reserve System grew out of the work of the National Monetary Commission (1908–1911), chaired by Senator Nelson Aldrich. Legislators had never before had as much information about financial operations as the commission's 42 reports provided. Congress knew that the problems identified by the National Monetary Commission had to be addressed. The path that the reform would take, however, was still unknown.

Democrats and Republicans envisioned solutions to reform differently. Various special interest groups, including bankers from large city institutions and bankers from small banks in the country, also had different views on reform.

The Aldrich Plan was the first specific proposal for reform. It was included in the commission's final report to Congress in March 1912. The Aldrich Plan called for the formation of a National Reserve Association, a kind of central bank. It did not address, however, the need for the building of reserves. Although the plan had the approval of the city bankers and might have passed a Republican-controlled Congress, it never had the opportunity to become law. Woodrow Wilson, the Democratic candidate, won the 1912 Presidential election, and the Democrats gained control of both the House and the Senate.

Soon after the election, a Congressional subcommittee began drafting a new banking plan that was in keeping with the outlook of the incoming administration. The Republicans generally preferred a single, privately owned central bank. The Democrats, however, favored a system of regional banks owned by the government.

After lengthy hearings, discussions, and modifications, the Democrat-inspired bill passed Congress as the Federal Reserve Act and was signed into law by President Wilson on December 23, 1913. The law created the Federal Reserve System, or the Fed, the topic of this chapter.

The Federal Reserve Act has proved to be one of the most important pieces of legislation passed during Wilson's term in office. From the beginning, the Fed had the authority to deal with the nation's inelastic currency and stockpile of reserves. While the Fed failed to prevent the Great Depression, it has since been strengthened to become a powerful central banking system.

system by supervising and regulating state banks. Local currencies were generally stable, and bank failures were few. Financial stability earned for the United States a high credit rating among European creditors.

Central banking, however, faced opposition. Many state banks, as profit-making institutions, opposed a central bank because it was often in direct competition with them. The central bank also restricted the right of local banks to issue local currency. As a major holder of local bank notes, the central bank could demand redemption in gold or silver specie for notes that were issued. This potential demand angered local bankers, who often preferred to print more money than they could back. It also angered small businesspeople and debtors, who

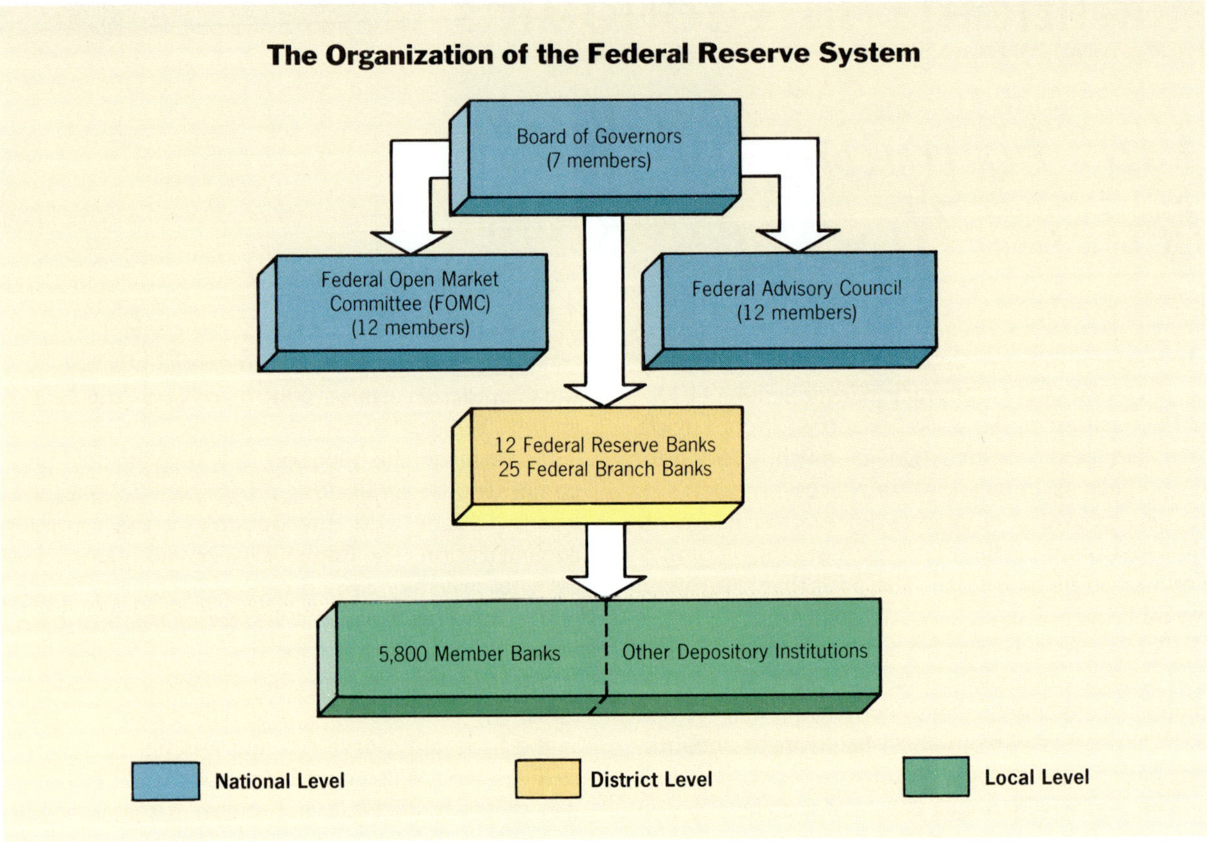

favored a growing money supply that would stimulate business and provide cheap money.

The opponents of central banking found a champion in President Andrew Jackson (1829–1837). In 1833, Jackson vetoed a bill that would have extended the bank's charter for another 20 years. Jackson's veto ended central banking in the United States until 1913, when the Federal Reserve System was established.

The Role of Economic Panics. Sectional fears and rivalries made the chartering of another central bank during the 1800s impossible. Even the depressions, or panics, of 1873, 1884, and 1893 failed to ◆ revive the central bank. The Panic of 1907, which caused the collapse of many banks and endangered the entire monetary system, however, broke the historic resistance to central banking. In response to the panic, Congress established in 1908 the National Monetary Commission.

The Commission identified two major causes of the Panic of 1907. First, during periods of prosperity and panic, the nation's monetary system had no mechanism for expanding the money supply. During prosperity, business expansion was restricted because consumers and businesses competed for a fixed supply of loanable funds. During financial-panic runs, sound banks were driven into bankruptcy because they had nowhere to turn to get emergency cash.

Second, the system of **pyramided reserves** failed. The system worked this way. As a safety precaution, virtually all smaller, local banks deposited some of their reserves with larger city banks. The larger city banks deposited some of their own cash reserves in the largest commercial banks in the nation's financial centers such as New York, Chicago, or San Francisco. These financial center banks used part of these deposits to extend loans and held the rest as reserves.

◆ **A sharp decline on the New York Stock Exchange that began in March 1907 sparked the Panic of 1907. The panic resulted in increased business failures, runs on banks, and widespread public alarm.**

During periods of prosperity, the larger banks received more deposits and had more funds to loan. At such times, the system of pyramided reserves encouraged business expansion. During times of depression, however, financial-panic runs obliged the smaller banks to withdraw their deposits from the larger banks. The reserves of the larger banks could not cover the sudden demand for cash because the larger banks loaned out most of the deposits. Consequently, many banks and businesses went bankrupt, and many individual depositors lost their savings.

To solve these two major causes of the Panic of 1907, the Commission proposed the reestablishment of a central bank. After lengthy debates, Congress passed the Federal Reserve Act in 1913, creating a central bank called the Federal Reserve System, or the Fed. The Fed's stated goals were "to furnish an elastic currency, [and]... to establish a more effective supervision of banking in the United States."

The Organization of the Federal Reserve System

The Federal Reserve, organized as it is on both national and state levels (see the chart on page 246), is unlike any other banking system in the world.

The National Level. The Fed makes its most important decisions at the national level. The Fed's two most important decision-making bodies are the Board of Governors and the Federal Open Market Committee.

The Board of Governors is the most important body in the Federal Reserve System. The board supervises the Fed's banking services, and its policies regulate the money supply. The President of the United States appoints, and the Senate confirms, the seven members of the Board of Governors.

Ideally, the governors represent different sections of the country and different economic interests such as agriculture, industry, commerce, and finance. The 14-year terms of the governors are staggered so that one governor is appointed every two years. The board's chairperson serves a four-year term. The long terms of office and staggered appointments are designed to free the governors from pressures that may be exerted by the executive and legislative branches of the federal government.

The Federal Open Market Committee (FOMC) is composed of 12 members. The seven members of the Board of Governors and the president of the Federal Reserve Bank of New York are permanent members of the FOMC. The remaining four members are presidents of district Federal Reserve banks who serve one-year terms on a rotating basis. The FOMC meets eight times a year to discuss the buying and selling of government securities. The sale and purchase of government securities by the Fed is known as open-market operations.

The District Level. Each of the Fed's 12 district banks services a designated region of the United States (see the map on page 248). In addition, 25 branch offices of the district Federal Reserve banks are located throughout the nation. All banks chartered by the federal government are members of the Fed, or **member banks.** About 5,800 of the nation's 15,000 federally chartered commercial banks are member banks and about 1,000 large state-chartered commercial banks have voluntarily joined the Fed.

The member banks in each Federal Reserve district elect six of the nine directors of the Federal Reserve Bank in their district. No more than three of the six directors can be bankers. The Board of Governors selects the remaining three directors.

The Federal Open Market Committee (FOMC) is directing the purchase of foreign currency.

Features of the System

Though its responsibilities and services are similar to those of central banks in other countries, the Fed has many unique aspects.

Common Elements. There are three common elements to central banks throughout the world. First, central banks lend money to private banks and the government.

Second, central banks hold cash reserves. These cash reserves represent a fund of ready cash for short-term borrowing by banks or by the government. The cash reserves are an emergency fund, guaranteeing that money is available when needed.

Third, central banks are nonprofit institutions. Their task is to hold large amounts of cash to make loans to banks and to the government. Their goal is to stabilize the national monetary and banking systems.

Unique Features. The Federal Reserve System in the United States has several features that distinguish it from central banks in other nations. These distinctive features include the ownership and control of the Fed by the member banks, the lack of a single central bank, and membership in the Fed.

In most other countries, the government owns all or a majority of the central bank stock, giving the government control of the bank. In the United ◆ States, however, member banks rather than the government own stock in the Federal Reserve banks in their respective districts. This privately held stock, which cannot be resold to other investors, allows the Fed to operate with a high degree of independence within the government.

In most nations, the national government establishes uniform central bank policies. Under the Federal Reserve System, however, the district banks have some flexibility in designing policies that fit

◆ Report topic: Whether it is important for the Federal Reserve System to stay independent of government.

DECISION MAKERS IN THE ECONOMY

Martha R. Seger

On May 31, 1984, President Reagan nominated Martha R. Seger, a professor of finance at Central Michigan University, to the Federal Reserve Board of Governors. She was to replace departing board member Nancy Teeters, the first female member in the Federal Reserve Board's 70-year history. The Senate did not approve Seger's appointment immediately. President Reagan then exercised his executive power to make appointments during a recess without Senate confirmation. His executive order sent Seger to the Fed for a year. She later received Senate approval, at which time her term was extended to the full 14 years.

During Seger's confirmation hearings, she reported that her views on monetary matters were influenced by many different schools of economic thought. In general, however, she supports President Reagan's supply-side policies and disapproves of government regulation on the grounds that it usually does not provide long-term solutions to economic problems.

Seger has argued that the Fed can allow faster growth of the money supply and lower interest rates without giving rise to runaway inflation. She also urged the Fed to cut the discount rate, which it did in the spring of 1986.

Seger is a strong advocate of an easy-money policy. This position often put her at odds with former Fed Chairman Paul Volcker. Volcker believed that tighter measures were needed to keep the economy in check. In Volcker's view, controlling inflation is the Fed's top priority, even in periods of lower inflation. Seger, on the other hand, believes that the Fed can safely pursue a policy that will encourage economic growth.

the unique needs of their districts. Further, the Fed is insulated from the pressures of the federal executive and legislative branches of the government by the long, overlapping terms of office. It is also insulated from public pressures because its governors are not elected officials.

In most other countries, there is a single central bank. In the United States, the decision to create 12 separate Federal Reserve banks was based on the traditional fear of a centralized national bank dominated by a few influential financiers. The Fed's decentralized structure protects the nation's monetary and banking systems from direct government control and allows each bank to respond to regional needs.

In most nations, membership in the central bank is usually compulsory for all depository institutions. All national banks are required to join the Fed. For state-chartered banks, membership in the Fed is voluntary. In fact, only about 40 percent of the commercial banks in the nation are members.

Section 1 Review See Answers, p. A 46.

DEFINE central bank, pyramided reserves

IDENTIFY National Monetary Commission

1. **Summarizing Ideas** Name and describe the three distinct periods in the development of central banking in the United States.
2. **Understanding Ideas** What are the two major decision-making bodies in the Federal Reserve System?
3. **Comparing Ideas** What features distinguish the Federal Reserve System from central banks in other nations?
4. **Interpreting Graphics** Study the flow chart on page 246. From your reading and the chart, describe the four flows from the Board of Directors illustrated on the chart.

See Suggested Assignments, p. TM 55.

See Key Study Questions and Key Understandings, p. TM 56.

2 The Federal Reserve System and its services strengthen the United States economy.

See Suggested Teaching Strategies, p. TM 56.

The Fed provides seven major services that strengthen the nation's monetary and banking systems. ◆ These services include clearing checks, extending loans to banks and to the government, transferring funds nationwide, supervising and regulating member banks, serving as the government's fiscal agent, distributing paper currency, and regulating the money supply. These seven services are classified into two groups of services: the Fed's services to banks and the Fed's services to government.

The Fed's Banking Services

The main services the Fed provides for banks are clearing checks and making loans to banks.

Clearing Checks. Americans write about 40 billion checks every year. The Fed keeps track of these billions of monetary transfers through the service of **check clearing**, which is a method of crediting and debiting checking accounts.

Computer technology has reduced the time it takes for checks to clear through the banking system. The Fed's advanced communications network allows it to transfer electronically large sums of money over the wires rather than through the mail. The flow chart on page 251 illustrates check clearing and highlights the Fed's role in the process.

Loans to Banks. New currency and the money reserves of member and nonmember banks provide the Fed with a pool of cash. The Fed loans money from these cash reserves to banks and the government, usually for periods of from one day to several weeks. Banks often need short-term loans when their depositors make large and unexpected withdrawals, leaving the banks with a temporary shortage of cash.

Most Federal Reserve loans are granted only for seasonal factors, natural disasters, and financial emergencies. Seasonal factors are the fairly predictable annual events that deplete cash reserves in banks. For example, the cash reserves of small rural banks are often reduced during planting or harvesting seasons when farmers withdraw their cash to fund farm operations. Similarly, the Christmas season typically involves high withdrawals from deposits and, thus, reduces cash reserves in banks. In

The 12 Federal Reserve Banks handle approximately 85 percent of all the banking system's check-clearing services.

◆ Class activity: Have the students list the ways in which the Fed is a banker's bank.

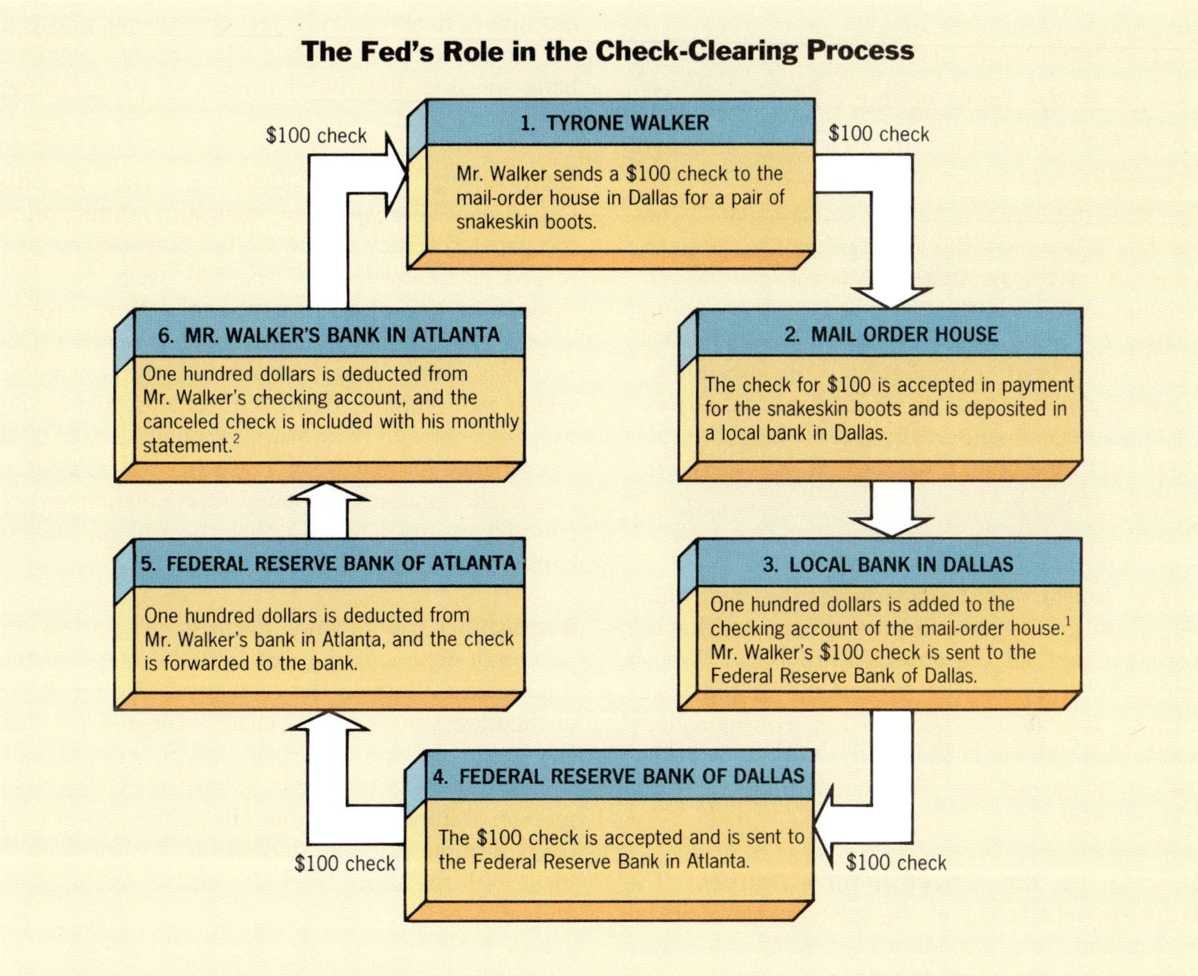

1. The electronic transfer of funds has greatly shortened the time it takes for checks to clear.
2. Some banks do not return canceled checks to the check writer.

each case, the Fed lends money to banks to replenish their cash supply.

In the aftermath of such natural disasters as ◆ floods, hurricanes, tornadoes, and earthquakes, cash withdrawals and the demand for new loans from area banks are high. To ensure adequate cash for cleanup and repair operations, the Fed loans money to federal relief agencies and to local banks.

In financial emergencies, the Fed serves as a "lender of last resort" by making emergency loans to banks. Under special circumstances, the Fed also extends loans to corporations or individuals if they are unable to obtain funding from other financial institutions. In determining which emergency loans to make, the Fed assesses the effect of the impending emergency on the national or regional economy. It then makes only those loans it considers vital to the economic well being of the region or nation. Banks and businesses that borrow often from the Fed become subject to federal audits and supervision.

The Fed's Services to the Federal Government

Each year the government raises and spends about $1 trillion. The Treasury Department and the Federal Reserve work together to manage the government's complex financial activities.

◆ **After natural disasters, the President may classify a region as a disaster area, qualifying residents for low-interest government loans.**

Economics Reporter

What Is the Issuing Bank of a Federal Reserve Note?

One of the chief features on all Federal Reserve notes is the seal of a Federal Reserve Bank. The seal is located on the front side of a note, to the left of the portrait. The letter on the seal identifies which of the 12 Federal Reserve banks issued the note. The letters and the Federal Reserve Bank each represents are as follows: **A,** Boston; **B,** New York; **C,** Philadelphia; **D,** Cleveland; **E,** Richmond; **F,** Atlanta; **G,** Chicago; **H,** St. Louis; **I,** Minneapolis; **J,** Kansas City; **K,** Dallas; and **L,** San Francisco.

The Secretary of the Treasury is the chief financial officer for the government and sees to it that the Treasury pays all the government's bills. Through the Internal Revenue Service and the United States Customs Service, the Treasury Department collects taxes. Through the Bureau of the Mint and the Bureau of Engraving and Printing, it produces coins and currency.

Serving as the Government's Banker. The Treasury Department is the government's banker. As a result, the Fed's duties are similar to those provided by banks to individuals. First, the Fed serves as the depository for federal revenues. Government moneys are deposited at the Fed by the Treasury. Second, the Fed holds a checking account for the Treasury on which the Treasury writes checks to cover tax refunds, Social Security payments, and all other government payments. Third, the Fed serves as a federal bookkeeper, recording the millions of deposits and withdrawals of federal funds, and the purchase and sale of government securities. Finally, the Fed serves as a financial adviser to the government, helping the legislative and executive branches of government develop a coordinated economic program.

Supervising and Regulating Member Banks. The Fed also acts as the government's watchdog for banking problems. Each of the 12 Federal Reserve banks has a staff of bank examiners that supervises the financial activities of member banks. These examiners monitor loans and investments and conduct audits of bank records. The Fed also regulates bank mergers and the chartering of bank holding companies.

Distributing Paper Currency. The Treasury Department's Bureau of Engraving and Printing prints the paper currency of the United States, most of it in Federal Reserve notes. The Fed issues the notes through its 12 Federal Reserve banks. New currency is put into circulation for two major reasons. One reason is simply to replace old and worn-out notes, which are eventually destroyed. Banks regularly ship worn-out notes to their district Federal Reserve Bank in exchange for new ones. The other reason is to increase the amount of money in circulation by expanding the pool of cash that the Federal Reserve banks can loan within their districts.

Regulating the Money Supply. The most important function of the Fed and the one that has the greatest effect on the economy is the regulation of the money supply. On behalf of the Fed, the Federal Reserve Bank of New York buys and sells United States government securities on the open market. Trading in securities allows the Fed to regulate the money supply and to provide the government with the cash it needs to finance public goods and services.

See Suggested Assignments, p. TM 56.

Section 2 Review See Answers, p. A 46.

DEFINE check clearing

1. **Summarizing Ideas** What services does the Federal Reserve provide to the **(a)** federal government and **(b)** to banks?
2. **Interpreting Ideas** For what purpose does the Fed buy and sell government securities?
3. **Understanding Ideas** How does the Federal Reserve regulate its member banks?
4. **Seeing Relationships** How does the Fed assist in distributing paper money?
5. **Interpreting Graphics** Study the flow chart on page 251. What is the Federal Reserve's role in clearing Mr. Walker's check?

◆ Ask the students to examine a dollar bill and determine which Federal Reserve Bank issued it. Then have the students review the map on page 248 and determine which Federal Reserve Bank services their community.

See Key Study Questions and Key Understandings, p. TM 57.

3 The Federal Reserve's monetary policy promotes economic growth and stability.

See Suggested Teaching Strategies, p. TM 57.
The services provided by the Federal Reserve System make the monetary and banking systems more efficient and sound. The major function of the Fed, however, is to regulate the money supply and to formulate a monetary policy that promotes economic growth and stability.

The Money Supply

Economists focus much of their attention on the **money supply**, the amount of money in circulation. The size of the money supply influences interest rates, consumer activity, and international trade.

The M1. Economists often disagree on what should be included in a measure of the nation's money. The two most common measures of the money supply are called M1 and M2. The narrower and simpler measure of the money supply is **M1.** M1 counts all the currency in circulation, the value of all traveler's checks, all checking deposits, and all checking-type accounts such as NOW and Super-NOW accounts in financial institutions. Checking and checking-type accounts represent nearly 70 percent of the M1 total (see the graph on this page).

The M2. A broader measure of the money supply is **M2.** M2 includes money market accounts, money-market mutual fund shares, and other savings deposits that allow people easy access to their funds, as well as the money counted in M1. Money market accounts, for example, allow savers to write a limited number of checks and an unlimited number of personal withdrawals. Deposits in money market accounts today are nearly as large as all the checking and checking-type deposits included in M1. In addition, many people have invested in money-market mutual funds. Finally, the development of automatic teller machines (ATMs) has allowed savings accounts to serve many of the same purposes as checking accounts. ATMs make possible the transfer of funds from savings to checking accounts electronically.

Components of the Money Supply

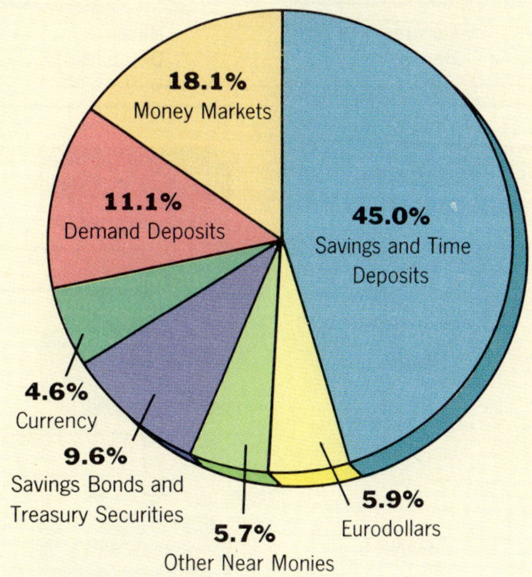

Source: *Economic Report of the President, 1986*

The M3 and the L. M3 is an even broader measure of the money supply than M2. M3 includes the money in the M2 and all time deposits over $100,000. When economists speak of the **L** as a measure of the money supply, they have added savings bonds, short-term Treasury securities, and other types of near moneys to the total count.

Monetary Policy

The **monetary policy** formulated by the Fed regulates the amount of money and credit available in the economy. By regulating the money supply and the interest rates charged for credit, the Fed influences **aggregate demand,** or total spending, in the economy. The Fed, while coordinating its monetary policy with other federal actions, follows either an easy-money policy or a tight-money policy.

Easy-Money Policy. The goal of an **easy-money policy** is to expand the money supply, increase aggregate demand, and promote economic growth. The lowering of the interest rates that banks charge for loans encourages people and businesses to borrow.

The Money Creation Process

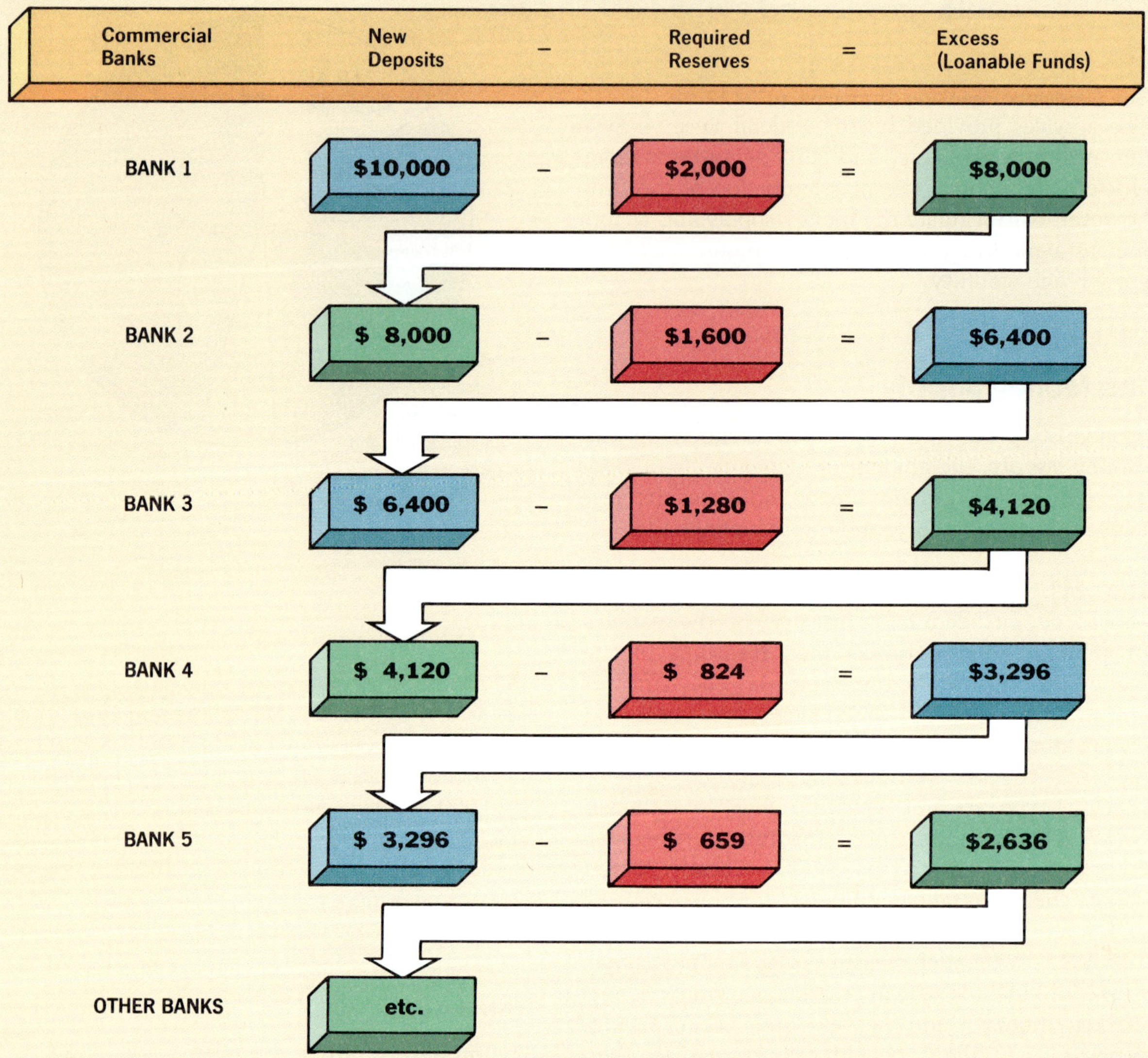

Increased borrowing and increased spending, in turn, stimulate economic growth as businesses increase production. Businesses then expand by borrowing and investing new capital. The Fed usually adopts an easy-money policy during a slowdown of the business cycle because the economy needs stimulation to move it toward recovery. The table on page 257 shows an example of the recent growth of the money supply.

Tight-Money Policy. Higher interest rates and a reduced money supply characterize a **tight-money policy.** By restricting the money supply and the use of credit, the Fed attempts to reduce the primary cause of demand-pull inflation, which is too much money chasing too few goods, and to stabilize prices. When less money is available and credit is expensive, aggregate demand falls and business activity slows.

Components of Monetary Policy

◆ The key components of the Fed's monetary policy are the reserve requirement, the discount rate, and open market operations. The Fed also has other formal and informal ways to affect aggregate demand in the economy.

The Reserve Requirement. One key part of the Fed's monetary policy is its **reserve requirement,** the percentage of money deposited in checking and savings accounts that must be held by banks either in their own vaults or at the district Federal Reserve Bank. The reserve requirement is a percentage of the member bank's total net transaction accounts. The percentage requirements change annually according to a formula specified in the Monetary Control Act of 1980. The Fed does not often change the reserve requirement because frequent changes create uncertainty in the banking system. Frequent changes would also make it more difficult for banks to make long-term loans and investments.

The Fed can increase or decrease the money supply and influence aggregate demand through its control of the reserve-requirement percentages that it sets for member and nonmember banks. When the Fed lowers the percentage, banks need to hold a smaller portion of their deposits as reserves. The result is that banks can extend more loans (see the chart on page 254). With a larger supply of loanable funds, interest rates fall, adding money to the money supply. The combination of more money and easier credit produced by the easy-money policy serves to increase aggregate demand and production in the overall economy.

By raising the percentages of the reserve requirement, on the other hand, the Fed forces banks to hold a larger portion of their deposits as reserves. Banks cut back on their loans, contracting the money supply. As the supply of loanable funds shrinks, interest rates rise. As a result, aggregate demand and production slow down. The Fed uses such a tight-money policy to fight inflation.

During 1986, the reserve requirement was 3 percent on all funds on deposit up to $31.7 million and 12 percent on funds over that amount. Banks are permitted, however, to hold fewer reserves on time deposits and other accounts that are less liquid than checking accounts. For example, the reserve requirement on some long-term CDs is as low as 1 percent.

The Discount Rate. A second component of the Fed's monetary policy is the **discount rate,** the interest rate that the Fed charges for the use of its money. Altering the discount rate has been a key tool in the Fed's fight against the inflation of the 1980s.

The Fed uses the discount rate to encourage or discourage borrowing by banks and governments. The Federal Reserve extends short-term loans to banks to help them maintain sufficient cash reserves. Banks may borrow from the Fed, however, only after they have exhausted alternative methods of meeting temporary cash shortfalls.

Lowering the discount rates encourages banks to borrow, increasing the reserves that banks can loan to businesses and individuals. Conversely, increasing the discount rate discourages borrowing from the Fed. Changes in the discount rate directly affect the interest rates that banks and other financial institutions charge. The banks and other lenders

Text continues on page 258.

The Discount Rate and Prime Rate, 1976–1986

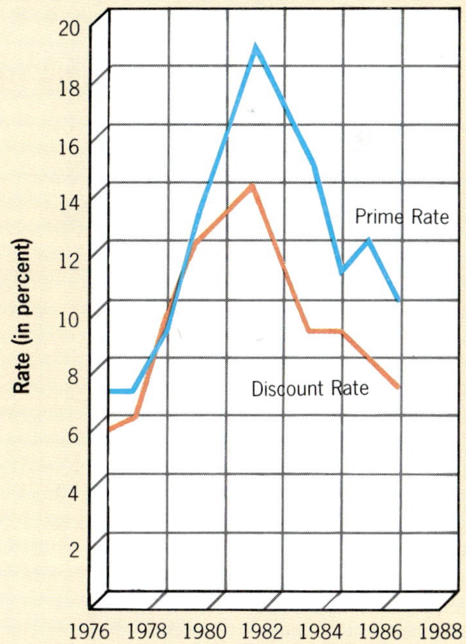

Sources: *Statistical Abstract of the United States, 1986*
Federal Reserve Bulletin

◆ **Point out to the students that the federal government can also use fiscal policy to regulate the economy.**

BUILDING ECONOMIC SKILLS

READING ABOUT ECONOMICS

Understanding Statistics

Statistics are numerical data. Statistics are often presented in the form of a table or a chart that organizes the statistics into columns and rows, by topic. The data in each column and row pertain to one topic. Where columns and rows cross, or intersect, the data are related. Economists use statistical tables and charts to organize large amounts of data and to present it compactly. Statistical tables permit students of economics to analyze numerical data easily, to see relationships, and to make comparisons.

How to Read Statistics

To read statistics, follow these guidelines.

1. **Identify the type of data.** Identify the title of the table or chart. Note any headings for columns or rows and any other headings or labels.
2. **Examine the components.** Note the specific statistics presented in each column or row. Read down each column and across each row.

Selected Financial Institutions in the United States, 1984

Assets (in millions)	Insured Commercial Banks	S & Ls	Mutual Savings Banks[1]	Credit Unions[2]
Less than $1.0	11	70	—	7,346
$1–$4.9	320	130	—	4,688
$5–$9.9	1,150	135	1	1,284
$10–$24.9	4,064	422	7	1,051
$25–$49.9	3,761	600	3	403
$50–$99.9	2,741	671	57	266
$100–$499.0	1,956	1,034	136	139
$500 or more	478	329	63	7
Totals	14,481	3,391	267	15,144

[1]Excludes federally chartered mutual savings banks.
[2]Excludes nonfederally insured state-chartered credit unions and federally insured corporate credit unions.

Source: *Statistical Abstract of the United States, 1986*

3. Relate numbers and values. Identify the quantities in which each category is recorded. Quantities are often given in parentheses beneath the heading.

4. Look for relationships. Note changes in statistics and trends over time. Note any comparisons between data in the columns.

5. Read footnotes. Footnotes often note the source of the statistical data, and explain any changes in recording procedures that may make comparisons over time difficult. A blank space usually indicates that data was not available, or no activity took place. Footnotes also explain any symbols that are used.

Applying the Skill

Study the statistics in the chart on page 256. The chart shows information about selected financial institutions in the United States in 1984. The chart has five columns. The first column indicates Asset Size. The size is stated in millions. The next four columns indicate the kinds of financial institutions selected for inclusion on the chart. Note the superscripts, which alert you to additional information contained in footnotes. Take time to read these footnotes.

Next pay attention to the rows. Each row tells you one size category and indicates how many of each kind of financial institution has assets of that size.

Now see if you can answer these questions.

1. What asset-size category has the most insured commercial banks? *If you answered $10–$24.9 million, you have read the chart correctly.*

2. What is the total number of the selected credit unions shown? *15,144*

3. Compare the number of selected credit unions with assets less than $1 million with the credit unions that have assets more than $1 million. Which number is greater? *To arrive at this answer, subtract 7,346 from 15,144. The balance is 7,798.*

Growth of the Money Supply, 1975–1985 (in billions)

Year	M1	M2	M3	L
1975	291	1,023	1,172	1,368
1976	310	1,164	1,312	1,516
1977	335	1,287	1,473	1,704
1978	363	1,389	1,646	1,910
1979	389	1,631	1,804	2,116
1980	415	1,631	1,989	2,325
1981	442	1,794	2,236	2,597
1982	481	1,954	2,447	2,855
1983	528	2,189	2,702	3,176
1984	559	2,372	2,995	3,540
1985*	582	2,445	3,076	(NA)

*as of May, 1985
NA = data not available

Source: *Statistical Abstract of the United States, 1986*

Practicing the Skill See Answers, p. A 46.

Study the statistical table above. Then on a separate sheet of paper, answer the following questions.

1. What is the subject of the data in the table?
2. What specific information about the money supply is given?
3. For what years is the information given?
4. In what value is the information recorded?
5. What additional information is given in the footnotes?
6. The data in the table indicates that from 1975 to 1985 the money supply **(a)** increased, **(b)** decreased, **(c)** remained constant.
7. In which year did one of the measurements of the money supply not show an increase from the previous year? Which measure was it?

pass the cost of the Fed's discount rate on to their customers by raising the prime rate. All interest rates are calculated on the **prime rate,** the rate of interest that banks charge on loans to their best business customers (see the graph on page 255).

Open Market Operations. The most important of the Fed's tools is **open market operations,** the buying and selling of government securities. The Federal Open Market Committee (FOMC) makes decisions to buy or sell government securities based on the monetary policy set by the Board of Governors. The Federal Reserve Bank of New York conducts the transactions through about 35 private securities dealers, who buy and sell billions of dollars worth of government securities in a single day for individuals, businesses, and banks.

When the Fed wants to pump money into the economy, it buys back government securities. Much of the buy-back money that is paid to individuals and businesses is deposited into bank accounts, increasing cash reserves and loan pools. When the government buys securities directly from a bank, the banks' reserves are similarly increased. Either way, the money supply expands, aggregate demand increases, and production rises.

By selling government securities, the Fed contracts the money supply. The cash withdrawn from the private sector is held by the Fed, reducing the ◆ money in circulation, shrinking bank reserves, and decreasing aggregate demand.

Other Controls. In addition to its primary tools, the Fed can restrict aggregate demand in the United States economy through informal and other formal controls on credit. **Moral suasion** refers to the unofficial pressures that the Fed exerts on the banking system. Moral suasion can be a direct appeal to individual banks through letters and conferences, public announcements through press releases, or testimony before Congressional committees. By using moral suasion, the Fed attempts to channel the lending policies of all banks in a desirable direction.

The Fed also places direct controls on credit. The Securities Exchange Act of 1934 authorizes the Board of Governors to set **margin requirements,** the percentage of cash an investor must have to buy stocks, options, warrants, and convertible bonds. If the margin requirement is set at 60 percent of the stock's value, the investor must put up 60 percent of the investment's purchase price in cash. The remaining 40 percent can be purchased with credit. The goal of margin requirements is to prevent the occurrence of wild price fluctuations caused by the extreme use of credit in the purchase of securities.

A high margin requirement discourages investment in the stock market and investor borrowing from banks. Very low margin requirements, on the other hand, make stock investing and investor borrowing popular. Since the stock market crash of 1929, the Fed has generally set relatively high margin requirements.

A second direct control on credit is the Fed's power to regulate consumer credit in times of national emergency. During World War II and the Korean War, for example, the Fed tightened credit by requiring high down payments and shorter repayment schedules for consumer installment loans. These credit policies made credit more expensive and reduced demand for consumer durables. The Fed coordinates its consumer credit policies with its monetary policies of easy or tight money.

See Suggested Assignments, p. TM 57.

Section 3 Review See Answers, p. A 47.

DEFINE money supply, monetary policy, aggregate demand, reserve requirement, discount rate, prime rate, open market operation, margin requirement

1. **Summarizing Ideas** **(a)** What is the general purpose of monetary policy? **(b)** What are the three key components of monetary policy?
2. **Understanding Ideas** Why is M2 a broader measure of the money supply than M1?
3. **Seeing Relationships** When the Federal Reserve sells securities, is the amount of money in circulation increased or decreased? Why?
4. **Contrasting Ideas** **(a)** What is the difference in the goals of an easy-money policy and a tight-money policy? **(b)** How does each policy accomplish its goal?
5. **Interpreting Graphics** Study the graph on page 255. **(a)** During what year was the prime rate at its highest level? **(b)** What was the prime rate in 1986? **(c)** What has been the overall trend since 1981 with each rate?

 ◆ Report topic: How the Fed uses its three monetary tools.

See Key Study Questions and Key Understandings, p. TM 58.

4 Monetary policy in the United States economy has limitations.

See Suggested Teaching Strategies, p. TM 58.

The Fed must consider several limitations when establishing a monetary policy. The five most important considerations are difficulties in forecasting business activity, time lags in the formulation and implemention of monetary policies, judgments in the setting of priorities and in the weighing of trade-offs, the lack of coordination among government agencies in the formulation of economic policies, and the lack of consensus among government leaders about the goals of monetary policy.

Economic Forecasting and Time Lags

Economic forecasts are predictions of future levels of business activity. Economic forecasts are used by government policymakers to develop and revise national economic policies. Forecasters rely on a set of criteria to help them predict changes in business cycles. Forecasts, hypothetical as they are, provide the assumptions on which policies are made, and incorrect forecasts can lead to inappropriate policies.

Problems with time lags are related to the problems of economic forecasting. Time lags are the inevitable delays that occur before government agencies implement their policies. Three types of time lags disrupt the effectiveness of monetary policy. First, collecting and studying the tremendous amount of economic data needed for analysis and action by the Federal Reserve sometimes takes months. Second, once the data has been studied, time-consuming discussions occur before agreement on an appropriate monetary policy is reached.

Third, the impact of the monetary policy often takes months before it is fully felt throughout the economy. Consumers and businesses need time to adjust to tight-money or easy-money policies. Aggregate demand and subsequent business activity seldom react instantly to actions by the Fed.

Economic forecasting helps the Fed determine what discount rate Federal Reserve Banks should charge commercial banks for loans.

The Impact of the National Debt on the American Economy

In 1791, the new government of the United States assumed the debts of the original 13 states. The nation's first "national debt" totalled $75 million. By 1981, the debt had risen to $1 trillion. In 1986, the debt had doubled to almost $2 trillion. The rapid growth of the national debt during the 1980s has made it a major economic issue.

Myths and Misconceptions

Some economists argue that myths and misconceptions have increased public alarm over the debt. These misconceptions concern the size, benefits, and repayment of the debt.

Size of the Debt. First, some economists argue that the size of the national debt has been grossly exaggerated. They note that in constant dollars—dollars adjusted for inflation—the "real" national debt has grown at a moderate pace over the years (see the graph on the left, below).

These same economists further point out that the national debt as a percentage of the GNP was higher during the 1940s and 1950s than it is today (see the graph on the right, below). These figures

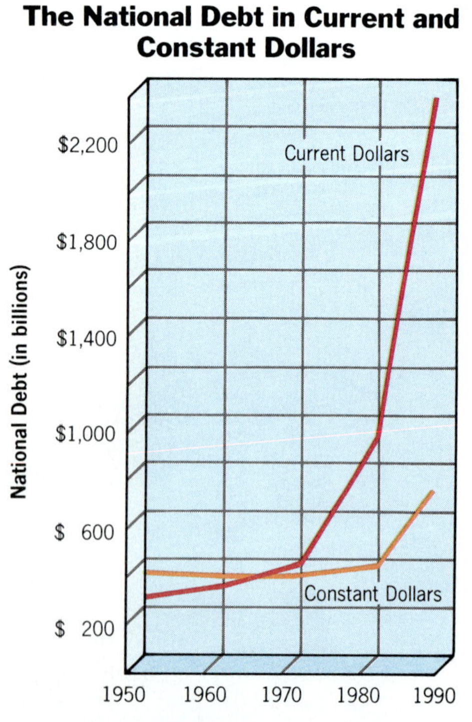

Source: *Economic Report of the President, 1986*

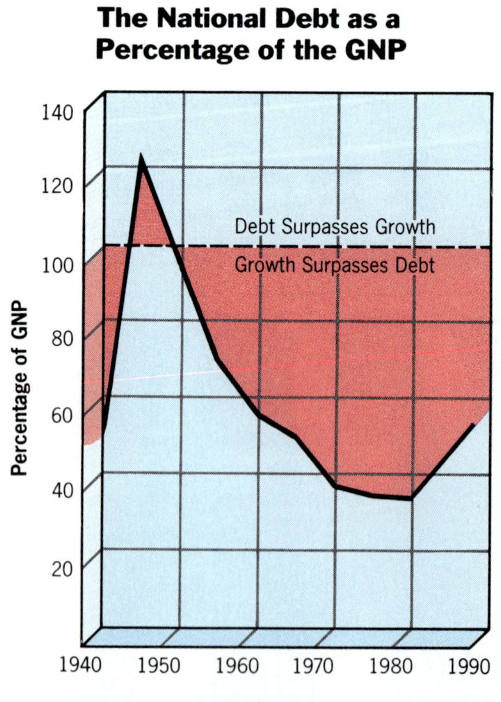

Source: *Economic Report of the President, 1986*

show that the overall growth in the economy surpassed the growth of the national debt. These economists concede, however, that the large deficits of the 1980s have caused the percentage to rise during the decade.

Benefits of the Debt. The nation has derived four important economic benefits from deficit spending. First, deficit spending has enabled the government to provide adequate public goods such as national defense and welfare payments to needy individuals. Second, deficit spending has allowed the government to hold taxes down, thus encouraging consumer spending and business investment.

Third, high government spending stimulates economic growth. Economists generally acknowledge the positive effects that deficit spending has had on the economic recovery of the mid-1980s. Finally, about 90 percent of all federal securities that are used to service the debt are purchased by Americans, who receive additional income because of the debt. In this investment sense, the national debt is really a national asset.

Public Debt. The last misconception is the common belief that the national debt must eventually be paid off. This misconception stems from individuals' experiences with personal debts such as installment loans and home mortgages.

Harmful Effects of the National Debt

Many economists who criticize the growth of the national debt believe it will have a negative impact on growth and stability in the American economy. They point to five major consequences of the debt. These are tighter credit markets, additional budgetary trade-offs, higher taxes, higher inflation, and an increasing dependence on foreign capital.

Tight Credit Markets. By 1986, the American economy had used about $6.5 trillion in credit. Higher government borrowing decreases the pool of loanable funds in the overall economy. As this credit pool shrinks, consumers and businesses are less able to obtain loans. Further, as competition for loanable funds increases between the public and private sectors, interest rates tend to rise.

Budgetary Trade-Offs. The growth of the national debt has forced the government to devote a larger percentage of federal receipts to interest payments on the debt. Before World War II, the federal government used less than 1 percent of the federal budget to service the debt. By 1985, it was spending close to 14 percent of the budget—some $129 billion—on interest payments. Higher spending on interest payments means that less money is available for other programs. Then budgetary trade-offs have to be made.

Higher Taxes and Higher Inflation. A likely result of an expanding national debt is higher taxes. Taxes levied on future generations will, in part, be used to service the growing interest payments on the national debt. The national debt contributes to inflation because deficit spending pumps billions of dollars into the economy, increasing aggregate demand. The danger of "too much money chasing too few goods"—the major cause of demand-pull inflation—is present.

Dependence on Foreign Capital. About 11 percent of all government securities are purchased by foreign investors, who are attracted to them as "safe" investments. While the government has been able to make good use of the money derived from foreign sources, it must guard against the dangers that accompany a dependence on foreign capital.

The first danger is that the interest earned on foreign investments is likely to leave the country and contribute very little to the American economy. The result is a drain of United States currency to other nations, and a decline in total spending in domestic markets.

The second danger is that foreign investors could choose to stop investing in government securities. As a result, the government would have to borrow a larger share of loanable funds in the American economy. This would further tighten credit and reduce aggregate demand and production.

Paul Volcker (above) resigned as chairman of the Fed in August 1987. President Reagan nominated economist Alan Greenspan to take Volcker's place.

National Priorities and Trade-offs

A third limitation on monetary policy is that it cannot do more than it is designed to do. Monetary policy is designed primarily to fight either inflation or unemployment and recession. It is especially ineffective, however, when it is used to battle stagflation. As an economic condition, stagflation is characterized by high unemployment rates and high inflation rates. The Fed, therefore, must determine whether to attack unemployment or inflation and then to devise an appropriate monetary policy.

In addition, certain economic policies used to remedy one problem may make another problem worse. For example, an easy-money policy fights the problems of recession and unemployment, but often causes an increase in inflation. Conversely, a tight-money policy is effective in combating inflation, but it decreases business activity and contributes to recession and unemployment.

Lack of Coordinated Economic Policies

A fourth limitation to the Fed's actions is that there is no guarantee that the economic policies of other government agencies will target the same economic problem identified by the Fed. This lack of coordination among government agencies hinders stabilization and sends mixed signals to the market.

During the early 1980s, for example, some economists felt that the government's monetary policies and its fiscal policies (see Chapter 16) seemed to contradict one another. The Fed's tight-money policy, targeting inflation as the nation's chief economic worry, sought to reduce the money supply and aggregate demand. At the same time, however, Congress and the President set a fiscal policy that approved massive tax reductions and federal spending hikes. The fiscal policy increased total spending in the economy.

The conflicts generated by the two policies caused heated debates between President Ronald Reagan and Paul Volcker, the Fed's chairman. The contradictions, however, led to agreements among Federal Reserve officials, Congressional leaders, and the President to consult regularly about the economy and how best to solve economic problems.

Disagreements Over Policy Goals

A final limitation to monetary policy effectiveness is the disagreement some economists have about the Fed's policy goals. Monetarists are economists who believe economic growth and stability result from a steady growth of the money supply. Monetarists reject the Fed's use of easy-money and tight-money policies. Monetarists argue that the Fed's manipulation of the money supply and aggregate demand hurts more than helps the economy. Monetarists believe that the Fed should increase the money supply by a fixed amount each year rather than to respond to short-term ups and downs in the economy.

The disagreement over the goals of United States monetary policy underscores the fact that there are still many uncertainties in the study of economics. It is almost impossible, therefore, for the Federal Reserve and other government agencies to develop policies that consistently solve the complex economic problems of the nation.

CASE STUDY

Paul Volcker's War on Inflation

Paul Volcker was appointed chairman of the Federal ◆ Reserve Board of Governors in 1979 by President Carter and reappointed to a second term in 1983 by President Reagan. Volcker resigned his post in 1987. During his first term, Volcker built a reputation for his firm and decisive battle against inflation.

During the late 1970s and early 1980s, the United States experienced double-digit inflation. The Fed targeted inflation as the nation's single most important economic problem. Chairman Volcker and the Board of Governors agreed that a tight-money policy was needed to decrease the money supply and restrict the use of credit. The Fed, therefore, increased the discount rate to make credit more expensive. The Fed's policies reduced aggregate demand. By 1982, the reduction in the rate of inflation was well underway.

The Fed's victory over inflation, however, had a price. The tight-money policy discouraged borrowing from the Fed, thus reducing the reserves that banks could loan to private businesses and individuals. The higher discount rate helped push the prime rate to almost 19 percent. Interest rates for other types of loans rose as high as 23 percent. Total spending declined. Many borrowers found the cost of credit too expensive. Producers were forced to cut back on production. Workers were laid off and business bankruptcies increased dramatically. The construction industry, real estate, and manufacturers of such consumer durables as automobiles were particularly hard hit by business failures.

In the mid-1980s, the Fed shifted its emphasis from price stability to economic growth. The Fed's shift to an emphasis on economic growth reflected its concerns for sectors of the economy that had suffered during the recession of the early 1980s. Its shift also reflected concern for the financial hardships faced by industries such as agriculture and petroleum that were suffering from the drop in inflation that had occurred in the early 1980s.

To spur spending, the Fed lowered the discount rate to 7 percent. By 1986, many banks had dropped their prime rates to 8.5 percent. In addition, the M1 was allowed to rise above targeted levels.

See Suggested Assignments, p. TM 58.

◆ Report topic: The current members of the Federal Reserve Board.

Section 4 Review See Answers, p. A 47.

IDENTIFY Paul Volcker

1. **Summarizing Ideas** What are the five limitations the Fed must consider in establishing a monetary policy?
2. **Comprehending Ideas** **(a)** What are economic forecasts, and why are they important? **(b)** What is meant by the phrase *time lag* as it refers to economic forecasting? **(c)** Why does monetary policy involve trade-offs?
3. **Understanding Ideas** Why is monetary policy ineffective in battling stagflation?
4. **Evaluating Ideas** Which of the limitations to monetary policy do you consider the most serious? Why?

CHAPTER 11 SUMMARY

Before 1913, central banking had a stormy history in the United States. After the end of the Second Bank of the United States in 1836, sectional fears and rivalries made the chartering of another central bank impossible during the 1800s. Repeated panic runs and other banking problems led to the creation of the Federal Reserve System in 1913.

The Federal Reserve System, or the Fed, acts as the central bank of the United States. The Fed is composed of 12 district Federal Reserve banks. The actions of the Federal Reserve banks are coordinated by a central decision-making authority in Washington, D.C., called the Board of Governors.

The Federal Reserve System provides a number of banking services in the United States economy. Its most important function is to devise and implement a monetary policy that regulates the money supply, credit, and aggregate demand for the nation.

Through its monetary policy, the Fed attempts to promote economic growth and economic stability through the goals of stable prices and full employment. The Fed's three major tools of monetary policy are reserve requirements, the discount rate, and open market operations. The Fed's actions, however, are limited by several factors, and easy solutions to the nation's economic problems have not been found.

CHAPTER 11 REVIEW

For Answers to Chapter 11 Review, see p. A 48.

Reviewing Economic Terms

With each definition or description below, match one of the following terms.

a. money supply
b. open market operation
c. tight-money policy
d. check clearing
e. reserve requirement
f. discount rate
g. margin requirement
h. easy-money policy

_____ **1.** Program aimed at reducing inflation by restricting borrowing and the use of credit.
_____ **2.** Method of crediting and debiting checking accounts.
_____ **3.** Amount of money in circulation.
_____ **4.** Buying and selling of government securities by the Federal Reserve.
_____ **5.** Percentage of cash required of an investor to buy stocks, options, warrants, and convertible bonds.
_____ **6.** Interest rate that the Federal Reserve charges member banks for the use of its money.
_____ **7.** Percentage of money deposited in checking and savings accounts that must be held by banks as part of the Fed's monetary policy.

Exercising Economic Skills

1. **Understanding Statistics** Study the chart on page 256. **(a)** In which asset-size category is the largest number of S & Ls found? **(b)** mutual savings banks? **(c)** credit unions? **(d)** State a conclusion you can reach from the statistics shown on the chart about each of the three types of financial institutions.
2. **Applying for a Mortgage** Study the feature on pages 523–525. Then visit several different types of lending institutions and ask for a mortgage application for each institution. **(a)** What do the applications have in common? **(b)** How are they different? **(c)** What seems to be the most important type of information on a mortgage application?

Thinking Critically About Economics

1. **Summarizing Ideas** **(a)** What functions does a central bank serve? **(b)** What are the Federal Reserve's seven services? **(c)** What is the major function of the Federal Reserve? **(d)** What are five limitations that the Federal Reserve considers when establishing a monetary policy?
2. **Organizing Ideas** **(a)** How many districts make up the Federal Reserve System? **(b)** How many Federal Branch banks are in the Federal Reserve System?
3. **Contrasting Ideas** Why are the policy decisions of the Board of Governors of the Federal Reserve System sometimes in conflict with the actions of Congress and the executive branch?
4. **Interpreting Ideas** **(a)** Why is it important to have a "lender of last resort"? **(b)** Explain the three basic reasons that Federal Reserve loans are granted?

Extending Economic Knowledge

1. Contact a local bank that is a member of the Federal Reserve System to find out how the bank borrows from the Fed. **(a)** Have bank officers outline for you the procedures they must follow to obtain a short-term loan and **(b)** the terms of repayment of the loan. Report your findings to the class.
2. Obtain information about how the Fed supervises its member banks. (Many pamphlets on the activities of the Federal Reserve are available.) Find out **(a)** how bank examiners check a bank's activities, **(b)** when examiners are called in to examine a bank's operations, and **(c)** what is done when a bank does not meet Fed specifications.
3. Research the monetary policies of the Federal Reserve during the 1920s. **(a)** Would the Fed's actions be characterized as an easy-money or a tight-money policy? Why? **(b)** How did the Fed's policies change with the onset of the Great Depression in the 1930s? **(c)** What further steps might the Federal Reserve have taken to avoid or soften the impact of the Great Depression?

Using Primary Sources

The Federal Reserve Act of 1913 established the Federal Reserve System (the Fed). One of the primary functions of the Fed is to supervise and regulate the nation's banking system. As you read the following excerpts from the Federal Reserve Act, note how the Federal Reserve Board, later called the Board of Governors, is empowered to directly affect banking activity in the United States. How does the Federal Advisory Council keep the lines of communication open between the Fed's Board and its banks?

The Federal Reserve Act

Sec. 10. A Federal Reserve Board is hereby created which shall consist of seven members, including the Secretary of the Treasury and the Comptroller of the Currency,* who shall be members ex officio, and five members appointed by the President of the United States, by and with the advice and consent of the Senate. In selecting the five appointive members of the Federal Reserve Board, not more than one of whom shall be selected from any one Federal Reserve district, the President shall have due regard to a fair representation of the different commercial, industrial, and geographical divisions of the country. . . .

Sec. 11. The Federal Reserve Board shall be authorized and empowered:

(a) To examine at its discretion the accounts, books and affairs of each Federal Reserve Bank and of each member bank and to require such statements and reports as it may deem necessary. . . .

(d) To supervise and regulate through the bureau under the charge of the Comptroller of the Currency the issue and retirement of Federal Reserve notes, and to prescribe rules and regulations under which such notes may be delivered by the Comptroller to the Federal Reserve agents. . . .

(f) To suspend or remove any officer or director of any Federal Reserve Bank. . . .

(g) To require the writing off of doubtful or worthless assets upon the books and balance sheets of Federal Reserve banks.

(h) To suspend, for the violation of any of the provisions of this Act, the operations of any Federal Reserve Bank, to take possession thereof, administer the same during the period of suspension, and, when deemed advisable, to liquidate or reorganize such bank.

(j) To exercise general supervision over said Federal Reserve banks.

Sec. 12. There is hereby created a Federal Advisory Council, which shall consist of as many members as there are Federal Reserve districts. Each Federal Reserve Bank by its board of directors shall annually select from its own Federal Reserve district one member of said council. . . .

The Federal Advisory Council shall have power, by itself or through its officers, (1) to confer directly with the Federal Reserve Board on general business conditions; (2) to make oral or written representations concerning matters within the jurisdiction of said board; (3) to call for information and to make recommendations in regard to discount rates, . . . note issues, reserve conditions in the various districts, the purchase and sale of gold or securities by Reserve banks, open-market operations by said banks, and the general affairs of the Reserve banking system. . . .

* Later amendments to the act gave the President the power to appoint all seven members of the Board of Governors.

Source Review

For Answers to Source Review, see p. A 49.

1. What is the Federal Reserve Board called today? How were the seven members to this board originally chosen? How are they chosen today?
2. How does the Federal Reserve Act ensure fair representation to different groups in the decision-making process? Ideally, what types of groups are represented on the Board of Governors?
3. List several specific powers that the board has that promote the security of the banking system.
4. What is the Federal Advisory Council? How are its members chosen? Why are its members an important link between the Board of Governors and the 12 Federal Reserve banks?

AVIS
bloomingdale's
TWA
GIMBELS
APPLESEED'S
ann taylor
Saks Fifth Avenue
AMOCO
Neiman-Marcus
CHASE MANHATTAN
CITIBANK
Brooks Brothers
SECURITY NATIONAL BANK
VISA

CHAPTER 12

See Chapter Overview, p. TM 60.
See Chapter Objectives, p. TM 60.
See Introducing the Chapter, p. TM 60.
See Extending Economic Knowledge on text p. 286.

Saving, Borrowing, and Using Credit

If you decide to use credit, the benefit of making the purchase now should outweigh the financial and psychological costs of using credit.

Federal Reserve Bank of Minneapolis

1 People in the United States have many ways to save money.

- Benefits From Saving Money
- Savings Rates
- Types of Savings Accounts
- Time Deposits
- Retirement Accounts

2 Borrowing money and using credit are important financial decisions.

- Borrowing Money
- Buying on Credit
- Federal Regulation of Credit
- Loan and Credit Debt

3 Saving, borrowing, and using credit stimulate economic growth and promote economic stability.

- Stimulating Economic Growth
- Promoting Economic Stability

CHAPTER 12 STUDY GUIDE

Chapter Focus

In the United States, savers have many options. Savers make their savings choices based on value, safety, and convenience of access. Financial institutions use savings deposits to form a pool of money for loans and credit to individuals and businesses. Saving, borrowing, and using credit have both negative and positive effects on the flow of money and the overall economy.

As you study the chapter, look for the details that support each of the following statements.

1. People in the United States have many ways to save money.
2. Borrowing money and using credit are important financial decisions.
3. Saving, borrowing, and using credit stimulate economic growth and promote economic stability.

See Preteaching Vocabulary, p. TM 60.

Terms to Know

The following terms, while not the only terms emphasized in this chapter, are basic to your understanding of saving, borrowing, and using credit. Determine the meaning of each term, either by using the Glossary or by watching for context clues as you read the chapter.

interest	installment loan
savings rate	mortgage
liquidity	credit rating
time deposit	credit bureau
maturity	finance charge
credit	annual percentage rate
principal	bankruptcy
collateral	usury

See Key Study Questions and Key Understandings, p. TM 61.

1 People in the United States have many ways to save money.

See Suggested Teaching Strategies, p. TM 61.

Freedom of choice in the free enterprise economy of the United States means that people are free to do as they please with the income at their disposal. They may spend it or save it, consume it or not consume it. **Spending,** the consumption of disposable income, and **saving,** the nonconsumption of disposable income, are equally important to a strong economy.

Benefits From Saving Money

People save money for four main reasons. They save for a down payment on an automobile or a house and to finance a major purchase such as a television set. They set money aside regularly to meet large annual or semiannual bills such as property taxes or automobile insurance payments. They save to have a ready reserve to meet unexpected expenses such as medical or home repair bills. Finally, they save for major expenses in the future such as college tuition payments or to meet retirement needs. Some people save because they want to leave money to their children. Still others have a need to amass wealth. Whatever the reasons for saving, depositors reap ◆ two benefits with their savings.

Security. Depositing money in a financial institution provides physical security by protecting savers' money from losses due to fire, theft, or other catastrophes that might take place in the home. Most financial institutions are protected by state and federal deposit-insurance plans. These insurance plans protect savers' money from losses when the financial institutions close. The plans provide for a reimbursement of up to $100,000 of depositors' money for each account. Almost all financial institutions carry insurance plans to take the risk out of saving money in their institution.

Interest. The fee that financial institutions pay for the use of depositors' money is **interest.** Interest rates on savings vary according to the type of account chosen and the lending institution in which the money is placed. Interest rates also fluctuate

◆ People tend to save more money when employment opportunities are uncertain.

across the nation, reflecting the general availability of money in the economy. When money is scarce, the interest rates are usually high. When more money is available, interest rates are lower. The top chart on this page shows how much interest a saver receives on a $10,000 savings account that pays 10 percent interest.

Each financial institution determines the specific interest rate for each of its various accounts according to the amount and length of deposit, the prevailing interest rates across the nation, and the current interest rate being charged for loans. A financial institution charges interest on loans to make money. It pays interest on savings deposits to attract a pool of money it can lend. A financial institution makes a profit by charging more interest on loans than it pays on deposits.

Calculating Interest

Year	Interest Income	Deposit Value
0	0	$10,000
1	$1,000	$11,000
2	$1,100	$12,100
3	$1,210	$13,310
4	$1,331	$14,641
5	$1,464	$16,105

Note: Interest income is calculated at a simple interest rate of 10%, compounded annually and reinvested.

Savings Rates

One of the measures economists use to analyze savings behavior is **savings rate,** the percentage of disposable income deposited into savings accounts. The single most important determinant of personal savings in the United States is income. High-income households tend to save more money than low-income households. As a result, the average rate of personal savings for the nation is high when wages and employment are high. In contrast, the average rate of personal savings is lower during depressions, recessions, and periods of high unemployment.

Two other economic factors that have key effects on the savings rate are the availablility of consumer goods and rising prices. When consumer goods are adequate to meet consumer demands and prices are lower, people tend to spend their money. At such times, savings rates are relatively low. When consumer demand is greater than the supply of consumer goods and prices are high, people cannot readily purchase the goods they need or want. At such times, savings often increase.

Rising prices also affect the savings rate. When prices rise, the savings rate decreases proportionately because consumers must spend more of their incomes to satisfy their needs and wants. When prices reach a certain high level, however, the savings rate generally increases because people choose to save their money rather than to pay the high prices.

A comparison of the personal savings rate of various nations shows that people in the United States save less than people in other industrialized nations. The chart below shows the average percentage of disposable income saved in selected countries around the world.

Economists cite two key reasons for the relatively low savings rate in the United States. First, home ownership in the United States is very important

Selected National Savings Rates, 1985

Nation	Savings Rate
Belgium	15.0%
Canada	12.3%
Finland	4.5%
Federal Republic of Germany (West)	11.6%
Italy	19.7%
Portugal	26.7%
Spain	7.2%
United States	6.3%

◆ Since deregulation, banks have been free to offer competing interest rates.

Typical Interest Rates on Savings

Type of Account	Qualifications and Requirements	Interest Rate
Statement (Passbook)	No minimum deposit or balance	5.05%
NOW	$1,000 minimum deposit and balance	5.25%
Money Market	$1,000 to $49,999 balance $50,000 or more	5.35% 5.55%
Certificates of Deposit	$500–$49,999 deposit; 6-month maturity $50,000 or more $500–$49,999 deposit; 12-month maturity $50,000 or more $500–$49,999 deposit; 24-month maturity $50,000 or more	6.00% 6.20% 6.25% 6.45% 6.60% 6.80%
Super Certificates	$100,000 or more; 15- to 30-day maturity 31- to 90-day maturity 91- to 180-day maturity 181- to 364-day maturity 365-day maturity	5.70% 5.75% 5.85% 6.10% 6.30%

Note: Interest survey taken in Orlando, Florida, October 29, 1986.

and represents a sizable investment. To buy a home, many Americans deplete their savings to make a down payment. Second, businesses in the United States offer a large number and variety of consumer goods which attract consumer dollars, especially with advertising. In nations with fewer available consumer goods, saving is the main alternative to spending money.

Types of Savings Accounts

Financial institutions have devised many types of savings accounts to meet the different needs of savers. Among these are passbook savings, NOW, and money market accounts. The chart on this page provides a means of comparing interest rates on these various accounts.

Regular Savings Accounts. A common type of savings account among financial institutions is a regular savings account, which is sometimes called a passbook account because depositors receive a book in which all account transactions are recorded. When opened at a credit union, a regular savings account is called a share account. A statement savings account is identical to a passbook account, except monthly statements rather than passbooks are used to record transactions.

Most regular savings accounts require no minimum deposit. Some financial institutions, however, charge a monthly service fee if the amount of money in the account falls below a certain level or if no transactions have occurred in the account within a specified length of time. Some depositors favor regular savings accounts because they have **liquidity,** a condition that indicates the ease with which the accounts can be converted into cash with little or no loss in interest payments. The fixed-interest rate on regular savings accounts, however, is relatively low compared to the interest on other types of savings accounts.

NOW and Super-NOW Accounts. A second type of savings account is the negotiable order of withdrawal, or NOW account. NOW accounts are offered at most commercial banks, savings banks, and savings and loan associations across the nation. The share drafts offered by credit unions are similar to NOW accounts.

A NOW account is an interest-bearing savings account and a checking account. The holder of a NOW account can write checks on the amount deposited in the account and collect interest on the money remaining in the account. Usually the holder of a NOW account must keep a minimum balance in the account in order to receive interest payments and free checking privileges.

NOW accounts, like regular savings accounts, have a high degree of liquidity. NOW accounts are easy to use, and they offer low fixed-interest rates. Until 1986, the government limited NOW interest rates to 5.25 percent. Even with deregulation, interest rates on NOW accounts remain below rates on many other savings plans.

Like NOW accounts, super-NOW accounts are interest-bearing savings accounts on which checks may be drawn. Super-NOW accounts, however, require a $2,500 minimum initial deposit and balance. Super-NOW accounts offer higher fixed-interest rates than passbook or NOW accounts.

Money Market Accounts. Another type of savings account that pays interest and allows easy access to the savings is a money market account. It offers variable interest rates that are usually higher than those of regular savings or NOW accounts. Money market interest rates fluctuate with changes ◆ in interest rates on Treasury bills, which are interest-bearing securities issued by the federal government. The interest paid by money market accounts is often linked to Treasury bills because financial institutions invest the money deposited in money market accounts in Treasury bills. The financial institution passes on to the depositor part of the interest it collects from the government on the Treasury bill and keeps the rest as profit.

Money market accounts have a fair amount of liquidity. Savers can make withdrawals from the accounts in person at any time without penalty, but they are usually restricted to three checks a month. Other restrictions vary among financial institutions, and the investor needs to be aware of them.

Time Deposits

A savings account that requires the saver to leave money in the account for a specific amount of time is called a **time deposit.** Certificates of deposit, government bonds, and individual retirement accounts are all time deposits.

Certificates of Deposit. A certificate of deposit (CD) represents money deposited for a specified length of time called the **maturity.** The most popular CDs have a maturity of six months. Other CDs may have a maturity of 12, 18, 24, 30, or 60 months. The longer the maturity of a CD, the higher the interest rate paid. The maturity of a CD is established at the time of purchase. The interest rate is also established at purchase and stays constant through maturity. A CD carries a financial penalty for early withdrawal of any amount before the maturity date. Some CDs, particularly those paying high interest, require a minimum deposit. The minimum deposit may vary from $250 to $100,000. CDs are popular because of the high fixed-interest rates they offer. Purchasers of CDs give up liquidity in favor of the high interest rates.

Government Bonds. The federal government issues bonds to raise money for government programs. Economists often consider government bonds as a type of savings because the purchasers assume little risk. Bonds are guaranteed by United States government funds on deposit.

The most common type of government bond issued by the United States government is the Series EE savings bond. By 1985, the value of outstanding EE savings bonds in denominations from $50 to $10,000 was more than $80 billion. Savers purchase the bonds for less than their face value and redeem them at their face value at maturity. Savers can purchase a $50 Series EE government savings bond for $25 and redeem it at its 10-year maturity date for $50. If a bondholder keeps the savings bond beyond its maturity date, the bond continues to earn interest until redeemed.

Other Treasury Investments. The United States Treasury Department issues Treasury bills, notes, and bonds. Each has a different required minimum purchase and maturity. The minimum purchase for a Treasury bill is $10,000. Maturity dates ranging from three months to one year may be selected. Treasury notes require investments of $1,000 to $5,000 and have maturities that range from two years to five years. Treasury bonds also have minimum investment amounts similar to those of Treasury notes, but Treasury bonds have maturities that start at 10 years.

◆ **Class activity: Bring bank information to class to help students decide which types of accounts would best suit their needs.**

As time deposits, Treasury bills, notes, and bonds have high interest rates, but they also carry penalties for early withdrawal. Interest on all three types of investments is exempt from state and local taxes, but not from federal income tax.

Retirement Accounts

Retirement accounts are long-term, tax-sheltered time deposits. People open retirement accounts to plan for financial security after the age of 59. Two types of retirement plans are the Keogh (KEE-oh) Plan and the Individual Retirement Account (IRA). Established in 1972, the Keogh Plan allows the self-employed to save as much as 15 percent of their incomes up to a maximum of $30,000 a year.

Established in 1975, the IRA allows an employee to save in ways similar to the Keogh Plan. An employee's contribution to an IRA is limited to $2,000 per year, but if the employee's spouse is not employed, the maximum amount allowable is increased to $2,250. In households where both spouses are employed, the maximum contribution is $4,000 each year. Each year's IRA contribution can be made in installments or in a lump sum. An employee can also choose not to contribute during certain years. Withdrawals from either plan cannot be made until the savers reach age 59.5, and early withdrawals mean substantial penalties. The money in the retirement accounts must be withdrawn by age 72.

How individuals spend their retirement years is determined in part by their financial security.

The tax law enacted in 1986 took away most of the tax deductions attached to individual retirement accounts. Savers liked IRAs because they did not have to pay income tax on the money in the account until they withdrew it during retirement. The tax advantage occurred because the income of most savers was lower during their retirement years.

The 1986 tax law, which had no major effect on Keogh Plans, has had a substantial impact on IRAs beginning in 1987. Regulations continue as before for an individual who earns less than $25,000 a year or spouses who have a combined gross income of $40,000 or less. IRAs also remain in effect for individuals with an income higher than $25,000 or spouses with a combined income higher than $40,000 if they are not covered by a pension, profit-sharing, or annuity plan. The major change affects individuals earning more than $25,000 a year and couples earning more than $40,000, who *are* covered by pension, profit-sharing, or annuity plans. For them, the new law means that no deduction from taxable income is now allowed if income is more than $35,000 for individuals and more than $50,000 for married couples.

CASE STUDY

Enjoying the Golden Years

Today, people in the United States are living longer than ever before. A baby born in 1984, for example, has a life expectancy of almost 75 years. At the same time, people are retiring earlier. In 1960, 43 percent of the Americans who were 65 years old were still working. In 1984, however, only 24 percent of American 65-year-olds were active members of the labor force.

As the trends toward longer lives and earlier retirements continue, many Americans can look forward to spending almost as many years in retirement as they spend working. Because retirees frequently receive no wages or salaries, the retirement years can be a time of poverty and deprivation. Careful financial planning, however, can ensure a rewarding and comfortable retirement. In order to have enough income to meet their wants and needs for 20 or 30 years, individuals must start formulating this plan years before they retire.

Consider the example of Mr. and Mrs. Tracy Fitzmier, who are both 65 years old and retired. Before retirement, Mr. Fitzmier was a mechanical engineer at Lankiewicz Engineering. Mrs. Fitzmier was self-employed as a free-lance graphics illustrator. When employed, the Fitzmiers had a joint income of $50,000.

Today, the couple's monthly expenses include a $650 mortgage payment, $150 in property taxes, $350 for food, $200 for utilities, $200 for routine maintenance on their home, $150 for medical, life, and homeowners insurance, and $300 for state and federal income taxes. These fixed expenses total $2,000.

Thanks to careful financial planning, the Fitzmiers are enjoying a comfortable retirement. They receive combined social security benefits of $780, and Mr. Fitzmier receives $700 per month from a company pension plan. In addition, the couple has $50,000 in IRAs that are invested in mutual funds, which pay monthly dividends of $400. The couple also has $30,000 invested in six-month Treasury bills that presently yield $250 a month. Because Mrs. Fitzmier was self-employed, she was eligible to invest in a Keogh plan. Today, she receives a monthly interest check of $300 on her $45,000 investment. The Fitzmiers' monthly retirement income totals $2,430, which is more than sufficient to meet their $2,000 monthly fixed expenses and enough for recreation and for emergency expenses.

The couple can enjoy income from their investments indefinitely because they are not disturbing the principal. Even though they must withdraw all money from their IRAs and their Keogh plan by the time they reach age 72, the Fitzmiers can put the funds in other income-producing investments.

If the Fitzmiers had not planned for their retirement long before they reached retirement age, their current situation would be completely different. Their income would include the $780 in social security benefits as well as the $700 from Mr. Fitzmier's pension plan. The couple might also have saved the $30,000 that yields $250 in monthly interest. Their total income, however, would be only $1,730—$270 less than their monthly fixed expenses.

Under such circumstances, the Fitzmiers would be forced to make difficult choices. They could, for example, try to find work that would not jeopardize their social security payments. They could further modify their lifestyle by selling their house and moving into a small apartment. Such a choice would save on mortgage costs, property taxes, and maintenance, but it would add rent to their budget. The couple could also draw on their savings to meet monthly expenses. By using their principal, however, the Fitzmiers would also receive lower interest payments until they had spent the entire $30,000. Under their current budget, they would use up their savings in less than 10 years.

Modifying their lifestyles or drawing on the principal of their investments are not attractive alternatives for retired Americans. Nevertheless, without adequate financial planning, many retirees are forced to make these unpopular choices. Such choices can transform the golden years into the nightmare years.

See Suggested Assignments, p. TM 61.

Section 1 Review See Answers, p. A 49.

DEFINE spending, saving, savings rate, liquidity

1. **Summarizing Ideas** **(a)** What savings options are available to savers? **(b)** What benefits do depositors receive from their savings? **(c)** For most savings accounts, what is the trade-off for a higher interest rate?
2. **Interpreting Ideas** What is one disadvantage of time deposits?
3. **Understanding Ideas** **(a)** What is a retirement account? **(b)** What is its purpose?
4. **Interpreting Graphics** Study the chart at the bottom of page 269. **(a)** Which country shown on the chart has the highest savings rate? **(b)** What is one conclusion you can draw about the nation with the highest savings rate?

◆ Have the students read "Accountants" on page 540 of *Careers in the Marketplace.*

BUILDING ECONOMIC SKILLS

WRITING ABOUT ECONOMICS

Expressing Economic Viewpoints

Being informed about and able to express a view on important economic issues is a valuable skill for citizens in a democratic society with an economy based on free enterprise. People in the United States today are concerned about many economic topics, issues, and problems. Some present-day concerns are:

- How much personal credit is too much?
- Will the decline in personal savings in the United States hinder future economic growth?
- Do current bankruptcy laws encourage business failures?

People in the United States want to know both sides of an issue, weigh the pros and cons, and formulate opinions of their own. The following guidelines will help you express your viewpoint.

How to Express a Viewpoint

To effectively express a viewpoint, follow these steps.

1. **Research the topic.** Note all sides to the topic and the evidence used to defend or refute an issue. Separate facts from opinions.
2. **Determine your position on the issue.** Collect data to support your position.
3. **State your position.** Write an opening, or introductory, paragraph that identifies the topic, issue, or problem. State your viewpoint.
4. **Support your position.** Compose additional paragraphs that provide data, or evidence, to support your viewpoint. Summarize your position and clearly restate your reasoning in a concluding paragraph.

Applying the Skill

Read the excerpt on page 275 by Karen Slater that appeared in the *Wall Street Journal.* The article is about credit bureau reports. The author expresses the viewpoint that consumers should know where their credit reports are, and what credit information is included in the reports. She notes the problems caused by insufficient information in credit reports.

Slater notes that married women who opened shared credit accounts with their husbands before the Equal Credit Opportunity Act took effect should check their credit reports. This is especially important for women who have been married a long time and who may have no separate records, or "credit identity," of their own.

The final two paragraphs concentrate on how consumers can exercise their right to know what data are in their credit reports. Slater notes the importance of the Fair Credit Reporting Act in this process. She also notes that a person's creditors, as well as the credit bureau, can be contacted should a credit dispute arise.

Practicing the Skill

Read the other passage on page 275, written by Jerrold Mundis, a novelist and contributor to the *New York Times Magazine.* Then on a separate sheet of paper, answer the questions and complete the activity.

1. What issue is the writer addressing?
2. Is the writer's viewpoint generally positive or negative toward "Debtors Anonymous"? Explain.
3. Use the guidelines on this page to prepare an essay expressing your viewpoint on this topic or on another of your choice.

Practicing the Skill Answers: 1. Self-help program for people in debt; 2. The writer's viewpoint is generally positive as the title, "A Way Back From Deep Debt," shows. 3. Essays will vary.

CREDIT BUREAU REPORTS

It's loan-application time. Do you know where your credit reports are?

Prospective lenders—even employers and landlords—certainly do. Unfortunately, most Americans neither have seen these records of their credit history nor understand how they are used. And that can lead to trouble.

Thus, consumer advocates and credit bureau officials say, people should examine their reports for accuracy every few years. It is particularly important that married women and young adults make sure their reports list accounts for which they are individually and jointly liable. . . .

Consumers can locate the bureaus in their area by asking local banks and stores. The bureaus are required by the federal Fair Credit Reporting Act to inform consumers about "the nature and substance" of the data in their reports. Most bureaus will mail a copy of the computer-printed report—for a fee of about $10. . . . [The] service is free if the individual has been turned down for credit in the previous 30 days because of information contained in that bureau's credit report. . . .

Women who have been married for many years and who primarily share accounts with their husbands have a special reason to check their reports for what they don't contain. Before the passage of the federal Equal Credit Opportunity Act in 1974, many credit bureaus lumped a married woman's credit history with that of her husband. Married women whose credit accounts were opened before the law became effective on June 1, 1977, may find that they have no credit identity of their own. . . .

Consumers should contact their creditors if it appears information isn't being properly reported to credit bureaus. Most other complaints should be directed to the bureaus themselves, which are obligated under law to reinvestigate items challenged by consumers. If the bureau continues to stand by a disputed item, the consumer can write a brief statement that will be incorporated in the credit report.

Karen Slater

A WAY BACK FROM DEEP DEBT

Debtors Anonymous is a 10-year-old self-help program, modeled on Alcoholics Anonymous, that provides moral support for those in debt. The organization is growing rapidly. Though precise figures are not available, Debtors Anonymous estimates that its membership has tripled in the last year—to about 4,000, with chapters in New York, Los Angeles, San Francisco, Washington, Boston, Chicago, Miami, Paris and other cities. . . .

How does Debtors Anonymous work? It offers techniques, strategies and "tools," but it is basically a process, a gradual change in perceptions and attitudes about money and self.

Admitting the problem is essential, and that's not easy, members say. Denial is nearly universal. It's the divorce, people tell themselves, it's the job market, late-paying accounts, taxes, the economy, interest rates, the new roof, high rents. Often an individual has to be driven right up against the wall, and through it, before being willing to face facts.

An incoming member is first encouraged to avoid taking on any new debt for that day. That concept is vital. Next week and next month are too much to think about, the program says, but anyone can abstain from incurring a new debt for one day—this day.

Income is the second area of consideration, and it is usually dealt with in two stages: first, stabilizing it to match monthly expenses; second, increasing it. Stabilization may involve seeking a moratorium from a creditor, taking in a roommate temporarily and similar options. Although the major concern is to avoid new debt, an increase in earnings is a logical extension—by taking on a part-time job, requesting a promotion, changing jobs, or aggressively seeking new business. . . .

Regular attendance at meetings is important. As in Alcoholics Anonymous, each chapter functions autonomously, but is linked together through the general organization. Members are welcome to attend the meetings of any chapter. . . .

The largest concentration of chapters is in New York and California, but new ones are being formed in other areas at a rate of about five a month.

Jerrold Mundis

See Key Study Questions and Key Understandings, p. TM 62.

2 Borrowing money and using credit are important financial decisions.

See Suggested Teaching Strategies, p. TM 62.

Borrowing is the transfer of a specified amount of money from a lender to a borrower for a specified length of time. Business people borrow money to begin or expand their businesses, and federal, state, and local governments borrow money to finance ◆ their programs and operations. **Credit** is the purchase of goods and services without the actual transfer of money on the promise to pay later. Even wealthy consumers consider the use of credit necessary when purchasing expensive items such as houses and automobiles.

Consumers borrow money and use credit for two main reasons. First, buyers can enjoy the use of an item while paying off the debt. They do not have to postpone purchases until they have saved enough money to pay for the items in cash. Second, consumers can extend payments for expensive items over a period of time. Payments for home mortgages typically run for 20 to 30 years. Houses are made affordable in this manner. Credit payments for televisions, major appliances, and other expensive items often run from one to five years.

The availability of credit has helped increase consumer spending in the United States.

Borrowing Money

The money borrowed is called a loan and the amount borrowed is called the **principal.** The amount paid by the borrower for the privilege of using the money is called the interest. Both the principal and the interest are included in the loan's repayment. Most loans are secured loans which require that borrowers put up collateral. **Collateral** is something of value offered by the borrower as a guarantee that the loan will be repaid. The house is the collateral in a mortgage loan and the automobile is the collateral in an automobile loan. Other loans are secured by other types of collateral. If the loan is not repaid according to the terms of the loan agreement, the lender may take the borrower's collateral. Unsecured loans requiring no collateral are rare and usually involve small amounts of money and short periods of time.

The interest rates charged by finance companies are often higher than those charged by banks and other depository financial institutions. For example, most states allow consumer finance companies to charge interest rates of 20 percent a year. Some states even allow interest as high as 36 percent. Consumers who use finance companies usually have a poor credit rating and cannot obtain a loan at a commercial bank or other banking institution.

A common consumer loan is an **installment loan.** Repayment of the principal and interest is divided into equal amounts according to the length of the loan period, typically 12, 18, 24, or 36 months. The length of repayment of the loan is important in determining the amount of the monthly payment. The longer the loan period is, the smaller the monthly amount the consumer must pay. However, a longer loan period means that the total interest payment, and the total amount that must be repaid, will be greater. Buyers with limited monthly incomes find loans with longer repayment periods and smaller installment payments attractive. Buyers who can afford higher monthly payments prefer the shorter loan period because it is less expensive.

◆ Have the students read "Applying For and Using Credit" on pages 525–526 of the *Everyday Economics Handbook* and answer the questions that follow.

• Have the students read "Applying For a Mortgage" on pages 523–524 of the *Everyday Economics Handbook* and answer the questions that follow.

The most common use of an installment loan is a home mortgage. A **mortgage** is an installment debt owed on land, buildings, or other real property. The mortgagee must repay the mortgage in installments for a fixed number of years, usually between 15 and 30 years. The loan is secured by the property, which is forfeited if the loan terms are not met.

Mortgage loans can generally be obtained at commercial and mutual savings banks, savings and loan associations, and credit unions. Mortgages can also be obtained at consumer finance companies. Loans at a finance company, however, often carry a much higher interest rate than loans from banks and other depository institutions.

The higher mortgage payments resulting from the double-digit interest rates of the early 1980s have added to the number of home foreclosures.

Buying on Credit

In the use of credit, no money changes hands directly. Rather than requiring money for a purchase, businesses allow customers to charge their purchases and to pay for them over a period of time. Customers who do not pay their charges in full each month pay interest on the unpaid principal until the full amount is repaid.

◆ **The Credit Rating.** Consumers who want credit must apply for it and must have their credit approved before the credit can be used. Financial institutions and businesses that extend credit to customers do so only when they are convinced that the credit terms will be met by the purchaser. The creditor evaluates information about the purchaser and assigns that person a credit rating. A **credit rating** is an estimation of the probability of repayment.

Creditors are particularly concerned about an applicant's 4-Cs—character, capacity to pay, capital, and credit history. An applicant who satisfies the 4-Cs is likely to receive a high credit rating, meaning the person is a good credit risk. An applicant who fails to satisfy the 4-Cs is usually assigned a low credit rating. The higher the credit rating a person has, the easier it is to get credit. Consumers can establish a good credit rating and increase the amount of credit available to them by repaying loans promptly.

The 4-Cs are important criteria for all lenders, but the importance a lender places on each of the elements varies. For example, a financial institution that is processing a mortgage application is concerned with an applicant's capital and the other factors that could affect repayment of a long-term loan. A retail store that issues a charge card, on the other hand, is more concerned with a customer's current income, which indicates the capacity to make monthly payments.

Many creditors consult a credit bureau to verify financial information about an applicant. A **credit bureau** is a business that specializes in collecting financial information about consumers. Consumer information comes from banks and other financial institutions, stores, and credit card companies. The credit bureau provides the information for a fee.

A low credit rating remains on a consumer's record for seven years and is very difficult to remove from a consumer's credit history. The grant of credit is a privilege that a business may refuse any time the creditor feels that nonrepayment is possible.

◆ Discussion topic: Why a good credit rating is essential to one's economic future.

■ Economics Reporter

What Is a "Smart" Card?

In today's society, credit cards are rapidly replacing money as a medium of exchange. Since 1983, the number of businesses accepting credit cards has increased by 50 percent. To help prevent fraud and credit abuse, many credit-card companies have begun issuing "smart" cards. Smart cards look like conventional credit cards, but contain one important difference—a microchip that details the user's credit history. In Europe, the cards are coded with the users' PIN (personal identification number). In the United States, smart cards are often used to guard against credit abusers. For example, the cards are programmed to stop any further granting of credit after established credit limits have been reached.

◆ **Credit Terms.** A charge account is a type of credit offered by businesses to their clients. It allows a customer to buy goods or services from the business and pay for them later. There are regular, revolving, and installment charge accounts.

In a **regular charge account** the customer is expected to pay in full for all purchases made within the 30-day billing period. The regular charge account has a specified credit limit such as $500 or $1,000. This credit limit is the maximum dollar amount of goods or services that can be purchased on credit. Interest is charged on any unpaid amount of the bill.

A **revolving charge account** adds a customer's additional purchases, up to a stated credit limit, to the previous month's balance. The customer must make a minimum monthly payment. Interest is charged on the unpaid balance and is often compounded daily on the average of the unpaid balance. In most states, the interest rate is 1.5 percent per month, or 18 percent per year. For both regular and revolving charge accounts, stores often issue their own charge cards.

People often purchase expensive items such as televisions, stereos, and major appliances through an **installment credit account.** They pay for the item in a number of equal payments spread over a period of time. The monthly payments on an installment credit account include an interest charge.

Credit cards are similar to charge cards except they are issued by banks, oil companies, or credit-card companies rather than stores. Credit-card users also pay an interest charge which is added to the monthly bill. Some credit-card companies charge a yearly fee that must be paid whether the card is used or not. This fee is usually between $15 and $50, although some credit-card companies charge as much as $200 a year for each card issued. In 1987 Citicorp, the nation's largest issuer of credit cards, lowered the interest rate but raised the yearly charge from $40 to $50 on its Preferred Mastercard and Visa cards. Sears, on the other hand, charges no annual fee for users of its Discover card.

Credit cards also have specific costs. Businesses that allow customers to purchase goods or services with a credit card must pay a certain percentage of the purchase total, usually about 4 percent, to the issuing bank or credit-card company. This is a service fee charged for use of the card. Businesses include this cost in the prices they charge all customers, credit-card and cash customers alike.

The **finance charge** is the total cost of credit expressed in dollars and cents. It includes interest, service charges, and any other miscellaneous fees. The **annual percentage rate** (APR) is the total cost of credit expressed as a yearly percentage. The APR is a better gauge of credit costs than monthly finance charges, because it can be used to compare credit costs among several businesses.

Critics claim that large credit-card companies gouge the public. For example, they charge 18 percent interest on credit-card balances. Yet banks pay only 5 percent or 6 percent interest on the deposits of their customers. The banks and credit-card companies justify their charges because of the number of high delinquencies by credit-card users, the lack of collateral for the loans, and the high costs of processing credit-card loans compared with other types of loans.

Credit Abuse. Credit abuse has increasingly become a problem for both consumers and businesses. Consumers sometimes take on more credit debt than they can handle. When repayment of loans and credit debts becomes a problem, consumers usually have only two courses of action.

They can seek credit counseling. Counseling on financial matters is available through most financial institutions, the National Foundation for Consumer

◆ Class activity: Have the students obtain information on the credit terms of several major credit-card companies.

◆ **Have the students read "Credit Managers" on page 541 of *Careers in the Marketplace.***

Credit, and private counseling services. Counselors advise consumers on ways to pay off present debts through a manageable repayment program and how to avoid recurring credit problems.

◆ Counselors sometimes advise people with severe credit problems to take out a debt consolidation loan. A debt consolidation loan involves borrowing money to repay several smaller loans and credit balances. But debt consolidation loans carry high interest rates because of the high risk creditors carry in making them. Others are counseled to file for bankruptcy.

Bankruptcy is a legal declaration of an inability to pay debts. The Bankruptcy Reform Act of 1978, which established the present-day bankruptcy code, governs the filing of bankruptcy. About 95 percent of the 500,000 bankruptcies filed each year are declared under Chapters 7 or 13 of the bankruptcy code. Most of the remaining 5 percent are filed under Chapter 11 of this code. For the number of bankruptcies between 1975 and 1984, see the graph on this page.

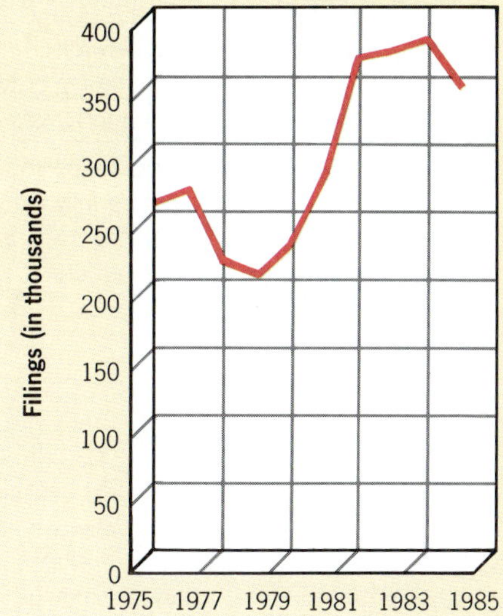

Source: *Statistical Abstract of the United States, 1986*

Bankruptcies filed under Chapter 7 of the code allow debtors to write off, or not repay, most of their debts. Debts that must still be paid are taxes, alimony, and student loans. The debtor's assets are sold to pay these debts.

Bankruptcies filed under Chapter 13 of the code allow debtors to repay a percentage of their debts to every creditor. The percentage to be repaid is determined by the financial situation of the debtor and the types of outstanding debts. Assets, however, remain in the debtor's possession. Bankruptcies filed under Chapter 11 allow individuals and businesses to delay payments while undergoing financial reorganization.

Declaring bankruptcy is generally the last resort for credit abuse, especially for individuals, because it has serious consequences. By law, bankruptcy information remains with an individual's credit history for 10 years, thus making it nearly impossible for the person to ever again borrow money or get credit.

The number of businesses filing for bankruptcy has more than doubled in the last 10 years.

Federal Regulation of Credit

Name of Law	Major Purpose	Provisions
Civil Rights Act of 1968	To outlaw discrimination by lenders in providing home mortgages.	Forbids lenders from rejecting a home loan application because of the applicant's race, national origin, religion, or sex.
Truth-in-Lending Act, 1968	To ensure borrowers that they are fully informed about the costs and conditions of credit.	Requires lenders to disclose all costs, finance charges and annual percentage rate, so that consumers can comparison shop for credit. Sets a $50 maximum for credit cards reported lost or stolen and eliminates all liability for purchases made after the loss is reported. Establishes a 3-day "cooling off period" within which consumers can cancel most credit contracts except first home mortgages. Regulates credit advertisements by requiring that all credit terms be advertised.
Fair Credit Reporting Act, 1971	To protect consumers against the use of inaccurate or outdated information that may be gathered by credit bureaus.	Entitles consumers to see a summary of their credit reports. Allows consumers to insist that disputed information be reinvestigated and corrected, and permits consumers to insert in the reports their own versions of the disputed information. Requires that most negative credit information be removed from the reports after 7 years, but permits bankruptcy information to remain in the report for 14 years.
Equal Credit Opportunity Act, 1974 and 1977	To expand the protection against discrimination in credit matters stated in the Civil Rights Act of 1968.	Prohibits discrimination in granting credit because of such personal factors as race, national origin, religion, sex, marital status, or public assistance. Requires that the same credit guidelines be applied to all applicants. Requires that applicants be notified of a decision on their credit application within 30 days.
Fair Credit Billing Act, 1975	To promote prompt correction of billing errors.	Sets up a procedure that allows consumers to challenge billing errors. Requires consumers to notify creditors of errors within 60 days and requires creditors to respond to that notification within 30 days. Permits unresolved disputes to be settled in court or through other legal means.
Fair Debt Collection Practices Act, 1977	To protect consumers from harrassment by professional collection agencies.	Outlaws harrassing telephone calls, contact with consumers' families and friends by intimidation and other threatening behaviors of collectors.

For businesses, bankruptcy may mean the end of the firm's existence, its reduction in size, or close regulation by various government agencies. Declaring bankruptcy, however, often has saved a business and given it time to rebuild much of its former strength.

For the creditor, the resolution to credit abuse is repossession. In cases where a borrower fails to repay a loan, the financial institution takes possession of the collateral. In cases where the debtor fails to pay for credit purchases, the creditor takes back the purchased item. In 1985, banks, stores, and credit-

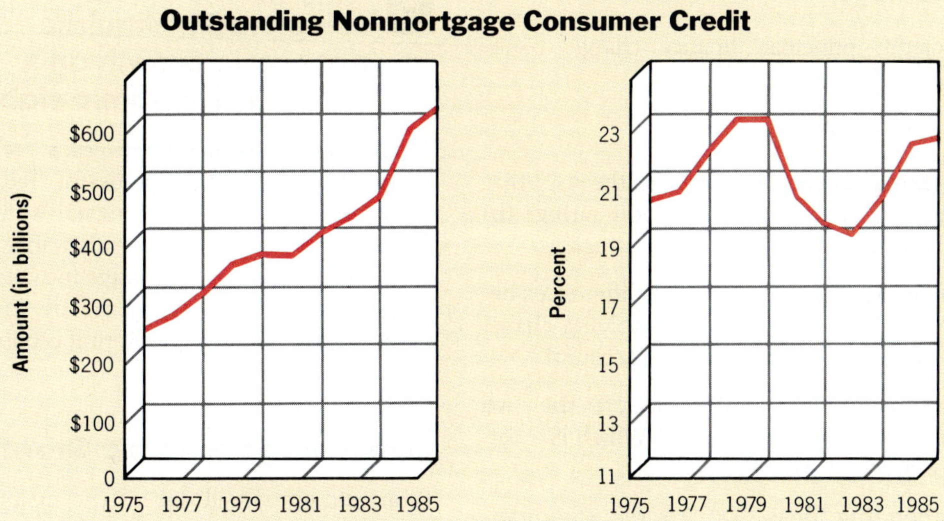

Source: *Statistical Abstract of the United States, 1986*

card companies repossessed nearly 3 percent of all purchases.

When a financial institution repossesses a house or land because the buyer cannot make the mortgage or loan payments, it is called a foreclosure. In 1985, United States banks foreclosed on over 5 percent of the mortgage loans.

Federal Regulation of Credit

Both the state and federal governments regulate credit. Most states, for example, have usury laws. **Usury** is the charging of illegally high interest rates. Usury laws set a limit on the amount of interest that can be charged for credit.

The federal government also has passed a number of laws to protect consumers from unfair credit practices. During the 1960s and 1970s, Congress passed a series of laws to more clearly define the rights and responsibilities of borrowers and lenders. The six most important credit protection laws are the Civil Rights Act of 1968, the Truth-in-Lending Act, the Fair Credit Reporting Act, the Equal Credit Opportunity Act, the Fair Credit Billing Act, and the Fair Debt Collection Practices Act. The chart on page 280 summarizes the major federal laws and their effects on consumer credit.

Loan and Credit Debt

Borrowing money and using credit has led to a large debt. The total outstanding loan and credit debt in the United States is more than $6 trillion. The federal government alone borrows $200 billion each year to pay for its spending programs. By 1987, the federal government's total outstanding debt, also called the national debt, totalled more than $2 trillion.

Businesses also have borrowed more money in recent years. In the 1980s, businesses have borrowed large sums of money to buy other companies, to finance new plants and equipment, and to modernize existing plants and equipment.

More than two thirds of consumer debt is in the form of long-term home mortgages. The other one third is in the form of nonmortgage consumer credit. Nonmortgage consumer credit includes loans for home improvements, college educations, major purchases such as automobiles and large appliances, and credit-card charges. For changes in nonmortgage consumer credit since 1975, see the graphs above.

The dollar amounts for credit have sharply increased over the last 15 years. But the portion of disposable income that goes toward consumer-credit payments has remained basically the same. Thus higher incomes have offset the increase in the use of consumer credit.

See Suggested Assignments, p. TM 62.

Section 2 Review See Answers, p. A 50.

DEFINE credit, principal, finance charge, bankruptcy, usury

IDENTIFY smart card

1. **Summarizing Ideas** **(a)** What are the 4-Cs that help creditors to determine a credit rating? **(b)** How does a consumer get a credit rating?
2. **Contrasting Ideas** What are the differences between a regular charge account, revolving charge account, and an installment charge account?
3. **Understanding Ideas** **(a)** What are the two measures of the cost of credit? **(b)** Which is a better gauge of credit cost? Why?
4. **Comprehending Ideas** **(a)** Describe the differences among Chapters 7, 11, and 13 of the bankruptcy code. **(b)** Why is declaring bankruptcy the last resort of credit abuse?
5. **Interpreting Graphics** Study the graph on page 279. **(a)** What was the trend in the number of bankruptcies between 1978 and 1981? **(b)** What inference can you make about the nation's economy between 1981 and 1983?

See Key Study Questions and Key Understandings, p. TM 63.

3 Saving, borrowing, and using credit stimulate economic growth and promote economic stability.

See Suggested Teaching Strategies, p. TM 63.

Saving, borrowing, and the use of credit help people to satisfy many of their personal wants and needs. These three uses of money also affect the nation's economy. The two major ways in which the uses of money affect the economy are by stimulating economic growth and by promoting economic stability.

Stimulating Economic Growth

Economic growth is one of the major goals of the United States. Economic growth occurs when the per capita output of goods and services in a nation increases during a specified period of time. During a period of economic growth, suppliers produce more goods and services, most of which consumers purchase. Essentially, money circulates more freely during periods of economic growth.

The flow chart on page 283 illustrates how saving, borrowing, and using credit help promote

Economic growth is dependent on bank financing. Bank financing, in turn, is dependent on sufficient levels of savings by individuals.

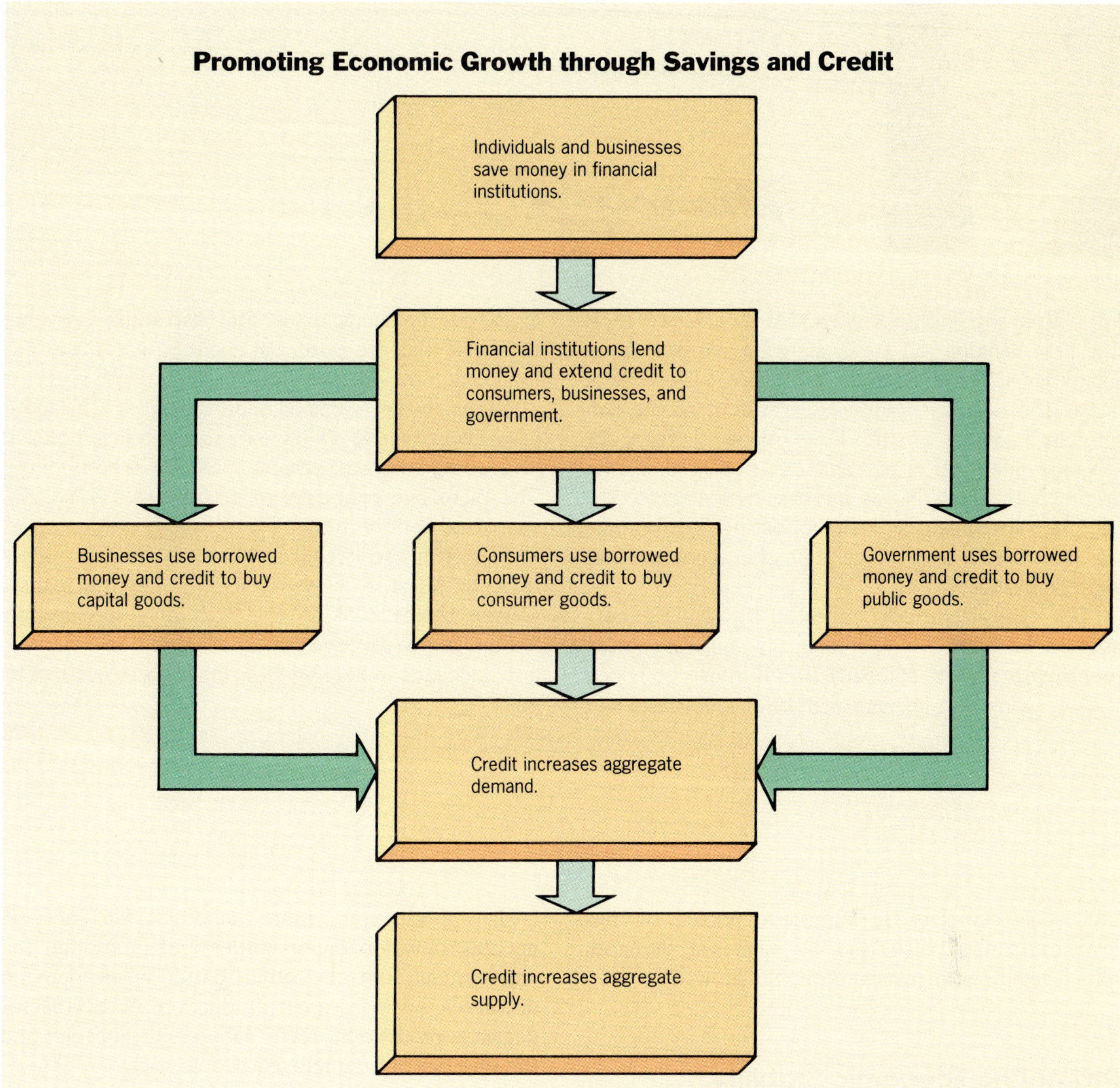

economic growth. The process begins with the pooling of financial resources through the money put into savings in financial institutions. Consumers save about 6 percent of their disposable incomes, while businesses, especially large corporations, save about 25 percent of their profits. Financial institutions then use the savings pool to make loans and extend credit to consumers and businesses.

Individuals use the borrowed money or the credit to buy consumer goods and services. Businesses use the borrowed money or the credit to buy such capital goods as new plants, equipment, and raw materials. Governments borrow money to provide schools, roads and bridges, and fire and police protection.

As businesses, individuals, and governments spend the borrowed money, it is spread throughout the economy. As more goods and services are purchased, demand increases. Businesses then increase their supply of goods to meet consumer demand. With the increase in supply, the economic growth

DECISION MAKERS IN THE ECONOMY

Marcy S. Lyons

Soon after she finished college, Marcy S. Lyons took her first banking job as an assistant national bank examiner for the United States Treasury Office. Today she is an assistant vice president at the San Francisco office of the First National Bank of Chicago. Her job is to seek out potential clients among companies that do business overseas, to create plans for financing their importing and exporting operations, and to maintain the accounts that she establishes.

The typical company targeted by Lyons generates at least $50 million annually in sales. After identifying such a company, Lyons must convince the company that her bank can offer innovative and attractive financing plans. She also must prove to the bank that the potential client is worth the risk involved in making the loan.

Lyons always keeps in mind that First Chicago is very conservative in its overseas lending policies. The companies she selects must be creditworthy. The plans she proposes must represent sound investment opportunities.

First Chicago has hired Marcy Lyons and people like her because it wants to become the leading United States bank in the area of trade finance. When Lyons succeeds in finding new clients, she also succeeds in helping First Chicago to achieve its goal.

process is complete. In summary, pooled savings lead to loans, which lead to increased demand, which results in increased economic growth.

Promoting Economic Stability

Economic stability is a companion goal to economic growth. A stable economy grows steadily, not in leaps and spurts with sharp periods of decline in between the leaps and spurts. Key indicators of a nation's economic stability are employment and price stability. The higher the rate of employment and the more stable the prices, the greater the economic stability.

High Employment. The rate of employment, or the percentage of people with jobs, is closely linked to economic growth. Economic growth spurs businesses to increase production. As businesses increase production, more laborers are needed, opening new job opportunities and promoting full employment. On the other hand, when demand decreases, businesses cut production. As businesses decrease production, fewer laborers are needed and the number of unemployed people rises.

By increasing demand in the overall economy, credit helps to keep production and employment levels high. When money is available for loans and credit, businesses and individuals buy goods and services. Buying stimulates production and helps ◆ ensure high employment.

Price Stability. Stable prices are those that remain relatively constant over a period of time. An adequate amount of money for loans and credit can have both positive and negative influences on price stability.

Often when consumers have money to spend, prices stabilize. Consumers borrow money or use

◆ **Various methods of "creative financing" have been popular in the 1980s. These loans often allow people who would not otherwise qualify to obtain credit.**

credit to buy more goods and services. Greater consumer demand encourages producers to increase the supply of goods available for purchase. When the supply of goods is sufficient to meet people's demands, prices reach a level acceptable to consumers and producers. Prices will remain at this level until such economic factors as reduced supplies or diminished demand cause them to change.

The availability of loan money and credit can also cause prices to rise. First, the buy-now attitude of people can force the prices of some goods to increase. When demand for goods is greater than the supply, prices increase.

Second, retailers who extend credit raise their prices to cover the paperwork and mailing costs associated with credit purchases. These higher prices apply to all customers, whether or not they use credit. Prices slowly increase throughout the economy until consumers and businesses cannot afford to buy the available goods and services.

See Suggested Assignments, p. TM 63.

Section 3 Review See Answers, p. A 50.

IDENTIFY Marcy S. Lyons

1. **Comprehending Ideas** Where do financial institutions get the financial resources that they use to extend loans and credit?
2. **Summarizing Ideas** What are the two ways in which the uses of money and credit affect the economy?
3. **Understanding Ideas** **(a)** How does the availability of money and credit affect prices? **(b)** What are two reasons that the availability of money for loans and credit causes prices to rise?
4. **Seeing Relationships** What is the general relationship **(a)** between the availability of money for loans and credit and economic growth? **(b)** between aggregate demand and employment? **(c)** When the availability of money for loans and credit increases demand in the overall economy, what two factors is it likely to affect?
5. **Interpreting Graphics** Study the flow chart on page 283. What types of goods do **(a)** consumers, **(b)** businesses, and **(c)** government buy with borrowed money and credit?

CHAPTER 12 SUMMARY

People in the United States can do many things with their money. People can save money, depositing it in several different types of savings institutions, to obtain physical security. Financial institutions protect savers' money from losses due to theft, fire, and other catastrophes. Each of these institutions offers services and savings accounts tailored to suit the many different reasons people save money. Besides security, another benefit of savings is interest.

High-income households tend to save more money than low-income households. The average rate of savings is high when employment is high, and low during depressions and recessions.

Finanical institutions have devised many types of savings accounts to meet the different needs of savers. Among these are passbook savings, NOW, and money market accounts. A savings account that requires a saver to leave money in the account for a specific amount of time is a time deposit. Retirement accounts are long-term, tax-sheltered time deposits.

Savings deposited by individuals and businesses form a pool that can be used to extend loans and credit to people and businesses. People borrowing money must decide from which institution to borrow and which repayment plan best suits their needs.

Money borrowed is called a loan and the amount borrowed is the principal. The amount paid by the borrower for the use of the money is the interest. A common consumer loan is an installment loan. The most common use for an installment loan is a mortgage on land, buildings, or other real property.

Consumers who want credit must apply for it. A credit rating is an estimation of the probability of repayment. Consumers can select from a variety of credit terms. Both the state and federal governments regulate credit rates and have passed legislation to protect consumers from unfair credit practices.

Saving, borrowing, and using credit have important influences on the United States economy. Banks pool savings and then lend the money to business and individuals. These loans are used to purchase capital and consumer goods, thereby spurring production and economic growth. Increased production, in turn, means an increased supply of consumer goods. A plentiful supply of goods leads to price stability. When savings lag, however, the pool of money available for loans decreases and the flow of money through the economy slows.

CHAPTER 12 REVIEW

For Answers to Chapter 12 Review, see p. A 51.

Reviewing Economic Terms

With each definition or description below, match one of the following terms.

a. interest
b. usury
c. maturity
d. liquidity
e. principal
f. credit
g. collateral
h. savings
i. borrowing

_____ 1. Nonconsumption of disposable income.
_____ 2. Payment by financial institutions for the use of depositors' money.
_____ 3. The ease with which a deposit can be converted into cash without penalty or loss of interest.
_____ 4. The amount that is borrowed as a loan.
_____ 5. Something of value guaranteed by the borrower as a repayment of a loan.
_____ 6. Charging an illegally high rate of interest.
_____ 7. Purchase of goods and services without the actual transfer of money on the promise to pay later.
_____ 8. Specified length of time for which time deposits are deposited.

Exercising Economic Skills

1. **Expressing Economic Viewpoints** Some people feel that a number of governments in Latin America are on the verge of default. These people feel that the United States should no longer lend the potential defaulters any money. Write an essay expressing your viewpoint about the United States continuing to make loans to Latin American governments that are in severe economic difficulty.
2. **Applying For and Using Credit** Study the feature on pages 525–526. Then review newspapers and magazines to find an advertisement for a credit card or another use of credit. Read the advertisement carefully and analyze its wording. **(a)** What are the specific terms mentioned in the advertisement? **(b)** What benefits to using credit are stressed? **(c)** What warnings, if any, are contained in the advertisement?

Thinking Critically About Economics

1. **Summarizing Ideas** **(a)** Why do people save money? **(b)** Why do people borrow money?
2. **Analyzing Ideas** **(a)** What two economic goals are affected by the availability of money and credit? **(b)** How do the goals of economic stability and economic growth conflict?
3. **Seeing Relationships** **(a)** What is the general relationship between the interest paid on a savings account and its liquidity? **(b)** Why do financial institutions charge a heavy penalty to withdraw funds from certain savings plans?
4. **Expressing Viewpoints** Defend or refute this statement: The government should encourage people to increase their savings.
5. **Interpreting Graphics** Study the graphs on page 281. **(a)** Describe the trend in the dollar value of outstanding nonmortgage consumer credit. **(b)** Describe the trend in outstanding nonmortgage consumer credit as a percentage of the consumer debt. **(c)** Based on these two trends and the 1985 figures shown on the graphs, what do you expect the trend to be in 1986 and 1987?

Extending Economic Knowledge

1. Visit a local bank and interview a loan officer. **(a)** Find out what criteria are used to determine a person's credit rating. **(b)** Which criteria does the bank consider the most important? Why?
2. Contact a local credit bureau to report on the credit bureau's activities. From that information, answer the following questions: **(a)** How do creditors contact a credit bureau? **(b)** How are your credit rights protected through this process? **(c)** What is the process a consumer must go through to protest inaccurate or false credit information?
3. Visit or write to a bank, savings and loan association, credit union, and finance company to gather interest rates and loan requirements for a new car loan. **(a)** Compare the interest rates each institution charges on new car loans. **(b)** List all the other loan requirements. **(c)** Select the loan that you think has the best terms. **(d)** Prepare a chart illustrating your findings to the class.

Using Primary Sources

The Equal Credit Opportunity Act (1974) guarantees that borrowers applying for credit are treated fairly by creditors. This historic act was the culmination of a decade of federal legislation designed to protect borrowers. The Equal Credit Opportunity Act Amendments of 1976 expanded on the protection of the original act. As you read the following excerpts from the Equal Credit Opportunity Act and its amendments, consider how this legislation supports equal access to credit. How did the 1976 amendments to the act broaden its scope?

Ensuring Fair Treatment for All Borrowers

Equal Credit Opportunity Act (1974)

Sec. 502. Findings and purpose

The Congress finds that there is a need to insure that the various financial institutions and other firms engaged in the extensions of credit exercise their responsibility to make credit available with fairness, impartiality, and without discrimination on the basis of sex or marital status. . . . It is the purpose of this Act to require that financial institutions and other firms engaged in the extension of credit make that credit equally available to all creditworthy customers without regard to sex or marital status. . . .

Sec. 701. Prohibited discrimination

(a) It shall be unlawful for any creditor to discriminate against any applicant on the basis of sex or marital status with respect to any aspect of a credit transaction. . . .

Equal Credit Opportunity Act Amendments (1976)

The Equal Credit Opportunity Act is amended to read as follows:

Sec. 701. Prohibited discrimination; reasons for adverse action

(a) It shall be unlawful for any creditor to discriminate against any applicant, with respect to any aspect of a credit transaction—

(1) on the basis of race, color, religion, national origin, sex or marital status, or age (provided the applicant has the capacity to contract);

(2) because all or part of the applicant's income derives from any public assistance program; or

(3) because the applicant has in good faith exercised any right under the Consumer Credit Protection Act [the larger act of which the Equal Credit Opportunity Act is a part].

(b) It shall not constitute discrimination for purposes of this title for a creditor—

(1) to make an inquiry of marital status if such inquiry is for the purpose of ascertaining the creditor's rights and remedies applicable to the particular extension of credit and not to discriminate in a determination of credit-worthiness;

(2) to make an inquiry of the applicant's age or of whether the applicant's income derives from any public assistance program if such inquiry is for the purpose of determining the amount and probable continuance of income levels, credit history, or other pertinent element of credit-worthiness . . . ;

(3) to use any . . . credit system which considers age if such system is demonstrably and statistically sound . . . , except that in the operation of such system the age of an elderly applicant may not be assigned a negative factor or value; or

(4) to make an inquiry or to consider the age of an elderly applicant when the age of such applicant is to be used by the creditor in the extension of credit in favor of such applicant. . . .

(d) **(1)** Within thirty days . . . after receipt of a completed application for credit, a creditor shall notify the applicant of its action on the application.

(2) Each applicant against whom adverse action is taken shall be entitled to a statement of reasons for such actions from the creditor.

Source Review

For Answers to Source Review, see p. A 51.

1. What category of borrowers does the 1974 Equal Credit Opportunity Act protect?
2. What additional categories of borrowers are guaranteed equal access to credit under the Equal Credit Opportunity Act Amendments of 1976? When is it unlawful for creditors to deny credit?
3. Under what conditions may a creditor ask about a borrower's marital status, age, or receipt of public assistance? How do these conditions protect the creditor?

BROADWAY
WALL ST

CHAPTER 13

See Chapter Overview, p. TM 64.
See Chapter Objectives, p. TM 64.
See Introducing the Chapter, p. TM 64.
See Extending Economic Knowledge on text p. 306.

Investment and Investors

This, then, is the duty of the man of Wealth: First, to set an example of modest, unostentatious living, shunning display or extravagance; to provide moderately for the legitimate wants of those dependent upon him ....

Andrew Carnegie

1 Investing money involves risk but contributes to economic growth.
- Financial and Real Investments
- The Risk Factor in Investments
- Real Investment and Economic Growth
- Planning for Personal Investment

2 People buy ownership in corporations by investing in corporate stocks.
- Profit and Loss in Stock Trading
- How Stocks Are Traded

3 Many factors help determine stock prices.
- The Determinants of Stock Prices
- Regulation of the Securities Industry

4 Bonds, futures, and real estate are alternative investment options open to investors.
- Corporate Bonds
- Government Bonds
- Futures Markets
- Real Estate Investments

CHAPTER 13 STUDY GUIDE

Chapter Focus

Chapter 13 examines the many ways people in the United States invest their money. The chapter looks at the reasons for investment and the planning that sound investment requires. The chapter concentrates on stock ownership, how and where stocks are traded, and what internal and external forces determine the price of a stock. The chapter also covers alternative investments: bonds, commodities, and real estate.

As you study the chapter, look for the details that support each of the following statements.

1. Investing money involves risk but contributes to economic growth.
2. People buy ownership in corporations by investing in corporate stocks.
3. Many factors help determine stock prices.
4. Bonds, futures, and real estate are alternative investment options open to investors.

Terms to Know

The following terms, while not the only terms emphasized in this chapter, are basic to your understanding of investment. Determine the meaning of each term, either by using the Glossary or by watching for context clues as you read the chapter.

investment
financial investment
real investment
economic infrastructure
venture capital
dividend
common stock
preferred stock
mutual fund
bull market
bear market
corporate bond
futures market
futures

1 Investing money involves risk but contributes to economic growth.

In the free enterprise system of the United States, freedom of choice allows people to use their money as they see fit. This freedom of choice extends to investment. **Investment** occurs when people exchange their money for something of value and expect to earn a profit from this purchase in the future. The two types of investment are financial investment and real investment.

Financial and Real Investments

The transfer of ownership of property from one person or group to another is **financial investment.** Although ownership of the property changes hands, financial investment produces no new goods. People make financial investments when they buy existing stocks, bonds, real estate, or other property. Both individuals and firms make financial investments, hoping to make a profit in the future from their investments. For example, two brothers buy a sizable plot of land. The brothers have bought the land as a financial investment. The brothers have created no new capital goods. They have bought the land, thinking that it will increase in value sometime in the future.

People who make financial investments must decrease their current consumption of goods and services because invested money cannot be spent on other goods. These investors make a trade-off, choosing to sacrifice some purchasing power in the present in exchange for the chance of increasing their purchasing power in the future.

Between 1980 and 1984, corporations offered $393,765,000 worth of new stocks and bonds for sale in an effort to raise operating capital.

Real investment occurs when investors use money to create a new capital good. Continuing the example mentioned above, the brothers decide to form a development company. The new company clears the land and constructs a condominium complex. The brothers have now created a new capital good, which is the condominium complex. The money spent on the complex now represents a real investment. In addition to individuals, firms and the government make real investments.

The Risk Factor in Investments

Most investments involve a risk because of the possibility that the investor will lose money. Certain investments, however, are safer than others.

The most risk-free way to earn a return on money is to deposit it in a savings account. Most deposits are protected by federal and state insurance plans. Savings accounts in savings and loan institutions that carry state insurance are riskier investments than those in institutions that carry federal insurance, as the panic runs on some state-insured S & Ls in 1985 illustrated. Savers also risk losing money if their accounts exceed $100,000, the maximum amount that federal or state insurance programs will guarantee. ◆ Federal bonds, notes, and bills are considered risk-free because they are backed by the federal government.

Making financial and real investments is riskier than depositing money in savings accounts because neither federal nor state insurance guarantees the investments. Many investors are willing to take the risk, however, because financial and real investments often offer higher returns than deposits in savings accounts.

Real Investment and Economic Growth

Real investment in the public and private sectors promotes economic growth. In the public sector, federal, state, and local governments make real investments when they improve the nation's **economic infrastructure,** that is, the roads, bridges, harbors, airports, other transportation facilities, and the public schools and universities. In the private sector,

◆ **Inform students that many people place money in different financial institutions so that no single account will exceed the amount insured.**

real investment stimulates capital accumulation, technological change, and entrepreneurship.

Capital accumulation is the expansion of the capital goods in an economy. Money spent to replace existing capital maintains the capital stock at its present level but does not add to economic growth. Capital accumulation, on the other hand, promotes economic growth.

The creation of new capital goods is related to the research and development of new products. Real investment by private firms and the government encourages the application of new technology to the production of goods and services. The result of this process is technological change. Technological changes in production methods increase productivity in the workplace. The rise of automation in the industrial and service sectors of the economy is an example of how technological change affects production.

The technological changes that occur in the United States economy are the result of research and development by major firms or by individual entrepreneurs. Entrepreneurs are willing to take risks to develop new products or production methods. Individuals who invest in enterprises operated by entrepreneurs also encourage productivity and growth.

By investing in new technology, businesses are often able to increase productivity.

Money that is invested in entrepreneurial enterprises is often called **venture capital,** or **risk capital.** Venture capital helps entrepreneurs develop an idea into a marketable product. Private venture-capital firms specialize in seeking out and financing promising businesses. These firms spend about $16 billion annually to support entrepreneurs and their projects.

The government also provides funding to entrepreneurs with promising businesses. The Small Business Administration, a federal agency, invests money in smaller-size firms by extending low-interest loans. Some state governments also pump venture capital into small businesses. Experts predict that virtually all states will have venture capital agencies within a few years.

Planning for Personal Investment

An individual desiring to make investments should devise a personal financial plan. Such a plan includes a spending and saving plan, an investment plan, a retirement plan, and an estate plan. The purpose of financial planning is to ensure that a person uses his or her money wisely.

Spending and Saving Plan. A **spending and saving plan** is another name for the personal or household budget and is the starting point for all financial planning. The spending and saving plan lists fixed expenses and flexible expenses. **Fixed expenses** are those payments that remain constant from month to month. Examples include payments for mortgages, rent, medical care, and insurance premiums. **Flexible expenses** vary from month to month. Examples include expenditures for food or recreation. The budget should also include the amounts a person is able to set aside for saving and investing.

Investment Plan. An **investment plan** is the way a person puts his or her money to work. To devise an investment plan, an investor must determine investment goals. Alternatives need to be identified. This step generally means getting professional advice from a banker, accountant, or stockbroker. Desirable features such as the relative safety, high return, or high liquidity of any potential investment also need to be identified.

Once an investor determines how his or her investment options satisfy the outlined goals, then a plan can be devised. An investment plan is often diversified. **Diversification** means that an investor combines several investment goals—security, high yield, growth—and chooses a variety of investments.

Retirement and Estate Plans. A **retirement plan** is a type of long-term savings plan. Individual Retirement Accounts (IRAs) and Keogh Plans, which allow individuals to set aside a portion of their incomes tax-free, are but two types of retirement plans. These were discussed in Chapter 12. A retirement plan varies depending on individual goals and lifestyle changes after retirement.

An **estate plan** provides for an orderly transfer of a person's property after death. Financial experts recommend an estate plan to guarantee that an inheritance is distributed to the designated heirs and to avoid heavy estate taxes.

See Suggested Assignments, p. TM 65.

Section 1 Review See Answers, p. A 52.

DEFINE investment, capital accumulation, venture capital, spending and saving plan, fixed expenses, flexible expenses, diversification

1. **Summarizing Ideas** **(a)** What are two types of investments? **(b)** How do financial investments and real investments differ?
2. **Understanding Ideas** **(a)** Why is a savings account the most risk-free way to save money? **(b)** Why are some investors willing to make financial and real investments?
3. **Comprehending Ideas** Why does real investment by private firms and by the government promote economic growth?
4. **Analyzing Ideas** **(a)** What is the economic infrastructure? **(b)** Why does real investment in the economic infrastructure spur economic growth?
5. **Seeing Relationships** How might a retirement plan and an estate plan be related?

See Key Study Questions and Key Understandings, p. TM 66.

2 People buy ownership in corporations by investing in corporate stocks.

See Suggested Teaching Strategies, p. TM 66.

Ownership in corporate stocks is a popular investment option as the graph on this page shows. Between 1965 and 1985, the number of stockholders increased from 20 million to 47 million, a 134 percent increase over the 20-year period.

Profit and Loss in Stock Trading

A number of important reasons lead people to invest in the stock market. The potential for profit, limited risk on the money invested, and the chance to become a part owner in a corporation all attract investors to the stock market.

The Potential for Profit. Stockholders make a profit in one of two ways. First, most stockholders receive regular **dividends** on the money invested in stocks. The company pays its dividends from profits

Stockholders in Public Corporations, 1965–1985

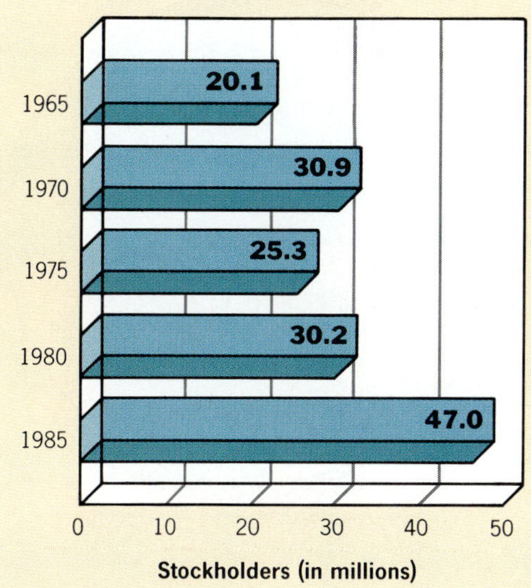

Source: New York Stock Exchange

after it pays all taxes and company expenses. Most corporations pay quarterly dividends; others pay dividends annually or semiannually.

Common stock offers variable dividends. When the company is making high profits, dividends on common stock are usually high. When the company's profits fall, dividends also tend to fall. The company's board of directors determines how much of the corporation's profits to distribute to shareholders of common stock. The directors can choose to withhold all dividends if they believe the company's profits are needed for plant expansion or for payments on the company's debts.

◆ **Preferred stock** offers fixed dividends that are paid from profits before the company pays any dividends on common stock. If the company is unable to pay this fixed dividend in full, it usually makes up the difference when the company's profits increase. At that time, the directors pay any arrears in dividends on preferred stock before they pay dividends on common stock.

Stocks in companies with high earnings that pay consistent dividends are called **income stocks.** Stocks that pay few or no dividends but that gain in value are called **growth stocks.**

Where Stocks Are Traded

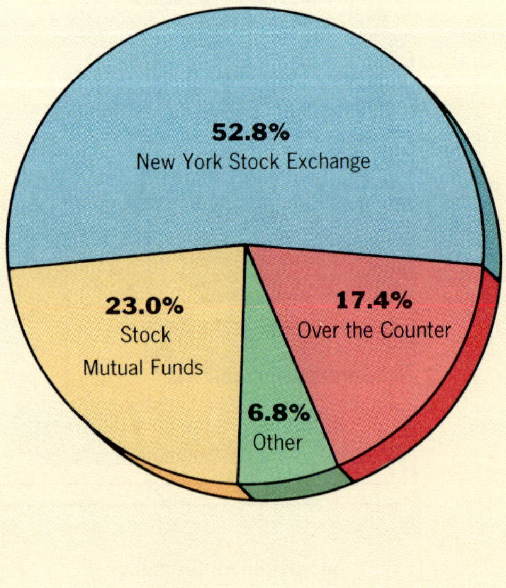

Source: New York Stock Exchange

A second way to earn a profit on a stock is by selling it at a higher price than the original purchase price. The difference between the higher selling price and the lower original buying price is the investor's **capital gain.** However, an investor who sells a stock at a price lower than the purchase price incurs a **capital loss.**

Limited Risk and Ownership. Owners of stocks are protected from some risks. Unlike the owners of sole proprietorships and partnerships, stockholders in corporations enjoy limited liability. The maximum amount of money a stockholder can lose is limited to the amount he or she invested in the stock. Limited liability protects the personal assets of stockholders even if the corporation goes bankrupt.

People also invest in stocks to become owners in the corporation. A certain amount of pride accompanies ownership because shareholders of common stock elect the corporation's board of directors and vote on important company matters. The number of votes a shareholder has is equal to the number of shares of stock he or she owns. Thus, 100 shares equals 100 votes.

Shareholders also must vote on **stock splits.** Stock splits usually occur when the directors determine that the price of a company's stock has become so high that it discourages potential investors from purchasing shares. The directors may decide, for example, to split the shares four for one. After the shareholders approve the four-for-one stock split, a shareholder will have four shares for every single share held before the split. A stock that previously sold for $100 will sell for about $25 after the split takes effect. Shareholders like stock splits because the price of their shares tends to rise following a split.

The actual power of small investors in shaping policy in public corporations is very limited, however, because the largest corporations have thousands of shareholders.

How Stocks Are Traded

The computer revolution and the biggest stock market boom in history during the mid-1980s have reshaped how stocks are traded, not only in the United States but also around the world. The com-

◆ **Have the students read "Investing In High-growth Stocks" on pages 528–529 of the *Everyday Economics Handbook* and answer the questions that follow.**

puter has speeded up the trading of stocks. At the same time, the vast infusion of money into the stock market has allowed some institutional investors to make huge profits.

Stock Exchanges. When people speak of the "stock market," they usually are referring to the New York Stock Exchange (NYSE). The NYSE, the largest stock exchange in the United States, was founded ◆ in 1792 on Wall Street in New York City as a place to buy and sell corporate stocks and government bonds.

Before the Civil War, other brokers founded the New York Curb Exchange, a name that arose because the brokers actually met on the street. In 1953, the name was officially changed to the American Stock Exchange (AMEX). Besides the NYSE and the AMEX, 10 regional stock exchanges are located in other United States cities. Major world cities such as Tokyo, Hong Kong, London, and Paris also have stock exchanges on which some United States firms are able to trade.

Changes in technology have continually improved the buying and selling of stocks on the NYSE. In 1867, the NYSE used the first stock ticker to give the prices of stocks traded. Office workers in New York skyscrapers tossed the paper from the tickers onto the streets below during parades, giving rise to the famous "ticker-tape parades." The trading of stock shares was improved nationwide with the invention of the telephone in the 1870s. The NYSE recorded its first million-share day in 1886 when 1.2 million shares were bought and sold.

The NYSE spent $200 million modernizing its equipment from 1980 to 1985. Huge computers in the exchange and in other locations throughout New York City connect with similar equipment in the nation's major brokerage firms. The computer link-up makes it possible to handle as many as 1,000 stock transactions a second and 450 million shares daily.

Selling Stocks. To have its stock traded on the NYSE, a company must meet rigorous standards concerning number of shareholders, number of shares, and minimum earnings. More than 1,500 companies now have their shares traded on the NYSE.

The NYSE provides a place for the trading of shares, but the exchange itself owns no stocks nor does it set prices for shares. Instead, the NYSE can be compared to an auction market, where investors determine the volume of stocks traded and at what price (see the graph on page 294).

Trading on the NYSE has increased over the years. In 1970, for example, 3,124,000 shares were traded. This total had jumped to 35,680,634 shares by 1986.

Stockbrokers, sometimes called **brokers,** link buyers and sellers of stock on the NYSE. Brokers work for brokerage firms, which are businesses that specialize in trading stocks and other securities. Brokerage firms buy "seats" on the NYSE, which allow representatives of the brokerages to buy and sell shares at the stock exchange. Prices for the 1,366 seats vary. In late 1986, the price of a seat was $580,000. The all-time high for a seat was $625,000 in 1929; the low was $4,000 in 1876 and 1878.

Major brokerage firms have branch offices throughout the United States. The firms employ thousands of brokers and many market analysts. A **market analyst** researches individual firms and evaluates their strengths and weaknesses. Brokers rely on reports of market analysts when advising clients about which stock to buy or sell. Brokers and brokerage firms earn a profit by collecting a commission, or fee, on each transaction.

◆ **Inform students that Wall Street originally ran parallel to a wall that the Dutch built to protect New Amsterdam from hostile Indians. George Washington took the oath of office as the first President of the United States on Wall Street, and the First Congress adopted the Bill of Rights on this historic site.**

◆ **Have the students read "Investing in the Stock Market" on pages 526–528 of the *Everyday Economics Handbook* and answer the questions that follow.**

◆ **The Over-the-Counter Market.** Stocks that are not listed on the NYSE or other stock exchanges are traded in the **over-the-counter (OTC) market.** The stocks of many smaller corporations are traded OTC because many corporations do not meet the standards set by the nation's stock exchanges. These stocks are sometimes called "unlisted stocks" or "OTC stocks."

Investors still need brokers to trade OTC stocks. First, sellers and buyers place buy or sell orders with their brokers. Second, the brokers consult the National Association of Securities Dealers Automated Quotations (NASDAQ) to find out the current price of the stock. If NASDAQ does not quote a price for a particular stock, the brokers telephone other brokers who might have clients who want to trade the stock. The brokers match their clients with suitable buyers or sellers and complete the OTC stock transactions, which then become a part of the public record.

The average number of shares traded daily on NASDAQ is 100 million shares. Even though NASDAQ has no trading floor like the NYSE, it is now the third largest exchange in the world after the NYSE and the Tokyo Stock Exchange.

Mutual Funds. A **mutual fund** pools the money of investors and purchases a variety of securities. Some mutual funds specialize only in bonds, others in growth stocks.

Mutual funds take some of the risk out of investing in stocks because professional managers choose the stocks that the fund purchases. The diversification of the mutual fund enables the fund managers to make up the losses on stocks in some companies with profits from others.

Institutional investors such as mutual funds control 33 percent of the total value of shares traded on exchanges in the United States. But they make 80 percent of the daily stock trades, many of which are in huge blocks of 500,000 or more.

Investment Banks. When corporations issue new stock, buy out controlling interests in another company, or trade large blocks of other stocks, they usu-

The number of commodity futures traded increased from 12,396,000 contracts in 1970 to 184,354,496 contracts in 1986.

DECISION MAKERS IN THE ECONOMY

Lilia Clemente

Born in the Philippines, Lilia Clemente has spent her working life in the United States as an investment specialist in foreign securities. After earning a master's degree from the University of Chicago, she became the first female investment officer at the Ford Foundation. She then founded her own investment advisory firm. Today Clemente is an investment officer at Paine Webber, where in 1983 she started the Atlas Fund, a stock mutual fund for investment in foreign stocks.

The Atlas Fund gained almost 40 percent in the year ending October 3, 1985, the highest gain recorded for a stock mutual fund that year. Under Clemente's guidance, the fund's net asset value per share has risen 33 percent since its beginning in 1983. This increase is 22 percent higher than the average increase for stock mutual funds in general.

As manager of the Atlas Fund, Clemente keeps abreast of economic, political, and social developments in 18 countries. She travels abroad some 10 weeks each year, collecting information from government officials, financial experts, and company executives. Her job is to determine which countries offer the right economic climate for investment. She also determines which companies within those countries are most likely to prove profitable. She then buys or sells stocks according to her assessments.

ally use an **investment bank.** Investment banks such as Morgan Stanley, First Boston, and Goldman Sachs specialize in the buying and selling of large blocks of stock. Some investment banks also do brokerage business, sell real estate, and conduct other financial business. They also earn a profit by collecting a commission on transactions.

At times, especially when large blocks of stock are traded, a number of investment banks work together to trade a corporation's stock in a process called **syndication.** Members of the **syndicate** spread the work, and risk, of reselling a large stock purchase.

Syndicates are often used when a major corporation issues new stock. Each investment bank in the syndicate agrees to buy a portion of the stocks at a price beneath its intended market value. The investment banks then resell the stocks to a number of different brokerage firms who, in turn, sell them to ◆ investors.

See Suggested Assignments, p. TM 66.

◆ **Have the students read "Actuaries" on page 540 of *Careers in the Marketplace.***

Section 2 Review

See Answers, p. A 52.

DEFINE dividend, common stock, stock split, stockbroker, market analyst, mutual fund, investment bank, syndicate

1. **Summarizing Ideas** What impact has technology had on the stock exchanges?
2. **Evaluating Ideas** What are the advantages of purchasing preferred stock?
3. **Analyzing Ideas** **(a)** What are the advantages of investing in a mutual fund? **(b)** Why do small investors have little power in shaping corporate policies?
4. **Interpreting Graphics** Study the graph on page 293. **(a)** What change in the number of stockholders occurred between 1970 and 1975? **(b)** What economic factor might explain the change between 1970 and 1975?

BUILDING ECONOMIC SKILLS

READING ABOUT ECONOMICS

Understanding a Financial Report

The financial section of a newspaper summarizes the daily performance of stocks and bonds. In addition, the financial section of many major newspapers provides information on commodities markets, world gold prices, foreign exchange rates, and other timely financial topics.

How to Read Financial Reports

Follow these steps when reading financial reports.

1. **Locate the financial section.** Newspapers such as *The Wall Street Journal* and the *New York Times* are the most important sources for vital financial information. Large-city newspapers often carry more extensive financial sections than small-city newspapers.
2. **Study the types of data provided.** Identify the headings under which data is categorized.
3. **Analyze the data.** Read all explanations of the data. A key is usually included at the end of each table. Also read any footnotes.
4. **Put the data to use.** Compare the current prices of stocks and bonds to earlier prices. Chart the performance of a stock, bond, commodity, mutual fund, or other investment over a period of time. Note changes or trends in the investment's prices. Compare its rate of return with other investment options. Consider future investment options.

Applying the Skill

Study the stock quotations from the New York Stock Exchange (NYSE) below as shown in Chart A. These quotations appeared in the financial sections of most daily newspapers on November 5, 1986. The key for reading the stock quotations, which is shown on page 299, is adapted from the key in the *New York Times.*

Now let us review some of the information in Chart A, using Citicorp stock as an example. The highest price paid for a share of Citicorp in the previous year was \$63.75. The lowest price paid was \$43.12. It paid an annual dividend of \$2.46 a share. Its yield was 4.8 percent. Its price-earnings ratio was 7. Shares traded were 3,896,000 on November 5, 1986. The highest price paid for a share of Citicorp stock on November 5, 1986, was \$51.50, and the lowest price was \$50.73. The closing price for a share was \$50.87.

Chart A

1	2	3	4	5	6	7	8	9	10	11
$63\frac{3}{4}$	$43\frac{1}{8}$	Citicrp*	2.46	4.8	7	3896	$51\frac{1}{2}$	$50\frac{5}{8}$	$50\frac{7}{8}$	$-\frac{5}{8}$
$71\frac{1}{4}$	$48\frac{3}{4}$	Exxon	3.60	5.1	9	12257	70	$69\frac{1}{8}$	70	$+\frac{5}{8}$
39	$19\frac{1}{8}$	Marriot*	0.13	0.4	23	2866	$31\frac{3}{4}$	$30\frac{5}{8}$	31	$-\frac{5}{8}$
$86\frac{3}{4}$	$47\frac{3}{4}$	Penney	2.48	3.1	14	4611	$81\frac{1}{4}$	$79\frac{5}{8}$	$80\frac{1}{4}$	$+\frac{3}{4}$
$72\frac{1}{4}$	$48\frac{5}{8}$	Xerox	3.00	5.2	13	3251	$58\frac{1}{8}$	57	58	$+\frac{3}{8}$

*On the NYSE, Citicorp stock is listed as Citicrp and Marriott stock is listed as Marriot.

Chart B

1	2	3	4	5	6	7	8	9	10	11
$63\frac{3}{4}$	$46\frac{1}{4}$	Citicrp*	2.46	4.5	8	8473	55	$53\frac{1}{8}$	55	$+2\frac{3}{8}$
$71\frac{1}{4}$	$48\frac{3}{4}$	Exxon	3.60	5.1	9	13399	$70\frac{1}{2}$	69	$70\frac{1}{2}$	$+1\frac{3}{8}$
39	$20\frac{5}{8}$	Marriot*	0.13	0.4	23	3838	$31\frac{3}{4}$	$30\frac{7}{8}$	$31\frac{3}{4}$	$+\frac{3}{4}$
$88\frac{3}{4}$	$52\frac{5}{8}$	Penney	2.48	3.0	14	3948	84	$82\frac{1}{2}$	84	+2
$72\frac{1}{4}$	$48\frac{5}{8}$	Xerox	3.00	5.0	13	19478	$60\frac{7}{8}$	$59\frac{3}{8}$	$60\frac{3}{8}$	+1

*On the NYSE, Citicorp stock is listed as Citicrp and Marriott stock is listed as Marriot.

	Key
1	***12-Month High:*** The highest price paid for the stock during the previous 52 weeks.
2	***12-Month Low:*** The lowest price paid for the stock during the previous 52 weeks.
3	***Stock:*** The company's name.
4	***Dividend:*** The annual return per share.
5	***Yield:*** The percentage return on the investment, calculated by dividing the annual dividend by the current price of the stock.
6	***Price-Earnings Ratio:*** The current stock price divided by the company's earnings per share; the lower the number is, the better is the ratio.
7	***Sales:*** The number of shares traded on that business day, in hundreds.
8	***High:*** The highest price paid for the stock during that business day.
9	***Low:*** The lowest price paid for the stock during that business day.
10	***Last:*** The final price, or closing price, paid for the stock during that business day.
11	***Net Change:*** The change in today's closing price from the previous business day's closing price.

Citicorp had a lower closing price on November 5, 1986, than it had on November 4, 1986. Its stock was down 1/8, or −$0.125.

Practicing the Skill

Study Chart B, showing the same selected stocks as Chart A. The stock quotations in Chart B appeared in the *New York Times* on December 3, 1986. Compare them with the quotations in Chart A, which appeared November 5, 1986. Then on a separate sheet of paper, answer the following questions.

1. **(a)** Which stock had a new 52-week high? **(b)** Which stocks had new 52-week lows? **(c)** What do the new high and lows tell you about the prices of those stocks in November and December of 1985?
2. **(a)** Did Citicorp's yield increase or decrease? **(b)** Did Citicorp's price-earnings ratio increase or decrease? **(c)** Do the new statistics indicate that Citicorp was a stronger or a weaker investment than it was on November 5, 1986?
3. **(a)** Which stock had the largest number of shares traded? **(b)** the least?
4. **(a)** Which stock had the largest net change? **(b)** the smallest?
5. Compare the statistics on both quotations and select a stock as an investment. Explain in detail why you selected the stock you did.

Practicing the Skill Answers: 1. (a) Penney; (b) Citicorp, Marriott, Penney; (c) whether they were higher or lower in price the previous year; 2. (a) decreased; (b) increased; (c) weaker; 3. (a) Xerox; (b) Marriott; 4. (a) Citicorp; (b) Marriott; 5. Answers will vary. Students might choose stocks for income or growth.

See Key Study Questions and Key Understandings, p. TM 67.

3 Many factors help determine stock prices.

See Suggested Teaching Strategies, p. TM 67.

The corporation's strength, investors' expectations, and external forces determine the supply and demand for stocks. The forces of supply and demand determine the price of a stock.

The Determinants of Stock Prices

Shares are traded in lots of 100. Less than 100 shares is an odd lot. Stock prices are quoted in eighths: a quotation at $38\frac{1}{8}$ means that the price for one share of stock is $38.12.

The stockbroker's task is to reconcile a "bid" price with an "asked" price and make a sale. For example, a buyer bids $37\frac{3}{8}$ or $37.37 a share, and the seller asks $38\frac{1}{8}$. If the stockbroker gets the buyer to agree to pay $0.50 more for a share and the seller to agree to sell for $0.25 less, a sale is made at $37\frac{7}{8}$, or $37.87. Demand for a stock pushes up the price. When many stocks are available for sale, thus increasing the supply of shares available, the price of the stock goes down.

Corporate Financial Strength. The corporation's financial strength is usually measured in terms of profits and losses. A company's quarterly earnings reports and its annual report are read carefully by investors, market analysts, and brokers. When investors have confidence in the quality products and long-term prospects of major corporations, they buy the stock issued by these corporations. Such stocks are called "blue chip" stocks, and they are in high demand during both economic upswings and downswings of the stock market.

The average price of the stocks included in the New York Stock Exchange's composite index of common stocks has increased from $45.70 in 1970 to $142.12 in 1986.

Investor Expectations. Investors' expectations about the future price of a stock affect the market price of a stock. Investors increase their demand for a stock when they expect it to increase in value, and investors tend to sell when they believe a stock's value will decrease in the future.

Investors, market analysts, and brokers watch fluctuations in the stock indexes, such as the Dow Jones Industrial Average. The Dow indexes changes in the prices of the stock of selected companies. When the Dow steadily rises over a period of time, a **bull market** exists.

A **bear market,** on the other hand, exists when the Dow averages fall for a period of time. The most serious bear market occurred from 1929 to 1932. This bear market was considered the beginning of the Great Depression. Investors lost confidence in stocks as an investment and "dumped" their stocks at any price. Bull markets and bear markets usually last from one to four years.

Financial experts also affect investors' expectations. Expert advice on individual firms or on the stock market itself is available through financial newspapers and magazines, investment newsletters, and other publications such as *The Wall Street Journal, Barron's, Forbes, Money,* and *Financial World.*

Economics Reporter

What Is Greenmail?

Greenmail has been called Wall Street's version of blackmail. The name is derived from the way an investor or a corporation attempts a hostile merger. A greenmailer looks for a company that has great cash potential and a low stock price, two indications that the company could be run more profitably. The greenmailers see themselves as interested investors who are willing to restructure the targeted company and increase profits. The company's top management, however, sees the greenmailers as the profit raiders of Wall Street.

Greenmailers will buy enough of a targeted company's stock to threaten a takeover or a proxy fight to gain control of the company. Greenmailers usually reap huge profits, as the targeted company's top management buys the shares back at a higher price. The issue of greenmail has not been resolved by business or government, and insurance companies have begun to offer greenmail-protection policies.

External Forces. Sometimes forces over which neither the firms nor the stock market have any control influence the price of stocks. For example, the price of Johnson & Johnson stock fell sharply in 1982 and again in 1986 after someone put poison in Tylenol capsules. Johnson & Johnson voluntarily withdrew Tylenol capsules from the shelves. Some investors, however, feared that Johnson & Johnson's profits would fall. These investors rushed to sell their Johnson & Johnson shares, contributing to a dramatic ◆ drop in the stock's price.

The sharp price increases for oil during 1973–1974 and again during 1979–1980 were partially responsible for the bear markets of 1974 and 1980. Investors viewed United States reliance on foreign oil and higher oil prices as negative external forces. As investors became more pessimistic about the chances for profit on the stock market, demand for stocks fell. By the mid-1980s, when the price of oil dropped dramatically, investor optimism rose, causing an increase in the demand for many stocks. Some experts attributed the record-breaking bull market of the mid-1980s to the sharp decline in oil prices.

Investors may determine that government statistics on unemployment, inflation, interest rates, and new housing starts will affect stock prices in a negative or positive fashion. National and international events, such as revolutions, assassinations of prominent world leaders, and elections can also affect investor confidence.

Regulation of the Securities Industry

Throughout the 1800s, stock exchanges in the United States took responsibility for monitoring trade in securities. This internal self-regulation created opportunities for abuse by unscrupulous securities dealers. In addition, listed corporations often offered investors misleading or fraudulent information about their securities to promote their sale.

During the 1900s, Congress passed a number of acts to regulate trading in securities. The two most important were the Clayton Antitrust Act (1914) and the Truth-in-Securities Act.

◆ **Discussion topic: How foreign policy influences the prices of certain stocks. (For example, stock prices in aerospace industries rise with political emphasis on stronger national defense.)**

The Ivan Boesky insider-trading case resulted in calls for stronger policing by the SEC.

◆ The Clayton Antitrust Act outlawed many monopolistic practices by big business. The act discouraged the formation of monopolies by forbidding corporations from buying stock in competing companies when such purchases could result in monopolistic control over an industry. Thus, the Clayton Act put limits on the types of stocks that corporations could purchase.

The Truth-in-Securities Act, also called the Federal Securities Act (1933), is the most important legislation affecting securities trading. The act originally required all companies to register their securities with the Federal Trade Commission (FTC). In 1934, the Securities Exchange Act established the Securities and Exchange Commission (SEC) to enforce the Federal Securities Act.

Companies register their securities by providing a detailed financial statement to the SEC and a prospectus to all potential investors. A **prospectus** is a fact sheet containing data on the company's finances. Investors use the prospectus to evaluate securities that are offered for sale. The SEC is empowered to levy heavy fines for violations of these requirements.

The SEC also regulates the procedures for the trading of securities. The SEC licenses all stock exchanges in the United States, ensuring that stock exchanges conform to certain rules and regulations when securities are traded. The SEC further regulates the activities of brokers and brokerage houses to guard against fraud and other unethical actions.

CASE STUDY

The SEC Crackdown on Insider Trading

In its role as chief federal watchdog agency over the stock market, the SEC has cracked down on professional rumor planting and inaccurate accounting practices by corporations. Each is illegal and each affects the price of stocks.

The SEC's enforcement efforts were strengthened in 1983 when the Justice Department established the Economic Crime Council to identify and convict people who commit financial crimes. The SEC has also become increasingly concerned about an illegal practice called insider trading.

Insider trading occurs when an investor uses information that is not available to the general public to make a profit on the purchase or sale of a stock. In many cases, the nonpublic information includes news about future mergers and acquisitions or a company's earnings report. This type of information gives the insider an unfair head start in deciding what to do with a stock.

In the process, it also undermines the confidence of other investors in the stock market. Investment bankers, corporate executives, accountants, stockbrokers, and lawyers often have access to insider information. It is illegal and unethical for them to pass on this information.

Insider traders use nonpublic information to make profits or to prevent losses on stocks. If the nonpublic information suggests that the stock's price will increase in the near future, insider traders buy the stock. Later, after the price has increased, they sell the stock. The profits made by insider traders take the form of capital gains. If, on the other hand, the nonpublic information will likely hurt the value of a stock, insider traders sell it quickly, allowing them to avoid capital losses.

The SEC has aggressively policed the stock exchanges in the United States for evidence of insider trading. In 1984, Congress passed legislation permitting the SEC to fine convicted insider traders $100,000 and to penalize them with additional amounts up to three times the profits they gained or the losses they avoided by trading on their illegal knowledge. The SEC's Division of Enforcement brought 13 insider trading cases to court in 1984 and 20 in 1985.

◆ **Remind the students that the Clayton Antitrust Act was designed to strengthen the Sherman Antitrust Act. The Sherman Act contained vague language, did not define what constituted a trust, and provided a loophole regarding restraint of trade. The Clayton Act listed specific illegal practices and declared that labor unions and farm organizations were not conspiracies in restraint of trade.**

The worst scandals over insider trading occurred in 1986. The managing director of a leading investment firm used insider information on takeover bids to make an illegal profit of $10.6 million, trading shares in 54 companies. He also illegally gave information on pending mergers to a risk arbitrageur, Ivan Boesky, who then made huge profits in trading shares in these companies.

◆ The SEC caught Boesky and forced him to pay a $100 million fine—$50 million in settlement for illegal profits and a $50 million penalty. The $100 million fine was only $6 million less than the SEC's budget for 1986. The SEC required Boesky to sell his securities holdings and barred him for life from trading on stock markets in the United States.

Some experts believe that inadequate federal funding hampers the SEC's Division of Enforcement. The division currently receives about one third of the annual SEC budget, money which must support a staff of 110 lawyers in Washington, D.C., and about 400 other officials in its nine regional offices. While the size of the SEC has been relatively constant, its responsibilities have mushroomed because of the great increase in the volume of shares traded, the increase in the number of securities dealers, and the increased sophistication of insider traders.

See Suggested Assignments, p. TM 67.

Section 3 Review See Answers, p. A 53.

DEFINE bull market, bear market, prospectus

IDENTIFY Dow Jones Industrial Average, greenmail, Ivan Boesky

1. **Summarizing Ideas** **(a)** What is the major determinant of stock prices? **(b)** What factors influence the demand for a stock?
2. **Organizing Ideas** In what ways is the securities industry regulated?
3. **Analyzing Ideas** How have actions against insider trading protected small investors?
4. **Evaluating Viewpoints** **(a)** How does a greenmailer try to gain control of a company? **(b)** Defend or refute this statement: Greenmail should be made an illegal activity.

◆ Report topic: How insider trading erodes public confidence in the stock market.

See Key Study Questions and Key Understandings, p. TM 68.

4 Bonds, futures, and real estate are alternative investment options open to investors.

See Suggested Teaching Strategies, p. TM 68.

Corporate bonds, government bonds, futures markets, and real estate are alternatives to investing in corporate stocks. Each investment alternative involves risk and the potential for profit.

Corporate Bonds

Corporations sell **corporate bonds** to raise large sums of money that might be difficult to obtain from a bank. Corporate bonds come in large units, such as $1,000, $5,000, or $10,000 each. The investor purchases a bond at face value, the value listed on the bond, and receives an annual interest payment at a rate also stated on the bond. On the maturity date, the investor collects the final interest payment and the principal, the amount of the original bond.

Corporate bonds are often compared to IOUs because they represent debt. Investors who purchase corporate bonds become creditors, not owners, of the corporation. Brokerage firms sell the corporate bonds to the public over the counter or on the bond markets of the NYSE or the AMEX.

Investors buy corporate bonds for several reasons. First, the bonds offer a fixed and often higher interest rate than that paid on savings accounts. Second, the fixed interest on bonds must be paid to bondholders in good times and in bad, unlike dividends on common and preferred stock. Third, corporate bondholders are paid off before stockholders should the company fail.

Government Bonds

Government bonds are similar to corporate bonds. Government bonds represent debt that the government must repay the investor. They carry fixed interest rates and are redeemable at a stated maturity date, which varies in length from 30 days to 30 years.

In contrast to corporate bonds, interest on bonds issued by the federal government, including savings bonds, Treasury bills, Treasury notes, and Treasury

Economics Reporter

What Is Programmed Trading?

In programmed trading, computerized programs direct the buying and selling of stocks and futures contracts. Programmed trading is based on changes in stock indexes such as Standard & Poor's 500—a daily index of the stock prices of 500 corporations in the United States. When the price of a futures contract rises above the index price, the computerized program automatically sells the futures contract and buys stock. Conversely, when the price of a futures contract slips below the index price, the computerized program automatically sells stock and buys futures contracts. Programmed trading often results in huge shifts in stock prices because of the amount of stocks being traded and the automatic nature of the trading.

bonds, is exempt from local taxes but not from federal income taxes. Backed by the federal government, government bonds are among the safest of all investments.

State, county, or local governments issue tax-exempt bonds. Investors who buy tax-exempt bonds do not have to pay federal income taxes or local income taxes on the interest they collect. The interest ◆ rate on tax-exempt bonds is generally lower than interest rates on corporate and federal bonds, but tax-exempt bonds remain a popular investment option because investors' interest is untouched by tax collectors.

Because interest rates on United States savings bonds are fixed at the time of purchase, bond values increase when interest rates fall.

State and local bonds have been safe investments since the Great Depression, but these bonds contain an element of risk. In the mid-1970s, for example, New York City was unable to sell its bonds because of its poor credit rating. Investors refused to buy the bonds because the risk of default was too high. Eventually, when New York City's financial situation stabilized, the bonds were sold.

In recent years, some local tax-exempt bonds have offered insurance to bondholders. Over 20 percent of all new municipal bonds, bonds issued by towns and cities, are insured. The interest rate for insured bonds is slightly lower than that of uninsured bonds, but the insurance removes the risk of default.

Futures Markets

Futures markets, or commodities markets, are organized much like stock markets. Instead of trading stock, investors trade different types of commodities called **futures.** Futures include agricultural products such as corn, wheat, soybeans, and oats. They include industrial goods such as steel and coal, and precious metals and gemstones such as gold, silver, and diamonds. The Chicago Board of Trade is the largest commodities market. Trading futures requires specialized knowledge about the commodities being sold and bought.

When businesspeople sell futures, they accept an investor's money today in exchange for a promise to deliver a commodity to the investor at a later date. The terms of a futures agreement are stated in a contract.

Selling futures includes two immediate benefits. First, the business can raise money quickly to help produce the commodity. In agriculture, for example, the money is used to raise capital to buy seed or fertilizer. Second, the business is guaranteed a market for its output, and payment is received prior to delivery of the commodity.

◆ **Federal bonds are tax-exempt until they are cashed. When the bonds are cashed, however, all interest must be reported as income.**

The major drawback to selling futures is that the commodity's price on the open market may rise far above that which is listed on the contract. If this occurs, the business must honor the contract, and deliver the commodity to the investor at the lower price.

Most investors, however, do not buy futures to purchase a commodity. They buy futures to resell the contracts for a higher price than they paid. Professional commodities traders are more likely to invest in futures markets than individual investors. Information on futures markets is published by the Commodities Futures Trading Commission and the National Futures Association.

Real Estate Investments

People also invest in real estate. Real estate is the physical land, the things that are natural to it such as minerals and trees, and the things people add such as buildings.

The chief advantage of investing in real estate is appreciation, which means that real estate grows more valuable over time. Investors in a house, apartment building, condominium, office building, and even vacant land tend to profit from the resale of their investments. Other advantages include the ability of the investor to collect rental income, claim certain tax deductions, and have pride of ownership.

Many of the disadvantages of real estate investments involve costs. Financial costs include local property taxes and income taxes on rental properties. In addition, real estate purchases are often expensive. Investors must often borrow money to purchase real estate, resulting in long-term mortgage payments. Finally, real estate investments entail expenses for repair, maintenance, and insurance protection.

The lack of liquidity is another disadvantage of real estate investment. **Liquidity** refers to the ease with which a property can be converted into cash. In prosperous times, when people have a steady income and are confident about the future, real estate tends to be much more liquid than during hard times. During economic upswings, people are more willing to make a major purchase such as real estate. During downswings in the economy, real estate becomes less liquid and sellers have much greater difficulty in selling real estate.

See Suggested Assignments, p. TM 68.

Section 4 Review See Answers, p. A 54.

DEFINE futures market

IDENTIFY programmed trading

1. **Summarizing Ideas** What are the chief advantages of investing in the four alternatives to corporate stocks?
2. **Comparing Ideas** Generally, how does the return on corporate bonds compare to the return on government bonds?
3. **Analyzing Ideas** Why is the futures market considered to be more of a risk than the purchase of common stock?

CHAPTER 13 SUMMARY

In the United States, people are free to make both financial and real investments. The transfer of ownership of property from one person or group to another is financial investment. In contrast, real investment involves using money to create new capital goods. Only real investment contributes to economic growth. Because all investments entail a certain amount of risk, a personal financial plan should be constructed before investments are made.

People invest in corporate stocks because of the potential for profit, the limited risk involved, and the chance to become a part owner in a corporation. Investors may choose either common stock, preferred stock, or mutual funds, all of which are traded on stock exchanges worldwide. While the New York Stock Exchange is the largest exchange in the United States, other stock exchanges, as well as an over-the-counter market, exist.

A corporation's strength, investors' expectations, and external forces, such as reports on inflation and unemployment, affect the supply and demand for stocks and, in turn, the prices of stocks.

In addition to corporate stock, many people invest in bonds, futures, and real estate. Both the government and corporations issue bonds, which are essentially IOUs. When investors buy futures, they pay money in exchange for a promise to receive a commodity at a later date. Real estate investment lacks liquidity, but investors generally realize a profit when they sell.

CHAPTER 13 REVIEW

For Answers to Chapter 13 Review, see p. A 54.

Reviewing Economic Terms

Supply the economic term that correctly completes each sentence.

1. The purchase of new capital goods is _____.
2. A pool of money investors used to purchase a variety of securities is a _____ _____.
3. A period of investor optimism marked by a steady rise in the Dow Jones Industrial Average is called a _____ _____.
4. Information on a company's finances is available to all potential investors in a _____.
5. The sale of an investment at a higher price than its original cost is a _____ _____.
6. Another term for venture capital is _____ _____.
7. When investors anticipate that stock prices will fall and the Dow Jones Industrial Average declines for a period of time, a _____ _____ exists.
8. When large blocks of stock are traded, investment banks work together in a process called _____.
9. Roads, public schools, airports, and port facilities are part of the _____ _____.

Thinking Critically About Economics

1. **Summarizing Ideas** **(a)** What is the difference between a financial investment and a real investment? **(b)** Why do most investments involve risk? **(c)** Why did Congress create the Securities and Exchange Commission to regulate the securities industry?
2. **Understanding Ideas** Why is the stock for some companies sold in the over-the-counter market rather than in one of the stock exchanges?
3. **Comprehending Ideas** Why are investment banks interested in forming syndicates to trade in stock?
4. **Seeing Relationships** What is the legal relationship between stockholders and the corporations that issue the stock?
5. **Comparing Ideas** What are some differences between growth and income stocks?
6. **Analyzing Ideas** Why would investors' expectations about the future cause the price of a stock to rise or fall?
7. **Interpreting Ideas** Why would an investor or market analyst want to look at *The Wall Street Journal* or *Forbes?*

Exercising Economic Skills

1. **Understanding a Financial Report** Check the financial section of a recent newspaper and study the NYSE quotations. **(a)** For the same six stocks as those listed on the chart on page 299, list the 12-month high; 12-month low; last, or closing price; and net change. **(b)** For each stock, compare the statistics on your list with the statistics on Chart B on page 299, and summarize the stocks' performance since December 3, 1986. **(c)** Decide which stock would have been the best investment and defend your choice in one or more paragraphs.
2. **Investing in the Stock Market** Study the feature on pages 526–528. Obtain a company's prospectus from a local stockbroker. Review the prospectus. Then in a paragraph summarize the information about the company contained in the prospectus.

Extending Economic Knowledge

1. By using a daily newspaper that reports activity on a stock exchange, follow a single stock for a period of one month. Pay particular attention to price changes, volume, dividends (if any), highs, lows, and price/earnings ratios. Make a chart to illustrate stock information.
2. Read accounts of the 1929 Stock Market Crash. Research federal regulations that were instituted to prevent another crash. Prepare a chart similar to the chart on page 280 that provides the following information: the name of the law or regulation and the date it was passed, its major purpose, its major provisions, and its major effects on the market.
3. Study newspaper and magazine accounts of the major insider trading scandals of the mid-1980s. Prepare a written summary of each scandal and its outcome.

Using Primary Sources

Andrew Carnegie (1835–1919) was a leading American industrialist, author, and philanthropist. In his most famous essay, "The Gospel of Wealth," Carnegie argued that the rich are the rightful "trustees" of society's wealth. This view was widely accepted during the nineteenth and early twentieth centuries. As you read the following excerpts, note Carnegie's reasons for the necessity of trustees. How did the trustees "invest" in the building of industrial America?

The Gospel of Wealth According to Andrew Carnegie

This, then, is held to be the duty of the man of wealth: To set an example of modest . . . living, shunning display or extravagance; to provide moderately for the legitimate wants of those dependent upon him; and, after doing so, to consider all surplus revenues which come to him simply as trust funds, which he is called upon to administer . . . as a matter of duty . . . in the manner which, in his judgment, is best calculated to produce the most beneficial results for the community—the man of wealth thus becoming the mere trustee and agent for his poorer brethren, bringing to their service his superior wisdom, experience, and ability to administer, doing for them better than they would or could do for themselves. . . .

Those who would administer wisely must, indeed, be wise; for one of the serious obstacles to the improvement of our race is indiscriminate charity. It were better for mankind that the millions of the rich were thrown into the sea than so spent as to encourage the slothful, the drunken, the unworthy. . . .

In bestowing charity, the main consideration should be to help those who will help themselves; to provide part of the means by which those who desire to improve may do so; to give those who desire to rise the aids by which they may rise; to assist, but rarely or never to do all. Neither the individual nor the race is improved by almsgiving. . . .

[The] best means of benefiting the community is to place within its reach the ladders upon which the aspiring can rise—free libraries, parks, and means of recreation, by which men are helped in body and mind; works of art, certain to give pleasure and improve the public taste; and public institutions of various kinds, which will improve the general condition of the people; in this manner returning their surplus wealth to the mass of their fellows in the forms best calculated to do them lasting good.

Thus is the problem of rich and poor to be solved. The laws of accumulation will be left free, the laws of distribution free. Individualism will continue, but the millionaire will be but a trustee for the poor, intrusted for a season with a great part of the increased wealth of the community. . . .

Such, in my opinion, is the true gospel concerning wealth, obedience to which is destined some day to solve the problems of the rich and the poor, and to bring "Peace on earth, among men good will."

Source Review

For Answers to Source Review, see p. A 55.

1. In Carnegie's view, who are the trustees of society's wealth? Why are they called trustees? What type of lifestyle should they live?
2. According to Carnegie, why is the trustees' ability to accumulate money important to society? How did the "captains of industry" use surplus wealth to build American industry?
3. Carnegie, as the period's leading philanthropist, donated hundreds of millions of dollars to various causes. According to Carnegie, what types of causes are worthy of support? How was Carnegie's philanthropy a type of investment in American society and culture?
4. Why does Carnegie believe that "indiscriminate charity" is an obstacle to the improvement of society? What rule does Carnegie believe should be followed when giving charity?

UNIT FOUR REVIEW

For Answers to Unit Four Review, see p. A 55.

Reviewing Economic Ideas

1. What are the functions of money in a market economy?
2. (a) When did the United States abandon the gold standard? (b) What was the main reason why the government abandoned the gold standard?
3. What is the purpose of deposit insurance?
4. What are the three main tools used by the Federal Reserve to control the money supply?
5. What forms of money are included in the measurement of M1?
6. When does the government adopt an easy-money policy?
7. (a) What is the average percentage of disposable income that is saved by people in the United States? (b) How does the United States savings rate compare to savings rates in other nations?
8. Why is real investment important?
9. (a) What does stock represent? (b) What is the difference between preferred stock and common stock? (c) What is a corporate bond?

Connecting Economic Ideas

1. **Summarizing Ideas** What are the trade-offs between putting money in a regular savings account and investing it in the stock market?
2. **Comprehending Ideas** Why are improvements in the economic infrastructure an investment in a nation's economic growth and economic equity?
3. **Seeing Relationships** How are (a) monetary policies and (b) the size of the money supply related to economic growth?
4. **Comparing Ideas** What are the similarities and differences in investing in savings deposits, time deposits, and stocks?
5. **Contrasting Ideas** (a) Why would members of large unions want to create credit unions? (b) Why did the United States create 12 separate Federal Reserve banks when other countries have only one?
6. **Analyzing Ideas** In what ways do interest rates affect economic activities in the United States?

Investigating Economic Issues

Reread the *Issues in Economics* feature on pages 260–261 and answer the following questions.

1. **Summarizing Ideas** According to some economists, what are some of the myths and misconceptions about the national debt?
2. **Comprehending Ideas** (a) According to some economists, what are the major consequences of the national debt? (b) What are the important economic benefits the nation has derived from deficit spending?
3. **Evaluating Viewpoints** Defend or refute the following statement: The negative impact of the national debt outweighs its benefits.
4. **Interpreting Graphics** Study the graphs on page 260. (a) Since 1950, what has been the trend in the national debt in current dollars? (b) In the same period, what has been the trend in the national debt as a percentage of the GNP? (c) State a generalization that explains these two trends.

Applying Economics

1. Research or survey financial institutions. Compile a list of investment or savings plans currently available. Propose a savings plan for a family of four—mother, father, and two children. This plan should include recommendations which will meet a variety of savings goals for that family. Your plan should show the relationship and advantage of each component to the goals of the family. Then prepare a report to present to the class that describes the investment or savings plan that you would recommend to the family.
2. Suppose you have $1,000 to invest in the stock market. Pick at least five stocks that are regularly traded on the New York Stock Exchange (NYSE) in which to invest. Study the financial section of the newspaper to determine what each stock sold for day by day. At the end of 30 days, calculate your gains and losses. Prepare a chart illustrating your trading activity to accompany your oral report to the class.

Using Primary Sources

Paul Craig Roberts (1939–) is a professor of political economy at the Center for Strategic & International Studies, Georgetown University. As you read the essay that appeared in *Business Week*, think about why Professor Roberts proposes to reduce the federal deficits and national debt through federal spending cuts. How would his proposal affect the role of government in the economy?

The Case for Spending Reduction

Falling interest rates are wrecking the deficit-reduction strategy of Senate Republicans and Federal Reserve Board Chairman Paul A. Volcker. This strategy promises lower interest rates in exchange for spending reductions or tax increases. At the Senate Finance Committee's showcase hearing on Jan. 2, three former chairmen of the Council of Economic Advisers testified that interest rates would fall two to three percentage points if the budget were significantly reduced. Volcker added to the pressure by telling Senate Republicans that lower interest rates were impossible unless the deficit was cut by at least $50 billion.

The problem with this strategy is that it is inconsistent with the facts. At the Finance Committee hearing, Senator Malcolm Wallop (R-Wyo.) observed that he had been listening to this argument for four years, during the course of which the budget quadrupled and interest rates fell by half. In recent months alone interest rates have declined two to three percentage points while the deficit increased by $50 billion. House Republican leader Robert H. Michel noted that Volcker has said many times in the past that lower interest rates depended on cuts in the deficit, but that interest rates had fallen despite the failure to reduce the deficit. Michel said that the result has been to make congressmen less concerned about the deficit, because none of its alleged harmful effects has, in fact, materialized.

As Treasury Dept. economists warned from the beginning, basing the case for spending reductions on the deficit theory of interest rates has proved to be a risky business. Not only do the facts not support this theory, but when interest rates fall anyhow, the result is to strip the deficit of any harmful consequences and make it more acceptable in people's minds.

Welfare statism. The case for spending reduction has to be faced head on. Government spending has to be cut because, far from being good for us, much of the spending is harmful. Crowding out is not a financial phenomenon caused by budget deficits. Rather, it occurs because government

(Text of article continues on page 590.)

Source Review

For Answers to Source Review, see p. A 57.

1. According to Professor Roberts, how should the government reduce the federal deficit and debt?
2. What is a "welfare state"? What does Roberts mean when he says that a welfare state exists in the United States?
3. According to Roberts, how is a welfare state harmful to private investment? to private property rights? to personal incentives and self-reliance? How does it "institutionalize" poverty?

Reading About Economics

Friedman, Milton. *Bright Promises, Dismal Performance: An Economist's Protest.* San Diego, California: Harcourt, Brace, Jovanovich, Publishers. A series of essays on economic activities, economic policies, and the Federal Reserve.

Hutchinson, Harry D. *Money, Banking and the United States Economy.* Englewood Cliffs, N.J.: Prentice-Hall, Inc., A general reference on money and banking topics.

Thomas, Gordon. *The Day the Bubble Burst: A Social History of the Wall Street Crash of 1929.* New York: Doubleday. A readable explanation of the financial causes of the crash.

Tobias, Andrew. *The Only Investment Guide You'll Ever Need*, rev. ed. New York: Bantam Books. A layman's guide to investment strategies.

See Unit Materials, p. TM 70.
See Multimedia Guide, p. TM 71.
See Applying Economics on text p. 380.

UNIT FIVE

SETTING AND MEETING ECONOMIC GOALS

GATE & SCALE

CHAPTER 14

See Chapter Overview, p. TM 72.
See Chapter Objectives, p. TM 72.
See Introducing the Chapter, p. TM 72.
See Extending Economic Knowledge on text p. 334.

Inflation, Recession, and Unemployment

Our Constitution is so simple and practical that it is possible always to meet extraordinary needs by changes in emphasis and arrangement without loss of essential form. That is why our constitutional system . . . is the most superbly enduring political mechanism the modern world has produced. . . .

Franklin D. Roosevelt

1 Inflation decreases the purchasing power of money.

- Price Fluctuations
- Measuring Price-Level Fluctuations
- Types of Inflation
- The Consequences of Inflation

2 Unemployment means that a portion of the labor force is nonproductive.

- The Labor Force and Employment
- Measuring Unemployment
- Types of Unemployment
- The Costs of Unemployment

3 Stagflation occurs when unemployment and inflation are high.

- Stagflation
- Causes of Stagflation

4 Business cycles show a pattern of economic upturns and downturns.

- Phases of the Business Cycle
- Causes of the Business Cycle
- Predicting the Business Cycle

CHAPTER 14 STUDY GUIDE

Chapter Focus

Chapter 14 presents an overview of three types of economic instability: inflation, recession and unemployment, and stagflation. It discusses the two types of inflation, demand-pull and cost-push, that decrease the purchasing power of money. The chapter also describes the four types of unemployment—structural, frictional, seasonal, and cyclical—and concludes with a discussion of the business cycle.

As you study the chapter, look for the details that support each of the following statements.

1. Inflation decreases the purchasing power of money.
2. Unemployment means that a portion of the labor force is nonproductive.
3. Stagflation occurs when unemployment and inflation are high.
4. Business cycles show a pattern of economic upturns and downturns.

See Preteaching Vocabulary, p. TM 72.

Terms to Know

The following terms, while not the only terms emphasized in this chapter, are basic to your understanding of inflation, recession, and unemployment. Determine the meaning of each term, either by using the Glossary or by watching for context clues as you read the chapter.

inflation
deflation
aggregate demand
disinflation
demand-pull inflation
cost-push inflation
employment rate
frictional unemployment
structural unemployment
full employment
seasonal unemployment
cyclical unemployment
stagflation
business cycle

See Key Study Questions and Key Understandings, p. TM 73.

1 Inflation decreases the purchasing power of money.

See Suggested Teaching Strategies, p. TM 73.

Price fluctuations often threaten the stability of the economy. The three types of price fluctuations that most affect the economy of the United States are inflation, deflation, and disinflation.

Price Fluctuations

Economists measure the changes in average price levels in the economy to assess economic health and stability. They use average price levels because in any period of inflation the prices of some goods are rising while the prices of some other goods are falling. For example, during the 1980s, the prices of compact discs and CD players decreased while the average price level of all goods increased.

Inflation is an increase in the average price level ◆ of all goods and services. **Deflation** is a decline in the average price level. Historically, inflation occurs when **aggregate demand,** the total spending by consumers, businesses, and government, increases faster than the supply of goods and services. As consumers compete for limited goods and services, prices rise to new and higher levels.

Deflation, on the other hand, occurs when the supply of goods and services increases more rapidly than spending. In such situations, sellers are forced to lower their prices to attract buyers. The most prolonged deflationary period in United States history occurred during the 1930s when high unemployment, coupled with wage reductions, caused aggregate demand and prices to fall.

In the early 1980s, **disinflation,** a reduction of inflation, not an elimination of it, occurred. In 1980, the inflation rate was 13.5 percent. In 1985, the inflation rate dropped to just 3.6 percent (see the top graph on page 315).

◆ The inflation rate is based on the national average. It may vary from one region to another because of differences in economic conditions.

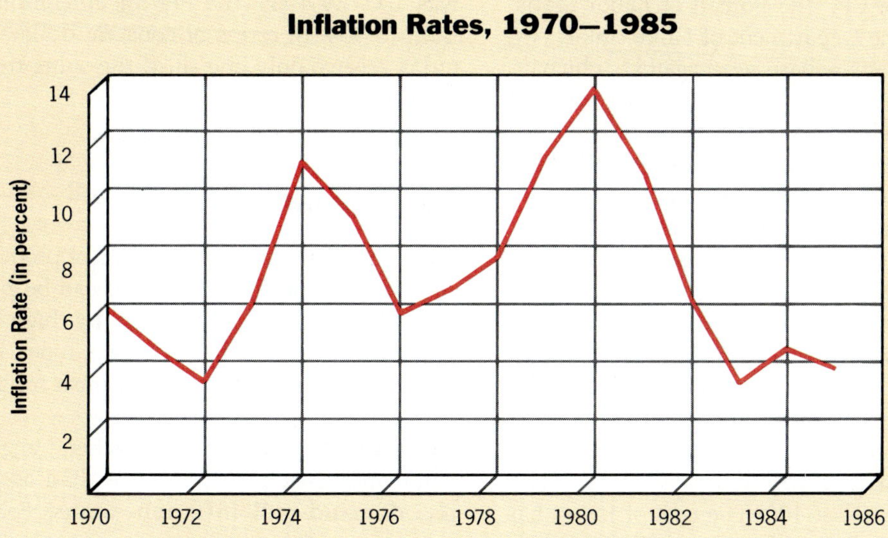

Source: *Economic Report of the President, 1986*

Measuring Price-Level Fluctuations

Inflation, deflation, and disinflation alter consumers' purchasing power and affect economic growth. To measure the rates of price-level fluctuations, economists use the Consumer Price Index (CPI) and the Producer Price Index (PPI).

Consumer Price Index. Changes in the prices paid by consumers for goods and services are measured by the **Consumer Price Index,** or CPI, which was begun in 1919. The Bureau of Labor Statistics ◆ publishes the CPI monthly. The graph below shows the CPI for the years 1950–1985.

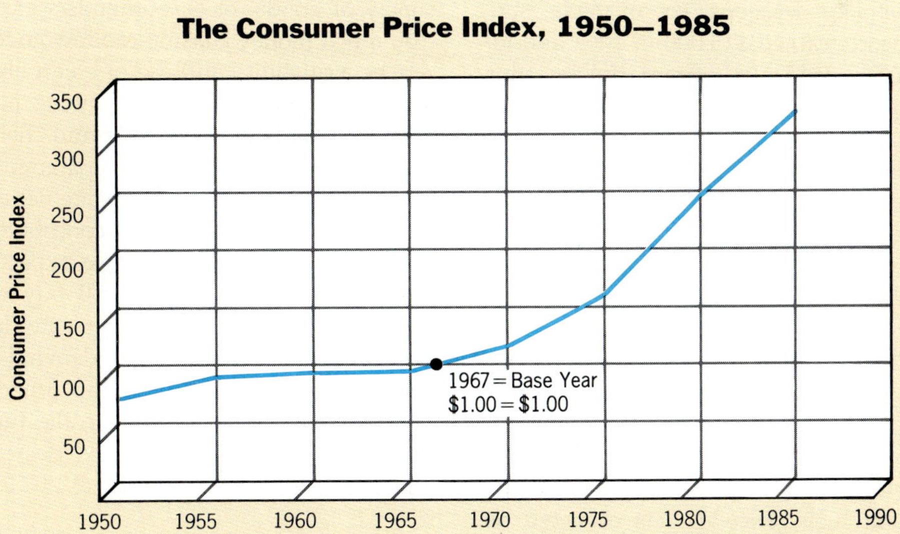

Source: *Economic Report of the President, 1986*

◆ **Class activity: Have the students research the prices of selected items between 1960 and the present.**

To arrive at the CPI, the Bureau of Labor Statistics, a branch of the Department of Labor, takes two steps. First, it selects a base year against which to measure price changes. The current base year is 1967. Second, it selects a sample of 400 of the most commonly purchased items. This sample, called the market basket, includes food, rent and home ownership costs, utilities, clothing, private and public transportation, entertainment, and health care. The bureau then samples prices of these goods and services every month in 85 areas across the nation. It also produces a separate CPI for 28 selected areas across the nation. A 1 percent increase during the month adds 1 index point to the CPI.

By the spring of 1986 the CPI was 326, an increase of 226 percent ($326 - 100 = 226$) from 1967, when the CPI was set at 100. The cost of living has more than tripled during the period. In monetary terms, an item that cost $1.00 in 1967 had an average cost of $3.26 in 1986.

The "Real Value" of the Dollar. The CPI is also used to arrive at the "real value" of money, that is, the value of current dollars after adjusting for price-level fluctuations. The real value of money is expressed in terms of constant dollars. The real value of money in the United States, as measured in constant dollars, is shown on the graph on page 317.

Understanding the difference between current dollars and constant dollars is important in many types of marketplace decisions. For example, suppose John Carpenter earned $15,000 in 1967 and received $30,000 in 1985. In current dollars, this $30,000 salary doubles Carpenter's 1967 wages. In constant dollars, however, the $30,000 salary represents a substantial decline in purchasing power because the value of the dollar in 1985 was less than half of what it was in 1967. To have a salary with purchasing power comparable to his 1967 salary, Carpenter would have to earn $48,500.

Producer Price Index. The **Producer Price Index** (PPI) also measures changes in the average prices of goods sold by producers in all stages of processing. PPIs are compiled for all commodities and for selected categories such as farm products, processed food, and fuels. Price data is collected on 2,800 goods. Price changes in the PPI, like in the CPI, are measured in relation to a 1967 base year. For example, in 1967 the PPI for all commodities was 100. By 1985, the PPI for all commodities had risen to 309. In terms of constant dollars, producers today receive only one third the value that they did in 1967.

Types of Inflation

Aggregate demand and the costs of production influence the rate of inflation. Prices can be *pulled up* by high demand, or *pushed up* by high production costs. Economists label the two types of inflation demand-pull inflation and cost-push inflation.

Demand-Pull Inflation. When aggregate demand increases at a faster rate than aggregate supply, **demand-pull inflation** occurs. Following the laws of supply and demand, prices increase when demand exceeds supply. As demand continues to increase, consumers pull the prices of goods even higher.

Demand-pull inflation usually results from an increase in the money supply, an increase in the availability and use of credit, and price expectations. The Federal Reserve System controls the money supply in the United States (see Chapter 11). When the Fed increases the money supply, aggregate demand increases and consumers, businesses, and governments purchase more goods. Demand-pull inflation results when spending outdistances the available supply of goods, or as economists explain, there is "too much money chasing too few goods."

The availability and use of credit also contributes to demand-pull inflation. Allowing people to "buy now and pay later," use credit and charge cards, and obtain easy credit terms for loans encourages consumption and increases aggregate demand.

Future price expectations contribute to demand-pull inflation as well. If people expect prices to increase in the future, they will buy now at lower prices, resulting in higher aggregate demand. Some economists call this type of demand-pull inflation **expectation inflation.** On the other hand, when people expect prices to drop in the future, they are likely to postpone buying and decrease aggregate demand, leading to deflation. ◆

Cost-Push Inflation. When producers raise their prices to cover higher production costs and to earn higher profits, **cost-push inflation** occurs. Higher

◆ **Social values also affect the economy. For example, many people now realize the long-term effect of credit abuse and are changing their buying habits. These changes may eventually lower the level of private debt and affect the overall economy.**

production costs oblige producers to raise prices even when demand has not increased. Producers' prices must be high enough to cover the costs of production and to earn a profit.

When OPEC increased the price of oil during the 1970s, for example, the United States entered a period of cost-push inflation. Price increases for this vital natural resource rippled through the economy, because oil is used to produce many products such as gasoline, home heating oil, plastics, record albums, and cosmetics.

Two different situations usually set cost-push inflation into motion. In one situation, higher costs for human resources result in a cost-push inflation called **wage-push inflation.** Laborers, particularly those represented by unions, bargain for wage increases that are greater than the inflation rate and a cycle called the **wage-price spiral** develops. Workers demand higher wages to stay ahead of inflation. Higher wages, in turn, force producers to raise their prices. Higher prices contribute to still higher inflation as workers demand even higher wages.

A second type of cost-push inflation is **profit-push inflation.** Profit-push inflation occurs when producers raise prices in order to raise their profits. During periods of inflation, most businesses increase their prices simply because other prices are rising. They also raise prices because people expect to pay higher prices for all goods and services. Firms in less competitive industries are better able to raise their prices than firms in industries where competition is strong.

The Real Value of the Dollar, 1950–1985

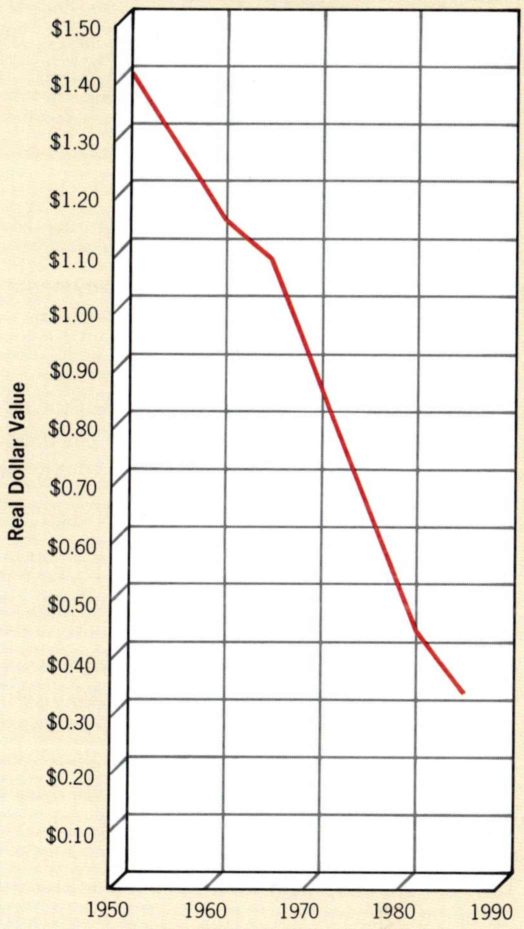

Source: *Economic Report of the President, 1986*

The Consequences of Inflation

Inflation benefits some people but has a negative effect on most people. In general, inflation benefits debtors, while it hurts consumers, workers, savers and investors, and businesspeople.

Effects on Consumers. Inflation decreases the purchasing power of the dollar. Some consumers are hurt more than others. For example, elderly people on fixed incomes, such as pensions, are able to purchase less when the value of the dollar declines.

Consumers whose incomes are tied to the CPI are better able to cope with inflation. Many labor contracts negotiated during the 1970s, for example, included **cost-of-living adjustments** (COLA), which automatically raise workers' wages when the inflation rate reaches a certain level. COLAs are also attached to some retirement plans, such as Social Security and federal pensions for military and civil service retirees.

Effects on Workers. Inflation also reduces the real wages of workers when pay increases fail to keep pace with inflation. The real wages of John Carpenter who earned $15,000 in 1967 dropped between 1967 and 1985, despite pay increases totalling $15,000, because inflation increased at a faster rate than his wages. Many employers during

Higher interest rates increase mortgage payments on homes purchased during inflationary periods.

the 1980s were more reluctant to include COLAs in negotiated contracts because of a need to cut production costs. As a result, many workers who had gained this benefit in the 1970s lost it.

Effects on Savers and Investors. The inflation rate affects the return that people receive from their savings and investments. For example, take a saver who deposited money in 1975 in a savings account that yielded 5.5 percent interest when the inflation rate was 9 percent. That same saver lost purchasing power when he withdrew the savings in 1980 when the inflation rate was 13.5 percent. High inflation also discourages saving, thus decreasing the funds available for borrowers.

During periods of high inflation people often seek types of investments that bring higher returns than savings accounts. For example, people might choose to invest in stocks, real estate, gold, or other commodities because the prices of these items tend to increase more dramatically than interest rates on savings accounts during periods of inflation.

Effects on Debtors and Creditors. Debtors are most likely to benefit from high inflation because the money they use to repay the loan is worth less than the money originally borrowed. When the inflation rate is 10 percent, for example, a person borrowing money for one year repays the loan with money that has 10 percent less purchasing power than the money borrowed.

◆ Conversely, creditors lose money during periods of inflation. Using the example above, the creditor incurs a loss because the money repaid has only 90 percent of the purchasing power of the money loaned. For this reason, creditors often protect themselves by charging interest rates high enough to cover increases in the inflation rate. In addition, certain types of long-term loans such as adjustable rate mortgages often carry rates of interest that are tied to the rate of inflation. The interest rates on these mortgages increase when the inflation rate is high and decrease when the inflation rate is low.

Effects on Businesses. Businesses that have issued long-term bonds with interest rates that are lower than the inflation rate benefit from inflation. High inflation rates, however, generally hurt all businesses because inflation increases the costs of production. Businesses that can pass these additional costs on to buyers survive, but businesses that produce goods or services where demand is elastic are likely to suffer declining sales because consumers will refuse to pay higher prices.

Effects on Nations. Inflation in Western industrialized nations has not increased as fast as it has in many developing nations. In some Latin American countries, for example, inflation is the most important economic problem. Bolivia's 9,000 percent inflation rate in 1984 was the world's highest. This type of runaway inflation, called **hyperinflation,** typically occurs just before the collapse of a nation's monetary system. Bolivia's monetary unit, the peso, was virtually worthless by the end of 1984. Hyperinflation in Bolivia's neighbor, Brazil, caused that nation's currency, the cruzeiro, to collapse in 1986.

See Suggested Assignments, p. TM 73.

Section 1 Review See Answers, p. A 59.

DEFINE inflation, deflation, disinflation, Consumer Price Index, Producer Price Index, demand-pull inflation, wage-price spiral

1. **Seeing Relationships** How does inflation affect the relationship between aggregate demand and the supply of goods and services?
2. **Analyzing Ideas** Why might a creditor be more unhappy with inflation than a debtor?
3. **Interpreting Graphics** Study the graphs on page 315. What generalization can you make about the Consumer Price Index, 1970–1985?

◆ Extremely high interest rates may offset the advantage of paying back a loan with cheaper dollars. One way to avoid this problem is to refinance a major purchase such as a home if lower interest rates become available.

See Key Study Questions and Key Understandings, p. TM 74.

2 Unemployment means that a portion of the labor force is nonproductive.

See Suggested Teaching Strategies, p. TM 74.

The two most important elements of economic stability, price stability and a productive labor force, are interwoven and often affected by the same forces. The government keeps a close watch on unemployment because one of the most important economic goals in the United States is full employment.

The Labor Force and Employment

Economists calculate the employment rate in the United States to gauge the health of the economy. The **employment rate** is the percentage of the labor force, all Americans 16 years of age or older, that is employed. In 1985, for example, 178 million Americans were 16 or older. About 109 million Americans were employed in civilian jobs and in the armed services, an employment rate of approximately 61 percent ($109 \div 178 = 0.61$). By mid-1986, the number of employed workers had grown to more than 110 million, about 98.5 percent of which were members of the civilian labor force. The remaining 1.5 percent, or 1.7 million people, were employed in the armed services. Economists and the government also keep records on the **labor force participation rate,** the percent of the population 16 years of age or older that is employed or actively seeking employment. In 1985, the labor force participation rate was 65.7 percent.

Measuring Unemployment

Traditionally, **unemployment,** the number of people who do not have jobs but are actively seeking employment, has been one of the most visible problems in the American economy. Compared with unemployment rates in other nations, however, United States totals are relatively low (see the graph on this page). In 1985, for example, the Bureau of Labor Statistics reported that there were about 8.4 million unemployed persons in the civilian labor force, a rate of approximately 7.4 percent.

Civilian Unemployment Rates of Selected Industrialized Nations

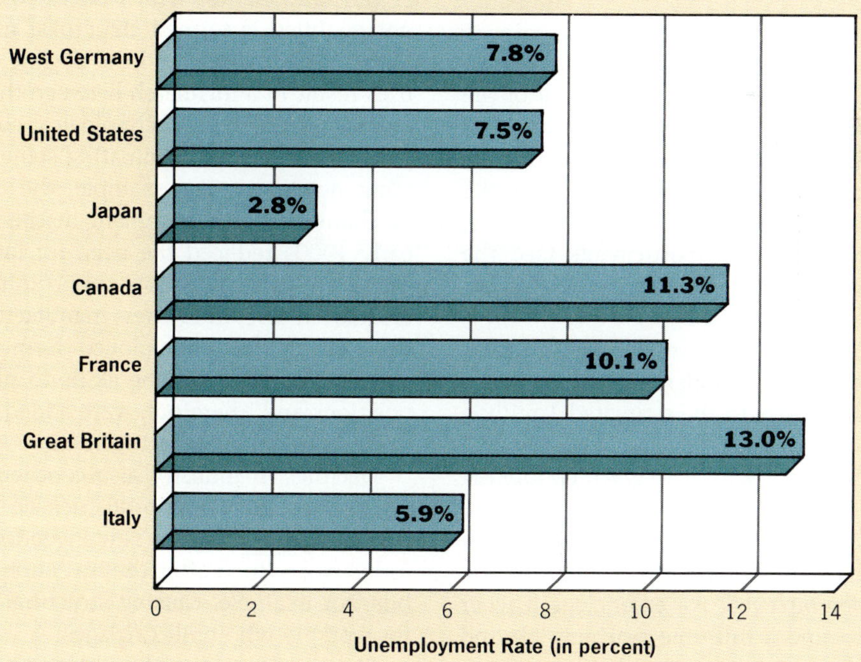

Source: *Economic Report of the President, 1986*

Unemployment Rates in the Civilian Labor Force, 1950–1985

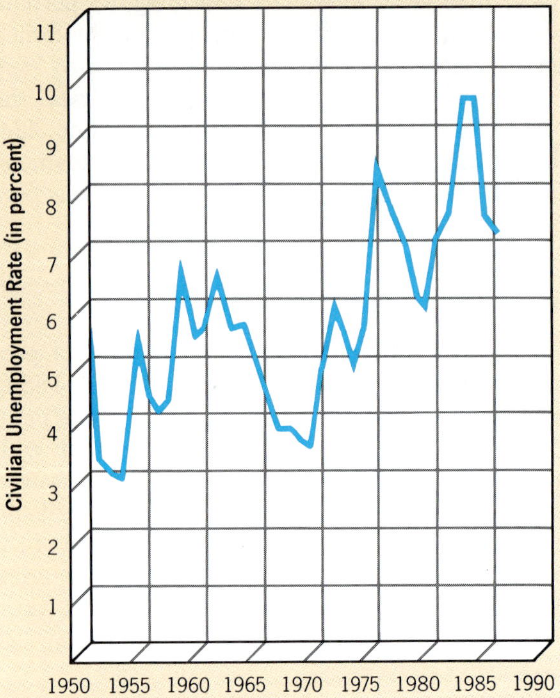

Source: *Economic Report of the President, 1986*

The Bureau of Labor Statistics has developed two measures of unemployment. They are a count of the people in the labor force who are presently out of work and the percentage of the labor force that is unemployed (see the graph above). In addition, the government measures unemployment by the age, sex, and race of labor force participants (see the graph on page 321) and by the reasons for unemployment.

Government statistics, however, do not measure hidden unemployment or underemployment. Hidden unemployment refers to the estimated 1 million unemployed people, many of whom at one time held productive jobs, but who have given up looking for jobs.

Laborers who work at jobs beneath their skill level, or who are unable to get a full-time job, are classified as underemployed. For example, a teacher who is unable to find a full-time teaching job and ends up working as a waiter in a fast-food restaurant is considered underemployed.

Types of Unemployment

To better analyze the reasons for unemployment, government statisticians divide it into four categories according to cause. The categories of unemployment are frictional unemployment, structural unemployment, seasonal unemployment, and cyclical unemployment.

Frictional Unemployment. Unemployment that results when workers are temporarily between jobs is **frictional unemployment.** Frictional unemployment rates count people who have decided to leave one job to look for another as well as new entrants and re-entrants into the labor force. In 1985, about one half of the 8.4 million unemployed persons were classified as frictionally unemployed. ◆

Economists consider frictional unemployment to be a normal part of a healthy and changing economy. It reflects workers' freedom of choice in the labor market, as workers select the jobs that are most satisfying to them. Frictional unemployment also is a signal that some new jobs in new industries are available.

Structural Unemployment. Unemployment that occurs when changes in the economy eliminate jobs or generate jobs for which unemployed workers are not qualified is termed **structural unemployment.** Shifts in technology and the decline of entire industries result in a mismatch between the available jobs and workers' skills. Technological changes alter the production process, eliminating some jobs while creating new ones. For example, the development of mechanized farm equipment in the late 1800s and early 1900s reduced the need for farm laborers. At the same time, new job opportunities were being created in the industries manufacturing the farm equipment. The unemployed farm workers, however, did not possess the skills to fill the industrial positions and, therefore, were added to the count of structurally unemployed workers.

Declines in industry also contribute to structural unemployment. Some industries decline because of technological change or new inventions. The carriage industry declined after the invention of the automobile, for example, causing structural unemployment for workers who built carriages.

Some industries decline because of the depletion of major natural resources in a region. Industries in

◆ Have the students read "Employee-Benefits Managers" on page 542 of *Careers in the Marketplace.*

Unemployment Rates by Age, Sex, and Race

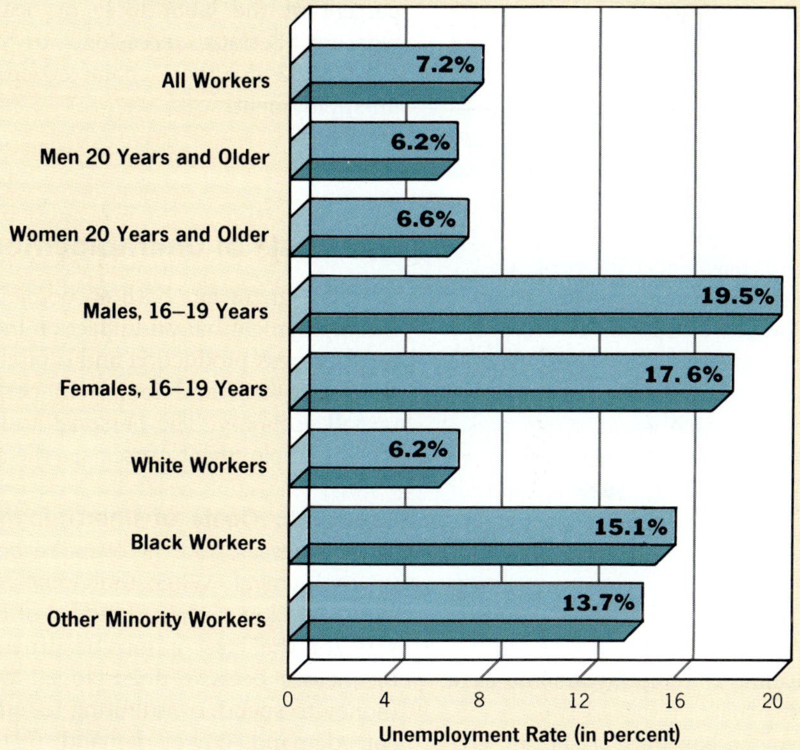

Source: *Economic Report of the President, 1986*

Appalachia,* for example, enjoyed high employment and prosperity during the late 1800s and early 1900s because the land offered timber and minerals, especially coal. As these resources were used up, however, lumbering and mining firms left the region. Workers who were tied to the area by family, tradition, or lack of education joined the ranks of the structurally unemployed. Today, Appalachia remains a region of high structural unemployment.

Many economists believe that frictional and structural unemployment are natural occurrences in an economy. Because economists regard some unemployment as unavoidable and as a sign of a healthy economy, they consider the employment of about 95 percent of the labor force as **full employment.**

* Appalachia is a region that includes parts of Georgia, Alabama, Tennessee, Kentucky, North Carolina, Virginia, West Virginia, and Pennsylvania.

◆ Have students use a map of the United States to point out what types of unemployment are most common in particular regions.

Seasonal Unemployment. When people are out of work for a part of the year because of changes in the seasons, economists classify the unemployment as **seasonal unemployment.** Agricultural workers are particularly susceptible to seasonal unemployment. Spring, summer, and fall are busy seasons for many farmers because most crops can only be planted, cultivated, and harvested during warm weather. At these times, the need for farm labor is high. During the winter, however, many farm workers temporarily lose their jobs. Seasonal unemployment is also common for workers in the construction and tourist industries.

Cyclical Unemployment. Unemployment resulting from economic downturns is **cyclical unemployment.** In such instances, unemployment ◆ runs in cycles. Responding to declining sales, producers reduce their output and workers are laid off. Higher unemployment, however, further reduces

Economics Reporter

What Is Unemployment Compensation?

Unemployment compensation is the money provided by state governments to persons who are laid off from their jobs. Under state guidelines, the unemployed who are eligible, collect between 25 and 55 percent of lost wages for 26 weeks in the form of direct cash payments. The program is both federally and state funded. Employers pay federal and state taxes for 86 percent of the program, with the remaining funds coming from state budgets. Each state devises its unemployment-insurance program. In the past, some states provided an additional 13 weeks of benefits to the unemployed who were actively seeking work. Congress restricted these extended benefits in 1981. Today only Alaska, Louisiana, and Puerto Rico have extended benefits.

aggregate demand, leading to more layoffs and even higher unemployment.

Cyclical unemployment has been a serious economic problem in the United States throughout the 1900s. In 1933, during the Great Depression, unemployment reached its all-time high, about 25 percent of the labor force or nearly 12.8 million workers. Serious recessions in 1974–1975 and 1980–1982 also were characterized by high cyclical unemployment.

During the height of the recession of the early 1980s, the number of people receiving unemployment compensation averaged more than 4 million.

The Costs of Unemployment

Unemployment has both economic and social costs. Unemployment has an impact on income and spending, business production and capital investment, and the short-term and long-term performance of the overall economy. The personal and social problems that unemployment causes are the social costs.

Economic Costs of Unemployment. Individuals, businesses, and the overall economy suffer from unemployment. When individuals are unemployed, they must lower their standard of living to compensate for the loss of income. Unemployment hurts businesses because unemployed workers have less money to spend, contributing to a decrease in aggregate demand. Lower demand, in turn, forces businesses to cut back their production and, therefore, their workforce. During the 1980–1982 recession, for example, plants in the United States were operating at just two thirds of their capacity.

Unemployment slows long-term growth in the economy because businesses are hesitant to invest in capital goods such as new machinery and plants when unemployment is high and aggregate demand is low. Even after the economy has recovered, businesses are often unprepared to increase output because plant modernization had been postponed.

Social Costs of Unemployment. The social costs of unemployment include the personal and social problems that affect unemployed workers, their families, and their communities. Prolonged unemployment can result in personal depression and family tensions. It often results in necessary and dramatic changes in lifestyle and the emotional and physical stress these changes bring. Families must cut back spending, often getting by on the bare necessities, and are often forced to move in search of employment. Unemployment can also contribute to higher crime rates and other social problems.

HIGHLIGHTS IN ECONOMICS

The Great Depression

In the 1920s, many middle-income and upper-income Americans rode a great wave of prosperity. The flow of United States goods and services reached an all-time high. Industrial production rose 50 percent in the decade. Many businesspeople were satisfied with their profits. Many workers were content with wage gains that gave them the opportunity to purchase automobiles and household appliances. Investors in the stock market rejoiced the most because almost any stock purchase rapidly increased in value. A few grumbles could be heard. Among the grumblers were many farmers who complained about low prices for their livestock and crops and the high price of land.

On Tuesday October 29, 1929, the stock market collapsed. Prosperity gave way to despair and frustration. Recession, depression, and finally almost a complete breakdown of the American economy followed. The breakdown completely devastated world economies.

From 1929 to 1933, the American economy—and the economies of other industrial nations worldwide—suffered a complete collapse. The GNP of the United States dipped from $104.4 billion to $56 billion. Industrial production dropped 50 percent. Wholesale prices plunged 33 percent. Consumer prices fell 25 percent. Unemployment rose from 1.5 million to about 12.5 million. So severe was the Great Depression that it took 11 years for the production of consumer goods to equal the 1929 pre-crash level.

The short-term and long-term causes of the Great Depression are still debated. The Great Depression caused tremendous misery for many. It also led to a strengthening of the Federal Reserve System and to banking and other monetary reforms.

Since the end of World War II, dips called recessions have bothered the economy, but nothing like the Great Depression has reoccurred. Stocks have fluctuated in value many times, but no stock market crash has taken place. Savers, investors in stocks and bonds, and borrowers have learned well the lessons taught by the Great Depression.

CASE STUDY

The Plight of the Migrant Worker

During the mid-1970s, the Labor Department estimated that there were a total of 1 million "seasonal agricultural laborers" in the United States. About 80 percent, or 800,000 of these workers, lived in permanent homes and traveled to and from their jobs each day. The remaining 20 percent, or 200,000 workers, were migrant workers who left their homes for months at a time to travel from one area to another in search of work. Most migrants work in agriculture, although some work in industry, construction, and lumbering.

Seasonal unemployment is a traditional problem for migrant workers, particularly during "off seasons." Droughts, floods, infestations, and other natural disasters worsen the problem of seasonal unemployment. In addition, while moving from one job to another, migrant workers have no guarantees of employment once they have arrived at a destination.

In recent years, the number of migrant farm workers in the United States has declined, in part because of mechanization. Harvesting machines, for example, have reduced the need for migrant workers in Georgia, Virginia, Maryland, and Delaware.

While migrant workers have been declining in number in recent years, their economic status has been improving. For example, today many seasonal farm workers are permitted to join unions, a right won during the 1960s when Cesar Chavez organized agricultural workers into the United Farm Workers (UFW). By the mid-1970s, the Teamsters also were representing agricultural workers.

State and federal legislation also has helped improve the economic status of migrant workers. For example, in the mid-1970s the California legislature

Many migrant workers do not have skills that are transferable to other industries. Thus when natural conditions such as droughts or freezes disrupt the harvest, migrant workers often cannot find alternative employment.

Adequate housing for migrant workers is one of the principal concerns of the unions representing farm workers. The quality of migrant housing varies greatly from employer to employer.

passed the Agricultural Labor Relations Act to help protect the economic rights of migrant workers. Under this act, the California Agricultural Labor Relations Board (ALRB) investigates claims of company unionbusting activities and management's failure to comply with provisions outlined in contracts. At the national level, minimum wage and social security laws have been revised to include migrant and other agricultural workers.

Despite the progress, state and federal authorities find it difficult to enforce the laws and regulations. Migrant housing and working conditions, for example, have improved little since reform legislation was passed. Child labor, though illegal, is still common and the education of these child workers is often neglected. As a result, the children of migrant workers, like their parents, have a narrow range of marketable skills. In addition, migrant workers are sometimes the victims of local prejudices because of cultural, racial, or income differences.

Section 2 Review See Answers, p. A 59.

DEFINE employment rate, unemployment, frictional unemployment, structural unemployment, full employment, cyclical unemployment

1. **Comprehending Ideas** Why is some measure of underemployment included in unemployment data?
2. **Analyzing Ideas** Why is it difficult to enforce laws that protect the rights of migrant workers?
3. **Interpreting Graphics** Study the graphs on pages 320 and 321. **(a)** What does the graph on page 320 tell you about the unemployment rate between 1982 and 1985? **(b)** What do the unemployment statistics on the graph probably not show? **(c)** According to the graph on page 321, what group has the highest unemployment? the lowest?

See Suggested Assignments, p. TM 74.

BUILDING ECONOMIC SKILLS

THINKING ABOUT ECONOMICS

Evaluating Economic Decisions

The landslide victory of Franklin Delano Roosevelt (F.D.R.) in the Presidential election of 1932 was, in large measure, a popular response to his remedies for the Great Depression. Assisted by a handpicked brain trust—an advisory group of economists and other scholars—F.D.R. set in motion a new course for the economy of the United States.

The economic decisions made by F.D.R. and the brain trust have been debated since the 1930s.

How to Evaluate Economic Decisions

To evaluate economic decisions, follow these steps.

1. **Determine the nature of the decision or decisions that have to be made.** Take into account any economic, social, or political conditions that existed at the time of the decision.
2. **Identify the alternatives available.** Note the possible options, or policy choices, the decision maker had.
3. **List the possible costs and benefits of each alternative.** Note that many alternatives have both short-term and long-range effects.
4. **Evaluate the alternatives.** Weigh the costs against the benefits.
5. **Analyze the results of the decision.** Determine whether the economic decision was a good one or a bad one. Note that the long-range effects may not have been evident to the decision maker at the time the decision was made. Recognize that your economic values, biases, or frame of reference, may affect your evaluation of the economic decision.

Applying the Skill

F.D.R. believed that a New Deal was necessary to end the Great Depression and to reform the American brand of capitalism. The cornerstones of his reform legislation were outlined in F.D.R.'s First Inaugural Address. This address was delivered to the American people on March 4, 1933. Read the excerpts from the address on page 327.

The economic decision to expand the role of government in the American economy meant that government would create jobs for the unemployed. It would help determine prices for agricultural products. It would protect property owners from foreclosures. It would provide immediate relief to the needy. Finally, it would regulate vital industries such as utilities and banking.

What alternative actions did F.D.R. have? The President could have made no changes in the moderate course followed by President Hoover, who had rejected many federal assistance programs during his tenure as President. By 1933, however, the unemployment rate had reached 25 percent of the labor force. In addition, the depression was three years old, and no end to it was in sight.

F.D.R. believed that the benefits—a lower unemployment rate, more stable agricultural prices, relief for the needy and for property owners, and long-term stability for the nation's banking system—far outweighed the short-term and long-term costs.

How good was F.D.R.'s New Deal for the United States? This question is still debated today. Most economists agree that the New Deal relief and reform measures brought many benefits to the economy. They believe that the benefits have exceeded the costs.

FIRST INAUGURAL ADDRESS

This great nation will endure as it has endured, will revive and will prosper. So, first of all, let me assert my firm belief that the only thing we have to fear is fear itself—nameless, unreasoning, unjustified terror which paralyzes needed efforts to convert retreat into advance. . . .

Our greatest primary task is to put people to work. This is no unsolvable problem if we face it wisely and courageously. It can be accomplished in part by direct recruiting by the Government itself, treating the task as we would treat the emergency of a war, but at the same time, through this employment, accomplishing greatly needed projects to stimulate and reorganize the use of our natural resources.

Hand in hand with this we must frankly recognize the overbalance of population in our industrial centers and, by engaging on a national scale in a redistribution, endeavor to provide a better use of the land for those best fitted for the land. The task can be helped by definite efforts to raise the values of agricultural products and with this the power to purchase the output of our cities. It can be helped by preventing realistically the tragedy of the growing loss through foreclosure of our small homes and our farms. It can be helped by insistence that the Federal, State, and local governments act forthwith on the demand that their cost be drastically reduced. It can be helped by the unifying of relief activities which today are often scattered, uneconomical, and unequal. It can be helped by national planning for and supervision of all forms of transportation and of communications and other utilities which have a definitely public character. There are many ways in which it can be helped, but it can never be helped merely by talking about it. We must act and act quickly.

Finally, in our progress toward a resumption of work we require two safeguards against a return of the evils of the old order; there must be a strict supervision of all banking and credits and investments; there must be an end to speculation with other people's money, and there must be provision for an adequate but sound currency.

These are the lines of attack. . . .

Franklin Delano Roosevelt

Practicing the Skill See Answers, p. A 60.

Research one of the following economic decisions. Then on a separate sheet of paper, evaluate the economic decision by answering the questions below.

- **The Immigration Reform and Control Act (1986):** Legislation granting amnesty to illegal aliens already residing in the United States.
- **Workfare Legislation:** Decisions of some states during the 1980s to require some welfare recipients to work for their benefits.
- **Fair Labor Standards Act (1938):** The federal government's 1938 decision to establish a minimum wage in the United States.
- **Executive Order No. 11246 (1965):** The federal government's decision to support affirmative action in hiring.

1. **(a)** What decision was made? **(b)** What relevant historical conditions existed at the time the decision was made?
2. List the possible alternatives available to the decision maker.
3. **(a)** What were the costs and benefits of each policy alternative? **(b)** Why did the policymaker select one alternative over another?
4. In your view, was the decision a "good" or "bad" one? Explain your answer.

See Key Study Questions and Key Understandings, p. TM 75.

3 Stagflation occurs when unemployment and inflation are high.

See Suggested Teaching Strategies, p. TM 75.

During the 1970s and early 1980s, high unemployment rates and high inflation rates simultaneously plagued the American economy, an economic situation called **stagflation.**

Stagflation

From 1970 to 1982, inflation averaged 7.8 percent, while the unemployment rate averaged 6.7 percent. In addition, during the recessions of 1974–1975 and 1980–1982, inflation and unemployment were particularly high. The graph on this page illustrates the aspects of this period of stagflation.

In the early 1980s, stagflation ended as unemployment and inflation declined. The unemployment rate, for example, dropped from almost 10 percent in the early 1980s to about 7 percent in 1985. Similarly, the inflation rate dropped from 13.5 percent in 1980 to less than 4 percent in 1985.

Causes of Stagflation

Economists are still unsure about the causes of stagflation, but they cite a number of economic factors that contributed to the economic instability of the 1970s and early 1980s. Government policies, inflationary expectations, the changing size of the labor force, and production disincentives are the four most important factors usually cited.

Government Policies. The roots of stagflation date back to the massive federal spending programs instituted in the late 1960s to support the Vietnam War and the Great Society program. The government chose to finance these expenditures by issuing new currency rather than by raising taxes. As more money flooded into the economy, aggregate demand increased, and people bid up prices throughout the economy.

Inflation and Unemployment Rates, 1960–1985

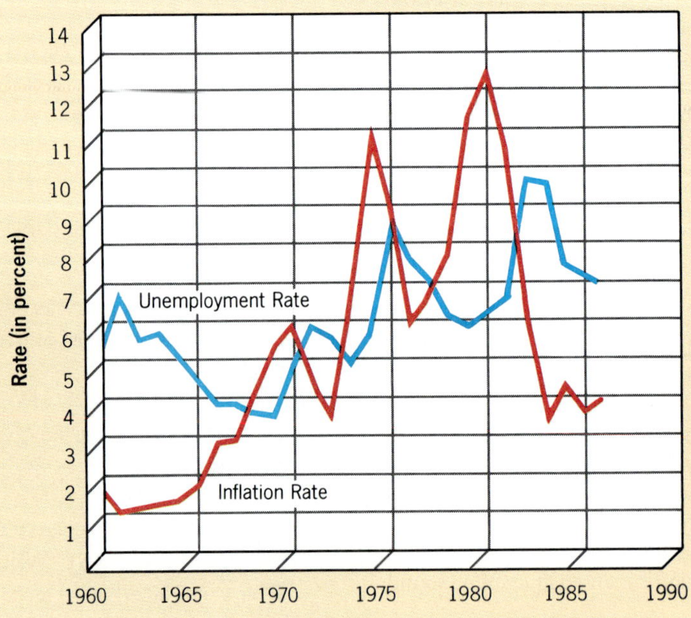

Sources: *Economic Report of the President, 1986*
Statistical Abstract of the United States, 1986

Government policies during the 1970s continued to contribute to stagflation. For example, the minimum wage more than doubled between 1970 and 1981, rising from $1.45 per hour to $3.35. The rise in the minimum wage increased the amount of money available and encouraged people to spend more. Higher minimum wages also increased production costs, forcing businesses to increase their prices and to lay off employees. Other legislation that fueled higher prices and higher unemployment included new regulations on businesses and higher social insurance taxes.

At the same time, people lost confidence in the government's ability to control inflation. In the 1970s, the wage and price controls of the Nixon administration and the voluntary wage and price guidelines of the Carter administration failed to bring price stability. The popular belief that inflation was beyond control and would continue for many years fueled this crisis of confidence.

Businesses are more vulnerable to failure during periods of stagflation.

Inflationary Expectations. During the 1970s and early 1980s, consumers, workers, and businesspeople began to expect inflation to increase. These inflationary expectations had a number of important consequences. Consumers, for example, increased their present demand for goods in order to avoid higher prices in the future. Workers bargained for higher wages and cost-of-living adjustments in order to keep pace with inflation. Businesses raised their prices, responding to higher labor costs, higher consumer demand, and the prevailing belief that the prices of all goods would increase.

Size of the Labor Force. A third factor contributing to stagflation was the growth in the labor force. Between 1970 and 1982, the total labor force grew from 85 million to 112 million workers, an increase of 27 million workers. As the number of wage earners increased, so did aggregate demand and prices. Even during the unemployment peak in 1982, when nearly 11 million Americans were out of work, more than 101 million people were employed and were maintaining high aggregate demand.

Production Disincentives. Further contributing to stagflation in the 1970s and 1980s were a number of **production disincentives,** or causes of production slowdown. One key disincentive in the 1970s was the skyrocketing cost of oil, which increased from $1.80 a barrel in 1971 to $35 a barrel in 1982. Businesses that relied on oil for power or as an ingredient in their product were forced to raise prices and, eventually, to cut back on production.

A second production disincentive was the high cost of labor, as workers increased wage demands in an attempt to keep up with inflation. Third, producers were generally pessimistic about future business activity. Many businesses saw no end to stagflation and postponed or cancelled plans for investments in new plants or equipment or in the research and development of new products.

See Suggested Assignments, p. TM 75.

Section 3 Review See Answers, p. A 62.

DEFINE stagflation, production disincentive

1. **Contrasting Ideas** What is the difference between the inflation and unemployment during the 1970s and 1980s and that of earlier periods in United States history?
2. **Analyzing Ideas** **(a)** How does an expectation of inflation affect economic behavior? **(b)** How does this behavior affect inflation?
3. **Interpreting Graphics** Study the graph on page 328. Why is there no stagflation in 1984–1985?

See Key Study Questions and Key Understandings, p. TM 76.

4 Business cycles show a pattern of economic upturns and downturns.

See Suggested Teaching Strategies, p. TM 76.

Inflation, unemployment and recession, and stagflation indicate economic instability. Economists study the phases and the causes of the business cycle to better understand and predict price and employment fluctuations.

Business cycles are the fluctuations in business activity that occur in a market system. These fluctuations are measured by increases or decreases in the real **Gross National Product** (GNP). The GNP is the total market value of all goods and services produced by the economy in a one-year period. The real GNP is the GNP adjusted for inflation. While fluctuations in the real GNP are inevitable, the duration of upturns or downturns varies, lasting from a few months to several years.

Phases of the Business Cycle

The business cycle can be divided into four stages or phases: expansion, or recovery; peak; contraction, or recession; and trough. The graph on this page illustrates the business cycle and its phases.

Expansion of the business cycle is a period of growth. For example, between 1940 and 1944 the real GNP increased from $773 billion to $1.38 trillion, indicating a period of economic expansion. This tremendous growth was mainly due to high government spending for military goods during World War II.

Periods of expansion eventually hit a **peak,** or a high point, during which the economy is generally prosperous. High aggregate demand encourages producers to more fully utilize plant capacity and to hire workers.

Following the peak is a period of business slowdown known as a **contraction,** which is the same as a recession. Technically, a recession is a decline in the real GNP for two consecutive quarters, a six-month period. Prolonged recessions are called depressions.

The final stage in the business cycle is the **trough,** which indicates that aggregate demand, production, and employment are at their lowest point. After the trough, the economy rebounds into another period of recovery, or expansion. ◆

The Business Cycle Model

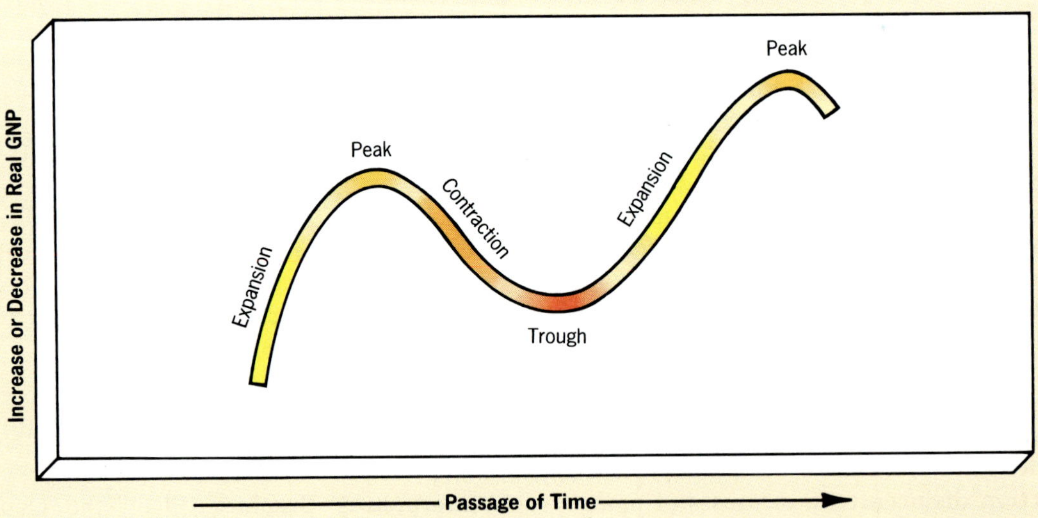

◆ Report topic: In what phase of the business cycle the United States economy is currently operating.

Causes of the Business Cycle

The factors that affect aggregate supply and demand cause the fluctuations of the business cycle. Many economists agree that the level of business investment, the availability of money and credit, expectations about future economic activity, and other external factors have the most impact on the business cycle.

Business Investment. Businesses invest in capital goods such as new machinery to increase their production. High levels of business investment promote expansion in the business cycle, while low levels of investment contribute to contractions.

Business investment is important to expansion for three reasons. First, by purchasing new capital goods, businesses create a demand for these goods, encouraging producers of capital goods to expand production. Second, businesses use the new capital to modernize production methods and promote efficiency. Third, business investment, particularly in the research and development of new capital goods, stimulates technological change and results in higher output at lower production costs.

Money and Credit. The availability of money and credit also affects the business cycle. The amount of money in circulation depends mainly on the policies of the federal government. People generally borrow more money to make purchases when interest rates for loans are low. When interest rates are high, borrowing tends to fall. Thus, aggregate demand fluctuates as the availability and affordability of credit rises and falls.

Expectations. People's expectations about economic activity in the future shape their economic behaviors in the present. For example, if consumers believe that the nation is heading for a recession, they may decide to limit their purchases in order to save money for the hard times ahead. The resulting decline in aggregate demand forces a contraction of the business cycle. When consumers believe that the future will be prosperous, however, they increase spending, which encourages higher production and employment and results in an expansion in the business cycle.

Business expectations, like consumer expectations, contribute to fluctuations in the business cycle. When firms believe that the future will be prosperous, they are more willing to invest in new capital or to hire additional workers. Such actions contribute to expansion in the business cycle. Conversely, a pessimistic view of future business activity causes firms to decrease investment and hiring, spurring a contraction of the business cycle.

The need to retrain displaced workers increases during periods of contractions and troughs in the business cycle.

External Factors. Changes in the world's economic or political climate also affect the business cycle in the United States. The sharp increase in world oil prices in 1973–1974, and again in 1979–1980, contributed to recessions in 1974–1975 and 1980–1982. Price-fixing by the OPEC oil cartel was the primary external factor that caused price shocks throughout the United States economy. Conversely, the dramatic decline in oil prices in the mid-1980s strengthened the expansion phase of the business cycle.

Warfare is another external factor that affects the business cycle. Large government expenditures for national defense have traditionally strengthened business activity in the United States. For example, periods of expansion accompanied the nation's

DECISION MAKERS IN THE ECONOMY

Jeno Paulucci

Jeno Paulucci is a genius at making money. He made one fortune on Chun King Foods and another on Jeno's, Inc., a producer of frozen pizzas. He will probably make another on Heathrow, a planned community for wealthy people that he is developing north of Orlando, Florida. He may make perhaps yet another on Pizza Kwik, a chain of pizza delivery shops. Paulucci joins his business acumen with a belief in social responsibility and uses his wealth, talent, knowledge, and prestige to bring about social change.

Paulucci has helped many people who are less fortunate than he. One New Year's Eve in Hibbing, Minnesota, he handed out free pizzas to the unemployed. On another occasion, acting as a middleman, he helped a struggling Indian group to sell moccasins to a Sears, Roebuck & Company buyer in Chicago. He also has made a practice of hiring the poor and the handicapped in his manufacturing establishments.

Paulucci himself grew up poor, the son of an immigrant miner who was often sick and unemployed. Now that Paulucci has become wealthy and successful, he is committed to putting some of what he has achieved back into the system. Of many business executives, Paulucci has this to say: "They think their only job is earnings per share, and taking care of their own perks and golden parachutes. They don't realize that part of their duty . . . is to participate."

involvement in World War I, World War II, and the Korean and Vietnam wars.

Predicting the Business Cycle

Economists try to predict the fluctuations of the ◆ business cycle. Such predictions are important to business decision makers because predictions of future business activity influence their plans for plant expansion or modernization, future production levels, and hiring. Similarly, government decision makers rely on economic forecasts when they devise taxation and spending policies for the coming fiscal year.

Economists often rely on three types of economic indicators to determine in which phase of the business cycle the economy is and in which direction it is heading. The three types are leading indicators, coincident indicators, and lagging indicators. All three are sets of statistics collected by the Commerce Department.

Leading Indicators. Leading indicators are statistics that illustrate in what direction the economy is headed. Among the most important leading indicators are changes in the number of businesses that open or that fail, the number of building permits issued, the number of orders for new capital and consumer goods, the layoff rate and length of the average workweek in manufacturing, the price for raw materials, the size of business inventories, stock prices, and the size of the money supply.

Favorable changes in leading indicators, such as larger orders for capital or consumer goods, or lower

◆ Economists often have different theories and opinions and may rely on different sets of statistics when formulating economic forecasts.

layoff rates, indicate expansion in the business cycle. Unfavorable changes, such as a decline in the number of building permits issued or higher inventories of goods, indicate a contraction in the business cycle. Usually, upturns or downturns in the business cycle occur 3 to 12 months after favorable or unfavorable changes in the leading indicators appear.

Coincident Indicators. Coincident indicators are sets of statistics that change as the economy moves from one phase of the business cycle to another. The most important coincident indicators are the level of personal income, the sales volume of businesses, and business production levels.

During economic upturns, personal incomes, sales volume, and production levels are high. During economic downturns, personal incomes, sales volume, and production levels are low. Coincident indicators are useful because they tell economists that an upturn or downturn in the economy has arrived. It is difficult to use coincident indicators to predict future economic activity. Coincident indicators are a reflection of the present economic situation rather than indications of movement along the business cycle.

Lagging Indicators. Lagging indicators are statistics that change months after an upturn or downturn in the economy has begun. Important lagging indicators include the unemployment rate, the use of consumer installment credit, and the number and size of business investments in new plants and equipment.

Lagging indicators are useful in predicting the duration of economic upturns or downturns. For example, if the unemployment rate begins to decrease 9 months after a recession starts, economists know that the trough has passed and the economy has moved into recovery. Similarly, higher levels of consumer borrowing and business investment indicate that groups in the private sector are more confident about their economic futures and that expansion is beginning.

Despite the use of leading, coincident, and lagging indicators, economic forecasting is an inexact science. At times, economic indicators give mixed and conflicting signals. In addition, economists are unable to isolate all of the factors that contribute to an upturn or a downturn in the economy.

See Suggested Assignments, p. TM 76.

Section 4 Review

See Answers, p. A 62.

DEFINE business cycle, Gross National Product

1. **Comprehending Ideas** **(a)** How are fluctuations in business activity measured? **(b)** By sequence, describe the phases of the business cycle.
2. **Summarizing Ideas** Name the three types of indicators that economists use to predict the business cycle and give an example of each.
3. **Interpreting Ideas** The number of new business permits and orders for new capital goods are examples of what type of economic indicator?
4. **Analyzing Ideas** What role do expectations play in the dynamics of a business cycle?
5. **Interpreting Graphics** Study the graph on page 330. What stage of the business cycle would a nation be in when unemployment is high and aggregate demand and production are at their lowest point?

CHAPTER 14 SUMMARY

Inflation, deflation, and disinflation are types of price fluctuations that disrupt the economy. Economists use both the Consumer Price Index (CPI) and the Producer Price Index (PPI) to measure the amount of price fluctuations, including demand-pull and cost-push inflation, in the economy at a given time. Although a few people benefit from high inflation, most people are hurt as the real value of money decreases.

Four major types of unemployment exist: frictional unemployment, structural unemployment, seasonal unemployment, and cyclical unemployment. Although some frictional and structural unemployment indicates a vibrant economy, unemployment in general has great economic and social costs.

In the 1970s and 1980s, the American economy experienced stagflation, a new type of price instability. Stagflation combines high unemployment and high inflation.

The American economy is subject to the four phases of the business cycle: expansion, peak, contraction, and trough. Economists can predict the occurrence or duration of a particular phase by analyzing leading, coincident, and lagging indicators.

CHAPTER 14 REVIEW

For Answers to Chapter 14 Review, see p. A 62.

Reviewing Economic Terms

Supply the economic term that correctly completes each sentence.

1. The total spending by consumers, businesses, and government is the ______ ______.
2. When changes in technology result in the elimination of jobs, ______ ______ results.
3. Stagflation exists when both high levels of unemployment and ______ exist at the same time.
4. High labor costs are a ______ for producers to increase investment.
5. When there is a decline in real GNP for two consecutive quarters, a ______ is said to exist.
6. A low point in the economic cycle is called a ______.
7. When workers are temporarily between jobs, ______ ______ occurs.
8. Simultaneous high unemployment and high inflation rates characterize ______.

Exercising Economic Skills

1. **Evaluating Economic Decisions** Review newspapers and newsmagazines for an article that describes a national, state, or local decision with economic implications. Read the article. Then evaluate it, using the following questions to guide your evaluation. **(a)** What decision was made? **(b)** What relevant conditions existed at the time the decision was reached? **(c)** What were the benefits and costs of the decision? **(d)** What impact, if any, has the decision had? **(e)** In your view, was the decision a "good" or "bad" one? Present your findings to the class in a written or oral report.
2. **Investing in High-Growth Stocks** Study the feature on pages 528–529. Then contact a local stockbroker. Ask: **(a)** What are five high-growth stocks you are currently recommending or watching? **(b)** What type of business does each stock represent? **(c)** Why have you included each of these stocks on your list? **(d)** What factors in the economy do you feel will promote the growth of each of these stocks? Present a report on your findings to the class.

Thinking Critically About Economics

1. **Summarizing Ideas** **(a)** Why do price fluctuations threaten the stability of the economy? **(b)** Why is keeping unemployment low important in achieving stability in the economy? **(c)** What are the causes of stagflation? **(d)** Why is the business cycle important to the study of economics?
2. **Comparing Ideas** **(a)** What is the difference between current dollar and constant dollar measurements? **(b)** Which type of dollar is a more significant measure of economic growth? Why?
3. **Analyzing Ideas** How can a leading economic indicator, such as the average workweek in manufacturing, help predict future changes in the real GNP?
4. **Using Economic Imagination** Why would an investor favor government policies aimed at reducing inflation instead of unemployment?

Extending Economic Knowledge

1. Study the help wanted advertisements for the past month by looking in the Sunday newspapers for the past four weeks. **(a)** State a generalization about the number and types of jobs available. **(b)** How might the number and types of want ads tell you something about the state of the economy? **(c)** How are the numbers and types of job openings you found related to current trends in the economy?
2. Construct a time line of the major periods of economic growth and recession in the history of the United States. Include major events or inventions that may be related to these periods. Prepare a report on how one of these events or inventions directly influenced a period of growth or a period of recession.
3. Find statistics on the national Consumer Price Index from 1967 to the present that are broken down by spending categories (food, housing, energy). **(a)** Prepare a chart illustrating the types of expenses that have risen more or less than the average. **(b)** In a paragraph, answer the question: What do you think accounts for the different rates of price changes for different categories?

Using Primary Sources

Thomas Sowell (1930–) is a leading economist in the United States. Many of his books examine racial and ethnic minorities in the American economy. They also examine the strengths of the market economic system. In *Markets and Minorities* (1981), Sowell comments on the cost of discrimination in the labor market. As you read the following excerpts about the economics of discrimination, consider how both the discriminator and the victim suffer. Why is discrimination more prominent in markets where competition is weak?

The Economics of Discrimination

The economics of discrimination involves . . . questions about what kind of economic conditions tend to increase or decrease discrimination. Economics takes as axiomatic [truth] the proposition that more of anything is demanded at a low price than at a high price. Discrimination is no exception. A pair of twins might be equally racist, but, if one was an employer of violinists and the other an employer of basketball players, they would face very different costs of excluding blacks. Their subjective *prejudices* might be identical, but economics would predict that the differing costs would produce different amounts of overt [open] *discrimination*. . . .

Looked at another way, there are costs to the discriminator, as well as the victim. . . . Foregone opportunities to make money—as employer, landlord, seller, lender, etc.—put a price on discrimination. Economic competition means that the less discriminatory transactors acquire a competitive advantage, forcing others either to reduce their discrimination or to risk losing profits, perhaps even being forced out of business. This in turn means that in *less* competitive situations . . . *more* discrimination would exist, because its costs would be less.

At one extreme, a firm operating under a guaranteed cost-plus pricing arrangement—a regulated public utility, for example—would have zero costs of discrimination. All the extra costs entailed by refusing to hire qualified members of particular groups would be passed on to a consuming public with no alternative supplier. Conversely, any savings made by dropping discrimination would be savings to the consumers but not to the public utility, whose profit rate is fixed by the government regulatory commission. Zero discrimination costs in this situation would imply more discrimination in the sense of more severe restrictions on the kinds of jobs available to minorities. . . . For example, in the era before civil rights legislation, telephone companies not only refused to hire blacks in high-level positions, but even as linemen or operators. Moreover, restrictions applied not only to blacks but to Jews, Catholics, and others.

By contrast, a highly competitive industry such as entertainment has traditionally had a disproportionate over-representation of whatever minorities were having difficulties making a career in other fields. Vaudeville, then the record industry, and today television, have been dominated by performers from an ethnic minority background. This is obvious in the case of black performers, but no less true of others, including many whose anglicized names conceal their ethnic identity.

Source Review

For Answers to Source Review, see p. A 63.

1. According to Thomas Sowell, how does the "cost" of discrimination affect employment opportunities for people?
2. Why does Sowell state that discrimination involves costs for both the victim and the discriminator?
3. Why does Sowell say that there are "zero costs" of discrimination in a regulated public utility? Why does he believe that the costs of discrimination are less severe in highly competitive industries?

CHAPTER 15

See Chapter Overview, p. TM 78.
See Chapter Objectives, p. TM 78.
See Introducing the Chapter, p. TM 78.
See Extending Economic Knowledge on text p. 356.

Measures and Causes of Economic Growth

A society has one higher task than to consider its goals, to reflect on its pursuit of happiness and harmony and its success in expelling pain, tension, sorrow, and the ubiquitous curse of ignorance. It must also, so far as this may be possible, ensure its own survival.

John Kenneth Galbraith

1 The real per capita Gross National Product is the most widely used measure of economic growth.

- The Gross National Product
- Economic Growth
- Comparing Economic Growth

2 Other indicators of economic growth aid in the economy's measurement.

- Net National Product
- National Income
- Personal Income
- Disposable Income

3 Economic growth results from the wise use of the factors of production.

- Natural Resources
- Human Resources
- Capital Resources
- Technology
- Entrepreneurship
- Environmental Factors

4 Economic growth in a nation entails both benefits and costs.

- Benefits of Economic Growth
- Costs of Economic Growth

CHAPTER 15 STUDY GUIDE

Chapter Focus

Chapter 15 discusses the many factors responsible for economic growth in the United States. The chapter also analyzes the costs and benefits of economic growth. It discusses various indicators used to measure economic growth and the wise use of the factors of production.

As you study the chapter, look for the details that support each of the following statements.

1. The real per capita Gross National Product is the most widely used measure of economic growth.
2. Other indicators of economic growth aid in the economy's measurement.
3. Economic growth results from the wise use of the factors of production.
4. Economic growth in a nation entails both benefits and costs.

See Preteaching Vocabulary, p. TM 78.

Terms to Know

The following terms, while not the only terms emphasized in this chapter, are basic to your understanding of economic growth. Determine the meaning of each term, either by using the Glossary or by watching for context clues as you read the chapter.

Gross National Product	national income
net exports	indirect business tax
money GNP	personal income
real GNP	disposable income
implicit GNP price deflator	capacity utilization rate
real per capita GNP	
economic growth	
depreciation	
Net National Product	

See Key Study Questions and Key Understandings, p. TM 79.

1 The real per capita Gross National Product is the most widely used measure of economic growth.

See Suggested Teaching Strategies, p. TM 79.

Economic growth is a major goal in the United States economy. Although economists use many methods to analyze how much the economy is growing, most economists rely on the Gross National Product to measure growth.

The Gross National Product

The **Gross National Product,** or GNP, is the dollar value of all new, final products that are produced in a nation each year. The Bureau of Economic Analysis, a branch of the Commerce Department, gathers the statistics to calculate the GNP each year.

Calculating the GNP. The GNP includes only new and final goods and services that are produced. The GNP excludes the dollar value of previously counted items, such as used cars or secondhand items purchased at a garage sale. In addition, the GNP does not include the cost of intermediate goods, the parts or components of the final good.

For example, automobile manufacturers purchase goods such as air conditioning systems and radios from other companies to install in new automobiles. The market value of these goods is not reflected in the GNP, however, because the cost of intermediate goods is included in the price of the final good—the new car. Counting the value of both intermediate and final goods in the GNP would distort the true value of the nation's total output because many goods would be counted twice, once when they are produced and once after they have been incorporated into a finished product.

The GNP includes three types of final goods and services. They are consumer goods (C), investment or capital goods (I), and government goods (G). The ◆

◆ Have the students read "Understanding Mutual Funds" on pages 530–531 of the *Everyday Economics Handbook* and answer the questions that follow.

market value of C + I + G, plus net exports (F), is the GNP. **Net exports** represent the value of all goods and services that a country sells to other countries less the value of the goods and services that the country buys from other countries.

Consumer goods are goods and services that consumers purchase for immediate use, such as clothing, movie tickets, home appliances, and consumer durables such as television sets, cars, refrigerators, or CD players. Over 63 percent of all spending in the United States is for consumer goods. Economists refer to the purchase of consumer goods as personal consumption expenditures.

Capital goods are goods that businesses buy to produce other products. Plants and machinery are examples of capital goods. Investment spending also includes unsold inventories of goods and new construction. Existing plants and facilities and the purchase of stocks or bonds are not counted as investment spending because these types of investments merely transfer existing assets from one person to another. About 16.5 percent of all spending in the United States is for capital goods.

Government goods are goods that national, state, or local governments purchase. School buildings, office supplies, military hardware, and space satellites are all types of government goods. About ◆ 20 percent of all spending in the nation is for government goods.

Money and Real GNP. The GNP can be expressed as money GNP and real GNP. The **money GNP** is the current dollar value of the nation's output with no adjustment for inflation. The money GNP in 1985 was $3,993 billion, as shown in the graph to the right. In contrast to the money GNP, the **real GNP** is adjusted for inflation.

Economists use the **implicit GNP price deflator** to calculate the real GNP. The implicit GNP price deflator measures price changes in the GNP by estimating the average price level of all consumer, capital, and government goods and services produced in a given year. Like the CPI and PPI, the implicit GNP price deflator uses a base year as a starting point for comparisons of the GNP's real value. In the mid-1980s, the base year for the implicit GNP price deflator was 1982. In that year the implicit GNP price deflator was set at 100.

The implicit GNP price deflator increases when prices for C, I, and G increase. In 1983, for example, the implicit GNP price deflator was 103.8, illustrating a 3.8 percent price increase for the year.

To calculate the real GNP, economists divide the money GNP by the implicit GNP price deflator, and then multiply this total by 100. For example, in 1984 the money GNP was $3,774.7 billion. The implicit GNP price deflator was 108.1. Thus, the real GNP for 1984 was $3,492 billion ($3,774.7 billion ÷ 108.1 × 100 = $3,492 billion).

■ Economics Reporter

Who Is Simon Kuznets?

More than any other person, economist Simon Kuznets is known as the father of the GNP. In his book, *National Income and Its Composition: 1919 to 1938,* Kuznets developed the concepts and measurement procedures that led to the government's current techniques for measuring national economic performance. In addition to his work in economic performance measurements, Kuznets studied the factors that affect economic growth in different countries. It was for this work that he won the Nobel Prize in Economics in 1971.

Money GNP versus Real GNP

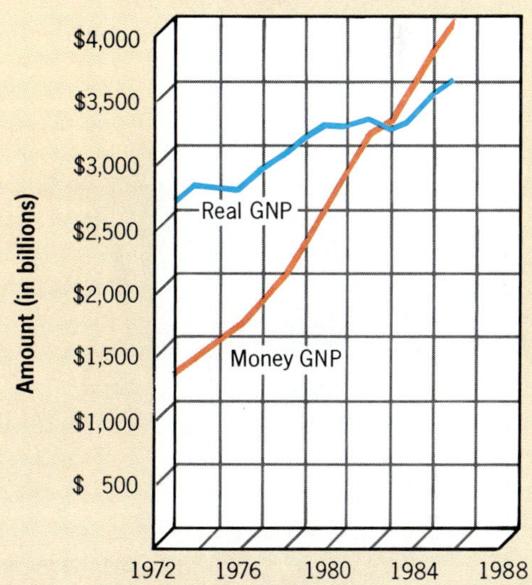

Source: *Economic Report of the President, 1986*

◆ Private industries bid on government contracts to produce government goods.

Although the nation's real GNP has been rising since the 1940s, periodic recessions have resulted in temporary declines in the real GNP. The graph on page 339 shows that the real GNP declined during the recessions of 1974–1975 and 1980–1982. During the same years, however, the money GNP continued to increase.

The Real Per Capita GNP. Economists divide the real GNP by the total population to calculate the **real per capita GNP.** Like the real GNP, the real per capita GNP in the United States has increased in most years since World War II. Between the mid-1950s and the mid-1980s, for example, the real per capita GNP increased from about $9,000 to nearly $15,000, representing an increase of over 60 percent. The increase in the real per capita GNP is one important indication that the material well-being, or standard of living, for the average American has improved.

Economic Growth

Economic growth occurs when the real per capita GNP increases. Consider the following example. Country A and Country B both produce $10 billion in output and have populations of 1 million people in 1990. The real per capita GNP for each nation is $10,000. Each country increases its real GNP to $30 billion between 1990 and 2010. During this 20-year period, however, Country A's population increases to 3 million while Country B's population remains at 1 million. The real GNP in each country has increased by $20 billion. Yet, only Country B experiences economic growth because its real per capita GNP rose by $20,000, from $10,000 in 1990 to $30,000 in 2010 ($30 billion ÷ 1 million = $30,000). Country A, on the other hand, did not experience economic growth because the increases in GNP merely matched the increases in population. Thus, the per capita GNP in Country A was the same in 2010 as it was in 1990 ($30 billion ÷ 3 million = $10,000).

Because of the United States trade deficit, net exports as a percentage of GNP have declined in recent years.

Comparing Economic Growth

Comparing economic growth, standards of living, and other economic data among the nations of the world is difficult because nations measure growth in different ways. In addition, statistical data is collected and recorded with varying degrees of accuracy. Economists usually compare growth among nations by looking at their real GNPs and per capita money GNPs.

Real GNP. The highly industrialized, developed countries of the world keep a detailed account of growth in their GNPs. Japan, for example, experienced a 10 percent growth rate in its real GNP for each of the five years during the 1961–1965 time period. By the 1981–1985 period, however, Japan's real GNP increased by less than one half of its previous total.

Per Capita Money GNP. Another commonly used comparison of economic growth and general well-being is the **per capita money GNP.** Economists often use the per capita money GNP, rather than the per capita real GNP, because reliable data on inflation are often unavailable. The World Bank reported that in 1983 per capita money GNPs ranged from $80 per year in Bhutan to $30,070 in the United Arab Emirates.

Using per capita money GNP to judge economic growth and the well-being of people has certain drawbacks. Many developing nations, for example,

The wealth derived from oil distorts per capita money GNP data in the oil-producing countries of the Middle East. The majority of people in these countries are not as prosperous as the data suggests.

have per capita GNPs of less than $1,000. Yet, lower prices, a reliance on subsistence agriculture, the use of barter rather than money for exchanges, and lower taxes increase the purchasing power of money in some developing nations.

At the other extreme, the United Arab Emirates, Kuwait, and Saudi Arabia all have higher per capita money GNPs than the United States and many other industrialized nations. The bulk of the wealth in these three oil-producing nations is in the hands of a small minority of the people, however, and the general share of each country's wealth is relatively small. Conversely, in the United States and other developed countries, the large middle class controls much of the wealth, a distribution of income which means that the people in general enjoy a high standard of living.

Section 1 Review See Answers, p. A 63.

DEFINE net exports, consumer good, capital good, government good, implicit GNP price deflator, real per capita GNP, per capita money GNP

IDENTIFY Simon Kuznets

1. **Summarizing Ideas** What four components comprise the Gross National Product?
2. **Interpreting Ideas** If sales of used cars were included in the measurement of GNP, why would it not be an accurate measurement of productivity?
3. **Interpreting Graphics** Study the graph on page 339. It shows that the money GNP has surpassed the real GNP. What does this indicate?

See Suggested Assignments, p. TM 79.

BUILDING ECONOMIC SKILLS

THINKING ABOUT ECONOMICS

Analyzing Economic Viewpoints

Economic issues are often complex, bringing into conflict one or more economic goals. As a result, economic questions rarely have simple answers. It is important for students of economics to be able to analyze economic viewpoints by distinguishing fact from opinion and analyzing evidence offered in support of the opinion. By breaking a viewpoint down into its component parts, students can assess its validity and reasonableness.

How to Analyze Viewpoints

To effectively analyze economic viewpoints, follow these steps.

1. **Identify the main idea.** List specific details and examples used to support the main idea.
2. **Determine the type of supporting evidence.** Distinguish between facts and opinions in the

TAX-REVISION SLEIGHT OF HAND

BY ROGER GARRISON

Tax revision represents one more play in the shell game of hiding the costs of government. While it has some desirable features, it is really an attempt to shift the costs of government back to corporations, which pay taxes whose costs are only indirectly borne by the American people.

Politicians have only four ways of financing government spending: money creation, deficits, indirect taxes and direct taxes. Predictably, the government will use all four methods in some combination, periodically making adjustments so that the political costs of raising money through any one method don't become too great.

The costs that count—for the purpose of predicting the behavior of politicians—are those perceived by voters. Direct taxes impose costs that are easily perceived. Costs associated with the other alternatives . . . are relatively difficult for voters to perceive. Therefore, an institutional environment such as ours, which lacks effective fiscal and monetary constraints, will favor money creation, deficit financing, and less so, indirect levies over direct taxation.

But given enough experience with either deficits or inflation, voters will begin to perceive the real costs of such obscured government financing. During the 1970s, the government relied on money creation as a means of financing. Eventually, voters came to recognize the high costs of inflation. In response to this, politicians shifted away from money creation and into deficit financing. However, its costs, though only partially and sometimes incorrectly understood, also recently have been seen as high. This would suggest that another shift in the way government will be financed is due. But memories of inflation are too fresh for money creation to be attractive right now. Enter tax revision, which aims to shift taxation from individuals to corporations.

A greater reliance on corporate taxes is the easiest route for politicians to take now—at least until memories of inflation and high deficits have sufficiently faded.

I do not suggest that politicians deliberately calculate . . . how best to hide the costs of government from the voters. But they do respond to the political incentives they face—which are to provide a high level of government spending while minimizing the perceived costs of that spending.

In the longer run, institutional reforms are needed to change fundamentally the political incentives. Debt-ceilings, Gramm-Rudman, and even a balanced budget amendment still allow politicians to pay lip service to fiscal prudence while they avoid spending cuts.

To advocate that these alternative means of financing government be held in check is not to support a tax increase. It is to suggest that taxes be more direct. Eliminating corporate taxes also would allow the voters to perceive more clearly the costs of government and could induce officials actually to reduce spending.

viewpoint. In general, a viewpoint's strongest support comes from facts.

3. **Consider how the details are used.** Decide whether the supporting evidence is used logically. Note any fallacies in reasoning (Chapter 9, pages 206–207). Identify any bias.

Applying the Skill

Read the viewpoint on page 342 in which Roger Garrison discusses the tax revision signed into law in 1986. The author has made two main points. The first is that the tax revision was politically motivated. That is, raising taxes on corporations was the least offensive way to raise revenues for the government. The second main point is that direct taxes on citizens permit citizens to more clearly see how government costs are rising. His economic viewpoint has a clear bias, which favors reducing the government's role in the economy.

Garrison's economic viewpoint fails, however, to consider the question of "fair" distribution of the tax burden. It also fails to report that corporate taxes, as a percentage of the government's total revenue, have declined markedly in recent years.

Practicing the Skill See Answers, p. A 63.

Read the article to the right from the August 25, 1986, issue of *Time*. Then on a separate sheet of paper answer these questions.

1. **(a)** What is the thesis of the economic viewpoint? **(b)** What evidence does the author provide to support the viewpoint?
2. **(a)** What facts are provided in the viewpoint? **(b)** What opinion does the author present?
3. Who is the author?
4. Does the author make a logical argument in defense of his or her viewpoint? Are there any fallacies contained in the viewpoint? Explain.
5. What bias, or point of view, is presented in the viewpoint?

THE MAKING OF A MIRACLE

BY GEORGE J. CHURCH

They said it couldn't be done . . . Scrap the gargantuan federal tax code and write a simpler, fairer one. How naive! Drastically reduce top tax rates to their lowest levels in 58 years by throwing out special breaks and deductions that have accrued over the past four decades. No way! Let the free market determine how people spend and invest their money rather than allow shills for favored industries to use the tax code to tinker with the economy? Get real! Such a drastic overhaul would amount to putting the public interest ahead of special interests—in this case nearly every interest with enough clout to hire a lobbyist. And everybody knows the political process does not work that way.

Except that once in a great while the process does work that way. Thus it was with tax reform, a political miracle that was brought to the verge of fruition by an amazingly varied group of conservatives and liberals, Republicans and Democrats. . . .

The Tax Reform Act of 1986 is one of the few pieces of legislation that can truly be called historic. It will affect nearly every one of the 99.6 million individuals and 3 million corporations that pay federal income taxes, plus some businesses that now pay no tax but will have to start coughing up. It reverses the whole direction that federal taxation has been following for decades: instead of adding exceptions and deductions, it wipes them out by the hundreds; instead of shifting the tax burden from business to individuals, it switches the load the other way. The bill marks a long step toward the reformers' ideal of using the code simply to raise revenue rather than for social and economic engineering. Altogether, it is easily the most fundamental revision of taxation since World War II. . . .

But how lasting will the victory be? There is an uncomfortable chance that future Presidents and Congresses will begin riddling a fairly rational tax system with deductions and special breaks all over again. Sometimes the goals that social and economic tinkerers try to achieve through the tax code seem worthy, and many groups of taxpayers can make a plausible case for special treatment. . . . To resist those pressures will require not just a one-time public embrace of reform. It will demand a lasting commitment to a system designed simply to raise revenue while treating everyone alike so far as possible. For now, the political system has proved . . . that it can fix a problem that has been festering for decades.

See Key Study Questions and Key Understandings, p. TM 80.

2 Other indicators of economic growth aid in the economy's measurement.

See Suggested Teaching Strategies, p. TM 80.

While the GNP is the broadest measure of economic activity in a nation, other measures of economic growth and of the people's standard of living also exist. These measures include the Net National Product, national income, personal income, and disposable personal income. Each of these measures is related to the GNP.

Net National Product

Every year businesses spend money to buy new capital goods. Some of these capital goods add to the nation's capital stock. Other capital goods are purchased simply to replace broken down or obsolete machinery, equipment, or other capital. The value of capital that is used up each year to keep a nation's capital stock intact is **depreciation.**

The Components of National Income

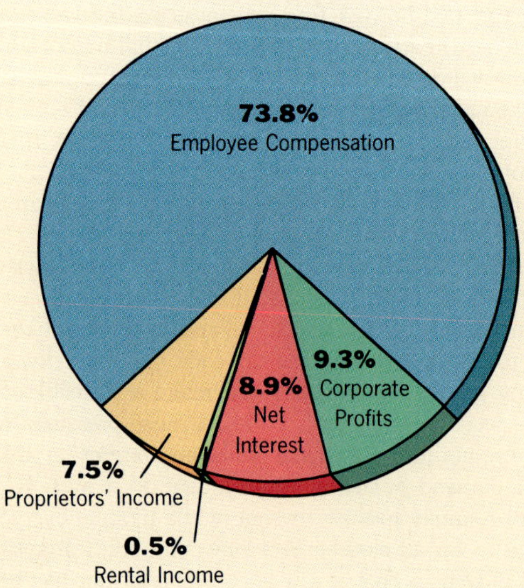

Source: *Economic Report of the President, 1986*

The **Net National Product,** or NNP, is the GNP minus depreciation. In 1985, for example, the GNP was $3,993 billion. Depreciation was $438 billion. Thus, the NNP was $3,555 billion ($3,993 − $438 = $3,555).

Economists often view the NNP as a better indicator of the economy's annual production than the GNP because the NNP recognizes that some capital wears out in the production process. Depreciation is sometimes called capital consumption to note that some capital is consumed, or rendered nonproductive, each year.

National Income

Another measure of the economy's health is the national income. **National income,** or NI, is the total amount of income that everyone in the economy earns. The key word in this definition is "earn." People are the suppliers of the factors of production. As such, they earn income in exchange for their contribution to the production process.

Sources of National Income. The NI can be calculated in two ways. One way is to identify the sources of the national income, and add the dollar amounts of each together (see the graph on this page). NI includes five sources of income.

Wages and salaries represent the largest source of NI. In 1985, for example, total compensation to employees was about $2.4 trillion, nearly three fourths of the NI. Proprietors' income is the income that self-employed individuals earn. Farmers and sole proprietors are examples of self-employed people. In 1985, proprietors' income accounted for $242 billion of the NI, or 7.5 percent of the total.

Rental income is income that property owners receive in exchange for the use of their property, whether land, buildings, or equipment, by another party. Rental income is the smallest component of the NI. It contributed just $14 billion to the NI in 1985, or less than 1 percent of the total.

Corporate profits represent the income corporations earn when business receipts are greater than the costs of production. Corporate profits accounted for $299 billion, or 9.3 percent, of the NI in 1985.

Net interest is the amount of interest that individuals receive from firms. Net interest contributed $288 billion to the NI in 1985, or 8.9 percent of the total.

Indirect Business Taxes. A second way to calculate the NI is to subtract **indirect business taxes** from the NNP. The government levies indirect business taxes on a firm's output rather than on the firm itself. The major types of indirect business taxes are sales taxes, excise taxes, customs duties, and license fees. The producer figures these taxes into the cost of the product and passes the tax costs on to the consumer.

The NI does not include indirect business taxes because the government receives the income. Money is withdrawn from the private sector and does not count as earned income. In 1985, for example, $339 billion in indirect business taxes was subtracted from the NNP to form the NI.

Personal Income

The total amount of income that individuals receive before paying taxes is called **personal income,** or PI. Personal income differs from NI, which represents the total amount of income that people earn. In 1985, the NI was about $3.2 trillion, and the PI was $3.3 trillion.

Economists use a two-step process to calculate the PI. The first step is to deduct from NI money that is not received by individuals. For example, corporate profits are deducted because corporations, rather than individuals, use these profits. Some profits are used to pay corporate taxes. Other moneys are spent on research and development and new capital. Similarly, employer Social Security contributions are deducted because these contributions leave the private sector and are automatically deposited in the federal government's Social Security trust fund.

The second step in the process is to add in other sources of income that individuals receive. Some of this income is earned. Earned income includes dividend payments that corporations make to individuals. Other income is classified as income received rather than income earned. Income received adds to an individual's income, but it does not represent an exchange for any current productive activity. Private and public transfer payments are income received. The most important type of private transfer payment comes from company pension plans. Public transfer payments include benefits for veterans, Social Security payments, and unemployment benefits paid directly to individuals.

Disposable Income

A final measure of the overall health of the economy is the nation's level of **disposable income** (DI), which is PI less personal taxes. In 1985, for example, the PI was $3,294 billion and personal taxes were $493 billion. Thus, disposable income in the United States was $2,801 billion ($3,294 − $493 = $2,801).

DI is an important factor in determining the people's standard of living because DI most accurately reflects how much income people can use to satisfy their wants and needs. Individuals are free to spend or to save their disposable income. People in the United States tend to spend the greater part of their income. Personal consumption expenditures accounted for over 95 percent of DI in 1985, while people saved under 5 percent of their DI. ◆

See Suggested Assignments, p. TM 80.

Section 2 Review

See Answers, p. A 64.

DEFINE depreciation, Net National Product (NNP), national income (NI), indirect business tax, personal income, disposable income

1. **Interpreting Ideas** Why is Net National Product (NNP) considered a more accurate measurement of an increase in productivity than Gross National Product (GNP)?
2. **Comprehending Ideas** Why are transfer payments included in personal income, but not in national income?
3. **Interpreting Graphics** Study the graph on page 344. Why does employee compensation account for such a large share of national income?

See Key Study Questions and Key Understandings, p. TM 81.

3 Economic growth results from the wise use of the factors of production.

See Suggested Teaching Strategies, p. TM 81.

All production stems from the use of the five factors of production: natural resources, human resources, capital resources, technology, and entrepreneurship. To achieve and sustain economic growth, nations must make wise use of these factors of production.

◆ Discussion topic: How the Tax Reform Law of 1986 affects families in which both the husband and wife work.

In addition, environmental factors often influence economic growth. The wise use of these factors explains much of the success of the United States in achieving economic growth.

Natural Resources

The United States is endowed with plentiful natural resources. Despite this abundance, the economic problem of scarcity is always present for two reasons. First, the United States must depend on other nations to supply certain resources. When world tensions disrupt international trade, the economy of the United States suffers. Shortages of key resources such as oil create bottlenecks in the production process because shortages in one phase of production delay the entire process. During the Arab oil embargo of 1973–1974, for example, the fuel shortage forced many factories to close temporarily. New discoveries of some resources, new methods of extracting or using existing resources, and the development of substitute goods help overcome resource shortages.

Second, people often abuse and waste natural resources. ◆ For much of the 1800s and the early 1900s, inexpensive natural resources in the United States such as oil, coal, and timber were used as if the supply would last forever. In addition, strip mining, overharvesting of trees, or overgrazing ruined some of the land. As the prices of some vital resources increased during the 1970s and 1980s, however, individuals, firms, and the government became more conscious of the importance of conservation and the efficient use of natural resources.

One sign of this new concern was the move to use renewable rather than nonrenewable resources. Renewable resources are resources that can be used over and over again or that can be naturally replenished by nature. Solar, wind, and geothermal power, which became popular sources of energy during the rapid climb in oil prices in the 1970s, are examples of renewable resources. Congressional approval of tax credits in 1978 to encourage investment in alternative energy sources demonstrated the government's commitment to renewable resources. Nonrenewable resources, on the other hand, are natural resources that are destroyed during the production process. Nonrenewable energy resources include oil, coal, and natural gas.

Human Resources

Human resources, or labor, represent the contributions of workers to production. The quantity and the quality of workers determine how human resources affect a nation's economic growth.

Quantity of Workers. The number, or quantity, of workers in the labor force affects productivity. If a worker shortage exists, a nation's economy cannot operate at full capacity.

Throughout the history of the United States, the size of the labor force has expanded. In 1900, the labor force stood at 29 million workers. By 1986, the labor force had risen to about 118 million workers. The two major reasons for this expansion are population growth and the increased participation by women in the labor force.

Population growth in the United States has furnished an ample supply of workers since the founding of the nation. The relatively high birth rate and the large number of immigrants who came to the United States during the 1800s and early 1900s increased the population. Between the mid-1800s and World War I, for example, about 35 million immigrants entered the United States.

The population growth rate has declined significantly in recent years, but the United States, with more than 240 million people, is the fourth most populous nation in the world.

The role of women in the economy has also changed over the years. Between 1900 and 1986, women workers, as a percent of the labor force, jumped from 19 percent to 44 percent. This dramatic increase of women working outside the home reflects changing economic needs and social attitudes in the United States during the 1900s.

Quality of Workers. The quality of workers refers to how effective, or productive, workers are. Many factors, including education and training, health, and attitudes toward work, affect worker productivity.

Nations invest in a productive work force in many ways. For example, many governments invest in public education, job-training programs, and health-care facilities to increase worker productivity. Investments in workers, or human capital, are as important to economic growth as investments in capital goods and technology.

◆ **President Theodore Roosevelt was one of the first public officials to recognize the need for conservation. During his administration, Congress created wildlife sanctuaries and national parks.**

● Have the students read "Purchasing Agents" on page 543 of *Careers in the Marketplace.*

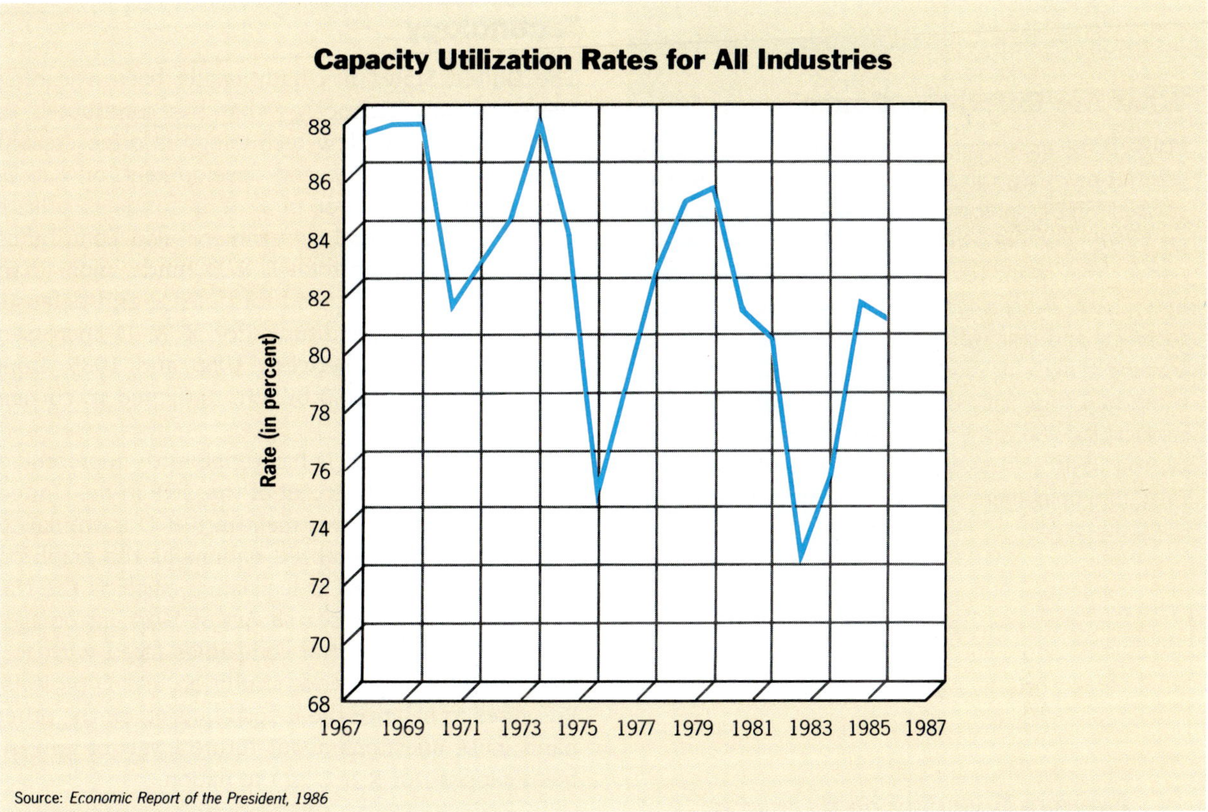

The United States has traditionally supported programs and services to improve the quality of the labor force. For example, public education has increased the literacy rate to 99 percent. About 80 percent of all students graduate from high school, and 20 percent graduate from college. Public and private sources provide funds for job-training and retraining programs. In addition, because of tougher competition from abroad during the 1980s, unions and management have worked to eliminate inefficient production techniques and wasteful practices.

Capital Resources

Capital resources, including real capital and money capital, are vital to a nation's economic growth. Throughout most of the 1900s, the United States had a greater level of capital resources per worker than any other nation. In 1979, however, Japan surpassed the United States in the amount of capital per worker. Japan's success in acquiring additional capital stems from the willingness of the Japanese to save money. Private-sector saving in Japan is roughly double the rate of saving in the United States. The large pool of savings in Japan has been used mainly for capital formation.

The utilization of existing capital is another crucial element in achieving economic growth. On the average, firms in the United States use more of their productive capacity during periods of prosperity, when aggregate demand is high. They use less productive capacity during periods of recession, when aggregate demand is low. ●

Every month the government calculates **capacity utilization rates** to show how much of the nation's total capital goods are being used to produce goods. The graph on this page shows the capacity utilization rate for all industries in the United States. Capacity utilization dropped during the recessions of 1974–1975 and 1980–1982. In 1982, for example, industries operated at only 72 percent of ◆ capacity. The underutilization of capital resources is an economic waste like unemployment and underemployment.

◆ The capacity utilization rate in May 1986 was 78.8 percent.

Economics Reporter

What Are Enterprise Zones?

Many state governments have established enterprise zones to promote economic growth in distressed geographical areas. Entrepreneurs are provided with incentives to invest in the zones. Among the incentives are reductions in local property taxes, license fees, and state business taxes; technical and managerial assistance; subsidized job training programs; modifications in business regulations; and financial assistance in the form of venture capital and loans. Enterprise zones are chosen on the basis of such factors as the area's poverty rate, unemployment rate, crime rate, and housing conditions.

Average Spending on Research and Development

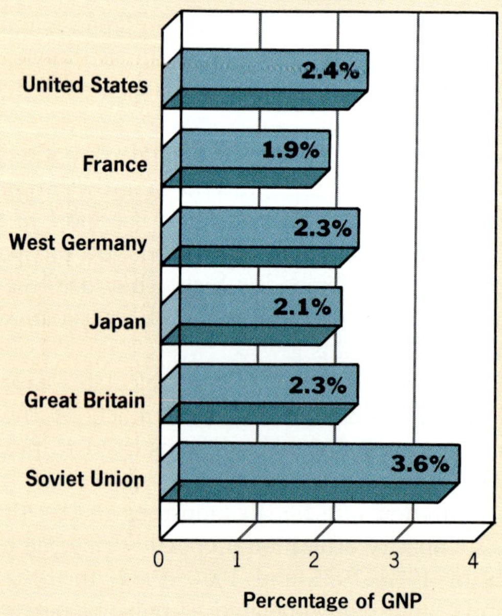

Source: *Statistical Abstract of the United States, 1986*

Technology

The United States has traditionally been a leading source of new technology that has contributed to economic growth. New technology is often created as a result of research and development, or R & D. The largest contributor of R & D funds is private industry. The federal government also contributes a large share of the total R & D funds, more than half of which are targeted for defense and defense-related areas. Expenditures for R & D increased nearly eight times between 1960 and 1985, from $13.5 billion to $106.6 billion, measured in current dollars.

Investment in R & D has consistently represented from 2 percent to 3 percent of the GNP in the United States. The rate of investment in R & D is similar to that of other industrialized nations as the graph on this page shows. Recent legislation, such as the National Cooperative Research Act of 1984, encourages R & D and permits rival companies faced with foreign competition to work jointly on R & D projects. Pressures to balance the federal budget, on the other hand, raise questions about future levels of government support for R & D in the nation.

Entrepreneurship

Entrepreneurship is a vital factor in promoting economic growth. Entrepreneurs such as Cyrus McCormick, Charles Goodyear, John D. Rockefeller, and Cornelius Vanderbilt contributed to the rise of American industry during the 1800s. The tradition of entrepreneurship continued into the 1900s through the work of Henry Ford, George Eastman, Edwin H. Land, Steven Jobs, and countless others. ◆

In recent years, venture capitalists have encouraged entrepreneurship by raising money nationwide to invest in promising new businesses. This venture capital enables entrepreneurs to develop and market their ideas. Many state and local governments provide venture capital to new businesses in their areas. By 1986, venture capitalists were investing about $17 billion annually in promising business ventures in the private sector.

Business incubators, or businesses that gather several new businesses in the same facility, also offer support to entrepreneurs. Business incubators allow new firms to save money by sharing various services and expenses. Between the mid-1970s and

◆ **Report topic: Have the students prepare written reports on prominent entrepreneurs.**

Economic growth in the United States is spurred by the quality and diversity of the country's human resources and by a commitment to entrepreneurship and technology.

mid-1980s, more than 100 business incubators formed throughout the United States. Because of the high success rate, experts predict the number of business incubators to increase in the future.

The teaching of entrepreneurial skills has gained popularity in recent years. About 250 colleges and universities offer courses in entrepreneurship. In addition, millions of employees in the private sector study entrepreneurial skills.

Environmental Factors

Environmental factors may either contribute to or detract from a nation's economic growth. In many developing nations, environmental factors have traditionally been unfavorable, but in the United States, economic, social, and political components favor economic growth.

Text continues on page 352.

The Underground Economy—What It Means to a Nation

The term *underground economy* refers to the unreported business activity in a nation. The underground economy has two major segments. One is unreported legal business activity. The other is unreported illegal business activity. Combined, the unreported income generated from legal and illegal sources in the American economy jumped from about $25 billion in 1965 to more than $400 billion in the mid-1980s.

Legal and Illegal Segments of the Underground Economy

The legal segment of the underground economy includes wage earners who fail to report all or part of their income to the government. Tax avoidance is the chief motive. The self-employed form the single, largest group who underreport income from legal sources. The self-employed include sole proprietors and members of partnerships, whether doctors, lawyers, plumbers, carpenters, contractors, and others who offer marketable services. The self-employed include those who sell goods on city streets or at roadside stands in the countryside. Wage earners and some people who earn income from interest, dividends, rents, and royalties also underreport income. Economists estimate that the legal segment represents about two thirds of the underground economy in the United States.

"Working off the books," as this unreported business activity is called, relies on cash transactions. Cash exchanges of goods and services are easily hidden from the Internal Revenue Service (IRS).

The other segment of the underground economy includes people who are engaged in illegal business activities. Drug trafficking, prostitution, fraud, gambling, and other illegal activities generate the other one third of unreported income. Record keeping for illegal activities is concealed from the authorities, not only to avoid paying taxes but also to avoid criminal prosecution.

Impact of the Underground Economy on the Nation's Economy

The rapid growth of the underground economy during the 1970s and 1980s has caused economists to study its impact on the nation's economy. Most often, economists focus on how the underground economy affects taxation and economic growth.

Taxation. Tax avoidance is the most important reason for the growth of the underground economy in the United States. By the mid-1980s, tax experts have estimated that an additional $100 billion in taxes could have been collected annually if all legal sources of income in the underground economy had been reported.

Economists point out that the $100 billion in annual tax losses represent about one half of the annual federal deficit. Getting people to comply with tax laws is a major step toward balancing the federal budget. Economists also point out that honest taxpayers are obliged to pay higher taxes because others are avoiding their responsibilities.

Economic Growth. Close to $500 billion worth of unreported business activity takes place in the American economy. The published Gross National Product (GNP), however, does not include the dollar value of these transactions in its statistics on total output in the economy. For this reason, some economists maintain that the GNP is far larger than the official data indicate.

Economic growth occurs when the nation's real per capita GNP increases. You read in Chapter 15 that the United States has experienced steady economic growth throughout its history. Yet, by adding $300 billion or so in legal but unreported business activity to the GNP, the real per capita GNP increases significantly. In addition, economists argue that some gains made in employment and worker productivity are "hidden" in the underground economy.

The International Underground Economy

The underground economy is not uniquely American. It exists under a variety of names in virtually all nations. In West Germany it is called the "shadow economy"; in the Soviet Union, the "second economy"; in Italy, the "submerged economy." In many industrialized nations, the output of goods and services produced in the underground economy represents 10 to 15 percent of the official GNP. In some nations, such as Israel, Italy, and South Africa, the underground economy represents a considerably larger percentage of the GNP.

Nations have tried different approaches to weeding out tax evaders. In the United States, the IRS favors more thorough federal auditing of tax returns to catch tax cheats, many of whom are also found out by tips sent to the IRS from acquaintances and co-workers. The IRS estimates that for every dollar spent in the audit process, $10.40 in new tax revenues is generated. Discussions about instituting a general tax amnesty were also under way by the mid-1980s. Tax amnesty allows tax evaders to pay on delinquent tax bills without incurring financial or criminal penalties.

In other countries, the crackdown on the underground economy is more dramatic than in the United States. In Israel, for example, "tax commando" raids have resulted in the arrest and prosecution of tax evaders. In the Soviet Union, one prominent businessman in the second economy was executed by firing squad in 1984. This execution was a part of a larger anticorruption campaign. Despite these efforts, the underground economies in many nations continue to grow.

Most flea markets in the United States do not belong to the underground economy. The government requires that they keep detailed sales records.

DECISION MAKERS IN THE ECONOMY

Philip B. Crosby

In 1979, Philip B. Crosby formed a company designed to teach corporations how to improve the quality of their products. This company, Philip Crosby Associates, already has achieved success.

Crosby began his career in 1953 as a radar-equipment inspector. He later worked as the quality manager for Martin Marietta's Pershing missile program and then as the director of quality control at ITT. During these years, he developed a theory of quality that differs from most traditional ones. Whereas most theorists assume that a certain number of defects are inevitable, Crosby stresses the idea that no defects are acceptable. Crosby reasons that the best way to achieve quality is to prevent errors in the first place.

A number of major corporations have sent representatives to Philip Crosby Associates' classes, which are taught at Quality College in Winter Park, Florida, and at other locations throughout the world. Mattel, for example, reports that Crosby's principles of manufacturing efficiency have helped the company save $7.5 million in two years. IBM has hired Philip Crosby Associates to train a group of staff members who in turn will train other company employees. General Motors now contracts for 20 percent of Crosby's business. All of these corporations believe that Philip Crosby's ideas are increasing their productivity and profitability.

A number of economic factors encourage growth in the United States economy. Competitive markets, for example, promote efficiency, the price system directs resources into profitable areas, and voluntary exchange permits individuals to pursue private goals in the marketplace. In addition, the nation's economic infrastructure provides basic facilities that private firms could not possibly afford to produce.

Social factors refer to people's attitudes about work and success. For example, workers in the United States traditionally follow the work ethic, which places a high value on hard work. They also value material success, and the drive to succeed motivates people to work hard and to produce. Finally, the status and prestige of an individual tends to rise along with his or her business successes.

◆ Political factors affect the stability of the business environment, and the United States has enjoyed remarkable political stability. The government has defended citizens from foreign aggression, protected the individual's right to own private property, and enforced contracts. In addition, the government forms its tax and regulatory policies with an eye toward fairness to all citizens. Combined with high spending for social capital, the government provides a favorable environment for saving, investing, working, and producing.

See Suggested Assignments, p. TM 81.

Section 3 Review See Answers, p. A 64.

DEFINE capacity utilization rate

IDENTIFY enterprise zone, Philip B. Crosby

1. **Comprehending Ideas** Under what classification of the factors of production are **(a)** machinery and buildings, **(b)** workers, and **(c)** raw materials such as ore?
2. **Summarizing Ideas** **(a)** An investment in public education is an investment in what factor of production? **(b)** Does this investment improve the quantity or quality of this resource?
3. **Interpreting Graphics** Study the graph on page 347. What do the dips in utilization rates on the graph mean?

◆ The political system of the United States provides people the freedom to choose where they will work and the free enterprise system provides incentives for success.

See Key Study Questions and Key Understandings, p. TM 82.

4 Economic growth in a nation entails both benefits and costs.

See Suggested Teaching Strategies, p. TM 82.

Throughout the history of the United States, the goal of economic growth has been constant. Economic questions concerned the achievement of growth, not the desirability of growth. People concentrated on finding the right mix of the factors of production to promote growth. In recent years, however, economists have begun to examine both the benefits and the costs of economic growth.

Benefits of Economic Growth

Many benefits are associated with economic growth. The standard of living improves when the real per capita GNP increases owing to the production of more goods and services.

Social benefits are positive side-effects of economic growth. Economic growth creates jobs. Higher employment rates, in turn, benefit society in other ways. Crime rates tend to decline during prosperous times, and the wealth that society gains during periods of growth stimulates creative work in science, technology, and the arts.

Federal, state, and local government revenues increase during periods of economic growth. The federal government collects additional income taxes because individuals and firms make more money. State and local governments earn higher revenues from income taxes, sales taxes, and excise taxes resulting from higher sales of goods and services.

Increased government revenues allow the government to better meet the needs of the people. Additional revenues enable the federal government to finance national defense, upgrade the economic infrastructure, and maintain adequate social programs. State and local governments finance education, health care, and other social programs. In many cases, the investments that government makes contribute to future economic growth.

Economic growth in the United States affects the nation's economic position in the world. A growing economy enables the United States to extend more economic aid to developing countries. Aid not only promotes economic growth in developing countries but also strengthens the global economic system.

Politically, economic growth adds to the prestige of the United States and reinforces the position of the United States as the world's leading capitalist nation. Likewise, economic growth in the United States demonstrates the effectiveness of the free market economic system. This positive example is especially important to developing countries in Africa, Asia, Latin America, and the Middle East, which are still forming their economic and political institutions.

Costs of Economic Growth

In recent years, economists have become more aware of the costs of economic growth. The four major types of costs are resource depletion, social costs, uneven growth, and sacrificed consumption.

Resource Depletion. Economic growth involves the use of additional natural resources. The use of nonrenewable resources such as oil or coal is a major concern because they are destroyed during the production process. As resources are used up, shortages occur. Lower supply results in higher prices.

Technology and conservation efforts have slowed resource depletion somewhat. Through new production methods, people use resources more efficiently today than in the past. Improved technology permits a less wasteful extraction of resources such as coal and oil. Finally, conservation efforts have increased in response to higher resource prices. In effect, wasting resources has become uneconomical.

Social Costs. The social costs of economic growth focus on the deterioration of the quality of life for people. Quality of life differs from standard of living in that quality of life includes the nonmaterial aspects of living.

One of the major social costs of economic growth is pollution. Pollution affects the natural environment—the quality of the air, water, and land. A social cost of a growing economy is more pollution. ◆ Pollution threatens the balance of nature and presents a hazard to plant, animal, and human life. The smog that periodically engulfs some cities is an extreme example of the hazards of air pollution. Careless disposal of nuclear waste products and other hazardous substances threatens water and land.

Another type of social cost involves the social environment. Economic growth, for example, encour-

◆ Discussion topic: The benefits and costs of economic growth.

While many segments of the economy are growing, the United States steel industry is experiencing a decline because of strong foreign competition.

ages **urbanization**, the movement of people from rural areas to the cities. Urbanization accompanied economic growth and the rise of industries during the 1800s and the early 1900s.

While urban life has social benefits, it also has social costs such as overcrowding, and a more hurried lifestyle. The hectic lifestyles of some urban dwellers contribute to increased levels of stress that can lead to heart disease and stroke. Large urban populations also tend to strain existing facilities such as schools, police and fire protection, and recreation facilities. In addition, the working environments in urban centers rely on the assembly-line method of production. The division of labor employed on the assembly line creates repetitious and often monotonous jobs that offer few psychic rewards.

Uneven Growth. Economic growth affects different areas of the country in varying ways. During periods of economic growth, production in some geographic areas lags. For example, many Americans did not share in the recovery of the mid-1980s. Farmers went bankrupt, and steelworkers in the Ohio Valley lost their jobs. Traditional pockets of poverty remained in rural Appalachia and in urban slums.

Economic growth also affects different groups of people in different ways. During periods of growth, for example, the rate of technological change increases. The new technology increases efficiency, but it also contributes to structural unemployment. The number of manufacturing jobs has dropped in recent years, a decline due in part to mechanization in the workplace. Other groups that share little in the nation's economic growth include migrant workers and other laborers with little education and few marketable skills.

Sacrificed Consumption. The final cost of economic growth is sacrificed consumption. Individuals and firms must save a portion of their incomes to finance the investments in R & D, new capital, job-training programs, and other elements that contribute to growth. This saving represents an investment in the future. Saving also means people sacrifice some present consumption. For example, an individual who deposits money in a savings account or buys a savings bond cannot spend that money on movie tickets or a compact disc.

CASE STUDY

Acid Rain and the Social Costs of Economic Growth

Acid rain is a form of pollution that affects the air, soil, and water. As industries burn coal, oil, or gas, the factory smokestacks release sulfur and other pollutants into the atmosphere. In the atmosphere, the chemicals in the pollutants combine with the chemicals in water vapor, and fall to the ground as acid rain or other precipitation.

Acid rain became a controversial international issue during the 1980s. The Canadian government believed that acid rain was ruining forests, streams, and lakes in the southeastern part of Canada. The Canadians insisted that the United States clean up the source of the problem—the heavy industrial plants in the Ohio Valley. The United States government argued that there was little evidence that acid rain was harmful to the ecosystem or that American industries were responsible for the deaths of Canadian streams and lakes.

In 1986, the National Research Council, which is associated with the National Academy of Sciences, completed an extensive report on the effects of acid pollutants. The National Research Council concluded that acid rain was responsible for some environmental decay in the northeastern United States and in adjoining southeastern Canada.

Negotiations between the United States and Canada resulted in a compromise solution in 1986. The United States government agreed to spend $2.5 billion between 1986 and 1990 to develop clean-coal technology, because the burning of coal is responsible for most sulfuric compounds in acid rain. United States firms agreed to spend an additional $2.5 billion. The government, however, refused to impose stricter sulfur-emission controls on heavy industries. Industrial firms estimated that compliance with additional controls would cost about $20 billion.

The compromise drew praises and complaints. The United States and Canadian governments, electric utilities, and the National Coal Association praised the compromise as an effective long-term solution to the acid rain problem. Critics of the plan, including environmental groups such as the Sierra Club, argued that the plan did not set specific targets for the reduction of emissions from the plants.

See Suggested Assignments, p. TM 82.

Section 4 Review See Answers, p. A 64.

DEFINE urbanization

IDENTIFY acid rain

1. **Summarizing Ideas** What are the benefits of economic growth?
2. **Interpreting Ideas** Why is pollution considered to be a social cost of production?
3. **Seeing Relationships** Why must an increase in spending on capital or on research and development result in reduced consumption?

CHAPTER 15 SUMMARY

Economists use the Gross National Product, which is the dollar value of all new and final goods produced in a given year, to measure economic growth. Economists divide the GNP into money GNP and real GNP. Unlike money GNP, real GNP is adjusted for inflation. By dividing the real GNP by the total population, economists can calculate the real per capita GNP. The real per capita GNP is the most effective measure of economic growth. To compare the economic growth of different countries, however, economists usually use per capita money GNP because figures on inflation rates are often unreliable.

Net National Product, national income, personal income, and disposable personal income are also useful in calculating economic growth. Of these measures, disposable personal income is the most accurate gauge of how much income individuals can use to satisfy their needs and wants.

Nations must make wise use of the five factors of production—natural resources, human resources, capital resources, technology, and entrepreneurship—in order to achieve and sustain economic growth. Traditionally, the United States has been very successful in using these factors.

In recent years, economists have begun to analyze both the benefits and costs of economic growth. The benefits include higher standards of living, social benefits such as higher employment, increased government revenues, and worldwide economic prestige. The costs include resource depletion, social costs such as urban overcrowding and hectic lifestyles, uneven growth in different regions of the country, and sacrificed consumption.

CHAPTER 15 REVIEW

For Answers to Chapter 15 Review, see p. A 65.

Reviewing Economic Terms

Supply the economic term that correctly completes each sentence.

1. The measurement of all new, final goods and services produced in a nation in one year is called the _____ _____ _____.
2. When the real per capita GNP increases, _____ _____ occurs.
3. The government's calculation of how much of a nation's capital goods are being used to produce goods is the _____ _____ _____.
4. A measurement of the well-being of individuals in a nation that most accurately reflects the resources people can use to satisfy needs and wants is the _____ _____ _____ _____.
5. The nation's personal income (PI) less personal taxes is its _____ _____.
6. Goods that businesses buy to produce other products are _____ _____.

Exercising Economic Skills

1. **Analyzing Economic Viewpoints** Review newspapers and newsmagazines to find an article stating an economic viewpoint. Read the article. **(a)** What is the main idea of the article? **(b)** What opinion does the author present? **(c)** What evidence does the author provide to support his or her viewpoint? **(d)** Evaluate the author's defense of his or her viewpoint. Prepare a report for class discussion.
2. **Understanding Mutual Funds** Study the feature on pages 530–531. Then suppose you are the manager of a mutual fund for investors and you have three clients of diverse backgrounds and different financial goals. The first client is a retired couple with a small amount of money to invest and whose financial goals are security and income. Your second client is a young college graduate with a good job whose goals are long-term economic growth. Your third client is a millionaire seeking short-term, high yield investments. Study the three chief kinds of mutual funds. In a paragraph, explain which of the mutual funds you would recommend for each of your clients.

Thinking Critically About Economics

1. **Summarizing Ideas** **(a)** Why are measures of economic growth and standards of living difficult to compare among nations? **(b)** Why is disposable income an important indicator of a nation's economic health, and of an individual's standard of living? **(c)** Explain how economic growth is inhibited by a scarcity of natural resources.
2. **Understanding Ideas** **(a)** What is the most significant measurement of economic well-being? **(b)** Why is it not always a reliable indicator?
3. **Comprehending Ideas** What are the social costs of economic growth, and why have they become so important?
4. **Interpreting Ideas** What is meant by the phrase "the cost of capital accumulation is reduced consumption"?
5. **Analyzing Ideas** Defend or refute this statement: The United States should allocate more resources to the technology necessary to eliminate acid rain.

Extending Economic Knowledge

1. Choose a product that is produced in your area. Report on the role that each of the factors of production plays in its production. Which factor of production do you think has the greatest influence in determining the price of the product? Why? Present your findings to the class.
2. Using line graphs, illustrate the changes in GNP, NNP, NI, and PI in the United States since World War II. (Information is available in the *Economic Report of the President* or *Statistical Abstract of the United States.*) In a paragraph, describe the similarities and differences among the trends shown by the statistics on the graphs.
3. Research the economy of a developing nation in Africa, South America, or Asia. (A developing nation has a per capita GNP of less than $500.) Prepare a report that identifies **(a)** which factors of production are missing or undeveloped, **(b)** how they can be supplied or developed, and **(c)** what can be done to improve the standard of living of the people.

Using Primary Sources

Lee Iacocca is a prominent American business leader. In his best-selling book *Iacocca: An Autobiography*, Iacocca supports the establishment of an industrial policy to promote economic growth in the United States. As you read the following excerpts, consider how Iacocca defines the term *industrial policy*. Why does Iacocca believe an industrial policy is important to the future of the United States economy?

From *Iacocca: An Autobiography*

These days, "industrial policy" is a loaded term. It's like yelling "fire!" in a crowded theater. A lot of people panic whenever they hear the phrase.

Don't they want America to be strong and healthy? Sure they do. But they want it to happen without any planning. They want America to be great *by accident*. . . .

As I see it, industrial policy means restructuring and revitalizing our so-called sunset industries—the older industries that are in trouble. Government must become more active in helping American industry meet the challenge of foreign competition and a changing world.

Almost everyone admires the Japanese, with their clear vision of the future; the cooperation among their government, banks, and labor; and the way they lead from their strengths. But whenever somebody suggests that *we* ought to follow their lead, the image suddenly shifts to the Soviets and their five-year plans. . . .

Is planning un-American? We do a great deal of planning at Chrysler. So does every other successful corporation. Football teams plan. Universities plan. Unions plan. Banks plan. Governments all over the world plan—except ours.

We're not going to make progress until we give up the ridiculous idea that any planning on a national level represents an attack on the capitalist system. Because of this fear, we're the only advanced country in the world without an industrial policy. . . .

Here's my six-point program that could form the basis for a new industrial policy.

First, we should provide for energy independence by 1990 by taxing foreign energy, both at the port and at the pump, in order to restore the conservation ethic and rekindle investments in alternative sources of energy. . . .

Second, we should provide for specific limits to Japan's market share for certain critical industries. . . . At this point in our history, we can't afford a trading partner who insists on the right to sell but who refuses to buy.

Third, as a nation, we've got to face reality on the costs and funding mechanisms for federal entitlement programs. . . . We can't continue to pay out more than we take in, and that will mean some very painful adjustments.

Fourth, America needs more engineers, scientists, and technicians. On a per capita basis, Japan graduates about four times as many engineers as we do. . . . Special education grants and loans should be provided for high-technology fields of study. . . .

Fifth, we need new incentives to increase research and development efforts in the private sector and to accelerate factory modernization and productivity in critical industries. . . .

Finally, we need to establish a long-term program for rebuilding America's arteries of commerce—our roadways, bridges, railroads, and water systems. . . .

. . . I am *not* proposing a welfare system for every company that gets into trouble. *We need a program that kicks in only when troubled American companies have agreed to equality of sacrifice among management, labor, suppliers, and financial backers.* It worked for Chrysler, and it can work for the rest of America.

Source Review

For Answers to Source Review, see p. A 66.

1. How does Lee Iacocca define industrial policy? Why does he believe the United States needs an industrial policy?
2. According to Iacocca, why is there resistance to an industrial policy in the United States? How might an industrial policy change the role of government in the economy?
3. List the six elements that Iacocca believes should form the basis of an industrial policy for the United States.
4. How might the six-point plan affect the goals of economic efficiency, economic equity, economic freedom, economic security, economic stability, and economic growth discussed in Chapter 1?

CHAPTER 16

See Chapter Overview, p. TM 84.
See Chapter Objectives, p. TM 84.
See Introducing the Chapter, p. TM 84.
See Extending Economic Knowledge on text p. 378.

The Nation's Fiscal Policy

Next, let us turn to the problems of our fiscal policy. Here the myths are legion and the truth hard to find.

John F. Kennedy

1 The government uses fiscal policy to promote economic growth and stability.

- Keynesian Theory and Fiscal Policy
- Discretionary Fiscal Policy
- Nondiscretionary Fiscal Policy
- Fiscal Policy and the Business Cycle
- The Multiplier Effect

2 The use of fiscal policy in the United States economy has certain limitations.

- Timing Problems
- Political Constraints
- Unpredictable Economic Behaviors
- Lack of Coordination

3 Supply-side economics is an alternative to demand-management economics.

- Supply-Side Economics
- Supply-Side Policies
- The Laffer Curve
- Limitations of Supply-Side Economics

CHAPTER 16 STUDY GUIDE

Chapter Focus

Chapter 16 presents fiscal policy. The chapter begins with a discussion of demand-side, or demand management, economics and explains how fiscal policy lessens the fluctuations of the business cycle. The chapter concludes with an analysis of supply-side economics.

As you study the chapter, look for the details that support each of the following statements.

1. The government uses fiscal policy to promote economic growth and stability.
2. The use of fiscal policy in the United States economy has certain limitations.
3. Supply-side economics is an alternative to demand-management economics.

See Preteaching Vocabulary, p. TM 84.

Terms to Know

The following terms, while not the only terms emphasized in this chapter, are basic to your understanding of fiscal policy. Determine the meaning of each term, either by using the Glossary or by watching for context clues as you read the chapter.

fiscal policy
demand-side economics
discretionary fiscal policy
tax incentive
investment tax credit
nondiscretionary fiscal policy
automatic stabilizer
public transfer payment
multiplier effect
supply-side economics
Say's Law
Reaganomics

See Key Study Questions and Key Understandings, p. TM 85.

1 The government uses fiscal policy to promote economic growth and stability.

See Suggested Teaching Strategies, p. TM 85.

The federal government's use of taxes, government spending, and transfer payments to promote economic growth and stability is **fiscal policy.** The major tools of fiscal policy include taxation, tax incentives, and government spending. In addition, automatic stabilizers built into the federal tax system and spending programs are a part of fiscal policy. Like monetary policy, fiscal policy regulates aggregate demand.

Keynesian Theory and Fiscal Policy

Economic upturns and downturns are a normal part of the business cycle in a market economy. Before the Great Depression of the 1930s, economists generally agreed that business fluctuations should be allowed to run their normal course in the marketplace without government interference. During periods of recession and high unemployment in the past, for example, laborers were expected to work for lower wages. Economists viewed high unemployment as a signal from the marketplace that wages were too high. Economists argued that as wages dropped, employers would hire more workers, leading to full employment.

Keynesian Theory. During the Great Depression, economists began to question this traditional theory of full employment. In 1936, John Maynard Keynes published his monumental work, *The General Theory of Employment, Interest, and Money.* With this book, he presented a theory that revolutionized economic thinking on the subject of economic stabilization in capitalist economies.

In *The General Theory,* Keynes stated that changes in aggregate demand cause fluctuations in the business cycle. He argued that when aggregate demand decreases, businesses produce fewer goods and lay off workers, causing a contraction in the business cycle and a slowdown in growth of the Gross National Product (GNP). When aggregate demand increases, on the other hand, he argued that businesses produce more goods and hire additional workers, causing an expansion and a speedup in the business cycle and speeding the growth of the GNP.

Keynes developed the model for calculating GNP to explain the relationship between the GNP and aggregate demand. This model states that the GNP equals the total market value of all consumer goods (C), investment goods (I), government goods (G), and net exports (F) produced in a one-year period. This model can be represented mathematically as $GNP = C + I + G + F$.

Keynes reasoned that marketplace forces alone are not enough to increase aggregate demand during economic downturns. Instead, he argued that active government involvement was necessary to combat unemployment and sluggish business activity. Many economists during the 1930s accepted Keynes's theories. In time, these economists became known as ◆ **Keynesian economists.**

The Keynesians favor the use of fiscal policy to regulate aggregate demand in the economy. Thus, the Keynesians advocate **demand-side economics,** or **demand-management economics.**

Keynesian Theories in Action. The use of fiscal policy and monetary policy was given a boost when Congress passed the Employment Act of 1946. One key provision of the Employment Act was a pledge to promote "maximum employment, production, and purchasing power" in the United States economy. In effect, this historic legislation defined economic growth and stability as responsibilities of the federal government. Thus, the Keynesians in the United States had both the theoretical and the legal justification to use fiscal policy to fight recessions, unemployment, and inflation.

The Keynesians have influenced government policies on taxation and federal spending in every administration since the 1930s. The two types of fiscal policy that have evolved since this time are discretionary fiscal policy and nondiscretionary fiscal policy. Each is used to influence the level of aggregate demand to combat unemployment and inflation.

Discretionary Fiscal Policy

Congressional actions that change taxes and government spending in response to economic instability in the economy are referred to as **discretionary fiscal policy.** When unemployment is high, the government uses discretionary fiscal policy to increase aggregate demand and create more jobs. When inflation is high, discretionary fiscal policy works to decrease aggregate demand and slow increases in prices.

The theories of British economist John Maynard Keynes (1883–1946) have had a major influence on the fiscal policies of most Western nations.

Taxation. Congress often uses taxation to regulate aggregate demand in the private sector. To reduce unemployment, Congress decreases taxes, a move that increases people's disposable incomes and allows firms to retain more of their profits. Additional money in the private sector means more total spending, or higher aggregate demand.

To reduce inflation, Congress increases taxes. Higher taxes decrease individual disposable incomes and corporate profits. Higher taxes slow business activity and reduce the chances of "too much money chasing too few goods," the major cause of demand-pull inflation.

Tax Incentives. The second tool of discretionary fiscal policy is tax incentives. **Tax incentives** are

◆ Report topic: Why many economists accepted Keynesian theories in the 1930s.

special tax breaks that the government extends to businesses to encourage investment in new capital.

One major tax incentive is the **investment tax credit.** The investment tax credit permits firms to deduct from their corporate income taxes a percentage of the money they spend on new capital. To reduce unemployment, Congress raises the investment tax credit, encouraging businesses to spend more money on expansion and thereby increase aggregate demand. To reduce inflation, Congress decreases the investment tax credit to restrict business activity and lower aggregate demand.

Suppose Congress sets the investment tax credit at 40 percent in a given year and that Miller Engineering invests $1 million in new capital. Under these conditions, Miller Engineering is able to deduct $400,000 from its income taxes ($0.40 \times \$1{,}000{,}000 = \$400{,}000$). Thus, the real cost of the new capital is only $600,000 because of the $400,000 in tax savings ($\$1{,}000{,}000 - \$400{,}000 = \$600{,}000$). Conversely, if the investment tax credit is 10 percent, a $1 million investment in new capital results in just $100,000 in tax deductions ($0.10 \times \$1{,}000{,}000 = \$100{,}000$). A lower investment tax credit is a disincentive to business investment.

Government Spending. The third tool of discretionary fiscal policy is government spending. To reduce inflation, Congress decreases government spending, resulting in lower aggregate demand and slower business activity.

To reduce unemployment, on the other hand, Congress increases government spending for government goods. Higher spending on education, national defense, and the nation's infrastructure increases aggregate demand and employment opportunities in the private sector.

In addition, government spending on public works programs reduces unemployment directly, while stimulating total spending in the economy. The public works programs of the 1930s, such as the Civilian Conservation Corps (CCC), Public Works Administration (PWA), and the Works Progress Administration (WPA) are examples of the government increasing spending to decrease unemployment.

At the peak of its activity in 1936, more than 4 million people were working for the Works Progress Administration (WPA). Between 1935 and 1943, the WPA spent more than $11 billion on construction projects.

◆ In general, liberal politicians oppose cuts in government spending that will affect social programs, while conservatives oppose cuts in defense spending.

Nondiscretionary Fiscal Policy

Nondiscretionary fiscal policy is automatically activated by certain built-in features of the federal tax and spending programs known as **automatic stabilizers**. These stabilizers are considered automatic because they provide a constant injection of money into the economy. This money helps maintain a certain level of aggregate demand during upturns and downturns in the business cycle. Economists identify two major types of automatic stabilizers: public transfer payments and the progressive income tax.

Public Transfer Payments. Tax dollars are redistributed to nonproductive sectors of the economy through **public transfer payments.** The term nonproductive in this context means that no goods or services are created in exchange for these government payments. Today, these payments form a safety net of social programs for the people in the United States.

◆ One important type of public transfer payment is unemployment compensation. During periods of recession and high unemployment, state governments automatically increase payments to the temporarily unemployed, thus stabilizing aggregate demand. As the unemployment rate drops, state governments are able to reduce the amount of money they pump into the economy.

Many federal public transfer payments also stabilize aggregate demand. Social security payments and veteran's benefits provide income to the elderly and the disabled. Welfare programs such as Aid to Families with Dependent Children (AFDC), the food stamp program, and nutrition programs provide help to the poor. Likewise, health insurance through Medicare and Medicaid injects billions of dollars into the economy each year.

Progressive Income Taxes. The second type of automatic stabilizer is the progressive income tax. The personal income tax and corporate income tax are both progressive taxes in that higher incomes are taxed at higher rates. During periods of prosperity, the higher incomes of individuals and firms place them in higher tax brackets. By being placed in a higher tax bracket, individuals are paying a higher percentage of their incomes in taxes. Higher taxes mean that individuals' disposable incomes, their income after taxes, do not increase by the same percentage as their incomes. By lessening the increase in disposable incomes, the higher tax rates lessen the increase in aggregate demand that rapidly rising incomes might cause and further reduce the possibilities of high inflation.

During recessions and depressions, on the other hand, incomes tend to fall. Many individuals and firms are taxed at lower rates because they are in lower tax brackets. The lower tax rates lessen the possibility of a disastrous drop in aggregate demand.

Using Fiscal Policy to Smooth Out the Business Cycle

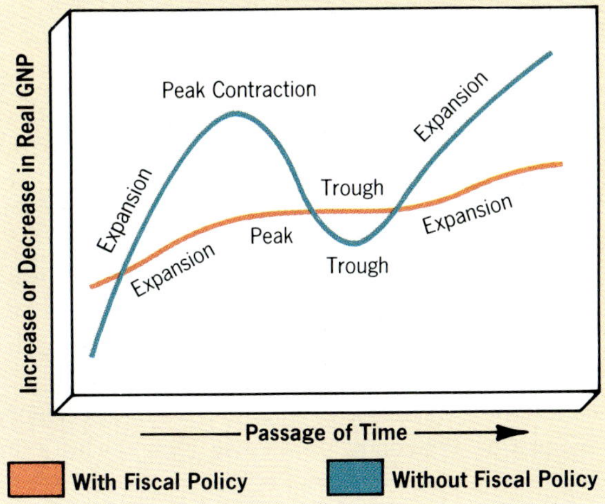

Fiscal Policy and the Business Cycle

The graph on this page illustrates the impact of fiscal policy on the business cycle. The blue line represents the business cycle when it operates independently of fiscal policy. The red line represents the business cycle when it is regulated by fiscal policies.

The unregulated business cycle has sharper fluctuations than the regulated business cycle. During periods of unregulated expansion, the optimism of the people snowballs, or multiplies rapidly. A high-rising optimism causes rapid increases in private sector spending, resulting in a corresponding increase in aggregate demand. On the other hand, during periods of unregulated contraction, pessimistic attitudes snowball, allowing aggregate demand to fall just as rapidly as it rose.

◆ Have the students read "Buying Insurance Policies" on pages 531–532 of the *Everyday Economics Handbook* and answer the questions that follow.

■ Economics Reporter

What Is the Council of Economic Advisers?

The role of professional economists in public decision making before World War II was small. After World War II, a provision of the Employment Act of 1946 established the Council of Economic Advisers. The major function of this council was "to develop and recommend to the President national economic policies." The impact of the Council of Economic Advisers on national policies through the years has varied. For example, the council had little direct influence on the policies of President Truman or President Eisenhower. Yet, during the 1960s, the council was an effective advocate for the tax cut of 1964 and for the tax surcharge of 1968. Since the 1960s, the Council of Economic Advisers has helped stabilize the nation's fiscal policies.

Economists explain the snowballing of economic activity by examining the multiplier effect. One of the major goals of fiscal policy is to regulate the snowballing that the multiplier effect causes.

The Multiplier Effect

The **multiplier effect** explains how small changes in income ripple through the economy and eventually cause a much larger change in spending. The multiplier effect takes spending habits into account. The multiplier effect is activated as soon as people receive new income. They spend a fraction of it and save a fraction of it. Economists call the fraction that is spent the **marginal propensity to consume** (MPC). The fraction saved is the **marginal propensity to save** (MPS). As the MPC increases, the total income of the nation increases because a larger portion of people's new income is spent and respent in the economy. As the MPC declines, total income in the nation declines because less money is in circulation.

To illustrate the impact of the MPC and MPS on the nation's total income, suppose workers in the United States receive $10 billion in tax cuts in a given year. Also assume that the MPC is 90 percent and the MPS is 10 percent.

According to the multiplier effect, the initial tax cut of $10 billion ripples through the economy. Workers who receive the $10 billion spend $9 billion ($0.90 \times$ \$10 billion = \$9 billion), and save $1 billion ($0.10 \times$ \$10 billion = \$1 billion). Individuals and firms that receive the $9 billion, in turn, spend $8.1 billion, and save $900 million. At this point, total spending has increased $17.1 billion. The workers have spent $9 billion and the individuals and firms that received this money have spent $8.1 billion ($9 billion + $8.1 billion = $17.1 billion).

The multiplier effect does not stop at this point, however. Instead, when the individuals and firms spend the $8.1 billion, those receiving the money spend $7.29 billion and save $810 million, further increasing total spending. Economists use the formula $1 \div 1 - \text{MPC} = \text{Multiplier}$ to calculate the multiplier effect. In our example, the formula would be $1 \div 1 - 0.90 = 1 \div 0.1 = 10$. To calculate the effect of a tax cut on total spending, economists multiply the initial tax cut by the multiplier. In this example, by the time the initial injection of $10 billion has rippled through the economy, it has generated $100 billion in new spending (\$10 billion $\times$ 10 = \$100 billion).

In contrast, if the MPC were only 0.5, the multiplier effect would be much lower. ($1 \div 1 - 0.50 = 1 \div 0.5 = 2$). In such a case a $10 billion tax cut would increase total spending by only $20 billion. Policymakers need to be aware of the multiplier effect when deciding how much to increase or decrease taxes or tax incentives.

The MPC tends to be high during periods of prosperity because people are optimistic about future business activity and are willing to spend a larger percentage of their additional incomes on goods and services. In prosperous times, therefore, small increases in income will trigger large increases in spending, contributing to demand-pull inflation in the economy.

During periods of sluggish business activity, on the other hand, the MPC is low because people are pessimistic and reluctant to spend new income. During recessions, policymakers must be aware that large increases in income are needed to produce enough spending to increase aggregate demand.

See Suggested Assignments, p. TM 85.

Section 1 Review

See Answers, p. A 66.

DEFINE fiscal policy, investment tax credit, automatic stabilizers, multiplier effect, marginal propensity to consume, marginal propensity to save

IDENTIFY Council of Economic Advisers

1. **Understanding Ideas** Is an investment tax credit an example of a discretionary or nondiscretionary type of fiscal policy?
2. **Interpreting Viewpoints** According to Keynes, what would be the effect on the business cycle if aggregate demand increased?
3. **Interpreting Ideas** If a nation's marginal propensity to consume is 80, and $10 million are injected into the economy, what is the resulting increase in total spending?
4. **Analyzing Ideas** If taxes were cut and federal spending increased, what would be the effect on aggregate demand?

See Key Study Questions and Key Understandings, p. TM 86.

2 The use of fiscal policy in the United States economy has certain limitations.

See Suggested Teaching Strategies, p. TM 86.

Although fiscal policy regulates aggregate demand in the economy, certain limitations exist. The four most important limitations include timing problems, political constraints, unpredictable economic behaviors in the private sector, and the lack of coordination among government policies.

Timing Problems

For fiscal policy to be effective, it must be administered in proper doses and at the proper time. Timing problems revolve around economic forecasting, problem identification, and spending inflexibility.

Forecasting Problems. Economic forecasting is an inexact science. Economists rely on economic indicators to predict future levels of business activity, but interpretations of this data often vary. The uncertainties about future economic problems often lead policymakers to take a "wait and see" position.

Identification Problems. Time lags occur between the time that the government identifies an economic problem and the time its stabilization policies have an impact on the economy. Time lags in developing and implementing fiscal policy affect its effectiveness in dealing with immediate and pressing economic problems.

Inflexibility Problems. One time lag results from the budgetary process in the United States. The current process, which outlines specific taxation and spending policies, takes more than a year to formulate and approve. The budgetary process begins with economic forecasting and other studies by the Office of Management and Budget, the Council of Economic Advisers, and other Presidential advisers. The process ends with formal Congressional approval of the federal budget. ◆

A second time lag involves the amount of time that tax or spending policies take to ripple through the economy once they are approved. For example, suppose the government injects $50 billion into the economy by reducing taxes and increasing government expenditures. The full effects of this injection will not be felt for another six months, perhaps

Text continues on page 368.

Economics Reporter

What Is the Office of Management and Budget?

The Office of Management and Budget (OMB) was established in 1970 to replace the old Bureau of the Budget. It is the largest department within the Executive Office of the President. The OMB, which is headed by a Director who reports to the President, serves four main functions. First, the OMB assists the President in preparing the budget submitted to Congress each year by reviewing budget requests from the various government agencies and making recommendations to the President. Second, the OMB supervises the administration of the budget. Third, the OMB reviews the structure and operation of the executive branch and recommends reforms for greater efficiency and effectiveness. Finally, the OMB clears and coordinates all proposed legislation coming from the various executive departments and agencies.

◆ If Congress does not approve the budget proposed by the President, the process of budget approval is more complex and may result in extensive time lags.

BUILDING ECONOMIC SKILLS

THINKING ABOUT ECONOMICS

Interpreting Statistics

You were introduced to the skill of reading statistical tables in Chapter 11, pages 256–257. Students of economics are often required to interpret the statistics included in tables and use the information as the basis for a generalization.

How to Interpret Statistics

To interpret statistics, follow these steps.

1. **Identify the type of data.** Note the chart's title, as well as all headings, subheadings, and labels.
2. **Examine the components.** Note the specific statistics given under each title or heading. Note the source of the statistics. Economic statistics are often found in reference books such as *Statistical Abstract of the United States, Statistical History of the United States, Economic Report of the President, Historical Statistics of the United States,* and various Census Bureau reports.
3. **Identify relationships among the data.** Note the features that are common to the data. Note trends. Determine similarities and differences as well as any cause-effect relationships among the data.

United States Gross National Product, 1940–1980

Year	Gross National Product*	Sectors of the Economy			
		Business	Households and Institutions	Government	Other
1940	100.0	89.4%	2.4%	7.8%	0.4%
1945	212.4	81.3%	1.9%	16.6%	0.2%
1950	286.4	89.9%	2.2%	7.3%	0.6%
1955	400.1	88.5%	2.3%	8.5%	0.7%
1960	506.5	87.3%	2.7%	9.3%	0.7%
1965	691.1	86.6%	2.8%	9.8%	0.8%
1970	992.7	84.3%	3.3%	11.7%	0.7%
1975	1,549.2	84.0%	3.3%	11.6%	1.1%
1980	2,631.7	84.7%	3.2%	10.4%	1.7%

*In billions

Source: *Statistical Abstract of the United States, 1986.*

4. **Read footnotes.** Remember to pay attention to asterisks or other symbols that refer to footnotes.

5. **Generalize from the data.** Make a general statement from the information. The generalization must be based on the facts, but cannot go beyond the facts at hand. You can begin formulating a generalization by looking for clue words or phrases in textbook content related to the content of the table. Clue words in content include most, least; many, few; often, rarely; usually, it is uncommon; and always, never.

Applying the Skill

Study the statistical table on page 366. The title indicates that the subject of the table is the United States GNP. The time period is 1940 to 1980. The chart is divided into sectors of the economy. One conclusion that you can draw from the statistics is that the business sector has consistently accounted for more than 80 percent of the GNP. Notice also that between 1940 and 1945, government expenditures jumped from 7.8 percent of the GNP to 16.6 percent. Recall that during these years the United States was embroiled in World War II. One interpretation that you can make from these statistics is that during wartime, government spending tends to contribute a greater percentage to the GNP.

Notice that government expenditures fell to 7.3 percent of the GNP in 1950, indicating that government tends to decrease its spending after a war. You may also use the statistics to generalize about the government's role in the GNP in the 1970s. You can calculate that government spending increased from $116 billion in 1970 to $273 billion in 1980. As a percentage of GNP, however, government spending fell from 11.7 percent in 1970 to 10.4 percent in 1980, indicating a de-emphasis of the government's role in the American economy.

Sources of Personal Income, 1945–1985

Year	Personal Gross Income*	Wages and Salaries	Other Income
1945	$ 172.4	$ 117.5	$ 54.9
1955	$ 319.3	$ 212.1	$ 107.2
1965	$ 565.3	$ 363.7	$ 201.6
1975	$1,363.7	$ 814.6	$ 549.1
1985	$3,443.3	$1,960.7	$1,482.6

*In billions
Source: Data adapted from *Economic Report of the President, 1986.*

Practicing the Skill See Answers, p. A 66.

Study the statistics on this page. Then on a separate sheet of paper answer these questions.

1. **(a)** What is the subject of the table? **(b)** What is the source of the table?

2. **(a)** What was the personal gross income (PI) in 1945? **(b)** What was the PI in 1985?

3. **(a)** In which 10-year period did the PI increase the most? **(b)** Since 1945, what has happened to other income as a percentage of the personal gross income?

4. Use 1945 and 1985 statistics to calculate the total increase in **(a)** personal gross income, **(b)** wages and salaries, and **(c)** other income.

5. **(a)** What generalization can you make about the growth in personal gross income? **(b)** its components?

DECISION MAKERS IN THE ECONOMY

Ray Rodriguez directs the Institute for Business and Industrial Training (IBIT), a job-training program in Colorado Springs, Colorado. IBIT operates on an annual budget of $2.8 to $3 million, part of which comes from the federal government's Job Training Partnership Act fund. The rest comes from private businesses. IBIT's purpose is to train or retrain workers for jobs that are available locally.

Rodriguez and his staff assess hiring trends in the area in order to determine the institute's basic approach. Just a few years ago, IBIT emphasized training for high-tech jobs because high-tech firms were moving into Colorado and providing many employment opportunities. Recently these jobs have become much less plentiful, and Rodriguez has had to look elsewhere for IBIT's training focus.

What Rodriguez now has IBIT emphasize are jobs in small businesses. To encourage startups in small businesses and to help newly formed small businesses, Rodriguez has his staff seek out well-established companies that have work to be performed by contract. The staff then finds or creates a small business to do the job. If the plan is to form a small business, IBIT determines which of its trainees have skills that match the requirements of the job. It then offers the trainees a chance to put their skills to use.

The IBIT-sponsored small business may set up shop in IBIT's headquarters. All the small businesses there share facilities and expenses and have access to entrepreneurial expertise. This type of arrangement typically is called a "business incubator."

Ray Rodriguez and IBIT are performing an important service for the economy of Colorado Springs by helping the community make better use of its human resources.

more, because it takes time for this money to be spent and respent in the economy.

A third type of timing problem involves government spending programs. For example, to fight recession the government may decide to inject money into the economy by rebuilding the nation's economic infrastructure or by increasing the national defense installations. These types of building projects take years to plan and implement. Thus, the additional spending will have little immediate effect on a stagnant economy. Further, the government's commitment to massive long-term spending programs may well extend into an expansion phase of the business cycle. Such an extension could result in inflation.

Political Constraints

Fiscal policy is more vulnerable to political pressures than monetary policy because fiscal policy is established by Congress and the President, the elected representatives of the people. These elected officials, unlike the Fed's Board of Governors, can be voted out of office if they make unpopular taxation and spending decisions. Thus, political as well as economic concerns affect the formulation of fiscal policy in a free enterprise economy.

Restrictive Fiscal Policy. Restrictive fiscal policy increases taxes and reduces government spending. Restrictive fiscal policy reduces inflation by reducing aggregate demand. Restrictive fiscal policy tends to be unpopular with the people. Higher taxes, for example, reduce wage earners' disposable incomes. Higher taxes also are a disincentive to work, save, invest, or increase the production of goods or services. Economists often refer to the negative side effects of restrictive fiscal policy as a "fiscal drag" on the economy.

In addition, lower government spending often means cutting specific programs. Elected representatives realize that the beneficiaries of dismantled programs are likely to remember unpopular economic decisions on election day.

Expansionary Fiscal Policy. Expansionary fiscal policy decreases taxes and increases government spending to stimulate business activity in the economy. Expansionary fiscal policy increases aggregate demand. Expansionary fiscal policy is often popular because people's disposable incomes rise as taxes fall.

Still, political constraints on expansionary fiscal policy exist. First, some people oppose a larger role for the government in the economy. Believing that the market, rather than the government, should ensure long-term growth and stability, these Americans oppose new government spending. Second, people have become more concerned about the massive budgetary deficits that resulted from lower taxes and higher government expenditures during the 1980s. Pressures for a balanced federal budget make policymakers more cost-conscious when spending tax dollars.

Unpredictable Economic Behaviors

When devising fiscal policies, policymakers rely on certain economic principles, or laws, that are based on logic and time-tested "truths" about economic behaviors. Policymakers have no guarantees, however, that the people will react traditionally to fiscal policies.

For example, the government institutes a tax cut of $50 billion to stimulate consumer spending during a serious recession. The policymakers expect the MPC to be 80 percent and the MPS to be 20 percent. Under these conditions, total income in the economy should rise by $250 billion as a result of this government injection of $50 billion ($5 \times \$50$ billion $= \$250$ billion).

Policymakers, however, overestimated the people's optimism about the economy. The people decided to spend only 50 percent and save 50 percent of their new incomes. The multiplier then is only 2, and the total income of the nation increases by just $100 billion ($2 \times \$50 = \$100$ billion).

In short, fiscal policy can increase people's ability to buy goods and services by increasing their disposable incomes. But fiscal policy cannot force people to actually spend their new incomes.

Lack of Coordination

A fourth limitation is that coordination among government agencies in the formulation of fiscal policies is often lacking. At the national level, fiscal policy needs to be coordinated with monetary policy to achieve agreed upon goals. For example, if inflation is the most important economic problem, monetary and fiscal policies should work to reduce aggregate demand. The Fed needs to institute a tight-money policy, while Congress and the President need to agree on a restrictive fiscal policy. If recession and unemployment are the primary concerns, an easy-money policy and an expansionary fiscal policy are needed.

In addition, it is important for tax and spending policies on the local and state levels to be coordinated with federal stabilization efforts. In many cases, such coordination is not present. For example, local and state governments tend to increase their expenditures for education and other services during periods of prosperity because tax revenues are high and credit is usually easy to obtain. High spending by local and state governments during prosperity tends to increase aggregate demand and fuel inflation. At the same time, the federal government may be following a restrictive fiscal policy to reduce inflation.

During recessions, local and state governments tend to cut spending, resulting in less aggregate demand. At the same time, the federal government's ◆ expansionary fiscal policy is pumping money into the economy. The coordination of state and local policies with those of the federal government, however, is an issue that needs delicate handling and voluntary compliance in order not to upset the constitutional mandates of federalism.

◆ **Have the students read "Urban and Regional Planners" on page 544 of *Careers in the Marketplace.***

The Influence of Government Policies on Unemployment and Inflation, 1960–1970

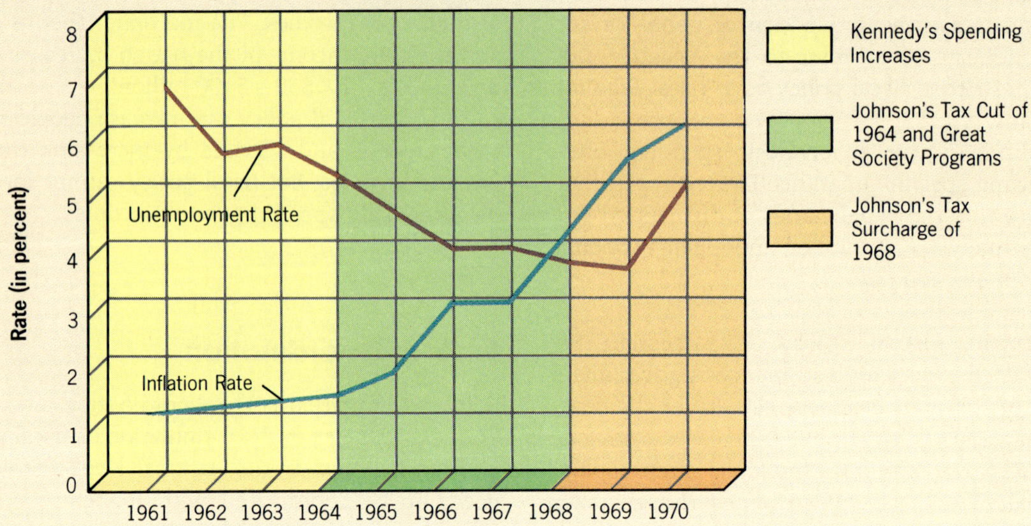

Source: *Economic Report of the President, 1986*

CASE STUDY

Keynesian Fiscal Policy During the Kennedy and Johnson Years

The election of President John F. Kennedy in 1960 was, in part, a response to his pledge to "get the country moving again." When Kennedy took office in 1961, unemployment stood at about 7 percent, a high percentage for the time. On the advice of his Council of Economic Advisers, many of whom were Keynesians, Kennedy aimed a two-pronged attack on unemployment.

First, during 1961 and 1962, he convinced Congress to increase federal spending to increase aggregate demand. Second, in 1963, he submitted a massive tax reduction bill to Congress. President Lyndon B. Johnson carried on the battle for massive tax cuts after Kennedy's assassination in November of 1963. By early 1964, Congress had approved a $10-billion tax reduction.

The economy responded to higher government spending and the massive tax cut much as the Keynesians had predicted. Aggregate demand increased. Also, the multiplier effect took hold as consumer spending and business investment snowballed. Economists estimate that the GNP increased by nearly $25 billion in 1965 alone because of the tax cut of 1964. Further, unemployment continued to drop, as the graph above shows.

During the mid- to late-1960s, inflationary pressures built up in the economy. One major cause of this inflationary pressure was high government spending on the Vietnam War and on President Johnson's Great Society programs.

Despite recommendations made by the Council of Economic Advisers to increase taxes, President Johnson resisted higher taxes until 1968. Johnson believed that asking for higher taxes in 1966 or 1967 might weaken the people's support for the Vietnam War or for his Great Society antipoverty legislation. In the meantime, inflation continued to rise during the late 1960s as the graph on this page shows.

In 1968, however, President Johnson was obliged to take action against inflation and reduce aggregate demand. First, he introduced a 10 percent tax surcharge, which was a temporary increase in personal and corporate income taxes. Second, Johnson cut some government spending programs. Third, he suspended the investment tax credit.

The time lag between the recognition of inflationary pressures in late 1965, and the introduction of the 1968 tax surcharge and other policies, reduced the effectiveness of fiscal policy. Inflation had already gained momentum. People's expectations of even higher inflation compelled them to "buy now." Further, the inflexibility of long-term government spending programs, especially for national defense and the expanded social programs, continued to increase aggregate demand.

The ineffectiveness of fiscal policy during the late 1960s damaged the credibility of the Keynesian economic stabilization model. It also contributed to the electoral defeat of the Democratic Party in the Presidential race of 1968.

See Suggested Assignments, p. TM 86.

Section 2 Review See Answers, p. A 67.

IDENTIFY Office of Management and Budget, Ray Rodriguez

1. **Summarizing Ideas** What are the four most significant limitations of fiscal policy in regulating aggregate demand?
2. **Interpreting Ideas** Explain the effects of a restrictive fiscal policy.
3. **Seeing Relationships** What behavior of consumers must be accurately predicted in order to accurately forecast the effect of a tax cut?
4. **Interpreting Graphics** Study the graph on page 370. How did **(a)** President Kennedy's spending increases and **(b)** President Johnson's Great Society program and tax cut affect unemployment and inflation?

See Key Study Questions and Key Understandings, p. TM 87.

3 Supply-side economics is an alternative to demand-management economics.

See Suggested Teaching Strategies, p. TM 87.

Demand-management stabilization policies are designed to fight inflation or recession, not both at the same time. During the 1970s, however, stagflation combined a stagnant economy with inflation. Economists and government policymakers were obliged to look for alternative stabilization models. Under these conditions the supply-side school of economic thought gained support during the late 1970s and 1980s.

Supply-Side Economics

Originated in western Europe during the 1700s, **supply-side economics** refers to government actions that provide incentives for producers to increase aggregate supply.

Some prominent economists, including Adam Smith, believed that high taxes and excessive regulations on businesses were obstacles to economic growth. The leading advocate of supply-side thought during its early years, however, was the French economist Jean-Baptiste Say (1767–1832). Say supported Adam Smith's thesis that self-interest motivates people to work, save, and invest; to produce; and to become entrepreneurs. Say was convinced that most types of government intervention in the economy were harmful to economic growth.

In addition to developing Say's Law, Jean-Baptiste Say was the first economist to divide the factors of production into land, labor, and capital.

The economic problems of the United States during the 1960s were complicated by social and political unrest.

President Ronald Reagan faced the problem of a growing federal deficit during his terms in office.

Say is best known as the author of **Say's Law.** Simply stated, this economic law declared that supply creates its own demand. Economic growth, therefore, rests on producers' willingness and ability to increase total production, or aggregate supply, in the overall economy.

Supply-side economics is aimed at promoting high employment and lowering inflation simultaneously. The supply-side model became an attractive alternative to fighting stagflation.

In contrast to demand-side economics, supply-side economics fights unemployment by providing incentives to firms to increase production. More production, in turn, means more jobs and lower unemployment. Supply-side economics fights inflation by increasing the aggregate supply of goods. As aggregate supply increases, the chance of "too much money chasing too few goods" is reduced (see the chart on page 373).

Supply-Side Policies

President Reagan used many of the ideas of the supply-side economists when formulating his economic policies during the 1980s. The three most important components of the President's supply-side policies included (1) tax cuts on personal and corporate incomes, (2) spending cuts on social programs, and (3) regulatory reform. Combined, these policies are sometimes called **Reaganomics.**

Tax Cuts. Supply-side economists favor tax cuts as an incentive for individuals and firms to invest. They argue that tax cuts increase individuals' disposable incomes and corporations' profits, and that some of this extra money will be invested. The long-range goal is to expand and modernize the nation's capital stock to increase the aggregate supply of goods and services. In contrast, the Keynesians use tax cuts to increase immediate consumption, or aggregate demand, in the economy.

The Economic Recovery Act of 1981 was the largest tax cut in the history of the United States. It reduced personal and corporate taxes by 25 percent over a three-year period. The Reagan administration supported this massive tax cut to stimulate investment and long-term economic growth. ◆

Two Opposing Views of Managing Fiscal Policy

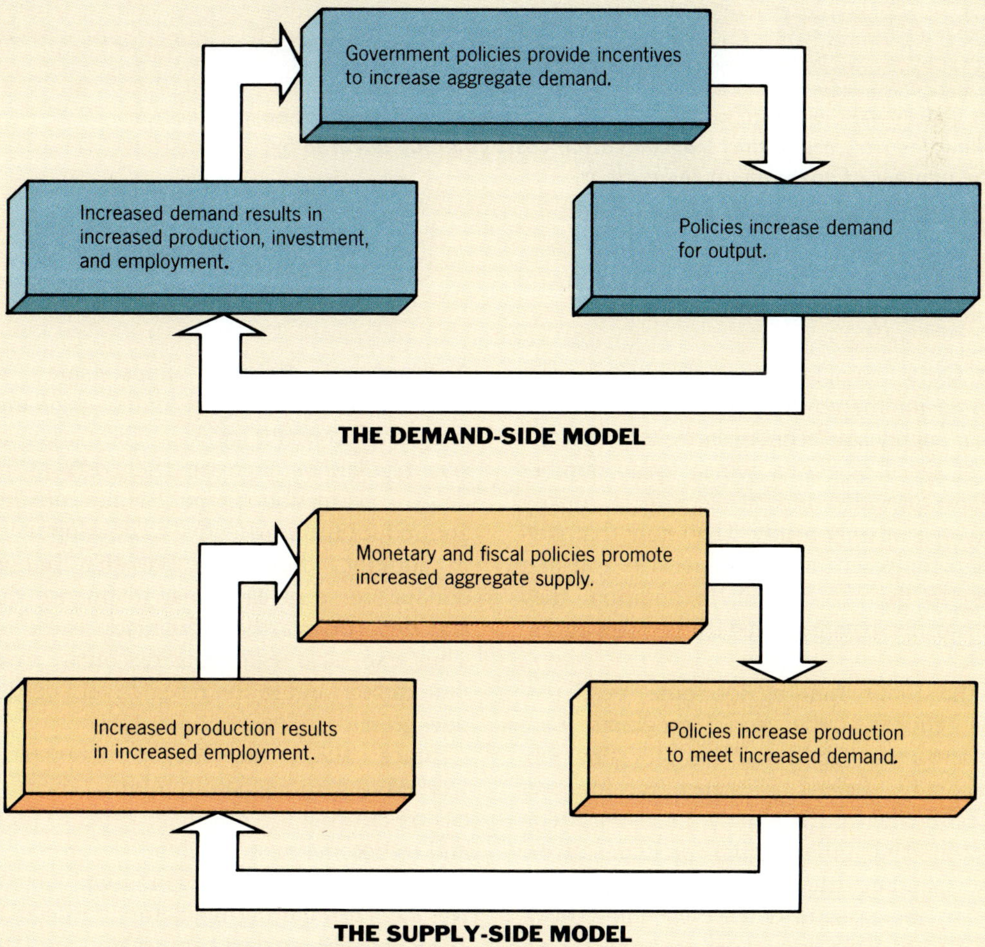

◆ The Economic Recovery Act of 1981 allowed each worker to open an Individual Retirement Account.

Adhering to government regulations is expensive. Proponents of deregulation of the trucking industry argue that transportation costs could be lowered by reducing the number of government regulations.

Spending Cuts. Supply-side economists support a reduced role for the government in the economy. In particular, supply-side economists believe that the safety net of social programs, which today number over 10, have provided income security to many people who are not truly needy. They note that government transfer payments are expensive and add significantly to the tax burden. In addition, they argue that transfer payments reduce people's incentive to work.

During the 1980s, funding for some social programs was reduced. Other social programs were eliminated altogether. Child-nutrition programs, job-training programs, federal assistance for low-cost housing, health care for the elderly under the Medicare program, and other social programs were among the spending cuts. These cuts were more than offset by increases in defense spending, however. From 1981 to 1986, annual expenditures for national defense nearly doubled from $168 billion to about $300 billion.

Regulatory Reform. Supply-side economists view many types of government regulations as obstacles to economic growth. They argue that excessive regulations increase the costs of production, delay construction on public and private projects, and reduce firms' incentive to develop new products. In addition, they point out that billions of tax dollars are spent each year to finance the agencies and departments that administer these regulations. Thus, excessive regulations discourage investment in new capital, and in the research and development of new goods.

Since 1981, the Reagan administration has ◆ worked toward regulatory reform. These reforms focus on creating incentives for firms to produce more and to become more efficient.

In 1981, President Reagan issued Executive Order No. 12291, requiring regulatory agencies to conduct a cost-benefit analysis for many proposed regulations. This analysis is then submitted to the Office of Management and Budget (OMB) for approval. The

◆ **Discussion topic: Statistics show that Presidents tend to concentrate on foreign policy during the first two years of their administration and domestic policy during the last two years of their administration. How does this pattern affect the economy at home and abroad?**

regulatory agency must prove that the benefits exceed the costs before the regulation is enacted.

Funding for many regulatory agencies was cut during the Reagan administration. The Consumer Product Safety Commission, the Federal Trade Commission, the Environmental Protection Agency, as well as other agencies, operated with reduced budgets.

The Reagan administration continued the deregulation of many industries that began in the late 1970s. Included in the industries that have experienced further deregulation are trucking, airline, telecommunications, and banking. Supply-side economists argue that competitive industries are more efficient than noncompetitive ones.

The Laffer Curve

Much of the economic theory that supports supply-side economics is embodied in the Laffer Curve. The **Laffer Curve,** which was developed by Arthur B. Laffer, illustrates how tax cuts affect tax revenues and economic growth. The graph on this page shows the Laffer Curve.

At either extreme of the Laffer Curve, government revenues are zero. A zero-percent tax rate generates no revenue because there are no taxes. When the tax rate is 100 percent, the government collects no revenue because individuals and firms would refuse to work or produce if the government took their total output. The government, therefore, must find a tax rate between these two extremes. This tax rate should maximize government revenues, while not discouraging work, investment, or production.

According to the Laffer Curve, two tax rates will generate the same amount of tax revenue. For example, the revenue that the government collects at point **A** is the same as that which it collects at point **E.** The low tax rate at point **A,** however, is an incentive to work, invest, or produce. At point **E,** however, the tax rate is higher. Thus the higher tax rate is a disincentive to work, invest, or produce.

Supply-side economists use the Laffer Curve to illustrate the Laffer effect. The **Laffer effect** states that tax cuts can increase the government's tax revenues because at lower tax rates, individuals and firms have a greater incentive to work, invest, and

Economics Reporter

Who Is Arthur B. Laffer?

Arthur B. Laffer, known as the "guru of the tax revolt," is the leading proponent of supply-side economics. The basis of Laffer's supply-side theory is that higher taxes slow productivity by decreasing profits and thereby remove the incentive to invest and produce. Lower taxes, on the other hand, stimulate productivity and eventually result in more revenue for the government. Laffer devised his famous Laffer Curve to make this theory more understandable to the public.

The story is told that Laffer first drew the curve on a dinner napkin in a restaurant while attempting to explain the theory. Laffer, who has become a bit of a celebrity because of the Laffer Curve, is often asked to draw his curve on a napkin and to autograph the drawing. In addition to his university teaching, Laffer does consulting work for various types of businesses, the government, and political candidates.

The Basis of Supply-Side Economics

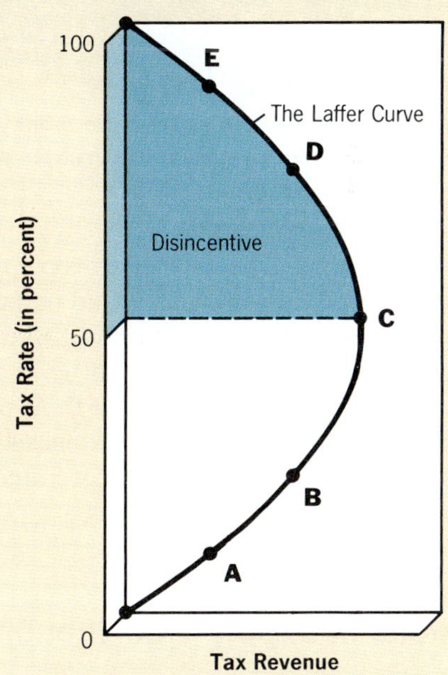

Supply-side economists believe that the money saved through tax cuts will spur new technological research and greater production.

produce. The government then collects more revenue because it is taxing higher incomes and outputs. For example, a tax cut at point **E** on the Laffer Curve results in higher tax revenues at point **D.** A further tax cut increases tax revenues at point **C.** At point **C,** individuals and firms have sufficient incentives to work and produce. In addition, the government collects the highest possible tax revenues.

Limitations of Supply-Side Economics

Just as limitations to the demand-management approaches to growth and stability exist, marketplace realities limit the effectiveness of supply-side economics. Critics of the supply-side model often question five major assumptions of supply-side theory.

The first assumption of supply-side economics is that economists can identify where the economy is placed on the Laffer Curve. Policymakers assumed that tax rates in the early 1980s were too high when they approved the Economic Recovery Act of 1981. Critics argue that economists have no foolproof way of recognizing precisely where on the Laffer Curve the economy is.

A second assumption of supply-side economics is that economists can predict the economic behaviors of people. Critics point out the limitations of this assumption. For example, supply-side economists assumed that individuals and firms would invest the money gained through tax cuts during the early 1980s. Many people chose, however, to spend the money gained through the tax cuts, increasing aggregate demand and contributing to higher inflation.

A third assumption of supply-side economics is that people will view supply-side policies as equitable, or "fair." Critics of the 1981 tax cuts argue that the wealthy benefited more from this legislation than the poor. Critics point out that the tax cuts reduced taxes at a fixed percentage, rather than by the person's ability to pay. They further point out that the spending cuts fell most heavily on social programs for the poor, the unemployed, and other traditionally disadvantaged groups.

A fourth assumption of supply-side economics is that new tax revenues resulting from the Laffer effect would be sufficient to balance the federal budget. By the mid-1980s, however, the annual federal deficits were topping $200 billion. In addition, between 1981 and 1986 the national debt doubled from $1 trillion to $2 trillion. Critics point to these facts to refute the assumption.

A fifth assumption of supply-side economics is that the "costs" of operating many regulatory agencies and commissions outweigh the "benefits" received through the regulations they were created to enforce. Supply-side policies cut the budgets for many of these agencies. Some economists believe that the supply-side regulatory reform has gone too far, however. These critics fear that the regulatory reforms of supply-side economics have weakened many "benefits," such as promoting a clean environment, product safety, and fair competition.

Critics point to the difficulty of determining the effects of government policies on the performance of the economy because many factors contribute to growth and stability. They say it is a mistake to "blame" the high inflation rate of the early 1980s solely on the 1981 tax cut. They point to people's inflationary expectations and the second OPEC price shock as contributory "fuels" for the fires of inflation. They also say that crediting supply-side theory for the low inflation of the mid-1980s is an error. They argue that other factors, such as the worldwide oil glut, also contributed to the disinflation of the period.

See Suggested Assignments, p. TM 87.

Section 3 Review See Answers, p. A 67.

DEFINE supply-side economics, Say's Law

IDENTIFY Arthur B. Laffer

1. **Summarizing Ideas** What were the three main components of President Reagan's supply-side policies in the early 1980s?
2. **Interpreting Viewpoints** How do supply-side proponents view the effects of government regulation on economic growth?
3. **Interpreting Graphics** Study the graph on page 375. What relationship does the Laffer Curve illustrate?

CHAPTER 16 SUMMARY

The federal government uses fiscal policy, based upon the theories of John Maynard Keynes, to regulate aggregate demand and promote economic growth and stability in the economy. Taxation, tax incentives, and government spending are types of discretionary fiscal policy. Automatic stabilizers such as public transfer payments and the progressive income tax are considered nondiscretionary fiscal policy. When deciding how to implement fiscal policy, policymakers must consider the multiplier effect.

Despite its advantages, fiscal policy has several limitations. Timing problems often occur because it takes time to implement policy. Political constraints arise because elected officials make fiscal policy. These officials are often reluctant to initiate unpopular policies. Policies sometimes achieve undesirable effects because economic behavior is often unpredictable. Finally, agencies within the federal government fail to coordinate federal fiscal policies. In addition, state and local governments often have fiscal policies that differ from federal fiscal policies.

In recent years, a school of economic thought called supply-side economics has influenced public economic policy. Supply-side economics concentrates on providing incentives to increase the nation's total output, or aggregate supply. Just as in demand-side economics, certain factors limit the effectiveness of supply-side economics.

CHAPTER 16 REVIEW

For Answers to Chapter 16 Review, see p. A 67.

Reviewing Economic Terms

With each definition or description below, match one of the following terms.

a. fiscal policy
b. public transfer payment
c. demand-side economics
d. automatic stabilizers
e. multiplier effect
f. supply-side economics
g. Say's Law

_____ **1.** Policies that stimulate economic growth by increasing aggregate demand.
_____ **2.** Term that explains the results of an injection of money into the economy that creates an even larger increase in aggregate demand.
_____ **3.** Policies that stimulate the production of goods and services.
_____ **4.** Government spending and tax programs.
_____ **5.** Policies that stimulate aggregate demand during an economic downturn.
_____ **6.** Redistribution of tax dollars to nonproductive sectors of the economy.

Exercising Economic Skills

1. **Interpreting Statistics** Using the *Statistical Abstract of the United States, Statistical History of the United States,* or the *Economic Report of the President,* select a table that provides economic information. **(a)** From which source did you select the table? **(b)** What is the subject of the table? **(c)** What generalization can you make about the data shown on the table?
2. **Buying Insurance Policies** Study the feature on pages 531–532. Then suppose you have purchased a new compact automobile for $8,000 and are shopping for an insurance policy that carries the lowest coverages allowed in your state. **(a)** Call at least three insurance companies to learn the costs of a policy for your new car. Be sure to give the agents your age, sex, and other pertinent information. **(b)** Prepare a chart illustrating the differences in costs. Make sure that you find out the terms of each policy so you are certain that you are comparing the costs of similar policies with similar coverages.

Thinking Critically About Economics

1. **Seeing Relationships** According to Arthur Laffer's theory, what is the relationship between tax rates and the incentive to produce?
2. **Interpreting Viewpoints** According to John Maynard Keynes, how would stimulating aggregate demand reverse a downturn in the business cycle?
3. **Interpreting Ideas** How does the progressive income tax act as an automatic stabilizer in a period of high wage inflation?
4. **Analyzing Ideas** How can business regulation be a disincentive for investment?
5. **Analyzing Viewpoints** Considering the Laffer effect, how might a tax cut actually increase total tax revenues?

Extending Economic Knowledge

1. Survey parents, teachers, and other adults to determine their marginal propensities to consume and save. Ask: If you received an additional $50 a week in income, what percentage of that additional income would you save and what percentage would you spend? Determine an average marginal propensity to save and an average marginal propensity to consume for the people in your survey. **(a)** What is the multiplier? **(b)** Assuming that your sample population is representative of the adult population of the United States, what would be the total increase in aggregate demand in the economy if 50 million adults received $2,500 in additional income this year?
2. Research at least three of the New Deal programs devised to counter the Great Depression. **(a)** How were these expansionary fiscal policy programs intended to stimulate the economy? **(b)** In your opinion, did they work? Defend your answer.
3. Study the provisions of the Tax Reform Act of 1986 that pertain to business investment and production. Then in an essay, answer this question: Does the overall effect of the act encourage or discourage economic growth? Defend your answer.

Using Primary Sources

John Maynard Keynes (1883–1946) was an English economist. In his monumental work, *The General Theory of Employment Interest and Money* (1936), Keynes supported a strong role for government in stabilizing the economy. At the same time, Keynes reaffirmed his support for many of the economic freedoms that exist under capitalism. As you read the following excerpts, think about how Keynes viewed government intervention in the economy. Why did he continue to support the free enterprise system?

Steps Toward Full Employment

. . . I see no reason to suppose that the existing system seriously misemploys the factors of production which are in use. . . . When 9,000,000 men are employed out of 10,000,000 willing and able to work, there is no evidence that the labour of these 9,000,000 men is misdirected. The complaint against the present system is not that these 9,000,000 men ought to be employed on different tasks, but that tasks should be available for the remaining 1,000,000 men. It is in determining the volume, not the direction, of actual employment that the existing system has broken down.

The central controls necessary to ensure full employment will, of course, involve a large extension of the traditional functions of government. Furthermore, . . . the free play of economic forces may need to be curbed or guided. But there will still remain a wide field for the exercise of private initiative and responsibility. Within this field the traditional advantages of individualism will still hold good.

Let us stop for a moment to remind ourselves what these advantages are. They are partly advantages of efficiency—the advantages of decentralisation and of the play of self-interest. The advantage to efficiency of the decentralisation of decisions and of individual responsibility is even greater, perhaps, than the nineteenth century supposed; and the reaction against the appeal to self-interest may have gone too far. But, above all, individualism, if it can be purged of its defects and abuses, is the best safeguard of personal liberty in the sense that, compared with any other system, it greatly widens the field for the exercise of personal choice. It is also the best safeguard of the variety of life, which emerges precisely from this extended field of personal choice, and the loss of which is the greatest of all the losses of the homogeneous totalitarian state. For this variety preserves the traditions which embody the most secure and successful choices of former generations; it colours the present with the diversification of its fancy; and, being the handmaid of experiment as well as of tradition and of fancy, it is the most powerful instrument to better the future. . . .

The authoritarian state systems of today [Keynes wrote in 1936] seem to solve the problem of unemployment at the expense of efficiency and freedom. It is certain that the world will not much longer tolerate the unemployment which, apart from brief intervals of excitement, is associated—and, in my opinion, inevitably associated—with present-day capitalistic individualism. But it may be possible by a right analysis of the problem to cure the disease whilst preserving efficiency and freedom.

Source Review

For Answers to Source Review, see p. A 68.

1. According to John Maynard Keynes, how can the government affect consumption? What is the complaint about the present system?
2. What in Keynes's view will ensure full employment?
3. How does Keynes view "individualism"?

UNIT FIVE REVIEW

For Answers to Unit 5 Review, see p. A 68.

Reviewing Economic Ideas

1. What rate of employment is considered to be full employment? Why?
2. What are the four phases of a business cycle?
3. **(a)** What does the Gross National Product (GNP) measure? **(b)** What are the four spending components of the Gross National Product (GNP)?
4. Why are transfer payments not considered to be a part of the Gross National Product (GNP)?
5. What category of the factors of production would include water and air?
6. If the marginal propensity to consume is 90, what is the multiplier used to determine the aggregate effect of an infusion of money into the economy?
7. Would a proponent of a supply-side economic policy be in favor of more or less regulation of business?
8. What is the Laffer Curve?

Connecting Economic Ideas

1. **Using Economic Imagination** If the federal government identified an inadequate level of capital investment as a problem of economic growth, what fiscal policy tool could it use to attack the problem?
2. **Evaluating Ideas** **(a)** What might be the social costs of a policy aimed at decreasing the rate of inflation? **(b)** Why might this policy be chosen despite the cost?
3. **Analyzing Ideas** Why are fiscal policy actions often inadequate to cope with the problem of cyclical unemployment?
4. **Seeing Relationships** How do President Reagan's regulatory reform policies give encouragement to entrepreneurship?
5. **Interpreting Ideas** How can a supply-side policy that promotes production be a stimulant to aggregate demand?
6. **Comparing Ideas** What are the similarities and differences between Keynesian theories of demand-management and the supply-side theory of economic growth? Is the goal the same? Are the assumptions about behavior similar?

Investigating Economic Issues

1. **Understanding Ideas** **(a)** What are the two segments of the underground economy? **(b)** What is included in each segment? **(c)** What effect has the underground economy had on taxation? **(d)** on economic growth?
2. **Summarizing Ideas** **(a)** What method does the IRS most often use to catch tax evaders? **(b)** Why does the IRS feel that this method is successful? **(c)** What is a general tax amnesty? **(d)** Why might amnesty be more successful than other approaches to tax evasion?

Applying Economics

1. **(a)** List examples of government activities in your community that contribute to economic growth. **(b)** Which of these activities could be done without government funds by the private sector? **(c)** Why do you think that the government has become involved in these activities? **(d)** In an attempt to decrease government spending, which activities would you recommend the government turn over to private enterprise? Present your answers to the class.
2. Construct charts illustrating the levels of Gross National Product (in constant dollars), inflation, and unemployment in the United States from 1960 to the present and answer these questions. **(a)** How is the growth or change in the three measurements similar or different over this period? **(b)** What explanation can you give for periods in which there seem to be similar changes in the levels?
3. Research the major changes in federal tax laws since World War II. **(a)** Which tax provisions have been aimed at stimulating the economy? **(b)** Which provisions have been aimed at slowing down economic activity? **(c)** Which policy changes have been aimed specifically at business? **(d)** Which changes have been aimed at influencing consumer behavior? **(e)** Would you consider the majority of the nation's efforts to stimulate the economy "Keynesian" or "supply-side" policies? Why? Present your findings to the class.

Using Primary Sources

The underground economies in capitalist, socialist, and Communist nations have expanded in recent years. As you read the following report from *Business Week* magazine, consider why these underground economies have developed. What are the costs and benefits of the underground economies to a nation?

The Underground Economy: An International Phenomenon

In Britain, it's called the black economy; in Germany, the *Schattenwirtschaft*, or shadow economy; in the Soviet Union, the second economy; in South Africa, the unrecorded sector; in Israel, the *kalkala schora;* and in Italy, the *economia sommersa*, or submerged economy. But whatever its name, the underground economy overseas is even bigger than in the U.S.

Italy's subterranean economy amounts to at least 25% of that country's GNP, say economists. And it has become such an integral part of production that Italy's above-ground economy would have a hard time without it. Entire industries have grown up outside Italy's recorded economy. Naples is one of Italy's biggest glove-making centers, but until recently, you would not have known it from official statistics. There was no record that a single pair was made there. Throughout Italy, small groups of workers manufacture items from shoes to industrial components in kitchens and garages.

Under Italian law, companies with fewer than 15 employees are virtually unregulated, so many companies have been splitting into smaller units. And it is in these smaller units that the underground economy flourishes and that productivity runs high. "In the morning I do the work my job imposes on me," says an engineer who moonlights in the submerged economy. "In the afternoon I do the work I like, using all the imagination I have at my disposal."

A mystery in cement. Germany's *Schattenwirtschaft* is far less visible than Italy's. But, spurred by rising taxes, it now represents about 10% of the GNP. Economists suspect

(Text of article continues on page 591.)

Source Review

For Answers to Source Review, see p. A 69.

1. Why do underground economies exist?
2. What are some of the "costs" of the underground economies mentioned in the reading? How do these costs compare to those that exist in the United States?
3. What are some of the "benefits" of the underground economies in these nations? How do these benefits compare to those in the United States?

Reading About Economics

Baxandall, Rosalyn, Linda Gordon, and Susan Reverby, eds. *America's Working Women.* New York: Random House. A compilation from diaries, journals, and letters of working women.

Garraty, John A. *Unemployment in History: Economic Thought and Public Policy.* New York: Harper & Row. A general history of unemployment and the public's perception of it in different societies from early recorded history to the present.

Maurer, Harry. *Not Working: An Oral History of the Unemployed.* New York: Holt, Rinehart and Winston. Interviews by an investigative journalist with a large variety of anonymous unemployed people in the United States.

Stein, Walter J. *California and the Dust Bowl Migration.* Contributions in American History, No. 21. Westport, Conn.: Greenwood Press. Studies not only the "Okies" but also the general problem of migratory agriculture in the West, state politics, federal policies, labor unions, and social relations in rural California.

Terkel, Studs. *Working: People Talk About What They Do All Day and How They Feel About What They Do.* New York: Pantheon. Portrayal of workers' satisfactions and frustrations.

1 DEUTSCHE MARK 1950
50 FRANCS 1953
REPUBLIQUE
ONE PENNY 1967
10 FRANCS MADAGASCAR
NEW PENCE
10 CENTS
MAGYAR NÉP
NORGE 1972
REPUBLICA ARGENTINA
NEDERLAND
1971
1965

See Unit Materials, p. TM 89.
See Multimedia Guide, p. TM 89.
See Applying Economics on text p. 462.

UNIT SIX

INTERNATIONAL ECONOMICS

CHAPTER 17

See Chapter Overview, p. TM 90.
See Chapter Objectives, p. TM 90.
See Introducing the Chapter, p. TM 90.
See Extending Economic Knowledge on text p. 408.

International Trade

Economists have achieved more nearly unanimous agreement about the principles of international trade than about any other aspect of our subject [economics].

Paul A. Samuelson

1 Specialization leads to economic interdependence and international trade.
- Absolute and Comparative Advantage
- Balancing Payments and Trade

2 Foreign exchange markets set the values of national currencies.
- Foreign Exchange Markets
- Foreign Exchange Rates

3 Many types of trade barriers work to restrict international trade.
- Trade Barriers
- Free Trade Versus Protectionism

4 The nations of the world often cooperate to improve international trade.
- United States Cooperation
- World Regional Trade Organizations
- International Trade Agreements
- Changes in International Trade

You may wish to have the students refer to the *World Economic Data File* on pages 481–498 of THE REFERENCE LIBRARY as they study Chapter 17.

CHAPTER 17 STUDY GUIDE

Chapter Focus

Chapter 17 discusses international trade. The chapter analyzes the role of specialization in international trade and examines how nations finance their trade with other nations. The chapter concludes by explaining the trade barriers that work to lessen international trade and how nations are cooperating to expand trade.

As you study the chapter, look for the details that support each of the following statements.

1. Specialization leads to economic interdependence and international trade.
2. Foreign exchange markets set the values of national currencies.
3. Many types of trade barriers work to restrict international trade.
4. The nations of the world often cooperate to improve international trade.

See Preteaching Vocabulary, p. TM 90.

Terms to Know

The following terms, while not the only terms emphasized in this chapter, are basic to your understanding of international trade. Determine the meaning of each term, either by using the Glossary or by watching for context clues as you read the chapter.

absolute advantage
comparative advantage
balance of payments
import
export
balance of trade
fixed exchange rate
foreign exchange rate
floating exchange rate
tariff
revenue tariff
protective tariff
embargo
protectionism
most-favored-nation status

See Key Study Questions and Key Understandings, p. TM 91.

1 Specialization leads to economic interdependence and international trade.

See Suggested Teaching Strategies, p. TM 91.

International trade is the voluntary exchange of goods and services between people in different nations. For thousands of years people have benefited from international trade, which provides them with products not available in their homeland. By the mid-1980s, international trade amounted to about $2 trillion annually.

At the basis of international trade are the concepts of specialization and economic interdependence. When individuals or businesses produce a single or very narrow range of products, it is called **specialization.** Many individuals and businesses specialize because by concentrating their efforts on the production of a narrow range of products they are able to increase productivity.

Specialization, however, leads to a decrease in self-sufficiency. If individuals and businesses concentrate on the production of specific goods and services, they must rely on other people to furnish the remaining products that are needed to satisfy their wants and needs. Economists call such dependence **economic interdependence.**

The same process of specialization and economic interdependence takes place on a national level in international trade. As people in various nations specialize to use their resources better, the nations become less self-sufficient. The political and business leaders of these nations turn to international trade to fulfill some of their wants and needs.

Absolute and Comparative Advantage

The world's resources are unevenly distributed. Each nation has a different quantity and quality of natural, human, and capital resources. The unequal distribution of resources affects what and how much goods and services a nation can produce.

Two concepts help people to decide which goods and services to produce for export. The two concepts are absolute advantage and comparative advantage.

Absolute Advantage. The distribution of resources often gives a nation an absolute advantage in the production of a particular product. **Absolute advantage** means that, using the same resources, one nation can produce a product at a lower cost than can a second nation.

Brazil, for example, enjoys an absolute advantage over the United States in coffee production. Brazil's resources—especially its land, climate, and inexpensive labor force—enable it to produce large quantities of coffee at a relatively low price compared to the costs for coffee production in the United States. Thus, it is to Brazil's advantage to export coffee to the United States.

The United States, on the other hand, enjoys an absolute advantage over Brazil in many other areas, particularly in the production of manufactured goods. The United States has well-tapped natural resources, a highly skilled labor force, and well-developed means of production for consumer and capital goods. Thus, it is to the advantage of the United States to export manufactured goods to Brazil.

Comparative Advantage. Although nations have an absolute advantage in the production of numerous goods and services, they generally specialize in the production of those items in which they have a comparative advantage. A **comparative advantage** is the advantage that arises from being able to produce a product at a lower opportunity cost relative to other products.

A nation determines its areas of comparative advantage by calculating the economic benefits received from producing various goods and services. The nation then chooses to specialize in the production of those goods and services that provide the greatest economic benefits. In other words, the nation specializes in those products that can be produced at the least expense relative to the other products that the nation might produce.

While Japan has a comparative advantage over many nations in the production of cars, Japan also imports cars from the United States.

◆ Some nations—particularly in the Third World—have vast natural resources but lack the capital and technological assets to utilize them.

It is important to understand the difference between absolute advantage and comparative advantage. A nation's absolute advantage is measured in relation to other nations. A nation has an absolute advantage in the production of a product any time it can produce that product at a lower cost than can another nation. A nation's comparative advantage is measured in relation to all of the goods and services the nation produces. A nation has a comparative advantage in those products that have the lowest opportunity costs.

Consider the situation of two imaginary nations, Bitoland and Micoland. Both nations can produce color television sets and CD players. If both nations devote all of their resources to manufacturing television sets, Bitoland can produce 1 million television sets, while Micoland can produce only 100,000 television sets. Using resources in this manner results in a production ratio of 10 to 1 for Bitoland.

On the other hand, if both nations devote all of their resources to manufacturing CD players, Bitoland can produce 100,000 CD players, while Micoland can produce only 50,000 CD players. Using resources in this manner results in a production ratio of 2 to 1 for Bitoland. Bitoland has an absolute advantage over Micoland in the production of both goods.

Even though Bitoland has an absolute advantage in the production of both goods, it is in the nation's best interest to specialize in the production of color television sets. Bitoland's decision to produce color television sets rather than CD players is based on the size of Bitoland's comparative advantage in the case of each product.

Bitoland's advantage over Micoland in the production of color television sets is sizable—10 to 1. The nation's advantage over Micoland in the production of CD players, however, is not as large—2 to 1. Thus, it is in Bitoland's best interest to export color television sets and import CD players.

Conversely, even though Micoland does not have an absolute advantage in the production of either product, the size of its disadvantage is much smaller in the case of CD players. Thus, it is in Micoland's best interest to specialize in the production of CD players and import color television sets.

By specializing in the production of the product that it can produce most efficiently, each nation is

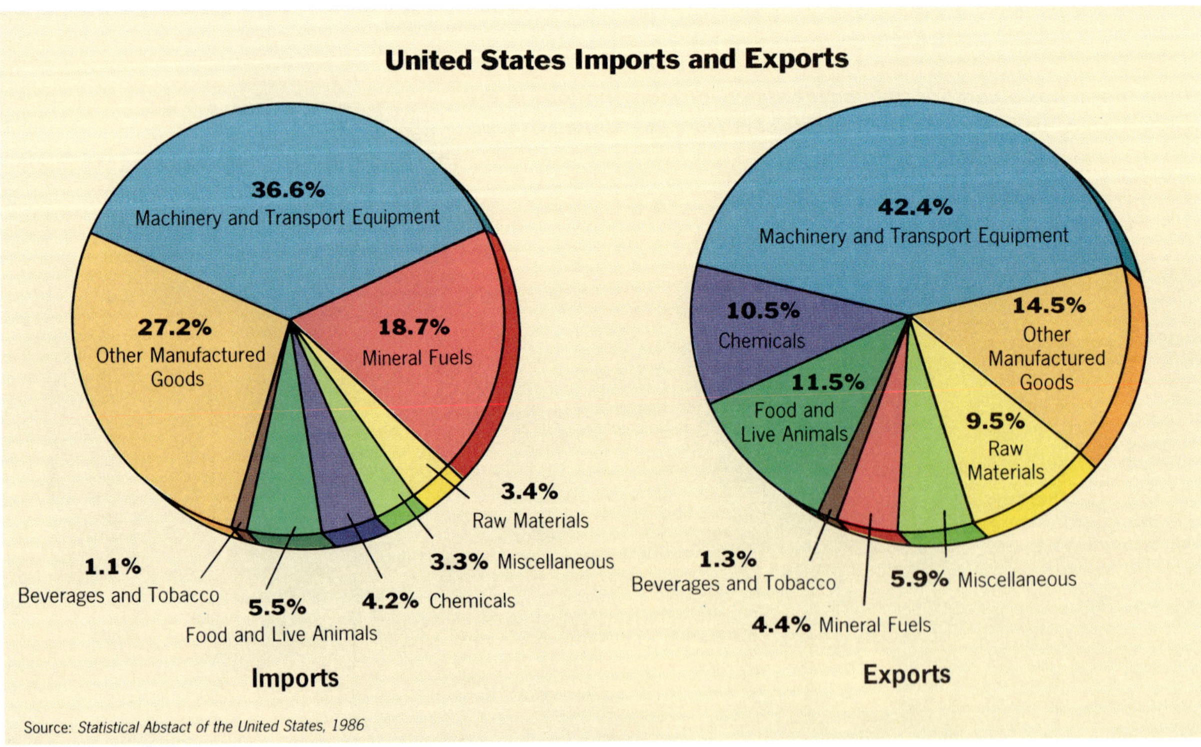

able to make the best use of its available resources. International trade then allows each nation to enjoy the most products at the lowest opportunity costs.

Balancing Payments and Trade

The flow of goods and money into and out of a nation is very important to international finance. This flow of goods and money also is an indicator of a nation's economic health. Nations seek a favorable balance of payments and trade.

Balance of Payments. A nation's **balance of payments** is an accounting record of all payments that a nation's residents, firms, and government make to other countries and all the monetary receipts they receive from other countries. In the United States, the Department of Commerce calculates the balance of payments quarterly. The balance of payments is useful to decision makers because it summarizes the economic relationship of the United States with the rest of the world.

Many types of transactions are figured into a nation's balance of payments. These transactions are grouped under the headings current account and capital account.

The **current account** portion of the balance of payments tallies a nation's inflow and outflow of money. Imports and exports represent the largest and most important part of the current account (see the graphs on page 388).

The goods that are bought from other countries are called **imports.** The goods that are sold to people in a foreign country are called **exports.** The United States is the world's leading importer and exporter of goods and services. In 1985, for example, the nation imported $358 billion worth of foreign goods and services and exported $214 billion worth of United States-made goods. The export from the United States accounted for 11 percent of all international trade, a drop from 15 percent in 1965. Japan's exports, which were valued at $177 billion, accounted for 9 percent of the world's total trade, double its 1965 total. Economists conclude that Japan may soon challenge the United States as the world's leading exporter of goods and services.

The **capital account** portion of the balance of payments records the movement of capital between nations. For example, suppose an American firm builds a $50 million factory in another country. The cost of the factory—$50 million—is recorded as an outflow of capital on the United States' capital account. If, on the other hand, a foreign firm builds a plant in the United States, the cost of the plant is recorded as an inflow of capital on the United States' capital account. Other transactions recorded in the capital account include the purchase of foreign securities such as bonds or stocks.

A nation's balance of payments is rarely at a break-even point. The total outflow of money in a given year usually does not equal the total inflow of money. When a nation's total expenditures abroad are greater than its receipts from other nations, a balance of payments deficit, or **unfavorable balance of payments,** occurs. In other words, more money flows out of the country than flows into it. The United States has consistently experienced a balance of payments deficit since the early 1950s. ◆

A balance of payments surplus, on the other hand, results when a nation's total expenditures abroad are less than its receipts from other countries. In other words, more money flows into the country than flows out of it. A balance of payments surplus is also called a **favorable balance of payments.**

Economics Reporter

What Is the Gray Market?

A gray marketer buys brand name goods overseas and brings them back to the United States for resale. Discount retailers then sell the gray-market products below the authorized distributors' markup and exclude the standard warranty. The gray market damages the retail market. The sellers of gray-market products benefit from the authorized distributors marketing campaigns without paying their share of promotion costs. Gray-marketers also do not provide any warranties to consumers. Uninformed purchasers of gray-market products stand to lose the most. Authorized domestic dealers usually refuse to fix defective gray-market products. A law in New York now requires that all shops selling gray-market products describe the product and the warranty accurately.

◆ Report topic: Policies the United States might implement to correct the unfavorable balance of payments.

Balance of Trade. The difference between the value of a nation's imports and exports is that nation's **balance of trade.** The balance of trade is the single most important factor in determining the nation's overall balance of payments. Like the overall balance of payments, the balance of trade can be a deficit or a surplus (see the graph below).

A **trade deficit,** or **unfavorable balance of trade,** occurs when the value of a nation's exports is less than the value of its imports. The chart on this page shows how in recent years the trade deficits incurred by the United States have grown dramatically. In 1985, the United States had the world's largest trade deficit, about $144 billion.

A **trade surplus,** on the other hand, occurs when the value of a nation's exports is greater than the value of its imports. A trade surplus is often called a **favorable balance of trade.** In 1985, some industrialized nations such as Japan, West Germany, and Canada enjoyed trade surpluses. In 1985, Japan's $40 billion trade surplus was the largest in the world.

The United States Balance of Trade

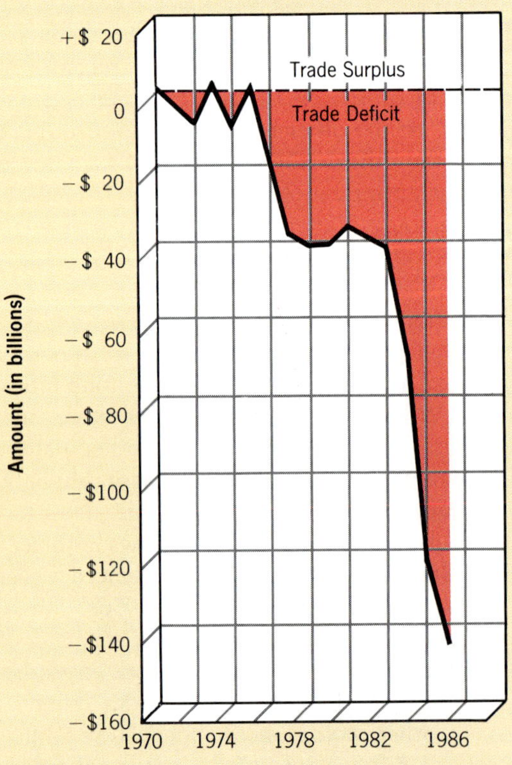

Source: *Economic Report of the President, 1986*

The United States Trade Deficit. Economists have listed many causes for the growing United States trade deficit. One major cause is a rise in the cost of imported oil. During the 1970s and early 1980s, the OPEC cartel increased the price of oil from less than $2 a barrel to $35 a barrel. The United States depended heavily on foreign oil. In 1980, foreign oil accounted for 40 percent of American imports. The price increase (see the graph on page 391) forced the United States to spend much more money abroad. Despite recent oil-price reductions, foreign oil still accounts for nearly 20 percent of all United States imports.

Rising productivity in other nations has also contributed to the trade deficit. Some nations, such as Japan, South Korea, Singapore, and Hong Kong, have increased their productivity at a faster rate than the United States. In 1985, for example, Japanese firms exported about $50 billion more in goods to the United States than American firms exported to Japan. These nations have lower production costs, including labor, than the United States, making their imports less expensive for Americans to purchase than American-made goods.

The flooding of American markets with low-cost imports is coupled with the strong United States dollar, providing a third explanation for the trade deficit. In the mid-1980s, the dollar rose in value in relation to other currencies. This rise in value made American-produced goods more expensive in foreign markets. As a result, foreigners purchased fewer United States goods, and United States consumers purchased more foreign goods. ◆

A fourth explanation for the rising trade deficit is that the United States lacks a coordinated industrial policy. No central authority helps steer firms into profitable areas. Instead, United States businesses are free to produce what they wish and market their goods where they wish. The government places on them just a few restrictions, such as armaments and high-tech goods. Some nations give more direction to firms, particularly to those firms that sell goods in international markets. Japan's Ministry of International Trade and Industry (MITI), for example, coordinates the nation's output of goods and services.

◆ **Have the students read "Buying a New Car" on pages 533–535 of the *Everyday Economics Handbook* and answer the questions that follow.**

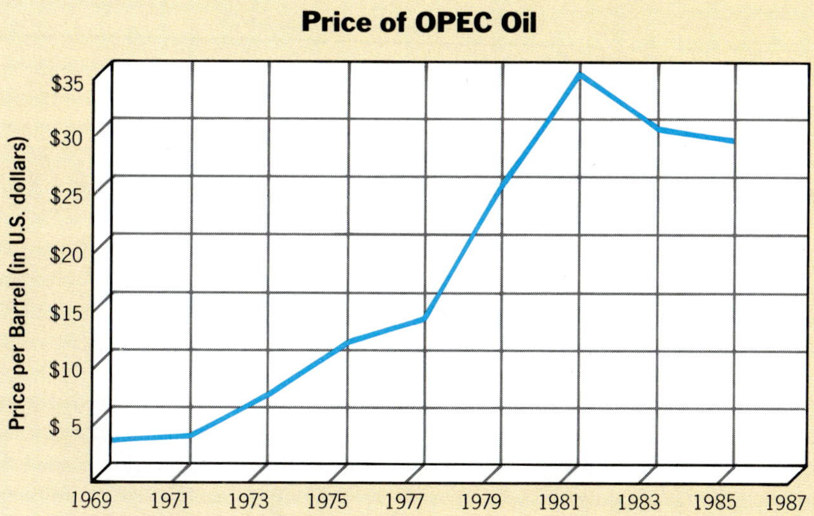

CASE STUDY

MITI—Coordinating Japan's Industrial Policy

The Ministry of International Trade and Industry (MITI) is a Japanese government agency. Its role is to coordinate the nation's industrial policy, a master plan for economic development. MITI employs different means to increase the production and sale of Japanese goods.

MITI's first duty is to determine which Japanese industries are the most important to the nation's economic well-being. MITI makes a priority list of industries from most to least important to the national economy. The automotive industry ranks high on the priority list, for example, because it satisfies domestic needs for transportation, and it produces the nation's leading export.

MITI's second role is to provide financial and technical assistance to private firms. For example, MITI provides financial assistance for research and development to encourage technological progress. MITI funds were used to help develop computer technology. MITI also aids in capital formation, helping firms to acquire capital for use in the production process. Extending low-interest loans to firms seeking new capital is another important part of MITI's duties.

The third function of MITI is to steer the nation's production into profitable areas. Often, MITI suggests that weak industries shift product lines. To help with production shifts, MITI assists in the retraining of workers and helps firms acquire additional capital.

Although MITI has little authority to demand compliance with its administrative guidance, Japanese firms tend to follow MITI's recommendations for the good of the firm and of the nation. Many nations are using MITI as a model for similar agencies in their nations.

See Suggested Assignments, p. TM 91.

Section 1 Review See Answers, p. A 71.

DEFINE international trade, absolute advantage, comparative advantage, trade surplus

1. **Seeing Relationships** How does specialization lead to interdependence among nations?
2. **Understanding Ideas** When is a nation's balance of trade said to be unfavorable?
3. **Interpreting Graphics** Study the chart on page 390. **(a)** During which years did the United States show a trade surplus? **(b)** In what year did the United States trade deficit exceed $140 million?

BUILDING ECONOMIC SKILLS

READING ABOUT ECONOMICS

Comparing Economic Interpretations

An economic interpretation is an economist's judgment about, or explanation of an event, problem, issue, or other situation. Economists often disagree about the causes and effects of these economic happenings. Disagreements among economists occur, in part, because different economists bring to their interpretations different points of view and frames of reference. Comparing economic interpretations involves careful analysis of the similarities and differences between arguments.

How to Compare Economic Interpretations

To compare two or more economic interpretations, follow these steps.

1. **Determine the nature of the source.** Note the source of each interpretation. Note whether the interpretation is a primary or secondary source.
2. **Read each source carefully.** Identify the central points of the interpretations including the author's main thesis, supporting evidence, and conclusions. Determine each author's point of view. Note similarities and differences between interpretations. You can do this by constructing a table. The chart on this page provides an example for you.

Practicing the Skill See Answers, p. A 71.

Locate two economic interpretations of an economic event or occurrence. Then on a separate sheet of paper, follow the directions on page 393.

Two Interpretations of United States Trade Policy

Similarities and Differences	Reagan Interpretation	Culbertson Interpretation
Main Thesis	"Free trade" in international markets benefits all nations' economies.	Positive action is needed to bring the nation's trade into balance.
Supporting Evidence	Historic trends indicate that free trade enhances human progress and peace, job creation and other economic benefits.	Free trade has led to a sharp rise in cheap imports. Cheap imports are derived from wage competition, not economic efficiency because poverty wages and other substandard working conditions prevail.
Conclusions	Open world markets are desirable.	New political machinery is necessary.
Assumptions	The United States can persuade its trading partners to abide by existing international trade agreements.	Selective trade restrictions will not lead to trade wars or other disruptions in world trade.

EXCERPT A: From a Speech to Business and Government Leaders

And let me say at the outset that our trade policy rests firmly on the foundation of free and open markets, free trade.

I, like you, recognize the inescapable conclusion that all of history has taught, the freer the flow of world trade, the stronger the tides for human progress and peace among nations. . . . [Free markets] produce more jobs, a more productive use of the nation's resources, more rapid innovation and a higher standard of living. They strengthen our national security because our economy, the bedrock of our defense, is stronger. . . .

There are some well-meaning in motive who have proposed bills and programs that are truly protectionist in nature. These proposals would raise the costs of goods and services that American consumers across the land would have to pay.

They would invite retaliation by our trading partners abroad, would in turn lose jobs for those American workers in industries that would be the victims of such retaliation, would rekindle inflation, would strain international relations, and would impair the stability of the international financial and trading systems.

The net result of these counterproductive proposals would not be to protect consumers or workers or farmers or businesses. In fact, just the reverse would happen. We would lose markets. We would lose jobs. And we would lose our prosperity. . . . Our commitment to free trade is undiminished. We will vigorously pursue our policy of promoting free and open markets in this country and around the world. We will insist that all nations face up to their responsibilities of preserving and enhancing free trade everywhere. . . .

President Ronald Reagan

EXCERPT B: From an Article in *The New York Times*

The first requirement of a reasonable trade policy is to give up the quixotic crusade for "free trade" . . . and get in step with the rest of the world and with economic reality. The sharp rise in imports and in the trade deficit must be quickly halted and reversed. That will not happen naturally. Positive action to bring the nation's trade into balance by limiting its imports is essential. A healthy nation must control its imports and balance its trade budget. . . . We need to replace the unrealistic objective of "free trade" with the constructive goal of "balanced trade." . . .

Why is unregulated trade destructive? Don't United States consumers benefit from the availability of low-priced foreign goods? In a very short-term sense, consumers obviously do benefit from cheaper goods. But the important distinction is between lower prices that result from genuine economic efficiency in the exporting country, and lower prices that result from poverty wages, substandard working conditions, low environmental and labor standards, tax advantages and government subsidies.

Trade based on the latter is, in effect, wage competition between the two countries and has nothing to do with genuine economic efficiency. . . . International wage competition would undercut the standards of living of high-income nations. . . .

To achieve the required management of foreign trade, the United States will need new political machinery, probably an agency in the executive branch that could provide continuity, impartiality, judgment, a long-term view and the highest expertise.

Thinking realistically about trade policy requires clearing away some confusions. It would be misleading to call the required import restraints "barriers to trade" or "protectionism." Rather, these policies prevent destructive foreign trade, allowing constructive trade to be developed. . . .

Professor John M. Culbertson

1. **(a)** Construct a chart, as shown in the example on page 392. **(b)** Fill in the chart with information from your two sources.

2. **(a)** Write a brief statement about how the two interpretations are similar. **(b)** Also tell how they are different.

See Key Study Questions and Key Understandings, p. TM 92.

2 Foreign exchange markets set the values of national currencies.

See Suggested Teaching Strategies, p. TM 92.

More than 160 nations, each with its own government and national currency, exist in today's world. National currencies are generally accepted in payment for goods and services within a nation's borders. To conduct international trade, however, nations must have a way of determining the values of their currencies in relation to one another. Foreign exchange markets and foreign exchange rates allow nations to make this comparison.

Foreign Exchange Markets

Individuals, businesses, and governments exchange foreign currencies. **Foreign exchange markets** are networks of major commercial and investment banks that link the economies of the world. Traditionally, the most important function of foreign exchange markets is to convert one currency into an equivalent amount of a second currency. This currency conversion is needed for three types of transactions: international trade, tourism and travel, and international investing.

Economics Reporter

What Are International Pirates?

International pirates are individuals who steal technological secrets and flood world markets with imitations of brand name goods. The United States government has estimated that 130,000 jobs are lost annually because of brand name piracy operations. The computer industry alone claimed to have lost $4 billion in computer sales in 1984. To defend American business interests, the United ◆ States is enforcing the antipiracy laws and making trademark copying a criminal offense. It is also imposing quotas on countries that condone piracy. Nations around the world helping the United States in the fight against international pirates are Taiwan (the Republic of China), Korea, China (the People's Republic), and Singapore.

In the mid-1980s, however, these traditional types of transactions represent just 10 percent of the business conducted on foreign exchange markets. The other 90 percent involves the speculative buying and selling of national currencies. In foreign exchange markets, money is purchased just like other goods. About $150 billion changes hands each day on foreign exchange markets. The graph on page 395 identifies the major trading centers and the daily volume of exchange.

Foreign Exchange Rates

The conversion of national currencies would be impossible without **foreign exchange rates.** Foreign exchange rates state the price of one currency in the currencies of other nations.

In the United States, foreign exchange rates are expressed in two ways. The first is the United States dollar value for each unit of foreign currency. In November 1986, for example, the Australian dollar was worth $0.64 in United States currency. The British pound was worth $1.42, and the Canadian dollar was worth $0.72. The second expression of the foreign exchange rate is in terms of units of foreign currency for each United States dollar. In November 1986, it took 3.7 Saudi Arabian riyals or 164 Japanese yen to equal $1.00 in United States currency.

Two types of foreign exchange rates have been used since World War II: the fixed exchange rate and the floating exchange rate. In a **fixed exchange rate,** the currency of one nation is fixed, or constant, in relation to other currencies. The fixed exchange rate was used from 1944 to 1973.

Fixed Exchange Rates. The fixed exchange rates of the postwar period were a result of the Bretton Woods Conference of 1944. At the conference, 44 Allied nations agreed that each nation should define its currency in terms of either gold or United States dollars. The United States, for example, fixed the dollar's value at 1/35 ounce of gold. The Bretton Woods Conference also established the International Monetary Fund (IMF) to oversee the fixed exchange rate system, to stabilize national currencies when necessary, and to promote trade. Today, about 125 nations are members of the IMF.

The system of fixed exchange rates added stability to the international monetary system in two

◆ Many goods, particularly watches and designer clothes sold in open-air markets, are products of international pirates.

Daily Business at the World's Major Trading Centers

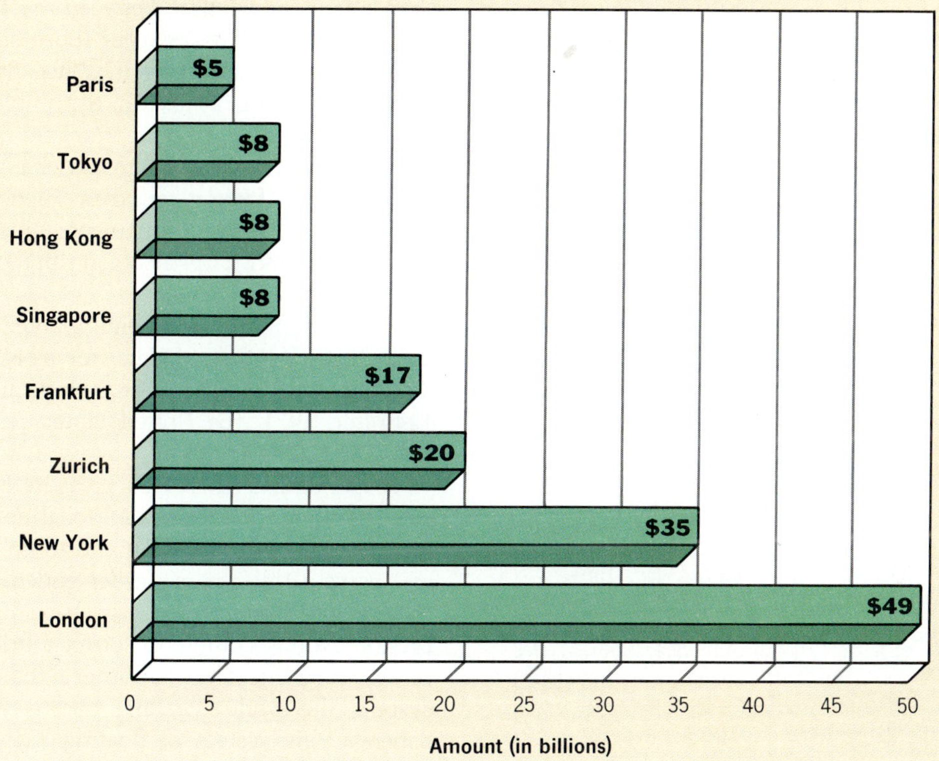

Source: *The New York Times,* May 4, 1986

Individuals who buy and sell foreign currency make a profit by speculating on fluctuations in exchange rates and interest rates.

important ways. First, fixed exchange rates benefited firms that imported and exported goods because these firms knew precisely how much foreign goods cost in relation to their own currencies. Second, fixed exchange rates reduced the number of currency devaluations.

Devaluation occurs when a government reduces the value of its currency in relation to other currencies. During the worldwide depression of the 1930s, governments intentionally cheapened their money to make their exports less expensive in foreign markets and thus stimulate domestic output and employment. Between the 1940s and 1960s, however, the IMF was able to regulate currency devaluations.

Foreign Currency Exchange Rates*

Country	Currency Unit	Value per unit in U.S. $	Units per U.S. $
Australia	Dollar	0.6641	1.5058
Austria	Schilling	0.0736	13.51
Brazil	Cruzado	0.0663	15.09
Britain	Pound	1.4710	0.6798
Colombia	Peso	0.0045	224.0
Denmark	Krone	0.1369	7.3070
Finland	Mark	0.2098	4.7665
France	Franc	0.1557	6.4240
Hong Kong	Dollar	0.1285	7.7835
Indonesia	Rupiah	0.0006	1634.50
Italy	Lira	0.0007	1354.50
Japan	Yen	0.0063	158.12
Kuwait	Dinar	3.4229	0.2922
Pakistan	Rupee	0.0580	17.25
Singapore	Dollar	0.4610	2.1695
South Korea	Won	0.0115	869.20

*As of January 7, 1987

The End of Fixed Exchange Rates. By the early 1970s, changing economic conditions made fixed exchange rates impractical. Between the 1940s and the 1970s, the United States spent enormous amounts of money overseas, resulting in a negative balance of payments by the 1960s. In the public sector, expenditures for the Vietnam War and other defense-related activities and foreign aid channeled billions of dollars into foreign countries. High private-sector spending on foreign investments, imported goods, and tourism and travel also contributed to the negative balance of payments.

When foreign governments wanted to exchange their United States dollars for gold, the United States was obliged to honor their requests. Between 1949 and 1971, the United States redeemed more than $16 billion in gold.

Responding to increased pressure by France and other nations to redeem additional dollars for gold, President Nixon ordered an end to gold redemption in August 1971. Nixon's order ended the fixed exchange rate system that had been created at the Bretton Woods Conference. After a brief and unsuccessful experiment with another fixed exchange rate system, the world's leading trading nations established a new system of floating exchange rates in 1973.

Floating Exchange Rates. With a **floating exchange rate,** the forces of supply and demand are allowed to determine the value of a currency. As a result, the values of currencies are constantly changing. ◆

For example, in the mid-1980s the demand for United States dollars in foreign exchange markets was high for several reasons. First, foreign investors wanted to buy dollars to invest in United States firms and securities. Second, United States dollars were viewed as among the most secure in the world because they were backed by a strong government. Dollars were also considered stable because the inflation rate was low, less than 4 percent. Finally, speculators and other investors continually bid up the dollar's price in foreign exchange markets. As a result, the United States dollar appreciated in value.

When a currency appreciates, economists say that the currency is "stronger." The "strong" dollar, however, had a negative effect on the ability of United States firms to export goods. Goods made in the United States became more expensive in foreign

◆ **Class activity: Have the students select a foreign currency and chart its value in relation to United States currency during a two-week period.**

In an attempt to increase exports to countries such as Japan, the United States took actions to weaken the strong dollar in the mid-1980s.

markets, and foreign-made goods became less expensive in United States markets. For this reason, fewer people bought goods made in the United ◆ States, contributing to a negative balance of trade.

To understand how a strong dollar affects exports, consider the following example. Six French francs equal $1.00 in United States currency. At this exchange rate, a $15,000 American-made automobile costs 80,000 francs in France. If the demand for the dollar increases, the dollar will appreciate and more francs will be needed to buy $1.00 (see the chart on page 396).

If the exchange rate doubles, 12 francs would equal $1.00. Such an increase in the value of the dollar would mean that the American-made automobile would cost 180,000 francs. Naturally, fewer French consumers would be willing or able to purchase the American-made automobile. All United States firms would then be forced to decrease their exports to France because the rise in the value of the dollar would double the cost of all American-made goods exported to France.

Depreciation means that one nation's currency has lost value, or gotten weaker, in relation to the currencies of other nations. As with devaluation, depreciation improves a nation's trade standing. In the above example, the lower value of the French franc would make French products less expensive in the United States.

Governments sometimes intervene in the present system of floating exchange rates. Through their central banks, national governments sometimes buy or sell their own currency. If, for example, a nation's currency is appreciating too quickly, the government sells currency on foreign exchange markets to increase supply and slow the increase in the currency's value.

If, on the other hand, a nation's currency is depreciating too quickly, the government buys its own currency on foreign exchange markets to decrease the supply and prevent the currency's value from dropping at too rapid a rate. Because governments have stepped in periodically to influence the value of their currencies, some economists refer to the present system of foreign exchange rates as managed float.

See Suggested Assignments, p. TM 92.

Section 2 Review See Answers, p. A 71.

DEFINE devaluation, floating exchange rate

1. **Summarizing Ideas** How did the foreign exchange rate for the dollar between 1944 and 1973 differ from the foreign exchange rate for today's dollar?

2. **Expressing Ideas** How does a "strong dollar" affect trade?

3. **Interpreting Graphics** Study the graph on page 395. **(a)** In what money market is the daily trading volume the greatest? **(b)** On what continent are the most major trading centers located? **(c)** Why do you think they are located there?

◆ Popular entertainers and television personalities have participated in a national campaign to encourage Americans to purchase goods "made in the U.S.A."

See Key Study Questions and Key Understandings, p. TM 93.

3 Many types of trade barriers work to restrict international trade.

See Suggested Teaching Strategies, p. TM 93.

◆ International trade allows people to specialize in the production of goods and services that they produce best. From an economic viewpoint, international trade is a positive force in promoting economic efficiency and growth. Yet, because of economic and political factors, nations often restrict the free exchange of goods across national borders.

Trade Barriers

Specific governmental actions that protect domestic industries and jobs from foreign competition are called **trade barriers.** The three major types of trade barriers are tariffs, import quotas and voluntary restrictions, and embargoes.

Tariffs. Any tax on imports is a **tariff.** Tariffs can be either revenue tariffs or protective tariffs. A **revenue tariff** is used to raise money for the government. Throughout the 1800s, revenue tariffs were

Average Tariff Rates in the United States Since 1820

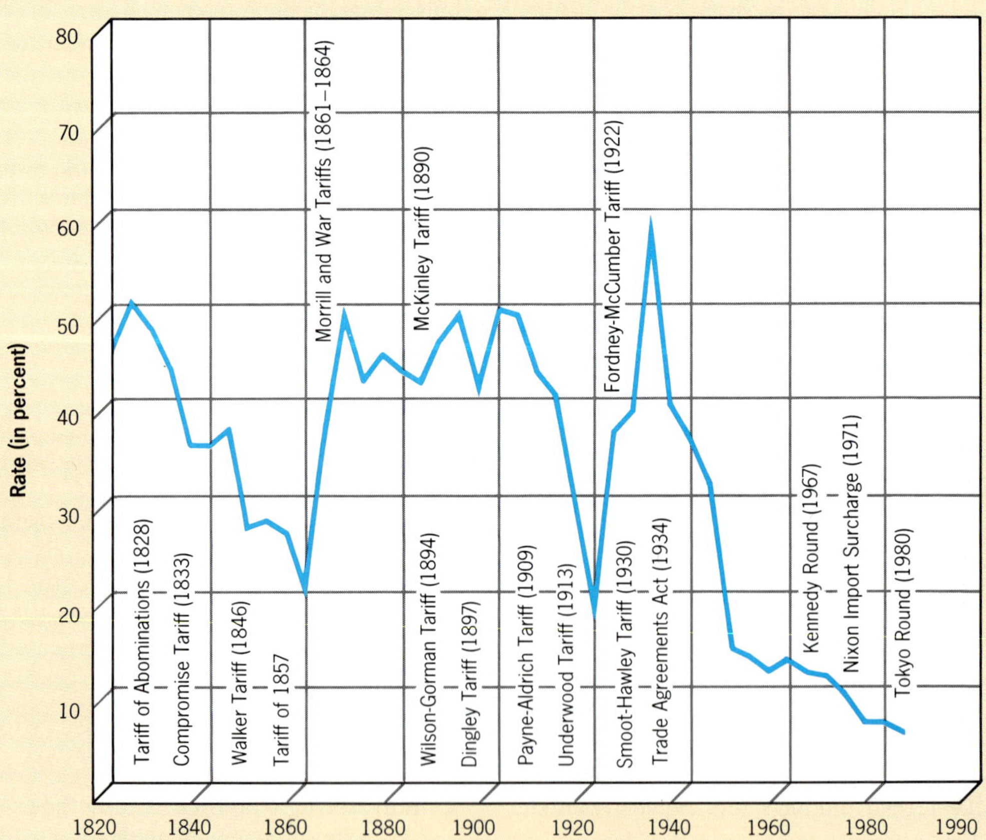

Sources: *Historical Statistics of the United States, Colonial Times to 1970*
Statistical Abstract of the United States, 1986

◆ **Have the students read "Import-Export Managers" on page 542 of *Careers in the Marketplace.***

the major source of income for the United States government. After the United States government adopted the income tax in 1913, however, the need for revenue tariffs declined. Today, less than 2 percent of the federal government's receipts come from tariffs (see the graph on page 398).

A **protective tariff** protects domestic industries from foreign competition. By raising the prices of imported goods, protective tariffs reduce people's demand for foreign goods.

A protective tariff works this way. Suppose that a South Korean firm sells a motorcycle for $3,000 and that a comparable American-made motorcycle costs $4,000. The $1,000 price difference would cause many buyers in the United States to purchase the South Korean model. If the United States government places a 50-percent protective tariff on South Korean motorcycles, however, the imported motorcycle's price would jump to $4,500 (50% × $3,000 = $1,500; $1,500 + $3,000 = $4,500). Thus, the protective tariff makes the Korean model more expensive than the American-made motorcycle and encourages consumers in the United States to buy the American model.

The United States has used protective tariffs for many years. The McKinley Tariff Act of 1890, for example, set such high tariffs that many foreign competitors were totally excluded from American markets. The extremely high Smoot-Hawley Tariff of 1930 decreased imports by almost 60 percent and had a negative impact on all international trade.

Since World War II, the United States has reduced its use of protective tariffs. Some exceptions to this policy still in effect in the mid-1980s, however, include a 50-percent tariff on large Japanese motorcycles, a 35-percent tariff on Canadian cedar roofing shingles, and a 25-percent tariff on Japanese small trucks.

Import Quotas and Voluntary Restrictions. The United States government can also use import quotas and voluntary trade restrictions. Both regulations help domestic businesses sell their products by limiting the quantity of a specific product that can be imported. An **import quota,** which sets a fixed amount for an import, is a law. A **voluntary trade restriction** is a binding agreement between two nations that does not require Congressional legislation.

Economics Reporter

What Are Free-Trade Zones?

Free-trade zones are areas in which goods or services may be bought and sold without being subjected to taxes, duties, and certain government regulations. One type of free-trade zone is the free port. In free ports, goods may be imported free of customs duties as long as the goods are not sold outside of the zone. About 30 operational free-port zones exist in the United States. About 350 operate worldwide. ◆

Free zones also exist for banks dealing in international finance. The free zones allow banks to provide services to multinational corporations without being subjected to local and state taxes and certain banking regulations.

Import quotas and voluntary restrictions are sometimes directed at specific goods from specific nations. In 1981, for example, United States automakers insisted that the government protect their industry from Japanese competition. In that year, Japan agreed to limit the number of auto imports to the United States to about 1.7 million automobiles each year. In 1985, a new agreement was reached, raising the quota to 2.3 million cars a year.

Quotas and restrictions also are imposed on a particular product regardless of the country of origin. The Mandatory Oil Import Quota of 1959, for example, restricted the amount of oil that American firms could import. The major goal of this quota, which was in effect until 1973, was to encourage domestic production of oil and thereby reduce United States dependence on foreign sources of oil.

Embargoes. A law that cuts off imports from and exports to specific countries is an **embargo.** Historically, embargoes have been enacted for political rather than economic reasons. President Jefferson's Embargo Act of 1807, for example, was a politically motivated embargo, designed to stop French and English raiding of United States merchant ships.

◆ Between 1973 and 1983, the value of goods handled by United States free-trade zones increased from $3 million to $7 billion.

For reasons of national defense, United States manufacturers are not allowed to sell various types of computer goods to certain countries.

Recent embargoes have also been used for political purposes. The United States placed a total trade embargo on Cuba in 1961. This embargo, which was partially lifted in 1977, was in response to Fidel Castro's Communist revolution in Cuba. Similarly, in 1985, the United States announced a trade embargo on Nicaragua to protest the policies of the Sandinistas leadership in that country.

Embargoes are sometimes limited to a specific product or group of products. In 1973–1974, the OPEC nations placed an oil embargo on the United States and other Western nations in retaliation for United States and Western support of Israel during the 1973 Yom Kippur War. In 1980, President Carter stopped grain sales to the Soviet Union. This limited embargo, lifted in 1981, was in response to the Soviet invasion of Afghanistan in 1979. In 1985, President Reagan placed a partial embargo on the sale of certain military and computer goods and technology to the Republic of South Africa. This move was designed to pressure the South African government into ending apartheid—a political, economic, and social system based on racism.

Other Trade Barriers. Other trade barriers including licensing requirements and extensive paperwork interrupt the free flow of goods between countries. Some nations require firms to obtain a license before they can import goods. By restricting the number of licenses, these nations ensure that fewer foreign goods enter the nation.

In some nations, paperwork delays also interfere with trade. In Japan, for example, imports undergo extensive testing and inspection as well as other time-consuming and expensive paperwork. Many exporters choose not to export their products to Japan because of the numerous regulations and required paperwork.

Free Trade Versus Protectionism

Advocates of **free trade** believe that international trade should be free of most government regulation. They believe that exports and imports should flow freely between nations in accordance with existing trade agreements. Other people believe in

protectionism—the use of trade barriers between nations to protect domestic industries. Both free-trade advocates and protectionists have a number of arguments to support their views.

The Infant Industries Argument. Protectionists offer six economic arguments to support trade restrictions. First, they argue that a nation's new, or "infant," industries should be protected from foreign competition until they are able to establish themselves. By restricting trade in goods produced by these new industries, the government allows the "infants" to build up a strong domestic market. Today, many developing nations use this argument to restrict imports.

Free-trade advocates believe that trade barriers allow industries to remain inefficient because less competition means that businesses have less reason to be efficient. Free-trade advocates also claim that these temporary protective measures are likely to be extended indefinitely because of the political pressures that businesses exert on government.

The Job Protection Argument. A second argument in favor of protectionism is based on job protection. Protectionists claim that reducing foreign competition allows more United States businesses to compete in the domestic market and guarantees jobs for more United States workers.

Free-trade advocates claim that trade restrictions actually reduce the employment of United States workers. They note that trade barriers historically have caused other nations to erect barriers to United States trade. These barriers hurt United States business in the world market and cost workers their jobs.

Labor unions in the United States are among the strongest supporters of protectionism, claiming that imports rob American workers of jobs.

Discussion topic: How protectionism affects the laws of supply and demand in the marketplace.

The Standard of Living Argument. In a third argument, protectionists believe that trade barriers help to protect the high wages and standard of living in the United States. Trade barriers between nations are needed, they claim, because cheap labor in other nations gives those nations an unfair advantage in world markets. For example, measured in 1984 constant dollars, the average hourly wage for manufacturing workers was $1.23 in Brazil, $1.36 in South Korea, $6.35 in Japan, and $12.59 in the United States. Without trade restrictions, protectionists claim that wages in the United States would have to be lowered to make United States products more competitive in price.

The advocates of free trade believe that the high wages and high standard of living in the United States can be maintained without trade barriers existing between nations. They claim that United States businesses can afford to pay high wages and still produce competitively priced products because United States laborers are more efficient than workers in other nations.

The Specialization Argument. The fourth economic argument focuses on specialization. Protectionists argue that free trade encourages businesses to overspecialize. They further claim that overspecialization makes a nation's economy vulnerable to changing world demand. To avoid overspecialization, these protectionists urge nations to encourage businesses within the nations to produce a wide variety of products. They also urge nations to protect those businesses in which the nations lack an absolute or comparative advantage.

Free-trade advocates believe that free trade benefits the world economy. They believe that competition guarantees the best product at the best price. Free-trade advocates recognize that an economy based on a single product is in a vulnerable position. They point out, however, that the United States economy is highly diversified. They claim that the failure of a few industries in the United States would not affect the nation's world position.

The National Security and Fair Trade Arguments. People in favor of trade restrictions offer two final arguments to support the establishment of barriers. Unlike the other four protectionist arguments, however, free-trade advocates agree to certain points of these final two arguments.

First, some industries must be protected from foreign competition and failure because they are vital to national security. In the United States, protected industries would include steel and heavy industries, defense-related industries, advanced technology businesses, and energy-based industries. Protectionism makes the United States less dependent on foreign firms during times of national emergency. Free-trade advocates agree that vital industries must be protected, but they claim that nonvital industries seeking protection abuse this argument.

Second, protectionists argue that few if any nations allow free trade. Protectionists feel that the United States should establish barriers that match those imposed by other nations. Free-trade advocates agree that some nations violate fair trade "rules," but the free-trade advocates oppose retaliation by the United States. Instead, free-trade advocates support negotiations to dismantle all trade barriers.

Rarely is a government's trade policy completely protectionist or completely free trade. Usually the policy is based on a variety of international and domestic economic and political factors. Often, the government protects some industries while allowing free trade in others. In the United States, government officials closely watch the nation's international trade situation, so they can be ready to take the necessary steps to guarantee the nation's economic strength. ◆

See Suggested Assignments, p. TM 93.

Section 3 Review

See Answers, p. A 71.

DEFINE trade barrier, revenue tariff, protective tariff, free trade

IDENTIFY free-trade zone

1. **Summarizing Ideas** Describe the three types of trade barriers.
2. **Comprehending Ideas** How do protective tariffs affect the price of imported goods?
3. **Interpreting Graphics** Study the graph on page 398 and answer the following questions. **(a)** In which year did the United States have the lowest and highest average tariffs? **(b)** What economic conditions in the United States in 1982 and 1930 might explain the tariff levels?

◆ Discussion topic: How the elimination of trade barriers may affect economic conditions in the United States.

As the boxes in this Tokyo warehouse attest, countries usually have trade agreements with many nations.

See Key Study Questions and Key Understandings, p. TM 94.

4 The nations of the world often cooperate to improve international trade.

See Suggested Teaching Strategies, p. TM 94.

The economic, as well as the political benefits, of international trade motivate nations to reduce trade barriers. In recent years, international cooperation has improved international trade. Some examples of trade cooperation among nations are national trade legislation, regional trade organizations, and international trade agreements.

United States Cooperation

The adverse effects that the Smoot-Hawley Tariff Bill (1930) had on international trade caused the United States and some other nations to rethink their protectionist policies. In the United States, the government moved to lower tariffs as early as 1934.

The Reciprocal Trade Agreements Act of 1934. With the election of President Franklin D. Roosevelt, the United States undertook an ambitious plan to restore vigor to international trade. The

Reciprocal Trade Agreements Act of 1934 identified protective tariffs as the leading obstacle to trade and sought to reduce tariffs in two ways. First, it gave the President the authority to reduce tariffs by as much as 50 percent, provided that other nations made similar trade concessions.

Second, it allowed Congress to grant most-favored-nation status to United States trading partners. When the United States lowers tariffs with one partner granted **most-favored-nation status**, all nations with the same status benefit. The United States, for example, grants most-favored-nation status to both Canada and Australia. A 20-percent tariff on wheat applies to both nations. When the United States lowers the 20-percent tariff to a 10-percent tariff for Australia, the tariff reduction for wheat automatically applies to Canada.

Congress has the final authority to grant and to revoke most-favored-nation status to United States trading partners. Before the Korean War in the early 1950s, for example, the Soviet Union enjoyed most-favored-nation status. Congress revoked

The trade deficit and the loss of jobs to foreign competition have put pressure on the government to rethink United States trade policies.

DECISION MAKERS IN THE ECONOMY

Reverend Leon Sullivan ◆

Reverend Leon Sullivan, a black Baptist minister in Philadelphia, is a vehement opponent of the South African system of apartheid. As a means of combating racial discrimination in businessess in South Africa, he introduced the Sullivan Principles in 1977.

The Sullivan Principles consist of six requirements for businesses. They must desegregate all parts of the workplace. They must provide equal employment practices for all employees. They must offer equal pay for equal work to all employees. They must develop programs to train nonwhites for supervisory, administrative, clerical, and technical jobs. They must work to increase the number of nonwhites in managerial and supervisory positions. They must also work to improve the quality of their employees' lives outside the workplace.

All United States companies operating in South Africa were asked to adopt the principles voluntarily. By October 1985, 175 United States companies had agreed to follow Sullivan's guidelines, and he had begun to urge companies in Great Britain, France, and Germany to comply as well.

Sullivan also began to question whether stronger measures than the original principles are needed to eliminate apartheid. Although Sullivan would still prefer to bring about change through the original principles, he now believes that more stringent economic measures may be necessary.

Sullivan's most recent call is for all foreign corporations to leave South Africa unless apartheid is abolished by May 1987.

this privilege, however, during the Korean War. In the mid-1980s, some American businesspeople were lobbying Congress to restore most-favored-nation status to the Soviet Union. By the beginning of 1987, that status had not yet been restored.

The Trade Expansion Act of 1962. The Trade Expansion Act of 1962 renewed and expanded the Reciprocal Trade Agreements Act of 1934. The 1962 act encouraged further tariff reductions and provided for worker retraining programs and other benefits to workers and firms hurt by foreign competition. These benefits are called **trade adjustment assistance.** The Trade Expansion Act of 1962 gave Presidents Kennedy and Johnson enough authority to push for important free-trade reforms during the 1960s.

The Trade Reform Act of 1974. The Trade Reform Act of 1974 further increased the President's authority to cut tariffs and expand benefits to displaced workers. Under the provisions of this act, the President was empowered to eliminate any tariff of 5 percent or less, and to cut by 60 percent any tariffs greater than 5 percent. The act also increased financial and other benefits to displaced workers, firms, and geographical areas that were especially hard hit by foreign competition. Congress regularly voted for additional trade adjustment funding during the 1980s.

World Regional Trade Organizations

Many nations have formed regional trade organizations and reduced or eliminated trade barriers

◆ Point out that many nations have imposed economic sanctions on the Republic of South Africa to pressure government leaders to abandon apartheid.

among member nations. The benefits of these reductions in trade barriers, however, are usually limited to the member nations.

The European Communities. The world's largest regional trade organization is the European Communities (EC), or the Common Market. The EC was organized in 1967, when three trade organizations—the European Economic Community, the European Coal and Steel Community, and the European Atomic Energy Community—merged. France, West Germany, Italy, Belgium, Luxembourg, the Netherlands, Great Britain, Denmark, Ireland, Greece, Spain, and Portugal all belong to the EC.

The members of the EC have agreed that trade barriers should be reduced and eventually eliminated, and that laborers and capital should be allowed to move freely across members' national borders. During the mid-1980s, EC leaders committed their nations to the complete elimination of trade barriers by 1992.

EC membership has benefited the economies of member nations. EC nations have achieved steady growth and rising standards of living.

The Council for Mutual Economic Assistance. Under the leadership of the Soviet Union, several Communist nations of Eastern Europe founded a regional trade organization called the Council for Mutual Economic Assistance (COMECON) in 1949. COMECON was originally composed of the Soviet Union, Bulgaria, Czechoslovakia, East Germany, Hungary, Poland, and Romania. Since its founding, Cuba, Mongolia, and Vietnam have been admitted. Yugoslavia participates on a limited basis.

Like the EC, COMECON has worked to reduce trade barriers among its members. It has traditionally been dominated by the Soviet Union.

Third World Regional Trade Organizations. Since 1960, regional trade organizations have also been created in many developing nations. In Latin America, the Central American Common Market (CACMO) was founded in 1960, and the Latin American Free Trade Association (LAFTA) was established in 1980. Many of Latin America's nations, including Argentina, Bolivia, Brazil, Chile, Colombia, Mexico, Paraguay, Peru, Uruguay, and Venezuela, are members of LAFTA.

Elsewhere in the Third World, similar organizations have been started. An Arab trade association, the League of Arab States, was founded in 1945. In Africa, the Central African Economic and Customs Union and the Afro-Malagasy Union for Economic Cooperation (UAMCE) were organized in 1964, and the Economic Community of West Africa (ECOWA) in 1976. Other African "customs unions," organizations with goals similar to regional trade organizations, also have been founded.

In addition to reducing trade barriers, these Third World regional organizations often discuss issues relating to industrialization, the use of scarce resources, the environment, tourism, and other topics related to economic development.

International Trade Agreements

The most important international trade agreement of the post-World War II period is the General Agreement on Tariffs and Trade (GATT), a multinational ◆ agreement. In 1947, 23 non-Communist nations signed this agreement. GATT membership has since risen to about 90. GATT members pledge to treat all members equally and to work toward the reduction of tariffs and the elimination of quotas.

GATT members meet periodically in meetings called "rounds" to discuss issues in international trade. Two of the most celebrated rounds of GATT talks were the Kennedy Round, which concluded in 1967, and the Tokyo Round which was completed in 1979. Each round resulted in substantial tariff reductions and opened talks on related issues.

In the 1980s, growing concern about nontariff trade barriers such as quotas, voluntary restrictions, export subsidies, and licensing requirements were also included in GATT negotiations. The GATT rounds in Geneva, Switzerland (1982), and in Punta del Este, Uruguay (1986), reaffirmed nations' support for free trade despite the rising tide of protectionism in the world.

Changes in International Trade

In the 1980s, telecommunications have revolutionized the way international trade is conducted. In addition, changes in the location and international

◆ **Have the students read "Interpreters" on page 542 of *Careers in the Marketplace.***

◆ Report topic: Whether a Toyota or Nissan produced at a plant in the United States should be considered "American-made."

ownership of firms have transformed world trade. These two changes have blurred the traditional definitions of imports and exports.

Multinational Investments. In recent years, more foreign firms have built plants in the countries with which they do business. The decision to build in foreign nations benefits a multinational corporation and the host nation. The corporation is able to avoid some shipping fees, protective tariffs, and quotas. The host nations benefit from additional employment opportunities and higher revenues from taxes on incomes, profits, and properties.

During the 1980s many foreign firms have located plants in the United States. Nissan, for example, builds cars and trucks in Tennessee. Honda builds them in Ohio, and Mazda has announced plans to build a factory in Michigan.

Joint Multinational Ownership. Under a joint ownership arrangement, two firms from different countries agree to build and operate a plant. The profits from a joint venture are shared by both countries, usually according to a written agreement or treaty.

Joint ventures during the mid-1980s united some of the world's leading corporations. General Motors and Toyota, for example, agreed to jointly produce economy cars at a new plant in California. The Boeing Corporation teamed with the Japanese Aircraft Development Corporation in 1986 to develop more sophisticated and fuel-efficient aircraft. RCA Corporation and Japan's Sharp Corporation agreed to build satellites together in the United States. Such recent changes in international trade have created new trade issues. One such issue is whether goods produced by joint ventures in the United States should ◆ be considered "American-made."

New types of trade agreements that distort free trade have also been formulated in the 1980s. For example, about 90 nations have imposed performance requirements on multinational corporations that build plants in their countries. Performance requirements stipulate that the corporation export a certain percentage of its output. Such requirements protect domestic industries. In a 1986 agreement between Toyota and the government of Taiwan, for example, the Toyota Corporation is obliged to eventually export up to 50 percent of the cars it produces in Taiwan.

See Suggested Assignments, p. TM 94.

Section 4 Review

See Answers, p. A 72.

DEFINE most-favored-nation status, trade adjustment assistance

IDENTIFY Reverend Leon Sullivan

1. **Summarizing Ideas** What are the main provisions of the Reciprocal Trade Agreements Act of 1934?
2. **Comprehending Ideas** What is the purpose of a regional trade organization?
3. **Interpreting Ideas** **(a)** What are two important changes in international trade in the 1980s? **(b)** How have these changes aided trade?

CHAPTER 17 SUMMARY

International trade allows individuals and businesses to specialize. It also causes worldwide economic interdependence. The value of specialization is determined by the absolute and comparative advantage that businesses hold. Nations, however, judge the strength of their international trade in terms of balance of trade and balance of payments.

The money needed to carry on international trade is generated through foreign exchange markets. These markets also allow business transactions. Historically, a variety of trade barriers have been used to regulate international trade. Tariffs and trade agreements protected domestic industries from foreign competition. Embargoes blocked foreign trade for political and economic reasons. Today, however, there has been a worldwide move to eliminate trade barriers.

Since the Great Depression there has been a steady move toward international cooperation among trading nations. The United States has led this cooperation with the passage of such laws as the Reciprocal Trade Agreements Act, the Trade Expansion Act, and the Trade Reform Act. Other world nations have formed regional trade organizations to eliminate trade barriers and foster cooperation. Nations have also entered into formal trade agreements aimed at reducing restrictions and guaranteeing the free flow of goods and services across national borders. When nations trade with one another, they are more able to specialize in the production of the goods that they produce best.

CHAPTER 17 REVIEW

For Answers to Chapter 17 Review, see p. A 72.

Reviewing Economic Terms

With each definition or description below, match one of the following terms.

a. import
b. export
c. tariff
d. quota
e. embargo
f. devaluation
g. comparative advantage
h. balance of payments
i. exchange rate

_____ **1.** The complete restriction on imports from or exports to a specific country.
_____ **2.** A good bought from other countries.
_____ **3.** A good sold to people in foreign countries.
_____ **4.** A restriction on the number of imported goods.
_____ **5.** The relative values of two currencies.
_____ **6.** The production of those goods and services with the least opportunity cost.
_____ **7.** An accounting of all payments sent to and received from other nations.
_____ **8.** A reduction by the government of the value of its currency in relation to other world currencies.

Exercising Economic Skills

1. **Comparing Economic Interpretations** Reread the excerpts on pages 176–177 of this textbook. Construct a chart, as shown in the example on page 392, to compare the interpretations and fill in the chart with information from the excerpts. **(a)** In a paragraph, tell how the two interpretations are similar. **(b)** In a second paragraph, tell how the interpretations are different.
2. **Buying a New Car** Study the feature on pages 533–535. Then suppose you are in the market for a new car. Select two models of automobiles to purchase and consult information on each model in *Consumer Reports.* Compare **(a)** the features offered, **(b)** the incidence of repair record, **(c)** the price, and **(d)** the magazine's evaluation for each model. **(e)** Write a report identifying which automobile you would buy, defending your choice. Prepare a chart to accompany your report to the class.

Thinking Critically About Economics

1. **Summarizing Ideas** **(a)** Why do nations engage in international trade? **(b)** Why do nations restrict the free exchange of products across national borders? **(c)** What are some recent examples of international cooperation?
2. **Understanding Ideas** How are **(a)** paperwork and **(b)** licensing requirements barriers to trade?
3. **Seeing Relationships** What is the relationship between a nation's level of specialization and its economic interdependence?
4. **Interpreting Ideas** If a nation's currency is too strong, what can the nation do to improve the competitiveness of its exports?
5. **Using Economic Imagination** Why does a nation that has an absolute advantage in the production of almost all products still gain from international trade?
6. **Interpreting Viewpoints** Why do some people favor the development of an industrial policy for the United States?

Extending Economic Knowledge

1. Research the exchange rates of the Japanese yen, the British pound, the French franc, the Canadian dollar, and the West German mark with the United States dollar since 1980. Prepare a graph to accompany your report to the class.
2. Survey a retail establishment. Select one imported item and one similar item produced domestically. **(a)** Which product has a higher price? Why? **(b)** Which product would you most likely buy? Why? Present your answers in a report to the class.
3. Research the United States policy on import limitations on foreign automobiles. Prepare a speech that calls for either increased limits on the importation of foreign automobiles into the United States or the elimination of such limitations. In preparing a speech favoring increased limitations, be sure to consider the effects of protectionist legislation on the overall economy. In preparing a speech seeking the elimination of limitations, be sure to consider the effects on the economy of increased competition by foreign automakers.

Using Primary Sources

The 1986 *Economic Report of the President* analyzes many types of issues. It also presents statistical data on economic activity and explains the present administration's policy initiatives. As you read the following excerpts, consider why President Reagan supports free and fair trade. What issues in international trade does he say are particularly important to the United States?

Free and Fair Trade

The President's Trade Policy Action Plan is based on the concept of free and fair trade. The guiding principle behind this policy is that opening foreign markets to enable greater U.S. sales is preferable to closing U.S. markets to foreigners.

An important goal of the President's Trade Policy Action Plan is to begin a new round of Multilateral Trade Negotiations under the auspices of GATT [General Agreement on Trade and Tariffs]. . . . U.S. objectives in the new round center on extending GATT discipline to areas where international rules are limited or nonexistent. . . . [Two] areas of particular interest are . . . services, [and] intellectual property rights. . . .

Trade in services is growing rapidly. Many activities fall in this category—tourism, transportation, insurance, banking, advertising, engineering design, data processing, and the transmission of information. The United States has . . . a skilled work force and a high rate of innovation to serve the large domestic market. A U.S. goal is to establish the right of entry in foreign markets and also to establish the principle of national treatment or nondiscrimination against foreign providers of services. . . .

The protection of intellectual property is of growing importance to the United States. U.S. research creativity has resulted in the successful introduction of many new products and processes. . . . A priority for the U.S. Government is to establish wider international agreements protecting intellectual property. Some U.S. concerns deal with the lack of patent, copyright, trademark, and trade secret protection or compulsory licensing provisions.

Another important objective of Administration trade policy is to ensure that markets remain open and that competition takes place under internationally agreed trading rules. Countries should be expected to live up to their international commitments regarding market access. The Administration has increasingly emphasized the standard of fair trade, because reduced market access generally reduces the profitability for U.S. exporters, worsens the U.S. terms of trade, and results in a lower U.S. standard of living. . . .

Unfair practices often extend beyond issues covered by GATT. However, U.S. actions embody the principle that nations benefiting from the current trading system have an obligation to apply to other areas of international commerce the spirit of open trading relationships established for merchandise trade. Negotiated settlements appear possible in some areas as like-minded nations recognize their own self-interest in moving toward a more open world economy. . . .

Source Review

For Answers to Source Review, see p. A 73.

1. President Reagan supports fair trade. What is fair trade? Why does the United States support fair trade policies? Ultimately, why does the Reagan administration believe that fair trade is beneficial to all nations?
2. What "guiding principle" underlies the President's Trade Policy Action Plan?
3. What two areas of concern does the President want future rounds of GATT to deal with? Why are these areas important to the American economy?
4. Why is the protection of "intellectual property" a priority of the U.S. Government?
5. What view about market access does the administration take?

CHAPTER 18

See Chapter Overview, p. TM 96.
See Chapter Objectives, p. TM 96.
See Introducing the Chapter, p. TM 96.
See Extending Economic Knowledge on text p. 436.

Economic Growth in the Developing World

. . . [T]he government has to create mechanisms for economic development; it cannot allow the processes of redistribution and fragmentation to continue unchecked because they are obstacles to development. . . .

Marina Ottaway

1 Developing nations share many common economic traits.

- Low Per Capita GNP
- Limited Resources
- Rapid Population Growth
- Traditional Agricultural Economies

2 Obstacles to economic growth exist in developing nations.

- Scarcity and Resource Use
- Noneconomic Obstacles

3 Decision makers seek to overcome obstacles to economic growth.

- Decision-Making Models
- Planning for Economic Development

4 Domestic and international funds finance economic development in developing nations.

- Domestic Savings
- Private Sources of Capital
- Foreign Aid
- International Development Organizations

You may wish to have the students refer to the *World Economic Data File* on pages 481–498 of THE REFERENCE LIBRARY as they study Chapter 18.

CHAPTER 18 STUDY GUIDE

Chapter Focus

Chapter 18 examines the economies of the world's developing nations. Despite the great variety of peoples and cultures, developing nations share many characteristics and face many of the same obstacles to economic growth. The chapter also discusses how leaders in the developing nations undertake economic development.

As you study the chapter, look for the details that support each of the following statements:

1. Developing nations share many common economic traits.
2. Obstacles to economic growth exist in developing nations.
3. Decision makers seek to overcome obstacles to economic growth.
4. Domestic and international funds finance economic development in developing nations.

See Preteaching Vocabulary, p. TM 96.

Terms to Know

The following terms, while not the only terms emphasized in this chapter, are basic to your understanding of developing nations. Determine the meaning of each term, either by using the Glossary or by watching for context clues as you read the chapter.

economic development
developed nations
developing nations
subsistence agriculture
one-crop economy
capital formation
default
nationalization
expropriation
development plan
green revolution
land reform
economic assistance
military assistance

See Key Study Questions and Key Understandings, p. TM 97.

1 Developing nations share many common economic traits.

See Suggested Teaching Strategies, p. TM 97.

◆ There are more than 160 nations in the world, each at a different stage of economic development. **Economic development** is a broad term that includes the size and sophistication of a nation's industrial, service, and agricultural sectors.

The industrialized nations of the world, which economists often classify as **developed nations,** have a high level of economic sophistication. Only about 30 nations, among them the United States, Canada, Japan, New Zealand, Australia, the Soviet Union, and most of the nations of eastern and western Europe, are considered developed nations. The combined populations of the developed nations compose about one quarter of the world's population.

The remaining world nations, about 130, are classified by economists as **developing nations.** Three fourths of the world's population live in developing nations. The developing nations are characterized by a low per capita Gross National Product (GNP), limited resources, a rapid population growth rate, and agricultural economies with traditional lifestyles.

Low Per Capita GNP

A nation's per capita GNP, a frequently used indicator of the standard of living, is the average dollar value of its annual total output for each person. The per capita GNP is calculated by dividing the nation's total GNP by its population.

Economists often subdivide developing nations into low-income and middle-income nations according to the per capita GNP. In the 1980s, the per capita GNP of low-income developing nations was $420

◆ Protectorates and colonies are not included in the number of nations in the world.

or less. For middle-income developing nations, it ranged between $420 and $5,669. In contrast, the developed nations had per capita GNPs of $5,670 or more (see table on this page and map on page 425).

Since the 1950s, the average real per capita GNP for low-income developing nations has increased at a faster rate than that of the middle-income developing nations and the developed nations. The average annual increase of real per capita GNP for low-income nations climbed from 1.6 percent between 1955 and 1970 to 4.9 percent between 1980 and 1984. Annual increases in the real per capita GNP for middle-income developing nations and developed nations slowed during the 1970s and 1980s, and actually declined for the middle-income developing nations between 1980 and 1984.

Limited Resources

The scarcity of resources in the developing nations is the result of both natural and historic forces. Natural forces that affect the uneven distribution of resources include climate, arable land, water resources, mineral deposits, and other gifts of nature. For example, in Libya, Mali, Niger, and other developing nations bordering the Sahara Desert, less than 4 percent of the land is arable, due chiefly to the lack of rainfall. On the other hand, in tropical Africa where rainfall is plentiful, the soil is drained of its fertility and is unsuitable for most types of agriculture.

Historic forces that affect uneven resource distribution include the decisions and actions of people. For example, many of today's developing nations are former European colonies. From the 1500s to the mid-1900s, the European powers used colonies to supply raw materials to the industries of the homeland. In turn, the European powers made only limited investments in the colonial economic structures. In some ways, this colonialism retarded economic development in much of Asia, Africa, and Latin America, especially after these nations gained independence (see Highlights in Economics, page 414).

Rapid Population Growth

The **population growth rate,** or the annual percentage of increase in a nation's population, is higher in most developing nations than it is in the developed nations. Since 1965, the population-growth rate of many of the developing nations in Latin America, the Middle East, Africa, and Asia has been nearly 3 percent. This growth rate is about three times higher than the rate of the developed nations. The world's population increased by more than 2 billion people between 1950 and 1985. Almost 90 percent of this increase occurred in the developing nations.

Per Capita GNP of Selected Nations

Nation	Per Capita GNP in 1984 $US
Bolivia	$540
Chile	$1,700
China	$310
Egypt	$720
El Salvador	$710
Ethiopia	$110
France	$9,760
Ghana	$350
Haiti	$320
Hungary	$2,100
India	$260
Israel	$5,060
Italy	$6,420
Kenya	$310
Mexico	$2,040
Nicaragua	$860
Nigeria	$730
Pakistan	$380
Peru	$1,000
Philippines	$660
Saudi Arabia	$10,530
Singapore	$7,260
Soviet Union	*
Tanzania	$210
Thailand	$860
Turkey	$1,160
United Kingdom	$8,570
United States	$15,390
Yugoslavia	$2,120
Zaire	$140

*Data not available
Source: The World Bank World Development Report, 1986

HIGHLIGHTS IN ECONOMICS

The Third World's Struggle for Economic Independence

The colonialism that has dominated the history of many Third World nations has left them a difficult legacy. Through colonialism, the people of the Third World have glimpsed the wonders of modern technology and the bustle of modern economic activity. The high standard of living enjoyed by the developed world has left Third World people with rising expectations. Yet the colonial powers did little to help their colonies modernize. When the colonies began to achieve independence after World War II they found that the legacies of the past had left them ill-equipped economically for successful competition.

At the time of their political independence, the new Third World nations had hardly begun to develop economically. Colonial powers tended to invest in their colonies only as necessary to produce and export a particular crop or raw material. The economic activities of colonial powers provided few jobs for members of colonial populations. They also generated little capital beyond the amount that made its way back to the colonial powers.

Furthermore, the people of the newly independent nations had little education and little experience in either business or politics. In most colonies, less than one fourth of the population had received any formal education. Few people had held managerial positions in business or received any technological training on the job.

Local populations had been governed by outsiders for years, perhaps had never noted, and certainly had never tried to organize a modern political and economic system. Suddenly independent, the people had little to work with except nationalistic pride and in some cases resentment against the system that oppressed them.

Colonialism, however, set a goal for Third World achievement by providing a glimpse of how developed economies work. Many Third World nations are still trying to reach this goal.

Traditional Agricultural Economies

Most people in the developing nations still rely on subsistence agriculture for survival. In **subsistence agriculture,** families grow just enough to meet basic needs, producing no crop surpluses to trade. A few developing nations, however, have been able to produce surpluses of agricultural products to sell in international markets. These surpluses are usually in such commercial plantation crops as coffee from Colombia and Brazil, rubber from Malaysia, cocoa from Ghana and the Ivory Coast, and sugar from the Caribbean nations. These cash crops are generally raised solely for export by the producers, who are usually the traditional landed elite.

In the developing nations, tradition largely determines the answers to the basic economic questions of what and how much to produce, how to produce, and who should produce. Subsistence agriculture reinforces a traditional lifestyle because people are tied to the land and remain relatively isolated from the outside world. Custom often plays the most important role in shaping people's religious beliefs and practices, the size of families, and the role of women in society—all of which have economic implications for developing nations.

See Suggested Assignments, p. TM 97.

Section 1 Review See Answers, p. A 74.

DEFINE population growth rate, subsistence agriculture

1. **Comprehending Ideas** **(a)** What is included in the economic definition of economic development? **(b)** How many nations do economists classify as *developed?* **(c)** How many do they classify as *developing?*
2. **Interpreting Ideas** What has been the impact of colonialism on Third World nations?
3. **Analyzing Ideas** Why is a high population growth rate a hindrance to economic growth in developing nations?
4. **Interpreting Graphics** Study the chart on page 413. Using the criteria on pages 412–413, classify the nations on the chart into three categories: low-income developing nations, middle-income developing nations, and developed nations.

See Key Study Questions and Key Understandings, p. TM 98.

2 Obstacles to economic growth exist in developing nations.

See Suggested Teaching Strategies, p. TM 98.

Two major obstacles that hinder rapid progress in developing nations are the scarcity and underutilization of resources and adverse environmental factors. ◆

Scarcity and Resource Use

To achieve economic growth and development, a nation must be able to increase its total per capita output of goods and services. But to increase the output of goods and services, a developing nation must improve the quantity and quality of the factors of production. This improvement, in turn, relies on the effective utilization of resources. The scarcity and underutilization of technology, entrepreneurship, and natural, human, and capital resources affect the potential for growth in the developing nations.

In cotton, sugar, and coffee, Peru's agricultural output is high enough to provide a surplus for export.

◆ Environmental factors such as drought, bitter winters, hurricanes, and forest fires may destroy crops and natural resources in a short time, yet economic recovery from such disasters may require several years.

Natural Resources. Most developing nations lack the variety of natural resources that the United States and the Soviet Union enjoy. As a result, developing nations tend to specialize in the production of one or a few goods, usually agricultural products or raw materials. While specialization promotes international trade (see Chapter 17), it can also lead to one-crop economies.

Concentration on the production of a single item is a **one-crop economy.** In the definition of one-crop economies, economists use the term "crop" to include many nonagricultural products, such as minerals.

One-crop economies are often unstable because the entire economy rests on the world price of a single commodity. For example, the oil glut of the mid-1980s caused world prices for oil to drop from more than $35 a barrel in the early 1980s to less than $10 a barrel in the spring of 1986. The oil-price drop crippled the economies of most oil-producing nations (see the Case Study, page 418). Similarly, the drop in world sugar prices from about $0.30 a pound in 1980 to less than $0.03 a pound in 1985 caused economic hardship in many Caribbean and Central American sugar-producing nations.

Human Resources. The quantity and the skill level of workers determine the effectiveness of human resources. Most developing nations have an ample quantity of workers because of their high population growth rates. Substandard education and job training, an inadequate diet, and the low level of medical care, however, often result in low worker productivity. In addition, high unemployment and underemployment, a result of unstable economies, plague developing nations.

Most developing nations recognize the importance of a long-term investment in human resources. For this reason, many developing nations are spending more money on primary and secondary education. Shortages of funds, however, limit the number of schools and qualified teachers. As a result, education in some developing nations is available only to people living in urban areas.

Capital Resources. Capital is essential to economic growth, but it is in short supply in most developing nations. Capital, transformed into plants, machinery, and other equipment, increases worker productivity.

A basic economic goal of many developing nations is **capital formation,** the accumulation of the financial resources and capital goods necessary for sound economic development. Three major obstacles—the lack of savings, the lack of private investment, and the rapid deterioration of the existing capital stock—hinder capital formation in the developing nations.

The first obstacle, the lack of savings, occurs because people in developing nations find it difficult to put off present consumption. Many people are already living at a subsistence level. After meeting their immediate needs for food, shelter, and clothing, they have nothing left to put into savings.

With insufficient domestic savings, the financing of capital formation must come from private capital. Investors, however, shy away from investing in corporations from developing nations. First, they fear that business leaders may be inexperienced and make mistakes about what goods to produce or what types of capital to use in the production process. Second, incentives to invest in markets where the domestic population has little or no money to spend on consumer goods is lacking. Third, the economic, political, and social environment in many developing nations is in a period of change. Investors fear to put their money in situations where instability is present. Finally, the lack of roads, railroads, and utilities discourages investment spending because the shortcomings of the economic infrastructure impede the production and distribution of finished products.

Capital goods often deteriorate more rapidly in developing nations than in developed nations. Mechanical breakdowns occur because of human error or because workers are unable to read operation and maintenance manuals. With a scarcity of trained mechanics, repairs to broken machinery are delayed. Furthermore, spare parts for many machines are in short supply and delays occur in securing replacements, which are often available only from manufacturers in other nations. Even with competent workers, normal wear and tear on machinery is expected. The lack of spare parts also limits the long-term operation of capital goods. Fuel shortages and resistance to change also have hindered progress in some developing nations.

Technology and Entrepreneurship. The same forces that account for the gap in capital formation between the developing nations and the developed nations also account for the gap in technology and entrepreneurship. The lack of savings and private investment retards the growth of technological change and the formation of an entrepreneurial class in the developing nations.

Technology and entrepreneurship also suffer from insufficient financial support from the government. Many developing nations make large expenditures for national defense. The emphasis on political development leaves little money in the national budgets to finance economic development and such social needs as universal public education.

Businesspeople and government officials in developing nations debate the question of how to achieve economic development by producing the most appropriate goods and services. To compete in world markets, production output in developing nations must match the production output of the developed nations, making technology necessary. Technology appropriate for developing nations such as India, however, is different from technology appropriate for the highly industrialized nations. Most developing nations now recognize that trying to copy the rapid industrialization of the Western model may not be the best way to achieve their economic goals.

In many developing nations, some people work in modern factories while others choose to work in more traditional industries.

CASE STUDY

The Limits of Oil

The economic health of Nigeria, one of 13 OPEC nations, and Mexico, an independent oil producer, relies on the production of oil. Both Nigeria and Mexico are among the world's leading oil-producing nations. Oil accounts for 95 percent of Nigeria's total exports and 70 percent of Mexico's. The dependence on oil gives both nations one-crop economies.

During the late 1970s and early 1980s, when oil commanded a high price on the world market, Nigeria and Mexico experienced economic growth. For example, in 1981 Nigeria, as a member of OPEC, produced 2 million barrels of oil a day, receiving nearly $40 for each barrel. Similarly, as an independent producer, Mexico sold oil for more than $35 on the spot market. By 1983, an oil glut occurred, causing the price of oil to decline. By 1986, the price of oil had dropped to about $10 a barrel. The economic impact on Nigeria and Mexico was immediate, demonstrating the instability of one-crop economies.

The oil glut affected the economies of Nigeria and Mexico in two important ways. First, lower oil prices reduced government revenues, forcing the governments to reduce expenditures for public goods. In Nigeria, the government halted construction on a steel plant, postponed plans to build a new capital city, and put off the upkeep of roads and schools. In Mexico, government spending on public works, education, and other social services also declined.

Second, the drop in revenue from oil production made Nigeria, Mexico, and other developing nations put off their loan payments. During the 1970s and early 1980s, lenders were eager to extend credit to oil-producing nations. Between 1978 and 1986, the total debt (principal plus interest) rose by about $100 billion (see the graph on page 419).

The failure of oil-producing nations to meet repayment schedules alarmed banks and governments in developed nations because it threatened default. **Default** occurs when a nation wipes its foreign debts off its books. By 1986, developing nations owed a staggering $1 trillion to developed nations.

Developing nations have taken different approaches in coping with their growing foreign debts. Nigeria has limited foreign debt payments to 30 percent of the value of its exports. Mexico repeatedly has rescheduled debt repayments, extending them for longer periods of time, as well as reducing the size of each payment. Both nations have also begun to develop more diversified economies to avoid the weaknesses of a one-crop system.

Noneconomic Obstacles

In the United States, the economic, political, and social environment has contributed to economic growth. In the developing nations, however, environmental forces have often created obstacles to economic development.

Inadequate Economic Infrastructure. In many developing nations, the economic infrastructure is inhospitable to economic development. Developing nations lack well-developed communication systems and systems of roads, railroads, bridges, harbors, and airports. Inadequate systems for communication and the transport of goods and services disrupt and impede business activity. Inadequate schools and a shortage of teachers restrict the number of literate workers, technicians, scientists, and entrepreneurs who are needed to shape economic progress in developing nations.

In addition, some developing nations lack a stable monetary and banking system, discouraging savings and investments. For example, in the early 1980s, extremely high inflation rates in Bolivia and Brazil rendered their currency worthless. Nationalization and expropriation of private property also discourage savings and investment. In **nationalization,** the government assumes ownership and control of a business, after compensating the former owner. On the other hand, in **expropriation,** the government takes control of a firm or industry without compensating the owner. Developing nations have nationalized or expropriated many types of enterprises such as mines, farms, oil refineries, and factories.

Nations with histories of nationalizing or expropriating properties lose domestic and foreign investment because investors fear the loss of their investment. For example, when the socialist government in Tanzania nationalized many private banks

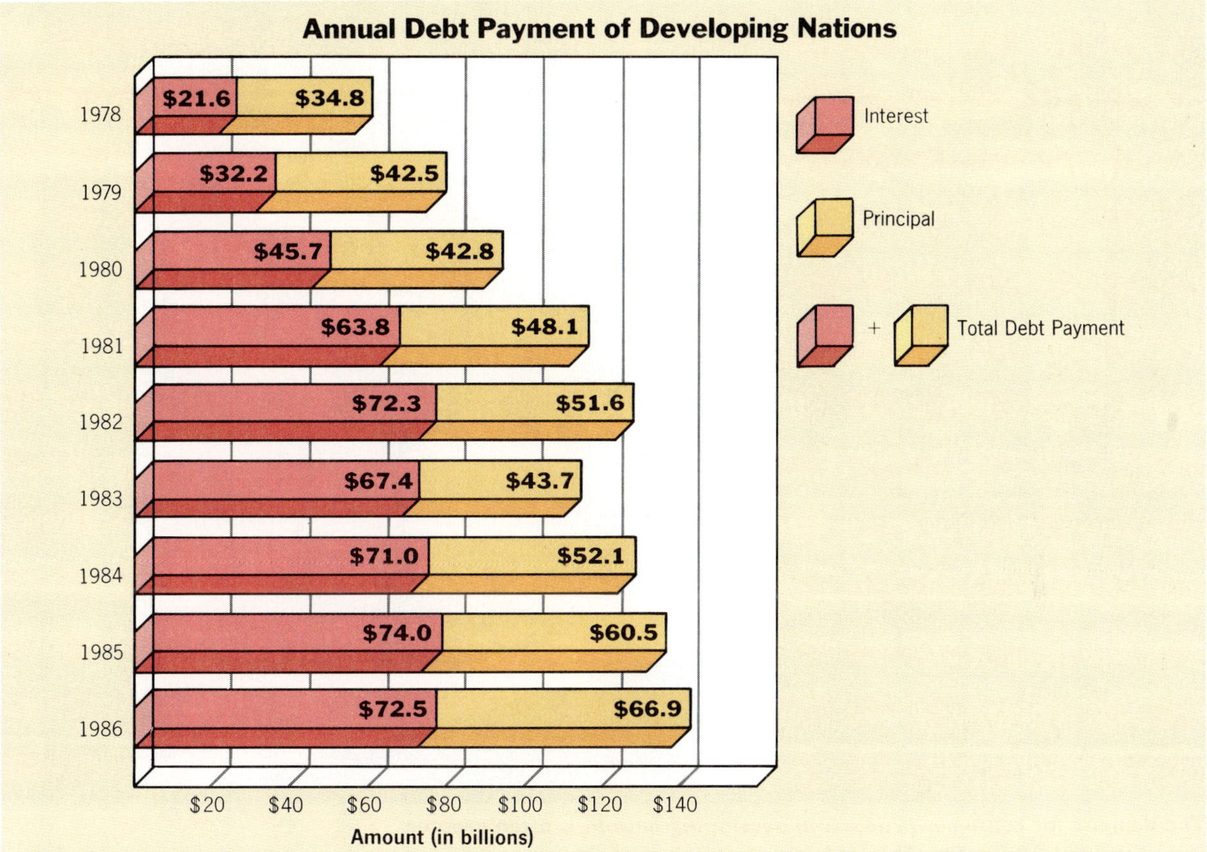

Source: *World Economic Outlook, 1985,* International Monetary Fund

and industrial firms, frightened investors sent their money out of the country, and foreign investors looked elsewhere for investment opportunities.

Political Instability. The frequent political instability in some developing nations is another disincentive to savings and investments. Domestic and foreign investors need to be assured that their investments are secure and that there is a reasonable chance to make a profit on them. Revolutions, civil wars, and riots indicate political instability and hinder economic development.

During the 1980s, power struggles in Angola, Mozambique, Nicaragua, El Salvador, Ethiopia, and Sri Lanka have disrupted normal business activity. The Iran-Iraq War that began in 1981 has resulted in the destruction of capital resources, including oil refineries, pipelines, and merchant ships. In each of these countries, huge sums of money have been spent on military goods rather than on consumer goods and the capital investments that result in economic progress.

Social and Cultural Obstacles. In some developing nations, the social and cultural environment restricts economic development. National traditions, attitudes toward work, rigid class structures, and rising expectations often interfere with a nation's economic planning and development.

Strong cultural customs lead people to resist changes in traditional production methods. Predominantly agricultural areas, which many developing nations are, remain more bound by tradition than nations that are predominantly urbanized. In recent decades, however, education and increased contacts with the developed world have weakened some resistance to economic change.

A relatively weak work ethic limits economic progress in some developing nations. The strong work ethic established in most developed nations

◆ Have the students read "Hotel Managers" on page 542 of *Careers in the Marketplace.*

The demand for consumer products in developing nations is often greater than the available supply. This undersupply tends to increase prices.

has stressed the value of discipline in work habits. For example, Japan's strong work ethic is tied to *bushido,* a centuries-old attitude based on self-discipline and loyalty to superiors.

The rising expectations of people, who expect their material well-being to improve quickly, is a potentially disruptive social force that impedes economic progress in some developing nations. Contact ◆ with the developed world through the mass media has taught people in many developing nations that a better life is possible for them. When these rising expectations cannot be matched by immediate improvements, the people are often stirred to agitation and revolution.

Finally, a rigid class structure in some developing nations limits opportunities for people to improve their economic well-being. An inability to climb the social and economic ladder reduces the incentive to become better educated. Furthermore, the ruling class often opposes change because the present social system guarantees them a privileged position.

See Suggested Assignments, p. TM 98.

Section 2 Review

See Answers, p. A 74.

DEFINE one-crop economy, capital formation, default, nationalization, expropriation

1. **Comprehending Ideas** **(a)** What must a developing country do to achieve real economic growth? **(b)** What major obstacles hinder rapid progress and potential for growth in the developing nations?
2. **Summarizing Ideas** What is the danger of a nation's dependence on a one-crop economy?
3. **Seeing Relationships** What is the relationship of education to a nation's potential for economic development?
4. **Interpreting Graphics** Study the graph on page 419. What generalization can you make about the overall debt of developing nations between 1977 and 1986?

See Key Study Questions and Key Understandings, p. TM 99.

3 Decision makers seek to overcome obstacles to economic growth.

See Suggested Teaching Strategies, p. TM 99.

Because decision makers in the developing nations operate within different types of economic systems and have established different goals for their nations, developing nations follow different paths to economic growth and development.

Decision-Making Models

Some leaders in developing nations use the socialist model of decision making, and some use the capitalist model.

The Socialist Model. Decision making in the socialist model, which is associated with Communist governments, is centralized in the hands of the government. For example, a central planning agency called the *Gosplan* dictates how resources in the Soviet Union are used. A number of developing nations, including Cuba, Nicaragua, Angola, and Vietnam have adopted the socialist model of decision making.

The most important advantage of central planning is that the government can direct resources and production toward specific economic goals. The major disadvantages of central planning are the inefficiency, resistance to change, and occasional corruption of the bureaucracy that formulates and implements the central plan.

Regardless of what economic decision-making model a developing nation employs, education is a basic necessity for economic growth.

In many developing nations, the electronics industry has helped reduce unemployment and spur economic growth by opening parts-assembly plants.

The Capitalist Model. In a decentralized market economy, private individuals make most of the decisions. The economic progress of the United States, western Europe, and Japan has demonstrated that economic development is possible through decentralized decision making. For this reason, the economies of many developing nations now use a capitalist model of decision making. For example, some of the most successful developing nations in East Asia, such as Singapore, Taiwan, South Korea, and Hong Kong, rely on the capitalist model.

In recent years, more developing nations have moved toward the capitalist model of decision making. During the mid-1980s, for example, Prime Minister Rajiv Gandhi of India has removed many bureaucratic restrictions on economic growth. Similarly, in the 1980s a reduced government role in the economies of Guinea, Ghana, Malawi, and Zimbabwe has led to freer markets and increased production. In China, Deng Xiaoping has established reforms that have resulted in substantial growth in China's industrial and agricultural sectors.

The major advantage of the capitalist model of decision making is free enterprise. Freedom of enterprise encourages individuals to become entrepreneurs. Freedom of enterprise also encourages businesses to invest in new capital and technology. Individuals work and produce because it is in their own self-interest to do so.

The major disadvantage to decentralized decision making is that there are few direct controls on the use of resources in the economy. The government, for example, may believe that businesses should invest more in capital goods to spur future economic growth. Businesses, however, may choose to produce additional consumer goods to meet consumer demands rather than invest capital in capital goods for future economic growth and stability. ◆ In the capitalist model, the government exercises its influence on the economy indirectly through taxing, subsidies, and various regulations. Commanding adherence to its wishes is an action that many governments in a free enterprise economy seldom take.

◆ **The wide variety of goods available to consumers in the United States provides Americans with one of the highest standards of living in the world.**

Planning for Economic Development

Whether developing nations prefer the socialist or capitalist models of decision making, they must formulate development plans. A **development plan,** an outline of how a nation's resources should be used to meet its economic goals, is essential to economic progress. In socialist economies, central planners in the government bureaucracy dictate the development plan. In capitalist economies, where the mix of public and private decision making varies from country to country, elected representatives of the government and private-sector executives together devise the development plan.

Trade-offs. Inevitably, because scarcity prevents the developing nations from satisfying all of their economic needs and wants, they make trade-offs in their development plans. For example, a developing nation may need a new irrigation system for one region of the country and a new road for another region. Lacking the resources to meet both needs, the government makes a choice. If the irrigation system receives funding, the new road is the trade-off. In such a case, decision makers consider the road to be the "second-best" use of resources, so the road becomes the opportunity cost of building the irrigation system.

Production Possibilities. To recognize the realities of trade-offs and opportunity costs in the developing world, note the range of economic choices in the production possibilities curve on the graph on this page. The graph charts one major type of production decision faced by all developing nations—whether to produce more capital goods or more consumer goods.

The production possibilities curve **AD** illustrates all of the possible production combinations of consumer and capital goods for a hypothetical country. The horizontal axis shows units of consumer goods and the vertical axis shows units of capital goods. At point **A,** 9 units of capital goods and 0 units of consumer goods are produced, meaning all resources are channeled into the production of capital goods. At point **D,** 9 units of consumer goods and 0 units of capital goods are produced because all resources are devoted to the production of consumer goods.

Decision makers realize that all production decisions have a cost. For example, suppose a developing

Trade-offs and Production Possibilities in Developing Nations

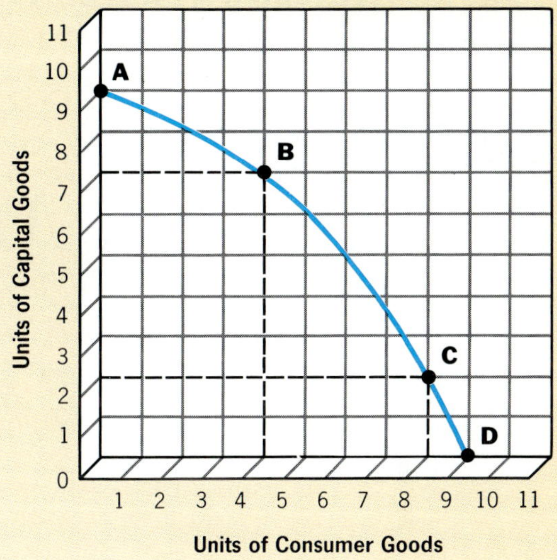

country's development plan focuses on the production of capital goods. At point **B,** 7 units of capital goods are produced, while only 4 units of consumer goods are produced. In this case, the opportunity cost of producing 7 units of capital goods is the 3 units of consumer goods that cannot be produced $(7-4=3)$.

On the other hand, suppose the decision makers in the hypothetical country decide to concentrate on the production of consumer goods. At point **C,** 8 units of consumer goods are produced, and only 2 units of capital goods are produced. The opportunity cost of producing 8 units of consumer goods is 6 units of capital goods $(8-2=6)$.

The graph shown above is a simplified model of the trade-offs and opportunity costs involved in making production decisions. The model assumes that nations can devote all of their resources to just two types of goods—consumer or capital goods. In reality, there are other production choices, including the choice of spending money on military or nonmilitary goods, or investing more heavily in agricultural or industrial capital. The graph also assumes a constant level of resources. In reality, a nation's production possibilities change as its resource levels change.

Text continues on page 426.

INTERPRETING THE VISUAL RECORD

Analyzing Economic-Data Maps

An economic-data map is a map that provides information on economic topics such as the distribution of resources, membership in international economic organizations, levels of economic development, population density, and information on manufacturing, agriculture, and trade. Like economic charts and graphs, economic-data maps are visual representations of economic information.

How to Analyze Economic-Data Maps

To effectively analyze an economic-data map, follow these steps.

1. **Read the map's title.** The title states the economic topic of the map.

2. **Study the map key, or legend.** The legend explains the map's symbols and color code.

3. **Note all labels.** The names of national and geographic features, key terms, and other information are often written on the map.

4. **Note relationships.** Study the data on the map. Record key data. On resource maps, identify the quantity, variety, and location of resources. On population density maps, identify population clusters. On economic activity maps, note locations that rely on manufacturing, agriculture, or services.

5. **Use the map's information.** Formulate generalizations or draw conclusions from the data.

Applying the Skill

Study the map on page 425. The title indicates that the map's subject is level of economic development of world nations as determined by per capita GNP. Note the legend. Its color code establishes levels of per capita GNP. Review the definition of per capita GNP given in the textbook on page 340. Per capita GNP is used to determine a nation's level of economic development. Study the map to see what generalizations you can form from its data. One generalization is that many nations with the lowest per capita GNP are in Africa and Asia. Another generalization is that most of the nations with a per capita GNP greater than $5,000 are in the Northern Hemisphere. A third generalization is that several of the oil-producing nations have higher per capita GNPs than surrounding nations. Several other generalizations also may be formed from the data on the map.

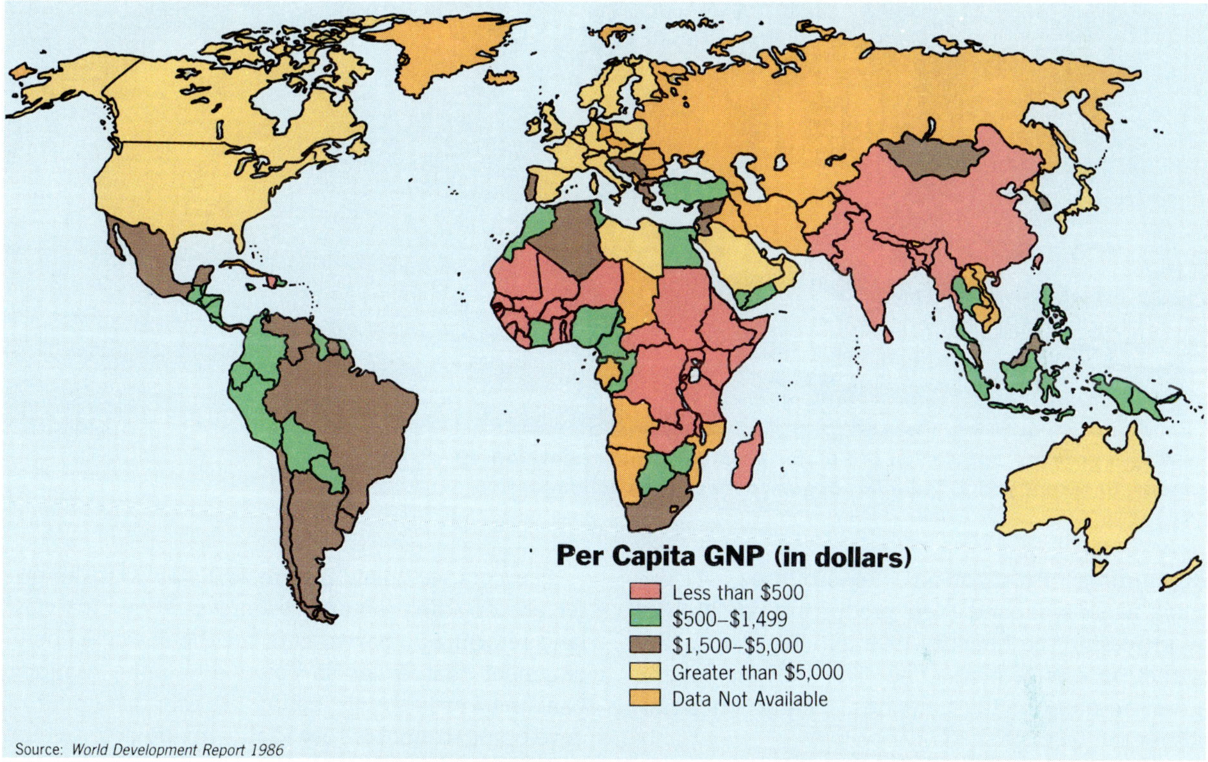

Practicing the Skill See Answers, p. A 75.

Study the economic-data map on the bottom of page 478 of the textbook's atlas. Then on a separate sheet of paper, answer the following questions.

1. **(a)** What is the title of the map? **(b)** What does the map show?

2. **(a)** What five categories of the percentage of the labor force in agriculture are listed in the legend? **(b)** Which color represents the lowest percentage of the labor force employed in agriculture? **(c)** Which color represents the highest percentage? **(d)** For how many nations is data unavailable?

3. **(a)** What nations devote less than 26 percent of the labor force to agriculture? **(b)** Form a generalization to note the location of these nations.

4. **(a)** On which continent do many nations devote more than 75 percent of the labor force to agriculture? **(b)** Form a generalization to note the location of these nations.

5. What generalization can be made about the number of nations in which more than 50 percent of the labor force is employed in agriculture?

Feeding a growing population is a major problem in many developing nations. In recent years, India has begun to meet the challenge.

Expanding Production Possibilities. Developing nations expand their production possibilities by increasing the quantity or improving the quality of their factors of production. The successes of the "green revolution" illustrate how production possibilities can be expanded.

The **green revolution** is the application of modern capital and technology—advanced machinery, fertilizers, irrigation systems, pesticides, and pest-resistant and high-yielding hybrid seeds—to agriculture. Since 1945, the green revolution has expanded production possibilities in agriculture in many developing nations. The results of the green revolution in these countries has been impressive. For example, by the mid-1980s India, once a major food *importer*, became a food *exporter*.

Increasing the amount of land under cultivation and the number of laborers working the land also raises agricultural production. In many developing nations, the traditional landed elite has owned most of the arable land, some of which is unused. Some economic planners believe that land reform is essential to increased agricultural output. **Land reform** is the redistribution of arable land from a few major landowners to a larger number of the peasants who work the land.

See Suggested Assignments, p. TM 99.

Planners view land reform as a way to make better use of scarce natural resources. They also view land reform as a partial cure for the massive unemployment that exists in some developing nations. Land reform is slowly taking place in a number of developing countries, especially in Mexico, Central America, and South America.

Section 3 Review See Answers, p. A 75.

DEFINE development plan, land reform

1. **Comprehending Ideas** What is the chief characteristic of **(a)** the socialist model of economic decision making? **(b)** the capitalist model? What are the advantages and disadvantages of **(c)** central planning? **(d)** decentralized planning?
2. **Interpreting Ideas** What role do incentives play in **(a)** the capitalist model of decision making? **(b)** the socialist model?
3. **Analyzing Ideas** Why is the green revolution particularly important to developing nations seeking economic growth?

See Key Study Questions and Key Understandings, p. TM 100.

4 Domestic and international funds finance economic development in developing nations.

See Suggested Teaching Strategies, p. TM 100.

To finance economic development, developing nations rely on domestic and international funds. Domestic savings are the most important source of domestic funds. Foreign sources of funds come from foreign businesses and private nonprofit organizations, foreign governments, and international development organizations.

Domestic Savings

In some developing nations, domestic savings are a major source of funding for economic development. Developing nations have undertaken some impressive development projects such as roads, railroads, dams, and schools without foreign funding, even though many people in developing nations exist at a subsistence level.

The construction of the Trans-Gabon Railway, now two thirds complete, is one example of a development project financed entirely through domestic savings. Begun in the mid-1970s, this multibillion-dollar project cuts through dense tropical forests to link the coastal capital of Libreville with the nation's interior. Gabon's investment in sophisticated capital goods, especially its rail-laying machine, has contributed to the project's success. The massive hydroelectric plant constructed jointly by Paraguay and Brazil is another development project funded with domestic funds.

In most developing nations, however, domestic savings alone are insufficient to finance economic development. For this reason, many developing nations seek international capital from private sources and foreign aid.

Private Sources of Capital

Several major sources of private capital are available to developing nations. Among the sources are banks, multinational corporations, and nonprofit organizations.

This McDonald's in Bangkok, Thailand, is an example of the growing influence of multinational corporations in many developing nations.

The Impact of Multinational Corporations on the Developing World

A multinational corporation, often called a multinational or MNC, is a firm located in an industrialized country that produces or sells goods in other countries. Multinationals have a corporate headquarters and some production facilities in one country and other plants called subsidiaries in other countries.

Traditionally, multinationals have allowed their subsidiaries to make many types of production decisions. During the 1930s, however, a trend toward centralized decision making developed. Centralization allows the corporate headquarters to control resources closely and to coordinate its "global strategy" for the production and sale of its goods.

Advantages of Foreign Location

◆ Multinationals invest in foreign countries for four major reasons. First, MNCs locate in certain areas to reduce production costs. Most often, natural and human resources are less expensive in another country. Second, foreign investment is a way to reduce corporate taxes. For example, some nations offer generous tax breaks to attract MNCs. Third, MNCs produce goods outside their home country location to avoid such trade barriers as import quotas and protective tariffs. Finally, MNCs operate outside their home country to expand more readily the markets for their goods.

Multinationals invest in developed and developing nations. For example, many MNCs whose headquarters are located outside the United States have built plants in the United States. Nestlé (Switzerland), Volkswagen (Germany), Seagrams (Canada), and Nissan (Japan), are just a few foreign firms that produce goods in the United States.

American multinationals also invest heavily abroad. By 1984, American MNCs had about $233 billion invested in their subsidiaries and in other firms worldwide. In 1985, American MNCs spent over $42 billion on new capital in foreign countries, mostly in the developing world.

Multinationals in the Developing World

Economists continually debate the degree of influence that multinationals have on the economies of developing countries. Their debate centers on three important topics. They ask about employment opportunities for people in the developing nations. They look at their potential for stimulating economic growth. And they examine their influence in changing the quality of life for people in the developing countries.

Employment Opportunities. Supporters of multinationals argue that foreign investments increase employment opportunities in host nations. New jobs are created in the MNC plants, for example. In addition, jobs in other domestic industries result because MNCs need the goods and services of local suppliers, contractors, distributors, and others.

Critics of MNCs counter that jobs in the developing world are lost because of the multinationals. First, some local competitors are driven out of business by the larger, more efficient MNCs, costing some workers their jobs. Second, some MNCs build capital-intensive plants even in areas where the economy is labor-intensive and wages are low. For example, a Japanese firm recently built a robotized plant in India that did not expand job opportunities for the people in India.

The jobs that are created in developing nations by MNCs are usually positions that require few skills.

◆ Have the students read "Applying For A Passport" on pages 535–536 of the *Everyday Economics Handbook* and answer the questions that follow.

Critics further argue that MNCs often neglect to train local workers for skilled jobs or management positions.

Economic Growth. Supporters of multinationals argue that they promote economic growth in developing countries. First, MNCs add factors of production to the local economy. Second, MNCs have access to international financial markets. They can borrow money easily at the lowest possible rates. Third, they create global markets for the output of workers in developing nations. In recent years, MNCs have even distributed competing goods produced by local firms. For example, during the mid-1980s, Caterpillar Tractor Company marketed lift trucks produced by South Korea's Daewoo Company.

Critics counter that multinationals stifle economic growth in developing nations. They argue that MNCs drive competing firms out of business. When MNCs borrow money from local banks, critics claim that the supply of funds for other business loans is reduced. The shortage of loan funds then limits business expansion in other areas. MNCs have the power to stop producing goods and services when it is no longer in their best interests. For example, the recent consolidation of N.V. Phillips Company (Netherlands) resulted in the closing of 40 plants around the world.

Quality of Life. Supporters argue that multinationals improve the quality of life for people in the developing nations. The supporters point to higher employment and the increase in national income, with the subsequent rise in the standard of living. They also note that MNCs produce and market quality goods for local markets. Finally, supporters point to an increase in tax revenues from property taxes, corporate taxes and personal income taxes collected from the governments of the developing nations. Higher tax revenues for developing nations translate into more schools, hospitals, roads, and other facilities that help to improve the quality of life.

Critics counter that the social costs associated with the presence of multinationals in developing nations outweigh the benefits. They point out that MNC investments in developing countries have resulted in increases in pollution and corruption. Further, critics note that the benefits derived from MNC investments in developing countries are often unevenly distributed, widening the gap between the rich and the poor.

Reactions by Developing Nations

The size and the power of MNCs (see the chart on page 431) have led many developing countries to establish policies to balance their own national interests with the corporate interests of the MNCs.

Some developing nations have required multinationals to form joint partnerships with local firms. The requirement of joint partnerships gives local businesspeople some control over production decisions. At the same time, the joint partnerships enable local businesspeople to learn modern management techniques and skills. The requirement also helps to prevent the outflow of resources from the host nation.

Some developing nations have used the multinationals to stimulate the creation of local businesses. For example, during the 1950s and 1960s, the Japanese government sent students abroad to study technical and management skills. Foreign experts were also recruited to instruct Japanese workers and the management of Japanese firms. Partly as a result of this investment, Japan's postwar industries were able to compete with firms in other industrial nations.

In a further reaction to multinationals, developing nations have enacted many laws and regulations. Some have formulated strict tax codes to reduce the possibilities of corporate tax cheating. Some have passed regulations requiring MNCs to export a certain percentage of their output in order to protect their local manufacturers. Others have regulations that state that a certain number of local workers must be trained for skilled jobs, including plant management positions.

The ultimate reaction of developing nations to MNCs is the threat to nationalize, or take over, the ownership and operation of multinational subsidiaries. Some socialist nations of the Third World have nationalized foreign multinational subsidiaries. The major drawback to nationalization in a developing nation is that it reduces further investment in the nation—either domestic or foreign.

Banks and Multinational Corporations. Banks and multinational corporations (MNCs) are the major suppliers of private capital to developing nations. Banks extend loans to businesses and to governments in developing nations, and earn a profit by collecting interest payments on these loans. Multinational corporations also pump money and technology into the developing nations and earn profits from the sale of their output in local and international markets. The construction of new plants and the use of advanced machinery funded by the MNCs in turn, add to the host nation's capital goods (see the chart on page 431).

Political and economic instability, however, often discourages banks and MNCs from extending credit or investing in developing nations. Banks fear loan defaults by nations that are already heavily in debt, while MNCs fear the loss of capital investments due to political turmoil. Nevertheless, banks and MNCs have continued making loans in developing nations (see the graph below).

The Foreign Debt of Non-Oil-Producing Developing Nations

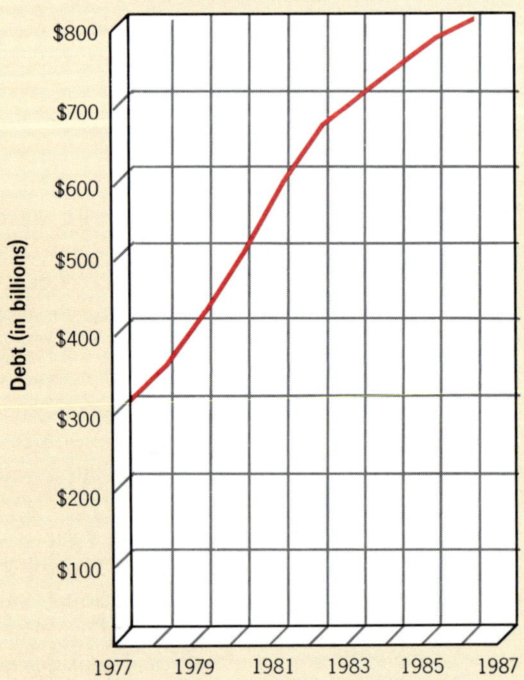

Source: *World Economic Outlook, 1985,* International Monetary Fund

Nonprofit Organizations. For many years, nonprofit organizations have supported development projects and supplied emergency aid to developing nations. The United States Peace Corps, for example, whose goal is to teach skills that increase worker productivity, provides agronomists, engineers, teachers, and other specialists to developing nations. More than 120,000 Americans have served in the Peace Corps, which was founded in 1961 by President John F. Kennedy. Today, about 6,000 American Peace Corps volunteers work in 60 nations.

Many other nonprofit organizations also provide aid to developing nations. For example, the International Red Cross and the Save the Children Fund provided food and medical assistance to famine victims in the Sudan, Ethiopia, and other sub-Saharan nations during the 1980s.

Foreign Aid

Foreign aid is the money, products, and services that governments extend to other nations. Each year foreign governments supply billions of dollars worth of economic assistance, military assistance, and emergency assistance to developing nations.

Forms of Assistance. Financial and technical aid, loans, and cash grants that contribute directly to economic development are known as **economic assistance.** Supplying the services of specialists such as engineers, scientists, teachers, and physicians is also considered economic assistance.

In 1984, foreign governments provided about $37 billion in economic assistance to developing nations. More than three fourths of all economic assistance comes from the developed nations, many of which are members of the Organization for Economic Cooperation and Development (OECD). OPEC nations and nations with centrally planned economies provided the remainder of the economic assistance.

Loans, cash payments, or technical training supplied to the military in developing nations are known as **military assistance.** Often a developed country extends military assistance to an allied nation, thus making military assistance an important part of the developed nation's foreign policy. The United States and the Soviet Union supply military assistance to many allies in the developing nations.

Finally, governments extend emergency assistance—food, medical supplies, clothing, and other goods that sustain life—at times of crisis. In 1985, for example, the United States provided emergency aid to famine victims in sub-Saharan Africa and to earthquake victims in Mexico.

Reasons for Extending Foreign Aid. The United States remains by far the largest source of foreign aid in the world. Like other developed nations, it extends foreign aid for economic, political, and humanitarian reasons.

First, foreign aid benefits international trade. The economic and social improvements made possible through foreign aid inject more money into the world economy. The stabilizing effects of foreign aid reduce political strife that often disrupts international trade. In addition, foreign aid often benefits the supplier because the aided countries often spend money on exports from that developed country.

Developed nations often extend foreign aid to induce developing nations to open their doors to multinational corporations from the developed nations. The profits earned by these multinational corporations go back to the developed nations. Thus foreign aid serves the economic self-interest of the developed nations.

Economics Reporter

What Is the Agency for International Development?

The Agency for International Development (AID) is an agency of the United States government that conducts programs to help developing nations use their human and capital resources to their best advantage. The assistance programs include population and health planning, technical assistance, and agricultural and educational programs. The agency was established by the Foreign Assistance Act of 1961 and is under the control of an administrator who reports to the President and the Secretary of State.

Developed nations sometimes grant foreign aid for political reasons because the aid promotes the nation's foreign policy. After World War II, for example, the United States channeled billions of dollars in military and economic aid to friendly European nations to stop the spread of Communism. By funding economic and physical rebuilding, the Truman Doctrine and the Marshall Plan improved postwar conditions while helping establish democracy and capitalism in Allied nations.

Multinationals: A Statistical Story

Multinational	Gross Sales*	Nation	GNP*
General Motors (U.S.)	$96.4	Brazil	$272.0
Exxon (U.S.)	$86.7	South Korea	$ 80.7
Royal Dutch/Shell (Neth.)	$81.7	Nigeria	$ 69.5
Mobil (U.S.)	$56.0	Argentina	$ 56.5
Ford (U.S.)	$52.8	Philippines	$ 41.6
IBM (U.S.)	$50.1	Egypt	$ 32.2
du Pont (U.S.)	$29.5	Iraq	$ 25.2
General Electric (U.S.)	$28.3	Tanzania	$ 5.0

*In billions

Sources: *Statistical Abstract of the United States, 1986; Fortune* (August 4, 1986)

Class activity: Have each student choose a developing nation and research the types, sources, and amounts of foreign aid that it is currently receiving. Students should use their information to construct a chart for the bulletin board.

In addition to foreign aid, many developing nations receive direct assistance in the form of famine relief, agricultural assistance, and support for education from various agencies and humanitarian groups.

During the 1960s, the United States established the Alliance for Progress to aid Latin American nations. Like the Marshall Plan, the Alliance for Progress programs were designed in part to improve the well-being of the people in Latin America and in part to promote democracy and oppose the spread

DECISION MAKERS IN THE ECONOMY

Barber Conable

In June 1986, Barber Conable became president of the World Bank, having served previously for more than 20 years as a United States Congressman from New York. During this time, he became an expert on United States tax policy and often spoke out in favor of free trade. Conable also became the ranking Republican member of the House Ways and Means Committee.

As president of the World Bank, Conable helps to set and implement the policies through which the institution lends $15 billion a year to developing nations. This job is not easy, particularly because many of these countries are already so deep in debt that they cannot repay loans on schedule.

In the past, the World Bank provided funds for agriculture and for such specific improvements as dams, roads, and ports. Now it has begun to offer new kinds of loans on the condition that receiving nations carry out specific economic reforms. By requiring these reforms, it hopes to convince banks in developed nations that the money they invest will be safe.

Developing nations have to agree to changes such as cuts in budget deficits and reduced taxes, changes that may actually hurt their economies temporarily. Lender banks, meanwhile, must trust that reforms will be effective, long before they can see any results.

To convince both debtors and lenders of the validity of the World Bank's plan is one part of Barber Conable's job. He also has to see that agreed-upon conditions go into effect.

of Communism. Often, foreign aid leads to further political and military cooperation among nations.

A final major motive for granting foreign aid is the reduction of human suffering. Nonprofit organizations, governments, and many international organizations have a humanitarian motive for providing ◆ foreign aid.

Effectiveness of Foreign Aid. Foreign aid has improved the standard of living and quality of life for millions of people in the developing nations. Still, experts question whether people in the developing nations are receiving the maximum benefit from foreign aid.

Some experts, for example, believe that closer supervision by the developed nations can improve the effectiveness of aid programs. Such supervision is often strongly opposed by the people and governments of the developing nations, who view it as interference with their economic freedom. Nevertheless, governments and international development organizations are now attaching stipulations to some loans and other forms of assistance in an attempt to direct the use of economic resources more efficiently in developing nations.

International Development Organizations

International organizations are a major source of funding and often serve as a vehicle to distribute foreign aid. The largest international organizations are the World Bank, the International Monetary Fund, and the United Nations.

◆ Discussion topic: Whether the United States should provide foreign aid to countries with military dictatorships.

The Mexican economy is heavily dependent on oil production. With the recent drop in oil prices, Mexico has found it difficult to meet its loan obligations.

The World Bank. The World Bank was founded by leading non-Communist nations at the Bretton Woods Conference in 1944 to promote economic progress in the developing nations. The World Bank consists of the International Bank for Reconstruction and Development (IBRD) and its affiliates, the International Development Association (IDA) and the International Finance Corporation (IFC). Today, the World Bank has nearly $130 billion in outstanding loans and is extending about $15 billion in new loans each year.

With 144 members, the International Bank for Reconstruction and Development (IBRD) is the largest part of the World Bank. The IBRD raises funds for its loans by borrowing money in the money markets of the developed nations. IBRD loans, with interest rates near the market rates, must be paid back within 20 years.

Over the years, IBRD loans have been directed at certain types of development. During the 1950s and 1960s, for example, the IBRD granted loans mainly for such internal improvements as roads, railways, and port facilities. During the 1970s, the IBRD stressed loans for agricultural development. In the 1980s, IBRD loans have focused on economic reorganization rather than on building projects.

The 131-member International Development Association (IDA) makes loans only to the lowest-income developing nations. The IDA gets its funds through contributions from developed nations and from IBRD earnings. To be eligible for IDA loans, a nation's annual per capita GNP must be $790 or less. About 90 percent of the IDA loans, however, are to developing nations with annual per capita GNPs of $400 or less. The IDA specializes in long-term, usually 50-year, no-interest loans. Because of the easy

◆ Report topic: How the role of the United Nations has changed since 1945.

lending terms, the IDA is often called the "soft-loan window" of the World Bank.

The 124-member International Finance Corporation (IFC) encourages private investment in developing nations. To achieve this goal, the IFC works closely with domestic businesses and foreign firms. IFC negotiations and advice help clear the way for the establishment of multinational corporations on foreign soil.

The International Monetary Fund. Also founded at the 1944 Bretton Woods Conference, the International Monetary Fund (IMF) has made hundreds of short-term loans to member nations. The IMF is not so much a development bank, however, as it is an agency whose primary goal has been to help developing nations with balance of payments deficits (see Chapter 17).

Recently, however, the IMF has begun making loans to help developing nations repay foreign debts. In 1985, for example, the IMF, in return for promised economic reforms, loaned Argentina $1.2 billion to repay loans. The IMF has made other large loans to debtor nations, including Brazil and Mexico.

The United Nations. The United Nations (UN), established as the world's leading international peacekeeping organization in 1945, is also concerned with economic development. Most of its 160 members are developing nations of the Third World.

The UN promotes economic development through the programs of its specialized agencies. The United Nations Development Program (UNDP) coordinates the efforts of agencies such as the Food and Agriculture Organization (FAO), the World Health Organization (WHO), and the United Nations Industrial Development Organization (UNIDO).

The UN has financed thousands of development projects in education, health, agriculture, and industry. UN funding comes from its member nations, of ◆ which the United States is the largest contributor.

Regional Organizations. Other regional organizations extend credit to nations within certain geographic locations. Major organizations such as the Inter-American Development Bank, the African Development Bank, and the Asian Development Bank, make loans to nations in their respective regions.

See Suggested Assignments, p. TM 100.

Section 4 Review See Answers, p. A 75.

DEFINE foreign aid, economic assistance

IDENTIFY Barber Conable

1. **Comprehending Ideas** What are the major sources of funds available to developing nations for economic development?
2. **Summarizing Ideas** What are the major roadblocks to private investment in developing nations by multinational corporations?
3. **Evaluating Viewpoints** Defend or refute this statement: It is in the best interests of the United States to supply foreign aid to developing nations.

CHAPTER 18 SUMMARY

Three out of four people in the world live in developing nations. Developing nations share such characteristics as low per capita GNP, limited resources, rapid population growth rates, and traditional agricultural or one-crop economies. Developing nations have abundant human resources. But the scarcity of such other factors of production as natural and capital resources, technology, and entrepreneurship restricts their economic growth. They also share social, cultural, and political obstacles to economic growth and development.

Decision makers in the developing nations seek to overcome the obstacles to economic development. These decision makers often use either a socialist or a capitalist model of decision making. Regardless of the model decision makers use, however, they must establish development plans to guide the use of their scarce resources. In creating these development outlines, planners must consider all the production possibilities and trade-offs in a proposed course of action.

Developing nations rely on both domestic and foreign funds to finance economic development. Domestic savings is a surprisingly important source of funds in many nations, but most seek foreign capital as well. Banks, multinational corporations, and nonprofit organizations supply vast amounts of private capital for development. Money and training from foreign governments and international organizations also are crucial to economic progress in developing nations.

CHAPTER 18 REVIEW

For Answers to Chapter 18 Review, see p. A 76.

Reviewing Economic Terms

Supply the economic term that correctly completes each sentence.

1. The international organization designed to help nations with balance of payments deficits is the _____ _____ _____.
2. The model of economic decision making that values central planning is called the _____ model.
3. The fear that assets will be taken without compensation through _____ deters multinational firms from investing in some nations.
4. The application of modern capital and technology to agriculture is called the _____ _____.
5. A term that includes gifts of money, products, and services from one nation to another is called _____ _____.
6. An outline of how a nation's resources should be used to meet its specific economic goals is its _____ _____.
7. The bureau of the United States government that conducts programs to help developing nations best use their human and capital resources is the _____ _____ _____ _____.

Exercising Economic Skills

1. **Analyzing Economic-Data Maps** Review history and geography textbooks and encyclopedias to find an economic-data map. Make a copy of the map. Then answer these questions. **(a)** What is the title of the map? **(b)** What information is illustrated on the map? **(c)** What special symbols or colors are used on the map and what does each represent? **(d)** From the information on the map, what generalization or conclusion can you state?
2. **Applying for a Passport** Study the feature on pages 535–536. Then answer the following questions. **(a)** In your community, where can you apply for a passport? **(b)** What documents do you need to obtain one? **(c)** Select a nation in each of the following areas to include on a travel itinerary: Central America, the Middle East, and Asia. For each country you are to visit, determine if you need a visa in addition to your passport.

Thinking Critically About Economics

1. **Summarizing Ideas** **(a)** What are the characteristics common to developing nations? **(b)** What two major obstacles hinder progress in developing nations? **(c)** Where do developing nations acquire the funds for economic development?
2. **Seeing Relationships** Why are rising expectations a potential hindrance to progress?
3. **Using Economic Imagination** How might economic development directed by central planners affect people whose lives have been dominated by traditional ways?
4. **Evaluating Viewpoints** Defend or refute this statement: For a developing nation, a capitalist decision-making model is the most effective in implementing a development plan.
5. **Interpreting Charts** Study the chart on page 431. **(a)** What is being compared on the chart? **(b)** From information contained in the chart, what generalization can you make about the comparative economic strength of the listed multinationals and nations?

Extending Economic Knowledge

1. Research a multinational company that is headquartered in the United States. **(a)** In what other countries does the MNC have major business operations? **(b)** For each nation in which the MNC operates, explain why you think the MNC located a branch of its operation there. **(c)** What do you think the benefits to each foreign nation are?
2. Select a low-income developing nation. Research its resources and evaluate the quality and quantity of its factors of production. **(a)** What are its potential strengths? **(b)** What are its problems? **(c)** What changes must be made for this nation to develop? Report your findings to the class.
3. Select a developing nation, research its economic planning, and analyze its decision-making model. **(a)** What type of model is it? **(b)** Who makes the economic decisions? **(c)** Evaluate recent economic growth of the nation you selected and report to the class.

Using Primary Sources

Barbara Ward (1914–1981) was a noted economist from England, who wrote extensively on economic growth and development in the Third World. In *The Rich Nations and the Poor Nations* (1962), Ward commented on the need for a strong profit incentive, and equal economic and political opportunities if the Third World is to make economic progress. As you read the following excerpts, note the connection between saving and science. Why does she believe that "saving and science" are important keys to economic growth in the developing world?

The Keys to Economic Growth

Saving and science are the keys to the revolution of economic growth. Technology is applied science and it results in a great increase in productivity; and productivity is a shorthand way of saying that with the same amount of work we can produce more results, or that we can produce the same results in shorter time and with less effort. Technology, in short, enables us to reinforce the workings of man's hand and brain so that the final output is much greater than could be produced by his own natural unaided efforts. . . .

Technology in all its forms is expensive. The cost of a fully developed technology is formidable [extensive]. Let us take one example—the building of a large power station to open up a new region to electrification. The preliminaries—levelling the site, constructing roads to it, putting in possibly a branch line to bring in fuel, assembling materials, machines, and generators—are all expensive. Then follows the costly construction period. But if the electricity is to have its full effect, the consequences are more expensive still. Power-lines have to be built, consumer industries developed, trade schools are needed to train both electricians and skilled workers for the new factories. The magnet of more work draws in migrant workers needing housing and urban services. And so it goes on, every step swallowing up capital and setting in motion new demands for still more capital. In other words, . . . technology is the key to producing more output with less use of resources—productivity—then capital or saving—is the only key to technology. . . . Without saving, there is no economic growth. . . .

Where is this massive injection of capital to come from? We have to remember that developing countries are, by definition, poor. The process of saving, therefore, will be rugged. . . .

We can say, broadly speaking, that there are two chief ways in which capital can be coaxed or induced to leave the circle of consumption and be drawn into the creation of more capital goods. [First] it can be done by the operation of private enterprise in which the profits which are made by enterprise are then available for further investment. . . . [Second], the state intervenes by taxation—directly through income taxes, indirectly through sales taxes. . . . Among the poorer communities it is virtually certain that the state will play a major part in raising more capital for development.

All economics is a matter of choice—of allocating scarce resources to alternative and competing needs. . . . And in this field of development it is very easy to make the wrong choices—choices which, in spite of a vast expenditure of money, do not lead to sustained growth. . . .

Source Review

For Answers to Source Review, see p. A 77.

1. How does Barbara Ward define technology? What is the relationship between technology and productivity?
2. Ward comments that technology is expensive. What costs, for example, are connected with electrification?
3. According to Ward, why is saving important to technological change?
4. In what two ways can developing countries use capital to create more capital?

See Chapter Overview, p. TM 102.
See Chapter Objectives, p. TM 102.
See Introducing the Chapter, p. TM 102.
See Extending Economic Knowledge on text p. 460.

CHAPTER 19

Comparative Economic Systems

There is, however, a noneconomic criterion that is of the utmost importance in choosing between capitalism and socialism . . . individual freedom.

William J. Baumol and Alan S. Blinder

1 The private sector answers the basic economic questions under capitalism.

- Origins of Capitalism
- Capitalism Today

2 The government assumes a larger role in the economy under democratic socialism.

- Origins of Socialism
- Sweden, a Model of Democratic Socialism Today
- Democratic Socialism in the Third World
- The Tanzanian Model

3 The government is the dominant decision maker under authoritarian socialism.

- The Theories of Karl Marx
- The Rise of Communism
- The Soviet Economy Today

4 Some Communist nations have loosened the government's control over the economy.

- Communism in Yugoslavia
- Communism in Hungary
- Communism in the People's Republic of China

You may wish to have the students refer to the *World Economic Data File* on pages 481–498 of THE REFERENCE LIBRARY as they study Chapter 19.

CHAPTER 19 STUDY GUIDE

Chapter Focus

Chapter 19 expands upon the discussion begun in Chapter 1 of the three basic types of mixed economic systems in the world today. The three types of mixed economic systems examined are capitalism, democratic socialism, and authoritarian socialism, or Communism. The loosening of government control in some of the nations practicing authoritarian socialism is also analyzed.

As you study the chapter, look for the details that support each of the following statements.

1. The private sector answers the basic economic questions under capitalism.
2. The government assumes a larger role in the economy under democratic socialism.
3. The government is the dominant decision maker under authoritarian socialism.
4. Some Communist nations have loosened the government's control over the economy.

See Preteaching Vocabulary, p. TM 102.

Terms to Know

The following terms, while not the only terms emphasized in this chapter, are basic to your understanding of economic systems. Determine the meaning of each term, either by using the Glossary or by watching for context clues as you read the chapter.

capitalism

mercantilism

laissez-faire capitalism

socialism

democratic socialism

authoritarian socialism

See Key Study Questions and Key Understandings, p. TM 103.

1 The private sector answers the basic economic questions under capitalism.

See Suggested Teaching Strategies, p. TM 103.

Economists and political scientists have devised many ways to classify nations. Nations, for example, can be grouped by level of economic development, using the per capita GNP to distinguish developing nations from developed nations. Nations also can be classified according to their economic system.

As was discussed in Chapter 1, most nations of the world have a mixed economic system. Mixed economic systems combine elements of the pure-market model and the pure-command model. Depending on the degree of government control, mixed economies can be classified as practicing either capitalism, democratic socialism, or authoritarian socialism, also called Communism.

Origins of Capitalism

In the economic system called **capitalism,** individuals in the private sector own and control the factors of production. Decentralized decision making guides most economic activity in capitalistic economic systems.

Capitalism became the dominant type of economic system in Europe and the United States during the 1800s. The origins of capitalism, however, date back to ancient Greece and Rome where individuals controlled the means of production.

Nationalism's Influence. The stage was set for the rise of capitalism in Europe with the financial successes of merchants during the 1100s, when merchants helped break the stranglehold of the landed nobility on the economy. As trade increased, people began to invest money in businesses with the goal of making a profit. New nation-states such as France, Spain, and England developed from 1200 to 1500. The rise of nations created a need for national currencies and a banking system, two key institutions of capitalism. The rise of cities and specialized trades further increased the use of money.

Mercantilism's Influence. During the 1600s and the 1700s, the governments of major European nations directed their economies by a doctrine called mercantilism. Leaders used **mercantilism** to regulate the economy and to accumulate greater wealth for the nation. Wealth was measured in terms of gold, silver, and an excess of exports over imports. Government leaders practiced mercantilism by granting trading monopolies, raising tariff barriers, and establishing colonies to supply European industries with necessary raw materials.

Adam Smith's Influence. By the mid-1700s, many Europeans believed that mercantilism interfered with economic growth. Reforming economists urged governments to grant individuals more economic freedom.

One of the most influential of the economists opposed to mercantilism was Adam Smith. In 1776 Smith wrote *An Inquiry into the Nature and Causes of the Wealth of Nations,* which argued that economies would prosper without government interference. Smith wrote that the profit motive would make a free economic system efficient. He said that competition in the marketplace would eliminate inefficient businesses. Later, this type of economic system became known as a free enterprise, or capitalistic, system.

Smith advocated a type of capitalism known as **laissez-faire capitalism,** after the French words best translated as "let the people do as they please." Under laissez-faire capitalism, individuals make all economic decisions, and the government does not interfere.

Capitalism Today

In the twentieth century, capitalism functions with some degree of government control. The amount of government control, however, varies from country to country. In the United States, the government intervenes in the economy only on a limited basis. In

Government intervention in economic planning and business development is much more common in Japan than in the United States.

Japan and South Korea, on the other hand, the government has a great deal of say in how the economy is run. The major characteristics of capitalism are outlined in the chart on page 450.

The features and goals of capitalism in the United States are presented in Chapter 1. In most respects, the capitalism that exists in the United States is similar to the type of capitalism that is found in Japan and South Korea. Both types of capitalism value private property and the profit motive. The one major difference involves the government's role in economic planning. Although the government of the United States regulates the economy in many ways, it is not directly involved in economic planning and decision making.

In contrast, the governments of Japan and South Korea are very involved in economic planning. The economies of Japan and South Korea rely on an alliance of government planners and private industrialists to direct the flow of resources and final goods.

In capitalist nations, the cost of labor strongly affects prices. South Korea's prices are relatively low because the cost of labor is low.

Capitalism in Japan. The Ministry of International Trade and Industry (MITI) is the chief economic planning agency in Japan (see the case study on page 391). MITI encourages the production of certain goods and discourages the production of others. For example, during the 1950s and 1960s, MITI encouraged the private sector to produce steel. MITI arranged for tax advantages, low-interest loans, subsidies, and other incentives to make investment in the steel industry more attractive. Today, Japan is a leading steel producer in the world. Similar incentives have been extended to Japan's automotive, ◆ computer, and electronics industries.

Capitalism in South Korea. The government-financed Korea Development Institute, South Korea's version of MITI, is the chief economic planning agency in South Korea. The agency brings government planners together with people in business to devise and implement the nation's development policy.

Like MITI, the Korea Development Institute extends financial incentives to businesses to direct the allocation of resources and the production of goods. In the mid-1970s, for example, incentives were provided to the automotive, shipbuilding, steel, chemical, and other heavy industries. By the mid-1980s, South Korean shipbuilders produced 15 percent of the world's new ships. South Korea also was exporting automobiles.

Other countries that have economic systems based on capitalism are Singapore and the Republic of China (Taiwan). Free enterprise has been remarkably successful in transforming these small countries into hubs of international commerce.

See Suggested Assignments, p. TM 103.

Section 1 Review

See Answers, p. A 77.

DEFINE mercantilism

IDENTIFY Adam Smith

1. **Comprehending Ideas** **(a)** How did the rise of nationalism contribute to the development of capitalism? **(b)** Describe ownership, control, and decision making in a capitalist economy.

2. **Understanding Ideas** **(a)** Under mercantilism, how was a nation's wealth measured? **(b)** How did government leaders practice mercantilism?

3. **Summarizing Ideas** What was Adam Smith's criticism of mercantilism?

4. **Contrasting Ideas** What is the major difference between the capitalist model of Japan and that of the United States?

◆ Report topic: The social benefits and costs of the Japanese philosophy of business.

See Key Study Questions and Key Understandings, p. TM 104.

2 The government assumes a larger role in the economy under democratic socialism.

See Suggested Teaching Strategies, p. TM 104.

Socialism is a broad term used to describe many types of noncapitalist economic systems. In general, socialism includes government ownership of at least part of the means of production.

Socialists believe that public ownership of industries protects workers from harsh working conditions and low pay. Socialists also believe that central planning is necessary in order to channel resources into socially desirable areas. One of the goals of central planning is to oversee the redistribution of wealth in a nation so that no one is too wealthy or too poor. In most democratic socialist nations, governments levy high personal and corporate income taxes to ensure that the wealth of the nation is not concentrated in the hands of a few people.

Origins of Socialism

During the early stages of the Industrial Revolution, the quality of life for workers deteriorated. Long working hours, low pay, child labor, and hazardous working conditions created an oppressive workplace environment. Overcrowded tenements, industrial pollution, and the lack of adequate sanitation and medical facilities reduced the quality of the workers' physical and social environments.

Under these conditions, reformers began to question the capitalist system. Some reformers favored an end to capitalism and the establishment of an economic system that would provide a more equal distribution of wealth. Collectively, these reformers were called socialists. Some socialists called for violent revolutions to topple the capitalists. Other socialists supported a peaceful, evolutionary transition from capitalism to socialism.

Those socialists who believed in peaceful change have adapted their economic and political ideals to changing economic and political conditions during the 1900s. One of these adaptations is democratic socialism.

Sweden, a Model of Democratic Socialism Today

Under **democratic socialism**, the people retain basic human rights and some control over economic planning through the election of government officials. The major characteristics of democratic socialism are outlined in the chart on page 450. European countries practicing democratic socialism are Great Britain, France, and Sweden. ◆

In France, the government-owned transit system provides fast, efficient train service. Such service is a positive aspect of democratic socialism.

◆ Have the students read "Travel Agents" on page 544 of *Careers in the Marketplace.*

Industry Ownership. Sweden is one of Europe's leading democratic socialist nations. The Swedish government owns about 10 percent of the industries in Sweden. The government controls the shipbuilding, telecommunications, and steel industries, and it owns part of the national railway network, broadcasting systems, and hydroelectric facilities. The remaining 90 percent of Sweden's industry is in the hands of private firms. The automotive industry, for example, includes private firms such as Volvo.

Workers' Freedoms. Swedish workers enjoy many of the economic freedoms that exist in capitalist economies. In some respects, the power of workers is even greater in Sweden than in the United States or Japan. For example, workers are entitled to representation on the board of directors of major corporations and share in corporate decision making.

Economic Planning. Economic planning in the Swedish economy is the responsibility of people who represent public and private interests. Representatives of the government, industry, agriculture, and labor formulate annual plans that set production and employment targets.

Only about 10 percent of Tanzania's labor force is employed in industry or commerce.

Taxation in Sweden. Taxes in Sweden are among the highest in Europe, absorbing about one half of all income that individuals and firms earn. The government uses the tax revenues to finance a wide assortment of social programs, including comprehensive health insurance, unemployment insurance, retirement benefits, free education through college, subsidized public housing, and child care. The standard of living in Sweden is one of the highest in the world.

The high taxes that Swedish workers pay are a constant source of controversy. High taxes force workers to demand higher wages, which increase the prices of goods produced for domestic and international markets. In addition, tax revenues have not been able to meet the rising costs of social programs. As a result, the government has had to borrow heavily to meet its economic and social goals.

Democratic Socialism in the Third World

Since the 1940s, dozens of developing nations, mostly in Africa, the Middle East, Asia, and Latin America, have set up economic systems based on democratic socialism. Democratic socialists in developing nations support some public ownership of the means of production, some central planning, and a more equal distribution of wealth. Developing nations that practice democratic socialism include Angola, Mozambique, and Tanzania.

Two factors have made democratic socialism popular in the Third World. First, democratic socialism is compatible with traditional values that exist in some parts of the world. Many African peoples, for example, value cooperation to achieve tribal goals and hold common property for community use. Thus, the concepts of public ownership of property and planning for the welfare of the community are well accepted in many developing nations.

Second, from the end of World War II in 1945 through the 1970s, European colonial powers such as Portugal, France, and Great Britain granted independence to the developing nations. Leaders in many of the newly independent nations view democratic socialism—with its emphasis on equal distribution of wealth and public ownership of the means of production—as a preferable alternative to capitalism, the economic system of their former rulers.

The Tanzanian Model

The economy of the Republic of Tanzania in East Africa is an example of democratic socialism in a developing nation. Tanzania is one of the most stable of the world's developing nations. Two major forces account for this stability. First, the nation's one-party political system has restricted opposition movements. Second, President Nyerere provided steady and honest leadership for 23 years.

Shortly after gaining independence from Great Britain in 1961, Julius K. Nyerere was elected president. During his administration, which lasted until 1985, Nyerere worked to create a democratic socialist state. In contrast to the democratic socialist states of Europe, however, Tanzania has only one political party—the Revolutionary Party of Tanzania.

Tanzanian democratic socialism is based on three policies: nationalization, villagization, and *ujamaa* (oo·jah·MAH). Nationalization refers to the process of a government buying industries from private owners. Once purchased, these nationalized industries are controlled by the government. Villagization involves the relocation of peasants from scattered farms into more centralized villages. *Ujamaa,* the Swahili word meaning familyhood, is the name given to the government policy aimed at encouraging villagers to farm their land collectively.

Nationalization Policy. President Nyerere nationalized some of the country's major factories, service industries (such as banking and insurance), and major importers and exporters of goods. This policy put some of the most important industries under public ownership and control.

Villagization Policy. The government's massive villagization program resettled more than 9 million peasants in new villages during the 1970s. By the mid-1980s, about 90 percent of the population lived in villages and towns. One goal of villagization has been to bring people together so that government services can be provided more efficiently. A second goal has been to advance the policy of ujamaa.

Collectivization Policy. The government's policy of ujamaa encourages the peasants to farm collectively and assist each other in local development projects. The results, however, have been disappointing. Peasants have continued to farm private plots and sell their products to earn individual profits.

Economic Planning Policy. More than 80 percent of the population of Tanzania work on the land. Since 1964, the government's Five-Year Plans have emphasized agricultural development. Since the 1970s, national boards called *parastatals* have controlled imports and exports. In addition, the government controls the only official union—the National Union of Tanganyika Workers (NUTA). Unlike most unions, NUTA is not permitted to strike.

Tanzania's socialist planning emphasizes services to rural populations. Social programs are mainly concerned with emphasizing nutrition, sanitation, disease control, and maternal and child care. Since independence, the number of hospitals, rural health centers, and physicians has increased sharply. As a result, the infant mortality rate has dropped by nearly 50 percent, and life expectancy has increased from 35 years to 52 years.

The government also constructs some low-cost housing, water and irrigation systems, schools, and other facilities. Today, Tanzania boasts a 79-percent literacy rate, the highest in Africa. Personal, corporate, and export taxes, in addition to foreign aid, pay for most social programs.

Tanzanian Problems. Tanzania still has major economic problems, some of which are the result of external forces. For example, higher prices for imported oil and lower prices for agricultural exports have forced Tanzania to borrow money. Today the nation has a heavy foreign debt. Ujamaa has been a failure. In addition, many educated Tanzanians have left the country.

See Suggested Assignments, p. TM 104.

Section 2 Review See Answers, p. A 77.

DEFINE socialism, democratic socialism

IDENTIFY Julius K. Nyerere

1. **Comprehending Ideas** What conditions in capitalist nations motivated the socialist reformers?
2. **Summarizing Ideas** What is the evidence that democratic socialism has improved the standard of living in Tanzania?
3. **Interpreting Ideas** What is the trade-off for the broad scope of social programs in Sweden?

BUILDING ECONOMIC SKILLS

WRITING ABOUT ECONOMICS

Composing a Comparative Essay

You have already been introduced to the skill of composing an essay in Chapter 5 on pages 110–111. Students of economics are sometimes required to compose a special type of essay called a comparative essay. A comparative essay notes the similarities and differences between two or among more than two courses of action, programs, and issues. An example of an essay directive that demands a comparative essay response follows.

ESSAY DIRECTIVE: Compare and contrast central planning in the Soviet Union with central planning in the People's Republic of China.

How to Compose a Comparative Essay

Review the steps for composing an essay that are listed on page 110. Instead of using a structured overview, however, you will learn how to use an outline and a chart to organize the information for your essay.

Applying the Skill

Read and respond to the following essay directive.

ESSAY DIRECTIVE: Contrast how the United States and Soviet economic systems answer the basic economic questions.

Two Economic Systems Answer the Basic Economic Questions

Basic Economic Questions	Capitalism in the United States	Communism in the Soviet Union
1. What to produce and in what quantity?	The private sector decides. Consumer demand affects many production decisions.	The government decides. Central planning directs the flow of most resources and sets production quotas.
2. How to produce goods and services?	Businesses decide. Professional managers determine the best mix of the factors of production. Entrepreneurs devise new production techniques.	The government decides. Plant managers have limited say in how to produce. Entrepreneurship is stifled by centralized planning.
3. Who gets what is produced?	Consumption is determined by income. Most income is generated through wages, interest, rents, and profits in the private sector. Government transfer payments supplement some incomes.	Consumption is determined by income and by association with the Communist party. The government regulates consumption by setting wages. Limited private enterprise exists in agriculture and in some services.

Study the chart shown on page 446. This chart has organized the information to be used in the essay. The outline below has been derived from the information on the chart and shows the basic parts of the essay. The sample essay on this page shows the completed essay.

I. Introduction

II. Contrasts in the Two Economies

  A. What to produce and in what quantity?

  B. How to produce goods and services?

  C. Who gets what is produced?

III. Conclusion

Practicing the Skill See Answers, p. A 78.

Read again the directive in column one on page 446. On a separate sheet of paper, answer the questions and complete the following activities.

1. List the informational terms in the directive.
2. List the performance terms in the essay directive.
3. Draw a chart with three columns headed "Nations," "Similarities," and "Differences." Fill in the chart, using information available in Section 3 and Section 4 of this chapter.
4. Prepare an outline based on the chart.
5. Write a comparative essay in response to the directive.

SAMPLE ESSAY

Introduction

The economies of the United States and the Soviet Union answer the basic economic questions in different ways. In the American brand of capitalism the private sector, which is comprised of individuals and firms, determines the answers to the basic questions. Under Communism, the Soviet government makes most production and distribution decisions.

Contrasts in the Two Economies

In the American economy individuals and firms, rather than the government, determine what and how much to produce. Businesses, for example, respond to consumer demand for goods and services in a capitalist system. In the Soviet economy, government planners channel most resources to firms and establish production quotas to ensure certain levels of output.

In the American economy, businesses rather than government bureaucrats decide how to produce goods and services. Professional managers determine the best mix of the factors of production, while entrepreneurs develop new production techniques. In the Soviet economy, plant managers have limited say in the purchase and use of resources. In addition, central planning stifles entrepreneurship.

The final difference between the two economies involves the consumption of goods and services. In both economic systems, the consumption decisions of the people are determined by their incomes. In the American economy, most income is generated through wages, interest and dividends, rents, and profits in the private sector. Government transfer payments such as Social Security and Aid to Families With Dependent Children, supplement some incomes. In the Soviet economy, however, the government directly regulates consumption by controlling wages in state-run firms. Further, ranking members in the Communist party have traditionally been given preferential treatment in the purchase of scarce commodities.

Conclusion

Most of the economic freedoms that exist in the American economy are absent in the Soviet economy. Under Communism, the power of the government, rather than the power of the market, determines the answers to the three basic economic questions.

See Key Study Questions and Key Understandings, p. TM 105.

3 The government is the dominant decision maker under authoritarian socialism.

See Suggested Teaching Strategies, p. TM 105.

Authoritarian socialism is the type of economic system that is closest to the pure-command model. The major examples of authoritarian socialism are the Soviet Union and the People's Republic of China.

Authoritarian socialism, or **Communism,** is a type of socialism in which the government owns and controls nearly all of the means of production. The German philosopher Karl Marx outlined the theories of authoritarian socialism in *The Communist Manifesto* (1848) and in *Capital* (1867).

The Theories of Karl Marx

Karl Marx wrote that economic factors determine political and social change. Marx viewed history as a series of class struggles between the oppressors, who owned the means of production, and the oppressed, who supplied the labor.

The Rise of the Bourgeoisie. Marx's view of the Middle Ages, for example, was that a small group of feudal lords owned the land and oppressed the serfs who worked the land. Gradually, with the expansion of trade and the growth of cities, a class of merchants arose. As these merchants, whom Marx called the **bourgeoisie,** became more powerful, they challenged the nobility's role in society. Marx believed the bourgeoisie had triumphed over the nobility and set up capitalistic economic systems in many parts of Europe by the late 1700s.

The Rise of the Proletariat. Marx did not see the rise of the bourgeoisie as the end of the class struggle. Instead, during the early Industrial Revolution, he saw the bourgeoisie taking control of the means of production and becoming the oppressors of the working class. The working class, whom Marx called the **proletariat,** provided the labor needed for the production process in return for very low wages.

Marx saw all profits going to the bourgeoisie who used the funds to build new factories, where they exploited even more members of the proletariat. According to Marx, the capitalistic system continued

The ideas of Karl Marx were first implemented by V. I. Lenin, founder of Soviet Communist ideology. The bust in the right-hand photograph is of Lenin.

In December 1982, the All-Union Communist Party Congress met to commemorate the 60th anniversary of the founding of the Soviet Union.

to concentrate wealth in the hands of the bourgeoisie. In Marx's view, the class struggle would continue to intensify until the proletariat would overthrow the bourgeoisie in a violent revolution.

Destruction of Capitalism. Marx then saw the victorious proletariat organizing a government known as the **dictatorship of the proletariat,** which would oversee the final destruction of capitalism. Marx believed that once capitalism was destroyed, the proletariat would create a classless society. In this classless society, everyone would be equal and all people would share ownership of the means of production.

In his theory, Marx stated that the dictatorship of the proletariat would be a temporary government. He saw workers in all nations toppling the bourgeoisie and establishing an ideal worldwide society. When this happened, Marx said people would no longer need governments. Then the ideal Communist society would have been created, and governments would merely wither away.

Economics Reporter

What Is *The Communist Manifesto?*

The Communist Manifesto, published in 1848, is a political pamphlet written by Karl Marx and Friedrich Engels. In the pamphlet, Marx and Engels outlined the program of revolutionary change advocated by the Communist League, an international workers' organization dedicated to the establishment of a Communist society. According to *The Communist Manifesto,* throughout history, the members of the working class, who owned nothing but their labor, had been locked in a class struggle against the ruling class, who owned the factors of production. The only way to end this struggle was for the working class to overthrow the ruling class and establish a society based on Communism.

A Simplification of History. Marx believed that the victory of the proletariat was the inevitable conclusion of capitalism. Marx, however, simplified history and ignored political forces by attributing almost all events to a class struggle. Marx also incorrectly believed that capitalism would lead to deteriorating standards of living for the working class. Furthermore, Marx did not foresee the steadily rising economic status that workers in industrialized nations such as the United States have enjoyed throughout the 1900s.

In addition, the government of the Soviet Union, which has practiced Communism since 1917, has not withered away. Soviet society is not the classless society that Marx envisioned. Instead, the leaders of the Soviet Communist party enjoy special privileges and make up the intellectual, political, and social elite of the nation. The majority of the people also have standards of living below those of capitalist nations. ◆

The Rise of Communism

During the early 1900s, numerous revolutionary groups formed in Russia. The Bolsheviks, later called Communists, were one of these opposition groups. Under the leadership of Vladimir Ilyich Lenin, the Bolsheviks in 1917 overthrew the existing government in Russia and proclaimed Russia the world's first Communist nation.

War Communism. The early years of Communism were ones of political and economic experimentation. Lenin's first experiment is known as the period of War Communism, 1918–1921. It was a time of civil war and great hardship following Russia's defeat in World War I and the overthrow of Czar Nicholas II. Under War Communism, Lenin abolished private property, broke up large estates in rural areas, and redistributed land to the peasants. In cities, the Communist government expropriated factories and allowed the workers to run them. A forced-labor policy relocated scarce labor resources to important industries.

War Communism ultimately failed because the peasants had no incentive to produce crops when the government confiscated crops to feed the army and urban workers. Furthermore, untrained industrial workers knew little about managing factories in the cities. As a result of War Communism, agricultural and industrial output fell dramatically, unemployment was high, and famine claimed millions of victims.

◆ Discussion topic: The theories of Karl Marx suggest that a utopian society will result from class struggles. Why have Communist countries failed to create utopian societies?

Comparison of Economic Systems ◆

	Capitalism	Democratic Socialism	Authoritarian Socialism/ Communism
Ownership of Natural and Capital Resources	Individuals own the great majority of natural resources.	Governments own some of the leading industries including health care, energy, railroads, banking, and raw materials. The governments usually acquire these industries through nationalization or expropriation.	Nearly all industries are government owned. The government forbids most types of private enterprise. Small "kitchen gardens" are permitted in some rural areas, along with small family-owned and family-operated enterprises. Other private shops and services operate under strict government regulation.
Economic Freedoms of Workers	Workers are free to choose jobs that fit their qualifications. Some workers join unions to bargain collectively with management for better wages, benefits, and other types of work-related compensation.	Workers get to choose jobs that fit their qualifications. Many workers join powerful unions that bargain with private firms and governments for better wages, benefits, and other types of work-related compensation.	Workers' freedom to choose employment is restricted by the government. Workers carry a "labor pass," which states where they work. The government must approve any transfer of jobs. Entrepreneurship is discouraged by rigid bureaucracies. Unions are strictly controlled by the government, and strikes are prohibited.
Central Planning in the Economy	The majority of economic decisions are made by the private sector. Governments influence economic activity through tax credits, subsidies, other financial incentives, low-interest loans, and regulations. In capitalist nations such as Japan and South Korea the government takes a more active role in economic decision making.	Governments are involved in planning the uses of resources and directly control all production in large, state-owned facilities. Some governments also suggest that private firms use their resources in certain ways.	Almost all economic decisions are made by a single political party. Specific economic plans are devised by government agencies in charge of planning for a specific industry. Plant managers at the local level are given some flexibility in how to maximize production.
Taxes and Social Programs	Many social programs, such as unemployment compensation, social security, welfare, and health care, are financed through tax receipts.	Progressive tax rates are sometimes extremely high. The high tax rates finance an extensive network of social programs, including free medical care, higher education, pensions, and unemployment compensation.	Government revenues from income, excise, and sales taxes are used to finance a comprehensive network of social programs, including low-cost public housing, free health care and education, and retirement pensions.
Type of Political System	Nations are mainly democratic.	Western European nations tend to be democracies, while other nations lean toward totalitarianism.	Most nations have a one-party totalitarian government. While elections are held, the single political party preselects all candidates for public office.
Examples	United States Republic of China (Taiwan) Singapore Japan South Korea Switzerland	France Sweden Great Britain Spain Mozambique Tanzania Algeria	Soviet Union Cuba Bulgaria Albania Hungary Poland The People's Republic of China

◆ **Class activity: Have the students rank European countries on a scale between pure capitalism and authoritarian socialism.**

The New Economic Policy. In 1921, Lenin embarked on the New Economic Policy (NEP), which restored some private incentives. Peasants were allowed to sell surplus crops on open markets for profit, and small private firms were allowed to open in the cities. Under the NEP, thousands of entrepreneurs revived the economy. Larger enterprises, however, remained in the hands of the government.

Stalin's Harsh Rule as Dictator. Lenin's successor, Joseph Stalin, abolished the NEP and its decentralized decision-making system. Stalin instituted strict central planning and eliminated all private property in rural and urban areas.

Beginning with Stalin's leadership in 1928, a series of Five-Year Plans established long-term economic goals and allocated scarce resources. Under the plans, Stalin and his successors set quotas for increased industrial and agricultural production. Workers who failed to meet quotas were punished severely.

The Soviet government emphasized heavy industries such as steel, concrete, machinery, chemicals, and mining at the expense of consumer-oriented industries. Shortages of basic necessities such as clothing resulted.

The harsh realities of life under Joseph Stalin's rule are mostly ignored in Soviet history books.

Under Stalin's rule, productive workers were expected to instruct their fellow workers on methods to increase output.

In agriculture, the government instituted **collectivization,** a policy of complete expropriation of land to form large state-run farms. Many peasants resisted collectivization fiercely, so the government sent them to work as laborers in factories or in the mines. Resistance was strongest in the Ukraine, the Volga region, and the North Caucasus. Resisters in these areas were denied membership in the collectives and were deported to labor camps in Siberia. Exact numbers are not known, but it is estimated that millions of lives were lost in the deportation process and in the labor camps.

The Soviet Economy Today

As the largest authoritarian socialist nation in the world, the economy of the Soviet Union is second only to the United States in total output. The basic characteristics of authoritarian socialism are outlined in the chart on page 450.

Central Planning. Government bureaucrats direct the flow of resources and final products in the Soviet Union. Long-term goals are embodied in the Five-Year Plans, while short-term annual plans keep the economy heading toward its long-term goals.

The process of creating annual economic plans is complex. The chart on this page traces the five stages that the plan must pass through before production begins. The diagram also shows the basic organization of the Soviet economy. The government carries out the policies and programs that the Communist party's leadership dictates. The Communist party, not the government, is the real power in the Soviet Union.

Production. Soviet central planners have emphasized the production of different types of goods and services over the years. Under Stalin, industrial goods and military goods were favored at the expense of consumer goods and agricultural goods. ◆

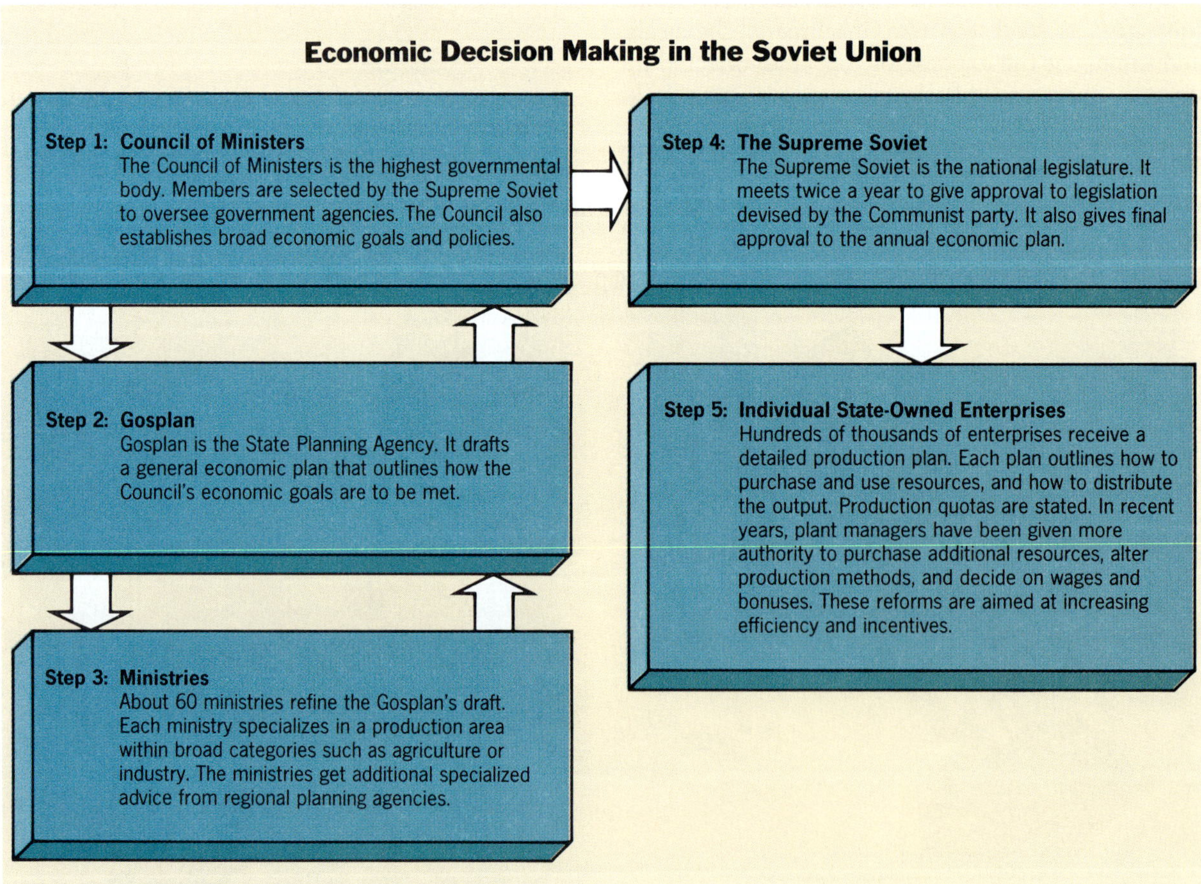

◆ **Even today, Soviet citizens wait in line for hours to purchase items such as small appliances and certain foods.**

After Stalin's death in 1953, central economic plans gradually included more consumer goods. While industrial and military goods are still the top priority, the Soviet government is producing more consumer goods and services. The variety of consumer goods and services available, however, is far less than those available in capitalist nations.

Agriculture continues to lag behind the other sectors of the Soviet economy. Agricultural productivity is low because of shortages of capital, the lack of incentives, and a harsh climate in some parts of the nation. About 20 percent of the Soviet labor force is employed in agriculture compared to only 2 percent to 3 percent in the United States. Despite the large agricultural labor force, however, the Soviets must import large quantities of food each year.

Future Challenges of Soviet Socialism. The Five-Year Plan for 1986–1990 addresses some of the weaknesses in the Soviet economy. The Communist Party and its General Secretary, Mikhail Gorbachev, have a number of special concerns.

Gorbachev wishes to improve the nation's capital stock. Much of the Soviet Union's industrial capital dates back to Stalin's era, and agricultural capital is primitive compared to that in the United States. The latest Five-Year Plan calls for more investment in new industrial capital, with computers a high priority. Agriculture has a relatively low priority.

The party also wants to improve productivity among Soviet workers. Current labor productivity is low because of high absenteeism, alcoholism, and a lack of incentives. The Communist party is calling for workers to practice more discipline and for the central planners to provide additional incentives, such as higher wages, bonuses, and paid vacations.

Soviet products do not sell well in international markets because production quotas have contributed to the mass production of shoddy goods. To increase the incentive to produce quality merchandise, the leadership of the Communist party plans to tie factory payrolls to the sale of products, giving higher wages to workers whose products sell well.

Finally, the Communist party leadership is streamlining some inefficient elements of the bureaucracy and weeding out corruption in the party ranks. It will encourage innovative management by giving plant managers more authority to make production decisions.

Mikhail Gorbachev (below) realizes that Soviet factories will have to be modernized to compete successfully in world markets.

Economics Reporter

What Is a Foreign Currency Store?

The Soviet government controls all retail stores in the Soviet Union. Most stores carry basic consumer goods, but not luxury items. Items such as color television sets and hand-held electric hair dryers, commonly found in stores in the United States and other nations with free enterprise systems, are almost nonexistent in Soviet stores. The Soviet government does, however, maintain a few stores that deal exclusively in luxury imports. Unlike the regular retail stores, these stores, often called foreign currency stores, do not accept Russian currency. Instead, the shops, which are open only to certain designated Communist party members and officials, accept money from nations with strong currencies.

CASE STUDY

Soviet Reforms in Authoritarian Socialism

Traditionally, private property and free enterprise in the Soviet Union have been prohibited. The Communist party has made all economic decisions. The only official exception to the prohibition of private property has been in agriculture, where laborers from collective farms have been allotted small kitchen gardens adjacent to their homes. The government has allowed the farmers to grow produce on these plots and to sell it in local farmers' markets where the laws of supply and demand determine prices. Even though these private plots account for only 2 percent of Soviet farmland, they produce 30 percent of the vegetables, milk, and eggs and 60 percent of the potatoes and fruit available in the nation.

Despite official prohibitions, Soviet citizens have devised elaborate schemes to acquire scarce goods and services. An illegal underground economy, or **black market,** thrives in the Soviet Union. In these black markets, Soviet citizens with enough money can purchase designer blue jeans and other luxury items that are unobtainable in government stores.

In addition, residents can bypass the often inefficient government bureaucracy and make arrangements on the black market to have automobiles repaired, plumbing fixed, or apartments painted. Although hiring service people from the black market is illegal and far more expensive than using government-paid workers, the black-market workers usually provide faster service and do better work. The black market has become so lucrative that economists estimate that it made up between 10 percent and 15 percent of the Soviet GNP in 1985.

Under the leadership of Mikhail Gorbachev, the Soviet government has instituted economic reforms to lessen black-market trading. In November 1986, for example, the Supreme Soviet, the legislative body of the Soviet Union, passed a law legalizing many of the free enterprise activities that were already a part of the black market. The comprehensive reforms, effective May 1, 1987, have legalized 29 kinds of private enterprise, including the manufacture of toys, clothing, shoes, furniture, and the repair of household appliances and automobiles. The law also has allowed individuals to charge for tutoring students in music, shorthand, and languages. By legalizing these practices, the Soviet government officially has recognized that it could not stamp out the black market.

Before the law was passed, Soviet citizens paid no taxes on black-market income because they did not report it. With legalization, however, the authorities will prosecute anyone who does not pay taxes on the newly legalized income.

The Soviet reforms mark a slight turn away from authoritarian socialism. Many economists, however, believe that the Soviet Union is unlikely to pass additional reforms within the next few years.

See Suggested Assignments, p. TM 105.

Section 3 Review See Answers, p. A 78.

DEFINE authoritarian socialism, bourgeoisie, proletariat, collectivization, black market

IDENTIFY Karl Marx, *The Communist Manifesto,* Vladimir Ilyich Lenin, Joseph Stalin

1. **Summarizing Ideas** What did Stalin do to remake the Soviet economy when he took power?
2. **Interpreting Graphics** Study the chart on page 452. Trace the flow of ideas from the establishment of broad economic goals to the implementation of detailed production plans.

See Key Study Questions and Key Understandings, p. TM 106.

4 Some Communist nations have loosened the government's control over the economy.

See Suggested Teaching Strategies, p. TM 106.

The Communist nations of the world share certain characteristics. They all have one-party totalitarian political systems. The government and Communist party control the economy. Many belong to the same international organizations, such as the Council of Mutual Economic Assistance (COMECON), a regional trade organization.

Since the 1950s, Communist nations have adapted authoritarian socialism to meet their own needs. Some nations follow the highly centralized authoritarian socialism of the Soviet Union. Other Communist nations permit individuals to make some economic decisions. The governments of these Communist nations, however, own most of the ◆ means of production.

Communism in Yugoslavia

At the end of World War II, Yugoslavia modeled its political and economic systems after those of the Soviet Union. President (Josip Broz) Tito, who ruled Yugoslavia from 1945 until his death in 1980, soon changed direction. After breaking away from the Soviet Union in 1948 to protect Yugoslavia's political independence, Tito modified Yugoslavia's authoritarian socialism to boost production and to improve his nation's standard of living.

Yugoslavian Modifications. The authoritarian socialism of Yugoslavia differs from that of the Soviet Union in several ways. First, most Yugoslavian farmers own their own land. Second, the Yugoslavian government has relinquished ownership and control of the factories. Workers, rather than government bureaucrats, answer most of the basic economic questions. Third, in Yugoslavia, the forces of supply and demand rather than the government determine the prices of most goods and services.

Participatory Socialism. One of the most outstanding features of Yugoslavia's brand of authoritarian socialism is its system of participatory socialism, or workers' self-management. Like a corporation's board of directors in the United States, elected workers' councils in Yugoslavian industries decide what to produce. The councils also select plant managers, determine workers' salaries, plan for investment in new capital, and decide how to market the final good.

Problems in Yugoslavia. The Yugoslavian economy has its share of problems. Unemployment and inflation are high. The rising number of strikes, which technically are illegal, indicate some dissatisfaction with the system. In addition, Yugoslavia remains a one-party totalitarian political system.

Communism in Hungary

Like Yugoslavia, Hungary followed the Soviet pattern of authoritarian socialism after World War II. In 1968, however, Hungary adopted the New Economic Mechanism (NEM). This strategy reduced the government's role in the economy, allowing the market a greater role in allocating scarce resources.

The New Economic Mechanism. Under the NEM, plant managers make most production decisions in the large state-owned enterprises in Hungary. In addition, smaller privately owned businesses, such as restaurants and fashion boutiques, operate for profit. Today, private enterprise in Hungary represents 25 percent to 30 percent of the nation's GNP, a percentage far higher than in Yugoslavia, where private enterprise accounts for about 11 percent of the GNP. The Hungarian government also supports the "second economy" as a way to increase the nation's total output and personal income. In the second economy, workers are free to get second jobs to supplement their income.

Problems of Economic Stability. Economic problems, however, remain a constant threat to the stability of Hungary's economy. Aging capital in the large state-owned factories and farms hampers productivity. Fear of Soviet reprisals makes the Communist party and government bureaucrats hesitant to institute further reforms in the direction of free enterprise. Hungarians have one of the highest standards of living in Eastern Europe. Hungary's standard of living, however, is far below that of the democratic socialist countries in Western Europe.

◆ Have the students read "Vacationing in Foreign Countries" on pages 537–538 of the *Everyday Economics Handbook* and answer the questions that follow.

Communism in the People's Republic of China

The People's Republic of China, like Hungary and Yugoslavia in Eastern Europe, has also moved toward a more market-responsive authoritarian socialism. The move is a response to the failures of overcentralized economic planning.

The Chinese Communists came to power in 1949 after a long and bloody civil war. Mao Zedong, head of the Chinese Communist party, assumed leadership of the new government. The economic history of the People's Republic of China can be divided into two periods. In the first period, under strict authoritarian socialism, China launched the Great Leap Forward program and the Cultural Revolution. The second period has been characterized by a more market-responsive authoritarian socialism.

The Great Leap Forward. In 1953, the Chinese Communists launched the first Five-Year Plan, which stressed industrial development. With the aid of the Soviet Union, China recorded some economic successes. Impatient with progress in industry and agriculture, however, Mao pushed for more rapid industrial and agricultural development. This push characterized the Second Five-Year Plan (1958–1962). The policies embodied in this plan were referred to as the Great Leap Forward.

One goal of the Four Modernizations is to increase productivity in China's vast commune system.

The Great Leap Forward established types of collective farms called people's communes to increase the agricultural output of China. On people's communes, peasants were sometimes required to live in barracks and eat in common dining halls. Work was done in small units of 20 to 30 people called production brigades. The peasants were guaranteed jobs. The system was called the **iron rice bowl.** Under the iron rice bowl system, workers received the same low wage regardless of their productivity. Government planners determined what, how much, and how communes produced. All output was delivered to the government.

In the industrial sector of China, the Great Leap Forward stressed steel and other heavy industries. Millions of small backyard furnaces were built to expand steel production, while light industries were neglected.

The policies of the Great Leap Forward caused economic ruin for China. Agricultural and industrial output fell. Central planners misallocated resources, while the iron rice bowl system reduced worker productivity. In the early 1960s, the government abandoned the Great Leap Forward.

The Cultural Revolution. After a brief economic recovery from 1961 to 1965, China's economy was again plunged into chaos. The chaos lasted from 1965 to 1975 during a period called the Cultural Revolution.

The Cultural Revolution was a violent movement aimed at safeguarding the Communist system against counterrevolution. Leaders of the Cultural Revolution denounced factory managers, scientists, teachers, college professors, and other professional people as counterrevolutionaries, and many factories and schools closed. The Cultural Revolutionaries killed thousands of people. The Cultural Revolution made it impossible for China to implement the Third (1965–1969) and Fourth (1970–1974) Five-Year Plans. ◆

The Four Modernizations. The end of the Cultural Revolution and the death of Mao Zedong in 1976 marked the beginning of the market-responsive period. A more rational program of economic development called the Four Modernizations began at this time. The Four Modernizations target modernization in agriculture, industry, science and technology, and defense as the nation's goals.

◆ **The United States reestablished contact with China in 1972 when President Nixon made an official visit to the world's most populous nation. On January 1, 1979, China and the United States established full diplomatic relations.**

Images of the capitalist world stand in sharp contrast to the more traditional patterns of daily life that are common in much of China.

DECISION MAKERS IN THE ECONOMY

Deng Xiaoping

As the head of government in the People's Republic of China, Deng Xiaoping is dedicated to the task of modernizing his country. He has instituted economic reforms that combine some characteristics of capitalism with a Communist philosophy of government. Deng's goal is to transform his nation, now primarily agricultural, into a modern industrial power. He also hopes to raise the annual per capita income from $300 to $800 by the year 2000.

Deng believes in the complete authority of the Communist party. In his view, no group or person should have the right to challenge the Communist party's leadership. Deng also believes in central planning, in public ownership of most property, and in the need to prevent society from polarizing into rich and poor economic classes.

On the other hand, Deng has recognized the economic failures of the Communist system. He has seen that the more productive capitalist system succeeds by providing workers with an incentive to work. His reforms represent an attempt to supply this incentive.

In 1978, Deng Xiaoping became China's leader. Deng's brand of Chinese socialism combines state planning with market incentives to achieve the Four Modernizations affecting agriculture and industry.

Under Deng Xiaoping, the most significant agricultural reform has been the establishment of the **contract responsibility system.** This system permits peasants to lease state-owned land for periods as long as 30 years. Under the contract responsibility system, peasants pay rent by delivering a certain portion of their crop to the government. The remainder of the crop can then be sold for profit in open markets. The government encourages individuals to build homes on their plots, raise animals, and acquire tractors and other capital that will improve productivity.

Deng has also instituted reforms in the industrial sector. In the Sixth Five-Year Plan (1981–1985), for example, Deng has redirected production into light industries that produce televisions, refrigerators, radios, and other consumer goods. This move to light industries has established a better balance between the production of consumer goods and capital goods.

The government has also extended to industry the contract responsibility system used in agriculture, a move that began in 1985. Under this arrangement, central planners set broad production goals and some production quotas, but plant managers can hire and fire workers—a challenge to the iron rice bowl system. Further, managers determine what goods to produce beyond their quotas. Anything produced above the quota can be sold for profit. The government levies a progressive income tax on profits, but plant managers can use after-tax profits for reinvestment or workers' pay raises and bonuses.

The government also has created **free-trade zones** in southern China and offered tax incentives to foreign corporations to invest in these zones. The free-trade zones reflect Deng's belief that foreign capital, technology, and management will strengthen the Chinese economy.

China's economy has responded favorably to Deng's market-oriented reforms. Agricultural and industrial output rose substantially. Not only are more goods produced, but China has a greater variety of consumer goods available.

◆ **Deng Xiaoping has encouraged diplomatic relations with the United States because he wanted China to increase trade with and learn from the West. He believes that the goals of China's modernization plan would have been achieved earlier if economic ties with the United States had been strong.**

China's Seventh Five-Year Plan (1986–1990) is committed to Deng's reforms. Important goals include plant self-management and the reduction of direct government controls over the economy. The new plan also stresses the importance of education as a long-term investment in human capital. In April 1986, China's first law on compulsory education went into effect.

Future Challenges of Chinese Socialism. The reforms of Chinese socialism have caused a variety of problems. Under the iron rice bowl system, workers were guaranteed jobs, but under the contract responsibility system, unproductive workers often lose their jobs. Now that firms in China are allowed to fail as well as succeed, increasing unemployment has resulted.

Some leaders of the Communist party have attempted to block reforms that they believe will erode their privileged positions. Corruption involving party officials, private entrepreneurs, and foreign firms has increased as the opportunity to make money grows. Central planners must learn how to control corruption and break down resistance to change if China's economic development is to continue in an orderly fashion.

Price increases have resulted from the lifting of price controls, making inflation another of the many challenges facing Chinese officials. Thus China's version of authoritarian socialism is still changing.

See Suggested Assignments, p. TM 106.

Section 4 Review See Answers, p. A 79.

DEFINE iron rice bowl, contract responsibility system, free-trade zone

IDENTIFY Deng Xiaoping

1. **Analyzing Ideas** What role does the second economy play in the Hungarian economy?
2. **Interpreting Ideas** Why is the economic system of the People's Republic of China described as market-responsive?
3. **Using Economic Imagination** What new problems may the People's Republic of China face as it attempts to mix Communism with market incentives?

CHAPTER 19 SUMMARY

Economists divide mixed economic systems into three major types based on whether individuals or governments answer the basic economic questions and make economic decisions. The three economic systems are capitalism, democratic socialism, and authoritarian socialism.

Capitalism, under which individuals and private-sector firms answer the basic economic questions, is the economic system of the United States. Japan and South Korea also have capitalist economies, but the Japanese and South Korean governments take a more active role in economic planning than the government of the United States.

Governments in democratic socialist countries own at least part of the means of production and are actively involved in economic planning. Sweden is a leading example of a nation practicing democratic socialism. Many developing nations of the Third World, such as Tanzania, have also chosen democratic socialism. In the developing nations, however, democratic socialist governments generally assume more authoritative roles in economic planning than the governments of democratic socialist countries such as Sweden.

Under authoritarian socialism, or Communism, which was originated by Karl Marx, the government controls almost all the means of production and makes almost all economic decisions. The Soviet Union is the leading example of a nation practicing authoritarian socialism.

Under the leadership of Mikhail Gorbachev, the Soviet Union has undertaken a number of economic reforms that indicate a slight turn away from authoritarian socialism. A farther turning away is not expected in the next few years.

In China, the market-responsive system began in 1976 with the Four Modernizations and has continued under the leadership of Deng Xiaoping.

Many Communist nations are modifying their authoritarian socialist economic systems. Leaders of Yugoslavia, Hungary, and the People's Republic of China are instituting reforms that make their economic systems more responsive to the forces of the marketplace. These reforms have given individuals more power to make economic decisions by decreasing the importance of central planners.

CHAPTER 19 REVIEW

For Answers to Chapter 19 Review, see p. A 79.

Reviewing Economic Terms

With each definition or description below, match one of the following terms.

a. capitalism
b. mercantilism
c. socialism
d. proletariat
e. collectivization
f. Great Leap Forward

_____ **1.** The name that was given to the first Chinese five-year plan.

_____ **2.** The working class who provided labor at very low wages and were exploited by the bourgeoisie.

_____ **3.** An economic system characterized by the private ownership of the means of production.

_____ **4.** An economic system characterized by the public ownership of some of the means of production.

_____ **5.** The policy of the Soviet government that expropriated peasant land to form large state-run farms.

Exercising Economic Skills

1. **Composing a Comparative Essay** Read the following essay directive and complete the activities below. *Based on the information in this chapter, compare and contrast the economic philosophies of Adam Smith and Karl Marx.* **(a)** List the informational terms in the directive. **(b)** List the performance terms in the directive. **(c)** Develop a table illustrating the information from the chapter on which you would base your essay. **(d)** Organize the information in the table into an outline.
2. **Vacationing in Foreign Countries** Study the feature on pages 537–538. Then suppose you are planning a trip to various parts of the world. Select a nation to include on your itinerary in each of the following areas: South America, Africa, Europe, the Middle East, and Asia. Contact a travel agent for information and compare the requirements and regulations of travel in each nation. Present your findings to the class.

Thinking Critically About Economics

1. **Summarizing Ideas** **(a)** What is the basic difference in the capitalist economies of the world? **(b)** How does capitalism differ from socialism? **(c)** Why is authoritarian socialism close to a pure-command model? **(d)** What is the basic difference in the Communist economies of the world?
2. **Interpreting Ideas** Why does democratic socialism appeal to developing nations such as Tanzania?
3. **Evaluating Ideas** **(a)** What are the goals of the current Soviet five-year plan? **(b)** Do these goals move the Soviet Union closer or farther away from the pure socialist ideal? **(c)** Under Mikhail Gorbachev, how will individual incentives improve in the Soviet Union?
4. **Expressing Viewpoints** How will the Four Modernizations proposed by Deng Xiaoping strengthen the Chinese economy?

Extending Economic Knowledge

1. Find information about China's Great Leap Forward. Compare the information you collect about China's modernization with Japan's industrialization after World War II. Then answer these questions. **(a)** The Japanese have adopted Western techniques in their society. Does it seem to you that China plans to do the same? Explain. **(b)** Do you feel that China can modernize as rapidly as Japan? Why or why not?
2. Research Japan's MITI and develop a plan for a similar United States government agency. **(a)** What should be its goals? **(b)** What policies should it promote to strengthen the U.S. economy? **(c)** How will it implement its programs and policies? Develop a chart to show the organization of your agency.
3. Find books, magazines, and newspapers about Europe in 1867 when Karl Marx wrote *Capital.* **(a)** What were working conditions like? **(b)** Do you agree with Marx that workers were exploited? Why or why not? **(c)** Were the ideas of Marx unique, or did he borrow them from other people? Explain.

Using Primary Sources

Lou Yumin is a successful peasant farmer in the People's Republic of China. She, her husband, and her three children grow vegetables for sale in private markets. As you read this eyewitness account, note how agricultural practices have changed since the responsibility system in agriculture was instituted. Why does Lou Yumin believe the responsibility system has changed things for the better?

The Responsibility System in Chinese Agriculture

I'm 41. My husband and I are residents of Evergreen township, one of the major vegetable-growing bases on the outskirts of Beijing [Peking].

We raise a dozen kinds of vegetables, and every morning we have to pick what's ripe and decide what will sell at the best prices in the market. . . .

All production matters used to be arranged by our production brigade strictly according to the higher state plan. The state purchased everything we grew, transported it and sold it through retail shops. This had some good and bad points. It did guarantee the vegetable supply and automatically controlled prices. But the complicated procedures often caused delays, so produce got stale and there was a lot of spoilage. City people complained a lot.

And, under the old policy, good workers and lazy ones were paid the same. . . . The present system's better. Each family in our village contracts land from the brigade (our family has 0.43 hectare [approximately one acre]). This year we have been allowed to sell our vegetables independently if we like, and we're all happy about this. In the past I never bothered to plan my work or figure out how to do it better. I just did whatever our brigade leaders ordered. Now I think about everything—what we should grow, when to apply fertilizer, when to harvest, etc.

My husband is strong and experienced. He's our family "market research" specialist, making frequent trips to the vegetable trading center set up by our village's Industrial-Agricultural-Commercial Company. There he finds out what's selling well or poorly. . . .

Now, the harder we work, the more money we get. In the first six months of this year we sold 14,000 yuan* worth of vegetables to our village's trading center. Deducting our production costs, that gave us a net income of 10,000 yuan, making us one of the best-off families in the village. We also earned a bonus for every 100 yuan of vegetables we sold, for an extra 470 yuan.

We're still not satisfied, and try to improve our methods. In slack seasons we attend technical classes sponsored by the brigade, which also sends technicians to help us in the fields and provides fertilizer and fine strains of seed. Many new techniques, such as covering fields with thin plastic sheets, are now widely practiced in our village. My family has built greenhouses and wind shields to grow more cucumbers, tomatoes and other summer vegetables even when the weather turns cold.

---

* In United States currency, a yuan is worth about 26 cents.

Source Review

For Answers to Source Review, see p. A 80.

1. According to Lou Yumin, how did production and distribution of goods occur in the past? What were the strengths and weaknesses of the control by the production brigades?
2. What reforms have been made in Chinese agriculture in recent years?
3. How has free enterprise encouraged Lou Yumin and her husband?

UNIT SIX REVIEW

For Answers to Unit Six Review, see p. A 81.

Reviewing Economic Ideas

1. What funding factor makes the Trans-Gabon railway so unique?
2. How does a nation determine its areas of competitive advantage?
3. What was the effect of the Trade Reform Act of 1974?
4. What is the negative effect of having a strong dollar?
5. How have the GATT rounds been successful in promoting free trade?
6. Name three regional trade organizations and explain how each has helped trade in its regions.
7. What four social factors work against a nation's economic planning and development?

Connecting Economic Ideas

1. **Comprehending Ideas** How will failing prices affect the value of the currency of a nation that is dependent on a single commodity for its income?
2. **Understanding Ideas** **(a)** Why does the socialist decision-making model often appeal to people in a country with a low per capita GNP? **(b)** Why are many developing countries less likely to choose capitalism than socialism?
3. **Summarizing Ideas** How does the promotion of international trade help the People's Republic of China develop its economy?
4. **Seeing Relationships** **(a)** Why might a developing country, dependent on exports, protect itself against imports with tariffs or quotas? **(b)** How might the tariffs or quotas of a developed country hurt developing countries?
5. **Interpreting Viewpoints** **(a)** How does foreign aid promote international trade? **(b)** How does the United States gain from providing foreign aid to developing countries?
6. **Analyzing Ideas** **(a)** How might the Smoot-Hawley Tariff of 1930 have contributed to the problems of the Great Depression? **(b)** If you were a free-trade advocate, how would you defend your position against the Smoot-Hawley Tariff?

Investigating Economic Issues

Reread the *Issues in Economics* feature on pages 428–429 and answer the following questions.

1. **Comprehending Ideas** **(a)** What is a multinational? **(b)** Why do multinational firms invest in foreign countries? **(c)** What three topics do economists cover when they attempt to determine the influence that the multinationals have on developing nations' economies?
2. **Understanding Ideas** In what ways have developing nations sought to control multinationals in their countries?
3. **Summarizing Viewpoints** How do critics of multinationals counter the idea that multinationals increase employment opportunities in developing nations?
4. **Interpreting Viewpoints** How do supporters of multinationals defend the idea that multinational corporations stifle economic growth in developing nations?

Applying Economics

1. Select three of the 10 top trading partners of the United States. List the major items traded with the United States and the yearly dollar values of those items. With which of these countries, if any, does the United States have **(a)** a favorable balance of trade? **(b)** an unfavorable balance of trade? Chart your findings.
2. Select 10 low-income developing nations. For each nation, research and record statistics on its standard of living (per capita GNP, literacy, infant mortality, exports, imports). See the World Economic Data File on pages 481–498 for some of this data. Then study the role of government in economic decision making in each country and divide the nations into capitalist economies and socialist economies. **(a)** Describe any trading patterns that emerge from your findings. **(b)** State a generalization or conclusion that you can draw from your research. **(c)** Make a recommendation on how the United States could improve its balance of trade. Report your findings to the class.

Using Primary Sources

Peter F. Drucker (1909–) is a noted American economist, who has written numerous books about business management and business operations. As you read the following excerpts from an essay in his book *Toward The Next Economics and Other Essays* (1981), consider how multinational corporations (MNCs) could enhance economic development in Third World nations.

A Plan for Integrating the Third World in the World Economy

... [T]he most advantageous strategy for the developing countries would seem to be [to implement] a policy that uses the multinationals' integrating ability to develop large productive facilities with access to markets in the developed world.... As Taiwan and Singapore have demonstrated, it can make much more sense to become the most efficient large supplier worldwide of one model or one component than to be a high-cost small producer of the entire product or line. This would create more jobs and provide the final product at lower prices to the country's own consumers. And it should result in large foreign-exchange earnings....

I would suggest a second integration requirement.... [This] would be a requirement by the developing country that the multinational integrate the managerial and professional people it employs in the country within its worldwide management development plans. Most especially it should assign an adequate number of the younger, abler people from its affiliate in the developing country for three to five years to managerial and professional work in one of the developed countries.... [It] is people and their competence who propel development; and the most important competence needed is not technical, i.e., what one can learn in a course, but management of people, marketing, finance, and first-hand knowledge of developed countries....

A policy of self-sufficiency is not possible even for the best-endowed country today. Development, even of modest proportions, cannot be based on uneconomically small, permanently high-cost facilities, either in manufacturing or in farming.... The integration of the productive capacities of developing countries into the world economy is the only way out. And the multinational's capacity across national boundaries would seem the most promising tool for this.

Source Review

For Answers to Source Review, see p. A 82.

1. How do MNCs enable developing countries to enter world markets?
2. Why is it important for managers and other professionals from developing countries to work in developed countries? How can MNCs aid in this process?
3. According to Drucker, is economic self-sufficiency possible today? How are the MNCs able to integrate the economies of the world?

Further Reading

Gorbachev, Mikhail S. "Remarks on US–USSR Trade," *Harvard Business Review*, vol. 64, no. 3 (May-June 1986), pp. 55–58. A recap of a speech by the general secretary of the Communist party of the Soviet Union, in which he reiterates the need to develop cooperation among nations of differing social systems and ideologies.

Polland, Sidney. *European Economic Integration 1815–1970.* San Diego: Harcourt Brace Jovanovich. A literate survey of European economics that provides a good overview of the type of industries that Marx mentions in *Capital.*

Schumpeter, Joseph A. *Capitalism, Socialism and Democracy.* New York: Harper & Row. The classic examination of capitalism, Marxism, and socialism and the relationship of each to democracy.

Smith, Adam. *An Inquiry into the Nature and Causes of the Wealth of Nations.* New York: Random House. This classic work, written in 1776, outlines the theory of laissez-faire capitalism.

State of the World
1986
Lester R. Brown
and William U. Chandler
Christopher Flavin
Cynthia Pollock
Sandra Postel
Linda Starke
Edward C. Wolf
A Worldwatch Institute Report on Progress Toward a Sustainable Society
PROVISIONAL PROJECTIONS OF THE POPULATION OF STATES, BY AGE AND SEX: 1980 TO 2000
National Data Book and Guide to Sources
STATISTICAL ABSTRACT OF THE UNITED STATES 1986
106th Edition
World Resources 1986
An Assessment of the Resource Base that Supports the Global Economy
With Data Tables for 146 Countries
World Resources Institute
International Institute for Environment and Development
The United States Government Manual 1985-86
A Statistical Abstract Supplement
State and Metropolitan Area Data Book
1986
U.S. Department of Commerce
BUREAU OF THE CENSUS
CURRENT POPULATION REPORTS
Money Income of Households, Families, and Persons in the United States: 1984
THE WORLD ALMANAC AND BOOK OF FACTS
1987
World Development Report 1986
World Population 1983
Recent Demographic Estimates for the Countries and Regions of the World

THE REFERENCE LIBRARY

WASHINGTON
Seattle
Tacoma
Olympia
Spokane
Columbia River
Portland
OREGON
Salem
Eugene
IDAHO
Boise
Snake River
MONTANA
Helena
Billings
NORTH DAKOTA
WYOMING
Casper
Cheyenne
NEBRASKA
CALIFORNIA
Sacramento
San Francisco
Oakland
San Jose
Fresno
Bakersfield
Pasadena
Los Angeles
San Bernardino
Long Beach
Santa Ana
Anaheim
San Diego
NEVADA
Reno
Carson City
Las Vegas
Great Salt Lake
UTAH
Ogden
Salt Lake City
Colorado River
COLORADO
Denver
Colorado Springs
Pueblo
ARIZONA
Phoenix
Mesa
Tucson
NEW MEXICO
Santa Fe
Albuquerque
Amarillo
Lubbock
El Paso
TEXAS
Rio Grande
PACIFIC OCEAN
MEXICO
ARCTIC OCEAN
U. S. S. R.
ALASKA
CANADA
Anchorage
Juneau
Bering Sea
Gulf of Alaska
0 300 miles
0 300 kilometers
PACIFIC OCEAN
Honolulu
HAWAII
Hilo
0 100 miles
0 100 kilometers

THE UNITED STATES
National capital
State capitals
0
500 miles
0
500 kilometers
CANADA
ATLANTIC OCEAN
Gulf of Mexico
THE BAHAMAS
CUBA
Straits of Florida
Lake Superior
Lake Michigan
Lake Huron
Lake Erie
Lake Ontario
St. Lawrence River
Hudson River
Mississippi River
Ohio River
Red River
Lake Okeechobee
MINNESOTA
WISCONSIN
MICHIGAN
IOWA
ILLINOIS
IND.
OHIO
MISSOURI
KENTUCKY
TENN.
ARKANSAS
MISS.
ALABAMA
GEORGIA
FLORIDA
LA.
SOUTH CAROLINA
NORTH CAROLINA
VIRGINIA
W. VA.
PA.
NEW YORK
N.J.
DEL.
MD.
VT.
N.H.
MAINE
MASS.
R.I.
CONN.
Fargo
Duluth
St. Paul
Minneapolis
Green Bay
Milwaukee
Madison
Lansing
Flint
Detroit
Chicago
Gary
Des Moines
Cedar Rapids
Davenport
Omaha
Lincoln
Peoria
Springfield
Indianapolis
Toledo
Cleveland
Columbus
Dayton
Cincinnati
Erie
Buffalo
Rochester
Syracuse
Albany
Montpelier
Concord
Augusta
Portland
Boston
Providence
Hartford
New York City
Newark
Trenton
Philadelphia
Dover
Baltimore
Annapolis
Washington, D.C.
Harrisburg
Pittsburgh
Charleston
Richmond
Norfolk
Roanoke
Frankfort
Louisville
Lexington
Abilene
Topeka
Wichita
Jefferson City
St. Louis
Springfield
Knoxville
Nashville
Winston-Salem
Raleigh
Tulsa
Oklahoma City
Memphis
Little Rock
Huntsville
Birmingham
Atlanta
Macon
Columbia
Charleston
Montgomery
Columbus
Jackson
Shreveport
Mobile
Biloxi
Tallahassee
Jacksonville
Baton Rouge
New Orleans
Dallas
Fort Worth
Waco
Beaumont
Houston
Austin
San Antonio
Galveston
Corpus Christi
Orlando
Tampa
St. Petersburg
Fort Lauderdale
Miami
Key West

United States Population Density

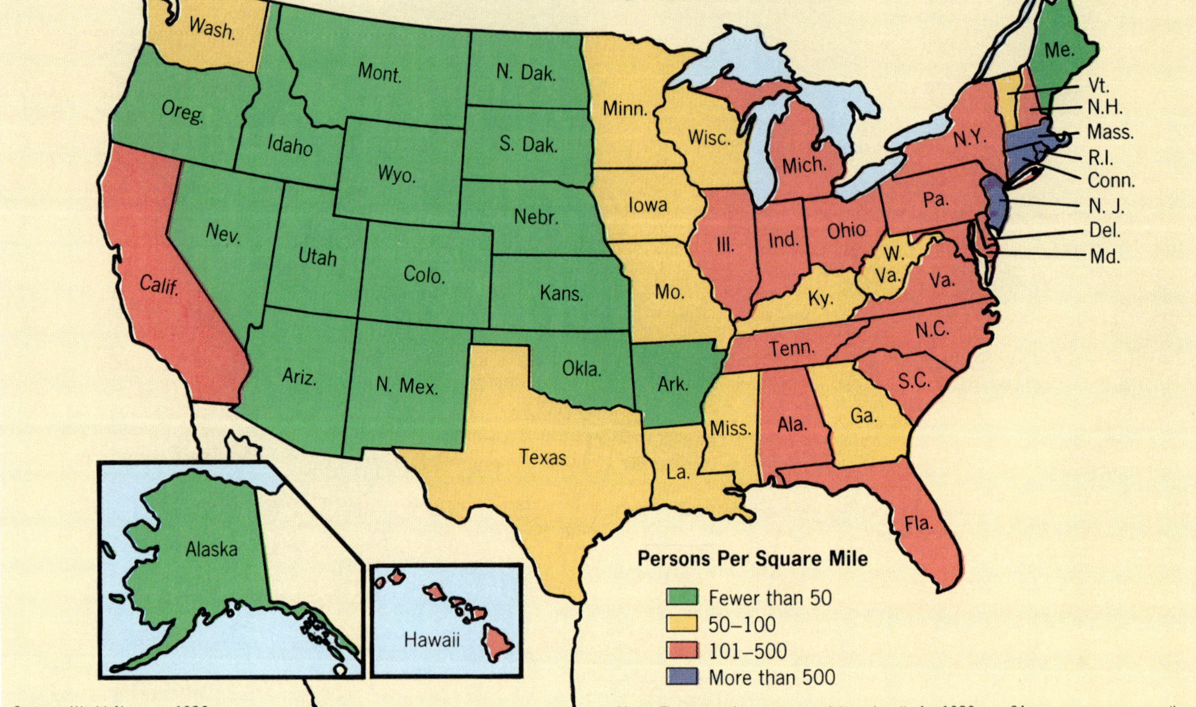

Source: *World Almanac, 1986*

Note: The national average population density for 1980 was 64 persons per square mile.

Rural and Urban Population Growth of the United States, 1900–1980

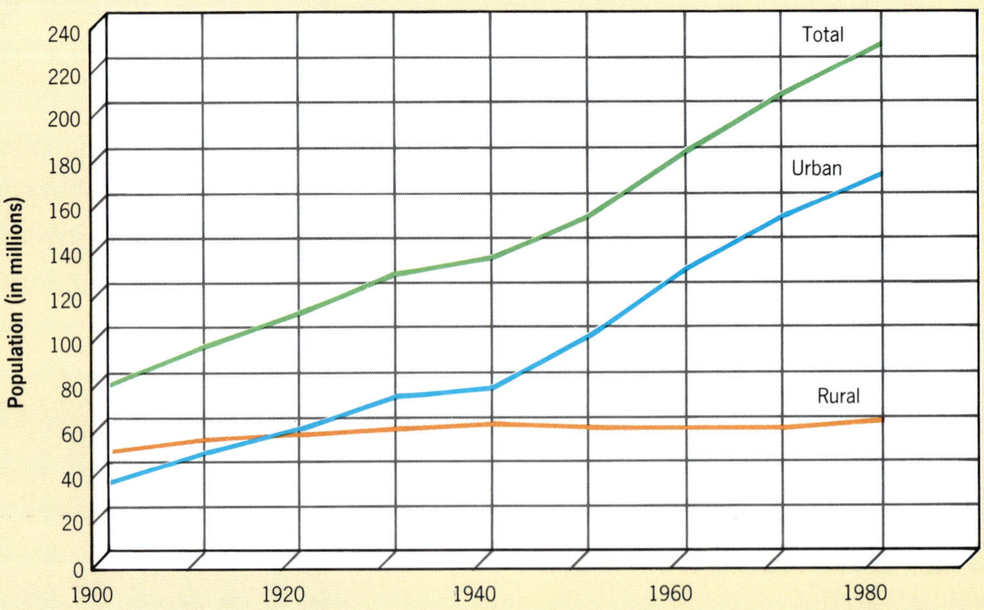

Sources: *Historical Statistics of the United States, Colonial Times to 1970; Statistical Abstract of the United States, 1986;* Population Reference Bureau

1987 Estimates (April): Total—243,200,000; Urban—186,600,000; Rural—56,600,000.

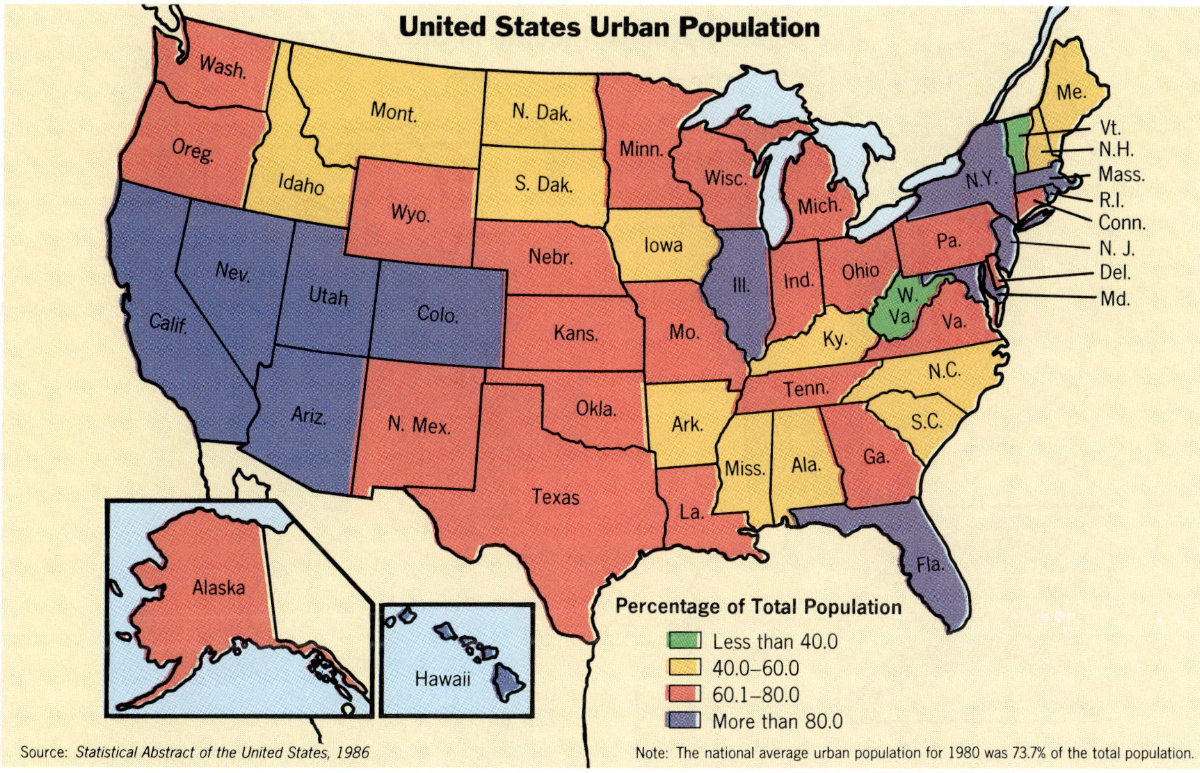
United States Urban Population
Wash.
Oreg.
Calif.
Nev.
Idaho
Mont.
Wyo.
Utah
Ariz.
Colo.
N. Mex.
N. Dak.
S. Dak.
Nebr.
Kans.
Okla.
Texas
Minn.
Iowa
Mo.
Ark.
La.
Wisc.
Ill.
Mich.
Ind.
Ohio
Ky.
Tenn.
Miss.
Ala.
Ga.
Fla.
S.C.
N.C.
Va.
W. Va.
Pa.
N.Y.
Me.
Vt.
N.H.
Mass.
R.I.
Conn.
N. J.
Del.
Md.
Alaska
Hawaii
Percentage of Total Population
Less than 40.0
40.0–60.0
60.1–80.0
More than 80.0
Source: *Statistical Abstract of the United States, 1986*
Note: The national average urban population for 1980 was 73.7% of the total population.

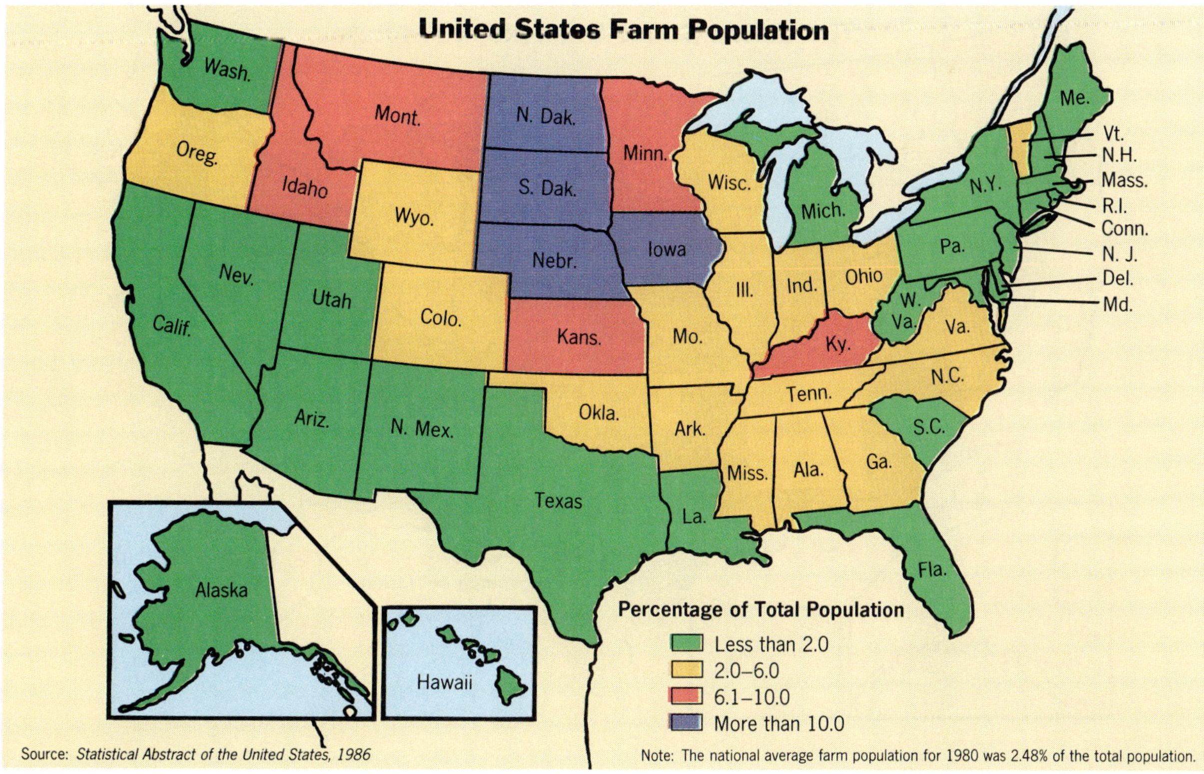
United States Farm Population
Wash.
Oreg.
Calif.
Nev.
Idaho
Mont.
Wyo.
Utah
Ariz.
Colo.
N. Mex.
N. Dak.
S. Dak.
Nebr.
Kans.
Okla.
Texas
Minn.
Iowa
Mo.
Ark.
La.
Wisc.
Ill.
Mich.
Ind.
Ohio
Ky.
Tenn.
Miss.
Ala.
Ga.
Fla.
S.C.
N.C.
Va.
W. Va.
Pa.
N.Y.
Me.
Vt.
N.H.
Mass.
R.I.
Conn.
N. J.
Del.
Md.
Alaska
Hawaii
Percentage of Total Population
Less than 2.0
2.0–6.0
6.1–10.0
More than 10.0
Source: *Statistical Abstract of the United States, 1986*
Note: The national average farm population for 1980 was 2.48% of the total population.

Per Capita Personal Income in Current Dollars

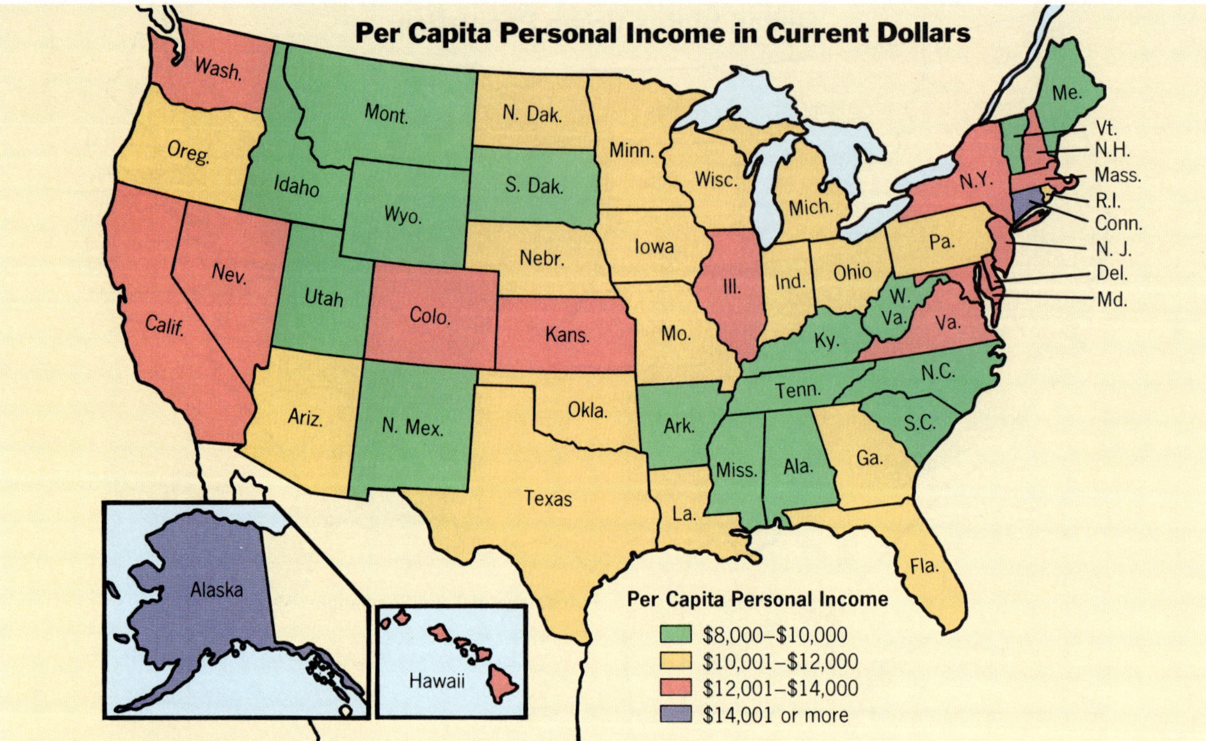

Source: *Statistical Abstract of the United States, 1986*

Note: The national average per capita personal income for 1983 was $11,687 in current dollars.

The United States Unemployment Rate

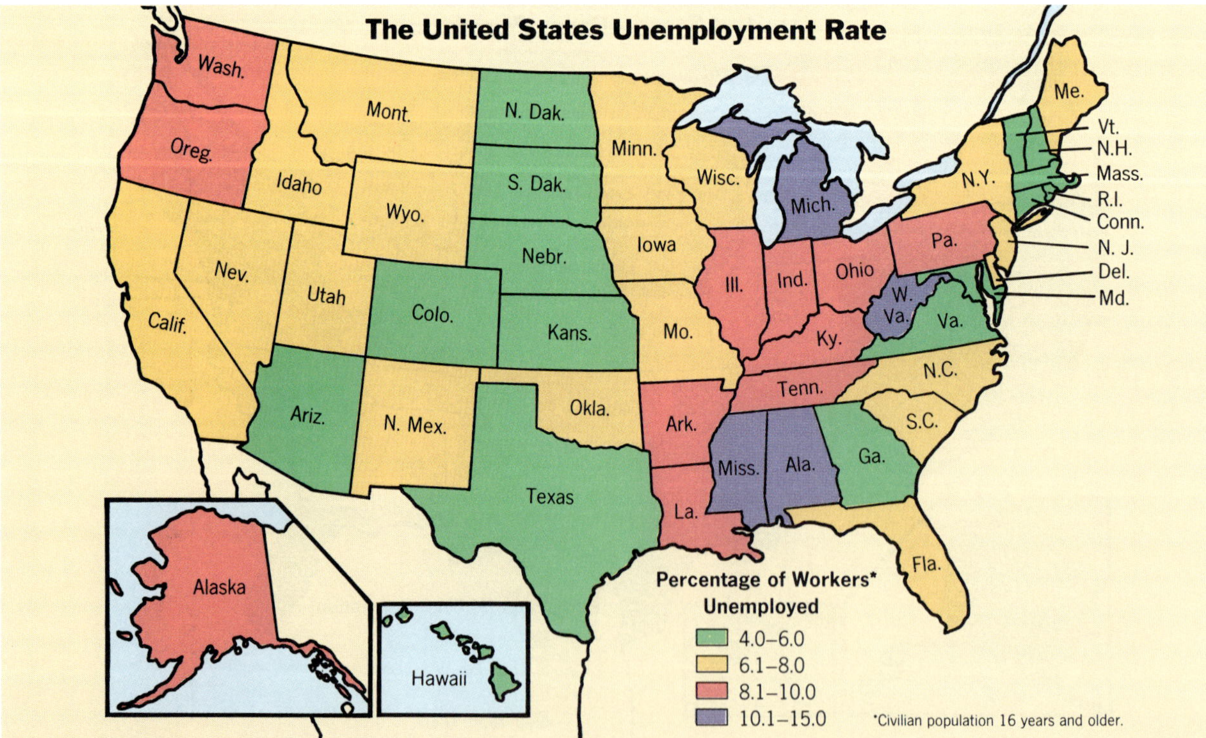

Source: *Statistical Abstract of the United States, 1986*

Note: The national average unemployment rate for 1984 was 7.5%.

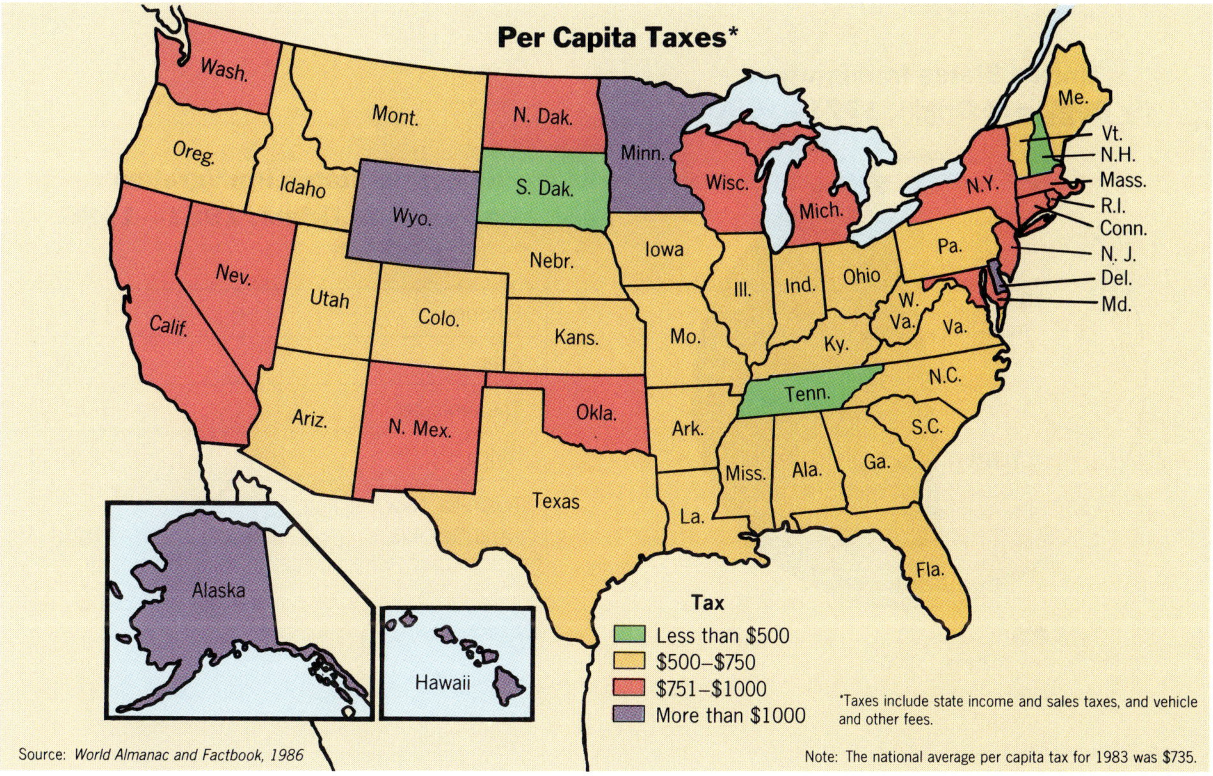

*Taxes include state income and sales taxes, and vehicle and other fees.

Source: *World Almanac and Factbook, 1986*

Note: The national average per capita tax for 1983 was $735.

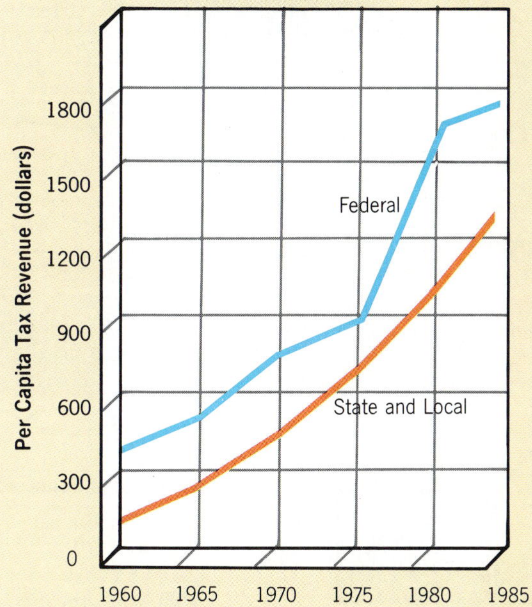

Source: *Statistical Abstract of the United States, 1987*

United States Immigration by Region of Origin, 1971–1980

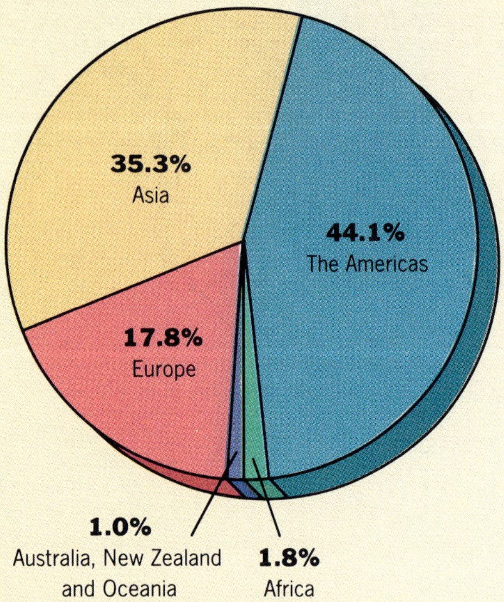

Source: *World Almanac, 1985*

United States Immigration by Region of Origin, 1981—1985

Europe	11.2%
Asia	48.0%
The Americas	37.3%
Africa	2.8%
Australia, New Zealand and Oceania	0.7%

Source: *Statistical Abstract of the United States, 1987*

Minorities as a Percentage of the Total Population

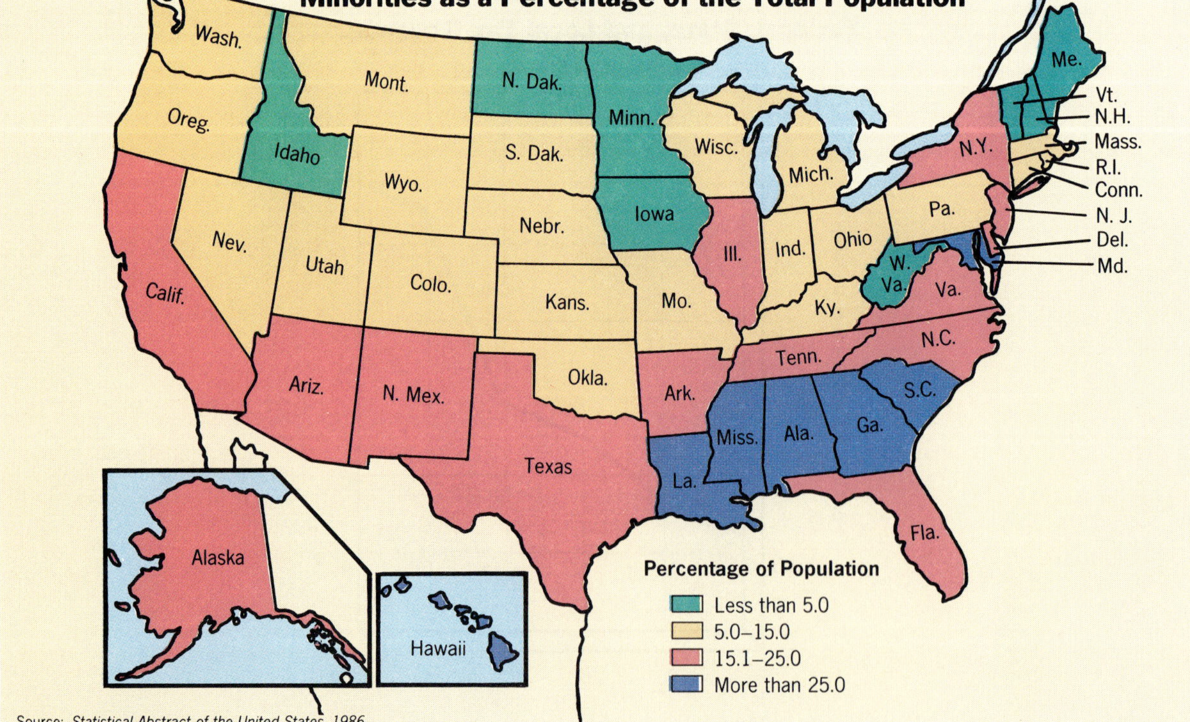

Source: *Statistical Abstract of the United States, 1986*

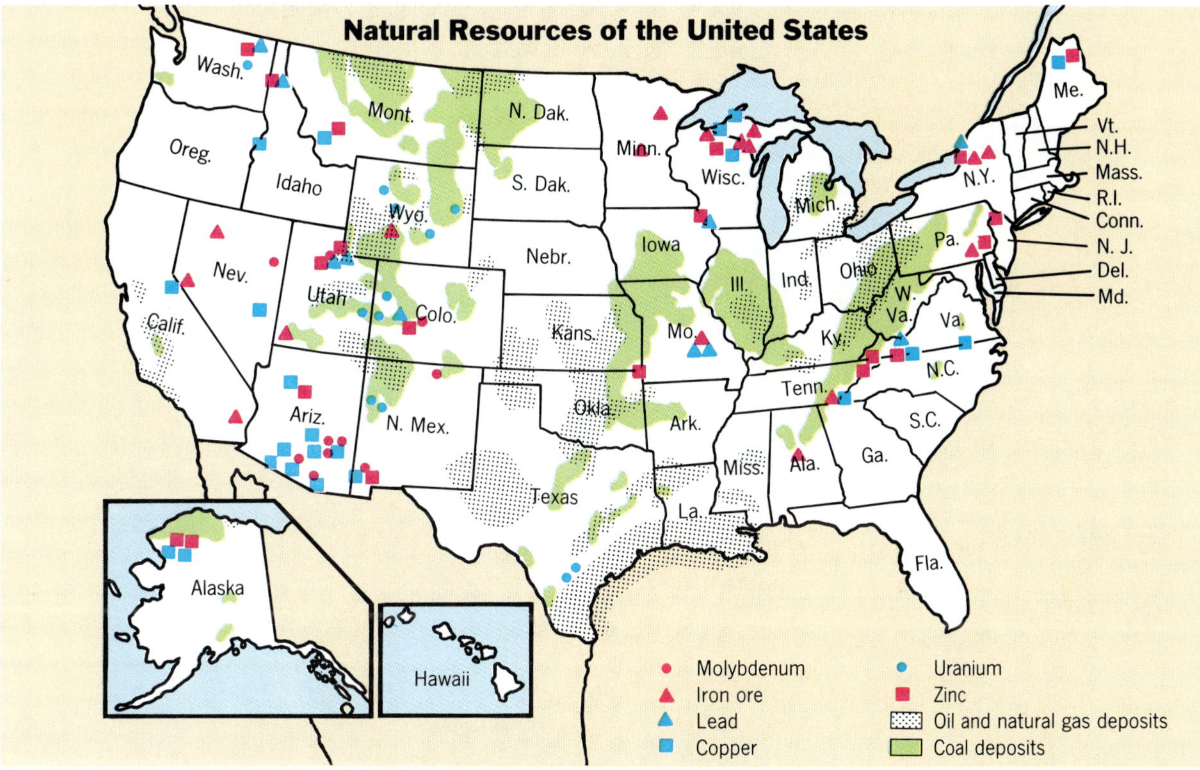

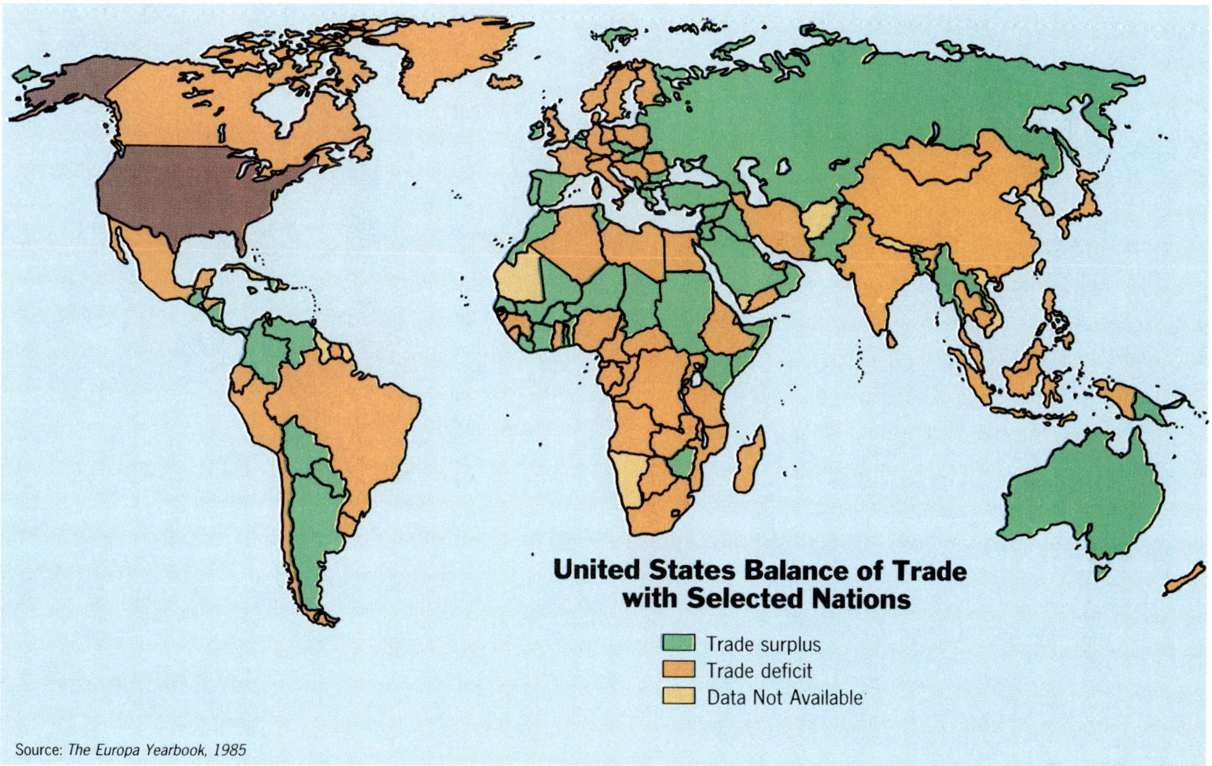

Source: *The Europa Yearbook, 1985*

ARCTIC OCEAN
U.S.S.R.
Bering Strait
Yukon River
Alaska (United States)
Bering Sea
Gulf of Alaska
Mackenzie River
Baffin Bay
Greenland (Denmark)
ICELAND
Hudson Bay
CANADA
NORTH AMERICA
Newfoundland
St. Lawrence River
Ottawa
Great Lakes
Missouri River
Ohio River
Mississippi River
UNITED STATES
Washington, D.C.
Rio Grande
NORTH PACIFIC OCEAN
NORTH ATLANTIC OCEAN
North Sea
UNITED KINGDOM
Dublin
London
IRELAND
DENMA
NETH.
BELG.
Paris
SWITZ.
FRANCE
PORTUGAL
Lisbon
Madrid
SPAIN
Rabat
Algiers
MOROCCO
ALGERIA
Gulf of Mexico
THE BAHAMAS
Havana
CUBA
HAITI
DOMINICAN REPUBLIC
Puerto Rico (U.S.)
Hawaii (United States)
MEXICO
Mexico City
JAMAICA
BELIZE
GUATEMALA
HONDURAS
EL SALVADOR
NICARAGUA
Managua
Caribbean Sea
COSTA RICA
PANAMA
Panama Canal
TRINIDAD AND TOBAGO
Caracas
VENEZUELA
GUYANA
SURINAME
FRENCH GUIANA
Bogotá
COLOMBIA
Quito
ECUADOR
Amazon River
SOUTH AMERICA
PERU
Lima
La Paz
BOLIVIA
Sucre
Brasília
BRAZIL
PARAGUAY
Asunción
CHILE
Paraná River
Santiago
Buenos Aires
URUGUAY
Montevideo
ARGENTINA
Falkland Islands (U.K.)
Strait of Magellan
SOUTH ATLANTIC OCEAN
SOUTH PACIFIC OCEAN
ESTERN SAMOA
American Samoa (U.S.)
INTERNATIONAL DATE LINE
Nouakchott
MAURITANIA
MALI
CAPE VERDE
SENEGAL
THE GAMBIA
GUINEA-BISSAU
GUINEA
Niger River
SIERRA LEONE
BURKINA FASO
LIBERIA
IVORY COAST
GHANA
TOGO
BENIN
EQ. GUINEA

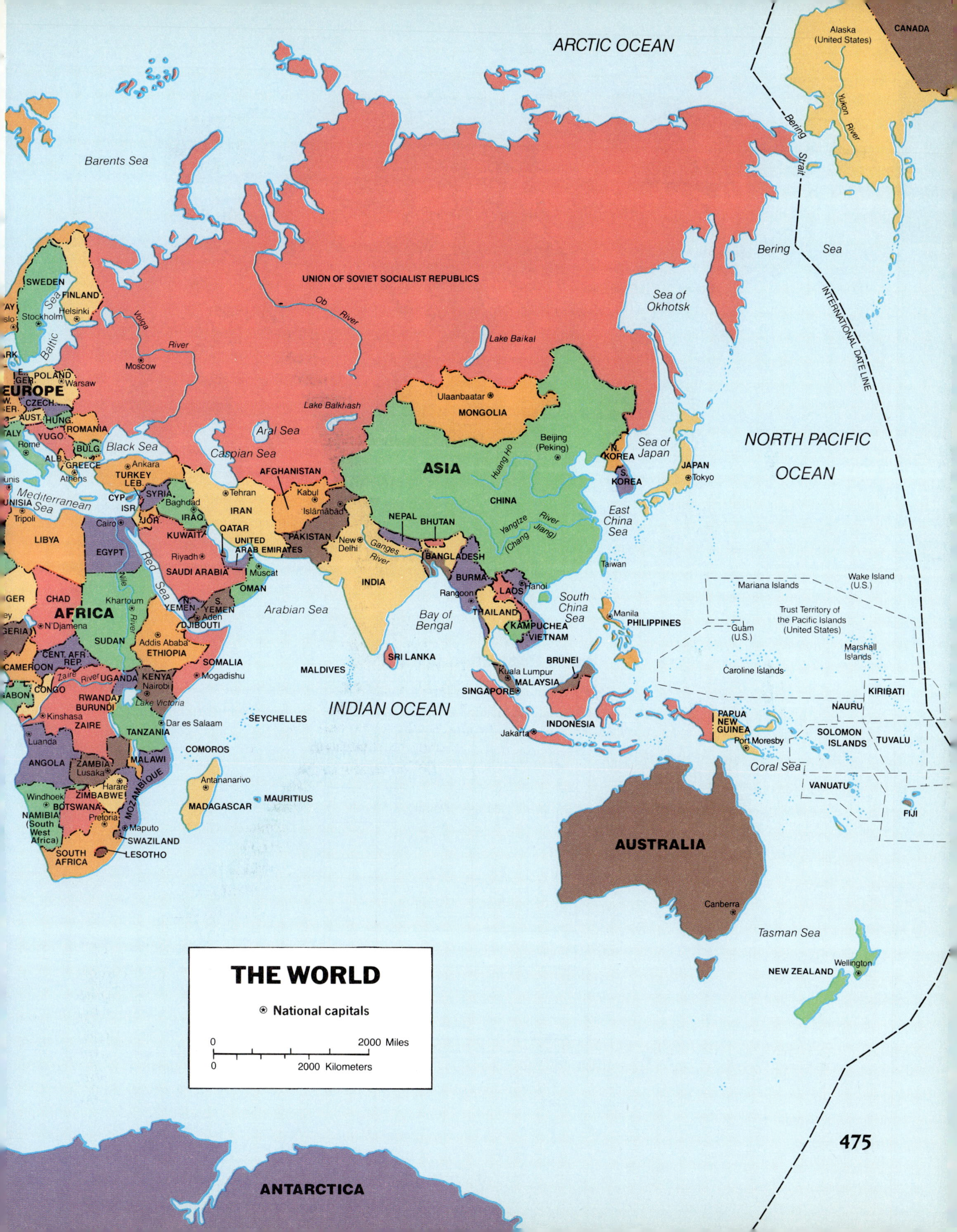
THE WORLD
National capitals
0 2000 Miles
0 2000 Kilometers
ARCTIC OCEAN
Barents Sea
Alaska (United States)
CANADA
Yukon River
Bering Strait
Bering Sea
INTERNATIONAL DATE LINE
UNION OF SOVIET SOCIALIST REPUBLICS
Ob River
Volga River
Moscow
Lake Baikal
Sea of Okhotsk
Lake Balkhash
Aral Sea
Caspian Sea
Black Sea
Ulaanbaatar
MONGOLIA
ASIA
Beijing (Peking)
Huang Ho
CHINA
Yangtze River (Chang Jiang)
N. KOREA
S. KOREA
Sea of Japan
JAPAN
Tokyo
NORTH PACIFIC OCEAN
East China Sea
Taiwan
SWEDEN
FINLAND
Helsinki
Stockholm
Baltic Sea
POLAND
Warsaw
EUROPE
CZECH.
AUST.
HUNG.
ROMANIA
YUGO.
BULG.
ALB.
GREECE
Athens
Rome
Ankara
TURKEY
CYP.
LEB.
SYRIA
ISR.
JOR.
Mediterranean Sea
Tripoli
LIBYA
Cairo
EGYPT
Baghdad
IRAQ
KUWAIT
Tehran
IRAN
QATAR
UNITED ARAB EMIRATES
Riyadh
SAUDI ARABIA
Muscat
OMAN
AFGHANISTAN
Kabul
Islāmābād
PAKISTAN
NEPAL
BHUTAN
New Delhi
Ganges River
INDIA
BANGLADESH
BURMA
Rangoon
LAOS
Hanoi
THAILAND
KAMPUCHEA
VIETNAM
South China Sea
Manila
PHILIPPINES
Arabian Sea
Bay of Bengal
SRI LANKA
MALDIVES
BRUNEI
Kuala Lumpur
MALAYSIA
SINGAPORE
INDONESIA
Jakarta
INDIAN OCEAN
SEYCHELLES
COMOROS
MAURITIUS
Antananarivo
MADAGASCAR
Red Sea
N. YEMEN
S. YEMEN
Aden
DJIBOUTI
Khartoum
Nile River
CHAD
AFRICA
N'Djamena
SUDAN
Addis Ababa
ETHIOPIA
SOMALIA
Mogadishu
CENT. AFR. REP.
CAMEROON
Zaire River
UGANDA
KENYA
Nairobi
CONGO
RWANDA
BURUNDI
Lake Victoria
Kinshasa
ZAIRE
TANZANIA
Dar es Salaam
Luanda
ANGOLA
ZAMBIA
Lusaka
MALAWI
MOZAMBIQUE
Harare
ZIMBABWE
Windhoek
BOTSWANA
NAMIBIA (South West Africa)
Pretoria
Maputo
SWAZILAND
LESOTHO
SOUTH AFRICA
Mariana Islands
Wake Island (U.S.)
Trust Territory of the Pacific Islands (United States)
Guam (U.S.)
Marshall Islands
Caroline Islands
KIRIBATI
NAURU
PAPUA NEW GUINEA
Port Moresby
SOLOMON ISLANDS
TUVALU
Coral Sea
VANUATU
FIJI
AUSTRALIA
Canberra
Tasman Sea
NEW ZEALAND
Wellington
ANTARCTICA

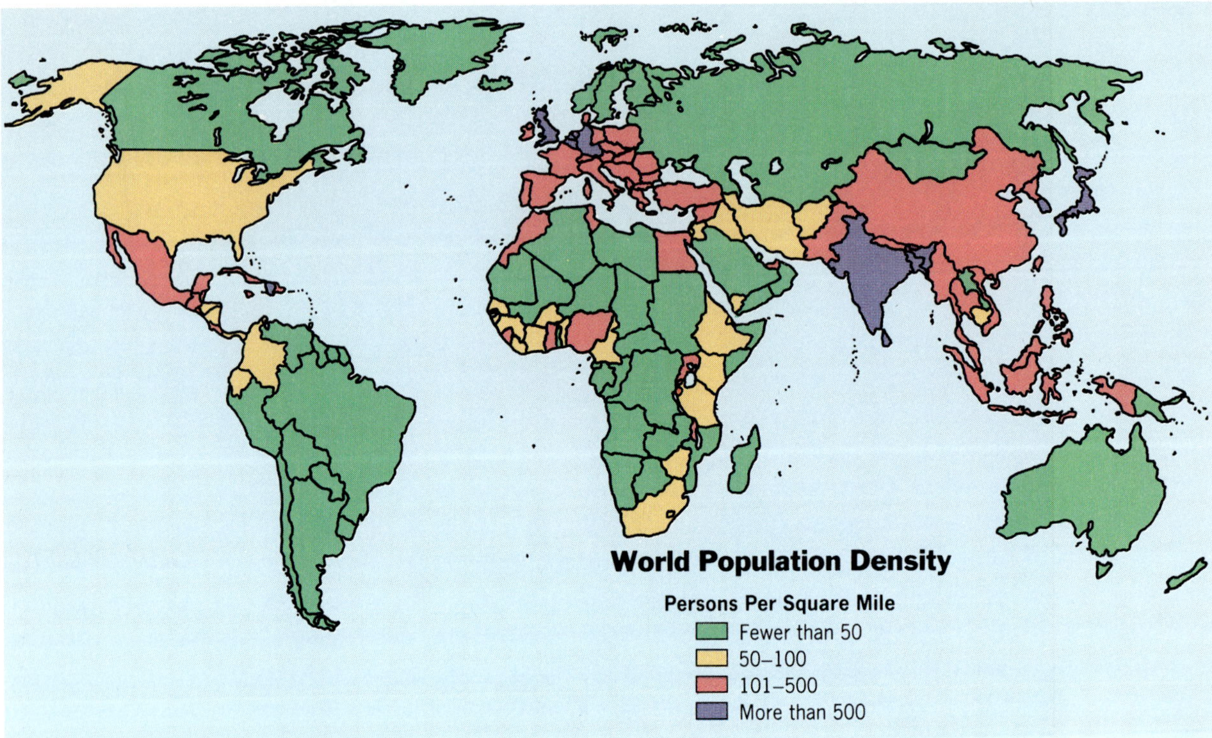

World Population Density

Source: *Statistical Abstract of the United States, 1986*

World Population Growth

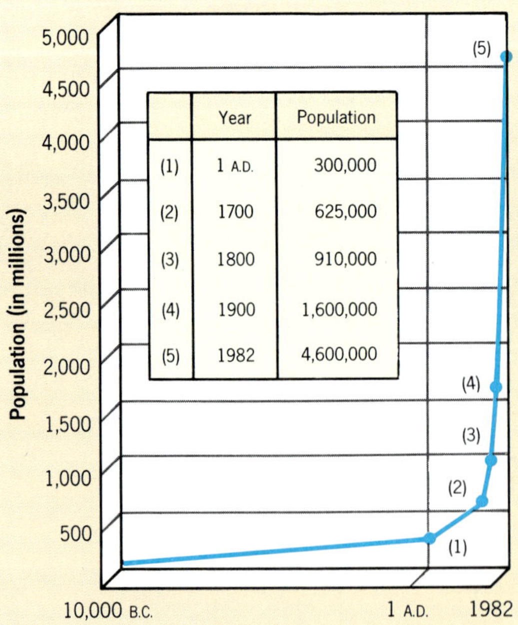

	Year	Population
(1)	1 A.D.	300,000
(2)	1700	625,000
(3)	1800	910,000
(4)	1900	1,600,000
(5)	1982	4,600,000

Source: *World Almanac, 1985*

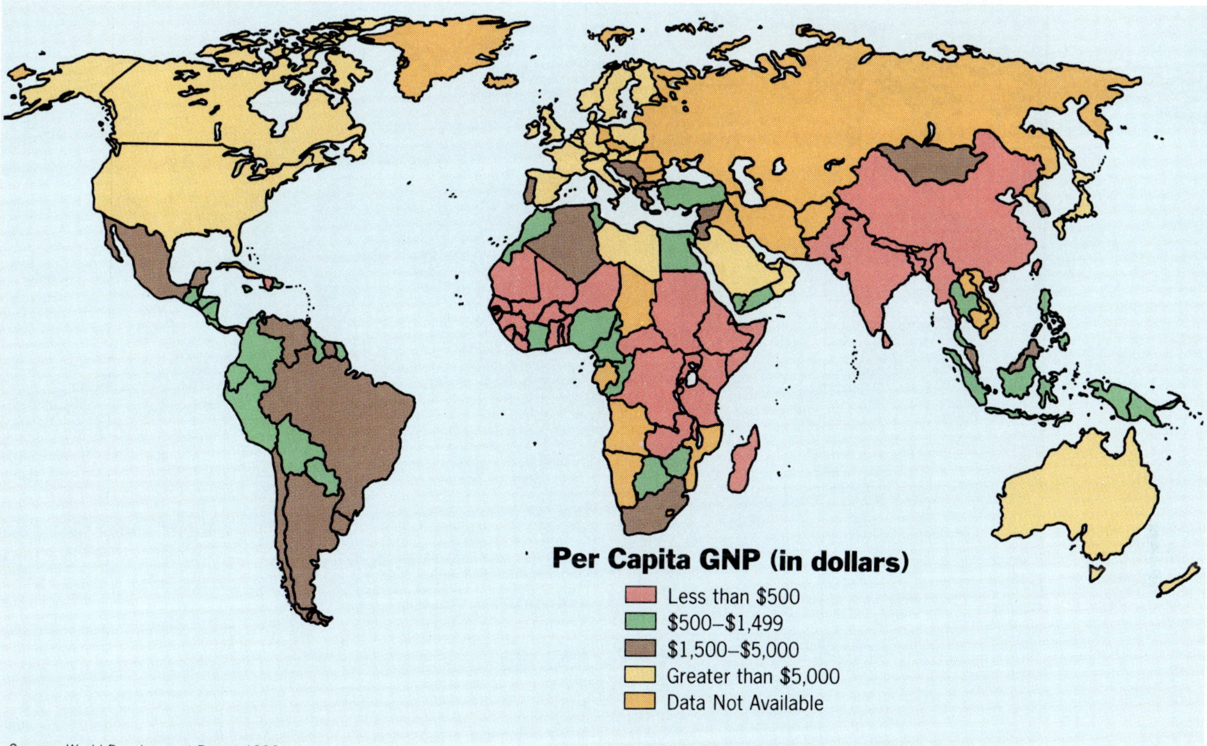

Source: *World Development Report 1986*

Population Growth Rates of the Fastest- and Slowest-Growing Nations

Fastest-Growing Nations	Population (in millions)	Annual % Growth
Kenya	18.5	4.1
Saudi Arabia	10.4	3.4
Syria	9.7	3.4
Nigeria	85.2	3.4
Iraq	14.2	3.3
Rwanda	5.6	3.3
Malawi	6.6	3.2
Tanzania	20.5	3.2

Slowest-Growing Nations	Population (in millions)	Annual % Growth
Afghanistan	14.2	−0.2
West Germany	61.5	−0.2
Denmark	5.1	−0.1
Hungary	10.7	−0.1
East Germany	16.7	0.0
Sweden	8.3	0.0
Britain	56.0	0.0
Austria	7.6	0.0

Source: *The World Almanac and Book of Facts, 1985*
Note: The world average population growth rate is 1.7%

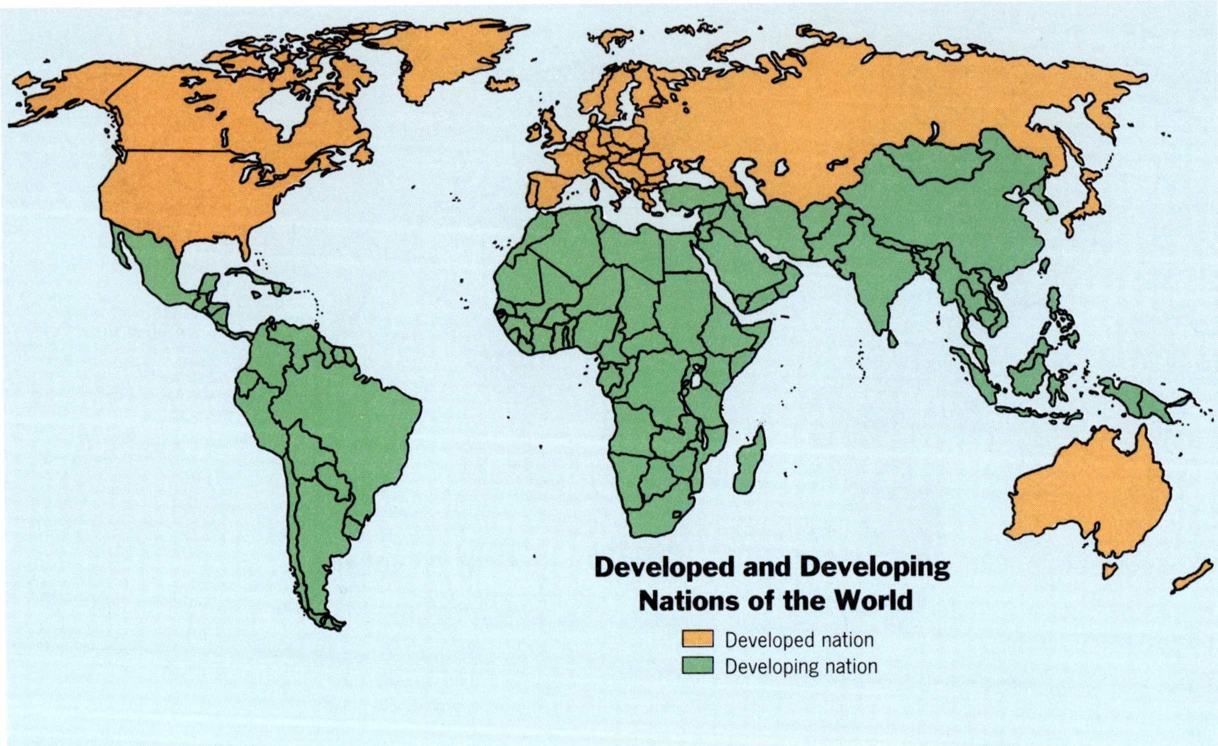

Source: *Statistical Abstract of the United States, 1986*

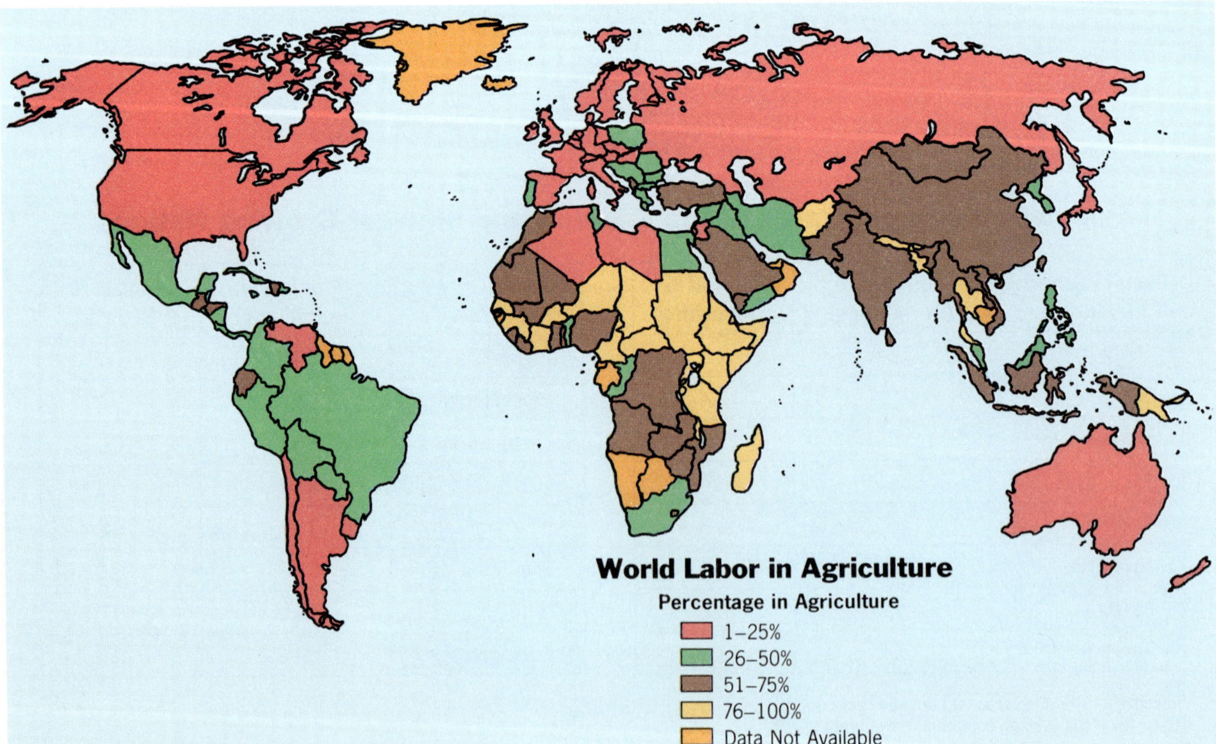

Source: *World Resources, 1986*

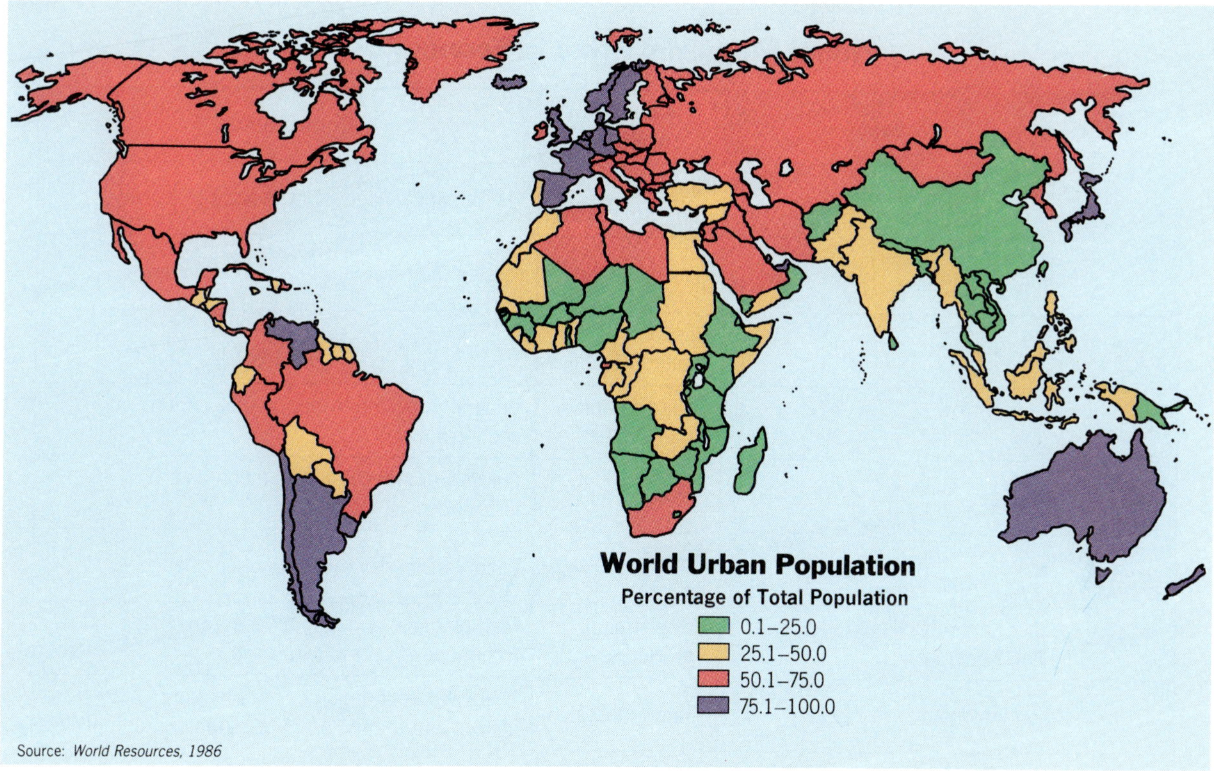

Source: *World Resources, 1986*

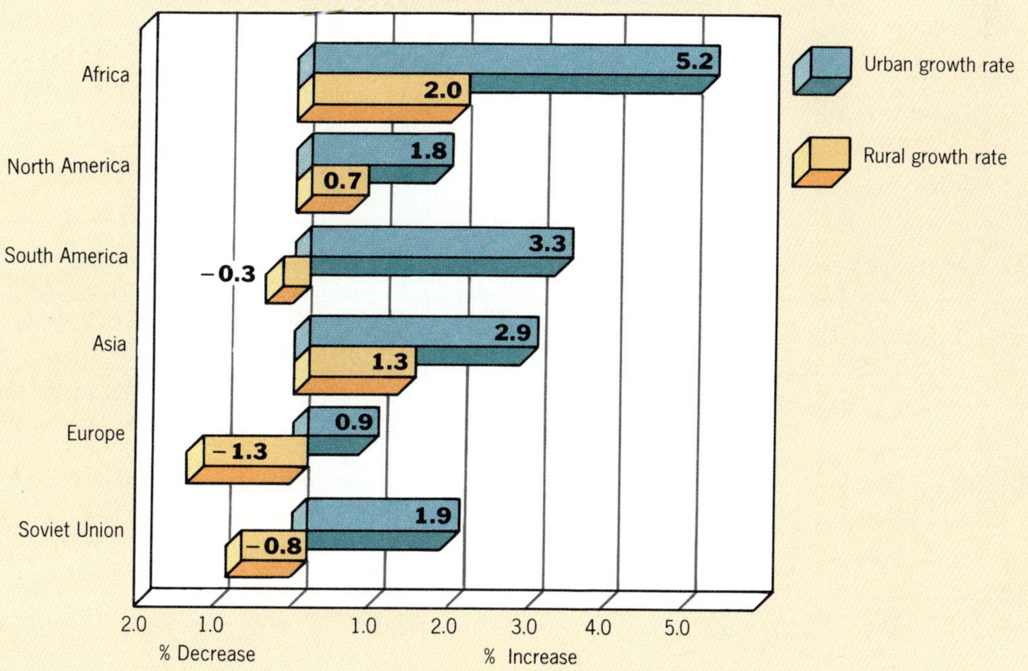

Source: *World Resources 1986*, Table 3.1, p. 248

Nobel Memorial Prize in Economics

Year	Recipient		Country of Birth	Contribution
1969	Frisch Ragnar Jan Tinbergen	(1895–1973) (1903–)	Norway The Netherlands	Mathematical analysis of economic activity
1970	Paul Samuelson	(1915–)	United States	Raising the level of analysis in economics
1971	Simon Kuznets	(1901–1985)	Russia (United States) ◆	National income accounting
1972	Kenneth Arrow Sir John Hicks	(1921–) (1904–)	United States Great Britain	General equilibrium theory and welfare economics
1973	Wassily Leontief	(1906–)	United States	Analysis of industrial production and distribution
1974	August von Hayek Gunnar Myrdal	(1899–) (1898–1987)	Austria Sweden	Theory of money and economic change
1975	Leonid Kantorovich Tjalling Koopmans	(1912–) (1910–)	Soviet Union The Netherlands	Mathematical and statistical approaches to optimal resource allocation
1976	Milton Friedman	(1912–)	United States	Theory of economic consumption, monetary history and theory, and price stabilization policy
1977	James Meade Bertil Ohlin	(1907–) (1899–1979)	Great Britain Sweden	International trade and capital movements
1978	Herbert Simon	(1916–)	United States	The role of corporations and decision-making processes
1979	Theodore Schultz Arthur Lewis	(1902–) (1915–)	United States Great Britain	Underdevelopment and the role of education in advancing the economy
1980	Lawrence Klein	(1920–)	United States	The application of econometrics to public policy and economic and social change
1981	James Tobin	(1918–)	United States	Analysis of financial markets and investment choices
1982	George Stigler	(1911–)	United States	Industrial organization research
1983	George Debreu	(1921–)	France (United States) ◆	Development of a mathematical model of supply and demand
1984	Sir Richard Stone	(1913–)	Great Britain	Development of methods for measuring the performance of national economies
1985	Franco Modigliani	(1919–)	Italy (United States) ◆	Theories of savings and corporate finance
1986	James Buchanan	(1919–)	United States	Application of economic theory to political decision making
1987	to come	(19 –)	to come	to come

 ◆ Indicates naturalized citizenship of prize winner.

WORLD ECONOMIC DATA

NATION/ Capital/ Population/ Urbanization	Land Use	Natural Resources	Major Industries	Exports	Imports	Monetary Unit/ Per Capita Income (in U.S. $)
AFGHANISTAN Kabul 15,425,000 18.5%	75% deserts, wasteland, other; 12% cultivated; 10% pasture; 3% forests	natural gas, oil, coal, copper, talc, lead, salt, zinc	textiles, soap, furniture, shoes, fertilizer, carpets	fruits, nuts, natural gas, carpets	food supplies, petroleum products	afghani $160
ALBANIA Tiranë 3,020,000 39.3%	43% forests; 21% arable; 19% pastures; 12% other; 5% cropland	oil, gas, coal, chromium	textiles, clothing, lumber, extractive industries (chrome and oil)	asphalt, bitumen, petroleum products, metals, ores, electricity, oil, vegetables	machinery, machine tools, iron and steel products, textiles, chemicals	lek $900
ALGERIA Algiers 22,817,000 66.6%	80% deserts, wasteland; 16% pastures; 3% cultivated; 1% forests	oil, natural gas, iron ore, phosphates, uranium, lead, zinc, mercury	petroleum, mining, automotive plants, food processing	petroleum and gas	capital goods, semifinished goods, food	dinar $2,410
ANDORRA Andorra la Vella 49,000 NA*	Mostly pasture	hydroelectric power, mineral water	tourism, sheep, timber, tobacco	agricultural products	consumer goods	French franc or Spanish peseta NA
ANGOLA Luanda 8,164,000 24.5%	44% forests; 22% pastures; 1% cultivated; 33% other	petroleum, diamonds, iron, phosphates, copper, gold	mining, fish processing, brewing, tobacco, sugar processing, textiles, cement	oil, coffee, diamonds, sisal, fish, iron ore, timber, cotton	machinery and electrical equipment, wine, bulk iron, steel, metals, vehicles	kwanza $500
ANTIGUA AND BARBUDA St. John's 82,000 NA	54% arable; 18% wasteland, built on; 14% forests; 9% unused; 5% pastures	Negligible	tourism, construction, manufacturing	clothing, rum, lobsters	fuel, food, machinery	East Caribbean dollar $1,990
ARGENTINA Buenos Aires 31,186,000 84.6%	57% agricultural; 25% forests; 18% mountains, wasteland, other	lead, zinc, tin, copper, iron, manganese, oil, uranium	food processing, motor vehicles, textiles, chemicals, printing	wheat, corn, oilseed, hides, wool	chemicals, machinery, fuel	austral $2,230
AUSTRALIA Canberra 15,793,000 86.8%	58% pastures; 6% arable; 2% forests; 34% other	bauxite, coal, iron ore, copper, tin, silver	mining, industrial and food processing equipment, food processing	coal, wool, iron ore, lamb, meat, dairy products	manufactured raw materials, capital equipment, consumer goods	dollar $11,740
AUSTRIA Vienna 7,546,000 56.1%	38% forests; 26% pastures; 20% cultivated; 16% wasteland, other	iron ore, petroleum, timber, coal, aluminum, cement, copper	foods, iron and steel, machinery, textiles, chemicals, electrical equipment	iron and steel products, machinery and equipment, lumber, textiles, chemicals	machinery and equipment, chemicals, textiles and clothing, petroleum, food	schilling $9,140

*NA: Information is not available.

WORLD ECONOMIC DATA

NATION/ Capital/ Population/ Urbanization	Land Use	Natural Resources	Major Industries	Exports	Imports	Monetary Unit/ Per Capita Income (in U.S. $)
THE BAHAMAS Nassau 235,000 65.0%	70% built on; 29% forests; 1% cultivated	salt, aragonite, timber	banking, tourism, cement, oil refining, lumber, salt production, rum	pharmaceuticals, cement, rum, crayfish	food, manufactured goods, mineral fuels	Bahamian dollar $7,950
BAHRAIN Manama 422,000 78.6%	95% deserts, wasteland, other; 5% cultivated	oil, natural gas, fish	petroleum processing and refining, aluminum smelting, offshore banking	petroleum	machinery and transport equipment, consumer goods, live animals	dinar $10,000
BANGLADESH Dhaka 104,205,000 11.9%	66% arable; 18% uncultivated; 16% forests	natural gas, uranium	jute manufacture, food processing, cotton textiles	raw and manufactured jute, leather, tea	food grains, fuels, raw cotton, fertilizer, manufactured products	taka $130
BARBADOS Bridgetown 253,000 42.2%	60% cropland; 30% built on, unused, wasteland; 10% meadows	Negligible	tourism, sugar milling, light manufacture	sugar, sugar cane byproducts, electrical parts, clothing	food, consumer durables, fuels, machinery	dollar $4,560
BELGIUM Brussels 9,868,000 89.2%	28% cultivated; 28% wasteland, other; 24% pastures; 20% forests	coal	engineering, processed food and beverages, chemicals, basic metals, textiles, glass	cars, petroleum products, chemicals	fuels, food, chemicals	franc $8,610
BELIZE Belmopan 168,000 52.0%	46% forests; 38% agricultural; 16% wasteland, other	arable land, timber, fish	sugar refining, garments, timber and forest products, furniture, rum, soap, cigarettes	sugar, garments, seafood, molasses, citrus fruits, wood and wood products	machinery and transport equipment, food, manufactured goods, fuels, chemicals	dollar $1,200
BENIN Porto-Novo 4,141,000 38.5%	80% arable; 19% forests, game reserves; 1% nonarable	offshore oil	palm oil and palm kernel oil processing, textiles, beverages	palm products, cotton, agricultural products	thread, cloth, clothing, construction materials, iron, steel, fuels	Communauté Financière Africaine franc $270
BHUTAN Thimphu 1,446,000 4.5%	70% forests; 15% deserts, wasteland; 15% agricultural	timber, hydroelectric power, coal	cement, chemical products, mining, distilling, food processing	agricultural and forestry products, coal	textiles, cereals, vehicles, fuels, machinery	ngultrum and Indian rupee $250
BOLIVIA La Paz 6,358,000 43.7%	47% deserts, wasteland, other; 40% forests; 11% pastures; 2% cultivated	tin, natural gas, petroleum, zinc, tungsten, antimony, silver, iron ore	mining, smelting, petroleum refining, food processing, textiles, clothing	tin, natural gas, silver, tungsten, zinc, antimony, gold, coffee, sugar, bismuth	food, chemicals, capital goods, pharmaceuticals	peso $540
BOTSWANA Gaborone 1,104,000 19.2%	94% Mostly deserts; 6% arable	diamonds, copper, nickel, salt, soda ash, potash, coal	livestock processing, diamond mining, copper, nickel, coal, salt, soda ash	diamonds, cattle, animal products, copper, nickel	food, vehicles, textiles, petroleum products	pula $960

WORLD ECONOMIC DATA

NATION/ Capital/ Population/ Urbanization	Land Use	Natural Resources	Major Industries	Exports	Imports	Monetary Unit/ Per Capita Income (in U.S. $)
BRAZIL Brasília 143,277,000 72.7%	60% forests; 23% built on, wasteland, other; 13% pastures; 4% cultivated	iron ore, manganese, bauxite, nickel, uranium, tin, gemstones	textiles, chemicals, cement, lumber, iron ore, steel, motor vehicles	soybeans, coffee, transport equipment, iron ore, steel products	petroleum, machinery, chemicals, fertilizers, wheat, copper	cruzado $1,710
BRUNEI Bandar Seri Begawan 240,000 64.0%	75% forests; 22% wasteland, other; 3% arable	oil, natural gas	crude petroleum, liquified natural gas, construction	crude oil, liquified natural gas, petroleum products	machinery and transport equipment, food, beverages	dollar $7,300
BULGARIA Sofia 8,990,000 68.6%	41% arable; 33% forests; 15% other; 11% agricultural	bauxite, copper, lead, zinc, coal, lignite, lumber	food processing, machine and metal building, electronics, chemicals	machinery, agricultural products, fuels, mineral raw materials	fuels and minerals, machinery, chemicals	lev $6,295
BURKINA FASO Ouagadougou 7,094,000 7.9%	50% pastures; 21% fallowland; 10% cultivated; 9% forests; 10% wasteland	manganese, limestone, marble, gold, antimony, copper, nickel	agricultural processing, brewing, bottling, bricks	livestock, peanuts, shea nut products, cotton, sesame	textiles, food, transport equipment, machinery, fuels	Communauté Financière Africaine franc $160
BURMA Rangoon 37,651,000 30.0%	62% forests; 28% arable (12% cultivated); 10% other	oil, copper, asbestos, marble, limestone	agricultural processing, textiles, footwear, wood, petroleum refining	teak, rice, peas, base metals, ores	machinery and transport equipment, building material	kyat $180
BURUNDI Bujumbura 4,807,000 2.5%	37% arable; 23% pastures; 10% scrub forests and forests; 30% other	nickel, uranium, rare earth oxide, peat, cobalt, copper	blankets, shoes, soap, assembly of imports, public works, food processing	coffee, tea, cotton, hides, skins	textiles, food, transport equipment, petroleum products	franc $220
CAMEROON Yaoundé 10,009,000 42.4%	50% forests; 18% meadows; 15% other; 13% fallowland; 4% cultivated	oil, natural gas, bauxite, iron ore, timber	crude oil production, food processing, sawmilling	crude oil, cocoa, coffee, timber, aluminum, cotton, natural rubber, bananas	consumer goods, machinery and transport equipment, alumina for refining	Communauté Financière Africaine franc $800
CANADA Ottawa 25,644,000 75.0%	44% forests; 4% cultivated; 2% pastures; 50% wasteland, other	nickel, zinc, copper, gold, lead, molybdenum, potash, silver, fish, forests	minerals, food products, wood and paper products, transport equipment	transport equipment, wood and wood products, ores, crude petroleum	transport equipment, crude petroleum, communication equipment, textiles, steel	dollar $13,280
CAPE VERDE Praia 318,000 6.1%	NA	salt, basalt, limestone, kaolin	salt mining	fish, bananas, salt, flour	petroleum products, corn, rice, textiles, machinery	escudo $350
CENTRAL AFRICAN REPUBLIC Bangui 2,744,000 45.7%	15% cultivated; 5% forests; 80% other	diamonds, uranium, timber	sawmilling, brewing, diamond mining and splitting	cotton, coffee, diamonds, timber	textiles, petroleum products, machinery, electrical equipment	Communauté Financière Africaine franc $260

WORLD ECONOMIC DATA

NATION/ Capital/ Population/ Urbanization	Land Use	Natural Resources	Major Industries	Exports	Imports	Monetary Unit/ Per Capita Income (in U.S. $)
CHAD N'Djamena 5,231,000 21.6%	35% pastures; 17% arable; 2% forests and scrubland; 46% wasteland, other	petroleum, uranium, natron, kaolin	agricultural and livestock processing, natron	cotton, meat, fish, animal products	cement, petroleum, flour, sugar, tea, machinery, textiles, motor vehicles	Communauté Financière Africaine franc $88
CHILE Santiago 12,261,000 83.4%	47% mountains, deserts, other; 29% forests; 15% pastures; 9% arable	copper, timber, iron ore, nitrates, precious metals, molybdenum	copper, food and fish processing, iron and steel, paper and forestry products	copper, molybdenum, iron ore, paper products, steel products, fishmeal, fruits	petroleum, sugar, wheat, capital goods, vehicles	peso $1,700
CHINA Beijing 1,045,537,000 21.0%	76% deserts, wasteland, other; 11% cultivated; 13% forests	coal, iron, petroleum, mercury, tin, tungsten, antimony, hydroelectric power	iron, steel, coal, machine building, armaments, textiles, petroleum	manufactured goods, agricultural products, oil, minerals	grain, chemical fertilizer, steel, industrial materials, machinery and equipment	yuan $310
COLOMBIA Bogotá 29,956,000 67.4%	72% forests and savanna; 14% pastures; 9% other; 5% cropland	petroleum, natural gas, coal, iron ore, nickel, gold, copper, emeralds	textiles, food processing, clothing, footwear, beverages, chemicals, metal products	coffee, coal, fuel oil, cotton, tobacco, sugar, textiles, cattle, hides	transport equipment, machinery, industrial metals, raw materials, fuels	peso $1,390
COMOROS Moroni 420,000 14.0%	48% cultivated; 29% uncultivated; 16% forests; 7% pastures	Negligible	perfume distillation	perfume oils, vanilla, copra, cloves	rice, food, cement, fuels, chemicals, textiles	Communauté Financière Africaine franc $250
CONGO Brazzaville 1,853,000 39.5%	63% forests; 31% meadows; 4% wasteland, other; 2% cultivated	petroleum, wood, potash, lead, zinc, uranium, phosphates	crude oil, cement, sawmilling, brewing, cigarettes, sugar milling	oil, lumber, tobacco, veneer, plywood, coffee, cocoa	machinery, transport equipment, manufactured consumer goods, iron and steel	Communauté Financière Africaine franc $1,140
COSTA RICA San José 2,714,000 45.9%	60% forests; 30% agricultural; 10% wasteland, other	hydroelectric power	food processing, textiles, clothing, construction materials, fertilizer	coffee, beef, bananas, sugar, cocoa	manufactured products, fuels, machinery, transport equipment, chemicals, food	colon $1,190
CUBA Havana 10,221,000 71.8%	35% cultivated; 30% pastures; 15% forests; 20% wasteland, other	cobalt, nickel, iron, copper, manganese, salt, forests	sugar milling, petroleum refining, food and tobacco processing	sugar, nickel, shellfish, tobacco, coffee, citrus	capital goods, industrial raw materials, food, petroleum	peso $1,530
CYPRUS Nicosia 673,000 49.5%	60% arable; 15% forests; 25% wasteland, other	copper, pyrites, asbestos, gypsum, lumber, salt, marble, clay earth pigment	mining, beverages, footwear, clothing, cement	food, beverages, cement, clothing	manufactured goods, machinery and transport equipment, fuels, food	pound $3,210

WORLD ECONOMIC DATA

NATION/ Capital/ Population/ Urbanization	Land Use	Natural Resources	Major Industries	Exports	Imports	Monetary Unit/ Per Capita Income (in U.S. $)
CZECHOSLOVAKIA Prague 15,542,000 66.3%	53% agricultural; 36% forests; 11% other	coal, coke, timber, lignite, uranium, magnesite	iron and steel, machinery and equipment, cement, sheet glass, motor vehicles	machinery, equipment, manufactured consumer goods, fuels, minerals	fuels, minerals, metals, machinery, equipment, agricultural and forestry products	koruna $8,280
DENMARK Copenhagen 5,097,000 85.9%	64% arable; 11% forests; 8% pastures; 17% other	oil, gas, fish	food processing, machinery, equipment, textiles, clothing, electronics, construction	meat, dairy products, industrial machinery and equipment	industrial machinery, transport equipment, petroleum, textile fibers	krone $11,170
DJIBOUTI Djibouti 304,000 50.0%	89% deserts, wasteland; 10% pastures; 1% cultivated	None	transit trade, port, railway, services, live cattle and sheep	hides, skins, coffee transit	almost all domestically needed goods	franc $1,168
DOMINICA Roseau 74,000 NA	67% forests; 24% arable; 2% pastures; 7% other	timber	agricultural processing, tourism, soap, cigars	bananas, coconuts, lime juice and oil, cocoa, reexports	machinery and equipment, food, manufactured articles, cement	East Caribbean dollar $1,034
DOMINICAN REPUBLIC Santo Domingo 6,785,000 55.7%	45% forests; 20% built on, wasteland; 17% pastures; 14% cultivated; 4% fallowland	nickel, bauxite, gold, silver	tourism, sugar processing, nickel mining, gold mining, textiles, cement	sugar, nickel, coffee, tobacco, cocoa, gold, silver	food, petroleum, industrial raw materials, capital equipment	peso $970
ECUADOR Quito 9,647,000 47.7%	55% forests; 11% cultivated; 8% pastures; 26% wasteland, other	petroleum, fish, timber	food processing, textiles, chemicals, fishing, petroleum	petroleum, fish products, coffee, cocoa, bananas	agricultural and industrial machinery, industrial raw materials, building supplies	sucre $1,150
EGYPT Cairo 50,525,000 46.5%	97% deserts, wasteland, other; 3% cultivated	petroleum, natural gas, iron ore, phosphates, manganese, limestone, talc	textiles, food processing, chemicals, petroleum, construction, cement	crude petroleum, raw cotton, cotton yarn, fabric	food, machinery and equipment, fertilizer, wood	pound $720
EL SALVADOR San Salvador 5,105,000 43.0%	32% cropland; 31% nonagricultural; 26% pastures; 11% forests	hydroelectric and geothermal power	food processing, textiles, clothing, petroleum products	coffee, cotton, sugar, shrimp	machinery, intermediate goods, petroleum, construction materials, fertilizer, food	colon $710
EQUATORIAL GUINEA Malabo 359,000 59.7%	NA	timber, petroleum	fishing, sawmilling	cocoa, coffee, wood	food, chemicals, textiles	Communauté Financière Africaine franc $420
ETHIOPIA Addis Ababa 43,882,000 17.6%	55% pastures; 10% cropland, orchards; 6% forests; 29% wasteland, other	potash, salt, gold, copper, platinum	cement, sugar refining, cotton textiles, food processing, oil refining	coffee, hides, skins	food, animals, beverages, chemicals, rubber, paper	birr $110

WORLD ECONOMIC DATA

NATION/ Capital/ Population/ Urbanization	Land Use	Natural Resources	Major Industries	Exports	Imports	Monetary Unit/ Per Capita Income (in U.S. $)
FIJI Suva 715,000 41.2%	NA	timber, fish, gold, copper	sugar refining, tourism, gold, lumber, small industries	sugar, copra	manufactured goods, food, machinery, fuel	dollar $1,850
FINLAND Helsinki 4,931,000 66.9%	58% forests; 8% arable; 34% other	forests, copper, zinc, iron, farmland	metal manufacturing, shipbuilding, wood processing, copper refining, food, textiles	timber, paper, ships, machinery, clothing, footwear	food, petroleum, chemicals, transport equipment, iron, steel, machinery	finnmark $10,770
FRANCE Paris 55,239,000 77.2%	34% cultivated; 24% pastures; 27% forests; 15% wasteland, other	coal, iron ore, bauxite, fish, forests	steel, machinery and equipment, textiles, clothing, chemicals, automobiles, food processing	machinery and transport equipment, chemicals, food, agricultural products	crude petroleum, machinery and equipment, agricultural products, chemicals	franc $9,760
GABON Libreville 1,017,000 40.9%	75% forests; 15% savanna; 1% cultivated; 9% wasteland, other	oil, manganese, uranium, gold, wood, iron ore	petroleum production, sawmilling, food and beverage processing, mining	crude petroleum, wood, minerals	mining and road building equipment, electrical equipment, transport vehicles	Communauté Financière Africaine franc $3,690
THE GAMBIA Banjul 774,000 20.9%	55% cultivable, built on, other; 25% uncultivated savanna; 16% swampland; 4% forest park	fish	peanut processing, tourism, brewing, soft drinks	peanuts and peanut products, fish, palm kernels	textiles, food, tobacco, machinery, petroleum products, chemicals	dalasi $170
GERMAN DEMOCRATIC REPUBLIC East Berlin 16,692,000 78.2%	43% arable; 27% forests; 15% pastures; 15% other	lignite coal, potash, uranium, copper, natural gas	metal fabrication, chemicals, light industry, brown coal, shipbuilding	machinery, transport equipment, fuels, raw materials	machinery, transport equipment, fuels, raw materials, food	ostmark $9,800
GERMANY, FEDERAL REPUBLIC OF Bonn 60,734,000 86.1%	33% cultivated; 29% forests; 23% pastures; 15% wasteland, other	iron, coal, potash	iron, steel, coal, cement, chemicals, machinery, ships, vehicles, machine tools	manufactures, agricultural products, fuels, raw materials	manufactures, fuels, agricultural products	mark $11,130
GHANA Accra 13,552,000 39.6%	60% forests and bushland; 19% agricultural; 21% other	gold, timber, industrial diamonds, bauxite, manganese, fish	mining, lumbering, light manufacturing, fishing, aluminum	cocoa, wood, gold, diamonds, manganese, bauxite, aluminum	textiles, manufactured goods, foods, fuels, transport equipment	cedi $350
GREECE Athens 9,954,000	40% pastures; 29% arable; 20% forests; 11% wasteland, other	bauxite, lignite, manganese, oil	food and tobacco processing, textiles, chemicals, metal products	tobacco, minerals, fruits, textiles	machinery and automotive equipment, petroleum, manufactured goods	drachma $3,770

WORLD ECONOMIC DATA

NATION/ Capital/ Population/ Urbanization	Land Use	Natural Resources	Major Industries	Exports	Imports	Monetary Unit/ Per Capita Income (in U.S. $)
GRENADA St. George's 86,000 NA	44% cultivated; 17% unused; 12% forests; 4% pastures; 23% built on, wasteland, other	land, fish	agriculture, forestry, fishing	cocoa beans, nutmeg, bananas, mace	food, machinery and transport equipment, oil, building materials	East Caribbean dollar $940
GUATEMALA Guatemala 8,600,000 41.4%	57% forests; 10% pastures; 14% cultivated; 19% other	oil, nickel, rare woods, fish, chicle	food processing, textiles, clothing, furniture, chemicals, metals	coffee, cotton, sugar, meat, bananas	manufactured products, machinery, transport equipment, chemicals, fuels	quetzal $1,160
GUINEA Conakry 5,734,000 22.2%	10% forests; 15% cultivated; 75% unused	bauxite, iron ore, diamonds, gold, uranium, hydroelectric power, fish	bauxite mining, alumina, diamond mining, light manufacturing and processing	bauxite, alumina, diamonds, coffee, pineapples, bananas, palm kernels	petroleum products, metals, machinery, transport equipment, food, textiles	syli $330
GUINEA-BISSAU Bissau 875,000 27.1%	8% arable; 92% other	petroleum, bauxite, phosphates	agricultural processing, beer, soft drinks	peanuts, palm kernels, shrimp, fish, lumber	food, manufactured goods, fuels, transport equipment	peso $180
GUYANA Georgetown 771,000 32.2%	66% forests; 22% wasteland, other; 8% savanna; 3% pastures; 1% cropland	bauxite, gold, diamonds, hardwood timber, shrimp, fish	bauxite mining, sugar and rice milling, timber, fishing, textiles, gold mining	bauxite, sugar, rice, shrimp, molasses, timber, rum	manufactures, machinery, food, petroleum	dollar $510
HAITI Port-au-Prince 5,870,000 28.0%	44% unproductive; 31% cultivated; 18% pastures; 7% forests	bauxite	sugar refining, textiles, flour milling, cement manufacturing, bauxite mining, tourism	mangos, coffee, light industrial products, sisal, essential oils, sugar	consumer durables, food, industrial equipment, petroleum products, construction materials	gourde $320
HONDURAS Tegucigalpa 4,648,000 39.9%	36% wasteland and built on; 30% pastures; 27% forests; 7% cropland	forests, gold, silver, copper, lead, zinc, iron, antimony, coal, fish	agricultural processing, textiles, clothing, wood products	bananas, coffee, lumber, meat, petroleum products	manufactured products, machinery, transport equipment, chemicals	lempira $700
HUNGARY Budapest 10,624,000 57.0%	70% agricultural; 18% forests; 12% other	bauxite, brown coal, natural gas	mining, metallurgy, engineering, food processing, textiles	fuel, raw materials, semifinished products, machinery and equipment	fuels, raw materials, semifinished products, machinery and equipment	forint $2,100
ICELAND Reykjavík 244,000 88.9%	22% pastures; 78% other	fish, hydroelectric and geothermal power, diatomite	fish processing, aluminum smelting, diatomite production, hydroelectricity	fish, animal products, aluminum, diatomite	machinery and transport equipment, petroleum, food, textiles	krona $9,040

WORLD ECONOMIC DATA

NATION/ Capital/ Population/ Urbanization	Land Use	Natural Resources	Major Industries	Exports	Imports	Monetary Unit/ Per Capita Income (in U.S. $)
INDIA New Delhi 783,940,000 25.5%	50% arable; 22% forests; 23% deserts, wasteland, other; 5% pastures	coal, iron ore, manganese, mica, bauxite, chromite	textiles, food processing, machinery and transport equipment, cement, jute	engineering goods, textiles, clothing, tea	machinery and transport equipment, petroleum, edible oils, fertilizer	rupee $260
INDONESIA Jakarta 176,764,000 25.3%	64% forests; 24% wasteland, other; 12% small holdings and estates	oil, tin, natural gas, timber, bauxite, copper	petroleum, textiles, mining, cement, chemical fertilizer, timber	petroleum and natural gas, timber, rubber, coffee, tin, palm oil, tea, copper	rice, wheat, flour, cereals, textiles, chemicals, iron and steel products, machinery	rupiah $540
IRAN Tehran 46,604,000 55.0%	51% deserts, wasteland; 30% cultivable; 11% forests; 8% pastures, other	petroleum, natural gas, coal, chromium, copper, iron, lead, manganese, zinc, barite	crude oil production and refining, textiles, cement, food processing, metal fabricating	petroleum, carpets, fruits, nuts	machinery, military supplies	rial $2,160
IRAQ Baghdad 16,019,000 70.6%	68% deserts, wasteland; 18% cultivated; 10% pastures; 4% forests	oil, natural gas, phosphates, sulfur	crude petroleum	mineral fuels, lubricants	food, live animals, cereals, chemicals, machinery	dinar $2,410
IRELAND Dublin 3,624,000 57.0%	51% pastures; 29% wasteland, other; 17% arable; 3% forests	zinc, lead, natural gas, copper, gypsum, limestone, dolomite, peat, silver	food products, textiles, clothing, chemicals, machinery and transport equipment	food, computers, live animals, machinery, chemicals, clothing	machinery, petroleum, chemicals, semifinished goods, cereals	pound $4,970
ISRAEL Jerusalem 4,208,000 90.7%	40% pastures; 20% cultivated; 4% forests; 36% deserts, other	copper, phosphates, bromide, potash, clay, sand, sulfur, bitumen, manganese	food processing, diamond cutting and polishing, textiles and clothing, chemicals, metal products	polished diamonds, citrus, textiles and clothing, processed foods, fertilizer	military equipment, rough diamonds, oil, chemicals, machinery, iron and steel	shekel $5,060
ITALY Rome 57,226,000 71.7%	50% cultivated; 21% forests; 17% pastures; 12% wasteland, other	mercury, potash, marble, sulfur, natural gas, fish	machinery and transport equipment, iron and steel, chemicals, food processing	textiles, chemicals, footwear	petroleum, machinery and transport equipment, food, metals, wool, cotton	lira $6,420
IVORY COAST Abidjan 10,500,000 42.0%	52% pastures, fallowland, wasteland; 40% forests; 8% cultivated	petroleum, diamonds, manganese	food and lumber processing, oil refining, automobile assembly, textiles, soap	cocoa, coffee, tropical woods, cotton, bananas, pineapples, palm oil	manufactured goods and semi-finished products, consumer goods, raw materials	Communauté Financière Africaine franc $610
JAMAICA Kingston 2,288,000 53.8%	23% pastures; 21% arable; 19% forests; 37% wasteland, other	bauxite, gypsum, limestone	tourism, bauxite mining, textiles, food processing, light manufacturing	alumina, bauxite, sugar, bananas, citrus, rum, cocoa	fuels, machinery, transportation and electrical equipment, food, fertilizer	dollar $1,150

WORLD ECONOMIC DATA

NATION/ Capital/ Population/ Urbanization	Land Use	Natural Resources	Major Industries	Exports	Imports	Monetary Unit/ Per Capita Income (in U.S. $)
JAPAN Tokyo 121,402,000 76.5%	69% forests; 16% arable; 12% wasteland, other; 3% grasses	fish	metallurgical and engineering industries, electrical and electronic industries	machinery, motor vehicles, iron and steel	fuels, manufactures, food, machinery	yen $10,630
JORDAN Amman 2,756,000 64.4%	88% deserts, wasteland, other; 11% agricultural; 1% forests	phosphates, potash, shale oil	phosphate mining, petroleum refining, cement production, light manufacturing	fruits, vegetables, phosphates, fertilizers	crude oil, petroleum, textiles, capital goods, motor vehicles	dinar $1,570
KAMPUCHEA (CAMBODIA) Phnom Penh 5,996,000 15.6%	75% forests; 25% other	forests, iron, copper, rubber, kapok, gold, manganese	textiles, paper, plywood, oil products	rice, rubber, haricot beans	agricultural products, mineral products, textiles, metals, chemicals	riel $90
KENYA Nairobi 21,044,000 16.7%	66% grassland; 21% forests; 13% agricultural	gold, limestone, diotomite, salt, barytes, magnesite, feldspar, sapphires	consumer goods, agricultural processing, oil refining, cement, tourism	petroleum products, coffee, tea, sisal, livestock products, pyrethrum	machinery, transport equipment, crude oil, paper, iron and steel products	shilling $310
KIRIBATI Tarawa 63,000 32.0%	NA	fish, phosphates	mining, fishing	phosphates, copra	food, fuel, transport equipment	Australian dollar $417
KOREA, NORTH Pyongyang 20,543,000 63.8%	74% forests and brush; 17% arable; 9% wasteland, other	coal, lead, tungsten, zinc, graphite, magnesite, iron, copper, gold, phosphates	machine building, electric power, mining, metallurgy, textiles, food processing	minerals, metallurgical products, agricultural products, manufactures	petroleum, machinery and equipment, coking coal, grain	won $1,170
KOREA, SOUTH Seoul 43,285,000 65.3%	66% forests; 23% arable; 11% other	coal, tungsten, graphite	textiles, clothing, food processing, chemicals, steel, electronics, shipbuilding	textiles, clothing, electrical machinery, footwear, steel, ships, fish	machinery, oil, steel, transport equipment, textiles, organic chemicals, grains	won $2,110
KUWAIT Kuwait 1,771,000 93.7%	99% deserts, wasteland, other; 1% cultivated	petroleum, fish, shrimp	crude petroleum production, petroleum refining, petrochemicals, retail trade	petroleum	machinery and transport equipment, live animals, food	dollar $16,720
LAOS Vientiane 3,679,000 15.9%	60% forests; 8% agricultural; 32% wasteland, other	tin, timber, gypsum, hydroelectric power	tin mining, timber, green coffee, electric power	electric power, forest products, tin concentrates, coffee, opium, tobacco	rice, food, petroleum products, machinery, transport equipment	kip $220
LEBANON Beirut 2,675,000 80.4%	64% deserts, wasteland, other; 27% agricultural; 9% forests	limestone, iron	service industries, food processing, textiles, cement, oil refining, chemicals	vegetable products, precious metals and stones, machinery	precious metals and stones, machinery and electrical apparatus, mineral products	pound $884

WORLD ECONOMIC DATA

NATION/ Capital/ Population/ Urbanization	Land Use	Natural Resources	Major Industries	Exports	Imports	Monetary Unit/ Per Capita Income (in U.S. $)
LESOTHO Maseru 1,552,000 5.8%	10% cultivated; 6% forests; 64% pastures; 20% other	diamonds, minerals, water, agricultural and grazing land	None	labor, wool, mohair, wheat, cattle, peas, beans, corn, hides, skins	corn, building materials, clothing, vehicles, machinery, medicines	loti $530
LIBERIA Monrovia 2,307,000 39.5%	40% forests; 30% rain forests, swamps; 20% agricultural; 10% other	iron ore, rubber, timber, diamonds, gold	rubber processing, food processing, construction materials, furniture	iron ore, rubber, diamonds, lumber, logs, coffee, cocoa	machinery, transport equipment, petroleum products, food	dollar $470
LIBYA Tripoli 3,876,000 64.5%	93% deserts, wasteland, other; 6% agricultural; 1% forests	petroleum, natural gas, gypsum	petroleum, food processing, textiles, handicrafts	petroleum	manufactures, food	dollar $8,520
LIECHTENSTEIN Vaduz 28,000 NA	NA	hydroelectric power	electronics, metal manufacturing, textiles, ceramics, pharmaceuticals	electronics, metals, machinery, precision instruments, artificial teeth	NA	Swiss franc $15,000
LUXEMBOURG Luxembourg 367,000 81.8%	15% wasteland; 33% forests; 27% pastures; 25% other	iron ore	banking, iron and steel, food processing, chemicals, metal products, engineering	iron and steel products	minerals, metals, food, machinery	franc $11,350
MADAGASCAR Antananarivo 10,227,000 21.8%	58% pastures; 21% forests; 16% wasteland, other; 5% cultivated	graphite, chrome, coal, bauxite, ilmenite, tar sands, semiprecious stones	agricultural processing, textiles, glassware, cement, auto assembly	coffee, vanilla, sugar, cloves	raw materials, intermediate goods, food	franc $260
MALAWI Lilongwe 7,292,000 12.0%	34% arable; 25% forests; 6% meadows; 35% other	limestone, uranium	agricultural processing, sawmilling, cement, consumer goods	tobacco, tea, sugar, peanuts, cotton, corn	manufactured goods, machinery, transport equipment	kwacha $180
MALAYSIA Kuala Lumpur 15,820,000 31.5%	26% forest reserves; 20% cultivated; 54% other	tin, petroleum, timber, copper, iron	rubber and palm oil processing and manufacturing, light manufacturing, electronics, tin mining and smelting, logging	natural rubber, palm oil, tin, timber, petroleum, light manufactures	machinery, transport equipment, basic manufactures, fuels and lubricants	ringgit $1,980
MALDIVES Malé 184,000 20.7%	NA	fish, tourism	fishing, tourism, coconut processing, garment industry, woven mats, shipping	fish, coconut oil	NA	rufiya $462
MALI Bamako 7,898,000 20.8%	75% sparse pastures, deserts; 25% arable	gold, phosphates, kaolin, salt, limestone, bauxite, iron ore, manganese, lithium	small local consumer goods and processing	livestock, peanuts, dried fish, cotton, skins	textiles, vehicles, petroleum products, machinery, sugar, cereals	Communauté Financière Africaine franc $140

WORLD ECONOMIC DATA

NATION/ Capital/ Population/ Urbanization	Land Use	Natural Resources	Major Industries	Exports	Imports	Monetary Unit/ Per Capita Income (in U.S. $)
MALTA Valletta 354,000 85.4%	45% agricultural; 55% wasteland, other	limestone, salt	tourism, ship repair, clothing, building, food processing, manufacturing	clothing, textiles, ships, printed matter	machinery and transport equipment, fuels, food	lira $3,010
MAURITANIA Nouakchott 1,691,000 34.6%	90% deserts; 10% pastures	iron ore, gypsum, fish	iron ore and gypsum mining, fish processing	iron ore, processed fish, gum arabic, gypsum, cattle	food, consumer goods, petroleum products, capital goods	ouguiya $450
MAURITIUS Port Louis 1,020,000 56.8%	50% agricultural; 39% forests; 11% built on, wasteland, other	hydroelectric power, fish	food manufacturing, textiles, clothing, chemicals, metal products, transport equipment	sugar	food, petroleum products, manufactured goods	rupee $1,090
MEXICO Mexico 81,709,000 70.0%	40% pastures; 22% forests; 12% cropland; 26% wasteland, other	petroleum, silver, copper, gold, lead, zinc, natural gas, timber	processing of food, beverages, tobacco, chemicals, basic metals and metal products	cotton, coffee, nonferrous minerals, shrimp, petroleum, sulfur, salt, cattle, meat	machinery, equipment, vehicles, intermediate goods	peso $2,040
MONACO Monaco 28,000 NA	NA	scenic beauty	chemicals, food processing, precision instruments, glassmaking, printing	pharmaceuticals, plastics, microelectronics	NA	French franc NA
MONGOLIA Ulaanbaatar 1,942,000 55.9%	90% pastures, deserts; 10% forests	coal, copper, molybdenum, tungsten, phosphates, tin, nickel, zinc, wolfram	processing of animal products, building materials, mining	livestock, animal products, wool, hides, fluorspar, nonferrous metals, minerals	machinery and equipment, petroleum, clothing, building materials, sugar	tugrik $2,760
MOROCCO Rabat 23,667,000 43.9%	51% deserts, wasteland, other; 32% arable, pastures; 17% forests, esparto grasses	phosphates, iron, manganese, lead, zinc, fish	mining and mineral processing, food processing, textiles, construction, tourism	phosphates	petroleum products	dirham $670
MOZAMBIQUE Maputo 14,022,000 19.4%	56% forests; 30% arable; 14% wasteland, other	coal, iron ore, natural gas, copper, heavy minerals, bauxite	food processing, chemicals, petroleum products, beverages, textiles, cement, glass, asbestos	cashews, shrimp, sugar, tea, cotton	refined petroleum products, machinery, transportation goods, spare parts	metical $150
NAURU Yaren District 8,000 0.0%	80% phosphate deposits; 20% other	phosphates	phosphate mining	phosphates	food, fuel, water	Australian dollar $20,000
NEPAL Kathmandu 17,422,000 5.8%	38% mountains, wasteland, other; 32% forests; 16% agricultural; 14% pastures	quartz, water, timber, hydroelectric potential	small rice, jute, sugar, oilseed mills, matches, cigarettes, brick factories	rice and other food, jute, timber, manufactured goods	manufactured consumer goods, fuel, construction materials, fertilizer, food products	rupee $160

WORLD ECONOMIC DATA

NATION/ Capital/ Population/ Urbanization	Land Use	Natural Resources	Major Industries	Exports	Imports	Monetary Unit/ Per Capita Income (in U.S. $)
NETHERLANDS Amsterdam; The Hague 14,536,000 92.5%	70% cultivated; 8% forests; 22% wasteland, other	natural gas, oil	food processing, metal and engineering products, electrical and electronic machinery and equipment	food, machinery, chemicals, petroleum products, natural gas, textiles	machinery, transport equipment, crude petroleum, food, chemicals, raw cotton	guilder $9,520
NEW ZEALAND Wellington 3,305,000 83.7%	50% pastures; 16% forests; 10% parks and reserves; 3% cultivated; 21% wasteland, other	natural gas, iron, sand, coal, timber	food processing, wood and paper products, textile production, machinery, transport equipment	beef, wool, dairy products	petroleum, cars, trucks, machinery and electrical equipment, iron and steel	dollar $7,730
NICARAGUA Managua 3,342,000 59.4%	50% forests; 7% arable; 7% pastures; 36% wasteland, other	gold, silver, copper, tungsten, arable land, timber, livestock, fish	food processing, chemicals, metal products, textiles and clothing, petroleum, beverages	cotton, coffee, chemical products, meat, sugar, seafood	food and nonfood agricultural products, chemicals and pharmaceuticals, transport equipment	cordoba $860
NIGER Niamey 6,715,000 16.2%	7% pastures; 3% arable; 2% forests; 88% other	uranium, coal, iron, tin, phosphates	cement, bricks, rice, cotton, oil pressing, slaughterhouse, uranium production	uranium, livestock, cowpeas, onions, hides, skins	petroleum products, primary materials, machinery, vehicles and parts, electronic equipment	Communauté Financière Africaine franc $190
NIGERIA Lagos 105,448,000 23.0%	35% forests; 24% arable; 41% deserts, wasteland, other	petroleum, tin, columbite, iron ore, coal, limestone, lead, zinc	mining, processing of oil palm, peanuts, cotton, rubber, petroleum, wool, hides, skins, textiles, cement	oil, cocoa, palm products, rubber, timber, tin	machinery and transport equipment, manufactured goods, chemicals, wheat	naira $730
NORWAY Oslo 4,165,000 80.3%	21% forests; 2% pastures; 3% arable; 74% other	oil, copper, gas, pyrites, nickel, iron, zinc, lead, fish, timber, hydroelectric power	oil, gas, food processing, wood pulp, paper products, metals, chemicals	oil, natural gas, metals, chemicals, machinery, fish and fish products, pulp and paper, ships	machinery, fuels, lubricants, transport equipment, chemicals, food, clothing, ships	krone $13,940
OMAN Muscat 1,271,000 8.8%	Mostly deserts, wasteland, and built on	oil, copper, asbestos, marble, limestone, chromium, gypsum	crude petroleum production	petroleum, reexports, processed copper	machinery, transport equipment, manufactured goods, food, livestock, lubricants	rial $6,490
PAKISTAN Islamabad 101,855,000 29.8%	40% arable; 3% forests; 57% wasteland, nonarable	land, natural gas, limited petroleum, poor quality coal, iron ore	cotton textiles, steel, food processing, tobacco, engineering, chemicals, natural gas	rice, cotton, textiles	petroleum, cooking oil, defense equipment	rupee $380
PANAMA Panama 2,227,000 51.9%	24% arable; 20% exploitable forests; 56% other forests, wasteland, other	copper, shrimp, mahogany forests	food processing, beverages, petroleum products, construction materials, clothing	petroleum products, bananas, shrimp, sugar	petroleum products, manufactured goods, machinery and transport equipment, chemicals	balboa $1,980

WORLD ECONOMIC DATA

NATION/ Capital/ Population/ Urbanization	Land Use	Natural Resources	Major Industries	Exports	Imports	Monetary Unit/ Per Capita Income (in U.S. $)
PAPUA NEW GUINEA Port Moresby 3,395,000 14.3%	70% forests; 3% cultivated; 2% pastures; 25% other	gold, copper, silver, gas	sawmilling and timber processing, copper mining, fish canning	gold, copper, coffee, palm oil, logs, cocoa, copra, coconut oil, tea	machinery and equipment, fuels and lubricants, food and live animals, chemicals	kina $710
PARAGUAY Asunción 4,119,000 41.5%	52% forests; 24% pastures; 22% wasteland, other; 2% cropland	iron, manganese, limestone, hydroelectric power, forests	meatpacking, oilseed crushing, milling, brewing, textiles, light consumer goods	cotton, oilseeds, meat products, tobacco, timber, coffee, essential oils, tung oil	fuels and lubricants, machinery and motors, motor vehicles, beverages, tobacco, food	guarani $1,240
PERU Lima 20,207,000 67.4%	55% forests; 14% pastures; 2% cropland; 29% wasteland, other	minerals, metals, petroleum, forests, fish	mining, petroleum, fishing, textiles, clothing, food processing, cement	fishmeal, cotton, sugar, coffee, copper, iron ore, gold, refined silver, lead, zinc	food, machinery, transport equipment, iron and steel semimanufactures, chemicals	sol $1,000
PHILIPPINES Manila 58,091,000 39.6%	53% forests; 30% arable; 5% pastures; 12% other	timber, petroleum, nickel, iron, cobalt, silver, gold	textiles, pharmaceuticals, chemicals, wood products, food processing	coconut products, sugar, logs, lumber, copper concentrates, bananas, garments, nickel	petroleum, industrial equipment, wheat	peso $660
POLAND Warsaw 37,546,000 59.2%	49% arable; 27% forests; 14% other agricultural; 10% other	coal, sulfur, copper, natural gas, silver	machine building, iron and steel, extractive industries, chemicals, shipbuilding	machinery and equipment, fuels, minerals and metals, manufactured consumer goods	machinery and equipment, fuels, minerals and metals, agricultural and forestry products	zloty $2,100
PORTUGAL Lisbon 10,095,000 31.2%	49% arable; 31% forests; 6% pastures; 14% wasteland, other	fish, forests (cork), tungsten, iron, uranium ore	textiles, footwear, wood, pulp, paper, cork, metalworking, oil refining	cotton textiles, cork, canned fish, wine, timber, resin, machinery, appliances	petroleum, cotton, industrial machinery, iron and steel, chemicals	escudo $1,970
QATAR Doha 305,000 88.0%	Mostly desert, wasteland, and built on	petroleum, natural gas, fish	oil production and refining	petroleum	machinery and transport equipment, manufactures, food, live animals	riyal $27,000
ROMANIA Bucharest 22,830,000 54.8%	44% arable; 27% forests; 19% other agricultural; 10% other	oil, timber, natural gas, coal	mining, forestry, construction materials, metal production and processing, chemicals	machinery and equipment, fuels, minerals, metals, manufactured consumer goods	machinery and equipment, fuels, minerals, agricultural and forestry products	leu $5,200
RWANDA Kigali 6,489,000 5.1%	33% cultivated; 33% pastures; 9% forests; 25% other	gold, cassiterite, wolframite	mining, tin, cement, agricultural processing, beer, soft drinks, soap, furniture	coffee, tea, cassiterite, wolframite, pyrethrum	textiles, food, machines, equipment, capital goods, steel, petroleum products	franc $280
ST. CHRISTOPHER AND NEVIS Basseterre; Charlestown 40,000 NA	40% arable; 33% wasteland, built on; 17% forests; 10% pastures	scenic beauty	sugar processing, tourism, cotton, salt, copra	sugar	food, manufactures, fuel	East Caribbean dollar $820

WORLD ECONOMIC DATA

NATION/ Capital/ Population/ Urbanization	Land Use	Natural Resources	Major Industries	Exports	Imports	Monetary Unit/ Per Capita Income (in U.S. $)
ST. LUCIA Castries 123,000 NA	50% arable; 23% wasteland, built on; 19% forests; 5% unused; 3% pastures	forests, beaches, minerals, mineral springs	garments, electronic components, beverages, corrugated boxes, tourism, lime processing	bananas, cocoa	food, machinery, equipment, fertilizer, petroleum products	East Caribbean dollar $1,105
ST. VINCENT AND THE GRENADINES Kingstown 103,000 NA	50% arable; 44% forests; 3% pastures; 3% wasteland, built on	scenic beauty	food processing	bananas, arrowroot, copra	food, machinery, equipment, chemicals, fertilizers, minerals, fuels	East Caribbean dollar $781
SAN MARINO San Marino 23,000 92.4%	74% cultivated; 22% pastures; 4% built on	building stones	light manufacturing, tourism, postage stamps	postage stamps, building stones, lime, wood, chestnuts, wheat, wine	consumer manufactures	Italian lira NA
SÃO TOMÉ AND PRINCIPE São Tomé 108,000 24.0%	NA	agricultural products, fish	light construction, shirts, soap, beer, fisheries, shrimp processing	cocoa, copra, coffee, palm oil	food products, machinery and electrical equipment, fuels	dobra $260
SAUDI ARABIA Riyadh 11,519,000 73.0%	98% deserts, wasteland, other; 1% agricultural; 1% forests	oil, natural gas, iron ore, gold, copper	crude petroleum production and refining, petrochemicals, cement, steel rolling	petroleum and petroleum products	manufactured goods, transport equipment, construction materials	riyal $10,530
SENEGAL Dakar 6,980,000 42.4%	40% agricultural; 13% forests; 47% built up, wasteland, other	fish, phosphates	fishing, agricultural processing, light manufacturing, mining	peanuts and peanut products, phosphate rock, fish, petroleum products	food, consumer goods, machinery, transport equipment, petroleum	Communauté Financière Africaine franc $380
SEYCHELLES Victoria, Mahé Island 67,000 37.0%	54% arable; 17% forests; 29% other	fish, copra, spices	tourism, processing of coconut and vanilla, fishing, small-scale manufacture of consumer goods	fish, copra, cinnamon bark	manufactured goods, food, tobacco, beverages, machinery and transport equipment	rupee $2,320
SIERRA LEONE Freetown 3,987,000 28.3%	65% arable; 27% pastures; 4% swamps; 4% forests	diamonds, rutile, bauxite, iron ore, gold, chromite	mining, beverages, textiles, cigarettes, construction goods, oil refining	diamonds, iron ore, palm kernels, cocoa, coffee	machinery and transport equipment, manufactured goods, food, petroleum products	leone $310
SINGAPORE Singapore 2,584,000 74.2%	31% built on; 22% agricultural; 47% other	rubber, lumber, fish, petroleum	petroleum refining, electronics, oil drilling equipment, rubber processing	manufactured goods, petroleum, rubber, electronics	capital equipment, manufactured goods, petroleum	dollar $7,260

WORLD ECONOMIC DATA

NATION/ Capital/ Population/ Urbanization	Land Use	Natural Resources	Major Industries	Exports	Imports	Monetary Unit/ Per Capita Income (in U.S. $)
SOLOMON ISLANDS Honiara 283,000 9.0%	NA	forests, agricultural land, marine shell, minerals, water	fish canning	copra, timber, fish	NA	Australian dollar $520
SOMALIA Mogadishu 7,825,000 34.1%	32% pastures; 14% scrubland, forests; 13% arable; 41% deserts, other	uranium, iron ore, tin, gypsum, bauxite	sugar refining, tuna, beef canning, textiles, iron rods, petroleum refining	livestock, hides, skins, bananas	textiles, cereals, transport equipment, machinery, construction materials	shilling $260
SOUTH AFRICA Pretoria 33,241,000 55.9%	86% deserts, wasteland, other; 12% arable; 2% forests	gold, chromium, antimony, coal, iron ore, manganese, nickel, phosphates, tin, uranium, gem diamonds	mining, automobile assembly, metalworking, machinery, textiles, iron and steel	gold, coal, diamonds, corn, uranium, mineral and agricultural products	machinery, motor vehicle parts, petroleum products, textiles, chemicals	rand $2,340
SOVIET UNION Moscow 279,904,000 66.3%	35% forests; 17% pastures; 10% cultivated; 38% other	fossil fuels, hydroelectric power, timber, manganese, lead, zinc, nickel, mercury	diversified, highly developed capital goods industries	petroleum, natural gas, metals, wood, agricultural products, manufactured goods	grain, agricultural products, machinery, equipment, steel products, consumer manufactures	ruble $7,120
SPAIN Madrid 39,075,000 77.4%	41% arable and cropland; 27% pastures; 22% forests; 10% other	coal, lignite, iron ore, uranium, mercury, pyrites, fluorspar, gypsum, zinc, lead	textiles, clothing, food, beverages, metals and metal manufactures, chemicals, shipbuilding	iron and steel products, machinery, automobiles, fruits and vegetables, textiles	fuels, machinery, chemicals, iron and steel, vegetables, automobiles	peseta $4,440
SRI LANKA Colombo 16,638,000 21.1%	44% forests; 31% wasteland, other; 25% cultivated	limestone, graphite, mineral sands, gems, phosphates	processing of rubber, tea, coconuts, consumer goods	tea, rubber, petroleum products, textiles, coconuts	petroleum, machinery, transport equipment, sugar, textiles, textile materials	rupee $360
SUDAN Khartoum 22,932,000 29.4%	37% arable; 33% deserts, wasteland, other; 15% pastures; 15% forests	oil, iron ore, copper, chrome, industrial minerals	cotton ginning, textiles, brewing, cement, edible oils, soap, distilling	cotton, gum arabic, peanuts, sesame	textiles, petroleum products, food, transport equipment, manufactured goods	pound $360
SURINAME Paramaribo 381,000 45.7%	76% forests; 16% built on, wasteland, other; 8% unused	forests, hydroelectric power, fish, shrimp, bauxite, iron ore, minerals	bauxite mining, alumina and aluminum production, lumbering, food processing	alumina, bauxite, aluminum, rice, wood and wood products	capital equipment, petroleum, iron and steel, cotton, flour, meat, dairy products	guilder $2,980
SWAZILAND Mbabane 692,000 26.3%	Mostly cropland or pastures	asbestos, coal, clay, tin, diamonds, hydroelectric power, forests	mining, pulping	sugar, asbestos, wood and forest products, citrus, canned fruit	motor vehicles, chemicals, petroleum products, food	lilangeni $900

NATION/ Capital/ Population/ Urbanization	Land Use	Natural Resources	Major Industries	Exports	Imports	Monetary Unit/ Per Capita Income (in U.S. $)
SWEDEN Stockholm 8,357,000 85.8%	55% forests; 7% arable; 2% pastures; 36% other	zinc, iron, lead, copper, silver, gold, forests, hydroelectric power	iron and steel, precision equipment, wood pulp and paper products, processed foods	machinery, motor vehicles, paper products, pulp and wood, iron and steel products, chemicals	machinery, petroleum and petroleum products, chemicals, motor vehicles, food, iron and steel, clothing	krona $11,860
SWITZERLAND Bern 6,466,000 60.4%	43% pastures; 24% forests; 33% wasteland, other	hydroelectric power, salt, timber	machinery, chemicals, watches, textiles, precision instruments	machinery and equipment, chemicals, precision instruments, metal products, textiles, food	machinery and transport equipment, metals and metal products, food, chemicals, textile fibers	franc $16,330
SYRIA Damascus 10,931,000 47.4%	48% arable; 29% pastures; 21% deserts; 2% forests	crude oil, phosphates, chrome, manganese, rock salt, marble, gypsum	textiles, food processing, beverages, tobacco, petroleum	petroleum, textiles and textile products, tobacco, fruit, and vegetables, cotton	petroleum, machinery, metal products, textiles, fuels, foods	pound $1,620
TAIWAN Taipei 19,601,000 66.0%	55% forests; 24% cultivated; 6% pastures; 15% wasteland, other	coal, natural gas, limestone, marble, asbestos	textiles, clothing, chemicals, electronics, food processing, plywood, sugar milling, cement	textiles, electrical machinery and equipment, general machinery and equipment, telecommunications equipment	machinery and equipment, crude oil, chemicals, basic metals, food	dollar $2,980
TANZANIA Dar es Salaam 22,415,000 14.8%	45% forests; 37% pastures; 4% arable; 1% cropland; 13% other	hydroelectric power, iron, coal, gemstones, gold, natural gas, nickel	agricultural processing, diamond mining, oil refining, shoes, cement, textiles	coffee, cotton, sisal, cashews, meat, cloves, tobacco, tea, coconut products	manufactured goods, machinery and transport equipment, cotton piece goods, crude oil, food	shilling $210
THAILAND Bangkok 52,438,000 15.6%	56% forests; 24% cropland; 20% other	tin, rubber, natural gas, tungsten, timber, fisheries	agricultural processing, textiles, wood and wood products, cement, tin and tungsten mining	rice, sugar, corn, rubber, tin, tapioca, textiles, garments, integrated circuits	machinery and transport equipment, fuels and lubricants, base metals, chemicals	baht $860
TOGO Lomé 3,118,000 20.1%	50% arable; 50% other	phosphates, limestone, marble	phosphate mining, agricultural processing, cement, handicrafts, textiles	phosphates, cocoa, coffee, palm kernels	consumer goods, fuels, machinery, tobacco, food	Communauté Financière Africaine franc $250
TONGA Nuk'alofa 104,000 50.0%	77% arable; 3% pastures; 13% forests; 7% other	fish	tourism	copra, bananas, coconut products	food, machinery, petroleum	pa'anga $580
TRINIDAD AND TOBAGO Port-of-Spain 1,204,000 22.6%	42% cropland; 58% grasses, forests, built on, wasteland, other	oil, gas, petroleum, asphalt	petroleum, chemicals, tourism, food processing, cement	petroleum and petroleum products, ammonia, fertilizer, chemicals, sugar	crude petroleum, machinery, fabricated metals, transport equipment, manufactured goods	dollar $7,150

WORLD ECONOMIC DATA

NATION/ Capital/ Population/ Urbanization	Land Use	Natural Resources	Major Industries	Exports	Imports	Monetary Unit/ Per Capita Income (in U.S. $)
TUNISIA Tunis 7,424,000 56.8%	43% deserts, wasteland, other; 28% cropland, tree crops; 23% range; 6% forests	oil, phosphates, iron ore, lead, zinc	mining, manufacturing, services	crude petroleum, textiles, phosphates, chemicals	machinery, petroleum, transport equipment, iron and steel	dinar $1,270
TURKEY Ankara 51,819,000 48.1%	35% cropland; 25% pastures; 23% forests; 17% other	antimony, coal, chromium, mercury, copper, borate, oil	textiles, food processing, mining, steel, petroleum	cotton, tobacco, fruits, nuts, metals, livestock products, textiles, clothing, cement	crude oil, machinery, transport equipment, metals, pharmaceuticals, dyes, plastics, rubber	lira $1,160
TUVALU Funafuti 8,000 30.0%	Mostly wooded	copra	copra	copra	food, mineral fuels	Australian dollar $450
UGANDA Kampala 15,158,000 14.4%	45% forests, grasses; 21% cultivated; 13% parks and reserves; 21% inland waters, swamps	copper, cobalt, limestone	agricultural processing, cement, copper smelting, corrugated iron sheet, shoes	coffee, cotton, tea	petroleum products, machinery, cotton piece goods, metals, transport equipment, food	shilling $230
UNITED ARAB EMIRATES Abu Dhabi 1,326,000 77.8%	Almost all deserts or wasteland	oil, natural gas	petroleum production	crude oil, gas, reexports, dried fish, dates	food, consumer and capital goods	dirham $21,920
UNITED KINGDOM London 56,458,000 91.7%	50% pastures; 30% arable; 13% wasteland, other; 7% forests	coal, oil, gas, tin, limestone, iron, salt, clay, chalk, gypsum, lead, silica	machinery and transport equipment, metals, food processing, paper and paper products, textiles	manufactured goods, machinery, fuels, chemicals, semifinished goods, transport equipment	manufactured goods, machinery, semifinished goods, food, consumer goods	pound $8,570
UNITED STATES Washington, D.C. 240,856,000 74.2%	32% forests; 27% pastures; 19% cultivated; 22% wasteland, other	coal, copper, lead, molybdenum, phosphates, uranium, bauxite, gold, iron, mercury	steel, motor vehicles, aerospace industries, telecommunications, electronics, consumer goods	machinery, chemicals, transport equipment, agricultural products	crude and partially refined petroleum, machinery, transport equipment	dollar $15,390
URUGUAY Montevideo 2,947,000 85.0%	84% agricultural; 16% forests, wasteland, other	soil, hydroelectric power, minor minerals	meat processing, wool, hides, textiles, footwear, leather apparel, tires, cement	wool, hides, meat, textiles, leather products, fish, rice, furs	fuels and lubricants, metals, machinery, transport equipment, industrial chemicals	peso $1,980
VATICAN CITY Vatican City 737 NA	100% built on	None	postage stamps, tourism, printing, production of mosaics	None	None	lira NA

WORLD ECONOMIC DATA

NATION/ Capital/ Population/ Urbanization	Land Use	Natural Resources	Major Industries	Exports	Imports	Monetary Unit/ Per Capita Income (in U.S. $)
VENEZUELA Caracas 17,791,000 85.7%	21% forests; 18% pastures; 4% cropland; 57% wasteland, other	petroleum, natural gas, iron ore, gold, bauxite, minerals, hydroelectric power	petroleum, mining, construction, food processing, textiles, steel, aluminum	petroleum	machinery and transport equipment, chemicals, food	bolívar $3,410
VIETNAM Hanoi 61,994,000 20.3%	50% forests; 14% cultivated; 36% other	phosphates, coal, manganese, bauxite, apatite, chromate, forests	food processing, textiles, machine building, mining, cement, chemical fertilizer, glass	agricultural and handicraft products, coal, minerals, ores	petroleum, steel products, railroad equipment, chemicals, medicines, raw cotton, fertilizer	dong $300
WESTERN SAMOA Apia 165,000 21.5%	65% forests; 24% cultivated; 11% wasteland, other	hardwood forests, fish	timber, tourism, light industry	copra, cocoa, timber, mineral fuels, bananas	food, manufactured goods, machinery	tala $770
YEMEN, NORTH Sanaa 6,339,000 20.0%	79% deserts, wasteland, other; 20% agricultural; 1% forests	petroleum, rock salt, coal, copper, oil	cotton textiles, leather goods, handicrafts, fishing, aluminum products	qat, cotton, coffee, hides, vegetables	textiles, manufactured consumer goods, petroleum products, sugar, grain, flour	rial $550
YEMEN, SOUTH Aden 2,275,000 39.9%	1% arable; 99% deserts, wasteland, other	fish, petroleum	petroleum refining	food, live animals, fish, petroleum	machinery and transport equipment, food, live animals, petroleum	dinar $550
YUGOSLAVIA Belgrade 23,284,000 46.3%	34% forests; 32% arable; 25% pastures; 9% other	coal, copper, bauxite, timber, iron, antimony, chromium, lead, zinc, asbestos, mercury	metallurgy, machinery and equipment, oil refining, chemicals, textiles, wood processing	raw materials and semimanufactures, consumer goods, equipment	raw materials, semi-manufactures, equipment, consumer goods	dinar $2,120
ZAIRE Kinshasa 31,333,000 44.2%	45% forests; 22% agricultural; 33% other	cobalt, copper, cadmium, petroleum, industrial and gem diamonds, gold, silver, zinc, manganese	mining, mineral processing, consumer products, processed food and beverages	copper, cobalt, diamonds, petroleum, coffee	consumer goods, food, mining, machinery, transport equipment, fuels	zaire $140
ZAMBIA Lusaka 7,054,000 49.5%	61% woodland, grasses; 13% forests; 10% grazing; 6% marsh; 10% other	copper, cobalt, zinc, lead, coal, emeralds, gold, silver, uranium, hydroelectric power	copper mining and refining, transport, construction, food, beverages, chemicals, textiles, fertilizer	copper, zinc, cobalt, lead, tobacco	machinery, transport equipment, food, fuels, manufactures	kwacha $470
ZIMBABWE Harare 8,984,000 24.6%	40% arable; 60% grazing	coal, chrome, asbestos, gold, nickel, copper, iron ore, vanadium, lithium	mining, steel, textiles, chemicals, vehicles	gold, tobacco, asbestos, cotton, copper, tin, chrome, nickel, meat, clothing, sugar	machinery, petroleum products, wheat, transport equipment	dollar $760

Sources: *World Factbook, 1986; World Development Report, 1986; World Almanac and Factbook, 1986; World Resources, 1986; The Europe Yearbook, 1987; Kaleidoscope.*

Chronology of Economic Events

1776

- Adam Smith, a Scottish economist, writes *An Inquiry into the Nature and Causes of the Wealth of Nations.*

1787

- The United States Constitution is adopted by the Constitutional Convention.

1789

- The United States Treasury Department is established.

1791

- Congress charters the First National Bank of the United States.

1792

- The New York Stock Exchange (NYSE) is established.
- Congress establishes a national coinage system.
- Philadelphia shoemakers form the nation's first craft union.

1813

- Congress charters the Second Bank of the United States.

1833

- Central banking in the United States ends until 1913.

Chronology

1848
- Karl Marx and Friedrich Engels write *The Communist Manifesto.*

1863
- Congress issues paper money called greenbacks.
- Congress passes the National Banking Act.

1867
- Karl Marx writes *Capital.*
- The New York Stock Exchange introduces the first stock ticker.

1869
- The transcontinental railroad is completed.
- Gold speculation triggers "Black Friday," one of the worst financial disasters in United States history.
- The Knights of Labor is founded.

1870
- John D. Rockefeller and his associates form the Standard Oil Company of Ohio.

1873
- The Coinage Act ties paper money to gold.

1882
- John D. Rockefeller develops the Standard Oil Trust.

1886
- The American Federation of Labor is founded.

1887
- Congress passes the Interstate Commerce Act.

1890
- Congress passes the Sherman Antitrust Act.
- Congress passes the McKinley Tariff.

1900
- The Gold Standard Act values all coins and paper money in terms of gold.

1901
- The United States Steel Corporation is formed by J. P. Morgan.

1906

- Congress passes the Pure Food and Drug Act.
- Congress passes the Employer's Liability Act.

1908

- The National Monetary Commission is formed.

1913

- Congress creates the Federal Reserve System.
- The 16th Amendment to the Constitution allows Congress to levy an income tax.

1914

- Congress creates the Federal Trade Commission.
- Congress passes the Clayton Antitrust Act.

1917

- The Russian Revolution begins.
- The United States enters World War I.

1918

- World War I ends.
- Lenin begins War Communism in the Soviet Union.

1919

- The Bureau of Labor begins publishing the Consumer Price Index (CPI).

1921

- Lenin begins the New Economic Plan (NEP) in the Soviet Union.
- The Budget and Accounting Act is passed empowering the President to formulate and present an annual federal budget for Congressional action.

1928

- The Soviet Union announces the first five-year plan for economic growth.

1929

- The stock market crashes, and the Great Depression begins.

1930

- The Hawley-Smoot Tariff becomes the highest tariff in United States history.

Chronology

1933

- A bank holiday stops panic runs on United States banks.
- The International Monetary and Economic Conference meets in London.
- The United States abandons the gold standard.
- The Federal Securities Act regulates securities trading.

1934

- The Securities Exchange Act regulates the stocks and securities industry.
- The Trade Agreements Act speeds the process of establishing new trade with foreign countries.

1935

- The Committee of Industrial Organizations (CIO) is formed.
- Congress passes the Social Security Act.

1936

- John Maynard Keynes publishes *General Theory of Employment, Interest, and Money.*

1938

- The first minimum wage-and-hours law is enacted by Congress.

1941

- The United States enters World War II and begins a great industrial expansion.

1944

- The International Monetary Fund and the World Bank are created to promote monetary stability in the world.

1945

- World War II ends.

1947

- The Taft-Hartley Act makes provisions for right-to-work laws.
- The General Agreement on Tariffs and Trade (GATT) is signed by 23 non-Communist nations.
- Congress establishes the Congressional Budget Office (CBO).
- The Federal Mediation and Conciliation Service (FMCS) is established to mediate labor disputes.

1948

- The Organization of American States (OAS) is established to develop better political and economic relations among countries of the Americas.

1950

- The Celler-Kefauver Act strengthens the Clayton Antitrust Act by tightening control over mergers that might reduce competition.

1953

- The People's Republic of China begins its first five-year plan for economic growth.

1955

- The American Federation of Labor and the Congress of Industrial Organizations merge to form the AFL–CIO.

1957

- Six European nations (France, Belgium, Luxembourg, The Netherlands, Italy, and West Germany) form the European Economic Community (Common Market).

1958

- Mao Zedong begins the second five-year plan, or the Great Leap Forward, to bring China into the modern age.

1960

- Venezuela and the oil-producing nations of the Middle East create the Organization of Petroleum Exporting Countries (OPEC).
- President John F. Kennedy creates the Alliance for Progress to help stimulate the economies of Latin America.
- The Latin American Common Market is formed.
- President John F. Kennedy creates the Peace Corps to aid underdeveloped nations of the world.

1962

- Congress passes the Trade Expansion Act, which expanded the Reciprocal Trade Agreements Act of 1934.

1963

- The Equal Pay Act mandates that female workers who do the same job as males receive the same pay.

1964

- The Equal Opportunity Act creates both the Job Corps and the Neighborhood Youth Corps Work Training programs.
- The Civil Rights Act protects citizens from discrimination based on race, age, sex, religion, and national origin.
- The Equal Employment Opportunity Commission helps minority citizens receive equal employment.

1965

- President Lyndon Johnson establishes an affirmative action policy through Executive Order 11246.

1967

- The Age Discrimination Act protects workers from 40 to 65 against age discrimination.

1970

- The Environmental Protection Agency is formed.
- The Occupational Safety and Health Administration (OSHA) is created to regulate working conditions.

1971

- The United States stops giving gold for dollars, and the government devalues the dollar.

1973

- Great Britain is admitted to the Common Market.
- The Arab oil embargo creates an energy crisis in the United States and causes a worldwide economic ripple effect.
- The Youth Employment and Demonstration Projects Act increases the government's commitment to the Job Corps.

1978

- The Electronic Funds Transfer Act paves the way for computer systems to handle many banking functions.

1980

- The Depository Institution Deregulation and Monetary Control Act eliminates many traditional differences between the various types of financial institutions.

1981

- The public debt of the United States reaches $1 trillion.
- Japanese automakers agree to voluntary import quotas.
- The socialist government of Francois Mitterand nationalizes many private banks and industrial firms in France.
- Congress passes the Economic Recovery Act, the largest tax cut in United States history.
- President Ronald Reagan issues Executive Order No. 12291, which requires government agencies to conduct a cost-benefit analysis on proposed regulations.
- The Tax Equity and Fiscal Responsibility Act strictly enforces existing tax laws.
- The Professional Air Traffic Controllers Organization (PATCO) begins a strike. President Ronald Reagan invokes the Taft-Hartley Act, firing all 12,000 of PATCO's members for refusing to go back to work.
- Iraq and Iran, both OPEC members, begin a war in the Middle East.

1982

- The Job Training Partnership Act provides for the retraining of displaced workers.

1984

- The Deficit Reduction Act establishes stricter tax record-keeping procedures and closes some tax loopholes.
- Courts force the breakup of the American Telephone and Telegraph Company (AT&T), one of the largest natural monopolies in the United States.

1985

- The Gramm-Rudman-Hollings Balanced Budget and Emergency Deficit Reduction Control Act requires the government to operate within a balanced budget.

1986

- The Supreme Soviet legalizes many free enterprise activities in the Soviet Union.

1986

- A report of the National Research Council concludes that acid rain is responsible for some environmental pollution.
- Wall Street is rocked by the worst instance of insider trading in the history of stock trading.
- The Tax Reform Act significantly changes the tax system in the United States.
- The public debt of the United States reaches $2 trillion.
- The Federal Deposit Insurance Corporation (FDIC) adopts a policy that promises to rescue all banks in the event of bank collapse.
- A federal district court rules that a part of the Gramm-Rudman-Hollings law is unconstitutional.
- President Ronald Reagan proposes the elimination of the Interstate Commerce Commission (ICC).

1987

- People Express merges with Continental Airlines.

Everyday Economics Handbook

The most important element of the American free enterprise system is the individual consumer. Choices made by consumers in a free market direct the course of the nation's economy. It is essential, then, that Americans learn to be wise and responsible consumers. The Everyday Economics Handbook has been designed to help you become such a consumer. This reference guide contains helpful tips on a wide range of subjects from reading the want ads to investing in high-growth stocks. Learning about your rights and responsibilities as a consumer will help you become an effective contributor to the economic health of the nation.

1 PREPARING A PERSONAL BUDGET

May be used with page 24.

Economics is a study of choices—the choices people make in order to satisfy their needs and wants. Such choices are necessary because people's needs and wants are greater than the economic resources available to satisfy them. For consumers, preparing a personal budget is essential to making wise economic choices.

A budget is a money plan. It identifies the amount of money a consumer can expect to earn and spend during a given period of time. Preparing a personal budget is not a difficult task, but it does take time and planning.

Handbook

Assessing Your Budget Needs

The best place to start when preparing a budget is to assess your budget needs. This can be done by studying your income and expenses for a given period of time, such as one month.

Traditionally, consumers plan their personal budgets on a monthly basis because the payments for many expenses, such as rent, electricity, and telephone service, are due each month. To begin to assess your budget needs, keep detailed records of the money you earn and the money you spend during a one-month period. You may wish to save cash-register and credit-card receipts and other bills to help you. At the end of the month, record your findings on a piece of paper. Divide the paper into two columns. Label the first column, "Income." Label the second column, "Expenses." Then, list your income and expenses for the month under the proper column. You will begin to see a pattern of earning, spending, and saving money. This pattern reflects your budget needs and can be used as the basis for your personal budget.

Estimating Your Income

Once you have assessed your budget needs, you now are ready to prepare your personal budget. First, write the name of the month that the budget is for at the top of a piece of paper. Then, divide the paper into two columns, as you did when assessing your budget needs. Under the "Income" column, record your estimated income for the month. Be sure to include the money you expect to earn from part-time jobs, as well as the money you expect to receive from allowances or gifts.

Estimating Your Expenses

Under the "Expenses" column, list the expenses that you anticipate you will have during the month. It is important to be as detailed as possible. List all the expenses that you think you will have, including those for personal items and other small purchases.

When listing expenses, it often is helpful to divide the expenses into two categories—fixed expenses and flexible expenses. Fixed expenses are those in which the amount paid remains the same from month to month. Fixed expenses might include monthly rent payments or car payments. Flexible expenses are those in which the amount paid changes from month to month. Among flexible expenses are the amounts spent on food, clothing, medical care, and medicines.

Your expenses may not be very high until you live away from home. When you live independently, however, you probably will find that your highest monthly expenses will fall into the same general categories as those of other consumers. These categories are housing, food, clothing, and transportation.

Housing Expenses. The costs of housing are high, regardless of whether you rent an apartment or own a house or condominium. For most people, the major housing expense is the monthly rent or mortgage payment. When preparing a budget for housing expenses, however, it also is important to list the expenses of utilities. Utilities are essential services such as electricity, gas, water, telephone service, and garbage disposal. Additional housing expenses include home repairs, property insurance, property taxes, furniture, decorating, maintenance equipment, and cleaning supplies.

Food Expenses. The highest food expenses for most consumers are for groceries. Meals and snacks purchased away from home also should be listed under food expenses. If you eat dinner in a restaurant twice a month, for example, money to pay for the meals should be reflected in your food budget.

Clothing Expenses. Clothing costs involve more than the price of new clothes. Dry cleaning and laundry bills, shoe repairs, and mending supplies also should be listed under your clothing expenses.

Transportation Expenses. Transportation costs may range from bus and subway fares to the expenses of automobile ownership—monthly car payments, gas and oil, repairs, insurance, car washes, and accessories.

Other Expenses. Aside from the major expense categories of housing, food, clothing, and transportation, most consumers also must include other expense categories in their budgets. These categories vary among consumers, depending on their needs. Such expense categories might include, for example, health care, life insurance policies, education, and entertainment.

Savings. One other category should be listed under monthly expenses in every consumer's budget. This category is savings. The main goal of a money plan is to help consumers make wise economic decisions. An important part of being a wise consumer is saving money.

Saving money is important because inflation and unforeseen expenses sometimes can ruin even the most carefully planned budget. Many items in your budget, such as medical bills and home and auto repairs, tend to increase in cost over time. In addition, expenses for the unexpected, such as flood damage and automobile accidents, can never be anticipated. For these reasons, it is useful to set money aside each month for a contingency fund, which can be used for those occasions when something unplanned happens.

Saving money is important for other reasons, too. Many people save for certain items they cannot buy right away, but saving money to satisfy short-term goals is not the only reason for saving. It also is important to save for the future to help assure a comfortable standard of living in later years. The interest and dividends from savings investments also can supplement your earned income.

Revising Your Budget

If a budget is to accurately plan for your needs, wants, and priorities, it must be revised periodically. Revision is necessary because your income and expenses change over time. Income often changes significantly with a new job or promotion. Likewise, expenses change as you get older.

One useful way of assessing the need for budget revision is to make an annual budget. After you have kept a budget for a number of months, prepare an annual budget listing all income and expenses for one year. An annual budget will help you get an overall picture of your financial situation and decide whether you are allocating enough funds for savings. It can also help you decide whether to seek a higher paying job to meet increased expenses or decrease expenses to combat inflation.

Everyday Economics Review

1. Why are personal budgets traditionally based on one-month time periods?
2. What general expense categories should be included in your personal budget?
3. Why is it important to revise your budget from time to time?

Everyday Economics Review Answers: 1. Most payments are due each month. 2. housing, food, clothing, and transportation; 3. Income and expenses change.

2 SHOPPING WISELY

May be used with page 46.

Buying and selling goods in a free market is the cornerstone of the American free enterprise system. It also is the means by which consumers satisfy their needs and wants. In order to satisfy the greatest number of needs and wants with limited resources, today's consumers must be wise shoppers.

Preparing to Shop

Even before going to a store, you can take several steps to help prepare you to shop.

Defining Your Needs and Wants. One of the most important parts of being a wise shopper is defining the needs or wants that you wish to satisfy by purchasing a product. Suppose that you are in the market for a video cassette recorder (VCR). You may want the VCR only to use its basic capability of playing video cassettes. Such a VCR, however, is quite different from one that can record television shows, has a remote control tuner, and is cable ready. By defining your needs and wants and setting priorities ahead of time, you will be better able to make a wise buying decision.

Setting a Spending Limit. Many of the buying decisions that you make depend on the amount of money that you have to spend. To make the best decisions on how to spend limited income, it is a good idea to set a spending limit before going to the store. In this way, you will be better prepared to buy a product that not only will satisfy your needs and wants, but also will be compatible with your budget.

Doing Your Homework. Before making a major purchase, it may be helpful to consult one or more consumer publications. Magazines such as *Consumer Reports* provide useful information on a wide variety of products. It may be worth a trip to the library to research the facts about the features and product histories of items you wish to buy.

Deciding Where to Shop. Deciding where to shop also is a part of being a wise shopper. One way to decide where to shop is to pay attention to advertisements that appear in newspapers or are broadcast on the radio and television. If you know that a product is on sale at a certain store, you may wish to start your shopping trip there. It also may be a good idea to consider shopping at a discount store. Discount stores often buy products in large quantities and can sell them at reduced prices. Before making a decision about where to shop, however, you may wish to phone several stores to make sure that the item you are looking for is in stock and to check on its price.

Deciding When to Shop. Deciding when to shop also can affect buying decisions. Car dealers, for example, often put new cars on sale in the spring or summer to help clear their showrooms for next year's models. Many holiday items go on sale after the first of the year. Being aware of sale patterns can help save money.

Other, more personal factors also should be considered in decisions about when to shop. Avoid going shopping when you are tired because tired shoppers tend to buy products on impulse so that they can get home faster. Avoid going to the grocery store when you are hungry because hungry shoppers tend to buy more than they planned.

How to Shop Wisely

Along with advanced planning, making the best buys for your needs requires careful shopping.

Reading Food Labels. When food shopping, it is especially important that you read food labels carefully. One of the first things you should notice is the brand of the product. You probably are familiar with many well-known name brands of foods. The same foods, however, often are available in house brands or generic brands. House brands are the brands produced and marketed by a grocery store and carry the house-brand label. Generic brands have no name labels. They usually are packaged in black and white and carry the word "generic." Some house and generic brands contain the same ingredients as more expensive name brands, making them the better buys.

Food labels also should be read for information about a product's contents. Most food labels list the ingredients found in the product, often giving the exact amounts of sodium, fat, and preservatives. These labels can be especially helpful to people who have allergies or who are on restricted diets. Many labels also list the amounts of vitamins and nutrients per serving, the number of calories per serving, and a date after which the product should not be purchased.

Reading Product Descriptions. Before making a purchase, it also is a good idea to read an item's product description. Most product descriptions contain information about the care of a product. Clothing items, for example, contain information about whether they should be washed or dry cleaned. If an item can be washed, most product descriptions recommend the kind of soap to use; whether the item should be washed in cold, warm, or hot water; and whether it should be dried in a dryer or on a clothesline.

Some product descriptions also contain information about a product's proper use and warnings about its misuse. An electrical product such as a space heater, for example, may contain information about how to use the product most efficiently by taking advantage of various settings. It also may contain warnings about placing the heater away from nearby objects.

When reading product descriptions, also be sure to note whether the product must be assembled or if it will need batteries to operate. These facts also may affect your buying decision.

Comparing Product Features. Using all of the information available, carefully compare the various features of a product when in the store. Before purchasing an item, be certain that it will perform all of the tasks you expect of it. To help you, ask the sales clerk to clarify exactly what the product can do. Ask about the product's warranties or guarantees. If practical, ask for a trial use.

Quality Considerations. High-quality items have features that make them more attractive to consumers. Such items may last longer, look nicer, and perform better. Consumers usually are willing to pay more for high-quality products and services.

Quality, however, is often difficult to measure. Certain brand name products, for example, penetrate the market by appealing to consumer tastes

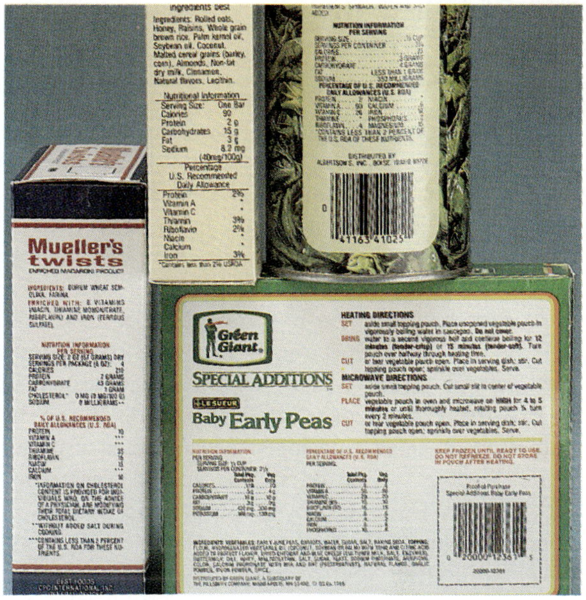

and preferences. Although such products become popular to own, it is important to remember that popularity is not the same as quality. Before buying any product, check the label and product description as well as the overall appearance to help get an accurate idea of the product's quality.

Quantity and Price Considerations. If you use large quantities of an item that can be stored easily and is nonperishable, you often can save money by buying the item in a larger size. You can tell if you are getting the most for your money by checking the unit prices marked on the product or on the store shelf. A unit price is the price of a product by unit, weight, or volume. The unit price of a certain brand of canned fruit, for example, may be \$0.49 an ounce. The unit price of the same brand of fruit packaged in a larger can may be \$0.44 an ounce. By checking the unit prices, you can be sure that the larger can is the better buy.

Everyday Economics Review

1. Why is it important to define specific needs and wants before going shopping?
2. What information can be obtained by reading food labels and product descriptions?
3. What is the unit price of a product?

Everyday Economics Review Answers: 1. You will be able to make wise buying decisions. 2. the product brand, contents, ingredients, and often the amount of vitamins, minerals and calories per serving, and the expiration date; 3. the price by unit, weight, or volume.

Handbook

3 READING THE WANT ADS

May be used with page 70.

When you are looking for a job, the classified section of the newspaper will be invaluable. Better known as the want ads, the classified section contains ads for jobs in businesses in the local area. It may also contain selected ads from businesses across the country.

In searching for the best possible job available, it is helpful to consult more than one newspaper, especially if you live in a large metropolitan area where more than one newspaper is likely to be published. Besides studying the want ads from your city's leading newspapers, you might also study newspapers from nearby suburbs and towns. If you are willing to relocate, it also would be a good idea to consult out-of-town newspapers. Most large newsstands or bookstores stock a selection of out-of-town newspapers. Public libraries also carry a good selection of out-of-town papers. Usually, the Sunday paper has the largest "Help Wanted" section.

How to Use the Want Ads

To find the want ads, check the listing of contents on the first or second page of the newspaper. After locating the help wanted section, refer to the jobs that interest you by checking under the headings that list specific job classifications. Want ads usually are listed in alphabetical order by job classification. Such job classifications might include accounting, administration, bookkeeping, clerical, computer programming, data processing, education, engineering, financial, insurance, marketing, medical, printing, sales, secretarial, and word processing.

Concentrate on the listings in which you are most interested, but do not limit your search to one heading. You may find that a job you are looking for is listed under one or more different categories. Openings for a cook, for example, may also be listed under bakers, chefs, and restaurants. By reading through other categories, you also may be able to uncover interesting job openings in related fields. It is helpful to read the want ads thoroughly the first few weeks of a job search to become familiar with the categories that pertain to your specialties and interests.

Everyday Economics Review

1. How are jobs listed in the classified section?
2. Why should you read several sections of the want ads when beginning a job search?

4 APPLYING FOR A JOB

May be used with page 76.

If you are like many Americans, you will spend a significant portion of your life working. A job influences your sense of personal fulfillment. A job provides you with income. For these reasons, learning good job-application techniques is important.

A job differs from a career. In general, a career is a long-term professional goal that includes many different jobs. For people who are interested in jobs rather than careers, job-application techniques are usually streamlined. Most jobs, such as assembly-line work or jobs in fast food restaurants, require that an applicant follow two steps: finding a job

Everyday Economics Review Answers: 1. in alphabetical order by job classification; 2. to become familiar with job categories that pertain to your specialities and interests.

opening and obtaining an interview. In contrast, for most people entering a professional career, a job search includes four basic steps. These are choosing a career, preparing a résumé, finding a job opening, and obtaining an interview.

Choosing a Career

The first step in a job search is to decide which occupational field or fields you have an interest in and which are suited to your abilities. Your high school and college counselors will be able to provide you with information about different careers and assist you as you consider career choices. Another source of information is *The Occupational Handbook,* published annually by the United States Department of Labor. This reference book provides growth projections and describes work conditions and salaries for hundreds of different occupations.

Preparing a Résumé

The second step in finding a job is preparing a résumé, which is a written summary of your career qualifications. It is important that your résumé be prepared carefully and attractively. Be sure that your résumé provides accurate information, has visual appeal, and is free of grammatical and typographical errors. Prospective employers receive their first impressions of you when they read your résumé.

As a general rule, a résumé can be divided into five sections: heading, career objective, employment history, education, and special interests.

Heading. The heading of your résumé should include your name, address, and telephone number. If you wish, you may label the heading with the word *Résumé.*

Career Objective. The career objective should briefly describe your career goal, usually in one to two sentences. This part of a résumé is optional. It is best to state a career objective if you have a specific job choice in mind. If you feel that you qualify for several different jobs, you may not want to include it.

Employment History. The section for employment history provides a summary of the kinds of jobs you have held. A résumé describes your employment history chronologically, beginning with the most recently held position. For each position, include the dates you held the job, your job title, and a brief description of your job responsibilities. Include important accomplishments and emphasize what you are now qualified to offer prospective employers.

Education. A description of your education starts with a listing of the schools you have attended, beginning with high school. In addition to college and graduate schools, a résumé may include professional seminars and other types of postgraduate training. For each school, list the degrees, licenses, or certificates that you earned and the dates you earned them. In addition, be sure to include any honors and scholarships you received.

Special Interests. In the special interests section of your résumé, list your hobbies and extracurricular activities. This section can be especially important if you are young and have limited work experience. Special interests often indicate that you enjoy working with other people and have strong leadership abilities.

Finding a Job Opening

Once your résumé is prepared, you are ready for the third step in the job search process— finding a job opening. Among the numerous approaches you may want to use to help you are networking, unsolicited campaigning, answering want ads, and using employment and school placement services.

Networking and Unsolicited Campaigns. Networking and unsolicited campaigning are two of the most successful means of finding a job. Networking is the process of telling people you know that you are looking for a job and asking them to inform you of available positions. It is a means of establishing contacts in the business world. An unsolicited campaign is one in which you write directly to a company for which you think you might like to work, even though the company has not advertised an opening. Your letter should describe the contri-

butions you think you could make to the company and should include a copy of your résumé.

Answering Want Ads. A popular approach to finding a job opening is to answer want ads in newspapers and trade and professional journals. When you decide to answer an ad, the most important thing to do is read the ad carefully and then to follow its directions. If an ad asks you to call in person, do not make a phone call or send a letter asking for the job. If an ad asks for an application by letter and gives a deadline for the receipt of the applications, be sure that your letter will arrive before the deadline. In your letter, identify the ad you are answering and cite your specific attributes that make you qualified for the job. Do not, however, make the letter unnecessarily long. Be concise and to the point as you discuss your qualifications.

Before answering a want ad, try to make sure that the job matches your qualifications, as well as your interests. If an employer advertises for a person with a master's degree in business administration and 10 years of experience as a comptroller, and you have a bachelor of arts degree in business and two years of experience in banking, you probably are not the right person for the job. It cannot hurt to send a résumé to a company advertising a job in which you are interested. However, your time and resources are limited. Try to concentrate your efforts on job possibilities for which you are best suited.

Employment Agencies and Placement Centers. Employment agencies and school placement centers also may be helpful to you in finding a job opening. Employment agencies are paid a fee by employers to place people in special positions. An agency also might require that you pay them a fee, as well, if placed in a job. School placement centers provide lists of job openings. Some even keep your transcripts and references on file and try to "match" you with an employer.

Obtaining an Interview

The fourth step in most job searches is obtaining an interview. Once a prospective employer receives your résumé, he or she may contact you to arrange an interview. When called for an interview, be sure that you are neatly dressed and arrive on time. If you look and feel your best, you will feel more confident as you meet your prospective employer.

During the interview, try to focus on three major objectives: to learn about the position, to listen carefully, and to answer questions clearly. Explain how your qualifications would meet the requirements of the job. You also may wish to take an opportunity to ask more about the company.

When the interview is over, be sure to thank the interviewer for his or her time. The next day, you also may wish to write a note to the interviewer expressing your thanks and your continued interest in the job.

◆ Everyday Economics Review Answers: 1. choosing a career, preparing a résumé, finding a job opening, and obtaining an interview; 2. Prospective employers receive their first impressions of you. 3. learning about the job, listening carefully, and answering questions.

◆ Everyday Economics Review

1. What are the four basic steps in a job search?
2. Why is it important for your résumé to be prepared carefully?
3. What major objectives should you focus on during a job interview?

5 INTERPRETING WARRANTIES

May be used with page 115.

As a wise consumer, you should be sure that the products you buy are durable and in excellent condition. Manufacturers generally are required by law to provide a warranty, or written guarantee, of the condition of their products. A warranty specifies the manufacturer's obligations to the consumer; contains information about the quality and attributes of the product, including its expected lifespan; and explains the manufacturer's plan to assure product performance.

Warranties and the Law

Warranties are subject to both federal and state laws. In many states, warranties are governed by the Uniform Commercial Code, which monitors trade rules and regulations. The Magnuson-Moss Warranty Act, passed by Congress in 1975, states that the seller of a product must explain the terms of the warranty at the time of purchase and that the manufacturer must specify if and how the warranty is limited.

What Warranties Cover

Most warranties cover the materials from which a product is made, as well as the quality of work used to make it. Should defects be found in either of these areas, the product normally will be repaired or replaced.

Be aware, however, that warranty coverage may not include all parts of a product. Specific limitations of the warranty often are written in small print. An automobile warranty, for example, may exempt rust. A microwave oven warranty may cover the oven's internal working parts but may exempt its case or its mechanical parts. Be sure to read the entire warranty carefully before purchasing a product.

Most warranties do not cover repairs that might be necessary due to normal wear, misuse, abuse, negligence, or accident. In such cases, the warranty may be void.

Most warranties are valid only for a specific time period. After the time period expires, the warranty no longer applies. Normally, the longer the warranty period, the better the quality of the product. The warranty period usually starts at the time of purchase. In the case of certain appliances, however, such as those that must be installed in the home, the warranty may start on the first day of actual use.

When a Product Is Defective

If you find that a product covered by a warranty is defective, you have certain rights. The extent of these rights depends on the manufacturer and the terms of the warranty.

Some warranties require that you return the product to the manufacturer for repair or replacement. Others require that you return the item to the place of purchase. Some warranties offer to repair the defective merchandise. Others offer to replace it. Still others offer to refund the purchase price.

Almost all warranties require that you present a proof of purchase before any corrective action can be taken. Because of this requirement, it is a good idea to check the warranty when you first purchase a product to see what will be required if it is found to be defective. Label and save any boxes, receipts, or other items required by the warranty.

Everyday Economics Review ●

1. What is a warranty?
2. What do warranties generally cover?
3. What recourse does a consumer have when a product covered by a warranty is found to be defective?

● Everyday Economics Review Answers: 1. a written guarantee; 2. materials, and quality of work; 3. Answers will vary.

AT&T

ACCOUNT NUMBER	STATEMENT CLOSING DATE	PAYMENT DUE DATE	PAGE
XXX-XXX-XXX-XX	May 13, 1987	June 12, 1986	1

FOR LONG DISTANCE CUSTOMER SERVICE CALL 1-800-222-0300
FOR EQUIPMENT CUSTOMER SERVICE CALL 1_800-555-1212

Previous Balance	Payments	Adjustments	Current Charges	Balance Due
75.00	-75.00	-3.50	+59.08	$55.58

DETAIL OF CURRENT TRANSACTIONS

No	Date	Time	To/From		Area-Number	Mins	Call Type*	Amount
Direct Dialed Calls								
1	Apr 15	1104P	to Richmond	CA	415 278-xxxx	39	N/Wknd-60%Discount	7.50
3	Apr 17	235P	to Portland	OR	503 283-xxxx	25	N/Wknd-60%Discount	5.02
3	Apr 19	935A	to Richmond	CA	415 278-xxxx	23	Day	6.75
4	Apr 23	230P	to Richmond	CA	415 278-xxxx	58	N/Wknd-60%Discount	9.75
							Subtotal.........	29.12
Operator Handled Calls								
6	Apr 16	1034A	to	CA	415 555-1212		Directory Assistance	Free
7	Apr 24	1130P	to	OR	503 555-1212		Directory Assistance	Free
8	May 9	845A	to	CA	713 555-1212		Directory Assistance	.60
							Subtotal..........	.60
							Total Long Distance Call Charges...	29.72

Equipment Charges
9 May 13 AT&T Telephone Equipment Rental from May 13 to Jun 12 16.00
Total Equipment Charges.... 16.00

Other Charges and Credits
10 Apr 17 Credit for REACH OUT® America Monthly Service at $10.50 from Apr 17 through May 12 7.75C
11 Apr 19 AT&T Long Distance Gift Certificate Purchase 20.00
Total Other Charges......... 12.25
Federal Tax......... 1.11
Total Current Charges......... $59.08

Payments and Adjustments
12 May 8 Payment - Thank you for paying promptly............. 75.00C
13 May 9 Previous Bill Credit for Cut-Off on Call to 415 278-xxxx 3.50C

Give the perfect gift for Father's Day. AT&T Long Distance Gift Certificates. To order call 1 800 222-8555. For information about our other products call 800 222 0300.

---------------------------------Tear Here---------------------------------

Account Number	Statement Closing Date	Payment Due Date	Balance Due	Amount Enclosed
XXX-XXX-XXXX-XX	May 13, 1987	June 12, 1987	$55.58	

Please return this portion with your payment. Make check payable to AT&T. Moving? For the free AT&T MOVE PLANNER, 40 pages of moving tips and more, 1 800 222-0300.

JANE DOE
ANYSTREET
ORLANDO, FL 32809

AT&T
P.O. BOX 109104
Atlanta, GA 300100000

6 CHOOSING A LONG-DISTANCE TELEPHONE SERVICE

May be used with page 123.

For many years, American Telephone and Telegraph Company (AT&T) was the major supplier of long-distance telephone service in the United States. By 1980, AT&T owned 22 local telephone subsidiaries across the country and provided a comprehensive, nationwide telecommunications service.

The AT&T Divestiture

In 1982, the United States Department of Justice brought suit against AT&T's vast holding network. After a long process of legal wrangling, AT&T offered to give up its local holdings. This action resulted in the divestiture, or breakup, of AT&T on January 1, 1984.

The AT&T divestiture had far-reaching repercussions in the telecommunications industry. AT&T's high long-distance revenues subsidized its local operations, making low-cost local service the norm. When local telephone companies became independent and no longer had the benefit of AT&T's long-distance revenues, they were forced to increase the prices they charged for local service.

Another result of the divestiture was that all long-distance carriers—including AT&T's competitors—were given access to special long-distance equipment. This access meant that other companies could now profitably compete with AT&T in the long-distance telephone business.

New Choices in Long-Distance Service

Today, more than 500 companies offer long-distance telephone service in the United States. The seven largest suppliers are Allnet, AT&T, GTE Sprint, International Telephone & Telegraph Corporation (ITT), MCI Communications, U.S. Telecom, and Western Union.

The added competition in the long-distance market means new opportunities for consumers—opportunities that consumers should consider before choosing a long-distance service.

Discounts. Many long-distance companies offer premiums, or initial discounts, to new customers. Most also offer discounts on monthly telephone bills that total a certain amount. One major supplier, for example, gives a 15 percent discount if the consumer makes $20 or more in long-distance calls during the month.

Credit Cards. Many companies supply their customers with free telephone credit cards. Such credit cards allow callers to make long-distance calls away from home, but to charge the calls to their home phones. Credit-card calls usually are cheaper to make than operator-assisted calls or collect calls.

Better Quality. Many long-distance carriers are competing for new business by offering better quality in their long-distance connections than their competitors offer. Some companies will permit you to test the quality of their services by making a sample call on their lines.

Other Services. Most long-distance companies also offer a wide range of additional services to customers. Among these services are a 24-hour customer service number; two or more free directory-assistance calls per month; paying only for calls made, with no monthly bill unless calls are placed that month; lower long-distance rates at night and on weekends; and special rates on calls to foreign countries. By comparing the services and rates offered by the various companies, consumers can select the service that best suits their needs—and their budgets.

Everyday Economics Review

1. What was the result of the AT&T divestiture?
2. What special services do many long-distance companies offer consumers?

7 UNDERSTANDING YOUR RIGHTS AS AN EMPLOYEE

May be used with page 150.

Before you start any new job, you should discuss your job description and the company's benefits with your employer. Ask your employer to explain the responsibilities of the position and the hours you will be expected to work. Your salary is based on the responsibilities of your job, as well as on

benefits such as sick leave, vacation pay, and health insurance provided by your employer.

This discussion normally is part of your job interview and provides you with an opportunity to ask questions and understand the terms and conditions of your employment. Be sure to clarify any unclear issues at this time. Most often, you will begin a new job with this type of verbal agreement. Sometimes, employers also will ask you to sign a written contract outlining your duties, responsibilities, and salary. Other conditions of your employment and company procedures will be clarified for you during your first few weeks of work.

Further Clarification of Benefits

When you start your job, you will be assigned a lunch hour and will soon become familiar with the day-to-day schedule your job requires. You may have breaks; you will become familiar with company holidays; and you may be enrolled in health insurance, life insurance, dental insurance, and pension programs. Some companies will give you a policy manual outlining your benefits and responsibilities. In addition to clarifying your benefits, it also is important that new employees fully understand the deductions that will be taken from their paychecks on a regular basis.

Everyday Economics Review Answers: 1. lowered the cost of local service, increased the price of long-distance service, and long-distance carriers were given access to special equipment; 2. discounts, credit cards, better service, and a variety of customer services.

Payroll Deductions

Employers make payroll deductions for federal and state income taxes, Social Security taxes, insurance plans, and, in some cases, pension plans and other optional programs. Your earnings before deductions are called your gross pay. Your earnings after deductions are called your net pay.

Federal Income Tax Forms. When you begin a new job, you will be asked to fill out a federal income tax form. On the form, you will be asked to indicate the number of dependents you want to claim and whether you are married or single. The amount withheld from your gross pay for federal income taxes will be based on the information you provide on this form.

Social Security. Congress passed the Social Security Act in 1935 to provide workers with disability and accident insurance, unemployment compensation, and old-age retirement benefits. Although not all categories of workers are covered by Social Security, most are. If you are covered under the Social Security program, FICA taxes also will be deducted from your gross pay.

Laws and the American Worker

Historically, your rights as an American worker have been defined and preserved by the interaction of the employers, employees, labor unions, and the government. Some of these rights include the right to belong to a labor union; the right to a minimum wage; the right to freedom from employment discrimination because of age, sex, color, or national origin; and the right to work in a safe environment.

The National Labor Relations Act. In addition to the Social Security Act, one of the earliest worker-oriented legislative initiatives by the federal government was the National Labor Relations Act, or Wagner Act. The Wagner Act was passed by Congress in 1935. This law guaranteed employees the right to belong to a union and to engage in collective bargaining. Many states have also passed right-to-work laws, which outlaw the closed shop, a situation in which workers must join a union in order to keep their jobs.

The Fair Labor Standards Act. The Fair Labor Standards Act, passed by Congress in 1938, is the legislation that grants workers the right to a minimum wage. Not all employers are obligated to pay this minimum wage, but most companies with a relatively large number of employees are affected by the law. The Fair Labor Standards Act also sets the standard workweek at 40 hours and grants employees who are paid on an hourly basis the right to overtime pay.

The Civil Rights Act. The Civil Rights Act was signed into law by President Lyndon Johnson in 1964. This law protects a person's freedom to vote, to use public places, and to seek employment. Title VII of this act broadens the scope of employee rights by preventing employers from discriminating against individuals on the basis of race, color, religion, sex, or national origin. Under this law, employees cannot be discriminated against in matters of hiring, compensation, employment privileges and opportunities, or union membership. Employers cannot advertise in a discriminatory manner and employment agencies may not fail to recommend a person for a certain job for prejudicial reasons.

The Equal Employment Opportunity Commission. The Equal Employment Opportunity Commission (EEOC) administers Title VII of the Civil Rights Act. The commission encourages employers and employment agencies to settle discriminatory charges on a voluntary basis. The commission also can help an injured party file a discrimination suit in a court of law.

Employment Rights for Minorities and Women

In the 1970's, the federal government began to pass laws to further assure employment rights for minorities and women. As part of this effort, the government adopted a program called affirmative action. Affirmative action seeks to make up for past discrimination by requiring that certain employers set hiring and fair employment goals for minorities and women.

Safety Measures. Employees also have the right to work in a safe environment. To this end, safety measures have been passed by the government to help eliminate hazards in the workplace. Many such laws concern the use of protective clothing and glasses, standards for safe equipment, and other matters that affect the safety of the individual at work. The Occupational Safety and Health Administration (OSHA), a division of the United States Department of Labor, oversees compliance with these laws and promotes safe and healthful working conditions.

Everyday Economics Review

1. What should you discuss with your employer before starting a new job?
2. What deductions will be made in your paycheck?
3. List four of your rights as an American worker.

8 UNDERSTANDING CONTRACT OBLIGATIONS

May be used with page 182.

A contract is an agreement between two or more parties that is enforceable by law and is used to regulate terms of trade. Both verbal and written agreements are contracts. A verbal agreement, however, is binding only if it involves a relatively small sum of money over a short period of time and does not involve a real estate purchase.

As a consumer, you probably will enter into a variety of different contracts. Some of the more common types of contracts are those involving an installment purchase; the buying and selling of real estate; a personal loan; the purchase of stocks or bonds; the use of a credit card; the purchase of an automobile; a rental agreement; agreements for such services as appliance maintenance and lawn care; and all types of insurance policies.

Contract Criteria

An agreement qualifies as a contract only when it meets four basic criteria. First, an offer and a promise to accept the offer must be made. The promise to accept the offer is especially important. A letter to you from a credit-card company offering you a credit line of $2,000 for a $25 annual fee would not represent a valid contract unless you paid the $25 or used the card, thereby accepting the offer.

Second, all parties to the agreement must be competent. Contracts signed by minors, people who are mentally incompetent, or people under the influence of alcohol or drugs are not legal or binding. Third, the terms of the agreement must be lawful. For example, you cannot legally collect money on a promise to deliver a stolen automobile or on a threat of blackmail. Fourth, an element of "bargain for exchange" must be present. This means that the agreement must contain reciprocal promises. These can involve money, goods, promises to do something, or promises not to do something. If one person agrees to deliver something and gets nothing in return, there is no contract.

Before You Sign a Contract

Before you sign a contract, be sure to take the following precautions. First, read the contract

Everyday Economics Review Answers: 1. job description and responsibilities, and company benefits; 2. federal and state income taxes, social security taxes, insurance and pension plans, and optional programs; 3. the rights to belong to a labor union, to a minimum wage, to freedom from discrimination; and to a safe work environment.

thoroughly. Although you may think the legal terminology in the document is beyond your comprehension, you may find that the contract is less complicated than you thought. If you find any part of the contract unclear, it is a good idea to contact a lawyer who will be able to fully explain the terms of the contract.

Second, be sure you agree with the terms of the contract. Try to understand what you are being asked to promise by the document. Also be sure to specify the obligations of the other parties.

Third, make certain you understand your options for terminating or changing the contract. It is very difficult to change a contract once it has been signed, unless it has specific provisions for a trial period. In some cases, the terms of a contract can change when other conditions change. A real estate contract, for example, may specify that the interest rate on a loan will fluctuate with changes in the market. Before signing a contract, be sure that you understand all of the circumstances under which it could be changed.

Fourth, make certain that you know what will happen if you default on your promise. If you are unable to pay your debts, most contracts state that your obligation still stands. As a result, you could lose the title to your house or car, for example. Some contracts also state that if you die during the life of the contract, your heirs are obligated to repay the debt.

Handbook

Everyday Economics Review

1. What criteria must contracts meet?
2. What should you consider before signing a contract?

9 UNDERSTANDING TAX REFORM

May be used with page 209.

Taxes have a tremendous impact on the lives of all American consumers. We pay many different kinds of taxes, including sales taxes, property taxes, excise taxes, and income taxes. In turn, tax money pays for many different kinds of public goods and services.

The Power of Government to Levy Taxes

The power of the government to levy taxes dates back to 1788— the year that the Constitution was ratified. The Constitution originally specified that taxes collected by the government had to be apportioned uniformly among the states according to population. When a law levying an income tax was passed by Congress in 1894, the Supreme Court found it to be unconstitutional because it did not meet this requirement.

The increasing costs of government in the growing nation, however, led many to support an income tax. This support eventually resulted in the adoption of the Sixteenth Amendment in 1913. The Sixteenth Amendment gave Congress the power to "lay and collect taxes on incomes from whatever source derived."

The Tax Reform Act of 1986

The Sixteenth Amendment is the basis of the income tax as we know it today. However, many issues concerning taxes have changed in the years following 1913. The primary tax issue of the 1980s was the emphasis on tax reform. Many supporters of reform cited inequities in the tax system, numerous tax loopholes, and overly complicated tax regulations as reasons for reform.

The Tax Reform Act of 1986 resulted from this tax reform movement and is the most significant tax legislation since 1913. The law was designed to completely restructure the tax code to make it more equitable for all sectors of the economy. Among other changes, the new tax law reduced the number of tax brackets. It also changed the tax status of IRAs and certain other tax shelters, real estate investments, and deductions on consumer debts.

Changes in Tax Brackets. The old income tax law had 16 tax rates that applied to single taxpayers within 16 different income levels. Married taxpayers and qualifying widows and widowers were subject to 15 tax rates that applied to 15 different income levels. Because there were so many tax brackets, inflation often pushed low- and middle-income families into tax brackets designed for upper-income families.

Everyday Economics Review Answers: 1. An offer and a promise to accept the offer must be made, all parties to the agreement must be competent, the terms of the agreement must be lawful, an element of "bargain for exchange" must be present; 2. Read the contract; be sure you agree with the terms and understand your options for terminating or changing the contract; make certain you know what will happen if you default.

The new tax law reduced the number of tax brackets, eventually to two. In 1987, the law went into effect on a transitional basis. The number of tax brackets was reduced to five. These brackets ranged from a minimum tax rate of 11 percent to a maximum rate of 38.5 percent. By 1988, the new tax law will reduce the number of tax brackets from five to two. One bracket will be at a rate of 15 percent. The other will be at a rate of 28 percent. Some people in lower-income groups will pay no taxes at all. Some people with very high incomes will pay more in taxes.

In the short-term, these changes will not represent a simplification of the tax law. Americans will need to adjust to the changes that applied in 1987, and to a different set of changes that will apply in 1988. In the long run, however, policymakers hope that the new law with only two tax brackets will be much less complicated and confusing for taxpayers.

IRAs and Other Tax Shelters. The Tax Reform Act of 1986 made significant changes in the status of IRAs and other tax shelters. A tax shelter is a special investment plan in which the amount invested is not taxed until it is withdrawn from the plan. The Individual Retirement Account, or IRA, has been a particularly popular tax shelter since it was established in 1975. The IRA is an account into which employees may contribute up to $2,000 of income per year. If the employee's spouse is not employed, the maximum contribution is $2,250. The employees do not pay taxes on this money or on the interest it earns until they withdraw it from their accounts at retirement.

Under the new tax law, the rules determining who qualifies for the tax advantages of this type of plan have been changed. For people who do not have other pension or retirement programs at work, the rules do not change. These employees still may contribute to an IRA and deduct their contributions from their income taxes. People who do have other pension programs at work, however, will qualify for these benefits only if they have individual incomes of less than $25,000 for single people or combined incomes of less than $40,000 for married people filing joint income tax returns. For those who qualify, their tax deduction is proportionately reduced as taxable income increases to $35,000 for single people and $50,000 for married people. After these higher levels of income have been reached, contributions to IRA accounts will no longer be tax deductible.

People who do not qualify under these guidelines still will be able to set aside money in IRAs. They also will be able to defer taxes on this money until their retirement. However, they will not be able to deduct their contributions from their income taxes.

Another popular form of sheltering money from taxes is the 401(k) program, or the Deferred Income Plan. This plan is one in which an employee and his or her employer make deposits into the employee's retirement program. Taxes are deferred on the money in the account until the employee's retirement. Under the old tax law, an employer was able to deposit up to $30,000 a year in this account. Under the new tax law, however, the upper limit on employer contributions will be $7,000 per year and will be reduced proportionately if the employee has any other tax shelter plan.

Real Estate Investments. Home ownership and other real estate investments received favorable treatment under the old tax law. Under the new law, mortgage interest will still be tax deductible. However, this advantage does not apply for more than two homes owned by the same taxpayer.

Deductions on Consumer Debt. Beginning in 1987, allowable deductions for the interest on consumer debts such as car loans and credit card accounts will be phased out over a five year period. The allowable deduction on consumer debt will be reduced from 65 percent in 1987 to 0 percent in 1991. As a result, many future investment decisions made by American consumers will be shaped more by the marketplace than by the tax code.

Everyday Economics Review

1. Why was the Sixteenth Amendment passed?
2. What problems in the tax codes led many to support tax reform in the 1980s?
3. How will the number of income tax brackets change under the new tax law in 1987 and 1988?
4. What changes does the new tax law make in IRAs? Real estate investments? Deductions for consumer debts?

Everyday Economics Review Answers: 1. gave Congress the power to levy an income tax; 2. inequities, loopholes, and tax regulations; 3. will be reduced from 5 to 2; 4. The tax deduction for IRAs is reduced as income increases. The interest on primary residence is still deductible. The interest on consumer debt will be phased out over the next five years.

10 KEEPING A CHECKING ACCOUNT

May be used with page 230.

Today, one of the easiest ways to pay bills and transfer money to others is through the use of a personal checking account.

Opening A Checking Account

If you have money to deposit, you can open a checking account at any bank or savings and loan institution. Most institutions offer different kinds of checking accounts. In most cases, the right account for you depends on the amount of money that you plan to keep in the account.

The traditional checking account has no minimum or monthly balance requirements. For most of these accounts, however, the customer must pay monthly service charges and check-printing fees. In addition, the amount in the account does not earn interest.

An alternative to the traditional checking account is the NOW account. The NOW account is an interest-bearing savings and checking account. The customer can write checks on the amount deposited and collect interest on the amount remaining. However, the customer usually must keep a minimum monthly balance in the account in order to receive the interest and free-checking privileges. This minimum balance amount can be quite high. The minimum balance on a special NOW account called a super-NOW account is $2,500.

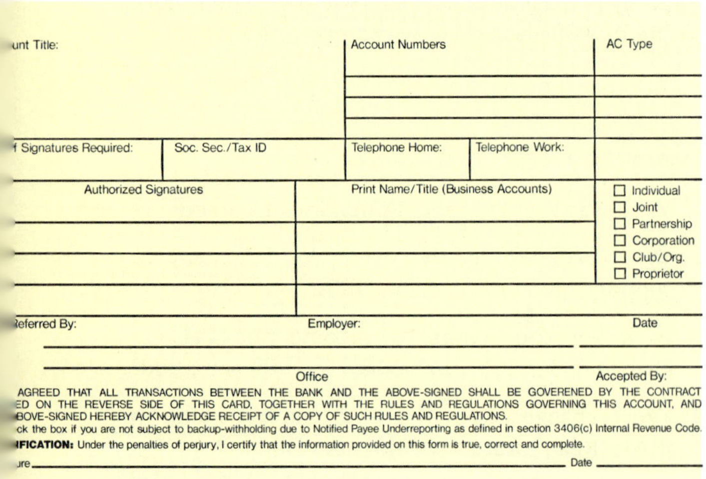

unt Title: | Account Numbers | AC Type

f Signatures Required: | Soc. Sec./Tax ID | Telephone Home: | Telephone Work:

Authorized Signatures | Print Name/Title (Business Accounts)

☐ Individual
☐ Joint
☐ Partnership
☐ Corporation
☐ Club/Org.
☐ Proprietor

ʀeferred By: | Employer: | Date

Office | Accepted By:

AGREED THAT ALL TRANSACTIONS BETWEEN THE BANK AND THE ABOVE-SIGNED SHALL BE GOVERENED BY THE CONTRACT ED ON THE REVERSE SIDE OF THIS CARD, TOGETHER WITH THE RULES AND REGULATIONS GOVERNING THIS ACCOUNT, AND BOVE-SIGNED HEREBY ACKNOWLEDGE RECEIPT OF A COPY OF SUCH RULES AND REGULATIONS.

ck the box if you are not subject to backup-withholding due to Notified Payee Underreporting as defined in section 3406(c) Internal Revenue Code.

IFICATION: Under the penalties of perjury, I certify that the information provided on this form is true, correct and complete.

ure ______ Date ______

Writing and Cashing Checks

A signed check represents money. For this reason, it is important that you follow special procedures both in writing and cashing checks.

Writing Checks. Most checks are printed with the account owner's name, address, and telephone number appearing in the upper left corner and the check number in the upper right corner. Checks are numbered consecutively to help people keep track of what checks they have written.

Near the check number is a place for you to write the date. Across the center of the check are words "Pay to the Order of" and a blank space. In this space, write the name of the person or business to whom you are writing the check. This person or business is known as the payee. To the right of the payee's name are places in which to write the amount of the check in numerals. The amount also should be spelled out in words on the next line.

In the lower left corner of the check is a line labeled "Memo." Use this line to record any information that might be helpful to you about the check, such as what the check was for.

In the lower right corner of the check is a space for you to sign your name. Without your signature, the check cannot be cashed. Across the bottom of the check you will see the name of the bank or S&L in which you have the account. You also will see a series of numbers. The first series is the bank's identification number. The second series is your checking account number.

Cashing Checks. When you receive a personal check from another person, it must be endorsed before it can be cashed. To endorse the check, simply sign your name on the back.

To receive the amount of the check in cash, you must go to the bank in person. There, the teller probably will ask you to write your account number on the check before giving you the cash.

To deposit the check in your checking account, you must fill out a deposit slip. Deposit slips usually are provided to you with your checks. Your name, address, telephone number, and checking account number are printed on the front of the deposit slip, as they appear on your checks. In the center of the deposit slip are spaces in which you must write the date and add up the total amount of the deposit.

If you are depositing several checks, these should be listed separately on the reverse side of the slip. If you are receiving some of the money you deposit back in cash, you should indicate the amount and sign the deposit slip on the line provided.

You may deposit checks through the mail or in person at the bank. If you are sending an endorsed check through the mail, however, it is best to write your account number and the words, "For Deposit Only" beneath your signature. Taking this precaution could prevent someone else from cashing your check.

Recording Your Transactions

Each time that you write or deposit a check, it is important that you keep a record of the transaction. Most banks and S&Ls provide you with a record book for this purpose. In the record book, you should note the check number, date, payee, and amount of each transaction. You also should keep track of your current balance. After writing a check, the amount of the check should be deducted from your balance. After making a deposit, the amount of the deposit should be added to your balance.

Balancing Your Checking Account

To help you verify the amount of money you have in your checking account, your bank or S&L will send you a checking account statement each month. This statement normally includes your balance at the beginning of the month, a listing of the transactions made during the month, and your balance at the end of the month. It also includes an explanation of any special charges made against your account during the month, such as service charges or check-printing fees, as well as any monthly interest added to your balance.

Many banks also include the checks that you wrote and that were cashed by the payees in your monthly statement. These checks are known as cancelled checks. In addition, if you did not receive receipts at the time that you made deposits in your account, many banks also include your deposit slips in your statement.

When you receive your monthly bank statement, it is important that you make sure that the balance you have recorded agrees with the bank's version of your balance. The easiest way to balance your checking account is to follow the directions on the back of the bank's statement. If you find a discrepancy, go back through your record book to verify that you have entered the amounts of all checks correctly. Also, make certain that you have noted which checks have not been cashed. Any time that you cannot reconcile a discrepancy in your records and the bank's statement, call the bank for assistance.

Everyday Economics Review

1. What are the different kinds of checking accounts?
2. What information must be filled in when you write a check?
3. How do you endorse a check?

Handbook

11 APPLYING FOR A MORTGAGE

May be used with page 277.

A loan is a promise to pay a debt, carrying with it the legal responsibility or obligation to do so. A mortgage is a type of a loan. Consumers apply to banks for mortgages in order to finance purchases of property. Most often we associate mortgages with the purchase of a house.

Real Estate Agreements

Most consumers in the housing market use the services of a real estate agent to help them find a house to buy. First, a real estate agent will qualify a person as a buyer by reviewing total income and helping determine how much money the consumer can afford to spend on housing. Then the agent will help find an affordable house that will meet the person's needs.

When deciding to purchase a certain house, a buyer will make a bid on the house to the seller. If the seller agrees to the price, both parties sign a real estate agreement. The price of the house and any special conditions of the sale will be specified in

Everyday Economics Review Answers: 1. traditional checking accounts, NOW accounts, and super-NOW accounts; 2. the date, the name of the person or business to whom you are writing the check, the amount of the check in numbers, the amount of the check spelled out, and your signature; 3. Sign your name on the back.

writing in the agreement. Once the agreement is signed, the house is said to be "under contract." During this time, the seller of the house may not sell it to anyone else while the buyer awaits mortgage approval.

The Lending Institution

Any bank, savings and loan, or other lending institution may grant a mortgage. Wise consumers should shop around for the lowest interest rate before deciding on a lending institution.

When visiting various lending institutions, prospective buyers should gather information about the different types of mortgages available. The most common mortgage is the conventional mortgage. This type of loan is made for a stated period of time, such as 20 years, at a fixed rate of interest. The borrower makes a fixed monthly installment payment that includes repayment of both principal and interest.

Today, several alternatives to the conventional mortgage exist. One of the most popular is the variable rate mortgage (VRM). The VRM is a loan in which flexible interest rates are built into the mortgage. If interest rates drop, the borrower pays less toward interest and more toward principal in his or her fixed installment payments. All interest on mortgages of any type is tax deductible.

After a consumer decides to apply for a certain kind of mortgage, the lending institution must qualify the buyer. This process normally takes several weeks or months. During this time, the lending institution will verify the borrower's income, employment history, current salary, and credit rating. The lending institution then tells the borrower whether the mortgage has been denied or approved.

Closing

Soon after a loan has been approved, the buyer, seller, real estate agent, representatives of the lending institution, and other people involved in the purchase of the house meet to sign the legal papers necessary to close the original agreement. This meeting is referred to as the "closing." The closing usually is the last step in what can be a long process of buying a house.

Everyday Economics Review

1. What is a mortgage?
2. What is specified in a real estate agreement?
3. What will a lending institution verify before approving a loan?

12 APPLYING FOR AND USING CREDIT

May be used with page 276.

As a consumer, one of the most valuable assets you have is credit. Using credit provides a means of making purchases now and paying for them in the future. Most consumers use credit to buy houses, automobiles, appliances, and other large purchases.

How Credit is Extended

Credit can be extended to you by a financial institution or by a vendor selling a product. Financial institutions extend credit by issuing loans such as mortgages, short-term notes, and bank cards such as Visa and Mastercard. Many vendors such as stores and oil companies extend credit by issuing charge cards or credit cards. To apply for most types of credit, you must fill out an application listing such credit information as your place of employment, income, and outstanding debts. If your application is approved, the institution will assign you a credit limit, or amount that you may spend using credit each month.

The Advantages of Credit

One of the most important advantages of credit is that it is convenient. It allows you to buy what you need when you need it. Suppose, for example, that you need to buy a new refrigerator but do not have the cash to buy it right away. If you have the ability to pay over time, the use of credit may be a wise and convenient choice.

Using credit also permits you to take advantage of sales, helping you to save money. In addition, it is much easier to return a defective product that has been purchased using credit rather than cash.

The Disadvantages of Credit

Although credit has many advantages, it also has disadvantages that a wise consumer should consider. The most obvious disadvantage is that credit is not free. For this reason, it is very important that you understand the terms of any credit arrangement you make. The Consumer Credit Protection Act, or "Truth in Lending Act," requires that consumers be informed in writing of the finance charge, total transaction cost, and annual percentage rate associated with the use of credit. Despite this act, however, the real cost of using credit can be deceptive. When interest rates are high and payments are extended over a long period of time, the actual cost of credit increases significantly.

Consumer Credit Ratings

When you first apply for credit, most financial institutions or vendors assign you a credit rating based upon the information provided on your credit application. A credit rating is an estimation of the probability that you will repay your debts. Even if you are assigned a good credit rating and your

Everyday Economics Review Answers: 1. a loan on a house; 2. the price of the house and special conditions of the sale; 3. the borrower's income, employment history, current salary, and credit rating.

CREDIT BUREAU
CONFIDENTIAL REPORT

FOR

DATE RECEIVED	DATE MAILED	WATCH CRITERIA
01/19/87		
TIME		IN FILE SINCE
11:09		6/85

REPORT ON (NAME)	SOCIAL SECURITY NUMBER	SPOUSE'S NAME
ECONOMICS, F.E.	345-AG-0010	

CURRENT ADDRESS	MKT. AREA	SPOUSE SOCIAL SECURITY NO.
5338 RED CLIFF TR., CHICAGO, IL 60611	16 CH.	

PRESENT EMPLOYER AND ADDRESS	CLOCK #	POSITION	DATE VERIFIED	SINCE	INCOME BASIS
U.S. Government, Chicago, IL	0543	Clerk	10/85	June 1985	$27,500

BIRTH DATE	NUMBER OF DEPENDENTS INCLUDING SPOUSE	OWNS/RENTS/BOARDS	TEL. NO.

FORMER ADDRESSES	FROM:	TO:
4344 AQUA VISTA DR., GRAY'S LAKE, FL 32897	7/61	6/85

FORMER EMPLOYER AND ADDRESS	CLOCK #	POSITION	DATE VERIFIED	SINCE	INCOME BASIS

SPOUSE'S EMPLOYER AND ADDRESS	CLOCK #	POSITION	DATE VERIFIED	SINCE	INCOME BASIS

CAUTION: For Consumer's Use Only
Federal Law prohibits
use for credit granting

SUBSCRIBER NAME	SUBSCRIBER CODE	DATE OPENED	ECOA	HIGH CREDIT	DATE CLOSED VERIFIED	PRESENT STATUS: BALANCE OWING	AMOUNT PAST DUE	NPPD	PAYMENT PATTERN				TYPE ACCOUNT & MOP
ACCOUNT NUMBER	COLLATERAL		TYPE LOAN	CREDIT LIMIT	TERMS	MAXIMUM DELINQUENCY: DATE	AMOUNT	MOP	HISTORICAL STATUS: NO OF MONTHS	30–59	60–89	90 +	REMARKS
FNB CHGO VISA	B9850019	2/83	I	$50	2/86P	$0	$0	0	11111111				R01
000-00000				$2000	X10								

Handbook

credit is approved, the businesses continue to rate your credit behavior as you make purchases on credit. Any misuse of your credit is reported to credit bureaus, which keep records of consumer credit ratings. If you fail to make payment on a loan, for example, the lender will report that information to a credit bureau. If you default on several loans, you will have a very poor credit rating and will find it difficult, if not impossible, to obtain credit in the future.

Everyday Economics Review

1. How is credit extended?
2. What are the advantages and disadvantages of credit?
3. Why is it important for you to maintain a good credit rating?

13 INVESTING IN THE STOCK MARKET

May be used with page 296.

The stock market is the organization through which corporate stock certificates are bought and sold. Corporations issue shares of stock in order to finance capital investment. Investors buy shares of stock because, if a corporation makes a profit, the stock can yield high dividends, or cash payments.

Types of Stock

Shares of stock are divided into two types, common stock and preferred stock. The type of stock issued by a corporation depends on the legal organization of the corporation and the decisions made within the corporation as the market changes.

Everyday Economics Review Answers: 1. by financial institutions or by vendors selling a product; 2. advantages: convenience; taking advantage of sales; returning a defective product is easier; disadvantages: it is not free; real cost can be deceptive; actual cost may increase significantly; 3. Misuse of credit will make it difficult to obtain credit in the future.

Common Stock. Owners of common stock receive dividends at a variable rate. When the corporation's profits are high, dividends are high. When the corporation's profits fall, dividends also fall. If a corporation is operating at a loss, it does not pay any dividends on common stock.

Preferred Stock. Owners of preferred stock receive dividends at a fixed rate, regardless of the rise or fall of the corporation's profits. In addition, owners of preferred stock receive their dividends first, before the owners of common stock do.

The Advantages and Disadvantages of Stock Investments

Consumers buy stock as long-term or short-term investments. As long-term investments, stocks can provide a hedge against inflation, are a means of increasing capital, and can provide future income.

People who buy and sell stock for short-term gain are called speculators. The object of speculation is to buy low and sell high in order to make a "quick profit." This type of investing is extremely risky because prices in the stock market are highly volatile in the short-term. As often as investors sell at a high price and earn a profit, they may be forced to sell at a low price and lose money.

Influences on Stock Prices

Almost any economic or political event can affect stock prices in the short term. An increase in the unemployment rate or the election of an unpopular foreign leader can cause stock prices to plummet. The passage of a law in Congress to reduce taxes or the announcement of a falling interest rate can cause stock prices to rise.

Stock prices also are influenced by news about specific corporations. The announcement that a corporation reached a new sales goal, for example, can cause the price of its stock to rise. Rumors of problems in a corporation, however, can cause its stock prices to fall.

Purchasing Stock

Consumers thinking about purchasing stock should follow these guidelines. (1) Look for stock in a growth industry, such as computers and electronics, as opposed to industries in which growth has peaked. (2) Look for corporations with higher-than-average growth rates. (3) Read business periodicals and newspapers to identify corporations with good overall performances. (4) Avoid corporations with large deficits. (5) Look for corporations with consistent dividend increases.

Everyday Economics Review

1. What is the difference between common stock and preferred stock?
2. Why is short-term stock investment risky?

14 INVESTING IN HIGH–GROWTH STOCKS

May be used with page 294.

The goal of a stock market investment is to achieve a high rate of return, either as the result of short-term speculation or over the long-term. Investments in high-growth stocks represent investments over the long-term.

Long-Term Investment and Economic Change

High-growth stocks are stocks in corporations that have high rates of growth over time, despite changes in the economy. The growth rates of such corporations are higher than the growth rates of other corporations, or of the economy as a whole.

When the economy is expanding, many stocks can be categorized as growth stocks. When the economy is contracting, or going through a recession, many stocks lose their growth status. High-growth stocks should be able to withstand recessions and remain in the high-growth category, despite economic downturns. Stocks that achieved high rates of growth despite the recession of the 1960s, for example, were IBM and Xerox.

By definition, growth stocks pay no or few dividends at first. Instead, they grow in value over time. Making money in the business world requires investing money over the long-term. Growing businesses typically invest in capital such as facilities and equipment, new marketing and distribution devices, research and development, and product or service improvement. For this reason, expanding companies normally do not make significant dividend payouts. A person investing in a high-growth stock should not do so with hopes of short-term gain, but in hopes of increased long-term value.

Finding the Right High-Growth Stock

Finding the right high-growth stock is the most difficult task involved in making this type of investment. It is not difficult to identify stocks and companies that have had high growth rates in the past. Knowing whether or not this growth will continue, or if another lower-growth stock or new stock will "take off," is not quite as simple.

Selecting a company with a high-growth potential means choosing a company with significant present earnings. Earnings must be great enough to create profits to reinvest in expansion. In fact, some stock market theoreticians believe the single most important factor in selecting a high-growth stock is choosing one with a high rate of retained earnings and reinvestment relative to the size of the firm.

Other criteria for selecting a high-growth stock should be: the market potential for a company's product or service; the possibilities a company has to benefit from technological change or a restructuring of the economy; freedom from government interference; strong managerial leadership; and relatively low wage requirements.

Everyday Economics Review Answers: 1. Owners of common stock receive dividends at a variable rate. Owners of preferred stock receive dividends first and at a fixed rate. 2. Prices are volatile in the short-term.

Everyday Economics Review Answers: 1. When the economy is expanding, many stocks can be categorized as high-growth stocks. During recessions, many stocks lose their growth status. (Answers continued below.)

No matter how carefully an investor chooses high-growth stock, a possibility of investing in a stock that loses money always exists. Although stockbrokers, annual reports, and financial periodicals help inform consumers, high-growth stocks always represent moderate risks. When investing in such stocks, an individual should be in a financial position to sustain a loss.

Everyday Economics Review

1. How can a long-term investment be affected by changes in the economy?
2. Why is it difficult to identify high-growth stocks?
3. What are the criteria for selecting a high-growth stock?

D-2 The Orlando Sentinel, Tuesday, January 20, 1987

N.Y. Stock Exchange

A

Stock	Div	PE	Sales hds	High	Low	Close	Chg.
AAR s	.50	20	1335	u28	27	28	+1
ADT	.92	..	132	29⅜	28¾	28⅞	— ½
AFG s	.12i	10	1225	35	34	35	— ¼
AGS		21	706	32⅞	31	32⅞	+ 1⅜
AMCA		..	19	7⅜	7¼	7⅜	+ ⅛
AMR		14	9484	60½	57¼	60⅜	+ 2
ANR pf	2.67	..	2	26¼	26¼	26¼	— ¾
ARX	.71t	11	91	11¾	11⅜	11⅝	.....
ASA	2a	..	1614	u42⅛	41	42⅛	+ 2½
AVX		..	1070	14⅞	14⅜	14⅞	+ ¼
AZP	2.72	9	2763	31¼	30⅞	31⅛	+ ⅛
AbtLb s	.84	23	4317	52⅜	50⅝	52⅛	+ ⅝
AccoWd	.56	19	124	29⅜	29	29⅜	+ ½
AcmeC	.40	..	261	11½	11⅛	11½	+ ⅜
AcmeE	.32b	19	79	7⅜	7⅛	7⅜	+ ⅛
AdaEx	3.42e	..	177	21⅝	20⅞	21⅜	+ ⅛
AdmM s		..	15	16	15¾	16	+ ⅛
AdvSys	.62t	15	268	19½	18⅞	18⅞	.....
AMD		..	8827	18½	17½	18½	+ 1⅛
Adobe		..	36	8¼	8⅛	8¼	+ ⅛
Adob pf	1.84	..	87	17¼	17⅛	17¼	.....
Adob pf	2.40	..	52	20	19½	20	+ ⅝
Advest	.12a	10	302	13⅞	13⅝	13⅞	.....
AetnLf	2.64	9	2716	61	59¾	60¾	+ ⅛
AetL pf	3.94e	..	52	52½	52⅛	52⅛	+ ⅛
AfilPb s	.44	39	91	81½	79¾	81¼	— ½
AflPb wi		..	29	41⅝	40½	40⅝	— 1½
Ahmns s	.46	7	14965	21⅛	20⅛	21	.....
Aileen		..	109	4½	4⅛	4¼	— ⅛
AirPrd s	.80	503	3893	40¼	38⅞	40¼	+ 1
AirbFrt	.60	22	136	31⅞	31¾	31¾	— ⅛
Airgas n		..	7	8¾	8¾	8¾	+ ¼
Airlse n	.49e	..	33	19⅛	18⅞	19	+ ⅛
AlMoan	1.60c	..	838	13-32	⅜	⅜	.....
AlaP dpf	.87	..	39	10⅝	10½	10½	.....
AlaP pf	11	..	z60	108½	108½	108½	.....
AlaP pf	8.28	..	z20	94½	94½	94½	.....
AlskAir	.16	18	1718	u24	22¾	23¾	+ ¾
Albrto s	.21	33	171	22½	22	22⅛	— ⅜
AlbCulA	.21	28	138	19⅛	18¾	18⅞	— ½
Albtsns	.84	16	634	46½	46	46⅛	— ⅛
Alcan	.80	..	6438	31⅞	31¼	31¾	— ¼
AlcoStd	1.28	18	274	47⅞	46⅝	47	— ⅞
AlexAlx	1	135	1155	28⅞	28¼	28¼	— ¾
Alexdr		127	45	43½	43⅛	43⅛	— ⅜
AlgCp wi		..	75	68½	68½	68½	— ½
AlgInt		..	219	15⅜	14⅞	15¼	+ ¼
AlgIn pr		..	1	13⅜	13⅜	13⅜	— ¼
Algl pfC		..	15	54⅜	53¾	54⅜	— ⅛
AllgPw	2.92	12	1241	47¾	47⅛	47½	+ ¼
AllenG	.56	16	264	16¾	16⅜	16½	.....
Allen pf	1.75	..	34	23⅛	23	23⅛	+ ¼
AlldPd		12	46	36⅛	35½	35⅝	— ¾
AldSgnl	1.80b	..	5345	44⅜	43⅝	43⅞	— ⅝

Stock	Div	PE	Sales hds	High	Low	Close	Chg.
Boeing	1.20	12	12475	51	49⅜	50¾	— ¼
BoiseC	1.90	24	1500	u71	69½	70¾	+ ⅜
BoltBer	.10	36	712	50¼	47¾	50	+ 1¾
Borden	s1.12	18	2354	51⅞	50¼	51⅜	+ ¼
BorgWa	1	16	1274	40½	39¾	40¼	— ¼
Bormns	.20e	9	114	19¾	19½	19¾	+ ⅛
BCelts n		..	73	15¾	15¼	15¾	+ ¼
BosEd s	1.78	10	894	26¾	26½	26¾	+ ⅛
BosE pr	1.17	..	160	11½	11	11⅜	— ⅜
BosE pr	1.46	..	31	16⅜	16	16⅜	.....
Bowatr	.80	23	4558	35⅝	34⅞	35½	+ ⅛
BrigSt	1.60	18	70	39½	38½	39½	+ ½
BrGas pp		..	2027	11	10⅞	10⅞	— ⅛
BristM	2.80	22	4737	u91⅜	88⅞	91⅜	+ 1
BritPt	2.44e	17	1640	49⅝	49¼	49⅝	+ ⅛
BritTel	1.33e	15	523	34	33⅝	34	+ ¼
Brock n		..	93	9½	9⅜	9⅜	.....
Brckw s	.88	..	97	27½	26¾	27⅛	+ ⅛
BkyUG	s1.66	14	305	25⅞	24⅞	25¾	+ ¾
BwnSh	.40	20	42	21⅛	20⅜	21⅛	+ ½
BrwnGp	1.50	17	99	37½	37	37½	— ¼
BrwnF	.80	28	1100	54⅛	52⅜	53⅞	— ¼
Brnswk	.60	15	1417	38½	37½	38	+ ⅛
BrshWl	.56	27	185	31¾	30¾	31⅝	+ ⅜
Buckeye n		..	417	22¼	21¾	22	— ⅛
Bundy	.80	11	5	26	25¾	26	+ ¼
BunkrH	2.16	..	24	23⅛	22¾	23⅛	+ ¼
BKInv	n1.10e	..	86	20⅞	20¾	20⅞	+ ⅛
BurlnCt		16	1113	23⅝	22	23⅝	+ 1¾
BurlInd	1.64	22	2592	u46⅜	43¼	46⅜	+ 2⅜
BrlNth	2	11	4123	63⅝	61⅞	63½	+ ⅞
BrlNo pf	.55	..	4	8⅞	8¾	8¾	— ¼
Burndy		..	1051	u16	14⅛	15½	+ 1⅛
ButlrIn	.52	38	793	19¼	19	19⅛	— ⅛

C

Stock	Div	PE	Sales hds	High	Low	Close	Chg.
CBI In	.60	18	607	31¾	30¾	31¾	+ ⅞
CBI pf		..	138	53½	53	53½	+ 1
CBS	3	16	642	137¾	136¼	137¾	— ⅛
CCX		..	49	4½	4⅜	4½	.....
CIGNA	2.60	..	2095	60⅛	59½	60	— ⅛
CIG pf	2.75	..	104	31¾	31⅝	31¾	+ ⅛
CIG pf	4.10	..	894	58	57¾	57⅞	— ⅛
viCLC		..	12	15-16	⅞	15-16	+ 1-16
CNA Fn		14	520	57⅝	57	57⅜	— ⅝
CNAI	1.24	..	74	13¾	13⅜	13½	.....
CNW		1238	299	25¼	24¾	24¾	— ¼
CNW pf	2.12	..	36	29½	29¼	29½	+ ½
CPC Int	2.48	21	767	86¾	85⅜	86⅝	+ ⅜
CPC wi		..	2	43¾	43½	43¾	+ ¾
CP Ntl	1.60	11	60	32⅞	32½	32⅝	— ⅜
CRIIM	3.35e	12	90	24	23¾	24	+ ⅛
CRI II	n1.70	..	76	20¾	20⅝	20¾	+ ⅛
CRSS	.34	15	56	16¼	16⅛	16⅛	— ⅜
CSX	1.16	12	2174	32⅜	31¾	32⅜	.....
CTS	1	..	187	32⅝	32½	32½	— ⅛
C 3 Inc		..	1397	13⅜	12½	13¼	+ ⅝
Cabot	.92	13	273	24½	23⅝	24⅜	+ ⅛
Crane s	1.20	22	1037	39¼	38⅛	39	+ ⅜
CrayRs		30	5174	u108¾	100¼	108¾	+ 7¼
CrmpK	1.28	15	30	39½	39¼	39¼	— ¼
CrwnCk		16	92	118¾	117	117½	— 1½
CrysBd		33	631	19⅞	19⅝	19⅝	— ⅛
Culbro	.80a	15	6	41⅛	41	41⅛	+ ⅛
Culinet		..	1781	8⅛	7⅝	8	.....
CumEn	2.20	..	522	72⅜	71½	72	+ ⅛
Cumn pr	3.50	..	5	58	58	58	.....
CurInc	1.10a	..	1	12¾	12¾	12¾	.....
CurtW	1.60	..	2	55¾	55½	55¾	+ ⅝
Cyclops	1.10	14	29	72	71½	71½	— ¾

D

Stock	Div	PE	Sales hds	High	Low	Close	Chg.
DCNY	2.15e	9	117	55¼	54½	55	— ½
DPL	2	18	2707	28¼	27¾	28¼	+ ¼
Dallas	.66	135	30	14⅞	14½	14⅞	+ ¼
DamonC	.20	..	50	14¼	14	14⅛	.....
DanaCp	1.28	16	489	34⅞	34¼	34⅝	— ⅛
Danahr		12	106	14¼	13⅞	14¼	+ ¼
Daniel	.18	..	117	8½	8⅜	8½	.....
DataGn		182	4750	38⅜	35½	38¼	+ 1⅜
Datapt		..	263	5¾	5⅜	5⅝	— ⅛
Datpt pf	4.94	..	5	31⅛	31	31⅛	— ⅛
DtaDsg	.24	6	48	6⅜	6⅛	6⅛	— ⅛
Dayco	.40	48	103	31⅞	31⅝	31¾	— ¼
DaytHd	.92	15	2320	43⅜	42¼	42¾	— ⅝
DPL pf	7.48	..	z100	86⅞	86⅞	86⅞	+ ¼
DPL pf	7.70	..	z330	u90	89	90	+ 1½
DeanF s	.46	20	110	30⅛	29¼	29⅝	— ⅜
DecCa	n.13e	..	9	15¾	15¾	15¾	.....
DIC		13	292	10⅞	10½	10⅞	+ ⅛
Deere	.25	..	1405	26¼	25½	26⅛	+ ⅛
DelmP	2.12	12	1960	33⅞	33½	33¾	— ⅛
DeltaAr	1	31	5285	u55⅜	52¼	55	+ 2
Deltona		..	104	6¼	5⅝	6¼	+ ½
DlxCh s	.64	27	1057	37¾	36¼	37⅝	+ ⅛
DensMf	1.20	39	237	u31¼	30⅝	31¼	+ ⅜
DeSoto	1.40	19	15	u43	42⅝	42⅞	+ ⅛
DetEd	1.68	7	1745	18⅜	18	18⅜	+ ¼
DetE pf	9.32	..	z300	96½	95½	96½	+ 1½
DetE pf	7.45	..	z1720	83¾	83	83	.....
DetE pf	7.36	..	z200	82	82	82	+ ¼
DE pfF	2.75	..	6	26½	26⅛	26⅛	— ¼
DE prR	3.24	..	27	29½	29	29	— ½
DE pfQ	3.13	..	33	28½	28¼	28½	.....
DE pfP	3.12	..	5	28⅛	28⅛	28⅛	— ½
DE pfB	2.75	..	4	26⅜	26⅛	26⅜	.....
DE prO	3.40	..	65	29	28¾	28⅞	.....
DE pfM	3.42	..	17	29⅛	29	29⅛	— ¼
DE prL	4	..	116	28⅞	28¾	28⅞	+ ⅛
DetE pr	2.28	..	24	24½	24⅜	24½	+ ⅛
Dexter s	.60	18	259	23⅝	23⅜	23⅜	— ¼
DiGior	.64	11	146	24¼	24⅛	24⅛	.....
DiaBth	.20	35	377	12¾	12¼	12⅜	— ¼
DiamS	.70r	..	1987	14⅝	14½	14½	.....
DiaSh pf	4	..	123	41	40⅜	40⅞	+ ½
DiaSO	2.80e	..	399	17¼	16⅝	17	— ¼
DianaCp	.30	18	2	11½	11½	11½	+ ⅛
Diebold	1.20	20	1069	53⅜	52¼	53¼	+ ⅞
Digital s		22	17227	u143¾	135	143	+ 6
Disney s	.32	28	5983	51	49½	51	+ 1
DEI	1.44	..	176	26¼	25¼	26¼	+ 1
DivrsIn		11	13	6⅛	6	6⅛	+ ⅛
Dome g	.06	..	4211	9⅝	9⅜	9⅜	+ ⅛
DomRs	2.96	12	1639	47⅝	46¾	47½	+ ⅜
Donald	.66	13	69	38	36¼	38	+ 1⅝
Donley	1.28	17	394	66	64½	65¾	+ ¼
Dorsey s	.64	14	239	24½	23½	24¼	+ 1
Dover	.92	20	613	52	51	51⅝	— ⅝
DowCh	2	52	6408	u70⅛	67	70⅛	+ 2⅛
DowJn s	.56	26	977	u47⅞	45	47½	+ 1¾
Downey	.12i	4	244	20⅞	20⅜	20⅝	— ⅛
Dravo	.50	43	155	19¼	18½	19¼	+ ¾
Dresr	.40	204	4984	u25¼	24¼	24½	.....
DrexB	2	..	32	24½	24⅛	24½	+ ⅜
Dreyfs	s.28a	20	2870	36	33⅞	35½	+ ⅞
duPont	3.20	15	7297	96⅜	94¼	95⅜	— ⅝
duPnt pf	3.50	..	3	50	50	50	.....
duPnt pf	4.50	..	9	63⅝	63⅝	63⅝	— ⅜

Stock	Div	PE	Sales hds	High	Low	Close	Chg.
FlaStl	.80	9	313	25⅛	24⅝	24⅝	— ¾
FlwGen		..	247	5½	5¼	5⅜	+ ⅛
Flower	.56	21	97	26¾	26½	26⅝	+ ⅛
Fluor	.40	..	1114	14	13⅜	13⅞	— ⅛
FooteC	2.20	14	80	54½	54¼	54¼	— ⅜
FordM	s2.60	6	7599	70⅜	68⅞	70¼	+ ¼
FtDear	1.36	..	23	16	15⅞	15⅞	.....
FtHowd	1	22	886	54¼	53	53⅞	— ⅜
FostWh	.44	21	358	14½	14⅛	14⅜	.....
Foxbro	.25e	..	136	25⅞	25½	25⅞	.....
Franc n		..	766	12	11¾	11⅞	+ ⅜
FrnkR s	.24	27	395	u41¼	38⅝	41¼	+ 1⅞
FMEP	2.20	..	224	16¼	16⅛	16¼	+ ⅛
FMGC	.05e	56	333	13	12¼	12⅞	+ ⅞
FMOG	.85e	3	150	5⅞	5½	5¾	.....
FrptMc	2e	69	1178	19⅞	19½	19⅞	+ ¼
FMRP	n2.40	..	148	20⅞	20½	20⅝	+ ⅛
FruhfB		..	258	5⅝	5⅜	5½	.....
Frhf pfA	3.68	..	413	22⅛	21⅞	22⅛	+ ⅛
Fuqua s	.24	11	1556	27½	25¾	27¼	.....

G

Stock	Div	PE	Sales hds	High	Low	Close	Chg.
GAF s	.10	16	1412	40⅛	39½	40	+ ⅜
GATX	1.50	19	168	37½	36⅝	37½	+ ¾
GATX pf	2.50	..	5	46	46	46	.....
GCA		..	772	2	1⅞	2	+ ⅛
GEICO	1.08	14	146	121½	117⅜	121⅛	— ⅜
GEO		..	99	2⅜	2¼	2⅜	+ ⅛
GF Cp		..	17	5⅝	5⅜	5⅝	+ ⅛
GTE	3.66	..	4551	61¼	60⅝	61	.....
GTE wi		..	22	41¼	40⅞	41¼	+ ⅜
GTE pf	2	..	9	33	32¾	33	.....
GTE pf	2.48	..	23	30⅜	29⅞	30⅜	+ ⅜
Gabeli n		..	882	9½	9¼	9¼	— ⅛
GalHou		..	86	2½	2¼	2½	— ⅛
Gannett	s.92	25	2665	41	40¼	41	+ ¼
Gap s	.50	24	1039	38⅝	37¾	38	— ⅝
Gearht	.20i	..	790	2½	2¼	2½	+ ⅛
Gelco		..	155	20⅞	20¾	20¾	+ ⅛
Gelco pf		..	374	16⅜	16¼	16¼	— ⅛
GemII C		..	841	u15⅛	14⅜	15	+ ⅛
GemII I	1.33e	..	147	15	14⅞	15	+ ⅛
GnCorp	1.50b	18	273	79¾	77¾	79¾	+ 1⅜
GAInv	2.51e	..	106	19⅜	19	19⅛	— ⅛
GCinm	.60	14	726	47	46¼	46¾	— ⅛
GCin pf	.66	..	5	46⅛	46⅛	46⅛	— ⅜
GnData		38	233	9⅞	9½	9¾	+ ⅛
GenDev		8	305	19⅞	19¼	19⅜	— ¾
GnDyn	1	9	607	75½	74⅛	74¾	— ½
GenEl	2.52	17	16228	u95⅝	93⅜	94⅞	+ ⅞
GnHme		7	49	8⅞	8½	8⅝	+ ⅛
GHost s	.24	12	415	14⅞	14¼	14⅝	— ⅜
GnHous	.24	35	37	10½	10⅛	10½	+ ⅜
GnInst	.25	42	1666	21⅛	20⅜	20⅞	.....
GnMill	s1.28	19	2169	45⅞	44⅞	45¼	— ⅛
GMot	5e	7	10134	70	68	70	+ 1¼
GM E	.40	15	3557	30¼	28⅞	30¼	+ ½
GM H	.45e	..	277	40¾	40⅛	40½	+ ¼
GNC	.16	..	99	5⅝	5¼	5½	+ ⅛
GPU		9	1976	24⅜	23¾	24¼	.....
GenRe s	.88	22	2819	57⅞	56½	57¾	— ⅛
GnRefr		8	98	18½	17¾	18½	+ ⅝
GnSignl	1.80	40	272	49⅜	47¾	48⅜	+ ⅛
GTFI pf	1.30	..	z200	17¼	17¼	17¼	.....
Gensco		..	366	4⅛	3⅞	4⅛	+ ⅛
GnRad		..	793	10⅜	9¾	10⅛	— ⅛
GenuPt	1.28a	21	282	48⅜	47⅜	48⅜	+ ⅜
GaPac	1	20	4988	44½	42¾	44⅜	+ 1⅜
GaPc pf	2.24	..	52	47¾	47½	47½	— ¼
GaP prB	2.24	..	4	u47⅞	47½	47⅞	+ ⅞
GaPc prC	2.24	..	1	46½	46½	46½	— ½
GaPwr pf	2.30	..	23	26⅞	26⅜	26⅞	+ ⅛
GaPwr pf	2.47	..	67	27⅜	27⅛	27⅛	— ¼
GaPw pf	1.91e	..	100	22⅝	22⅝	22⅝	+ ⅝
GaPw pf	3	..	17	29½	29	29¼	.....
GaPw pf	3.44	..	10	30⅜	29¾	30⅜	.....
GaPw pf	3.76	..	99	31	30½	30½	— ½
GaPw pr	2.56	..	7	27⅛	27	27	— ⅛
GaPw pf	2.52	..	21	26½	26¼	26¼	— ½
GaPw pf	2.75	..	8	27⅞	27⅝	27¾	— ⅛

Handbook

2. It is difficult to determine if growth will continue, or if a lower-growth stock will "take off."
3. choosing a company with earnings and reinvestment relative to the size of the firm, market potential, possibilities from technological or economic change, freedom from government interference, strong management, and low wages.

15 UNDERSTANDING MUTUAL FUNDS

May be used with page 338.

One of the most popular investment choices for consumers today is mutual funds. A mutual fund is a fund in which investors' money is pooled to purchase a variety of securities.

As investments, mutual funds have a number of advantages. Most important, mutual funds are managed by professional financial experts who know market trends, thus freeing investors from the time and effort required to purchase securities on their own. Such management also helps limit the risks of investment. In addition, mutual funds enable investors to buy a variety of securities with a minimal amount of money because the funds allow investors to pool their capital.

Kinds of Mutual Funds

Stock market, money market, and bond market securities are three different types of securities available through a mutual fund.

Stock Market Mutual Funds. Buying stocks in a mutual fund has several advantages. Buying several different kinds of stock minimizes the risk of loss by spreading the investment out over several possible outcomes—a process known as diversification. For their stock investments, many consumers prefer to pool their money with a number of other people, invest in several different stocks, and hire a professional manager to manage their investments.

Money Market Mutual Funds. Money markets are markets in which investors lend money on a

short-term basis to banks, businesses, and governments. Money market certificates generally pay the current interest rate, called a yield. A money market mutual fund is a mutual fund investing in a variety of short-term money market instruments. The typical interest rate for such funds often is relatively high. In addition, because they are for the short-term, money market mutual funds enable investors to switch to other investments as market conditions change.

Bond Market Mutual Funds. Bond markets are markets in which investors lend money to governments and corporations for a relatively long period of time and at a fixed rate of interest. Investors generally invest in bond markets when the interest rate is high and is expected to drop, because the bond's yield is guaranteed at a high rate. Bond market mutual funds, or bond funds, are funds in which investments are made in a variety of bonds.

How to Invest in Mutual Funds

Investors can buy a mutual fund from a stockbroker, an insurance salesperson, or on their own. Some mutual funds require consumers to pay a sales commission. By law, this commission cannot be more than 8.5 percent. Other funds, called "no-load" funds, do not charge sales commissions. However, all mutual funds charge consumers with a professional management fee.

Investors who want to invest in a mutual fund on their own, may subscribe to a mutual fund advisory service, or study the publications of such services in the library. Charges for advisory service publications range from $20 to $120 per year.

Everyday Economics Review

1. What are the advantages of investing in a mutual fund?
2. What is diversification?
3. Describe three types of mutual fund investments.

16 BUYING INSURANCE POLICIES

May used with page 363.

Careful financial planning should include plans for the unexpected. As a consumer, different types of insurance policies can help protect you and your family in times of crisis.

Kinds of Insurance Policies

Many different kinds of insurance policies are available today to meet a variety of needs. Among the most important are automobile insurance, homeowner's or renter's insurance, medical insurance, disability insurance, and life insurance.

Automobile Insurance. Two basic types of automobile insurance—collision insurance and liability insurance—are available. Collision insurance pays for damages to your car if you are involved in an accident. Most collision policies include a deductible, or specified amount of the repair cost that you must pay despite your insurance coverage. Liability insurance pays for the medical expenses of those injured in an accident and for damages to property.

Homeowner's and Renter's Insurance. Like automobile insurance, two kinds of homeowner's or renter's insurance—property insurance and liability insurance—are available. Property insurance will pay for the replacement or repair of a dwelling or other structure on your property, as well as its contents. If you are renting an apartment and do not own the structure, it still is a good idea to buy insurance on the contents of your apartment. Liability insurance pays for the medical expenses of persons injured on your property.

Medical and Disability Insurance. Traditionally, medical insurance was available only as part of a major medical insurance plan, which pays for medical expenses billed by the doctors and hospitals of your choice. Not all medical services are covered, however, and some that are include deductibles. Today, another form of medical insurance, known as Health Maintenance Organizations (HMOs), is available. HMOs pay for medical expenses billed by the

Everyday Economics Review Answers: 1. They are managed by financial experts who know market trends. Because investors pool capital, a variety of securities can be purchased with a minimum investment. 2. Buying several different kinds of stock spreads the investment out over several possible outcomes. 3. stock market, money market, and bond market mutual funds.

Handbook

doctors and hospitals designated by the organization. Often, these plans cover medical expenses such as yearly examinations and well-baby care in an effort to prevent future medical problems. Disability insurance provides income assistance to those who become disabled and can no longer work.

Life Insurance. Life insurance pays benefits to the families of people who die. Two kinds of life insurance available are term insurance and whole life insurance. Term insurance expires after a specified period of time. Individuals who have young children or large mortgages often invest in term insurance because it is relatively inexpensive and will allow a surviving spouse to raise children and pay off a mortgage or other large debts. Whole life insurance covers you throughout your life and offers dividends that are generally used to pay for more insurance after the policy has been in effect a certain number of years. In most cases, whole life insurance is more expensive than term insurance.

How to Buy Insurance

Different kinds of insurance, especially medical, disability, and life insurance, usually are offered as part of an employer's benefits package. When you buy other kinds of insurance individually, be sure that the insurance company from which you buy is an established company with a reputation for making payments readily and in full. If you need more than one kind of insurance, shop around to find the company that can offer you the best insurance package.

Everyday Economics Review

1. What is the purpose of insurance policies?
2. What are the major kinds of insurance policies?

Everyday Economics Review Answers: 1. to protect you and your family in times of crisis; 2. automobile, homeowner's or renter's, medical, disability, and life insurance.

17 BUYING A NEW CAR

May be used with page 390.

Buying a car involves making a number of decisions. These decisions simplify the process and result in maximum satisfaction and savings. To help you in this decision-making process, you should consider several factors before even visiting an automobile showroom. Among these are the size and style of the car you want to buy; the amount you can afford to spend; and whether you want a foreign or domestic car.

Size and Style

When you consider the size and style of the car you want, you will be defining how you plan to use your car and the models that you will consider as you shop. Large families often prefer larger cars. Single persons or couples often prefer smaller cars. People who do a lot of traveling often want larger cars for comfort. At the same time, however, smaller cars get better gas mileage and are very practical for short distances such as commuter trips and shopping excursions. If you use your car to transport materials for your business, you will find that some models suit your needs better than others. You can choose from a variety of models—sedans, station wagons, hatchbacks, jeeps, vans, and pickup trucks.

Style often is a matter of personal preference. Most models will be available in a variety of colors. The basic lines and design of the cars also will vary. In some cases, you may be able to save money if you are flexible about color and design extras such as pinstripes because dealers often will accept a lower price for models that they have in stock.

What You Can Afford to Spend

When deciding what you can afford to spend on a car, you must consider the total price of the car as well as options, initial fees, and maintenance costs.

CHEVROLET Division of General Motors Corporation GM

MODEL: 1987 S10 BLAZER 4WD — VEHICLE IDENTIFICATION NUMBER: 1GNCT18RXH8130224 0038532

DEALER TO WHOM DELIVERED: DON MEALEY CHEVROLET INC. ORLANDO FL — 26-339 AM3030 JC

DELIVERED TO DEALER AT (IF DIFFERENT FROM ABOVE) ORLANDO FL — FINAL ASSEMBLY POINT: SHREVEPORT, LA. USA

THE FOLLOWING ITEMS ARE STANDARD ON THIS MODEL AT NO EXTRA CHARGE UNLESS REPLACED BY OPTIONAL EQUIPMENT:

* 13.2 GALLON FUEL CAP	* FOLD DOWN ENDGATE AND LIFT REAR GLASS	* TWO STAGE LEAF TYPE REAR SPRINGS	* HEADLAMP WARNING BUZZER
* DELCO FREEDOM BATT	* FLUIDIC WINDSHIELD WIPERS/WASHERS	* FRONT STABILIZER BAR	* ELECTRONIC FUEL INJECTED ENGINE
* 15 INCH TIRES AND WHEELS	* FULL INTERIOR TRIM	* POWER DISC/DRUM BRKS	* COLUMN MOUNTED SMART SWITCH
* STEEL BELTED TIRES	* RH LH SUNSHADES	* TWO DOME LAMPS	* EZ-ENTRY RH SEAT
* TINTED GLASS (ALL)	* SIDE WINDOW DEFOGGER	* LOCKABLE GLOVE COMPT	
* INSIDE HOOD RELEASE		* DUAL OUTSIDE MIRRORS	

MANUFACTURER'S SUGGESTED RETAIL PRICE OF THIS MODEL INCLUDING DEALER PREPARATION: 11,588.00

MANUFACTURER'S SUGGESTED RETAIL DELIVERED PRICE FOR OPTIONAL EQUIPMENT INSTALLED ON THIS VEHICLE BY MANUFACTURER

AJ1	DEEP TINTED GLASS	200.00
AM7	FOLDING REAR SEAT	359.00
A78	RECLINING SEAT BACKS	74.00
B32	FRONT COLOR-KEYED FLOOR MATS	16.00
B33	REAR COLOR KEYED FLOOR MATS	12.00
B93	DOOR EDGE GUARD MOLDINGS	18.00
C60	AIR CONDITIONING-FRONT	NO CHARGE
D45	EXT.BELOW-EYE-LINE-MIR-BRIGHT	87.00
D55	CONSOLE	114.00
E55	TAILGATE BODY	NO CHARGE
H04	REAR AXLE - 4.11 RATIO	38.00
LL2	2.8 LITER EFI V6 GAS ENGINE	295.00
MX0	4-SPD. AUTO. TRANS. W/OVERDRIVE	735.00
NK2	20 GALLON FUEL TANK	51.00
N33	COMFORTILT STEERING WHEEL	121.00
N40	POWER STEERING	275.00
N90	CAST ALUMINUM WHEELS	252.00
QJL	P205/75R15 OOR SB RAD W/L FT/RR	167.00
TT4	HALOGEN HEADLAMPS	24.00
UX1	ELEC TUNED AM STEREO, FM STEREO RAD W/SK&SC,CASS TAPE, W/SEARCH & REPEAT, GRAPH EQUAL & CLOCK	604.00
V54	LUGGAGE CARRIER - PAINTED	126.00
YC2	TAHOE EQUIPMENT	657.00
YL7	ANNIVERSARY SAVINGS SPECIALS	NO CHARGE
ZK5	FULL SIZE OOR SPARE TIRE	76.00
ZQ2	OPERATING CONVENIENCE PACKAGE	344.00
ZY8	SPECIAL TWO-TONE PAINT	177.00
21U	21 LIGHT BLUE 28 GALAXY BLUE	NO CHARGE
23E	HDD4 BLUE SPL CUS CLO HI BK BKT	NO CHARGE

THIS GM PRODUCT, INCLUDING ALL COMPONENTS, IS PRODUCED FOR CHEVROLET BY VARIOUS GM OPERATIONS AND SUPPLIERS TO GM WORLDWIDE.

Compare this vehicle to others in the **FREE GAS MILEAGE GUIDE** available at the dealer

OPTIONS SUBTOTAL	4,822.00
DESTINATION CHARGE	340.00
TOTAL AMOUNT	16,750.00

CITY MPG — Gas Mileage — HIGHWAY MPG

Options. All vehicles are manufactured with standard equipment. The list price of the car is the base price without options. Options are added features that are not necessary for the operation of the car. You will have many options to choose from, but you should know that each increases the price of the car. Among the options available on many cars are leather interiors, electronic dashboards, AM-FM stereo radios and tape decks, rear window defoggers, chrome styling, automatic window controls, whitewall tires, and a variety of technical equipment.

After you have identified the base price of the car, consider the options you want one at a time. It may be a good idea to rank the options in order of priority, listing those most important to you first. Then, list the prices of the options. This may help you identify those options that will meet your needs and that you can afford, as well as those that you are willing to give up. When budgeting for options, also keep in mind that you will need to consider the costs of initial fees and the continuing costs of owning a car.

Initial Fees and Continuing Costs. Initial fees are one-time charges for items such as sales tax, title, and original license plates. These costs usually are not included in the base price of the car.

The amount for sales tax may be more than you expect. Sales taxes are set at given percentage rates that vary from state to state. In many cases, the sales tax on an automobile adds up to hundreds of dollars.

In addition to initial fees, the continuing costs of owning a car must be considered when thinking about your budget. These include insurance premiums, safety and performance records, repair and maintenance costs, license plate renewal, and gas mileage. This type of information for most models of American and foreign cars may be found in publications such as *Consumer Reports,* which is available at your local library or newsstand.

Once you have compared the prices of different car models and options, compare the prices offered at different car dealers before making a final buying decision. You may find that certain dealers can make you a better offer for the basic car that you want than others can. It is a good idea to shop around, work with salespeople, and compare your options until you are satisfied that you are buying the car you want at the best possible price.

Foreign Cars

In the 1960s, the most popular imported car was the Volkswagen. It was known as an economy car because it was relatively affordable, easy to repair, and less expensive to operate because it got good gas mileage.

In the years that followed, many other foreign cars began to compete with Volkswagen in the American car market. Over time, the foreign cars became more and more popular in the United States. Many consumers came to believe that the smaller, more economical foreign cars had significant advantages over the larger American-made cars.

When gasoline prices skyrocketed in the 1970s, American manufacturers began an effort to downsize American cars. Almost every major American

Handbook

auto company produced what they called a "compact" model to compete with imported vehicles.

Most American car manufacturers, however, believed that high gasoline prices were temporary. From the sales of American-made compact models, the manufacturers had reason to believe that Americans would not continue to purchase smaller cars when the price of gasoline went down. As a result, many American manufacturers failed to invest in the styling, safety features, and special options that might have made compact cars more desirable to the American buyer. This trend provided increased opportunities for foreign automobile competition in American markets. The strength of the United States dollar in foreign markets also meant that foreign cars were relatively less expensive for consumers than they otherwise might have been. Some of the manufacturers that gained a significant hold in the American market as a result were Toyota, Honda, Mitsubishi, and Nissan.

American automobile makers began to take foreign competition more seriously in the 1980s. A new effort to produce stylish cars with downsized engines, better safety features, better gas mileage, and unique high-tech features was made. In addition, certain Japanese car manufacturers began to build their cars in American plants. In this way, American companies were able to profit from foreign competition more directly.

Whether you decide to purchase an American-made car or a foreign car, you have a wide range of choices as a consumer. Keep in mind that your overall goal is to buy a car that suits your needs, as well as your budget.

Everyday Economics Review

1. What should consumers keep in mind when deciding on the size and style of a car?
2. What costs does the total price of a car include?
3. What impact has foreign competition had on American car manufacturers?

18 APPLYING FOR A PASSPORT

May be used with page 428.

Many consumers spend years budgeting for a vacation. After such careful planning, it is important that you take all of the steps necessary to make sure that your vacation is enjoyable as well as economical. If you are planning a vacation to another country, one of the first things to do is to apply for a passport.

Everyday Economics Review Answers: 1. how you plan to use the car, how many people will use it, and personal preference; 2. the car's price, options, initial fees, and maintenance costs; 3. In the 1970s, American manufacturers failed to design desirable compact cars. In the 1980s, an effort was made to produce compact cars with features attractive to American buyers.

Handbook

Who Needs a Passport

A passport is a document that provides identification for people who travel in foreign countries. Passports are issued by government officials to their citizens upon request. A passport identifies the holder as a citizen of the nation that issued the document. It also requests protection for the citizen while he or she is traveling in other countries.

Any American planning to travel abroad must obtain a passport issued in his or her name in order to enter most foreign countries. A few countries, however, do not require Americans to have passports. These countries are Canada, Mexico, Bermuda, and most of the West Indies. Americans traveling in these countries only need proof of their citizenship such as a birth certificate, naturalization papers, or a voter's registration card.

How to Apply for a Passport

American passports are issued by the Department of State in Washington, D.C. A passport must be applied for in person. You may apply to officials of the Department of State in Washington, D.C., and several other cities across the country; clerks of federal courts and certain state courts; designated state judges; designated postal employees; and United States diplomatic officials abroad.

When you apply for a passport, you will be required to show proof of your citizenship. For citizens born in the United States, this proof should be in the form of a birth certificate. American citizens who were born in other countries but who claim citizenship due to the citizenship of their parents also must show a special government certificate to prove their citizenship. If this certificate is not available, documentation of the parents' citizenship would be acceptable. Naturalized citizens must show proof of citizenship by providing a naturalization certificate.

In addition to proof of citizenship, you also must provide two identical photographs of yourself. The photographs should be recent, should show a good likeness of your face, and should be two inches by two inches.

After you present these items to the passport official, you will be asked to fill out a passport application and pay a passport fee. Once everything is submitted, it usually takes from three to four weeks to receive your passport.

Passports are valid for 5 years for children and 10 years for adults. If you have been issued a passport in the past and want to obtain a new one, you may apply by mailing a special application along with your old passport and supporting documents to the nearest passport office.

Visas

In addition to a passport, some countries require foreign travelers to have a visa. A visa is a special stamp that government officials of foreign countries put on a traveler's passport. Without a visa, some countries deny travelers entry. For information about obtaining a visa, write to the Department of State or to the American consular office in the country you are planning to visit.

Everyday Economics Review

1. What is a passport?
2. How does an American citizen obtain a passport?

Everyday Economics Review Answers: 1. an identification document for people traveling in foreign countries; 2. apply in person to officials of the Department of State, clerks of federal courts and certain state courts, designated state judges or postal employees, or United States diplomatic officials abroad.

19 VACATIONING IN FOREIGN COUNTRIES

May be used with page 455.

Tourism is as much a business as any other form of free enterprise. In the last two decades, countries, states, and cities have become increasingly aware that travelers from other places create jobs in hotel, motel, restaurant, resort, and other tourist places and that tourism is an industry of importance. The hotel, motel, restaurant, and resort industries bring money and economic activity into their areas. Many foreign countries have attempted to attract visitors from the United States, just as the United States attempts to attract foreign visitors. Were you to see some interesting publicity and decide to take your next vacation outside of the United States, you might begin planning your trip with the help of a travel agent.

Planning your Trip

Travel agents can describe what you would see on a typical excursion of the country or group of countries you wish to visit. A trip to Canada, for example, would be the choice of some consumers. Other people would prefer to visit several different countries in Europe. A wide selection of options provides the consumer the opportunity to travel to almost any destination of his or her choice.

In addition to information concerning points of interest, travel agents sell tours. For a fee, a travel agent will make all the necessary arrangements prior to your departure date. Transportation, hotel accomodations, meals, and guided tours of specific points of interest are items generally included in the price of a tour. However, the wise consumer will verify what is or is not included. Some tours, for example, may be less expensive but may not include all meals or transportation fees after you reach your destination.

Preparing for Your Departure

Once you have selected a destination and have made satisfactory arrangements for your trip, you should consider several other aspects of traveling in a foreign country before your departure. It is a good idea to verify through your travel agent, or from numerous books available on travel, what specific documents or other information you need before your departure. To travel almost anywhere in the world, for example, you will need a passport. Many countries also have special medical requirements. Obtaining information on the exchange of currency and the customs regulations of the specific country or group of countries you plan to visit also will prevent unnecessary delays once you are ready to leave the United States.

Medical Requirements. As a student, you probably have been required to have certain vaccinations and inoculations to protect you from specific illnesses. When you travel abroad, these vaccinations and inoculations continue to protect you from diseases. However, different countries require different inoculations. Verify the specific requirements of the country you wish to visit and make arrangements for these inoculations to be administered prior to your departure.

Although almost all foreign countries have physicians who speak English, it is wise to anticipate some medical needs before you leave on your trip. If you take a specific medication, be sure to have your prescription filled before you leave. Also, any medical records pertaining to specific medical problems should be available in case of the need for emergency medical treatment.

Exchange of Currency. Because a trip abroad usually consists of a tour lasting several days or weeks, you will need to plan your budget accordingly. Your tour will probably be paid for before your departure date. Some hotels and restaurants in foreign countries may accept American dollars and major credit cards. However, most of your other expenses will be paid for with the currency of the country you are visiting.

Exchange rates allow the consumer to exchange units of one monetary system for equivalent units of another monetary system. These rates vary from country to country and from day to day. The rates of exchange are posted for consumers at many American banks and airports, where currency may be conveniently exchanged. Currency also may be exchanged at banks and other designated areas in foreign countries. In some foreign countries, especially Third World nations and Communist nations, travel is restricted to designated areas. In such countries currency also is limited and must be accounted for as you enter the country and again when you leave.

Customs. Once you have exchanged American dollars for the currency of the country you will be visiting, you will be ready for the trip you have planned. While traveling in a foreign country, you will have the opportunity to purchase a variety of interesting souvenirs. Large items may be shipped to your home address. You may choose to carry other items back with you. Whenever you cross the border of a foreign country or return to the United States, however, you must declare these items at customs.

Customs offices are located at border crossings, seaports, and international airports throughout the world. Customs officials are responsible for inspecting items brought into a country by travelers. When you go through customs, officials look through your luggage, searching for goods on which a customs duty may be due. The officials also search for goods that may be illegal.

Although going through customs can be a time-consuming process, it is not always the case. Keep in mind, too, that going through customs also protects the consumer. Some plants and animals, for example, must be isolated for a specified time before being cleared through customs. This process is a safeguard against disease or other problems that could harm people and plant life.

Everyday Economics Review

1. How can a travel agent be helpful to a consumer planning a trip?
2. Why is it important to allow extra time to obtain a passport, visa, and medical documents?
3. Where can a consumer exchange American dollars for foreign currency?

Everyday Economics Review Answers: 1. They can describe your trip and if you buy the tour, make all arrangements. 2. to prevent unnecessary delays once you are ready to leave the United States; 3. many American banks and airports, banks and other designated areas in foreign countries.

Careers in the Marketplace

Planning for a career is one of the most important steps a student can take to plan for the future. Careers in the Marketplace has been designed to describe several career options in fields related to economics. For further information about these and other careers, you may wish to consult the latest edition of the *Occupational Outlook Handbook*, published by the United States Department of Labor. The *Handbook* contains detailed descriptions of a variety of jobs, including working conditions, qualifications, current salaries, and job outlooks.

Accountants

May be used with page 273.

Accountants prepare, analyze, and verify the financial reports used by company and government officials to make financial decisions. The four largest fields in accounting are public accounting, management, government accounting, and internal auditing.

Most employers require a bachelor's degree in accounting or a related field to fill entry-level positions. Many prefer applicants with a master's degree in business administration. Certification and licensing also are important in this field. Certified public accountants (CPAs), for example, must have a certificate and license issued by the state. To obtain these credentials, candidates must pass the Uniform CPA Examination. Most states also require candidates to have some public accounting experience.

Actuaries

May be used with page 297.

Actuaries assemble and analyze the statistics related to insurance plans in order to maintain a plan's financial stability. They calculate the probabilities of death, sickness, injury, unemployment, and property loss to determine the claims an insurance company can expect and the premium rates the company should charge.

Most actuaries work for insurance companies, with the majority working for life insurance companies. Companies prefer applicants with a bachelor's degree in mathematics, statistics, or actuarial science. Actuaries also are expected to pass a series of exams offered by the professional actuarial societies. Those who pass the first few exams while still in school often have the best employment opportunities.

Air Traffic Controllers

May be used with page 160.

Air traffic controllers guide the flight paths of aircraft within assigned airspace. Their main goal is to maintain air safety. They also work to direct air traffic with a minimum of delays. Many controllers work in airports, monitoring the flow of air traffic in and out of the area. Others work in enroute radar stations, guiding air traffic between airports.

Air traffic controllers work for the federal government. They are selected through the civil service system and must pass a written exam, as well as physical and psychological tests. Applicants with college degrees or previous experience as air traffic controllers, pilots, or navigators have the best job opportunities.

Banking Officers

May be used with page 236.

Banks, savings and loans, and other financial institutions have one or more officers who oversee various aspects of the institution's business. Among these are branch managers, treasurers, controllers, mortgage loan officers, credit and collection managers, foreign-exchange traders, and international banking officers.

Most banking officer positions are filled by employees who have worked their way up through a financial institution's management training program. Applicants for such training programs usually are college graduates in business, economics, or liberal arts. Applicants with a master's degree in business administration have the best job opportunities.

Consumer Safety Inspectors

May be used with page 186.

Consumer safety inspectors work to protect the public from health and safety hazards. The inspectors periodically check businesses that produce foods, drugs, and certain other products to see that the companies are in compliance with current regulations. The consumer safety inspectors discuss their observations with company officials and submit formal reports of their findings.

The vast majority of consumer safety inspectors are employed by the federal and state governments. Some, however, work for businesses such as insurance companies and manufacturing firms. To qualify, most applicants are required to have a college education as well as specific product knowledge. Government inspectors also must pass a written civil service exam.

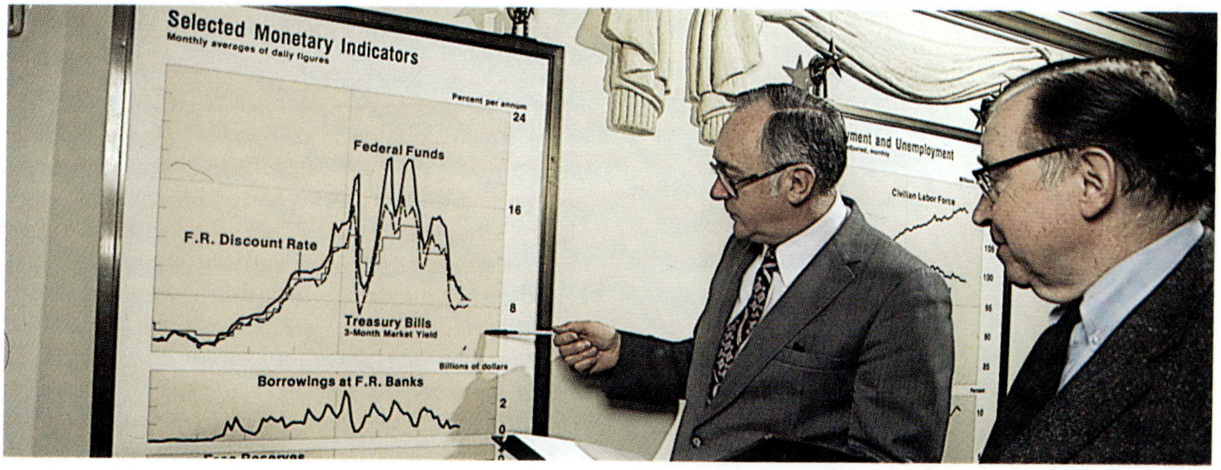

Credit Managers

May be used with page 279.

Credit managers make the final decision as to whether to accept or reject an application for credit from an individual consumer or a business. Working with a company's credit investigators, credit managers study the information provided on a credit application and review the applicant's background and credit history before making a decision about extending the company's credit.

Many credit managers, especially those who handle consumer credit, are employed by retail trade companies such as department stores. Others are employed by manufacturing firms and financial institutions. Employers prefer to hire college graduates with a degree in business or economics. Many prefer those with a master's degree in business administration.

Customs Inspectors

May be used with page 200.

Customs inspectors enforce the laws governing imports and exports. They work at airports, seaports, and border crossing points throughout the nation. When commercial cargoes enter or leave the United States, the inspectors examine, count, weigh, gauge, measure, and sample the shipments to ensure that all merchandise is declared, determine the proper amount of tax to be paid, and search for illegal or dangerous items. Customs inspectors also check the luggage of foreign travelers.

Customs inspectors work for the federal government. The standard qualifications for the position are a combination of education and experience. Applicants also must pass a written civil service exam.

Economists

May be used with page 29.

Economists study the way a society uses its resources to provide goods and services that meet the needs and wants of its people. Some economists are theoreticians. Most, however, are concerned with the practical application of economic theory to fields such as finance, labor, agriculture, and health.

Many economists work in private businesses such as manufacturing, market research, advertising, and investment firms. Many work for the government, analyzing economic conditions and assessing the impact of government policies. Some economists also teach in colleges and universities. A bachelor's degree in economics is required for most entry-level positions, but graduate training is needed for advancement. A Ph.D. is required for most top positions in business and education.

Electricians

May be used with page 153.

Electricians assemble, install, and maintain the wiring for electrical systems that operate lighting and machinery. Most electricians specialize either in construction or maintenance, although some electricians work in both categories.

Electricians should have average strength, good vision, agility, and dexterity. High school or vocational school courses in electricity, electronics, mechanical drawing, science, and mathematics all provide a good background for electrical work. Most electricians learn their trade by completing a four-year apprenticeship program that includes both classroom instruction and on-the-job training.

Employee-Benefits Managers

May be used with page 320.

Employee-benefits managers oversee the benefits programs that a company provides for its employees. Most employee-benefits managers are primarily concerned with an organization's health insurance and pension plans. In recent years, however, managers have become increasingly involved in coordinating a variety of other benefits offered by employers, including everything from additional insurance programs, stock options, and profit-sharing plans to company cafeterias, employee discounts, and fitness programs.

Most employers seek benefits managers with college degrees in personnel administration or labor relations. The top positions are filled by those who have experience in personnel and, particularly, in designing benefits programs.

Hotel Managers

May be used with page 420.

Hotel managers are responsible for the profitable operation of hotel establishments. They oversee the front office, housekeeping, food service, and recreational activities of a hotel. They also manage the accounting, personnel, sales, maintenance, and security departments. Seeing to the comfort of hotel guests, along with coping with unexpected problems, are important parts of the job.

Experience in hotel work is the best qualification for the position of hotel manager. Many employers also look for applicants who have a bachelor's degree in hotel and restaurant administration or specialized credits from a junior college or technical school.

Import-Export Managers

May be used with page 398.

Import-export managers oversee the buying and selling of products and raw materials between companies in the United States and companies in other nations. Import managers purchase foreign products or raw materials for their American companies through buyers who live abroad. They see that the goods meet customs regulations and are shipped and received on time. Export managers supervise the work of sales representatives who live abroad. Orders for American products from foreign customers are processed through the managers. In some companies, managers handle both imports and exports.

Most businesses require applicants to have a college degree to qualify for entry-level positions. Some also require managers to have a master's degree in business administration and to be fluent in a foreign language.

Interpreters

May be used with page 406.

Interpreters translate the words of a speaker from one language to another. Simultaneous interpreters translate a speaker's words as he or she is speaking, even before an entire sentence is completed. The audience listens to the interpreter through earphones during the speech. Consecutive interpreters translate sentences or passages after the speaker pauses. Once the interpreter translates the passage, the speaker resumes the speech.

Many interpreters work for the government in the United States and abroad. Larger companies, especially multinational corporations, also hire interpreters. Most employers require interpreters to have a college degree in a foreign language. Training from a foreign school and travel abroad also is desirable.

Labor Relations Specialists

May be used with page 156.

Labor relations specialists serve as liasons between a company's management officials and its employees. Most often, they work in companies that employ unionized labor. In such companies, the specialists advise top management about union-management relations. An important part of the job is to provide the information needed by management to negotiate contract agreements.

The position of labor relations specialist requires extensive knowledge of labor law and collective bargaining trends. Entry-level positions usually are filled by college graduates majoring in labor relations or personnel administration. Those with advanced degrees, usually labor lawyers, fill the top labor relations positions.

Mail Carriers

May be used with page 173.

Mail carriers deliver and collect mail to households and businesses along planned routes. A carrier may travel the route on foot, by car or truck, or a combination of both.

Mail carriers are employed by the United States Postal Service. To qualify, a person must be an American citizen or have been granted permanent resident-alien status. The minimum age requirement is 18, but 16-year-olds with a high school diploma may apply. Applicants must pass a physical exam and a written test that checks their speed and accuracy at organizing and memorizing numbers and names. Applicants also must have a driver's license and a good driving record, and must pass a road test.

Market Researchers

May be used with page 51.

Market researchers collect, analyze, and interpret data to provide companies with information about the needs and desires of the buying public. Researchers are trained to develop forecasts of consumer motivations and buying habits. On the basis of these forecasts, they propose strategies for the marketing campaigns of current products and suggest areas of expansion into new markets.

Market research trainees usually have a bachelor's degree in business or economics with additional training in statistics and research. For higher level positions, many companies prefer applicants with a master's degree in business administration.

Purchasing Agents

May be used with page 347.

Purchasing agents are responsible for buying the goods and services needed to run a business. They see that these products are available in the proper quantity, are of acceptable quality, arrive when needed, and are purchased at a reasonable price. To be effective, purchasing agents must understand the needs of their company, as well as the needs of the suppliers from whom they buy products.

The best opportunities for purchasing agents are for those who have a master's degree in business administration. Entry-level jobs often are filled by those with a bachelor's degree or by graduates of associate degree or vocational programs. This is especially true in companies that require purchasing agents to have special technical knowledge about their business.

Stockbrokers

May be used with page 106.

Stockbrokers help individuals and organizations invest money in the securities market. Brokers relay their customers' orders to buy and sell stocks to the floor of a securities exchange, where the transactions are made. They also offer customers financial advice and prepare individual financial portfolios.

Most stockbrokers work for large brokerage and investment firms. Some also are employed by banks and other credit institutions. Employers usually hire brokers who are college graduates with degrees in business or economics. To qualify to work, brokers must meet state licensing requirements. They also must register at the exchanges where they will operate and pass a test approved by the Securities and Exchange Commission, the National Association of Securities Dealers, or the exchanges.

Systems Analysts

May be used with page 104.

Systems analysts plan and develop methods for computerizing businesses or improving existing computer systems. Analysts first define the goals of a customer's computer system. They then plan a system to meet those goals. If the plan is accepted, the analysts decide on the equipment, personnel, and procedures needed to set up the system and to put it on line.

Many systems analysts work for computer companies. Others work for businesses such as manufacturing firms, banks, and consulting firms, or for government agencies. Most employers prefer applicants with a college degree in computer science or a related field. Some, however, require a graduate degree or advanced scientific training.

Tax Auditors

May be used with page 196.

Tax auditors verify the accuracy of an organization's financial records to check for discrepancies that might exist between the records and the organization's tax returns. To be effective, tax auditors must be knowledgeable about current tax laws as well as overall economic conditions.

Many tax auditors are employed by the Internal Revenue Service. Others work for large business firms to help ensure that the company is doing its best to comply with the law. Most employers require applicants for entry-level positions to have a college degree in business or accounting. The federal government requires a college degree that includes a minimum of 24 semester hours in accounting or auditing.

Tellers

May be used with page 234.

Tellers are the most visible employees of a bank, savings and loan, or other credit institution. They cash checks and process deposits and withdrawls for customers. Tellers also may carry out specialized duties, handling savings bonds, utility payments, or foreign currency exchanges, for example.

Employers look for tellers who are friendly and attentive and who have good clerical and mathematical skills. Almost all tellers have at least a high school education. To be considered for promotions into managerial positions, college courses or special training courses usually are required.

Tool-and-Die Makers

May be used with page 143.

Tool-and-die makers produce the tools, dies, and guiding and holding devices that are used in metal-working and plastic-working machines. Toolmakers produce jigs and fixtures that hold metal, as well as gauges and other measuring devices. Diemakers construct metal forms, or dies, to shape metal. They also produce metal molds for diecasting and for molding plastic.

Most workers learn tool-and-die making through a company's apprenticeship program. Such a program usually consists of four to five years of shop training as well as classroom training in mathematics, mechanical drawing, and blueprint reading. Most companies that offer apprenticeships require applicants to have a high school or vocational school education.

Travel Agents

May be used with page 443.

Travel agents are specialists who make travel arrangements for their clients. Whether planning a family's vacation or arranging an international business trip, travel agents consider a client's travel goals, tastes, and budget when making travel arrangements. Depending on the client's needs, the agents may make arrangements for airline reservations, ground transportation, hotel accommodations, guided tours, and restaurant reservations.

Most travel agencies require applicants to have a high school or vocational school degree, although some prefer a college degree. Many travel agents gain valuable experience for the job by traveling themselves.

Urban and Regional Planners

May be used with page 369.

Urban and regional planners develop programs for the revitalization and future growth of an area's communities. Planners study the current facilities of an area as well as the projected impact of changes such as population growth. In this way, they estimate a community's long-term needs for housing, schools, transportation, industrial sites, and other facilities.

Many urban and regional planners are employed by local government planning agencies. Others work for state and federal agencies, or for consulting firms, market research firms, and land developers. Most employers require at least two years of graduate study in urban or regional planning for entry-level positions.

Glossary

This Glossary contains many of the terms you need to understand as you study economics. After each term, there is a brief definition or explanation of the meaning of the term as it is used in the textbook. The page number in parentheses after each definition refers to the page in the textbook where the boldfaced term can be found.

The definitions in this Glossary do not always provide all the information about these terms as they are currently used by economists. Therefore, you may find it useful to turn to the page(s) listed in the parentheses to read more about any of the terms. You may also consult a more comprehensive reference work in economics, a dictionary, or your teacher.

A

ability-to-pay principle Criterion of tax fairness which holds that people with higher incomes and wealth should pay higher taxes, while those with lower incomes or wealth should pay lower taxes. (**196**)

absolute advantage Ability of one nation to produce a product at a lower cost than a second nation, given the same resources. (**387**)

aggregate demand Total spending in the economy. (**253, 314**)

annual percentage rate (APR) Total cost of credit expressed as a yearly percentage. (**278**)

antitrust legislation Laws designed to monitor and regulate big business, prevent monopolies from forming, and break up existing monopolies. (**136**)

arbitration Process in which a neutral third party to a labor dispute, an arbitrator, offers specific terms in the settlement of a contract. (**158**) *See also* **mediation.**

articles of incorporation Application for a corporate charter with a state in which a corporation will have its headquarters. (**103**)

authoritarian socialism Economic system in which the government owns or controls almost all of the means of production. Practiced in nations with economies that are closest to the pure-command model (**30, 448**); also known as **Communism.**

automatic clearing house service (ACH) System that transfers money from a customer's bank account to a creditor's bank account. (**236**)

automatic stabilizers Built-in features of federal tax and spending programs that activate non-discretionary fiscal policy. (**363**)

automatic teller machine (ATM) Automated device that handles many routine banking tasks. (**235**)

B

balance of payments Accounting record of all payments that a nation's residents, firms, and government make to other countries and all the monetary receipts it receives from other countries. (**389**) *See also* **unfavorable balance of payments.**

Glossary

balance of trade Difference between the value of a nation's imports and exports. (**390**)

bank failure Condition in which government regulators close a bank that has insufficient assets on deposit to cover its accounts. (**237**)

bankruptcy Legal declaration of an inability to pay debts. (**279**)

barter Exchange of goods and services without using money. (**222**)

bear market Condition in the stock market noted for investor anticipation that prices will fall and marked by a steady decline in the Dow Jones Industrial Average. (**301**)

benefits-received principle Criterion of tax fairness which holds that people who benefit directly from certain public goods and services should pay for them. (**196**)

black market Illegal underground economy. (**454**)

board of directors A group of individuals elected by shareholders who set the policies and goals of a corporation. (**103**)

borrowing Transfer of a specified amount of money from a lender to a borrower for a specific length of time. (**276**)

bourgeoisie According to Karl Marx, merchant class who took control of the means of production during the early Industrial Revolution and exploited the working class, or proletariat. (**448**)

budget deficit Financial situation that occurs when government expenditures are greater than government revenues. (**208**)

budget surplus Financial situation that occurs when government revenues are greater than government expenditures. (**208**)

bull market Condition in the stock market noted for investor optimism that prices will rise and marked by a steady rise in the Dow Jones Industrial Average. (**301**)

business cycle Sequential rise and fall of the economy. (**185, 330**) *See also* **contraction; expansion; peak; trough.**

C

capacity utilization rate Information calculated by the government to show how much of the nation's total capital goods are being used to produce goods. (**347**)

capital Money, tools, machinery, equipment, and inventory used in the production process. Referred to as **capital resources** in text. (**23**)

capital account Portion of the balance of payments that records the movement of capital between nations. (**389**)

capital accumulation Expansion of capital goods in the economy. (**292**)

capital formation Accumulation of the financial resources and capital goods necessary for sound economic development. (**416**)

capital gain Sale of an investment at a higher price than its original cost. (**294**)

capital good Building, structure, machinery, or tool that is used in the production process. (**23**)

capital loss Sale of an investment at a lower price than its original cost. (**294**)

capital resource Money or capital good that is used to produce a consumer product. (**23**)

capital-intensive Economy that produces goods through machine power rather than through human and animal power. (**143**)

capitalism Economic system in which individuals own and control the factors of production and intervention by the government is limited. Practiced in nations with economies that are closest to the pure-market model. (**30, 440**)

central bank Depository for a nation's funds and a place where banks bank. (**244**)

check clearing Method of crediting and debiting checking accounts. (**250**)

circular flow model Chart that shows how the exchanges are made in **resource market, product market,** and **income** payments. (**37**)

collateral Item of value offered by a borrower as a guarantee that a loan will be repaid. (**99, 276**)

collective bargaining Process in which union representatives speak for all their members in an effort to negotiate a contract with management. (**158**)

collectivization Policy of the Soviet government that completely expropriated peasant land to form large state-run farms. (**452**)

collusion Condition in which leaders of competing firms set production levels or prices for products, presenting a clear danger to free competition. (**132**)

Glossary

command economy Economic system that relies on central planners in the government to determine basic economic goals. (**29**)

commercial bank Financial institution that lends money; accepts savings and checking deposits; and transfers money among businesses, other banks and financial institutions, and individuals. (**230**)

commodity money Item that has a value of its own and is also used as money. (**224**)

common stock Share of ownership in a corporation that offers a variable dividend determined by the corporation's board of directors and gives a stockholder a voice in how the corporation is run. (**103, 294**)

Communism *See* **authoritarian socialism.**

comparative advantage Ability of one nation to produce an item at a lower opportunity cost relative to other products than a second nation. (**387**)

competition Economic rivalry that exists among businesses selling similar products. (**33, 68**)

competitive advertising Information that tries to persuade consumers that a product is better than substitute goods. (**127**)

complementary good Item that is commonly used with another item. (**55**)

conglomerate combination Merger between two or more companies producing or marketing different products. (**112**)

consumer Person who buys goods and services. (**22**)

consumer good Good that a consumer buys. (**22, 339**)

Consumer Price Index (CPI) Government measure that charts changes in the prices paid by consumers for goods and services. (**315**)

consumption Expenditures by consumers on final goods and services. (**339**)

contract Legally binding agreement, either oral or written, between people to buy and sell goods and services. (**33**)

contract responsibility system Agricultural reform in China after 1978 permitting peasants to lease state-owned land and sell a certain portion of their crops on the open market. (**458**)

contraction Phase in the business cycle characterized by a down that occurs after a peak. (**330**)

cooperative Business that is owned by the people who use its services. (**116**)

corporate bond Certificate, offering a fixed interest rate, issued by a corporation in exchange for money borrowed from investors. (**103, 303**)

corporate charter License granted by a state government that gives a business the right to operate as a corporation. (**103**)

corporate income tax Progressive federal levy on a corporation's profits. (**198**)

corporation Business organization that is owned by stockholders and is treated by law as if it were an individual person. (**102**)

cost of production Wages and salaries, rents, interest, and payments to other entrepreneurs and resource suppliers. (**61**)

cost-of-living adjustment (COLA) Clause in a labor contract that provides for an automatic raise in workers' wages when the inflation rate reaches an agreed-upon level. (**317**)

cost-push inflation Increase in the price level of all goods and services that occurs when producers raise their prices to cover higher production costs and to earn higher profits. (**316**)

credit Purchase of goods and services without the actual transfer of money on the promise to pay later. (**276**)

credit bureau Business that specializes in collecting financial information about consumers. (**277**)

credit rating Estimation of the probability that a borrower will be able to repay a loan. (**277**)

credit union Cooperative in which members pool their savings and borrow money at low rates of interest. (**116, 231**)

currency Coins and paper money. (**225**)

current account Portion of the balance of payments that tallies a nation's inflow and outflow of money. (**389**)

customs duty Levy on imported goods brought into the United States from another country (**200**); also known as a **tariff.**

cyclical unemployment Situation that occurs when people are out of work because of economic downturns. (**321**)

D

debit card Plastic card that can be inserted into a point-of-sale terminal allowing a buyer to transfer funds from the buyer's account to the seller's account to pay for purchases. (**236**)

debt ceiling Legislation that limits how much the federal government can borrow. (**210**)

default Action by which a nation fails to pay its foreign debts, wiping them off the books. (**418**)

deficit spending Government policy of appropriating more money for its programs than it is able to cover from revenues. (**208**)

deflation Decline in the average price level of all goods and services. (**314**)

demand Amount of a good or service a consumer is willing and able to buy at various prices during a given period. (**33, 46**) *See also* **law of demand.**

demand curve Graph that plots the information from the demand schedule to illustrate the inverse relationship between price and the quantity demanded. (**48**)

demand deposit Funds payable on demand to the holder of a check (**226**); also known as a **checking account.**

demand schedule Table that shows the inverse relationship between the price of a good or service and the quantity consumers demand. (**48**)

demand-pull inflation Increase in the price level of all goods and services that occurs when aggregate demand increases at a faster rate than aggregate supply. (**316**)

demand-side economics Fiscal policy to regulate aggregate demand in the economy; advocated by Keynesian economists (**361**); also known as **demand-management economics.**

democratic socialism Economic system in which the government owns some of the factors of production, but individuals maintain basic human rights and have control over economic planning through the election of government officials. (**31, 443**)

depreciation Value of capital that is used up each year to keep a nation's capital stock intact. (**344**)

deregulation Process by which the government lifts some of its restrictions on an industry. (**234**)

derived demand Need for workers that results from a shift in consumers' tastes and preferences and a subsequent demand for new goods and services. (**147**)

determinant of demand Nonprice factor that affects demand, such as consumer tastes and preferences, the size of the market, people's income, the prices of related goods, and consumer expectations. (**51**)

determinant of supply Nonprice factor that affects supplies of a good, such as technological improvement, resource prices, taxes and subsidies, prices of other goods, price expectations, and market competition. (**64**)

devaluation Reduction of the value of a nation's currency in relation to the currencies of another nation. (**396**)

developed nation Country with a high level of industrialization and economic sophistication. (**412**)

developing nation Country with a low level of industrialization and economic sophistication characterized by a low per capita GNP, limited resources, a rapid population growth rate, and a traditional lifestyle. (**31, 412**)

development plan Outline of how a nation's resources should be used to meet its economic goals. (**423**)

dictatorship of the proletariat According to Karl Marx, the government organized by workers that would oversee the final destruction of capitalism and the creation of a classless society. (**449**)

differentiated oligopoly Type of imperfect competition in which a few producers dominate the production of similar products. (**132**)

diminishing marginal utility Law which states that as more units of a product are consumed, demand for the product declines. (**47**)

discount rate Interest that the Federal Reserve charges member banks for the use of its money. (**255**)

discretionary fiscal policy Government actions that change taxes and government spending in response to instability in the economy. (**361**)

disinflation Reduction of inflation. (**314**)

disposable income (DI) Personal income less income taxes. (**345**)

diversification Variety of investments combining

several investment goals—security, high yield, and growth. (**293**)

dividend Payment by a corporation to a shareholder. (**103, 293**)

E

easy-money policy Expansion of the money supply by the Federal Reserve to increase aggregate demand and promote economic growth. (**253**)

economic assistance Financial and technical aid, loans, and cash grants that governments extend to other nations and that contribute directly to economic development. (**430**)

economic development Process of growth and basic change in all sectors of a nation's economy. (**412**)

economic efficiency Economic goal of making the best use of scarce resources. (**34**)

economic equity Economic goal of ensuring that all members of a society share equally in the costs and benefits of the free enterprise system. (**34**)

economic freedom Economic goal of maintaining freedom of choice in the market. (**34**)

economic growth Economic goal of increasing the amount of goods and services each worker in the economy can produce. (**35, 340**)

economic infrastructure Real investments in the nation's public sector such as roads, bridges, harbors, airports, and public schools and universities. (**291**)

economic institutions Households, families, corporations, government agencies, banks, labor unions, and cooperatives. [Individual institutions are discussed in the textbook in the contexts in which they apply.]

economic interdependence Condition in which individuals and businesses concentrate on the production of specific goods and services and must rely on other people to furnish the remaining products needed to satisfy their wants and needs. (**386**)

economic rent Payment to a factor in excess of what is necessary to keep it at its present occupation or use. (**37–38**)

economic security Economic goal of protecting all members of society from poverty, business and bank failures, medical emergencies, and other situations that would have a negative effect on their economic well-being. (**34**)

economic stability Economic goal of achieving **full employment** and **price stability.** (**35**)

economic system Organized set of procedures a nation uses in producing and distributing goods and services. (**27**)

economics Study of the choices people make in an effort to satisfy their wants and needs. (**22**)

economies of scale Benefit received by large firms that are able to take advantage of mass production techniques to lower per unit production costs. (**137**)

elastic demand Condition that exists when a small increase in a good's price causes a major decrease in the quantity demanded. (**49**) *See also* **inelastic demand.**

elastic supply Condition that exists when producers significantly change production in response to relatively small increases or decreases in the product's price. (**62**) *See also* **inelastic supply.**

elasticity of demand Degree to which changes in a good's price affect the quantity demanded by consumers. (**49**)

elasticity of supply Degree to which a good's supply is affected by changes in price. (**62**)

electronic home banking Link between a bank computer and a home computer, on which an individual's bank records can be accessed and many transactions completed. (**237**)

embargo Law that cuts off imports from and exports to specific countries. (**399**)

employment rate Percentage of the employed labor force 16 years of age or older. (**319**)

entrepreneur Person who attempts to start a new business or introduce a new product. (**24**)

entrepreneurship Risk-taking and organizational abilities involved in starting a new business or introducing a new product to consumers. (**24**)

equilibrium point Intersection on a graph where the supply curve and demand curve for a product meet. (**84**)

estate plan Provision for an orderly transfer of property after death. (**293**)

estate tax Levy on the assets of a person who has died. (**200**)

estimated tax payment Installment payment that individuals and businesses make to the government, based on an approximation of how much they will owe the government at the end of the year. (**198**)

exchange Trading goods and services produced by people located elsewhere. (**37**)

excise tax Levy on the production or sale of a particular good or service. (**200**)

expansion Phase in the business cycle characterized by growth. (**330**)

expectation inflation Increase in the price level of all goods and services that occurs when people buy more because they believe prices will increase in the future; a type of **demand-pull inflation.** (**316**)

export Good or service that is sold to another country. (**389**) *See also* **net exports.**

expropriation Process by which a government seizes ownership and control of a business or property without compensating the former owner. (**418**) *See also* **nationalization.**

externality Negative side-effect, or social cost, of a producer's or consumer's actions on people not connected with the production or consumption of the good. (**88**)

F

factor of production Resource used to produce goods and services. (**23**)

favorable balance of payments Condition in which a nation's total expenditures abroad are less than its receipts from other nations. (**389**)

favorable balance of trade *See* **trade surplus.**

federal budget Federal government's plan for the use of government revenues. (**203**)

fiat money Item that has value because a government decree, or fiat, states that it has value. (**225**)

finance charge Total cost of credit expressed in dollars and cents. (**278**)

financial investment Transfer of ownership of property from one person or group to another without creating new goods. (**290**)

fiscal policy Program of the government designed to stabilize the business cycle and reduce unemployment through the use of federal taxing and spending powers. (**185, 360**) *See also* **monetary policy.**

fixed cost Expense which a business incurs that does not vary with changes in output (**69**); also known as **overhead.**

fixed exchange rate System in which the currency of one nation is fixed, or constant, in relation to the currency of another nation. (**394**)

fixed expenses Costs that remain constant from month to month. (**292**)

flexible expenses Costs that vary from month to month. (**292**)

float time Period between purchase and payment when a credit card is used. (**236**)

floating exchange rate System in which supply and demand determine the value of a nation's currency. (**396**)

foreign aid Money, products, and services that governments extend to other nations. (**430**) *See also* **economic assistance**; **military assistance.**

foreign exchange market Network of major commercial and investment banks linking world economies and whose major function is to convert one currency into an equivalent amount in a second currency. (**394**)

foreign exchange rate Price of one nation's currency in relation to the currency of another nation. (**394**) *See also* **fixed exchange rate**; **floating exchange rate.**

franchise Contract in which a company known as a **franchiser** agrees to let another person or group known as a **franchisee** establish an enterprise using its name to sell goods or services. (**115**)

free enterprise system Economic system in which business is conducted freely with only limited government intervention. (**31**)

free market system *See* **free enterprise system.**

free trade Policy advocating the lifting of government regulations on international trade. (**400**)

free-trade zones Areas in China where foreign corporations are offered tax incentives to invest and build in return for providing capital, technology, and management to strengthen China's economy. (**458**)

frictional unemployment Situation that occurs when workers are temporarily between jobs. (**320**)

full employment Lowest level of unemployment

that is possible in an economy, generally occurring when about 95 percent of the labor force has jobs. (**35, 321**)

future Commodity traded on the futures market. (**304**)

futures market Trading in which contracts are made to sell securities or commodities such as agricultural products, industrial goods, and gold and silver at a future date. (**304**)

G

general partnership Business owned by two or more individuals who enjoy equal decision-making authority and who have unlimited liability. (**100**)

geographic monopoly Condition in which a firm is the only producer or seller of a good or service in a specific location. (**126**)

gift tax Levy on the transfer of any gift of value, such as money or other personal property. (**200**)

gold standard Monetary system in which paper money is fully backed by and convertible into gold. (**228**)

good Physical object that can be purchased. (**22**)

government good Item that national, state, and local governments purchase. (**339**)

government monopoly Condition in which government at any level owns and operates a monopoly. (**126**)

grant-in-aid Transfer payment from the federal government to state or local governments. (**201**)

green revolution Application of modern capital and technology to agriculture in developing nations. (**426**)

Gross National Product (GNP) Dollar value of all new, final products produced in a nation each year; increases or decreases measure business cycles. (**330, 338**) *See also* **money GNP; per capita money GNP; real GNP; real per capita GNP.**

growth stock Share of ownership in a corporation that pays few or no dividends but gains in value. (**294**)

H

horizontal combination Merger between two or more companies that produce the same good or service or dominate one phase of a service or of a good's production. (**108**)

housing cooperative Business that is formed by members who buy the buildings in which they live. (**116**)

human resource Anyone who works. (**23**)

hyperinflation High and uncontrollable increase in the price level of all goods and services that typically occurs just before the collapse of a nation's monetary system. (**318**)

I

implicit GNP price deflator Measure of price changes in economic output that estimates the average price level of all consumer, capital, and government goods and services produced in a given year. (**339**)

import Good or service that is bought from another country. (**389**)

import quota Law that sets a fixed amount of goods to be imported. (**399**) *See also* **voluntary trade restriction.**

incentives Factors that motivate and influence human behavior. (**80**)

income Money payments that households receive from business firms and the government in exchange for the households' resources. (**37**)

income effect Increase or decrease in purchasing power brought on by changes in prices. (**47**)

income stock Share of ownership in a corporation that has high earnings and pays consistent dividends. (**294**)

indirect business tax Government levy on a firm's output rather than on a firm itself. (**345**)

individual income tax Levy based on an individual's income, including wages or salaries, interest, dividends, and tips. (**198**)

industrialization Process by which a nation's economy is transformed from an agricultural one to one based on the mechanization of all major forms of production. (**142**)

inelastic demand Condition that exists when a change in a good's price has little impact on the quantity demanded. (**50**) *See also* **elastic demand.**

inelastic supply Condition that exists when producers are unable or unwilling to increase or decrease the supply of a product regardless of price. (**63**) *See also* **elastic supply.**

inflation Increase in the average price level of all goods and services. (**314**) *See also* **cost-push inflation; deflation; demand-pull inflation; disinflation; expectation inflation; hyperinflation; profit-push inflation; stagflation; wage-push inflation.**

informative advertising Information intended to provide consumers with the price, quality, and special features of specific products. (**127**)

installment credit account Credit account often used to purchase expensive items such as appliances; payments are spread over a period of time. (**278**)

installment loan Common type of consumer loan with repayment of the principal and interest divided into equal amounts according to the length of the loan period. (**276**)

interdependence *See* **economic interdependence.**

interest Predetermined amount of money a borrower must pay for the use of borrowed funds. (**103, 268**)

interest group Organization of citizens having common interests and goals. (**188**) *See also* **lobbyist.**

international trade Voluntary exchange of goods and services between people in different nations. (**386**)

investment Condition in which people exchange their money for something of value and expect to earn a profit from the purchase in the future. (**290**)

investment bank Financial institution frequently used by corporations when they issue new stock, buy out controlling interests in another company, or trade large blocks of other stocks. (**297**)

investment plan Economic program outlining how a person puts his or her money to work. (**292**)

investment tax credit Incentive that permits businesses to deduct from their corporate income taxes a percentage of the money spent on new capital. (**362**)

iron rice bowl System in China under which workers received the same low wages regardless of their productivity. (**456**)

K

Keynesian economists Experts in economics who favor government action to combat unemployment and sluggish business activity. (**361**)

L

L Measure of the nation's money supply that includes the M3 and savings bonds, short-term Treasury securities, and other near moneys. (**253**)

labor Mental and physical talents people contribute to the production process. Referred to as **human resources** in text. (**23**)

labor force All people who are at least 16 years old and are working or looking for work. (**142**)

labor force participation rate Percentage of the population 16 years of age or older who are employed or actively seeking employment. (**319**)

labor union Organization of workers that negotiates with employers for better wages, improved working conditions, and job security. (**150**)

labor-intensive Economy that produces goods through human and animal power. (**143**)

Laffer Curve Graph developed by economist Arthur B. Laffer that illustrates how tax cuts affect tax revenues and economic growth. (**375**)

Laffer effect Principle which states that tax cuts can increase the government's tax revenues because individuals and firms have a greater incentive to work, invest, and produce at lower tax rates. (**375**)

laissez-faire capitalism Form of capitalism in which individuals make all the economic decisions and the government does not interfere (**441**)

land One of the factors of production referring to any part of natural resources. Referred to as natural resources in text. (**23**)

land reform Redistribution of arable land from a few major landowners to a larger number of the peasants who work the land. (**426**)

law of demand Principle which states that an increase in price causes a decrease in the quantity demanded, while a decrease in price causes an increase in the quantity demanded. (**46**)

law of diminishing returns Law which states that as more of one resource is added to a fixed supply of other resources, the output per unit of input may increase for a time, but eventually the rate of increase of productivity will diminish. (**70**)

law of supply Principle which states that producers supply more products when they can charge higher prices and fewer products when they must charge lower prices. (**60**)

liability Debt or amount of money owed by a business. (**99**)

limited partnership Business owned by two or more individuals, at least one of whom joins the partnership as an investment, rarely takes an active role in business decisions, and has limited liability. (**100**)

liquidity Condition that indicates the ease with which accounts or property can be converted into cash with little or no loss in interest payments or capital. (**270, 305**)

lobbyist Person hired by an interest group to express the group's point of view to policymakers. (**189**)

M

M1 Narrowest measure of the nation's money supply that includes all currency in circulation, the value of all traveler's checks, and all checking accounts. (**253**)

M2 Measure of the nation's money supply that includes the money counted in M1 as well as money market accounts, money-market mutual fund shares, and other savings deposits that allow people easy access to their funds. (**253**)

M3 Measure of the nation's money supply that includes the money in the M2 and all time deposits over $100,000. (**253**)

manorialism Command economy of the Middle Ages in Europe in which the head, or lord, of the manor had absolute control over the use of human, natural, and capital resources on the manor. (**29**)

margin requirement Percentage of cash required of an investor to buy stocks, options, warrants, and convertible bonds. (**258**)

marginal cost Variable expense incurred by producing one more unit of output. (**69**)

marginal propensity to consume (MPC) Fraction of additional income that people spend. (**364**)

marginal propensity to save (MPS) Fraction of additional income that people save. (**364**)

market Place where goods or services are exchanged freely (**29**); also known as a **marketplace.**

market analyst Individual who researches individual firms and evaluates their strengths and weaknesses. (**295**)

market economy Economic system that relies on individuals to answer basic economic questions. (**29**)

market equilibrium Condition in which supply and demand for a product are equal, making the prices charged for a product relatively stable. (**84**)

market failure Disruption of the stability of a market economy, including inadequate business competition, the negative side effects of business, the inability or unwillingness of private enterprise to produce public goods, inadequate knowledge of market conditions, and immobility of the factors of production. (**186**)

market structure Term used to describe competition in the marketplace. (**122**)

marketing cooperative Business that collects, processes, and ships goods for its members. (**116**)

maturity Length of time a bond, certificate of deposit (CD), or loan must run to draw full interest or on which the principal must be paid in full. (**271**)

mediation Process in which a neutral third party, or mediator, listens to the arguments of labor and management in a labor dispute and suggests ways to reach an agreement. (**158**) *See also* **arbitration.**

medium of exchange Any item that sellers will accept in payment for goods and services. (**222**)

member bank Federal Reserve System member. (**247**)

mercantilism Economic doctrine calling for government regulation of the economy in order to accumulate greater wealth for the nation. (**441**)

merger Business arrangement in which one company absorbs another. (**108**) *See also* **conglomerate combination**; **horizontal combination**; **vertical combination.**

military assistance Loans, cash payments, or technical training supplied to the military that governments extend to other nations. (**430**)

minimum wage Lowest compensation that employers can legally pay a worker for a job. (**149**)

mixed economy Economic system that combines elements of the pure-market and pure-command models. (**30**)

monetary policy Program of the Federal Reserve Board designed to control the nation's money supply and credit. (**185, 253**) *See also* **fiscal policy.**

money Any item that people commonly accept in exchange for goods or services. (**222**)

money GNP Current dollar value of a nation's economic output with no adjustment for inflation. (**339**)

money supply Amount of money in circulation. (**253**) *See also* **M1**; **M2**; **M3**; **L.**

monopolistic competition Condition that occurs when these four factors exist: a good or service has numerous buyers and sellers, similar but differentiated products are offered for sale, buyers are well informed about differentiated products, and firms can easily enter or leave an industry. (**127**)

moral suasion Unofficial pressure that the Federal Reserve exerts on the banking system to channel its lending policies in a desirable direction. (**258**)

mortgage Installment debt owed on land, buildings, or other real property. (**277**)

most-favored-nation status United States policy that automatically extends any trade benefits granted one nation to another nation with the same status. (**404**)

multiplier effect Term that explains how small changes in income ripple through the economy and eventually cause a much larger change in spending. (**364**) *See also* **marginal propensity to consume**; **marginal propensity to save.**

mutual fund Pool of money from investors to purchase a variety of securities. (**296**)

mutual savings bank Financial institution originally set up to serve savers who wished to make small deposits that were not welcomed by larger banks. Such institutions' major business is from savings deposits and home loans. (**231**)

N

national bank Financial institution chartered by the federal government. (**228**)

national debt Total amount of money that the federal government owes to its creditors. (**209**)

national income (NI) Total amount of money that everyone in an economy earns. (**344**)

nationalization Process by which a government assumes ownership and control of a business or property after compensating the former owner. (**418**) *See also* **expropriation.**

natural monopoly Condition in which a single firm most efficiently produces or sells a good or service. (**125**)

natural resource Item provided by nature that can be used to produce goods and provide services. (**23**)

near money Assets such as savings accounts and time deposits that are not usually considered part of the nation's money supply. (**226**)

need Good or service such as food, clothing, and shelter that is necessary for survival. (**22**)

net exports Value of the goods and services that a country sells to other countries less the value of the goods and services that the country buys from other countries. (**339**)

Net National Product (NNP) GNP less depreciation. (**344**)

nondiscretionary fiscal policy Government actions activated automatically by certain built-in features of the federal tax and spending programs. (**363**) *See also* **automatic stabilizers.**

nonprice competition Condition in which firms within an industry compete in areas other than price. (**127**)

nonprofit organization Business that provides goods and services without seeking profits for distribution to individual members. (**117**)

Glossary

O

oligopoly Type of imperfect competition in which only a few large firms control an industry. (**132**)

one-crop economy System of production in which a nation concentrates on a single item. Economists also use the term *crop* to include nonagricultural products such as minerals. (**416**)

open market operation Buying and selling of government securities by the Federal Reserve. (**258**)

opportunity cost Value of what a person gives up to get something else. (**24, 223**)

over-the-counter market (OTC) Method of trading stocks not listed on the New York Stock Exchange or other stock exchanges. (**296**)

overhead *See* **fixed cost.**

P

panic run Situation that occurs when many depositors withdraw their deposits from a banking or lending institution at the same time. (**239**)

partnership Business that is owned and controlled by two or more people. (**100**) *See also* **general partnership; limited partnership.**

partnership contract Document that outlines the distribution of profits and losses, details the specific responsibilities of each partner, and provides for adding or dropping partners and dissolving the partnership. (**100**)

peak Phase in the business cycle when expansion reaches its highest point; high point in a period of expansion. (**330**)

per capita money GNP Measure used to compare economic growth and the standard of living when reliable data on inflation are unavailable. (**340**)

perfect competition Type of industry that is the most competitive because it has many buyers and sellers, none of whom control prices. (**122**)

personal identification number (PIN) Confidential number keyed into an ATM that allows customers to use ATMs 24 hours a day. (**235**)

personal income (PI) Total amount of money that an individual receives before paying taxes. (**345**)

population growth rate Annual increase in a nation's population, expressed as a percentage. (**413**)

preferred stock Share of ownership in a corporation that offers a fixed dividend paid from profits before dividends on common stock. (**103, 294**)

price ceiling Government regulation that prohibits prices from rising above a certain maximum level. (**88**)

price floor Government regulation that prohibits prices from falling below a certain minimum level. (**88**)

price leadership Condition in which the largest firm in an industry controls the price of a good, often by setting a price for a new product, hoping that competing firms will set similar prices. (**132**)

prices Amounts of money that people pay in exchange for a unit of a particular good or service. (**55**)

price stability Condition achieved when the overall price level of the goods and services available in the economy is relatively constant. (**35**)

price system Economic system based on the principles that everything bought and sold in a market has a price and that price is a good measure of what products should be produced, how they should be produced, and for whom they should be produced. (**76**)

primary boycott Organized effort by strikers and sympathizers to stop buying a firm's products until a strike is resolved. (**159**)

prime rate Interest that a bank charges on loans to its best business customers. (**258**)

principal Amount of money originally borrowed. (**103, 276**)

private property Goods that are owned by individuals or businesses rather than by the government. (**31**)

privatization Sale of government property or the relinquishment of certain government services to private businesses. (**179**)

producer Person who makes the goods and provides the services that satisfy consumers' wants and needs. (**22**)

Producer Price Index (PPI) Government measure that charts changes in the average prices of goods sold by producers in all stages of processing. (**316**)

product Term referring to either a good or a service. (**22**)

product differentiation Market structure that results when sellers emphasize the differences among competing products in order to increase sales. (**127**)

product market Total exchanges of goods and services in an economy. (**37**)

production disincentive Cause of slowdown in industrial output that contributes to stagflation. (**329**)

production possibilities curve Graph that shows all the possible combinations of two goods or services that can be produced within a given time. (**25**)

productivity Amount of output of goods and services produced per input of productive resources used. (**70**)

profit Amount of money that remains after all the costs of production have been paid. (**30, 60**)

profit-push inflation Increase in the price level of all goods and services that occurs when producers raise prices in order to raise their profits. (**317**)

progressive tax Levy that takes a larger percentage of income from a high-income person than from a low-income person (**195**); also known as an **automatic stabilizer.**

proletariat According to Karl Marx, working class who provided labor at very low wages. (**448**)

property tax Levy that individuals and firms pay on their assets. (**201**)

proportional tax Levy that takes the same percentage of income from individuals at all income levels. (**195**)

prospectus Fact sheet containing data on a company's finances; used by investors to evaluate securities offered for sale. (**302**)

protectionism Policy advocating the use of trade barriers to protect domestic industries. (**401**)

protective tariff Tax on imports designed to protect domestic industries from foreign competition. (**399**)

public good Good or service that the government provides for everyone. (**179**)

public transfer payment Redistribution of tax dollars to the nonproductive sectors of the economy (**363**); also known as an **automatic stabilizer.**

purchasing cooperative Retail store that is owned and operated by its customers. (**116**)

purchasing power Amount of money that individuals have available to spend on goods and services. (**47**)

pure monopoly Condition in which a single firm controls the total production or sale of a good or service. (**122**)

pure oligopoly Type of imperfect competition in which a few producers dominate the production of an identical product. (**132**)

pyramided reserves System designed to avoid economic panics by requiring local banks to deposit some of their reserves with larger city banks. Larger city banks deposit some of their own reserves in the largest banks, which in turn use some of these deposits to extend loans while holding the rest in reserve. (**246**)

R

Reaganomics Supply-side economic policy of President Ronald Reagan that has three important components: tax cuts on personal and corporate incomes, spending cuts on social programs, and regulatory reform. (**373**)

real GNP Dollar value of a nation's economic output adjusted for inflation. (**339**)

real investment Condition in which investors use money to create a new capital good. (**291**)

real per capita GNP Real GNP divided by the total population. (**340**)

regional banking System in which financial institutions expand outside their home state to states whose legislatures permit such expansion. (**234**)

regressive tax Levy that takes a larger percentage of income from a low-income person than from a high-income person. (**195**)

regular charge account Credit account in which all purchases made within the 30-day billing period must be paid in full by the customer. (**278**)

related good Item whose demand is connected to the demand for other items related to it. (**55**) *See also* **complementary good**; **substitute good.**

representative money Item that has value because it can be exchanged for something valuable. (**225**)

reserve requirement Percentage of money deposited in checking and savings accounts that must be held by banks either in their own vaults or at the district Federal Reserve Bank. (**255**)

resource market Exchange of resources between households—the individuals who own the factors of production—and business firms and the government—the users of these resources. (**37**)

retirement plan Long-term savings program designed to provide income after a person has stopped working. (**293**)

revenue Money a business takes in from the sale of the goods it produces. (**61**)

revenue tariff Tax on imports designed to raise money for the government. (**398**)

revolving charge account Credit account in which a customer's additional purchases, up to a stated credit limit, are added to the previous month's balance; the customer must make a minimum payment each month. (**278**)

S

sales tax Levy on the sale of some goods or services. (**195**)

saving Nonconsumption of disposable income. (**268**)

savings Amount of income that is not spent on consumption or direct taxes. (**269**)

savings and loan association Financial institution that lends money and accepts deposits but, unlike a bank, loans most of its money for home mortgages and is an association of customers. (**230**)

savings rate Percentage of disposable income deposited into savings accounts. (**269**)

Say's Law Economic principle formulated by Jean-Baptiste Say which declares that supply creates its own demand. (**372**)

scarcity Condition that results from the imbalance between the relatively unlimited wants and the relatively limited resources available to satisfy those wants. (**2, 22**)

seasonal unemployment Situation that occurs when people are out of work for a part of the year because of changes in the seasons. (**321**)

secondary boycott Organized effort by strikers and sympathizers to stop buying the products of any firm that does business with a company whose employees are on strike. (**159**)

service Action or activity done for others for a fee, such as the work of lawyers and teachers. (**22**)

service cooperative Business that provides services to its members. (**117**)

shortage Condition in which the quantity of a good demanded exceeds the quantity supplied at the price offered. (**84**)

Social Security tax Levy withheld by employers and sent to the government, which places the taxes in two special trust funds: one for retirement and disability insurance and the other for hospitalization insurance. (**198**)

socialism Broad term used to describe many types of noncapitalist economic systems in which the government owns all or part of the means of production. (**443**) *See also* **authoritarian socialism; democratic socialism.**

sole proprietorship Business owned and controlled by one person. (**98**)

specialization Process by which individuals or businesses produce a single or very narrow range of products. (**386**)

specie Gold or silver coins. (**225**)

spending Consumption of disposable income. (**268**)

spending and saving plan Personal or household budget that is the starting point for all personal financial planning. (**292**)

stagflation Condition that results when high unemployment rates and high inflation rates simultaneously plague the economy. (**328**)

standard of living Economic measurement of well-being, usually by the average amount of goods an individual can consume over a given period of time. (**35**)

standard of value Measure of the relative value of a good or service derived from comparing the prices of products. (**223**)

stock Certificate of ownership in the corporation. (**102**)

stock split Increase in the number of shares of a company that occurs when the company's directors and shareholders declare that each old share can be converted into a specified number of new shares. (**294**)

stockbroker Person who links buyers and sellers of stocks and bonds; also known as a **broker.** (**295**)

stockholder Individual who invests in a corporation by buying shares of stock. (**102**)

store of value Function of money allowing it to be saved for later use, providing the money is nonperishable and keeps its value over time. (**223**)

strike Halting of production by unions when an agreement cannot be reached with management through collective bargaining, mediation, or arbitration. (**158**)

structural unemployment Situation that occurs when changes in the economy eliminate jobs or generate jobs for which unemployed workers are not qualified. (**320**)

subsidiary Company that retains its corporate identity after its acquisition by another company. (**112**)

subsidy Government grant of money or benefits to private businesses or individuals to reduce production costs and increase supply. (**67, 181**)

subsistence agriculture Type of farming in which just enough is grown to meet basic needs. (**414**)

substitute good Item that can be used to replace the purchase of other items when prices rise. (**55**)

substitution effect Tendency of consumers to replace an expensive product with a lower-priced product. (**47**)

supply Quantity of goods and services that producers offer; directly related to the prices producers charge. (**60**)

supply curve Graph that plots the information found in a supply schedule to illustrate what quantity of a product producers are willing to supply at various market prices. (**61**)

supply schedule Table that lists each quantity of a product that producers are willing to supply at various market prices. (**60**)

supply-side economics Fiscal policy that provides incentives for producers to increase aggregate supply. (**371**) *See also* **Reaganomics.**

surplus Condition in which the quantity of a good produced exceeds the quantity demanded at the price offered. (**84**)

syndicate Group of investment banks that spreads the work and risk of marketing a new stock issue or reselling a large stock purchase in a process called **syndication.** (**297**)

T

tariff Any tax on imports. (**398**) *See also* **customs duty; protective tariff; revenue tariff.**

tax Mandatory payment that individuals and firms make to the government to cover the costs of public goods and services. (**194**) *See also* **progressive tax; proportional tax; regressive tax.**

tax break Deduction that a person is allowed to subtract from gross income. (**203**)

tax incentive Special tax break that the government extends to businesses to encourage investment in new capital. (**361**) *See also* **investment tax credit.**

tax rate Percentage of a person's income that is taken by the government. (**195**)

tax return Record of a person's taxable income and any payments or refunds that are due the government. (**198**)

technological monopoly Condition in which a single firm captures market control by developing new production technology or creating an entirely new product. (**125**)

technology Use of science to create new products or more efficient ways to produce products. (**23, 64**)

tight-money policy Restriction of the money supply and the use of credit by the Federal Reserve to reduce the primary cause of demand-pull inflation and to stabilize prices. (**254**)

time deposit Savings account requiring that the money be left in the account for a specific amount of time. (**271**)

total cost Sum of the fixed and variable costs of production. (**69**)

trade adjustment assistance Government program that provides for worker retraining and other benefits to workers and firms hurt by foreign competition. (**405**)

trade barrier Specific government action that protects domestic industries and jobs from foreign competition. (**398**) *See also* **protectionism.**

trade deficit Condition in which the value of a nation's exports is less than the value of its imports (**390**); also known as **unfavorable balance of trade.**

trade surplus Condition in which the value of a nation's exports is greater than the value of its imports (**390**); also known as a **favorable balance of trade.**

trade-off Sacrifice made when a resource used to produce one item cannot be used to produce another. (**24**)

traditional economy Economic system whose economic activities are based on tradition—the customs, habits, laws, and religious beliefs that were developed by the group's ancestors. (**27**)

transfer payment Redistribution of government money from one group of citizens to another. (**180**)

trough Phase in the business cycle when aggregate demand, production, and employment reach their lowest point. (**330**)

trust Huge monopoly created through a merger and cutthroat competition in the United States after the Civil War. (**136**)

U

unemployment Situation that occurs when people do not have jobs but actively seek employment. (**319**) *See also* **cyclical unemployment; frictional unemployment; seasonal unemployment; structural unemployment.**

unfavorable balance of payments Condition in which a nation's total expenditures abroad are greater than its receipts from other nations. (**389**)

unfavorable balance of trade *See* **trade deficit.**

urbanization Movement of people from rural areas to cities. (**354**)

usury Charging of interest at a rate higher than the law allows. (**281**)

utility Amount of satisfaction that an individual receives from consuming a product. (**47**) *See also* **diminishing marginal utility.**

V

variable cost Cost, usually associated with labor and raw materials, that varies with changes in output. (**69**)

venture capital Money invested in high risk but promising new businesses (**65**, **292**); also known as **risk capital.**

vertical combination Merger between two or more companies that are involved in different phases of a service or of a good's production. (**112**)

voluntary trade restriction Agreement between two nations, usually binding, that sets limits on the quantity of a specific product that can be imported. (**399**)

W

wage and price control Government measure, usually imposed only during wartime, that sets limits on increases in wages and prices. (**185**)

wage rate Hourly, weekly, monthly, or yearly pay that a worker receives. (**148**)

wage-price spiral Condition in which workers, particularly those represented by unions, bargain for pay increases that are greater than the inflation rate, leading to higher inflation. (**317**)

wage-push inflation Increase in the price level of all goods and services that occurs when higher costs for human resources lead producers to raise prices; helps set cost-push inflation in motion. (**317**)

want Good or service that a person consumes beyond what is needed for survival. (**22**)

Index

Page numbers in italics that have *m, c, g, p, f, ps,* or *fn* before them refer to maps *(m)*, charts or tables *(c)*, graphs *(g)*, photographs *(p)*, features *(f)*, primary source readings and chapter opening quotes *(ps)*, or footnotes *(fn)*.

A

Index

B

Index

C

Index

Index

D

E

F

G

J

K

L

M

N

Index

O

P

Index

S

Index

T

Index

U

V

Index

W

Y

Z

Index

(Continuation of article from text page 177.)

from only about one-third of federal spending and without raising taxes. It's an impossible task.

Airbrushed picture. The Hill's—and the President's—frustration is understandable. In 1985, to the surprise of many, Congress actually made some tough choices. When the year began, Congress thought it was dealing with a fiscal 1986 budget deficit of $230 billion. Yet when the final returns are in, the 1986 deficit could hit $220 billion, largely because the economy grew much more slowly than expected. The lawmakers are on a treadmill. They make cuts in popular spending programs, yet the deficit keeps rising.

They've got to keep trying. The Supreme Court left the Gramm-Rudman targets intact, and Congress will try to meet them one way or another. In August, the Office of Management & Budget and the Congressional Budget Office will take a "snapshot" of both the economy and the enacted levels of federal spending. If the picture shows that Congress will come within $10 billion of its $144 billion deficit target, the lawmakers will be off the hook, at least for this year. And already, it is widely expected that the OMB will produce a picture that has been sufficiently airbrushed to preserve the budget targets. The Administration will be tempted to forecast an economic boom for the second half and assume $10 billion to $20 billion in administrative spending cuts and deferrals.

If the effort works, Congress and the President will have found a way to claim that they are complying with Gramm-Rudman. But those numbers will be no more than past budget estimates. If Congress fails to make the hard choices, and if the President continues to send unrealistic budgets to Capitol Hill, the deficit will remain unacceptably high. Estimates are that Congress would have to cut spending by at least an additional $30 billion this year to meet the Gramm-Rudman target. Next year the target will be $108 billion. It only gets worse.

(Return to text page 177.)

(Continuation of article from text page 309.)

spending pre-empts real resources from being used more efficiently and effectively in the private sector. Some economic studies have concluded that each dollar of federal spending reduces private investment by roughly 22¢.

Government spending crowds out private investment. More important, government spending, particularly transfer payments and entitlements, crowds out incentives and undermines both private property rights and self-reliance. The main problem created by the growth of spending is the transformation of the U.S. from a free society in which private property rights are respected to a welfare state in which the productive elements of society have only a residual claim to what is left of their income and wealth after all levels of government are finished redistributing it to the politically deserving.

As scholars increasing document, when governments make the redistribution of income more important than the production of income, people reallocate their energies from economic to political action. The enormous growth in special-interest lobbies, which many members of Congress lament, parallels the growth in the proclivity of government to take from some to give to others.

The growth of government has brought about an enormous transformation in the nature of U.S. society. Over most of our country's history there was neither an income tax nor a welfare system. This was a period during which the economy simultaneously absorbed millions of penniless immigrants, many of whom could not even speak the language, and rapidly reduced the poverty rate.

The setup. Now poverty has been institutionalized by government poverty programs, and its rate no longer declines. In the U.S. today, only the illegal poor—aliens who do not qualify for the government's transfer and welfare programs—are consistently able to work themselves out of poverty. By undermining private property rights, a welfare state restricts opportunities for all. Those who, despite the government, are determined to succeed, move into the underground economy, which is growing together with the growth of government.

For four years, many Republicans have framed the budget problem in the wrong way. By making the deficit the issue, Republicans can be trapped by the implication that it does not matter how much the government spends as long as it does not run a deficit. So far, this way of thinking has produced three tax increases on the heels of the 1981 reduction in taxes.

Strangely, Republicans keep setting themselves up for the repudiation of their own policy by downplaying the role that economic growth can play in reducing the deficit. By discounting growth, Republicans are left only with austerity. And by assuming that a tax increase is a substitute for a spending cut, Republicans guarantee that new taxes will be back on the agenda when cutting spending runs into trouble.

(Return to text page 309.)

(Continuation of article from text page 381.)

that a good portion of the "unemployed" labor force in Germany is actually working. Industrial production is running at about 80% of capacity, and Enno Langfield, an economist with the Institute for the World Economy in Kiel, says that the current level of production means that only about 1.4 million are out of work, not the officially recorded 2 million.

The underground economy may also explain the mystery of the missing cement. Official numbers on construction show declines, while sales of building materials are on the rise. "Obviously, someone is using the cement for something," says an official with the German Manual Trades Industry Assn. In France, it appears that 50% of the cement that leaves factories vanishes into thin air as far as official records go. The *travail au noir* in France represents about 10% to 15% of the country's official output.

In Britain, more and more construction companies offer two prices for home repairs—one with an invoice and one without. Gerald Mars, a social anthropologist at Middlesex Polytechnic, says that the black economy's construction companies are driving out the others. "A lot of small-scale builders are going bust or going black."

For the elite. The underground economy in Japan is largely a middle- and upper-class phenomenon. White- and blue-collar workers shoulder most of the tax burden because taxes are withheld from their pay, and there is little opportunity to get into underground activities. But businessmen, professionals, and farmers evade taxes on a huge scale. Takatsugu Nato, of Nikon University, calculates that 86% of salaried workers pay full taxes compared with 36% for businessmen and professionals. The shadow economy in 1981 amounted to 15% of Japan's GNP, up from 13% in 1980, he says.

In Israel, underground transactions involve products from potatoes to diamonds, and some estimates put the amount at 30% of the country's GNP. Government officials try to stamp out unreported activity, and newspapers periodically carry reports about "tax commando" raids on dentists' and doctors' offices. A major gynecology clinic in Jerusalem was closed last month after a government raid found that its doctors had gone for years without reporting large portions of their incomes. Income tax rates that reach 60%, customs fees, and the value-added tax combined with runaway inflation to make evasion prevalent.

South Africa may have the biggest underground economy in the industrial West. According to Leon Louw, director of the Free Market Foundation in Johannesburg, it could amount to 50% of the official gross domestic product. He contends that millions of blacks, especially those in the "independent homelands" are working, but not being counted in the official numbers.

In contrast to the market economies, the Soviet Union's huge second economy exists primarily to provide goods and services that official channels cannot deliver. The second economy probably adds 20% to the country's GNP. It exists everywhere. At open-air *tolkuchkas,* or markets, individuals negotiate trades in autos, food, and books. A family moves into an apartment building, finds it unlivable, and has to pay workers to level the floors and fix the pipes. A woman gives an official a set of handmade porcelain to obtain a place for her mother at a prestigious cancer hospital.

1,000 spare wrenches. The industrial sector in the Soviet Union has its second economy, too. A factory in Kursk, listed officially as making desktop calculators, also turns out spare parts for cars. *Shabashniks,* or moonlighting workers, form work brigades and rent themselves out at triple or quadruple the prevailing wage at construction projects that have fallen behind schedule. In one case, they were paid from funds officially recorded as payment for spare wrenches.

In China, the central government has given up hope of being able to provide jobs for its vast army of unemployed youths, which some put at 20 million. The government now allows workers to sell private-plot farm goods in free markets, set up repair businesses, and form co-ops. And their production goes largely unrecorded.

(Return to text page 381.)

ACKNOWLEDGMENTS *(continued)*

Brace Jovanovich, Inc.: From "The General Theory of Employment" (Retitled: "Steps Toward Full Employment") in *The General Theory of Employment, Interest, and Money* by John Maynard Keynes. © 1973 by The Royal Economic Society. *China Reconstructs:* From "Vegetables for City People" (Retitled: "The Responsibility System in Chinese Agriculture") by Lou Yumin in *China Reconstructs,* Vol. XXXV, No. 1, January 1986, pp. 11–12 (North American Edition). *City News Publishing Company:* From the speech "America's Entrepreneurial Environment, The New Industries" (Retitled: "The Entrepreneurial Explosion") by Bernard A. Goldhirsh, President, Goldhirsh Group, as reprinted in *Vital Speeches of the Day,* April 15, 1985, Vol. LI, No. 13, pp. 402–06. Copyright © 1985 by City News Publishing Company. *Dow Jones & Company, Inc.:* From "Sometimes the Biggest Mistake Is Saying No to a Future Success" by Michael M. Miller in the *Wall Street Journal,* December 15, 1986, p. 32. © 1986 by Dow Jones & Company, Inc. All rights reserved. From "When It Comes to Credit Bureau Reports, The More Consumers Find Out the Better" by Karen Slater in the *Wall Street Journal,* April 26, 1985. © 1985 by Dow Jones & Company, Inc. All rights reserved. *The Economist Newspaper Ltd.:* From "OPEC: Harmony, for How Long?" (Retitled: "A Change in Direction for OPEC") from *The Economist,* August 9, 1986, pp. 51–52. © 1986 by The Economist Newspaper Ltd. *FORTUNE:* From "Reagan's Budget: Selling Off the Government" by Lee Smith in *FORTUNE,* March 3, 1986, p. 70. Copyright © 1986 by Time, Inc. All rights reserved. *Roger W. Garrison:* From "Tax-Revision Sleight of Hand" by Dr. Roger Garrison in the WALL STREET JOURNAL, Friday, October 3, 1986, p. 28. *Harcourt Brace Jovanovich, Inc.:* From "Created Equal" (Retitled: "Capitalism, Freedom, and Equality") from *FREE TO CHOOSE: A Personal Statement* by Milton and Rose Friedman. Copyright © 1979, 1980 by Milton and Rose D. Friedman. *Harper & Row, Publishers, Inc.:* From "Multinationals and Developing Countries" (Retitled: "A Plan for Integrating the Third World in the World Economy") in *Toward the Next Economics and Other Essays* by Peter F. Drucker. Copyright © 1974, 1981 by Peter F. Drucker. *Harvard University Press:* From "Administration of Wealth" (Retitled: "The Gospel of Wealth According to Andrew Carnegie") in *The Gospel of Wealth and Other Timely Essays* by Andrew Carnegie, edited by Edward C. Kirkland. Copyright © 1962 by the President and Fellows of Harvard College. Published by the Belknap Press of Harvard University Press, Cambridge, Massachusetts. Originally published in *North American Review,* June 1889. *Houghton Mifflin Company:* From pp. 135–37 and 148–49 in *American Capitalism* by John Kenneth Galbraith. Copyright © 1952, 1956 by John Kenneth Galbraith. *Macmillan Press Ltd., London and Basingstoke:* From "The Substance of Economics" (Retitled: "Economics and Economic Laws"), Chapter II, in *Principles of Economics,* Ninth (Varorium) Editions, Volume 1, by Alfred Marshall, with annotations by C. W. Guillebaud. *McGraw-Hill, Inc.:* From " 'Shadow economy' translates into every language" (Retitled: "The Underground Economy: An International Phenomenon") in "Economics" in *Business Week,* April 5, 1982, p. 14. © 1982 by McGraw-Hill, Inc. From "We Should Cut the Deficit — But Not Because of Interest Rates" (Retitled: "The Case for Spending Reduction") in "Economic Watch" in *Business Week,* February 11, 1985, p. 68. © 1985 by McGraw-Hill, Inc. From "The Budget Is Congress' Problem Again" by Howard Gleckman in *Business Week,* July 21, 1986, p. 68. © 1986 by McGraw-Hill, Inc. *The New York Times Company:* From "Toward a Rational Trade Policy: Control Imports Through Bilateral Pacts" by John M. Culbertson in "Forum" in *The New York Times,* Sunday, August 11, 1985. Copyright © 1985 by The New York Times Company. From "A Way Back from Deep Debt" by Jerrold Mundis from *The New York Times* (Magazine), January 5, 1986, pp. 22–6. Copyright © 1986 by The New York Times Company. From "New York Stock Exchange Issues; Consolidated Trading" in *The New York Times,* November 5, 1986, pp. 41–4 and December 3, 1986, pp. 41–3. Copyright © 1986 by The New York Times Company. *W. W. Norton & Company, Inc.:* From "The Economics of Development" (Retitled: "The Keys to Economic Growth") in *The Rich Nations and The Poor Nations* by Barbara Ward. Copyright © 1962 by Barbara Ward. *Random House, Inc.:* From "Things: The Throw-away Society" (Retitled: "The Economics of Impermanence") in *Future Shock* by Alvin Toffler. Copyright © 1970 by Alvin Toffler. *TIME:* From "The Making of a Miracle" by George J. Church in *TIME,* August 25, 1986. Copyright 1986 by Time Inc. All rights reserved. *Arthur Zelvin:* From "A Job Hot Line Can Help the Pink-Slip Blues" (Retitled: A Job Hot Line") by Arthur Zelvin, President, Shareholder Reports, Inc., in "Manager's Journal" in the *Wall Street Journal,* February 2, 1987, p. 24.

COVER: Comstock (l, tr); FPG International (br).

GRAPHIC ART: The maps and charts on the following pages were prepared by Danmark and Michaels, Inc., Orlando, Florida: 13, 25, 26, 37, 48, 49, 50, 52, 53, 54, 61, 63, 64, 65, 68, 70, 83, 84, 85, 86, 102, 104, 105, 109, 123, 143, 144, 145, 150, 160, 171, 172, 174, 184, 197, 199, 200, 202, 205, 208, 209, 210, 232, 237, 246, 248, 251, 253, 254, 255, 260, 279, 281, 283, 293, 294, 315, 317, 319, 320, 321, 328, 330, 339, 347, 348, 363, 370, 373, 375, 388, 390, 391, 395, 398, 419, 423, 425, 430, 452, 468, 469, 470, 471, 472, 473, 476, 477(t), 478, 479. All others, HBJ.

PHOTOGRAPHS: Positions of photographs are shown in abbreviated form as follows: (t) top, (c) center, (b) bottom, (l) left, and (r) right.

Contents: pages *v,* Ted Clutter/Photo Researchers; *vi,* Milton and Joan Mann/Cameramann International; *vii,* Robert M. Friedman/Frozen Images; *viii,* David R. Frazier; *ix,* Robert Isear/Photo Researchers; *x,* Ellis Herwig/The Picture Cube; *xi,* Alex Webb/Magnum Photos; *xii,* J. Zehrt/FPG International; *xiii,* Dave Schaefer/Monkmeyer Press Photo Service; *xiv,* Doug Menuez/Stock, Boston; *xv,* Steve Elmore/The Stock Market of NY; *xvi,* Susan Van Etten/The Picture Cube; *xvii,* Richard Laird/The Stock Shop; *xviii,* Jeffrey D. Smith/Woodfin Camp & Associates; *xix,* C. Kaldor/FPG International; *xx,* Arthur d'Arazien/The Image Bank; *xxi,* Dennis J. Cipnic/Photo Researchers; *xxii,* Robert Frerck/Odyssey Productions; *xxiii,* Lenore Weber/Taurus Photos.

Illustrated Overview: pages 2(tl), HBJ Photo/Earl Kogler; 2(bl), Randy Matusow/Archive Pictures; 2(tr), G. Marche/FPG International; 2(br), Paul Conklin; 3(tl), D.C. Lowe/FPG International; 3(bl), H. Wendler/The Image Bank; 3(r), Chuck Keeler, Jr./Frozen Images; 4, Vince Streano/After Image; 5(tl), William Strode; 5(bl), Frank Fisher/After Image; 5(r), HBJ Photo/Earl Kogler; 6(tl), James H. Simon/The Picture Cube; 6(bl), Dick Luria/FPG International; 6(r), Paul Shambroom/ Photo Researchers; 7(tl and tr), HBJ photo/Earl Kogler; 7(br), John Running/Black Star; 8(l), Tom Tracy/The Stock Shop; 8(tr), Trev Kyle/West Stock; 8(br), 9(tl), HBJ Photo/Earl Kogler; 9(bl), Miro Vintoniv/Stock, Boston; 9(r), Barton Silverman/Leo deWys, Inc.; 10(tl), Gabe Palmer/The Stock Market of NY; 10(bl), Dick Luria/The Stock Shop; 10(r), Erich Hartmann/ Magnum Photos; 11(tl), HBJ Photo/Earl Kogler; 11(bl), R.P. Kingston/Stock, Boston; 11(r), Cezus/Alpha, FPG International; 12(tl), Chuck Keeler, Jr./Frozen Images; 12(bl), Jonathan Barkan/The Picture Cube; 12(tr), Tom Tracy/The Stock Shop; 12(br), Ted Horowitz/The Stock Market of NY; 13(l), Adam Woolfitt/Woodfin Camp & Associates; 13(c),

Paul Conklin; 13(r), Joseph Nettis/Photo Researchers; 14(tl), NASA/FPG International; 14(bl), Bernard Gotfryd/Woodfin Camp & Associates; 14(r), Cliff Hollenbeck/After Image; 15(l), P. Ryan/Black Star; 15(tr), Milton and Joan Mann/Cameramann International; 15(br), James A. Cudney/Nawrocki Stock Photo; 16(tl), John Marmaras/Woodfin Camp & Associates; 16(bl), Peter Turnley/Black Star; 16(tr), Blaine Harrington/The Stock Market of NY; 16(br), Tass/Sovfoto; 17(t), Ulrike Welsch/Stock, Boston; 17(c), Robert Frerck/Odyssey Productions; 17(b), M. VanderWall/Leo deWys, Inc.

Unit One: pages 18–19, Robert Langlotz/Black Star; 20, Ted Clutter/Photo Researchers; 23, Jim Whitmer/Nawrocki Stock Photo; 24, Michael Pugh Photography; 28(tl), Paul Conklin; 28(tr), Robert Frerck/Odyssey Productions; 28(c), John Launois/Rapho, Black Star; 28(b), Adam Woolfitt/Woodfin Camp & Associates; 30, Granger Collection; 32, Granger Collection; 33, Fred Ward/Black Star; 35, Phil Schofield/West Stock; 36, Jeffry W. Myers/West Stock; 38, Robert Frerck/Odyssey Productions; 44, Milton and Joan Mann/Cameramann, International; 47, Mimi Forsyth/Monkmeyer Press Photo Service; 51, Jim Knowles/Picture Group; 58, Robert M. Friedman/Frozen Images; 62, Cary Wolinsky/After Image; 67, Courtesy, Genentech, Inc.; 69, David R. Frazier; 71, John Troha/Black Star; 74, David R. Frazier; 77, Stuart Cohen/The Stock Market of NY; 80, Andrew Popper; 81(b), John Marmaras/Woodfin Camp & Associates; 81(inset), Wm. S. Nawrocki/Nawrocki Stock Photo; 85, Paul Shambroom/Photo Researchers; 87, Freda Leinwand; 88(l), Robert M. Friedman/Frozen Images; 88(r), D. Goldberg/Sygma Photos.

Unit Two: pages 94–95, William Strode/Woodfin Camp & Associates; 96, Robert Isear/Photo Researchers; 99, José A. Fernandez/Woodfin Camp & Associates; 100, Erich Hartmann/Magnum Photos; 106, Courtesy, Portia Isaacson; 107, AP/Wide World Photos; 112, Sepp Seitz/Woodfin Camp & Associates; 114, Robert Frerck/Odyssey Productions; 115, Ron Sherman/After Image; 116(l), Chuck Fishman/Woodfin Camp & Associates; 116(r), Stuart Cohen/Stock Boston; 120, Ellis Herwig/The Picture Cube; 125, HBJ Photo/Peter A. Burg; 126, Courtesy, Tennessee Valley Authority; 128, Courtesy, TBS; 129, Robert Frerck/Woodfin Camp & Associates; 130, Culver Pictures; 131, Bettmann Archive; 132, Dan McCoy/Rainbow; 140, Alex Webb/Magnum Photos; 143, T.M. Wathen/Quadrant; 146(l), Mark Godfrey/Archive Pictures; 146(r), Peter Vadnai/The Stock Market of NY; 148, Jon Feingersh/The Stock Market of NY; 151, Charles West/The Stock Market of NY; 152(l), Granger Collection; 152(r), Wally McNamee/Woodfin Camp & Associates; 153, Milton and Joan Mann/Cameramann, International; 154, Eli Reed/Magnum Photos; 158, Robert McElroy/Woodfin Camp & Associates; 159, United Steelworkers of America.

Unit Three: pages 166–167, PHOTRI; 168, J. Zehrt/FPG International; 171, William Rivelli/The Image Bank; 178, David R. Frazier; 180(l), Gerhard Gscheidle/Peter Arnold, Inc.; 180(r), Rhoda Sidney/Leo deWys, Inc.; 181, Cynthia Johnson/Gamma-Liaison; 185, Fred Ward/Black Star; 186, Scott Thode/International Stock Photo; 187, Paul Conklin; 188(l, r), J.L. Atlan/Sygma Photos; 192, Dave Schaefer/Monkmeyer Press Photo Service; 197, Philip Jon Bailey/The Picture Cube; 200, Stacy Pick/Stock, Boston; 201, Milton and Joan Mann/Cameramann, International; 203, Charles O'Rear/Woodfin Camp & Associates; 204, Dennis Brack/Black Star; 211, Paul Conklin; 212, Cynthia Johnson/Gamma-Liaison.

Unit Four: pages 218–219, Roger Tully/After Image; 220, Doug Menuez/Stock, Boston; 223, T.J. Florian/Nawrocki Stock Photo; 224, Thomas Hopker/Woodfin Camp & Associates; 227, Milton and Joan Mann/Cameramann, International; 229 (tl, tr), Patrick Grace/Photo Researchers; 229 (bl, br), W.S. Nawrocki/Nawrocki Stock Photo; 234, HBJ Photo/Peter A. Burg; 235, Philip Amdal/West Stock; 236, Ellis Herwig/The Picture Cube; 238, Andrew Popper; 242, Steve Elmore/The Stock Market of NY; 247, Dennis Brack/Black Star; 249, Eric Smith/Gamma-Liaison; 250, Milton and Joan Mann/Cameramann, International; 259(l), Mike Mazzaschi/Stock, Boston; 259(r), Jan Staller; 262, Dennis Brack/Black Star; 266, Susan Van Etten/The Picture Cube; 272, Stacy Pick/Stock, Boston; 276, Ken Sexton/Nawrocki Stock Photo; 277, Phil Huber/Black Star; 279, Freda Leinwand; 282, Eugene Richards/Magnum Photos; 284, Stan Wan; 288, Richard Laird/The Stock Shop; 291, W.S. Nawrocki/Nawrocki Stock Photo; 292, Gabe Palmer/After Image; 295, Jon Riley/The Stock Shop; 296, Robert Frerck/Odyssey Productions; 297, Maggie Steber; 300, John Coletti/The Picture Cube; 302, David Burnett/Contact Press Images, Woodfin Camp & Associates; 304, Brett Froomer/The Image Bank.

Unit Five: pages 310–311, George Hall/Woodfin Camp & Associates; 312, Jeffrey D. Smith/Woodfin Camp & Associates; 318, George Hall/Woodfin Camp & Associates; 322, Andrew Sacks/Black Star; 323, Culver Pictures; 324, David York/The Stock Shop; 325, Milton and Joan Mann/Cameramann, International; 329, Freda Leinwand; 331, Andrew Sacks/Black Star; 332, JFP and Associates of Florida; 336, C. Kaldor/FPG, International; 340, Dennis Brack/Black Star; 341, Anthony Howarth/Woodfin Camp & Associates; 349(tl), Bob Stern/International Stock Photo; 349(tr), Dick Luria/After Image; 349(bl), Milton and Joan Mann, Cameramann, International; 349(br), Vadnai/The Stock Market of NY; 351, Benn Mitchell/The Image Bank; 352, Printed with permission from Philip Crosby Associates, Inc., Winter Park, FL.; 354, Dennis Brack/Black Star; 358, Arthur d'Arazien/The Image Bank; 361, BBC Hulton/Bettmann Archive; 362, Bettmann Archive; 368, Jim Cooke/Picture Group; 371, Culver Pictures; 372, Copyright, 1986, Universal Press Syndicate. Reprinted with permission. All rights reserved; 374, Craig Aurness/Woodfin Camp & Associates; 376(l), James Stoots, Jr., Lawrence Livermore National Laboratory; 376(r), Franklin Wing/Stock, Boston.

Unit Six: pages 382–383, Luis Villotta/The Stock Market of NY; 384, Dennis J. Cipnic/Photo Researchers; 387, Owen Franken/Stock, Boston; 395, Earl Young/After Image; 397, Milton and Joan Mann/Cameramann International; 400, Hank Morgan/Rainbow; 401, C. Fitch/FPG International; 403, Milton and Joan Mann/Cameramann International; 404(l), Robert Frerck/Odyssey Productions; 404(r), Sepp Seitz/Woodfin Camp & Associates; 405, Stephen Ferry/Gamma-Liaison; 410, Robert Frerck/Odyssey Productions; 415, Steve Vidler/Leo deWys, Inc.; 417(tl), Roz Joseph/OMNI Photo Communications; 417(r), Ted H. Funk/FPG International; 417(bl), Dagmar Fabricius/Stock, Boston; 420, Milton and Joan Mann/Cameramann International; 421, James A. Sugar/Black Star; 422, Pankaj Shah/The Stock Market of NY; 426, Elihu Blotnick/OMNI Photo Communications; 427, James B. Cudney/Nawrocki Stock Photo; 432(tl), Anthony Suru/Black Star; 432(tr), Dave Forbert/Shostal Associates; 432(b), Robert Frerck/Woodfin Camp & Associates; 433, Mike Greenlar/Picture Group; 434, Alon Reininger/Woodfin Camp & Associates; 438, Lenore Weber/Taurus Photos; 441, Michal Heron/Woodfin Camp & Associates; 442, Griffiths/Magnum Photos; 443, Patrick Zachmann/Magnum Photos; 444, Hans Paul/Lehtikuva, Woodfin Camp & Associates; 448(l), Bettmann Archive; 448(r), Tass/Sovfoto; 451(t), Granger Collection; 451(b), Wide World Photos; 453(t), Wally McNamee/Woodfin Camp & Associates; 453(b), Martti Kainulainen/Lehtikuva, Woodfin Camp & Associates; 456, Owen Franken/Stock, Boston; 457(t), Alon Reininger/Contact Press Images, Woodfin Camp & Associates; 457(bl), Lenore Weber/OMNI Photo Communications; 457(cr) Richard J. Quataert/Taurus

Photos; 457(br), Vince Streano/The Stock Market of NY; 458, Contact Press Images/Woodfin Camp & Associates; 464, Leo Touchet/Woodfin Camp & Associates.

The Reference Library: page 499, Granger Collection; 500, Fred Ward/Black Star; 501, Bettmann Archive; 502, Culver Pictures; 503, UPI/Bettmann Newsphotos; 504, Eric Kroll/Taurus Photos; 505, S. Ray/Alpha, FPG International; 506, Larry Downing/Woodfin Camp & Associates; 509, Mimi Forsyth/Monkmeyer Press Photo Service; 511, HBJ Photo/Earl Kogler; 512, Rick Friedman/Black Star; 514, Jim Pickerell/Black Star; 516(t), Reprinted with permission of AT&T. All rights reserved; 516(b), B.J. Ullmann/Taurus Photos; 517, HBJ Photo/Earl Kogler; 519, Gabe Palmer/The Stock Market of NY; 522, Sun Bank, National Association; 524, Larry Smith/DPI; 525, Peter Russell Clemens/International Stock Photo; 527, Catherine Ursillo/Leo deWys, Inc.; 528, HBJ Photo/Earl Kogler; 529, *The Orlando Sentinel;* 530, Jon Feingersh/The Stock Market of NY; 532, HBJ Photo/Earl Kogler; 533, Don Mealey Chevrolet, Inc., Orlando, FL.; 534, Gabe Palmer/After Image; 535, HBJ Photo/Peter A. Burg; 536, Cliff Feurner/The Image Bank; 537, Randa Bishop/DPI; 540, Milton and Joan Mann/Cameramann, International; 541, Milton and Joan Mann/Cameramann, International; 542, Will McIntyre/Photo Researchers; 543, Robert McElroy/Woodfin Camp & Associates.